Livy
The Fragments and *Periochae*

Livy

The Fragments and *Periochae*

*Edited with an Introduction,
Translation, and Commentary by*

D. S. LEVENE

Volume II
Periochae 1–45

Great Clarendon Street, Oxford, OX2 6DP,
United Kingdom

Oxford University Press is a department of the University of Oxford.
It furthers the University's objective of excellence in research, scholarship,
and education by publishing worldwide. Oxford is a registered trade mark of
Oxford University Press in the UK and in certain other countries

© D. S. Levene 2023

The moral rights of the author have been asserted

All rights reserved. No part of this publication may be reproduced, stored in
a retrieval system, or transmitted, in any form or by any means, without the
prior permission in writing of Oxford University Press, or as expressly permitted
by law, by licence or under terms agreed with the appropriate reprographics
rights organization. Enquiries concerning reproduction outside the scope of the
above should be sent to the Rights Department, Oxford University Press, at the
address above

You must not circulate this work in any other form
and you must impose this same condition on any acquirer

Published in the United States of America by Oxford University Press
198 Madison Avenue, New York, NY 10016, United States of America

British Library Cataloguing in Publication Data
Data available

Library of Congress Control Number: 2023933547

ISBN 978–0–19–888853–6 (Pack)
ISBN 978–0–19–287122–0 (Vol. I)
ISBN 978–0–19–287123–7 (Vol. II)

Printed and bound by
CPI Group (UK) Ltd, Croydon, CR0 4YY

Links to third party websites are provided by Oxford in good faith and
for information only. Oxford disclaims any responsibility for the materials
contained in any third party website referenced in this work.

Contents

Abbreviations	vii
Introduction	xi
i. Introduction	xi
ii. The *Periochae* and Orosius	xiv
iii. The *Periochae* and Livy	xxii
iv. The *Periochae* and Orosius Revisited (also Augustine, Eutropius…)	xxviii
v. The Narrative of the *Periochae*	xxxii
(a) Form, Structure, and Voice	xxxii
(b) Content	xl
(c) Style	lii
vi. Authorship and Composition	lv
vii. Reading the *Periochae*	lx
viii. The *Periochae* and the Articulation of Livy's Text	lxxiv
ix. Note on the Text	lxxix
Appendix: Subdivisions of the *Periochae*	lxxxii
Sigla	lxxxiii
TEXT AND TRANSLATION	1
Periochae 1–45	2
COMMENTARY	71
Book 1	73
Book 2	94
Book 3	114
Book 4	125
Book 5	136
Book 6	148
Book 7	154
Book 8	167
Book 9	179
Book 10	191
Book 11	198
Book 12	226
Book 13	248
Book 14	279
Book 15	302

Book 16	320
Book 17	339
Book 18	355
Book 19	377
Book 20	409
Book 21	452
Book 22	462
Book 23	478
Book 24	491
Book 25	497
Book 26	507
Book 27	515
Book 28	525
Book 29	534
Book 30	549
Book 31	559
Book 32	569
Book 33	576
Book 34	581
Book 35	587
Book 36	594
Book 37	597
Book 38	604
Book 39	616
Book 40	625
Book 41	631
Book 42	646
Book 43	652
Book 44	659
Book 45	666
Bibliography	673
General Index	707
Index of Latin	723

Abbreviations

AE	R. Cagnat et al. (eds.), *L'Année épigraphique* (Paris, 1888–).
BarrAtl	R. J. A. Talbert (ed.), *The Barrington Atlas of the Greek and Roman World* (Princeton: Princeton University Press, 2000).
Beloch, *GG*	K. J. Beloch, *Griechische Geschichte* (2nd edn, Berlin: De Gruyter, 1912–27).
Beloch, *RG*	K. J. Beloch, *Römische Geschichte bis zum Beginn der punischen Kriege* (Berlin: De Gruyter, 1926).
Bingham	W. J. Bingham, *A Study of the Livian 'Periochae' and Their Relation to Livy's 'Ab Urbe Condita'*. Unpublished diss., University of Illinois at Urbana-Champaign, 1978.
BTCGI	G. Nenci, G. Vallet, et al. (eds), *Bibliografia topografica della colonizzazione greca in Italia e nelle isole tirreniche* (Pisa: Scuola Normale Superiore, 1977–2012).
CAD	*The Assyrian Dictionary of the Oriental Institute of the University of Chicago* (Chicago: The Oriental Institute, 1956–2010).
CAH[2]	*The Cambridge Ancient History* (2nd edn, Cambridge: Cambridge University Press, 1971–2005).
Carandini, *Atlas*	A. Carandini with P. Carafa (eds), *The Atlas of Ancient Rome* (tr. A. Campbell Halavais, Princeton: Princeton University Press, 2017).
CIL	T. Mommsen et al. (eds), *Corpus Inscriptionum Latinarum* (Berlin: Georg Reimer, 1853–).
CNH	L. Villaronga (ed.), *Corpus Nummum Hispaniae ante Augusti Aetatem* (Madrid: José A. Herrero, 1994).
De Sanctis	G. De Sanctis, *Storia dei Romani* (2nd edn, Florence: La Nuova Italia, 1956–69). [Page numbers of 1st edn in square brackets.]
Degrassi	A. Degrassi, *Inscriptiones Italiae* XIII, 1 (Rome: La Libreria dello Stato, 1947).
Degrassi, *Fast. Ann.*	A. Degrassi, *Inscriptiones Italiae* XIII, 2 (Rome: La Libreria dello Stato, 1963).
FGrH	F. Jacoby (ed.), *Die Fragmente der griechischen Historiker* (Berlin: Weidmann, 1923–30; Leiden: Brill, 1940–58).
FHG	K. Müller, *Fragmenta Historicorum Graecorum* (Paris: Ambroise Firmin-Didot, 1841–72).
FRHist	T. J. Cornell et al. (eds), *The Fragments of the Roman Historians* (Oxford: Oxford University Press, 2013).
Funari	R. Funari (ed.), *Corpus dei papiri storici greci e latini. Parte B. Storici latini. 1. Autori noti. Vol. 1. Titus Livius* (Pisa: Fabrizio Serra, 2011).
GL	H. Keil (ed.), *Grammatici Latini* (Leipzig: Teubner, 1855–80).
GRF	G. Funaioli (ed.), *Grammaticae Romanae Fragmenta*, vol. 1 (Leipzig: Teubner, 1907).

H-S	J. B. Hofmann and A. Szantyr, *Lateinische Grammatik: Syntax und Stilistik* (Munich: C. H. Beck, 1965).
IG	*Inscriptiones Graecae* (Berlin: Georg Reimer, 1873–).
IGRRP	R. Cagnat *et al.* (eds), *Inscriptiones Graecae ad Res Romanas Pertinentes* (Paris: E. Leroux, 1906–27).
ILLRP	A. Degrassi (ed.), *Inscriptiones Latinae Liberae Rei Publicae* (2nd edn, Florence: Biblioteca di studi superiori, 1963–5).
ILS	H. Dessau (ed.), *Inscriptiones Latinae Selectae* (Berlin: Weidmann, 1892–1906).
K-S	R. Kühner and C. Stegmann, *Ausführliche Grammatik der Lateinischen Sprache: Satzlehre* (Hanover: Hahnsche Buchhandlung, 1914).
Krebs-Schmalz	J. P. Krebs and J. H. Schmalz, *Antibarbarus der Lateinischen Sprache* (7th edn, Basel: Benno Schwabe, 1905).
LSJ	H. G. Liddell, R. Scott, and H. S. Jones, *A Greek–English Lexicon* (9th edn, Oxford: Oxford University Press, 1940).
LTUR	E. M. Steinby (ed.), *Lexicon Topographicum Urbis Romae* (Rome: Edizioni Quasar, 1993–2000).
Mommsen, *StR*³	T. Mommsen, *Römisches Staatsrecht* (3rd edn, Leipzig: S. Hirzel, 1887–8).
Mommsen, *StrR*	T. Mommsen, *Römisches Strafrecht* (Leipzig: Duncker & Humblot, 1899).
MRR	T. R. S. Broughton with M. L. Patterson, *The Magistrates of the Roman Republic* (New York: American Philological Association, 1951–86).
OCD⁴	S. Hornblower, A. Spawforth, and E. Eidinow (eds), *The Oxford Classical Dictionary* (4th edn, Oxford: Oxford University Press, 2012).
OGIS	W. Dittenberger (ed.), *Orientis Graeci Inscriptiones Selectae* (Leipzig: S. Hirzel, 1903–5).
OLD	*Oxford Latin Dictionary* (Oxford: Clarendon Press, 1968–82).
ORF³	H. Malcovati (ed.), *Oratorum Romanorum Fragmenta Liberae Rei Publicae* (3rd edn, Turin: G. B. Paravia & C., 1953).
P.Oxy.	*The Oxyrhynchus Papyri* (London: Egypt Exploration Fund, 1898–).
Peter	H. Peter, *Historicorum Romanorum Reliquiae* (2nd edn, Leipzig: Teubner, 1914).
Pinkster	H. Pinkster, *The Oxford Latin Syntax* (Oxford: Oxford University Press, 2015–21).
Polybios-Lexikon	A. Mauersberger *et al.* (eds), *Polybios-Lexikon* (2nd edn, Berlin: Akademie Verlag, 1998–2006).
RDGE	R. K. Sherk, *Roman Documents from the Greek East* (Baltimore: Johns Hopkins University Press, 1969).
RE	A. E. von Pauly *et al.*, *Pauly's Real-Encyclopädie der classische Altertumswissenschaft* (Stuttgart: J. B. Metzler, 1894–1963).
Rhodes-Osborne	P. J. Rhodes and R. Osborne (eds), *Greek Historical Inscriptions 404–323 BC* (Oxford: Oxford University Press, 2003).

Rossbach	O. Rossbach (ed.), *T. Livi Periochae Omnium Librorum. Fragmenta Oxyrhynchi Reperta. Iulii Obsequentis Prodigiorum Liber* (Leipzig: Teubner, 1910).
RRC	M. H. Crawford, *Roman Republican Coinage* (Cambridge: Cambridge University Press, 1974).
Rüpke, *FS*	J. Rüpke and A. Glock, *Fasti sacerdotum: A Prosopography of Pagan, Jewish, and Christian Religious Officials in the City of Rome, 300 BC to AD 499* (Revised edn, tr. D. M. B. Richardson, Oxford: Oxford University Press, 2008).
SEG	*Supplementum Epigraphicum Graecum* (Leiden: A. W. Seijtoff, 1923–71; Amsterdam: J. C. Gieben, 1976–2001; Leiden: Brill, 2002–).
SIG	W. Dittenberger (ed.), *Sylloge Inscriptionum Graecarum* (3rd edn, Leipzig: S. Hirzel, 1915–24).
SGDI	H. Collitz and F. Bechtel (eds), *Sammlung der griechischen Dialekt-Inschriften* (Göttingen: Vandenhoeck & Ruprecht, 1885–1915).
TLL	*Thesaurus Linguae Latinae* (Leipzig: Teubner, 1890–).
Torelli, *Fontes*	M. R. Torelli, *Rerum Romanarum fontes ab anno CCXCII ad annum CCLXV a. Ch.* (Pisa: Giardini, 1978).
Via Aurelia	*La Via Aurelia* (Rome: De Luca, 1968).
W-M	W. Weissenborn, H. J. Müller, and O. Rossbach, *Titi Livi: Ab Urbe Condita Libri* (Berlin: Weidmann, 1880–1924, latest edition of each volume reprinted 1965).
Waddington	W. H. Waddington, *Inscriptions grecques et latines de la Syrie* (Paris: Firmin Didot, 1970).
Woodcock	E. C. Woodcock, *A New Latin Syntax* (London: Methuen & Co., 1959).

Abbreviations of titles of journals are taken from *L'Année Philologique*. Abbreviations of ancient texts and authors are taken from LSJ for Greek texts and *TLL* for Latin, with some adaptations: notably *Per.* is used as the abbreviation for the Livian *Periochae* (with P. as its author), and *EpOxy* to designate the Oxyrhynchus Epitome of Livy. Cassius Dio is abbreviated to Dio, Jerome to Jer., Josephus to Jos., Xenophon to Xen. Also, particular works are sometimes identified by title (for example with Dionysius' *Antiquitates Romanae* or Plutarch's *Moralia* or Seneca's *Dialogues* or Claudian or Priscian) where LSJ or *TLL* prefers to leave them either unspecified or specified only by number: in those cases I have created my own (I hope reasonably clear) abbreviations for the titles. Conversely, Florus' so-called *Epitome* and Orosius' *Historiae Adversus Paganos* are abbreviated to 'Flor.' and 'Oros.' respectively, with the title omitted.

Introduction

i. Introduction

There are four ancient epitomes of Livy that survive at least in part: (i) the *Periochae*,[1] which survives almost complete; (ii) the epitome surviving on a third-century papyrus containing Books 37–40 and 48–55, known as the Oxyrhynchus Epitome; (iii) the rump epitome or contents-listing which is attached to the beginning of the *Periochae* and which is traditionally labelled A; and (iv) the *Liber Prodigiorum* of Julius Obsequens, a summary anthology of omens and prodigies in Livy. I will leave a full discussion of the Oxyrhynchus Epitome for Volume 3, and of Obsequens for Volume 4; for a discussion of the A *Periochae*, including a demonstration that it is identical with neither the *Periochae* proper nor the Oxyrhynchus Epitome, see the introduction to the commentary of *Per.* 1 (73–5).

The very fact that Livy was so often summarized is interesting and revealing. One obvious explanation is the length of Livy's text, which made direct access to it difficult and time-consuming, but that alone is not sufficient, since the alternative might have been merely to ignore his work. The canonization in the first century of Livy, along with Sallust, as the iconic Roman historian, goes further towards explaining why Livy was summarized rather than simply ignored; but perhaps no less important is that the Republic, the period for which Livy was (thanks to his canonization) perceived as the authoritative source, became central to the Roman consciousness of history in the late Empire, supplying the richest crop of exemplary figures and anecdotes through which many of the writers of that period conceptualized their historical traditions.[2] As I shall discuss below (xlv–xlvi), the *Periochae*, though representing something far more than a string

---

[1] Only a minority of the MSS refer to it as the *Periochae* (others refer to it as *Epitoma* or *breviarum*), but they include the oldest complete MSS, N and P, and it has remained the conventional title for the work, though it can hardly be asserted securely that it was the original one. For the significance see Bingham 8–9; cf. Bessone (1984), 42–3; Jal (1984), ix–xi. Other works titled 'Periochae' are recorded as having been composed for the plays of Menander, the epics of Homer and Virgil, and the plays of Terence. Formally, as Bessone argues, the distinction from an 'epitome' appears to be that 'Periochae' connotes something closer to a *hypothesis* or 'argument', a brief summary of the work, not an abridged history, but that hardly fits the *Periochae* as we have it (cf. below), and it may be that the terms were ascribed loosely, either by the author or whichever copyist first applied the title to the work.

[2] See Felmy (2001), 35–64, though he arguably overstates the extent to which historical writers of the period substituted such exemplary readings of history for the more analytic historical consciousness found in the historiography of earlier periods.

of *exempla*, nevertheless is structured in ways that strongly recall that way of understanding history.

There is, however, a fifth epitome of Livy whose existence has often been hypothesized, even though not a single word of it survives. Ever since Niebuhr it has been widely argued that a large number of Livy-dependent writers—not just the surviving epitomes, but also Eutropius, Florus, Orosius, and many others—are all dependent on a single source, namely an epitome of Livy made relatively close to his time, in the first century AD.[3] This epitome, it is argued, is the text that is mentioned in a famous poem of Martial (14.190 = T 23).[4] The scholars in question have argued that it, or something very like it, is the source of the *Periochae* and also for the other later writers. The later writers often overlap substantially with one another in content and wording, but also diverge from one another, each including details which are not in the other. In many cases it is either demonstrable or probable that the shared material cannot go back to Livy himself: hence (so it is argued) both the shared material, and that which is not shared, must have appeared in the lost epitome. In particular, it has been widely believed that the *Periochae* itself was derived from this epitome, rather than the author working directly from Livy's text. Almost all of this, however, is controversial—notably, most recent scholars who have addressed the issue have denied that Martial's poem is referring to an epitome at all,[5] while the majority of recent scholars on the *Periochae* have denied its dependence on the 'lost epitome' (if such a work even existed), and preferred to see the author working directly from Livy.[6]

There are different threads that need to be untangled if we are to assess this argument. As a first step, one needs to recognize that the question of the existence of an early epitome which is the source for later writers is largely separate from the question of whether we should interpret Martial 14.190 as referring to that epitome. Such an epitome may have existed even if Martial is referring to something completely different, while, conversely, even if Martial is referring to an epitome, that does not imply that any later writer actually employed it—or any other epitome—as a source. The one point of contact between the two is that the existence or otherwise of epitomes of historical authors is a necessary prerequisite if one is to interpret Martial as referring to an epitome: were Livian epitomes unknown in first-century Rome, it would make it less likely that a reader of Martial would understand his poem as referring to one.

---

[3] Niebuhr (1846), 58–9 proposed this in passing: the idea was subsequently expanded and elaborated by e.g. Zangemeister (1882), Ay (1894), Sanders (1898), 18–51, Drescher (1900), Sanders (1904), Schmidt (1968), esp. 31–2, 43–7, Bessone (1977), (1982), (1984), (2015). Which authors depend on the epitome is highly contested—notably, it is often suggested that the Oxyrhynchus Epitome, Obsequens, and Cassiodorus are based on a different, more chronicle-like epitome—but all accept that the *Periochae* derives from it.

[4] It is also sometimes suggested that Stat., *Silv.* 4.7.53–6 = T 21 refers to a Livy epitome, but see *ad loc.*

[5] So e.g. Ascher (1968–9), Butrica (1983), Roberts and Skeat (1983), 25–7, Jal (1984), xxxiv–xxxix, Leary (1996), 255–6, Harnett (2017), 201; *contra* Sansone (1980–1). See further T 23n.

[6] So e.g. Begbie (1967), Jal (1984), xxvi–lv.

So the first question is whether we have any evidence independent of Martial for an epitome of Livy in the first century AD: and there is very clear evidence that there was. Plutarch (*Marc.* 11.4 = C 53) attributes to Livy a comment on the battle at Nola during the Second Punic War which is not found in Livy's actual text: namely that as a result of the battle the Romans developed a new confidence, since they now knew that Hannibal could be beaten. A remarkably similar idea, though more succinctly expressed, is found in *Periochae* 23.10: that this was the first battle that gave the Romans hope in the war.[7] It looks highly probable that there is a connection; but the *Periochae* is unlikely to have taken it from Plutarch, and it is also extremely unlikely that both authors took it from some unrelated third party and then independently ascribed it to Livy. Accordingly, by far the most probable conclusion is that it comes from some text which the *Periochae* employed as a source in its Livy summary, and which Plutarch could quote as coming from 'Livy': an epitome is overwhelmingly the most likely possibility.

Hence we can reasonably assume that the idea of a Livy epitome would have been a comprehensible possibility for the readership of Martial's poem. That does not, of course, show that Martial is referring to it; but that is the most natural interpretation of the poem. I would concede that it is not *impossible* that it refers to some other form in which Livy's text might have been condensed, but Sansone's argument for an epitome seems to fit the wording better than any other reading (Sansone (1980–1)): as Martial explains, the volume he is offering as a gift is not 'the whole of Livy', but it is nevertheless 'huge Livy reduced' (*artatur*) onto a parchment codex. This fits neither a volume written in tiny script (so e.g. Ascher (1968–9)) nor a multiplicity of codices (Harnett (2017), 201)—such volumes would still be 'the whole of Livy', and (*contra* Harnett) Martial indicates that his gift is not that—nor a selection of excerpts from speeches such as that described in T 24 (which would not be naturally described as 'Livy reduced'). For a fuller discussion see T 23n.

So we have an excellent reason not only to accept the hypothesis of a lost first-century AD epitome of Livy, but also to see it as a text that was available to and used by the surviving *Periochae*. But the scholars of the late nineteenth and early twentieth centuries went further: they argued that both the *Periochae* and other works of summary history in the Livian tradition were not deriving their material from Livy directly, but they were simply employing this epitome. Hence, as I noted above, numerous overlaps of wording between the *Periochae* and those other historians, combined with the inclusion of separate details in those sections, are held to be the result of all of them depending on the lost epitome but selecting different material from it. The fact that the *Periochae* frequently offers versions of history that are at variance with Livy's own is similarly held to be the result of its dependence on an

---

[7] Cf. also the similar thought in Oros. 4.16.12: that too could depend on the first-century epitome, but it is at least as probable that it is the result of Orosius' own dependence on the *Periochae* (cf. below).

epitome, although in that particular case it is less obvious how the argument is meant to be working. The majority of the cases where the *Periochae* varies significantly from Livy are the result of adopting a popular version of events which Livy happens not to share (below, li–lii), and there is no reason to assume an intermediate source to explain it. If the original epitomizer could introduce an alternative version when summarizing Livy, the *Periochae* could have done the same without the intervention of such an earlier epitomizer.[8] For the same reason, even when two or more of the Livy-derived writers share the same non-Livian version of an event, this does not indicate dependence on an intermediate source: if one writer can introduce such a version, then two can, at least if (as is often the case) the version was better-known and more popular than Livy's own.

ii. The *Periochae* and Orosius

So in order to assess the extent of the *Periochae*'s alleged dependence on the lost epitome, we need, first, to examine the places where we find those areas of overlap with other sources. The author whose text shows by far the greatest affinity to the *Periochae* is Orosius: Table 1 sets out all of the places (forty-seven in total) where the *Periochae*'s wording and Orosius' coincide to a significant degree:

Table 1

	Periochae	Orosius
1.	2.3 cum adversus reges, qui contractis Veientum et Tarquiniensium copiis bellum intulerant, exercitum duxisset, in acie cum Arrunte filio Superbi commortuus est	2.5.2 ipse deinde Veientum Tarquiniensiumque bello cum Arrunte, Superbi filio, congresso sibi commortuoque procubuit.
2.	2.13 Popilia virgo Vestalis ob incestum viva defossa est.	2.8.13 Popilia virgo ob crimen stupri viva defossa est.
3.	2.14 trecentos et sex armatos, qui ad Cremeram praeter unum ab hostibus caesi sunt.	2.5.9 omnes ibidem trucidati sunt, uno tantum ad enuntiandam cladem reservato.[9]
4.	3.6 petitis per legatos et adlatis Atticis legibus ad constituendas eas proponendasque X viri pro consulibus sine ullis aliis magistratibus creati altero et trecentesimo anno quam Roma condita erat, et ut a regibus ad consules, ita a consulibus ad X viros imperium translatum.	2.13.2 ipso autem trecentesimo anno, hoc est olympiade nonagesima quinta, potestas consulum decemviris tradita constituendarum legum Atticarum gratia magnam perniciem reipublicae invexit.

[8] As noted by Jal (1984), xlvii.
[9] Despite the lack of shared vocabulary, these passages present a unique and unparalleled version of a very famous story, and hence are likely to be related: see *Per.* 2.14n.

THE *PERIOCHAE* AND OROSIUS   xv

	Periochae	Orosius
5.	3.7–9 hi X tabulis legum positis cum modeste se in eo honore gessissent et ob id in alterum quoque annum eundem esse magistratum ⟨placuisset, duabus tabulis⟩ ad decem adiectis cum complura inpotenter fecissent, magistratum noluerunt deponere et in tertium annum retinuerunt, donec inviso eorum imperio finem adtulit libido Appi Claudi. 8. qui cum in amorem Virginiae virginis incidisset, summisso, qui eam in servitutem peteret, necessitatem patri eius Virginio inposuit. qui rapto ex taberna proxima cultro filiam occidit, cum aliter effici non posset ne in potestatem stuprum inlaturi veniret. 9. hoc tam magnae iniuriae exemplo plebs concitata montem Aventinum occupavit coegitque X viros abdicare se magistratu.	2.13.5–7 duabus tabulis legum ad decem priores additis, agentes insolentissimo fastu plurima, die, quo deponere magistratus mos erat, cum isdem insignibus processerunt. 6. maximam etiam Appii Claudii libido auxit invidiam, qui ut Verginiae virgini stuprum inferret, prius servitutis causam intulit; quamobrem adactus Verginius pater dolore libertatis et pudore dedecoris protractam ad servitutem filiam in conspectu populi pius parricida prostravit. 7. qua populus necessitate atrocitate permotus et periculo libertatis admonitus montem Aventinum occupavit armatus. nec tueri libertatem armis destitit, nisi postquam se coniuratorum conspiratio ipsis quoque honoribus abdicavit.
6.	5.7 cum Galli Senones Clusium obsiderent et legati a senatu missi ad conponendam inter eos et Clusinos pacem pugnantes contra Gallos starent in acie Clusinorum, hoc facto eorum concitati Senones urbem infesto exercitu petierunt.	2.19.5 igitur Galli Senones duce Brenno exercitu copioso et robusto nimis cum urbem Clusini, quae nunc Tuscia dicitur, obsiderent, legatos Romanorum, qui tunc conponendae inter eos pacis gratia venerant, in acie adversum se videre pugnantes: qua indignatione permoti, Clusini oppidi obsidione dimissa, totis viribus Romam contendunt.
7.	8.5 Minucia virgo Vestalis incesti damnata est.	3.9.5 Minucia virgo Vestalis ob admissum incestum damnata est.
8.	11.1 cum Fabius Gurges cos. male adversus Samnites pugnasset et senatus de removendo eo ab exercitu ageret, Fabius Maximus pater deprecatus hanc fili ignominiam eo maxime senatum movit quod iterum se filio legatum pollicitus est, idque praestitit.	3.22.6–7 Fabius Gurges consul male adversum Samnitas pugnavit. namque amisso exercitu victus in urbem refugit. 7. itaque cum senatus de summovendo eo deliberaret, pater eius Fabius Maximus ignominiam filii deprecatus legatum se filio iterum ultro obtulit.
9.	12.2 legati ad eos a senatu, ut de his iniuriis quererentur, missi pulsati sunt. ob id bellum his indictum est.	4.1.2 missi Tarentum a Romanis legati, ut de inlatis quererentur iniuriis, pulsati ab isdem auctas insuper iniurias rettulerunt. his causis bellum ingens exortum est.
10.	14.6 Sextilia, virgo Vestalis, damnata incesti viva defossa est.	4.2.8 Sextilia virgo Vestalis convicta damnataque incesti ad portam Collinam viva defossa est.

	Periochae	Orosius
11.	17.1 Cn. Cornelius consul a classe Punica circumventus et per fraudem, veluti in conloquium evocatus, captus est.	4.7.9 ubi ab Hannibale quasi ad conloquium pacis evocatus Punica fraude captus atque in vinculis necatus est.
12.	17.4 Atilius Calatinus cos. cum in locum a Poenis circumsessum temere exercitum duxisset, M. Calpurni, tribuni militum, virtute et opera evasit, qui cum CCC militibus eruptione facta hostes in se converterat.	4.8.1–2 Calatinus consul Camerinam Siciliae urbem petens temere in angustias deduxit exercitum, quas Poenorum copiae iam dudum praestruxerant. 2. cui cum omnino nulla vel obsistendi vel evadendi facultas esset, Calpurni Flammae virtute et opera liberatus est, qui lecta trecentorum virorum manu insessum ab hostibus tumulum occupavit et in se Poenos omnes pugnando convertit, donec Romanus exercitus obsessas angustias hoste non urguente transiret.
13.	20.8 eo bello populum R. sui Latinique nominis DCCC milia armatorum habuisse (Fabius) dicit.	4.13.6 quo facto in utriusque consulis exercitu octingenta milia armatorum fuisse referuntur, sicut Fabius historicus, qui eidem bello interfuit, scripsit.
14.	20.9 exercitibus Romanis tunc primum trans Padum ductis Galli Insubres aliquot proeliis fusi in deditionem venerunt.	4.13.11 primi trans Padum Romanas duxere legiones. pugnatum est ibi cum Insubribus Gallis.
15.	21.3 Hannibal superato Pyrenaeo saltu per Gallias, fusis Volcis, qui obsistere conati erant ei, ad Alpes venit et laborioso per eas transitu, cum montanos quoque Gallos obvios aliquot proeliis reppulisset, descendit in Italiam et ad Ticinum flumen Romanos equestri proelio fudit. in quo vulneratum P. Cornelium Scipionem protexit filius, qui Africani postea nomen accepit.	4.14.4–6 Pyrenaeos montes transgressus inter ferocissimas Gallorum gentes ferro viam aperuit et nono demum die a Pyrenaeo ad Alpes pervenit; ubi dum montanos Gallos, repellere ab ascensu obnitentes, bello superat atque invias rupes igni ferroque rescindit, quadriduum commoratus quinto demum die cum maximo labore ad plana pervenit. 5. fuisse tunc exercitum eius in centum milibus peditum et viginti milibus equitum definiunt. 6. Scipio consul Hannibali primus occurrit commissoque proelio apud Ticinum ipse graviter vulneratus per Scipionem filium admodum praetextatum, qui post Africanus cognominatus est, ab ipsa morte liberatus evasit.
16.	21.5 Cn. Cornelius Scipio in Hispania contra Poenos prospere pugnavit duce hostium Magone capto.	4.14.9 alter tunc Scipio, frater consulis Scipionis, in Hispania plurima bella gessit, Magonem quoque Poenorum ducem bello vicit et cepit.

	Periochae	Orosius
17.	22.8 post quae cum a nobilibus adulescentibus propter <u>desperationem consilium de relinquenda Italia</u> iniretur, <u>P. Cornelius Scipio tribunus militum, qui Africanus postea</u> vocatus est, <u>stricto</u> supra capita deliberantium <u>ferro</u> iuravit pro hoste se habiturum eum qui <u>in verba sua non iurasset</u>, effecitque ut omnes non relictum iri a se Italiam <u>iureiurando adstringerentur</u>.	4.16.6 usque adeo autem ultima <u>desperatio</u> reipublicae apud residuos Romanos fuit, ut senatores <u>de relinquenda Italia</u> sedibusque quaerendis <u>consilium ineundum</u> putarint. quod auctore Caecilio Metello confirmatum fuisset, nisi <u>Cornelius Scipio tribunus tunc militum, idem qui post Africanus, destricto gladio</u> deterruisset ac potius pro patriae defensione <u>in sua verba iurare coegisset</u>.
18.	23.6 <u>L. Postumius praetor a Gallis cum exercitu caesus est</u>.	4.16.11 <u>L. Postumius praetor</u> adversus <u>Gallos</u> pugnare missus <u>cum exercitu caesus est</u>.
19.	23.10 <u>Claudius Marcellus praetor Hannibalis exercitum</u> ad Nolam <u>proelio fudit</u> et vicit, <u>primusque tot cladibus fessis Romanis meliorem spem belli dedit</u>.	4.16.12 <u>Claudius Marcellus ex praetore</u> proconsule designatus <u>Hannibalis exercitum proelio fudit primusque post tantas reipublicae ruinas spem fecit Hannibalem posse superari</u>.
20.	25.5–8 <u>Tib. Sempronius Gracchus pro cos. ab hospite suo Lucano in insidias deductus a Magone interfectus est</u>. 6. <u>Centenius Paenula</u>, qui <u>centurio</u> militaverat, cum <u>petisset</u> a senatu ut sibi exercitus daretur pollicitusque esset, si hoc impetrasset, <u>de Hannibale victoriam</u>, <u>VIII milibus acceptis militum dux factus</u> conflixit acie cum Hannibale et cum exercitu <u>caesus est</u>. 7. Capua obsessa est a Q. Fulvio et Ap. Claudio coss. 8. Cn. <u>Fulvius praetor male adversus Hannibalem pugnavit</u>. in quo proelio XX milia hominum ceciderunt; ipse cum equitibus CC effugit.	4.16.15–17 <u>Sempronius Gracchus proconsule ab hospite suo Lucano</u> quodam <u>in insidiis inductus occisus est</u>. 16. <u>Centenius Paenula centurio</u> decerni sibi ultro bellum <u>adversum Hannibalem petiit</u>: a quo cum octo milibus militum, quos <u>in aciem eduxerat, caesus est</u>. 17. post hunc <u>Cn. Fulvius praetor ab Hannibale victus</u> amisso exercitu <u>vix evasit</u>.
21.	26.2 <u>Capua capta est a Q. Fulvio</u> et Appio Claudio coss. <u>principes Campanorum veneno sibi mortem consciverunt</u>.	4.17.12 <u>Capua capta est a Q. Fulvio</u> proconsule; <u>principes Campanorum veneno mortem sibi consciverunt</u>.
22.	27.4 Claudius <u>Marcellus</u> T. Quintius Crispinus cos. speculandi causa progressi e castris <u>insidiis ab Hannibale circumventi sunt</u>. Marcellus <u>occisus</u>, Crispinus fugit.	4.18.8 <u>Hannibal utrumque consulem Marcellum et Crispinum insidiis circumventos interfecit</u>.
23.	30.1 <u>bina</u> hostium <u>castra</u> expugnavit, <u>in quibus XL milia hominum ferro ignique consumpta sunt</u>.	4.18.19 <u>in utrisque castris quadraginta milia hominum igni ferroque consumpta sunt</u>.

	Periochae	Orosius
24.	30.6 nobilissimumque egit <u>triumphum</u>, quem Q. <u>Terentius</u> Culleo senator <u>pilleatus secutus est</u>.	4.19.6 <u>triumphans</u> urbem ingressus est; <u>quem Terentius</u>, qui postea comicus, ex nobilibus Carthaginiensium captivis <u>pilleatus</u>—quod insigne indultae sibi libertatis fuit—triumphantem post currum <u>secutus est</u>.
25.	39.6 tamquam iungente fortuna circa idem tempus duo funera maximorum virorum, <u>Hannibal a Prusia, Bithyniae rege</u>, ad quem victo Antiocho confugerat, <u>cum</u> dederetur <u>Romanis</u>, qui ad exposcendum eum T. Quintium Flamininum miserant, <u>veneno mortem consciit. Philopoemen</u> quoque, <u>dux Achaeorum</u>, vir maximus, <u>a Messeniis occisus</u> veneno, cum ab his in bello captus esset.	4.20.29 isdem etiam diebus <u>Hannibal apud Prusiam Bithyniae regem</u>, cum a Romanis reposceretur, <u>veneno se necavit</u>, Philopoemenes, dux Achivorum a Messanis captus occisusque est.
26.	48.14 <u>provocatorem barbarum</u> tribunus militum <u>occidit</u>.	4.21.2 <u>barbarum provocantem</u> singulariter congressus <u>occidit</u>.
27.	56.8 <u>bellum servile in Sicilia ortum</u>.	5.6.3 <u>in Sicilia bellum servile ortum</u> est.
28.	61.2 <u>Cn. Domitius procos. adversus Allobrogas ad oppidum Vindalium feliciter pugnavit</u>.	5.13.2 <u>Gnaeus quoque Domitius proconsule Allobrogas Gallos iuxta oppidum Vindalium</u> gravissimo bello vicit.
29.	64.2 <u>o urbem venalem et cito perituram, si emptorem invenerit</u>.	5.15.5 <u>o urbem venalem et mature perituram, si emptorem invenerit</u>!
30.	67.4 <u>in triumpho</u> C. Mari <u>ductus ante currum eius Iugurtha cum duobus filiis et in carcere necatus est</u>.	5.15.19 qui <u>in triumpho ante currum cum duobus filiis</u> suis actus et mox in carcere strangulatus est.
31.	68.4 in quo caesa traduntur hostium milia CXL, capta LX.	5.16.17 <u>centum quadraginta milia eorum tunc in bello caesa, sexaginta milia capta dicuntur</u>.
32.	69.4 <u>idem</u> Apuleius <u>Saturninus</u> trib. pleb. C. <u>Memmium</u>, candidatum consulatus, quoniam adversarium eum actionibus suis timebat, <u>occidit</u>.	5.17.5 <u>idem Saturninus Memmium</u>, virum acrem et integrum, fieri consulem timens, orta subito seditione fugientem per P. Mettium satellitem informi stipite conminutum <u>interfecit</u>.
33.	69.5 in cuius causam et C. Marius, homo varii mutabilis ingenii consiliique semper secundum fortunam, transierat.	5.17.6 Marius consul accommodato ad tempus ingenio consensui bonorum sese inmiscuit.

THE *PERIOCHAE* AND OROSIUS   xix

	Periochae	Orosius
34.	71.1 M. <u>Livius Drusus trib. pleb.</u>, quo maioribus viribus senatus causam susceptam tueretur, <u>socios et Italicos populos spe civitatis</u> Romanae sollicitavit	5.18.2 <u>Livius Drusus, tribunus plebi, Latinos omnes spe libertatis</u> inlectos cum placito explere non posset, in arma excitavit.
35.	71.3 <u>incertum a quo domi occisus est.</u>	5.18.7 Drusus tantis malis anxius <u>domi suae incerto quidem auctore interfectus est.</u>
36.	72.1 Italici populi <u>defecerunt: Picentes, Vestini, Marsi, Paeligni, Marrucini, Samnites, Lucani.</u>	5.18.8 Igitur <u>Picentes Vestini Marsi Paeligni Marrucini Samnites Lucani</u> cum adhuc occultam <u>defectionem meditarentur.</u>
37.	74.1 <u>Cn. Pompeius Picentes proelio fudit.</u>	5.18.17 <u>Cn. Pompeius Picentes</u> gravi <u>proelio fudit.</u>
38.	77.4 C. <u>Marius</u> pater cum <u>in paludibus Minturnensium lateret, extractus est</u> ab oppidanis, et cum missus ad occidendum eum servus natione Gallus <u>maiestate tanti viri perterritus</u> recessisset.	5.19.7 <u>Marius</u> fugiens cum persequentum instantia circumsaeptus esset, <u>in Minturnensium paludibus sese abdidit</u>; e quibus infeliciter luto oblitus ignominioseque <u>protractus</u>, turpi autem spectaculo Minturnas deductus contrususque in carcerem percussorem ad se missum <u>solo vultu exterruit.</u>
39.	78.1 <u>iussuque eius, quidquid civium R. in Asia fuit uno die trucidatum est.</u>	6.2.2 crudeli praecepit <u>edicto, ut per totam Asiam quicumque inventi essent cives Romani sub una die omnes necarentur.</u>
40.	82.4 L. Valerius <u>Flaccus cos.</u>, collega Cinnae, missus ut Syllae succederet, propter avaritiam invisus exercitui suo a C. <u>Fimbria, legato ipsius, ultimae audaciae homine, occisus est.</u>	6.2.9 interea <u>Fimbria</u> Marianorum scelerum satelles, <u>homo omnium audacissimus, Flaccum consulem, cui legatus ierat,</u> apud Nicomediam <u>occidit</u>
41.	86.5 L. <u>Damasippus praetor ex voluntate C. Mari cos.</u> cum <u>senatum contraxisset</u>, omnem quae in urbe erat nobilitatem <u>trucidavit.</u> ex cuius numero Q. Mucius Scaevola pont. max. fugiens in vestibulo aedis Vestae occisus est.	5.20.4 <u>Damasippus praetor</u> incentore Mario consule Q. Scaevolam C. Carbonem L. Domitium P. Antistium <u>in curiam</u> quasi ad consultandum <u>vocatos</u> crudelissime <u>occidit.</u>
42.	90.5 L. Manlius procos. et M. <u>Domitius legatus ab Hirtuleio quaestore proelio victi sunt.</u>	5.23.3 <u>Domitius ab Hirtuleio</u> Sertorii <u>duce cum exercitu oppressus est.</u>
43.	95.2 <u>IIII et LXX gladiatores Capuae ex ludo Lentuli profugerunt</u> et congregata servitiorum ergastulorumque multitudine <u>Crixo et Spartaco ducibus.</u>	5.24.1 <u>gladiatores septuaginta et quattuor Capuae a ludo Cn. Lentuli diffugerunt.</u> qui continuo <u>ducibus Crixo</u> et Oenomao Gallis <u>et Spartaco</u> Thrace Vesuvium montem occupaverunt

	Periochae	Orosius
44.	106.2 A quibus <u>Cotta et Titurius, legati</u> Caesaris, <u>circumventi insidiis cum</u> exercitu cui praeerant <u>caesi sunt</u>.	6.10.1 <u>Cottam et Sabinum legatos</u> apud Eburonas <u>cum tota funditus legione insidiis circumventos interfecit</u>.
45.	110.1 C. Caesar <u>Massiliam, quae portas cluserat, obsedit</u> et <u>relictis in obsidione urbis eius legatis</u> C. Trebonio et D. Bruto <u>profectus in Hispaniam</u> L. Afranium et M. Petreium, legatus Cn. Pompei, cum VII legionibus ad Ilerdam in deditionem accepit omnesque incolumes dimisit, <u>Varrone</u> quoque, legato Pompei, <u>cum exercitu in potestatem suam</u> redacto.	6.15.6–7 mox Alpes transvectus <u>Massiliam venit, ad quam oppugnandam, cur receptus non esset, Trebonium</u> cum tribus legionibus <u>relinquens, ad Hispanias contendit</u>, quas <u>L. Afranius et M. Petreius</u> et M. Varro Pompeiani duces cum legionibus obtinebant. ibi multis proeliis Petreium Afraniumque superatos <u>conposita pactione dimisit</u>. 7. in ulteriore vero Hispania duas legiones a M. Varrone suscepit.
46.	111.1 pulsus urbe <u>Miloni exuli</u>, qui fugitivorum exercitum contraxerat, <u>se coniunxit</u>. <u>uterque</u>, cum bellum <u>molirentur, interfecti sunt</u>.	6.15.8 <u>se Miloni exuli iunxit</u>; cumque <u>ambo</u> servorum manu Capuam oppugnare <u>molirentur, occisi sunt</u>.
47.	116.3 ex his causis conspiratione in eum facta, cuius <u>capita fuerunt</u> M. Brutus et C. Cassius et ex Caesaris partibus Dec. Brutus et C. Trebonius, <u>in</u> Pompei <u>curia occisus est XXIII vulneribus</u>.	6.17.1 <u>auctoribus Bruto et Cassio</u>, conscio etiam plurimo senatu, <u>in curia viginti et tribus vulneribus confossus interiit</u>.

First of all, it is worth noting that the similarities in most of the examples listed in the table cannot be the result of the *Periochae* and Orosius independently drawing on Livy. In most of the cases where Livy's original survives, the shared language is not found in Livy's text (nos. 1, 2, 5, 6, 7, 16, 17, 18, 19, 20, 21, 23, 25); moreover, even when Livy's text does not survive, the restricted scale of the narrative in the *Periochae* and Orosius makes it all but impossible that they could independently be drawing on precisely the same few phrases from Livy's grand large-scale account. Either one is drawing on the other, or they are independently drawing from the same abridged history.

A very simple example of where the *Periochae* and Orosius appear on the face of things to be drawing independently on the same source comes with the passage discussed above in the context of demonstrating that the *Periochae* based itself on an epitome of Livy: namely the account of Marcellus' second victory at Nola in 215 (no. 19 in the table above). The wording of the *Periochae* and Orosius here is very close, and both share the comment on the battle which is not found in Livy himself. But neither, on the face of things, can depend on the other: the *Periochae* gives the location of the battle, but Orosius does not, while Orosius correctly reports Marcellus' status as proconsul, whereas the *Periochae*, apparently erroneously (but see *Per.* 23.10n. for a possible justification), calls him *praetor*. The most natural conclusion would appear to be that Orosius separately drew on the same Livian epitome as the *Periochae* did, but drew different elements from it.

A similar example comes with the heroic deed of M. Calpurnius Flamma during the First Punic War (no. 12). Here Orosius' version is considerably longer, and he includes many details that are not in the *Periochae*. But the *Periochae*'s language is closely reflected in Orosius, even if Orosius has more information: manifestly there is some relationship between the two texts. But that relationship cannot simply be that the *Periochae* is dependent on Orosius, since it has two pieces of information which Orosius does not: Calpurnius' *praenomen*, and the fact that he was *tribunus militum*. Here too one might naturally hypothesize that they were separately drawing on a shared source. Or one might note the account of Fimbria's murder of L. Valerius Flaccus (no. 41): there is significant overlap (notably the very similar descriptions of Fimbria's character), but here too each text has pieces of information which is not in the other (the *Periochae* gives Flaccus' full name, his consular colleague, and the fact that he succeeded Sulla in command, while Orosius mentions the location of the murder and Fimbria's being a supporter of Marius). Another instance is the deaths of Caelius and Milo (no. 46), where only the *Periochae* reports Caelius being expelled from Rome, while only Orosius mentions the attack on Capua.

Examples like this explain why the hypothesis of a 'lost epitome' as a source for both the *Periochae* and Orosius attracted so much support for so long: it is by far the neatest and easiest explanation, since each has details not in the other, and indeed one of the passages in question is one where we happen to have firm independent evidence, as discussed above, for the *Periochae* drawing on a first-century epitome. We can add that at certain points where the wording of Orosius and that of the *Periochae* do not overlap, such as *Per.* 33.5–34.1 and Orosius 4.20.10–14, they select exactly the same set of events to narrate in the same order, even though Livy narrates a number of other episodes between them which they overlook.[10]

However, generalizing from the individual instances here, either to the positive conclusion that the 'lost epitome' was a (or the) primary source for both the *Periochae* and Orosius, or to the negative conclusion that the Periochist and Orosius never consulted Livy directly, is problematic. With regard to the former, there is a consideration that is often overlooked: just how few instances there are of significant overlap between the *Periochae* and Orosius. Forty-seven examples may appear a lot when set out in a table like the one above, but they represent only a tiny proportion—less than 5 per cent—of the total narrative of the *Periochae*, and an even smaller proportion of the rather lengthier narrative of Orosius (which, admittedly, covers a far wider range of topics than the *Periochae* does, including numerous events that do not form part of Livy's text). Were these two

---

[10] Zangemeister (1882), 99, Ay (1894), 70.

authors both making significant use of an earlier epitome, one would surely expect a far greater overlap in their narrative details, if not necessarily in the exact language that they used.

This argument would not, of course, preclude one of the two authors making extensive use of the epitome, while the other one employed it only intermittently. I am not going to address the question of Orosius' sources here, which have recently been effectively re-examined by Peter Van Nuffelen, who has demonstrated that Orosius constructed his narrative not by following one source at a time, as was traditionally assumed, but by blending multiple sources even within a single episode (Van Nuffelen (2012), 93–114). One of Van Nuffelen's examples is the Curtius episode narrated in Livy 7.6.1–6: Van Nuffelen suggests that Livy's own text is one of the sources blended into Orosius' version (3.5: see Van Nuffelen (2012), 99–102), and I tentatively suggested that the three occasions when Orosius cites Livy by name indicate direct use of his text (Volume I, xxx). If we accept (as we should) Van Nuffelen's argument for Orosius' manner of working with his sources, it also undermines the provisional conclusion above, namely that shared wording combined with unique details in each individual source suggests the joint use of a Livian epitome. An alternative and (following Van Nuffelen) better conclusion would be that Orosius employed the *Periochae* as a source, but selected some material from it while adding information from other sources. That Orosius did indeed base himself on the *Periochae* is something that I will be demonstrating in more detail below; but what I will now be seeking to demonstrate is that the *Periochae*'s own working methods were not dissimilar to Orosius': the author of the *Periochae* did indeed employ Livy directly, but blended him with material taken from other sources, and the 'lost epitome' was simply one of those sources.

iii. The *Periochae* and Livy

There is an obvious difficulty about proving that the *Periochae* is sometimes dependent on Livy directly, rather than indirectly via an epitome of Livy. If we hypothesize that the *Periochae*, in using that epitome (as it sometimes demonstrably does), transfers material from it more or less verbatim, then anything that might appear to point to the *Periochae*'s use of Livy might equally be an example of the lost epitome using Livy, and the *Periochae* merely reproducing it.

But while that is a theoretical possibility if we simply consider these as texts in the abstract, it is far less plausible if we think of the cultural contexts of their production and reception. The closer that the *Periochae*'s wording is to the 'lost epitome's', the harder it is to make sense of the existence and survival of the *Periochae* at all: what reason can we imagine for someone to write an epitome of a narrative history, whose wording is largely drawn from that of a previous epitome of that same narrative history? Even if we assume that the *Periochae*'s justification was its abridgement of that earlier epitome, it is still difficult to understand why the author of the *Periochae* would care to spend time on it, or why it would supersede the earlier work so completely, especially given that the likely dating of the *Periochae* (see below) places it after the rise of the codex, and hence a time where even an unabridged epitome could comfortably be compassed within a single volume.[11]

And there are a considerable number of places where the *Periochae* is not merely summarizing Livy, or even reproducing Livy's words (something it regularly does, even if less frequently than one might have supposed), but appears to be engaging with his text in a creative way, the sort of creativity which only makes sense if the author has the actual text of Livy in front of him. It is hard to imagine that these are all merely the accidental consequence of reproducing the words of an earlier epitomizer. That argument might make sense if there were only a handful of instances, but, with dozens of examples on offer, it is *a priori* unlikely, for the reasons set out above, that the author of the *Periochae* would have reproduced so much of the text of his predecessor. And there are indeed many examples on offer; they are discussed in detail in the course of the commentary, but I will offer some brief illustrations here.

One feature of the *Periochae*'s summary of Livy is that even when the author draws the language of his summary from Livy, he does not always do so from the most obvious parts of Livy. As I will discuss later (below, liii–liv), aspects of his writing verge on pastiche, regularly introducing Livian turns of phrase at times when Livy himself happens not to use the phrase in question. This suggests at the very least a keen sense of Livy's characteristic writing style, and hence a knowledge of Livy's actual text. One example of this is particularly revealing. At 45.2 the *Periochae* uses the unusual phrase *editisque mandatis*, a phrase hardly found outside Livy, and which Livy himself uses just twice in his surviving work—but the second time he uses it is a passage of Book 45 that occurs not long after the episode which is being summarized by the *Periochae*. The most natural explanation for the *Periochae*'s use of that phrase here is that the author's reading of Book 45 as a whole drew (perhaps unconsciously) his attention to it.

There is a more focused form of this habit of introducing language from other parts of Livy's text. Very often the author of the *Periochae* will summarize Livy using language taken not from the point when the episode he is describing

---

[11] The closest and most obvious parallel, cited by Wölfflin (1900a), 2, is Paul the Deacon's abridgement of Festus, *De Significatione Verborum*, itself generally argued to be an abridgement (and adaptation) of the massive *De Significatione Verborum* of the Augustan antiquarian Verrius Flaccus. But the difference from what is hypothesized for Livy, the presumed 'lost epitome', and the *Periochae* is huge, partly because Paul was writing in the very different literary and cultural context of the court of Charlemagne, but more importantly because Paul shows no awareness of Verrius' original work underlying Festus: his dedicatory letter refers to the work of Festus alone, which at twenty volumes was itself long enough to make abridgement seem worthwhile. The *Periochae*, by contrast, is overtly structured around and makes constant reference to Livy's original.

originally appeared in the narrative, but from some later point when Livy refers back to the same episode. So, for example, the punishment of the troops defeated at Cannae is described by Livy in Book 23, and the *Periochae*, accordingly, includes a notice of the punishment in that book (23.8). But the language—and indeed, the substance—of the punishment is not taken from Livy Book 23, but from Livy's reference in Book 25 to the penalties that had been imposed on the Cannae army (25.5.10). The *Periochae*'s account of the birth of Servius Tullius (1.B.3) takes its wording not from Livy's narrative in Book 1, but from a reference back to the story in Book 4 (4.3.12). When the *Periochae* describes Marcius saving the Roman position in Spain after the killing of the Scipio brothers in Book 25 (25.11), the language comes from Livy's account of Scipio Africanus' reference back to it in Book 26 (26.41.5). More subtly, the description of the victory of L. Aemilius Regillus in Book 37 conflates the language of Livy's account of it in Book 37 with the reference back to it in Book 40 (37.58.3, 40.52.4). These are relatively exceptional, in as much as they draw material not from later in the same book of Livy, but from a different book altogether: rather more of these allusions to later (or, occasionally, earlier) passages come from the same book (examples include 5.1, 9.4, 23.13, 30.5, 37.4, 39.8, 42.1, 44.1). But the basic principle is the same in all of these cases: the *Periochae* is not simply working through Livy selecting and abridging his text, but is looking synoptically at Livy and relating different parts of his text to one another. Only someone with a strong sense of Livy's text would think to draw on a passage in Book 25 when summarizing an episode in Book 23.

These are, admittedly, relatively simple examples, and of themselves would not suggest any very sophisticated reading of Livy on the part of the author. More significant, however, is that sometimes the later passages from which the *Periochae* draws its summary are ones that offer a different perspective on Livy's narrative. For example, when the *Periochae* reports the tribunes' indignation at the unprecedented year-round campaign during the siege of Veii (5.1), the language used comes from the response to the tribunes by Appius Claudius, noting that they had no right to complain about the novelty of their military service, given that the pay the soldiers were receiving was no less novel (5.4.3). The description of Marcius bolstering the Roman position in Spain after the death of the Scipios, as noted above, comes from Africanus' speech in Book 26; however, one notable point about Africanus' speech is its pointed (and, as appears from Livy's narrative, unjust) failure to credit Marcius. The *Periochae*'s description not only restores Marcius to his rightful place, but obliquely draws attention to Africanus' injustice in excluding him. Along similar lines, the *Periochae*'s account of Q. Marcius Philippus' invasion of Macedonia during the Third Macedonian War apparently treats it as a success (44.1), but the language comes from a later account of it in Livy, where it is scathingly and ironically regarded as a failure (44.20.2).

Moreover, even when the author draws on aspects of Livy's language taken from the same episodes as he is summarizing, he often does so in a way that is surprisingly nuanced and pointed, and which suggests not merely a reproduction of but a critical engagement with the original. So, for example, Livy gives two alternative versions of the constitutional position of Fabius Maximus after the battle of Lake Trasimene: in the version he appears to endorse in his main narrative he has Fabius as dictator, but then he appends an alternative version, which he claims is more correct, in which Fabius was only acting dictator (22.31.8–11). The *Periochae*'s narrative, as one would expect, has Fabius as dictator, which is the mainstream version not only in Livy but elsewhere in the tradition—yet the language in which the *Periochae* describes his dictatorship is taken from Livy's alternative version (22.4): the author appears to be signalling his awareness of Livy's constitutional discussion even while overtly ignoring it.

The *Periochae*'s account of the Caudine Forks defeat in Book 9 is similar. Livy has a notorious discussion of the legal basis for the Roman repudiation of the treaty (9.5.1–5), arguing that the agreement struck by the defeated consul was not a *foedus* but a *sponsio*. The *Periochae* treats it, apparently uncomplicatedly, as a *foedus*, which is the view of the vast majority of the historical tradition (9.1), but introduces a phrase from Livy, including the specific word *spoponderant*, which in Livy is premised on the opposite interpretation. In the same way, Livy at the end of the episode doubts whether the Romans' legalistic repudiation of the agreement did indeed clear the state of wrongdoing (9.11.13). The *Periochae* overtly expresses no such doubts, but when the consul proposes his plan to repudiate the agreement, the author uses an adaptation of the very phrase in which Livy expressed doubt, as if alerting the reader to the potential problems with the consul's position. Or one might note the *Periochae*'s description in Book 2 of how Horatius Cocles at the bridge held off the attacking Etruscans alone, as indeed he does in most versions of the story (2.5). But in Livy Horatius is not alone, but has two companions—and the language used by the *Periochae* specifically alludes to the places where Livy described Horatius being assisted by those companions.

Sometimes the *Periochae* alludes to the wider context in Livy not so much by direct use of Livy's language, but rather by the inclusion of a detail which is apparently superfluous to the story as the *Periochae* narrates it, but points the reader to a complicating feature of the narrative. An example is 34.3, where the author notes that Flamininus reaches a settlement with Nabis of Sparta *qualem ipse volebat* ('in the manner he personally wanted'). If one reads the *Periochae* in isolation from Livy, this looks odd—why would anyone doubt that Flamininus wanted the settlement that he himself agreed to? Only knowledge of the Livian context, in which Flamininus is resisting the harsher terms desired by his Greek allies, explains the phrase.

All of these examples suggest direct use of Livy by the *Periochae*. Were there just one or two of them, they could possibly be explained as merely tralatician: the author of the *Periochae* unwittingly inserted material from an earlier epitome which was making clever allusions to Livy. But so many examples make that improbable, for the reason explained above: were the *Periochae* doing little more than constantly and inertly repeating the language of an earlier epitomizer, it is hard to explain why the author would bother producing his text at all. The simplest and most economic explanation is that the author of the *Periochae* was well acquainted with Livy's original text, and that at least some of the time he was working from it directly.

There is another consideration which leads to the same conclusion. The *Periochae* not only shows signs of dependence on Livy's original text: it also contains various nods to other classic authors, above all Cicero and Valerius Maximus. So, for example, the *Periochae*'s account of Tarquinius Priscus' challenge to Attus Navius (1.B.2) follows the language of Cicero, *Div.* 1.32 rather than the account in Livy 1.36.3–6. Livy gives no explicit explanation for the honouring of the Roman ambassadors killed at Fidenae, so the *Periochae*, which does offer an explanation (4.5), takes it almost verbatim from Cicero, *Phil.* 9.4. The *Periochae*'s summary account of the abolition of debt-bondage at Rome (8.10) takes its wording from the summary of the same event in Cicero's own abridged history of Rome at *Rep.* 2.59. Indeed, occasionally the *Periochae*'s narrative reflects Cicero not only in wording, but even in its facts: thus the description of the killing of Spurius Maelius (4.4) derives from the version of the story in Cicero, *Sen.* 56 (where it is ordered by Cincinnatus), rather than Livy's (where Ahala alone is responsible).

Especially interesting is a cluster of passages which depend closely on a single passage of Cicero: *Off.* 1.39–40, which is drawn on by the *Periochae* in three separate places: 13.7, 18.5, and 22.8. Since Livy's original text survives only with the last of these, it obviously cannot be demonstrated conclusively that this is an example of the direct use of Cicero by the *Periochae*: it is theoretically possible that it is Livy who employed Cicero's language in Books 13 and 18, and the *Periochae* is simply following Livy. Against that, however, is that Livy certainly narrated the stories in question at far greater length than either Cicero or the *Periochae* did, and it seems a vanishingly improbable coincidence that Livy incorporated the language of Cicero into his full-length accounts, and that the *Periochae*, in condensing Livy, just happened to select the very places where Livy had drawn on Cicero. Far more probable is that it is the author of the *Periochae* who had recourse to Cicero's language in creating his summary of Livy.

In the case of Valerius Maximus the case is even clearer, since Valerius postdates Livy and indeed appears to have employed him regularly as a source: but in a number of places the *Periochae*'s language is far closer to Valerius' than it is to Livy's. That is the case, for example, with Camillus' removal of the statue of Juno from Veii to Rome (5.3: cf. Val. Max. 1.8.3), or Manlius Torquatus' return to Rome after the Latin War (8.4: cf. Val. Max. 9.3.4), or the prayer of Aemilius Paullus at the time of Pydna (44.3:[12] cf. Val. Max. 5.10.2). On other occasions, though the language is not distinctively from Valerius, the elements of Livy's narrative chosen

---

[12] This passage is exceptional within the *Periochae* for other reasons: cf. below.

for summarizing by the *Periochae* mirror very closely the selection that had previously been made by Valerius, as with the triumph of Livius Salinator and Claudius Nero after their victory at the Metaurus (28.2: cf. Val. Max. 4.1.9), and the contentious censorship of the same two figures (29.14–15: cf. Val. Max. 2.9.6).

Of course, it is theoretically possible, as with the elements which were suggested above to show direct dependence on Livy, that these allusions to Cicero and Valerius derive from the earlier epitome; but, as also with Livy, their sheer number makes that improbable. And here there is a further consideration also. There is at least one passage in the *Periochae* which derives neither from Livy nor from Cicero nor from Valerius, but from Julius Paris' summary of Valerius, namely the account of Antiochus' release of Scipio Africanus' son before the battle of Magnesia (37.3: cf. Paris 2.10.2). Since Paris is himself writing in later antiquity, his language cannot have reached the *Periochae* via the lost epitome of Livy, which must have pre-dated Plutarch. The *Periochae* must have drawn on Paris directly.

Thus, even in terms of its sources alone, the *Periochae* is far from being simply a condensation of Livy. While articulating itself around Livy's narrative and the structure of Livy's text, it draws on other sources also. And, as noted above, this has implications for its use of Livy. It seems highly unlikely that the author of the *Periochae* would make direct use of at least two completely extraneous authors, and yet would never have recourse to the text of the author he was purportedly summarizing.

So we have good reason to believe that the author of the *Periochae*, far from simply abridging an earlier epitome, or indeed simply abridging Livy himself, was doing something far more complicated. At least on the evidence of his summary of the surviving Livian books, he based himself on Livy's own text, but, when constructing the abridgement, he at different times had recourse to other texts, either the earlier epitome which had itself summarized Livy, but also apparently extraneous sources like Cicero and Valerius Maximus, both widely read in later antiquity.

When described in this way, the process may sound strange, but it probably should not. I consider myself more than averagely knowledgeable in the text of Livy, but if I am searching for a passage whose location I have forgotten, or where I roughly know its location but want to remind myself quickly of its general sense, rather than reading through the entire Latin text, I will often have recourse to other tools—to the indices and summaries that are contained in various modern published texts and translations of Livy, or indeed sometimes to the *Periochae* itself. I do so in full knowledge that those indices and summaries (and even more the *Periochae*) may not be entirely reliable, but I weigh up the likely investment of time to find what I need in the original text against the probability that those secondary sources may be wrong on the specific question which I seek to answer. I have not surveyed my colleagues on this question, but I would be very surprised if they do not do the same thing. People employ whatever tools they have to hand,

and that is likely to have been at least as true in antiquity as it is today—indeed, more so, given the lack of many of the resources, both printed and electronic, that we can nowadays use to orient ourselves within Livy's text.

So it is of little surprise that the author of the *Periochae* supplemented his own reading of Livy by drawing on an earlier epitome—indeed, it would be of more surprise had he austerely insisted on ignoring the latter. It may seem more strange that he had recourse to Cicero and Valerius, but that is easily explicable when one recalls the blurring in later antiquity between Livy's actual text and the general traditions of Republican history, which I discussed in the Introduction to Volume I (xxi–xxii). The *Periochae* often adjusts Livy in the light of familiar traditions about the Republic, even when those familiar traditions are not reflected in Livy's own writing (I discuss this in more detail below, l–lii). His drawing of texts that related Republican history independently of Livy is part of the same phenomenon. More generally, the use of Cicero and Valerius alongside Livy makes sense in terms of the highly textualized culture of late antiquity, the period in which the *Periochae* was almost certainly composed (below, lv–lvi). Much of the Latin literary culture of the time was centred on the creation of texts through the allusive reworking of other texts. The practice of epitomizing in many genres is just one aspect of that; others include the popularity of centos,[13] and the growth of the commentary tradition, and even 'original' works such as Ammianus or the *Historia Augusta* which engage constantly through a patchwork of allusions with a large variety of predecessors.[14] That the *Periochae* shows something of the same texture is a sign of its own connections with the literary culture of the day.

iv. The *Periochae* and Orosius Revisited (also Augustine, Eutropius…)

The above discussion has established that the *Periochae* made direct use both of Livy and of an early epitome of Livy, and that it also incorporated material from other writers into the texture of his work. Orosius shows every sign of having done the same (above, xx–xxii). So, with that in mind, we need to reconsider the relationship between the *Periochae* and Orosius. The forty-seven passages listed above where their wording overlaps shows that either one used the other, or they were both dependent on a third source. With most of them it is hard to distinguish between these possibilities, but there are a number which strongly indicate Orosius' use of the *Periochae*.

---

[13] See Formisano and Sogno (2010) for the cento as a particular instance of late antique textualization.

[14] For the strongly allusive texture of Ammianus, see esp. Kelly (2008); for the *Historia Augusta* esp. Rohrbacher (2016).

One clear example is *Per.* 23.6 = Oros. 4.16.11 (no. 18 in Table 1). *cum exercitu caesus est* is one of the *Periochae*'s standard phrases (22.2, 25.6, 27.1, 33.5, 53.2, 65.5, 80.2, 103.1, 110.5; cf. 25.10, 50.12, 106.2). Orosius, by contrast, uses the phrase nowhere except here (though cf. 4.20.23), and it appears nowhere else in surviving Latin apart from Front., *Princip. Hist.* 3 (though see Livy 28.19.2, 28.41.14 and Frontin., *Strat.* 2.5.24 for related language). This makes it overwhelmingly likely that Orosius took it from the *Periochae*.

Another instance is *Per.* 25.5–8 = Oros. 4.16.15–17 (no. 20). Here Orosius and the *Periochae* are extremely close to one another in wording, structure, and length over a series of separate notices. The similarity in length makes it very unlikely that both can have abstracted their narrative from a putatively longer epitome while arriving at such similar wording. The *Periochae* is, moreover, drawing on a relatively narrow section of Livy (25.16–21), which the author follows sequentially: Orosius has exactly the same sequence, with one exception, namely the omission of the notice about the siege of Capua (*Per.* 25.7: the omission is easily explicable, since Orosius' account of the Second Punic War in general shows little interest in that aspect of it). It seems far less probable that the *Periochae* drew on Orosius and then inserted a brief notice about Capua at the appropriate point than that the *Periochae* summarized a passage of Livy and then was used as a source by Orosius.

A more interesting example is *Per.* 3.6 = Oros. 2.13.2 (no. 4). In this case Orosius does have information that the *Periochae* does not, namely the dating of the decemvirate by Olympiads. But, as noted above, this is easily explicable in terms of Orosius' regular compositional practice, and in this case his particular interest in chronological markers would make it very natural to supplement the Livian date reproduced by the *Periochae* with an Olympiadic one taken from a separate source. More significant is that there is an oddity in Orosius' account. He refers to the decemvirs being commissioned 'to establish Attic laws' (*constituendarum legum Atticarum gratia*), which appears a bizarre misreading if he were deriving his account from Livy, who does indeed speak of 'Attic laws' being brought back from Athens as a model for the decemvirs to use (3.32.6), but does not suggest that the laws that the decemvirs themselves actually created were in any sense 'Attic'. But an examination of the *Periochae* explains how Orosius reached that conclusion. The *Periochae* says *adlatis Atticis legibus ad constituendas eas*, which appears to mean literally 'with Attic laws brought in order to establish them [sc. the laws]'. This translation, however, makes no sense: instead *eas* needs to be understood as the equivalent of *tales* 'similar laws' (see commentary *ad loc.*). It is easy to see, however, how Orosius could have misinterpreted this to mean that the decemvirs literally established 'Attic laws'. The oddity of Orosius' account is entirely explicable on the assumption that he was basing it on the *Periochae*.

Even on occasions when Livy's original does not survive, there are clear indications of Orosius' use of the *Periochae*. One such example is *Per.* 17.4 = Oros.

4.8.1–2 (no. 12). Here there are a number of verbal overlaps between the *Periochae* and Orosius, as noted in the table above—but Orosius incorporates into his narrative the phrase *qui lecta trecentorum manu insessum ab hostibus tumulum occupavit*, which has no parallel in the *Periochae*, but is taken verbatim from Flor. 1.18.13. There are, however, no verbal parallels between Florus and the *Periochae* in this section, nor any other parallels between Florus and Orosius; moreover, Florus, unlike the *Periochae* and Orosius, mistakenly assigns the episode to Caiatinus' dictatorship rather than his consulship. Hence it is highly improbable that all three authors could have been drawing on a single source, or that the *Periochae* and Orosius were separately drawing on Florus, and even less so that the *Periochae* could be drawing on Orosius while coincidentally omitting exactly the words that corresponded to Florus. The most straightforward explanation is that Orosius had the texts of both the *Periochae* and Florus in front of him, and that he incorporated a phrase from the latter into a narrative derived from the former.

But the most interesting example of all is *Per.* 11.1 = Oros. 3.22.6–7 (no. 8). As argued in the Commentary (see *ad loc.*), the correct reading in both the *Periochae* and Orosius is not the commonly accepted *iturum*, but the *iterum* supported by all the major MSS of the *Periochae* and a number of those of Orosius: this alludes to the fact that this was the second time that the elder Fabius accompanied his son as his *legatus*, although neither text has referred to the first occasion in its earlier narrative. This is extremely unlikely to come from a shared source such as an epitome. We can imagine that one author, in drawing on this hypothetical epitome, artfully retained a mention of Fabius' second legateship without mentioning the first; we can even imagine that a second author, reading a predecessor who used this artful device, decided to retain it. But it seems implausible that two separate authors will have hit on the same artful device independently of each other. We could in theory attribute the artful device to the prior epitome, but that too seems unlikely. The earlier epitome is (*ex hypothesi*) much longer than either the *Periochae* or Orosius, and so will have included more details of the campaigns, and thus would have referred to Fabius' first legateship explicitly, since (according to Zonar. 8.1.10) the legateship of the father was the fundamental cause of the son's initial defeat.

Accordingly, either Orosius or the *Periochae* must have derived this episode from the other, and there is a strong presumption that the *Periochae* must have been the original, since Orosius, for the only time in his text, uses the *Periochae*'s standard phrase *male adversus...pugnasset*.

No other author's work shows as strong an overlap with the *Periochae* as Orosius does, and accordingly it is harder to work out any potential relationships. Eutropius is perhaps the closest, but precise parallels with the *Periochae* are both fewer in number than between the *Periochae* and Orosius, and mostly less close linguistically even when they exist.[15] There is, however, one passage that seems to imply that Eutropius may have been dependent on the *Periochae* much as Orosius was. As noted above, the *Periochae*, in the context of the Roman settlement with Nabis of Sparta, says that Flamininus made the peace *qualem ipse volebat* ('in the manner he personally wanted'); it was argued above that this is an allusion to the fact that, in Livy, Flamininus disputed the terms of the settlement with his Greek allies, who wanted harsher terms. Interestingly, exactly the same idea, albeit in quite different wording, appears in Eutr. 4.2.2: 'he received his surrender on the terms he wanted' (*quibus voluit condicionibus in fidem accepit*). The oblique allusion is, however, much more plausibly originating with the *Periochae* than with Eutropius: the *Periochae* is premised on a single prior text in which that story is told and to whom he could be alluding, whereas Eutropius purports to be writing an independent account, and subtle hints at untold parts of the story are not at all like his usual manner.

If the *Periochae* predated Eutropius, who wrote between AD 364 and 380, it necessarily follows that it predated Augustine as well. Direct verbal overlaps between the *Periochae* and Augustine are even rarer than they are in Eutropius (though see *Per.* 4.4 and 11.6 and Aug., *Civ.* 3.17, with commentary *ad locc.*). There is, however, one clear instance where Augustine appears to have adopted the language of the *Periochae* in a manner that strongly suggests that he is making direct use of it (cf. Felmy (2001), 109–10). At *Per.* 2.1 the author has a subtle reworking of Brutus' expulsion of Collatinus which suggests that Brutus was acting cannily and manipulating Collatinus into resigning the consulship; Augustine (*Civ.* 2.17) reworked this into a version where Brutus was not only the prime mover, but was actually acting in opposition to the people (see commentary *ad loc.*).

Another text that appears to have made intermittent use of the *Periochae* is the anonymous *De Viris Illustribus*; for the most part there is insufficient overlap between them to suggest that one is dependent on the other, but an exception is the account of the trial and exile of Scipio Africanus (*Per.* 38.8–9 = *Vir. Ill.* 49.17–18). Here the wording of the two texts is very close, but the *Periochae* derives part of its phrasing, as often (cf. above) from the 'wrong' text of Livy: an earlier reference to Gracchus' enmity with Scipio Africanus is transferred into an account of Gracchus' formal intercession as tribune on behalf of Scipio

---

[15] In addition to the example discussed in the text, the following parallels may be observed: *Per.* 7.5 = Eutr. 2.5; *Per.* 7.8 = Eutr. 2.6.4; *Per.* 9.4 = Eutr. 2.9.2; *Per.* 13.2 = Eutr. 2.12.2; *Per.* 15.4 = Eutr. 2.16; *Per.* 20.8 = Eutr. 3.5 (also Oros. 4.13.6: see above); *Per.* 21.1 = Eutr. 3.7.2; *Per.* 31.3 = Eutr. 4.1; *Per.* 37.7 = Eutr. 4.4.3; *Per.* 51.3 = Eutr. 4.12.1; *Per.* 52.6 = Eutr. 4.16.2; *Per.* 55.5 = Eutr. 4.17.1; *Per.* 59.1 = Eutr. 4.19; *Per.* 67.4 = Eutr. 4.27.4 (also Oros. 5.15.19: see above); *Per.* 68.4 = Eutr. 5.2.2; *Per.* 77.1 = Eutr. 5.4.2; *Per.* 89.6 = Eutr. 5.9.1; *Per.* 95.2 = Eutr. 6.7.2 (also Oros. 5.24.1: see above); *Per.* 116.3 = Eutr. 6.25 (also Oros. 6.17.1).

Asiaticus—and in this case the *Periochae* has a metatextual hint at the use of the earlier passage by including the word *antea* (see *ad loc.*). *Vir. Ill.* employs the same phrase, but without the *antea*. The best way of making sense of this is that *Vir. Ill.* is working from the *Periochae*, and is failing to recognize (or is uninterested in reproducing) the Livian intertext.

v. The Narrative of the *Periochae*

(a) Form, Structure, and Voice

One further theory concerning the *Periochae* can be mentioned at this point: namely the theory associated above all with Alfred Klotz,[16] that the text does not have a single author in any meaningful sense, because it grew by accretion, with a fairly brief original text then supplemented by later writers.

In principle there is no reason why this could not have occurred. There is no doubt that texts of this sort did exist in antiquity and later, especially texts within what may broadly be referred to as the 'commentary' tradition, where each commentator on a text builds on material assembled by his predecessors;[17] it would not have been especially surprising if the *Periochae* had developed in the same way. Such a hypothesis would have the advantage of providing a straightforward explanation for the large disparity in the lengths of the summaries in different books of the epitome (Volume I, xxviii–xxix with Fig. 1): some books received more elaboration by later hands than others did. It also readily explains how so many places could arise where the version of the *Periochae* varies from Livy's own, since the elaborators of the spare original could easily be introducing details from other sources altogether (Klotz suggested that a collection of *exempla* lay behind much of it). However, there are other possible explanations for both of those disparities (cf. e.g. below, li–lii); and there are even more significant points that tell against Klotz's theory. Part of the evidence against it is the very patchiness of the *Periochae* (cf. below): there are numerous episodes in Livy which receive no notices at all, which tells against the idea that the original core could have been some form of brief contents-list which was then elaborated. Just as important is the distinctive and consistent style in which the *Periochae* is written,[18] with formulaic phrases constantly recurring (see below), but a still more important part of it is the narrative consistency of the work: the text shows consistent biases and

---

[16] Klotz (1913), (1936); the idea was originally proposed by Otto Jahn in the introduction to his edition (Jahn (1853), x–xiii).

[17] An example is the commentary on Horace that comes down to us under the name of Pomponius Porphyrio: its core is indeed the commentary of Porphyrio, but it has been repeatedly supplemented and edited by a series of other hands (see Zetzel (2018), 151–3).

[18] So e.g. Wölfflin (1877), 339; cf. more broadly Brunt (1980), 478 on the way authors of historical epitomes tended to maintain a fairly consistent style.

interests which are most naturally explained by the hypothesis of a single author, as I shall discuss shortly.[19]

Moreover, and perhaps most important of all, the *Periochae* as a whole appears to be written for a reader who is seeking a coherent narrative of Roman history, and the text supplies such a narrative: in this respect it is very unlike the three other surviving ancient epitomes of Livy, all of which are far more piecemeal and which could not be read as a narrative with anything like the same ease.

It is true that on a superficial reading the *Periochae* appears highly atomized. A great deal of the work is structured around a series of brief 'notices', each 'notice' wrapping up an entire story into a self-contained sentence which recounts what appears to be a discrete episode in Roman history (though there are exceptions, where a story is narrated in far greater detail: examples include 35.1 and much of Books 48 and 49). As Love observes, moreover, there are aspects of certain of its notices which appear to encourage an atomized reading (Love (2019), 84–5): her example is Nabis in Books 32–35, who is carefully identified as *Lacedaemoniorum tyrannus* on each of his four appearances (32.7, 34.3, 34.7, 35.3), as if assuming a reader who was simply looking at this one episode and who could not be expected to recall him from the earlier episodes, even though they occurred just a few lines before.

But reading through the sequence of notices shows the art with which they are created. First is the very fact that many of the notices are self-contained, revealing a final outcome to each episode: that may appear an obvious method of summary, but it is very unlike the 'A' *Periochae*, whose oblique notices could not be read easily in such a fashion (cf. the introduction to *Per.* 1 for further discussion). Moreover, on those occasions when a notice manifestly fails to indicate the final outcome of a story, a further notice will provide a satisfactory conclusion. So, when renegade troops occupy Rhegium at 12.5, we are told of the fate of those troops at 15.2. The episode of Mago's invasion of Italy at 28.10 and 29.3 is rounded off with his death at 30.7. The Spanish rebel Viriathus is introduced at 52.6, but we are told of his murder at 54.5; the slave revolt in Sicily in the 130s begins at 56.8–9 and concludes at 59.2. Spartacus' revolt takes place at 95.2, with Spartacus himself and Crixus named as the leaders; we are then told of the death of Crixus at 96.1 and that of Spartacus himself, along with the remainder of his army, at 97.2. When it comes to larger-scale elements of Livy's narrative, the *Periochae* follows them through multiple books; for example Caesar's conquest of Gaul, which is described in a series of notices between 103.10 and 108.4. This is not to say, of course, that the *Periochae* provides anything like a comprehensive distillation of Livy's narrative, since it demonstrably omits numerous episodes from it. But those omissions are generally invisible to the reader who has no independent

---

[19] Heyer (1875), 650–1 already made this point briefly in response to Jahn's theory; also Wölfflin (1877), 340–1.

knowledge of Livy's text: at most the *Periochae* slyly includes a hint to an aspect that is not overtly present (cf. above, xxv).

Indeed, even the point that Love observes as apparently suggesting a less coherent narrative, the provision of apparently extraneous information as if addressed to those who are reading that notice in isolation, when examined in more detail, reveals patterns which suggest a more coherent approach to the narrative rather than a less coherent one. First, it should be noted that Nabis is an outlying case: most characters are not constantly reintroduced in this fashion.[20] So, for example, L. Cornelius Cinna is first mentioned as 'L. Cinna', as an ambassador to the Marsi during the Social War (76.4); he is then reintroduced as 'L. Cornelius Cinna cos.' at the beginning of Book 79 (79.1), leaving it unclear to the reader whether or not he is the same L. Cinna (a point that matters little to the narrative). But on every one of his ten subsequent appearances between then and his final mention at 84.1, he is simply 'Cinna', apart from 83.4, where he is 'L. Cinna', formally marking his election to his final consulship. Moreover, the author of the *Periochae* sometimes uses 'extraneous' information of the sort Love discusses, not to fragment the narrative, but rather to mark its progress. The case of Philip V of Macedon is an especially interesting one. He is first introduced when he makes an alliance with Hannibal at 23.11, where he is *Macedoniae rex*. He is then regularly (though not uniformly) referred to as *Macedoniae rex* or *Macedonum rex* through the period of the First Macedonian War, and then again is reintroduced in that fashion at the start of the Second Macedonian War (31.1). But from then onwards he is always simply *Philippus*, or occasionally *Philippus rex*, except on two occasions when his full title is mentioned, once as a formal marker of Flamininus as victor over him at the time of his triumph (34.8), and once when mentioning the conflict of his sons over the succession to his kingdom (40.2). In this way, the author of the *Periochae*, by ostentatiously implying that Philip needs constant reintroduction, marks the First Macedonian War as secondary to the Hannibalic War with which it was concurrent, but once Philip is the primary antagonist, the knowledge of his position is assumed.

This ability of the *Periochae* to be read as a coherent narrative presumably explains why it continued to be copied and read and survives to this day, and why it was drawn on by so many other late antique writers of history (above): in many respects, despite its overt orientation as a summary of Livy, it reads in a manner not altogether different from other abridged narrative histories in antiquity, such as Florus, Eutropius, or Festus.[21] And like those histories, the *Periochae* has a

---

[20] For the reasons the *Periochae* might have done this in the case of Nabis see 34.8, 35.3nn.

[21] For an examination of the *Periochae*'s qualities as an independent narrative cf. Jal (1984), lxxxiii–lxxxvii. More recently Love (2019) has engaged in a revisionist examination of various abridged post-Livian histories, placing the *Periochae* and the Oxyrhynchus Epitome side by side with Florus, Eutropius, and Festus as works which each present meaningful and distinctive narratives in their own right.

distinct slant and its own particular set of interests, which do not always coincide with Livy's. This can be seen on a large scale with the construction of the narrative. For example, Livy speaks of the Samnite Wars as a single sequence which began with the First Samnite War in the late 340s and only ended with the defeat of Pyrrhus (who allied himself to the Samnites) in the 270s; but within that he marks a clear division between the First and the Second War, and he sees the power of the Samnites comprehensively broken during the Third War with the Roman victory at Aquilonia, even though fighting still continued after that point. The *Periochae*, by contrast, elides the First War into the Second, by failing to record the peace treaty that ended the First or the *casus belli* which began the Second (for detailed discussion see 8.1n. and 8.9–12nn.); with regard to the Third War it plays down Papirius Cursor's victory at Aquilonia (10.8), while the later victory by Curius Dentatus, who for other writers achieved the decisive victory over the Samnites, is treated as though it came in a different war altogether (11.4n.). Instead he narrates a version in which the decisive victory is the intervening one achieved by Fabius Gurges (11.1n). Another example occurs within the Second Punic War: Livy explicitly describes the war as being in the balance prior to Scipio's victory at New Carthage (26.37), and his narrative in Book 25 and Book 26 reflects that, with major successes in both books balanced by significant defeats. The *Periochae* offers a very different dynamic: it largely suppresses or minimizes the victories in Book 25 and the defeats in Book 26, and so makes the end of Book 25 more of a turning point in the war than Livy had.[22]

Another aspect of the strong narrative movement of the *Periochae* is how often the author links together different episodes. A particularly striking instance is at 52.7, where the account of the rule of Alexander Balas refers back to the assassination of Demetrius Soter (48.19), and does so with a phrase (*sicut ante dictum est*) which self-consciously refers to the *Periochae*'s earlier description. At other times there is simply a repetition of the earlier point: so, for example, the prosecution of Claudius Pulcher's sister (19.6) mentions his defeat at 19.2. Scipio Nasica's (alleged: see *ad loc.*) dedication of the temple of the Magna Mater (36.2) refers back to his receiving of the image of the goddess at 29.7; Glabrio's triumph at 37.8 refers (in identical language) to the expulsion of Antiochus from Greece (36.1) that qualified him for it; the description of Scipio Aemilianus' games at the capture of Carthage (51.6) alludes back to the victory of his father, Aemilius Paullus, over Macedon. Decimus Brutus' conquest of Lusitania (55.6) is mentioned again when he defeats the Iapydae (59.12). When Pompey is first introduced (85.3) there is an allusion to his father's capture of Asculum during the Social War (74.1). Other connections are marked by parallel language: so, for example, Marcellus' winning of the *spolia opima* at 20.9 uses a virtually identical phrase to that used of

---

[22] On Livy's nuanced treatment of the turn in the war in Books 25 and 26, cf. Levene (2010a), 15–16, *contra* Burck (1962), 13–26.

Cossus' winning of them at 4.6, or the repeated selection of M. Aemilius Lepidus as *princeps senatus* is recorded in a sequence of books (43.6, 46.6, 47.4, 48.7), or the parallel movements of Scipio and Mago at 28.8 (cf. 28.10) use identical phrasing. Some of these may reflect allusions in Livy himself, but manifestly not all of them do: for example, the account of Glabrio's triumph at Livy 37.46.3–4 does not refer back to the details of his victory in Book 36.

And still more are not directly marked at all, but the author highlights particular events and allows them effectively to be juxtaposed to related events, as they would not have been in Livy, simply because of the abbreviation of his narrative. Thus, proportionate to the length of his text, he pays rather more attention to the First Macedonian War than Livy does (23.11, 24.4, 26.4, 27.8, 28.1, 29.5); it seems plausible to suggest that this is precisely because it can more effectively act as a preliminary to the Second War in the *Periochae* than it does in Livy, where more than a book separates the two. With the later books, where Livy's original text does not survive, it is harder to be certain whether the *Periochae*'s emphasis is its own or whether it reflects that of Livy, but the very fact of the abridgement means that similar events are placed in closer proximity than they ever could have been in Livy: thus the revolutionary tribunate and killing of Saturninus (Book 69) occurs eight books and more than twenty years after that of Gaius Gracchus (Book 61), but the compression of the *Periochae* leaves them only a couple of pages apart.

The *Periochae* shows an interest in shaping its narrative in other ways also. More than 10 per cent of the books are given dramatic closural force by ending on a death (14.8, 18.5, 30.7, 48.19, 55.7, 60.10, 71.3, 83.8, 88.3, 91.3, 92.4, 116.8, 121.2, 124.3, 133.3, 140.2, 142.2–3). Of course, it is probable that some of these were inherited from Livy, but manifestly not all of them were, since in the one case where the corresponding book of Livy has survived (30.7) the *Periochae* has rearranged Livy's order so as to make a death the final element of the book (see further below). Also with regard to the shaping of books, the author at least some of the time seems concerned to provide an internal sense of narrative movement within them: so while some books (e.g. Book 15) are narrated in a very disjointed fashion, others (e.g. Book 22, or Book 58, or Book 112) maintain a strong connection between the separate notices in the book so as to give the effect of a fluid narrative across the book.

The *Periochae*'s concern for shaping its narrative within the book helps explain one further feature of it, namely its occasional willingness to change Livy's narrative order.[23] A regular reason for the *Periochae* to do this is to tidy up the narrative by unifying separate events into a single notice. So, for example, at 4.8 three episodes concerning Fidenae, which are separated in Livy (not least because they

---

[23] As Bingham 390–2 argues, this is better seen as a sign of the author's command of the Livian text than his ignorance of it, since he is able to unify under a single heading disparate parts of that text.

THE NARRATIVE OF THE *PERIOCHAE* xxxvii

occur in separate years), are united in a single notice; at 8.6 the same is done with two colony foundations from different years. The story of Coriolanus, which in Livy is broken by the story of the vision of Latinius, is treated by the *Periochae* at a single point after the Latinius story (2.11). At 2.7 the *Periochae* moves the arrival at Rome of the first Appius Claudius to a time after the battle of Lake Regillus, and then rolls it into a single notice with the foundation of the Claudian tribe, which in Livy occurs later. Moreover, in this last case the repositioning makes for a telling juxtaposition, since the next notice (2.8) relates to the first secession of the plebs: the appearance on the stage of the famously anti-plebeian Claudians receives an immediate response (see further the Commentary *ad loc.*). The antithesis of the Claudians here, for the *Periochae*, is the conciliatory Menenius Agrippa who brings the plebs back to the city, and here too the *Periochae* rearranges its material, so as to include his death, which occurs later in Livy. Effectively the *Periochae*, by its arrangement, not only makes Livy less piecemeal, but also provides a structure of its own which represents Livy's account of class conflict in a different fashion from Livy's own.

As this last example indicates, not all of the *Periochae*'s rearrangements can be explained by its habits of summary: some suggest broader narrative aims. The victory in the war with Antiochus III in Book 37 is followed immediately by Scipio Asiaticus receiving his honorific *cognomen* (37.5), which in Livy does not occur until the end of the book: this sequence provides a stronger narrative arc to that war. As noted above, the *Periochae* transfers the death of Mago to the end of Book 30 in order to create closure to that book (30.7). The *Periochae* will sometimes move an event, not in order to create a single combined notice, but in order not to break up some other narrative sequence, for example at 6.5, where a land law is moved to appear after the law permitting plebeian consulships, which has been the primary focus of the preceding notices. Likewise, in Book 22 two anecdotes from the dictatorship of Fabius Maximus are placed outside the main narrative of his conflict with Minucius, whereas in Livy they are interwoven with it (22.5–6): the Fabius-Minucius conflict is thus tightened.[24] A more complex example is 23.13, where the corruption of Hannibal's troops is recorded not during his stay in Capua in the winter of 216/15, but after the second battle of Nola and Hannibal's treaty with Philip in the summer of 215: the reasons for the complexity are that the *Periochae* does not associate the corruption with Capua, but also that Livy's own chronology in 216/15 is far from transparent, and it may be that the *Periochae*'s displacement to a later point in the narrative has something to do with that (see *ad loc.*).

An extreme example of such displacement within the *Periochae* is when an episode is moved from one book to another. Usually this is readily explicable for

---

[24] A complication in this case is that App., *Hann.* 14–15 has the same order as the *Periochae*, which may suggest that narrating the story in this fashion was more broadly embedded within the tradition: see *ad loc.*, and also below for the *Periochae*'s frequent inclusion of non-Livian versions of events.

much the same reasons as before: the author of the *Periochae* unites two disparate parts of a story into a single notice, but in this case the two parts originally appeared in separate books, so one of them ends up in the 'wrong' book. This is what happens at 11.2 (the plague that leads the Romans to send an embassy to Epidaurus was actually in Book 10), at 38.5 (the debate over Manlius Vulso's triumph was in Book 38, but the triumph itself was in Book 39), and at 19.1, where Metellus' victory at Panormus was actually in Book 18 (or so I would argue: see 18.5n. and 19.1n.), but it is only mentioned in the context of his triumph in Book 19. In one case, however, the displacement is more startling and less easy to explain: the transfer of Aemilius' prayer from Book 45 after his Macedonian campaign to Book 44 at the start of it. It is possible that this is simply an error, perhaps based on a misreading of Livy (who has Aemilius refer to the prayer retrospectively), but it may be explicable ideologically—that in the world-view of the late fourth century such a prayer would make far more sense at the start rather than at the end of a campaign: for full discussion see 44.3–4n.

There is one sub-category of displacement which should probably not be considered displacement at all, but rather a different kind of practice. The *Periochae* routinely concludes its books formulaically with a notice in the form *res praeterea continet* or *praeterea…referuntur*, a summary reference to 'other things' that the Livian book contains, but which it is not summarizing in detail. Considerably more than a third of the books end in such a manner; in addition, on a further dozen or so occasions the same formula is used at other points in the book. In the early books the events so summarized are mainly (though not invariably) Roman wars against a list of foes with no other details given; later on in the *Periochae* it becomes more common to include material of other sorts, such as the doings of foreigners. But while this might be formally regarded as 'displacement', it differs from those discussed earlier in its self-consciousness and openness. The use of *praeterea* (or occasionally *item* or *quoque*: 40.3, 60.10) acts as a signal to the reader that the material in question may well be appearing out of chronological or narrative order, and the fact that in the great majority of cases it is at the end of the summary means that it appears to summarize the remaining material that has not been included in the separate notices: that is illusory, since there are invariably many items in Livy that neither appear in those notices nor are mentioned in this 'round-up'[25] final summary, but it provides for many of the books of the *Periochae* an impression of completeness. It is interestingly analogous to what Livy himself does with his end-of-year annalistic summaries, where he rounds up material from all parts of the year (see Levene (2010a), 48–52). However, it also carries a further implication (though sometimes a misleading one: see above): that the other material in each book's summary *is* included in broadly

---

[25] My own phrase: Jal (1984), lxi (on the suggestion of J.-P. Chausserie-Laprée) engagingly refers to them as 'phrases de liquidation'.

chronological order. But in that context it is also noteworthy that the *Periochae* does not structure its narrative around consular dates (see further below, xlvi): the chronology is in general implicit rather than explicit, which in turn leaves the author the opening to violate it tacitly in the interests of his narrative sequence without the chronological displacement becoming apparent to the reader.

These 'round-up' notices also have another effect: of reminding the reader of the *Periochae*'s relationship to Livy's original text. That relationship is, of course, constantly kept in front of the reader's eyes by the paratextual inclusion of the headings that inform us of the Livian book-number (assuming, as is overwhelmingly probable, that these headings are not merely an artefact of the manuscript tradition, but were present in the original); the *praeterea* formulae are another example. But in addition to those, there are a number of places where the *Periochae*'s notice, rather than, in its usual fashion, narrating in its own voice the historical events, is explicitly framed as coming from Livy. In some cases this marks a digression from Livy's own narrative, very plausibly (though in the cases where we have lost Livy's full text this cannot be certain) episodes which Livy himself marks as digressive. This is the case, for example, with the Alexander digression (9.7): see also 16.1 (the origins of Carthage), 38.3 (the origins of the Gallogrecians), 103.11 (the geography of Gaul), 104.1 (the ethnography of Germany—a passage which even mentions where in the book Livy inserted it). Related to this is the use of the device on occasions where Livy may not have overtly marked the episode as digressive, but where there is an analytic element—for example the causes or origins of a war—which the *Periochae* highlights as being discussed by the author: so the introduction of luxury to Rome (39.2), and the origins of the Second Punic War (21.1), the Second Macedonian War (32.1), the Third Punic War (48.2), the Achaean War (51.7), or the Caesar–Pompey civil war (109.1);[26] in the last case the attribution to the author then extends to 109.2, the actual narrative of the first events leading up to the war.

Sometimes there may be a distancing effect: the *Periochae* only rarely introduces Livy's descriptions of prodigies and omens (cf. below), and on some (though not all) of those occasions the prodigies are ascribed to Livy's narrative rather than simply being narrated (32.1, 35.2, 60.4, 68.7)—this may be the result of the author's Christian slant (see further below). But at other times the reason is less obvious: a statement is referred to Livy rather than the direct narrative voice, for example at 28.1, 40.2, 42.2, 59.9, 71.2, 72.4, 112.1, 132.3, 134.3, 135.1, 140.1, 141.1, 142.1. We can see certain patterns: some of these refer to events that are entirely external to Rome, and so may have appeared digressive to the author of the *Periochae*, even if Livy himself did not present them in that way. There is also

---

[26] Cf. also 39.8 on the origins of the Third Macedonian War: here, however, it is appended to the *res…praeterea* formula, referring to fighting in Spain.

a noticeably increased use of the formula in the hyper-laconic final books, where the entire summary of the book is contained in one or two notices; the author compensates for the increasingly jejune narrative by attributing what is there to Livy. But the effect of these overall is to keep the readers constantly aware that, underlying the text they are reading, there exists Livy's text, which gives the summary history an authority which it might not have possessed on its own.

(b) Content

In addition to the distinctive form of the work, the author of the *Periochae* has a very consistent and distinctive set of interests, which are by no means identical to Livy's own. One of those interests is his almost obsessive focus on landmarks in the growth of the Roman state.[27] The material is almost all taken from Livy (but there are exceptions: see e.g. 37.1n.), but the balance is very different from Livy's: more often than not Livy will refer to these points in passing, but for the *Periochae* they become a dominant theme of the narrative. So the *Periochae* records almost every example of the expansion of tribes (2.7, 6.2, 7.6, 9.3, 10.5; cf. 19.11),[28] and almost every colonial foundation mentioned in Livy's surviving text (for exceptions see 9.3 and 10.6nn.). Not only the fact of each census, but the number of citizens counted is meticulously recorded, detailing the material growth of the citizen body—and on one occasion where the numbers fell rather than grew (27.5: see *ad loc.*) the author offers an explicit explanation for the discrepancy where Livy himself provided no such explanation. And, more generally, the author is often interested in 'firsts', at least in the first half of the work.[29] He records the occasions when political offices were created (1.B.7, 4.2, 7.1, 8.9, 11.5), or when they were first held by plebeians (6.4, 18.4, 59.5). He records the first time that Romans campaigned in particular areas, or fought against particular enemies (16.2, 20.3, 20.9, 37.1, 60.2; cf. 19.3), and other transformative moments in military and political history (4.10, 5.1, 17.2, 19.7, 24.6, 59.3, 74.3, 129.3), or in Roman law (8.7, 67.3, 68.6) or culture (7.2, 16.4, 34.5). But such moments become noticeably rarer after Book 20, and rarer still in the last century of the Republic, no doubt in part because there were fewer such innovations then, but also because such innovations as did occur are more easily associated with a narrative of decline rather than one of growth or development.[30]

---

[27] Chaplin (2010), 456–8.
[28] Cf. Bingham 415–16; the one exception, which he notes, is that the *Periochae* omits the foundation of the Maecian and Scaptian tribes recorded at Livy 8.17.11.
[29] Cf. Bingham 407–9, though, as he observes, the *Periochae* is not comprehensive in this, since there are several places where Livy refers to something as an innovation which the *Periochae* does not record. In some cases this may be because the innovation was of a kind that was of less interest to the *Periochae*: for example, the *Periochae*'s relative lack of interest in religious ritual (see below) makes it unsurprising that it fails to record the first *lectisternium* (Livy 5.13.6).
[30] Chaplin (2010), 457–8 acutely observes that innovations in the last eighty or so books are not only fewer in number, but also marked by a change in vocabulary: instead of using forms of *primus*,

Another matter in which the *Periochae* is particularly interested, as Chaplin argues (Chaplin (2010), 458–60) is the influence on events of speeches and letters, which are frequently introduced as causal or explanatory factors to a degree that is surprising, given the abridgement of the events in question: there are over forty-five speeches explicitly mentioned by the *Periochae* (see the list in Bingham 423–5), and a number of letters play a key role also (e.g. 18.1, 33.7, 99.4). Chaplin suggests also that this may help explain the remarkable expansion of Books 48 and 49, since a good portion of the *Periochae*'s narrative of those books is framed through speeches and debates (Chaplin (2010), 460). However, there is a danger of circularity in this argument, since there are many places where Livy's text contains speeches which the *Periochae* could have used as the basis for an expansion of its narrative along similar lines to what it does in Books 48 and 49: examples include the debates over the legality and morality of Hannibal's war on Rome in Book 21, or the treatment of Capua and Syracuse in Book 26, neither of which are mentioned at all by the *Periochae*; while there are also parts of the expansive narrative in Books 48 and 49 which are entirely unconnected with speeches. It is preferable to argue that the *Periochae*'s concentration on those books comes about for different reasons (cf. below, xlviii–l), but that, given the author's interest in speeches, it becomes very natural to frame the issues at stake in those books around the speeches in them.

Conversely, the author of the *Periochae*, with certain limited exceptions, does not share Livy's fascination with religion. Most obviously, the omens and prodigies which Livy frequently records in his surviving books, and which Obsequens shows continued to be recorded in the lost books, are largely omitted by the *Periochae*. A few exceptions come in cases where Livy himself explicitly shows a prodigy or omen predicting future events (1.B.6, 5.10, 22.2, 25.3, 32.1, 35.2; cf. 14.2, 19.2, 55.5, 68.7, 117.1); a few well-known stories of divine activity, mainly from the early period of Roman history, are included also (1.B.2, 1.B.3, 5.2, 2.10, 7.4, 11.2, 26.1, 26.3, 60.4). But the vast majority are omitted; and the same is true with other varieties of religious behaviour. Livy records temple foundations fairly meticulously in his surviving books; the *Periochae* does not, with just a handful of exceptions, mostly associated with dramatic historical events—the key temple of Jupiter Capitolinus (1.B.5, 2.4; cf. 98.4), the temple of Diana on the Aventine founded by Servius Tullius (1.B.3), the temple of Aius Locutius[31] after the Gallic sack (5.11), the temple of Aesculapius (11.2), and the temple of the Magna Mater (29.6–7, 36.2). Among other famous stories, the *Periochae* mentions the moving of Juno to Rome after the fall of Veii and the associated dedication to Delphi (5.3), the *devotiones* of the Decii (8.3, 10.7), and the foundation of Roman drama as

---

the *Periochae* begins to adopt variants on the phrase *quod numquam antea factum erat* (59.3, 67.5, 89.3, 89.6, 107.3, 129.3), and the bulk of these relate to events that 'appear to signal something rather more sinister than additions to the republican constitution'.

[31] Attributed by the *Periochae* to Jupiter: for an explanation see *ad loc.*

part of an expiation for a plague (7.2). The activities of priests are occasionally mentioned, especially when they have political consquences (e.g. 19.8, 47.1, 86.5, 117.2); and a few dramatic acts of piety (19.10, 22.3, 49.5) or impiety (29.8, 39.4, 40.5, 42.1, 103.2). But this represents only a tiny proportion of Livy's religiously themed episodes in the surviving books; and as for the lost books, not only Obsequens, but a significant proportion of the fragments (FF 4, 12, 18, 19, 20, 32, 33, 38, 40, 47, 59, 64) show that Livy's interest was maintained there. Even if, as is plausible, we accept that the interest in religion in the fragments is in part an accident of survival, it is revealing that only one—F 12—is reflected in the *Periochae*. The one exception—the one issue of religion in which the *Periochae* shows a consistent (indeed, one might suspect, prurient) interest—is the punishment of Vestals, which he records meticulously (2.13, 8.5, 14.6, 20.5, 22.11, 28.3, 63.3; cf. 41.1), sometimes even adding details that were not present in Livy.

This might be thought to be related to the different religious circumstances under which the *Periochae* was written. There is good reason, as I shall argue below (lv–lvi), to believe that the author was Christian: in addition to the considerations I mention there, one might observe his emphasizing that the image of the Magna Mater was a stone (29.6: see 29.6–7n.), a detail taken from Livy, but which was highlighted by some Christian writers for the purpose of anti-pagan polemic; moreover, the few reports of prodigies and omens which the author includes are typically not told in the narrator's voice, but are attributed to Livy (above, xxxix). One should not overstate this: at certain times the *Periochae* appears to accept the presence of divine activity (11.2: cf. also 26.3: see *ad locc.*), and it is in any case a mistake to assume that most upper-class Christians in the later fourth century would find something objectionable in traditional Roman religious ideas and practices in the same way Christian polemicists like Arnobius or Augustine did (see Cameron (2011), *passim*). But it is plausible to assume that, even if not objectionable, Livy's records of omens and religious activity would simply appear less salient from the perspective of that later period, when so much of it would seem of largely antiquarian interest.

Another distinctive aspect of the *Periochae*'s narrative is its tendency to focus on individuals (cf. Bessone (1977), 221–2). An extremely high proportion of its notices are structured around a protagonist, who is named at the beginning of the sentence, typically along with an identifying word or phrase to place him (or, less often, her) in the Roman political or social structure. There are of course occasional exceptions: the account of the *lex Canuleia* does not mention the eponymous tribune who passed it (4.1: nor does it even mention him indirectly by naming the law); the same is true of the obscure *lex de ambitu* recorded at 47.2. A handful of victories are included without the names of the victorious generals (8.6, 8.8, 10.2, 15.1, 15.4, 15.6, 20.1, 20.6, 20.10); the reports of censuses do not usually name the censors, and the few exceptions (1.B.3, 13.4, 14.4, 18.4, 29.15, 59.5, 98.2, 115.3) arise when the census report is appended to some other activity of the censor. But the overall impression of the narrative is less of the accomplishments of the Roman people *en masse*, and rather that the Roman state was built on a series of actions performed by major individuals. It is of a piece with this that the *Periochae* shows a considerable interest in triumphs: not that it records anything close to the number that Livy or other parts of the historical tradition do, but it contains a good number of them, especially in the middle Republic (interestingly, it ignores them in the early books, and also most of those in the late Republic: apart from those celebrated by Marius, Pompey, and Caesar).[32] Triumphs are perfectly calibrated to combine the *Periochae*'s interest in the growth of Rome with its focus on leading individuals, and the author, accordingly, often includes them at times when Livy mentions them only in passing and places little emphasis on them.

This practice may appear so obvious and natural as to require little comment, but not all summary historians organized their work in this way.[33] Eutropius does it less than the *Periochae*, Florus considerably less than either. Nor would it follow inevitably from Livy's narrative, not least because Livy himself, even though he usually names generals and politicians when describing the actions in which they were involved, often shows less interest than one might expect in individual actors; and the Oxyrhynchus Epitome is noticeably less assiduous at naming individual Romans than the *Periochae* is.

Related to this is that the author has an unusual interest in certain particular figures in Roman history.[34] His focus on Scipio Africanus is particularly obvious.[35] Naturally Scipio is prominent in Livy's original text, but the *Periochae* accentuates that. Between Scipio's introduction in Book 21 and his death in Book 39 the *Periochae* introduces him at almost every point when Livy's narrative gives him the opportunity to do so, even on relatively minor matters (such as his aedileship at 25.1, or his legateship to his brother at 37.1); and at one point, his supposed meeting with Hannibal at the court of Antiochus (35.1), the *Periochae* narrates the entire conversation with a fullness that comes close to that of Livy's original text. We can contrast, for example, Aemilius Paullus, who is introduced for his victory in Macedon and his subsequent triumph in Books 44 and 45, along with his death at 46.11, but whose earlier career, including his first consulship and the associated triumph, along with certain contentious interventions which Livy describes (notably his unsuccessful attempt to prevent Cn. Manlius Vulso's triumph over the Gallogrecians: 38.45.1–50.3; but cf. also 43.2), is entirely ignored.

In the case of Livy's lost books, of course, it is more difficult to determine how far the *Periochae*'s patterns of inclusion and omission of key figures matches their

---

[32] Cf. Chaplin (2010), 456–7.
[33] Cf. Bessone (1982), 1246–7, Horster (2017), 38–40.
[34] Cf. Chaplin (2010), 460–3, who aptly refers to this as 'tracking'.
[35] Cf. Chaplin (2010), 460–1, Levene (2015b), 322–5. More generally on the iconic position of both Scipio Africanus and Scipio Aemilianus in late antiquity (though without reference to the *Periochae*) see Felmy (2001), 186–227.

prominence or otherwise in Livy's original text. One interesting case is Cicero. He is mentioned only occasionally: he thwarts the Catilinarian conspiracy in 102.4, and the *Periochae* mentions his exile and return (103.9, 104.3); his absence from Pharsalus is recorded (111.4), as is his death (120.3).[36] Oddly, despite the *Periochae*'s general interest in speeches, not a single speech by Cicero is referred to, although it seems unlikely *a priori* that Livy would not have at least mentioned them, even if he might have baulked at attempting to create his own versions of them.[37] But the fact of Cicero's literary production appears to matter to the *Periochae* in a broader sense. Arguably the *Periochae* (whether or not reflecting Livy) makes Cicero more prominent than an actual record of his political achievement in the absence of his writings would justify—it can, after all only be on the assumption that Cicero is of unusual interest as a person that his failure to appear at the battle of Pharsalus would be thought worthy of comment in so abridged a narrative, and one might also suspect that the sole mention of Quintus Cicero (in the context of his service under Caesar in Gaul: 106.3) is explained by the literary fame of his brother.

In other cases, too, one might hypothesize a particular interest in certain leading figures on the part of the *Periochae* even with respect to the books that are lost. Scipio Aemilianus has a prominence in the text which virtually matches that of his adopted grandfather, beginning with his famous victory in single combat in Spain (48.14; cf. 48.12), continuing through his assistance with the legacy of Masinissa (50.6), and then his elevation to the command in the Third Punic War (50.10, 51.1–6, 52.5), and his later command at Numantia (56.7, 57, 59.1), and finally his support for the killing of Tiberius Gracchus and his own suspicious death (59.8, 59.11–12). The focus may seem at first sight unsurprising, but the way in which almost the entire narrative in the *Periochae* of Books 51 and 57 centres on this single figure is exceptional. It seems improbable, at least to judge by the surviving text, that any one figure could have dominated a book of Livy to quite that degree: the way in which Livy typically shifts between domestic and foreign events, and between different areas of conflict and command abroad, more or less precludes him from so intense a focus on a single person. Similarly, the *Periochae* focuses the whole of Book 58 on Tiberius Gracchus, but the vastly more far-reaching programme of Gaius Gracchus is treated more diffusely, mentioned intermittently through Books 60 and 61, but interspersed with a lot of

---

[36] Slightly different is 70.1, where Cicero is (unusually) cited as the source for the acquittal of M. Antonius.

[37] Other Latin historians make references to Cicero's speeches, even though not creating versions of them: so Sall., *Catil.* 31.6 refers to Cicero's *First Catilinarian*, and Vell. 2.64.3 describes the *Philippics*. In Greek, Cassius Dio is considerably more expansive; he puts a lengthy speech of his own composition into the mouth of Cicero after the assassination of Caesar at 44.23–33, and an even longer one (effectively a version of the *Second Philippic*) at the opening of the following year (45.18–47); he refers in addition to various of his other speeches: for example to the *Third Catilinarian* at 37.34.3, to the *Catilinarians* in general at 37.42.1, to his speeches *Post Reditum* at 39.9.1, his speech *De Domo Sua* at 39.11, to the *Pro Milone* at 40.54.

unrelated material. Tiberius' career is presented as a self-contained tragedy, Gaius' is not.

We can suspect a similar reworking of Livy's interests with the figures who formed the 'First Triumvirate'. Pompey and Caesar are both dominant figures in the *Periochae*, which is not surprising; but Crassus is a substantially diminished figure in the text, appearing just four times: his victory over Spartacus (97.1), his consulship with Pompey in 70 (97.6–7), at the forming of the 'First Triumvirate' (103.6), and his death at Carrhae (106.4). While any account of the period is certain to have given far more emphasis to Pompey and Caesar than to Crassus, it seems improbable, though not of course impossible, that Crassus's role can have been so disproportionately small in Livy by comparison with them.

The *Periochae* thus centres its narrative on certain people; but those people receive relatively little direct characterization (though see Levene (2015b), 313–18)—the bulk of the narrative reads simply as a summary of their most famous achievements, along with (in some cases) various exemplary anecdotes associated with them. The *Periochae*'s approach may well, in fact, have been influenced by the Roman exemplary tradition, which was one of the most prominent ways in which history was consumed and understood within Roman society, and which itself had the tendency to break down history into discrete episodes, each centred on an individual whose actions could be deployed in a moral lesson.[38] This is not to suggest that every notice in the *Periochae* is structured as a moral *exemplum*. A few are explicitly framed as such (2.5, 18.2, 38.4, 55.1); considerably more can be implicitly read in that manner, not least because they provide the same details and the same outcomes as are found in Valerius Maximus and other writers who cite stories for their exemplary value. But the vast majority of notices do not fall into those categories, but simply record characters engaging in actions without offering the kind of details of either the personal qualities or the decisions that led to that particular outcome, such as would enable an ethical lesson to be drawn from the stories. In some cases the *Periochae*, while not offering an *exemplum* directly, provides enough information to remind the reader of a famous story whose exemplary lessons were well known; but in many others there is not even that much, especially since we cannot reasonably assume that the mere fact that a story appears in (for example) Valerius Maximus means that it was well known more broadly, even given Valerius' apparent popularity in later antiquity: there are far more stories in Valerius than can have been maintained as part of general historical knowledge among the educated population. But in any case the suggestion is less that the *Periochae* reads as a series of linked *exempla*— it clearly does not—but rather that the habits of exemplary thought encouraged

---

[38] For the tendency of *exempla* to be constructed around individual heroes, cf. Walter (2004), 52–3; more generally on the complex way such *exempla* functioned within Roman culture, see esp. Langlands (2018).

the author to structure his understanding of Roman history in terms of the individual actors engaging in events which under the right circumstances might sometimes produce episodes with exemplary value for their audiences.

In this context it is worth observing another unusual but less-noticed aspect of the *Periochae*: its lack of interest in chronology.[39] The author never offers a consular date,[40] and only rarely does he provide an AUC date (3.6, 31.2, 47.11, 49.1, 49.5): to judge by the first two of these, he does so only on occasions when Livy himself, exceptionally, provided such a date (3.33.1, 31.5.1). In this respect he is not only unlike Livy himself, but also unlike most of the other Latin epitomists and summarizers: the Oxyrhynchus Epitome, Obsequens, Orosius, and (to a lesser extent) Eutropius all repeatedly date events either by the consuls or by AUC dates, and even Florus, who is less concerned than any of these to follow chronological sequence, occasionally does so. Horster (2017), 36–7 suggests that this detaches the *Periochae* from the existing historiographical tradition, and gives it closer affinities with biographical and exemplary works: this is somewhat overstated (Sallust's *Jugurtha*, widely read in the fourth century, is an excellent precedent for a work of Latin historiography that was neither biographical nor chronologically focused), but she is surely right to suggest that this aspect of the work's texture serves to highlight the sequence of famous episodes and leaves the reader less concerned about the precise period in which they occurred. However, Horster's further proposal ((2017), 37–8) that the *Periochae*'s well-known interest in 'firsts' (above, xl) somehow relates to the lack of chronology is more puzzling. Granted that the innovations so recorded are not strictly 'dated', they give a cumulative impression of change and development which has an historical force of its own: for example, a large portion of them centre around the expansion of political offices to plebeians, and so speak (rightly or wrongly) to the gradual social equalizing of the early Republican classes.

The focus of the *Periochae* on simple stories centred around famous individuals would appear at first sight to link to another distinctive aspect of the text: the simplicity of its ethics. To many readers of Livy (myself included), this is the respect in which the *Periochae* is most disappointing. Ethics are at the centre of Livy's history, but what makes him especially attractive to modern sensibilities is the complexity and balance of his implied ethical judgements: people often are shown as drawing on multiple considerations in their choices of action, some good, some bad; people do good things for bad reasons and bad things for good reasons; and in either event the outcomes of their actions are often counter to

---

[39] Noted by Love (2019), 61.
[40] Jal (1984), lxxxviii treats those occasions when the *Periochae* describes both consuls of the year acting in tandem (e.g. 9.1, 22.7, 25.4, 25.7, 26.2, 28.2, 33.6, 48.11, 49.9, 55.1, 83.4, 97.6, 108.3) as if they provided consular dates; but while it is obviously possible to read these passages as indirectly dating the events, from a narratological perspective this functions very differently from naming the consuls as a dating formula (cf. Bessone (1977), 267).

what they expected or hoped for. Virtually all of this complexity vanishes in the *Periochae*. Often no explanations are given at all; when they are given, they are more often than not described in monocausal terms, single causes leading to single effects. When certain individuals have good and bad sides, only one is presented; complicating factors are either ignored or treated as entirely separate. So (to take one notorious example) the *Periochae*'s interest in Scipio Africanus does not extend to those actions of his which Livy presents as morally problematic: the atrocities committed by his legate Pleminius in Locri have, for the *Periochae*, nothing to do with Scipio himself, while the consequent accusations against him, which Livy explicitly says were partially valid and which led to a Senatorial investigation against him, are, for the *Periochae*, simply false (29.8–9: see Levene (2015b), 323–4). The same is true of many other stories: the way, for example, that the rise of Tarquinius Priscus fails to mention the key role played by the ambivalent Tanaquil (1.B.2), or how the story of Manlius Torquatus' defence of his father against the tribune prosecuting him becomes a simple story of filial loyalty (7.3), though Livy himself directly denies its exemplary value and is suspicious of the inherent violence, or the way the strategy of Fabius Maximus in his dictatorship, unlike in Livy, is treated as obviously correct, and Minucius' opposition assumed to be the result of mere slander (22.4). These moral simplifications can be paralleled in many other writers in the later Latin historical tradition: it is those, and not the intricate ethical balance of Livy, which appears to have struck a chord in most of the authors who looked back to the Republic from the perspective of the second century AD and later.

One might argue, of course, that the ethical flattening of the *Periochae* is simply a by-product of its general abridgement. It is certainly true that, even leaving ethical questions aside, many of the complex stories in Livy are collapsed by the *Periochae* into an uncomplicated and easily comprehensible dynamic. An egregious example is the revolt and recapture of Syracuse in Books 24 and 25, where the multiple poles of Syracusan and Sicilian opinion, and the convolutions of the city's changing relationship with both Carthage and Rome, are turned by the *Periochae* into a straightforward sequence of events which completely misrepresents the dynamic of Livy's narrative. According to the *Periochae*, Hieronymus defected from Rome to Carthage, but was assassinated by his own people; Marcellus then besieged Syracuse, and captured it three years later (24.1, 24.3, 25.9). One would never know from this that, on Livy's account, the Syracusan break from Rome, although begun by Hieronymus, is not finalized until after Marcellus arrives in Sicily, and in the intervening period Livy repeatedly presents it as a serious possibility that Syracuse might remain in alliance with Rome.[41] And there are innumerable other examples: complex battles reduced to a simple

---

[41] Admittedly Livy's account of the Syracusan revolt contains certain causal inconsistencies that make it hard to explain the behaviour of the different actors at every point: for an analysis and explanation, see Levene (2010a), 321–6.

victory or defeat, hard-fought laws which are simply passed without comment. But narrative simplification is hardly a sufficient explanation for the *Periochae*'s consistent ethical simplicity, because even simple narratives may have complicated ethical valences. The stories in the *Periochae* are often little shorter than some of the *exempla* in Valerius Maximus, whose work is far more ethically complex than appears at first sight. To achieve a minimal level of ethical complexity, a narrative needs only to contain a couple of details that point the reader in more than one direction. Yet the *Periochae* usually does not even do that.

It is, however, possible to argue that, at least some of the time, the *Periochae* itself offers some measure of ethical complexity in a different way, even while falling far short of Livy's intricate and agonized ethical balancing. One point is that with certain exemplary stories, especially those that are familiar and ingrained in the Roman historical imagination, some level of ethical complexity is almost unavoidable. An example might be Manlius Torquatus' execution of his son (8.2): the act itself is so shocking that even in the absence of detail it would naturally raise ethical questions in the minds of many readers, and in fact the *Periochae* does include some of the details that make the execution appear counterintuitive, notably the fact that the son was victorious, and it also invites the reader to see it as controversial, by noting the resentment that it aroused among the youth at Rome (8.4). Moreover, even in less stark cases, Rebecca Langlands has persuasively argued that the Roman practice of moral reasoning via the contemplation of *exempla* cannot avoid a fundamental complexity in almost every case, since it is always contestable whether the person seeking to apply the *exemplum* to his own life is in fact in the same position in all relevant respects (Langlands (2011)). A further point along not dissimilar lines is that the *Periochae*'s method of allusive interaction with Livy's original text sometimes, as I described, specifically incorporates references to complicating elements of Livy which on the face of things the *Periochae* excludes (above, xxiv–xxv; see also below, lxi–lxiii for the broader significance of this in our understanding of the text). Hence the minority of readers who can recognize the original text underlying the *Periochae*'s account have their attention drawn to some of the complexities of the original, which the *Periochae* effectively incorporates by brief hints rather than explicit detail.

But perhaps most interesting of all is that, on rare occasions, the *Periochae* directly confronts those ethical questions which for the bulk of its narrative are avoided. Most obvious in this respect is its account of the Third Punic War in Books 48–51, which is described at far greater length and in far greater detail than anything else in the entire work, and where ethical questions are at the heart of the author's treatment. The Third Punic War, in the tradition most famously associated with Sallust (but which extended both before and after him), became the central ethical moment in all of Republican history, with the Roman victory over Carthage marking the pivotal moment when the Romans, released from the pressure of external threats, turned in on themselves and broke morally.

It is thus immensely significant that here, and only here, the author of the *Periochae* slows down and explores in detail both the justification for the war and the debate over it at Rome—and, crucially, he does so in a way which gives strong weight, in a very Livian manner (whether or not Livy himself treated it in precisely this way), to an ethically intricate complex of considerations that drew the Romans into war (see the commentary *ad locc.* for fuller discussion). A series of accusations are made against Carthage: that the army ostensibly assembled to protect them in their border dispute with Masinissa was in fact for use against Rome (48.2); that, contrary to the terms of the treaty agreed with Rome after the Second Punic War, the Carthaginians had an army and also wood to be used for a fleet (48.3; cf. 47.12); that a fleet was actually being built and a military levy being held (48.9); that Carthage had both an army and a fleet (48.16); and finally that they had a fleet, had taken an army outside their borders, had attacked Masinissa, and had refused his son Gulussa entry to the city (49.3). But every one of these accusations is put into someone else's mouth and is not presented in the authorial voice. It is true that the some of the accusations are made by the Roman *legati*, who (unlike Cato and Gulussa) have no obvious ulterior motive, but the different accusations, though overlapping, each have a slightly different scope which makes it difficult to assess the precise level of Carthaginian culpability. Only one of these accusations is confirmed in the authorial voice—the Carthaginians' attack on Masinissa (48.18)—and here their culpability is muddied by the fact that the army they used is suggested to have been assembled to repel a Numidian invasion (48.2).

Apart from the question of whether the Carthaginians had committed military actions in violation of the treaty with Rome, the political actions of both sides come under scrutiny in ways that complicate the narrative of Carthaginian culpability. When Roman ambassadors seek to broker an agreement between Carthage and Masinissa, one which appears favourable to Carthage, and the Carthaginian senate is ready to accept it, it is derailed by a single official who rouses the people to attack the ambassadors (48.4). Later, after Rome declares war on Carthage, the Carthaginians seek to protect themselves by surrendering and throwing themselves on Rome's mercy (49.6), only for the Romans, under the prompting of Cato, to deliberately push the Carthaginians towards war with an outrageous demand that appears to be designed as one which Carthage could not possibly accept (49.7–8).

And it is indeed the role of Cato that attracts the most attention from the author. The *Periochae* repeatedly alludes to his long-running debate with Scipio Nasica on the necessity for the destruction of Carthage (48.2, 48.10, 48.16, 49.2); the grounds for each man's opinion is not offered directly, but the general basis on which they are disputing is indicated by the fact that on the last occasion the *Periochae*, unusually, offers a direct characterization for each (49.2): Cato 'was considered the wisest man in the state' (*sapientissimus vir in civitate habebatur*),

1 INTRODUCTION

Nasica (erroneously conflated by the *Periochae* with his father: cf. 36.2) 'had even been judged the best man by the Senate' (*optimus vir etiam iudicatus a senatu erat*). This marks the debate as being one between prudence and ethics, which is indeed, in outline, the basis for the debate in the tradition. It is true that in the traditional account Nasica's ethical concerns were not (or not primarily), as the *Periochae* appears to imply (cf. esp. the reference to *iustam causam* at 48.16), the justice or otherwise of the war with Carthage, but the ethical effects on Rome herself were Carthage to be destroyed, but the two are not mutually exclusive, and, as noted above, the very fact of the *Periochae*'s focus on the Third Punic War suggests a recognition of its traditional position as a turning point in Roman ethical behaviour, which any reader of Sallust would know. It is highly probable that Livy's original account, too, made some sort of reference to that theme, and that, as at other times (cf. above), a reader who knew it would be alerted to it by the *Periochae*'s narrative, especially the repeated insistence on the Cato–Nasica debate as a central feature of the story.

Of course, the author's interest in ethical complexity should not be overstated. Books 48 and 49 are entirely exceptional within the summary, and even though it is likely that the author attributed particular significance to the Third Punic War, as noted above, one should be careful not to make this the sole reason behind the unusual expansiveness of the narrative in these books—it is, after all, not only African matters which receive unusually detailed attention here (cf. Bessone (2015), 434), and there may be some measure of arbitrariness, here and elsewhere, in the author's decision to focus on certain things at the expense of others. But the narrative here does at least demonstrate that the absence of elements of ethical complexity elsewhere in the *Periochae* is not because of a deep-seated aversion to that manner of analysis.

Another distinctive aspect of the *Periochae*'s account is that its summaries of Livy often involve a significant degree of not merely abridgement, but actively rewriting factual information in Livy's narrative. The simplest kind of rewriting relates to Livy's own alternative versions. As is well known, Livy often appends to his main narrative a secondary, different version of the story in question, but these the *Periochae* almost invariably removes; only on rare occasions does the author himself present both of Livy's alternative accounts (39.5; cf. 60.9). But from time to time the author substitutes Livy's secondary account for that of his main narrative: so at 8.1 the Latin envoy Annius is killed falling from the Capitol, while at 10.7 the Etruscans and Umbrians are present at Sentinum along with the Gauls and Samnites. A more complex instance is 45.6, where Livy provides two versions of Prusias' appearance before the Senate, but the *Periochae* has a single story which unites elements from each one; similarly at 34.5 the *Periochae* combines elements from both of Livy's versions of the reform of seating at the games.

More common still is where the author supplies from his general knowledge a factual detail which is not present in Livy, although it is not incompatible with him: the *Periochae* simply makes it explicit. So at 1.B.3, when Livy describes Servius Tullius' foundation of the famous temple of Diana, the *Periochae* adds that it was on the Aventine. With both the punishment of a Vestal at 2.13 and the decimation of the army by Appius Claudius (2.15), the *Periochae* describes the manner of punishment, although Livy does not. At 5.9 the *Periochae* describes the Gallic siege of the Capitol as lasting six months, something not mentioned by Livy, but recorded in other sources; the torque taken from the Gaul by Manlius Torquatus at 7.5 is described as *aureus*, not mentioned by Livy, but part of the regular stereotype of Gallic dress. At 33.5 the praetor Sempronius Tuditanus is defeated in Spain; Livy does not record his opponents, but the *Periochae* asserts that they were the Celtiberi, which may well be true, and is at any rate not incompatible with Livy's account.

The most striking moments of rewriting in the *Periochae*, however, are those where the *Periochae* not merely supplements Livy's version, but substitutes for it an alternative version which is incompatible with Livy's own, albeit often only in certain details. To give just a few of the many examples: at 2.5 Porsenna is engaged in sacrifice when Mucius attempts to assassinate him, as in the version in Valerius Maximus 3.3.1, rather than paying his soldiers, as in Livy. In Livy the funeral of Menenius Agrippa is paid for out of small private contributions; the *Periochae* substitutes the version found in D.H., *AR* 6.96.1–3, where it is paid for from the public treasury. In Livy, there is little overlap in personnel between the first and second college of decemvirs, but in *Per.* 3.7, in common with much of the rest of the post-Livian tradition (Flor. 1.17(24).1, Pompon., *Dig.* 1.2.2.4, Eutr. 1.18, *Vir. Ill.* 21.1–2), the same men served in both colleges. The shrine founded after the Gallic attack in commemoration of the divine warning of that attack is dedicated to Aius Locutius in Livy, as in most other sources, but the *Periochae* offers an alternative tradition (5.11), found also in Juv. 11.111–16, according to which it was dedicated to Jupiter. Manlius Torquatus in Livy threatens the tribune with a knife, but in the *Periochae*, as in every other version of the story, it is with a sword (7.3). In the *Periochae* (26.1) Hannibal marches on Rome at the Porta Capena, as in Val. Max. 3.7.10 and Fest. 354L, rather than the Porta Collina, as in Livy. The princes who fight for the kingdom in Scipio's gladiatorial contest at New Carthage are not cousins, as Livy has them, but brothers, as in other versions (28.5: cf. Val. Max. 9.11.ext.1, Sil. 16.527–56, Zonar. 9.10.3). With the death of Cicero, Livy's version of which is preserved by the elder Seneca (F 61: see *ad loc.*), the *Periochae* adds the (popular but fictional) story that Cicero's assassin was his former client Popillius, and has both of Cicero's hands (rather than only his right hand) nailed to the Rostra after his death (120.3).

All of these, while apparently odd if one thinks of the *Periochae* merely as a summary of Livy, make a lot more sense if one recalls what was argued in Volume I (xxi–xxii): that 'Livy', for the writers of late antiquity, was not simply the text we have, but effectively stood in for the entire tradition of Republican history. The author of the *Periochae* acknowledges the central cultural status of Livy's text by summarizing it, but simultaneously does so also by adjusting it so that it aligns with the version of history that he prefers: paradoxically, this maintains Livy's status by ensuring that his authority remains in line with accepted understandings of the Republic. That there is some tension here is obvious, especially if one remembers that much or all of Livy's text still existed, and the *Periochae*, as I explained above, at various times tacitly alludes to particular details in it, including occasions where the author marks for the informed reader his own distance from the version of the story in Livy.[42] Livy is at one and the same time acting in two different ways for the *Periochae*: first as the canonical author whose work the *Periochae* overtly attaches itself to and organizes itself around, but also as the authority justifying the *Periochae*'s own narrative of Roman history, which presents itself as 'Livy' and yet is designed to be read independently of him.[43]

(c) Style

The *Periochae*'s Latin style is itself more interesting than has often been appreciated. Admittedly, the style has a strongly formulaic side, though that, for the purposes of our present enquiry, is itself useful, since in its very consistency it offers additional evidence, beyond that presented above, for seeing the text as a product of a single person rather than one which has accumulated by accretion (Wölfflin (1877), 339–40). One example of the formulae that the *Periochae* employs was discussed above (xxxviii–xxxix): the *res praeterea continet* or *praeterea referuntur* formula used to summarize extra material in many of the books. Others include the many variants on the phrase *feliciter/infeliciter/prospere/parum prospere/ bene/male/dubio eventu/vario eventu adversus X pugnavit/bellum gestum/res gestas*, or *(com)pluribus ducibus* or *cum exercitu caesus est* or *in deditionem venerunt/ accepti sunt/accepit* or *in potestatem venit/redegit*. Still other formulae are derived from Livy's own—for example the census formula (*censa sunt civium capita*) or the formula for colonial foundations (*colonia deducta est* etc.)—but they are more prominent in the *Periochae* precisely because those episodes are given a disproportionate attention in its narrative (above, xl).

Apart from lexical formulae such as these, the *Periochae*'s sentences regularly fall into a broader syntactic pattern, one which follows naturally from its tendency to break down many events into atomized notices. Many sentences are simple declarative sentences, with no subordinate clauses, succinctly recounting a single

---

[42] For an instructive parallel, compare Doody (2009) on the late antique *Medicina Plinii*, a collection of medical extracts largely (but not entirely) drawn from Pliny's *Natural History*. Much as with the *Periochae* and Livy, Doody argues that the *Medicina* acquires its authority from Pliny, but at the same time reorganizes his material and constantly marks its distance from him.

[43] Cf. Horster (2017), 26–7.

event. But with many of those which are not, they take the form of a single causal, temporal, or participial phrase which sets out the background information to an event, followed by a main clause which describes the event itself. That pattern can then be further elaborated—a second main clause joined paratactically, for example, or a relative clause providing more background to the person who forms the centre of attention in the sentence (cf. above, xlii–xliii) but the basic underlying structure remains the same. A remarkably high proportion of sentences in the *Periochae* follow this pattern, and the reason is obvious: it maintains the focus on the key event in the notice while at the same time offering sufficient explanatory material to make some sense of it.

Naturally not all sentences fall into these two patterns; especially in the cases where the *Periochae* offers a more connected and less atomized narrative, such as the lengthier Books 1, 48, and 49, there is a wider range of syntax on offer; in the case of the latter two books, one may suspect that some of this may even replicate the syntax of Livy's original text, in the same way that, in the summaries of the surviving books, the unusually detailed account of the meeting of Scipio and Hannibal at 35.1 is demonstrably drawn, in syntax as well as vocabulary, from Livy (see *ad loc.*). The same may be true on other occasions where the *Periochae*'s narrative slows down enough to offer some elements of fine detail, such as the account of Scipio Aemilianus restoring military discipline at Numantia (57.1–3) or the episode of the two brothers who killed one another in the civil war (79.2). In a number of other cases the *Periochae* offers a more elaborate sentence structure even without basing it on Livy himself, as at 9.1; and we may suspect that this also happens with some parts of the later books where the events are told too quickly to be simply a transcription of Livy's syntax, such as the account of the massacres perpetrated by Marius and Cinna at 80.5. But these are rare exceptions in the *Periochae*: overall, no one would ever mistake the simple and repetitive syntax of the summary for the sinuous and complex sentences that fill out Livy's narrative.

But although syntactically the *Periochae* is nothing like Livy, when it comes to the shorter phrases out of which these formulaic sentences are composed, a very different picture emerges: the *Periochae* appears to be constantly striving to make those as Livian as possible, at times almost to the point where they read as a pastiche of Livian vocabulary shoehorned into a very un-Livian sentence-structure. Partly this is achieved simply by adopting Livy's own vocabulary from whatever episode happens to be under consideration, selecting phrases that will suit the need, sometimes with minor alterations and substitutions. Sometimes, as noted above (xxiii–xxiv), the phrases in question are taken from the 'wrong' section of Livy, not the episode being summarized but a later reference back to it. This procedure, as I discussed above, gives the author opportunities for certain kinds of sly allusions, but it has another potential attraction as well. When Livy refers back to an earlier point in his narrative, he usually does so briefly, and hence they become a useful model for the *Periochae*'s own abridgement.

But at other times the Livian phrases are not employed with regard to the story being summarized at all, but are adopted from a completely unrelated part of the work. This is the case, for example, with *foedus restitutum* (9.5: cf. Liv. 10.3.5), *praealtam voraginem* (7.4: cf. Liv. 22.2.5, 44.8.6), *agro perpercit* (22.6: cf. Liv. 32.15.5), and *editis mandatis* (45.2: cf. Liv. 33.35.3, 45.20.2; also above, xxiii). In all these cases the phrase, though only occurring once or twice in the surviving books of Livy, is virtually unknown in Latin literature outside his text: the author's knowledge of Livy is fine-grained enough to identify rarities of that sort and incorporate them into his own 'Livian' work[44] (though it is of course possible that the phrases became more common and hence more typically 'Livian' in the later books). More often the phrases incorporated are more widespread in Livy's surviving work: in these cases they are not necessarily unknown elsewhere, but are very typical of his writing, to the point that a writer seeking to imitate his manner might naturally pick them up. Livian quirks of that sort in the *Periochae* include the ending of sentences in *-que* (2.12, 5.9, 29.7, 40.5; cf. 54.3, 93.3), or the forming of the pluperfect passive out of the perfect participle + *fuerat* (25.3, 29.14, 38.4; cf. 52.8) or the inversion of the *nomen* and *cognomen* (4.6); others include the pairing of *incendo* and *diruo* (5.10), or the phrases *locum iniquum* (7.11), *in praesidio relicti* (7.12), *ferocem...victoriis* (22.4), and *ad ultimum* (1.B.7, 40.2; cf. 11.6, 50.5, 96.4).

The *Periochae*'s Livian pastiche is, however, far from complete even at the level of phrases and vocabulary. Not infrequently, instead of employing distinctively Livian language, the author will use phrases or grammatical structures that are associated with the late Republic and early imperial period in general, rather than Livy in particular. The language in these instances is far less common in writers of late antiquity, so it still appears to be the case that the author is making a conscious effort to 'archaize' his language and match it to the period of his source material, but in a more generic fashion, rather than the very precise focus on Livy that I have been discussing up to now. Examples include *leges constituere* (3.6, 8.7), *permagna* (21.4), *fortuna...abstulisset* (27.5), and *innumerabilem pecuniam* (38.10).

But more significant still is that the *Periochae* is not consistent even in this broadly archaizing manner. While on the whole the author maintains a style that would be, if not very sophisticated, nevertheless an acceptable representation of Latin of Livy's day, he occasionally slips into more contemporary language, incorporating Latin idioms from his own time of writing that, as far as we know,

---

[44] It is interesting to compare this linguistic practice of the *Periochae* with the Virgilian centos composed by several writers around the same period (for the parallel between centos and epitomes cf. esp. Formisano and Sogno (2010), 380). The parallel is of course not exact, since the *Periochae* does not subvert the Livian text to the point of reusing his words in an entirely non-Livian narrative, but the way in which the original Livian phrases are repurposed into a new context is nevertheless strikingly similar.

would never have been used in the Augustan or early imperial period (cf. Wölfflin (1877), 349). An obvious example is his use of *amplio* to refer to increasing the number of people appointed to a political office (1.B.2, 2.7, 3.5, 10.3, 15.7, 20.7, 32.5, 89.4), which is not the way Livy employs the term, and which is not found in any writer before the second century AD (Wölfflin (1900a), 1). *perseverare in accusatione* (7.3) is a phrase specifically used by late antique commentators, and never found in any writer before the fourth century; the same is true of *victoriam restituere* (8.3). *spes evadendi* (9.1) is a common phrase of the fourth century, never found in any writer of classical Latin. *togam accipere* (26.3) is likewise a phrase used in the fourth century to describe men reaching adulthood, but is not found in Livy or any other classical writer; similarly *successorem relinquere* (40.6) to describe the transfer of power in a monarchy.

Most revealing of all, however, is the occasional use of phrases which are not merely generic fourth-century diction, but are associated specifically with Christian theological discourse. Examples include *in visu* (2.10) to refer to a vision seen in a dream, or *seminarium* + genitive of a crime (39.4). There are two especially striking instances, where Christian theological language seems to be applied by the *Periochae* in a context of interest to Christians. One is the description of the Seleucid monarch Antiochus IV Epiphanes as *vilissimum regem* (41.3): the language recalls the Latin translation of Daniel 11:20, a passage which obliquely alludes to the Seleucid monarchy. Antiochus himself was a central figure in the Jewish (and hence Christian) memory of the period, as the chief antagonist at the time of the Maccabean revolt, and that appears to lie behind the language of the *Periochae* here (see further *ad loc.*).

Perhaps even more remarkable is the account of the death of Regulus at 18.5. Since Livy's original does not survive, we cannot be certain how closely the *Periochae* reflects it, but it contains one key phrase that Livy is extremely unlikely to have used: *fide custodita*. This phrase appears in Cicero, but with a completely different meaning; otherwise it is used by no pagan writer, but employed widely by Christians in the context of loyalty to Christianity, especially in narratives of martyrdom. It can hardly be a coincidence that Regulus repeatedly appears in Christian theological writings as a pagan prototype of Christian martyrdom: hence that is the lens through which the *Periochae*, using Christian theological language, presents the story of Regulus' steadfast death (see *ad loc.* for more detailed discussion).

vi. Authorship and Composition

In the light of the discussion above, therefore, what can we tell about the author of the *Periochae*? Two immediate data points are apparent. First, the author wrote before AD 380, since his work was used by Eutropius (above, xxx–xxxi). Second, the author was manifestly a Christian, as evidenced by the occasional use of

Christian theological language.[45] There is, nevertheless, no sign of strong aversion to (as opposed to a moderate lack of interest in) pagan religious practices, and a general orientation towards an admiration of the virtues of the Roman Republic, at least before the conflicts of its last century; this suggests the Christian culture of the later fourth century or afterwards, when the profession of Christianity was a more conventional position for an upper-class Roman, and less likely to be associated with oppositional polemic, at least in non-theological writers.

Putting those considerations together, we can assign the writing of the text to the third quarter of the fourth century AD (i.e. c.350–75).

There are also some indications of where it was written. There are three occasions when the author makes a slight alteration to Livy's geography in a manner which appears to suggest an acquaintance with the area in question. At 21.4 the *Periochae* has Hannibal successfully cross the Apennines: a change to Livy, where the attempted crossing is a failure. In Livy, however, Hannibal never actually appears to cross the Apennines at all, despite being on one side of them at the end of Book 21, and on the other side shortly after the start of Book 22: the *Periochae* misrepresents Livy, but his narrative offers a more plausible version of the geography of Hannibal's campaign than Livy's does. Secondly, at 29.3 the Carthaginian Mago lands in Italy, not, as in Livy, between the Ligurian tribe called the Albingauni and Genoa, but at the town of Albingaunum. In this case it is impossible to say which version is correct, but the *Periochae*'s version does at least show knowledge of the existence of a town of that name, information which it could not have derived from the surviving books of Livy, in which the town is never mentioned. Thirdly, at 39.3, the *Periochae* records a victory over the Ligurians as being *cis Apenninum* (sc. on the south-west—Roman—side of the Apennines). This happens to be correct, in as much as the campaign which Livy describes took place entirely in north-western Italy south-west of the Apennines. Yet Livy himself does not identify it in this way: the geographical designation comes from the *Periochae* alone.

There are other places where the *Periochae* changes Livy's geography, but those appear to show ignorance rather than knowledge (23.4—possibly a scribal error— and 28.6).[46] The three passages mentioned in the last paragraph all reveal the

---

[45] An additional (though minor) point in support of this is that there are some signs that the author may have known Greek: he reports a Greek etymology at 60.8 (though that may have been inherited from Livy), and uses Greek forms for certain place-names (see 9.3, 14.6, 25.2nn.; cf. 22.2n.). This was an increasingly rare skill among upper-class Italians in this period (Cameron (2011), 527–66), but much commoner among Christians (who sought out Greek for religious reasons) than pagans (Cameron (2011), 534–5).

[46] Jal (1984), xxv–xxvi takes *Per.* 89.9, where Nola is mistakenly said to be in Samnium rather than Campania, to show that the author was not Italian at all. But this assumes far too high a level of geographic awareness in someone who lived before the resources of modern travel and geographical tools: a northern Italian might well be in error concerning a town of southern Italy. Indeed, Livy himself shows some surprising failures of geographical knowledge, even in relation to northern Italy, his

opposite. With the first, it is possible that the correction to Livy was inherited—a similar account of Hannibal's crossing is given in Nepos and Silius Italicus—and the second may depend on an alternative source. But the third is more a clarification than a correction, and all three, as will probably have been noticed, relate to the same general geographic region, namely the north-western part of the Italian peninsula. It seems a reasonable hypothesis that the author was acquainted with—and very possibly based in—that region.

But the author had to have had access to a library with a reasonably complete text of Livy (though see below), which cannot have been that easy to come by (cf. Volume I, xxi). Perhaps he was a wealthy man who owned his own copy, as Symmachus did; but if not, he would have had to read it in either a private or a public library, and the most obvious place to find one in that part of Italy was the imperial Western capital, Milan. If the author was working in Milan, it would also make it easy to explain how the text came soon afterwards to be in the hands of Augustine, who taught in Milan from AD 384 to 387, and thence of Orosius, Augustine's protégé. It might also explain how it was known to Eutropius, who was active in the imperial court of the Eastern empire, and who is likely to have visited Milan in the course of his official career—a likelihood that becomes a near-certainty if, as is probable, he is the Eutropius with whom Symmachus corresponded (*Epist.* 3.46–52: see esp. 3.50, referring to Eutropius' presence in Italy).

Locating the composition of the *Periochae* in Milan is of course speculative, but it is informed rather than random speculation: it makes the best sense of the evidence we have for the date of the author, the geographic features of the text, the resources necessary for its composition, and its subsequent circulation.

There is another aspect of the *Periochae* which may assist us in understanding its composition: namely the variation in the lengths of the books. I discussed this in the Introduction to Volume I, in the context of its rough correlation with the broader record of the citation of Livy's work (xxviii–xxix). As noted there, the average length of books in the *Periochae* varies dramatically by decade, from 262 words per book in the Fifth Decade to 56 words per book in Books 121–142. But for our purposes here, the more interesting point is the variation *within* individual decades. Within the Fifth Decade itself, the length of the books varies between 84 words for Book 43 and 715 words for Book 49.[47] Admittedly, that decade is an

---

own native region (Levene (2010a), 71–3): we should not rule out that the error may have originated with him rather than the *Periochae*.

[47] A note for the statistically minded reader: the standard deviation of the book-lengths (in words) in the *Periochae* of the Fifth Decade is 193.32; in the First Decade, where the average book-length is very similar, the standard deviation is less than half that: 95.47 (though that would be increased to 143.01 if we hypothesize that Book 1 was originally twice its current length). Conversely, the Civil War books (Books 109–116: cf. Volume I, xxx–xxxi) are relatively uniform, with a standard deviation of 32.21, whereas in the Ninth Decade, with an almost identical average book-length, the standard deviation is 58.95.

outlier, given the *Periochae*'s exceptional focus on the Third Punic War (see above, xlviii–l), but other decades show remarkable variations also, even if not over so wide a range: the Ninth Decade, for example, varies between 34 words for Book 87 and 254 words for Book 89.

Much of this may simply be, if not random, at least the reflection of the private interests and focus of the author, some of which may be understandable, but much of which is not easily explicable.[48] For example, within the Third Decade, the shortest book in Livy—Book 29—generates the longest book in the *Periochae* (384 words); conversely, one of the longest books in Livy, Book 21, is the shortest in that decade in the *Periochae* (127 words). Few modern readers would regard Book 29 as more attractive or interesting than Book 21, and there are signs that Livy himself was straining to extend it to an appropriate length (Levene (2010a), 30), but for the author of the *Periochae* it offered a number of points of interest—a central focus on his hero Scipio, for example (cf. above, xliii), and also on Masinissa, another figure to whom the author pays particular attention. But these are not sufficient to explain why, for example, the dispute between Livius Salinator and Claudius Nero during their censorship is extended to the same length as Hannibal's crossing of the Alps and the battles of Ticinus and Trebia all added together, and it may be that the author simply was taking more care or paying more attention to the details of the text when he came to summarize that part of the history.

There is, however, one particular point where the variation in text-length may reveal something more interesting about the composition of the history. Book 36 is the shortest summary in the Fourth Decade (53 words), less than half the length of any other book in that decade—it is in fact the shortest summary of any of Livy's surviving books. A less quantifiable (but nevertheless true) point is that it is also the summary of the surviving books that has the least connection to Livy's actual narrative (cf. esp. 36.1n.). In terms of its length and lack of detail, the summary of this book thus resembles those of a significant number of the later books, which are similarly jejune and vague in what they purport to reproduce from Livy, and it is reasonable to hypothesize that whatever caused the brevity of this summary may be present in the case of those other summaries also.

The summary of Book 36 offers two key pieces of evidence which may assist in those other cases. First, it is unusual, in that its phrasing is entirely unrelated to Livy's: while the *Periochae* often does not employ Livy's words, it is surprising for it to do so nowhere in an entire book. Second, the only part which provides more than minimal detail—namely the dedication of the temple of Magna Mater—relays not Livy's version of events, but one drawn from a

---

[48] Cf. Horster (2017), 44 on the lack of correlation between the lengths of books in Livy and those in the *Periochae*.

different source (36.2n.). That combination of brevity, vagueness, and non-Livian provenance makes it plausible that in this case the author was not working directly from a complete text of Livy, but from one that was in whole or in part defective, and that he was obliged to supplement his own summary from other material, presumably including an earlier summary or contents-list (which he would have needed in order to determine the general scope of the book). This separates these books from those which he is summarizing more fully, where there are strong reasons to believe that he was working directly from Livy's text, even if at times he introduces non-Livian material (see above, xxii–xxviii).

We can therefore reasonably conclude that the library where the author of the *Periochae* was working did not have a complete text of all the books of Livy. This is not especially surprising: as I argued in Volume I (xxix–xxx), a complete text of Livy must have been a rare thing in the fourth century, and manifestly the history did not circulate as a single unit. But the absence of Book 36 alone also suggests something else: that the author was working, at least in part, from a text of Livy that was preserved on papyrus scrolls rather than codices, since it is unlikely that a codex, which would in principle be able to contain an entire decade of Livy, would be missing just one book from the middle of the decade, or even an entire book from the beginning of a pentad.

A similar consideration may help explain the sudden brevity of a book like 53 or 81 or 87 or 91, which are so much shorter than the books around them; it may even explain the absence of Books 136 and 137 from the *Periochae*, though the brevity of all the *Periochae* in that part of the work may suggest that the author had no access to any of those books, in which case we need a different explanation for the complete disappearance of Books 136 and 137. (Conceivably, not only was the author of the *Periochae* working from a defective set of Livy, but so was the author of the epitome he was using to supplement his defective set...)

However, there is a further point to make about the author's working methods. The *Periochae*'s non-Livian version of the Magna Mater temple (36.2) is already anticipated at 29.7, where it presents a version of the oracle commanding the importation of the goddess which assumes the same story as in Book 36. As discussed at 29.7n., we cannot tell whether the *Periochae*'s account of the oracle was itself directly derived from a non-Livian version, or whether the author himself rewrote the oracle in order to make it harmonize with his account of Book 36; but, even if the former is the case, it is clear that he is making an effort to select sources that are coherent with one another, which in turn indicates that he was deliberately seeking to harmonize his narrative between the books he possessed and those he happened not to, rather than making an arbitrary patchwork of his different sources.

vii. Reading the *Periochae*

All of the discussion above shows something of the interesting 'doubleness' of the *Periochae*.[49] As has long been known,[50] and as I discussed above (esp. xxxix–l), the *Periochae* is a text which is doing two different things—things that are certainly not incompatible, but nevertheless have some tension between them. On the one hand it is very self-consciously and visibly abridging the work of Livy, and in that sense presenting itself *as* Livy, but at the same time it is seeking to ensure that it can be read as a narrative independent of and at some points incompatible with Livy's actual text. That tension is, of course, not something unique to the *Periochae*—the vast majority of epitomizing texts in antiquity show something similar, a self-conscious dependence on their original sources, while enabling themselves to be read independently of those sources. Indeed, a similar tension is arguably present in every work in every medium which seeks to recreate an established classic in a new form, representing itself as something that can be experienced in its own right while firmly anchoring itself to an original. One does not have to reach back to antiquity to find those: I am old enough to remember when British children were introduced to Shakespeare via the prose narratives of Charles and Mary Lamb; in my daughter's generation it is not uncommon for children to encounter classics first through graphic novel versions, which proclaim themselves with the title and author of the original work even while diverging substantially from that work in both form and content.

This has a further, more radical and surprising dimension still. But in order to understand this, we need to consider more generally the concept of allusion in historiography, and its distinctive nature.

Until recently it has rarely been appreciated that the distinctive ontological status of historiography—that it purports to be representing reality—means that many, perhaps most, cases of allusion in the historians require the reader to take an entirely different theoretical stance towards them from those we adopt when reading most other writers. I previously discussed this issue at some length,[51] focusing in particular on two separate types of allusion. The first is the case where the historian alludes to another historical text which relates to a different historical event, and I argued that in such cases we are invited to see not merely a

---

[49] Some of the material in this section derives from a paper I prepared for a panel on 'Allusion and Intertextuality in Classical Historiography' organized by John Marincola at the Annual Meeting of the American Philological Association in San Antonio in January 2011; subsequently I placed it unrevised on the Internet as a 'Working Paper' for the journal *Histos* (Levene (2011)). I do not intend to remove that paper from the journal's website, since it has occasionally been cited during the last decade, and I believe it is important for scholarly continuity that such citations can be readily followed; but all future references to this material should be made to the version in this volume, not to the 'Working Paper'.

[50] Cf. e.g. Zangemeister (1882), 90–1, Bingham 472–5, Jal (1984), xc.

[51] Levene (2010a), 82–163.

relationship between texts, but simultaneously a real-life connection between different events.[52] When (as is perhaps most common) the events of the text alluded to predated the events of the alluding text, the implicit assumption is that we can see a form of historical development and indeed direct influence between the two sets of events. There is very often the further implication that the later people are actively aware of and responding to the actions of their predecessors, treating them as models for imitation, and that likewise implies a real-life historical relationship.[53] Even in the less common case, where the events of the later text precede the events of the earlier, a similar—and even more challenging—dynamic is assumed: the later author implies that the events he recounts at the very least prefigured, and may have influenced, the later events written about by his predecessor.[54]

The second case I considered is a more tightly controlled one: the case where the earlier author not merely wrote about the same events, but was actually the later writer's source for those events—my example was of course Polybius and Livy, the best-known and most studied instance of such a relationship where both authors survive more or less intact.[55] It has been traditional to treat the phenomenon of 'sources' as quite separate from the phenomenon of 'allusion' or 'intertextuality', but I argued that such a separation makes no sense in theory, and is manifestly false in practice. Livy not only uses Polybius as a source, but he evokes his text to the reader exactly as he does with his allusions to authors who wrote about other matters, and reworks him so as to self-consciously correct and respond to his version of history. The reworkings do not merely provide us with a window into Livy's aesthetic preferences or political ideology, but they imply something about reality itself as Livy saw it: that Polybius in key respects misunderstood or misrepresented the events that he was describing, and that Livy will provide us with a superior account of them. My conclusion (p. 162): 'Any time that Livy uses Polybius he is effectively alluding to him. Any time that Livy changes Polybius he is effectively responding to him in an act of creative imitation.'

All of this I still believe to be true, and it provides an indication of some of the respects in which allusion and intertextuality in historians needs to be conceptualized in rather different terms from that in other genres, where there is no assumed correspondence to reality, or at best such correspondence is an incidental rather than intrinsic feature of the text. And much the same features are observable in the *Periochae* here. As I noted above (xxvi–xxvii), two of the author's identifiable extraneous sources, Cicero and Valerius Maximus, were widely read

---

[52] Compare O'Gorman (2010), who argues further that such allusions implicitly undermine the historian's claim to be recounting a singular event; also Damon (2010), who notes the blurring of such episodes into occasions where the historian has no specific textual model in mind, but refers to the past events themselves as prefiguring the ones about which he is writing.
[53] Cf. Damon (2010), 385–6.
[54] See Clauss (1997), 180–2; cf. O'Gorman (2010), 238–9.
[55] Cf. the similar arguments in relation to Ammianus put forward by Kelly (2008), 222–55.

in antiquity, and as such are likely to have been known to a good proportion of his readers. But the manner of the *Periochae*'s engagement with Livy's own text, as described above, suggests that the same is true even of his use of Livy. The *Periochae*, summarizing Livy, does not merely use Livy's text as a source; it engages with him, critiques him, even sometimes challenges him, or makes sly jokes at his expense. In other words, the *Periochae*'s use of Livy is in certain respects not unlike Livy's use of Polybius. Livy is the *Periochae*'s source, but Livy is also the *Periochae*'s intertext, a text with which the *Periochae* engages systematically, in a manner which, at least some of the time, self-consciously marks the similarities and differences. And in doing so, just like Livy with Polybius, the *Periochae* shows the author's attitude not only to Livy and to Livy's text, but also to the underlying history which Livy is narrating, and which the *Periochae* is in some form reproducing: he marks for us the places where he is changing or improving on Livy, the places where Livy (on his account) got the history wrong.

So in this respect (but cf. below, lxviii–lxxiv) the *Periochae* treats Livy, albeit only for a select audience, in much the same way as Livy treated Polybius, presumably also for a relatively select audience. And in doing so, it marks not only its attitude to Livy's history as a text, but to the real-life history which Livy was narrating and which the *Periochae* narrates in its turn.

There is one potential objection to this argument. If the *Periochae* is engaging in a programme of allusive adaptation which can only be appreciated if one has Livy's original text to hand, that seems odd, if one considers, as I argued above that one should, the cultural context of the summary. The *Periochae*, as I said, presents itself in a dual fashion: as a summary of Livy, but also as a self-contained history of Rome which it articulates around Livy's book-structure but which can be (and often has been) read as a coherent narrative in its own right. This suggests that the *Periochae* positions itself for a readership which will use it not as an ancillary to Livy, but rather as a substitute for him—and, accordingly, a readership which is highly unlikely to be acquainted with the original text of Livy. This does not appear to sit easily with the idea that the author repeatedly makes sly allusions to Livy which can only be appreciated by a reader of the original text.

This objection, however, rests on a fallacy, albeit a widespread one: that authors, ancient or modern, assume an audience which is effectively monolithic in its knowledge and interests, and address their texts so that everything in them can be appreciated by that monolithic audience. One might imagine that such an assumption could hardly survive reflection on well-known artefacts of our own popular culture (any adult who has watched a good selection of children's films knows how many sly allusions in them are introduced which the ostensible primary audience could never understand); nevertheless all too many scholars appear to proceed without making the connection. It is altogether probable that the author of the *Periochae* saw his sly critiques of and nods to and hints at Livy's original text as something that could be appreciated only by a very select minority of his readers, which would be completely invisible to the majority. Such an appeal to a learned minority is intrinsic to much of the intellectual culture of later antiquity, with its textualized focus and its constant (and sometimes competitive) reliance on detailed textual knowledge by an intellectual elite.[56] Admittedly, as I argued in Volume I (xix–xxi), Livy is not Virgil or Cicero: his text was not widely known even among the educated. But that would not preclude there being a small intellectual subset of aficionados who would appreciate the games being played by the author (or at least those games which related to parts of Livy they were familiar with). It is even possible that he included them as private jokes that he did not necessarily think anyone apart from himself would recognize. Scholars have, after all, sometimes been known to have a sense of humour, which leads them to add private jokes to their work purely for their own amusement. I have even been known to do this myself.

However, what I have discussed above is only one aspect of the distinctive nature of allusion in historiography; in my earlier writing, I believe that I underplayed the extent to which it differs from that in other genres, and accordingly the extent to which it has to be 'retheorized' if we are to make sense of its role.[57]

Historians, as I said, believed themselves and their predecessors to be representing reality. One corollary of that is that, when using a predecessor as a source, they are far more restricted in their ability to rework that source than are their counterparts in almost all other literary genres.[58] Admittedly their licence is demonstrably far greater than one might guess from looking at modern historical practice. The precise extent of that licence is controversial, but no one doubts that historians were prepared to rewrite and invent material in a way that no reputable modern historian would feel free to do. But it is not the licence given to historians, but the constraints on them, that are important for my argument here; for it is likewise the case that no scholar—even A. J. Woodman, the person who has argued most vigorously and systematically for the greatest licence for historical invention—denies that the historians were to some significant degree constrained by their belief that there was a historical core that needed to remain unaltered. Woodman uses the phrase 'hard-core facts' to describe the historical substratum which no historian could plausibly change.[59]

---

[56] Especially illuminating in this regard is Rohrbacher (2016), esp. 76–86, arguing that the bizarre jokes and distortions of the *Historia Augusta* make sense within such shared intellectual practices, offering the audience humorous challenges to recognize what is going on.

[57] Cf. Levene (2015a), 209–15, where I have discussed this question in more detail with specific regard to Livy and Polybius.

[58] See, however, Elliott (2015), arguing that a parallel process may be identified in epic, particularly in historical epic. Her primary example is Ennius, and she suggests that not only does he contribute significantly to the Romans' sense of their own past, but even his reworkings of Homer express a form of ontological commitment of their own: that the Romans he is describing really did replay the (supposedly historical) Trojan War.

[59] Woodman (1988), 88–94.

Now, it is true that, on Woodman's account, the scope of such 'hard-core facts' is relatively narrow, and the 'facts' are best conceived in relatively general terms. So an historian could not deny that (e.g.) Hannibal was defeated by Scipio at the battle of Zama, but he was not tied to any *particular* account of what happened at Zama, and it would be theoretically open to him to rewrite the events of the battle completely from those he found in his source, perhaps basing himself on a stereotype of the way battles (or major battles, or Roman–Carthaginian battles, or any other subset that might seem relevant) would be expected to play themselves out, rather than specific evidence that he might possess about how this battle in particular did play itself out. And (though Woodman does not make this explicit) it is clear that it is precisely the awareness that such licence was taken in the past that would justify a new historian taking the same licence; for if one was aware that the account found in a predecessor might be no more than plausible reconstruction on that historian's part, then it would surely be legitimate to substitute an arguably more plausible reconstruction of one's own in its place.

But the existence of such licence does not mean that it was always taken: in many, perhaps most, cases it is clear that it was not. While an historian *could* (in theory) completely rewrite the events of the battle of Zama, in practice no surviving historian actually *did* completely rewrite the events of the battle of Zama. This is not to say that all accounts are identical; for example, Appian offers a version of the battle in which Scipio and Hannibal engaged in single combat (a version which had previously appeared in the epic of Silius Italicus, though in this case the 'Scipio' is a phantom conjured up by Juno, in imitation of the fake Turnus whom Aeneas pursues in *Aeneid* Book 10), followed by a further single combat between Hannibal and Masinissa. But even here the broad structure of the fighting and the moves of the different parts of the two armies are more or less the same.

And in practice the variants are often even slighter than this, and historians stick closely to their predecessors' accounts not only in outline, but in exact detail: at many of the places where Livy's work overlaps with Polybius, he follows him in immense detail, with only relatively minor changes. If one compares, for example, Flamininus' proclamation of Greek freedom at the Isthmian Games in Polybius (18.46.4–16) with that in Livy (33.32.4–33.4), the overlap between the two is remarkable. It is true that one can note various minor changes that Livy has made. He glosses for his Roman audience the practice of the heraldic announcement from the arena; he removes from Polybius the dull practical reason that some people wished the proclamation repeated (that they had not heard it the first time),[60] and instead focuses entirely on the desire of people to see the messenger for themselves (something Polybius had offered only as his personal speculation, but which Livy turns into unchallenged fact). Livy increases the sense of

---

[60] Walsh (1961), 184, Tränkle (1977), 138.

detachment from the athletics, suggesting not merely (as in Polybius) that there was little attention paid to them, but that the games themselves were truncated.[61] He also slightly downgrades the role of Flamininus,[62] removing an explicit mention of him in the praise of the selflessness of Rome, as well as suppressing the uncomfortable adulation implicit in the address to him as σωτῆρ. But the evocation of Polybius does more than simply allow us to mark Livy's changes: it invites the reader to recognize the limitations of Polybius' perspective. For Polybius the sound of the cheering after the second announcement is merely unimaginably loud; Livy gives it a more specifically political turn by using it as a sign of the Greek desire for liberty—but the allusion to Polybius also sets up an ironic dig at the Greeks, given that Polybius says that the loudness would be incomprehensible to his contemporaries, and Livy was well aware that Greece ultimately lost her liberty to Rome in Polybius' own lifetime. And the comments on the selflessness and virtue of the Romans, which Polybius had praised in his own voice, are transferred by Livy into the mouth of the Greeks, here too indicating Polybius as an authentic representative of Greek attitudes, but—once again, with hindsight—allowing the authorial voice to remain agnostic on the superlative justness of Roman imperial power.

So it would hardly be true to suggest that Livy has reproduced Polybius inertly; but at the same time, the close overlap between his account and Polybius' is obvious. It might indeed appear that it is too obvious to be worth discussing: clearly Livy has based himself on Polybius, but is there anything more than that to be said? I would suggest that, especially in the context of an examination of 'allusion', the phenomenon of one historian closely reproducing another in this way is more important than it is generally given credit for.

Modern scholars and readers—except, naturally, in the context of Quellenforschung, and in particular in the context of attempting to burrow back from a surviving historical text to its source in order to test its historical reliability—have tended to respond to the phenomenon of close historical reproduction with embarrassment. After all, if Livy spends the great bulk of his account of Flamininus' proclamation reproducing Polybius, and if (as happens to be the case here) Polybius survives independently of Livy, what is the point of reading Livy at all? Hence, in the scholarly literature on such passages, the concentration (I profess myself as guilty of anyone else of this) on the relatively few points where Livy demonstrates independence of Polybius, in style and analysis if not necessarily in the content of what is described, in order to rescue him from perceived irrelevance by showing that he has the originality that one would generally require of a canonical writer. And the same is even more obviously true of the *Periochae*, and, even apart from the perception of brevity and superficiality (cf. above), helps

---

[61] Walsh (1961), 184.
[62] Tränkle (1977), 166.

explain its neglect, especially with regard to its summary of the surviving books of Livy. Why would anyone read the *Periochae*'s brief summary of Livy's account of the Hannibalic War when they could read Livy's original? And even if they have not the time to read Livy's original, there is still the sense that the time that one does have could be better spent on something else, rather than reading a text that advertises its own dependence.

But that anxious focus on the minority of differences rather than the majority of similarities seriously misrepresents the balance of Livy's text, and (more significantly) the literary world-view that made possible both Livy's reproduction of Polybius, and the *Periochae*'s reproduction of Livy. Livy often clung closely to his sources in a way which no modern historian would, and this represents a significant difference between ancient and modern historiography which has been far less studied than the imaginative invention which has been the focus of so much scholarship. Just as the licence for historians to invent something new is far greater than would be permitted today, so too was the licence to produce an account which was so close to the original that nowadays it would often be vilified as plagiarism.[63] Similarly, the practice of producing an abbreviated history by massively condensing an existing history in the manner of the *Periochae* would nowadays be considered an unprestigious form of historical writing, and would be unlikely to acquire a readership in the event that anyone chose to do it. Yet in antiquity this was manifestly not the case:[64] the *Periochae* was circulated and survived; indeed, in the parallel case of Justin and Pompeius Trogus, the abridgement entirely superseded the original.

In the case of Livy and Polybius, one possible way of understanding this phenomenon while still retaining the idea of authorial authenticity would be to argue that even the retention of a large portion of the original account can be seen as, effectively, an authorial choice. Since (it may be argued) Livy *could* have diverged significantly from Polybius had he wished—could, indeed, have invented a scene of his own, basing himself on nothing more than his own imaginative reconstruction—one might argue that even if he happened not to do so in this particular case, but instead stuck closely to Polybius' original, that was nevertheless his choice just as much as invention would have been, and it can accordingly be treated as if it were his own original creation.

This argument, however, assumes that the only constraint on Livy is his ideological or aesthetic choices; and that is questionable for the reasons I gave above.

---

[63] This point should not be overstated: Mülke (2010) argues that epitomators were considered suspect in antiquity as actual or potential falsifiers of the original work. But he generalizes this from relatively few examples, none historiographic, and moreover, even if this generalization is accepted, Mülke also acknowledges that such suspicions went hand in hand with an awareness that epitomized works attracted a wide public because of the greater ease of reading them.

[64] Cf. Horster (2017), 25–6. In general on the ancient practice of summarizing and abridging works as a literary-sociological phenomenon, see the essays in Horster and Reitz (2010), esp. Dubischar (2010) for a general survey.

For even if we do not regard the Polybian account of the proclamation of Greek freedom as a 'hard-core fact' in Woodman's sense, namely an event so firmly planted in the popular consciousness that it would be impossible to present an alternative version while still maintaining plausibility,[65] the very fact that Livy chose to maintain it largely intact strongly suggests that he is *treating* it as if it were a 'hard-core fact'. I suggested above that Livy's corrections of Polybius point to his belief in the greater truth of his own account over Polybius'. But it would appear to follow from this that in the places where Livy fails to correct Polybius, but instead reproduces him, he is accepting the truth of Polybius' account, at least in that respect. Hence also there is a practical constraint that prevents him from altering the substance of Polybius, namely that he believes Polybius' account to be true. His grounds for that belief were likely to have been different from a modern historian's—they were presumably less strongly founded in presumptions about the evidence available to his source and the methodology which the source used. But the unchanged reproduction of Polybius' original, while it is certainly an allusion, as I argued above, is an allusion with a distinctive ontological status: it not only refers to Polybius' account, but signals acceptance of its truth. It is hard to detach the allusion to the text of Polybius from the external reality which Livy is relaying, since the two here effectively coincide.

This then leads to a further problem about analysing this allusion according to our normal literary procedures. If Livy's allusion to Polybius is not the product of choice on his part—or at least, is only 'chosen' in the sense that it is governed by his prior commitment to the truth of Polybius' account—then in what sense can we see this as an 'allusion' by Livy at all? Granted that Livy has framed the Polybian material in a new analysis and has changed some details, the bulk of what we read in Livy was compelled upon him by his generic commitment, not taken on as a result of his desire to evoke and respond to Polybius in particular. The difficulty can be seen if we try to construct a historicizing reading of Livy here, relating the details of his text to his position as a writer in the early Augustan period. Such historicist readings are nowadays commonplace: we often assume automatically that our task as critics is to explain our text as the product of a particular author writing at a determinate time. Yet here that is highly problematic. Nothing that Livy relays unchanged from Polybius can, it might appear, be legitimately regarded as a product of the early Augustan period, since it is a creation of a Greek writer of the middle Republic, which Livy is reproducing unchanged for no other reason than that he regards it as true.

---

[65] It may however be noted that the later versions of this story (e.g. Val. Max. 4.8.5, Plu., *Flam.* 10.3–11.2, App., *Mac.* 4) do not diverge from Polybius in any more substantial respect than Livy's does, which *may* imply that Polybius' version achieved broadly canonical status. The only significant variant is the anecdote relayed by both Valerius and Plutarch, that the Greek cheers were so overwhelming that birds fell from the sky; and this represents a detachable addition to rather than a correction of Polybius' account.

Now this point should not be overstated; for Livy does after all have some measure of freedom even within his acceptance of the truth of Polybius' account: he does, as I noted above, make a number of changes at the margins, and even in the places where he felt unable to do that, he could, if nothing else, have abridged it considerably, and in that sense the reproduction of details from Polybius represents a choice he made.

But if we now return from Livy's use of Polybius to the *Periochae*'s use of Livy, we can see the same issue even more acutely: for the very nature of the *Periochae*'s project means that its freedom to make changes to its original is in certain ways considerably more constrained than Livy's. In this case the presence of the prior text in the later one is overt: the later text precisely defines itself around that relationship, articulating itself as a book-by-book summary of its predecessor. Indeed, the two texts are so closely related to one another that people rarely read the *Periochae* as a text in its own right: it is read for what it tells us about the text of Livy (or about the subject of Livy's narrative) rather than as an independent entity. And for the same reason it would appear that to attempt to analyse the *Periochae*'s summary of Livy as an 'allusion' to Livy in its totality (as opposed to those occasions when the *Periochae* self-consciously points to its changes of the original) is unlikely to produce a meaningful result. The *Periochae*'s narration is governed not by its choices, but by the prior narration of Livy and its own prior decision to summarize that narrative.

Against that, however, if we *do* decide to read the *Periochae* against the grain of tradition, and consider it as an independent text rather than as a window (if an opaque window) into Livy, we can easily find places where, even within the general fidelity to Livy, the author appears to be asserting something of his own. Consider, for example, the *Periochae*'s handling of the same episode I have been discussing, namely Flamininus' proclamation of the independence of Greece in Book 33. What in Livy, as in Polybius before him, was an iconic and revealing scene in the history of Roman–Greek relations, is reduced to a brief subordinate participial phrase—*Graecia liberata*. Instead the *Periochae* focuses nearly half its account of the book on an episode which in Livy is (relative to the length of his text) much briefer and on the face of things less consequential, namely the flight of Hannibal from Africa to the court of Antiochus III. For a work on the scale of the *Periochae*, after all, the 'freedom of Greece' is not an iconic and world-changing moment, but a short-lived phenomenon which vanishes within a couple of pages. The iconic character of Hannibal is far more pertinent within the centuries of Roman history, even if his great days are now behind him; it is worth comparing *Per.* 35, more than half of which is devoted to the single scene where Scipio and Hannibal meet for the first time since Zama, and *Per.* 39, where the author makes a point of recording Hannibal's death.

So the *Periochae* can certainly be read as a narrative in its own right. Its balance and structure can be (and frequently are) substantially adjusted, because the general project of retelling Livy, unlike Livy's reworking of Polybius, is governed by the desire to abridge his text into a more manageable and readable format. Abridgement necessarily and constantly involves a degree of selectivity: even *Per.* 35.1, the narrative section of the surviving books with the greatest pretensions to comprehensiveness, is still shorter than Livy's original text. And in that respect, it makes sense to read the *Periochae*, as indeed I have above, in a historicist fashion, as a distinctive product of the third quarter of the fourth century AD. When the *Periochae* chooses from the broad text of Livy what to narrate and what to omit, when it chooses what to narrate briefly and what to narrate more fully, one can see it as reflecting, at least in large part, the interests of an author from a particular background from a particular period: I gave various examples of this in the discussion above. Hence, paradoxical though it may sound from our modern perspective, it in one way arguably makes more sense to read the *Periochae* as an independent narrative than it does to read Livy himself as one: for the *Periochae*'s project of selection and compression means that almost every moment of its text shows a level of independent choice which, on the argument above, it is harder to ascribe to Livy.

Nevertheless, with that said, it obviously makes no sense to ignore the Livian provenance of the material. The content of the *Periochae* is to a large extent predetermined by the author's project of summarizing Livy. It declares its relationship to Livy overtly and constantly: it frames itself entirely as a summary of Livy, as a text that is secondary to Livy's original. Livy hints at the extent of his relationship to Polybius (cf. Levene (2010a), 161–2), but he neither is nor suggests that he is parasitic on his text in the way in which the *Periochae* marks its own secondariness to Livy, organizing its structure around the associated Livian books, and repeatedly referring to the contents of Livy's text (above, xxxix). That self-conscious secondariness is of course normal in the case of epitomizing texts, but it means that the intertextual engagement with Livy's original that I have described above has a very different texture from Livy's own intertextual engagement with his sources.[66] Even though, as I discussed above, the allusive programme of Livy's work is arguably more insistently present than the *Periochae*'s is, it can only be recognized as such by an informed reader who recognizes the sources on which Livy is drawing: the uninformed reader—which in fact means every modern reader, since almost all of Livy's sources apart from Polybius are lost—will be more likely to see Livy's narrative as self-sufficient. By contrast, no reader of the *Periochae* can ignore the presence of Livy behind the narrative, even with those books of Livy that are lost. This means that any allusions to other authors are intrinsically subordinated to the overarching presence of Livy, even in those cases when the other author's version of a story has supplanted Livy's own.

---

[66] Cf. Love (2019), 50–1. More generally on epitomizing as a form of intertextuality, cf. Formisano and Sogno (2010), 376–8.

Hence we can read a meaningful narrative in the *Periochae*, but the meaning we read is not the product of any one author. It is a combination of two authors: Livy himself, who determines the content, and the author of the *Periochae*, who selects, compresses, and adjusts and perhaps even (by his own lights) improves[67] within that content. But in fact even that analysis understates the various contributions; for we have already seen that Livy himself, when composing certain parts of his text, is constrained by his prior acceptance of the historicity of Polybius' account—an account which the author of the *Periochae* is highly unlikely to have read, but which nevertheless lies two stages behind his own narrative. Any interpretation of it as a narrative has to treat it not as free composition, nor even as one text alluding to another in the sense in which we generally analyse such allusions in works where the author is presumed to have a freer hand to select and rework his source texts. Instead we need to treat the alluding text as— in effect—a collaboration, but a collaboration across time by authors who may be assumed to be unacquainted with one another. In consequence, while the overall narrative of the *Periochae* has an ideological valence, it is not solely the ideology of the historical moment when the text was produced (although it is that in part). It simultaneously reflects a dynamic ideological system across centuries of Roman history.

And moreover, the contributors to that dynamic system are not only the authors in the direct chain of influence that leads from Polybius to Livy and thence to the *Periochae*. As I noted above, when the *Periochae* changes Livy's narratives, very often it does so in order to make Livy align more closely with the versions that are apparent in other texts of the later Empire. In that respect, the *Periochae* is not only 'collaborating' with Livy, but is reflecting, continuing, but also transforming the wider historical memory of the Roman Republic as it passed through the centuries of the Empire and as paganism gave way to Christianity.

The study of such historical memories, as maintained collectively in the wider community, has been the centre of much scholarship in recent decades, not least because the ability to share stories about the community's past is arguably central to every society's conception of itself as a unit.[68] When it comes to Rome, we do

---

[67] Cf. Mülke (2010), 74–83 for epitomators claiming the independent value of their own work over the original.

[68] Central to the development of the study of collective memory is Halbwachs (1980: originally published in 1950); however, Halbwachs's primary focus was on the social construction of memories within individuals or small groups, and he wanted to draw a sharp division between such collective memories and the broader consciousness of the past such as is found in a national history (see esp. Halbwachs (1980), 78–87). Later scholars have argued that such a division cannot be justified: see e.g. Burke (1989), arguing for social memories in Halbwach's sense and the written records which together make up a society's 'history' as different manifestations of the same essential phenomenon, the ways in which a society collectively remembers its past, which however vary from culture to culture both in the manner and in the richness of content which is remembered. Along similar lines, Jan Assmann has articulated a theoretical development whereby collective memories (or, as he calls them, cultural

not, of course, have access to many of the ways in which those stories were shared and maintained, since the entire oral dimension of story transmission is not available to us; but we can see them in many other media, iconographic and textual, and historiography is a central component of that.[69] Although Livy was, as I have discussed, seen as the iconic historian of the Republic, the length—and hence relative unreadability—of his work meant that the role of his actual text in that transmission was less central than those of its briefer epigones such as the *Periochae* (or Orosius or Ampelius or Eutropius or Florus). All of these together, along with other places, both older and newer, in which the stories were represented and alluded to, together constitute different aspects of that collective historical memory of the Republican past in the Roman Empire. But although the memories are collectively maintained, there are nevertheless differences of emphasis and interpretation, and those differences, too, form part of that constantly evolving dynamic tradition which connects the society of the present with their remembered or constructed past.

Allusivity in its traditional sense is usually treated as independent of that collective memory,[70] but the argument above should show that, when it comes to historiography, the two are intimately connected. The *Periochae* is, as noted above, highly constrained in its allusive engagement to its source text by the very fact that it accepts the essential authority of that text.[71] That authority is not, of course, in itself specific to historiography, since some form of it is intrinsic to the activity of epitomizing itself, even with a fictional text—without such authority, the new text could not claim the appropriate relationship to the original one (the 'arguments' attached to Greek tragedies in our manuscripts reflect the authority of the original play even though there is no claim to an external historicity of the

---

memories) are created from different combinations of an oral and ritual practice with written texts to create the historical self-consciousness of a community (see e.g. Assmann (2006), (2011), 15–121). Cf. also Cubitt (2007), who wants to distinguish 'social memory' from 'collective memory', seeing the latter as the artificial self-conception of a supposedly discrete community, whereas the former is a shared sense of the past which nevertheless reflects the constantly shifting dynamics of social relations: it is social memory above all, he argues, that has an intimate connection with (though is not identical to) history properly practised (see esp. Cubitt (2007), 26–49, 199–249). There has been a vast output of scholarship related to the broader question, touching on every discipline from history to archaeology to anthropology to sociology to media studies and much else: for a useful survey see Olick, Vinitzky-Seroussi, and Levy (2011).

[69] See Walter (2004) for a comprehensive analysis of the role of different media of memory in maintaining historical traditions during the Republic itself; also the essays in Sandberg and Smith (2018), esp. Sandberg (2018). Cf. Hölkeskamp (1996), (2001), (2016) (the last two focusing particularly on topography and monuments), and Pina Polo (2004), both of whom emphasize the centrality of aristocratic culture in originally constructing those traditions. For social memory across the whole of Roman history, extending up to (and beyond) the time of the *Periochae* itself, see e.g. the essays in Galinsky (2014), (2016), Galinsky and Lapatin (2015); for historical memories of the Republic specifically, see Felmy (2001), Gowing (2005), Gallia (2012).

[70] Note, however, Roller (2013) (cf. also Hölkeskamp (2018)), who specifically examines the relationship between the social memory embodied in non-literary media in a manner closely analogous to intertextuality, although he prefers the term 'intersignification'.

[71] Cf. Love (2019), 47–8.

events depicted in those plays). But with historiography, as discussed above, there is the additional constraint of the fundamental truth (or so it is assumed) of the events described by the historian. When the *Periochae* reproduces Livy's narrative; it does so out of fidelity not only to Livy's text, but also to the 'facts' of Republican history. By the time of late antiquity, Livy was the prime representative of that history, but far from the only one, since various of the stories were enshrined in the collective memory of the Roman community. Narratives such as Livy's or the *Periochae*'s served to fix them in a broader historical framework, associating different stories and characters with one another and linking better-known figures and stories to less-known ones.

But although the historical memory of the Republic was formally identified with Livy, that broader stream of collective memory often diverged from the specifics of his text. That tension is central to explaining the many occasions when the *Periochae* changes Livy's original: it effectively realigns the text of Livy with the historical memory, which is now relabelled as 'Livy', by attributing the latter to the former. And this has a consequence for the process of allusion. As I argued above, reproducing one's historical source without changing it is a consequence of accepting the truth of the events underlying that historical source, and as such, even if an 'allusion', it is not one that can readily be analysed in historicist terms by reference to the choices of the author. Usually that problem only appears in cases where the original's version is unchanged; but the *Periochae* ensures that the same is true even when Livy's text is changed, since it attributes the putatively true version to him, replacing the putatively false or incomplete version which he actually wrote. This alignment of Livy's text with the 'true' history is admittedly not total, since, as I argued above, the *Periochae* sometimes discreetly hints at the changes it is making to the original; but, as I also argued, only a small minority of the readership could ever have recognized those hints. For other readers, the constant and insistent allusion to Livy is present by implication in every portion of the *Periochae*, even those parts which in fact diverge from Livy (since those readers, by definition, would not have read Livy's original text), but it is not an interpretable one. The *Periochae*'s allusive relationship with Livy simply guarantees for readers that the *Periochae*, like Livy himself, is reproducing the 'true' history of Rome, which they themselves would know because different elements of it formed part of the collective historical memory of their society.

That historical memory is itself not the product of a particular era, although it is also not entirely fixed: it is, in effect, transhistorical. The story of Flamininus' liberation of Greece begins with Polybius, but then is told across centuries of Roman history, including both Livy and the *Periochae*. The significance of that story at Rome does not lie solely in any particular author's adaptation of it— though of course it is at various times adapted in some of its details, as I have shown; it needs to be understood as a feature of the Romans' conception of their own history that remains constant (at least in part) across time. This is not to say, of course, that we should see it as a fixed and deterministic part of Roman culture, because even while the core of the story remains constant to be drawn on by successive authors, there is a changing penumbra; and different stories and different aspects of each story fade in and out.[72] Nor should we assume that 'Roman ideology' or 'Roman culture' is itself a discrete and self-contained thing. To mention only the most obvious point, Greeks writing under the Roman empire, like Plutarch or Appian, may well be assumed to be working in a tradition that is partly different: it is intrinsically unlikely that Flamininus' 'liberation' of Greece had the same resonance in then-liberated-but-subsequently-conquered Greece as it did in the city of Rome (or indeed in imperial Milan). Nevertheless, the substantial narrative core of Roman history cannot be narrowly pinned down to a single author or a single time and place;[73] and our readings of the texts in which that history is represented need to take that into account.

Such an approach to literary texts runs counter to many of our assumptions about the way in which meaning through allusion is generated. As I noted above, contemporary interpreters of ancient historiography (as of other literary texts) have tended to work from broadly historicist assumptions, whereby we abstract the contribution of each particular writer and seek to interpret it as a product of its time. But once we understand that allusion in ancient historiography can often be generated less by a decision to allude, but rather more by a prior commitment to represent the work of an earlier author (often founded in a presumption of that work's historicity), it makes more sense to adopt a broader, transhistorical approach side by side with that historicism, and to see the episodes not as a product of a single writer, but as part of the developing traditions of Roman historical culture and Roman historical memory.

Polybius, Livy, the *Periochae*, and many other texts, all form part of that transhistorical reading; the major difference is that in some ways the *Periochae*, for all its dependence on Livy, offered a more independent reworking of it than he did. That seems odd and paradoxical to us, but it should be emphasized that this does not mean that the *Periochae* is 'more worth reading' than Livy. Whether something is 'worth reading' of course depends on the interests and aims of the reader;

---

[72] On the theory underlying this, cf. Cubitt (2007), 14–20.
[73] Hans-Joachim Gehrke has influentially developed the idea of 'intentional history' in the context of (especially) Greece, whereby the collective memory of the community is developed by historians and others in a fashion which supports the particular needs of a community to maintain its identity at a certain time (see e.g. Gehrke (2001), or the essays in Foxhall, Gehrke, and Luraghi (2010)). The potency of this model is obvious, but there are dangers in it also. One is that it often leads to a narrowly political conception of why certain stories predominate and others do not: see the important caveats about the excessive politicization of memory studies offered by e.g. Confino (1997). But a second problem is that it can lead to too strong an emphasis on immediate material circumstances and too little on the conservatism through which a society links itself to its ancestors via the perpetuation of its historical beliefs of their ancestors even in the absence of a contemporary material need to do so: cf. Shils (1981) for the hold of tradition in shaping a society; also Schudson (1989) for the past having its own force which prevents it from simply being rewritten by a new generation.

and most of the things in Livy that a modern reader finds most attractive are absent from the *Periochae* (cf. above, xlvi–xlviii). Livy is intense, dramatic, and above all often profound; the *Periochae* is curt, uninvolving, undramatic, and rarely if ever shows even the slightest elements of profundity. This in one sense should not especially surprise us: profundity is a gift granted to few. The *Periochae* is more often clever than profound, since cleverness is far more widespread a gift than profundity (as any participant in the modern university system can easily attest). In another sense, ascribing profundity to Livy, a text and an author whose independence (or so I am arguing) is severely constrained, may seem surprising; but that is perhaps because of our post-Romantic association of profundity with individual genius. In reality, there is no reason to accept that as an automatic association: any student of the Babylonian Talmud will be well aware how deeply thought a text may be, despite being the product of no single thinker, and in any case Livy, for all the constraints upon him, is nevertheless a vastly more prominent contributor to his own text than are any of the individuals whose thoughts collectively make up the Talmud.

viii. The *Periochae* and the Articulation of Livy's Text

One of the primary questions that people have sought to determine from an examination of the *Periochae* is the structure of Livy's work in the portion which is lost. Livy's surviving work is, famously, divided into sections of five and ten books, commonly known as 'pentads' and 'decades'. Some such structure is more or less guaranteed by Livy himself, who marks a strong break at the ends of Book 5 and Book 20 and Book 30, as is demonstrated not only by clear narrative caesurae at those points (the Gallic sack in Book 5, the beginning and end of the Hannibalic War in Books 21 and 30), but also by prefatory material at the beginning of Books 6, 21, and 31, all of which directly indicate a structural break in the work. There is no comparable preface at the beginning of Book 26 or Book 36, and the beginning of Book 41 is lost, but it is not hard to find respects in which Livy appears to have marked those as structural turning points also: both Book 26 and Book 36, contrary to Livy's usual practice, begin with a new consular year, and Book 36 opens with the preliminaries of a major new war with Antiochus III, while Books 25 and 26 contain a number of episodes which collectively mark a major turning point in the Hannibalic War, including the Roman defeat in Spain in Book 25 followed by the rise of Scipio Africanus in Book 26, and Hannibal's march on Rome at the opening of Book 26 (cf. Levene (2010a), 15–16). Book 40 ends with the death of Philip V of Macedon and the accession of Perseus, who starts to prepare for the Third Macedonian War in Book 41, while Book 45 contains the settlement following Rome's victory in that war. It fits this general pattern that the *Periochae* indicates that there was prefatory material in Book 16, introducing the history of Carthage as a prelude to the First Punic War (*Per.* 16.1n.).

However, even in the surviving books there is one place where it is hard to see a significant break at the five-book boundary, namely Book 10/11, because the Third Samnite War demonstrably is not concluded in Book 10, but continues into Book 11. It is true that, as Stadter argues, the victory of Papirius at Aquilonia is represented as the effective conclusion of the Samnites' ability to prosecute the war in a substantial manner (10.44.8), and the book concludes with a detailed account of Papirius' triumph (10.46.1–9).[74] Nevertheless the basic fact is that Book 11 contained further fighting against and indeed defeats at the hands of the Samnites, before further major victories were achieved by Fabius Gurges and Curius Dentatus, and it is hard to imagine that Livy presented those as unimportant. In this case it is arguable that Book 6–15, covering the conquest of Italy between the Gallic Sack and the First Punic War, should be seen as a more coherent unit than either Books 1–10 or Books 11–20,[75] for all that, once Livy was being transmitted in codex form, it became natural to conceptualize these books in terms of 'the First and Second Decades', shown not only by the extant MSS (cf. Volume I, xxix–xxx), but also by the references to Livy's 'decades' in both the *Acta Sancti Sebastiani Martyris* (C 51) and the letter of Pope Gelasius (F 4), even though neither the First nor the Second Decade is as coherently unified as either the Third Decade or the Fourth Decade are.[76]

That separation between the tradition of manuscript copying and the narrative conception, or (to put it differently) between the clearly decade-based structure of some sections and narratives that cut across decades elsewhere, is revealing when we come to the far more difficult task of discerning a structure within Books 46–142. There are, admittedly, times when we can easily see the possibilities for articulating around pentads or decades, or places where key structural moments are identified at five-book boundaries. Books 71–80 neatly encompass the Social War:[77] according to the *Periochae*, Book 71 began with the campaign for Italian citizenship conducted by Livius Drusus, while Book 80 contained the conclusion of the war with the granting of citizenship; it also contained the death of Marius, which, even if it was not literally at the end of the book in the manner the *Periochae* suggests (cf. above, xxxvi), nevertheless could easily be presented as a key turning point in the history. Books 81–90, similarly, centre on Sulla,[78] beginning with his

---

[74] Cf. Stadter (1972), 294 (= Chaplin and Kraus (2009), 99–100).

[75] So, rightly, Syme (1959), 30 = (1979), 403; cf. Wille (1973), 54–6.

[76] It is worth observing that after the rise of the codex, Greek historians, too, were regularly copied in volumes containing five or ten books, even when nothing in the internal structure of their works obviously justified that arrangement: see Irigoin (1997), 132–3.

[77] Stadter (1972), 294–5 (= Chaplin and Kraus (2009), 100–1). Syme (1959), 31–2 (= (1979), 405), in a confusing and not altogether coherent argument, denies any break at all between Book 70 and Book 71 on the basis that the first part of the tribunate of Livius Drusus was in Book 70; but that overstates the problem, since the *Periochae* clearly suggests that Livy confined his programme for Italian citizenship to Book 71. But in any case by the end of the paragraph Syme appears to have recanted, and sees a new beginning in Book 71 after all.

[78] Stadter (1972), 295–6 (= Chaplin and Kraus (2009), 101); cf. Chaplin (2010), 462 for the *Periochae*'s particular interest in—and even sympathy towards—Sulla. Syme (1959), 33 (= (1979),

sack of Athens, containing his march on Rome and his dictatorship, with his death coming in Book 90. Book 120 contained—and very possibly ended with—the death of Cicero, while the *Periochae* includes a note at the beginning of Book 121 that it was published after the death of Augustus: if we hypothesize how this entered the text of the *Periochae*, the most likely possibility is that it derives from a prefatory note inserted by Livy himself, explaining why he withheld this and subsequent books after completing them (since he cannot plausibly have written more than twenty books in the three years of life that were left to him).[79] Hence this too looks like a book which marked a new segment of the work.

However, not all of the lost books can be so easily fitted into such a structure. Most obviously, as noted in Volume I (xxx–xxxi), the Civil War books, Books 109–116, circulated as an eight-book edition. This, of course, does not demonstrate that Livy himself presented them as a unit, but at the very least they must have been sufficiently self-contained that they made sense in those terms, and *Per.* 109 begins the book by noting that it 'recounts the causes and beginnings of the Civil War' (109.1: *causae civilium armorum et initia referuntur*), which at least gives the impression that Livy offered introductory material to the war in that book, if not necessarily a preface *per se* (compare the language it uses of the opening of the Second Macedonian War: *Per.* 31.1). Other examples: the Third Punic War crosses a decade boundary, running from Books 48 to 51. The tribuneships of Gaius Gracchus do the same (Books 60–61). Hypothesizing that the primary unit of Livy's structure is not the pentad or the decade, but the pentakaidekade (sc. fifteen books), as Wille (1973) does (with further five- or ten-book subdivisions within it), deals with the first problem, but certainly not the second, since Book 60 is at the boundary of two pentakaidekades also;[80] Wille's thesis also requires that we see a primary division in Book 75, in the centre of the Social War, and making that more significant than the fact that the Social War, as noted above, occupies the decade 71–80. Wille (1973), 84–109 has an elaborate argument for his thesis, based around what he argues Livy saw as the primary theme of each fifteen-book group, with a central character associated with each group (Scipio Aemilianus in Books 45–60, Marius in Books 61–75, Sulla in Books 76–90,

---

406) sees the break with Sulla's abdication, which he claims was in Book 89, rather than his death in Book 90; but there is in any case nothing explicit in the *Periochae* to say in which book Livy placed the abdication, which is at least as likely to have been in Book 90 as Book 89 (see *ad loc.*).

[79] For the relationship between this note and the political attitude of Livy to Augustus see *ad loc.*

[80] As noted already by Nissen (1872), 556, raising the pentakaidekade possibility only to argue against it. This point also tells decisively against Crosby (1978), who, building on Wille, suggested that the primary organization of the history was in groups of thirty books which are secondarily broken down into units of fifteen. Wille (1973), 82–3 seeks to solve the problem with an elaborate but far-fetched argument which makes Gracchus' career as tribune far less significant to Livy's account of Roman history than is either suggested by the *Periochae* or can be considered *a priori* plausible.

Pompey in Books 91–105, Caesar in Books 106–120),[81] but the idea that one can separate Marius-centred books from Sulla-centred ones, or Pompey from Caesar, in so neat a way makes little sense even in principle, and is certainly not supported by the balance of events recorded in the *Periochae* (cf. Luce (1977), 19–20).

Admittedly, it can hardly be conclusively demonstrated that Livy did not see things in the way that Wille claims, but, given the intrinsic malleability of perceived historical structures and the human ability to observe patterns in them, there is virtually no pattern for which we could not find some justification, especially in the case of books that do not survive and to which we have access only through a summary whose emphases are demonstrably different from Livy's own. However, in addition to the objection noted above, two fundamental points tell against Wille's argument: the strong preface at the beginning of Book 21, which clearly marks 21–30 as a primary unit, and the ancient eight-book edition of Books 109–116, which, even if (as is likely) it does not originate with Livy himself, nevertheless was accepted by people who, unlike us, were able to read the books in question, and, as noted above, clearly thought that it made sense to think of them as a unit. When combined with the problematic lack of an apparent break after Book 60, and the apparent coherence of Books 71–80 as a narrative unit (see above), it seems unlikely that seeing Livy's history as a series of fifteen-book units is the key to understanding the structure of his history.

An interesting alternative is offered by T. J. Luce:[82] he argues that the pentadic structure was retained by Livy, but was handled in a completely different way. Luce argues that, instead of wars or other major events, the structure was marked by placing key events on either side of the boundary between the pentads or decades: thus the Third Punic War comes to a climax in Book 50 with the conclusion coming in Book 51, the bulk of Gaius Gracchus' career as tribune is in Book 60 but the end of his tribuneship and his death in Book 61, Pompey's Mithridatic command beginning in Book 100 but his final defeat of Mithridates in Book 101, Caesar's final victories in Book 115 but his assassination in Book 116. This meets the objection above, since on this model the decades and pentads do not have to mark off key events from one another, but effectively unite them at the boundary. Luce's thesis, however, creates a new problem, namely how such a structure could plausibly be perceived by readers, especially since Luce offers no parallels for it that would contribute to its recognizability. It is hard to imagine that readers would perceive a pentad- and decade-based structure to Livy's surviving books had he postponed the battle of Zama to Book 31, or the battle of Cynoscephalae to Book 36 or Pydna to Book 46; similarly the hexadic structure of Tacitus' *Annals*

---

[81] The claim that Livy's structure was articulated around leading individuals was anticipated by Nissen (1872), 551–5, but in a much more fluid form, since Nissen did not believe that Livy had a rigid formal structure for his work (cf. below, lxxviii); he did, however, argue that the deaths of those individuals were a central way in which Livy punctuated and structured his narrative.

[82] Luce (1977), 9–24, elaborating and expanding a suggestion originally made by Walsh (1961), 6.

would appear to disappear completely if the last years of Tiberius' reign had been in Book 7 rather than Book 6 and if the accession of Nero had been in Book 14 rather than Book 13. Moreover, the eight-book Civil War edition is still hard to explain on his hypothesis.

Given all of this, it may well be the case that Livy did not have a single structuring device for his entire work—and indeed, it may be argued that to do so became increasingly hard as he came closer to his own day and devoted relatively more books to fewer years (the last half of his history—Books 71-142—covers around eighty years in more than seventy books), combined with the fact that the expansion of the empire required Livy to narrate several overlapping series of events in different parts of the world.[83] A more sensible interpretation would be to say that, while Livy clearly had a fondness for five- and ten-book structures, and was able to maintain them in the earlier parts of his work, the exigencies of his history, as Roman politics and the exercise of Roman power became more diffuse and complex, necessitated that he sometimes employed other structural units as the work progressed.[84] But what those structural units were is in many cases opaque, since our primary evidence is the *Periochae*, which demonstrably distorts Livy's emphases at least as often as it reflects them. For example, if Livy marked any sort of structural break in the intervening period between Book 91, the first after Sulla's death, and Caesar's invasion of Italy in Book 109 (and, at least to judge by his practice in the surviving books, it seems improbable that he did not), it is completely invisible in the *Periochae*: every book in that set shows a narrative which continues the themes of the previous book and is then continued in the subsequent book, without any caesura apparent.[85]

A further issue with the structure of the history is the fact that the *Periochae* records that it contains the very irregular number of 142 books; but at the same time books 136 and 137 are missing. One might have guessed that Livy wrote 140 books and the numbering of the books in the *Periochae* MSS has gone awry, but that is manifestly not the case: an entire decade of history has dropped from the

---

[83] As rightly noted by Luce (1977), 17-19; as he felicitously observes, 'events and years would be viewed under increased magnification' (18).

[84] This thus adds a fifth structural possibility to the four offered by Luce (1977), 13: namely (a) Livy continued to use pentads and decades; (b) Livy structured thematically rather than by set numbers of books; (c) Livy ceased to use any structure at all; and (d) Livy structured by some other numerical scheme (such as hexads) after Book 45. Much of my argument here was anticipated by Nissen (1872), still perceptive on the central issue.

[85] Stadter (1972), 296-8 (= Chaplin and Kraus (2009), 101-5) seeks to identify breaks after Book 100 and Book 110, and thus also to deny the salience of the eight-book Civil War edition to the question; but his arguments are strained and at one point explicitly *a priori* ('If Livy before had organized by decades, there is every reason to think that he still did so in Books XCI-C' (Stadter (1972), 296 (= Chaplin and Kraus (2009), 102))). He (like Wille (1973), 107-8) also fails to observe that the Civil War edition is attested in the Lucan scholia (see Volume I, xxx), and hence is not merely an artefact of the *Periochae* or its source. The idea of a major structural break after Book 110, two books into that edition and at the time when Caesar had just crossed over to Greece to face Pompey, is thus doubly implausible.

Periochae along with those books, and that Livy did indeed cover the period is guaranteed by Censorinus' quotation of his introduction to the account of Augustus' celebration of the Secular Games in 17 BC, which he assigns to Book 136 (F 67).

A more elaborate version of the case for 140 books is offered by Barnes (1998), 211–12: he notes that Books 140–142 in the *Periochae* each cover around a year of history each (a slight misinterpretation: see *ad locc.*), whereas the books covering the period 29–12 BC each cover at least three years. He proposes, therefore, that this material originally appeared in Book 140 alone, but 'after the Periochae of CXXXVI and CXXXVII had been lost, it seems that someone, in a futile attempt to repair the loss, expanded the summary of Book CXL to cover three books (viz., the Periochae of CXL–CXLII)'. But Barnes's hypothetical scribal correction is highly improbable: one would expect a scribe bothered by the loss of Books 136 and 137 to expand the narrative into Books 136 and 137, rather than tacking two extra books onto the end with new numbering but leaving a gap at 136 and 137. And the problem that he finds with the slowing of the narrative in Books 140–142 is no problem at all. Earlier in the history Livy had allowed the events of a single year—42 BC—to extend over four books (121–124), so he manifestly had no problem slowing his narrative to that degree; and Books 140–142, according to the *Periochae*, focused on the campaigns of the current emperor, Tiberius, and his brother Drusus, and so Livy had both potential access to extensive information about them and a possible incentive to write about them at some length.

The most likely explanation for the *Periochae* recording 142 books, therefore, is that Livy wrote 142 books. He may well have intended to write more, perhaps to extend his history to the neater figure of 150 books, but if so, he died or ceased working before completing his plan; and the disappearance of Books 136 and 137 is coincidental.

ix. Note on the Text

The MS tradition of the *Periochae* is closely bound up with that of Florus: all of the oldest MSS of the *Periochae* (save, perhaps, the fragmentary MS B discussed below), and a lot of the more recent ones, append it to the text of Florus. Accordingly, any investigation of the relationships between the MSS needs to take full account of Florus as well as the *Periochae*: this lies beyond the scope of this edition, and in any case such an investigation has already been thoroughly done, first by R. A. Reid (1969) (cf. also Reid (1990)), and subsequently by M. D. Reeve (1988), (1991), who partly based himself on Reid's analysis, but also offered significant corrections to it. What follows below is a slightly modified summary of the conclusions of Reeve, who argues that only these MSS (all of which I have personally collated) need to be employed for the construction of a text of the *Periochae*.

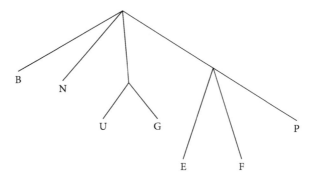

Fig. 1 Outline stemma derived from Reeve (1988 and 1991)[86]

The two oldest manuscripts of the whole of the *Periochae* are demonstrably independent of one another (cf. below). The first, N (Heidelberg Pal. Lat. 894, 62r–104v, https://digi.ub.uni-heidelberg.de/diglit/cpl894), was written early in the ninth century, probably at Lorsch: for fuller description, see Reid (1969), 13–14. The second, P (Paris B.N., Lat. 7701, 76r–104v, https://gallica.bnf.fr/ark:/12148/btv1b10510431j/f155.image.r=7701), was written in France in the twelfth century (Reid (1969), 18). P is substantially more corrupt than N,[87] but has received extensive correction from a second hand of the same date (P² in the apparatus),[88] which itself had access to either P's source MS or one related to it.[89]

Of approximately the same age as N is B (Bern A 92.10, 1r–1v), which is just a single leaf, containing *Per.* 6.2 *Sabatina*–8.1 *facerent*. Reeve (1988), 487 notes that it is possible that it could be the MS from which all the later MSS derive,[90] but too small a portion survives to make that anything more than a vague conjecture. I am, accordingly, tentatively treating it in the stemma above as an independent witness.

A further group of MSS, called α by Reid, includes all of Florus, but omits the whole of the *Periochae* after 7.12 *restituti sunt*; Reeve (1991), 456–7 (*contra* Reid

---

[86] This stemma includes only the seven MSS I have collated for this edition; in reality, the branches represented here by U and G and by E and F each contains many more MSS: see Reid (1969) for a full listing.

[87] At least until *Per.* 41.3 *successerat*, after which a new scribe appears to have taken over, and a marked improvement is noticeable in the care with which it was copied.

[88] I also occasionally use P¹ to record corrections by the first hand where it seems relevant to the text to keep them distinct from the copyist's original text.

[89] One unusual quirk of P² deserves notice. When the MS reports census figures and other large numbers, P² not only adds a bar over the thousands (a common convention which P generally ignores), but also, more unusually, inserts letters over the part of the number below 1,000. So, for example at *Per.* 18.4, where P reads CCXCVII ·DCCXCVII, P² adds the thousands bar over CCXCVII, and then, over DCCXCVII, writes *ti · ta · tem*: this abbreviation gives the last letters of the spelled-out form of the numbers (*septengenti, nonaginta, septem*). (My thanks to Bob Kaster for interpreting this convention for me, which I had never encountered previously.)

[90] The slender reed on which the hypothesis is based is that in 7.5 a verb is omitted in all MSS (see commentary *ad loc.*), and in B the omitted verb would have been at the end of a line.

(1969), 111–12) shows that its original source derived from the same lost MS as N and P do, and thus should be regarded as an independent witness to the part of the text it covers. The best MS of the group is U (Bern 249, 39v–42v, dating from the eleventh century: see Reid (1969), 9–10); Reeve also proposes using London, B.L. Harl. 2620 as an additional check on it, but on the arguments of Reid (1990), which Reeve does nothing to refute (except perhaps *ex cathedra* with a passing comment: Reeve (1991), 455), that MS belongs to the same subgroup of the α MSS as U. Hence it makes more sense to use an early representative of Reid's other subgroup, namely the tenth-century G (Paris B.N., N.A. Lat. 1767, 51r–55r, https://gallica.bnf.fr/ark:/12148/btv1b100323298/f53.image.r=1767, possibly written at Chartres: see Reeve (1991), 454).

There is a large number of later Italian MSS of the *Periochae*; Reeve argues that all of these are descendants of a lost manuscript owned by Petrarch. That manuscript shared key errors with P which are not shared by N, notably the loss of the end of *Per.* 48; and Reeve argues that it was in fact an ancestor of P, since there also are no significant errors shared by its Italian descendants which are not also present in P (Reeve (1991), 464–7). The Italian manuscripts derive remotely from it; so some representatives of the Italian tradition need to be included as a check on P when it differs from N, to confirm whether the reading is likely to have occurred in that shared source MS or is simply an error of P. Reeve proposed using two Florentine MSS, E (Laur. Edili 186, 41r–73v, from the second quarter of the fourteenth century: see Reid (1969), 35–6), and the fifteenth century F (Laur. 89 inf. 25 http://mss.bmlonline.it/s.aspx?Id=AWOMMi5CI1A4r7GxMRIq#/book: see Reid (1969), 31).[91]

Readings from these MSS are reported in the apparatus according to the following broad (but flexibly applied) principles based on the stemma above. All readings unique to B (where available) or N are recorded, except for minor orthographic variants[92] or obvious transcription errors that do not produce meaningful Latin. All places where either U and G together (where available), or at least two of P, E, and F, have a unique reading against the consensus of the other MSS are recorded, here too excluding minor orthographic variants. Places where all of the MSS agree except for only one of U, G, P, E, or F are *not* generally reported, since the latter may be presumed to represent only an idiosyncratic error of a particular copyist; the main exception is where these appear to offer a useful conjecture for a problematic passage.

---

[91] Misleadingly bound and catalogued under the title *Sexti Rufi Epitoma*.
[92] However, the apparatus is more liberal in its reporting of orthographic variation when it comes to proper names, since there is no guarantee that the Livian MSS that were drawn on by the author of the *Periochae* spelled names in the same way as our own MSS of Livy do, and the MSS of the *Periochae* may sometimes give us an indication of the forms of names that were used by the author. Certainly to automatically emend the spelling of names in the *Periochae* to conform with those in modern editions of Livy would be arbitrary and unjustified.

Other MSS are included in the apparatus only occasionally, when they appear to provide valuable conjectures; with one exception[93] I have not seen these MSS myself, but have relied on the reports of Jal, or occasionally Rossbach (not always first-hand). Rossbach in addition gave a surprising prominence in his apparatus to the *editio princeps* (*r* in the apparatus: it was printed at Rome *c*.1469 by Arnold Pannartz and Conrad Sweynheim as part of the *editio princeps* of the majority of Livy), which frequently adopts a text at variance with all of the chief MSS, but which appears to have no independent value; this too I have generally ignored except as a repository of conjecture.

Appendix: Subdivisions of the *Periochae*

The *Periochae* has traditionally (with one exception) been printed with no subdivisions within each book. This is often unimportant, since many of the books are short, and in those it is generally easy to locate a cited passage; but it becomes inconvenient with the longest books, such as 48 and 49. Moreover, even with shorter books, a large-scale commentary such as this one ideally requires a more precise way of referring to individual passages. The exception is Jal's Budé edition, the first and, to date, only edition of the *Periochae* to offer subdivisions. However, Jal's subdivisions are far from ideal from another point of view, since they simply number each individual sentence separately, with no attention paid to the articulation of the narrative.

Accordingly, I have created my own subdivisions in this edition. I appreciate that this will create inconveniences of its own to those who are using Jal, but Jal's subdivisions have not been widely accepted in the scholarly literature, and I thought it unfortunate under those circumstances to forgo the opportunity to create what appears to me a more rational way of dividing the text.

---

[93] Namely Vatican Pal. Lat. 895, 41r–73v (https://digi.vatlib.it/fview/MSS_Pal.lat.895), dated by its scribe to 1396 (see Reid (1969), 55–6), which I collated as a possible substitute for E at a time when, owing to the global pandemic of 2020–2021, I saw little immediate prospect of gaining access to materials from Florence. However, its readings are generally similar to those of E and F, but more carelessly copied; I see little point in reporting them systematically in the apparatus.

Sigla

B	Bernensis (Bibl. Urb.) A 92.10, f. 1r–v	9th century.[1]
N	Palatinus Lat. Heidelbergensis 894, f. 62r–104v	9th century.[1]
P	Parisinus Lat. 7701, f. 76r–104v	12th century.
E	Laurentianus Edili 186	14th century.[2]
F	Laurentianus Plut. 89 inf. 25	15th century.[1]
G	Parisinus Lat. N.A. 1767, f. 51r–55r	10th century.
U	Bernensis (Bibl. Urb.) Lat. 249, f. 39v–42v	11th century.
r	*editio princeps* (Rome: Pannartz & Sweynheim)	c.1469

Text and Translation

EX LIBRO I

A

1. adventus Aeneae in Italiam et res gestae. Ascani regnum Albae [Italiae] et deinceps Silviorum. Numitoris filia a Marte compressa nati Romulus et Remus. Amulius obtruncatus. 2. urbs a Romulo condita. senatus lectus. cum Sabinis bellatum. spolia opima Feretrio Iovi lata. in centurias populus divisus. Fidenates, Veientes victi. Romulus consecratus. 3. Numa Pompilius ritus sacrorum tradidit. porta Iani clausa. 4. Tullus Hostilius Albanos diripuit. trigeminorum pugna. Metti Fufeti supplicium. Tullus fulmine consumptus. 5. Ancus Marcius Latinos devicit, Ostiam condidit. 6. Tarquinius Priscus Latinos superavit, circum fecit, finitimos devicit, muros et cloacas fecit. 7. Servio Tullio caput arsit. Servius Tullius Veientes devicit et populum in classes divisit, aedem Dianae dedicavit. 8. Tarquinius Superbus occiso Tullio regnum invasit. Tulliae scelus in patrem. Turnus Herdonius per Tarquinium occisus. bellum cum Vulscis. fraude Sexti Tarquini Gabii direpti. Capitolium inchoatum. Termini et Iuventae arae moveri non potuerunt. Lucretia se occidit. Superbi expulsio. regnatum est annis CCLV.

B

1. Latinis victis montem Aventinum adsignavit, fines protulit, Hostiam coloniam deduxit, caerimonias a Numa institutas renovavit. regnavit annis XXIIII. 2. eo regnante Lucumo, Demarati Corinthi filius, a Tarquiniis, Etrusca civitate, Romam venit et in amicitiam Anci receptus Tarquini Prisci nomen ferre coepit et post

INCIPIT ·· TITILIVI · A · BERBECONDITA [ab urbe *superscripsit m. 2*] · LIBER · I *N* Incipit Titi Livii ab urbe condita ex libro primo Periocha *P* Incipit Titii Livii ab urbe condita ex libro primo *E* Incipit epytoma ex libris Titi Livii *F* DE TITO LIVIO AB URBE CUMDITA *G om. U* ‖ A.1 Ascanii *UG* Ascanius *NPEF* | Italiae *NPF* Italie *G² Y*talie *E* Italae *U* Itale *G del. r* | Amulius *P²E* Amullius *NPUGF* ‖ A.2 centurias *NPUGF* curias *Frobenius* | Veientes *N²PUGE²F* venientes *NE* ‖ A.3 ritus *NPEF* ritum *UG* ‖ A.4 Tullus Hostilius *UGE* Tullius Hostilius *NPF* | pugna *N²UGE²F* pugnam *NPE* | Mettii *Munich Lat. 6392², Vatican Lat. 1859* et Titi *NPUGEF* | Fufeti *NPG* Fufetii *F* Fufeo *U* sufeti *E* | Tullus *NUGEF* Tullius *P* ‖ A.5 Ostiam *NPUE* Hostiam *GF* ‖ A.7 Veientes *PUEF* Vegentes *NG* ‖ A.8 Turnus Herdonius *NPEF* Turnius Herdonius *U* Turnius Erdonius *G* | Gabii direpti *UG* Gabi directu *NPF* Gabii directu *E* directum *N²* | Termini *Guelferbytanus 175 et cett.* Cremonae *NP²UGF* Cremone *E* Cremoniae *P* Terminos *U²* Termonis *Pithoeus* | arae moveri *NP²* aremoveri *E* ea removeri *PF* arae removeri *UG* | expulsio *NUG* expulsi *PEF* | annis *NUG* annos *PF* an. *E* ‖

B.1 *ante* Latinis victis *inserit G* LIBER SECUMDUS | Hostiam *NPUGF* Ostiam *E* ‖ B.2 Lucumo Demarati *Jahn* Lucumo Demarathi *F* Buchomo Demarathi *N* Buchomede Marathi *P* Buchomode Marathi *E* Bochomodem Arabi *UG* Boccomodem *G²* Lucumo Damarati *Sigonius* | Etrusca *Jahn* et Etruscia *UG* Etrusciae *NPF* Etruscie *E* Etruriae *Sigonius*

BOOK 1

[A.]

1. Aeneas' arrival in Italy and his deeds. The reign of Ascanius in Alba and of the Silvii in turn. Romulus and Remus were born after the daughter of Numitor was raped by Mars. The killing of Amulius. 2. The city founded by Romulus. The review of the Senate. War fought with the Sabines. The *spolia opima* brought to Jupiter Feretrius. The people divided into centuries. Victory over the Fidenates and the Veians. Romulus deified. 3. Numa Pompilius handed down religious rites. The gate of Janus was closed. 4. Tullius Hostilius plundered the Albans. The fight of the triplets. The punishment of Mettius Fufetius. Tullus burned up by a thunderbolt. 5. Ancus Marcius defeated the Latins, founded Ostia. 6. Tarquinius Priscus overcame the Latins, built the Circus, defeated neighbouring peoples, built the walls and the sewers. 7. Servius Tullius' head caught fire. Servius Tullius defeated the Veians and divided the people into classes, dedicated the temple of Diana. Tarquinius Superbus seized the kingdom after killing Tullius. Tullia's crime against her father. Turnus Herdonius killed by Tarquinius. War with the Volsci. Gabii sacked through the deceit of Sextus Tarquinius. The Capitol begun. The altars of Terminus and Iuventas could not be moved. Lucretia killed herself. The expulsion of Superbus. There were kings for 255 years.

[B.]

1. He allocated the Aventine hill to the defeated Latins, extended the borders, founded the colony of Ostia, reintroduced the ceremonies started by Numa. He reigned twenty-four years. 2. During his reign Lucumo, the son of Demaratus of Corinth, came from the Etruscan community of Tarquinia to Rome and after being befriended by Ancus began to bear the name Tarquinius Priscus and

mortem Anci regnum excepit. hic temptandae scientiae Atti Navi auguris causa fertur consuluisse eum, an id de quo cogitaret effici posset; quod cum ille fieri posse dixisset, iussisse eum novacula cotem praecidere, idque ab Atto protinus factum. centum in patres adlegit, Latinos subegit, ludos in circo edidit, equitum centurias ampliavit, urbem muro circumdedit, cloacas fecit. occisus est ab Anci filiis, cum regnasset annis XXXVIII. 3. successit ei Servius Tullius, natus ex captiva nobili Corniculana, cui puero adhuc in cunis posito caput arsisse traditum erat. is censum primum egit, lustrum condidit, quo censa LXXX milia esse dicuntur, pomerium protulit, colles urbi adiecit Quirinalem, Viminalem, Esquilinum, templum Dianae cum Latinis in Aventino fecit. interfectus est a Lucio Tarquinio, Prisci filio, consilio filiae suae Tulliae, cum regnasset annis XLIIII. 4. post hunc L. Tarquinius Superbus neque patrum neque populi iussu regnum invasit. is armatos circa se in custodiam sui habuit. 5. bellum cum Vulscis gessit et ex spoliis eorum templum in Capitolio Iovi fecit. Gabios dolo in potestatem suam redegit. 6. huius filiis Delphos profectis et consulentibus quis eorum Romae regnaturus esset, dictum est eum regnaturum qui primum matrem osculatus esset. quod responsum cum ipsi aliter interpretarentur, Iunius Brutus, qui cum his profectus erat, prolapsum se simulavit et terram osculatus est; idque factum eius eventus comprobavit. 7. nam cum impotenter se gerendo Tarquinius Superbus omnes in odium sui adduxisset, ad ultimum propter expugnatam nocturna vi a Sexto filio eius Lucretiae pudicitiam, quae ad se vocato patre Tricipitino et viro Collatino obtestata ne inulta mors eius esset cultro se interfecit, Bruti opera maxime expulsus est, cum regnasset annos XXV. tum consules primi creati sunt L. Iunius Brutus L. Tarquinius Collatinus.

hic temptandae—factum *huc transtuli; post* renovavit (B.1) *NPUGEF post* centurius ampliavit *ponit Sigonius; post* regnasset annis XXXVIII *ponit Madvig sed quoque delevit* | Atti Navi *N* Atti Nevii *E²* Atinavi *UG* Ati Gnavi *P²* Actii Nevii *F* Etati Gnavi *P* Eati Navi *E* | ille *Vatican Pal. Lat. 895* illi *NPEF om. UG* | cotem *NPEF* cutem *UG* | ab Atto *NP* ab Actio *F* ab Ato *UG* abacto *E* | in patres allegit *NEF* in partes allegit *P* hic patres elegit *UG* | ludos *NUG* lucos *PEF* || B.3 Tullius *NPG²* Tullus *UGEF* | Corniculana *r* Coroinculana *UG* Corioniculana *NPEF* | Aventino *NP²UGF* Adventino *PE* | XLIIII *NPEF* LXIIII *UG* || B.4 is *NUG om. PEF* || B.5 potestatem suam *Munich Lat. 6392 et cett.* potestate sua *NPUGEF* || B.6 profectus erat *NPEF* profectus esset *UG* || B.7 Tricipitino *NPEF* Tricipicinio *U* Tricipicinio *G* | annos *NPE* annis *UGF*

received the kingdom after Ancus' death. It is said that in order to test the skill of the augur Attus Navius he consulted him as to whether the thing he was thinking could be accomplished. When Attus said that it could be done, he ordered him to cut a whetstone with a razor, and Attus straightaway did it. He incorporated a hundred new senators, he subdued the Latins, he put on games in the Circus, he increased the centuries of the *equites*, he surrounded the city with a wall, he built the sewers. He was killed by the sons of Ancus after reigning thirty-eight years. 3. Servius Tullius succeeded him, the son of a noblewoman from Cornicula who was a captive. It is recorded that when he was still a child in the cradle his head caught fire. He was the first to take a census, and completed the lustral cycle, in which 80,000 are said to have been counted, he enlarged the *pomerium*, he added the Quirinal, Viminal, and Esquiline hills to the city, he built (along with the Latins) the temple of Diana on the Aventine. On the advice of his daughter Tullia he was killed by Lucius Tarquinius, son of Priscus, after reigning forty-four years. 4. After him Lucius Tarquinius Superbus seized the kingdom without the authorization of either the Senate or the people. He kept armed men around himself as a bodyguard. 5. He waged war with the Volsci and from their spoils built a temple to Jupiter on the Capitol. He gained power over Gabii by deceit. 6. When his sons went to Delphi and enquired which of them would rule at Rome, the answer was given that the first one to kiss his mother would rule. Although they themselves understood the response differently, Junius Brutus, who had gone with them, pretended to fall over and kissed the ground. And the outcome ratified his action. 7. For although Tarquinus Superbus' tyrannical behaviour had led everyone to loathe him, in the end after reigning for twenty-five years he was expelled primarily through the efforts of Brutus because of the assault on the chastity of Lucretia by his son Sextus in an act of nocturnal violence: she summoned her father Tricipitinus and her husband Collatinus and after calling them to witness that her death should not be unavenged, she killed herself with a knife. Then the first consuls were elected: Lucius Junius Brutus and Lucius Tarquinius Collatinus.

EX LIBRO II

1. Brutus iureiurando populum adstrinxit neminem Romae regnare passuros. Tarquinium Collatinum collegam suum propter adfinitatem Tarquiniorum suspectum coegit consulatu se abdicare et civitate cedere. 2. bona regum diripi iussit, agrum Marti consecravit, qui campus Martius nominatus est. adulescentes nobiles, in quibus suos quoque et fratris filios, quia coniuraverant de recipiendis regibus, securi percussit. servo indici, cui Vindicio nomen fuit, libertatem dedit; ex cuius nomine vindicta appellata. 3. cum adversus reges, qui contractis Veientum et Tarquiniensium copiis bellum intulerant, exercitum duxisset, in acie cum Arrunte filio Superbi commortuus est; eumque matronae anno luxerunt. 4. L. Valerius consul legem de provocatione ad populum tulit. Capitolium dedicatum est. 5. Porsenna, Clusinorum rex, bello pro Tarquiniis suscepto cum ad Ianiculum venisset, ne Tiberim transiret virtute Coclitis Horati prohibitus est, qui, dum alii pontem Sublicium rescindunt, solus Etruscos sustinuit et ponte rupto armatus in flumen se misit et ad suos transnavit. accessit alterum virtutis exemplum in Mucio. qui cum ad feriendum Porsennam castra hostium intrasset, occiso scriba, quem regem esse existimaverat, comprehensus impositam manum altaribus, in quibus sacrificatum erat, exuri passus est dixitque tales CCC esse ⟨...⟩. quorum admiratione coactus Porsenna pacis condiciones ferre bellum omisit acceptis obsidibus. ex quibus virgo una Cloelia deceptis custodibus per Tiberim ad suos transnavit et cum reddita esset, a Porsenna honorifice remissa equestri statua donata est. 6. adversus Tarquinium Superbum cum Latinorum exercitu bellum inferentem Aulus Postumius dictator prospere pugnavit. 7. Appius Claudius ex Sabinis Romam transfugit. ob hoc Claudia tribus adiecta est numerusque tribuum ampliatus est, ut essent XXI. 8. plebs cum propter nexos ob aes alienum in Sacrum montem secessisset, consilio Meneni Agrippae a seditione revocata est. idem Agrippa cum decessisset, propter paupertatem publico impendio elatus est. tribuni plebis quinque creati sunt. 9. oppidum Vulscorum Corioli captum est virtute et opera Cn. Marci, qui ob hoc Coriolanus vocatus est. 10. T. Latinius, vir de plebe, cum in visu admonitus ut de quibusdam religionibus ad senatum perferret id neglexisset, amisso filio pedibus debilis factus, postquam

EX LIBRO II *N* ex libro secundo *PEF* LIBER TERCIUS *G om. U* || 1 consulatu se abdicare *NPEF* consulatus abdicare *UG* || 2 fratris *NPUGEF* sororis *Sigonius* || 3 Arrunte *NUG* Arunte *PEF* | commortuus *NUEF* cum mortuus *PG* | 4 L. Valerius *NPUGEF* P. Valerius *Sigonius* | 5 Coclitis *r* Coclis *NPGEF* cordis *U* | Sublicium *P²EF* Sublicum *NPUG* | ponte *PUGEF* fonte *N* | transnavit *NPEF* transnatavit *UG* | accessit alterum *NUG* alterum accessit *PEF* | *post* esse *lacunam indicavi* coniuratos in mortem ipsius regis *add. r* | condiciones (-iti- *EF*) *NPEF* condicione (-iti- *G*) *UG* | ex quibus *NPEF om. UG* | Cloelia *N²EF* Coelia *NP* Caelia *UG* | transnavit *NPEF* transnatavit *UG* | a Porsenna *F* Porsenna *NPE* Porsennae *UG* || 6 Postumius *F* Postumus *NPUGE* || 8 secessisset *NPEF* successisset *UG* | Meneni *NPEF* Menni *UG* | elatus *NPEF* elevatus *UG* || 10 Latinius *PEF* Latinus *NUG* | religionibus *UGF* regionibus *NPE* | id *Drakenborch et NPUGEF del. Rossbach* | pedibus *NUG om. PEF*

BOOK 2

1. Brutus bound the people with an oath that they should allow no one to be a king at Rome. He compelled his colleague Tarquinius Collatinus, who was under suspicion because of his relationship to the Tarquinii, to resign from his consulship and leave the community. 2. He ordered the royal property to be plundered, he consecrated a field to Mars, which was named the Campus Martius. He executed noble young men, including even his own and his brother's sons, because they had conspired to bring back the kings. He gave freedom to the slave informant, whose name was Vindicius; and *vindicta* [freeing by the rod] is called after him. 3. When he led an army against the kings, who had gathered forces from Veii and Tarquinia and had made war, he fell in battle along with Arruns, the son of Superbus; and the matrons mourned him for a year. 4. The consul Lucius Valerius brought to the people a law on the right of appeal. The Capitol was dedicated. 5. Porsenna, the king of the Clusini, waged war on behalf of the Tarquinii. When he came to the Janiculum, he was prevented from crossing the Tiber by the courage of Horatius Cocles, who held off the Etruscans by himself while other people were cutting down the Sublician Bridge, and once the bridge was broken he threw himself fully armed into the river and swam across to his people. A second model of courage was added in the case of Mucius: after entering the enemy camp in order to assassinate Porsenna, and after killing a scribe whom he had imagined to be the king, he was arrested, but, placing his hand on the altars on which they had been sacrificing, he let it burn away, and he said that there were three hundred similar ⟨...⟩. Porsenna was driven by his amazement at these to offer peace terms, and he gave up the war after taking hostages. One of these, a girl called Cloelia, after tricking the guards swam across the Tiber to her people, and when she was returned to Porsenna, she was sent back honourably by him and granted an equestrian statue. 6. The dictator Aulus Postumius fought successfully against Tarquinius Superbus who was attacking with an army of Latins. 7. Appius Claudius deserted to Rome from the Sabines. For this reason the Claudian tribe was added and the number of tribes increased to twenty-one. 8. When the plebeians seceded to the Mons Sacer because of those suffering debt-bondage, they were brought back from mutiny by the advice of Menenius Agrippa. When the same Agrippa died, he was buried at public expense because of his poverty. Five tribunes of the people were elected. 9. The Volscian town of Corioli was captured by the courage and efforts of Gnaeus Marcius, who for that reason was called Coriolanus. 10. When Titus Latinius, a plebeian, was warned in a dream to inform the Senate about some ritual matters but took no notice, he lost his son and was crippled in his feet, but after he was brought to the Senate in a litter and provided

delatus ad senatum lectica eadem illa indicaverat, usu pedum recepto domum reversus est. 11. cum Cn. Marcius Coriolanus, qui in exilium erat pulsus, dux Vulscorum factus exercitum hostium urbi admovisset, et missi ad eum primum legati, postea sacerdotes frustra deprecati essent ne bellum patriae inferret, Veturia mater et Volumnia uxor impetraverunt ab eo, ut recederet. 12. lex agraria primum lata est. Spurius Cassius consularis regni crimine damnatus est necatusque. 13. Popilia virgo Vestalis ob incestum viva defossa est. 14. cum vicini Veientes incommodi magis quam graves essent, familia Fabiorum id bellum gerendum depoposcit misitque in id trecentos et sex armatos, qui ad Cremeram praeter unum ab hostibus caesi sunt. 15. Appius Claudius cos. cum adversus Vulscos contumacia exercitus male pugnatum esset, decimum quemque militum fuste percussit. 16. res praeterea adversus Vulscos et Hernicos et Veientes et seditiones inter patres plebemque continet.

EX LIBRO III

1. seditiones de agrariis legibus fuere. 2. Capitolium ab exulibus et servis occupatum caesis his receptum est. 3. census bis actus est. priore lustro censa sunt civium capita CIIII milia DCCXIIII praeter orbos orbasque, sequenti CXVII milia CCCXVIIII. 4. cum adversus Aequos male gesta res esset, L. Quintius Cincinnatus dictator factus, cum rure intentus operi rustico esset, ad id bellum gerendum arcessitus est. is victos hostes sub iugum misit. 5. tribunorum plebis numerus ampliatus est, ut essent X, tricesimo sexto anno a primis tribunis plebis. 6. petitis per legatos et adlatis Atticis legibus ad constituendas eas proponendasque X viri pro consulibus sine ullis aliis magistratibus creati altero et trecentesimo anno quam Roma condita erat, et ut a regibus ad consules, ita a consulibus ad X viros imperium translatum. 7. hi X tabulis legum positis cum modeste se in eo honore gessissent et ob id in alterum quoque annum eundem esse magistratum placuisset,

---

11 Marcius (-ti- P) *NPF* Marcus *UGE* | Volumnia *PUGE* Volumina *N* Volunnia *F* || 13 Popilia *Zangemeister ex Oros. 2.8.13* Illia *NU* Illia *G* Ilia *PF* Ylian *E* Opillia *Hertz* Oppia *Liv. 2.42.1* || 14 vicini *N* vicini hostes *PUGEF* | gerendum *UG* gerendi *NPEF* || 16 *lacunam post* Veientes *indic. Jahn*

EX LIB III *N* ex libro tercio (-ti- *E*) *PE* Ex libro III *F* LIBER QUARTUS *G om. U* || 2 est *NPEF om. UG* || 3 CIIII milia *Vatican Lat. 3334, Vatican Lat. 7313 ex Liv. 3.3.9* VIII milia *NUG* octo milia *PE* octoginta milia *F* | CCCXVIIII *restituit Jahn ex Liv. 3.24.10* CCXVIIII *NPUGEF* || 4 arcessitus *NPE* accersitus *UGF* || 5 a primis *Paris Lat. 5743 et cett.* primis *NPUGEF* || 6 altero et trecentesimo *Aldinus* nono tricesimo (-gesi- *PUE* -gessi- *G*) *NPUEG* nono et trecentisimo *F* | ad *ante* consules *UGF om. NPE* | ita a consulibus *N²P²UGEF* ita consulibus *NP* || 7 hi *NPF* hy *E* in *UG* | eundem esse magistratum placuisset, duabus tabulis ad decem adiectis *Sigonius* eundem esse magistratum ad decem adiectis *NPEF* ad eundem magistratum decem adiectis *UG* eundem esse magistratum placuit. qui cum duabus tabulis ad decem adiectis *F* eundem esse magistratum placuisset *Aldinus*

the same information, he returned home having recovered the use of his feet. 11. After Gnaeus Marcius Coriolanus, who had been driven into exile, was made general of the Volsci and led an enemy army against the city, and first envoys then afterwards priests were sent to him and appealed in vain for him not to wage war on his homeland, his mother Veturia and his wife Volumnia persuaded him to retreat. 12. An agrarian law was passed for the first time. The ex-consul Spurius Cassius was convicted on a charge of aspiring to be king and was executed. 13. Popilia, a Vestal Virgin, was buried alive for unchastity. 14. Although the nearby Veiians were troublesome rather than dangerous, the household of the Fabii demanded to wage war with them, and sent 306 armed men for that purpose, all but one of whom were killed by the enemy at the Cremera. 15. The consul Appius Claudius, after fighting against the Volsci unsuccessfully because of his army's recalcitrance, had every tenth soldier executed by cudgelling. 16. The book also contains campaigns against the Volsci and the Hernici and the Veiians and civil conflict between the patricians and the plebeians.

BOOK 3

1. There were civil conflicts over agrarian laws. 2. The Capitol was seized by exiles and slaves, but was recovered after they were killed. 3. The census was performed twice: in the first cycle 104,714 citizens were counted, excluding orphans and widows, in the second it was 117,319. After a war against the Aequi had gone badly, Lucius Quintius Cincinnatus was made dictator, and although he was in the countryside busied with agricultural work he was summoned to take charge of the war. He sent the defeated enemy under the yoke. 5. The number of tribunes of the people was increased to ten, in the thirty-sixth year from the first tribunes of the people. 6. When Attic laws were sought out and brought in by envoys, in order to establish and promulgate ones like them decemvirs were elected in place of the consuls without any other magistrates, in the three hundred and second year after the foundation of Rome, and just as power had been transferred from the kings to the consuls, so now it was transferred from the consuls to the decemvirs. 7. These men established ten tables of laws; after they had conducted themselves moderately in that office and for that reason it was decided that there should be the same magistracy for a second year as well, and two tables were

duabus tabulis ad decem adiectis cum complura impotenter fecissent, magistratum noluerunt deponere et in tertium annum retinuerunt, donec inviso eorum imperio finem adtulit libido Appi Claudi. 8. qui cum in amorem Virginiae virginis incidisset, summisso, qui eam in servitutem peteret, necessitatem patri eius Virginio imposuit, qui rapto ex taberna proxima cultro filiam occidit, cum aliter effici non posset ne in potestatem stuprum inlaturi veniret. 9. hoc tam magnae iniuriae exemplo plebs concitata montem Aventinum occupavit coegitque X viros abdicare se magistratu. ex quibus Appius, qui praecipuam poenam meruerat, in carcerem coniectus est; ceteri in exilium sunt acti. 10. res praeterea contra Sabinos et Vulscos prospere gestas continet et parum honestum populi Romani iudicium, qui iudex inter Ardeates et Aricinos sumptus agrum de quo ambigebatur sibi adiudicavit.

EX LIBRO IIII

1. lex de conubio patrum et plebis a tribunis contentione magna patribus repugnantibus perlata est. 2. tribuni ⟨...⟩ plebis. aliquot annos res populi Romani domi militiaeque per hoc genus magistratus administratae sunt. item censores tunc primum creati sunt. 3. ager Ardeatibus populi iudicio ablatus missis in eum colonis restitutus est. 4. cum fame populus Romanus laboraret, Spurius Maelius eques Romanus frumentum populo sua impensa largitus est et ob hoc factum conciliata sibi plebe regnum adfectans a Servilio Ahala magistro equitum iussu Quinti Cincinnati dictatoris occisus est; L. Minucius index bove aurata donatus est. 5. legatis Romanorum a Fidenatibus occisis, quoniam ob rem publicam morte occubuerant, statuae in rostris positae sunt. 6. Cossus Cornelius tribunus militum occiso Tolumnio, Veientum rege, opima spolia secunda rettulit.

cum complura *NEF* cum cumplura *P* cum plura *UG* | inviso *Drakenborch* invito *NPUGEF* invicto *Aldinus* ‖ 8 in amorem *UG* in amore *NPEF* | summisso qui *F* summo qui *NP²E* summa qui *N²* sumno qui *P* sibique *UG* | servitutem *UG* servitute *NPEF* | qui *ante* rapto *UG om. NPEF* | effici *NUG* enim *PEF* ‖ 9 abdicare se magistratu *NPE* abdicare se a magistratu *F* abdicare magistratus *UG* | Appius *NPEF* Appius Claudius *UG* | sunt acti *NUG* acti *PEF* ‖ 10 praeterea (pret- *EF*) *PEF* praetera *N* Romanae *UG*

EX LIBRO IIII *NPF* EX LIBRO IIII° *E* LIBER QUINTUS *G om. U* ‖ 2 tribuni plebis *NPUGEF lacunam indicavit Sigonius* a tri. pl. *r* tribuni militares *Gruterus* tribuni mil. consulari potestate creati *Rossbach* tribuni militum consulari potestate promisce creati sunt ex patribus et plebe *exempli gratia propono ex Liv.* 4.6.8 | aliquot *EF* aliquod *N²* aliquid *NPUG* | annos *NPUGEF* menses *Bingham* | res populi Romani *NEF* res per populi Romani *P* res pro *UG* ‖ 3 Ardeatibus *Drakenborch ex vet. lib.* Ardeatinus *NPEF* Ardeatini *UG* Ardeatinis *Aldinus* | in eum *NPEF* in eis *UG* ‖ 4 eques (aeq- *G*) Romanus *NUGF* eques populi Romani *PE* | sua *NUGF* suo *PE* | ob hoc factum *UG* ob factum *NP* ob id factum *EF* | conciliata *Leiden Bibl. Publ. Lat.* 19 *et cett.* concitata *NPUGEF* | a Servilio Hahala magistro *F* a Servilio et Hala magistris *UG* ex Servilio et Ahala magistris *NP* xc Servilio et Ahala magistris *E* | iussu Quintii *F* iussi Quinti (-tii *U* -cii *G²*) *NPUG²* iussu Quintii et *E om. G* | L. *Sigonius* T. *NPUGEF* | index *r* vindex *NPUGF* iudex *E* ‖ 5 morte *NPEF om. UG* ‖ 6 Tolumnio *NP* Tolomnio *UG* Toluminio *E* Tolunnio *F*

added to the ten, they did many things tyrannically, and refused to give up the magistracy and kept it for a third year, until the lust of Appius Claudius brought an end to their loathsome power. 8. He had fallen in love with the virgin Virginia, and, by surreptitiously sending an agent to claim her for slavery, drove her father Virginius to an unavoidable action: Virginius seized a knife from a nearby shop and killed his daughter, since that was the only way of preventing her from coming into the power of a rapist. 9. The people were incited by an instance of so great a crime to occupy the Aventine hill, and they forced the decemvirs to resign their magistracy. Appius, the one of them who deserved the chief punishment, was thrown into prison, while the others were exiled. 10. The book also contains successful campaigns against the Sabines and the Volsci, as well as the highly dishonourable ruling of the Roman people, who were invited to judge between the Ardeans and the Aricini, but awarded themselves the territory under dispute.

BOOK 4

1. A law relating to the marriage of patricians and plebeians was carried by the tribunes amid intense controversy and against the patricians' opposition. 2. Tribunes ⟨...⟩ of the people. For several years the domestic and military affairs of the Roman people were controlled by this kind of magistrate. Likewise, censors were then elected for the first time. 3. The territory that had been taken from the Ardeans by the judgement of the people was restored to them after colonists were sent onto it. 4. When the Roman people were suffering from famine, Spurius Maelius, a Roman equestrian, lavished grain on the people at his own expense, and, after this action brought the people onto his side, he aspired to the kingship, but was killed by Servilius Ahala, the Master of the Horse, at the order of the dictator Quinctius Cincinnatus; the informant Lucius Minucius was rewarded with a gilded cow. 5. When Roman ambassadors were killed by the people of Fidenae, since they had been killed in the service of the state, their statues were placed on the Rostra. 6. The military tribune Cornelius Cossus brought the second set of

7. Mam. Aemilius dictator censurae honorem qui antea per quinquennium gerebatur, anni et sex mensum spatio finit; ob eam rem a censoribus notatus est. 8. Fidenae in potestatem redactae eoque coloni missi sunt; quibus occisis Fidenates cum defecissent, ab Mam. Aemilio dictatore victi sunt et Fidenae captae. 9. coniuratio servorum oppressa est. 10. Postumius tribunus militum propter crudelitatem ab exercitu occisus est. stipendium ex aerario tum primum militibus datum est. 11. res praeterea gestas adversus Vulscos et Fidenates et Labicanos continet.

EX LIBRO V

1. in obsidione Veiorum tabernacula militibus facta sunt. ea res cum esset nova, indignationem tribunorum plebis movit querentium non dari plebi nec per hiemem militiae requiem. equites tum primum equis suis mereri coeperunt. 2. cum inundatio ex lacu Albano facta esset, vates qui eam rem interpretaretur ex hostibus captus est. 3. Furius Camillus dictator X annis obsessos Veios cepit, simulacrum Iunonis Romam transtulit, decimam praedae Delphos Apollini misit. 4. idem tribunus militum cum Faliscos obsideret, proditos hostium filios parentibus remisit statimque deditione facta Faliscorum victoriam iustitia consecutus est. 5. cum alter ex censoribus C. Iulius decessisset, in locum eius M. Cornelius suffectus est. nec id postea factum est, quoniam eo lustro a Gallis Roma capta est. 6. Furius Camillus, cum dies ei ab L. Apuleio tribuno plebis dicta esset, in exilium abiit. 7. cum Galli Senones Clusium obsiderent et legati a senatu missi ad componendam inter eos et Clusinos pacem pugnantes contra Gallos starent in acie Clusinorum, hoc facto eorum concitati Senones urbem infesto exercitu petierunt fusisque ad Aliam Romanis cepere urbem praeter Capitolium, quo se iuventus contulerat; maiores natu cum insignibus honorum, quos quisque gesserat, in vestibulis

7 Mam. *Vatican Ottob. Lat. 2852* M. *NPUGEF* | mensum NP^2 mensium *PUGEF* | finit *UG* finito *NPEF* ‖ 8 in potestatem *UG* in potestate NPE^2F imperante *E* | eoque *London Burneianus 204 et cett.* eaque *NPUGEF* | Mam. Aemilio *Vatican Ottob. Lat. 2852* M. Aemilio (Em- *E*) *NPEF* Emilio *UG* ‖ 10 primum militibus *NUG* militibus primum P^2EF milibus primum *P* ‖ 11 Labicanos *Levene* Labscos NP^2FG Labascos *P* Lascos *U* Labiscos *E* Faliscos *Leiden Bibl. Publ. Lat. 19 et cett.*

EX LIBRO V *NF* Ex libro quinto *PE* LIBER VI *G om. U* ‖ 2 ex hostibus *NUG* ab hostibus *PEF* ‖ 3 Iunonis *Guelferbytanus 175, Leidensis Bibl. Publ. 19 om. NPUGEF* | Romam *UG* Romae (-me *PE*) *NPEF* ‖ 4 idem *r* item *NPUGEF* ‖ 5 in locum *NUGF* et in locum *PE* ‖ 6 ei *PUGEF om. N* | abiit *PEF* abit *NUG* ‖ 7 Galli Senones *NUGF* Senones Calli *P* Senones Galli *E* | componendam (conp- *N*) *NPEF* conponenda *UG* | starent *UG om. NPEF* | exercitu *NPEF* agmine *UG* | quo *Vatican Urb. Lat. 462 et cett.* in quo *NPUGEF* | contulerat *UEF* contulerunt *NP* cumtulerunt *G*

spolia opima after killing Tolumnius, king of the Veiians. 7. The dictator Mamercus Aemilius limited the office of the censorship, which had previously been held for five years, to a year and six months; for that reason he was blacklisted by the censors. 8. Fidenae was brought under Roman power and colonists were sent there; after they were killed and the Fidenates revolted, they were defeated by the dictator Mamercus Aemilius, and Fidenae was captured. 9. A slave conspiracy was crushed. 10. The military tribune Postumius was killed by his army because of his cruelty. That was the first time that payment from the treasury was given to the soldiers. 11. The book also contains campaigns against the Volsci and the Fidenates and the Labicani.

BOOK 5

1. In the siege of Veii tents were made for the soldiers. Since that was something new, it made the tribunes of the people angry, complaining that no respite from military service was being granted to the people even during the winter. That was the first time that the *equites* began to serve with their own horses. 2. When a flood occurred from the Alban Lake, a prophet who could interpret it was captured from the enemy. 3. The dictator Furius Camillus captured Veii, which had been besieged for ten years, and transferred the image of Juno to Rome, and sent a tenth of the booty to Delphi for Apollo. 4. When the same man, as military tribune, besieged the Falisci, he sent back to their parents the sons of the enemy who had been betrayed, and instantly achieved a victory through justice, when the Falisci surrendered. 5. When Gaius Julius, one of the censors, died, Marcus Cornelius was substituted in his place. But that was never done subsequently, since Rome was captured by the Gauls in that *lustrum*. 6. When a summons was issued for Furius Camillus by the tribune of the people Lucius Apuleius, he went into exile. 7. When the Senonian Gauls were besieging Clusium and envoys, who were sent by the Senate to arrange peace between them and the Clusini, stood fighting in the Clusini battle line against the Gauls, the Senones, infuriated by their behaviour, attacked the city with a hostile army and, after routing the Romans at the Allia, captured the city apart from the Capitol, where the young men had retreated. They slaughtered the older men, with the marks of honour

aedium sedentes occiderunt. 8. et cum per aversam partem Capitoli iam in summum evasissent, proditi clangore anserum M. Manli praecipue opera deiecti sunt. 9. coactis deinde propter famem Romanis descendere, ut M pondo auri darent et hoc pretio finem obsidionis emerent, Furius Camillus, dictator absens creatus, inter ipsum conloquium quo de pacis condicionibus agebatur cum exercitu venit et Gallos post sextum mensem urbe expulit ceciditque. 10. dictum est ad Veios migrandum esse propter incensam et dirutam urbem, quod consilium Camillo auctore discussum est. movit populum vocis quoque omen ex centurione auditae, qui cum in forum venisset, manipularibus suis dixerat: 'sta, miles, hic optime manebimus!'. 11. aedis Iovi [Capitolino] facta est, quod ante urbem captam vox audita erat adventare Gallos.

EX LIBRO VI

1. res adversus Vulscos et Aequos et Praenestinos prospere gestas continet. 2. quattuor tribus adiectae sunt, Stellatina, Tromentina, Sabatina, Arniensis. 3. M. Manlius, qui Capitolium a Gallis defenderat, cum obstrictos aere alieno liberaret, nexos exsolveret, crimine adfectati regni damnatus de saxo deiectus est. in cuius notam S. C. factum est, ne cui de Manlia gente Manli cognomen esset. 4. C. Licinius et L. Sextius tribuni plebis legem promulgaverunt ut consules ex plebe fierent qui ex patribus creabantur, eamque cum magna contentione repugnantibus patribus, cum idem tribuni plebis per quinquennium soli magistratus fuissent, pertulerunt; et primus ex plebe consul L. Sextius creatus est. 5. lata est et altera lex, ne cui plus quingentis iugeribus agri liceret possidere.

occiderunt *NPEF* ceciderunt *UG* || 8 aversam *NUG* adversam *PG²EF* | anserum *NPEF* anseris *UG* | Manlii *UG* Manili *NPE* Mallii *F* | deiecti *F* detecti *NPUGE* || 9 M pondo *NP* mille pondo *EF* decem pondo *UG* | et hoc *r* ut hoc *NPUGEF* || 10 sta miles *NPEF* aestimabiles *UG* || 11 aedis *NPUG* aedes (ed- *E*) *EF* | Iovi [Capitolino] *Levene* Iovi Capitolino *NPUGEF* Aio Locuto *Sigonius* | quod *NPEF* quo *UG* | adventare Gallos *NPEF* Gallos adventare *UG*

EX LIBRO VI *NPEF* LIBER VII *G om. U* || 2 Tromentina *Sigonius* Promentina *NPUGEF* | Sabatina *BNPEF* Sabitana *UG* hinc incipit *B* | Arniensis *BNPF* Armensis *UGE* || 3 Manlius *UGF* Manilius *BNPE* | deiectus *P²UGEF* defectus *BNP* | S.C. *BNPEF* sic *UG* | post factum est *add. F* ne patricii in Capitolio vel arce habitarent, et gens Manlia statuit | ne cui de Manlia gente *NUGEF* ne cuidem Anlia gente *B* nec cui de Manlia gente *P* | Manli (-lii U) cognomen *BNUEP* M. Manlii cognomen *F* Manlia cognomen *G* Marco cognomen *Aldinus* Marco nomen *Sigonius* || 4 C. Licinius *BNPEF* Cilicinius *UG*

that each had borne, as they sat in the entrance-halls of their homes. 8. And when they had already emerged on the top of the Capitol by a back route, they were betrayed by the noise of the geese and were thrown down, primarily thanks to Marcus Manlius. 9. Then, when the Romans were forced down by hunger, so that they would give 1,000 pounds of gold and purchase an end to the siege at this price, Furius Camillus, who had been elected dictator in his absence, arrived with his army right in the middle of the negotiations about the terms of peace, and expelled from the city and massacred the Gauls after six months. 10. It was said that there should be a migration to Veii because the city was burned and plundered; the proposal was, at Camillus' instigation, rejected. The people were also influenced by an omen, consisting of a remark heard from a centurion, who, arriving in the Forum, had said to his troops, 'Halt, soldiers; this is the best place for us to stay'. 11. A temple was built to Jupiter, because a voice was heard prior to the city's capture saying that the Gauls were approaching.

BOOK 6

1. The book contains successful campaigns against the Volsci and the Aequi and the Praenestini. 2. Four tribes were added, the Stellatina, Tromentina, Sabatina, Arniensis. 3. Marcus Manlius, who had defended the Capitol from the Gauls, after freeing those who were constrained by debt and releasing the debt-enslaved, was convicted on the charge of aspiring to kingship and was thrown from the Rock. As a mark against him a senatorial decree was passed forbidding anyone from Manlius' clan to use Manlius' last name. 4. Gaius Licinius and Lucius Sextius, tribunes of the people, proposed a law that the consuls, who were being elected from the patricians, might come from the plebeians. The same tribunes of the people passed that law amid intense controversy against the patricians' opposition, after being the sole magistrates for five years; and Lucius Sextius was elected the first plebeian consul. Another law was also passed banning people from possessing more than five hundred acres of land.

EX LIBRO VII

1. duo novi magistratus adiecti sunt, praetura et curulis aedilitas. 2. pestilentia civitas laboravit, eamque insignem fecit mors Furi Camilli. cuius remedium et finis cum per novas religiones quaereretur, ludi scaenici tunc primum facti sunt. 3. cum dies L. Manlio dicta esset a M. Pomponio tribuno plebis propter dilectum acerbe actum et T. Manlium filium rus relegatum sine ullo crimine, adulescens ipse, cuius relegatio patri obiciebatur, venit in cubiculum tribuni strictoque gladio coegit eum in verba sua iurare, se non perseveraturum in accusatione. 4. tunc omnia pretiosa missa sunt in praealtam voraginem urbis Romanae. in eam Curtius armatus sedens equo praecipitavit; †explet at†. 5. T. Manlius adulescens, qui patrem a tribunicia vexatione vindicaverat, contra Gallum provocantem aliquem ex militibus Romanis in singulare certamen descendit eique occiso torquem aureum detraxit, quem ipse postea tulit, et ex eo Torquatus vocatus est. 6. duae tribus adiectae, Pomptina et Publilia. 7. Licinius Stolo lege sua damnatus est, quod plus quingentis iugeribus agri possideret. 8. M. Valerius tribunus militum Gallum, a quo provocatus erat, insidente galeae corvo et unguibus rostroque hostem infestante occidit et ex eo Corvi nomen accepit, consulque proximo anno, cum annos XXIII haberet, ob virtutem creatus est. 9. amicitia cum Carthaginiensibus iuncta est. 10. Campani cum a Samnitibus bello urgerentur, auxilio adversus eos a senatu petito, cum id non impetrarent, urbem et agros populo Romano dediderunt. ob quam causam ea, quae populi Romani facta essent, defendi bello adversus Samnites placuit. 11. cum ab Aulo Cornelio cos. exercitus in locum iniquum deductus in magno discrimine esset, Deci Muris tribuni militum opera servatus est. qui occupato colle super id iugum, in quo Samnites consederant, occasionem consuli in aequiorem locum evadendi dedit; ipse ab hostibus circumsessus erupit. 12. cum milites Romani, qui Capuae in praesidio relicti erant, de occupanda ea urbe conspirassent et detecto consilio metu supplici a populo Romano defecissent, per M. Valerium Corvum dictatorem, qui consilio suo eos a furore revocaverat, patriae restituti sunt. 13. res praeterea contra Hernicos et Gallos et Tiburtes et Privernates et Tarquinienses et Samnites et Vulscos prospere gestas continet.

EX LIBRO VII *BNPEF* LIBER VIII *G om. U* || 2 et finis *NPEF* est finis *BUG* || 3 esset a M. *BN* esset a *UG* esset et a M. *PEF* | Pomponio *NP²UGE* Pompinio *B* Pompeio *P* | propter *BNPEF om. UG* | T. Manlium *E* T. Manilium *NPUGF* T. Mannilium *B* | non *EF om. BNPUG* || 4 ante tunc omnia *lacunam suspicit Gronovius* | explet at *BN obelis notavi* expleta *PE* exiit *UG* et expleta est *F* eaque expleta est *Aldinus* ita expletam *Jahn* ita expleta *Weissenborn* || 5 T. Manlius *Paris Lat. 7701 et cett.* Lucius Manilius *BNU* Lucius Manīlius *G* T. Lucius Manilius *PE* T. Lucius Manlius *F* | vindicaverat *BNPF* liberaverat *UGE* | ex *BNPEF* de *UG* | descendit *London Harleianus 3694 et cett. om. BNPUGEF* processit *Rossbach* || 6 Pomptina *London Harleianus Lat. 2620 et cett.* Pomptinia *NPUGEF* Pomptlinia *B* || 7 sua *Jahn ex Liv. 7.16.9* lata *BN* latia *PEF* data *UG* ab ipso lata *r* a se lata *Woodman* || 8 tribunus *NPUGEF* tribus *B* | galeae (-ee *E*) *BNPEF* Gallo *UG* | infestante *UGF* infestantem *BNPE* | Corvi *BNPE* Corvini *UGF* || 9 iuncta *BNPEF* firmata *UG* || 10 cum *BNPEF om. UG* | dediderunt *BNPEF* dederunt *UG* | facta essent *BPEF* essent facta *UG* acta essent *N* || 11 consederant *BNPEF* insederant *UG* | erupit *Leiden Bibl. Publ. 19 et cett.* eripuit *BNPUGEF* || 12 cum milites *BNPEF* commilitones (cum- *G*) *UG* | in praesidio relicti (pres- *BEF*) *BNPEF* relicti in praesidio *UG* | de *BNPEF* cum de *UG* | ea *BPF om. NUG* | per *N²UG om. BNPEF* | post restituti sunt *defecit UG*

BOOK 7

1. Two new magistracies were added, the praetorship and the curule aedileship. 2. The community suffered from plague, which the death of Furius Camillus made distinguished. When a cure and end to it was sought through new religious rites, theatrical performances were put on then for the first time. 3. When a summons was issued against Lucius Manlius by the tribune of the people Marcus Pomponius because of a levy that was carried out harshly, and because Titus Manlius his son had been sent to the countryside without any charge, the young man himself, whose exile formed the charge against his father, came into the tribune's bedroom and forced him at swordpoint to swear to his dictation that he would not persist in the prosecution. 4. Then everything valuable was thrown into a very deep chasm in the city of Rome; Curtius, sitting armed on his horse, threw himself into it; and in this way it was filled up. 5. The young Titus Manlius, who had defended his father from the tribune's harassment, went into single combat against a Gaul who was challenging any one of the Roman soldiers, and after killing him removed his golden necklet, which he afterwards personally wore, and consequently was called Torquatus. 6. Two tribes were added, the Pomptina and the Publilia. 7. Licinius Stolo was condemned under his own law, on the charge of possessing more than five hundred acres of land. 8. Marcus Valerius, a military tribune, killed a Gaul who had challenged him, with a raven settling on his helmet and assaulting the enemy with its talons and beak; in consequence he received the name Corvus, and was elected consul in the following year on account of his courage, although he was only twenty-three years old. 9. An agreement of friendship was made with the Carthaginians. 10. The Campanians were under pressure in a war with the Samnites, and sought help against them from the Senate; when they failed to obtain it, they surrendered their city and territory to the Roman people. For that reason it was decided that those things which had become the property of the Roman people should be defended by war against the Samnites. 11. When the army was led down onto unfavourable ground by the consul Aulus Cornelius and was in great danger, it was saved thanks to the efforts of the military tribune Decius Mus. He seized a hill over the ridge which the Samnites had occupied and gave the consul the chance to escape onto more favourable ground; and he himself, though surrounded by the enemy, broke out. 12. The Roman soldiers who had been left at Capua as a garrison conspired to seize the city and, when their plot was uncovered, they defected from the Roman people out of fear of punishment; but they were restored to their country by the dictator Marcus Valerius Corvus, whose advice had brought them back from their insanity. 13. The book also contains successful campaigns against the Hernici and the Gauls and the Tiburtes and the Privernates and the Tarquinienses and the Samnites and the Volsci.

EX LIBRO VIII

1. Latini cum Campanis defecere et missis legatis ad senatum condicionem tulerunt ut si pacem habere vellent alterum ex Latinis consulem facerent. qua legatione perlata praetor eorum Annius de Capitolio ita lapsus est ut exanimaretur. 2. T. Manlius consul filium, quod contra edictum eius adversus Latinos pugnaverat, quamvis prospere pugnasset, securi percussit. 3. laborantibus in acie Romanis P. Decius devovit se pro exercitu, et concitato equo cum in medios hostes se intulisset, interfectus morte sua Romanis victoriam restituit. 4. Latini in deditionem venerunt. T. Manlio in urbem reverso nemo ex iuventute obviam processit. 5. Minucia virgo Vestalis incesti damnata est. 6. Ausonibus victis et oppido ex is capto Cales [colonia deducta est] item Fregellae coloniae deductae sunt. 7. veneficium complurium matronarum deprehensum est, ex quibus plurimae statim epotis medicaminibus perierunt. lex de veneficio tunc primum constituta est. 8. Privernatibus, cum bellassent, victis civitas data est. 9. Neapolitani bello et obsidione victi in deditionem venerunt. Q. Publilio, qui eos obsederat, primo et imperium prolatum est et pro cos. triumphus decretus. 10. plebs nexu liberata est propter L. Papiri creditoris libidinem, qui C. Publilio debitori suo stuprum inferre voluerat. 11. cum L. Papirius Cursor dictator reversus in urbem ab exercitu esset propter auspicia repetenda, Q. Fabius magister equitum, occasione bene gerendae rei invitatus, contra edictum eius prospere adversus Samnites pugnavit. ob eam causam cum dictator de magistro equitum supplicium sumpturus videretur, Fabius Romam profugit, et cum parum causa proficeret, populi precibus donatus est. 12. res praeterea contra Samnites prospere gestas continet.

EX LIBRO VIIII

1. T. Veturius Spurius Postumius coss. apud furcas Caudinas deducto in locum artum exercitu, cum spes nulla esset evadendi, foedere cum Samnitibus facto et

---

1 *post* facerent *defecit B* || 3 medios *PEF* medio *N* || 6 et oppido ex is capto Cales *Rossbach* in oppidoexis Cales capto Cales colonia deducta est *NPEF* in oppidum Cales colonia deducta est *Aldinus* in oppidum ex iis captum Cales colonia deducta est *Sigonius* || 12 res *N* et res *PEF*

1 artum *Drakenborch ex* arctum *in codice Barberiniano inventum* tacitum *NPEF* iniquum *Aldinus*

BOOK 8

1. The Latins defected along with the Campanians, and, sending ambassadors to the Senate, offered the terms that, if the Romans wanted peace, they should select one of the consuls out of the Latins. After the end of this embassy their praetor Annius slipped down from the Capitol and lost his life. 2. The consul Titus Manlius executed his son because he had fought against the Latins contrary to his instructions, even though he had fought successfully. 3. When the Romans were struggling in the battle, Publius Decius devoted himself on behalf of the army: he spurred on his horse and rode into the middle of the enemy, and when he was killed, restored victory to the Romans by his death. 4. The Latins surrendered. When Titus Manlius returned to the city, none of the young men came out to meet him. 5. Minucia, a Vestal Virgin, was convicted of unchastity. 6. After the defeat of the Ausones and the capture of their town the colonies Cales and also Fregellae were founded. 7. Poisoning by a number of matrons was detected; several of them immediately died from drinking their own brews. That was the first time that a law on poisoning was established. 8. When the Privernates made war and were defeated, they received citizenship. 9. The Neapolitans, defeated by a war and a siege, surrendered. The man who had besieged them, Quintus Publilius, was the first both to have his command extended and to be decreed a triumph as proconsul. 10. The people was freed from debt-bondage as a consequence of the lust of the creditor Lucius Papirius, who had wanted to rape his debtor Gaius Publilius. 11. When the dictator Lucius Papirius Cursor returned to the city from his army in order to get new auspices, Quintus Fabius, the Master of the Horse, encouraged by the chance of a victorious campaign, fought successfully against the Samnites contrary to his orders. When the dictator seemed about to punish the Master of the Horse for this, Fabius fled to Rome, and although his case was unsuccessful, he was given up to the prayers of the people. 12. The book also contains successful campaigns against the Samnites.

BOOK 9

1. The consuls Titus Veturius and Spurius Postumius, when the army was led into a narrow spot at the Caudine Forks, since there was no hope of escaping, made a

sescentis equitibus Romanis obsidibus datis ita exercitum abduxerunt ut omnes sub iugum mitterentur; idemque auctore Spurio Postumio cos. qui in senatu suaserat ut eorum deditione quorum culpa tam deforme foedus ictum erat, publica fides liberaretur, cum duobus tribunis plebis et omnibus qui foedus spoponderant dediti Samnitibus non sunt recepti. 2. nec multo post fusis a Papirio Cursore Samnitibus et sub iugum missis receptisque sescentis equitibus Romanis qui obsides dati erant, pudor flagitii prioris abolitus est. 3. tribus duae adiectae sunt, Offentina et Falerna. Suessa et Pontia coloniae deductae sunt. 4. Appius Claudius censor aquam perduxit; viam stravit quae Appia vocata est, libertinorum filios in senatum legit. ideoque, quoniam is ordo indignis inquinatus videbatur, sequentis anni coss. in senatu legendo observaverunt quem ad modum ante proximos censores fuerat. 5. res praeterea contra Apulos et Etruscos et Umbros et Marsos et Paelignos et Aequos et Samnites, quibus foedus restitutum est, prospere gestas continet. 6. Cn. Flavius scriba, libertino patre natus, aedilis curulis fuit per forensem factionem creatus, quae, cum comitia et campum turbaret et in his propter nimias vires dominaretur, a Q. Fabio censore in quattuor tribus redacta est; eaque res Fabio Maximo nomen dedit. 7. in hoc libro mentionem habet Alexandri, qui temporibus his fuit, et aestimatis populi Romani viribus, quae tunc erant, colligit si Alexander in Italiam traiecisset, non tam ei victoriam de populo Romano fore quam de his gentibus quas ad orientem imperio suo subiecerat.

EX LIBRO X

1. coloniae deductae sunt Sora et Alba et Carsioli. 2. Marsi in deditionem accepti sunt. 3. collegium augurum ampliatum est, ut essent novem, cum antea quaterni fuissent. 4. lex de provocatione ad populum a †Murena† cos. tertio tunc lata est. 5. duae tribus adiectae sunt, Aniensis et Teretina. 6. Samnitibus bellum indictum

fides *Leiden Bibl. Publ. 19* fide *NPEF* ‖ 3 Offentina *PEF* Ofentina *N* Oufentina *Hertz* | Falerna *London Burneianus 204 et cett.* Faleria *NPEF* | Pontia *N²* Pontias *NPEF* ‖ 4 in senatu legendo *Vatican Urb. Lat. 392* in senatum *NPEF* in senatu citando *Rossbach* ‖ 5 Apulos et Etruscos *Paris Lat. 5744 et cett.* Apulos Etruscos *NPEF* (-schos *E*) ‖ 6 Cn. Flavius *Jahn* C. Flavius *N* Flavius *PF* Fabius *E* | censore *PEF* censo *N* | Fabio Maximi nomen dedit *F* Fabio Maximo dedit *NPE*

4 Murena *NPEF obelis notavi* Valerio *Aldinus* | tertio *Milan Ambrosianus S 16 sup., Ambrosianus C 109 inf.* pretio *NPEF* ‖ 5 Teretina *Levene* Terentina *r* Terentia *NP* Terrentia *EF*

treaty with the Samnites and gave six hundred Roman *equites* as hostages, and led away their army on the condition that all of them were sent under the yoke. By the authority of the consul Spurius Postumius (who had advised in the Senate that the public honour should be restored by the surrender of the men whose fault had led to such a twisted treaty being agreed), the same men, along with the two tribunes of the people and all who had vowed the treaty, were surrendered to the Samnites, who refused to accept them. 2. Not long after, when the Samnites were routed by Papirius Cursor and sent under the yoke, and the six hundred Roman *equites* who had been given as hostages were recovered, the shame of the earlier disgrace was wiped out. 3. Two tribes were added, the Offentina and the Falerna. The colonies of Suessa and Pontia were founded. 4. Appius Claudius the censor brought in water; he paved the road which is called the Appian, he chose the sons of freedmen for the Senate. For that reason, because the order seemed to be stained by the unworthy, the consuls of the following year when choosing the Senate oversaw it in the manner it had been done before the most recent censors. 5. The book also contains successful campaigns against the Apulians and the Etruscans and the Umbrians and the Marsi and the Paeligni and the Aequi and the Samnites, with whom the treaty was renewed. 6. The scribe Gnaeus Flavius, born from a freedman father, was elected curule aedile by the forum faction, which, since it was disrupting the assemblies and the Campus and was dominant in these because of its excessive strength, was reduced by the censor Quintus Fabius to four tribes; and in consequence he received the name Fabius Maximus. 7. In this book he mentions Alexander, who lived at that time, and, after reckoning the power of the Roman people at that moment, deduces that if Alexander had crossed into Italy, he would not have achieved the kind of victory over the Roman people that he did over those nations to the East which he made submit to his power.

BOOK 10

1. The colonies of Sora and Alba and Carsioli were founded. 2. The Marsi surrendered. 3. The college of augurs was expanded to nine, although previously there had been four. 4. A law concerning the right of appeal was then brought before the people for the third time by the consul ?Murena. 5. Two tribes were added, the Aniensis and the Teretina. 6. War was declared on the Samnites, and

est et adversus eos saepe prospere pugnatum est. 7. cum adversus Etruscos, Umbros, Samnites, Gallos, P. Decio et Q. Fabio ducibus pugnaretur et Romanus exercitus in magno discrimine esset, P. Decius, secutus patris exemplum, devovit se pro exercitu et morte sua victoriam eius pugnae populo Romano dedit. 8. Papirius Cursor Samnitium exercitum, qui de iureiurando obstrictus quo maiore constantia virtutis pugnaret, in aciem descenderat, fudit. 9. census actus est, lustrum conditum. censa sunt civium capita CCLXXII milia et CCCXX.

EX LIBRO XI

1. cum Fabius Gurges cos. male adversus Samnites pugnasset et senatus de removendo eo ab exercitu ageret, Fabius Maximus pater deprecatus hanc fili ignominiam eo maxime senatum movit quod iterum se filio legatum pollicitus est, idque praestitit. eius consiliis et opera filius consul adiutus caesis Samnitibus triumphavit; C. Pontium, imperatorem Samnitium, ductum in triumpho, securi percussit. 2. cum pestilentia civitas laboraret, missi legati ut Aesculapi signum Romam ab Epidauro transferrent, anguem, qui se in navem eorum contulerat, ⟨et⟩ in quo ipsum numen esse constabat, deportaverunt; eoque in insulam Tiberis egresso eodem loco aedis Aesculapio constituta est. 3. L. Postumius consularis, quoniam, cum exercitui praeesset, opera militum in agro suo usus erat, damnatus est. 4. pacem petentibus Samnitibus foedus quarto renovatum est. Curius Dentatus cos. Samnitibus caesis et Sabinis, qui rebellaverant, victis et in deditionem acceptis bis in eodem magistratu triumphavit. 5. coloniae deductae sunt Castrum Sena Hadria. triumviri capitales tunc primum creati sunt. censu acto lustrum conditum est. censa sunt civium capita CCLXXII milia. 6. plebs propter aes alienum post graves et longas seditiones ad ultimum secessit in Ianiculum, unde a Q. Hortensio dictatore deducta est; isque in ipso magistratu decessit. 7. res praeterea contra Vulsinienses gestas continet, item adversus Lucanos, contra quos auxilium Thurinis ferre placuerat.

---

8 quo maiore *London Burneianus 204 et cett.* suo maiore *NPE* (*ante* maiore *scripsit tum delevit E* iure constantia) suo more *N²* suo ut maiore *F* || 9 censa sunt civium capita *N* censa sunt capita *PF om. E*
1 iterum *NPE* iturum *F* || 2 missi legati *Paris Lat. 5744 et cett.* missis legatis *NPEF* | et *addidi om. NPEF* || 4 Samnitibus *Paris Lat. 5743 et cett. om. NPEF* || 5 Hadria *NPF* Adria *E* || 6 post *London Harleianus 3694, Milan Ambrosianus S 16 sup.* propter *NPEF* || 7 Thurinis *Vatican Lat. 5258, Vatican Lat. 7313* Tyrrhenis (-rre- *P*) *NEFP*

there were many successful battles against them. 7. When the Roman army was fighting under the leadership of Publius Decius and Quintus Fabius against the Etruscans, Umbrians, Samnites, and Gauls, and was in grave danger, Publius Decius, following his father's precedent, devoted himself on behalf of the army and by his death gave victory in the battle to the Roman people. 8. Papirius Cursor routed the army of the Samnites, which had gone into battle bound by an oath to make it fight with greater constancy of courage. 9. A census was performed and the cycle completed. 272,320 citizens were counted.

BOOK 11

1. When the consul Fabius Gurges had fought unsuccessfully against the Samnites and the Senate was discussing removing him from the army, Fabius Maximus his father appealed against such disgrace to his son; what especially influenced the Senate was his promise that he would once again be his son's legate, and he fulfilled his promise. His son, assisted by his advice and efforts, slaughtered the Samnites and triumphed; he executed the Samnite general Gaius Pontius after leading him in triumph. 2. When the community was suffering under a plague, envoys were sent to bring the image of Aesculapius to Rome from Epidaurus. They brought a snake, which had got itself onto their ship, and in which it was accepted that the god himself was present; and when it emerged onto the island in the Tiber a temple was founded to Aesculapius on that very spot. 3. The ex-consul Lucius Postumius was convicted, since he had made use of the soldiers' services on his own land when he was in command of the army. 4. When the Samnites sued for peace, the treaty was renewed for the third time. The consul Curius Dentatus, after slaughtering the Samnites and defeating the Sabines, who had revolted, and receiving their surrender, triumphed twice in the same magistracy. 5. The colonies of Castrum, Sena, and Hadria were founded. *Triumviri capitales* were then elected for the first time. The census was performed and the cycle completed; 272,000 citizens were counted. 6. The people, after major and lengthy mutiny over debt, finally seceded to the Janiculum, and were brought back from there by the dictator Quintus Hortensius; and he died during his office. 7. The book also contains campaigns against the Volsinienses, and also against the Lucani, against whom it had been decided to bring help to the Thurini.

EX LIBRO XII

1. cum legati Romanorum a Gallis Senonibus interfecti essent, bello ob id Gallis indicto, L. Caecilius praetor ab his cum legionibus caesus est. 2. cum a Tarentinis classis Romana direpta esset, duumviro, qui praeerat classi, occiso, legati ad eos a senatu, ut de his iniuriis quererentur, missi pulsati sunt. ob id bellum his indictum est. 3. Samnites defecerunt. adversus eos et Lucanos et Brittios et Etruscos aliquot proeliis a compluribus ducibus bene pugnatum est. 4. Pyrrhus, Epirotarum rex, ut auxilium Tarentinis ferret, in Italiam venit. 5. cum in praesidium Reginorum legio Campana cum praefecto Decio Vibellio missa esset, occisis Reginis Regium occupavit.

EX LIBRO XIII

1. Valerius Laevinus cos. parum prospere adversus Pyrrhum pugnavit, elephantorum maxime inusitata facie territis militibus. post id proelium cum corpora Romanorum qui in acie ceciderant Pyrrhus inspiceret, omnia versa in hostem invenit populabundusque ad urbem Romanam processit. 2. C. Fabricius missus ad eum a senatu ut de redimendis captivis ageret, frustra ut patriam desereret a rege temptatus est. captivi sine pretio remissi sunt. 3. Cineas legatus a Pyrrho ad senatum missus petiit ut componendae pacis causa rex in urbem reciperetur. de qua re cum ad frequentiorem senatum referri placuisset, Appius Claudius, qui propter valetudinem oculorum iam diu consiliis publicis se abstinuerat, venit in curiam et sententia sua tenuit ut id Pyrrho negaretur. 4. Cn. Domitius censor primus ex plebe lustrum condidit. censa sunt civium capita CCLXXXVII milia CCXXII. 5. iterum adversus Pyrrhum dubio eventu pugnatum est. 6. cum Carthaginiensibus quarto foedus renovatum est. 7. cum C. Fabricio consuli is qui ad eum a Pyrrho transfugerat polliceretur venenum se regi daturum, cum indicio ad regem remissus est. 8. res praeterea contra Lucanos [et] Bruttios Samnites Etruscos prospere gestas continet.

---

2 duumviro *Sigonius* et duumviro N^2 et duoviro *N* duoviro *PEF* ‖ 3 Brittios *NP* Brutios *EF* ‖ 4 Tarentinis ferret *N* ferret Tarentinis *PEF* ‖ 5 Regium *F* regnum *NPE*

1 invenit *F* venit *NPE* | populabundusque N^2F populabundosque *NP* populabundasque *E* | processit *r* praecessit *NPEF* ‖ 3 petiit *r* petit *NPEF* | cum *PEF* dum *N* ‖ 4 civium *N om. PEF* ‖ 8 [et] *NPEF delevi* | Bruttios *NP* Bructios *F* Brutios *E*

BOOK 12

1. When envoys of the Romans were murdered by the Senonian Gauls, and war was therefore declared against the Gauls, the praetor Lucius Caecilius was killed by them along with his legions. 2. When a Roman fleet was plundered by the Tarentines and the duumvir in charge of the fleet was killed, the envoys, who had been sent to them by the Senate to complain of these outrages, were assaulted. War was therefore declared on them. 3. The Samnites defected; in a series of battles under several generals the Romans fought successfully against them and the Lucani and the Bruttii and the Etruscans. 4. Pyrrhus, king of the Epirotes, came to Italy to bring help to the Tarentines. 5. When a Campanian legion was sent with its commander Decius Vibellius as protection for the Rhegini, they killed the Rhegini and seized Rhegium.

BOOK 13

1. The consul Valerius Laevinus fought unsuccessfully against Pyrrhus, when the soldiers were especially terrified by the unfamiliar appearance of elephants. When, after the battle, Pyrrhus looked upon the bodies of the Romans who had fallen in the line, he found them all facing the enemy. He marched on the city of Rome, plundering. 2. Gaius Fabricius was sent to him by the Senate to negotiate the ransoming of prisoners, and the king tried in vain to get him to abandon his country. The prisoners were returned without payment. 3. Cineas was sent as an envoy by Pyrrhus to the Senate and requested that the king should be received into the city to agree peace. When it was decided that the matter should be raised in a quorate meeting of the Senate, Appius Claudius, who had kept away from political debate for a long time because of his blindness, came into the Senate House and with his argument won the point that Pyrrhus' request should be rejected. 4. The censor Gnaeus Domitius was the first plebeian to complete the lustral cycle; 287,222 citizens were counted. 5. There was a second battle against Pyrrhus with doubtful success. 6. The treaty with the Carthaginians was renewed for the third time. 7. When a deserter from Pyrrhus to the consul Gaius Fabricius promised him that he would administer poison to the king, he was sent back to the king with the evidence. 8. The book also contains successful campaigns against the Lucani, the Bruttii, the Samnites, and the Etruscans.

EX LIBRO XIIII

1. Pyrrhus in Siciliam traiecit. 2. cum inter alia prodigia fulmine deiectum esset in Capitolio Iovis signum, caput eius per haruspices inventum est. 3. Curius Dentatus cos. cum dilectum haberet, eius, qui primus citatus non responderat, bona ⟨...⟩ vendidit. iterum Pyrrhum ex Sicilia in Italiam reversum vicit et Italia expulit. 4. Fabricius censor P. Cornelium Rufinum consularem senatu movit, quod is X pondo argenti facti haberet. lustro a censoribus condito censa sunt civium capita CCLXXI milia CCXXIIII. 5. cum Ptolemaeo, Aegypti rege, societas iuncta est. 6. Sextilia, virgo Vestalis, damnata incesti viva defossa est. coloniae deductae sunt Posidonia et Cosa. 7. Carthaginiensium classis auxilio Tarentinis venit, quo facto ab his foedus violatum est. 8. res praeterea contra Lucanos et Bruttios et Samnites feliciter gestas et Pyrrhi regis mortem continet.

EX LIBRO XV

1. victis Tarentinis pax et libertas data est. 2. legio Campana, quae Regium occupaverat, obsessa, deditione facta securi percussa est. 3. cum legatos Apolloniatium ad senatum missos quidam iuvenes pulsassent, dediti sunt Apolloniatibus. 4. Picentibus victis pax data est. coloniae deductae Ariminum in Piceno, Beneventum. 5. tunc primum populus Romanus argento uti coepit. 6. Umbri et Sallentini victi in deditionem accepti sunt. 7. quaestorum numerus ampliatus est, ut essent ⟨VI⟩.

3 Dentatus *EF* Dendatus *N* Demptatus *P* | cos. *Leiden Bibl. Publ. Lat. 19, Vesoniensis (Bibl. Urb.) 840* is *NPEF* | qui primus citatus non responderat, bona vendidit *Rossbach sed lacunam suspicor; eam post* bona *exempli gratia indicavi, fortasse rectius alibi* qui citatus non responderat, bona primus vendidit *NPEF* qui citatus non responderat, bona primum, mox eum vendidit *Lipsius* || 7 classis *PEF* clausis *N* || 8 Bruttios *NP* Brutios *EF*

1 data *Vatican Lat. 1859 et cett.* nata *NPEF* || 4 Ariminum *PEF* Ariminium *N* | Beneventum *r* Neventum *NP* eventum *EF* || 5 populus Romanus argento *F* populus pro argento *NPE* || 6 Salentini *Frobenius* [Sallentini *Sigonius*] Salleni *NPEF* || 7 ⟨VI⟩ *addidi Mattingly (1969) secutus* octo *add. Sigonius* ut essent *NPEF quamquam lacunam quoque notavit E*

BOOK 14

1. Pyrrhus crossed to Sicily. 2. When, among other prodigies, the statue of Jupiter on the Capitol was struck down by a thunderbolt, its head was found by the *haruspices*. 3. When the consul Curius Dentatus was holding a levy, he ⟨...⟩ sold the goods of the man who was the first to be summoned but had not responded. He defeated Pyrrhus who had returned from Sicily once more to Italy, and he drove him from Italy. 4. The censor Fabricius removed the ex-consul Publius Cornelius Rufinus from the Senate, on the grounds that he possessed ten pounds of silver plate. The cycle was completed by the censors and 271,224 citizens were counted. 5. An alliance was formed with Ptolemy, king of Egypt. 6. Sextilia, a Vestal Virgin, was convicted of unchastity and buried alive. The colonies of Posidonia and Cosa were founded. 7. A Carthaginian fleet came to help the Tarentines, a deed by which they violated the treaty. 8. The book also contains successful campaigns against the Lucani and the Bruttii and the Samnites and the death of King Pyrrhus.

BOOK 15

1. Peace and freedom was given to the defeated Tarentines. 2. The Campanian legion which had seized Rhegium was besieged, and after surrendering was executed. 3. After certain young men had assaulted the envoys from Apollonia who had been sent to the Senate, they were surrendered to the Apollonians. 4. Peace was given to the defeated Picentes. The colonies of Ariminum in Picenum and Beneventum were founded. 5. That was the first time that the Roman people began to use silver. 6. The Umbrians and the Sallentini were defeated and surrendered. 7. The number of quaestors was increased to six.

EX LIBRO XVI

1. origo Carthaginiensium et primordia urbis eorum referuntur. 2. contra quos et Hieronem, regem Syracusanorum, auxilium Mamertinis ferendum senatus censuit, cum de ea re inter suadentes ut id fieret, dissuadentesque contentio fuisset; transgressisque tunc primum mare exercitibus Romanis adversus Hieronem saepius bene pugnatum. petenti pax data est. 3. lustrum a censoribus conditum est. censa sunt civium capita CCLXXXXII milia CCXXXIIII. 4. Decimus Iunius Brutus munus gladiatorium in honorem defuncti patris primus edidit. 5. colonia Aesernia deducta est. 6. res praeterea contra Poenos et Vulsinios prospere gestas continet.

EX LIBRO XVII

1. Cn. Cornelius consul a classe Punica circumventus et per fraudem, veluti in conloquium evocatus, captus est. 2. C. Duillius consul adversus classem Poenorum prospere pugnavit, primusque omnium Romanorum ducum navalis victoriae duxit triumphum. ob quam causam ei perpetuus quoque honos habitus est, ut revertenti a cena tibicine canente funale praeferretur. 3. L. Cornelius consul in Sardinia et Corsica contra Sardos et Corsos et Hannonem, Poenorum ducem, feliciter pugnavit. 4. Atilius Calatinus cos. cum in locum a Poenis circumsessum temere exercitum duxisset, M. Calpurni, tribuni militum, virtute et opera evasit, qui cum CCC militibus eruptione facta hostes in se converterat. 5. Hannibal, dux Poenorum, victa classe cui praefuerat, a militibus suis in crucem sublatus est. 6. Atilius Regulus cos. victis navali proelio Poenis in Africam traiecit.

---

2 et *NF om. PE* | exercitibus *Weissenborn* equitibus *NPEF* || 3 CCLXXXXII milia CCXXXIIII *correxit Drakenborch ex Eutropio 2.18.2* CCCLXXXII milia CCXXXIIII *NP²E* CCCLXXXII ACCXXXIIII *P* CCCLXXXII milia ACCXXXIIII *F* CCXCII millia CCXXIII *Sigonius* || 4 gladiatorium *N* gladiatorum *PEF* || 6 Vulsinios *Sigonius* Vulsinos *NPEF*

2 revertenti *NF* reverenti *PE* | tibicine canente *N* tibicine canentes *N²P* tibicines canentes *EF* | funale *EF* furiale *P* furi *N* || 4 Calatinus *r* Calasinus *NPEF* || 6 Atilius—traiecit *in librum XVIII transponit P*

BOOK 16

1. The origin of the Carthaginians and the beginnings of their city are described. 2. Against them and Hiero, king of the Syracusans, the Senate voted that help should be sent to the Mamertines, although there was a dispute about the matter between those urging that it should happen and those protesting; Roman armies then crossed the sea for the first time, and fought effectively on several occasions against Hiero. He sought peace and was granted it. 3. The cycle was completed by the censors. 292,234 citizens were counted. 4. Decimus Junius Brutus was the first to put on a gladiatorial show in honour of his dead father. 5. The colony of Aesernia was founded. 6. The book also includes successful campaigns against the Carthaginians and Volsinii.

BOOK 17

1. The consul Gnaeus Cornelius was surrounded by a Carthaginian fleet and, lured as if to a negotiation, was treacherously captured. 2. The consul Gaius Duillius fought successfully against the Carthaginians' fleet, and was the first of all Roman generals to celebrate a triumph for a naval victory. For this reason he was also given the permanent honour of being preceded by a piper playing music and a torch when he went home from dinner. 3. The consul Lucius Cornelius fought successfully in Sardinia and Corsica against the Sardinians and Corsicans and Hanno, the general of the Carthaginians. 4. After the consul Atilius Calatinus rashly led his army into a position surrounded by the Carthaginians, he escaped by the courage and efforts of the military tribune Marcus Calpurnius, who made a sortie with 300 soldiers and drew the enemy onto himself. 5. Hannibal, the general of the Carthaginians, who had been in command of a defeated fleet, was crucified by his own soldiers. 6. The consul Atilius Regulus, after the Carthaginians were defeated in a naval battle, crossed to Africa.

EX LIBRO XVIII

1. Atilius Regulus in Africa serpentem portentosae magnitudinis cum magna clade militum occidit, et cum aliquot proeliis bene adversus Carthaginienses pugnasset, successorque ei a senatu prospere bellum gerenti non mitteretur, id ipsum per litteras ad senatum scriptas questus est, in quibus inter causas petendi successoris erat, quod agellus eius a mercennariis desertus esset. 2. quaerente deinde fortuna, ut magnum utriusque casus exemplum in Regulo proderetur, arcessito a Carthaginiensibus Xanthippo, Lacedaemoniorum duce, victus proelio et captus est. 3. res deinde a ducibus Romanis omnibus terra marique prospere gestas deformaverunt naufragia classium. 4. Tib. Coruncanius primus ex plebe pontifex maximus creatus est. Valerius Maximus Sempronius Sophus censores cum senatum legerent, XVI senatu moverunt. lustrum condiderunt, quo censa sunt civium capita CCXCVII milia DCCXCVII. 5. Regulus missus a Carthaginiensibus ad senatum ut de pace et, si eam non posset impetrare, de commutandis captivis ageret, et iureiurando adstrictus, rediturum se Carthaginem, si commutari captivos non placuisset, utrumque negandi auctor senatui fuit, et cum fide custodita reversus esset, supplicio a Carthaginiensibus de eo sumpto periit.

EX LIBRO XVIIII

1. Caecilius Metellus rebus adversus Poenos prospere gestis speciosum egit triumphum, XIII ducibus hostium et CXX elephantis in eo ductis. 2. Claudius Pulcher cos. contra auspicia profectus—iussit mergi pullos, qui cibari nolebant—infeliciter adversus Carthaginienses classe pugnavit, et revocatus a senatu iussusque dictatorem dicere Claudium Gliciam dixit, sortis ultimae hominem, qui coactus abdicare se magistratu postea ludos praetextatus spectavit. 3. A. Atilius Calatinus primus dictator extra Italiam exercitum duxit. 4. commutatio captivorum cum Poenis facta est. 5. coloniae deductae sunt Fregenae, in agro Sallentino Brundisium. lustrum a censoribus conditum est. censa sunt civium capita CCXLI milia DCCXII.

1 erat *London Harleianus Lat. 3694 et cett.* om. *NPEF* ‖ 4 Coruncanius *Sigonius* Coruncanus *NPE* Corruncanus *F* | Valerius Maximus Sempronius Stofus *Levene* M. Sempronius Stofus *N* M. Sempronius Val. Maximus C. Sempronius Stofus (-oph- *E*) *PEF* | legerent *EF* regerent *NP* | XVI *N* XIII *PEF* ‖ 5 senatui *EF* senatus *NP* | periit *EF* perit *NP*

2 Cl. Pulcher (-lce- *E*) *EF* C.L. Pulcher *NP* | profectus *NF* prospectus *PE* | Claudium Gliciam *Sigonius* Cl. Glauciam *EF* Cl. Glaucia *P* Cl. Claucia *N* ‖ 3 A. Atilius Calatinus *F* A. Atilius Calanus *N* Atillius Calanus *P* Attilius Culanus *E* ‖ 5 Brundisium *NE* Brundusium *PF*

BOOK 18

1. Atilius Regulus in Africa killed a snake of prodigious size, though with great losses of his soldiers. He fought effectively against the Carthaginians in a number of battles, but when the Senate did not send a successor to him while he was successfully conducting the campaign, he complained about it in a letter to the Senate, mentioning, among other reasons for seeking a successor, that his little farm had been abandoned by his hired men. 3. Then Fortune sought to make out of Regulus a major example of both kinds of luck; he was defeated and captured by Xanthippus, the general of the Spartans, who had been summoned by the Carthaginians. 3. After that, a shipwreck of the fleets disfigured the successes of all the Roman generals on land and sea. 4. Tiberius Coruncanius was the first plebeian to be elected *pontifex maximus*. When the censors Valerius Maximus and Sempronius Sophus reviewed the Senate, they removed sixteen from it. They completed the cycle, in which 297,797 citizens were counted. 5. Regulus was sent by the Carthaginians to the Senate to negotiate peace and, if he could not obtain it, an exchange of prisoners; he was bound by oath to return to Carthage if the exchange of prisoners was not acceptable. But he advised the Senate to refuse both, and after he kept faith and returned, he was tortured to death by the Carthaginians.

BOOK 19

1. Caecilius Metellus, after successfully campaigning against the Carthaginians, celebrated a spectacular triumph, in which thirteen enemy generals and 120 elephants were led. 2. The consul Claudius Pulcher, after setting out against the auspices (he ordered the chickens who refused to eat to be drowned), fought unsuccessfully against the Carthaginians with the fleet. He was recalled by the Senate and ordered to name a dictator: he named Claudius Glicia, a man of the lowest rank, who was forced to resign his office, but subsequently watched the games wearing a purple-bordered toga. 3. Aulus Atilius Calatinus was the first dictator to command an army outside Italy. 4. An exchange of prisoners was made with the Carthaginians. 5. The colony of Fregenae was founded, and of Brundisium in Sallentine territory. The cycle was completed by the censors. 241,712 citizens were counted.

6. Claudia, soror P. Claudi qui contemptis auspiciis male pugnaverat, a ludis revertens cum turba premeretur, dixit: 'utinam frater meus viveret ⟨et⟩ iterum classem duceret.' ob eam causam multa ei dicta est. 7. duo praetores tunc primum creati sunt. 8. Caecilius Metellus, pontifex maximus, A. Postumium consulem, quoniam idem et flamen Martialis erat, cum is ad bellum gerendum proficisci vellet, in urbe tenuit nec passus est a sacris recedere. 9. rebus adversus Poenos a pluribus ducibus prospere gestis, summam victoriae C. Lutatius cos. victa ad Aegates insulas classe Poenorum imposuit. petentibus Carthaginiensibus pax data est. 10. cum templum Vestae arderet, Caecilius Metellus, pontifex maximus, ex incendio sacra rapuit. 11. duae tribus adiectae sunt, Velina et Quirina.

EX LIBRO XX

1. Falisci cum rebellassent, sexto die perdomiti in deditionem venerunt. 2. Spoletium colonia deducta est. 3. adversus Liguras tunc primum exercitus promotus est. 4. Sardi et Corsi cum rebellassent, subacti sunt. 5. Luccia, virgo Vestalis, incesti damnata est. 6. bellum Illyriis propter unum ex legatis qui ad eos missi erant occisum indictum est; qui subacti in deditionem venerunt. 7. praetorum numerus ampliatus est ut essent IIII. 8. Galli transalpini, qui in Italiam inruperant, caesi sunt. eo bello populum Romanum sui Latinique nominis DCCC milia armatorum habuisse ⟨Fabius⟩ dicit. 9. exercitibus Romanis tunc primum trans Padum ductis Galli Insubres aliquot proeliis fusi in deditionem venerunt. M. Claudius Marcellus cos. occiso Gallorum Insubrium duce, Vertomaro, opima spolia rettulit. 10. Histri subacti sunt. iterum Illyrii cum rebellassent, domiti in deditionem venerunt. 11. lustrum a censoribus ter conditum est. primo lustro censa sunt civium capita CCLXX milia DCCXIII. libertini in quattuor tribus redacti sunt, cum antea dispersi per omnes fuissent, Esquilinam, Palatinam, Suburanam, Collinam. ⟨C. Flaminius censor viam Flaminiam⟩ muniit et circum Flaminium exstruxit. 12. coloniae deductae sunt in agro de Gallis capto Placentia et Cremona [in Italia].

6 ⟨et⟩ iterum *Madvig* iterum *NPEF* iterumque *London Harleianus 3694, Vatican Lat. 5258 r* ‖ 8 A. Postumium *Vatican Lat. 6803 et cett.* Aurelium *NPEF* ‖ 9 a *NP²F om. PE* | victoriae *Vatican Lat. 6803 et cett.* victoriam *NPEF* | Lutatius *N²PF* Lutarius *N* Luctatius *E* | ad Aegates (Eg- *E*) *PEF* Daegates *N* ‖ 10 ex incendio *N²PEF* et incendio *N*

1 Falisci—venerunt *in librum XIX transponit E* ‖ 5 Luccia *PEF* Lucia *N* ‖ 6 qui subacti *Levene* subactique *NPEF* ‖ 7 praetorum–9 venerunt *bis scripsit N* ‖ 8 eo *F* et *NPE* | DCCC milia *Mommsen* ACCC *NPEF* | habuisse ⟨Fabius⟩ dicit *Mommsen* habuisse dicit *NPEF* ‖ 11 ter *Madvig* per *NPEF* quater *vel* ter *Mommsen* | C. Flaminius censor viam Flaminiam *add. Sigonius om. NPEF* ‖ 12 agro de Gallis *Sigonius* agro Gallis *NPF* agro Gall *E add.* a *E²* agro a Gallis *r* | [in Italia (Yt- *E*)] *in NPEF initio libri XXI scriptum est;* initia *Sigonius;* huc transposuit *Gronovius;* seclusit *Rossbach*

6. Claudia, the sister of the Publius Claudius who had fought unsuccessfully after he spurned the auspices, while returning from the games was hemmed in by a crowd and said: 'I wish my brother were alive and were leading the fleet again.' For that reason she was punished with a fine. 7. This was the first time that two praetors were elected. 8. Caecilius Metellus, the *pontifex maximus*, kept the consul Aulus Postumius in the city when he wanted to set off to campaign, because he was also *flamen Martialis*; he refused to let him abandon the rites. 9. After successful campaigns against the Carthaginians by many generals, the consul Gaius Lutatius put the finishing touch on victory, defeating the Carthaginian fleet at the Aegates Islands. The Carthaginians sought and were granted peace. 10. When the temple of Vesta was on fire, the *pontifex maximus* Caecilius Metellus snatched the sacred objects from the flames. 11. Two tribes, the Velina and the Quirina, were added.

BOOK 20

1. When the Falisci rebelled, they were tamed on the sixth day and surrendered. 2. The colony of Spoletium was founded. 3. That was the first time that an army was deployed against the Ligurians. 4. When the Sardinians and Corsicans rebelled, they were subdued. 5. Luccia, a Vestal Virgin, was condemned for unchastity. 6. War was declared on the Illyrians because of the killing of one of the envoys who had been sent to them; they were subdued and surrendered. 7. The number of praetors was increased to four. 8. The Transalpine Gauls, who had invaded Italy, were slaughtered. In that war Fabius says that the Roman people had 800,000 armed troops, their own and those of Latin status. 9. When Roman armies had then for the first time been led across the Po, the Insubrian Gauls were routed in several battles and surrendered. The consul Marcus Claudius Marcellus killed Vertomarus, the general of the Insubrian Gauls, and brought home the *spolia opima*. 10. The Istrians were subdued. When the Illyrians once again rebelled, they were tamed and surrendered. 11. The cycle was completed three times by the censors. In the first cycle 270,713 citizens were counted. The freedmen were limited to four tribes—the Esquilina, the Palatina, the Suburana, and the Collina—although previously they had been scattered through all of them. The censor Gaius Flaminius built the Via Flaminia and constructed the Circus Flaminius. 12. The colonies of Placentia and Cremona were founded on territory captured from the Gauls.

EX LIBRO XXI

1. belli Punici secundi ortum narrat et Hannibalis, ducis Poenorum, contra foedus per Hiberum flumen transitum. a quo Saguntum, populi Romani civitas socia obsessa, octavo mense capta est. 2. de quibus iniuriis missi legati ad Carthaginienses, qui quererentur. cum satis facere nollent, bellum his indictum est. 3. Hannibal superato Pyrenaeo saltu per Gallias, fusis Volcis, qui obsistere conati erant ei, ad Alpes venit et laborioso per eas transitu, cum montanos quoque Gallos obvios aliquot proeliis reppulisset, descendit in Italiam et ad Ticinum flumen Romanos equestri proelio fudit. in quo vulneratum P. Cornelium Scipionem protexit filius, qui Africani postea nomen accepit. 4. iterumque exercitu Romano ad flumen Trebiam fuso Hannibal Apenninum quoque permagna vexatione militum propter vim tempestatium transiit. 5. Cn. Cornelius Scipio in Hispania contra Poenos prospere pugnavit duce hostium Magone capto.

EX LIBRO XXII

1. Hannibal per continuas vigilias in paludibus oculo amisso in Etruriam venit, per quas paludes quadriduo et tribus noctibus sine ulla requie iter fecit. 2. C. Flaminius cos., homo temerarius, contra auspicia profectus signis militaribus effossis, quae tolli non poterant, et ab equo quem conscenderat per caput devolutus, insidiis ab Hannibale circumventus ad Thrasymennum lacum cum exercitu caesus est. sex milia quae eruperant, fide ab Atherbale data, perfidia Hannibalis vincta sunt. 3. cum ad nuntium cladis Romae luctus esset, duae matres ex insperato receptis filiis gaudio mortuae sunt. ob hanc cladem ex Sibyllinis libris ver sacrum votum. 4. cum deinde Q. Fabius Maximus dictator adversus Hannibalem missus nollet acie cum eo confligere, ne contra ferocem tot victoriis hostem

---

1 ortum *Leiden Bibl. Publ. Lat 19, Milan Ambrosianus S 16 sup.* actum *NPEF* | transitum *Rossbach* transitus *NPEF* | Saguntum *N²* Saguntini *NPEF* | socia *Paris Lat. 5743, Guelferbytanus 175 om. NPEF* || 3 Volcis *Vatican Lat. 1859* Vulscis *NPEF* | ei *Vatican Lat. 1859 et NPEF* || 4 Apenninum *N* Appenninum *P²EF* Appenniums *P* | permagna vexatione *Jahn* per magnam vexationem *NPEF* || 5 Cn. *Paris Lat. 5744 et cett.* C. *NEF* G. *P*

2 C. Flaminius *N* Cesar Flaminius *PE* G. Flaminius *F* | Thrasymmenum *NP* Thrasymenum *F* Trasimenum *E* | eruperant *PF* ruperant *NE* || 3 et *ante* duae matres *add. N* | *post* mortuae sunt *add. N* quod subito et nimio quis gaudio moriatur || 4 ne contra *NF* nec contra *PE*

BOOK 21

1. He narrates the opening of the Second Punic War and the crossing of the River Ebro by Hannibal, the general of the Carthaginians, contrary to the treaty. Saguntum, a community allied to the Roman people, was besieged by him and captured in the eighth month. 2. Envoys were sent to the Carthaginians to complain about these outrages; when they refused to give satisfaction, war was declared on them. 3. Hannibal crossed a pass over the Pyrenees, and going through Gaul and routing the Volcae, who had tried to block him, came to the Alps. After a difficult crossing over them, in which he fought off in several battles the Gauls of the mountains who also stood in his way, he descended into Italy and routed the Romans in a cavalry battle at the River Ticinus. In the course of it the wounded Publius Cornelius Scipio was protected by his son, who afterwards received the name Africanus. 4. And Hannibal routed a Roman army for the second time at the River Trebia, and also crossed the Apennines, though with considerable trouble to his soldiers because of the violent storms. 5. Gnaeus Cornelius Scipio in Spain fought successfully against the Carthaginians, capturing the enemy general Hanno.

BOOK 22

1. Hannibal came into Etruria, after losing an eye through constant sleeplessness in the marshes: he journeyed through those marshes for four days and three nights without any rest. 2. The consul Gaius Flaminius, a reckless man, set off against the auspices, digging up the military standards which could not be raised, and falling head-first from the horse he had mounted. He was caught in a trap by Hannibal at Lake Trasimene and was slaughtered along with his army. Six thousand who had broken through were treacherously imprisoned by Hannibal after a pledge had been given by Atherbal. 3. When there was mourning at Rome at the news of the disaster, two mothers died of joy when their sons unexpectedly returned. A Sacred Spring was vowed on account of this disaster, in accordance with the Sibylline Books. 4. After this the dictator Quintus Fabius Maximus, who had been sent against Hannibal, refused to fight against him in open battle, in

adversis proeliis ⟨territos⟩ milites pugnae committeret, et opponendo se tantum conatus Hannibalis impediret, M. Minucius, magister equitum, ferox et temerarius, criminando dictatorem tamquam segnem et timidum effecit ut populi iussu aequaretur ei cum dictatore imperium; divisoque exercitu cum iniquo loco conflixisset et in magno discrimine legiones eius essent, superveniente cum exercitu Fabio Maximo discrimine liberatus est. quo beneficio victus castra cum eo iunxit et patrem eum salutavit, idemque facere milites iussit. 5. Hannibal vastata Campania inter Casilinum oppidum et Calliculam montem a Fabio clusus sarmentis ad cornua boum alligatis et incensis praesidium Romanorum, quod Calliculam insidebat, fugavit et sic transgressus est saltum. 6. idemque Q. Fabi Maximi dictatoris, cum circumposita ureret, agro pepercit, ut illum tamquam proditorem suspectum faceret. 7. Aemilio deinde Paulo et Terentio Varrone coss. et ducibus cum magna clade adversus Hannibalem ad Cannas pugnatum est, caesaque eo proelio Romanorum XLV milia cum Paulo cos. et senatoribus XC et consularibus aut praetoriis aut aediliciis XXX. 8. post quae cum a nobilibus adulescentibus propter desperationem consilium de relinquenda Italia iniretur, P. Cornelius Scipio tribunus militum, qui Africanus postea vocatus est, stricto supra capita deliberantium ferro iuravit pro hoste se habiturum eum qui in verba sua non iurasset, effecitque ut omnes non relictum iri a se Italiam iureiurando adstringerentur. 9. propter paucitatem militum VIII milia servorum armata sunt. captivi, cum potestas esset redimendi, redempti non sunt. 10. praeterea trepidationem urbis et luctum et res in Hispania meliore eventu gestas continet. 11. Opimia et Florentia, virgines Vestales, incesti damnatae sunt. 12. Varroni obviam itum et gratiae actae, quod de re publica non desperasset.

EX LIBRO XXIII

1. Campani ad Hannibalem defecerunt. 2. nuntius Cannensis victoriae, Mago, Carthaginem missus anulos aureos corporibus occisorum detractos in vestibulo

---

adversis proeliis ⟨territos⟩ milites *Levene* ⟨territos⟩ adversis proeliis milites *Madvig* adversus proeliis (pre- *F*) milites *NPEF* adversis proeliis militem *r* territum adversis praeliis militem *Aldinus* | pugnae *r* pugnare *NPEF* | effecit *PEF* efficit *N* || 5 Casilinum *Paris Lat. 5744 et cett.* Pasiolanum *N* Pasilianum *PEF* | quod Calliculam *Guelferbytanus 175 et cett.* quod Callicula (Gall- *EF*) *NPEF* | insidebat *r* insedebat *PEF* insedebant *N* || 7 Aemilio (Em- *E*) *PEF* Aemulio *N* | Terentio *NP* Terrentio *EF* || 8 post quae *F* postque *NPE* | relictum iri *F* relictu iri *NP* relicturi *E* || 11 Opimia *F* Opima *NPE* | virgines Vestales *N* Vestales virgines *PEF*

order not to commit his soldiers to a fight against an enemy who was fierce in consequence of his many victories, when they were terrified by their defeats. Instead, he merely blocked Hannibal's attempts by setting himself against him. But Marcus Minucius, the Master of the Horse, a fierce and reckless man, accused the dictator of being a cowardly sluggard, and ensured that his own power, by the command of the people, was made equal to the dictator's. When he fought in an unfavourable location with his half of the army, and his legions were in great danger, he was freed from danger by the arrival of Fabius Maximus with his army. He was overcome by that kindness and joined camp with him and hailed him as 'father', and ordered his soldiers to do the same. 5. Hannibal, after ravaging Campania, was shut in by Fabius between the town of Casilinum and Mount Callicula; he tied brushwood to the horns of oxen and set it on fire, and put to flight the Roman garrison which was occupying Callicula, and in this way crossed the pass. 6. And the same man spared the land of the dictator Quintus Fabius Maximus when he burned the surrounding area, in order to put him under suspicion of being a traitor. 7. Then, under the command of the consuls Aemilius Paulus and Terentius Varro, there was a fight against Hannibal at Cannae, and 45,000 Romans were killed in the battle, including the consul Paulus and ninety senators and thirty ex-consuls or ex-praetors or ex-aediles. 8. After this, when in despair some young nobles were forming a plan of leaving Italy, the military tribune Publius Cornelius Scipio, who was subsequently called Africanus, drew his sword over the heads of those debating and swore that he would consider as an enemy anyone who did not swear an oath to his dictation, and he ensured that all bound themselves by an oath that they would not abandon Italy. 9. 8,000 slaves were armed because of the lack of soldiers. Although there was the opportunity of ransoming prisoners, they were not ransomed. 10. In addition, the book contains the terror and mourning in the city and campaigns in Spain that were more successful. 11. Opimia and Florentia, Vestal Virgins, were convicted of unchastity. 12. Varro was met and thanked for not despairing of the state.

BOOK 23

1. The Campanians defected to Hannibal. 2. Mago was sent to Carthage to report the victory at Cannae, and poured out in the entrance-hall of their senate house

curiae effudit, quos excessisse modii mensuram traditur. post quem nuntium Hanno, vir ex Poenis nobilibus, suadebat senatui Carthaginensium ut pacem a populo Romano peteret, nec tenuit obstrepente Barcina factione. 3. Claudius Marcellus praetor ad Nolam, eruptione adversus Hannibalem ex oppido facta, prospere pugnavit. 4. Casilinum a Poenis obsessum ita fame vexatum est ut lora et pelles scutis detractas et mures inclusi essent. nucibus per Vulturnum amnem a Romanis missis vixerunt. 5. senatus ex equestri ordine hominibus CXCVII suppletus est. 6. L. Postumius praetor a Gallis cum exercitu caesus est. 7. Cn. et P. Scipiones in Hispania Hasdrubalem vicerunt et Hispaniam suam fecerunt. 8. reliquiae Cannensis exercitus in Siciliam relegatae sunt, ne decederent inde nisi finito bello. 9. Sempronius Gracchus cos. Campanos cecidit. 10. Claudius Marcellus praetor Hannibalis exercitum ad Nolam proelio fudit et vicit, primusque tot cladibus fessis Romanis meliorem spem belli dedit. 11. inter Philippum, Macedoniae regem, et Hannibalem societas iuncta est. 12. praeterea in Hispania feliciter a Publio et ⟨Cn. Scipionibus, in Sardinia a T.⟩ Manlio praetore adversus Poenos res gestas continet, a quo Hasdrubal dux et Mago et Hanno capti. 13. exercitus Hannibalis per hiberna ita luxuriatus ut corporis animique viribus enervaretur.

EX LIBRO XXIIII

1. Hieronymus, Syracusanorum rex, cuius pater Hiero amicus populi Romani fuerat, ad Carthaginiensis defecit et propter crudelitatem superbiamque a suis interfectus est. 2. Tib. Sempronius Gracchus procos. prospere adversus Poenos et Hannonem ducem ad Beneventum pugnavit servorum maxime opera, quos liberos esse iussit. 3. Claudius Marcellus cos. in Sicilia, quae prope tota ad Poenos defecerat, Syracusas obsedit. 4. Philippo, Macedonum regi, bellum indictum est, qui ad Apolloniam nocturno bello oppressus fugatusque Macedoniam cum prope inermi exercitu profugit. ad id bellum gerendum M. Valerius praetor missus.

---

2 quos *PEF* quo *N* | Hanno *r* Hannon *NPEF* | Barcina *Drakenborch* Barchina *r* Barcinae *N* Barchiane *P* Barchine *P²F* Bartine *E* ‖ 4 a Romanis *F* a Roma *NPE* ‖ 7 Hasdrubalem *PEF* Asdrubalem *N* ‖ 8 relegatae (-te *PE*) *PEF* religatae *N* ‖ 9 Graccus *EF* Graecus *NP* ‖ 12 Cn. Scipionibus, in Sardinia a add. *Jahn* | T. add. *Aldinus*, om. *NPEF* | praetore *Milan Ambrosianus C 109 inf., Vatican Lat. 6803* praetoribus (pret- *EF*) *NPEF* | quo *Aldinus* quibus *NPEF*

2 Tib. *NPE* T. *F* | Gracchus *N* Graccus *PEF* ‖ 4 M. *N* om. *PEF*

the golden rings removed from the bodies of the slain, which are recorded as exceeding a *modius*. After this report, Hanno, a member of the Carthaginian nobility, advised the Carthaginian senate to seek peace from the Roman people, but he did not win his argument, thanks to the objections of the Barcine faction. 3. The praetor Claudius Marcellus fought successfully at Nola, after making a sortie from the town against Hannibal. 4. Casilinum, under siege from the Carthaginians, was so tormented by starvation that the besieged ate thongs and leather (removed from shields) and mice; they survived on nuts sent down the River Vulturnus by the Romans. 5. The Senate was supplemented by 197 men from the equestrian order. 6. The praetor Lucius Postumius was slaughtered by the Gauls along with his army. 7. Gnaeus and Cornelius Scipio defeated Hasdrubal in Spain and took Spain under their control. 8. The remains of the army of Cannae were exiled to Sicily, and were not to depart from there until the war ended. 9. The consul Sempronius Gracchus slaughtered the Campanians. 10. The praetor Claudius Marcellus routed and defeated Hannibal's army in battle at Nola, and was the first man to give the Romans, exhausted by so many defeats, better hope of the war. 11. An alliance was formed between Philip, the king of Macedonia, and Hannibal. 12. The book also contains successful campaigns against the Carthaginians, in Spain by Publius and Gnaeus Scipio and in Sardinia by the praetor Titus Manlius, by whom the general Hasdrubal and Mago and Hanno were captured. 13. Hannibal's army indulged itself during its time in winter quarters to the point that its strength was physically and mentally emasculated.

BOOK 24

Hieronymus, king of the Syracusans, whose father Hiero had been a friend of the Roman people, defected to the Carthaginians and was killed by his own people because of his cruelty and arrogance. 2. The proconsul Tiberius Sempronius Gracchus fought successfully at Beneventum against the Carthaginians and their general Hanno, primarily through the help of slaves, whom he ordered to be freed. 3. In Sicily, which had almost entirely defected to the Carthaginians, the consul Claudius Marcellus besieged Syracuse. 4. War was declared on Philip, king of the Macedonians, who was defeated and routed at Apollonia in nocturnal fighting and escaped to Macedonia with his troops almost unarmed. The praetor

5. res praeterea in Hispania a P. et Cn. Scipionibus adversus Carthaginienses gestas continet. a quibus Syphax, rex Numidiae, in amicitiam adscitus, qui a Masinissa, Massyliorum rege pro Carthaginiensibus pugnante victus, in Hispaniam ad Scipiones cum magna manu transiit contra Gades, ubi angusto freto Africa et Hispania dirimuntur. 6. Celtiberi quoque in amicitiam recepti sunt. quorum auxiliis adscitis tunc primum mercennarium militem Romana castra habuerunt.

EX LIBRO XXV

1. P. Cornelius Scipio, postea Africanus, ante annos aedilis factus. 2. Hannibal urbem Tarenton praeter arcem, in quam praesidium Romanorum fugerat, per Tarentinos iuvenes, qui se noctu venatum ire simulabant, cepit. 3. ludi Apollinares ex Marci carminibus, quibus Cannensis clades praedicta fuerat, instituti sunt. 4. a Q. Fulvio et Ap. Claudio coss. adversus Hannonem, Poenorum ducem, prospere pugnatum est. 5. Tib. Sempronius Gracchus pro cos. ab hospite suo Lucano in insidias deductus a Magone interfectus est. 6. Centenius Paenula, qui centurio militaverat, cum petisset a senatu ut sibi exercitus daretur pollicitusque esset, si hoc impetrasset, de Hannibale victoriam, VIII milibus acceptis militum dux factus conflixit acie cum Hannibale et cum exercitu caesus est. 7. Capua obsessa est a Q. Fulvio et Ap. Claudio coss. 8. Cn. Fulvius praetor male adversus Hannibalem pugnavit. in quo proelio XX milia hominum ceciderunt; ipse cum equitibus CC effugit. 9. Claudius Marcellus Syracusas expugnavit tertio anno et †ingentem virum gessit††. in eo tumultu captae urbis Archimedes intentus formis quas in pulvere descripserat interfectus est. 10. P. et Cn. Scipiones in Hispania tot rerum feliciter gestarum tristem exitum tulerunt, prope cum totis exercitibus caesi anno octavo quam in Hispaniam ierunt. 11. amissaque eius provinciae possessio foret, nisi L. Marci, equitis Romani, virtute et industria contractis exercituum reliquiis, eiusdem hortatu bina castra hostium expugnata essent. ad XXVII milia caesa, †ex† mille octingentos, praeda ingens capta. dux Marcius appellatus est.

5 Scipiones *Jal secutus Wölfflin* Scipionem *NPEF* ǁ 6 Celtiberi—habuerunt *ante* 24.5 res praeterea *habet NPEF transposuit Aldinus* | auxiliis *Vatican Ottob. Lat. 2852 et cett.* auspiciis *NPEF*

2 Tarenton *NPEF* Tarentum *Milan Ambrosianus S 16 sup. et cett.* | praesidium Romanorum fugerat *huc transtulit Leid. Bibl. Publ. Lat. 19, post* simulabant *NPEF* | cepit *London Harleianus Lat. 3694 et cett.* petit *NPEF* ǁ 4 Q. Fulvio *PEF* que Fulvio *N* | Ap. Claudio *N* a P. Claudio *PEF* | Hannonem *PEF* Annonem *N* ǁ 5 Gracchus *NP* Graccus *EF* ǁ 6 VIII milibus *NP¹* VIII militibus *P*V̄Ī̄Ī̄Ī̄ militibus *EF* ǁ 7 Ap. Claudio *Gronovius* a P. Claudio *PEF* ab Claudo *N* ab Claudio *N²* ab Ap. Claudio *Aldinus* ǁ 9 ingentem virum gessit *NPEF sed valde suspicor; vid. comm. ad loc.; fortasse melius* ingentem thesaurum regis cepit ǁ 10 tristem *N* triste *N²PEF* | exitum *r* exitium *NPEF* ǁ 11 Marci *NE* Marti *P* M. *F* | ex mille octingentos *N; ex obelis notavit Jahn* ex mille octingentis *N²PEF* ad mille octingentos triginta capti *Sigonius ex Liv. 25.39.13* circa mille octingentos *Rossbach* | Marcius *N* Martius *PEF*

Marcus Valerius was sent to wage the war. 5. The book also includes the campaigns conducted in Spain by Publius and Gnaeus Scipio against the Carthaginians; they brought Syphax, king of Numidia, into an agreement of friendship. Syphax was defeated by Masinissa, king of the Massylii, who was fighting for the Carthaginians, and crossed with a great force to join Scipio in Spain opposite Cadiz, where Africa and Spain are separated by a narrow strait. 6. The Celtiberi were also received into an agreement of friendship; when their help was obtained, a Roman camp then for the first time had mercenary soldiers.

BOOK 25

1. Publius Cornelius Scipio, later Africanus, was made aedile before the proper age. 2. With the help of young Tarentines who pretended that they were going hunting by night, Hannibal captured the city of Tarentum, apart from the citadel, into which the Roman garrison had fled. 3. The *ludi Apollinares* were established on the basis of the prophecies of Marcius, which had predicted the disaster at Cannae. 4. There was a successful campaign by the consuls Quintus Fulvius and Appius Claudius against Hanno, the general of the Carthaginians. 5. The proconsul Tiberius Sempronius Gracchus was led into a trap by his Lucanian friend and was killed by Mago. 6. Centenius Paenula, who had served as a centurion, asked the Senate to give him an army and promised victory over Hannibal if his request was granted. He was given 8,000 soldiers and was made their general: he fought in a battle with Hannibal and was killed along with his army. 7. Capua was besieged by the consuls Quintus Fulvius and Appius Claudius. 8. The praetor Gnaeus Fulvius fought unsuccessfully against Hannibal; 20,000 men fell in that battle; he himself fled, along with 200 cavalry. 9. Claudius Marcellus stormed Syracuse in the third year and ?played a great man?. In the chaos of that city being captured Archimedes was killed, while he was concentrating on the figures which he had inscribed in the dust. 10. Publius and Cornelius Scipio in Spain had a tragic end to their long sequence of successes, when they were killed with almost their entire armies in the eighth year after their arrival in Spain. 11. Possession of the province would have been lost, had it not been for the gathering of the remnants of the armies through the courage and efforts of Lucius Marcius, a Roman *eques*, at whose encouragement two camps of the enemy were captured. Around 27,000 were killed, while 1,800 and a substantial amount of booty were captured. Marcius was called 'general'.

EX LIBRO XXVI

1. Hannibal ad tertium lapidem ab urbe Roma super Anienem castra posuit. ipse cum duobus milibus equitum usque ad ipsam Capenam portam, ut situm urbis exploraret, obequitavit. et cum per triduum in aciem utrimque exercitus omnis descendisset, certamen tempestas diremit; nam cum in castra redisset, statim serenitas erat. 2. Capua capta est a Q. Fulvio et Appio Claudio coss. principes Campanorum veneno sibi mortem consciverunt. cum senatus Campanorum deligatus esset ad palos ut securi feriretur, litteras a senatu missas Q. Fulvius consul, quibus iubebatur parcere, antequam legeret, in sinu posuit et lege agi iussit et supplicium peregit. 3. cum comitiis apud populum quaereretur cui mandaretur Hispaniarum imperium, nullo id volente suscipere, P. Scipio, P. filius eius qui in Hispania ceciderat, professus est se iturum, et suffragio populi consensuque omnium missus Novam Carthaginem expugnavit, cum haberet annos XXIIII videreturque divina stirpe, quia et ipse, postquam togam acceperat, cotidie in Capitolio erat et in cubiculo matris eius anguis saepe videbatur. 4. res praeterea gestas in Sicilia continet et amicitiam cum Aetolis iunctam bellumque gestum adversus Acarnanas et Philippum, Macedoniae regem.

EX LIBRO XXVII

1. Cn. Fulvius procos. cum exercitu ab Hannibale ad Herdoniam caesus est. 2. meliore eventu ab Claudio Marcello cos. adversus eundem ad Numistronem pugnatum est. inde Hannibal nocte recessit. Marcellus insecutus est et subinde cedentem pressit donec confligeret. priore pugna Hannibal superior, sequenti Marcellus. 3. Fabius Maximus cos. pater Tarentinos per proditionem recepit. 4. Claudius Marcellus T. Quintius Crispinus coss. speculandi causa progressi e castris insidiis ab Hannibale circumventi sunt. Marcellus occisus, Crispinus fugit. 5. lustrum a censoribus conditum est. censa sunt civium capita CXXXVII milia CVIII; ex quo numero apparuit quantum hominum tot proeliorum adversa fortuna populo Romano abstulisset. 6. in Hispania ad Baeculam Scipio cum Hasdrubale Hamilcaris conflixit et vicit. inter alia captum regalem puerum

2 Q. Fulvio *PEF* que Fulvio *N*

1 Herdoniam *Levene* Hieroniam *NPF* Ieroniam *E* Herdoneam *Sigonius ex vet. lib.* || 2 Numistronem *r* Numisionem *NPEF* || 3 Tarentinos N^2P^1F Tarentinus *NP* Tartentinos *E* || 6 Hamilcaris *Drakenborch* Amilcaris *Aldinus* et Hamilcare *NPF* et Amilcare *E* | et vicit *PEF* evicit *N* | regalem puerum *NE* puerum regalem *PF*

BOOK 26

1. Hannibal pitched camp at the third milestone from the city of Rome above the Anio. He himself rode right up to the Porta Capena itself with two thousand cavalry in order to survey the layout of the city. And, when the whole army on each side fell into line, a storm kept the contestants apart over a three-day period: for whenever he returned to camp, the weather immediately cleared. 2. Capua was captured by the consuls Quintus Fulvius and Appius Claudius. The leading Campanians committed suicide by poison. When the senate of the Campanians was bound to poles for execution, the consul Quintus Fulvius put away in his clothing without reading it the letter from the Senate which ordered him to spare them, and he ordered that it be done according to law and he completed the punishment. 3. When at an election the question was put to the people about to whom they should entrust the command in Spain, and no one wanted to undertake it, Publius Scipio, the son of the Publius who had fallen in Spain, announced that he would go, and after being sent by the vote of the people and the agreement of all he captured New Carthage; he was twenty-four years old and seemed to be of divine stock, both because he was on the Capitol every day after reaching adulthood, and because a snake was often seen in his mother's bedroom. 4. The book also contains campaigns in Sicily and the friendship agreed with the Aetolians and the war waged against the Acarnanians and Philip, king of Macedon.

BOOK 27

1. The proconsul Gnaeus Fulvius was slaughtered with his army by Hannibal at Herdonia. 2. The consul Claudius Marcellus had greater success in his battle against the same man at Numistro. Hannibal retreated from there by night; Marcellus pursued him and constantly pressed on him as he retired until they came into conflict. Hannibal was successful in the first battle, Marcellus in the second. 3. The consul Fabius Maximus, the father, retook the Tarentines through betrayal. 4. The consuls Claudius Marcellus and Titus Quintius Crispinus went out of their camp on a scouting mission and were caught in a trap by Hannibal. Marcellus was killed, Crispinus fled. 5. The cycle was completed by the censors. 137,108 citizens were counted; the number made it obvious how great a number of people had been stolen from the Roman people by the disasters of so many battles. 6. In Spain Scipio fought with Hasdrubal son of Hamilcar at Baecula and defeated him. Among other things, he sent a royal captive, a boy of exceptional

eximiae formae ad avunculum Masinissam cum donis dimisit. 7. Hasdrubal, qui cum exercitu novo Alpes transcenderat ut se Hannibali iungeret, cum milibus hominum LVI caesus est, capta V milia CCCC M. Livi cos. ductu, sed non minore opera Claudi Neronis cos., qui, cum Hannibali oppositus esset, relictis castris ita ut hostem falleret, cum electa manu profectus Hasdrubalem circumvenerat. 8. res praeterea feliciter a P. Scipione in Hispania et a P. Sulpicio praetore adversus Philippum et Achaeos gestas continet.

EX LIBRO XXVIII

1. res in Hispania prospere gestae a Silano, Scipionis legato, et ab L. Scipione fratre adversus Poenos, a Sulpicio procos. socio Attalo rege Asiae adversus Philippum, regem Macedonum, pro Aetolis referuntur. 2. cum M. Livio et Claudio Neroni coss. triumphus decretus esset, Livius, qui in provincia sua rem gesserat, quadrigis invectus est, Nero, qui in collegae provinciam, ut victoriam eius adiuvaret, venerat, equo secutus est, et in hoc habitu plus gloriae reverentiaeque habuit: nam et plus in bello quam collega fecerat. 3. ignis in aede Vestae neglegentia virginis, quae non custodierat, extinctus est; caesa est flagro. 4. P. Scipio in Hispania cum Poenis debellavit XIIII anno eius belli, quinto post anno quam ierat, praeclusisque in totum possessione provinciae eius hostibus Hispanias recepit; et a Tarracone in Africam ad Syphacem, regem Massyliorum, transvectus foedus iunxit. Hasdrubal Gisgonis ibi cum eo in eodem lecto cenavit. 5. munus gladiatorium in honorem patris patruique Carthagini Nova edidit, non ex gladiatoribus, sed ex his qui aut in honorem ducis aut ex provocatione descendebant; in quo reguli fratres de regno ferro contenderunt. 6. cum Gisia urbs obpugnaretur, oppidani liberos et coniuges rogo extructo occiderunt et se insuper praecipitaverunt. 7. ipse Scipio, dum gravi morbo implicitus est, seditionem in parte exercitus motam, confirmatus discussit rebellantesque Hispaniae populos coegit in deditionem venire. 8. et amicitia facta cum Masinissa, rege Numidarum, qui illi auxilium, si in Africam traiecisset, pollicebatur, ⟨cum⟩ Gaditanis quoque post discessum inde Magonis, cui Carthagine scriptum erat ut in Italiam traiceret,

---

7 oppositus esset *F* oppositus est *NPE* ‖ 8 Achaeos gestas *Vatican Ottob. Lat. 2852, Vatican Urb. Lat. 392* Ascreos *NPEF*

1 a Sulpicio *London Burneianus 204 et cett.* a L. Sulpicio *NPF* a ab Lulpitio *E* a P. Sulpicio *Rossbach* | socio *N om. PEF* ‖ 2 Claudio *F* L. *NPE* ‖ 4 debellavit *Frobenius* bellavit *NPEF* | preclusisque *PEF* perclusisque *N* | provintiae *N om. PEF* | Hispanias *N* Hispaniam *PEF* | Tarracone *Paris Lat. 5743 et cett.* Tarcone *E* Tharcone *NPF* ‖ 5 Nova edidit *Drakenborch* Novae dedit *NP* Nove dedit *EF* Nova dedit *Sigonius* ‖ 7 deditionem *EF* deditione *NP* ‖ 8 cum *add. Aldinus om. NPEF* | cui *Paris Lat. 5743 et cett.* cum *NPEF*

beauty, to his uncle Masinissa with gifts. 7. Hasdrubal, who had crossed the Alps with a new army in order to join Hannibal, was killed with 56,000 men, while 5,400 were captured under the leadership of the consul Marcus Livius, but with no less effort from the consul Claudius Nero: the latter, although he was facing Hannibal, abandoned his camp in such a way as to deceive the enemy, and after setting off with a select band of troops surrounded Hasdrubal. 8. The book also contains successes by Publius Scipio in Spain and the praetor Publius Sulpicius against Philip and the Achaeans.

BOOK 28

1. Successful campaigns are described against the Carthaginians in Spain by Silanus, Scipio's legate, and by his brother Lucius Scipio, and against Philip, king of the Macedonians, by the proconsul Sulpicius, allied to Attalus king of Asia, on behalf of the Aetolians. 2. When a triumph was decreeed to the consuls Marcus Livius and Claudius Nero, Livius, who had conducted the campaign in his own province, rode on a chariot, while Nero, who had come into his colleague's province to assist in his victory, followed on horseback, and in this mode had more glory and respect: for he had achieved even more in the war than his colleague had. 3. The fire went out in the shrine of Vesta through the negligence of the Virgin who had failed to guard it; she was flogged. 4. Publius Scipio completed the war against the Carthaginians in Spain in the fourteenth year of the war, and the fifth year after his own arrival, and with the enemy totally excluded from occupying the province, he recovered the Spanish territories. He crossed from Tarraco to Africa to meet Syphax, king of the Massylii, and made a treaty with him. While he was there, Hasdrubal the son of Gisgo dined with him on the same couch. 5. He put on a gladiatorial show in New Carthage in honour of his father and uncle, not using gladiators, but those who went to fight either to honour the general or in response to a challenge; in that show two royal brothers duelled over the kingdom. 6. When the city of Gisia was attacked, the townspeople killed their children and wives on a pyre they had built and threw themselves on top of them. 7. Scipio himself was afflicted by a serious illness; after his recovery he broke up a mutiny that had occurred in part of the army, and forced the rebellious peoples of Spain to surrender. 8. And having made an agreement of friendship with Masinissa, king of the Numidians, who promised him assistance if he crossed to Africa, and also with the people of Cadiz after the departure of Mago from that town (he had received letters from Carthage that he should cross into Italy),

Romam reversus consulque creatus. 9. Africam provinciam petenti contradicente Q. Fabio Maximo Sicilia data est, permissumque ut in Africam traiceret, si id e re publica esse censeret. 10. Mago, Hamilcaris filius, a minore Baleari insula, ubi hiemaverat, in Italiam traiecit.

EX LIBRO XXVIIII

1. ex Sicilia C. Laelius in Africam a Scipione missus ingentem praedam reportavit et mandata Masinissae Scipioni exposuit querentis quod nondum exercitum in Africam traiecisset. 2. bellum in Hispania finitum victore Romano, quod Indebilis excitaverat; ipse in acie occisus, Mandonius exposcentibus Romanis a suis deditus. 3. Magoni, qui Albingauni in Liguribus erat, ex Africa et militum ampla manus missa et pecuniae, quibus auxilia conduceret, praeceptumque ut se Hannibali coniungeret. 4. Scipio a Syracusis in Bruttios traiecit et Locros pulso Punico praesidio fugatoque Hannibale recepit. 5. pax cum Philippo facta est. 6. mater Idaea deportata est Romam a Pessinunte, oppido Phrygiae, carmine in libris Sibyllinis invento, pelli Italia alienigenam hostem posse, si mater Idaea deportata Romam esset. tradita est autem Romanis per Attalum, regem Asiae. lapis erat, quem matrem deum incolae dicebant. 7. excepit P. Scipio Nasica Cn. filius eius qui in Hispania perierat, vir optimus a senatu iudicatus, adulescens nondum quaestorius, quoniam ita responsum iubebat ut id numen ab optimo viro exciperetur consecrareturque. 8. Locrenses legatos Romam miserunt qui de impudentia Plemini legati quererentur, qui pecuniam Proserpinae sustulerat et liberos eorum ac coniuges stupraverat. in catenis Romam perductus in carcere est mortuus. 9. cum falsus rumor de P. Scipione procos., qui in Sicilia erat, in urbem perlatus esset, tamquam is luxuriaretur, missis ob hoc legatis a senatu qui explorarent an ea vera essent, purgatus infamia Scipio in Africam permissu senatus traiecit. 10. Syphax, accepta in matrimonium filia Hasdrubalis Gisgonis, amicitiam quam cum Scipione iunxerat renuntiavit. 11. Masinissa, rex Massyliorum, dum pro Carthaginiensibus in Hispania militat, amisso patre Gala de regno exciderat. quo per bellum saepe repetito aliquot proeliis a Syphace, rege Numidarum, victus in totum privatus est, et cum CC equitibus exul Scipioni se

---

9 si id e re publica *Jahn* si id de re publica *Leiden Bibl. Publ. Lat. 19* si de re p. *NPEF* si ex Rep. *Aldinus* || 10 Hamilcaris *NPF* Amilicaris *E*

1 Laelius *Paris Lat. 5744 et cett.* Caecilius (Cec- *E*) *NPEF* || 2 Indebilis *NPE* Indibilis *F* | Mandonius *F* Madonius *NPE* || 3 Magoni *F* Magonis *NPE* | Abingauni *N* in Galauni *PE* in Gallia *F* | conduceret *F* doceret *NPE* || 4 Bruttios *N* Brutios *PE* Bructios *F* || 6 a Pessinunte *F* a Pesimunte *E* Apes insinenute *NP* || 8 P. Lemini *NPE* P. Levinii *F* P. Pleminii *r* || 9 urbem *London Burneianus 204 et cett.* urbe *NPEF* || 10 accepta in matrimonium filia *NF* in matrimonium *P* accepta in matrimoni filia P^2 in matrimonium filia *E* | amicitiam *London Burneianus 204 et cett.* amicitiae (-tie *PE* -icici *F*) *NPEF*

Scipio returned to Rome and was elected consul. 9. When he sought Africa as his province against the opposition of Quintus Fabius Maximus, he was granted Sicily, and he was allowed to cross to Africa if he considered that in the interests of the state. 10. Mago, the son of Hamilcar, crossed into Italy from the smaller Balearic island, where he had wintered.

BOOK 29

1. Gaius Laelius, sent by Scipio from Sicily to Africa, brought back a great deal of booty, and set out for Scipio the instructions given by Masinissa, who complained that he had not yet brought his army across to Africa. 2. The war in Spain that Indebilis had stirred up was put to an end with a Roman victory; he himself was killed in the battle, while Mandonius was surrendered by his own people to the Romans, who were demanding this. 3. To Mago, who was at Albingaunum among the Ligurians, a substantial force of soldiers was sent, along with money for hiring reinforcements, and he was ordered to join forces with Hannibal. 4. Scipio crossed from Syracuse to the Bruttii and recovered Locri after the Carthaginian garrison was driven away and Hannibal was put to flight. 5. Peace was made with Philip. 6. The Idaean Mother was brought over to Rome from Pessinus, a town in Phrygia, after a prophecy was found in the Sibylline Books that a foreign enemy could be driven from Italy if the Idaean Mother was brought over to Rome. She was handed over to the Romans through the agency of Attalus, king of Asia. It was a stone, which the inhabitants called the mother of the gods. 7. Publius Scipio Nasica, son of the Gnaeus who had died in Spain, received her, after the young man (not yet of quaestorian rank) has been judged by the Senate as the best man: for the oracle had given the order that the deity should be received and dedicated by the best man. 8. The Locrians sent envoys to Rome to complain about the lawlessness of the legate Pleminius, who had stolen money from Proserpina and raped their children and wives. He was brought to Rome in chains and died in prison. 9. When a false rumour was brought to the city about the proconsul Publius Scipio, who was in Sicily, claiming that he was indulging himself, envoys were sent by the Senate to find out whether the accusation was true; Scipio, cleared of the ill report, crossed over to Africa with the permission of the Senate. 10. Syphax, after marrying the daughter of Hasdrubal son of Gisgo, repudiated the friendship which he had formed with Scipio. 11. Masinissa, king of the Massylii, had been deprived of his kingdom after the death of his father Gala while he was fighting for the Carthaginians in Spain. He repeatedly sought to regain the kingdom in war, but was defeated in a number of battles by Syphax, king of the Numidians, and was utterly excluded from it; and he joined Scipio as an exile with 200 cavalry, and with

iunxit et cum eo primo statim bello Hannonem, Hamilcaris filium, cum ampla manu occidit. 12. Scipio adventu Hasdrubalis et Syphacis, qui prope cum centum milibus armatorum venerant, ab obsidione Uticae depulsus hiberna communiit. 13. Sempronius cos. in agro Crotoniensi prospere adversus Hannibalem pugnavit. 14. inter censores M. Livium et Claudium Neronem notabilis discordia fuit. nam et Claudius collegae ecum ademit, quod a populo damnatus actusque in exilium fuerat, et Livius Claudio, quod falsum in se testimonium dixisset et quod non bona fide secum in gratiam redisset. idem omnes tribus extra unam aerarias reliquit, quod et innocentem se damnassent et posthac consulem censoremque fecissent. 15. lustrum a censoribus conditum est. censa sunt civium capita CCXIIII milia.

EX LIBRO XXX

1. ⟨...⟩ in Africa Carthaginienses et eundem Syphacem, Numidiae regem, Hasdrubalemque pluribus proeliis vicit adiuvante Masinissa; bina hostium castra expugnavit, in quibus XL milia hominum ferro ignique consumpta sunt. Syphacem per C. Laelium et Masinissam cepit. 2. Masinissa Sophonibam, uxorem Syphacis, filiam Hasdrubalis, captam statim adamavit et nuptiis factis uxorem habuit; castigatus a Scipione venenum ei misit, quo illa hausto decessit. 3. effectumque multis Scipionis victoriis ut Carthaginienses in desperationem acti in auxilium publicae salutis Hannibalem evocarent. isque anno XVI Italia decedens in Africam traiecit temptavitque per conloquium pacem cum Scipione componere, et cum de condicionibus pacis non convenisset, acie victus est. 4. pax Carthaginiensibus petentibus data est. Hannibal Gisgonem pacem dissuadentem manu sua detraxit, excusata deinde temeritate facti ipse pacem suasit. 5. Masinissae regnum restitutum est. 6. reversus in urbem Scipio amplissimum nobilissimumque egit triumphum, quem Q. Terentius Culleo senator pilleatus secutus est. Scipio Africanus incertum militari prius favore an populari aura ita cognominatus sit. primus certe hic imperator victae nomine a se gentis nobilitatus est. 7. Mago bello quo in agro Insubrum cum Romanis conflixerat vulneratus, dum in Africam per legatos revocatus revertitur, ex vulnere mortuus est.

11 Hamilcaris *NPF* Amilcaris *E* ‖ 13 Crotoniensi *F* Protoniensi *NPE* sed *P²* supra Pro *scribit vel* Cro ‖ 14 Claudium Neronem *F* Cl. Neronem *N* Ciceronem *PE* | gratiam *r* gratia (-cia *P*) *NPEF* | posthac *Jahn* postaec *N* postea *PEF*

1 *lacunam ante* in Africa *indicavi*; Scipio *post* vicit *add. F; alii alibi* | consumpta *PEF* consummata *N* | C. Lelium *EF* Cl. Aelium *N* Delium *P* ‖ 2 Sophonibam *Vatican Pal. Lat. 895 et alii* Sofonibam *NP* Sofonisbam *EF* ‖ 3 multis *F* multum *NPE* | isque *r* idque *NPEF* ‖ 4 dissuadentem *EF* suadentem *NP* ‖ 6 quem Q. *EF* quemque *NP* | Terentius *NP* Terrentius *EF* | pilleatus *NE* pilleator *PF* ‖ 7 quo in *Vatican Urb. Lat. 462 et cett.* quin *N* qui in *N²PEF*

him in the first part of the war killed Hanno, the son of Hamilcar, along with a substantial army. 12. Scipio was driven away from the siege of Utica by the arrival of Hasdrubal and Syphax, who had come with 100,000 armed men; he established secure winter quarters. 13. The consul Sempronius fought successfully against Hannibal in the territory of Croton. 14. There was a notorious dispute between the censors Marcus Livius and Claudius Nero; for Claudius removed his colleague's horse, because he had been convicted by the people and driven into exile, while Livius did the same to Claudius, on the grounds that he had offered false testimony against him and that his reconciliation with him was not sincere. Livius reduced all but one of the tribes to *aerarii*, on the grounds that they had convicted him despite his innocence but subsequently had made him consul and censor. 15. The cycle was completed by the censors. 214,000 citizens were counted.

BOOK 30

1. ⟨...⟩ in Africa in several battles defeated the Carthaginians and the same Syphax, king of Numidia, and Hasdrubal, with the assistance of Masinissa; he stormed two enemy camps, in which 40,000 men were killed by the sword or by fire. He captured Syphax through the agency of Gaius Laelius and Masinissa. 2. Masinissa, having captured Sophoniba, the wife of Syphax and daughter of Hasdrubal, immediately fell in love with her and arranged a marriage ceremony at which he took her as his wife. After being chastised by Scipio he sent her poison, and she perished after drinking it. 3. Scipio's numerous victories brought the Carthaginians, driven to desperation, to recall Hannibal to help save the state. And he departed Italy in the sixteenth year and crossed into Africa, where he tried to negotiate peace at a meeting with Scipio and when they could not agree on the terms of peace he was defeated in battle. 4. The Carthaginians petitioned for peace and were granted it. When Gisgo advised against peace, Hannibal physically restrained him, then, after apologizing for the rashness of what he had done, personally recommended peace. 5. Masinissa's kingdom was restored to him. 6. Scipio returned to the city and held a magnificent and distinguished triumph, which the senator Quintus Terentius Culleo followed in a freedman's cap. Scipio was surnamed Africanus, it is unsure whether it was originally through the support of the soldiers or by popular opinion. But at any rate he was the first commander to be distinguished by the name of the people he had conquered. 7. Mago was wounded in the war which he had fought with the Romans in the territory of the Insubrians, and died of his wound while returning to Africa after being recalled by envoys.

EX LIBRO XXXI

1. belli adversus Philippum, Macedoniae regem, quod intermissum erat, repetiti causae referuntur hae: tempore initiorum duo iuvenes Acarnanes, qui non erant initiati, Athenas venerunt et in sacrarium Cereris cum aliis popularibus suis intraverunt. ob hoc, tamquam summum nefas commisissent, ab Atheniensibus occisi sunt. 2. Acarnanes mortibus suorum commoti ad vindicandos illos auxilia a Philippo petierunt et Athenas obpugnaverunt, Athenienses auxilium a Romanis petierunt. 3. post pacem Carthaginiensibus datam paucis mensibus, quingentesimo quadragensimo anno ab urbe condita coeptum est bellum. cum Atheniensium, qui a Philippo obsidebantur, legati auxilium a senatu petissent, et id senatus ferendum censuisset, plebe, quod tot bellorum continuus labor gravis erat, dissentiente, tenuit auctoritas patrum ut sociae civitati ferri opem populus quoque iuberet. 4. id bellum P. Sulpicio cos. mandatum est qui exercitu in Macedoniam ducto equestribus proeliis prospere cum Philippo pugnavit. 5. Aboedeni a Philippo obsessi ad exemplum Saguntinorum suos seque occiderunt. 6. L. Furius praetor Gallos Insubres rebellantes et Hamilcarem Poenum bellum in ea parte Italiae molientem acie vicit. Hamilcar eo bello occisus est et milia hominum XXXV. 7. praeterea expeditiones Philippi regis et Sulpici cos. expugnationesque urbium ab utroque factas continet. Sulpicius cos. bellum gerebat adiuvantibus rege Attalo et Rhodiis. 8. triumphavit de Gallis L. Furius praetor.

3 post pacem Carthaginiensibus datam paucis mensibus, quingentesimo quadragensimo anno ab urbe condita coeptum est bellum *Levene ex Liv. 31.5.1* post pacem Carthaginiensibus [Carthaginensibus *F*, Cartaginensibus *E*] datam quadringentesimo anno ab urbe condita [condita *bis in F*] paucis mensibus. coeptum [ceptum *E*] est autem anno (anno *om. E*) quingentesimo quinto *NPEF* post pacem Carthaginiensibus datam quadragesimo anno paucis mensibus *Jahn* coeptum est autem anno quingentesimo quadragesimo ab urbe condita, post pacem Carthaginiensibus datam paucis mensibus *Weissenborn* post pacem Carthaginiensibus datam paucis mensibus coeptum est, ab urbe condita autem anno quingentesimo quinquagesimo *Hertz* post pacem Carthaginiensibus datam paucis mensibus *Rossbach* | ferri *Vatican Ottob. Lat. 2089* ferre *NPEF* | opem populus quoque *Leiden Bibl. Publ. 19* quoque opem populus *NPF* opem populus *E* || 4 Macedoniam *Vatican Pal. Lat. 805* Macedonia *NPEF* || 5 Saguntinorum *P²E* Aguntinorum *N* Sangunitorum *F* || 6 Insubres *F* Insubras *NP* in Subras *E* | Hamilcarem *NPF* Amilcarem *E* | Italiae *N om. PEF* | Hamilcar *NF* Hamilcal *P* Amilcar *E* | XXXV *N* XXXVI *PEF* || 7 et Rhodiis—32.3 Attalo *om. P sed restituit P²*

BOOK 31

The reasons for the renewal of the war (which had been interrupted) against Philip, king of Macedonia, are reported as follows: at the time of the initiations two young Acarnanians who had not been initiated came to Athens and entered the shrine of Ceres along with others of their countrymen. They were killed for this by the Athenians, on the grounds of having committed the ultimate sacrilege. 2. The Acarnanians, moved by the deaths of their countrymen, sought aid from Philip to avenge them and attacked Athens, while the Athenians sought aid from the Romans. 3. The war commenced a few months after the peace agreement with the Carthaginians, in the 540th year from the founding of the city. When envoys of the Athenians (who were being besieged by Philip) sought aid from the Senate, and the Senate voted to give it, the people disagreed, because the endless hardship of so many wars was unsparing; but the senators' authority ensured that the people, too, ordered that help should be granted to an allied community. 4. The war was entrusted to the consul Publius Sulpicius, who led his army into Macedonia and fought successfully with Philip in cavalry battles. 5. The Aboedeni, under siege by Philip, killed their families and themselves on the model of the Saguntines. 6. The praetor Lucius Furius defeated in battle the rebellious Insubrian Gauls and the Carthaginian Hamilcar who was stirring up war in that part of Italy. In the war Hamilcar and 35,000 men were killed. 7. The book also contains the campaigns of King Philip and the consul Sulpicius, and the attacks on cities that both men engaged in. The consul Sulpicius waged war with the assistance of King Attalus and the Rhodians. 8. The praetor Lucius Furius triumphed over the Gauls.

EX LIBRO XXXII

1. conplura prodigia ex diversis regionibus nuntiata referuntur, inter quae in Macedonia in puppe longae navis lauream esse natam. 2. T. Quintius Flamininus cos. adversus Philippum feliciter pugnavit in faucibus Epiri fugatumque coegit in regnum reverti. 3. ipse Thessaliam, quae est vicina Macedoniae, sociis Aetolis et Athamanibus vexavit, L. Quintius Flamininus, frater consulis, navali proelio Attalo rege et Rhodiis adiuvantibus Euboeam et maritimam oram ⟨…⟩ 4. Achaei in amicitiam recepti sunt. 5. praetorum numerus ampliatus est, ut seni crearentur. 6. coniuratio servorum facta de solvendis Carthaginiensium obsidibus oppressa est, duo milia D necati. 7. Cornelius Cethegus cos. Gallos Insubres proelio fudit. 8. cum Lacedaemoniis et tyranno eorum Nabide amicitia iuncta est. 9. praeterea expugnationes urbium in Macedonia referuntur.

EX LIBRO XXXIII

1. T. Quintius Flamininus procos. cum Philippo ad Cynoscephalas in Thessalia acie victo debellavit. 2. L. Quintius Flamininus, ille frater procos., Acarnanas, Leucade urbe, quod caput est Acarnanum, expugnata, in deditionem accepit. 3. pax petenti Philippo Graecia liberata data est. 4. Attalus ab Thebis ob subitam valetudinem Pergamum translatus decessit. 5. C. Sempronius Tuditanus praetor ab Celtiberis cum exercitu caesus est. 6. L. Furius Purpurio et Claudius Marcellus coss. Boios et Insubres Gallos subegerunt; Marcellus triumphavit. 7. Hannibal frustra in Africa bellum molitus et ob hoc Romanis per epistulas ab adversae factionis principibus delatus propter metum Romanorum, qui legatos ad senatum Carthaginiensium de eo miserant, profugus ad Antiochum, Syriae regem, se contulit bellum adversus Romanos parantem.

---

2 Flamininus *NP*² Flaminius *EF* ‖ 3 Flamininus *NP* Flaminius *EF* | post oram *lacunam indicavit Jahn* ‖ 5 seni *F* senio *NPE* ‖ 6 duo milia D *N* duo milia *PEF*

1 Flamininus *NP* Flaminius *EF* | Cynocephalas *N* Cinocefalas *PF* Cenocephalas *E* ‖ 2 Flamininus *NP* Flaminius *EF* ‖ 3 Grecia liberata *N sed* libertati *supra scribit N*² Grecia libera *PE* Graeciae libertas *F* ‖ 7 ab *Paris Lat. 14630, Vesoniensis (Bibl. Urb.) 840 om. NPEF*

BOOK 32

1. Several prodigies are recorded as having been announced from different regions, including a laurel tree that grew in Macedonia on the stern of a warship. 2. The consul Titus Quintius Flamininus fought successfully against Philip in the passes of Epirus, put him to flight, and forced him to return to his kingdom. 3. He himself harassed Thessaly, which borders on Macedonia, with the Aetolians and Athamanes as allies, while Lucius Quintius Flamininus, the consul's brother, with the assistance of King Attalus and the Rhodians ⟨...⟩ Euboea and the sea coast. 4. The Achaeans were received into an agreement of friendship. 5. The number of praetors was increased, so that six were elected. 5. A slave conspiracy formed for the purpose of freeing Carthaginian hostages was crushed, and 2,500 were killed. 7. The consul Cornelius Cethegus routed the Insubrian Gauls in a battle. 8. An agreement of friendship was made with the Spartans and their tyrant Nabis. 9. In addition, attacks on cities in Macedonia are recorded.

BOOK 33

1. The proconsul Titus Quintius Flamininus brought the war with Philip to an end with his defeat in battle at Cynoscephalae in Thessaly. 2. Lucius Quintius Flamininus, that brother of the proconsul, stormed the city of Leucas, the capital of the Acarnanians, and received the Acarnanians' surrender. 3. Philip's request for peace was granted and Greece was freed. 4. Attalus travelled from Thebes to Pergamum because of a sudden illness and died there. 5. The praetor Gaius Sempronius Tuditanus was slaughtered by the Celtiberi along with his army. 6. The consuls Lucius Furius Purpurio and Claudius Marcellus defeated the Boian and Insubrian Gauls; Marcellus held a triumph. 7. Hannibal strove in vain for war in Africa, and was denounced for it to the Romans in letters from the leaders of the opposing faction. Out of fear of the Romans, who had sent envoys to the Carthaginian senate about him, he fled in exile to Antiochus, king of Syria, who was preparing war against the Romans.

EX LIBRO XXXIIII

1. lex Oppia, quam C. Oppius tribunus plebis bello Punico de finiendis matronarum cultibus tulerat, cum magna contentione abrogata est, cum Porcius Cato auctor fuisset ne ea lex aboleretur. 2. is in Hispaniam profectus bello, quod Emporiis orsus est, citeriorem Hispaniam pacavit. 3. T. Quintius Flamininus bellum adversus Lacedaemonios et tyrannum eorum, Nabidem, prospere gestum data his pace, qualem ipse volebat, liberatisque Argis, qui sub dicione tyranni erant, finiit. 4. res praeterea in Hispania et adversus Boios et Insubres Gallos feliciter gestae referuntur. 5. senatus tunc primum secretus a populo ludos spectavit. ⟨id⟩ ut fieret, Sextus Aelius Paetus et C. Cornelius Cethegus censores intervenerunt cum indignatione plebis. 6. coloniae plures deductae sunt. 7. M. Porcius Cato ex Hispania triumphavit. 8. T. Quintius Flamininus, qui Philippum, Macedonum regem, et Nabidem, Lacedaemoniorum tyrannum vicerat Graeciamque omnem liberaverat, ob hoc [rerum factarum multitudinem] triduo triumphavit. 9. legati Carthaginiensium nuntiaverunt Hannibalem, qui ad Antiochum confugerat, bellum cum eo moliri. temptaverat autem Hannibal per Aristonem Tyrium sine litteris Carthaginem missum ad bellandum Poenos concitare.

EX LIBRO XXXV

1. P. Scipio Africanus legatus ad Antiochum missus Ephesi cum Hannibale, qui se Antiocho adiunxerat, conlocutus est, ut, si fieri posset, metum ei, quem ex populo Romano conceperat, eximeret. inter alia cum quaereret quem fuisse maximum imperatorem Hannibal crederet, respondit Alexandrum, Macedonum regem, quod parva manu innumerabiles exercitus fudisset quodque ultimas oras, quas visere supra spem humanam esset, peragrasset. quaerenti deinde quem secundum poneret, Pyrrhum, inquit, castra metari primum docuisse, ad hoc neminem loca elegantius cepisse, praesidia disposuisse. exsequenti quem tertium diceret, semet ipsum dixit. ridens Scipio 'quidnam tu diceres', inquit, 'si me vicisses?' 'tunc

---

1 C. Oppius *Vatican Ottob. Lat. 2089* Cn. Oppius *NF* Cn. Poppius *PE* | finiendis *Leiden Bibl. Publ. 19* fingendis *NPEF* | Porcius *N* Portius *PEF* || 3 Flamininus *NP* Flaminius *EF* | liberatisque *F* liberatosque *NPE* | finiit *Rossbach* finivit *Paris Lat. 5744* finit *NPEF* || 4 Boios *EF* Bolos *NP* || 5 spectavit id ut *Jahn* spectavit ut id *r* spectavit ut *NPEF* | C. Cornelius *Sigonius* L. Cornelius *NPEF* || 7 Porcius *N* Portius *PEF* | ex Hispania *N* de Hispania (Hysp- *E*) *PFE* || 8 Flamininus *NP* Flaminius *EF* | rerum factarum multitudinem (-ine *F*) *NPEF del. Rossbach*

1 P. Scipio—posuissem *ponunt post 34.9 concitare NPEF; huc transtulit Aldinus* | inquit si me *N* si me inquit (-uid *P*) *PEF*

BOOK 34

1. The *lex Oppia*, a law setting limits on the adornment of matrons which the tribune of the people Gaius Oppius had carried during the Punic War, was repealed amid great controversy, although Porcius Cato had proposed not abandoning the law. 2. He then set out for Spain and pacified Nearer Spain in a war which he had embarked upon at Emporiae. 3. Titus Quintius Flamininus completed the successful war against the Spartans and their tyrant Nabis, after giving them peace in the manner he personally wanted and after freeing Argos, which had been under the tyrant's control. 4. Successful campaigns in Spain and against the Boian and Insubrian Gauls are recorded. 5. The Senate then for the first time watched games while segregated from the people. The censors Sextus Aelius Paetus and Gaius Cornelius Cethegus, to the resentment of the people, intervened to make that happen. 6. Several colonies were founded. 7. Marcus Porcius Cato triumphed over Spain. 8. Titus Quintius Flamininus, who had defeated Philip, king of the Macedonians, and Nabis, tyrant of the Spartans, and had freed all of Greece, triumphed for three days on account of this. 9. The envoys of the Carthaginians announced that Hannibal, who had fled to Antiochus, was preparing war with him. And Hannibal had attempted to rouse the Carthaginians to war through the agency of Aristo of Tyre, who had been sent to Carthage without letters.

BOOK 35

1. Publius Scipio Africanus, sent as envoy to Antiochus, had a conversation at Ephesus with Hannibal, who had joined himself to Antiochus, in order to remove, if possible, the fear which he had conceived because of the Roman people. When, among other things, he asked who Hannibal believed was the greatest general, he replied Alexander, king of the Macedonians, because with a small force he had routed countless armies, and had traversed the furthest regions, which it was beyond human hope to visit. Then, when Scipio asked whom he would place second, he said that Pyrrhus had been the first to show how to lay out a camp, and in addition to this that no one took control of places and distributed his garrisons more effectively. When Scipio followed up by asking whom he would put third, Hannibal said it was himself. Scipio laughed and said 'What would you be saying if you had defeated me?' 'In that case', he said, 'I would have put myself above

vero me', inquit, 'et ante Alexandrum et ante Pyrrhum et ante alios posuissem.' 2. inter alia prodigia, quae plurima fuisse traduntur, bovem Cn. Domitii cos. locutam 'Roma, cave tibi' refertur. 3. ⟨cum⟩ Nabis, Lacedaemoniorum tyrannus, incitatus ab Aetolis, qui et Philippum et Antiochum ad inferendum bellum populo Romano sollicitabant, a populo Romano descivisset, bello adversus Philopoemenen, Achaeorum praetorem, gesto ab Aetolis interfectus est. 4. Aetoli quoque ab amicitia populi Romani defecerunt. 5. cum societate iuncta Antiochus, Syriae rex, bellum Graeciae intulisset, complures urbes occupavit, inter quas Chalcidem et totam Euboeam. 6. res praeterea in Liguribus gestas et apparatum belli ab Antiocho continet.

EX LIBRO XXXVI

1. Acilius Glabrio cos. Antiochum ad Thermopylas Philippo rege adiuvante victum Graecia expulit idemque Aetolos subegit. 2. P. Cornelius Scipio Nasica cos. aedem matris deum, quam ipse in Palatium intulerat, vir optimus a senatu iudicatus, dedicavit. 3. idemque Boios Gallos victos in deditionem accepit; de his triumphavit. 4. praeterea navalia certamina prospera adversus praefectos Antiochi regis referuntur.

EX LIBRO XXXVII

1. L. Cornelius Scipio cos. legato Scipione Africano fratre (qui se legatum fratris futurum dixerat, si ei Graecia provincia decerneretur, cum C. Laelio, qui multum in senatu poterat, ea provincia dari videretur) profectus ad bellum adversus Antiochum regem gerendum, primus omnium Romanorum ducum in Asiam traiecit. 2. Regillus adversus regiam classem Antiochi feliciter pugnavit ad Myonnesum Rhodiis iuvantibus. 3. filius Africani captus ab Antiocho patri remissus est. 4. victo deinde Antiocho ab L. Cornelio Scipione adiuvante Eumene, rege

---

3 ⟨cum⟩ *hic addidi; add. Jahn ante* a populo Romano *om.* NPEF | sollicitabant *Paris Lat. 5743, Vatican Ottob. Lat. 2852* sollicitabat (soli- *E*) NPEF | descivisset bello *N*² decivisse et bellum NPE descivisse et bello *F* descivit sed bello *Rossbach* | Philopoemenen *Aldinus* Philopomenen PF Phylopomenen *E* Filopomenen *N* || 5 Chalcidem *r* Calchidem *N* Colchidem PEF

1 ad Thermopylas *N* ad Termopilas *P* ad Termophilas *F* Atemophilas *E* | 3 idemque *F* itemque NPE

1 C. Lelio *PE* C. Lellio *F* Cl. Aelio *N* | Asiam *Vatican Ottob. Lat. 2089* Asia NPEF

Alexander and Pyrrhus and everyone else.' 2. Among other prodigies, a large number of which are recorded to have occurred, it is recorded that an ox belonging to the consul Gnaeus Domitius said 'Rome, beware!' 3. When Nabis, tyrant of the Spartans, defected from the Roman people, spurred on by the Aetolians, who were provoking both Philip and Antiochus into waging war on the Roman people, he was killed by the Achaeans after undertaking a war against Philopoemen, the general of the Achaeans. 4. The Aetolians also defected from their friendship with the Roman people. 5. After forming an alliance with them Antiochus, king of Syria, waged war against Greece, and seized several cities, including Chalcis and the whole of Euboea. 6. The book also contains the campaigns among the Ligurians and Antiochus' preparation for war.

BOOK 36

1. The consul Acilius Glabrio expelled Antiochus from Greece after defeating him at Thermopylae with the assistance of King Philip, and the same man subdued the Aetolians. 2. The consul Publius Cornelius Scipio Nasica dedicated the temple of the Mother of the Gods, whom he himself had brought to the Palatine after being judged the best man by the Senate. 3. And the same man received the surrender of the Boian Gauls after their defeat and triumphed over them. 4. In addition, successful naval conflicts against the prefects of King Antiochus are recorded.

BOOK 37

1. The consul Lucius Cornelius Scipio set off to wage war against King Antiochus, and was the first of all Roman generals to cross into Asia. His legate was his brother Scipio Africanus, who had said that he would be the legate of his brother if that man were allotted Greece as his province, when it appeared that the province was being given to Gaius Laelius, who had a lot of influence in the Senate. 2. Regillus fought successfully against the royal fleet of Antiochus at Myonnesus with the assistance of the Rhodians. 3. The son of Africanus was captured by Antiochus but was sent back to his father. When, subsequently, Antiochus was defeated by Lucius Cornelius Scipio, with the help of Eumenes, king of Pergamum

Pergami, Attali filio, pax data est ea condicione ut omnibus provinciis citra Taurum montem cederet. 5. L. Cornelius Scipio, qui cum Antiocho debellaverat, cognomine fratri exaequatus Asiaticus appellatus. 6. colonia deducta est Bononia. 7. Eumenis, quo iuvante Antiochus victus erat, regnum ampliatum. Rhodiis quoque, qui et ipsi iuverant, quaedam civitates concessae. 8. Aemilius Regillus, qui praefectos Antiochi navali proelio devicerat, navalem triumphum deduxit. M'. Acilius Glabrio de Antiocho, quem Graecia expulerat, et de Aetolis triumphavit.

EX LIBRO XXXVIII

1. M. Fulvius cos. in Epiro Ambracienses obsessos in deditionem accepit, Cephalloniam subegit, Aetolis perdomitis pacem dedit. 2. Cn. Manlius cos., collega eius, Gallograecos, Tolostobogios et Tectosagos et Trocmos, qui Brenno duce in Asiam transierant, cum soli citra Taurum montem non apparerent, vicit. 3. eorum origo, et quo modo ea loca quae tenent occupaverint, refertur. 4. exemplum quoque virtutis et pudicitiae in femina traditur. quae cum regis Gallograecorum uxor fuisset capta, centurionem, qui ei vim intulerat, occidit. 5. lustrum a censoribus conditum est. censa sunt civium capita CCLVIII milia CCCX. 6. cum Ariarathe, Cappadociae rege, amicitia iuncta est. 7. Cn. Manlius contradicentibus X legatis, ex quorum consilio foedus cum Antiocho conscripserat, de Gallograecis acta pro se in senatu causa triumphavit. 8. Scipio Africanus die ei dicta—ut quidam tradunt a Q. Petilio tribuno plebis, ut quidam a Naevio— quod praeda ex Antiocho capta aerarium fraudasset, postquam is dies venit, evocatus in rostra: 'hac die', inquit, 'Quirites, Carthaginem vici', et prosequente populo Capitolium escendit. inde ne amplius tribuniciis iniuriis vexaretur, in voluntarium exilium Liternum concessit. incertum ibi an Romae defunctus sit: nam monumentum eius utrobique fuit. 9. L. Scipio Asiaticus, frater Africani, eodem crimine peculatus accusatus damnatusque cum in vincula et carcerem duceretur, Tib. Sempronius Gracchus tribunus plebis, qui antea Scipionibus

---

4 Pergami Attali *vet. lib. Sigonii* Attali Pergami *NPEF* ‖ 7 Eumenis *N²* Eumenes *NPEF* ‖ 8 deduxit *N* reduxit *PEF* | M'. Acilius *Sigonius* M. Acilius (Acc- *E*) *NPEF*

1 Cephaloniam *F* Cephallaniam (Cefa- *N*, -ala- *E*) *NPE* ‖ 2 Manlius *N* Manilius *PEF* | Tolostobogios *Guelferbytanus 175* Tolos Bogios *N* Tholos Bogios *PEF* | Tectosagos *Aldinus* Toctos Agios *NF* Toctos Agyos *P* Toctosagias *E* | Trocmos *NF* Troctnos *P* Troanios *E* ‖ 3 quo modo *Jahn* quoniam *NF* qm̄ *PE* quando *Sigonius* quemadmodum *Gronovius* ‖ 4 fuisset *N* fuit *PEF* ‖ 6 Ariarathe *EF* Ariarthe (-thae *P*) *NP* ‖ 7 Manlius *NP* Manilius *EF* | in senatu causa *N* causa in senatu *PEF* ‖ 8 Q. Petilio *Madvig* Q. Petillio *Sigonius* P. Petilio *NPEF* | Quirites *F* quicaptes *NPE* | escendit *NP* ascendit *N²P²EF* | Liternum *Vatican Lat. 6803 om. NPEF*

and son of Attalus, peace was granted to him on the condition that he withdrew from all the provinces this side of Mount Taurus. 5. Lucius Cornelius Scipio, who had completed the war with Antiochus, was called Asiaticus, matching his brother in his surname. 6. The colony of Bononia was founded. 7. The kingdom of Eumenes, by whose help Antiochus had been defeated, was enlarged; likewise some communities were yielded to the Rhodians, who had also given help. 8. Aemilius Regillus, who had defeated Antiochus' prefects in a naval battle, conducted a naval triumph. Manius Acilius Glabrio triumphed over Antiochus, whom he had expelled from Greece, and over the Aetolians.

BOOK 38

1. The consul Marcus Furius in Epirus received the surrender of the Ambracians, whom he had besieged; he subdued Cephallonia, and gave peace to the Aetolians who had been tamed. 2. His colleague, the consul Gnaeus Manlius, defeated the Gallogrecians (the Tolostobogii and Tectosagi and Trocmi), who had crossed into Asia under the leadership of Brennus, since they alone on this side of Mount Taurus were failing to submit. 3. Their origin is described, and also how they took control of those places which they occupy. 4. An exemplary instance of virtue and chastity in a woman is also recorded: when she, the wife of the king of the Gallogrecians, was captured, she killed a centurion who had offered violence to her person. 5. The cycle was completed by the censors; 258,310 citizens were counted. 6. An agreement of friendship was made with Ariarathes, king of Cappadocia. 7. Gnaeus Manlius triumphed over the Gallogrecians after making a case in the Senate on his own behalf, despite the opposition of the ten legates on whose advice he had drafted the treaty with Antiochus. 8. Scipio Africanus was prosecuted—some record it was by the tribune of the people Quintus Petilius, according to others by Naevius—on the charge of defrauding the treasury of the booty captured from Antiochus. When the date of the trial came, he was arraigned at the *rostra*, but said 'On this day, Citizens, I defeated Carthage', and with the people in attendance he climbed the Capitol. Then, so as not to be troubled further by the attacks of the tribunes, he retired to voluntary exile in Liternum. It is unclear whether he died there or at Rome, for there was a monument to him in each place. 9. Lucius Scipio Asiaticus, Africanus' brother, was accused and convicted on the same charge of embezzlement; when he was being led in chains to prison, Tiberius Sempronius Gracchus, the tribune of the people, who had previously been the Scipios' enemy, interceded, and in return for the favour married

inimicus fuerat, intercessit et ob id beneficium Africani filiam duxit. 10. cum quaestores in bona eius publice possidenda missi essent, non modo in his ullum vestigium pecuniae regiae apparuit, sed ne quaquam tantum redactum quantae summae erat damnatus. conlatam a cognatis et amicis innumerabilem pecuniam accipere noluit; quae necessaria ei erant ad cultum redempta.

EX LIBRO XXXVIIII

1. M. Aemilius cos. Liguribus subactis viam Placentia usque Ariminum productam Flaminiae iunxit. 2. initia luxuriae in urbem introducta ab exercitu Asiatico referuntur. 3. Ligures quicumque citra Appenninum erant subacti sunt. 4. Bacchanalia, sacrum Graecum et nocturnum, omnium scelerum seminarium, cum ad ingentis turbae coniurationem pervenisset, investigatum et multorum poena sublatum est. 5. a censoribus L. Valerio Flacco et M. Porcio Catone, et belli et pacis artibus maximo, motus est senatu L. Quintius Flamininus, T. frater, eo quod, cum Galliam provinciam consul obtineret, rogatus in convivio a Poeno Philippo, quem amabat, scorto nobili, Gallum quendam sua manu occiderat sive, ut quidam tradiderunt, unum ex damnatis securi percusserat rogatus a meretrice Placentina, cuius amore deperibat. extat oratio M. Catonis in eum. 6. Scipio Literni decessit et, tamquam iungente fortuna circa idem tempus duo funera maximorum virorum, Hannibal a Prusia, Bithyniae rege, ad quem victo Antiocho confugerat, cum dederetur Romanis, qui ad exposcendum eum T. Quintium Flamininum miserant, veneno mortem consciit. Philopoemen quoque, dux Achaeorum, vir maximus, a Messeniis occisus veneno, cum ab his in bello captus esset. 7. coloniae Potentia et Pisaurum et Mutina et Parma deductae sunt. 8. praeterea res adversus Celtiberos prospere gestas et initia causasque belli Macedonici continet. cuius origo inde fluxit quod Philippus aegre ferebat regnum suum a Romanis imminui et quod cogeretur a Thracibus aliisque locis praesidia deducere.

10 missi essent *Gronovius* misissent *NPEF* misisset *Aldinus*

1 Placentia *Vatican Pal. Lat. 895* Placentiam *NPEF* || 2 in urbem *N om. PEF* || 3 subacti *P²F* sublacti *P* sublati *NE* || 4 ad ingentis *EF* adiungentis *NP* | pervenisset *F* pervenit sed *NPE* || 5 L. Valerio Flacco et M. Porcio Catone *Aldinus* M. Valerio Flacco M. Portio Catone *F* M. Valerio Flacco M. Valerio Catone *N* M. Valerio Flacho M. Valeo Catone *E* M. Valerio Flacco M. Naleo Catone *P²* M. Valerio Falcco M. Naleo Catone *P* | Flaminius T. frater *Jahn* Flaminius T. Quintii frater *r* Flaminius frater *NP* Flaminius frater *EF* | cum *F om. NPE* | Poeno *F* Poenio *NPE* || 6 iungente *F* lugente *NPE* | Flamininum *N²P* Flaminium *NEF* || 7 Potentia *Vatican Lat. 1859 et cett.* Polentia *NPEF*

Africanus' daughter. 10. When the quaestors were sent to take official possession of Asiaticus' property, not only was there no trace of the king's money among it, but the total sum realized fell short of the amount for which he had been convicted. He refused to accept the vast amount of money contributed by his relatives and friends, but they bought back what he needed for his way of life.

BOOK 39

1. The consul Marcus Aemilius, after subduing the Ligurians, joined to the Via Flaminia a road that extended from Placentia to Ariminum. 2. The introduction into the city of the beginnings of luxury by the army of Asia is recorded 3. All of the Ligurians this side of the Apennines were subdued. 4. The Bacchanalia, a nocturnal Greek rite, a seed-bed of all evils, was investigated after it turned into a conspiracy of a huge crowd of people; it was suppressed through the punishment of many. 4. Lucius Quintius Flamininus, the brother of Titus, was removed from the Senate by the censors Lucius Valerius Flaccus and Marcus Porcius Cato, the latter of whom was the greatest in the arts of both war and peace. The reason was that, when he was controlling the province of Gaul as consul, at a banquet at the request of the Carthaginian Philippus, a famous prostitute with whom he was in love, he had killed a certain Gaul with his own hand, or else, as others have recorded, had executed one of the condemned men at the request of Placentina, a whore for whom he was dying of love. The speech of Marcus Cato attacking him is extant. 6. Scipio died at Liternum and, as if fortune was linking two deaths of the greatest men around the same time, Hannibal committed suicide by poison: he had fled to Prusias, king of Bithynia, after the defeat of Antiochus, and Prusias was surrendering him to the Romans, who had sent Titus Quintius Flamininus to demand him. Also Philopoemen, general of the Achaeans, an outstanding man, was poisoned by the Messenians after being captured by them in war. 7. The colonies Potentia, Pisaurum, Mutina, and Parma were founded. 8. The book also includes successful campaigns against the Celtiberi and the beginnings and causes of the Macedonian war; the ultimate origin from which it sprang was Philip's resentment at the diminution of his kingdom at the hands of the Romans, and also that he was being compelled to remove his garrisons from Thrace and other places.

EX LIBRO XL

1. cum Philippus liberos eorum quos in vinculis habebat nobilium hominum conquiri ad mortem iussisset, Theoxena, verita pro liberis suis admodum pueris regis libidinem, prolatis in medium gladiis et poculo in quo venenum erat, suasit his ut imminens ludibrium morte effugerent et cum persuasisset, et ipsa se interemit. 2. certamina inter filios Philippi, Macedoniae regis, Persen et Demetrium, referuntur; et ut fraude fratris sui Demetrius fictis criminibus, inter quae accusatione parricidii et adfectati regni, primum petitus, ad ultimum, quoniam populi Romani amicus erat, veneno necatus est, regnumque Macedoniae mortuo Philippo ad Persen venit. 3. item res in Liguribus et Hispania contra Celtiberos a compluribus ducibus feliciter gestas continet. 4. colonia Aquileia deducta est. 5. libri Numae Pompili in agro L. Petilli scribae sub Ianiculo a cultoribus agri arca lapidea clusi inventi sunt et Graeci et Latini. in quibus cum pleraque dissolvendarum religionum praetor, ad quem delati erant, legisset, iuravit senatui contra rem publicam esse ut legerentur servarenturque. ex S. C. in comitio exusti sunt. 6. Philippus aegritudine animi confectus, quod Demetrium filium falsis Persei, alterius filii, in eum delationibus impulsus veneno sustulisset, et de poena Persei cogitavit voluitque Antigonum potius, amicum suum, successorem regni sui relinquere, sed in hac cogitatione morte raptus est. Perseus regnum excepit.

EX LIBRO XLI

1. ignis in aede Vestae extinctus est. 2. Tib. Sempronius Gracchus procos. Celtiberos victos in deditionem accepit, monimentumque operum suorum Graccurim, oppidum in Hispania, constituit; et a Postumio Albino procos. Vaccaei ac Lusitani subacti sunt. uterque triumphavit. 3. Antiochus, Antiochi filius, obses a patre Romanis datus, mortuo fratre Seleuco qui patri defuncto

---

2 filios Filippi Macedoniae regis *N* Philippi Macedoniae regis filios *PF* Phylippi Macedonie regis filiis *E* | fictis *NP* confictis *EF* | inter quae (que *P²*) *P²F* inter quem *NPE* interiit qui *N²* | adfectati regni *Frobenius* adfectatione (aff- *PEF*) regni *NPEF* | primum *r* primus *NPEF* || 3 ducibus *N om. PEF* || 5 a *London Burneianus 204 et cett. om. NPEF* | cum pleraque *Guelferbytanus 175 et cett.* cum plura que (quae *F*) *NPE* || 6 falsis *London Burneianus 204 et cett.* falsi *NPEF* | Perseus *EF* Persaeus *NP*

1 est *PEF* et *N* || 2 Graccurim *Dukerus* Gracchurim *Frobenius* Gracchorum (-cco- *PE*) *NPEF* || 3 qui—egit *post* 41.6 sollicitabat *ponunt NPEF huc ut transferret proposuit Drakenborch*

BOOK 40

1. When Philip ordered the children of those nobles whom he was keeping in prison to be sought out for execution, Theoxena, fearing the king's lust for her children, who were still quite young boys, brought out swords and a cup of poison, and advised them to escape the impending humiliation by their deaths; after persuading them, she killed herself as well. 2. The competition between Perseus and Demetrius, the sons of Philip, king of Macedon, is described, and how Demetrius, through the deceit of his brother, was first attacked with false charges, including accusations of parricide and designs on the kingship, and in the end was killed with poison, because he was a friend of the Roman people, and the kingdom of Macedonia came to Perseus after the death of Philip. 3. The book similarly contains successful campaigns among the Ligurians and in Spain against the Celtiberi by several generals. 4. The colony of Aquileia was founded. 5. Books of Numa Pompilius in Greek and Latin, locked in a stone chest, were found on the land of the scribe Lucius Petillius by people working the land. After the praetor, to whom they were brought, read in them several things that subverted religious practice, he took an oath to the Senate that it was not in the interests of the state that they be read and preserved, and they were burned in the *comitium* by decree of the Senate. 6. Philip was worn out by weariness of spirit because he had killed by poison his son Demetrius, driven to it by the false accusations against him made by his other son Perseus. He considered punishing Perseus and wanted to leave his friend Antigonus as successor to his kingdom instead of his son, but he was taken by death while considering this. Perseus received the kingdom.

BOOK 41

1. The fire went out in the temple of Vesta. 2. The proconsul Tiberius Sempronius Gracchus defeated the Celtiberi and received their surrender, and founded Graccuris, a town in Spain, as a monument to his deeds. In addition, the Vaccaei and Lusitani were subdued by the proconsul Postumius Albinus. Both men triumphed. 3. Antiochus, son of Antiochus, who had been given to the Romans as a hostage by his father, on the death of his brother Seleucus (who had succeeded on

successerat, in regnum Syriae ab urbe dimissus. qui praeter religionem, qua multa templa magnifica multis locis ⟨fecit⟩, Athenis Iovis Olympi et Antiochiae ⟨Capitolini⟩, vilissimum regem egit. 4. lustrum a censoribus conditum est. censa sunt civium capita CCLVIII milia DCCXCIIII. 5. Q. Voconius Saxa tribunus plebis legem tulit, nequis mulierem heredem institueret. suasit legem M. Cato; extat oratio eius. 6. praeterea res adversus Liguras et Histros et Sardos et Celtiberos a compluribus ducibus prospere gestas et initia belli Macedonici continet quod Perseus, Philippi filius, moliebatur. miserat ad Carthaginienses legationem et ab his nocte audita erat. sed et alias Graeciae civitates sollicitabat.

EX LIBRO XLII

1. Q. Fulvius Flaccus censor templum Iunonis Laciniae tegulis marmoreis spoliavit, ut aedem quam aedificabat tegeret. tegulae ex S. C. reportatae. 2. Eumenes, Asiae rex, in senatu de Perseo, Macedoniae rege, questus est, cuius iniuriae in populum Romanum referuntur. 3. ob quas bello ei indicto P. Licinius Crassus cos., cui mandatum erat, in Macedoniam transiit levibusque †expeditionibus† equestribus proeliis in Thessalia cum Perseo dubio eventu pugnavit. 4. inter Masinissam et Carthaginienses de agro fuit lis. dies his a senatu ad disceptandum datus. 5. legati missi ad socias civitates regesque rogandos ut in fide permanerent, dubitantibus Rhodiis. 6. lustrum a censoribus conditum est. censa sunt civium capita CCLXVII milia CCXXXI. 7. res praeterea adversus Corsos et Liguras prospere gestas continet.

qua *Drakenborch* quam *NPEF* | locis *Vatican Lat. 6803* sociis (-oti- *E*) *NPEF* | fecit *add. Rossbach* erexit *r om. NPEF* | et Antiochie *P* et Anthiochie *F* et Anthyochie *E* est Antiochiae *N* | Capitolini *add. Sigonius* || Voconius *Sigonius* Volonius *N* Velonius *PEF*

1 Lacinie *r* Lactasine *NE* iacta fine *P* laeta fine *P²* Locrensis *F* | edificabat *P* dedicabat *NF* dedicarat *E* || 3 expeditionibus *NPEF sed suspicatus obelis notavi: vid. comm.* | Perseo dubio eventu *Vatican Pal. Lat. 895* Perseo eventu *NPE* Perseo felici eventu *F* || 4 fuit lis. dies his a senatu ad disceptandum *Jahn* fuit dictis a senatu ad disceptandum *NPE* contentio fuit. dies eis a senatu ad disceptandum *F* fuit dies ad disceptandum a senatu *Aldinus* || 6 $\overline{\text{CCLXVII}}$ CCXXXI *N* $\overline{\text{CCXLVII}}$ CCXXXI *PF* $\overline{\text{CCLVII}}$ CCXXXI *E*

their father's death) was despatched from the city to take the kingdom of Syria. He behaved like the most worthless king, apart from in religion, which led him to build many spectacular temples in many places, including of Olympian Jupiter at Athens and Jupiter Capitolinus at Antioch. 4. The cycle was completed by the censors; 258,794 citizens were counted. 5. The tribune of the people Quintus Voconius Saxa passed a law that no one should make a woman his heir. Marcus Cato supported the law; his speech is extant. 6. The book also contains successful campaigns by several generals against the Ligurians and Istrians and Sardinians and Celtiberi, and the beginnings of the Macedonian war which Perseus, son of Philip, was preparing. He had sent an embassy to the Carthaginians which was heard by them at night; in addition he was inciting other Greek communities to revolt.

BOOK 42

1. The censor Quintus Fulvius Flaccus plundered the temple of Juno Lacinia of its marble tiles, in order to roof the temple which he was building. The tiles were returned by decree of the Senate. 3. Eumenes, king of Asia, complained in the Senate about Perseus, king of Macedonia, whose attacks on the Roman people are described. 3. War was declared on him because of these things, and the consul Publius Licinius Crassus, to whom the war had been entrusted, crossed into Macedonia and in a series of ?minor cavalry battles in Thessaly fought against Perseus with doubtful success. 4. There was a dispute over territory between Masinissa and the Carthaginians; they were given by the Senate a day for them to argue their cases. 5. Embassies were sent to allied communities and kings, asking them to remain loyal, although the Rhodians hesitated. 6. The cycle was completed by the censors; 267,231 citizens were counted. 7. The book also contains successful campaigns against the Corsicans and Ligurians.

EX LIBRO XLIII

1. praetores aliquot eo quod avare et crudeliter provincias administraverant damnati sunt. 2. P. Licinius Crassus procos. complures in Graecia urbes expugnavit et crudeliter corripuit. ob id captivi qui ab eo sub corona venierant ex S. C. postea restituti sunt. 3. item a praefectis classium Romanarum multa impotenter in socios facta. 4. res a Perse rege in Thracia prospere gestas continet [et] victis Dardanis et Illyrico, cuius rex erat Gentius. 5. motus qui in Hispania ab Olonico factus erat ipso interempto consedit. 6. M. Aemilius Lepidus a censoribus princeps lectus.

EX LIBRO XLIIII

1. Q. Marcius Philippus per invios saltus penetravit in Macedoniam et complures urbes occupavit. 2. Rhodii miserunt legatos Romam minantes ut Perseo auxilio essent, nisi populus Romanus cum illo pacem atque amicitiam iungeret. indigne id latum. 3. cum id bellum L. Aemilio Paulo, sequentis anni cos. iterum mandatum esset, Paulus in contione precatus ut quidquid diri populo Romano immineret in suam domum converteretur, et in Macedoniam profectus vicit Persen totamque Macedoniam in potestatem redegit. 4. antequam confligeret, praedixit exercitui ne miraretur quod luna proxima nocte defectura erat. 5. Gentius quoque, rex Illyricorum, cum rebellasset, a L. Anicio praetore victus venit in deditionem et cum uxore ac liberis et propinquis Romam missus. 6. legati Alexandrini a Cleopatra et Ptolemaeo regibus venerunt querentes de Antiocho rege Syriae quod is bellum inferret. 7. Perseus, sollicitatis in auxilium Eumene rege Pergami et Gentio rege Illyricorum, quia iis pecuniam quam promiserat non dabat relictus ab his est.

---

2 ex S.C. *F* et sic *P* et *N* et si *E* || 4 et *NPEF del. Gronovius* | Gentius *Vatican Pal. Lat. 895* Gento *N* Genio (Gae- *P*) *PEF*

1 in *PEF om. N* || 2 miserunt *N* misere *PEF* || 5 L. Anicio *N* Lacinio *PF* Licinio *E* || 6 Alexandrini *N* Alexandri *PE* Alexandriae *F* || 7 Perseus *PEF* Persaeus *N*

BOOK 43

1. Some praetors were convicted because they governed their provinces with greed and cruelty. 2. The proconsul Publius Licinius Crassus stormed several cities in Greece and brutally sacked them. For that reason the captives whom he had sold at auction were subsequently restored by decree of the Senate. 3. Likewise the commanders of Roman fleets did many things tyrannically against the allies. 4. The book contains successful campaigns by King Perseus in Thrace, defeating the Dardanians and Illyricum, whose king was Gentius. 5. An uprising which was started in Spain by Olonicus subsided after he was killed. 6. Marcus Aemilus Lepidus was chosen as *princeps* by the censors.

BOOK 44

1. Quintus Marcius Philippus made his way into Macedonia through trackless passes and took control of several cities. 2. The Rhodians sent envoys to Rome threatening to assist Perseus, unless the Roman people agreed peace and friendship with him; the threat was resented. 3. When the war was entrusted to Lucius Aemilius Paulus, consul for the second time in the following year, Paulus prayed at a public meeting that whatever disaster threatened the Roman people should be turned against his own home. Then, after departing for Macedonia, he defeated Perseus and brought the whole of Macedonia under his control. 4. Before the engagement he warned the army not to be amazed that the moon was going to be eclipsed on the next night. 5. When Gentius, the king of the Illyrians, also revolted, he was defeated by the praetor Lucius Anicius and surrendered, and was sent to Rome with his wife and children and relatives. 6. Ambassadors from Alexandria, from the rulers Cleopatra and Ptolemy, came complaining about Antiochus, king of Syria, because he was making war on them. 7. Perseus, after inciting Eumenes king of Pergamum and Gentius king of the Illyrians to assist him, was abandoned by them because he did not give them the money which he had promised.

EX LIBRO XLV

1. Perseus ab Aemilio Paulo in Samothrace captus est. 2. cum Antiochus, Syriae rex, Ptolemaeum et Cleopatram, Aegypti reges, obsideret et—missis ad eum a senatu legatis, qui iuberent ab obsidione socii regis absisteret, editisque mandatis—consideraturum se quid faciendum esset respondisset, unus ex legatis Popilius virga regem circumscripsit iussitque, ante quam circulo excederet, responsum daret. qua asperitate effecit ut Antiochus bellum omitteret. 3. legationes gratulantium populorum atque regum in senatu admissae, Rhodiorum, qui eo bello contra populum Romanum faverant, exclusa. postera die cum de eo quaereretur ut his bellum indiceretur, causam in senatu patriae suae legati egerunt; nec tamquam socii nec tamquam hostes dimissi. 4. Macedonia in provinciae formam redacta Aemilius Paulus, repugnantibus militibus ipsius propter minorem praedam et contradicente Servio Sulpicio Galba, triumphavit et Persen cum tribus filiis duxit ante currum. cuius triumphi laetitia ne solida ei contingeret, duorum filiorum funeribus insignita est, quorum alterius mors triumphum patris praecessit, alterius secuta est. 5. lustrum a censoribus conditum est. censa sunt civium capita CCCXII milia DCCCV. 6. Prusias, Bithyniae rex, Romam, ut senatui gratias ageret ob victoriam ex Macedonia partam, venit et Nicomedem filium senatui commendavit. rex plenus adulationis libertum se populi Romani dicebat.

2 obsidione socii *Paris Lat. 5744 et cett.* obsidione solo *NPF* obsidione sole *E* [obsidione] solo *Rossbach* | effecit *PEF* efficit *N* || 3 quaereretur *Aldinus* quereretur *NPEF* | egerunt *London Burneianus 204 et cett.* gerunt *NPEF* || 6 Prusias *PEF* Frusias *N*

BOOK 45

1. Perseus was captured by Aemilius Paulus in Samothrace. 2. Antiochus, king of Syria, was besieging Ptolemy and Cleopatra, the rulers of Egypt, and envoys were sent to him by the Senate to order him to raise the siege of the allied king; when they issued their instructions, he replied that he would consider what he should do, and Popilius, one of the envoys, drew a circle around the king with his staff, and ordered him to give a reply before stepping out of the circle. Through his bluntness he ensured that Antiochus gave up the war. 3. The envoys of the peoples and kings congratulating them were received into the Senate, but that of the Rhodians was kept out, because they had taken sides in the war against the Roman people. When on the following day there was a discussion about this, as to whether war should be declared on them, the envoys pleaded their country's case in the Senate; they were sent away as neither allies nor enemies. 4. Macedonia was reconstituted into a province, after which Aemilius Paulus triumphed, even though his own soldiers were hostile because of the smaller amount of booty, and Servius Sulpicius Galba objected. He led Perseus with his three children in front of his chariot. But, so that the joy of that triumph would not be be granted to him as unmixed, it was marked by the deaths of his two sons, one of whom died before his father's triumph, the other after it. 5. The cycle was completed by the censors. 312,805 citizens were counted. 6. Prusias, king of Bithynia, came to Rome to congratulate the Senate on the victory that had been achieved over Macedonia; he also entrusted his son Nicomedes to the Senate. The king, full of flattery, said that he was the freedman of the Roman people.

Commentary

Book 1

Book 1 of the transmitted *Periochae* is revealingly different from all of the others. It falls into two clear sections, conventionally known as A and B. B is written in the style and manner familiar from the remaining text, and can be attributed to the same author (P.). However, it is incomplete: it begins with the reign of Ancus Marcius, approximately halfway through Livy's book. A is quite different: it covers the whole book, but, unlike B (and the work of P. in general), it does not summarize Livy in the form of an abbreviated narrative. Instead, it looks more like a contents-list, with episodes from Livy's book listed in abrupt sentences or short participial phrases and noun phrases, and finite verbs regularly omitted. Moreover, not only the style, but also the vocabulary of the two sections differs (Wölfflin (1877), 338–9, Jal (1984), xvii). Most notably, A uses *devicit* three times to describe a victory, while P. never uses the word; A uses *bellare* of the Romans fighting a war, whereas P. only uses this word, like *rebellare*, to describe the activities of foreigners (8.8, 34.9, 49.8, 60.1). A twice uses *diripere* for the plundering of a nation, a word which is much rarer in P., and found in quite different contexts (2.2, 12.2); only at 79.4 and 82.5 is it used of a military sack.

The obvious explanation is that at some point the opening sections of the *Periochae* were lost, so an early copyist supplemented it from another source. That the copyist wrote it himself is ruled out by the overlap between A and B: it is hard to see why a copyist summarizing Livy to fill a gap in his manuscript would continue with his summary beyond the point where the existing manuscript commenced. Accordingly, A must represent an existing epitome or contents-list that the copyist had available for Book 1.[1] It has sometimes been hypothesized that it is the Oxyrhynchus Epitome,[2] which shares some of the same lapidary qualities, and indeed sometimes makes similar vocabulary choices: both *devincere* (twice) and *diripere* (of a military sack) appear in the surviving fragments. However, the Oxyrhynchus Epitome is not as close to A stylistically as might appear at first sight: in particular, it is far more willing than A is to employ subordinate clauses and coordinating conjunctions (Kornemann (1904), 79); moreover, since *devincere* and *diripere* are both common words in Livy, it is unsurprising that two summarizers might independently use the same vocabulary.

It is more likely that A is a quite different summary. Unlike both P. and the Oxyrhynchus Epitome, the author makes little effort to create a narrative that is self-contained and self-explanatory to a reader who was not already acquainted with the text or the story. He refers to the *regnum...Silviorum* (1.A.1), a phrase which would be opaque to someone who was unaware that, as Livy explains

---

[1] So, rightly, Sanders (1904), 174–5.
[2] Esp. Rossbach (1904); cf. also Rossbach xx–xxii; *contra* Kornemann (1904), 78–9.

(1.3.8), all of the later kings of Alba Longa took the name Silvius. The death of Amulius is reported (1.A.1), without any explanation of who he was or why he was killed. Each king is listed by his bare name, usually without any reference even to the fact that he was king: the reader is apparently expected to know. The 'fight of the triplets' and the 'punishment of Mettius' are introduced without comment in the reign of Tullus Hostilius (1.A.4), as are the killing of Turnus Herdonius and the suicide of Lucretia in the reign of Tarquinius Superbus (1.A.8; contrast 1.B.7). The miraculous fire around Servius Tullius' head is mentioned without any account of who he was or why it might be relevant to the story (1.A.7; contrast 1.B.3).

All of this suggests a text which is being used to orient the reader within a copy of Livy which is immediately to hand. This is also a natural explanation for its incorporation here by a scribe: were that scribe working in a library which happened to own a copy of Livy's first pentad which had a contents-list, it would be easy enough to copy that list for the first book, in order to supply a new beginning for the truncated *Periochae*. Admittedly, contents-lists are not especially common in Latin texts of the classical period,[3] but at least five texts are known to have had them: Scribonius Largus, *Compositiones*, Columella, Pliny, *Natural History*, Frontinus, *Strategems*, and Aulus Gellius. There are also some less certain examples, including Pliny's *Letters*: one branch of the MSS, whose oldest exemplar (M 462 in the Pierpont Morgan Library in New York) dates from the late fifth century AD, contains such a list.[4] There are no known examples in Latin historiography, but in Greek we may compare the indices that appear in MSS of Cassius Dio, which probably date from not long after the composition of the history, from the early third century AD.[5]

Bessone (2015), 428 argues that A is older than B, on two grounds: (i) that people will have needed to start indexing Livy fairly early in its transmission, but (ii) that once our *Periochae* began to circulate, the need for an index was lessened. The second of these arguments, however, is based on flawed reasoning: an orienting index attached to an MS of Livy has quite a different function from a narrative summary circulating independently of Livy, and even if the *Periochae* was usable as an index, not all libraries will have possessed a copy.

As to Bessone's first argument, even if correct, it would show only that *some* sort of index is likely to have existed early, not that it is identical with A—but in any case it appears that it is mistaken, since as Riggsby argues, the very fact that contents-listings were rare at Rome meant that readers did not expect to find

---

[3] See Riggsby (2007), (2019), 22–9, arguing for (and seeking to explain) the rarity of the practice (*contra* Bodel (2015), 28–35).

[4] Cf. Barwick (1936), who argues that it is likely that the index was included by Pliny when he first published his collection of letters (also Gibson (2014), 38–45, Bodel (2015), 23–6), but see *contra* Riggsby (2019), 26–7.

[5] So Mallan (2016), who further hypothesizes that they may even have been composed by Dio himself.

them, which in turn meant that people were less likely to create them in the first place; Riggsby also shows that paratextual material of this sort in general is not widely or consistently transmitted in Roman texts of this period. In late antiquity, however, such paratexts became far more common,[6] and it is accordingly most probable that A was created then.

Hence no conclusion can be drawn about the relative priority of the two summaries in terms of their composition. However, we can be reasonably certain that the loss of the opening of B and the incorporation of A took place early in the MS transmission of the *Periochae*, perhaps in the late fifth or early sixth century, since it appears that none of the MSS of Livy Book 1 that reached the Carolingian period contained such an index;[7] it must derive from a strand of the tradition that did not survive antiquity.

1.A.1 *Before the founding of the city*. Corresponds to Livy 1.1.1–6.2. A lists the events under four headings: (i) Aeneas in Italy (1.1.1–2.6); (ii) the kings of Alba Longa (1.3.1–11); (iii) the rape of Rea Silvia and birth of Romulus and Remus (1.4.1–2); and (iv) the killing of Amulius (1.5.7). The remarkable omission is the entire sequence of the miraculous rescue and secret upbringing of the boys, along with their restoration to their grandfather (Livy 1.4.3–5.6). However, although this omission is surprising from a modern perspective (it is, after all, one of the best-known stories from early Rome), it is less so in terms of the post-Livian readings of Romulus. The story of the uncle's attempt to kill the twins, and their rescue by a wolf, is similarly omitted from Eutr. 1.1 and Oros. 2.4.1–2. In Orosius' case it is clear that the omission suits his polemical ends, since he has no interest in showing the foundation of Rome as divinely favoured (he also, anomalously, has Romulus killing his grandfather Numitor rather than his great-uncle: 2.4.3). But this is not true of Eutropius, who in fact has the same balance as A: the divine parentage, but not the miraculous rescue. While it would not be true to say that the wolf story was of little interest to the Romans of later antiquity (it appears, among other places, in Flor. 1.1.1.3, Just. 43.2.5–7, *Vir. Ill.* 1.2–3, *Orig.* 20–1), it loomed less large as a key feature of the Romulus story. More important was his (alleged) parentage by Mars (see below), which appears in some form in all of these texts (apart from Orosius).

A's willingness to take the story back to Aeneas and Alba Longa, on the other hand, goes more against the grain of the later summary historians: apart from *Origo Gentis Romanae*, which is precisely concerned with pre-foundation myths, the tendency of the Latin abbreviators of Roman history is to begin with Romulus and ignore or downplay his precursors (so Florus, *Vir. Ill.*, Eutropius, Orosius). A's reading of Livy, by contrast, maintains it as a point of interest.

---

[6] Riggsby (2019), 216–22.
[7] Riggsby (2019), 29 observes that even the few contents-listings which are authorial are often erratically transmitted within the manuscript traditions of those authors.

adventus Aeneae: The same phrase (in the accusative) is in Livy 1.2.1; for *adventus in Italiam* cf. 1.7.8 (used, however, not of Aeneas but of the Sibyl).

regnum...Silviorum: Cf. Livy 1.3.10 *regnum...Silviae gentis*.

Albae: Locative. Livy calls the town Alba Longa on its introduction (1.3.4), but subsequently refers to it simply as Alba, as here. The MSS add *Italiae*, which seems oddly redundant in this context. The *editio princeps* accordingly deletes it; Rossbach hypothesizes that it was a gloss added by someone who wanted to distinguish it from another town of the same name, such as Alba Helviorum.

a Marte compressa: For *compressa* cf. Livy 1.4.2. Livy's account, however, is somewhat different from A's. Livy is not prepared to say that Rea Silvia was actually raped by Mars (cf. *Praef.* 8), or even to suggest it as a possibility: he offers two options, one that she believed that she was raped by Mars, the other that she merely invented it as an excuse (Levene (1993), 129). In A, by contrast, Mars' parentage of Romulus is given as an uncomplicated fact: this is a clear misreading of Livy, but it is an account of early Rome that was widely shared in the post-Livian tradition. *Vir. Ill.*, in similar language, says 'raped by Mars she gave birth to Remus and Romulus' (1.1: *a Marte compressa Remum et Romulum edidit*); Florus calls Romulus 'born of Mars' (1.1.1.1: *Marte genitus*); also (e.g.) Conon, *Narr.* 48, Polyaen. 8.2, Ael., *VH* 7.16. Eutropius is only slightly more equivocal: he speaks of Mars as 'the son of Rea Silvia...and, as far as was believed, of Mars' (1.1.1: *Reae Silviae...filius et, quantum putatus est, Martis*); similarly Lyd., *Mens.* 4.150. Other writers (Just. 43.2.3, *Orig.* 19.5–20.1; cf. also D.H., *AR* 1.77.1–3, Plu., *Rom.* 4.2[8]) offer different alternative versions, with divine parentage not excluded even if not necessarily endorsed; indeed, that is true even in Aug., *Civ.* 3.5, 18.21, who offers Genesis 6:1–4 as a possible parallel. Hence Livy's more rigorous scepticism was highly anomalous with regard to later historical readings of Romulus (cf. Wiseman (2002)); in consequence his epitomizer rewrites him so that he coalesces more firmly with the historical mainstream.

obtruncatus: Cf. Livy 1.5.7 *regem obtruncat*.

1.A.2 *Romulus*. Corresponds to Livy 1.6.3–16.8. A lists seven key events of the reign: (i) the founding of the city (1.6.3–1.7.3); (ii) the establishment of the Senate (1.8.7); (iii) the war with the Sabines (1.11.5–1.13.4); (iv) the vowing of the *spolia opima* (1.10.5–7); (v) the organization of the people into *curiae* (1.13.7: but see further below); (vi) the victories over Fidenae and Veii (1.14.4–15.5); (vii) Romulus' deification (1.16.1–8). A's headings, however, conceal some of the most familiar events of Romulus' rule. The killing of Remus is subsumed under the foundation, the story of Tarpeia (admittedly a story which Livy passes over fairly lightly: 1.11.6–9) under the Sabine war, the (possible)

---

[8] In *Fort. Rom.* 320B, however, Plutarch simply assumes the divine conception of Romulus as a fact.

assassination of Romulus under his deification. Even more strikingly, the rape of the Sabine women (1.9.4–16) is unmentioned; it too may be assumed to be part of the Sabine war,[9] but within the later tradition the rape was more prominent than the war. If, as argued above (73–4), A's text was written to orient the reader in Livy, rather than to be read independently, these conflations are to some extent justifiable, but it is still notable that the headings do not draw attention to the particular points in which many readers of Livy might be expected to be most interested. It may not be coincidental that the killing of Remus, the rape, and the (possible) assassination are the three most contentious aspects of Romulus' reign: A declines to headline them. A's sanitization of Romulus goes beyond other writers, for all that the difficulties of his reign are regularly softened or excused.[10] Since he does not noticeably sanitize the other kings, it is presumably the particular status of Romulus as the founder of the city which leads him to favour him.

The same may explain why his account of Romulus' political organization highlights the creation of the Senate and not the establishment of the Asylum (1.8.4–6). The latter, with its implication that the Romans arose from a mixed rabble, is more potentially problematic;[11] the Senate points to the creation of a fixed oligarchic hierarchy that would be more comfortable for a conservative readership. But it should also be acknowledged that A omits points which are not readily explicable in those terms, such as the invention of lictors (1.8.1–3). It may be that with some of these smaller notices there is simply a measure of arbitrary selection with what he includes and excludes.

urbs a Romulo condita: Cf. Livy 1.7.3: *condita urbs conditoris nomine appellata*.

senatus lectus: Livy does not use this term for Romulus' original creation of the Senate: instead he says *creat senatores* (1.8.7). However, *legere senatum / lectus senatus* is the standard technical term for the review of the senate by the censors (cf. *TLL* VII.2 1125.42–76), and Livy regularly uses it in that context in later books (23.22.3, 23.22.10, 27.11.12, 38.28.1, 39.42.5, 40.51.1, 40.53.1, 43.15.6). A's phrase assimilates Romulus' actions to later constitutional practice.

bellatum: Not used by Livy here, though it is not uncommon elsewhere in his work.

spolia opima: Cf. F 14n.

---

[9] That A was thinking in those terms appears from the fact that the war is listed before the dedication of the *spolia opima*. Strictly speaking that is the wrong way round, since the Sabine war does not begin until 1.11.5; but if the war was held to begin with the rape, then A's order is explicable.

[10] Of the other later Latin writers, only Eutr. 1.2 is to some extent similar to A: he too elides the death of Remus and the assassination into (respectively) the foundation and consecration, but he gives full weight to the rape, which forms the predominant part of his (brief) narrative.

[11] For the ambivalence underlying this legend, especially in Livy's formulation of it, see Dench (2005), 18–20, 101–4.

lata: Livy uses *fero* three times in quick succession in this passage to describe the dedication of *spolia opima* (1.10.6–7), alluding to the etymology which linked *fero* to Jupiter Feretrius (Paul., *Fest.* 81L; cf. Maltby (1991), 229).

in centurias populus divisus: In Livy Romulus divides the people into *curiae*, not *centuriae* (1.13.7 *populum in curias…divideret*); the general division of the people into *centuriae* does not happen until the time of Servius Tullius (1.42.5). Accordingly, Frobenius corrected *centurias* to *curias*, which has been followed by some later editors. However, Livy does speak of the creation of *centuriae* just a few lines later (1.13.8), albeit of the *equites* rather than of the population as a whole, and it is at least as likely that A has misread Livy as that it is an error of transmission; accordingly, the text should be retained.

Romulus consecratus: Livy does not use *consecratus* for the deification of Romulus; indeed, contrary to what A implies here, Livy does not indicate any sort of formal process of deification, but rather a spontaneous outpouring of prayers and supplications (1.16.3). *consecrare* is, however, a standard term for deification (cf. *TLL* IV 383.45–384.37), used not least of the formal processes to deify a deceased emperor. A thus assimilates Romulus to a familiar pattern in the imperial period (cf. Eutr. 1.2.2 *consecratus*, *Vir. Ill.* 3.1 *post consecrationem Romuli*).

1.A.3 *Numa*. Corresponds to Livy 1.18.1–21.6. The entire reign is summarized with the phrase *ritus sacrorum tradidit*; the only specific item mentioned is the closing of the temple of Janus (1.19.2–3). This is not an unreasonable summary of Livy, who focuses Numa's reign on religion to an unusual degree, omitting the secular reforms with which other historians also associated him (Levene (1993), 135). Nor is the singling out of the temple of Janus surprising, given the importance that Livy attaches to the peacefulness of Numa's reign and the key symbolic role of the closing of the temple within that (Levene (1993), 135–7). Other historians after Livy did not place quite as much emphasis on Janus within Numa's reign: indeed, Eutr. 1.3 does not mention it at all (as previously Dionysius of Halicarnassus had not), while Flor. 1.1.2.3 and *Vir. Ill.* 3.1 merely list it in passing.[12] A in this respect is closer to Livy himself than to the so-called 'Livian tradition'.

ritus sacrorum tradidit: Nothing close to this phrase is found in Livy, either in this book or elsewhere. Indeed, he never uses the phrase *ritus sacrorum* at all, a pleonastic locution which appears to have developed in the early empire as a general term for 'religious rites': it is first in Mart. 3.24.11, twice in Tacitus (*Ann.* 11.15.2, 16.8.2), and periodically thereafter (Min. Fel. 6, Solin. 1.10, Arnob.,

---

[12] Orosius does not mention Numa's reign at all in his summary of Rome under the kings, since its peaceful air would not suit his theme; but he subsequently refers to him twice in the context of the temple of Janus (3.8.2, 4.12.4), in order to illustrate how rare such peace was at Rome after his time.

Nat. 1.24.3, Amm. 23.6.33, 28.1.20). A summarizes in the language of his own day the overall tenor of Livy's text.

porta Iani clausa: Livy uses *clausus* twice in the passage, but of Janus himself, who stands metonymically for his temple: the word *porta* does not appear. A adds the clarification: without context the metonymy would be opaque.

1.A.4 *Tullus Hostilius*. Corresponds to Livy 1.22.1–31.8. A mentions four key episodes in the reign: the plundering of the Albans (1.22.3: but cf. below); the duel of the Horatii and the Curiatii (1.24.1–25.14); the punishment of Mettius Fufetius (1.28.1–11); Tullus' death by a thunderbolt (1.31.8). This covers many of the highlights of the reign, but also misrepresents it, by separating an integrated narrative into a number of discrete episodes. In Livy the plundering leads to war between Rome and Alba; it is that war which the duel of the Horatii and the Curiatii is intended to resolve. The resulting agreement between Rome and Alba is, however, violated by Mettius, the Alban dictator, who betrays the Romans in a battle against Fidenae and Veii; his punishment is in consequence of that betrayal. A's summary in addition omits the trial of Horatius for killing his sister (1.26.1–14), the Romans' destruction of Alba (1.29.1–6: but cf. below), and the incorporation of its population into Rome (1.30.1–3), Tullus' war with the Sabines (1.30.4–10), and the prodigies and plague that lead Tullus into *superstitio* and ultimately his death (1.31.1–7).

A's summary does, however, include a little more than is apparent at first sight. The phrase *Albanos diripuit* on the face of things refers, as noted above, to the plundering that is the *casus belli* between Rome and Alba. In Livy the plundering is mutual: both sides are equally culpable (1.22.3), and A's version accordingly misrepresents the case. However, it is also clear that Tullus is actively seeking a war with Alba, and to that degree has the greater responsibility (1.22.2–4); in that respect the summary is not an unreasonable one (cf. Flor. 1.1.3.2, *Vir. Ill.* 4.1, Oros. 1.4.9, and Zonar. 7.6.1, all of whom make Tullus unequivocally responsible for the war; contrast D.H., *AR* 3.2.1–4, where it is the Albans, not the Romans, who deliberately provoke war). Moreover, while *diripuit* when applied to a city as a whole clearly refers to plundering, not its destruction (*TLL* V 1261.80–1262.31),[13] there appears to have been a version of the sack of Alba in which not only its inhabitants, as in Livy, but also its wealth was transferred to Rome (Flor. 1.1.9): hence A's phrasing may hint at the ultimate end as well as the beginning of the war.

Albanos diripuit: *diripere* is a common word in Livy (cf. above), but he does not use it here: his phrase is *praedas...agerent* (1.22.3). A appears to like the word

---

[13] This is misunderstood by both Wölfflin (1877), 338 and Jal (1984), lxvii, who believe that A is (inaccurately) referring to the destruction of Alba at the end of the story rather than the plundering at the start.

(cf. above), but it is pointed here: it not only assigns responsibility to Tullus alone (cf. above), but accentuates the violence.

fulmine consumptus: A unique phrase: for *consumere* = 'burn up' see *TLL* IV 606.40–79. Livy 1.31.8 has *fulmine ictum… conflagrasse*.

1.A.5 *Ancus Marcius.* Corresponds to Livy 1.32.1–33.9. A mentions just two events of the reign: Ancus' victory over the Latins (1.33.1–5), and his foundation of Ostia (1.33.9). Livy's account of Ancus is admittedly brief, but these are by no means the most prominent events within it. More than half of Livy's account is given over to the institution of the fetial formula (1.32.5–14); Livy also highlights the expansion of the city after the defeat of the Latins and the incorporation of their people into Rome (1.33.2, 1.33.5–7), while the foundation of Ostia is mentioned as just one among several acts by which Roman power was expanded and key monuments built or restored (1.33.8–9).

A's selection from Livy thus appears at first sight arbitrary and misleading. However, the omission of the fetial formula is at least in part explicable. In Livy's own day this was not an inert piece of antiquarianism, but appears to have been highly topical, since it was a ritual employed—and possibly in part invented[14]—by Octavian in 32 in the context of declaring war against Cleopatra and Antony. While it continued to be used at least until the late second century AD (Dio 72.33.3), it was clearly of less interest to later writers: not only A, but also Flor. 1.1.4, Eutr. 1.5, and Oros. 2.4.11 have no mention of it in the context of Ancus; and while in *Vir. Ill.* 5.4 it does appear, it is reduced to a secondary element of the reign (cf. also 1.B.1n. for P.'s version). Conversely, Ancus' victory over the Latins, which is less prominent in Livy's account, is highlighted by not only A, but *Vir. Ill.* 5.1, Eutr. 1.5, and Oros. 2.4.11; while the foundation of Ostia is singled out by Flor. 1.1.4.2 as a sign of the Romans' farsighted imperialism, preparing themselves early on for overseas commerce (cf. also *Vir. Ill.* 5.3, Eutr. 1.5). This is a reading of Ancus' reign which predates as well as postdates Livy: Cic., *Rep.* 2.33.2–4 likewise focused on the defeat of the Latins and the foundation of Ostia as its key elements.

In short, A's version is less arbitrary than it appears to be: it derives its account from Livy, but reworks him to match more closely the priorities of the broader historical tradition.

devicit: Appears to have been one of A's favourite terms (cf. above): it is often used by Livy elsewhere, but not here.

Ostiam condidit: Cf. Livy 1.33.9 *Ostia urbs condita*.

---

[14] So Wiedemann (1986), 478–83; cf. Rüpke (1990), 106–7. Rich (2011b), 204–9 argues that Wiedemann overstates the case, but he concludes that, even if the relevant portion of the rite was not actually invented in 32, it probably was the product of 'antiquarian aetiological speculation' (209) which Octavian latched onto.

1.A.6 *Tarquinius Priscus*. Corresponds to Livy 1.35.2–38.7. A refers to four events of the reign: the defeat of the Latins (1.35.7), the creation of the Circus Maximus (1.35.8–9), the defeat of other neighbouring peoples (1.36.1–38.4), and the building of city walls and sewers (1.38.6). This omits a good portion of Livy's narrative, including what one might regard as the two most memorable parts of it: first, Tarquinius' arrival in Rome and his manoeuvres for the throne after Ancus' death (1.34.1–35.6), and second, his famous challenge to Attus Navius to prove the science of augury (1.36.3–6). Both of these receive something closer to their due in P. (see 1.B.2n.), as also in Flor. 1.1.5 and *Vir. Ill.* 6. Eutr. 1.6, on the other hand, is close to A, passing over these well-known anecdotes, and instead listing much the same set of accomplishments as A does: A may misrepresent Livy, but he accurately reflects one strand of the post-Livian tradition of the regal period.

As with Romulus (1.A.2n.), the effect of this selectivity may in part be to sanitize Tarquinius' rule, overlooking his unsavoury manipulations to acquire and maintain his position; but it also fits A's broader interest in the contribution of each king to the creation of Roman power and monuments (cf. 1.A.2n., 1.A.5n.).

finitimos: In Livy, the defeated peoples are the Sabines and the Prisci Latini; A does not feel any need to specify them (similarly Oros. 2.4.11 *omnes finitimos*).

devicit: See 1.A.5n.

1.A.7 *Servius Tullius*. Corresponds to Livy 1.39.1–46.1. A singles out four points in his career: (i) the omen that marked him for the throne (1.39.1–3), (ii) the defeat of Veii (1.42.2–3), (iii) the classification of Roman citizens by census (1.42.4–44.2), and (iv) the foundation of the temple of Diana (1.45.1–7). This is a reasonable summary of the reign—the events omitted are the expansion of city to accommodate the citizen body (1.44.3–5) and the distribution of captured land to the Roman people (1.46.1)—though it does not mention any other aspect of Servius' taking of power other than the omen, something to which Livy paid a considerable amount of attention (1.40.1–41.7), nor does it refer to what is for Livy the key feature of the foundation of the temple of Diana, namely the accompanying sacrifice which marked Rome for future power.

Servio Tullio caput arsit: The same phrase in Livy 1.39.1, though in *oratio obliqua*: *caput arsisse ferunt*.

devicit: See 1.A.5n.

1.A.8 *Tarquinius Superbus*. Corresponds to Livy 1.46.1–60.3. A singles out a number of events of the reign: (i) the seizure of the throne with assassination of Servius Tullius, along with Tullia's mutilation of her father's corpse (1.46.1–48.7), (ii) the murder of Turnus Herdonius (1.50.1–51.9), (iii) the Volscian war (1.53.2), (iv) the capture of Gabii by trickery (1.53.4–54.10), (v) the foundation of the Capitoline temple (1.55.1–9; cf. 1.53.3), (vi) the suicide of Lucretia (1.58.1–12), and (vii) the expulsion of Tarquinius (1.59.1–60.3). This covers most of the chief points of the reign: indeed, A is unique among post-Livian historical epitomizers in mentioning the episode of Turnus Herdonius, something to which Livy allotted a good deal of space, but which seems to have loomed much less large in the later historical tradition: cf. 1.B.4n. Nevertheless, there are some notable omissions. A does not mention the steps Tarquinius took to consolidate his tyranny (1.49.2–9), nor his incorporation of the Latins into Rome (1.52.1–6), nor the other works of building and colonization he undertook (1.56.1–4). Nor, most notably, does he cover much of the events that led up to the fall of Tarquinius' regime: the omen of the snake and the consequent mission to Delphi (1.56.4–13), the siege of Ardea at which the fatal wager was made between Collatinus and the Tarquinii (1.57.4–11). Indeed, while the suicide of Lucretia is referred to, A has no mention of its cause in her rape by Sextus Tarquinius: A does not whitewash the crimes (cf. below), but, as with the rape of the Sabines (1.A.2n.), he refers to the events while obscuring the most sordid details.

regnum invasit: *invadere* in the sense of illegitimately usurping an office first appears at Livy 40.57.1, but becomes increasingly common later: cf. *TLL* VII.1 114.21–59.[15] P. uses the same phrase (see 1.B.4n.).

scelus: Livy uses the word repeatedly of Tarquin's usurpation in general and of Tullia's vicious treatment of her father in particular: see 1.46.3, 1.47.1, 1.48.5, 1.48.9, and esp. 1.48.7.

direpti: The chief MSS read *directu*, though it is corrected to *direpti* in the later ones. Kornemann, noting that Gabii is not sacked in Livy, but is taken over by deception (1.54.10), proposed *Gabini recepti*; but *direpti* is easier palaeographically, and also not a misrepresentation of Livy's text (*contra* Bingham 100), since Livy does refer to 'plunder' being taken (1.54.10 *praedae*), in consequence of Sextus' confiscation of the property of the town's leaders. As at 1.A.4, A slants the story against the king by giving the impression of a greater level of violence than appeared from Livy.

inchoatum: Livy presents this somewhat differently: the implication of his text is that Superbus did not 'begin' the temple, which in his version had been begun by Tarquinius Priscus (1.38.7), but he completed pretty well everything except its dedication, which took place in the first year of the Republic (2.8.5–8). A's version downplays Tarquin's role in the foundation: it might seem less comfortable to have the dominant temple of the Roman state as wholly the product of tyranny.

---

[15] Briscoe (2008), 560 (presumably following *TLL* VII.1 114.21–2) mistakenly cites Sall., *Jug.* 20.6 *regnum iam animo invaserat* as a precedent, but the context there is Jugurtha as ruler of one kingdom planning an assault on another: hence *invadere* there means not 'usurp' but 'attack' (cf. *TLL* VII.1 109.23–42).

Termini: The chief MSS read *Cremonae* (*Cremoniae/Cremonia*), corrected in some of the later MSS to *Termini*, presumably on the basis of Livy 1.55.3–4. Pithoeus, followed by Rossbach and Jal, corrected to *Termonis*, *Termon* being the Greek form of the Latin Terminus (cf. D.H., *AR* 3.69.5, Plu., *Num.* 16.1), used as a Latin noun by Enn., *Ann.* 465–6 Sk. However, those lines of Ennius survive only because they were cited as an unusual usage by Fest. 498L (presumably here, as elsewhere, following the Augustan antiquarian Verrius Flaccus). While the corruption to *Cremonae* is slightly easier to explain if the original read *Termonis*, it seems highly unlikely that a late epitomizer of Livy would replicate a rare and archaic Grecism which did not appear in Livy's text. It is far more probable that A used the standard version of the name.

Iuventae: This is not here in Livy; but he refers to it later (5.54.7), and it is found in various other sources (D.H., *AR* 3.69.5, Flor. 1.1.7.8–9, Aug., *Civ.* 4.23). A appears to be summarizing based on his memory of the story rather than on Livy's text.

regnatum est: The phrase comes from Livy (1.60.3; cf. also 1.17.2 for *regnare* in the impersonal passive).

annis CCLV: Livy 1.60.3 has *annos ducentos quadraginta quattuor*. Either A's text has been corrupted, or he was drawing (directly or indirectly) on a corrupted version of Livy's figure, or he personally mistranscribed it. It is impossible to decide between these: hence the transmitted text should remain.

For the ablative *annis* (itself a Livian idiom) see Woodcock 37–8.

1.B.1 *Ancus Marcius*. The surviving portion of P. begins with Ancus, though the opening of the reign is manifestly lost, since the king is not mentioned by name. For the same reason, it is impossible to be certain how much of Livy is omitted, since P. demonstrably presents some aspects of the reign out of order (cf. below), and may have done the same with others.

Ancus' reign in Livy covers 1.32.1–35.1. Of this, P. mentions (i) assigning the Aventine to the defeated Latins (1.33.2), (ii) the expansion of Roman territory (1.33.9), (iii) the foundation of Ostia (1.33.9), (iv) the renewal of Numa's ceremonies (1.32.2), (v) Ancus' death (1.35.1). The last of these involves a reworking of Livy's order, since Livy does not mention the death until after his account of Tarquinius Priscus' arrival at Rome during his reign (1.B.2n.), but P. prefers to complete Ancus' reign before introducing the next king, even at the cost of some chronological dislocation. More striking is a second reordering: the removal of the reintroduction of Numa's religious rites from the beginning to the end of the account. This reflects a change of emphasis, towards Ancus as a military and political figure and away from his religious role, and this is reflected in other authors also (see 1.A.5n.); it also suggests that P. may, also like others, have omitted the fetial ceremony, which in Livy follows naturally from the discussion of

Ancus' religious revival, though it cannot be completely excluded that he mentioned it in the earlier, lost, portion of his account of the reign. The highlighting of the victory over the Latins and the foundation of Ostia is also in accord with the priorities of other authors (see 1.A.5n.).

One strand of the MS tradition marks this as the beginning of Book 2, and the real Book 2 in those MSS then becomes Book 3, and so on: this was presumably introduced by a scribe who noted the break in the narrative but failed to observe that the B material retells more fully the second half of the A material.

montem Aventinum adsignavit: Livy's phrase is *Aventinum…datum* (1.33.2); P. substitutes a choicer word, one which Livy employs on various other occasions; cf. also 125.4n.

fines protulit: A standard phrase to describe the expansion of Roman power (e.g. Cic., *Rep.* 3.18, August., *R.Gest.* 30.1), but never used by Livy in this context (it appears at 42.1.6 in a different sense). Livy's phrase (1.33.9) is *imperium prolatum*.

Hostiam: The form of the name in Livy, here and elsewhere, is Ostia; this is also the regular version elsewhere in literature and in all epigraphy. However, 'Hostia' (also Obseq. 28, 68; cf. Itin. Anton. 301,6) is probably not a careless error (whether scribal or authorial), but reflects the (false) etymology found at Isid., *Orig.* 15.7.4, which derived the name from *hostis* (cf. Maltby (1991), 437).

coloniam: Livy does not refer to Ostia as a colony on its foundation here, but he records it as such later (27.38.4–5, 36.3.6). When the town was originally settled is not clear, but, even if a settlement existed previously, it was probably only in the fourth century BC that a colony was founded on the site (Meiggs (1973), 20–3). However, by the late Republic it was widely held that Ancus founded it as Rome's first colony (Cic., *Rep.* 2.5.3, 2.33.3; cf. e.g. Plin., *Nat.* 3.56, Flor. 1.1.4.2, Ampel. 17.1, *Vir. Ill.* 5.3), something in which the people of Ostia appear to have taken great pride (*CIL* XIV 4338). As often, P. incorporates his broader knowledge into his summary.

deduxit: The technical phrase for founding colonies, regularly used by P. (*TLL* V.1 273.27–80); for the precise significance of the language, and especially the distinction between this and other forms of foundations, see Tarpin (2021), 25–42. Strictly speaking it refers only to the specific moment when the colony formally was recorded as having been founded (cf. Tarpin (2021), 20), but P. regularly uses it to cover all stages of the process of foundation: see Fronda (2011), 429–31; cf. 20.12n.

caerimonias a Numa institutas renovavit: Cf. Livy 1.32.2: *sacra publica ut ab Numa instituta erant facere*. *caerimonias…renovavit* is a unique phrase (though cf. Livy 3.55.6), but captures the general sense of Livy's narrative. P. may in part be reflecting Livy's language a few lines later (1.33.5), where he uses *caerimoniae*, not of the rites of Numa that Ancus reintroduced, but the rite that Ancus introduced himself for war on the model of Numa's rites in times of peace.

regnavit annis XXIIII: The wording is almost identical to Livy's (1.35.1: *regnavit Ancus annos quattuor et viginti*). For *annis* see 1.A.8n.

1.B.2 *Tarquinius Priscus*. P. highlights two elements from Livy's account of Tarquinius' reign: the episode recounting his arrival in Rome from Tarquinii, along with his subsequent change of name and his taking of the throne (1.34.1–35.6); and his testing of the augur Attus Navius (1.36.3–6). This is then followed by a brief list of some his other achievements: the expansion of the Senate (1.35.6), his defeat of the Latins (1.35.7), the creation of the Circus Maximus (1.35.7–9), the expansion of the centuries of the *equites* (1.36.7–8), the building of the city walls and sewers (1.38.6); P. then concludes with his death at the hands of the sons of Ancus (1.40.2–7).

As with Ancus Marcius (1.B.1n.), P. concludes Tarquinius' reign before introducing his successor, even at the cost of dislocating both the chronology and the order of Livy's text. The other events of the reign are listed in order, apart from the Attus Navius episode: assuming it does indeed belong in the text (see further below), P.'s summary of Livy highlights the two episodes on which Livy, too, laid the greatest stress. On the other hand, P. removes Tanaquil entirely, and has no mention of her key role in Tarquinius' rise (nor indeed in that of Servius Tullius: see 1.B.3n.); unlike the wicked Tullia and the virtuous Lucretia, both of whom have their place in P.'s text, Tanaquil is more uncomfortably ambivalent in Livy, since her ambitions and manipulations are transgressive in terms of Roman conceptions of gender roles, but are not put to obviously immoral ends (cf. Fox (1996), 132–5). P. avoids the problem by omission.[16] A greater oddity is that the war with the Latins is mentioned, which Livy refers to only briefly, but the war with the Sabines and the Prisci Latini is not, although that occupies a significant proportion of Livy's text: as often, P.'s summary involves an element of apparent arbitrariness.

eo regnante Lucumo...Romam venit: Close to the wording of Livy 1.34.1: *Anco regnante Lucumo...Romam commigravit*.

Demarati Corinthi filius: So too Livy 1.34.2 *Demarati Corinthii filius*.

Etrusca civitate: Livy does not identify Tarquinii as an Etruscan town on its introduction, presumably relying on his audience's general knowledge (though he does later mention in passing that Tarquinius' neighbours there were Etruscan: 1.34.5). P. makes more concessions to the reader's ignorance (cf. Bingham 96).

in amicitiam...receptus: A simpler paraphrase of Livy's *in familiaris amicitiae adduxerat iura* (1.34.12). P. uses the phrase again at 24.6, 32.4, 98.1; it is found in

---

[16] Flor. 1.1.5.1 likewise fails to mention Tanaquil in the context of Tarquinius, though, unlike P, he does give her her due in the accession of Servius Tullius (1.1.6.1–2). *Vir. Ill.* 6.4 allows Tanaquil the role of interpreting the omen that Tarquinius received on his way to Rome, but does not suggest the extent to which, in Livy, she is instrumental in fostering his ambitions.

Livy at 21.19.5, 43.6.9. More generally it is a common idiom in Cicero's letters and elsewhere.

Tarquini Prisci nomen ferre coepit: Livy 1.34.10 has *L. Tarquinium Priscum edidere nomen*. In Livy this happens before Tarquin has worked his way into Ancus' affections; P., perhaps simply for the sake of succinct phrasing, implies it was subsequent to that (Bingham 96). For the omission of Tarquinius' *praenomen* cf. 4.4n.

hic temptandae... protinus factum: In the MSS this sentence appears prior to the death of Ancus, and so refers to that king rather than to Tarquin. This reflects neither Livy's text nor the historical tradition: it is extremely unlikely that P. could have made so drastic an error in his summary. Madvig deleted the entire sentence as a gloss, but it is stylistically unexceptional for P.[17] As I discuss below, the language is closer to Cic., *Div.* 1.32 than to Livy (cf. Bingham 94–5), but the use of Cicero's language is not unparalleled in P.: see 4.4n., 5.11n., 8.10n., 13.7n., and 18.5n. for other episodes where P. appears to have rewritten Livy using phrasing taken from Cicero.

Accordingly, it is far more likely to be a textual transposition than a gloss.[18] As to where it should be placed, Sigonius moved it to after *centurias ampliavit*,[19] while Madvig inserted it parenthetically at the end of the entire reign; but it is better to put it before *centum in patres allegit*, not only because a shorter displacement is more likely than a longer one, but also because *hic* is likely to introduce the first episode of the reign after the king's introduction (cf. 52.8n.). On either version it is out of chronological sequence, and so highlighted as a key episode of the reign.

temptandae scientiae... causa: In Livy, as in most other sources (e.g. D.H., *AR* 3.71.2, Fest. 168L, Lact., *Inst.* 2.7.8, Zonar. 7.8.8), Tarquinius acts *eludens... artem* (1.36.4), mocking rather than testing Attus Navius. See, however, Cic., *Div.* 1.32 *cum temptaret scientiam*, which is probably the source of P.'s phrasing. P.'s use of Cicero's language does not necessarily mean that he is assuming the Ciceronian version of the story (*contra* Bingham 95), where Tarquinius' test is motivated simply by Attius' fame, rather than a conflict over the enlargement of the centuries of the *equites* (see Pease (1920–3), 146): note Flor. 1.1.5.3, where the story is the Livian one, but where Florus still speaks in terms of testing rather than mockery.

fertur: Livy, in similar language, attributes the story to others rather than narrating it in his own voice (1.36.4 *ut ferunt*, 1.36.5 *ferunt*); this is generally accepted to represent his unwillingness to endorse the historicity of the miracle (e.g. Levene

---

[17] Denied by Wölfflin (1877), 340, who argued that the introduction of the episode with *hic* rather than *is* was anomalous, but see *contra* Klotz (1936), 75–6.

[18] So, rightly, Jal (1984), 93, although he does not make the transposition in his actual text.

[19] Sigonius did this, however, as part of a much larger rearrangement of the section; like other early editors of the *Periochae*, he failed to realize that the A section and the B section represented different original texts, and so sought to conflate them into a single narrative; he also tried to match Livy's chronological order of Priscus' reign.

(1993), 19–20),[20] a distancing which P. here replicates (cf. 35.2n.). Although Cicero does narrate part of the story in *oratio obliqua*, the overall tenor of his account is quite different, since his entire argument depends on accepting the story as reliable.

consuluisse eum an id de quo cogitaret effici posset: Livy 1.36.4 has Tarquin speaking in *oratio recta: inaugura fierine possit quod nunc ego mente efficio*. Here too (cf. above) P.'s language is closer to Cic., *Div.* 1.32: *dixit ei cogitare se quiddam; id possetne fieri consuluit*, though *effici* may suggest that he has Livy's version in mind as well.

iussisse eum novacula cotem praecidere: Once again (cf. above) P. appears to have drawn his language from Cic., *Div.* 1.32 *dixit se cogitasse cotem novacula posse praecidi: tum Attum iussisse experiri*, rather than from Livy 1.36.4 *hoc animo agitavi…te novacula cotem discissurum*.

protinus: Livy 1.36.5 has *haud cunctanter*: Cic., *Div.* 1.32, by contrast, implies a slower and more elaborate process, as Tarquinius organizes a public demonstration in the Comitium.

centum in patres adlegit: Cf. Livy 1.35.6: *centum in patres legit*. *adlego* is rare in surviving Republican literature: it is first recorded by Varro, *Ling.* 6.66, then is used twice by Livy (10.6.6, 10.6.9), but then becomes increasingly common in the imperial period: see *TLL* I 1663.83–1665.63.

An alternative MS reading is *centum hic patres elegit*, but the phrasing that is closer to Livy's original is on balance to be preferred.

equitum centurias ampliavit: P. regularly uses *amplio* when recording expansions of offices or enlargements of groups: see 2.7, 3.5, 10.3, 15.7, 20.7, 32.5, 89.4. Livy never uses the word in this sense, but only in the quite different meaning of having a trial deferred (*TLL* I 2001.80–2002.3, *OLD s.v. amplio* 3a). The meaning 'increase' or 'enlarge' is occasionally found in the triumviral period (*Bell. Hisp.* 42.2, Hor. *Sat.* 1.4.32), but is primarily a later usage; and only in the early second century AD is it used specifically of increasing the numbers of a group (*OLD s.v. amplio* 1b).

In Livy the expansion of the centuries of the *equites* is closely linked with the story of Attus Navius (cf. above). P. separates them, treating the latter as a self-contained anecdote, unconnected to Tarquinius' political reforms, and to that extent aligns himself more closely with the Ciceronian than the Livian version.

urbem muro circumdedit: Livy does not actually describe Tarquinius building a wall. He prepares to do so at 1.36.1 (*muro quoque lapideo circumdare urbem parabat*—'he was preparing to surround the city with a stone wall'), but is interrupted by a war with the Sabines. When the war ends, he once again plans to do so, but Livy's language only talks about 'planning', not completing (1.38.6: *muro lapideo…urbem*

---

[20] *Contra* Davies (2004), 28–61; but see Levene (2006b), 422.

qua nondum munierat cingere parat—'He prepared to gird the city with a stone wall where he had not yet fortified it'). Only with his successor Servius Tullius does Rome finally receive a wall (1.44.3: *muro circumdat urbem*—'he surrounded the city with a wall'). P., on the other hand, suggests that Tarquinius actually completed the wall, and has no mention of a wall under Servius—though, interestingly, his language is closer to Livy's account of the latter, as if he were drawing attention to the discrepancy.

One should note that P.'s version is the commoner one in the tradition: in D.H., *AR* 3.67.4 Tarquinius builds the first wall around Rome, while Servius' role is only to extend that wall to enclose the Viminal and Esquiline, which he added to the city (*AR* 4.14.1); similarly in both *Vir. Ill.* (6.8, 7.6) and Eutr. (1.6.2, 1.7.1) Tarquinius builds the wall, Servius only adds a rampart and a ditch.

1.B.3 *Servius Tullius*. Corresponds to Livy 1.39.1–48.9. P. summarizes five episodes from his career: (i) the omen that marked him for the throne (1.39.1–3), (ii) his institution of the census (1.42.4–44.2), (iii) the extension of the *pomerium* and the addition of three hills to the city (1.44.3–5), (iv) foundation of the temple of Diana (1.45.1–7), and (v) his assassination at the hands of Tarquinius Superbus (1.46.2–48.9). Although in terms of length this is, as always, fuller than the version in A (see 1.A.7n.), in some respects it is less representative of Livy's text. Like A, P. does not discuss the details of Servius' rise to power other than the omen (contrast Livy 1.40.1–41.7); both of them refer to the dedication of the temple of Diana, but neither refers to the accompanying trick of the sacrifice which forms the centre of Livy's account. Unlike A, P. refers to the physical expansion of the city, but against that, he does not mention the defeat of Veii (1.42.2–3).

But the most notable difference is that P., unlike A, speaks of Servius' institutional reforms solely in terms of the invention of the census, ignoring the detailed classification of citizens which occupies much of Livy's account. This last is perhaps related to the fact that P. shows a particular interest in Livy's census reports, at least in the first half of the work (3.2, 10.9, 11.5, 13.4, 14.4, 16.3, 18.4, 19.5, 20.11, 27.5, 29.15, 38.5, 41.4, 42.6, 45.5, 46.5, 47.3, 48.1, 54.2, 56.4, 59.5, 60.5, 63.1, 98.2, 115.3): through them he marks the progressive growth of the Roman citizen body. The technicalities of Servius' classification, most of which was long obsolete by his day, were less pertinent to this theme. Eutr. 1.7 shares P.'s approach to Servius' reforms (cf. Ampel. 17.2, who singles out the 'first census' as the key event of Servius' reign), though the balance in Flor. 1.1.6.3 is closer to Livy's.

natus ex captiva nobili Corniculana: Livy presents this as his preferred version (1.39.5), though he acknowledges an alternative story whereby Servius was born as a slave from a slave mother (so Cic., *Rep.* 2.37, Val. Max. 1.4.1, Plin., *Nat.* 36.204, Plu., *Quaest. Rom.* 287F, *Fort. Rom.* 323A–B). P., as is his usual practice, tells only one of the stories. However, Livy himself later has a character allude to the version where Servius was born a slave (4.3.12: *Ser. Tullium…captiva Corniculana natum, patre nullo, matre serva*): P.'s language here is taken from that later passage rather than from the original introduction of the story in Book 1, but with the addition of *nobili* to realign it with Livy's main account (cf. 1.39.5 *nobilitatem*). P. teasingly alludes to the version of the story which on the face of things he excludes.

cui puero…caput arsisse traditum erat: Cf. Livy 1.39.1: *puero…caput arsisse ferunt*. P. not only uses Livy's phrasing, but, unlike A (cf. 1.A.7n.), also retains the distancing from the story implicit in the *oratio obliqua*.

in cunis: Livy 1.39.1 has only *dormienti*; P. offers an imaginative expansion, although in doing so he appears to misrepresent Livy's version, which seems to assume that Servius Tullius was older than an infant, in as much as Tanaquil says that he was already being brought up in a lowly status (1.39.3: *tam humili statu educamus*), but he was thenceforward (1.39.4: *inde*) given a royal education. Cic., *Rep*. 2.37 is even clearer than Livy in making Servius an older child (he has him serving at Tarquinius' table prior to the miracle), as is Zonar. 7.9.2 (he falls asleep on a chair, not a cradle: cf. D.H., *AR* 4.2.4). On the other hand, Val. Max. 1.6.1 uses the diminutive *puerulus* (cf. Plu., *Fort. Rom.* 323C βρέφους ὄντος), and it is possible that this lies behind P.'s reconstruction.

is censum primum egit: Livy 1.42.5 has *censum…instituit*. P.'s phrasing is almost identical to Ampel. 17.2 *Servius Tullius censum primum egit*, and one may be drawing on the other.

lustrum condidit: Livy 1.44.2 *conditum lustrum appellatum*: for the phrase see 11.5n.

quo censa LXXX milia esse dicuntur: The phrasing, including the 'distancing' *oratio obliqua*, is directly from Livy 1.44.2: *milia octaginta eo lustro civium censa dicuntur*.

pomerium protulit: Cf. Livy 1.44.3 *pomerium profert*. In Livy the enlargement of the *pomerium* is subsequent to and indeed consequent on the expansion of the city to encompass the three further hills; P. reverses the order and so treats them as if they were independent events.

adiecit: Livy 1.44.3 has *addit*. P. never uses *addere*, but regularly substitutes *adicere*, which may have seemed to him a choicer and more pointed word. Cf. also 19.11n.

in Aventino: This is not in Livy, who does not specify the location. The temple was, however, extremely famous: P. glosses Livy on the basis of his general knowledge (cf. 1.B.1n.).

Prisci filio: Livy 1.46.4 questions whether Tarquinius Superbus was the son or the grandson of Tarquinius Priscus, but prefers the former, which was supported by the majority of his sources (D.H., *AR* 4.6.1–7.5, patiently explains the chronological absurdities implicit in this version, but Livy appears unconcerned by them). As usual, P. mentions only Livy's preferred account and suppresses the discrepancy.

1.B.4 *Tarquinius Superbus seizes the throne.* P.'s summary of the first part of Superbus' reign (corresponding to Livy 1.49.1-6) emphasizes his formal illegitimacy, which likewise formed the centre of Livy's account. As an illustration of his tyranny, he mentions not the direct oppression of the senate and people, which is described by Livy at 1.49.4-6, and is the thing seized on by most other epitomizing historians, but his adoption of a bodyguard, which Livy gives less emphasis to (1.49.2), and which no other epitomizer remarks on, but which for Livy reflects the stereotype of the tyrant fearing usurpation.

This in one respect suggests an unusually acute reading of Livy's text: only in Republican terms would a bodyguard be perceived as a marker of a dangerous tyrant, since it became universal and hence unexceptionable for rulers under the Empire; other writers focus on the aspects of Superbus which more obviously separated good monarchs from bad ones in Roman imperial terms. However, what P. shares with most others—A is the exception (see 1.A.8n.)—is a failure to mention the extension of Superbus' control over the Latins, with the entrapment and killing of Turnus Herdonius. This forms the major theme of the first part of Livy's narrative of the reign (1.49.8–52.6), yet for P., as for others, it goes unmentioned: neither the Latin epitomizers nor Zonaras refer to it. There is no obvious reason why it dropped off the historical radar: it appears a gripping and pointed tale, and it may simply be that it is the consequence of what might be called negative feedback: as any individual historian or collector of anecdotes failed to mention it, its general prominence was reduced and so the likelihood of the next writer picking it up was diminished.

neque patrum neque populi iussu: Adapted from Livy 1.49.3 *neque populi iussu neque auctoribus patribus*. Livy's version is, however, very precisely phrased, distinguishing the *iussu* of a popular election from the general authority exercised by the Senate: the object is to indicate the legitimacy or otherwise of the rule in Republican terms (see Ogilvie (1965), 87). P. has less interest in such constitutional niceties.

regnum invasit: See 1.A.8n.

armatos circa se in custodiam sui habuit: P.'s 'summary' is actually longer than Livy's original phrase: 1.49.2 *armatis corpus circumsaepsit*.

1.B.5 *Achievements of Tarquinius Superbus.* Corresponds to Livy 1.53.1–56.3. P. refers to three events: the war against the Volsci (1.53.2), the building of the temple of Jupiter Capitolinus from the spoils (1.53.3, 1.55.1–56.1), and the capture of Gabii (1.53.4–54.10). None receives more than cursory recognition; the lengthy account of the stratagem by which Gabii was taken is reduced to *dolo*; the foundation of the temple is devoid of the significant omens surrounding it. Nor does P. refer to Tarquinius' other building works or the colonies he founded (1.56.1–3).

templum...fecit: This is formally placed in the correct sequence, in as much as Livy originally introduces the building of the temple directly following and consequent on the defeat of the Volsci. However, the bulk of his account of the building, including the most famous stories around it, are later in the text, following the capture of Gabii, and to that extent P. diverges from Livy's order.

dolo: Cf. Livy 1.53.4 *minime arte Romana, fraude et dolo*.

1.B.6 *Mission to Delphi*. Corresponds to Livy 1.56.4–13. P. summarizes the chief features of the story relatively fully: most of the later Latin historians, by contrast, have nothing of the episode at all (an exception is *Vir. Ill.* 10.1–3, for whom it forms part of the biography of Brutus; it is also in Dio fr. 11.10–12; cf. Zonar. 7.11.11–13), but move directly to the rape of Lucretia as the trigger of the fall of the monarchy. P. does omit the omen of the snake which prompts the consultation (1.56.4–5)—in Livy the question about the future rule is not the primary purpose of the visit. However, this omission smooths over a slight awkwardness in Livy's narrative, since Livy in fact never explains what response the oracle gave, but instead takes the story off on a tangent (see Levene (1993), 143–5).

consulentibus quis eorum Romae regnaturus esset: Livy 1.56.10 *has sciscitandi ad quem eorum regnum Romanum esset venturum*; P.'s phrasing instead follows Val. Max. 7.3.2 *Apollinem iuvenes consuluerunt quisnam ex ipsis Romae regnaturus videretur*; for P. drawing on Valerius' language cf. also e.g. 2.5n., 2.12n., 8.4n.

regnaturum: Livy carefully distinguishes the question asked to the oracle, which is expressed in terms of *regnum*, and the oracle's response, which refers instead to *summum imperium* (1.56.10), since Brutus will not hold the office of king, and so will not, strictly speaking, 'rule' at Rome: while *regnare* can be used metaphorically to refer to forms of power other than kingship, it would not usually be used of the constitutional power of magistrates under the Republic, except in a pejorative context to imply their illegitimacy (e.g. Cic., *Sull.* 21, *Mil.* 43, *Lael.* 41: see e.g. Allen (1953)). P. is less careful, presumably because by his time the distinction between kingship and constitutional Republican rule was less immediately obvious:[21] he merely repeats the term first used.

cum ipsi: 'Although they themselves'.

aliter: P.'s compression leads to a slight oddity of phrasing: the Tarquinii after all interpret the oracle's response according to its literal sense, and it is Brutus' interpretation that is deviant, though ultimately proved correct.

---

[21] See Felmy (2001), 99–105 on the way in which the image of Lucius Brutus as liberator in the late Empire shifted from seeing him as an opponent of monarchy to presenting him as an opponent of tyranny, thus enabling him to be used as a positive *exemplum* even for an emperor; esp. 103 on *Paneg.* 2.20.6, where Pacatus argues that Brutus' opposition to *regnum* should have been qualified in the light of the virtuous rule of Theodosius.

idque factum eius eventus comprobavit: P. explains the significance of the story in a rather heavy-handed way: Livy does not feel the need to do so, and one might have thought it would have been even more obvious to a reader of P.'s abbreviated account. For *factum... eventus comprobavit* ('the outcome ratified his action') cf. Plin., *Epist.* 4.8.3 *quod nunc eventus ita comprobavit* (see OLD *s.v. comprobo* 2).

1.B.7 *Rape of Lucretia; fall of the monarchy.* Corresponds to Livy 1.57.1–60.3. P. includes the main features of the story, while naturally omitting much of the detail: notably, he does not mention the siege of Ardea, nor the wager made there that led to the rape. In this, he is similar to other parts of the later historical tradition (though the full story appears in Ov., *Fast.* 2.721–852, *Vir. Ill.* 9.1–4 (cf. 8.5), Serv., *Aen.* 8.646). Flor. 1.1.7.11, too, omits the siege altogether, and while Eutr. 1.8 does mention it, he does not directly connect it to the rape. Especially relevant in this regard is Dio, for while he himself in his full text appears to have connected the siege of Ardea with the rape much as Livy does (fr. 11.13–19), Zonaras' epitome, although recounting the story at substantial length, dispenses with the context in Ardea and confines itself to the rape alone (7.11.14–17). It is perhaps unsurprising that the drama of violated sexuality is the sole focus; the military and political context ultimately can prove dispensable.

cum: Concessive.

ad ultimum: A phrase especially favoured by Livy: as often, P. employs Livian language in constructing his summary, even when it is not used in the passage being summarized.

expugnatam... pudicitiam: The language reflects Livy, who describes Lucretia's rape in an extended military metaphor: 1.58.5 *quo terrore cum vicisset obstinatam pudicitiam velut victrix libido, profectusque inde Tarquinius ferox expugnato decore muliebri esset*. P., however, compresses it into a somewhat more commonplace phrase, one also used of the rape of Lucretia in *Vir. Ill.* 9.3; see also e.g. Cic., *Cael.* 49, Porcius Latro *ap.* Sen., *Contr.* 2.3.1, Arnob., *Nat.* 5.22, Lact., *Inst.* 1.10.12, Ambr., *Paenit.* 2.5.38; cf. Cic., *II Verr.* 1.9.

patre Tricipitino: Livy refers to him here as Sp. Lucretius (1.58.6), although he provides the *cognomen* in passing later in the story (1.59.8). In most other versions of the story in which he appears, 'Tricipitinus' is the primary name used to identify him: e.g. Cic., *Rep.* 2.46, *Leg.* 2.10, *Vir. Ill.* 10.4, Serv., *Aen.* 6.818, 8.646. P. relies on his broader knowledge of the story, and highlights the form of the name with which he was most familiar (cf. 1.B.1n.).

obtestata: *obtestor* without a direct object is unusual, but not unparalleled: it is found at Livy 23.26.2; cf. also Sall., *Jug.* 49.4.

cultro se interfecit: Livy 1.58.10 is more dramatically pointed: *cultrum... in corde defigit*.

cum regnasset annos XXV: Livy 1.60.3: *Tarquinius Superbus regnavit annos quinque et viginti.*

tum consules primi creati sunt L. Iunius Brutus L. Tarquinius Collatinus: P. ends his first book, as Livy ended his, with the election of the consuls heralding the new Republic; and his language, too, comes from Livy: 1.60.3 *duo consules... creati sunt, L. Iunius Brutus et L. Tarquinius Collatinus*. *primi*, however, is not explicit in Livy: P. has a particular interest in marking the development of Rome through 'firsts' (cf. 11.5n.), and makes the point clear even when Livy himself did not.

Book 2

2.1 *Initial moves against the monarchy.* Corresponds to Livy 2.1.1–2.11. P.'s account focuses on two specific points: the oath against monarchy (2.1.9), and the removal of Collatinus from the consulship (2.2.3–11); he omits not only Livy's preamble about the timeliness of the move from monarchy to republic (2.1.1–6), but also the restoration of the Senate (2.1.10–11) and the institution of the *rex sacrificulus* (2.2.1–2). A comparable pattern can be seen in Flor. 1.3.1–3 and Eutr. 1.9.1–4, who report the removal of Collatinus but not the other constitutional moves, and in addition do not mention the oath.

The Collatinus episode does, however, reveal one apparent oddity about P.'s account (cf. Bingham 106–19). For P., Brutus not only enforces the oath, but compels Collatinus to abdicate. On the face of things this misrepresents Livy, where Collatinus' departure is not compelled by Brutus, nor is it even primarily because of him, but it is Collatinus' own decision at the prompting of the *primores civitatis*, and above all of his father-in-law Sp. Lucretius: he fears disgrace and ruin at the people's hands once his term of office has ended (2.2.8–10). P. appears closer to the account found in Cic., *Brut.* 53, *Off.* 3.40, Aug., *Civ.* 2.17, 3.16, and Obseq. 70 (see *ad loc.*), where Brutus directly acts to deprive his colleague of his office.

Yet it is notable that unlike Cicero (and Obsequens), who speaks of Brutus abrogating Collatinus' *imperium*,[22] P. agrees with Livy in having Collatinus himself resign, for all that in P. it is at Brutus' compulsion.[23] P. elsewhere transfers to Brutus actions which in Livy are the responsibility of the Senate as a whole (see 2.2n.), but with regard to the resignation of Collatinus, Brutus does play a key role in Livy:[24] it is he who calls an assembly and gives a speech in which he urges his colleague to resign in the interests of the state, and it is this speech which converts a vague sense of popular anger into a concrete proposal that Collatinus should remove himself (2.2.4–7), and he follows this up by passing a law expelling the entire *gens Tarquinia*—presumably including Collatinus—from the city (2.2.11). It is not hard to see how P. could have read Livy's Brutus as the prime mover in the whole affair, even if formally his role is more limited: in particular his speech—with its promise that, *if* Collatinus leaves, the security of his

---

[22] Cf. also Flor. 1.3.3, where Collatinus' office is abrogated, albeit by the people rather than Brutus (cf. below); this version appears to be implicit in Eutr. 1.9.3 as well.

[23] Ogilvie (1965), 238–9 argues that Livy's account, in which the final decision to leave is taken by Collatinus, is a deliberate refusal to accept the constitutionality of the annulment of Collatinus' consular *imperium* described in the Ciceronian version. Livy's version may derive ultimately from Piso, *FRHist* 9 F 20 (= fr. 19P): the final outcome of the story there is unclear, but the surviving fragment is more likely to point to resignation than annulment (Bauman (1966), 133–4, Astin (1967a), 318, 348; *contra* MRR I 1).

[24] Cf. Johner (1996), 42–3 for a typically acute reading of Livy's portrayal of Brutus' manipulative behaviour in this episode.

possessions will be guaranteed (2.2.7)—constitutes an implicit threat which could add up to virtual compulsion:[25] certainly Collatinus' stated concern that his property might be confiscated suggests that he saw it as such (2.2.10). It is noteworthy that at 4.15.4, Livy himself has Cincinnatus refer to Collatinus being 'ordered' (*iussum*) to resign, which implies the same dynamic as in P.: not an abrogation of Collatinus' power, as in Cicero, but also not a purely voluntary act on his part. Hence this is not a simply a question of P. employing a non-Livian source: rather it appears that he reads Livy in such a way as to bring his account closer to the version of events which on the face of things he rejects.

A further, though less marked, difference is between P. on the one hand, who places Brutus very strongly at the centre of events, and Florus (explicitly) and Eutropius (implicitly) on the other, where it is not Brutus who takes the lead, but the Roman people *en masse* who do so.[26] As noted above, P.'s focus on Brutus' role is an intelligent reading of Livy's subtle politics; but this is not to say that Florus' version is mistaken, since it is the people who start the entire process by showing hostility to the presence of Collatinus (2.2.3-4). Both versions are distillations of Livy's text, albeit very different ones. However, it is worth observing that Aug., *Civ.* 3.16 not only makes Brutus the author of Collatinus' expulsion, but explicitly contrasts him with the people, who did not care about Collatinus' connection to the Tarquins and thus made him consul (though at 2.17 he had blamed the people for tacitly conniving at Brutus' actions). It appears that Augustine interpreted the Brutus-centred strand of tradition represented by P. as meaning that Brutus alone was responsible.[27]

iureiurando populum adstrinxit neminem Romae regnare passuros: Largely taken from Livy 2.1.9 (cf. 2.2.5): *iure iurando adegit neminem Romae passuros regnare*. *iureiurando adigere* is found a number of times in Livy (also 10.38.9, 21.1.4, 22.38.2, 24.16.12, 26.27.15, 27.38.5, 31.17.9, 35.19.3, 40.41.8, 43.15.8), but is not used by P. He prefers *iureiurando astringere* (also 18.5, 22.8), which is not found in Livy at all, and is relatively rare elsewhere, though it is used by Cic., *Off.* 1.40, which P. is likely to have known (cf. 18.5n.): he may have regarded it as the choicer classical phrase.

---

[25] See Bauman (1966), 134-6, who, however, overinterprets Livy, taking the phrase *res tuas...cives reddent* (2.2.7) to be implying that Brutus had already proposed the confiscation of Collatinus' property and was now offering to have it restored: but *reddere* does not necessarily involve restoration of something lost (cf. *OLD s.v. reddo* 8).

[26] There is also an entirely different tradition found in Greek sources, where the removal of Collatinus is later, in response to the pro-Tarquinian conspiracy (D.H., *AR* 5.11-12, Plu., *Publ.* 7.4, Zonar. 7.12), but here too there are different possible interpretations: Brutus can be read as the primary actor (Dionysius, Zonaras), or the withdrawal can be seen as Collatinus' response to a more general popular hatred of him (Plutarch).

[27] See Felmy (2001), 109-13 for the way in which Augustine highlights the immorality of Brutus' role in the Collatinus affair.

Tarquinium Collatinum collegam suum propter adfinitatem Tarquiniorum suspectum coegit consulatu se abdicare: P.'s language here is closely reflected in Aug., *Civ.* 2.17: *Lucium Tarquinium Collatinum…collegam suum…propter nomen et propinquitatem Tarquiniorum coegit magistratu se abdicare*, probably the result of Augustine using P. as a source (cf. Introduction).

consulatu se abdicare et civitate cedere: Cf. Livy 2.2.10: *abdicavit se consulatu…civitate cessit*.

2.2 *Conspiracy to restore the Tarquins*. Corresponds to Livy 2.3.1–5.10. P. covers three points in particular: (i) the destruction of the royal property, along with the creation of the Campus Martius (2.5.1–4); (ii) the pro-monarchic conspiracy, and the subsequent execution of the conspirators (2.3.1–4.7, 2.5.5–8); and (iii) the rewarding of the slave who exposed the conspiracy (2.5.9–10). The details of the conspiracy are not mentioned—the stress is on the punishment, with the exemplary episode of the father executing his own sons; while the focus on the Campus Martius and the freeing of the slave both provide aetiologies for central features of later Roman society: a third aetiology provided by Livy, the creation of the Tiber island out of the discarded grain from the Campus Martius (2.5.3–4), goes unmentioned, perhaps because it is more of a curiosity. However, P.'s account is fuller than the other Latin summarizers: Flor. 1.3.5, *Vir. Ill.* 10.5, and Oros. 2.5.1 have Brutus' execution of the conspirators, but neither of the other points mentioned by P. Eutropius passes over all of this completely. With regard to the execution, there was a tradition going back at least to Virg., *Aen.* 6.819–23, and later taken up by Florus, Aug., *Civ.* 3.16, and Orosius, of seeing it as a reflection, not of Brutus' disinterested patriotism, as in Livy,[28] but of his ambition (cf. Felmy (2001), 113–16); P. does not go down either route, but treats it neutrally.

Two further aspects of P.'s treatment are noteworthy. One is the central role given to Brutus: as in the previous section (2.1n.), he is made the author of every one of these actions, although Livy himself associates him directly with only the execution of the conspirators: this focus on the individual rather than the collective reflects the broader habits of the 'exemplary' reading of Roman history in later antiquity (cf. the Introduction). Second is the apparent change to Livy's order of events: in Livy the plundering of the Tarquins' property is subsequent to the conspiracy, not prior to it. The reason for this may be the natural connection between the attack on the property and the deposition of Collatinus directly before: both represent stages in the total removal of the monarchy from the state. But the order

---

[28] Cf. D.H., *AR* 5.8 and Val. Max. 5.8.1, who present Brutus' actions in an even more laudatory light; *contra* Lushkov (2015), 55, who mistakenly believes that Dionysius' phrase σκληρὰ καὶ ἄπιστα (*AR* 5.8.1) represents his own judgement ('Brutus' actions are unequivocally cruel'), rather than the imagined response of his Greek audience. Plu., *Publ.* 6 is more equivocal, but ultimately comes down on the side of Brutus' virtue (*Publ.* 6.4).

can also be formally justified as a representation of Livy's text, since P.'s notice focuses on the punishment, which did indeed take place after the plundering of the property in Livy, and the conspiracy itself, which happened earlier, is, in accordance with P.'s regular sentence patterns (see below), summarized in a clause providing the background. This is not the only place in P. where his habits of summary lead to a change in Livy's original order (cf. e.g. 2.11n., 11.2n., 18.5n., 38.7n.).

bona regum diripi: Livy's description of the plundering at 2.5.1–2 is slightly different: *de bonis regiis...diripienda plebi sunt data*. P.'s phrasing, however, comes not from here, but from the summary at the end of the passage: *direptis bonis regum* (2.5.5).

agrum Marti consecravit, qui campus Martius nominatus est: Cf. Livy 2.5.2: *ager...consecratus Marti, Martius deinde campus fuit*. P., as often (cf. e.g. 1.B.1n., 1.B.3n., 2.1n.), substitutes a choicer word.

adulescentes nobiles: Cf. Livy 2.4.2 (cf. 2.3.6) *aliquot nobiles adulescentes conscii adsumpti*.

fratris filios: This is an error: Livy 2.4.1 describes the co-conspirators as the brothers of Brutus' wife. The fact that Livy emphasizes the youthfulness of those agitating for the return of the Tarquins (2.3.2–3, 2.3.6, 2.4.2; cf. above) presumably made it seem natural to P. that Brutus' sons conspired with their cousins rather than with their uncles. Moreover, D.H., *AR* 5.6.4 adds that the Aquilii, who also participated in the conspiracy, were the sons of Collatinus' sister; it is possible that P. arrived at his mistake by supplementing Livy with extra information, as he often does (cf. e.g. 1.B.1n., 1.B.3n.), but in this case inaccurately conflating the various relationships.

quia: One of the commonest sentence-patterns in P.: he records a point (in this case Brutus' execution of his sons), with a causal or temporal clause setting out the background that led up to it, thus providing, if only in outline, a causal sequence rather than simply a series of events.

securi percussit: Livy 2.5.8 has *securi...feriunt*; this is a standard phrase for execution (*OLD s.v. ferio* 3a), but still more common, especially in Republican contexts, is the phrase which P. substitutes here (*OLD s.v. percutio* 2b: cf. Martin and Woodman (1989), 158).

servo indici, cui Vindicio nomen fuit, libertatem dedit: The vocabulary is from Livy, but Livy's phrasing is somewhat different, referring to other rewards also: *praemium indici pecunia ex aerario, libertas et civitas data...Vindicio ipsi nomen fuisse* (2.5.9–10). P. focuses on the part of the story that gives the aetiology, but also offers a further word-play which was not in Livy at all, by juxtaposing the slave's name *V<u>indici</u>o* with his role in the story (*indici*): for the interest in puns on names in historiography see Woodman and Martin (1996), 491–3, with extensive bibliography; also Woodman (1998), 219–22.

ex cuius nomine vindicta appellata: Livy is more equivocal, offering the slave's name as one theory for the name of the ceremony, but not endorsing it (2.5.10: *ille primum dicitur vindicta liberatus; quidam vindictae quoque nomen tractum ab illo putant*). P., as often, rewrites Livy so as to endorse clearly its truth of the account.

2.3 *Death of Brutus in battle*. Corresponds to Livy 2.6.1–7.4. P. refers to Tarquin's assembling of his army (2.6.1–4), the battle in which Brutus fell in single combat with Arruns (2.6.5–9), and the mourning for him at Rome (2.7.4), but shows no interest in the ultimate result of the battle, with the enemy's surprising withdrawal, possibly at the prompting of a divine voice (2.6.10–7.3); this is the logical consequence of his consistent focus on Brutus up to this point (cf. 2.1n., 2.2n.). Brutus is similarly at the centre of Flor. 1.4.8 (dated to after the war with Porsenna), *Vir. Ill.* 10.6–7, Oros. 2.5.2, and also Eutr. 1.10, though he, unlike the other summarizers, does at least indicate the Roman victory after his death.

cum: Cf. 2.2n.

reges: Livy regularly uses *reges* to describe the family of the Tarquins, even though technically only Superbus was the *rex*: see e.g. 1.59.5, 2.2.7, 2.2.11, and cf. *OLD s.v. rex* 6b.

in acie cum Arrunte filio Superbi commortuus est: The wording is not from Livy, who never uses *commorior*; it is, however, close to Oros. 2.5.2 *cum Arrunte, Superbi filio, congresso sibi commortuoque procubuit*, who may be drawing on P. (see Introduction).

eumque matronae anno luxerunt: Cf. Livy 2.7.4: *matronae annum ut parentem eum luxerunt, quod tam acer ultor violatae pudicitiae fuisset*. Eutr. 1.10.1 has similar wording, but is much closer to Livy than either is to P. (1.10.1: *Brutum matronae Romanae, defensorem pudicitiae suae, quasi communem patrem per annum luxerunt*), indicating that he is not here drawing on Livy via P.; *Vir. Ill.* 10.7 *matronae anno luxerunt*, on the other hand, is closer to P., and one may derive from the other (see Introduction). For the change of Livy's *annum* to the ablative *anno* see 1.A.8n.

2.4 *Law on appeal; dedication of the Capitoline temple*. Corresponds to Livy 2.8.1–8. P. refers briefly to two episodes: Valerius Publicola's law granting the right to appeal to the people (2.8.2), and the dedication of the temple of Jupiter Capitolinus (2.8.6–8). The latter completes the story of the temple begun in 1.B.5, with its building under Tarquin, but P. does not mention the story of the conflict over its dedication, with the consul Horatius proceeding despite hearing that his son had died. The former loses the extensive political context which Livy supplies, where he explains that it was in response to accusations made against Publicola of aspiring to kingship (2.7.5–12). P.'s interest appears to be solely in recording two developments in the rise of Rome, rather than the tricky political background associated with them.

The omission of the story of Horatius might on the face of things appear surprising, given that it was a staple anecdote in exemplary contexts (Cic., *Dom.* 139, Val. Max. 5.10.1, Sen., *Cons. Marc.* 13.1–2, Symm., *Epist.* 3.6.3, Jer., *Epist.* 60.5.3, Serv., *Aen.* 6.8 = C 24, 11.2; also Plu., *Publ.* 14, Dio fr. 13.3–4), but P.'s lack of interest is shared by the rest of the Latin historical summarizers, none of whom even mentions the dedication of the Capitol, let alone Horatius' heroic forbearance. This appears to be one instance where the historiographic tradition diverged from the exemplary. Likewise, Publicola's conflicts, which themselves could be cited for exemplary purposes (Val. Max. 4.1.1; cf. Cic., *Rep.* 2.53, D.H., *AR* 5.19, Plu., *Publ.* 10–11, Dio fr. 13.2), largely disappear from the later Latin historians; Flor. 1.3.4 (calling him 'Horatius Publicola') and *Vir. Ill.* 15.5, like P., refer to the founding of the right to appeal but not the political controversy leading up to it; Eutropius and Orosius omit the episode altogether.

L. Valerius: Livy, like most other sources, gives Publicola's *praenomen* as Publius; accordingly, Sigonius (followed by most other editors) emended L. to P. However, he is called Lucius in not only in P., but in Eutr. 1.9.4 and 1.11.4, *Vir. Ill.* 15.1, and Cassiod., *Chron.* 97; hence P.'s version reflects a broader tradition, and the MS reading should be retained (Bingham 122).

legem de provocatione ad populum tulit: *Vir. Ill.* 15.5 is almost identical: *legem de provocatione a magistratibus ad populum tulit*; it is likely that here too, as in the previous sentence (cf. 2.3n.), one of the two is drawing on the other (cf. Introduction).

2.5 **War with Lars Porsenna.** Corresponds to Livy 2.9.1–15.7. P., unsurprisingly, concentrates entirely on the three great episodes of personal heroism, which form the heart not only of Livy's narrative, but of the memory of the war in the later Roman tradition (Ogilvie (1965), 255): the stories of Horatius Cocles (2.10), Mucius Scaevola (2.12), and Cloelia (2.13.6–11). While all three frequently appear independently as *exempla*, they became canonical jointly, as Flor. 1.4.3 indicates (*illa tria Romanis nominis prodigia et miracula*); cf. Livy 2.13.8, and note esp. Serv. auct., *Aen.* 8.648, who finds a covert reference to Scaevola in Virg., *Aen.* 8.646–51, where only Horatius and Cloelia are mentioned explicitly. Not only P., but also Flor. 1.4.1–8 and *Vir. Ill.* 11–13 focus their entire account of the war on them;[29] for the three cited in conjunction cf. also e.g. Manil. 1.779–81, Juv., 8.264–5, Claud., *In Eutr.* 1.449–51. The rest of the war is only narrated by P. in as

---

[29] Oros. 2.5.3, in a typically idiosyncratic take on the war, mentions Mucius and Cloelia but not Horatius: his slant is that these stories prove that Rome was in such dire straits that these two alone saved her. Eutr. 1.11 is perhaps even more of an outlier, since he refers to the war only in passing, and mentions none of the canonical acts of heroism during it.

far as is needed to provide context for those; thus he omits the Roman preparations for the siege (2.9.5–8), Publicola's luring the Etruscans into a trap (2.11), the attack on Aricia by Porsenna's son (2.14.5–9), and the final peace agreement (2.15: cf. below).

Porsenna, Clusinorum rex: Cf. Livy 2.9.1 *Porsennam, Clusinum regem.*

rescindunt: Cf. Livy 2.10.7 *rescindebant.*

solus Etruscos sustinuit: P. makes no reference to the support given to Horatius by Spurius Larcius and Titus Herminius (Livy 2.10.6–7; cf. e.g. D.H., *AR* 5.23.2–4, Plu., *Publ.* 16.4). This perspective is shared in much of the historical tradition: Larcius and Herminius are similarly removed from the story by (e.g.) Cic., *Parad.* 12, Val. Max. 3.2.1, Plin., *Nat.* 34.22, Frontin., *Strat.* 2.13.5, Flor. 1.4.4, *Vir. Ill.* 11. For P.'s phrasing cf. *Vir. Ill.* 11.1 *aciem hostium solus sustinuit*: this could be coincidental, since variations on *solus sustinet* are found in other places also: see e.g. Cic., *Rab. Post.* 41, Hor., *Epist.* 2.1.1, Flor. 1.34.2. However, it is also worth observing that in the context of Horatius the phrase may act as a tacit correction to Livy, who twice uses *sustinuit* in the passage (2.10.7, 2.10.10), but both times to describe points in the story where it is *not* solely Horatius who is holding the Etruscans back. This would not be the only time where P. draws on Livy's language partly in order to mark the change he makes to him (cf. Levene (2015b), 318–22).

ponte rupto: Cf. Livy 2.10.10 *rupti pontis.*

armatus in flumen se misit: Livy 2.10.11 has *armatus in Tiberim desiluit*; P.'s language derives more closely from Val. Max. 3.2.1 *armatus se in Tiberim misit* (cf. 1.B.6n., 2.12n., 8.4n.). The fact that one of the key details P. abstracts from Livy is Horatius being armed is significant: it emphasizes his heroism by showing that his retreat was not a flight from battle, but part of an orderly plan (and it also makes the swimming—see below—more remarkable). See Roller (2004), 18–19.

ad suos transnavit: From Livy 2.10.11 *ad suos tranavit*; the phrase also appears in *Vir. Ill.* 11.1. In Horatius' swimming P. focuses on another feature of the story that was of considerable cultural significance: see Roller (2004), 19–20.

alterum virtutis exemplum: Livy does not directly mark Mucius as an *exemplum*: despite his manifest interest in *exempla* (on which see esp. Chaplin (2000)), he does not usually identify them as such in the narrative voice.[30] P., too, does not generally point them up in his own voice (though this is not the only instance: see 18.2, 38.4, 55.1, the first of which may be taken over from Livy, as discussed *ad loc.*); he is, moreover, much less assiduous than Livy about showing characters adducing *exempla* or acting on them (though see 10.7, 31.5, 51.6). The reason he does so here may be precisely to highlight the war's traditional exemplary canon (cf. above): *alterum* places Mucius' deed directly in conjunction with Horatius'.

---

[30] Chaplin (2000), 50 n. 1 lists just eighteen examples in Livy's thirty-five surviving books.

castra hostium intrasset: Cf. Livy 2.12.5 *intrare, si possim, castra hostium volo*.

scriba, quem regem esse existimaverat: In Livy 2.12.7 Mucius' error is less blatant: he sees both the king and the scribe, does not know which is which, and does not dare to ask, so he selects one at random hoping for the best (so also Plu., *Publ.* 17.2). P. substitutes a commoner and simpler version, where Mucius merely mistakes the scribe for the king (e.g. Cassius Hemina, *FRHist* 6 F 20 = fr. 16P, D.H., *AR* 5.28.2, ps.-Plu., *Par. Min.* 305F (citing the supposed *Histories* of Aristides of Miletus: *FGrH* 286 F 2), *Vir. Ill.* 12.2, Aug., *C. Philos.* 2.107).

comprehensus: So also Livy 2.12.8 *comprehensum*.

altaribus, in quibus sacrificatum erat, exuri passus est: Livy 2.12.13 does not suggest that any sacrifice had in fact taken place: Porsenna was paying his soldiers when the assassination attempt took place (2.12.7), and no explanation is given for why there happened to be a hearth (*foculo*) kindled for sacrifice nearby. P. seems to assume the slightly different (and neater) version of the story found in Val. Max. 3.3.1, in which Porsenna is engaged in sacrificing when Mucius tries to kill him, and it is on that altar that Mucius places his hand: that P. depends in part on Valerius is suggested by the phrase *exuri passus est*, which is directly taken from him.

dixitque tales CCC esse ⟨...⟩: The transmitted text is unlikely, on several grounds. The bare phrase *tales CCC esse* is difficult Latin; the precision of the '300' is odd if all Mucius is saying (as he appears to be) is that there were many other Romans of comparable steadfastness; and it is rare for P. to offer a summary that is hard to follow without prior knowledge of the story (in Livy 2.12.15–16, as in other accounts,[31] these 300 are Mucius' fellow-conspirators against Porsenna). Putting these points together, the most likely conclusion is that a phrase defining the 300 more closely has dropped out of the MS tradition: thus the *editio princeps* suggests *coniuratos in mortem ipsius regis*—presumably a supplement offered by a copyist who was troubled by the anomaly.

quorum: sc. the 300 peers of Mucius.

admiratione: It is common in exemplary contexts for the viewer to marvel at the heroic deed, and in Livy 2.12.13, as in other accounts of Mucius, Porsenna is similarly overcome by amazement (Langlands (2018), 88–92: see esp. Val. Max. 3.3.1, where *admiratio* is likewise mentioned as the response). In P., however, the *admiratio* is the result not of Mucius' sacrifice of his hand, but rather the number of his (supposed) co-conspirators. The purport of the story is subtly deflected away

---

[31] See e.g. D.H., *AR* 5.29.3–4, Plu., *Publ.* 17.4, Flor. 1.4.5–6, Polyaen. 8.8, *Vir. Ill.* 12.5, Aug., *C. Philos.* 2.107. In some of these it is made explicit that Mucius is lying (cf. Langlands (2018), 55–6), which is not obviously true in Livy, although it is implicit in the introduction to the story, where Mucius is said to be acting *ignaris omnibus* (2.12.4), contrary to what he claims when speaking to Porsenna, and also in the fact that he is said to speak 'as if repaying the favour' to Porsenna (2.12.15 *quasi remunerans meritum*).

from Mucius' singular and famous act to the impression Porsenna receives of collective Roman heroism.³²

coactus…pacis condiciones ferre: Cf. Livy 2.13.2 *pacis condiciones ultro ferret Romanis*. However, Livy's account of the peace-terms (2.13.1–4) does not quite suggest that Porsenna was 'compelled' to them, since he successfully extracted not only hostages but also territory from the Romans (2.13.4). P. accentuates the Romans' heroism by making it dramatically successful in concluding the war.

bellum omisit: The language is from Livy 2.14.5 *omisso Romano bello*; however, P. misleadingly implies that this represented the end of the entire war, whereas in Livy Porsenna abandons his direct attack on Rome only to assault instead the allied Latin town of Aricia (2.14.5–9). The war in Livy does not formally reach its conclusion until the following year, when Porsenna is persuaded to come to terms, returning the territory and hostages that Rome had earlier ceded (2.15).

ex quibus virgo una Cloelia: Cf. Livy 2.13.6 *Cloelia virgo una ex obsidibus*. P. does not mention that in Livy Cloelia did not escape alone, but led other female hostages to freedom. There appears to have been a dispute about this point in antiquity (cf. Plu., *Publ.* 19.4): Livy's version is shared by e.g. D.H., *AR* 5.33.1, Polyaen. 8.31, but an alternative version, found in Val. Max. 3.2.2, Flor. 1.4.7, *Vir. Ill.* 13.1, has Cloelia crossing the river alone on horseback. Without directly contradicting Livy, P. aligns his account with the version that was familiar in other imperial Latin writers.

deceptis custodibus: Livy has *frustrata custodes* (2.13.6); P.'s phrase is used of Cloelia also in *Vir. Ill.* 13.1.

per Tiberim ad suos transnavit: Livy is briefer (2.13.6 *Tiberim tranavit*); P. repeats the phrase he (and Livy) had used of Horatius (cf. above), emphasizing the parallel between the two heroic acts. For Cloelia doing her heroic deed in imitation of Horatius' example cf. Roller (2004), 28–30.

equestri statua donata est: Cf. Livy 2.13.11 *novo generi honoris, statua equestri, donavere.*

2.6 *Battle of Lake Regillus*. Corresponds to Livy 2.19.3–20.13; P., as often, simply alludes to the victory (and also the presence of Tarquinius Superbus), with no further account of the events during it. More noteworthy is that he not only changes the order of events, describing the battle before the arrival of Appius Claudius in Rome (see 2.7n.), but he omits several other episodes which Livy described prior to the battle: in particular the death of Valerius Publicola (2.16.7), the revolt of Pometia and Cora (2.16.8–17.7), and above all the creation of the dictatorship in

---

³² Plu., *Publ.* 17.3–5 has Porsenna showing amazement ($\theta\alpha\upsilon\mu\acute{\alpha}\sigma\alpha\varsigma$) at both Mucius' burning of his hand and the other Romans who may follow him. In *Vir. Ill.* 12.5, like P., Porsenna responds primarily to the latter, but the context is very different, since Mucius has burned his hand not to impress Porsenna with his fortitude, but to punish himself for failing in the assassination attempt (a version of the story found in several other sources, including Val. Max. 3.3.1: see Langlands (2018), 149–50).

response to a threat of war with the Sabines and the Latins (2.18.1–11). The last is particularly surprising, given that P. is generally interested in marking 'firsts' as key moments in Rome's development (cf. 1.B.7n.).[33] Part of the reason for the omission may be that the dictatorship was not of continuing importance in Roman history: it was primarily a feature of the early and middle Republic, and was effectively obsolete by the end of the third century BC, though in the civil wars of the first century BC Sulla and then Caesar revived it in an entirely different form.[34]

adversus Tarquinium Superbum...prospere pugnavit: *prospere pugnare* is a Livian phrase (8.8.11, 22.34.5, 23.37.10, 27.29.8, 33.34.4, 35.22.8, 42.59.7). P., for whom *prospere* is a favourite word (see 3.10n., 13.1n.) employs it frequently. It is rarer in other writers, but see Vell. 2.79.4 (a passage describing Octavian's later victory at Mylae: cf. below), Plin., *Nat.* 11.55, Frontin., *Strat.* 4.1.39, Tac., *Hist.* 2.23.3, Gell. 3.8.1, Sulp. Sev., *Chron.* 1.26.5, 2.21.1. *prospere pugnare adversus*, however, is a phrase distinctive to P.: it appears also at 10.6, 17.2, 24.2, 25.4, 29.13, 47.8, 65.4, 73.4, 98.7, 110.5, but nowhere else other than Sulp. Sev., *Chron.* 2.21.1 (who uses *adversum*).

2.7 Arrival of Appius Claudius in Rome; creation of the Claudian tribe. Corresponds to Livy 2.16.3–5 and 2.21.7. P. omits the broader context of a war, opposed by Claudius, between the Sabines and Rome, culminating in a Roman victory (Livy 2.16.6); more strikingly, he transfers Appius Claudius' arrival in Rome from before the battle of Lake Regillus to after it (2.6n.). The immediate impetus for this may be that P.'s primary interest is in the creation of a new tribe (see below). Livy formally records this under Appius' consulship (2.21.7), which was indeed after the battle; however, the creation of the Claudian tribe was also mentioned at the time of Appius' arrival (2.16.5), and, as will be shown below, P.'s notice combines information from the two passages. It may have seemed natural to group together all of the material associated with Appius.

The rearrangement has also a wider effect, clarifying the narrative in two ways. First, it juxtaposes the battle, which was the last act in the story of the fall of the Tarquins, with the war against Lars Porsenna, a war which was likewise identified by P. as being on the Tarquins' behalf (2.5). Second, it juxtaposes the introduction of Claudius with the story of the first Secession of the Plebs (2.8n.), the first place where the patrician–plebeian conflict, which forms a major theme of the First Decade, reaches centre stage in Livy. The *gens Claudia* in Livy (and other authors) is famous for its viciously anti-plebeian character (see esp. Wiseman (1979),

---

[33] By contrast, Oros. 2.5.4 has the first dictatorship but does not mention Lake Regillus: he, unsurprisingly, highlights the invention of an institution proving the existence of dire threats to Rome over an actual Roman victory.

[34] Eutr. 1.12, however, presents the invention of the Republican dictatorship in contemporary terms, seeing it as the precursor of the power held by Roman emperors: a questionable claim; though cf. Tac., *Ann.* 1.1.1.

55–139, Vasaly (1987)); P. never mentions that stereotype (though it is implicit in the story of the prosecution of Claudia during the First Punic War: see 19.6n.), but he rearranges the text in such a way as to make sense to a reader who was aware of it. Livy implicitly assigns to Claudius a large degree of responsibility for the plebeian grievances that culminate in the Secession (Vasaly (1987), 205–9), and P.'s order hints at the same point.

Appius Claudius...Romam transfugit: Cf. Livy 2.16.4 *Attus Clausus, cui postea Appio Claudio fuit Romae nomen...Romam transfugit.*

Claudia tribus: Livy is generally assiduous about reporting the introduction of new tribes (6.5.8, 7.15.11, 8.17.11, 9.20.6, 10.9.14: see Oakley (1997), 440–1), and all but one of these are relayed by P. also (6.2, 7.6, 9.3, 10.5; cf. also 19.11): the enlargement of the number of tribes is a concrete illustration of the expansion of Rome, a matter in which he is keenly interested (cf. 11.5n.).

In this case, however, the issue is complicated. In this part of his history, as noted above, Livy has two notices concerning the tribes. At 2.16.5, in the context of Appius' arrival in Rome with his entourage, he says *his civitas data agerque trans Anienem; Vetus Claudia tribus, additis postea novis tribulibus qui ex eo venirent agro, appellata* ('Citizenship was granted to them, and territory on the other side of the Anio; it was called the Vetus Claudia tribe, with new tribesmen later added who came from that territory'). In 2.21.7, in a list of activities that occurred during Appius' consulship, he says *Romae tribus una et viginti factae* ('At Rome twenty-one tribes were created'). In isolation one might take the second passage to mean that the entire tribal system originated at this point, but that fits neither Livy's earlier notice about the creation of the Claudian tribe, nor the consensus of the historical tradition, which associated the creation of the tribes with Servius Tullius (D.H., *AR* 4.14.1–15.1, citing Fabius Pictor, *FRHist* 1 F 9 = fr. 9P, Cato, *FRHist* 5 F 17 = fr. 23P, Vennonius, *FRHist* 13 F 2 = fr. 1P; *POxy* 2088 = *FRHist* 109 F 1; cf. Livy 1.43.13, Paul., *Fest.* 506L). It is more likely that Livy meant only that twenty-one was now the total number after some unspecified new tribes had been created: P. clearly understood him this way.

If we put the two Livy passages together, it might be suggested that the Claudian tribe was created at the time of Appius' arrival, and some other tribe(s) at the time of his consulship—perhaps the Clustumina, the creation of which must have postdated the capture of Crustumeria, which Livy dates to the year of the battle of Lake Regillus (2.19.2). But P. must have inferred (and even perhaps had sources which stated directly) that the Claudian tribe was not formally created until Appius' consulship, and that Livy's original notice was out of chronological sequence.[35] His inference may indeed have been correct, although, if so, it is reasonable to suggest that both the Clustimina and the Claudia were created then

---

[35] Cf. D.H., *AR* 5.40.5, who, like Livy, records the creation of the Claudian tribe when he describes Claudius' migration to Rome, but who is explicit that it happened somewhat later.

(so e.g. Taylor (2013 (1960)), 36, Ogilvie (1965), 275, 292, Cornell (1995), 174–5; *contra* e.g. Beloch, *RG* 264–71, Badian (1962), 201).

For the tribes see further 19.11n.

adiecta est: Cf. 1.B.3n., 19.11n.

ampliatus est: See 1.B.2n.

XXI: The chief MSS of Livy 2.21.7 read *una et triginta*, but fourteen of Rome's thirty-five tribes are recorded by Livy as being created later, and editors generally accept the minority reading *una et viginti*: P.'s notice appears to confirm that this was the reading in the text he used. See Ogilvie (1965), 292–3.

2.8 *First Secession of the Plebs*. Corresponds to Livy 2.31.7–33.3 and 2.33.10–11. P. omits, save by implication (cf. also 2.8n.), all of the background to the story: the increasing conflicts between patricians and plebeians that Livy describes in detail at 2.23.1–24.8 and 2.27.1–30.7. Nor does he mention the sequence of wars interspersed with these: the threatened war with the Volsci and Hernici (which is aborted when the Latins refuse to join them and hand the envoys over to Rome: 2.22.1–7; cf. 2.16n.), or the further wars against the Volsci (2.24.8–25.6, 2.30.10–15, but see 2.16n.), the Sabines (2.26.1–3, 2.31.1–3), the Aurunci (2.26.4–6), and the Aequi (2.30.8–9, 2.31.4–6). The internal and external conflicts are reduced to the single moment of the secession, and the focus is on the exemplary figure of Menenius Agrippa, who was instrumental in resolving it, along with the institution of the tribunate. As often, at the heart of P.'s narrative is the constitutional development of Rome, as well as the virtuous individuals who made it possible.

P. also rearranges Livy's order: the death of Menenius Agrippa, which in Livy appears at 2.33.10–11, not only after the creation of the tribunate (2.33.1–3), but after the Volscian war and the capture of Corioli (2.33.4–9: see 2.9n.), is transferred to a point immediately after his resolution of the secession. This tidies up the story, and ensures that the virtues of Agrippa are at its centre.

cum: Cf. 2.2n.

propter nexos ob aes alienum: The same phrase appears at Livy 2.23.1, as part of the introduction to the whole sequence of class conflict that culminates in the secession. However, in Livy, by the time of the secession itself, the debt-crisis, though the ultimate trigger, spirals into a far wider set of grievances, including challenges to military conscription and complaints at arbitrary arrests and exercises of consular power. P. draws a more direct line than Livy does between the beginning and the climax of the story, a perspective shared by Flor. 1.17.23.1–2, Ampel. 25.1, Zonar. 7.14.6 (cf. Dio fr. 17.9), who likewise see the secession entirely through the lens of the debt-crisis.[36]

---

[36] By contrast, *Vir. Ill.* 18.2 does not mention debt, but speaks of *tributum et militiam*; Eutr. 1.13 speaks more vaguely of the people being oppressed by the senate and consuls.

in Sacrum montem secessisset: Cf. Livy 2.32.2 *in Sacrum montem secessisse*. P., as usual, omits the alternative version Livy cites from Piso (2.32.3 = *FRHist* 9 F 24 = fr. 22P), in which the secession is to the Aventine.

consilio Meneni Agrippae: P.'s abridgement elides the best-known part of the story: Menenius' parable of the body-parts dissenting from one another (Livy 2.32.9–12), although this forms the heart of most other accounts of the secession. The fact of Menenius' reconciliation of the people matters more to him than the means by which he did it.

publico impendio: This represents a change to Livy. *publicum impendium* is not a common phrase, but it appears at Livy 7.21.7 (cf. 22.23.8) in the sense of 'communally held funds', which appears to be its most natural sense (cf. *OLD s.v. publicus* 1a; *TLL* VII.1 543.37–8). But according to Livy, Menenius' funeral was not 'at public expense' in that sense, but was paid for by small contributions collected from the plebeians (2.33.11). P. seems instead to depend on an alternative version, relayed by D.H., *AR* 6.96.1–3 (cf. 9.27.3), where the Senate is shamed by the generosity of the people into providing the funds from the public treasury. That version downplays the idea that Menenius is primarily a plebeian favourite, and instead has him publicly recognized for his contributions to the state as a whole. Although P. is unusual in his direct preference for the story found in Dionysius, the idea that Menenius is honoured in his death by patricians and plebeians alike is commonplace in the later tradition. The source of the contributions is tacitly changed from the *plebs* to the *populus* in all other authors, undercutting any sense of faction (Val. Max. 4.4.2, Plin., *Nat.* 33.138, Apul., *Apol.* 18.10, *Vir. Ill.* 18.7); *Vir. Ill.* adds that the Senate specifically provided the burial site.

elatus est: Cf. Livy 2.33.11: *extulit eum plebs*.

tribuni plebis quinque creati sunt: Cf. Livy 2.33.2: *tribuni plebei creati duo...hi tres collegas sibi creaverunt*. Most of the other Latin epitomizers mention the creation of the tribunate (Flor. 1.17, Eutr. 1.13, *Vir. Ill.* 18.6). However, even though P.'s account is short, only he records the specific number, presumably because of his greater interest in constitutional details of this sort. As usual, he omits Livy's variant version, under which only two tribunes are chosen (2.33.3).

2.9 Capture of Corioli. Corresponds to Livy 2.33.5–9. The episode is of course primarily of interest because it introduces Coriolanus to the narrative, and is treated in similar terms by other late historical epitomizers: see e.g. Flor. 1.5.9, *Vir. Ill.* 19.1, Eutr. 1.14, 1.15.1. All of these, like P., eschew any military detail: the fact of the capture outweighs the actual deeds that won Coriolanus his eponym, which are barely mentioned.

virtute et opera: The phrase implies (correctly) that Coriolanus acted as a subordinate, not the commander: cf. 17.4, where P. uses it of the heroic military tribune Calpurnius Flamma. Some other sources (e.g. Eutr. 1.15.1 *qui Coriolos ceperat*;

Flor. 1.5.9) phrase it in such a way as to suggest that he led the army, as the *cognomen* would naturally indicate to later Roman ears.

2.10 *Dream of Latinius*. Corresponds to Livy 2.36.1–8. In P., as in Livy, this forms an interlude in the story of Coriolanus; however, in Livy it falls after Coriolanus has been forced into exile and allied himself with the Volsci, something which P. does not mention until afterwards (cf. 20.11n.). Related to this is that Livy integrates the story with the broader narrative (cf. Levene (1993), 154–6): the miracle of Latinius causes the Romans to repeat the *Ludi Magni*, which is where the Volsci, as planned by Coriolanus, deceive the Senate into provoking a war. P., unlike Livy—but like virtually every other source for the story[37]—treats it as a free-standing anecdote; but he goes further down that route than almost any other writer, removing all elements that might relate it to its historical context. Unusually, he does not mention the original religious violation which led to Latinius receiving the warning, the flogging of a slave at the games: most authors treat that as an integral part of the episode. For P. the point of the anecdote rests in the religious offence and punishment of Latinius alone (cf. below), rather than divine anger at the city as a whole because of the public violation of the games.

vir de plebe: Cf. Livy 2.36.2 *de plebe homini*.

in visu: In classical Latin, *visus* means not the dream itself, but the figure seen in the dream (*OLD s.v. visus* 2b); hence the phrase *in visu* in the sense of 'in a dream' or 'in a vision' is not found. Its first appearance is in Christian translations of the Bible, reflecting Greek phrases like ἐν ὁράματι (Daniel 7:13, quoted in Cypr., *Testim.* 2.26, Lact., *Inst.* 4.12.12, Firm., *Err.* 24.6) or ἐν τῇ ὁράσει (Revelations 9:17, quoted in Cypr., *Testim.* 3.59); it then becomes increasingly common among Christian writers of the later fourth and early fifth century.

id: The MSS reading is *et*, which is manifestly dittography after *perferret*. Rossbach simply deleted the word: but while *neglego* is sometimes used with an implied direct object (*OLD s.v. neglego* 2a), in this case the bare *neglexisset* is too abrupt to be idiomatic; accordingly, Drakenborch's *id* is a preferable reading.

neglexisset: P. implies that Latinius' failure to act on the warning was merely a matter of personal negligence. Livy, by contrast, emphasizes that Latinius was personally pious (2.36.3: *haud sane liber erat religione animus*), but that as a plebeian he feared that for him to approach the consuls would invite mockery. A similar explanation to Livy's, rooting the violation in the social divisions at Rome, appears in some other sources (Cicero, Dionysius of Halicarnassus, Valerius Maximus, Arnobius, Augustine), although others, like P., treat it as the

---

[37] It appears at Cic., *Div.* 1.55 (citing Fabius Pictor, *FRHist* 1 F 14 = fr. 15P, Cn. Gellius, *FRHist* 14 F 26 = fr. 21P, Coelius Antipater 15 F 48 = fr. 49P), Val. Max. 1.7.4, Min. Fel. 7.3, 27.4, Arnob., *Nat.* 7.39, Lact., *Inst.* 2.7.20, Aug., *Civ.* 4.26 (cf. 8.13), *C. Philos.* 2.77–8, 4.167–8, Macr., *Sat.* 1.11.3. D.H., *AR* 7.68–9 (albeit more loosely) and Plu., *Cor.* 24, like Livy, integrate it with the Coriolanus story.

fault of Latinius alone (Plutarch, Julius Paris, Lactantius, Macrobius). P. once again chooses the version which detaches the story most cleanly from its historical context.

amisso filio: Cf. Livy 2.36.4 *filium…amisit*.

pedibus debilis factus: Livy makes Latinius more severely handicapped: he is 'suffering in all his limbs' (2.36.8: *captus omnibus membris*). In P. the injury is specifically to his feet, presumably so as to make for a neater final reversal, when he uses his feet to return home.

postquam delatus ad senatum lectica: Cf. Livy 2.36.6: *in forum…lectica defertur. Inde in curiam…delatus*.

usu…recepto: An unusual phrase, not otherwise attested until the early fifth century.

domum reversus est: Cf. Livy 2.36.8: *eum…domum redisse traditum memoriae est*: here (contrast 1 B.3n.) P. narrates directly something which Livy placed in indirect speech.

2.11 *Coriolanus*. Corresponds to Livy 2.34.7–35.8 and 2.37.1–40.12. P. compresses the story to its barest bones: not only does he omit the problems with the grain supply in the year prior to Coriolanus' exile (2.34.1–6), which forms the background to the conflict which leads to the exile, but the exile is reduced to the mere fact recorded in a relative clause, with no hint at the reasons which led to it. Nor is there anything about the machinations that lead to the Volscian declaration of war, or indeed about Coriolanus' victories in that war. Everything is focused on the march on Rome and the series of appeals that culminate in his withdrawal. This reflects the common image of the story elsewhere, including in Livy's own later citations of it (7.40.12, 28.29.1, 34.5.9); cf. also Val. Max. 5.2.1a, 5.4.1 (along with Paris' summaries), Flor. 1.17.22.3, Ampel. 27.1, Plu., *Fort. Rom.* 318F, Eutr. 1.15; P., however, goes even beyond most of these in his removal of the background to the story (so e.g. Livy 28.29.1 has Scipio refer to Coriolanus' 'unjust condemnation, wretched and undeserved exile' (*damnatio iniusta, miserum et indignum exilium*); likewise Valerius Maximus, Florus, Ampelius, and *Vir. Ill.* give brief information about the reason for the exile).

One consequence of P.'s approach is that the order of events is distorted. In Livy, Coriolanus' exile comes prior to the story of Latinius (2.10n.), but P., as he does elsewhere (see e.g. 2.2n., 11.2n., 18.5n., 38.7n.), introduces the earlier part of the story only as background to the later part, and so unites things which in Livy were separated.

in exilium erat pulsus: Livy never uses this phrase, but it is found several times in Tacitus (*Hist.* 4.6.1, *Ann.* 4.20.1, 16.30.3), and occasionally in other writers (*TLL* X 1012.38–41, 46).

dux Vulscorum factus: Livy 2.39.1 has *imperatores...lecti*.

exercitum hostium urbi admovisset: Livy's version (2.39.5) is *ad urbem...ducit*.

legati: In Livy 2.39.11 they are *oratores*; but *orator* in the sense of 'envoy' is rare in post-Augustan Latin.[38] They are, accordingly, described as *legati* not only in P., but also in Val. Max. 5.4.1 and Eutr. 1.15.2. For the technical distinction between an *orator* and a *legatus* see Ogilvie (1965), 154; cf. *TLL* IX.2 893.45–894.49.

sacerdotes: Eutr. 1.15.2 and *Vir. Ill.* 19.4 omit these, moving straight from the *legati* to the successful appeal by the women.

bellum patriae inferret: Livy never uses this phrase, and it is rare in most other writers (though cf. Just. 38.8.11, Ampel. 40.4). It is, however, used several times by Cicero (*Catil.* 1.23, *Phil.* 2.24, *Div.* 2.114, *Off.* 3.95, *Lael.* 43—the last in the context of Coriolanus) and also by Vell. 2.20.4, 2.21.1, 2.82.4; for P. it may have had the flavour of late Republican or early imperial Latin.

2.12 *Spurius Cassius*. Corresponds to Livy 2.41.1–12; P. omits the brief account of the wars with the Volsci, the Aequi, and the Hernici which separate the story of Cassius from that of Coriolanus (2.40.12–14; but cf. 2.16n.). P.'s focus is on two points: the agrarian legislation, and the execution of Cassius. In Livy the two are intimately linked—it is precisely Cassius' offers to the people (not only the agrarian law, but also the offer to reimburse the price of the grain they had purchased) that rouse suspicion that he is really aspiring to become monarch. P. leaves the connection implicit rather than explaining it.

lex agraria primum lata est: Cf. Livy 2.41.3 *tum primum lex agraria promulgata*. P.'s wording, both here and in the sequel (see below), more closely reflects Val. Max. 5.8.2 *tribunus pl. agrariam legem primus tulerat*; even though Valerius actually offers a different version from Livy, having Cassius make his proposal as tribune rather than as consul.

primum: P. is, as often, keen to record 'firsts' (cf. e.g. 1.B.7n., 11.5n.).

regni crimine damnatus est necatusque: This is the single fact about Cassius that was most commonly mentioned in the historical tradition, namely that he was convicted of aspiring after *regnum*: cf. Livy 4.15.4; also Piso, *FRHist* 9 F 39 = fr. 37P = Plin., *Nat.* 34.30, Cic., *Dom.* 101, *Rep.* 2.49, 2.60, *Lael.* 36, *Phil.* 2.114, D.S. 11.37.7, D.H., *AR* 8.77.1, 8.78.3, 8.87.2, Val. Max. 5.8.2 (also the summary by Paris), Plin., *Nat.* 34.15, Flor. 1.17.

For the language, cf. Livy 2.41.10 *damnatum necatumque constat*. P. is, however, closer to Val. Max. 5.8.2 *adfectati regni crimine domi damnauit uerberibusque adfectum necari iussit*, despite the fact that, as before (cf. above), Valerius'

---

[38] Ammianus regularly uses it (14.10.14, 17.1.12, 25.7.5, 27.12.9, 29.5.8, 31.4.1), but as a deliberate archaism (De Jonge (1972), 110); cf. also e.g. Tac., *Ann.* 13.37.4.

version, in which Cassius was tried and executed by his father, is not the one preferred by Livy. P. leaves the matter open: his account is formally compatible with Livy's, but his language gives a nod to the Valerian version, which Livy had mentioned only to reject (2.41.10–11). To the Valerian language, however, P. adds a typically Livian stylistic quirk (albeit one not found in this passage of Livy): ending the sentence on -*que*, a device avoided by most classical Latin writers, but especially favoured by Livy (and also Tacitus: see Kraus (1992)).

2.13 *Execution of a Vestal*. Corresponds to Livy 2.42.11. This is the first of seven punishments of Vestal executions which P. records (the others being 8.5, 14.6, 20.5, 22.11, 28.3, 63.3; cf. 41.1); he appears to have had a certain interest in the phenomenon—indeed, proportionate to the length of his text, he shows somewhat more interest in them than Livy does (see Introduction, xlii). He omits, however, the civil conflict and divine signs which, according to Livy, led up to the execution (2.42.1–10, though see 2.16n.): Vestal unchastity is more of interest to him as a phenomenon in its own right than as a symbol of wider dysfunction at Rome. More generally, however, after the trial of Cassius (2.12n.), P.'s summary of the book is far patchier, and numerous episodes of all sorts are overlooked (see 2.14n., 2.15n.); this broader pattern may be as significant as the author's specific interests in determining the omissions.

For Vestals see further 14.6n.

Popilia: The chief MSS of P. read either *Illia* or *Ilia*, which is scarcely possible. The MSS of Livy read *Oppia*, and this is read by most early editors; but the name varies in other sources: D.H., *AR* 8.89.4 has Ὀπιμία, Jer., *Chron.* P. 108 (Helm) *Pompilia*, and Syncellus p. 483 Πόρπιλα, while Oros. 2.8.13 has Popilia.[39] The whole phrase in Orosius is very close to P. (*Popilia virgo ob crimen stupri viva defossa est*), suggesting either a common source or (more likely: see Introduction) that he has himself made use of P.; moreover, Jerome and Syncellus seem to depend on the same tradition. Accordingly, it is overwhelmingly likely that P.'s *Ilia* should be corrected to *Popilia*, as in Orosius: it introduces an unnecessary complexity to conflate the MS reading of P. with Livy and Dionysius so as to read *Opillia*, as Hertz, Rossbach, and Jal do. It is, moreover, a reasonable supposition that a strand of the textual tradition of Livy in the fourth century likewise read *Popilia* or *Pompilia* here, and is the ultimate source of the readings in all of the later writers (cf. Zangemeister (1882), 101).

viva defossa est: This information is not in Livy, who says only *poenas dederit* (2.42.11): P. has expanded either on the basis of another source or (more probably) of his general knowledge of how such executions were normally conducted (cf. 1.B.1n., 1.B.3n.).

---

[39] Jerome and Syncellus date it to 486 and Orosius to 478, but this is of little significance, given the uncertainties of Roman chronology at this time.

2.14 *Defeat of the Fabii at the Cremera.* Corresponds to Livy 2.48.7–50.11. At this stage of the book (cf. 2.13n.), P.'s summary is becoming increasingly patchy; he omits the whole of Livy's narrative in 2.43.1–48.6 (though cf. 2.16n.), covering wars with Veii (2.43.1–11, 2.44.6–47.12, 2.48.5–6) intertwined with renewed civil conflict at Rome (2.44.1–5, 2.48.1–4). The defeat at the Cremera was, however, an iconic moment in early Roman history, and could hardly be overlooked. P. gives no detail of the fighting, but focuses on two points: the number of the Fabii, and the death of all but one of them; the same balance is visible in Eutr. 1.16, and also *Vir. Ill.* 14 and Oros. 2.5.8–9, although both of these offer slightly more information about how the Fabii came to be trapped.

vicini: P. recognizes that Veii's proximity to Rome (around 15 km) was a key factor in the century or more of war between them, culminating in the town's destruction in the early fourth century (see 5.3). Livy, too, had noted this on their first introduction in his text (1.15.1); the slight oddity is that this is not in fact Veii's first introduction in P. (see 2.3), but it is the first time that he reports them challenging the Romans in their own right.

Most of the MSS add *hostes* after *vicini*, but it is almost certainly a gloss.

incommodi magis quam graves: Livy 2.48.7 has *adsiduus magis quam gravis*; P. substitutes a more general expression of inconvenience for Livy's precision about what aspect of the Veiian attacks caused trouble to Rome; but the opposition between *gravis* and *incommodus* also may have a mildly philosophical flavour which is absent from Livy. *incommoda* was used in Stoic contexts (especially by Seneca: see Griffin (1976), 295–6; cf. also Cic., *Fin.* 3.69) to translate the Greek δυσχρηστήματα or ἀποπροηγμένα—the 'dispreferred' things which had no absolute value but were nevertheless to be avoided: for the philosophical contrast with things that are *gravis* see e.g. Sen., *Cons. Helv.* 12.1; also e.g. *Rhet. Her.* 4.57.

No less important, however, is that P. includes Livy's comment at all, since it undercuts the Fabii's heroism by suggesting that their self-sacrifice was unnecessary: contrast e.g. D.H., *AR* 9.14.8 and Zonar. 7.17.3 (cf. Dio fr. 21), both of whom imply that the threat to Rome was rather greater. This is a relatively rare instance of P.'s summary retaining something of Livy's moral complexity.

id bellum…depoposcit: Livy does not directly use this phrase of the Fabii, but the vocabulary occurs a little afterwards, when the people imagine other families taking on other enemies: 2.49.1: *deposcant haec Volscos sibi, illa Aequos*. P.'s phrase is closer to Ampel. 20.2: *Fabii trecenti…bellum Veiens peculiariter sibi depoposcerunt*; cf. *Vir. Ill.* 14.1 *eos sibi hostes familia Fabiorum…depoposcit*.

trecentos et sex: Cf. Livy 2.49.4 *sex et trecenti milites*; cf. 2.50.11.

armatos, qui…praeter unum ab hostibus caesi sunt: The implication of P. is that the surviving Fabius was one of the 306 who formed the garrison. The majority view, however, is that the survivor was a boy who had been left at home (so Ov., *Fast.* 2.239–40, Eutr. 1.16.3, *Vir. Ill.* 14.6, Zonar. 7.17.4), and this is the implication of Livy

2.50.11 also: the surviving Fabius was *propter impuberem aetatem relictum*, and general considerations of probability, as well as the parallels in other writers, indicate that this means 'left behind on account of his youth'. However, this reading of Livy depends on a correction by Kreyssig (followed by Madvig and Ogilvie): the MSS read *prope puberem aetate relictum*. The MSS reading is linguistically improbable, and Kreyssig's emendation (on the basis of *Vir. Ill.* 14.6) overwhelmingly likely (see Ogilvie (1965), 365–6); but we may hypothesize that it (or something similar) was the reading of the text used by P., since on that reading it would be easier to interpret *relictum* as 'left alive' rather than 'left behind', an interpretation perhaps facilitated by the parallel of Thermopylae, whose narrative seems to have influenced memories of the Cremera (Ogilvie (1965), 359–60), and which similarly was said to have had a single survivor (Hdt. 7.229–31). P.'s version of the story is shared by Orosius, who speaks of *uno tantum ad enuntiandam cladem reservato* (2.5.9: 'only one preserved to announce the disaster'); it is possible that they derived it independently, but it may also be that one (probably Orosius: see Introduction) is partly dependent on the other.

2.15 *Appius Claudius decimates the army.* Corresponds to Livy 2.58.3–59.11. P.'s summary of the last part of Book 2 becomes increasingly perfunctory (cf. 2.13n., 2.14n.); from the last fifteen chapters he describes just one episode, namely Appius Claudius' disastrous command against the Volsci, culminating in his brutal punishment of his own army. Everything else both before and after this is omitted (though cf. 20.16n.): further operations against Veii (2.51.1–9, 2.53.1–3), the Volsci and Aequi (2.53.4–6, 2.63.2–6, 2.64.5–65.7), the Aequi alone (2.60.1–3, 2.62.1–2), and the Sabines (2.62.3–5, 2.63.7, 2.64.3–4); while at home P. omits further disputes between the Senate and people, centring especially on the tribunes' attempts to prosecute various senators (2.52.1–8, 2.54.2–10), on popular resistance to the levy (2.55.1–11), and on proposed reforms to the tribunate, culminating in violent attempts to exercise power by both the tribune Laetorius and the consul Appius Claudius (2.56.1–58.2). The last forms the background to the story summarized by P. here, as the prosecution and death of Appius in the following year (2.61.1–9) forms its sequel; but P. has nothing of either. In consequence, Livy's story, which focuses on the flaws of Appius quite as much as on his troops' culpability (cf. Vasaly (1987), 209–12), is turned in such a way as to substantially whitewash him: no reason is given for the army's *contumacia*, and at most he can be accused of exercising harsh military discipline.

This downplaying of Appius' violent hostility is matched elsewhere: thus Val. Max. 9.3.5 (likewise Paris' summary) and Flor. 1.17.2 mention only the troops' revolt, Valerius explaining that they did so out of anger against Appius' father; Frontin., *Strat.* 4.1.34 simply describes the fact of the punishment. Even Zonar. 7.17.5 gives no more reason for the troops' revolt than that Appius had 'opposed' (ἠναντιοῦτο) the people, and is far more critical of their reactions than of his actions. P.'s reworking of Livy thus aligns him with the broader historical tradition.

contumacia: Livy refers to Appius' troops acting *segniter, otiose, neglegenter, contumaciter* (2.58.7); but he subsequently also describes *contumacia* as a typical quality of Appius himself (2.61.6). P., in accordance with his generally one-sided approach to the story (cf. above), ascribes this to the soldiers alone.

fuste percussit: Livy does not specify the form of punishment (2.59.11), but this was the standard form of military execution, and was used in cases of decimation (cf. Plb. 6.38.3); P. once again expands Livy's information on the basis of his general knowledge (cf. e.g. 1.B.1n., 1.B.3n., 2.13n.).

A detailed description of the punishment is given by Plb. 6.37.1–3: the soldier to be executed was touched with a stick by an officer, and the other soldiers then cudgelled and stoned him to death. For discussion see esp. Jones (1972), 24: he describes it (not unfairly) as 'organized lynching', suggesting that it was designed to protect commanders from prosecution for having violated the soldiers' rights of appeal.

2.16 *Wars against Italian tribes; class conflict at Rome.*

res praeterea... continet: sc. *Liber*. P.'s standard phrase for his round-up of other events in the book, usually (but far from invariably) as his final notice (cf. Introduction, xxxviii–xxxix). Most commonly, at least in the first sixty books (his practice changes later: see 31.7n and 62.6n.), P. includes wars under this heading; it is rarer for him to use it to give additional details about specific events that occurred within the book (but for exceptions see e.g. 3.10n., 14.8n., 24.5–6n., 39.8n.). This is, however, the sole case where he employs it to cover a broad category of domestic material, namely the class conflict between patricians and plebeians. This may speak to his awareness that in the last portion of the book he skated over a good deal of such material (see 2.13n., 2.14n., 2.15n.); but it also is a sign that he has not yet settled down into the formulaic pattern of summarizing Livy that he employs in the bulk of the work—it is not the only time in the early books where he does something unusual under this heading (cf. 3.10n., 6.1n.).

adversus Vulscos et Hernicos et Veientes: This list is odd. P. had indeed previously omitted several wars with the Volsci (2.8n., 2.12n., 2.15n.) and Veii (2.14n., 2.15n.), some of which are described in detail by Livy. However, the Hernici are far less prominent in Livy's text: they (along with the Volsci) threaten war at 2.22.3–4, but their plans are betrayed and the war never transpires (see 2.8n.). They next appear in a brief notice of a war at 2.40.14 (cf. 2.12n.); but then they sign a treaty with Rome at 2.41.1, and their subsequent appearances in the book are as Roman allies (2.53.1–4, 2.64.10). Far more prominent are the wars, likewise omitted by P., against the Aequi and the Sabines (see esp. 2.8n., 2.15n.), yet they go unmentioned here. For this reason Jahn proposed a lacuna after *Veientes*, in order to allow for these other tribes; but it is more likely that P.'s selection of what to include and what to omit in these 'summary' statements is somewhat arbitrary.

Book 3

3.1 *Conflicts over agrarian laws*. P.'s summary of the opening sections of Book 3 is odd. There is a brief account at the very start of the book of the passing of an agrarian law (3.1.1–7), but it is relatively uncontentious, thanks to a compromise proposal by the consul Q. Fabius, that the land to be distributed should not be that currently occupied by patricians, but the land newly captured from the Volsci. From that point agitations over land cease; certainly there is nothing that would count as a *seditio*, let alone multiple *seditiones*. There are repeated conflicts between patricians and plebeians in the first half of the book (esp. 3.9.1–11.5, 3.14.1–15.3, 3.24.1–9, 3.25.1–4), but they do not relate to land-tenure, but instead to a proposal to limit the consuls' arbitrary power by creating a legal codification—the proposal that will ultimately result in the establishment of the decemvirate.

The most plausible explanation is simply carelessness on P.'s part. Just as with the last portion of Book 2, his account of the whole of the opening half of Book 3 is extremely patchy: among the many omissions are further internal conflicts (themselves in part linked to the conflict over legal codification), notably with the trial of Kaeso Quinctius (3.11.6–13.10) and the subsequent consulship of his father Cincinnatus (3.19.1–21.8); also a series of prodigies and a plague which devastates the country (3.5.14–7.8), and substantial accounts of wars with the Aequi (3.1.8–3.8, 3.4.1–5.13) and with the Volsci and Aequi working together (3.8.1–11, 3.22.1–23.7). Given that P. is manifestly skating over a great deal of Livy's text very rapidly, it is understandable that he might note constant references to class conflict, but mistakenly assume that it centred on the same issue as it did at the start of the book, especially since land-tenure was a problem that recurred repeatedly in Roman history, whereas the legal question was one that applied only at this period.

3.2 *Seizure and recovery of the Capitol*. Corresponds to Livy 3.15.4–18.11. As noted above (3.1n.; cf. also 3.3n.), P. omits (or misrepresents) virtually all of the portion of the book prior to this episode; with the episode itself, he focuses on the identity of the occupiers (though not mentioning their leader, Ap. Herdonius) and their defeat. He does not describe their subversive political programme of freeing the Romans' slaves, or the accompanying dissension in Rome, as the tribunes refuse to join the consuls in defeating the enemy; nor does P.—unlike Oros. 2.12.5–6 and Aug., *Civ.* 3.17[40]—mention the killing of the consul Valerius when the Capitol was retaken. The impression he gives is simply of a threat comprehensively neutralized.

---

[40] Orosius and Augustine also describe Herdonius as burning the Capitol: this is not in Livy, but adds to the sense of disaster that accompanies their account of the episode.

ab exulibus et servis occupatum: Cf. Livy 3.15.5 *exules servique...Capitolium et arcem occupavere.*

caesis his: In Livy 3.18.10 many of the occupiers are taken alive as well as many being killed; but Livy then comments that each was punished according to his status, which would have meant a form of execution in all cases (Ogilvie (1965), 428). Hence P.'s summary, even if giving the slightly misleading impression that the occupiers all died at the point when the Capitol was retaken, is not unreasonable overall.

An ablative absolute whose subject plays a different grammatical role elsewhere in the sentence is mostly avoided in classical Latin prose, but it is not uncommon in Caesar. See esp. Eden (1962), 104–6, who suggests that it arises because of the strong priority that Caesar gives to precise chronological ordering; a similar explanation may be given here, since P. is summarizing an entire narrative sequence into a single sentence.

receptum: Livy uses *recipero* three times in quick succession to describe the retaking of the Capitol (3.18.6, 3.18.7, 3.18.10); P. only uses *recipero* once (88.1n.), here (like Flor. 2.7.2) he substitutes the more commonplace *recipio*.

3.3 *Censuses.* Livy refers to two censuses in Book 3: at 3.3.9 and 3.24.10. These are the only census figures he records in the first pentad, apart from Servius Tullius' original census. In Livy they are not given any particular emphasis, but P., who had also relayed the figures associated with Servius Tullius (1 B.3n.), makes a point of including them, as he often does later also: he appears to have had a particular interest in such data, as a concrete illustration of the growth of Rome.

The notice is out of chronological order, in as much as the first census is recorded by Livy well before the seizure of the Capitol (3.2n.), but the second is in precisely the right place; the reason for the chronological disarrangement is that P. is grouping together material that is thematically linked (Bingham 146; cf. 2.7n., 20.11n.).

census bis actus est: cf. Livy 3.3.9 *census deinde actus.*

censa sunt civium capita: Livy's standard formula to report the census figures, regularly used by P. also.

CIIII milia DCCXIIII: The figure reported in the chief MSS of P. is 8,714;[41] Livy's figure is 104,714. Clearly P.'s figure is corrupt; the question is whether this is because he reproduced a corruption already found in the MS he was using as a source: if so, the transmitted figure should remain. However, the MS figure is so unfeasibly low in the context of the others recorded by P. from Livy that it seems

---

[41] In one of the Italian MSS (F) the figure is 80,714: this presumably represents a correction by a copyist who recognized the impossibility of the lower figure, which is recorded in all other strands of the tradition.

unlikely that he would have transmitted it unquestioningly, even had he found it in his source: his interest, as noted above, is in the growth of Rome, and he could have hardly have failed to observe that this would have meant a massive (albeit very temporary) contraction rather than growth. Accordingly, the MS reading should be emended to that found in Livy, as in a couple of the later MSS: the corruption from CIIII to VIII is not a difficult one.

praeter orbos orbasque: The same phrase appears in Livy 3.3.9, and a similar phrase at *Per.* 59.5 (see *ad loc.*); for a discussion of its significance see Scheidel (2009), who proposes that Livy wrote these books directly after Augustus' censuses in 28 and 8 respectively, and that he was drawing attention to the differences between those included under Augustus and those in the historical censuses he was reporting.

CXVII milia CCCXVIIII: Here too there is a variance between Livy and the MSS of P.: P.'s figure is 117,219, whereas Livy's figure is 117,319. In this case one cannot argue that P. would have found the figure 117,219 implausible had he read it in his text of Livy: indeed, it is even theoretically possible that 117,219 was the original version, and that it is the subsequent MS tradition of Livy that has been corrupted. However, the fact that Eutr. 1.16.3 reports the same figure as in the MSS of Livy strongly indicates that 117,319 is the correct reading in Livy; and it is, accordingly, on balance more probable that that is the original reading in P. as well.

3.4 *Dictatorship of Cincinnatus.* Corresponds to Livy 3.25.5–29.7. P. is vague about both the nature of the trouble that led Cincinnatus to be chosen as dictator, and the details of how he won his victory. Instead, he focuses on two moments in the story: that Cincinnatus was farming when he was summoned to the dictatorship, and that the defeated enemy were sent 'under the yoke'. Cincinnatus was a staple Roman *exemplum*, and the graphic image of his being summoned from his farm to the dictatorship is the heart of the anecdote for virtually every writer. It is less common to make passing the enemy beneath the yoke a focal point, but it is specifically commented on by Flor. 1.5.13 and Oros. 2.12.8, both of whom remark on the appropriateness of the farmer-soldier treating his defeated enemy like cattle; it is possible that a similar thought animates P.'s choice to mention it here, although nothing in his text explicitly signals the connection, and Livy himself had made nothing of that aspect—indeed, his explanation of what the 'yoke' consisted of (3.28.11) gives it a military rather than an agricultural cast.

cum adversus...res esset: See 2.2n.

male gesta res: P. uses *rem male gerere* also at 59.13 and 110.4; it is Livian, and moreover the natural obverse to P.'s favourite *res prospere gerere* (on which see 3.10n.).

Quintius: Here and elsewhere I have retained the MS spelling, as opposed to the *Quinctius* printed in editions of Livy. As noted by Briscoe (1985), 423, the MSS of Livy himself often have *Quintius*, but that is a stronger reason to print that spelling here than to regularize it to the Livian one, since it suggests that it may have been the orthography in the manuscripts of Livy that the author was using.

rure: 'In the country' (*OLD s.v. rus* 3b). The repetition *rure...rustico* looks mildly redundant, but it is a pointed figure ('derivative polyptoton'): see Wills (1996), 240–1.

intentus operi rustico: Cf. Livy 3.26.9 *operi...agresti intentus*. Most authors specify that Cincinnatus was ploughing (so e.g. Cic., *Fin.* 2.12, *Sen.* 56, Pers. 1.73–5, Colum. 1. *Praef.* 13, Flor. 1.5.12–14, Ampel. 18.4, Eutr. 1.17, *Vir. Ill.* 17.1, Veg., *Mil.* 1.3.5, Oros. 2.12.8; more obliquely Val. Max. 4.4.7); Livy is virtually unique in offering ploughing as only one possibility,[42] and P. prefers to replicate his vagueness rather than having recourse to the standard anecdote.

3.5 *Expansion of the tribunate.* Corresponds to Livy 3.30.5–7. P. gives nothing of the political background to this (it was agreed by the Senate in return for the tribunes not obstructing the levy), nor the condition set on it (that the current tribunes should not be eligible for re-election). As usual, his primary interest is in the development of the Roman constitution as a marker of the rise of Rome.

ampliatus est: Cf. 1.B.2n.

tricesimo sexto anno a primis tribunis plebis: Cf. Livy 3.30.7 *tricesimo sexto anno a primis tribuni plebis decem creati sunt*: P. retains Livy's vocabulary and word-order, even though not reproducing his syntax. A is omitted in the chief MSS of P., but the necessary restoration is made in some of the later ones.

3.6–9 *The decemvirate.* Having skated rapidly over the first part (see 3.1n.), P. offers a far more comprehensive summary of the episode which for Livy forms the heart of the book, namely the decemvirate. He touches on many of the chief points in Livy's story: the agreement to establish a commission for codifying Roman law (3.31.5–8, 3.32.6–33.7), the exemplary moderation shown by the decemvirs in administering the state while they codified the ten tables of laws (3.33.8–34.6), the decision to continue the decemvirate for a further year (3.34.7–35.11); the addition of two more tables (3.37.4; cf. 3.34.7), the arbitrary power exercised by the decemvirs in the second year of their rule (3.36.1–37.8), and their extension of their rule for a third year (3.38.1–2; cf. 3.36.9, 3.37.5). He then moves to the attempt by Appius Claudius to take Verginia by having her

---

[42] The only parallel is D.H., *AR* 10.24.1: τῶν κατ' ἀγρὸν ἔργων τι διαπραττόμενος. However, in that case the reason is that Dionysius has already told the story once before, in the context of Cincinnatus' first consulship, and there he did specify that Cincinnatus was ploughing (10.17.3).

falsely claimed as a slave, and Verginius' killing his daughter when the case is judged against her (3.44.1–48.9); then the seizure of the Aventine (3.50.2–51.11), the forced resignation of the decemvirs (3.51.11–54.6), and their punishment (3.56.1–57.6, 3.58.1–11).

This is not to say, of course, that P.'s summary reflects the complex dynamics of Livy's narrative of the decemvirate. Most obviously, he reduces the story of their fall to the single case of the crime against Verginia and the popular response to it. While to some extent Livy's account warrants this interpretation, since he introduces the Verginia episode by comparing it to the rape of Lucretia, noting that both led to the loss of power by the perpetrators,[43] the detailed narrative reveals many more political dimensions. Resistance to the decemvirs does not begin with Verginia: it starts when Rome is attacked by the Sabines and Aequi, and the Senate and people in different ways refuse to assist in repelling the invaders—the Senate, at least initially, refuses to meet, and the people to enlist (3.38.2–12), something that Livy comments could have been the first step on the road to the end of the decemvirate (3.38.10), except that the Senate fails to hold the line. Even in the Senate, though the decemvirs are ultimately successful in gaining support, they meet strong resistance, especially from L. Valerius Potitus and M. Horatius Barbatus (3.38.13–41.6). P., at least on the face of things (though see 3.7n., 3.10n.), omits the entire episode, along with the war's disastrous outcome, when the army deliberately brings about its own defeat, and the decemvirs arrange for the murder of Siccius when he speaks against them (3.41.7–43.7). P. has nothing of the way in which the death of Verginia is exploited by Verginius, Valerius, and Horatius to raise the army and the people against the decemvirs: the seizure of the Aventine is treated as though it were primarily a move made by the populace at Rome, rather than, as in Livy, an action initiated by the army in the field; nor does P. have any hint of the ambivalence of the Senate, who feel unable to support the decemvirate but still fear popular power. He moves directly from the resignation of the decemvirs to their punishment, with nothing of the details of the new constitutional settlement of the restored Republic, which Livy recounts in some detail (3.54.7–55.15). Indeed, it is noticeable that even with the chief villain of the piece, Appius Claudius, P. does not mention him until the Verginia episode, whereas Livy gives him the central role in the decemvirate from the beginning to the end.

The balance of the narrative in P. is not all that dissimilar to that found in much of the rest of the tradition. In particular, most other sources similarly omit the poorly conducted war and the ambivalent role of the Senate (only D.H., *AR* 11.3–27 has both; the war is in Zonar. 7.18.5). Conversely, the attempted rape of Verginia and her killing by her father is almost always the heart of the story; it is

---

[43] See esp. 3.44.1 *non finis solum idem decemviris qui regibus sed causa etiam eadem imperii amittendi esset* ('not only did the decemvirs have the same end as the kings, but also they lost their power for the same reason'). Cf. also 3.58.10–11.

also widely noted that the codification of laws was inspired by Greek codes (e.g. D.H., *AR* 10.55.5, Tac., *Ann.* 3.27.1, Flor. 1.17(24).3, Pompon., *Dig.* 1.2.2.4, *Vir. Ill.* 21.1, Aug., *Civ.* 2.16, Oros. 2.13.2, Zon. 7.18.2, Isid., *Etym.* 5.1.3–4), that the decemvirate went through at least two stages, with two extra tables added later but also with a turn to tyranny (e.g. Cic., *Rep.* 2.61–3, D.H., *AR* 10.58–60, Pompon., *Dig.* 1.2.2.4, 1.2.2.24, Oros. 2.13.3–5, Zonar. 7.18.4),[44] and that the decemvirs were ultimately punished (e.g. D.H., *AR* 11.46, Pompon., *Dig.* 1.2.2.24, Flor. 1.17(24).3, *Vir. Ill.* 21.3, Eutr. 1.18, Zonar. 7.18.11). Where P.'s version is more distinctive is in the secession to the Aventine: most sources who mention it treat it as primarily an action of the army, as in Livy (so e.g. Cic., *Corn.* F 49 (Crawford), *Rep.* 2.63.2, D.S. 12.24.5, D.H., *AR* 11.43, Pompon., *Dig.* 1.2.2.24, Eutr. 1.18, *Vir. Ill.* 21.3, Zonar. 7.18.9); apart from P., it is only in Oros. 2.13.7 that the people take the lead.[45]

3.6 adlatis Atticis legibus: Cf. Livy 3.32.6: *iam redierant legati cum Atticis legibus.*

constituendas: Livy uses not *constituere* but *condere* of the decemvirs' legal enactments (3.33.5, 3.34.1; cf. 34.6.8). Ogilvie (1965), 457 suggests that the phrase *iura condere* has 'a somewhat pejorative flavour'; but even if that was the case for Livy, it is unlikely to have been so for P., since similar phrases were becoming increasingly common in the fourth century, especially in Christian sources (see *TLL* IV 153.40–5; for the theological significance of *condere* also IV 154.30–55). Nevertheless, P. substitutes *constituere*: although Livy himself never uses phrases like *leges constituere* (though cf. 39.26.14), Cicero repeatedly does, and in general in the late Republic and early Empire they are far commoner than *leges condere* (cf. *TLL* IV 515.68–78, 522.39–43, 63–5); hence for P. it may have had the flavour of classical Latin, even if not derived from Livy himself.

eas: sc. *leges*. The pronoun is surprising. The most natural reading would take it to be referring to the 'Attic laws' mentioned in the previous phrase (for the grammar cf. 3.2n.); but on Livy's account, the Romans did not establish and promulgate 'Attic laws' *per se*, but rather a set of laws of their own that were partly modelled on those laws. Possibly P. has in mind a different version of the story, according to which the Twelve Tables were not an original composition by the decemvirs, but were the laws of Solon themselves, translated into Latin (so *Vir. Ill.* 21.1, Isid., *Orig.* 5.1.3); but *constituendas eas proponendasque* is not a natural way to describe the process of translation either. It is more probable that *eas* here

---

[44] Several sources include the turn to tyranny in the second year of the decemvirate, but not the two stages of compiling the laws: so e.g. D.S. 12.24.1–2, Flor. 1.17(24).1, Ampel. 29.2–3, Eutr. 1.18, *Vir. Ill.* 21.2.

[45] There is also an entirely different version, in which it is the decemvirs themselves, not the seceding troops or people, who occupy the Aventine (Flor. 1.17(24).3, Ampel. 25.2): see Mignone (2016), 24, arguing that it may 'reflect contemporary residential topography', since the Aventine in the second century AD was inhabited by many of the Roman elite.

120 COMMENTARY

effectively means *tales*: that meaning is not uncommon when *is* is used adjectivally (see *TLL* VII.2 472.80–473.43). It is not as regular a usage when, as here, *is* is a free-standing pronoun, but we may also compare the use of the interrogative *qui* to mean *qualis* (cf. Cairns (2012); also *OLD* s.v. *qui*[1] A.2): P., compressing the narrative, may have phrased a little loosely.

One might consider emending the text to *novas* (cf. Livy 3.33.5 *ad condenda nova iura*); however, there is an additional consideration that militates against this. Oros. 2.13.2 says that the decemvirate was created *constituendarum legum Atticarum gratia* ('in order to establish Attic laws'). This appears to reflect the same version as appears in P., with the additional consideration that in Orosius there is no possibility that this is the consequence of loose phrasing. The most plausible explanation is that Orosius is deriving his account in part from P. (cf. Introduction), and understandably interpreted him to mean that the laws the decemvirs created were 'Attic laws'; it is even possible that this is the ultimate source of the version in *Vir. Ill.* Also, that it grew out of an attempt to explain in what sense the Twelve Tables could have been 'Attic'.

proponendasque: Cf. Livy 3.34.2: *propositis decem tabulis…leges propositas*.

X viri…sine ullis aliis magistratibus creati: Cf. Livy 3.32.6: *placet creari decemviros…et ne quis eo anno alius magistratus esset*.

altero et trecentesimo anno quam Roma condita erat: The MSS reading is *nono trigesimo*; it is emended on the basis of Livy 3.33.1 *anno trecentensimo altero quam condita Roma erat*. This emendation is not certain: Oros. 2.13.2, which appears in part to be dependent on P. (cf. above), reads *ipso autem trecentesimo anno*, and this may have been P.'s reading also. But on balance it is more probable that P. correctly reflects Livy, and that either Orosius' version is corrupt or he has modified his source in order to make the chronology neater.

ut a regibus ad consules, ita a consulibus ad X viros imperium translatum: Cf. Livy 3.33.1: *ab consulibus ad decemviros, quemadmodum ab regibus ante ad consules venerat, translato imperio*.

3.7 **hi:** According to Livy, like most other sources,[46] the decemvirs who held office and ruled with exemplary restraint in the first year were not (for the most part) the same ones who ruled with arbitrary power in the second year and illegally prorogued their rule into a third. P., in common with much of the later Latin tradition (Flor. 1.17(24).1, Pompon., *Dig.* 1.2.2.4, Eutr. 1.18, *Vir. Ill.* 21.1–2), tidies up the story, implying that the same men continued in office throughout. Ironically, this version may in fact be closer to the historical reality, since the second college is widely argued to be an annalistic invention (so e.g. Beloch, *RG* 242–6, Ogilvie (1965), 461–2, Forsythe (2005), 222–5; *contra* Cornell (1995), 273–4), but even if this is the case, the coherence of the history

---

[46] e.g. Cic., *Rep.* 2.61, D.S. 12.24.1, D.H., *AR* 10.58.4, Oros. 2.13.1, Zonar. 7.18.4.

with the version here is more likely to be coincidence than because P. and the other summarizers had access to a more authentic tradition.

X tabulis...positis cum modeste...placuisset, duabus tabulis...adiectis cum...impotenter fecissent: P. elaborates his standard syntactic structure of providing a 'background' explanatory clause (2.2n.), in this case providing two *cum*-clauses and supplementing each one with further background provided in the ablative absolute. This piling up of clauses looks awkward from the standpoint of the classical periodic sentence, but P. has made some effort to provide structure by means of verbal parallels: *X tabulis–duabus tabulis, modeste se in honore gessissent–impotenter fecissent.*

positis: The term is not used of the decemvirate by Livy, but is well chosen: it encompasses both the physical erection of the tables of law in public (*TLL* X.1 2633.64–2634.24) and the creation of the legal code (*TLL* X.1 2655.2–20).

ob id: This slightly rewrites Livy's emphasis. On his account (as also in Pompon., *Dig.* 1.2.2.4), the primary reason for the reappointment of the decemvirs was because the original ten tables were perceived as inadequate (3.34.7), and the decent behaviour of the decemvirs in their first year was a secondary explanation of why the people were willing for this to happen (3.34.8). P.'s version is closer to that in D.H., *AR* 10.58.1 and (implicitly) Cic., *Rep.* 2.61, where an active preference for the rule of the decemvirate is the primary reason for its extension into a second year.

eundem esse magistratum placuisset, duabus tabulis ad decem adiectis: The primary MSS read *eundem esse magistratum ad decem adiectis*, which is impossible. The basic meaning of the sentence is, however, clear from Livy 3.37.4: *duae tabulae legum ad prioris anni decem tabulas erant adiectae*, and one of the Renaissance MSS (F) has *eundem esse magistratum placuit. Qui cum duabus tabulis ad decem adiectis*, presumably a restoration by a scribe who knew the story from Livy or elsewhere. This sentence is, however, ungrammatical, unless *et* were omitted before *ob id* earlier in the sentence; the *cum* is also awkward and unnecessary, and an easier and more plausible restoration along similar lines was made by Sigonius, simply adding *placuisset, duabus tabulis*.[47] Oros. 2.13.5, who may be partly deriving his account from P. (3.6n.), has *duabus tabulis legum ad decem prioris additis*.

impotenter: Cf. Livy 3.36.2 *impotentibus...consiliis*.

magistratum noluerunt deponere: For *deponere* (= 'surrender an office') see *TLL* V.1 578.29–44. *magistratum deponere* is used once by Livy (4.24.7), albeit not in the context of the decemvirate (but note 3.51.12 *deponerent insignia magistratus*);

---

[47] *placuisset* had been offered as a restoration in several Renaissance MSS, *duabus tabellis* in two others (see the reports in Jal's apparatus), but no one before Sigonius appears to have completed the entire phrase in this manner.

it is relatively rare elsewhere, but used of the decemvirate also by Oros. 2.13.5, who may be drawing it from P. (3.6n.).

retinuerunt: Cf. *OLD s.v. retineo* 7b.

inviso eorum imperio: The MSS read *invito*, which makes for strained and unlikely Latin. The Aldine edition proposed *invicto*, but far better is Drakenborch's *inviso*, following Livy 3.38.10 *invisum imperium*. Livy's phrase is striking (cf. W-M *ad loc.*), used nowhere else by him, and rare in other Latin writers: it appears in the context of the refusal of the Romans to assist the decemvirs in repelling the invasion of the Aequi and Sabines. On the face of things P. omits this part of the story altogether (see 3.6–9n.), but his language tacitly points the reader who happens to be acquainted with Livy towards it (cf. 11.1n. for P. alluding to a part of story which he does not overtly tell).

libido Appi Claudi: *libido* is used repeatedly by Livy as a central theme in the Verginia story, and he, like P., refers to it at the start as the prime explanation for the fall of the decemvirs (3.44.1 *ab libidine ortum*). For the specific phrase, cf. Livy 3.50.7 *libidinem Ap. Claudi*; it had previously been used by Cic., *Fin.* 2.66, and later appears in Oros. 2.13.6 (who may be deriving it from P.: see 3.6n.).

3.8 in amorem...incidisset: A relatively commonplace phrase (cf. *TLL* VII.1 898.30–4), not from Livy, who describes Appius' desires in terms which suggest a greater measure of perversity (e.g. 3.44.2 *stuprandae libido*, 3.44.4 *amore amens*).

Virginiae virginis: P. is far from the only writer who puns on Verginia's all too appropriate name:[48] Livy does much the same at 3.44.2 (*pater virginis, L. Verginius*), as does Cic., *Rep.* 2.63 and Ascon., *Corn.* 77C, though all three of these make the punning less heavy-handed by juxtaposing the name of the father rather than the daughter. Here too (cf. 3.6n., 3.7n.) Orosius is closest to P. (2.13.6: *Virginiae virgini stuprum inferret*), another indication of his dependence on him in this episode. For P.'s broader interest in word-play around names see 2.2n.

summisso, qui: The older MSS have *summo qui* or *sibique*; *summisso* is first found in the Renaissance MSS, presumably a scribal correction, but a highly plausible one: see *OLD s.v. submitto* 6b: 'to put forward by secret or underhand means (the agent of a misdeed)'. The usage is post-Livian. P., as often, rather than supplying a pronoun allows the subject of the participle to be assumed from the *qui*-clause (cf. also *inlaturi* below); for the construction cf. K-S 1.773.

eam in servitutem peteret: The phrase is a standard legal one: it appears regularly in the *Digest*. Livy uses it twice in metaphorical contexts in his later books (42.52.16, 45.22.6), but not here, employing instead *in servitutem adserere* (3.44.5), which appears not to be legal language *per se* (*contra* Briscoe (1981), 81),

---

[48] Her name may indeed have been invented precisely because of the role she plays in the story (so e.g. Ogilvie (1965), 477).

but rather an extension from the manumission formula *adserere in libertatem* (on which see *TLL* II 863.51–82). P. substitutes the more familiar version.

necessitatem patri eius Virginio imposuit: *necessitatem imponere* is a common phrase (*TLL* VII.1 657.4–12); it is not used by Livy here, but he does refer to the *necessitas* placed on Verginius (sc. of killing his daughter) at 3.48.7. Oros. 3.13.7, perhaps deriving it from P. rather than Livy (cf. 3.6n.), similarly speaks of the *necessitatis atrocitas*.

qui rapto ex taberna proxima cultro: A distillation of Livy 3.48.5: *seducit filiam…ad tabernas…atque ibi ab lanio cultro arrepto*. P. substitutes the commoner *rapto* for Livy's more choice verb, and does not think it necessary to specify the shop from which the knife came.

The α MSS include *qui* before *rapto*, which the other older MSS omit; it is more in P.'s manner to link the sentences with the relative clause.

filiam occidit: Livy 3.48.5 is more graphic: *pectus deinde puellae transfigit*.

3.9 **hoc tam magnae iniuriae exemplo plebs concitata:** P. roughly paraphrases Livy 3.49.1: *concitatur multitudo…atrocitate sceleris*.

montem Aventinum occupavit: The same phrase, perhaps derived from P. (3.6n.), appears in Oros. 2.13.7. As noted above (3.6–9n.), P. and Orosius are unusual in having the people, rather than the army, take the lead against the decemvirs. They also both go against Livy in having the key occupation be of the Aventine: in Livy, the army initially seizes the Aventine (3.50.13), but then soon afterwards moves to the Mons Sacer, where they are joined by the people (3.52.1–4). In this, however, P. is reflecting a wider tradition, since there was no consensus as to the site of the secession, and the Aventine was much more commonly associated with it than was the Mons Sacer.[49]

X viros abdicare se magistratu: Cf. Livy 3.54.5 *decemviri se…magistratu abdicarent*; 3.54.6 *decemviri prodeunt in contionem abdicantque se magistratu*.

Appius…in carcerem coniectus est; ceteri in exilium sunt acti: Cf. Livy 3.57.6: *in carcerem est coniectus*. Livy, however, presents the decemvirs' punishment slightly differently: not only Appius, but also Oppius is taken to prison (3.58.9), and both of them commit suicide there.

3.10 *Wars against Italian tribes; arbitration over Ardea and Aricia.* As often, P. concludes the book with a round-up in general terms of events that the rest of his account has not covered. Prior to this, however, he has omitted a long series of

---

[49] The Aventine is referred to as the site of the secession by Livy himself in a later passage (7.40.11); this version is also found in (e.g.) Cic., *Corn.* F 49 (Crawford), Sall., *Jug.* 31.17, D.S. 12.24.5, Pompon., *Dig.* 1.2.2.24, *Vir. Ill.* 21.3. Cic., *Rep.* 2.58, 2.63 has the opposite version to Livy, with the Mons Sacer seized first, and a move to the Aventine later. Mignone (2014), 140–7, (2016), 24–32, 40–3 plausibly argues that the association of the Aventine with the secessions was a late introduction into the tradition, invented on the model of Gaius Gracchus' flight to the Aventine in 121.

episodes from the last portion of Livy's book, notably the constitutional settlement following the fall of the decemvirs (3.55), the successful wars fought against the Volsci and Aequi and the Sabines (3.60.1–63.4; see also below), and various civil disputes between senate and plebs (3.63.5–66.2), culminating in a further attack by the Volsci and the Aequi, which the plebs refuse to join in repelling until they are rallied by the consul T. Quinctius Capitolinus (3.66.3–70.15; see also below). The activities of the decemvirate are at the centre of P.'s interest in Book 3, and, as with the first part of the book (3.1n.), he excludes most things that do not relate directly to them.

The mention of the arbitration over Ardea and Aricia is more unusual: P. may once again (cf. 2.16n.) be experimenting with different techniques near the start of his work, since elsewhere he rarely includes precise references to specific events under this heading. In this case, the final event that is added on is also the event that occurs at the very end of Livy's book (3.71–2). P., like Livy, closes with an episode that is far from creditable to the Romans, although in P. its closural force is diminished, even though he in fact follows Livy's narrative sequence, because he explicitly places it as part of a summary of events which is not assumed to be in chronological order.

res praeterea...continet: See 2.16n.

contra Sabinos et Vulscos: P.'s list of 'other' enemies the Romans fought against in the book is not as eccentric as the list in Book 2 (2.16n.), but still surprising. In the sections of Book 3 that P. has previously omitted, the Romans do defeat both the Volsci (3.8, 3.22.2–23.7, 3.60.1–61.10, 3.69.6–70.13) and the Sabines (3.61.11–63.4). However, in Livy the Volsci are regularly partnered by the Aequi, who had also fought against the Romans by themselves at the start of the book (3.1.8–3.8, 3.4.1–5.13)—indeed, the Aequi are arguably more prominent as enemies of Rome in this book than either the Sabines or the Volsci are. It may be that P. ignores the Aequi here because he had previously mentioned them in the context of Cincinnatus (3.4), so they came less readily to mind in the context of Roman victories he had overlooked; but it is no less likely that this simply represents a more or less arbitrary selection on his part (cf. 2.16n.).

res...prospere gestas: P.'s usual formula for summarizing success in war, used regularly by Livy and many other writers also (cf. *TLL* X.2 2217.23–9).

parum honestum populi Romani iudicium: Cf. Livy 3.71.2: *victoriam honestam...turpe domi...iudicium populi deformavit*. P. transfers the adjective from the contrasting phrase to the one which directly describes the episode under discussion.

agrum de quo ambigebatur: Cf. Livy 3.71.7: *agrum de quo ambigitur*.

sibi adiudicavit: Cf. Livy 3.72.5: *sibi controversiosam adiudicaret rem*. Livy here describes a hypothetical parallel offered by the opponents of the judgement; P. transfers it to the judgement itself.

Book 4

4.1 *The lex Canuleia.* Corresponds to Livy 4.1.1–6.4. In Livy the debate between the Senate and Canuleius over intermarriage between the classes is bound up with another issue, namely the access of the plebeians to the consulship, and the arguments for both are intertwined; indeed, consular access is, if anything, both more prominent in the argument and has more far-reaching narrative consequences, since it is that which leads to the establishment of the consular tribunate (4.2n.). P.'s account treats these as entirely independent questions.

lex de conubio patrum et plebis…perlata est: Cf. Livy 4.1.1 *de conubio patrum et plebis…rogationem promulgavit. legem perferre* is a standard phrase in Cicero and Livy for the passing of a law. It largely falls into disuse after the first century AD (see *TLL* X 1362.25–40), but P. uses it to evoke Livian Latin, even though Livy had used a different verb of the *lex Canuleia*.

patribus repugnantibus: This combination of words is never used by Livy, nor indeed elsewhere in surviving Latin literature—apart from P., who uses it three times (also 6.4, 50.10) as a useful shorthand for class conflict.

4.2 *Establishment of the consular tribunate and the censorship.* Corresponds to Livy 4.6.5–7.3 and 4.8.1–7; P. omits the appeal of the Ardeans against the removal of their land, which takes place between the establishment of the consular tribunate and the censorship, a story whose resolution he will tell immediately afterwards (4.7.4–7: see 4.3n.); he also omits any sense of the conflict (and the dispute in Livy's sources) over whether consular tribunes or consuls were to be appointed after the initial establishment of the office (4.7.7–12: see further below).

tribuni ⟨…⟩ plebis: The transmitted text is manifestly lacunose, as has been recognized since Sigonius, or indeed before.[50] That the missing portion concerned the establishment of the consular tribunate is guaranteed by the following sentence. The only substantial question concerns *plebis*: whether it is a later gloss seeking to explain the hanging *tribuni*, or whether it (or some form of it) stood in P.'s original. The latter is on balance preferable: it may be that P. wrote something along the lines of *tribuni militum consulari potestate promisce creati sunt ex patribus et plebe* (cf. Livy 4.6.8), and the lacuna came about precisely because the copyist was anticipating finding *plebis* with *tribuni*.

If so, P., as is his usual practice, highlights one of Livy's explanations for the establishment of the consular tribunate (namely its availability to plebeians: cf. also D.H., *AR* 11.60.5, Zonar. 7.19.3–5) over another (namely that it was to

---

[50] Hence the reconstruction *tribuni plebis aliquot annos fuere* offered by one Renaissance MS (F), with a new sentence beginning at *res populi Romani*: ingeniously simple grammatically, but impossible historically.

handle a military emergency: Livy 4.7.2). It is still highly controversial whether either of these explanations is correct, since neither seems to be fully supported by the evidence, nor is it clear what alternative explanation should replace them if both are rejected: for a summary of the problem see Oakley (1997), 371–6.

aliquot annos: As Livy makes clear, even after the establishment of the consular tribunate in 444, the Romans continued to elect consuls in some years. It is only in the period 408–367 that the consular tribunate became the norm, and even within that period consuls were chosen in 393–392. Hence, while strictly speaking one could say that P. is correct—there was a period of several years when Rome was controlled by consular tribunes—in the context of his sequential narrative he is clearly misleading, since that period did not begin at the time he is discussing here.[51] But it is in accord with that perspective that he omits the conflict over the continuation of the office (above).

item...tunc primum: P., here as elsewhere (cf. 11.5n.), uses *tunc primum* as a marker of strict chronology: the notice is closely related chronologically as well as thematically (as emphasized by *item*) to the previous one. In this case the chronology in Livy was slightly more extended than he implies: although the censorship was established immediately after the consular tribunate in Livy's text, it was in the following year. But Livy's narrative of these years is so abbreviated as to give an impression of the virtual simultaneity of the two institutions, and it is not implausible that their creation was in fact somehow interlinked.[52]

4.3 *Restitution of territory to the Ardeans.* Corresponds to Livy 4.9–11. In accordance with his usual practice of not leaving narratives unfinished, P. completes the story that he began in 3.10: here the original story was not obviously incomplete in itself, except in as much as the moral structure of P.'s narrative (like Livy's) would usually have wrongdoing by Rome either rectified or punished.

In this case, however, the completion of the moral narrative is left puzzlingly abridged on the level of literal action, since it is far from clear from P. how Rome's sending colonists to Ardea could constitute restoration of their territory to them. Only on reading the fuller narrative in Livy does it make sense. The population of Ardea had been depleted through a civil war, in which the Romans took one side and the Volsci the other. The Romans, victorious, restored the state, and sent out colonists to replenish the population and support them against future Volscian attacks—but the Senate secretly ruled that the colonists should be primarily

---

[51] Bingham 153–4, noting the error, proposed emending *annos* to *menses*; but, while this would be more in accord with the history as Livy reports it (since the first consular tribunes were compelled to resign their office before the year was out), the generalizing phrase *per hoc genus magistratus* looks very strange on that reading.

[52] For different views see e.g. Nilsson (1929), 4–5, Suolahti (1963), 22–3, Ogilvie (1965), 545, Forsythe (2005), 236. The nature of the link, if any, naturally depends on why the consular tribunate was established in the first place, which is controversial (above).

people from the region of Ardea, and that they should be assigned the land previously removed from them. P. omits all this, as well as the romantic story (thematically appropriate, in the context of the *lex Canuleia*) of the origins of the Ardean civil war in a proposed marriage across classes. The primary issue for him is the restitution of the territory; he may perhaps focus on the sending of colonists as the means by which it was accomplished because of his broader interest in colonization as a mode of the growth and expansion of Rome (cf. 11.5n.). How precisely these two points are connected is of less interest to him.

4.4 *Sedition of Maelius*. Corresponds to Livy 4.12.6–16.5. P. provides the basic outline of Livy's story; the famine, the campaign (and seditious aspirations) of Maelius, the dictatorship of Cincinnatus, the killing of Maelius by Ahala. All of these are central to the story as it appears in most other sources also; it seems to have had particular resonance in the last decades of the Republic, and Cicero repeatedly cites Maelius as an example of someone illegitimately seeking *regnum*, and Ahala as an example of justifiable killing in such a context (cf. Livy 6.19.2): this became especially pertinent in the case of Brutus, who claimed descent from Ahala and held up his ancestor as a model.[53] Of the major features of the story as it was handed down not only by Livy but elsewhere in Roman tradition, P.'s only substantial omission is the posthumous razing of Maelius' house (Livy 4.16.1; cf. e.g. Cic., *Dom.* 101, Varro, *Ling.* 5.157, D.H., *AR* 12.4.6, Val. Max. 6.3.1c, Quint., *Inst.* 3.7.20, *Vir. Ill.* 17.5); he substitutes the reward given to Minucius, which was less commonly mentioned. His other primary omissions concern the economics of Maelius' campaign: in Livy, Maelius was buying up and hoarding grain, and thus increasing both the price and his own power over the desperate populace when he distributed part of it; once Maelius was dead, the grain was brought to market at a low price. This sort of economic details was of less interest to P., as indeed it was to the rest of the historical tradition.

fame...laboraret: This phrase is not found in Livy, or anywhere else in Republican or Augustan Latin, but first appears in the middle of the first century AD, after which it becomes increasingly common; P. summarizes Livy with language that had become a virtual cliché by his own day. The same phrase is used by Aug., *Civ.* 3.17 in the context of Maelius: while Augustine could easily have come up with it independently, in combination with other verbal overlaps (see below), it may indicate dependence on P.

frumentum populo sua impensa largitus est: Cf. Livy 6.13.2 *largitiones frumenti facere instituit*. Also close to P. is Aug., *Civ.* 3.17: *multitudini frumenta largitus est* (cf. above).

---

[53] See esp. *RRC* no. 443/2: a coin issued by Brutus as moneyer in 54 BC, with the head of L. Junius Brutus on one side and Ahala on the other; also e.g. Cic., *Att.* 13.40.1, *Phil.* 2.26.

regnum adfectans a Servilio Ahala magistro equitum iussu Quinti Cincinnati dictatoris occisus est: This represents a significant change to Livy. In Livy (as also in D.H., *AR* 12.2.3–8), the killing was not on Cincinnatus' orders (though it was approved by him after the event), but came about when Ahala sought to arrest Maelius and Maelius resisted. P.'s version is, however, the commonest one in the later tradition: see esp. Flor. 1.17(26).7: *Quinctii dictatoris imperio in medio foro magister equitum Servius Ahala confodit* (though Ahala's opponent is mistakenly said to be Cassius rather than Maelius); Ampel. 27.2: *Maelius cum frumentaria largitione affectare regnum videtur, iussu Quinctii Cincinnati dictatoris a magistro equitum in rostris occisus est*; *Vir. Ill.* 17.5: *dictator dictus Spurium Maelium regnum affectantem a Servilio Ahala magistro equitum occidi iussit*; also Aug., *Civ.* 3.17, and Zonar. 7.20.4 (who offers the two as alternatives). The phrasing of Ampelius and *Vir. Ill.* is close to P.'s, and it may be that they depend upon each other or some other common source, but all ultimately appear to derive directly or indirectly from Cic., *Cato* 56: *dictatoris iussu magister equitum C. Servilius Ahala Sp. Maelium regnum occupantem interemit*: Cicero's version has effectively displaced Livy's from the tradition (cf. 1.B.2n., 2.1n., 13.7n., 18.5n.).[54]

a Servilio Ahala: The MSS do not give a *praenomen*. Rossbach includes it, but probably wrongly, since P. more commonly (though not invariably) omits it when he is giving both the *nomen* and *cognomen*, thus conforming to a more typically imperial mode of nomenclature (see Salway (1994), esp. 128–31).

L. Minucius index: On Livy's account, Minucius was not the usual sort of informant, an insider who turns against the conspiracy,[55] but the *praefectus annonae*, who discovered the conspiracy while searching out grain. P.'s failure to mention this is probably simply due to his abridgement, though it does have the additional consequence that Maelius' story is assimilated to a more conventional form of conspiracy narrative.

However, *MRR* I 57[56] argues that there was an alternative version of the story, according to which Minucius did indeed act as a private informant rather than in an official capacity; if so, it might be argued that P. used that version. *MRR* claims that this version is presupposed by Plin., *Nat.* 18.15, and is found in Cincius Alimentus (*FRHist* 2 F 4 = fr. 6P) and Piso (*FRHist* 9 F 26 = fr. 24P): both of the latter are cited by D.H., *AR* 12.4.2–5 for an account of the story under which there was no dictatorship, and Ahala killed Maelius as a private citizen. But while it is true that none of these explicitly associates Minucius with the office of *praefectus annonae*, none of them is incompatible with his holding some such office; the fact that they denied the dictatorship does not entail that they denied Minucius' office

---

[54] See esp. Panitschek (1989), 239–41, who discusses the development of the different versions of the story in light of the political changes of the late Republic and early Empire.

[55] For this stereotypical feature of Roman conspiracy narratives see Pagán (2004), 5–6.

[56] Some of the argument was originally put forward by Mommsen (1871), 259–60, 266–8 = (1879), 203–4, 213–16; later followed by (e.g.) Ogilvie (1958), 46, (1965), 550.

as well.[57] Admittedly, the *praefectus annonae* (as *MRR* puts it) 'is a very unlikely office at so early a date', but this does not prevent it (or some other post with equivalent responsibility) being firmly entrenched in the historical tradition by the second century BC. As De Sanctis II 16 [17] argues, while the story probably had little historical basis, the most likely reason Minucius appears in it at all was because someone of that name was associated with grain distribution in a time of crisis.[58]

Hence there is no reason to believe that P., in abridging Livy, was pointing to an existing alternative version. Indeed, the form of the story in P. supports the argument outlined above: it shows that an author may fail to mention Minucius' official position even when summarizing a version in which he actually did hold that position.

bove aurata donatus est: Cf. Livy 4.16.2, whose transmitted text reads *L. Minucius bove aurato extra portam Trigeminam est donatus*. However, Wiseman (1996), 59 = (1998), 202 argues that Livy's text should read something like *bove aurato ⟨et statua⟩* (an emendation originally proposed by Crévier), since the *bos auratus* was not a monument, as would be implied by giving it a location, but an ox with gilded horns intended for sacrifice. The phrase *bos auratus* was sufficiently common that Livy is unlikely to have thought that it was some sort of statue (see *TLL* II 1521.47–65), and indeed he himself uses it in an unambiguously sacrificial context at 25.12.13. P. has simply ignored the more commonplace honour in favour of the more distinctive one (*contra* Ogilvie (1965), 556, who takes this passage as confirming the integrity of Livy's text).

The feminine in P. is clearly a transcription error: the question is whether it is an error in the MS tradition of P., or the consequence of P. working from a defective text of Livy (or misreading Livy himself). Since there are no obvious considerations to weigh in one or other direction, the MS reading should remain by default.

4.5 *Roman ambassadors at Fidenae.* Corresponds to Livy 4.17.1–6. P. treats this as a self-contained event, whereas in Livy it is closely connected to the sequel (see 4.6n.), namely the war against Lars Tolumnius of Veii, with whom the Fidenates were

---

[57] Livy 4.13.7 cites the *libri lintei* as showing that Minucius was *praefectus annonae* in both the year of the conspiracy and the previous year. Since Livy knew of the *libri lintei* only through Licinius Macer, writing in the first century (see esp. Ogilvie (1958)), it is deduced that it is only in Macer that his part in the story involved his holding this office (so e.g. Mommsen (1871), 267–8 = (1879), 215–16). But the form of the citation in Livy suggests the opposite: that all his sources had Minucius as *praefectus annonae* (or at least an office with similar functions, even if a different title), but that only the *libri lintei* (which, according to Livy, in fact spoke only of *praefectus*, not *annonae*: see Ogilvie (1965), 552) gave the precise dates of his holding it.

[58] This is far more plausible than an alternative suggestion: that Minucius came into the story because the Greek version of his name (Μηνύκιος) was connected etymologically to 'informing' (μηνύειν) (so e.g. Münzer (1932), 1953–4, Wiseman (1996), 67–9 = (1998), 102–3). It is true that Dionysius repeatedly puns on the name in this way (*AR* 12.2.1. 12.4.3, 12.4.6), but such puns were commonplace in ancient historiography with people whose historicity is unquestionable (see 2.2n.).

allied, and who indeed, in Livy's version, was the person who ordered the ambassadors' murder. Cossus' killing of Tolumnius and winning the *spolia opima*, on Livy's account, is retribution for Tolumnius' treachery (4.19.3). However, P.'s isolation of these stories is not especially surprising: there was no consensus either about the historical context of the murder of the ambassadors or indeed of Cossus' killing of Tolumnius. With regard to the former, D.S. 12.80.6–8 places the murder more than a decade later, in the same year as the final defeat of Fidenae (426), and does not associate it with Tolumnius or Veii. Plin., *Nat.* 34.23 likewise does not mention Tolumnius, while Val. Max. 9.9.3 associates the killing solely with him and does not refer to Veii (Cic., *Phil.* 9.4–5 is the only other source who mentions both).

Cossus was even more mobile: while Livy, Serv., *Aen.* 6.841,[59] and (probably) D.H., *AR* 12.5 have him killing Tolumnius when he was a military tribune in 437, some other sources associate that, too, with 426, when he was *magister equitum*, and killed (apparently) the general of the Fidenates (Val. Max. 3.2.4; similarly Servius auct.: see n. 59 above), while Livy 4.20.5–11 famously reports Augustus' argument that it was to be attributed to Cossus' consulship in 428, a version followed by Festus p. 204L. Flor. 1.6.9 (who does not mention Cossus) appears to date the winning of the *spolia opima* a generation later, at the time of the Roman siege of Veii.

No surviving source other than Livy and *Vir. Ill.* 25 (which dates it to a nonexistent dictatorship of Quinctius Cincinnatus with Cossus as *magister equitum*)[60] associates the murder of the ambassadors with the war in which Cossus won the *spolia opima*.[61] Presumably it was precisely because of the fluidity of the chronology that the individual components were able to float as independent anecdotes, as they effectively do here.

legatis...occisis: See 2.2.n.

quoniam ob rem publicam morte occubuerant: Livy does not feel it necessary to give any explanation for the honour given to the ambassadors: P. takes one almost verbatim from Cic., *Phil.* 9.4: *qui ob rem publicam mortem obierant* (cf. Phil. 9.5: *ipsa mors ob rem publica obita honori fuit*; also Phil. 9.16, Tab. Siar. 1.18, Tac., *Ann.* 2.83.2, 3.6.1). However, for Cicero's *mortem obire* P. substitutes *morte*

---

[59] Note, however, that Servius auct. adds *consulari potestate*, thus dating it in 426, as Valerius Maximus does, albeit earlier in the year, before Cossus became *magister equitum*. Since much of the added material in Servius auct. derives from the commentary of (probably) Donatus, which was itself a source for Servius (cf. F 5n.), this suggests that Servius may have removed these words, either because he was unaware of the difference between a *tribunus militum* and a *tribunus militum consulari potestate*, or in a conscious correction of Donatus in order to align him with the Livian tradition.

[60] Most probably *Vir. Ill.* has conflated 428, when in one version Cossus won the *spolia opima* as consul and T. Quinctius Cincinnatus was his colleague, with 426, when (in another version) he won them as *magister equitum* under Mam. Aemilius Mamercinus (though Quinctius was consular tribune in that year also).

[61] *Contra* Flower (2000), 44–5 = Richardson and Santangelo (2014), 298, who claims that it was the memorial to the murdered ambassadors that in part accounts for the prominence of Cossus in Roman tradition.

occumbere, a rare phrase used (at most) only seven other times in surviving Latin, three of which are in Livy (1.7.7, 29.18.6, 38.58.6; also Cic., *Tusc.* 1.102, Lucan 4.165, Lact., *Inst.* 5.19.25; *CIL* III 14214 = *ILS* 9107; cf. *TLL* IX.2 380.46–9).[62] P. rewrites Livy using Cicero, while also rewriting Cicero into distinctively Livian Latin.

statuae in rostris positae sunt: Cf. Livy 4.17.6: *statuae publice in Rostris positae sunt*.

4.6 *Cossus wins the spolia opima*. Corresponds to Livy 4.19–20. For this episode see 4.5n.: as discussed there, P. treats it as an isolated event, whereas in Livy it was directly connected to the murder of the Roman ambassadors at Fidenae. P. also removes Livy's narrative of the war surrounding Cossus' exploit; like most others who refer to Cossus' deed, P. is more interested in the fact of his performing the feat than in any of the ancillary details (see further 20.9n., F 14n.). He also apparently ignores the variant tradition that Livy discusses in some detail, concerning Cossus' status when he won the *spolia* (4.20.5–11); this is P.'s usual practice when faced with variants, but see below for some qualifications.

Cossus Cornelius: For the omission of the *praenomen* cf. 4.4n. It is less usual for P. to invert the names, as he does here: in doing so he is adopting a stylistic device that began in the late Republic and which Livy often used, albeit more regularly when naming sources than for characters in his narrative (see Curschmann (1900), esp. 55–61 for Livy). It then came increasingly popular in the first and second centuries AD, but seems to have largely died out by the late Empire (Cameron (1985), 171). Livy does not himself invert Cossus' name anywhere in his narrative: P. is, as often, consciously archaizing.

Cossus Cornelius tribunus militum occiso Tolumnio, Veientum rege, opima spolia secunda rettulit: P. takes his language not from Livy's narrative of Cossus' actual exploit but from the conflation of two subsequent references to it: (1) the introduction to the digression about Augustus and the dispute over Augustus' status, with the alternative tradition which dated it to his consulship (Livy 4.20.5: *A. Cornelium Cossum tribunum militum secunda spolia opima Iovis Feretri templo intulisse*); (2) the reminder of the exploit during Mamercus Aemilius' later dictatorship (4.32.4: *Larte Tolumnio rege Veientium...occiso, spolia opima Iovis Feretri templo intulerit*; cf. 4.8n.)—this being the time when, according to the second alternative tradition, the exploit was actually performed (see 4.5n.).

The person reading P. independently of Livy will simply take the narrative at face value; however, P.'s language gives a nod to the alternative possibilities, which can be recognized by the (presumably small) minority of readers who are

---

[62] Livy 38.58.6, Cic., *Tusc.* 1.102, and Lact., *Inst.* 5.19.25 all have the commoner *mortem* as a variant reading, and this is sometimes accepted by editors, and indeed sometimes read even in the cases where there is no MS support. In all of them, however, the principle of *lectio difficilior* should apply.

acquainted with Livy's text, and the even smaller minority who might know the historical controversy outside Livy.

4.7 *Mamercus Aemilius' reform of the censorship.* Corresponds to Livy 4.24. P. touches on the chief points of Livy's account, although he does not discuss either Aemilius' rationale for making the change (the danger represented by holding office for the long term), or his practising what he preached when he resigned his dictatorship immediately on the law being carried (4.24.6–7). No other historian mentions this event: the only other reference to it is by Livy himself in Book 9 (9.33.4–9, 9.34.6–10), when the precise scope of Aemilius' law became a point of contention at the time of the censorship of Ap. Claudius Caecus (see below).

qui antea per quinquennium gerebatur, anni et sex mensum spatio finit: The phrasing is closer to Livy's later discussion in Book 9 than to the original narrative in Book 4: see esp. 9.33.6: *Mam. Aemilium dictatorem…qui quinquennalem ante et longinquitate potestatem dominantem intra sex mensum et anni coegisset spatium.*

4.8 *Capture, revolt, and recapture of Fidenae.* Corresponds to Livy 4.21.7–22.6, 4.30.5–6, 4.31.7–34.7. P. treats under a single heading three episodes concerning Fidenae which in Livy are separated: the original capture of Fidenae, the sending of colonists there, and the murder of those colonists followed by the defeat and capture of Fidenae. Uniting them in this way makes sense thematically, though it does mean that the first episode is treated out of sequence, since it occurred before Mamercus Aemilius' reform of the censorship (4.7n.; see Bingham 161). The other intervening episodes are omitted altogether, notably domestic scheming over plebeian access to the consular tribuneship and a debate over whether consuls or consular tribunes should be chosen (4.25), which would have complicated P.'s earlier narrative of a smooth transition into the consular tribunate (4.2n.), an account of a drought and the influx of foreign superstitions into Rome (4.30.7–11), and, most significantly, a war with the Aequi and Volsci narrated by Livy at some length (4.26.1–29.7; but see 4.11n.). The last was associated with the story of the dictator Postumius' execution of his son (4.28.5–7), but Livy argues that the latter is unhistorical (similarly D.S. 12.64.3), and it is not P.'s usual practice to include stories that Livy flatly rejects, even though in this case writers in the Roman exemplary tradition appear to have given it more credence (Val. Max. 2.7.6; Gell. 17.21.17, cf. 1.13.7).

As far as the wars with Fidenae go, P. omits all the details of the fighting and the double capture of the city, although these are elaborated by Livy with dramatic vividness: this is not unexpected, given the way P., like others of the Latin summary historians, regularly abridges such wars.[63] P. does, however, mention the

---

[63] Oros. 2.13.10 is almost as laconic; though note Flor. 1.6.7 (cf. Frontin., *Strat.* 2.4.19), who seizes (and expands) on the story of the Fidenates attempting to terrify the Romans by coming from the city armed with torches (cf. Livy 4.33.1–2).

crime with which the Fidenates renewed the war, which Livy explicitly parallels to their earlier murder of the Roman ambassadors (4.31.7; cf. 4.5n.). It is more interesting that, as before (4.5n.), he omits all mention of Veii, which was not only allied with Fidenae throughout, but which actually initiated the war in which they revolted (4.30.4, 4.30.12–31.6). The crimes, punishment, and conquest of Fidenae is, for him, a limited and self-contained story.

eoque: 'And thither'.

quibus occisis Fidenates cum defecissent: Cf. 2.2n.

4.9 *Slave conspiracy.* Corresponds to Livy 4.45.1–2. As with Books 2 and 3, P.'s coverage is very patchy: after the recapture of Fidenae more than a third of Book 4 is still to come, and P. barely touches on any of it (though cf. 4.11n.). He passes over the further disputes concerning plebeian elections to the consular tribunate and the choice between consuls and consular tribunes for election (4.35–36, 4.43.3–12; cf. 4.8n.), and above all an unsuccessful war against the Volsci, culminating in the prosecution of the commander (4.37.3–42.9, 4.44.6–10); he even omits Livy's account, bound up with the dispute over the consular tribunate, of the expansion of the quaestorship (4.43.3–12), a constitutional development of the sort that usually interests him (e.g. 2.8n.). Why he pauses to mention the slave revolt in particular is hard to determine: it is the sort of episode which created anxieties in Romans of all periods, as would be expected in any slave-holding society,[64] but it is still fairly insignificant in Livy's text. As often with minor notices, P.'s selection of episodes for inclusion involves a measure of arbitrariness.

4.10 *Murder of Postumius; salaries given to soldiers.* Corresponds to Livy 4.49.8–50.6, 4.59.10–60.8. Once again (cf. 4.9n.), P. is extremely patchy in his treatment of the last part of the book (though cf. 4.11n.). Among other things, he omits: a war with the Aequi and Labicani, initially unsuccessful because of contentions among the Roman commanders, but with the Romans ultimately victorious after the appointment of a dictator (4.45.4–47.7); several wars with the Volsci (4.51.7–8, 4.58.3, 4.59.1–10, 4.61.3–11); another with the Aequi and the Volsci together (this constantly hindered by class conflict in the city: 4.55.1–57.8); disputes over proposed agrarian laws (4.48, 4.49.11, 4.51.5–6, 4.53.2–7); and a plague and famine (4.52.1–8). Most notably, he omits the start of the war with Veii which will form the major theme of the first half of Book 5 (3.58.1–2, 3.58.6–10, 3.60.9–61.3).

What P. focuses on is two episodes which are separated in Livy's text, but which he implicitly links. In both cases he gives a bare summary of the central points:

---

[64] See e.g. de Ste. Croix (1981), 409–11, and several of the essays in Serghidou (2007), esp. Gamauf (2007). One can, however, overstate the pervasiveness of such anxieties: note the caution of (e.g.) Bradley (2001), McKeown (2007).

the killing of Postumius 'because of his cruelty' (but without saying what precisely Postumius' offence consisted in), and the decision to pay the Roman troops, again without offering any explanation why the decision was taken. However, *tum primum* suggests a connection between the events (see below), even though P. leaves it unexpressed on the surface. According to Livy, while the specific 'cruelty' for which Postumius was killed consisted of brutally executing some of his troops for insubordination, the insubordination was generated by a series of earlier incidents in which he showed contempt for them, starting with his violation of his promise to give the booty from a captured town to the soldiers (4.49.9–10, 4.50.1). The second episode in Livy likewise has as its starting point the distribution of booty, when the commanders who take Anxur turn over the wealth of the town to the soldiers: Livy says that 'this generosity of the commanders first reconciled the people to the senators' (4.59.10: *eaque primum benignitas imperatorum plebem patribus conciliavit*), and then describes the decision to pay the soldiers as a bonus added to that.

Livy does not explicitly connect the generosity of the leaders at Anxur with the ungenerosity Postumius had shown several years earlier, but the prominence of the theme of the soldiers' access to booty in this part of his narrative (see also 4.51.8, 4.53.10, 4.55.8) makes it not unreasonable to read his account in those terms. P., by implying that the response to a mutiny prompted by the 'cruelty' of Postumius was to provide stipends for the soldiers, points to the same link, even though only the small minority of readers who knew Livy's text would be able to appreciate exactly how the two were connected (cf. 4.6n.).

That these events were sometimes read in such a way is suggested by the only other continuous source for them, namely Zonar. 7.20.5–6. Although Zonaras is more sympathetic to Postumius and less to the soldiers than Livy is (there is no suggestion that Postumius acted cruelly, and the soldiers kill not only him, but the quaestor also), he too makes a direct causal connection between the army's violent response to Postumius and the plunder and pay received after the capture of Anxur: the latter is a reward for being willing to abandon their mutiny and return to their duty. Although Zonaras cannot have read Livy's version, he is abridging Dio, who might well have done.

propter crudelitatem: Cf. Livy 4.50.4: *crudelibus suppliciis*; also 4.49.14: *crudeles superbosque adversarios*.

stipendium ex aerario...militibus datum est: Cf. Livy 4.59.11: *stipendium miles de publico acciperet*.

tum primum: P. is, as often, interested in 'firsts' (cf. e.g. 1.B.7n.), but, in addition, he usually uses *tum primum* only when there is a close chronological connection between the event and the one before (see 11.5n.); this passage is one of only two exceptions, where he uses it of events which Livy separated from one another both chronologically and textually. It is, accordingly, likely that he is doing so here precisely in order to imply that the provision of stipends was a direct consequence of the murder of Postumius, even though Livy himself does not present it in those terms (but cf. above).

4.11 *Wars against Italian tribes.*

res praeterea gestas...continet: Cf. 2.16n.

Vulscos et Fidenates et Labicanos: As with the previous two books (cf. 2.16n., 3.10n.), there is a certain arbitrariness about the selection of tribes here. In Livy, the Romans do indeed fight against the Volsci a great deal (4.9.11–10.7, 4.37.3–42.9, 4.44.6–10, 4.51.7–8, 4.58.3, 4.59.1–10, 4.61.3–11); but they are sometimes partnered by the Aequi, who are not mentioned here (4.26.1–29.7, 4.55.1–57.8); the Aequi also fight in partnership with the Labicani (see below). The Fidenates also play a substantial role in the book, but all of those wars have in fact been covered by P. (4.6n., 4.8n.): the only respect in which they might be thought to qualify for a list of 'other things in the book' comes from the fact that P. failed to mention their involvement in the war against Veii in which Cossus won the *spolia opima*.

The final people mentioned is given in the MSS as *Labscos* or *Labascos*; Rossbach and Jal, following a number of the Renaissance MSS, read *Faliscos*, but they too appear only in the book as an ally of Veii in the war in 4.6; and while, given P.'s almost random listings, that would not be objectionable were the text secure, it is manifestly corrupt, and an easier emendation is *Labicanos*, since they do play a role in the book which would otherwise go unmentioned (4.45.4–47.7).

Book 5

5.1 *Year-round campaigning at Veii; cavalry start providing their own horses.* Corresponds to Livy 5.2–7. P. describes the complaints that the tribunes make about being required to be out in the field through the year, but he ignores (at least on the surface: see below) the lengthy—and successful—response to their arguments by Ap. Claudius, which constitutes the bulk of Livy's account (5.2.13–6.17). P.'s narrative, accordingly, is far more slanted towards the plebeian perspective than Livy's had been. Nor does P. make any overt connection between this decision and the cavalry using their own horses, although his language implies at least a chronological link (cf. below): Livy explains that it was the example of the cavalry which finally persuaded the people serving as infantry to be equally unselfish in prosecuting the campaign, whereas P.'s account seems to suggest that the people remained angry and unreconciled to the new circumstances of campaigning.

In this sense P. misrepresents Livy; more broadly, however, Livy's subsequent narrative shows that the reconciliation was only temporary, and the extended campaigning season remained a source of conflict (esp. 5.10.4–9). P. moves directly from the volunteering of the *equites* to the prodigy of the Alban Lake (5.2n.), omitting all of the contentions (and indeed partial military setbacks) that Livy describes in the intervening chapters (5.8–14), but the fact that he leaves the opening salvo of the tribunes unresolved and without response does to some extent give a fair picture of where internal relations at Rome stood when the siege of Veii reached its climax.[65]

tabernacula: Livy refers to them as *hibernacula* (5.2.1), but by the time of P. *hibernaculum* was no longer readily comprehensible: it is never found after the early second century AD, apart from a single instance in Claud., *Pan. Hon. IV* 322, who is presumably archaizing.[66] P. substitutes the commonplace *tabernaculum*, although it creates the misleading impression that this was the first time that Romans had ever used tents, rather than tents designed for winter: he relies on the following sentence to explain its particular significance here, namely that the troops would now be in the field year-round.

---

[65] We can compare the abridged narrative of Plu., *Cam.* 2.5–6, which likewise moves from complaints over winter campaigning to military setbacks to the Alban Lake prodigy, though with an obvious focus on Camillus, who is invisible at this point in P. (as he largely was in Livy), and without any note about the new circumstances affecting the cavalry; Oros. 2.19.1, as one might expect, similarly describes the miseries affecting the Roman army with their new campaign in winter, without suggesting that it had any positive effects. Flor. 1.6.8, by contrast, focuses only on the exceptional efforts undertaken by the Roman army to capture the city, which he implies were entirely voluntary.

[66] There is one possible epigraphic example from the end of the second century AD (*AE* 1995, 1790), but that reading depends on reconstructing the text so as to create an otherwise unattested abbreviation for this word: see the cautious commentary of Laporte (1995), 346.

ea res cum esset nova, indignationem...movit: Cf. Livy 5.2.1: *res nova militi Romano*; however, Livy does not refer to *indignatio* about *nova* in his own voice, but only when Appius Claudius in a speech challenges the reasoning of the tribunes, who appeared to expect that the novelty of military pay (cf. 4.10n.) should come without novel duties (5.4.3: *quonam modo igitur nunc indignari possunt, quibus aliquid novi adiectum commodi sit, eis laborem etiam novum pro portione iniungi?*). While P., as noted above, makes no direct reference to Appius' arguments, his comment that it was novelty that excited the tribunes' indignation signals, certainly to the reader who is aware of Livy's original text, one logical weakness in their case.

This sense of *movere* is commonplace; cf. *OLD s.v. moveo* 16b. *indignationem movere* is, however, a more distinctive phrase: it is found once in Livy (4.50.1), but it is otherwise relatively rare before the fourth century AD, after which it becomes increasingly common.

non dari plebi nec per hiemem militiae requiem: A rough paraphrase of Livy 5.2.7: *militem Romanum...ne hiemis quidem spatio quae omnium bellorum terra marique sit quies arma deponentem*. For *nec = ne...quidem* see *OLD s.v. neque* 2b.

equites tum primum equis suis mereri coeperunt: This is almost word for word from Livy 5.7.13: *tum primum equis suis merere equites coeperunt*. The phrase *tum primum* for P. has, however, an additional implication which is independent of its use by Livy, since it is a function of P.'s text rather than Livy's original: it (correctly) indicates a close chronological relationship between this notice and the one immediately before. See further 11.5n.

5.2 Prodigy of the Alban Lake. Corresponds to Livy 5.15. Crucially, P. omits the sequel (Livy 5.16.8–17.5), in which the Veiian seer's interpretation is confirmed by the Delphic Oracle, and the appropriate remedies are taken; connected with this is that he does not actually say what the interpretation was (sc. that if the Romans drew the water from the lake, they would be able to capture Veii: 5.15.11; cf. 5.16.9, 5.19.1), but moves directly from the prodigy to the dictatorship of Camillus and the fall of Veii. The juxtaposition of the prodigy and the capture of the seer with the capture of the city implies a connection between them, but P.— uniquely among sources for the event[67]—does not describe what that connection might be. The fact that the prodigy was (presumably successfully) interpreted matters more to him than the content of the interpretation.

cum...esset: See 2.2n.

---

[67] None of the other Latin summarizers mentions the prodigy, since they focus solely on the capture of the city. The longer accounts (Cic., *Div.* 1.100, 2.69, D.H., *AR* 12.10–12, Val. Max. 1.6.3 (including Paris' epitome), Plu., *Cam.* 3–4, Zonar. 7.20.7–9) all provide a more or less full indication of what the prodigy signified and how the Romans needed to act in response.

5.3 *Camillus captures Veii.* Corresponds to Livy 5.19.2–23.11, 5.25.4–10, 5.28.1–4. Once again, P. ignores all of the detail of the manner by which Veii was captured, apart from the fact that it was after a ten-year siege—a crucial detail for understanding the significance of Livy's account, since it symbolically links the fall of Veii to that of Troy (see esp. Kraus (1994b)). He does, however, focus on two elements of the aftermath: the transfer of Juno to Rome, and the gift made to Apollo, thus associating Camillus with piety. Livy had done the same, but, unlike P., had included extensive debate and conflict over the latter, with complicating contrasts between the pious Camillus and his less than fully pious fellow-countrymen (see Levene (1993), 187–91). In occluding this, P. reflects the tradition represented by Val. Max. 1.8.3 and 5.6.8, who, far from indicating internal conflict, treats the dedications after the fall of Veii as an exemplary instance of the piety of the state as a whole; similarly D.S. 14.93.2–5 and (apparently) App., *Ital.* 8.1 (Plu., *Cam.* 5–8 is in this respect closer to Livy). Avoiding any mention of the conflict also leads to a slightly misleading order in P.; in Livy, while the vow to send the gift to Apollo is made even before the final attack on Veii (5.21.2), its fulfilment is delayed until after the Faliscan war (see 5.4n.). P. simply attaches it directly to Veii's capture.

In addition, the debates over the gift to Apollo in Livy are bound up with the opening of the debate about a possible move from Rome to Veii (5.24.4–11), a debate which forms an important underlying theme in the book, but which P. ignores completely until its last (though admittedly most significant) appearance: see 5.10n.

Furius Camillus: For the form of the name see 4.4n.

simulacrum Iunonis Romam transtulit: Livy does not use either *simulacrum* or *transferre* in this context: P.'s language is closer to Val. Max. 1.8.3: *simulacrum Iunonis Monetae... in urbem translaturi* (cf. the epitomes of Paris and Nepotianus).

5.4 *Camillus and the Faliscan schoolmaster.* Corresponds to Livy 5.26–7; it is slightly out of the sequence in Livy's narrative (5.3n.). P. reflects the main contours of Livy's account, though as usual eschewing most of the detail: notably, he does not even identify the man who treacherously sought to hand over the children to Camillus as their teacher, nor does he refer to the man's punishment, although those were staple features of the story in every other version (D.H., *AR* 13.1–2, Val. Max. 6.5.1 (incl. Paris' epitome), Frontin., *Strat.* 4.4.1, Plu., *Cam.* 10, Polyaen. 8.7, Dio fr. 24.2–3, Flor. 1.6.5–6, *Vir. Ill.* 23.1–2, Jer., *Epist.* 87.3). He offers only enough to illustrate Camillus' ethically exemplary behaviour; compare the account he gives of the similar story of Pyrrhus' treacherous doctor (13.7n.), where, unlike most sources, he does not identify the traitor by name or give his position.

iustitia: Livy twice pairs *iustitia* with *fides* in describing the reason for the Faliscans' surrender (5.27.11, 5.28.1), but in the later exemplary tradition it was almost always, as here, only the former virtue which was cited: see Val. Max. 6.5.1 (also Paris' epitome), Frontin., *Strat.* 4.4.1, *Vir. Ill.* 23.2 (Plu., *Cam.* 10.6–7 similarly speaks of δικαιοσύνη, and Dio fr. 24.3 of πολέμιος δίκαιος).[68]

5.5 *Suffect censorship.* Corresponds to Livy 5.31.6–7. P. omits Livy's account of fighting with the Aequi (5.28.5–13, 5.29.3–6, 5.31.4), and with Volsinii and the Sapienati (5.31.5, 5.32.1–5), interwoven with further debates about the distribution of the land captured at Veii and the possibility of moving there (5.29.1–3, 5.29.6–30.9: cf. 5.3n.). Throughout this book, P. focuses on the two major themes of the capture of Veii and the Gallic sack (especially the latter), and ignores most things extraneous to them. The reason he nevertheless introduces this relatively minor notice from Livy's text is perhaps in part because it was overtly related, for reasons he explains, to the Gallic sack, but more importantly, because it is the type of constitutional point in which he is regularly interested.

cum alter ex censoribus C. Iulius decessisset, in locum eius M. Cornelius suffectus est. nec id postea factum est, quoniam eo lustro a Gallis Roma capta est: Cf. Livy 5.31.6–7: *C. Iulius censor decessit; in eius locum M. Cornelius suffectus—quae res postea religioni fuit quia eo lustro Roma est capta; nec deinde unquam in demortui locum censor sufficitur.* P. reproduces almost the whole of Livy's notice with only minor verbal changes, notably by succinctly conflating the sense of Livy's final clause into the *postea* earlier in his text, and adding the explanatory *a Gallis*.

5.6 *Exile of Camillus.* Corresponds to Livy 5.32.7–9. Livy juxtaposes it with the omen heard by M. Caedicius (5.32.6–7), but P. reserves that for later (5.11n.). The exile of Camillus is a central part of the dynamics of the story, and could hardly be omitted, but, in accordance with his general tendency to play down Livy's account of internal dissension at Rome in this part of the book (cf. 5.3n.), P. says nothing about the grounds for Apuleius' prosecution, which was over Camillus' treatment of the spoils from Veii. Most other sources include this detail (e.g. Val. Max. 5.3.2a, Plu., *Cam.* 12; cf. *Fort. Rom.* 324E, Flor. 1.17(22).4, Dio fr. 24.4, 24.6; cf. Zonar. 7.22.7–8, Eutr. 1.20.2, *Vir. Ill.* 23.4, Serv., *Aen.* 6.825); but P. is not unique in being uninterested in the precise reasons for Camillus being exiled: other examples include Cic., *Dom.* 86, Julius Paris (abridgement of Val. Max. 5.3.2a), and especially Aug., *Civ.* 2.17 and Oros. 2.19.3, for whom the fact of the exile is merely one sign of the problems Rome was labouring under at this time.

dies ei ab L. Apuleio tribuno plebis dicta esset: Cf. Livy 5.32.8: *die dicta ab L. Apuleio tribuno plebis.*

in exilium abiit: Cf. Livy 5.32.9: *in exsilium abiit.*

---

[68] The main exception is Flor. 1.6.5–6, who refers to *fides* alone. Surprisingly, the closest to Livy is Polyaen. 8.7, who speaks of both εὐσεβεία and δικαιοσύνη.

5.7 *Gauls attack Clusium, then defeat Rome at the Allia, and finally sack the city and murder the elders.* Corresponds to Livy 5.35.4–41.10. Livy moves directly from the exile of Camillus into a long digression about the history of the Gauls' migration into Italy (5.33.2–35.3), prompted by a report (5.33.1) of the embassy from Clusium; P. unsurprisingly omits that background, as irrelevant to his main story. Of the narrative of the sack, he, as usual, touches on the main highlights of the story: the appeal to the Senate from Clusium, the sending of ambassadors, the ambassadors' joining the Clusines in battle, the Gallic defeat of the Romans at the Allia, the retreat to the Capitol when the Gauls take the city, and the killing of the senators. What he fails to mention is, above all, the religious theme, which is central to Livy throughout this book (Levene (1993), 175–203), illustrated in this section in particular by the care the Romans show to preserve their sacred rites as the city is taken (esp. 5.39.10–11, 5.40.7–10; but cf. below). P. also substantially softens the Romans' moral failings, by having the ambassadors alone as the offending parties who prompt an immediate Gallic attack, whereas, for Livy, no less important is the fact that the Gauls, before attacking, send an embassy to Rome to complain, but not only does the Senate refuse to punish the ambassadors, but the people elect them to the consular tribunate, thus involving the whole state in the offence (5.36.8–37.3).

With regard to the second of these, P. is far from unique in implicitly confining the offence that the Romans commit to the actions of certain individuals or groups: it is Livy who is the outlier, in his determination to implicate the entire state (Luce (1971), 273–4, Levene (1993), 194). Plu., *Cam.* 18.1–3 (cf. *Num.* 12.6–7) has only one ambassador fighting, and the Senate and the fetials advocate his surrender, only to be overruled by the people; D.H., *AR* 13.12.1 likewise only has one ambassador, and the Senate delays responding to the Gallic request rather than turning it down outright. D.S. 14.113.4–7, like Plutarch, distinguishes the Senate's response from the people's, and in addition has the ambassadors merely getting caught up in a battle that had begun before they arrived (cf. the slightly different version of Dio fr. 25.1–2). Oros. 2.13.5, like P., confines the offence to the ambassadors alone; Flor. 1.7.6 goes further still, suppressing any sense that the ambassadors at Clusium even were involved in fighting. Only *Vir. Ill.* 23.5–7 has something of the same balance as Livy, both making it explicit that the ambassadors fought the Gauls *contra ius gentium*, and noting that they were not subsequently surrendered to the Gauls (though not explaining why).

In this respect P.'s reworking of Livy follows the contours of the broader historical tradition, rather than reproducing the emphases of the original. The same is not quite as obvious with his passing over the Romans' concern for religion on evacuating the city. This partly centred on a famous anecdote about L. Albinius assisting the removal of the sacred objects, and Plu., *Cam.* 20–1 describes it at even greater length than Livy had; cf. also Val. Max. 1.1.10, Flor. 1.7.11–12; *CIL* VI 1272 = *ILS* 51. But even here, P.'s presentation is not unique to him: both

Vir. Ill. 23.8 and Oros. 2.13.7, like P., have the Gallic massacre of the senators, but not the religious preservations.

cum Galli Senones Clusium obsiderent et legati a senatu missi ad componendam inter eos et Clusinos pacem pugnantes contra Gallos starent in acie Clusinorum: P.'s language is close to that of Oros. 2.19.5: *Galli Senones...cum urbem Clusini...obsiderent, legatos Romanorum, qui tunc conponendae inter eos pacis gratia uenerant, in acie aduersum se uidere pugnantes*: it looks as if one (probably Orosius: see Introduction) is partly dependent on the other.

For the structure of the sentence cf. 2.2n.

ad componendam inter eos et Clusinos pacem: This suggests a more neutral stance on the part of the Romans than Livy had. In Livy the ambassadors were there at the request of the Clusines, to warn the Gauls not to attack Clusium, on pain of coming to war with Rome as well, and it is in part their antagonistic stance that escalates negotiations into violence (5.36.1–5). Oros. 2.19.5 presents their mission in identical terms to P., as does Dio fr. 25.1, who is explicit that the Romans are negotiating peace after refusing direct aid to Clusium. *Vir. Ill.* 23.5 is closer to Livy, as is Flor. 1.7.6, with the crucial difference, however, that he does not have the ambassadors' mission leading them to violence (cf. above).

pugnantes contra Gallos starent in acie Clusinorum: The combination *pugnare* with *stare in acie* looks mildly pleonastic, but there is a distinction between them: the first phrase shows that they were directly engaging in the violence, the second that they were doing so as part of the opposing army (cf. *OLD s.v. sto* 11a).

urbem infesto exercitu petierunt: The MSS vary between *infesto exercitu* and *infesto agmine*. Both are common Livian locutions, but the entire phrase in P. reflects a different passage of Livy: see 3.7.4: *infesto agmine Romanam urbem petentibus*. That might incline one to read *agmine* here, but given that P.'s allusions to Livy are not always verbatim even in the passages he is summarizing directly, and given that *agmine* is only found in the α branch of the MS tradition and not in N or P or the Italian MSS, *exercitu* should be considered more probable *unless* it were demonstrably the case that N and the other MSS were more closely related to each other than to the α MSS; against this see Reeve (1991), 456–7.

cum insignibus honorum, quos quisque gesserat: Cf. Livy 5.41.2: *qui eorum curules gesserant magistratus, ut in fortuna pristinae honorumque ac virtutis insignibus morerentur &c.*; also *Vir. Ill.* 23.8: *in curulibus ac honorum insignibus.*

in vestibulis aedium sedentes: Cf. Livy 5.41.8: *in aedium vestibulis sedentes.* P. has no clear reference to the point which Livy sets out in some detail: that the senators effectively 'devote' themselves to death, and in doing so acquire a quasi-divine aura: contrast Flor. 1.7.14 and *Vir. Ill.* 23.8, where the point is explicit (also the ironical version of Oros. 2.19.7). However, this phrase in Livy comes precisely from the moment where the Gauls are awe-struck at the sight of the senators as though they were gods, and it is worth observing that, unlike in Livy, where the context makes it clear that the *aedium* are the senators' houses, the phrase in P. could equally mean 'in the vestibules of the shrines', where statues would be placed much as they were in aristocrats' houses (cf. Wiseman (1987), 395–6 = (1994), 99–100). Even though the religious undertones to the story are absent on the surface, P. allows them to creep in tacitly through the ambiguity of his borrowed language.

5.8 *Manlius and the geese.* Corresponds to Livy 5.47. P. passes over Livy's narrative of the first part of the Gallic occupation of Rome: the burning of the city, their first assault on the Capitol, Camillus' defeat of them at the head of an army at Ardea (and an accompanying defeat of the Etruscans by Roman troops based at Veii), and Fabius Dorsuo's escape from the besieged Capitol to perform his family rites on the Quirinal (5.42.1–46.3). The omission of the last of these is slightly surprising, since it was a staple anecdote in the exemplary tradition,[69] something which often correlates with P.'s including an episode. His failure to do so here may relate to his general downplaying of the religious side to the story (cf. 5.7n.).

He pauses to take note of the heroic defence of the Capitol by Manlius Capitolinus—not only the most famous story from the time of the Gallic sack, but also the prelude to Manlius' attempted seizure of power in the next book (6.3n.); he does not, however, include either Manlius' reward or the punishment of the guard who allowed the Gauls' approach, although these occupy almost as much space in Livy as the deed itself (5.47.7–10). This omission is not surprising: the story was an immensely popular one, but relatively few of the shorter accounts speak of any aspect of it except the saving of the Capitol itself.[70]

clangore anserum: Livy, too, speaks about the *clangor* of the geese waking Manlius (5.47.4). The word was standard in the anecdote (Colum. 8.13.2, Flor. 1.7.15, *Vir. Ill.* 24.4, Serv. *Aen.* 8.652, Isid., *Orig.* 12.7.52); but this may simply reflect the fact that it was a normal word to use of the sounds of geese in other contexts also (e.g. Plin., *Nat.* 18.363, Amm. 18.3.9: cf. *TLL* III 1262.47–51).

praecipue: This is a fair reflection of Livy's narrative, since he has Manlius playing the central role in the defence, but not the sole defender—he alone is woken by the geese in the first instance and holds off the Gauls, but then is joined by others (5.47.4–5). This is, however, not the view of the majority of the tradition. Some (especially Greek) sources have the geese waking up all of the defenders, though Manlius takes the lead in fighting them off (D.S. 14.116.6–7, D.H., *AR* 13.7.3–8.2, Plu., *Cam.* 27.3–4). Conversely, there is a version of the story where Manlius literally acts alone in his defence of the Capitol: that is the version which

---

[69] Esp. Val. Max. 1.1.11, along with Paris' summary, Flor. 1.7.16, Dio fr. 25.5–6, Ampel. 20.7, Min. Fel. 6.2; also App., *Gall* 6 = Cassius Hemina *FRHist* 8 F 22.

[70] Among the shorter versions, only *Vir. Ill.* 24.4 and Serv. auct., *Aen.* 6.852 refer to Manlius' reward for his actions, though it is found in the fuller narratives of D.H., *AR* 13.8.2–4, Plu., *Cam.* 27.5.

BOOK 5   143

Manlius, in Livy, subsequently uses to promote his own achievements (6.11.5, 6.15.11),[71] and which Livy much later puts into the mouth of another Manlius (38.17.9). It is this version which appears to dominate in much of the tradition, as the defence of the Capitol is ascribed to Manlius alone either explicitly (e.g. Plin., *Nat.* 7.103-4) or, more often, implicitly (e.g. Quadrig. *FRHist* 24 F 3 (*ap.* Gell. 17.2.14), Cic., *Dom.* 101, Virg., *Aen.* 8.652-6, Ov., *Fast.* 6.185-6, App., *Ital.* 9, Flor. 1.7.15, *Vir. Ill.* 24.4). Livy strikes a careful balance between these; P., despite the brevity of his account, is equally careful in reflecting that.

5.9 *Camillus saves Rome.* Corresponds to Livy 5.46.4-11 and 5.48.1-49.7. P. slightly rearranges Livy's order, recounting Camillus' election as dictator only at the time when he arrives to save Rome at the very point of surrender (Livy had narrated it prior to Manlius' defence of the Capitol). In almost all respects (but cf. below), P. follows the outlines of Livy's account very closely: the Romans forced by famine into negotiations, the agreement to pay the Gauls 1,000 pounds of gold to depart, the remarkable appearance of Camillus and his army before the ransom could be paid, and his defeat of the Gauls.

P.'s closeness to Livy is more interesting than it may appear, since this is one part of Roman history where the tradition failed completely to converge on any sort of consensus version. There was no agreement about Camillus' intervention and defeat of the Gauls: the idea that the Romans obtained some sort of victory to compensate for the humiliation of their submission is explicitly or implicitly denied by (e.g.) Plb. 2.18.2-3, 2.22.5 (followed by Plu., *Fort. Rom.* 325F-326A), Just. 28.2.4, 38.4.8, 43.5.8-9, Oros. 2.19.9. Among those who do accept a compensatory victory, some, unlike Livy, had it later, after the Gauls left with their ransom (D.S. 14.117.5, Eutr. 1.20.3, Serv., *Aen.* 6.825, Ruf. Fest. 6.1); one tradition ascribed the recapture of the gold to a much later figure than Camillus (Suet., *Tib.* 3.2), and another gave the victory to the people of Caere rather than the Romans (Str. 5.2.3). There are indeed traces of an even more radical version, in which the Gauls actually capture the Capitol, rather than being held off then bought off.[72] Much of the supposed evidence for this version is extremely flimsy (see esp. Cornell (1986), 247-8), but Lucan 5.27-8 'The Tarpeian seat burned by the torches of the Gauls' (*Tarpeia sede perusta / Gallorum facibus*) and Tert., *Apol.* 40.8 'The Senones seized the Capitol itself' (*ipsum Capitolium Senones occupaverunt*) make sense only on that reading: even if it was not an early tradition, at all events it was an accepted way of recounting the story in the imperial period.

In P., as in Livy, the impetus for the negotiated settlement is primarily the Romans' starvation, though for Livy the Gauls, too, are under pressure because of

---

[71] For Manlius in Livy as a quasi-historian offering alternative versions to Livy's own see Kraus (1994a), esp. 146-51.
[72] So esp. Skutsch (1968), 138-42, (1978), (1985), 405-8; Horsfall (1987); Williams (2001), 144-5; *contra* Cornell (1986), 247-8, Forsythe (2005), 254; cf. Malloch (2013), 356.

a plague in the city; but another version had the Gauls withdrawing because of trouble at home (Plb. 2.18.2–3, followed by Plu., *Fort. Rom.* 325F–326A), while in another popular version the ruse whereby the Romans threw down food to convince the Gauls that they had plenty of supplies (Livy 5.48.4) is successful, as it was not in Livy (so Ov., *Fast.* 6.349–94, Val. Max. 7.4.3, along with Paris' epitome, Lact., *Inst.* 1.20.33; cf. Flor. 1.7.17). Yet another version has the failure to capture the Capitol as making the Gauls simply give up (D.S. 14.116.7), another has the Gallic plague alone, rather than the Romans' lack of food, as the thing which makes the Gauls keen to settle (Plu., *Fort. Rom.* 324D), while Oros. 2.19.9 transfers the plague from the Gauls to the Romans in order to show the straits the latter had come to.

P. is not the only later writer to follow Livy's lead (Plu., *Cam.* 28–9 is identical in almost every relevant respect), but it is still noteworthy that he gives no space for any of the competing versions either by commission or omission. It may be precisely the lack of consensus which led P. to hew to Livy so closely: with no established alternative version, there was less incentive to adjust the original.

coactis...descendere, ut...darent et...emerent: Gronovius, followed by Rossbach, proposed adding *eo* before *descendere*, so as to make *ut...emerent* a final clause dependent on it, rather than being constructed after *coactis*. But this turns *descendere* from a literal to a metaphorical descent in a way that is unlikely for P., who tends to the concrete; the *variatio* in construction, with the switch from an infinitive to an *ut* clause, is unexceptionable (cf. H-S 817).

deinde: Cf. 18.2n.

post sextum mensem: Livy says nothing about the timing of the siege; P. introduces the information from elsewhere. That the Gallic siege lasted for six months is stated by Varro, *Vit. Pop. Rom.* fr. 61 (Riposati) *ap.* Non. p. 498M = p. 800L, Flor. 1.7.15, Oros. 2.19.13; an alternative reckoning gave it as seven months (Plb. 2.22.5, Plu., *Cam.* 28.2, 30.1, Polyaen. 8.7.2). The apparent divergence probably reflects nothing more than dependence on sources with different ways of describing partial months, since the standard account of the Gallic sack had the capture of Rome taking place shortly after the battle of the Allia, which was regularly dated to 18 July in both inscribed calendars and literary sources, including by Livy himself (6.1.11),[73] while the Gauls' departure was dated to 13 February (Plu., *Cam.* 30.1, Pol. Silv., *Fast.* (Degrassi, *Fast. Ann.* 263)). This could equally be interpreted as 'over six months' or 'nearly seven'.[74]

ceciditque: Cf. 2.12n.

5.10 *Proposed move to Veii forestalled.* Corresponds to Livy 5.50.8–55.2. P. omits most of Livy's account of the reconstruction of Rome (5.50.1–7, 5.55.3–5), apart

---

[73] For a full list see Degrassi, *Fast. Ann.* 484–5.
[74] Mommsen (1879), 328, though he is wrong to include Serv. *Aen.* 8.652 under this heading: his 'eight full months' (*octo integris mensibus*) is more likely to be a mere error.

from the building of the shrine to Aius Locutius, which he reserves for later (5.11n.): this may be in part because it is largely focused on religious renewal (cf. Levene (1993), 199), a theme which P. has consistently in this book placed much less emphasis upon than Livy had (cf. 5.7n., 5.8n.). He focuses instead on the episode which forms the climax not only of Livy's book, but of the entire pentad: Camillus' speech advocating that the people remain at Rome rather than migrating to Veii, followed by the omen of the centurion. For P., as for Livy, both of these are separately important: P. does, however, slightly change Livy's account, in as much as for Livy the people are moved by Camillus' speech, but the omen is what is decisive (5.55.1–2), whereas for P. it appears to be the other way round (cf. *Vir. Ill.* 23.10, who mentions only the speech, not the omen). However, although Livy explicitly states that the omen mattered more than the speech to the outcome, the balance of his narrative, with a lengthy and moving speech capped by a brief account of the omen, inevitably gives more emphasis to the former than to the latter. Since P., in accordance with his usual practice, does not give any sense of the content of the speech, he highlights it in a different way, by treating it as more decisive than Livy himself had.

propter incensam et dirutam urbem: *incendo* and *diruo* are a standard pairing in Livy (7.27.8, 9.45.17, 26.13.15, 28.11.9, 31.26.10, 42.54.6), much less common in other authors (but see e.g. *Bell. Hisp.* 16.2, Ascon. *Pis.* 14C, Just. 6.5.8, Serv. auct., *Aen.* 2.507, Oros. 7.9.6): cf. Oakley (1998), 264–5. Although Livy does not use the phrase on this occasion (though cf. 5.49.8 *incensam urbem*), P. summarizes his account in recognizably Livian Latin.

vocis...auditae: Cf. Livy 5.55.2: *qua voce audita.*

manipularibus: Although Livy generally assumes a manipular army (sometimes anachronistically: see esp. Oakley (1998), 452–3), the word *manipularis* is surprisingly uncommon in his work: it appears only at 7.34.15, 25.14.7, and 25.37.10. However, even in the late Republic and Empire, after the manipular army had ceased to exist, the term remained in use to describe a common soldier (see *TLL* VIII 315.57–70),[75] and it is presumably in that spirit that P. uses it (for the only time in his text) here: a word which was still comprehensible, but which captured the flavour of the middle Republic, even if not of Livy in particular.

sta, miles, hic optime manebimus: Livy himself phrases it differently: *signifer, statue signum; hic manebimus optime* (5.55.2); this version is followed by Val. Max. 1.5.1 (also Paris and Nepotianus' summaries) and Plu., *Cam.* 32.2. P. offers a more generic address, to the soldiers to hold their position rather than to a standard-bearer to set down his standard. This account is not unique to him,

---

[75] It also appears to have had a quite different technical military sense in the imperial period, referring specifically to the marines: see *TLL* VIII 315.70–84, and esp. Kienast (1966), 23 (*contra* Starr (1941), 59).

but is found also in Zonar. 7.23.8, where the centurion likewise addresses his troops in these terms (ἐνταῦθα στῆτε ... ἐνταῦθα γὰρ δεῖ ὑμᾶς μεῖναι).

One might indeed hypothesize that P.'s version was the original one: it recalls the phrase *Mars...sta* in the third line of the *carmen Arvale*, an ancient formula evoking Mars as the military protector of borders (see Norden (1939), 149–58). On this reading, the centurion's omen, addressed to a generic Roman soldier, simultaneously could be understood as referring to the war-god remaining with his city. But the allusion could also have been introduced into the story later, since this aspect of Mars remained resonant at least until the early Empire (see Woodman (1977), 278–9, discussing the reference to Mars as *stator* at Vell. 2.131.1). In any case, the religious overtones were probably lost by P.'s time: he is more likely to have preferred this version simply because it represented a tidier omen for the people remaining in Rome.

5.11 *Foundation of shrine*. Corresponds to Livy 5.50.5 (cf. 5.32.6–7). This is the one point where P. offers something of Livy's religious focus when it comes to the Gallic sack; and he does so out of sequence, recording the story neither at the point when the divine voice was originally heard, nor prior to Camillus' speech, the point when Livy records the shrine's foundation (cf. 5.7n., 5.11n.). It is perhaps related to this that he omits any idea of religious flaw or revival on the Romans' part, since, unlike Livy, he does not indicate that the voice was neglected when it originally occurred. He concludes the book with an indication of divine support for Rome, but without Livy's dynamic picture of the correlation of the gods' intervention the fall and rise of Roman virtue.

aedis Iovi: In Livy, as in most other sources (Cic., *Div.* 1.101, 2.69, Varro, *Ant. Div.* fr. 107 (Cardauns) (*ap.* Gell. 16.17.2), Plu., *Cam.* 14.2, *Fort. Rom.* 319A), the shrine is founded to Aius Locutius. The MSS tradition of P., on the other hand, uniformly reads *Iovi Capitolino*. It appears that either P. or his manuscripts are in error; other things being equal, one would be more likely to ascribe it to the latter, and so follow Sigonius in emending *Iovi Capitolino* to *Aio Locutio* (it is not unlikely that a scribe might misread an obscure god as a more popular one). However, there is a complication. Juv. 11.111–16 appears to ascribe the heavenly voice to Jupiter, not to Aius (cf. also Schol. *ad loc.*). This indicates that there was an alternative tradition which associated the voice with Jupiter (perhaps seeing Aius as a particular aspect of him), and that makes it less likely that the appearance of *Iovi* in the MSS of P. is merely a coincidental scribal error: it is more probable that P. is reflecting an alternative tradition.[76] On the other hand, *Capitolino* looks more dubious: nothing in Juvenal supports it, and it is less plausible that P.,

---

[76] This also tells against the suggestion of Heyer (1875), 648, that the *Periochae* has mistakenly transferred the name of Jupiter from the next section of Livy (5.50.6), where the gold rescued from the Gauls is placed in his shrine.

who described the original foundation of the temple of Capitoline Jupiter at 1.B.5 (cf. 2.4), would have offered a competing version of its foundation here. It is more likely to be a scribal gloss (or possibly a misreading of an alternative epithet in P.'s original), and should be deleted.

ante urbem captam vox audita erat adventare Gallos: P.'s phrasing conflates Livy 5.32.6 *vocem noctis silentio audisse clariorem humana, quae magistratibus dici iuberet Gallos adventare* with Cic., Div. 1.101 *non multo ante urbem captam vox exaudita est*; cf. 1.B.2n.

Book 6

6.1 *Wars against Italian tribes*. Once again (cf. 2.16n., 3.10n.), P. experiments with a different approach to summarizing: in this case he puts first, rather than last, the round-up of the wars that he omits in his sequential narrative.

res...prospere gestas continet: See 2.16n., 3.10n.

Vulscos et Aequos et Praenestinos: P. includes no wars in the book apart from those he lists in this opening summary: his detailed narrative touches solely on domestic matters. The Volsci are indeed once again prominent as enemies of Rome: the Romans successfully fight against them alone at 6.2.8–13 and 6.31.3–8, in partnership with the Latins and Hernici at 6.6.4–8.10 and 6.12.1–13.8, with the Latins alone at 6.32.4–11, and with the Praenestines at 6.22.3–24.11; the Praenestines, moreover, fight alone at 6.28.1–29.8. The Aequi, however, are almost entirely absent: they briefly fight at 6.2.14, but their only other appearance is when the Romans engage in a brief punitive raid on their territory (6.4.7–8), which is explicitly said by Livy *not* to be a war. On the other hand, P. does not mention the Latins, who, as well as fighting in partnership with the Volsci, take up the war on their own at 6.33.4–12, nor the wars against the Etruscans *en masse* at 6.3.1–10, 6.4.9–10, and 6.9.7–10.6, nor the Velitri (6.22.1–2, 6.36.1–5), nor the war against the Gauls with which the book concludes (6.42.4–9). All of these are more important than the Aequi in Book 6, yet the Aequi are listed, the others are not.

What is especially odd about the appearance of the Aequi here is that they were the most prominent tribe to have been omitted from the summaries of Books 2, 3, and 4 (2.16n., 3.10n., 4.11n.): yet, having overlooked them there, P. includes them here, despite the minimal role they play in Book 6. One might perhaps hypothesize that it is the very fact of their earlier exclusion that makes P. conscious of the fact that he has previously failed to do them justice as enemies of Rome, and so he needs to give them a nod before they disappear from Livy's narrative altogether, as they now more or less do (Oakley (1997), 411–12, though cf. 9.5n.). However, once again it may be idle to try to find a rationale behind P.'s largely random selections in these listings.

6.2 *Addition of new tribes*. Corresponds to Livy 6.5.8. P. omits not only the wars prior to this (6.1n.), but also Livy's account of further religious actions taken after the Gallic sack (6.1.9–12), and an abortive attempt at agrarian legislation (6.5.1–5). The addition of tribes, however, is a matter of particular interest to him (cf. 2.7n.), and so he takes note of it here.

adiectae sunt: Cf. 1.B.3n., 19.11n.

6.3 *Trial of Manlius Capitolinus*. Corresponds to Livy 6.11.2–10, 6.14.1–17.6, 6.18.1–20.14. Livy's account of Manlius' alleged sedition and trial is notoriously double-edged (Kraus (1994a), esp. 146–7, 197–8, 205–6, 210–12; cf. Oakley (1997), 476–81). He is far from sympathetic to Manlius, describing his actions and words in terms that suggest a dangerous demagogue; yet when it comes to the specifics of the charges against him that lead to his execution, he declines to endorse the validity of the case; moreover, he places a great deal of emphasis on the genuine sufferings of the indebted populace, sufferings which Manlius seeks to alleviate. This sets him apart from most sources, who see Manlius as an aspirant to tyranny who was justly punished (so e.g. Cic., *Sull.* 27, *Dom.* 101, *Rep.* 2.49, *Phil.* 1.32, 2.114, *ad Nep.* fr. 5 (*ap.* Amm. 21.16.13), D.S. 15.35.3, Val. Max. 6.3.1a (also Paris' epitome), Plin., *Nat.* 7.103–4, Plu., *Cam.* 36.2–7, *Quaest. Rom.* 285F, Dio fr. 26, *Vir. Ill.* 24.5–7, Paul., *Fest.* 112L, 135L).

However, Livy's ambiguity is reproduced by a small minority of later writers, who, like him, do not explicitly endorse the charge, and sometimes note the problems that his programme was intended to alleviate (so Ampel. 27.4, Serv. auct., *Aen.* 8.652; cf. App., *Ital.* 9). P. aligns himself with this tradition: not only does he make no comment on the validity of the charge, but he suggests that it was generated simply by Manlius' attempt to help debtors. In that regard he shows himself more sympathetic to Manlius than almost any other writer, including Livy himself.

obstrictos aere alieno liberaret: 'Was freeing those constrained by debt'. The phrase *aere alieno obstringere* is unusual, but there is a precedent with D. Brutus in Cic., *Fam.* 11.10.5 (cf. *TLL* IX.2 253.5–7); more importantly, the fact that the phrase *aere alieno liberare* is relatively common (e.g. Cic., *Fam.* 15.4.2, *Att.* 6.2.4, 14.18.1, *Phil.* 2.35, Sall., *Cat.* 40.4, Gaius, *Dig.* 15.1.27.8, Iavol., *Dig.* 24.1.50 pr.), makes P.'s overall meaning readily comprehensible, even though *aere alieno* in the first instance needs to be taken with *obstringere*, since *obstrictos* cannot by itself mean 'indebted'. Livy never uses either phrase, but he does speak of the centurion rescued by Manlius as *libraque et aere liberatum* (6.14.5): the meaning is quite different, since it is a technical legal phrase ('freed by balance and bronze': see Oakley (1997), 520–1), but P. may be evoking this passage with his language.

Bingham 174 suggests that P. diverges from Livy here: that whereas Livy has only a single person freed by Manlius from debt (namely the centurion at 6.14.3–8), P. (like Flor. 1.17(26).8 and *Vir. Ill.* 24.5) has multiple people rescued. However, while Livy speaks directly only of one person freed, he indicates Manlius had acted similarly to others: he produces at his trial numerous people whom he had helped (6.20.6), and this is also the implication of his putting up his Veian estate for auction precisely for that purpose (6.14.10; cf. 6.17.2), and his use of the plural *singulis* at 6.15.11. Hence P.'s summary of Livy is a reasonable reflection of his text, not an alternative version of the story.

damnatus de saxo deiectus est: Cf. Livy 6.20.12: *sunt qui per duumviros...auctores sint damnatum. tribuni de saxo Tarpeio deiecerunt*. P.'s phrasing is fairly close to Livy's, although the first word in Livy actually appears in a slightly different context.

S. C. factum est: In Livy 6.20.14 this is not a senatorial decree, but a decision made by the *gens*; so also Cic., *Phil.* 1.32, Plu., *Quaest. Rom.* 285F, Dio fr. 26.1, Paul., *Fest.* 135L; also *Vir. Ill.* 24.7 (but see below). Only in P. is it done by the Senate;[77] this may be a straightforward error on his part, or he may have come across it in a now lost version of the story. Most of the (relatively few) known cases of banning particular names to families took place in the late Republic and early Empire, and there the ban is enacted by senatorial decree (see the list at Oakley (1997), 567): it is altogether possible that some author of that time or later read the procedure back into the case of Manlius, instead of the obscure process of a gentile enactment (on which see Minieri (1995), esp. 156–65; cf. Smith (2006), 44–50).

Manli cognomen: This is a clear error: Livy 6.20.14, like Cicero, Plutarch, Dio, and Paulus (refs above), records this as a stricture against the *praenomen* Marcus, not the *cognomen* Capitolinus, and the accuracy of his account is assured by the fact that no subsequent Manlius is known with that *praenomen*, though there are several with the *cognomen* Capitolinus. Accordingly, the Aldine edition corrected the text to *Marco cognomen*, further corrected by Sigonius to *Marco nomen*. However, an identical error to P.'s appears in *Vir. Ill.* 24.7, and it is more likely that P. shared the mistake (indeed, perhaps even that one derived it from the other) than that a later copyist would have introduced it into the MS tradition.

6.4 *The Licinio-Sextian rogation on the consulship*. Corresponds to P. 6.34.1–42.14. P. moves directly from Manlius Capitolinus to the other major episode in Book 6; he omits not only various accounts of wars (see 6.1n.), but also conflicts between the Senate and people over debt relief (6.27.3–11, 6.31.2–4, 6.32.1–2), conflicts which not only replay some of the themes of the Manlius Capitolinus episode, but which form the prelude to the Licinio-Sextian rogations, since the question of plebeian debt leads into complaints about the absence of plebeian magistrates to stand up for their class, and the two issues become intertwined as Licinius and Sextius proceed with their campaign (6.34.1–4, 6.35.1–4, 6.36.11, 6.37.2, 6.39.2, 6.39.10). The issue of land reform, which Livy also binds up with the rest of Licinius' and Sextius' programme, is treated by P. as a separate question (see 6.5n.). At most, both of these may be alluded to implicitly by P. (see below); the question of plebeian access to the priesthoods is not present even implicitly (6.42.2), although Livy presents this as a stepping-stone towards the consulship. Most surprising is P.'s omission of the memorable story of the two daughters of

---

[77] One late MS, F, adds, after *factum est, ne patricii in Capitolio vel arce habitarent, et gens Manlia statuit*. This solves the problem very neatly, and the omission would be explained, equally neatly, by the scribe's eye jumping from one *ne* to the other. However, the text as printed here appears across all branches of the MS tradition, showing that F cannot be preserving the archetypal reading. Thus this additional phrase must be a supplement, presumably derived from Livy 6.21.13–14, by a scribe who noticed the inconsistency. As an emendation it is ingenious and plausible, and a solution along these lines cannot be ruled out, but it is on balance slightly more probable that P., as often, was simply offering a different version of the story.

M. Fabius Ambustus, one married to a patrician, one to a plebeian, a story which in Livy (as also in Dio fr. 29; cf. Zonar. 7.24.8) gives an intensely personal dimension to the question of plebeian consulships (6.34.5–11: cf. Kraus (1991)).

Instead of Livy's complex and wide-ranging account, P. homes in on the single issue of plebeian consulships, which he treats as something entirely self-contained, along with the unique (and unlikely: see von Fritz (1950), 8–10) political arrangement prior to it—the five-year period in which (supposedly) no curule magistrates were elected. This fits his consistent interest in constitutional innovations; it is also in accord with this interest that the final resolution of the story, with the election of the first plebeian consul, is much more clearly a highlight for him than it is for Livy, who unexpectedly treats it as something of an afterthought at the end of his book (6.42.9–11).[78] The balance of the narrative in Plu., *Cam.* 39, 42 is in this respect much closer to P., although Plutarch's inevitable focus on Camillus, both as a participant in the anti-plebeian conflict and as the ultimate promoter of reconciliation, gives his account a very different flavour.

C. Licinius et L. Sextius tribuni plebis legem promulgaverunt ut consules ex plebe fierent qui ex patribus creabantur: Cf. Livy 6.35.4–5: *creatique tribuni C. Licinius et L. Sextius promulgavere leges…tertiam, ne tribunorum militum comitia fierent consulumque utique alter ex plebe crearetur.* P. distils his summary from a section in which Livy recounts a series of proposals by Licinius and Sextius: not only the proposal over the consulship, but also debt relief and land reform. P. gives a nod to his omissions which can be recognized by the reader of Livy, although the majority of readers, with no access to Livy's text, will be unaware of them.

P.'s presentation of the law, however, involves a significant adjustment to Livy's version. Whereas, for Livy, the proposed law stated that one consul *must* be plebeian, P. seems only to suggest that consuls *may* be plebeian. (For *ut* + subjunctive used of a circumstance that is permitted but not required by the law cf. e.g. August., *R.Gest.* 14.1 *ut interessent consiliis publicis decrevit senatus*, where Augustus clearly cannot mean that Gaius and Lucius *must* be present at all senatorial meetings, but only that they *may*.)

Livy's account is supported by some other sources (Plu., *Cam.* 39.1, *Vir. Ill.* 20.1), but the bulk of the tradition presents the reform in a version closer to P.'s, allowing but not demanding plebeian consuls at every election (so Val. Max. 8.6.3, Gell. 17.21.27, Ampel. 25.4, Zonar. 7.24.13). Livy's version is admittedly the fullest, but leads to a notorious historical crux, since he himself records consular colleges in which there were no plebeians in several years after the law was passed (355, 353, 351, 349, 345, 343), though he does himself explain the discrepancy, by recording a challenge to the first of these consulships which was overruled on legalistic grounds (7.17.12–13; cf. Pompon., *Dig.* 1.2.2.26). P.'s version has the

---

[78] For the narrative games that Livy is playing here, with his refusal of a grand resolution to the conflict, see esp. Kraus (1994a), 330; cf. also Levene (1993), 210–11.

advantage of circumventing the problem, and may well even be historically correct.[79]

As to why P. elevated this version over Livy's, his concern is typically for the development of Roman institutions rather than precise questions of Roman constitutional law. Hence it is not surprising that he would prefer a version of the law which corresponded to the change that was actually made, not the change that Livy suggests should theoretically have resulted but in fact did not.

eamque cum magna contentione repugnantibus patribus...pertulerunt: Almost identical language is used by P. of the passing of the *lex Canuleia* in 4.1 (see *ad loc.*). Here too, Livy does not use *legem perferre* specifically of the passing of the law concerning the consulship, though it appears twice in the broader context of Licinius' and Sextius' measures (6.39.11, 6.42.2).

cum idem tribuni plebis per quinquennium soli magistratus fuissent: Although P.'s broad point reflects Livy (6.35.10: *Licinius Sextiusque tribuni plebis refecti nullos curules magistratus creari passi sunt; eaque solitudo magistratuum et plebe reficiente duos tribunos...per quinquennium urbem tenuit*), the summary is misleading in various ways. First, he implies that Licinius and Sextius were literally the only elected magistrates in the state, but Livy makes it clear that the remaining eight tribunes, and moreover the plebeian aediles, were also elected (6.35.9–10; cf. 6.36.7). Second, he implies that the passing of the law on the consulship immediately succeeded the five-year anarchy, but, at least on Livy's chronology, a further five years interceded before the tribunes finally achieved their end.

These errors are not unique to him: Zonar. 7.24.9–10 both implies that Licinius and Sextius were alone in their office, and directly states that the anarchy was brought to an end by Camillus' dictatorship in 367, after which the law was passed. Zonaras is summarizing Dio, and, while Dio's account does not survive complete, fr. 29.5–6 relates to the dictatorship of P. Manlius Capitolinus in 368. This suggests that Dio, like Livy, had a more extended chronology, which Zonaras, like P., compresses by omitting most of the stages between the anarchy and the final settlement. Rather than reflecting a separate tradition about the period, it appears more likely that the two summarizers independently saw compression of the chronology (and indeed the personnel) as a natural reflex when shaping their story.

---

[79] That the Licinio-Sextian law, contrary to what Livy states, allowed, but did not require, one plebeian consul, has often been proposed. For various accounts of how this might be reconciled with Livy's version see e.g. von Fritz (1950), 28, 32–3 (the requirement for a plebeian consul applied in the first year only); Staveley (1954), 208–11 (the law referred to consuls as 'praetors', and could thus be fulfilled by electing a plebeian to the new office of praetor (7.1n.)—the problem being that no plebeians are certainly known to have been praetors in this period); Richard (1979) (the historical tradition read back into the Licinian-Sextian law the provisions of the *lex Genucia* in 342). (Surprisingly, none of these supports their argument with reference to the manifest existence of an alternative tradition about the Licinian-Sextian law, as represented by a majority of the post-Livian sources.) Livy's account, with the law passed in more or less the terms he states, but then ignored in certain years, is accepted as likely or at least possible by (e.g.) Develin (1979a), 9–11, (1985), 176–85, Forsythe (2005), 266.

primus ex plebe consul L. Sextius creatus est: Cf. Livy 6.42.9: *L. Sextius de plebe primus consul factus.* For P.'s general interest in 'firsts' cf. 1.B.7n.

6.5 *Law limiting holding of land.* Corresponds to Livy 6.35.5, 6.39.2. P. introduces this notice out of sequence, since the law was passed prior to the law concerning the consulship. However, Livy presents it only briefly, and it is not altogether unreasonable, given that P.'s main interest is in the constitutional innovation that took place over the consulship (cf. 6.4n.), for him to separate this provision out and treat it as an afterthought to the main struggle. Doing so has one additional narrative effect: by placing it as a separate item at the end of the book, he prepares the reader for its aftermath in Book 7, where Licinius is convicted of violating his own law (see 7.7n.).

altera lex, ne cui plus quingentis iugeribus agri liceret possidere: Cf. Livy 6.35.5: *alteram...ne quis plus quingenta iugera agri possideret.* While P.'s *altera* makes this law second to the law on the consulship, in Livy the first law in the list is the one concerning debt, which P. passes over (the consular law is mentioned third): once again (cf. 6.4n.) P. uses Livy's language in a manner which, for the reader of Livy, draws attention to what he is passing over.

Book 7

7.1 Creation of the praetorship and the curule aedileship. Corresponds to Livy 7.1.1. Livy had actually referred to the creation of these offices at the end of the previous book (6.42.11, 6.42.13–14), but he reintroduces them at very opening of the new book, and in addition names their first holders (7.1.2), and P., accordingly, reserves his notice for this point.

duo novi magistratus adiecti sunt, praetura et curulis aedilitas: See Livy 7.1.1: *annus…insignis novis duobus magistratibus, praetura et curuli aedilitate*. For *adiecti sunt* see 1.B.3n.

7.2 Plague; death of Camillus. Introduction of theatre to Rome. Corresponds to Livy 7.1.8–2.13. P. summarizes the main outline of Livy's story: the plague, the death of Camillus, and the attempt to rectify it through 'new rites', and, in particular, the introduction of theatrical performances. However, he passes over the earlier attempt to solve the problem with a *lectisternium*—the third in Roman history, according to Livy (7.2.2), but thirds are much less interesting to P. than firsts. Nor, perhaps more surprisingly, does he have the final attempt to resolve the religious crisis via the ceremony of driving in a nail (7.3.1–8), though the aftermath of this, the attack on the dictator L. Manlius, is treated by P. under a separate heading (see 7.3n.). His interest in the remedies adopted by the Romans to the plague is above all, as often, in the possibility it offers to record an innovation, namely the beginning of Roman drama.

pestilentia civitas laboravit: *pestilentia laborare* is not used by Livy here, but is a standard phrase: see Livy 1.31.5, and cf. *TLL* VII.2 806.74–5.

eamque insignem fecit mors Furi Camilli: Cf. Livy 7.1.8: *eam pestilentiam insignem mors…M. Furi fecit*. For the form of name used, see 4.4n.

novas religiones: Livy elsewhere in his work twice uses the phrase *nova religio* (25.12.2) or *novae religiones* (30.2.9). In both cases, however, he appears to mean something rather different from P. Both of Livy's uses should be understood as 'new religious scruples' or 'new religious awe/fears'.[80] P., however, in context must mean 'new religious rites' (cf. *OLD s.v. religio* 9b). The phrase in this sense is not found before later antiquity, where it appears only in pejorative contexts (cf. Lact., *Epit.* 23.4, Arnob., *Nat.* 1.24.3, Serv., *Aen.* 8.187).[81] It is, accordingly, not unreasonable to assume that P. is importing similar overtones here, and that by this phrase he intends to capture something of Livy's hostility towards the theatre, which Livy

---

[80] *OLD s.v. religio* 2 and 6 respectively: I am not convinced that the *OLD* is correct to treat these as separate senses of the word.

[81] Note, however, that Val. Max. 2.4.4, recounting the origins of theatre in somewhat Livian terms, speaks of it having its origins in *exquisito et novo cultu religionis*.

treats as problematic from the start, since it is the result of *superstitio* (7.2.3, cf. 7.3.1: see Levene (1993), 212–13) and develops into something even more highly undesirable (7.2.13). Cf. also Aug., *Civ.* 1.32 (followed by Oros. 3.4.4–5), who, from his overtly Christian perspective, is even more explicit that the introduction of theatre was a blight on Rome.[82]

tunc primum: See 4.2n., 11.5n.

7.3 T. Manlius prevents the prosecution of his father. Corresponds to Livy 7.3.9–5.7. The anecdote was relatively popular (Cic., *Off.* 3.112, Val. Max. 5.4.3, 6.9.1 (both with Paris' summary), Sen., *Benef.* 3.37.4, App., *Sam.* 2, *Vir. Ill.* 28.1–2): the key aspect of it in almost every version, as in P., is the contrast between the dramatically violent way in which the son threatens the tribune on his father's behalf, and the fact that among the charges the tribune was bringing against the father was the mistreatment of the son. Livy, as often, uses this for intricate moral reflections: the son's behaviour was 'praiseworthy for its dutifulness, although not a good precedent for a citizen' (7.5.2: *quamquam non civilis exempli, tamen pietate laudabile*), and indeed is the consequence of his 'unrefined...and rustic spirit' (7.5.2: *rudis...atque agrestis animi*), something caused by the very maltreatment by his father to which the tribune objected; moreover, it relates in complex ways to Manlius' later violent behaviour in this book and the next (cf. Oakley (1998), 83–4). P., however, like every other source, treats it as an entirely praiseworthy episode:[83] Manlius behaves with exemplary loyalty towards his father, despite his father's maltreatment of him.

dies L. Manlio dicta esset a M. Pomponio tribuno plebis: Cf. Livy 7.4.1: *dies Manlio dicitur a M. Pomponio tribuno plebis*.

propter dilectum acerbe actum: Cf. Livy 7.3.9: *dilectu acerbo iuventutem agitavit*; also 7.4.2: *acerbitas in dilectu*. Although Livy is clear that this was a major factor in the popular resentment against Manlius, he does not explicitly state that this formed part of the tribune's charges against him, nor does any other source except P. claim this—the only other sources that mention specific charges apart from the maltreatment of his son are Cic., *Off.* 3.112 and Val. Max. 5.4.3, both of whom refer to his illegally extending his dictatorship, something about which Livy says nothing. P. may have access to an alternative tradition, but more probably he is simply inferring from Livy that this was an actual charge.

---

[82] For Augustine's attack on the theatre see e.g. Dox (2004), 11–29; also Barish (1981), 38–65, contextualizing it in relation to earlier Christian thought and broader Roman assumptions about acting. Such critiques predated Christians, as can be seen in Livy's own hostility, and non-Christians in the fourth century sometimes shared the Christians' concerns (see esp. Jul., *Ep.* 304B–D). On the other hand, the theatre continued to be immensely popular, including among Christians, and doubtless many saw the objections to it by intellectuals as merely carping. See Cameron (2011), 789–91.

[83] It is, for example, explicitly referred to as a *praeclarum exemplum* by Val. Max. 5.4.3.

rus relegatum: The phrase is not from Livy, but variants of it often come up with Manlius' story: so Val. Max. 6.9.1 (also Paris' epitome), *Vir. Ill.* 28.1, cf. Cic., *Off.* 3.112 (*relegasset et ruri habitare iussisset*); for other examples of the phrase cf. Cic., *S. Rosc.* 46, Oros. 5.16.8.

sine ullo crimine: Livy (in the mouth of Pomponius) says *nullius probri compertum*, but goes on to explain that the reason his father treated him in this way is the younger Manlius' lack of eloquence and dullness of wits (cf. Val. Max. 6.9.1, Sen., *Benef.* 3.37.4, *Vir. Ill.* 28.1). P. is not interested in any explanation which might get in the way of the simple moral he is drawing: cf. Val. Max. 5.4.3, where the young man is described as being 'of outstanding character' (*optimae indolis*: Paris' summary goes further, and says that he was sent to the country despite being *aptum militiae*); also App., *Sam.* 2, where his mistreatment is explained by his father's being a 'miser' (μικρολόγος).

cuius relegatio patri obiciebatur: The phrase is strictly speaking superfluous: the story would be perfectly comprehensible without it. By including it, P. accentuates the paradox of Manlius' virtuous act: he supported his father against the tribune even though the tribune was notionally acting in his support.

in cubiculum tribuni: Livy does not state that the scene took place in a *cubiculum*. However, the tribune is seated on a *lectus* (7.5.5), and while this could refer to furniture in a dining context (cf. e.g. Varro, *Ling.* 9.47), the fact that the *cubiculum* prototypically contained a *lectus*, was regularly used for meeting visitors, and was in particular the natural place for a meeting without witnesses (cf. Riggsby (1997), 41–51), would make this a reasonable inference by P.; alternatively, he could have taken the location directly from some other version of the story (Val. Max. 5.4.3 explicitly refers to the location as a *cubiculum*): cf. Bingham 178.

strictoque gladio: In Livy 7.5.3 and 7.5.5 the weapon is a *culter*, not a *gladius*, perhaps because it is more suited to concealment, or because it reinforces the point about Manlius' rustic upbringing if he carries a blade that might be in anyone's hands rather than the weapon of a Roman soldier.[84] It is, however, a *gladius* in every other version of the story (Cic., *Off.* 3.112, Val. Max. 5.4.3 (also Paris' epitome), Sen., *Benef.* 3.37.4, *Vir. Ill.* 28.2), and P. follows that here.

in verba sua iurare: 'To swear to his dictation' (*OLD s.v. iuro* 5a). Livy 7.5.5 has the less formulaic *in quae ipse concepisset verba iuraret* (cf. also 7.5.6 *adiurat in quae adactus est verba*).

non perseveraturum in accusatione: *perseverare in* is common at all periods of Latin (cf. *TLL* X 1700.65–1701.30), but *perseverare in accusatione* is found only in writers of later antiquity, primarily as a convenient summarizing phrase used by

---

[84] For the cultural associations of the *culter* see Ov., *Trist.* 5.7.19–20; also e.g. Livy 1.58.11, 3.48.5 (cf. 3.8).

commentators (e.g. Eugraph., *Ter. Andr.* 642, 663, Mar. Victorin., *In Gal.* 1180A, Jer., *In Ier.* 5.42).

7.4 Self-sacrifice of Curtius. Corresponds to Livy 7.6.1–6. This is a well-known story,[85] but one which Livy narrates in an unusual way: he says nothing about the chasm closing up after Curtius threw himself into it, nor does he indicate that the object of Curtius' self-sacrifice was to close it; instead Curtius acts in response to a prophecy saying that this would allow Rome to survive in perpetuity (see Levene (1993), 213–15). In this respect P.'s account is closer to the one that is relayed in most other sources (e.g. Procilius, Valerius Maximus, Pliny, ps.-Plutarch, Orosius, Suidas), emphasizing the miraculous closing of the chasm, but saying nothing about any meaning the prodigy might have had for Rome.

More distinctive is P.'s presentation of the story, which is surprisingly indirect. He assumes, rather than describing, the opening of the chasm,[86] and offers no explanation for why the Romans were attempting to fill it in this fashion. The reader who came to this without knowing anything of the story might well be puzzled; only existing knowledge of the story—or a very acute piece of inference—would allow one to see that P. is alluding to, without mentioning explicitly, an important premise found in Livy (and others: see e.g. Dionysius of Halicarnassus, Valerius Maximus, Ampelius, ps.-Plutarch, Augustine, Zonaras, Suidas), namely that the Romans received an oracle that they should close the chasm by throwing into it the most precious thing in the city—the answer to the riddle, of course, being that the courage of Curtius was the most precious thing that Rome possessed. Nor does he offer the story as the aetiology for the Lacus Curtius in the Forum, unlike Livy 7.6.6.[87]

Still more distinctive, however, is that the version of the story which P. is not narrating in detail, but allows the reader to recognize or infer, is not Livy's. Livy does not suggest that there was any real debate on the question of what precious object the Romans should use—Curtius comes up with the answer immediately. P., on the other hand, seems to assume a version in which the Romans are misled into trying various other sorts of precious objects before arriving on the right

---

[85] e.g. Procilius fr. 1P (in Varro, *Ling.* 5.148), D.H., *AR* 14.11, Val. Max. 5.6.2 (with Paris' epitome), Plin., *Nat.* 15.78, Ampel. 20.9, ps.-Plu., *Par. Min.* 306F–307A (= Aristides of Miletus, *FGrH* 286 F 11), Min. Fel., *Oct.* 7.3, Aug., *Civ.* 5.18, Oros. 3.5, Drac., *Laud. Dei* 3.407–13, Zonar. 7.25.1–6, Suid. Λ 491 (Adler).

[86] Some late MSS add an explanatory opening phrase: *cum telluris hiatu tota ad ultimum territa patria foret*; without accepting that, but adopting similar reasoning, Gronovius hypothesized a lacuna. However, P.'s carefully descriptive phrasing (*praealtam voraginem urbis Romanae*) presupposes that this was the first time he has mentioned the chasm; the MSS presumably represent an explanatory addition by a later copyist who was troubled by the anomalous narrative.

[87] This is less unusual, however: the aetiology is similarly omitted by (e.g.) Valerius Maximus, ps.-Plutarch, and Zonaras.

answer:[88] this story otherwise appears only in Dionysius of Halicarnassus, ps.-Plutarch, and the Suda. This is not the only time that P. assumes an unusual version of a story in which the Romans are misled by an oracle (see 11.2n.): it appears to be a story-pattern in which he had a particular interest, and which he liked offering tacitly as a minor puzzle to his readers.

praealtam voraginem: Livy himself refers to the chasm as a *vorago* (7.6.2); moreover, *praealta vorago* is a phrase he uses twice elsewhere (22.2.5, 44.8.6), albeit of eddies in water rather than of chasms in the ground. It is not found elsewhere in Latin: P., as often, writes in recognizably Livian Latin even when he does not draw on the specific passage of Livy.

in eam Curtius armatus sedens equo praecipitavit: Cf. Livy 7.6.5: *equo... insidentem, armatum se in specum immisisse.*

explet at: The MSS show a lot of confusion here. N and B both read *explet at*; while P (along with some of the Italian MSS) has *expleta*, and the α MSS read *exiit*; none of these are acceptable. The general sense is clear—the chasm was filled up after Curtius' self-sacrifice, but something is wrong with the Latin. *explet at* may have arisen from Manlius' *praenomen* in the next sentence, where the MSS wrongly read *Lucius*: it is likely that *expleta. T. Manlius* was corrupted to *expletat. Manlius*, and that *Lucius* was then mistakenly inserted as the *praenomen*. But since the bare *expleta* is hardly acceptable either, there must have been an earlier stage of corruption in which something dropped out: some late MSS read *et expleta est*; the Aldine edition read *eaque expleta est*, while Weissenborn offered *ita expleta*. Weissenborn's suggestion is the best from the point of view of explaining the corruption (haplography after *praecipitavit*), but P. does not elsewhere use *ita* as the equivalent of *itaque*, and the baldly laconic phrase is unlike his manner. The other proposals are further from the text and it is hard to choose between them. Accordingly, I have preferred to obelize.

7.5 Manlius and the Gaul. Corresponds to Livy 7.9.3–10.14. Prior to this, P. omits Livy's account of a war against the Hernici (7.6.7–9.2: but see 7.13n.), a war which (on Livy's account: see 7.6.8) was the first time a plebeian consul, namely L. Genucius, had conducted a war under his own auspices. P.'s general interest in 'firsts' (1.B.7n., 11.5n.) might make it seem surprising that he omitted it; on the other hand, Genucius' achievement is undercut by the fact that he is actually unsuccessful in the war, and his primary significance in Livy is that he becomes the occasion of carping by the patricians against his right to hold the consulship at all. P. is less interested in class conflict than Livy was, and after the Licinio-Sextian

---

[88] Cf. Langlands (2018), 51–2 on the Curtius story 'dramatising the realisation that true value lies not (only) in money and material wealth, but primarily in Rome's military power, which in turn depends of the soldiers themselves and on their courage and motivation'. The version which is assumed here accentuates that point.

laws (6.4n.) the issue largely disappears from his narrative, though it certainly does not from Livy's.

Instead, he moves on to the famous account of Manlius Torquatus' duel with a Gaul: an immensely popular story in the Latin tradition, though, oddly, barely present in surviving Greek sources.[89] The only full account apart from Livy's own, however, is a well-known fragment of Claudius Quadrigarius (*FRHist* 24 F 6). For the rest, the story is invariably distilled into at most three points, all of which are present in P.: (1) Torquatus' killing of the Gaul in single combat, (2) his taking the torque from his fallen enemy, which (3) becomes the origin of his *cognomen*. The fame of the story ensured its constant repetition as a brief anecdote, but the points of interest in it did not lend themselves to much variation,[90] nor did it have a great deal of traction as an exemplary model: it is interesting, for example, that Valerius Maximus only mentions the story in passing (3.2.6: even that reference is dropped by Paris in his summary).

adulescens: Livy does not describe Torquatus as an *adulescens* at the time of the duel, but had done so when he saved his father from prosecution (7.5.8: cf. 7.3n.), which he recorded in the previous year.

qui patrem a tribunicia vexatione vindicaverat: Cf. Livy 7.10.2: *qui patrem a vexatione tribunicia vindicaverat*: P., like Livy, explicitly makes the connection with the story mentioned not long before, perhaps in part because, until Manlius gets his *cognomen*, the name alone is not sufficiently distinctive.

contra Gallum provocantem aliquem ex militibus Romanis in singulare certamen descendit: Cf. Eutr. 2.5: *provocantem Gallum ad singulare certamen progressus occidit*.

descendit is omitted in the major MSS, but added by some of the later ones. While it is possible that P. used another verb (Rossbach hypothesizes *processit*, on the basis of Livy 7.26.2), Livy regularly uses phrases of the form *descendere in* as part of his battle descriptions; see Oakley (2005a), 159, and cf. F 23.8n. Admittedly, *descendere in certamen*, while classical, is not Livian (cf. *TLL* V.1 649.14–17), but Livy on one occasion in his surviving text uses the closely related *descendere ad certamen*—namely 7.14.6, not long after the passage here. It is not improbable (cf. above) that P. constructed his narrative using language that in general form, if not necessarily in all detail, recalls Livy.

torquem aureum detraxit: Cf. Livy 7.10.11: *corpus…uno torque spoliavit*. Livy does not specify that the torque was gold; but it is in Flor. 1.8(13).20, whose

---

[89] There are just two passing references: by Plu., *Mar.* 1.3 (= Posidon. fr. 264 (Edelstein-Kidd)), as part of a discussion of Roman names, and Zonar. 7.26.4, where it is mentioned at the time of Torquatus executing his son (cf. 8.2n.), though the latter alludes to it as something known, probably indicating that Dio had told the story in its chronological sequence.

[90] The partial exception is Oros. 3.6.2, who uses it as an illustration of Roman brutality: but he does so largely by omitting everything that made it distinctive (*atrocissimam pugnam Manlius Torquatus singulariter inchoavit*).

language appears to be closely related to P.'s (*singulari certamine Manlius aureum torquem barbaro inter spolia detraxit*); also Plin., *Nat.* 33.15, Gell. 9.13.3, Eutr. 2.5, Amm. 24.4.5. This presumably represents plausible expansion by the historical tradition, since Gallic torques were stereotypically golden (e.g. D.S. 5.27.3, Livy 24.42.8, 33.36.13 (= Val. Ant. *FRHist* 25 F 38), 36.40.12, 44.14.2, Str. 4.4.5, Quint., *Inst.* 6.3.79, Flor. 1.20.4, Justin. 43.5.7; cf. *CIL* XII 354 = *ILS* 3855).

7.6 *Addition of new tribes.* Corresponds to Livy 7.15.11. P. is, as ever, interested in the expansion of the tribes (cf. 2.7n.); prior to this, he has omitted a number of wars that Livy had described (but cf. 7.13n.). The most extensive is a renewed war with the Gauls under the command of C. Sulpicius Peticus (7.12.7–15.8): this is recounted by Livy in some detail, and receives a notice in various of the other later historians (Eutr. 2.5, Oros. 3.6.2; cf. *Vir. Ill.* 28.3, App., *Gall.* 1), but P., by comparison with these, has less of an interest in wars and more in domestic affairs (none of these mentions the addition of the tribes here, for example). He also omits Livy's brief notices of wars with the Tiburtines and Gauls (7.11.2–8), the Hernici (7.11.8, 7.15.9), the Tiburtines alone (7.11.10–12.4), the Tarquinienses (7.12.5–6, 7.15.9–10—the latter a Roman defeat); also incursions by the Privernates and Veliterni (7.15.11).

adiectae: Cf. 1.B.3n., 19.11n.

7.7 *Prosecution of Licinius Stolo.* Corresponds to Livy 7.16.9. Prior to this, P. omits a number of small notices of financial and legal measures (7.15.12–16.1, 7.16.7–8), as well as a war against the Privernates (7.16.3–6; but see 7.13n.). The prosecution of Stolo, however, though only referred to briefly by Livy, is of interest to him, because it forms an ironic aftermath to the Licinian-Sextian laws, which he recounted at the end of the previous book (cf. 6.5n.); the prosecution is similarly appended to the description of the laws at Plu., *Cam.* 39.5 and *Vir. Ill.* 20.3–4, and the fact of Licinius suffering under his own law elsewhere forms the basis of a moralizing anecdote in its own right (Val. Max. 8.6.3 (with Paris' epitome), Plin., *Nat.* 18.17, Colum. 1.3.11; cf. D.H., *AR* 14.12). Most of these, like Livy, have some reference to the device by which Licinius tried to circumvent the law (transferring the excess property to his son after emancipating him): P. (along with Columella and Plutarch) does not—the fact of the prosecution matters more to him than the legal question.

Licinius Stolo lege sua damnatus est: The MSS tradition here reads *lege lata* (or *lege data*), but that leads to a narrative oddity. For the anecdote to work, the reader has to recognize that this figure is the same one who passed the law in the first place; but he was referred to by P. as *C. Licinius* (6.4), and was not even named in the same sentence as the one in which the law was recounted; moreover, *lege lata* is an uncomfortably bald way of describing a law that had been passed some years earlier. Accordingly, Jahn emended the text to read *lege sua*, as in

Livy 7.16.9: *C. Licinius Stolo...sua lege damnatus est*; an alternative, proposed by A. J. Woodman *per litteras*, would be *lege ⟨a se⟩ lata*; along the same lines the *editio princeps*, followed by most other early editors, reads *lege ab ipso lata*.

quod plus quingentis iugeribus agri possideret: Livy does not repeat the terms of the law at this point, but P. does, using identical language to his (and Livy's) original account (see 6.5n.), thus confirming that the law at issue was the same. P., like Livy in the parallel passage (7.16.9), places the charge against Stolo in the subjunctive, reporting the allegation without vouching for its validity.

7.8 *Valerius and the Gaul*. Corresponds to Livy 7.26.1–12. Prior to this, P. omits a long series of wars (though cf. 7.13n.). The longest of these is once again (cf. 7.6n.) against the Gauls (7.23.2–24.10); there are others against the Tarquinienses and the Faliscans, extending throughout Etruria (7.17.2–9), the Tarquinienses alone (7.19.1–3, 7.22.4–5), against the Tarquinienses and the Caerites (7.19.6–20.8), the Tiburtines (7.19.1), the Faliscans (7.20.9, 7.22.4–5), and raids by Greek pirates (7.25.4, 7.25.12). On the domestic front P. omits conflicts between patricians and plebeians over the application of the Licinian-Sextian laws (7.17.10–18.10, 7.21.1–4, 7.24.11–25.2; cf. 6.4n.) and moves to debt relief (7.21.5–8): his interest in class conflict largely ceased once the Licinian-Sextian laws have passed (cf. 7.5n.). More important, in the light of the later narrative, is that he passes over Livy's brief notice about a Roman treaty with the Samnites (7.19.4: cf. 7.10n.).

The story of Valerius and the Gaul, however, could hardly be passed over: it formed a pair with the very similar story of Manlius (7.5n.), and even surpassed it in the interest shown by the later tradition, perhaps because of the intervention of the raven, with its supernatural overtones.[91] There are relatively full accounts not only in Livy, but also in D.H., *AR* 15.1, Gell. 9.11, Zonar. 7.25. As with Manlius, the story varies remarkably little between different sources (as noted by Gell. 9.11.1). Three points, all found in P., are central to the tradition: Valerius' single combat with the Gaul, the raven's assisting him in the fight, and this being the aetiology of his name. Fewer join P. (and Livy) in linking this directly to his unusually early consulship, but the connection is made by Val. Max. 8.15.5[92] and Eutr. 2.6.4.

M. Valerius tribunus militum: Cf. Livy 7.26.2: *M. erat Valerius tribunus militum*.

Gallum, a quo provocatus erat: This is slightly misleading, in as much as in almost all sources, including Livy, the Gaul does not challenge Valerius in particular, but issues a generic challenge to single combat, which Valerius takes up. Ampelius 22.2 uses similar language (*a Gallo provocatus*), which may point to a

---

[91] This is an important part of Livy's presentation (Levene (1993), 216–17); it is also explicit in Val. Max. 8.15.5, Gell. 9.11.6, Flor. 1.8(13).20, and may be at least an undercurrent in the story in others.

[92] Not, however, by Paris' epitome, which, interestingly, reports the early consulship as the chief point of the item, and does not mention the duel or the raven.

shared source or dependence of one on the other; but whether or not that is the case, the difference from Livy is more likely to be the consequence of slightly careless compression than a reflection of an alternative version.

insidente galeae corvo: Livy 7.26.3 has *corvus repente in galea consedit*. P.'s language is closer to Ampel. 22.2 (*corvus galeam eius insedit*: cf. above) and *Vir. Ill.* 29.2 (*corvus…galeae eius insedit*); cf. also Flor. 1.8(13).20 (*insidente galeae sacra alite*).

unguibus rostroque hostem infestante: Cf. Livy 7.26.5: *os oculosque hostis rostro et unguibus appetit*. *infestare* is not Livian: it is found only three times in Republican and Augustan Latin, first in *Bell. Alex.* 3.1, then twice (with a different meaning) in Ovid (*Am.* 2.11.18, *Met.* 13.731). It becomes increasingly widespread from the reign of Tiberius onwards: P. is using the language of his own day, rather than Livy's.

7.9 Diplomatic agreement with Carthage. Corresponds to Livy 7.27.2. P.'s interest in this brief notice is presumably generated by the future relations between the states; like Livy himself, P. 'has no need to draw attention to the ironies of this treaty' (Oakley (1998), 252: Oros. 3.7.1–3 is rather more heavy-handed).

amicitia…iuncta est: Livy 7.27.2 speaks of *foedus ictum*, though he goes on to note that the Carthaginian ambassadors had arrived seeking *amicitiam ac societatem*. While there was a distinction between *amicitia* and a *foedus*—broadly speaking, *amicitia* could refer to any friendly relationship between states, whereas a *foedus* was a formal legal agreement (see Heuss (1933), esp. 53–9)—P.'s formulation is not incorrect, since almost any *foedus* would lead to *amicitia* (though not vice versa). In any case, Livy himself often uses the terms *amicitia* and *amicus* loosely, applying them to allies under treaty as much as to informal relationships of non-aggression: see Matthaei (1907), esp. 186–7. P.'s preference for *amicitia* here may perhaps be because it helps point the irony that the future relationships of Rome and Carthage would be far from amicable (cf. above).

7.10 Beginning of Samnite War. Corresponds to Livy 7.29.1–32.1. P. moves to the Samnite Wars that will occupy much of the next four books, passing over without comment (but cf. 7.13n.) Livy's briefer accounts of wars against the Volsci (7.27.5–9, 7.28.6) and the Aurunci (7.28.1–4), as well as a few small notices of domestic events. Livy recounts the opening of the war in some detail, not surprisingly, since he explicitly describes it as the beginning of a new phase in Roman history, beginning a chain of wars that led from the Samnites through Pyrrhus to the Carthaginians (7.29.1–2: cf. 11.1n.). No other surviving source gives such emphasis to it—indeed, the opening of the Samnite War is only mentioned in a handful of places (Flor. 1.11.1–7, Oros. 3.8.1; cf. D.H., *AR* 15.3.2); but it is in accordance with this that P. gives it a relatively full notice, marking not only the war, but the means by which the Romans entered it: the Samnite attack on the Campanians, the Campanians' appeal to Rome, which is initially unsuccessful, until the Campanians manage to draw in the Romans by dint of surrendering themselves to Rome.

P. simplifies the story slightly, by omitting the role of the Sidicini, who, in Livy, were the Samnites' original target, until they brought in the Campanians by appealing to them for support. This is relatively inessential to the story; a more important and relevant omission by P. is the reason Rome initially refused help to the Campanians: that they themselves had a treaty with the Samnites, something on which Livy places a great deal of emphasis (7.31.1–2; cf. 7.19.4, 7.29.3, 7.30.4, 7.31.8). This not only explains Rome's first response, but also makes her later willingness to use the Campanians' surrender as a way to circumvent that treaty appear at best legalistic and at worst morally problematic. One may compare the debate—in some respects similar—over the morality and legality of the Roman position at the start of the First Punic War (cf. 16.2n.); here, as there, P., by ignoring the existence of the Samnite treaty, presents the issue in such a way as to avoid any complicating questions about the Romans' legal or moral position.[93]

bello urgerentur: *bello urgeri* is Livian, though not used in this passage: see 21.41.12; cf. 24.48.3, 29.1.20, 31.28.3.

auxilio...a senatu petito: Cf. Livy 7.29.7: *ab Romanis petere auxilium*; 7.30.1: *auxilium...a vobis petitum*.

urbem et agros populo Romano dediderunt: Cf. Livy 7.31.4: *populum Campanum urbemque Capuam, agros, delubra deum, divina humanaque omnia in vestram, patres conscripti, populique Romani dicionem dedimus*. Out of the list of things surrendered, P. focuses on those with a territorial dimension, since they have the most direct bearing on the subsequent confrontation with the Samnites: cf. Livy 7.31.7: *agrum urbemque per deditionem factam populi Romani*; also 7.31.10: *ut Capua urbe Campanoque agro abstinerent*.

ea, quae populi Romani facta essent: Cf. Livy 7.31.7: *agrum urbemque...factam populi Romani*.

7.11 *Heroic deed of P. Decius Mus.* Corresponds to Livy 7.34.1–37.3. P., having introduced the First Samnite War (7.10n.), surprisingly does not describe a single Roman military victory from it (though cf. 7.13n.). He passes over Valerius Corvus' initial victory in Campania (7.32–3); he also omits his final battle in Suessula (7.37.4–17). He even omits the aftermath to the episode here, in which the Romans take the opportunity to turn the tables and defeat the Samnites. Instead, he concentrates solely on Decius' story, an act of exemplary heroism of the sort P. describes elsewhere, with a soldier putting himself at risk for the sake of the entire army: see esp. the story of Calpurnius Flamma (17.4n.), with which

---

[93] Flor. 1.11.2 avoids the moral and legal question in a different way: he states that the Campanian surrender of themselves to Rome predated the Samnite treaty, and so took priority over it.

this was sometimes paired (Livy 22.60.11, Plin., *Nat.* 22.11, Frontin., *Strat.* 1.5.14–15 = 4.5.9–10). Moreover, the events here prefigure the following book, in which Decius will sacrifice himself even more spectacularly (8.3n.): cf. the explicit linking of the two episodes at Cic., *Div.* 1.51.

P. does not make that connection explicit (though cf. 10.7n.), but he does highlight the story here by, unusually, dividing it into two sentences, one in which he draws attention to the heroic significance of Decius' deed, the second in which he narrates what this heroism consisted of. He offers just enough narrative detail for the reader to be able to appreciate the outline of Decius' ploy, although not exactly how he accomplished it: the Romans caught with the Samnites occupying the ground above them, Decius regaining control for the Romans by seizing a still higher position, the escape of the main Roman army, and finally Decius extricating himself. This is a reasonable summary of the situation in Livy; of other accounts, *Vir. Ill.* 26.1–2 is even more jejune, with the same basic structure, but not even mentioning that Decius' actions ensured the escape of the main army; while the version of Frontin., *Strat.* 1.5.14 appears to envisage a different situation, one closer to that in the parallel story of Calpurnius (above): the primary function of Decius' detachment was to divert the Samnites away from the main army, rather than exploiting a superior position so as to block them from the pursuit.

in locum iniquum deductus: Livy 7.34.12 speaks of *iniquitate loci*, but with respect to Decius' position dominating the Samnites, not the Samnites dominating the Romans (cf. Frontin., *Strat.* 1.5.14 speaks of Cornelius being *iniquis locis deprenso*). *locus iniquus*, is, however, common in Livy's battle narratives (and even more so in Caesar's): cf. esp. 26.3.4: *in loca iniqua incaute deductum*. It is far less so in later antiquity: P. is once again writing in the manner of Livy, even when not replicating the specifics of Livy's text.

Deci Muris tribuni militum: Cf. Livy 7.34.3: *P. Decius tribunus militum*. Livy does not give Decius' *cognomen* (this was not his first appearance in the narrative: see 7.21.6), but does offer his *praenomen*. P., in accordance with his usual practice (cf. 4.4n.), introduces a major hero with *nomen* and *cognomen* alone (hence it is superfluous to add the *praenomen*, as Sigonius, followed by Rossbach, did).

occupato colle: Livy does not use the phrase in this episode, but has done so a few chapters earlier when speaking of the Samnites' attack on Capua (7.29.6); cf. also Frontin., *Strat.* 1.5.14 (*occupandum collem*).

occasionem consuli in aequiorem locum evadendi dedit: Cf. Livy 7.34.8: *spatium consuli dedit ad subducendum agmen in aequiorem locum*. P. paraphrases rather than replicating Livy's wording.

erupit. cum milites: The chief MSS read not *erupit* but *eripuit*. The majority of them supply no object, but the α group of MSS (see Introduction) reads *commilitones* instead of beginning the next sentence with *cum milites*, with the grammar preserved by inserting *cum* before *de occupanda urbe*. This is a possible reading, but, following the reading of a few of the later MSS, I, like previous editors, read *erupit* instead of *eripuit*. This is for two reasons. First, with three or four (apparently) independent MS groupings (B, N, P, and α), it is improbable that three will be corrupt, with only one preserving the correct text. Second, it is not in P.'s manner to attribute a crime committed by one set of Romans to the Romans collectively. *commilitones...cum de occupanda* in the α MSS should be understood as a copyist's attempt at emendation.

7.12 *Mutiny in Capua*. Corresponds to Livy 7.38.4–42.7. P.'s account is a reasonable distillation of Livy's long and complex narrative: the initial attempt to seize Capua, which is foiled when the plan is uncovered; the open defection of the conspirators, and finally the pacific intervention of Valerius Corvus, who offers the conspirators an amnesty if they abandon their mutiny. It is not the only possible distillation: note in particular the very different account of *Vir. Ill.* 29.3, which refers to Quinctius' reluctant leadership of the revolt, which plays a significant part in Livy, but P. does not mention Quinctius at all. *Vir. Ill.* also has the oppression of the Roman people by debt (barely present in Livy, but see 7.38.7; cf. also D.H., *AR* 15.3.6, App., *Samn.* 1.1–2) as the fundamental cause of the crisis, and its removal (not in Livy,[94] but see App., *Samn.* 1.2: cf. Oakley (1998), 362–3) as the solution. Livy himself, like D.H., *AR* 15.3.5 and App., *Samn.* 1.1, prefers to stress the enervating moral climate of Capua (7.38.5).

Unlike these, P. gives no reason for the defection; nor does he fill out the details of how a conspiracy that was, apparently, detected would not lead to immediate punishment[95] rather than accelerating into defection through the conspirators' fear of punishment (the answer in Livy is that the consul who discovers it acts behind the scenes to remove the ringleaders from Capua, but one cohort, recognizing that their plans have been detected, intercept those being removed and form an army with them; so also D.H., *AR* 15.3.13–15, App., *Samn.* 1.1). P.'s account has the bare events, but, as often, leaves a lot of the motivations without explanation.

cum: Cf. 2.2n.

in praesidio relicti erant: A common Livian phrase (though not used in this passage): see 1.14.9, 1.38.1, 24.19.5, 29.7.2, 29.9.8, 36.33.4, 39.31.11, 40.32.5. It is also found occasionally in the Caesarian corpus (*Gall.* 6.33.4, 6.38.1 (some MSS); cf. *Bell. Afr.* 11.4), but hardly ever in post-Augustan Latin. As often, P. summarizes Livy in Livian language.

conspirassent: Livy rarely uses *conspiro* or *conspiratio* (exceptions are 2.32.10, 3.36.9. 3.56.12, 5.11.9, 42.14.10). His preferred terms are *coniuro/coniuratio*, which appear repeatedly in his narrative of the mutiny (7.38.8, 7.39.6, 7.41.5,

---

[94] Livy (7.42.1) does refer to a tribunician measure found in some of his sources (*apud quosdam*) to ban the lending of money at interest; but that appears to be different from what is assumed in Appian and *Vir. Ill.*, which is a senatorial decree at Valerius' prompting to abolish existing debts.

[95] Note the very different version of Frontin., *Strat.* 1.9.1, which has the consul punishing the conspirators, and the conspiracy apparently never turning to open munity.

7.41.8, 7.42.3, 7.42.4). P. uses the two more or less interchangeably, though *coniuro* is slightly more common in his text.

detecto consilio: Cf. *TLL* V 793.83–794.71. *detegere consilium* is, however, relatively rare: prior to P., it is found once in Livy (27.45.1), then only in the *Acta* of the Arval Brethren (*CIL* VI 32346h), Suet., *Jul.* 17.1, and Just. 2.10.17. This is perhaps because *detegere* usually appears in the context of revealing the illicit (the *Acta* speak of *nefaria consilia*), and so tends to be used with less neutral objects.

furore: Livy does not use this term of the mutineers, but he similarly implies their irrationality by speaking of them as *insanientis* (7.39.10), and their actions as the product of *iras* (7.40.1); they themselves ultimately regard the mutiny as *rabies* (7.40.2). However, *furor* is used prominently by Livy to describe a later mutiny (e.g. 28.24.5, 28.24.10, 28.24.12, 28.25.12), and it is thence picked up by Tacitus in his account of the mutinies at the start of Tiberius' reign (*Ann.* 1.18.2: see esp. Woodman (2006), 312–19 = (2012), 304–11).

7.13 Wars against Italian tribes.

res praeterea…prospere gestas continet: Cf. 2.16n., 3.10n.

Hernicos et Gallos et Tiburtes et Privernates et Tarquinienses et Samnites et Vulscos: For the first time (cf. 2.16n., 3.10n., 4.11n., 6.1n.), P.'s list of wars he has omitted appears to be a relatively comprehensive reflection of Livy. Livy did indeed speak of successful wars against the Hernici (7.11.8, 7.15.9), the Gauls and Tiburtines (7.11.2–8), as well as the Gauls alone (7.23.2–24.10) and the Tiburtines alone (7.11.10–12.4, 7.19.1), the Privernates (7.15.11, 7.16.3–6), the Tarquinienses (7.12.5–6, 7.17.2–9, 7.19.1–3, 7.19.6–20.8, 7.22.4–5), the Samnites (7.32–33, 7.37.4–17: cf. 7.11n.), and the Volsci (7.27.5–9, 7.28.6). Peoples whom Livy describes the Romans as defeating but whom P. omits are the Faliscans (who fought in their own right at 7.20.9 and 7.22.4–5 and alongside the Tarquinienses at 7.17.2–9), the Aurunci (7.28.1–4), the Caerites, who fought alongside the Tarquinienses at 7.19.6–20.8, and the Veliterni, who fought alongside the Privernates at 7.15.11.

Moreover, the pattern of inclusion and exclusion seems less arbitrary than before: most of those included are more prominent in the narrative than those excluded. The chief exceptions are the Hernici and the Volsci. The former is easily explained: although Rome's victories over them are nothing but minor notices in Livy, they are preceded by a far longer account of an early Roman defeat at their hands (7.6.7–9.2), and while strictly speaking a defeat cannot come under the heading of *res…prospere gestas*, P. may have seen the wars with the Hernici as effectively a single unit, with their defeat of Rome being ultimately reversed. As for the Volsci, their inclusion may perhaps be because of their lengthy past history as enemies of Rome rather than because of their importance in Book 7: this is, moreover, their final appearance in P. (cf. 6.1n.), though they continue to play a minor role in Livy.

Book 8

8.1 Opening of Latin War: Latin embassy to Rome. Corresponds to Livy 8.3.2–5, 8.3.8–6.8. P. omits not only the fighting at the very beginning of the book, when the Romans rapidly deal with the Privernates, the Volsci, and the Antiates (8.1.1–6), but all of the complex preliminaries to the Latin revolt, which ultimately arises out of the First Samnite War. That war comes to a conclusion at the start of Book 8, when the Samnites refuse to fight the Romans any longer and instead petition for peace, asking only that they be allowed to continue to fight the Sidicini (8.1.7–8.2.4); the Sidicini fail to get help against the Samnites from Rome, and instead get it from the Latins and Campanians, who invade Samnium; the Samnites in their turn seek the Romans' help (8.2.5–3.1).

P. ignores the Samnites altogether, and consequently fails to bring to a close the First Samnite War whose beginning he had recounted in Book 7. This might seem a surprising omission, but, as we shall see (cf. 8.9–12nn.), it is of a piece with how he handles the opening of the Second Samnite War, where he overlooks all of its preliminaries, instead having the Romans engaging in battle with the Samnites with no explanation given. The upshot of both of these is to meld the two wars into one, and to ignore the decades of peace that separated them. In one sense this clearly misrepresents Livy; in another way, however, it is not an unfair reflection of the broader tenor of his narrative. Livy constructs the Samnite Wars as a continuous series stretching from their beginnings in the late 340s until the defeat of Pyrrhus in the late 270s. This is implicit at 7.29.1–2, where the war with Pyrrhus is said to have succeeded the Samnite War that had been 'waged with doubtful success' (*ancipiti Marte gestum*); it is stated directly several times in the later books. In 10.31.10 Livy speaks of himself having since Book 7 narrated forty-six years of 'continuous...wars' (*bella...continua*) with the Samnites. At 23.42.2 and 23.42.6 the Samnite envoys to Hannibal imply that they were constantly in arms against Rome up to their alliance with Pyrrhus; at 31.31.10 the Romans claim to have defended the Campanians against the Samnites for 'almost seventy years'; and the consul Varro in his appeal to the Capuans at 23.5.8 refers (albeit with manifest exaggeration) to 'almost 100 years' of Samnite wars.

Accordingly, P., instead of starting from the Samnites, begins his narrative of Book 8 at the point when the Latins and Campanians make the decision to revolt. Of their subsequent negotiations with Rome, he focuses on two points: first, their demand that one of the consuls should be Latin, and the second, Annius' fall as he leaves the Capitol. The first of these is later recalled by Livy himself in the context of the very similar demand allegedly made by the Campanians at the time of their revolt (23.6.8: compare Val. Max. 6.4.1a (also Paris' epitome), which appears to conflate the Campanian episode with the one here); it is similarly highlighted by Eutr. 2.7.1, and mentioned by Flor. 1.9.1. However, P. ignores the Latins' broader demands for citizenship and membership of the Senate, which are also referred to later by Livy (23.22.5–7) and are in Florus as well: P. mentions only the proposal that was obviously outrageous even in retrospect.[96]

As for Annius' fall, no other author refers to it, but it is a significant moment in Livy, since it acts as an omen which effectively gives sanction to the Roman position in the dispute: Livy draws the moral explicitly in the mouth of Torquatus (8.6.5–6). In Livy there is a suggestion (albeit not vouched for by the author: 8.6.1) that Annius directly blasphemes against Jupiter, and that his fall (and perhaps death: cf. below) is punishment for that. P. does not have any idea of blasphemy, nor any mention of the gods (unlike Livy, where Jupiter is a repeated point of reference in the debate): although he does not draw the conclusion explicitly, the manner in which he describes the fall suggests that, for him, it is symbolically important in a slightly different way. The Latins have, in his version, challenged a fundamental institution of Roman power; in response, their leader slips and falls at the place which is at the symbolic heart of that power.

condicionem tulerunt ut si pacem habere vellent alterum ex Latinis consulem facerent: Cf. Livy 8.5.4–5: *condiciones pacis feramus…consulem alterum Roma, alterum ex Latio creari oportet*. P. uses Livy's language, but rewriting and distilling it rather than exactly replicating it. For *condiciones ferre* = 'offer terms' see *TLL* IV 136.12–20; the construction with *ut* is not uncommon, though not used by Livy here (but cf. Livy 39.43.5).

legatione perlata: *legationem perferre* is not Livian: it is a rare phrase with no set meaning. At Quint., *Inst.* 7.4.36 it means 'complete an embassy' (cf. *OLD s.v. perfero* 5a); at Suet., *Claud.* 6.1 and Rufin., *Hist. Mon.* 1.1.25 it is 'go on an embassy' (with no particular sense of completion); at Apul., *Met.* 6.20 and Heges. 5.22.1 it is 'perform a commission' (cf. *OLD s.v. legatio* 2a). P. presumably is using the phrase in the first sense, since Livy is clear that Annius slipped as he left the Capitol after his embassy was over.

de Capitolio ita lapsus est: In Livy 8.6.2 Annius slips down the steps of the temple of Jupiter Capitolinus; but *de Capitolio lapsus est* implies a different version of the story, in which he actually fell off the hill (cf. Livy 5.46.2: *de Capitolio descendisset*; 5.48.4: *panis de Capitolio iactatus est*).

exanimaretur: Unusually, P. takes the final moment of the story not from Livy's main version, but from a variant which Livy himself declines to assert, though without completely ruling it out (8.6.3). Given P.'s considerably more dramatic image of Annius' slipping (above), it is hardly surprising that he prefers the

---

[96] The other proposals are likely to have been influenced by the Italian demands at the time of the Social War (cf. 71.1–2n.), and to have been anachronistically retrojected to the fourth century (see esp. Dipersia (1975)). With those, P., like Livy, is writing from a perspective where the key concessions were ultimately granted, and would not have seemed obviously unreasonable (cf. Levene (1993), 219–20, (2010), 40–1).

version in which he dies in consequence: he would be unlikely to have survived such a fall.

8.2 *Manlius Torquatus executes his son.* Corresponds to Livy 8.7. This famous story is distilled by P. virtually to its bare bones: Manlius' execution of his son for fighting against orders—with the pointed irony that he did so despite the fact that his son was actually successful. This was a standard distillation of the tradition, and precisely the same elements are drawn on by a number of other authors also: see e.g. Val. Max. 6.9.1, Frontin., *Strat.* 4.1.40,[97] Flor. 1.9.2, Aug., *Civ.* 1.23, *Schol. Bob. ad Cic. Sull.* 32. Sometimes the ironic fact of the son's victory is passed over (e.g. Sall., *Catil.* 52.30–1, cf. 9.4; *Vir. Ill.* 28.4); conversely, others fill out the narrative slightly by adding extra details, such as that the son fought because he was challenged by the enemy to do so (e.g. Val. Max. 2.7.6 (also Paris' epitome), Gell. 9.13.20, Serv., *Aen.* 6.824 (= C 36), Oros. 3.9.2, Aug., *Civ.* 5.18, Zonar. 7.26.3–4), or the even more ironic point (found exclusively in Greek sources: cf. Oakley (1998), 438–9) that he was crowned by his father for his victory prior to his execution for disobedience (so e.g. D.H., *AR* 8.79.2, Plu., *Fab.* 9.2; ps.-Plu., *Par. Min.* 308E (citing Aristeides of Miletus, *FGrH* 286 F 18), Zonar. 7.26.5 (cf. Dio fr. 35.2)). But P.'s version captures what virtually all post-Livian writers saw as the essence of the story: cf. below.

filium, quod contra edictum eius adversus Latinos pugnaverat, quamvis prospere pugnasset, securi percussit: Cf. Livy 8.7.15: *adversus edictum nostrum...in hostem pugnasti*. Even closer to P. here, however, is the language used by Livy in the story of Papirius Cursor and Fabius Rullianus at 8.35.5 *Q. Fabius, qui contra edictum imperatoris pugnavit*: see further 8.11n. By the standards of classical Latin grammar, one would expect *suum* rather than *eius*, but this substitution is not uncommon in later Latin (H-S 175–6).

More generally, P.'s phrasing is very similar to others within the Latin tradition: the story was regularly constructed around a standard linguistic model with only minor variations. See Sall., *Catil.* 52.30: *filium suum, quod is contra imperium in hostem pugnaverat, necari iussit*; Val. Max. 6.9.1: *filium victorem, quod adversus imperium cum hoste manum conseruerat, securi percussit*; Frontin., *Strat.* 4.1.40: *filium, quod is contra edictum patris cum hoste pugnaverat, quamvis victorem...securi percussit*; Flor. 1.9.2: *filium suum, quia contra imperium repugnaverat, quamvis victorem occiderit*; *Vir. Ill.* 28.4: *filium suum, quod contra imperium pugnasset, securi percussit*; Aug., *Civ.* 1.23: *filium, qui contra imperium in hostem pugnaverat, etiam victorem laudabiliter Torquatus occidit.*

For *prospere pugnasset* see also 2.6n.; for *securi percussit* 2.2n.

---

[97] However, Frontinus' next anecdote adds a further element, attested nowhere else: that the soldiers sought to mutiny on the younger Manlius' behalf, and he quelled it by voluntarily accepting the execution.

8.3 *Devotio of Decius.* Corresponds to Livy 8.9.1–11.1. P. has nothing of the explanatory preface to Livy's account (8.6.9–13), in which both Decius and Manlius receive a vision, warning them that one or other will have to sacrifice himself. Nor does he have any of the extensive detail that Livy offers of how the ritual was accomplished, including the key point that it involved formally sacrificing to the gods the enemy army along with oneself. Instead, he simply focuses on the fact of Decius' self-sacrifice at a time when his army was in trouble, with a brief description of his dramatically riding into the enemy ranks in order to ensure his death.

The story of Decius showed considerably more variation in the tradition than did that of Manlius and his son (8.2n.). There are many citations and retellings of the story,[98] especially in exemplary contexts. Not only do these sometimes vary from Livy's version,[99] but even when there is no factual discrepancy, different authors regularly selected different elements from it. For example, various sources (e.g. Cic., *Div.*,[100] Valerius Maximus, ps.-Plutarch, *Vir. Ill.*, *Schol. ad Juv.*, Zonaras) include the initial dream, which is not in P., or add something of the ritual detail which P. ignores (e.g. Valerius Maximus, Florus, Servius, Zonaras).

Nevertheless, the core image that we find in P., of Decius sacrificing his life for his army as he rides his horse into the enemy ranks, is widespread within the tradition. The reason is presumably that the story of a vicarious sacrifice of oneself on behalf of others is one with much wider cultural resonances (cf. the numerous parallels discussed by Versnel (1981); note also the parallel that Aug., *Civ.* 5.18 draws between the Decii and Christian martyrs). It mattered far more that the hero was sacrificing himself for his own side than that the opposing side was simultaneously being ritually dedicated to death. The same reason explains why P. emphasizes that the difficulties of the Roman army necessitated Decius' intervention (Versnel (1981), 140–5). Those narrative elements carried far more cultural significance than did most of the specific ritual details.

laborantibus in acie: *laborare* in the sense of an army being in trouble is both classical and Livian (*TLL* VII.2 807.51–67). *laborare in acie*, on the other hand, is

---

[98] So (e.g.) *Rhet. Her.* 4.57; Cic., *Sest.* 48, *Cato* 75, *Parad.* 12, *Fin.* 2.61, *Tusc.* 1.89, *Nat. Deor.* 2.10, 3.15, *Div.* 1.51 (cf. 2.136); Val. Max. 1.7.3, 5.6.5 (both with Paris' epitome, the first also with Nepotianus); Sen., *Epist.* 67.9; Plin., *Nat.* 22.9, 28.9; Frontin., *Strat.* 4.5.15; Plu., *An Vit. Inf.* 499B–C; ps.-Plu., *Par. Min.* 310A–B (citing Aristeides of Miletus, *FGrH* 286 F 19); Juv. 8.254–8 (with scholiast); Flor. 1.9.3; Ampel. 20.6; *Vir. Ill.* 26.4–5, 28.4; Serv., *Aen.* 6.824; Aug., *Civ.* 5.18; Oros. 3.9.3; Zonar. 7.26.6–8 (cf. Dio fr. 35.7–8).

[99] For example, in ps.-Plutarch the *devotio* takes place in a war against the Albans, not the Latins. The Juvenal scholiast has the Romans and the enemy fighting over Decius' body—in Livy there is no such struggle, and the body is unproblematically recovered after the battle (8.10.10). Oddest is Plutarch, where Decius sacrifices himself (to Kronos = Saturn) by burning himself on a funeral pyre on the battlefield, rather than by riding into the enemy ranks.

[100] In Cicero, however, the dream takes place much earlier, at the time of Decius' heroic deed during the First Samnite War (7.11n.).

not a Livian phrase; it is used in the context of Decius' *devotio* also by *Vir. Ill.* 26.4, but otherwise appears only in Sen., *Contr.* 1.8.4 (with a different meaning).

P. Decius: Some later MSS add the phrase *tunc consul cum Manlio*, and this reading is accepted by Rossbach, doubtless because P.'s most common practice is to say explicitly when a named individual is consul. However, there are various times when he does not do this (cf. e.g. 10.7, 10.8, 21.3), and it is also relatively unusual for P. to link separate anecdotes in this way. Given that the MS authority is also extremely weak (see the apparatus), we can be sure that the phrase merely derives from an explanatory gloss.

devovit se pro exercitu: Cf. Livy 8.9.9: *se devotum pro exercitu*. See also 10.7n.: despite the ubiquity of the Decii in the exemplary tradition, this specific phrase appears nowhere in Latin except these two passages of P. and the Livian passages from which they derive, along with Paris' epitome of Val. Max. 1.7.3—Paris appears to have drawn his language in this instance from Livy rather than Valerius.

concitato equo: Livy does not use this phrase of Decius; but cf. Val. Max. 5.6.5, Sen., *Epist.* 67.9.

in medios hostes se intulisset: Cf. Livy 8.9.9: *se in medios hostes immisit*; similar language is used of Decius in *Rhet. Her.* 4.57, Val. Max. 5.6.5, Sen., *Epist.* 67.9, *Schol. ad Juv.* 8.254.

Romanis victoriam restituit: P. goes beyond Livy in explicitly attributing the victory to Decius' *devotio*: although Livy strongly implies the efficacy of the consul's self-sacrifice, he does not directly state that it was successful, and approvingly but inconsistently quotes a view that attributes the victory entirely to Manlius' strategic skills (8.10.8: cf. Levene (1993), 222). A minority of sources (esp. Cic., *Nat. Deor.* 3.15, Dio fr. 35.7–8, Zonar. 7.26.8) are similarly reticent or even openly sceptical. However, P. follows the line taken by most others (e.g. Cic., *Div.* 1.51, Val. Max. 5.6.5 (cf. Paris, summary of Val. Max. 1.7.3), Frontin., *Strat.* 4.5.15, Flor. 1.9.3, *Vir. Ill.* 26.5, Aug., *Civ.* 5.18), when he explicitly states that Decius' sacrifice led to the victory.

victoriam restituere is not found in Livy, or indeed elsewhere in pre-fourth-century Latin. Strictly speaking it appears an incongruous phrase, since it implies the restoration of a victory which cannot yet have occurred, since the battle is still continuing. Nevertheless, as well as in this passage of P., it is found in Anon., *De Mach. Bell.* 18.7, and probably reflects the language of the fourth century, presumably arising on the model of common phrases in military contexts like *rem (pugnam, proeliam) restituere* (*OLD s.v. restituo* 3c), and understood as meaning 'bringing about the due victory'. For *re-* compounds being used without the implication of repetition cf. Berry (1996), 130–1.

8.4 *End of Latin War; return of Manlius to Rome.* Corresponds to Livy 8.11.12–12.1. P. rounds off the account of the war with a reference to Livy's final notice from it: the grim return of Manlius to Rome, where the young men refused to greet him (an anecdote also found in Val. Max. 9.3.4 (also Paris' epitome) and Oros. 3.9.4). This puts the final seal on the implied contrast between the admirable Decius and the problematic Manlius, accentuated by the fact that P. omits Livy's brief notice of the final battle with which Manlius wrapped up the war (8.11.11–12), leaving the impression that the credit for the victory belonged entirely to Decius. Valerius and Orosius, by contrast, like Livy, do credit Manlius with the victory, which for them shows how extreme the refusal of the Roman youth to acknowledge his return was.

in deditionem venerunt: Livy 8.11.12 has *dederunt se omnes Latini*; P. substitutes a different phrase, itself used quite frequently by Livy, but one which P. appears to prefer, employing it intermittently through his work: cf. 8.9, 20.1, 20.6, 20.9, 20.10, 28.7, 44.5, 126.

nemo ex iuventute obviam processit: Livy 8.12.1 is quite different: *seniores tantum obviam exisse constat, iuventutem...aversatam eum*. P. derives his phrasing instead from Val. Max. 9.3.4: *iuniorum nemo obviam processit* (cf. 1.B.6n., 2.5n., 2.12n.).

8.5 *Condemnation of a Vestal*. Corresponds to Livy 8.15.7–8. Prior to this, P. has omitted Livy's account of renewed fighting with the Latins, along with the final settlement that the Romans imposed (8.12.5–10, 8.13–14): for him, the grand victory accomplished (in his version) by Decius put an end to the war, and he shows no interest in what came after. He also leaves out the *leges Publiliae*, which granted various rights to the people (8.12.14–17): after the Licinian-Sextian laws, P. has largely ceased to show interest in patrician–plebeian conflict (7.5n., 7.8n.). He does, however, pause to note a prosecution of a Vestal, a subject in which he is particularly interested (cf. 2.13n., 14.6n.), a prosecution also recorded by Oros. 3.9.5, Jer., *Adv. Iovin.* 1.41, and the *Oxyrhynchus Chronicle* (*P.Oxy.* 12 col.3 = *FGrH* 255 F 6).

incesti damnata est: Nothing corresponds to this in Livy's language here (though cf. Oros. 3.9.5 *ob admissum incestum damnata est*). However, Livy had used the phrase for the first Vestal trial that he records in his work (2.42.11; cf. Sen., *Contr.* 1.3 pr., Sen, *Apocol.* 8.2, Quint., *Inst.* 7.8.3, Plin., *Epist.* 4.11.6, Oros. 2.4.2); P. did not do so on that occasion (see 2.13), but it now becomes his preferred formula (cf. 14.5, 20.5, 22.5, 63.5).

8.6 *Victory over the Ausones; foundation of colonies*. Corresponds to Livy 8.16 and 8.22.1–2. The only event intervening in Livy between the Vestal trial and the Ausonian war is the creation of the first plebeian praetor, Q. Publilius Philo (8.15.9). P.'s omission of this might seem slightly surprising: although Livy himself makes little of it, P. likes marking the development of the Republic with 'firsts' of this sort (cf. e.g. 1.B.7n.). But he does not do so automatically in all cases, and in this instance it may be relevant that he will shortly be citing Publilius in the context of an even more resonant 'first' (8.9n.).

The note unites two acts of colonization which are separated both chronologically and in Livy's text; some of the intervening material is introduced by P. in the two subsequent notices (8.7, 8.8nn.).

Ausonibus victis et oppido ex is capto: For the sentence structure, cf. 2.2n. P. regularly refers to victories over foreign peoples; he does not ordinarily add the capture of a town, a pointed piece of information which allows the reader to infer something which Livy makes explicit: namely that the town in question is Cales, where the Romans founded the first colony mentioned in the main clause. The point would be explicit if one accepted the MSS reading *in oppido*, but while P. sometimes speaks of colonies being founded *in agro* or the like (15.4, 19.5, 20.12, 60.7), *in oppido* would be anomalous: the town itself became the colony, the colony was not founded 'in' it. Rossbach's correction of *in* to *et* is accordingly to be preferred; the Aldine edition changed it to *in oppidum*, deleting *ex is capto*; Sigonius retained *in oppidum* but changed *capto* to *captum*; this is another possibility, but requires also retaining the repetitive *colonia deducta* from the MSS at this point (see below), since Fregellae was not founded in the captured town; overall, Rossbach's solution is the simplest and neatest.

item: Indicates that Fregellae is extraneous to the causal sequence in the earlier part of the sentence: it is another colony, but not related to the victory over the Ausones.

coloniae deductae sunt: Cf. 1.B.1n. The MSS add *colonia deducta* after *Cales*, but the repetition would be clumsy even for P., and the plural here hard to explain were the first phrase present.

8.7 *Poisoning trial.* Corresponds to Livy 8.18; P. omits a variety of minor notices from Livy 8.17, including an abortive Samnite war, a treaty with Alexander of Epirus, and a census in which two new tribes were added.

The story here is also recorded in Val. Max. 2.5.3, Aug., *Civ.* 3.17, and Oros. 3.10; all, like P., omit from Livy the expiatory acts performed in the wake of the trial (8.18.11–13). The emphasis in all three, as also in Livy, is on the magnitude of the alleged crime (Livy, Valerius, and Orosius give the number of those convicted). P. is more interested, as is typical of him (cf. 1.B.7n.), in the fact that this was Rome's first poisoning trial, a point which is only referred to in passing in Livy (8.18.11), and is not mentioned at all in Augustine or Orosius. From the rest of Livy's account of the way the crime was discovered and prosecuted, which both Valerius and Orosius describe in outline, P. gives only the moment of dramatic reversal, where the criminals drink their own poison.

veneficium complurium matronarum deprehensum est: Livy uses *deprehendo* twice in the passage (8.18.6, 8.18.8), once of the discovery of the criminals, once of the finding of the actual poison. P. uses it of the crime itself (cf. *TLL* V.606.18-55): for the subjective genitive with *veneficium* compare Sen., *Contr.* 9.6.8, 9.6.18, Gell. 12.7.7. P.'s phrasing here appears in part to distil Val. Max. 2.5.3 *veneficii quaestio...complurium matronarum patefacto scelere orta est.*

epotis medicaminibus perierunt: Cf. Livy 8.18.9 *epoto...medicamento... interierunt.*

lex de veneficio: Livy says *neque de veneficiis ante eam diem Romae quaesitum est* (8.18.11: 'there had not been a trial for poisoning at Rome before that day'), implying a *quaestio*, in other words an *ad hoc* special investigation and trial (cf. Val. Max. 2.5.3). The historicity of this procedure is problematic (for varying views cf. e.g. Mommsen, *StrR* 143, 172,[101] Strachan-Davidson (1912), vol. 1, 225-30, Oakley (1998), 595-7). However, there is little doubt that if this trial took place at all, it neither was conducted under nor resulted in a specific *lex de veneficio*, as P. misleadingly states (doubtless because he anachronistically misinterpreted Livy's language).

tunc primum: Cf. 4.2n, 11.5n.

constituta est: Cf. 3.6n.

8.8 *Citizenship granted to the Privernates.* Corresponds to Livy 8.19.4-21.10: P. reduces Livy's intricate narrative of the war and the debate over the Privernates' treatment to a bare notice of the fighting and the granting of citizenship. Those two points are enough, however, to allow the reader to see the chief point of the story: that the Romans, paradoxically, met rebellion with something that looks like a reward—a point which is reinforced by the fact that P., like Livy himself and Val. Max. 6.2.1 (cf. also Dio fr. 35.11), does not explain that the form of citizenship was *sine suffragio*, which arguably (though the matter is controversial) conferred a lesser status on its holders (cf. 12.5.n.).

Privernatibus...civitas data est: Cf. Livy 8.21.10 *Privernatibus civitas daretur.*

bellassent: Unlike Livy (cf. 1.A.2n.), P. treats this term, here as elsewhere (34.9, 49.8, 60.1), as the equivalent of *rebellare*—he never uses it of Romans, only of foreigners.

8.9 *Defeat of the Neapolitans; first proconsulship.* Corresponds to Livy 8.22.5-10, 8.23.10-12, and 8.25.5-26.7. In Livy the account of the war is broken up by the account of the dictatorship of M. Claudius Marcellus (8.23.13-17), the digression on Alexander of Epirus (8.24), and the preliminaries of the renewed war with the Samnites (8.23.1-10, 8.25.1-4; cf. 8.12n.). P. unsurprisingly omits the first two of

---

[101] Mommsen denied the historicity of such early *quaestiones* in general, but accepted this one, arguing that the defendants were female and so not subject to regular criminal procedure.

these; the omission of the third is more surprising, but it is of a piece with the way he ignored the end of the First Samnite War (8.1n.): no peace, for P., has been struck with the Samnites, and hence there is no need to describe a new war beginning. In Livy, the Samnites are allied to the Neapolitans/Palaepolitans (see below), which in fact is a major reason for the latter's surrender: they prefer Rome to their nominal allies. For P. the Neapolitan war has nothing to do with the Samnites: its interest is above all in its being the occasion of two 'firsts' (cf. below).

Neapolitani: Livy attributes the war not to Naples, but to its twin city Palaepolis—a city unattested in all literary and documentary sources apart from Livy himself and the record of Publilius' triumph in the *Fasti Capitolini*. Only at the very end of the story (8.26.6) does he switch to talking about Naples, with the sudden announcement that the seat of government had been moved there, and so the treaty was formed with them. P., like the only other account of this war, namely D.H., *AR* 15.5-6, speaks solely of Naples, and does not mention Palaepolis.

It is generally accepted that Livy's account of the war being against 'Palaepolis' is mistaken, though it is heavily disputed how far there may be a kernel of truth to it, and what precisely that kernel might consist of (for various interpretations see e.g. Mommsen, *CIL* X p. 170, Burger (1898), 14–16, De Sanctis II 286–8 [301–2], Beloch, *RG* 392–4, Gabrici (1948), De Caro (1974), Oakley (1998), 643–5). This is one case where P. appears more accurate than Livy; it is, however, impossible to tell whether he is so because he, like Dionysius, was drawing on alternative sources, or whether he on his own initiative substituted a familiar name for an unfamiliar one, inferring their identity from Livy's final comment about the treaty being with Naples (cf. Bingham 194).

bello et obsidione victi: On Livy's account, the Palaepolitans were not defeated in the siege at all, but voluntarily surrendered rather than submit to the depredations of their Samnite allies. Livy, however, comments that Publilius' triumph was granted on the basis that it was his successful siege of the city that forced the enemy to surrender (8.26.7), and P. appears to accept that at face value, flattening (as he often does) Livy's ambivalence and cynicism into something more uncomplicatedly laudatory.

As to whether the Palaepolitans were defeated *bello*, Livy does not record any Roman battlefield success in this war either. However, his account of the commencement of the siege at 8.23.10 is preceded by a lacuna of unknown length, and P.'s language may indicate that Livy after all described some sort of military victory here (*contra* Oakley (1998), 657–8).

primo: P., as usual (cf. 1.B.7n.), is interested in 'firsts', and in this case he accurately records both of those which Livy associated with this war, namely the proroguing of Publilius' *imperium* and his receipt of a triumph as proconsul (8.26.7; cf. 8.23.12).

imperium prolatum est: A surprising turn of phrase. Livy speaks of *prorogatio imperii* (8.26.7), which is the usual formula for extending a period of *imperium*.

imperium proferre generally refers to the geographical extension of power: it is used in that sense by Livy (1.33.9) and many other authors. However, *proferre* may be used of an extension of a period of time (*OLD s.v. profero* 10b), and P.'s language is comprehensible, even if unparalleled.

triumphus decretus: Cf. Livy 8.26.7 *Publilio triumphus decretus*.

8.10 *Abolition of debt-bondage at Rome.* Corresponds to Livy 8.28. P. omits the story of the brief Lucanian alliance with Rome, which is derailed when the Tarentines trick the Lucanians into rejoining the Samnites (8.27), another example of his melding the First and Second Samnite Wars by passing over the preliminaries of the latter (8.1n., 8.9n.).

Versions of this story appear in Cic., *Rep.* 2.59, D.H., *AR* 16.5.1–3, and Val. Max. 6.1.9 (also Paris' epitome); cf. Varro, *Ling.* 7.105. There is considerable variation between them: neither the date nor the personnel of the story is constant between the different versions (see Oakley (1998), 688–90); nor is there a consistent outcome, since in Valerius (and Paris) debt-bondage is not abolished, but the lustful creditor is punished, whereas in Livy and Cicero there is no reference to punishment, but only to the political change; Dionysius alone has both. P. follows Livy, though sketchily: the process whereby the attempted rape led to the abolition of *nexum* is left unclear (cf. below).

plebs nexu liberata est propter L. Papiri creditoris libidinem: Cf. Livy 8.28.1: *plebi Romanae velut aliud initium libertatis factum est...ob unius feneratoris simul libidinem, simul crudelitatem insignem*. However, P.'s phrasing seems to owe even more to Cic., *Rep.* 2.59: *sunt propter unius libidinem omnia nexa civium liberata*; and it may not be accidental that P. has nothing of the second motive that Livy gives for the story, namely Papirius' 'exceptional cruelty'. Livy's double explanation makes sense given his narrative: the people's immediate cause for outrage is not the attempted rape, but the flogging of Publilius because he resisted the rape. However, in Livy there is a manifest pattern of sexual violence leading to political change, notably with the rape of Lucretia in Book 1 and the attempted rape of Verginia in Book 3 (see e.g. Joplin (1990), Joshel (1992)), and P. accentuates that here, when he follows Cicero in focusing solely on the sexual aspect.

8.11 *Quarrel between Papirius Cursor and Fabius Rullianus.* Corresponds to Livy 8.30.1–35.9. The last twelve chapters of Book 8 in Livy describe the opening phases of the Second Samnite War (8.29–40). However, as already noted (8.1n., 8.9–10nn.), P. does not separate the Second Samnite War from the First, and, in accordance with that, he does not give any overall impression of how the new round of fighting progressed. Instead, he selects one anecdote to recount— admittedly one which Livy had narrated in unusual detail. For P., the story is primarily concerned with an exploration of Roman values, and the fact that it occurred during a war with the Samnites is mentioned only incidentally. Livy makes it explicit that the same themes are being explored as had come up earlier in the book with Manlius' execution of his son (cf. 8.2n.): he refers directly to Manlius' example at 8.30.13, 8.34.2, and 8.35.9. This point is not explicit in P., but emerges implicitly, through the repetition in the language that he uses of the two incidents (cf. below).

The story is told in several other sources also: a fragment from Papirius' *elogium* in the Forum Augustum (*ILS* 53), Val. Max. 2.7.8, 3.2.9 (both with Paris' epitome), Frontin., *Strat.* 4.1.39, Dio fr. 36.1–7, Eutr. 2.8.2–3, *Vir. Ill.* 31.1–3, 32.1. All of these (apart from the *elogium* and Dio, which are fragmentary) take more or less the same essential elements of Livy's lengthy and intricate story as P. does: Papirius' return to the city from the army to take the auspices, Fabius' fighting against his orders, winning a victory, Papirius' initial attempt to punish him, Fabius' flight to Rome, Papirius' pursuit of him there, and the successful appeal on his behalf. There are relatively few variations from this. Valerius divides the anecdote into two, the first focusing on the attempted punishment, the second on the initial fighting against orders (and Paris' summary of the former stops before Fabius' flight to Rome); the second passage also includes more detail about how Fabius achieved his victory. Frontinus does not explain the reason for Papirius' initial absence. Eutropius elides the two occasions (one in the camp, one in Rome) when Papirius attempted to exact punishment, and omits any reference to the auspices (though he does refer to the danger that Papirius himself was in because of popular anger over his actions, something found in no other source). Valerius, Frontinus, and the *De Viris Illustribus* refer to the key role played by Fabius' father in securing mercy, something prominent in Livy, but which P. passes over.

L. Papirius Cursor dictator reversus in urbem ab exercitu esset propter auspicia repetenda: Cf. Livy 8.30.2 *Papirius dictator...ad auspicium repetendum Romam profisceretur*, though P.'s phrasing is even closer to Val. Max. 3.2.9 *Papirio Cursore propter auspicia repetenda in urbem proficiscente*. Similar language is also found in *ILS* 53 *auspicii repetendi caussa Romam redisset* and *Vir. Ill.* 31.1 *ad auspicia repetenda Romam regressus*.

occasione bene gerendae rei invitatus: The language is mainly taken from Livy 8.30.4 *occasione bene gerendae rei inductus*; P. substitutes *invitatus* for *inductus*. The resulting phrase is not, as far as we can tell, Livian or indeed Augustan Latin, though versions of it are occasionally found in the early imperial period and later (Sen., *Benef.* 3.1.4, Flor. 1.40.4, Aug., *Civ.* 7.22).

However, in Livy this is only one explanation for Fabius' eagerness to fight: the other is that he was resentful of Papirius. P. selects the version which reflects better on Fabius (similarly, cf. *Vir. Ill.* 31.2 *opportunitate ductus*).

contra edictum eius prospere adversus Samnites pugnavit: Cf. Livy 8.35.5 *contra edictum imperatoris pugnavit*. That passage was also apparently drawn on by P. for his account of Manlius Torquatus' killing of his son earlier in the book, with the result that the two passages are very similarly phrased (8.2 *contra edictum eius adversus Latinos pugnaverat, quamvis prospere pugnasset, securi percussit*): see the comments *ad loc.* P. uses linguistic repetition to point a parallel which Livy makes explicitly in his text (see above). Frontin., *Strat.* 4.1.39 uses similar phrasing: *adversum edictum eius quamvis prospere pugnaverat*.

For *prospere...pugnavit* see also 2.6n.

Romam profugit: Cf. Livy 8.33.3 *clam ex castris Romam profugit*.

cum parum causa proficeret: P. takes the phrase from earlier in the story, in relation to the appeals on behalf of Fabius in the camp, rather than after his flight to Rome. However, the full context in Livy refers to neither *preces* nor the *causa* being effective (8.33.16 *parum precibus, parum causa proficerent*); the small minority of readers aware of the Livian context can admire the ingenuity with which P. transfers the phrase to the later moment where, as he immediately goes on to explain, it was *preces* that after all were effective.

populi precibus donatus est: Cf. Livy 8.35.5 *donatur populo Romano*; for the meaning of *donatus* here, cf. Oakley (1998), 743, citing *inter alia* Ov., *Pont.* 2.7.51 *culpa gravis precibus donatur saepe suorum*.

8.12 *Samnite War.*

res praeterea...prospere gestas continet: Cf. 2.16n., 3.10n.

contra Samnites: In his main narrative sequence P. does, as previously discussed, omit a good deal of the fighting with the Samnites in this book (see esp. 8.1n., 8.9n., 8.11n.). I argued that this arises from his melding the First and Second Samnite Wars into a single war. The effect of this final 'round-up' note, which mentions only the Samnites out of all the omissions that P. has made from Livy's book, is the same: the implication is of war against the Samnites continuing without relief in the background to all the events which P. has mentioned explicitly.

Book 9

9.1 *The Caudine Forks.* Corresponds to Livy 9.1.1–12.4. Livy launches immediately into the story of the Caudine Forks, which occupies around the first quarter of Book 9; P. starts his summary of the book the same way, and has it occupy a similar proportion of the text. P.'s summary covers a number of key points: the trapping of the army, the agreement made with the Samnites, the giving of hostages, the passing of the Roman army under the yoke. Then the scene moves to Rome, and to Postumius' argument for his own surrender so as to free the people from their obligation to the Samnites; and P. concludes with the surrender of Postumius and the tribunes, a surrender which the Samites refused to accept.

All of these points are in Livy, and many of them are found in other accounts of the episode as well.[102] There is, however, relatively little that counts as a pattern to the way the story is told, not because there are contradictory traditions, but rather because different authors chose different aspects to emphasize.[103] The one point universally shared is the humiliating fact of the Roman army sent under the yoke; but that apart, the selection varies dramatically. Even the Roman repudiation of the treaty and the surrender of Postumius and the tribunes, which one might have expected to be central to any telling, appears in some sources (Cicero, Florus, Gellius, Dio/Zonaras), but in others is either ignored altogether or present only by implication (Valerius Maximus, Orosius; Eutropius has the treaty repudiated, but nothing on the form the repudiation took). P.'s version appears to represent the core of the story found in Livy at least as well as any other source, and more closely than most.

In one interesting respect, however, P.'s presentation diverges substantially from Livy. A good deal of Livy's account is presented from a non-Roman perspective: in particular, Pontius' justification for continuing the war (9.1.3–11), his debate with his father over the appropriate treatment of the trapped Romans (9.3.4–13), and his angry response to the Roman repudiation of the agreement (9.11) are all presented at some length, as is the sympathetic response of the Capuans to the humiliated Romans (9.6.5–7.5). This perspective is maintained in several of the later sources: Dionysius, Valerius Maximus (with Paris), Florus, Appian, Dio, and Orosius all focus their accounts in whole or in part from a non-Roman point of view. P., by contrast, is wholly Romanocentric.

furcas Caudinas: Livy consistently calls them *furculae*, not *furcae*. *furcae* is, however, used elsewhere, such as Lucan 2.138, Val. Max. 5.1 ext. 5, 7.2 ext. 17,

---

[102] Other accounts of the Caudine Forks episode include Cic., *Inv.* 2.91, *Off.* 3.109, D.H., *AR* 16.1.4 (cf. 16.2), Val. Max. 7.2 ext. 17 (with Paris' epitome), Flor. 1.11.9–11, App., *Samn.* 4.2–7, Dio fr. 36.10–20 (cf. Zonar. 7.26.10–16), Eutr. 2.9.1, Oros. 3.15.2–7.

[103] There are a number of divergences of detail between Livy, Appian, and Dio/Zonaras (see Oakley (2005a), 8–10). None, however, affects the basic outline of the story, which is universally shared.

Amm. 25.9.11: it is interesting to note that Julius Paris' summary of the second Valerius passage (though not the first) makes the opposite change to P.'s, substituting *furculae* for Valerius' *furcae*. This is a useful illustration of how summarizers would form details of their summary (whether or not consciously) on the basis of the broader tradition, rather than on the specific text before them.

artum: Drakenborch, basing himself on the reading *arctum* in one late MS, proposed this correction of *tacitum*, which is found in the chief MSS, but which makes no sense in the context. The Aldine edition proposed *iniquum*, accepted by most other early editors, but *locus artus* is a Livian phrase (29.7.4), and it is characteristic of P. to employ Livian language, even when the phrase does not appear in the particular text he is summarizing.

cum spes nulla esset evadendi: Cf. Flor. 1.11.10: *unde non posset evadere*. The specific phrase *spes evadendi* is not found in classical Latin (though cf. Quint., *Inst.* 1 pr.20 *praesumpta desperatione quo velint evadendi*); it is, however, regularly found in the fourth century and later (e.g. Ambr., *Iac.* 1.8.36, *Fug. Saec.* 9.58, Amm. 19.6.4, Jer., *In Is.* 5.23.6, Julian., *In Iob.* 19.8–9, Serv. auct., *Aen.* 3.458, Serv., *Aen.* 9.723). P. falls naturally into the typical language of his day.

foedere: This diverges from Livy. Livy claims that the agreement made by the consuls at Caudium was not a *foedus*, but a *sponsio* (9.5.1–5): in other words, a personal guarantee by the consuls, not a legally binding treaty. He notes that the view that it was a *foedus* was both popularly believed and claimed by Claudius Quadrigarius in particular (9.5.2 = Quadrig., *FRHist* 24 F 13), but gives detailed arguments as to why this view was mistaken.

It is generally accepted that the idea of the *sponsio* in Livy is a late fabrication, constructed in order to give the fullest possible justification for the Roman repudiation of the treaty (e.g. Mommsen, *StR*³ 1.251 n. 1; Crawford (1973), Oakley (2005a), 31–4; *contra* Loreto (1989–90));[104] if it had indeed originally been only a *sponsio*, it is hard to see how the idea that it was a *foedus* became dominant in the tradition. Apart from Livy himself, App., *Samn.* 4.5 appears to have accepted it (his account is incomplete, but he draws attention to the absence of fetials at Caudium, and hence implies that no legally binding treaty was formed there). But other sources speak directly of a *foedus*: the word is used by Cic., *Inv.* 2.91, Flor. 1.11.11, Gell. 17.21.36, Oros. 3.15.7. P. appears to be following this more mainstream version, implicitly rejecting Livy's spurious legalism (but see further below).

sescentis equitibus Romanis obsidibus datis: Cf. Oros. 3.15.6 (perhaps dependent on P.): *sescentis autem equitibus Romanis in obsidatum receptis*.

---

[104] It was probably invented in the light of the Roman surrender at Numantia and the subsequent repudiation of that agreement, an event which parallels the story of the Caudine Forks so closely that it is likely to have influenced both the general structure and individual details in the latter narrative: see Oakley (2005a), 27–31, and cf. 56.3n.

idemque auctore Spurio Postumio cos.: The construction is odd, since Postumius himself is one of the people included in *idem*. P.'s compression of the story has (not for the only time) led him to a clumsy locution.

deforme foedus: A unique and striking phrase. P. puns on *foedus* = 'treaty', connecting it to *foedus* = 'foul', a connection regularly made in Roman linguistic writings (cf. Maltby (1991), 237–8); *foedus* = 'foul' was often paired with *deformis*, not least by Livy himself (27.31.5, 31.12.8; also e.g. Cic., *Tusc.* 4.35, 5.80, Sen., *Benef.* 4.32.3, Quint., *Inst.* 9.4.30, *Hist. Aug., Car.* 13.2). Similar word-play (though not as stark as in P.)[105] is found in Val. Max. 2.7.1 (*deformi se foederis ictu maculaverat*; cf. also Sil. 16.220). Valerius is describing the surrender at Numantia, which was regularly associated with the Caudine Forks (e.g. Cic., *Off.* 3.109, Vell. 2.1.5, Tac., *Ann.* 15.13.2, Flor. 1.34.7, App., *Hisp.* 83, Oros. 5.7.1; cf. n. 104 above); this might lead one to hypothesize that P. here is alluding to a text in which the Numantine surrender was described, possibly even Livy's own account of that surrender, on which Valerius could well be drawing (cf. 55.5n.).

ictum erat: The indicative suggests that this is the narrator's description, rather than being part of Postumius' argument: it is P. himself who is implying that the treaty was *deforme*.

publica fides liberaretur: This draws on Livy's comment at the very end of the Caudine Forks episode: *forsitan et publica, sua certe liberata fide* (9.11.13: 'with their own pledge at any rate released, and perhaps even the official one as well'). Livy is expressing doubt as to whether the surrender of the officials did indeed release Rome from the agreement with the Samnites. By using the same language in Postumius' argument, P. provides a subtle hint for the informed minority of readers that his claim to be releasing Rome from her obligations is not uncontentious.

foedus spoponderant: P.'s language derives from the fetials' words at the surrender of the guarantors at Livy 9.10.9: *foedus ictum iri spoponderunt*. Livy's phrase, however, in accordance with the legal line which he consistently takes through the episode (above), emphasizes that what Postumius and his colleagues had agreed was not a *foedus*, but a *sponsio*—they had pledged that a *foedus* would be struck, but had not struck such a *foedus* themselves. P. removes the future infinitive, thus maintaining, as he has done throughout, that what the Roman leaders agreed to was a *foedus*, while at the same time through the verb offering a hint at Livy's alternative reading.

dediti Samnitibus non sunt recepti: Cf. Gell. 17.21.36: *Samnitibus per fetiales dediti recepti non sunt*; P. may be drawing on Gellius directly, or both may depend on another source now lost.

---

[105] Oros. 3.15.7 makes the pun starker still: he refers to *huius foedissimi foederis macula*.

9.2 *Roman revenge for the Caudine Forks*. Corresponds to Livy 9.13.6–15.11. P. omits all of the preliminaries to Papirius' victory: in particular the Samnite capture of Satricum and Fregellae (9.12.5–8) and the successful campaign by Papirius' colleague Publilius (9.12.9–13.5). Even with Papirius' own battle, he has nothing of the campaign beyond the fact of victory, ignoring, among other things, the attempt by the Tarentines to make peace (9.14.1–5). Instead, he focuses his attention on the points which demonstrate the reversal which Papirius has accomplished: the passing of the Samnites under the yoke and the return of the Roman hostages, both described in language which reflects the original loss (see below).

The Roman revenge on the Samnites was of considerably less interest to the later tradition than was the original defeat and its immediate aftermath with the surrendering of the consuls. While all surviving continuous narratives complete the story with a reference to the final reversal accomplished by Papirius (D.H., *AR* 16.1.4, Flor. 1.11.11, Dio fr. 36.21–2 (cf. Zonar. 7.26.16), Eutr. 2.9.1, Oros. 3.15.8–9; cf. the *Oxyrhynchus Chronicle* (*FGrH* 255 F 10)), it is rarer for this part of the story to appear as an isolated anecdote: the only exceptions are Livy's own reference to Papirius' achievement in reversing the earlier defeat at 22.14.12 (cf. Chaplin (2000), 44 for the unusual way in which Caudium is converted into a positive *exemplum* here), along with the brief mention at Ampel. 18.7. Among the historical narratives, some, like P., having nothing more than the bare reversal (so Eutropius, Zonaras), whereas others (Florus, Orosius) at least gesture at a description of Papirius' prior campaign, although they too have nothing of Publilius.

sub iugum missis: Livy 9.15.8 quotes a variant version in which Pontius himself was sent under the yoke: this version appears also in D.H., *AR* 16.1.4, Flor. 1.11.11, Oros. 3.15.9, and possibly Quadrig. *FRHist* 24 F 16.[106] P., however, ignores it, keeping more closely to Livy's main narrative.

receptisque sescentis equitibus Romanis qui obsides dati erant: The language is not close to Livy (9.15.7: *equitibus reciperatis quos pignora pacis custodiendos Luceriam Samnites dederant*), but instead mirrors P.'s own phrase in the previous sentence where he reported the handing over of the hostages (9.1 *sescentis equitibus Romanis obsidibus datis*). The sense of reversal, which Livy also highlights (Oakley (2005a), 20), is accentuated by P. through his repeated language.

pudor flagitii: The phrase is not Livian, but is used twice by Tacitus (*Hist.* 3.34.2, *Ann.* 2.14.3; cf. *Ann.* 16.26.3), and otherwise only by Just. 44.4.2. It may be that Justin is employing Tacitean language, or that Tacitus is drawing on Justin's source Pompeius Trogus. Both phenomena occur (cf. Levene (2010b)), but on balance

---

[106] Oakley (2005a), 6 and 167 regards this reading of Quadrigarius as certain; but see *contra* J. Briscoe, *FRHist* III 308, who notes another possible context in which the fragment might have appeared.

the former is perhaps more likely in this case (Yardley (2003), 180), in which case P. may have seen the phrase as distinctively Tacitean, or else as reflecting the general language of early imperial historiography. For *flagitium* in the context of military failure, cf. *TLL* VI 842.23–32.

9.3 *Tribes and colonies*. Corresponds to Livy 9.20.6 and 9.28.7. After covering the opening sections of the book reasonably comprehensively, P. becomes far more patchy for the remainder. From the extensive narrative that Livy offers between Papirius' victory after the Caudine defeat and the censorship of Appius Claudius Caecus, P. selects just two brief notices to highlight. Both of them relate to matters in which he was consistently interested, namely the addition of tribes (2.7n.) and the founding of colonies (4.3n.), but even on this score he is lacking, mentioning two of the colonies founded at this time, but omitting two others, Luceria (9.26.3–5) and Interamna (9.28.8). Material omitted (though see 9.5n.) includes fighting against the Samnites and Satricans (9.16.2–10), the Samnites and Saticulani (9.21–22), the Samnites and the Sorani (9.23–24), the Samnites and the Lucerians (9.26.1–2), and finally the Samnites alone (9.27.1–28.6); also defeats inflicted on the Apulians and Lucanians (9.20.7–9) and on the Ausones (9.25), and a conspiracy against Rome at Capua, the investigation of which descended into the pursuit of grievances at Rome itself (9.26.5–22).

Offentina: The archetype reading in Livy is *Ufentina*. The epigraphical evidence, however, shows that the original name was *Oufentina*: *Ufentina* is rarely found (Fayer (1962), 191). The chief MSS of P. vary between *Ofentina* and *Offentina*. The latter should be read here, since it is commonplace in inscriptions (Fayer *loc. cit.*), and it is possible that this is the correct reading in Livy also.

adiectae sunt: Cf. 1.B.3n., 19.11n.

Pontia: Livy, like most classical Latin authors, calls it *Pontiae*, but the singular *Pontia* is not only the usual form in Greek (e.g. D.S. 19.101.3, Str. 5.3.6), but is found in Latin at Suet., *Tib.* 54.2 and, perhaps most importantly, at Jer., *Epist.* 108.7, which refers to it as a site of Christian pilgrimage. P. is probably using the form most current in his own day.

coloniae deductae sunt: Cf. 1.B.1n.

9.4 *Censorship of Appius Claudius Caecus*. Corresponds to Livy 9.29.5–30.2. As noted above (9.3n.), after the Caudine Forks P. skips rapidly over Livy's narrative; the censorship of Claudius is one of only two episodes from the remainder of the book that he treats in detail (cf. 9.6n.). Its interest to him is presumably in part that Appius himself was the most memorable and controversial figure of the period (13.3n.), and in part that his censorship introduced two major features of the Roman landscape, the Aqua Appia and the Via Appia, respectively Rome's first aqueduct and its first officially created road. Both of these building works are referred to by P., even as he fails to mention the feature of the censorship on which Livy himself places a great deal of emphasis, namely the removal of the rites of Hercules at the Ara Maxima from the Potitii, with the consequent divine punishment both to that family and to Appius himself.

This does not make P. unique, but it does place him on one side of a clear division in the traditions of Appius' censorship. Only two authors have both the Ara Maxima controversy and the building programme: D.S. 20.36, and *Vir. Ill.* 34.1–2, 6–8. Several authors describe nothing but the former (Val. Max. 1.1.17 (also the epitomes by Paris and Nepotianus), Fest. 270L, Lact., *Inst.* 2.7.15, Macr., *Sat.* 3.6.13, Serv., *Aen.* 8.179). There are also those who focus solely on the building (Cic., *Cael.* 34, *CIL* XI 1827 = *ILS* 54, Frontin., *Aq.* 5.1–3, Pompon., *Dig.* 1.2.2.36, Eutr. 2.9.2, Procop., *Goth.* 1.14.6–11). P., like these, is more interested in Appius' solid achievements than in a story of impiety and divine revenge which reflects far less well upon him; he similarly smooths over the problems in Appius' character when, like most others, he does not mention his contentious extension of his censorship beyond the statutory eighteen-month period, which Livy recounts in even greater detail (9.33.3–34.26).

What makes P. more of an outlier is his further reference to Appius' admission of the sons of freedmen to the Senate, something otherwise described only in D.S. 20.36.3 (mistakenly claiming it was the freedmen themselves) and Suet., *Claud.* 24.1. This was another 'first', although not explicitly mentioned by P. as one, with broader implications for questions of the extension of political power to those of lower social status, a matter in which he is at least intermittently interested (cf. e.g. 2.8, 6.4, 13.4, 18.4, 20.11, 74.3, 77.1, 84.5); it also, perhaps at least as importantly, ties the episode closely to the one remaining episode from the book which he will recount in detail, namely the aedileship of Cn. Flavius (9.6n.).

aquam perduxit: A surprisingly compressed phrase. Livy has *aquam in urbem duxit* (9.29.6), and variations of this are found in other sources (*CIL* XI 1187 = *ILS* 54 *aquam in urbem adduxit*; Frontin., *Aq.* 5.1 *aqua Appia in urbem inducta est*; *Vir. Ill.* 34.7 *aquam Anienem in urbem induxit*); others do not mention the destination, but identify the aqueduct in question (Pompon., *Dig.* 1.2.2.36 and Eutr. 2.9.2 both read *aquam Claudiam induxit*). However, P.'s compression is paralleled in Cic., *Cael.* 34 *aquam adduxi*, and *perducere* makes the phrase readily comprehensible, since *aquam perducere* has the technical sense of 'bringing in water' via a new construction (Rodgers (2004), 131–2; cf. *TLL* X 1285.9–45); it is repeatedly used in that sense by Frontinus, and one finds comparably bald phrasing to P.'s at Frontin., *Aq.* 128.1 *cum aquas perducerent* and Suet., *Aug.* 42.1 *perductis pluribus aquis.*

viam stravit: Cf. Livy 9.29.6 *viam munivit*. However, P.'s phrase is not a synonym: *viam munire* is a general term for the construction of a road, whereas *viam sternere* refers specifically to its being paved (Oakley (2005a), 373). It is widely believed that Appius' construction during his censorship involved only the former, and that the (many) texts, which, like P., refer to Appius 'paving' the road,[107] are simply in error (so e.g. Wiseman (1970), 140–1, Rodgers (2004), 145, Oakley (2005a), 373–5; Humm (1996), 698–70 is more cautious, but ultimately is not prepared to assert that Appius himself had the road paved). The primary reason for doubting that Appius paved the road is that Livy appears to refer to the first section, up to the temple of Mars, being paved for the first time sixteen years later (10.23.12), and to the paving continuing to Bovillae in 293 (10.47.4); Oakley also asserts ((2005a), 375) that Rome could not have afforded to pave the road in Appius' day.

However, there are reasons to question this argument. Briscoe (2008), 103 rightly observes that the paving in Livy 10.23.12 is said to be of a *semita*, which he suggests means 'a pedestrian path by the side of the road'.[108] Briscoe's argument may be reinforced: there is no example of *semita* used for a major road such as the *via Appia*, and many texts make it clear that the Romans regarded the two as entirely distinct (e.g. Plaut., *Cas.* 675, *Rud.* 212, Enn., *Trag.* 267 (Jocelyn), Cic., *II Verr.* 2.57, *Leg. Agr.* 2.96, Mart. 7.61.4, Serv., *Aen.* 4.405); for *semita* as a path by the roadside cf. Plaut., *Curc.* 287.

Livy 10.47.4 does refer to the *via* being paved in 293 between the temple of Mars and Bovillae, and the argument made above shows that this must refer to the road itself, not a side-path. But this would be compatible with the first section of the road being paved when Appius built it in 312, a side-path being paved to the same distance in 296, with the second section of the road paved in 293. The temple of Mars stood between the first and second milestone from the city (*CIL* VI 10234 = *ILS* 7213); I can see no reason to think that it would have been prohibitively expensive to pave the short section leading to it in 312, but affordable to do so in 296;[109] nor does it seem likely that a footpath to the side of the road would have been paved while the road itself was not.

While one cannot show definitively that this is the case, and it is after all possible either that P. and the other sources which talk of paving the road are simply in error, or else that Livy's phrasing at 10.23.12 was misleading, this scenario, which allows a significant degree of truth to all the sources (some of the Via Appia was paved by Appius, even if not all of it), is at least as plausible as any other. In

---

[107] D.S. 20.36.2, *CIL* XI 1187 = *ILS* 54, Pompon., *Dig.* 1.2.2.36, Eutr. 2.9.2, *Vir. Ill.* 34.6, Procop., *Goth.* 1.14.6–11.

[108] That Livy 10.23.12 refers to a footpath rather than the road proper had already been observed by Wiseman (1970), 144 and (more tentatively) Humm (1996), 699; but neither saw the implications for the paving of the Via Appia itself.

[109] Bernard (2018), 130–1, on the basis of the Hadrianic-era repair cost of the southern portion of the road recorded in *CIL* IX 6075 = *ILS* 5875, estimates the cost of paving the entire road from Rome to Capua at 15 million HS = 5 million person-days; on that basis, paving to the second milestone from the city would have cost around 212,265 HS = 70,754 person-days. As a point of comparison, Bernard notes that the Aqua Appia, started at the same time, most of which was underground, may have required 33,000 person-days (= 100,000 HS) for a single (Roman) foot of tunnel (Bernard (2018), 132–3).

either case we can see P. here, not contradicting Livy, but rather interpreting him on the basis of a widespread understanding of Appius' achievement.

libertinorum filios in senatum legit: Cf. Livy 9.46.10 *senatum primus libertinorum filiis lectis inquinaverat*. P. takes this information not from Livy's account of Appius' censorship (where Livy records controversy over Appius' selection of (allegedly) inferior men for the Senate, but does not give any details as to what made them unsuitable: 9.29.7, 9.30.1–2), but from his narrative of the aedileship of Cn. Flavius (cf. 9.6n.), where he mentions it in passing as part of the background to Flavius' election.

is ordo...inquinatus videbatur: *inquinatus* likewise derives from Livy 9.46.10 (quoted above: cf. Bingham 202): one of only two times the word appears in Livy's surviving text (the other being 29.37.11), and one of only two times it appears in P. (cf. 88.1n.).

indignis: The instrumental ablative is surprising, especially in a late antique author: they tend to be stricter than classical writers when it comes to omitting *a* or *ab* with groups of people (cf. H-S 122). It is presumably used in order to mark the fact that the sons of freedmen, about whom the complaint is made, are the means whereby Appius is deemed to have stained the Senate, not the ones who actively caused the stain. It is also worth pointing out the subversive ambiguity that emerges: precisely because the ablative is unexpected, the reader might also be tempted to read it as a dative after *videbatur*, with the implication that it is those who objected to senators with freedman parentage rather than the new senators themselves who were 'unworthy'.

in senatu legendo observaverunt: The chief MSS read *in senatu observaverunt*, which is meaningless. Most editions read *in senatu legendo*, found in one late MS; Rossbach tentatively suggested *in senatu citando* on the basis of Livy 9.30.2 *negaverunt eam lectionem se...observaturos et senatum extemplo citaverunt*. But since P. never otherwise uses *citare*, but employs *legere* elsewhere in this context, including earlier in this same note (also 18.4, 59.7), *legendo* is probably preferable, even if the MS authority is weak.

quem ad modum ante proximos censores fuerat: Cf. Livy 9.30.2 *eo ordine qui ante censores Ap. Claudium et C. Plautium fuerat*. *proximi censores* should refer to the censors before Claudius and Plautius, not Claudius and Plautius themselves. However, Livy uses the same phrase a few lines later (9.30.5), and although the most natural reading of those lines would likewise take it to refer to the previous censors (so Palmer (1965), 309), there is a good case to be made that he means Claudius and Plautius by it (Oakley (2005a), 399); this certainly appears to be the way P. interpreted it. Once again (cf. above), this constitutes evidence that P. is working directly from Livy's text, rather than from an earlier summary.

9.5 *Wars against Italian tribes*. P., unusually, inserts his familiar 'round-up' sentence (2.16n., 3.10n.) not at the end of the book, but when he still has some episodes to come. This may be in part because one of the things which he is still to mention is the entirely anomalous 'Alexander digression', which is itself presented out of narrative order (9.7n.). But it is also relevant that P. has still one episode in his chronological sequence to come, namely the story of Cn. Flavius (9.6n.), which is the last episode in Livy's book: the wars referred to in this passage thus represent something closer to a narrative than they would if the sentence were placed in its usual position at the very end (see below).

res praeterea...prospere gestas continet: Cf. 2.16n., 3.10n.

contra Apulos et Etruscos et Umbros et Marsos et Paelignos et Aequos et Samnites: After describing the beginning of Appius' censorship, Livy has further accounts of fighting against the Etruscans (9.32—although that hardly counts as a Roman success—9.35–36, 9.39.5–11, 9.40.18–20, 9.41.5–7), against the Etruscans and Umbrians together (9.37, 9.41.8–20), against the Marsi (9.41.4), the Paeligni (9.41.4), the Hernici (9.42.11–43.7), and the Aequi (9.45.5–18). Every one of these is mentioned in P.'s list apart from the Hernici: moreover, they are, unusually, listed in exactly the order they first appear in Livy's text.

By contrast, the wars prior to the censorship are much more patchily represented here (cf. 9.3n.): if one leaves out the special case of the Samnites (below), of the fighting between 9.15 and 9.29 only the Apulians are mentioned here (cf. 9.20.7–9): the Satricans, the Saticulani, the Sorani, the Lucerians, the Lucanians, and the Ausones are all omitted. This once again (cf. above) gives the sense that P. is directly looking to represent the narrative in Book 9 (cf. 7.13n.): this notice, placed between the censorship of Appius and the aedileship of Flavius, gives a fair reflection specifically of the wars that intervene between those points.

The exception is of course the Samnites. These are listed last, although they are the first Roman opponents who appear in the book, and are constantly in conflict with them, both before and after the censorship: the Romans are recorded as fighting against them, usually successfully, at 9.16.2–10, 9.21–24, 9.26.1–2, 9.27.1–28.6, 9.31, 9.38, 9.40.1–14, 9.42.6–7, 9.43.7–21, 9.44.5–16. Their position in the text thus in one sense breaks the chronology, but in another sense it reinforces it, since after the last of these wars, close to the end of the book, Livy records the renewal of the treaty between them and Rome, and P. does the same, putting a seal on the narrative of the fighting.

quibus foedus restitutum est: Cf. Livy 9.45.4 *foedus antiquum Samnitibus redditum*. *foedus restituere* is itself a Livian phrase, used by him at 10.3.5, but found nowhere else in surviving Latin literature. As often, P., even when not reproducing Livy's phrasing from the passage he is summarizing, employs Livian language.

9.6 Aedileship of Cn. Flavius. Corresponds to Livy 9.46. The balance of Livy's narrative is, however, rather different from P.'s. P., unlike Livy, shows little interest in anything about Flavius himself or what he did—he mentions neither his publication of the civil law code and the calendar, nor his controversy with the nobles over his dedication of a temple, nor the scene where he ostentatiously occupies his curule chair against the nobles who despised him. Instead, P. focuses entirely on the electoral politics: the composition of the electorate who selected Flavius for office, and the reforms of Fabius to prevent a similar election from taking place in the future. This is surprising, since the balance in later accounts of Flavius is quite different. It was above all his publication of the calendar and the civil law that attracted attention (Cic., *Mur.* 25, *De Orat.* 1.186, *Att.* 6.1.8, 18, Val. Max. 2.5.2 (also Paris and Nepotianus' summaries), Plin., *Nat.* 33.17, Pompon., *Dig.* 1.2.2.7, Macr., *Sat.* 1.15.9); the curule chair story was also relayed by Piso, *FRHist* 9 F 29 (*ap.* Gell. 7.9) and Val. Max. 2.5.2 (with Paris and Nepotianus), and the dedication of the temple of Concord by Plin., *Nat.* 33.19.

The contentiousness of his election forms a lesser aspect of later memories of him, though there is something of it in D.S. 20.36.6, Val. Max. 9.3.3 (also Paris' summary), and Plin., *Nat.* 33.18. There is also an entirely separate tradition of remembering Fabius' attacks on the rights of the lower classes, which is usually connected with his receiving the *cognomen* Maximus (Val. Max. 2.2.9 (with Paris' and Nepotianus' summaries), Plu., *Pomp.* 13.5, Ampel. 18.6, *Vir. Ill.* 32.1–2). However, no one save Livy and P. links Fabius' actions to the controversy over Flavius' election. On this occasion, P.'s interests are governed less by the existing traditions over Flavius than by his broader interest in class conflict at Rome.

Cn. Flavius scriba, libertino patre natus: Cf. Livy 9.46.1: *Cn. Flavius Cn. Filius scriba, patre libertino humili fortuna ortus*; P.'s *natus* is closer to Piso (*FRHist* 9 F 29: *Cn. Flavius...patre libertino natus*), who is likely to have been Livy's source— Livy substituted a word of higher register (Oakley (2005a), 603–4). That might suggest that P. is deliberately returning to Livy's predecessor rather than Livy himself. However, it is unlikely that P. could have had independent access to Piso (although he could have found this fragment in Gellius); and it is worth noting that his language is even closer to the phrase that Horace repeatedly uses of himself in *Sat.* 1.6 (ll. 6, 45, 46: *libertino patre natum*; cf. *Epist.* 1.20.20 *me libertino natum patre*)—with the additional complication that it is likely that Horace is himself alluding to Piso in this passage, and is associating himself, a *scriba* who was a freedman's son, with an iconic figure from Roman history whose status was identical (Woodman (2009), 158–60 = (2012), 113–15).

aedilis curulis fuit: Cf. Livy 9.46.1: *aedilis curulis fuit*.

per forensem factionem creatus: Cf. Livy 9.46.10: *Flavium dixerat aedilem forensis factio*.

comitia et campum turbaret: Cf. Livy 9.46.7: *forum et campum corrupit*.

in quattuor tribus redacta est: Cf. Livy 9.46.14: *in quattuor tribus coniecit*. For *redigere* (= 'bring into a (usually reduced) condition') see *OLD s.v. redigo* 7a: P. uses the same phrase in a similar context at 20.11.

nomen dedit: *nomen*, omitted by the main MSS, was inserted in the Renaissance: it is a clearly necessary supplement.

9.7 The Alexander Digression. Corresponds to Livy 9.17–19. This is a unique episode in Livy, and indeed in ancient historiography—a long exercise in counterfactual history. It is perhaps unsurprising that P. should have considered so unusual an episode worth mentioning in his summary. It is also unsurprising that he does so out of the sequence of the chronological narrative,[110] since Livy's argument, while formally needing to take place at a time in his history when Alexander was alive, is only very tenuously tied to the actual moment at which he introduces it.[111] Instead, P. removes it from the narrative sequence, and presents it as a notice of an additional point which was contained in Livy's book; he furthermore associates the argument with Livy personally in a way that is almost unparalleled in his work (see below).

Similar comparisons of Alexander with the Romans—and especially with Papirius Cursor, whose generalship forms the specific peg on which Livy hangs his discussion—are found at Plu., *Pyrrh.* 19.1, Jul., *Ep.* 51 (433C), Amm. 30.8.5, Oros. 3.15.10, Lyd., *Mag.* 1.38. That there is some relationship of these with Livy seems overwhelmingly likely: they could all depend on him directly or indirectly, or some could go back to a source which he himself used (cf. Oakley (2005a), 194–6). It is worth noting that Orosius cannot in this case be deriving his account from P. (cf. Introduction), since he makes the specific comparison with Papirius found in Livy, and P. does not.

in hoc libro mentionem habet Alexandri: sc. *Livius.* It is extremely unusual for P. to make Livy, rather than the book, the implied subject of a sentence: the only possible parallels are 20.8 and 21.1 (see *ad loc.*).[112] This gives the notice here the appearance of the thoughts of an individual, rather than, as is the case with most of P., the summary of a history which existed independently of Livy, even if he happened to be the one to relay it.

aestimatis populi Romani viribus: *vires aestimare* is a Livian phrase, though not used in this passage: cf. 34.27.1, 35.15.8. It is occasionally found elsewhere in Latin (e.g. Sen., *De Ira* 1.11.8; *Dig.* 29.1.36.3), but does not otherwise appear in P.

---

[110] *Contra* Bingham 205, who claims that 'the only possible explanation for its position at the end of the *Periocha* is that it is a later addition of the author after he had finished the summarization of the rest of the book'; we may compare (for example) *Per.* 23.13 (see discussion *ad loc.*) for P. introducing at the end of the book material that in Livy had formed a digressive discourse earlier in it.

[111] For the reasons Livy placed the digression here, see Oakley (2005a), 196–7.

[112] These parallels are, however, overlooked by Wölfflin (1877), 345, who uses the supposed uniqueness of the phrase as part of his argument that the entire notice should be deleted as a later interpolation. The claim of interpolation is moreover weakened by the fact that Wölfflin in this article is arguing that *all* of the (many) places where P. includes material after his *res praeterea…continet* summary formula are to be considered interpolations; his assumption of a crass uniformity in P.'s practice reaches the level of *petitio principii*.

colligit: Here too (cf. above) the subject is Livy. For *colligere* (= 'deduce') with the accusative and infinitive see *TLL* III 1617.75–1618.23.

si Alexander in Italiam traiecisset: Cf. Livy 9.17.9: *si…in Italiam traiecisset.*

fore: Strictly speaking this should be *futuram fuisse*, representing the apodosis of a past counterfactual conditional (Woodcock 235). It is hard to parallel the substitution of a future infinitive here, but the effect appears to be one of temporary vividness, as if Livy was himself a contemporary of Alexander, and was reasoning about the likely future effects of his hypothetical invasion. Wölfflin (1877), 312 claims the anomalous syntax as a reason to delete the entire sentence, but, even if we leave aside the broader problems with this argument (cf. n. 112 above), it is not clear why the grammatical oddity would be more likely in an interpolator than in P. himself.

ad orientem: Livy's argument for the superiority of the Romans to Alexander depends in part on the deployment of invidious stereotypes about the weakness of the Easterners over whom Alexander gained his famous victories (e.g. 9.17.16–17, 9.19.10–11). P. does not explicitly refer to those stereotypes, but his pointed reference to the fact that Alexander's victories were in the East allows them to be activated in the minds of readers who shared those prejudices, and provides the one concrete indication of why Livy regarded the Romans as superior.

Book 10

10.1 *Foundation of colonies.* Corresponds to Livy 10.1.1–2, 10.3.2, and perhaps 10.13.1 (see below). Livy begins the book with a series of relatively minor notices; apart from the colony foundations, he also mentions citizenship given to the Arpinates and Trebulani (10.1.3), the punishment of the Frusinates for conspiracy (10.1.3), a Roman attack on Umbria (10.1.4–6), a brief war with the Aequi (10.1.7–9), the invasion of Italy by the Spartan Cleonymus (10.2), and a treaty with the Vestini (10.3.1). Of these, P. mentions none apart from the foundations: these are not only the first point in Livy's book, but relate to a topic in which P. is consistently interested (see 4.3n.).

coloniae deductae sunt: Cf. 1.B.1n.

Carsioli: Livy has two contradictory reports of this foundation, one at 10.3.2, where he records it as being founded in 302/1, wrongly locating it on Marsic territory (cf. 10.2n.), and one at 10.13.1, where he records the foundation in 298 on the territory of the Aequi (for the discrepancy cf. Oakley (2005b), 69–70). It is conceivable that P. has both passages in mind, and it would certainly not be uncharacteristic for him to bring colonial foundations together under a single notice even when they were separated in Livy's text (see e.g. 8.6n.). However, on balance the likelihood is that he is looking only at the first passage, which is chronologically closer to the other foundations.

The MSS of Livy read *Carseoli*, which is the spelling found in most literary sources. However, the MSS of P. are consistent in reading *Carsioli*, which is also the form attested epigraphically (*CIL* IX 4067 = *ILS* 6538), and is likely to be correct (cf. Mommsen, *CIL* IX p. 382). That spelling should, accordingly, be retained here; it is possible that it is the original reading of Livy also.

10.2 *Defeat of the Marsi.* Corresponds to Livy 10.3.2–5. It is not clear why P. chooses this relatively minor point in Livy to summarize, when he ignores Livy's rather longer account of a war with the Etruscans, which immediately follows the fighting here (10.3.6–5.13). It is possibly connected with the resonant cultural image of the Marsi in Roman literature (on which see Dench (1995), esp. 159–73), but one should not overinterpret: P.'s selection of minor notices often appears to be little more than arbitrary (cf. e.g. 1.B.2n., 4.9n.).

in deditionem accepti sunt: Livy himself represents it differently: according to him (10.3.5), the Marsi were defeated in a single battle, driven into their cities, three of which were then rapidly captured; after which the dictator M. Valerius Maximus Corvus restored the treaty with them (*foedus restituit*), though punishing them with the loss of territory. Livy does not say that the Marsi surrendered.

It may be that P. here is simply summarizing Livy inaccurately (so Bingham 207), inferring the surrender from the account of a comprehensive defeat. But it is also possible that he is reflecting a non-Livian tradition in which the defeated Marsi surrendered to Rome: such a surrender would not comprise a treaty in itself (Heuss (1933), 61–2, Dahlheim (1968), 20–2), but a treaty might follow it as part of the new arrangements imposed by the Romans (cf. Heuss (1933), 78–83): hence this tradition would not necessarily be incompatible with Livy. It is admittedly unprovable whether P. is indeed reflecting such a tradition, but the possibility lends some small additional weight to the already strong likelihood[113] that the treaty made with the Marsi here was not an exact renewal of the earlier one (Livy 9.45.18), as a literal reading of Livy might be taken to imply, but one adapted to take account of the reduced status of the defeated party (so Oakley (2005a), 273; *contra* Badian (1958), 27–8).

10.3 *Enlargement of augural college*. Corresponds to Livy 10.6.3–9.2. The oddity of P.'s account is that the law in question, as recounted by Livy, involved increasing the number of both the pontifices and the augurs; but P. mentions only the latter. The reason is perhaps that Livy is himself puzzled by the number of augurs—why there should only have been four in the first place—and so focuses slightly more on that office than on the other (10.6.7–8): hence the summarizer's attention was drawn to it. It is also noteworthy that whereas, for Livy, this is above all part of the class struggle at Rome—plebeians were excluded from the colleges, and the new appointees were all to be drawn from them—P. completely ignores that side to it. P. is at least intermittently interested in the class struggles of the early Republic (cf. e.g. 9.4n.), but he is even more interested in the development of Roman institutions, and he treats the proposal here as an example of the latter rather than of the former.

ampliatum est: Cf. 1.B.2n.

quaterni: Livy himself has *quattuor* (10.6.6–7); but a substitution of the distributive for the cardinal number is a commonplace stylistic feature in post-Augustan prose (cf. H-S 212).

10.4 *Lex de provocatione*. Corresponds to Livy 10.9.3–6. P. had recorded the first of these laws (2.4n.), though not the second (Livy 3.55.4–5); his language draws in part on his notice there, tying the two together (see below): his interest is once again in the constitutional development of Rome.

---

[113] This is assuming that the war with the Marsi took place at all; for reasons to doubt its historicity, see De Sanctis II 324–5 [341], who rightly notes Livy's claim that the war was provoked by the foundation of Carsioli on Marsic territory; but Carsioli was not on Marsic territory, and may not even have been founded in that year (see 10.1n.). On balance De Sanctis's scepticism may go too far, given that Valerius' triumph over the Marsi appears also in the *Fasti Capitolini*, but he offers a salutary reminder of the fragility of our knowledge of the period.

lex de provocatione ad populum: Cf. Livy 10.9.3 *de provocatione legem tulit*. P.'s *ad populum* is not explicit in Livy's account here, but P. is reflecting his own language on the occasion of passing of the first of these laws (2.4 *legem de provocatione ad populum tulit*).

†Murena†: The MS reading is extremely puzzling. Livy is clear that the person who passed the law was M. Valerius Maximus Corvus—he makes a point of noting that all three laws *de provocatione* were passed by members of the same family (10.9.3). No prominent Roman by the name of Murena is known at that period, or indeed for another 150 years; even if we grant that P. sometimes introduces non-Livian material, this seems too far-fetched to represent an alternative tradition. But neither is it satisfactory merely to emend P. to *Valerius* or *M. Valerius* to conform with Livy, as the Aldine edition and subsequent editors do—there is no easy way of seeing how such a corruption could have occurred.[114] The most likely explanation is that some other name, perhaps representing a non-Livian tradition, or else some longer phrase, is concealed within P.'s transmitted text, but since no other account of this law survives, it is impossible to say which name or phrase it is. Accordingly, it seems most prudent to obelize.

tertio tunc lata est: Cf. Livy 10.9.3: *tertio ea tum post reges exactos lata est*. However, *tunc* in P. has a rather different force from Livy's *tum*. As usual in P., it marks chronology: it shows that the event in question took place at the same time as the one in the previous notice (cf. 4.2n., 11.5n.). Livy has already noted the chronological juxtaposition with the enlarging of the priesthoods, when he observed that the two took place in the same year (10.9.3 *eodem anno*); the *tum* is superfluous for that purpose, and instead reinforces the point in *tertio*—that this was the time when the third of the *leges de provocatione* was passed.

The chief MSS of P. read *pretio*; two late MSS make the necessary emendation on the basis of Livy.

10.5 *Addition of new tribes.* Corresponds to Livy 10.9.14: as always, this is a topic in which P. is especially interested (2.7n.).

adiectae sunt: Cf. 1.B.3n., 19.11n.

Teretina: The MSS of P. read *Terentia*; those of Livy 10.9.14 read either *Terentina* or *Tarentina*. Mommsen (1857) demonstrated, partly on the basis of Fest. 498L and *CIL* III 4464, that the correct spelling is *Teretina*, and Oakley (2005b), 150 accordingly argues that this is the correct reading of Livy also. It follows that the same text should be read here: there is no reason to suspect that the word had already been corrupted in P.'s text of Livy, and it is easy to see how a later scribe might have altered *Teretina* into a name of a more familiar form.

---

[114] *Contra* Begbie (1967), 334, who refers to it as 'an easy manuscript corruption'.

10.6 *Opening of the Third Samnite War*. Corresponds to Livy 10.11.11–12.9, 10.14.1–15.6, 10.16.1–18.8, 10.20.1–21.6. P. places into a single notice the fighting with the Samnites that separates the opening of the war from the assembling of the coalition that the Romans will face at Sentinum (10.7n.). In the course of this, he not only (inevitably) passes over the details of the fighting, but also omits wars with the Umbrians and Etruscans (10.10.1–11.6, 10.18.9–19.22), and the beginnings of the coalition of these and others with the Samnites that will ultimately come together in the year of Sentinum (10.16.3–8, 10.18.1–4, 10.21.11–15), as well as the electoral politics centring on Fabius Rullianus and Decius Mus (10.13.2–13, 10.22.1–26.7), and Appius Claudius Caecus (10.15.7–12). P. even omits the foundation of colonies, something which is usually of interest to him: he mentions neither the colony of Narnia (10.10.1–5), nor Minturnae and Sinuessa (10.21.7–10). All of these are subsumed into a bare mention of Roman victories; only with Sentinum and Aquilonia (10.7–8nn.) will P. revert to a more varied set of stories.

adversus eos saepe prospere pugnatum est: Cf. 2.6n.

10.7 *Battle of Sentinum; devotio of Decius*. Corresponds to Livy 10.26.7–30.10. The primary feature remembered about Sentinum was the *devotio* of the younger Decius; this is directly said by Livy to be in imitation of his father (10.28.12–13, 10.28.15; cf. 10.30.9), which is the aspect on which P., likewise, focuses. This is unsurprising: by far the most common way for the younger Decius to be cited in the later tradition was in tandem with his father (e.g. Cic., *Sest.* 48, *Dom.* 64, *Tusc.* 1.89, 2.59, *Cato* 75, *Nat. Deor.* 3.15, *Parad.* 1.12, *Schol. Bob.* p. 131 (Stangl), Sen., *Benef.* 6.36.2, Plin., *Nat.* 28.12, Frontin., *Strat.* 4.5.15, Juv. 8.254–8 (with scholia), Ampel. 20.6, ps.-Plu., *Par. Min.* 310B (citing Aristeides of Miletus, *FGrH* 286 F 19)), or else he was specifically said, as here, to be imitating his father (so Cic., *Fin.* 2.61, *Div.* 1.51, Val. Max. 5.6.6, Sen., *Epist.* 67.9, Flor. 1.12.7, *Vir. Ill.* 27.3, Zonar. 8.1.6).

Etruscos, Umbros, Samnites, Gallos: According to Livy's main narrative, the battle of Sentinum was fought only against the Samnites and the Gauls, since the Etruscans and Umbrians had been drawn away from their allies by a Roman counterattack against Etruscan territory (10.27.6;[115] cf. 10.27.11, also Plb. 2.19.5–6, Frontin., *Strat.* 1.8.3, Oros. 3.21.3). However, Livy later reports (10.30.5) that some earlier sources had all four nations present at the battle, and this

---

[115] Accepting Gundermann's supplement of *Etruscos* ⟨*et Umbros*⟩ at 10.27.6, where the MSS only has *Etruscos*; for reasons to prefer that reading see Oakley (2005b), 315.

occasionally is found in the later tradition also (Ampel. 18.6, implicitly Cic., *Tusc.* 1.89).[116] This appears to be the version that P. is following here (interestingly, listing first the two which Livy himself said were not present, as if to highlight their importance).

The likelihood is that Livy's main account is correct (see e.g. De Sanctis II 339 [357], Harris (1971), 72–3; *contra* Firpo (2002), 96–8): the claim of the Romans fighting four nations in a single battle looks, as Livy himself implies, like an attempt to magnify the Roman achievement by exaggerating the size of the enemy army. It is true that the record of Fabius' triumph in the *Fasti Capitolini* includes the Etruscans, as does Livy's account of the same triumph (10.30.8), but it is likely that this is the consequence either of additional fighting by Fabius, or because he took the credit for the victories of the propraetor Fulvius (Oakley (2005b), 289).

in magno discrimine: The phrase is used once by Livy, but in a rather different context (*Praef.* 8, though cf. also 6.36.7, 10.39.7, 25.41.9, 29.7.1, 31.32.1). P. uses it on just two other occasions (7.11, 22.4).[117] Interestingly, the first of these is the occasion when our Decius' father risked his life to rescue his army during the First Samnite War, an episode which prefigured his later *devotio* (cf. 7.11n.). The allusion allows the reader to connect the son to his father's entire heroic career, not merely the specific moment of *devotio*.

P. Decius, secutus patris exemplum, devovit se pro exercitu: Cf. Livy 10.28.14: *se legionesque hostium pro exercitu populi Romani Quiritium devoveret*. Moreover, P. graphically illustrates the fact that Decius was following his father's example by employing exactly the same language as he had in 8.3 (see *ad loc.*). With the participial phrase, P. appears to be drawing directly on Val. Max. 5.6.6 *patris exemplum secutus*; cf. also *Vir. Ill.* 27.3 *exemplum patris imitatus*, Schol. ad Juv. 8.254 *exemplo patris*.

morte sua victoriam eius pugnae populo Romano dedit: Livy's own account is more complex (see Levene (1993), 236): as with the *devotio* of Decius' father, he attributes the victory in part to the *devotio*, but also in part to the strategic skills of Fabius. Here too, as with that earlier *devotio* (8.3n.), P. makes the *devotio* itself the sole effective agent; and in this he is following the dominant tradition: compare e.g. Val. Max. 5.6.6, Sen., *Benef.* 6.36.2, Frontin., *Strat.* 4.5.15, ps.-Plu., *Par. Min.* 310B (= Aristeides of Miletus, *FGrH* 286 F 19), *Vir. Ill.* 27.4.

---

[116] Compare *Vir. Ill.* 27.3, who says that Decius' *devotio* took place when the four nations conspired against Rome: he does not say directly that all four were present at Sentinum, although the general tenor of his narrative implies their presence (otherwise it is hard to see why they are mentioned in the context of the *devotio*). Cf. *Vir. Ill.* 32.3, where Fabius is said to have triumphed over the Gauls, Umbrians, Marsi, and Etruscans—the Marsi presumably appearing here because the author conflated them with the Samnites: ethnic identities of the central Apennine peoples, always problematic to some degree, were increasingly fluid in the imperial period (compare Dench (1995), 175–217).

[117] In the later books he regularly employs *cum magno discrimine* (104.5, 112.4, 113.6, 115.4).

Once again (cf. above), P. recalls the earlier *devotio* by employing similar language: cf. 8.3 *morte sua Romanis victoriam restituit*.

10.8 Battle of Aquilonia. Corresponds to Livy 10.38–42; P. makes no mention of the less prominent episodes of fighting against the Samnites (and, to a lesser extent, the Etruscans) that took place between Sentinum and Aquilonia, which occupy Livy 10.31–7.

As for the battle itself, there is little consistency in the tradition. Perhaps the most distinctive features of Livy's account are the religious ceremonies with which, according to him, the Samnites bound themselves prior to the battle, and the story of the deceitful chicken-keeper. Oros. 3.22.1–4 has both of these, though the latter is in a radically different form from Livy's, one which suits better his critique of Roman paganism: in his version, the chicken-keeper announces a bad omen, which Papirius ignores, but nevertheless wins the battle. Val. Max. 7.2.5 (also Paris' epitome) has only the chicken-keeper story; a surviving fragment of Dio's account (fr. 36.29) refers to the Samnite ceremonies, although the section of Zonaras deriving from Dio barely mentions the battle at all (8.1.9). There are also references to other aspects of the battle in Plin., *Nat.* 14.91 and Frontin., *Strat.* 2.4.1.

P. records the victory, and also refers to the Samnite ceremonies, but in far less critical terms than Livy does (cf. also below): he has none of the lurid details which Livy uses to give a sense of alien and corrupt religious practices (cf. Levene (1993), 237–8). He does not mention the story of the chicken-keeper, perhaps because it did not lend itself readily to summary: the manner whereby Papirius 'converted' the omen from a negative one to a positive one would be incomprehensible to his audience unless more details were given than he typically allows himself space for (cf. Linderski (1993), 60–1).

Papirius Cursor: Cf. 4.4n. for the form of name used here.

de iureiurando obstrictus: Cf. Livy 10.38.12: *ea detestatione obstrictis*. *iureiurando obstringere* appears a number of times in classical Latin, though not in later periods (Caes., *Gall.* 1.31.7, Hor., *Ars* 179–80, Val. Max. 5.3 ext. 3, 9.2 ext. 6, Tac., *Ann.* 1.14.4, 4.31.3, Paul., *Fest.* 207L, Just. 5.10.11, 14.4.3). However, *de iure iurando obstringere* is never otherwise found; *de* with *obstringere* is rare in any context, but it appears twice in the *Digest* (Mod., *Dig.* 26.7.32.3, Ulp., *Dig.* 39.5.12). P. gives the Samnites' oath a legalistic cast (cf. *OLD s.v. obstringo* 7).

constantia virtutis: The phrase is not Livian, but it is classical (*Bell. Hisp.* 17.1; it is otherwise found in Just. 15.3.9 and Firm., *Err.* 6.9). It gives the Samnites' oath a very different characterization from that found in Livy (cf. above), marking it as a route to achieving courage rather than, as in Livy, a cruel manner of binding them through superstition—cf. especially Livy 10.41.1–5, where he describes the Samnites as compelled by their oath to stand and face the Romans, but in a manner far short of true courage.

in aciem descenderat: Cf. 7.5n.

10.9 *Census*. Corresponds to Livy 10.47.2. Following the battle of Aquilonia, P. omits the bulk of the material which in Livy concludes the book: further victories over the Samnites (10.43–44, 10.45.9–14), and the Etruscans and Faliscans (10.45.1–8, 10.46.10–12), and the triumphs and dedications made by the victorious commanders (10.46.1–9, 10.46.13–16). He also omits the beginning of the story of the bringing of Aesculapius to Rome (10.47.6–7), reserving it for Book 11 (see 11.2n.). The reason he includes the census is, however, clear: he is regularly interested in census data. He recorded both of the censuses that Livy recorded in Book 3 (cf. 3.3n.), and while he omitted the data from 9.19.2, that was mentioned by Livy only in the context of the Alexander digression (cf. 9.7n.), rather than at the time it was taken.

lustrum conditum: Livy 10.47.2: *lustrum conditum eo anno est*: for the phrase see 11.5n.

censa sunt civium capita: Livy 10.47.2 has *censa capitum*, but at other times he uses the phrase here: see 3.3n.

CCLXXII milia et CCCXX: There are two problems with the figure here. One is that it is different from the figure given by all the MSS of Livy himself, which is 262,321. The second is that the 'thousands' figure is identical to that recorded for the next census in Book 11 (11.5). It could be that the passage here has been corrupted from the figure in *Per.* 11, but that would not explain the variation between the 'hundreds' figure in P. and that in Livy. Hence it is more likely to be a double corruption in the other direction: first the figure in *Per.* 10 was mistranscribed from Livy (or correctly transcribed from a corrupt MS of Livy, or correctly transcribed from a good MS and then corrupted in the transmission of P.), then the real figure in *Per.* 11 was replaced by a false repetition of the 'thousands' column in *Per.* 10. For the corruption of census numbers in both P. and the MS tradition of Livy see Beloch (1877), 227–33, esp. 232 on the tendency in the MSS of P. for the numbers in one list to be transferred to a neighbouring one.

Book 11

11.1 *Continuation of the Samnite Wars.* Livy appears to indicate that a decisive victory in the Third Samnite War was achieved by Papirius Cursor in Book 10 (10.38.1, 10.42.5–6, 10.44.6–8), and that the period afterwards was one where the Samnites, while still at war with Rome, had ceased to pose as serious a threat.

P.'s reading of Livy, however, adopts quite a different balance. He is far more perfunctory on Cursor's successes, and instead places the responsibility for the major victory onto the campaigns of Fabius Gurges and (to a lesser extent) Curius Dentatus in Book 11; note that he omits all previous references to triumphs over the Samnites, including Papirius' spectacular one from Livy 10.46.2–8, but records ones for both Gurges and Dentatus. On the other hand, he does not treat the fighting against the Samnites subsequent to this as part of the same sequence, but rather as a rebellion of an already defeated subject population (see 12.3n.).

The result is to give a smoother and steadier upward path through the war; Fabius' initial setback is to be seen against the background of an ongoing campaign in which he is ultimately the primary victor (with Dentatus left to pick up the final pieces: cf. 11.4 below), not as an astonishing loss in a war which the Romans had all but won. Florus has an even more lacunose account to a similar effect; in his case the final victory over the Samnites is implied to be the consequence of the *devotio* of the younger Decius at Sentinum, since he moves directly from that victory to the Tarentine War and Pyrrhus (1.12–13).[1] A different version is found in Eutr. 2.9, who has a single brief narrative of what he describes as a forty-year period, highlighting just three episodes: the Caudine Forks and Fabius Gurges, both involving initial Samnite victories which are dramatically reversed in the Romans' favour, and finally the ultimate victory of Curius Dentatus and Cornelius Rufinus.

So it is common for post-Livian historians to tidy up the Samnite Wars into a much less messy and more linear picture, but P.'s highlighting of Fabius Gurges as 'the' victor is a distinctive reading of the tradition. It does however appear to be that of Serv. auct., *Aen.* 1.720, who refers to Fabius' dedication of a shrine to Venus *post peractum bellum Samniticum* ('after the Samnite War had been brought to a close').[2] Most importantly, it is much the same balance as is found in Oros. 3.22.1–10, who similarly downplays Papirius' victory and makes no mention of

---

[1] Flor. 1.11.8 refers in passing to the 'son of Fabius' as one of those contributing to the victory over the Samnites, so he must presumably have been at least aware of a role for Gurges, but his narrative leaves it entirely open what that role might have been.

[2] As noted by Ziolkowski (1992), 167–71, *contra* Richardson (1980), 58–9, Servius' account of the foundation of the temple appears to be confused, since in Livy 10.31.9 the temple was vowed by Gurges some years earlier, but that does not affect the point at issue: indeed, Ziolkowski speculates that the source of the confusion might precisely have been an attempt by Fabius Gurges to present himself as the true victor of the Samnite Wars.

his triumph, but is even more emphatic than P. about the decisive nature of Fabius Gurges' victory, saying that it put an end to the whole of the forty-nine years of Samnite Wars (3.22.10),[3] and who does not suggest that Dentatus fought the Samnites at all. Part of this is the result of Orosius' overtly Christian slant to Roman history, since he orders the sequence of events so as to imply that Fabius Gurges' initial defeat was the result of excessive deference to pagan religion.[4] But the similarity with P. suggests something broader: that there was an historical tradition of the dynamic of the Samnite Wars, one that was intrinsically dependent on Livy's narrative and yet not identical to him; one which could be transmitted from individual to individual while retaining a meaning that did not depend on any individual. It was not the only strand of tradition—Florus and Eutropius show some of the other possibilities—but it is one that carried a particular force: that the true victory over the Samnites came as a result of a father's willingness to stand up for his son's honour and to submit himself to his command. Neither Livy nor P. nor Orosius can rightly be called the author of that story: Livy provides the details but not the teleological interpretation, P., and to a lesser extent Orosius, was bound to the historical details found in Livy, and indeed to the tradition of interpreting those details of which both P. and Orosius formed part.

cum: Cf. 2.2n.

Fabius Gurges cos.: Q. Fabius Maximus Gurges, consul in 292 (*RE* 112, *MRR* I 181). Livy gave his name as *Q. Fabius Maximi filius Gurges* when recording his election at the end of Book 10 (10.47.5; cf. 10.31.9), but as *Maximus* on his first introduction at 10.14.10; *Fabius Gurges* is likewise the name given in Val. Max. 5.7.1, Serv., *Aen.* 1.720, and Oros. 3.22.6. Eutr. 2.9.2 calls him Q. Fabius Maximus, while the Greek sources generally omit his *cognomen*. P. (like Valerius, Servius, and Orosius), as usual, omits Fabius' *praenomen*: see 4.4n.

According to Macr., *Sat.* 3.13.6, the name *Gurges* (= 'whirlpool') was applied to him because he 'had devoured his inheritance', but Macrobius comments that he would prefer to pass over the matter, because his later virtue made up for his earlier vices. Nothing of this is in P. or any other surviving narrative historian, nor (presumably) in Livy, since he said nothing of it at Gurges' first appearances in Book 10. However, it is worth noting that the basic structure of Gurges' career in P., as someone whose earlier faults are redeemed by later success, is the same.

male adversus Samnites pugnasset: The only relatively full source for this is Zonar. 8.1.11–12, according to whom the reason for the defeat was that Fabius was in a rush to complete the campaign before his father, who was serving as his legate, should arrive. He then mistook an advance party of Samnites for the main

---

[3] Orosius had however constructed the history differently at 3.8.1, where (drawing on Livy 7.29.1–2) he said that Pyrrhus attacked Rome while the Samnite War was *ancipiti statu*.
[4] Fear (2010), 15–16, 144.

body of the army, rushed carelessly in pursuit of them in loose formation, and encountered the full Samnite army arrayed for battle. His carelessness also led to excessive post-battle casualties, since doctors and medical supplies were left behind in the rush forwards. Zonaras, presumably following Dio, is thus unequivocal about Fabius' failings (cf. also the briefer version in Suid. Φ 3 (Adler), referring to his actions as θρασύτερον ἢ ἀσφαλέστερον); P.'s phrasing leaves Fabius' degree of responsibility for his defeat open, since *male pugnare* could imply simple lack of success rather than direct culpability.

male adversus...pugnare is one of P.'s standard phrases for a defeat, the reverse of his favourite *prospere adversus...pugnare* (2.6n.); it is used also at 25.8, 48.15, 63.1, 73.1, 96.2, 96.6, 119.2. Like that phrase, it is rarely found outside P., the chief exception being Orosius' account of this very defeat (3.22.6), where he is likely to be drawing the phrase from P. himself: see the Introduction.

senatus...ageret: The action against Fabius is similarly attributed to the Senate by Oros. 3.22.7 and Suidas Φ3 (Adler), who, like P., present it as an action for removing him from his command. Dio fr. 36.30 (cf. Zonar. 8.1.13), on the other hand, says that he was sent for and accused before the people: the implication of his version is that he was on trial before them. If the story is to be taken at face value, both versions appear legally problematic. The legal authority to remove a holder of *imperium* from his office rested not with the Senate, but with the people (Mommsen, StR³ I 628–30).⁵ Conversely, a holder of *imperium* could not, despite what Dio implies, be put on trial (Mommsen, StrR 352–4). The abrogation of *imperium* by the people could presumably be a prelude to placing an official on trial before them, but in this case, since the abrogation was unsuccessful, no trial could ever have been reached.

The simplest solution is proposed by Bauman (1968), 43–5, who argues that the action to remove Fabius' command, as was constitutionally proper, took place before the people, but that Dio confused this action with the trial that was to follow.⁶ In which case, Fabius Rullianus' speech took place at the *contio* where the motion to remove his son's *imperium* was raised, and P. (presumably in this case following Livy) mistakenly attributes it to the Senate.

But that raises another problem. At least to judge by later practice, at a *contio* Rullianus could speak only if called upon by the presiding magistrate. It was not in the interests of a presiding magistrate to call on an opponent who might

---

⁵ Mommsen further claims that there are no examples in the pre-Gracchan period of a magistrate, as opposed to a pro-magistrate, being threatened with abrogation of his *imperium*. However he does not discuss the case of Fabius Gurges, which appears to be a clear counter-example; Bauman (1968) rightly argues that there is no meaningful legal distinction between a magistrate and a pro-magistrate in this context.

⁶ As Bauman (1968), 38 n. 9 and 44 n. 43 notes, Plu., *Marc.* 27.3–4 made a similar mistake in the case of Marcellus, treating a bill of abrogation as if it were an actual trial. The mistake was an understandable one, since if the abrogation were successful, the prosecution itself would be likely to be a foregone conclusion.

undermine the case he was trying to make, especially an opponent with the *auctoritas* of Rullianus.

It is true that in the later Republic presiding magistrates did sometimes seek to trap opponents by having them speak at a *contio* under disadvantageous circumstances; it is also true that sometimes this tactic backfired and the opposing speaker was successful at making his case (Morstein-Marx (2004), 161–72). We might envisage some such sequence of events here. But this leads to a further question: for it should be emphasized how far the proceedings here are historically exceptional. As is noted by Rosenstein (1990), 37–41, it is astonishingly rare that unsuccessful Roman commanders were faced with the loss of their command or punishment for their mismanagement of it, and the few attested examples almost all relate to cases of egregious misbehaviour, not mere incompetence. There is no parallel for the proceeding against Fabius Gurges here, which strongly suggests that if it occurred at all, it was not initiated in consequence of outrage at the defeat, but was engineered by a political opponent of his father or himself (more probably the former, given the length of time he had had to accumulate enemies).

So we have to imagine a situation under which Fabius' opponent would reach for the virtually unprecedented weapon in his arsenal of having a command abrogated for what appear (in Roman terms) minor offences, and yet allow his enemy a platform from which to shoot the charges down. According to Dio, indeed, Gurges was not permitted to speak in his own defence (a point which Bauman uses to demonstrate that this was indeed a *contio*, not a trial, where self-defence would have been possible). Why would the magistrate who barred Gurges from speaking allow his father to do so?

Given our general ignorance of the politics of the early third century, it is possible to construct many speculative scenarios that could make sense of this. Perhaps, for example, we are to see the proceeding against Gurges as some sort of staged demonstration rather than a genuine attempt to abrogate his office; or perhaps Rullianus and his supporters managed (legally or not) to hijack their opponent's *contio* in some way; or perhaps Zonaras' narrative omits some crucial point of culpability in Gurges' actions that made his opponents believe that their case against him was watertight. But it is worth considering two other possibilities also.

The first is that Dio is after all wrong and P. correct to see this as a Senatorial proceeding: for while later abrogations were certainly done through the assembly, the only recorded precedent prior to Fabius Gurges, namely the consular tribunes of 402 BC (Livy 5.9), likewise was said to have been engineered by the Senate, albeit using quite different legal mechanisms (see Bauman (1968), 41–3). Indeed, as Bauman notes, even at a later period the attempt to revoke Scipio Africanus' command in 204 BC began (and ended) with a Senatorial debate on whether the issue of abrogation should be referred to the people (Livy 29.19.6). Perhaps that was all that took place here, and P. (like Orosius and Suidas) is over-dramatizing it as a debate on which the revocation of command actually hung. If so, Rullianus' participation is unproblematic, since in the Senate as a senior consular he could have spoken as a matter of right. On balance that seems a more palatable suggestion than to attempt to reconstruct an entire political background to make sense of Dio.

The more radical alternative is that of Münzer (1909b), 1810–11 (cf. also Salmon (1967), 274–5, Grossmann (2009), 160–1): that while (perhaps) an attempt to abrogate Gurges' command really took place, the circumstantial details about his father's role in his rehabilitation are the construction of a later period,[7] possibly simply because of the centrality of Rullianus in earlier episodes of the war (so Grossmann), or else based on the life of Scipio Africanus, who similarly served as his brother's legate when (according to one version—see 37.1n.) the latter's ability at command was questioned, and of Q. Fabius Maximus Cunctator, who famously yielded to his son's authority while serving under him as legate (e.g. Quadrig., *FRHist* 24 F 57, Livy 24.44.9–10, Plu., *Fab.* 24.1–2). Certainly the two fathers, both named Q. Fabius Maximus and both five times consul, were sometimes confused: see Val. Max. 2.2.4, who ascribes to Rullianus the story of Fabius Cunctator yielding to his son (24.5–6n.), and note also Val. Max. 4.1.5 and Polyaen. 8.15, telling an anecdote about Fabius and his son that could fit either father equally (cf. also 27.3n.).

Münzer's suggestion may seem unnecessary. Certainly, while we should not underestimate the ability of Roman historians to invent narrative details, we should also not assume that a story is invented merely because of its similarity to a later story, since in real life events often occur which are remarkably similar to earlier events (cf. Woodman (1983b)). And in this case the historical problems with the transmitted narrative are not sufficiently intractable to render such a solution essential. But it is a salutary reminder of the limitations of our knowledge of the early third century that we cannot rule out Münzer's answer with any degree of probability.

removendo eo ab exercitu: This phrase is not found in Livy for the act of removing a general from his command, and it is rare elsewhere: the only parallel is Nep., *Pel.* 1.3, a non-Roman context (though it is used at *Bell. Afr.* 54.4 of a general cashiering one of his staff officers; cf. also Cic., *II Verr.* 1.38). In Roman contexts the usual phrase is *imperium* (or *magistratum*) *abrogare* (*TLL* I 138.35–139.5). The phrase here appears to be modelled on the common *removere ab re publica*; hence although P., unlike Dio, does not suggest that Fabius was on trial, he uses

---

[7] The historicity of the elder Fabius' intervention had earlier been doubted by Bruno (1906), 81, on the basis that (on her view) it contradicts Dio/Zonaras' account, according to which Fabius had already been his son's legate prior to his defeat. But even if this is indeed a significant contradiction (which, as Bruno herself observes, is doubtful), it depends on a disputed textual emendation (see below).

language that implicitly makes Fabius' military disgrace analogous to the loss of civil rights such as would only follow a trial.

Fabius Maximus pater: Q. Fabius Maximus Rullianus (*RE* 114), who had been five times consul (322, 310, 308, 297, 295). P.'s account of his career is (as ever) abridged, but he refers to his problems as *magister equitum* in Book 8 (325), to his censorship in Book 9 (304), and to his victory at Sentinum in Book 10 (295). He associates with the censorship the acquisition of the name Maximus, thus identifying that censor with the father here. By allowing the reader (correctly) to assume the identity of these names, P. brings out, without having to state it explicitly, the key point needed for the story: that Fabius Maximus' military and political distinction is being used as a guarantor for his son in the future. For his legateship here cf. also Val. Max. 5.7.1, Plu., *Fab.* 24.3.

deprecatus…ignominiam: The phrase is Livian, used twice by him (5.9.3, 27.20.13) in the context (as here) of the abrogation of a magistracy; cf. Cic., *Phil.* 11.17, in the not dissimilar story of Scipio Africanus requesting to be sent as his brother's legate.

maxime: A pun on Fabius' *cognomen*: as often in Roman writings, a character is shown to act in accordance with his name. The pun may be P.'s own, rather than being derived from Livy (cf. 2.2n.).

iterum: The oldest MSS (N and P), as well as some of the later MSS, read *iterum*, which must, accordingly, have been the reading of the archetype, but in certain of the Renaissance MSS this is emended to *iturum*, a reading accepted by Rossbach and Jal. Cf. the similar phrasing at Oros. 3.22.7 (see Introduction); Orosius' MSS vary between *iturum* and *iterum*, but the former appears on the face of things more likely given the perceived clumsiness of the double adverb *iterum ultro* and the fact that another *iterum* appears in the next line to explain the corruption.

However, in P. there is no reason to suspect the Latinity of the transmitted text (for *polliceor* with a predicative phrase cf. Quint., *Inst.* 2.5.5 *se magistratum eloquentiae pollicetur*). Even more pertinently, *iterum* is far more meaningful and pointed in this context, because it appears from Zonar. 8.1.10 (following Dio) that Maximus was already acting as his son's legate from the start of the campaign, though he did not take part in the fighting, as his son went ahead in order that he and not his father should get the credit (cf. above). It is far more likely that we have here a hint at this back-story rather than that a later copyist's error just happened to coincide with an historical version known from elsewhere—or alternatively than that the later copyist was aware of Dio's version and corrected the text accordingly (cf. 3.7n. for another instance of P. hinting at a story which he does not tell in detail; also 44.3n. for P. referring to someone holding an office for the second time when he did not mention the first occasion).

If *iterum* is accepted here, then the corollary is that we should look more carefully at the possibility that it is the correct reading in Orosius also. The linguistic objection to the double adverb can be put aside; for while *iterum ultro obtulit* is an unlikely phrase in classical Latin, it is not unlikely for Orosius: compare e.g. 4.6.7 *iterum infelicius victi sunt*. Moreover, if *iterum* is indeed correct in the first line, its repetition in the second appears artful rather than awkward.

Indeed, other things being equal, the MSS traditions would appear to support the reading of *iterum* in both Orosius and P. Where we have two related texts, one reading *iterum* in its major MSS, and the other having its MSS split between *iterum* and *iturum*, the most natural conclusion is that *iterum* is correct in both but that one MS tradition has been partly corrupted, rather than that the MS traditions of both authors independently introduced the identical corruption. For other implications of reading *iterum* here, see the Introduction.

idque: i.e. he obtained the right to serve as his son's legate. That Gurges was allowed to retain his command is left unstated but is naturally assumed.

eius consiliis et opera...adiutus: P. implies that the primary thing Gurges received from his father was advice and support. Dio fr. 36.31, by contrast, has the father leading the army to an immediate victory on his own account, and subsequently effectively taking over the leadership from his son even while pretending to be merely an adviser, while Oros. 3.22.8 has him winning the victory by leading a dramatic charge against the enemy. P. is closer to Val. Max. 5.7.1, who explicitly says that the father was too old and infirm to do anything more than serve *animo sine corpore*—although Valerius also lays more emphasis on the value of the father's advice, saying that he was seen as the *auctor* of the subsequent triumph. Eutr. 2.9.2 is in the same tradition but more vague, linking the victory to the arrival as the father as legate, while leaving open what precisely the father might have done to ensure this. Just as P. did not directly blame the son for his initial defeat, here he gives the least credit to the father and the most to the son for the decisive victory over the Samnites.

consiliis et opera: The combination in the ablative of *consilium* and *opera* in the context of giving assistance is extremely common in Cicero (especially in the letters), but usually with the singular *consilio*, and usually (though not always) with *opera* appearing first. See Cic., *Fam.* 1.9.17, 3.13.1, 5.8.5, 7.17.2, 13.57.1, *Att.* 3.11.2, 7.3.7, 12.36.2, *II Verr.* 4.30, *Rep.* 2.51, *Lael.* 51. It is sometimes found in other Republican and early imperial authors (see Plaut., *Mil.* 137, *Pseud.* 17, *Trin.* 189, Livy 9.10.4, and esp. Varro, *Ling.* 5.87, where *legati* are defined as *qui lecti publice, quorum opera consilioque uteretur peregre magistratus*), but less commonly in later writers (though note Julian., *Dig.* 27.10.7 pr. and cf. the slightly different phrases in Plin., *Paneg.* 93.3 and Suet., *Dom.* 17). Given that the point of the story centres on Fabius' role as *legatus*, P.'s use of this (for him) archaic phrase (perhaps adapting Livy's wording) hints at the etymology as found in Varro.

consul...caesis Samnitibus triumphavit: This took place in the following year (291), with Gurges fighting the last part of the campaign as proconsul rather than consul, as is confirmed by the *Fasti Capitolini* (Degrassi 72–3 and 544) and Dio fr. 36.31. P. has, as often, tidied the story by conflating episodes which Livy, writing annalistically, presumably kept separate.

C. Pontium, imperatorem Samnitium, ductum in triumpho: The general view is that this is the C. Pontius who defeated the Romans thirty years earlier at the Caudine Forks; it is also felt that his capture and display here is so neat as to be historically suspect.[8] While little from this period is beyond suspicion historically, it should be noted that neither P. nor Oros. 3.22.8–9 (the only other source) identifies this Pontius as the victor of the Caudine Forks, though Orosius might be read as doing so implicitly (unlike P., he had named the Caudine victor 'Pontius' at 3.15.3). It is certainly possible that the same man led the Samnites (or some portion of them: see 11.4n.) for thirty years; it is no less possible that this is a son or grandson of the same name.[9] Livy might have resolved the question (or not: see Levene (2010a), 73–4); but in the absence of his text, to conclude *both* that this is the same Pontius *and* that his capture is accordingly too neat to be true is one assumption too many. If the neatness is indeed suspect, that is a reason for rejecting the identification, not for rejecting the historicity.

securi percussit: For the phrase cf. 2.2n.; for the form of execution see Mommsen, *StrR* 916–18.

Beard (2007), 128–32 shows that, although Roman writers often spoke as if the execution of the defeated general following a triumph was the norm, there are surprisingly few securely attested examples of this taking place and rather more of the enemy being spared. While executions did occasionally occur, she argues that the 'norm' was largely hypothetical, assumed but rarely put into practice, such that each general could appear all the more merciful when he rose above it.

It is therefore possible that the execution here is an invention, created by the later tradition on the model of the assumed (but rarely practised) norm. If so, P. is unlikely to be the inventor, but he uses the death to provide a sense of closure appropriate to the true ending of the Samnite Wars (cf. above).

11.2 *The bringing of Aesculapius to Rome.* In Livy the story opens at the very end of Book 10 (10.47.6–7), in a final notice for the year 293 mentioning the plague and its interpretation as requiring the summoning of Aesculapius from Epidaurus, though it is also stated there that the mission to Epidaurus was postponed. P. omits any mention of it from Book 10, and allows the reader to assume that it all took place in Book 11.

---

[8] So e.g. De Sanctis II 344–5 [363], Salmon (1967), 274–5, Oakley (2005a), 40, Grossmann (2009), 166. *Contra* Bruno (1906), 100–1 (though she argues, less plausibly, that the victory was not won by Gurges himself but by the consuls of 291), Tullio (1993), 2–4.

[9] On the semi-dynastic nature of Samnite politics see Salmon (1967), 82–4, Scopacasa (2015), 215–18. Note that, according to an anecdote in Cic., *Sen.* 41, the father of the victor at Caudium, whom Livy 9.1.2 calls 'Herennius Pontius', was also called C. Pontius.

The story was immensely famous. Although Plu., *Quaest. Rom.* 94 offers it as merely one of three possible options to explain the location of the temple of Aesculapius at Rome, so showing that (at least to an early imperial Greek writer) it was not the only available account,[10] it became by far the dominant version. The most detailed narratives are in Ov., *Met.* 15.622–744, Val. Max. 1.8.2 (cf. also the epitomes by Paris and Nepotianus), and *Vir. Ill.* 22; but it is also referred to by (e.g.) Livy 29.11.1, Ov., *Fast.* 1.289–94, Str. 12.5.3, Plin., *Nat.* 29.16, 29.74, Claud., *Cons. Stil.* 3.171–3, while the scene of the arrival of the snake in Rome is depicted on a medallion from the mid-second century AD as well as a relief dating from perhaps the same period (see von Duhn (1886), Besnier (1902), 175–83). It became especially potent in the polemic of Latin Christians, who seized both on the bizarre image of the serpent and on the plague that generated the transfer of a god of healing: see Arnob., *Nat.* 7.44–8, Lact., *Inst.* 2.7.13, 2.16.11, Aug., *Civ.* 3.17, 10.16, Oros. 3.22.5.

On the episode (the first of a series of introductions of foreign cults to Rome over the following century) see Besnier (1902), 152–83, Schmidt (1909), 31–46 (over-sceptical), D'Ippolito (1988). One common interpretation is to see the introduction of the cult as a conciliatory gesture towards the Greek cities of Italy following the Roman victories over the Samnites (so Gagé (1955), 150–1, Scheid (1985), 97–8, Orlin (1997), 106–8); but it is far from clear why, in a polytheistic world where syncretism of foreign gods was commonplace, importing a Greek god from Epidaurus would have had a significantly conciliatory effect towards Italian Greek cities.

It is more likely that the move to import foreign gods to Rome, often from far afield, reflects the Roman awareness of religious alternatives as they came more frequently into contact with a range of foreign communities: indeed, starting around 300 there is a noticeable move by the Romans in a variety of areas to draw upon the culture of mainland Greece. See Feeney (2016), 117–18: as he notes, the decision to transfer Aesculapius in particular shows the Romans' 'discriminating religious knowledge', since the cult of Aesculapius was one which was regularly taken from one Greek state to another. It is probable in any case that the god was already known in Latium prior to this introduction (Beard, North, and Price (1998), vol. 1, 69–70): the distinctive feature here is that the introduction comes from a distant rather than a local source, one which was recognized as the centre of the cult. But, as Padilla Peralta (2020), 109–14 rightly observes, a key part of the decision to introduce the god must have been the internal social and political dynamics in Rome itself: faced with a devastating plague, the Roman leadership made a high-profile demonstration to the people

---

[10] Likewise Fest. 98L, while differing in the details, has a broadly similar explanation to the first in Plutarch: the site was chosen because it was conducive to good health. For discussion of the possible significance of the location see Graf (1992), esp. 160–7, who argues that the primary consideration was the separation of the temple from the human world.

that it was able to mount an effective communal response in the same way that other communities were doing.

pestilentia civitas laboraret: Cf. 7.2n. Livy 10.47.6–7 places both the plague and the consultation of the Sibylline Books in 293, implying that the mission to Epidaurus was in 292 and hence the dedication of the temple in (at the earliest) 291 (see below). This is contradicted by Valerius Maximus, who describes the plague as running for three years prior to the consultation of the Sibylline Books[11] and the transfer of the cult to Rome. Livy does mention a plague in 295 (10.31.8), but none in 294, and he does not connect the former with the eventual consultation of the Sibylline Books. It is possible that Valerius is drawing on a source which had a three-year plague and that Livy has suppressed any mention of it in 294 (cf. Oros. 3.21.7–8, who describes a major plague in the years between the battles of Sentinum and Aquilonia); alternatively (and perhaps more likely) Livy presented the plague in 293 as continuing for a further two years up to 291, ceasing after the dedication of the temple, and Valerius has merely back-dated the start. See Schmidt (1909), 35.

P. has in any case distorted this chronology, since he not only, unlike Livy, starts the story in Book 11, but places it after the triumph of Fabius Gurges in 291, so implying that not only the mission, but the plague, took place then. Oros. 3.22.5, like P., tells it as a single story, but places it between the victory at Aquilonia and Gurges' initial defeat, as if it all happened in late 293 and early 292, which is probably closer to the truth (though he also has ideological reasons for narrating it here: cf. above, 198–9).

legati: The mission was led by Q. Ogulnius Gallus (*MRR* I 182).

Aesculapi signum: No other source specifies that the Romans were ordered to bring the *signum* from Epidaurus: others, including Livy 10.47.6, have the order being 'to bring Aesculapius'. The most natural interpretation of *signum* in this context would be 'statue', which would also be a reasonable way of understanding the command 'to bring the god', given the way in which cult images were commonly spoken of and treated as if they actually were the gods themselves, rather than merely representing them (see e.g. Gordon (1979), 7–8, Steiner (2001), esp. 79–134, 157–84, Rüpke (2010)). P. is spelling out what is implicit in other sources, which hints at a version of the story involving some oracular misdirection (cf. 7.4n. for his interest in stories of this sort). The cult statue of Aesclepius at Epidaurus was famous, huge, and exceptionally valuable:[12] it is inconceivable either that the Epidaurians would actually have been willing for the Romans to take it, or even

---

[11] Besnier (1902), 166–8 misinterprets Valerius as meaning that the plague ran for three years before the departure of the embassy, not before the consultation of the books, and so concludes that the embassy departed two years after the consultation, i.e. in 291.

[12] According to Paus. 2.27.2 it was half the size of Pheidias' giant statue of Zeus in Olympia, and like it was made of ivory and gold.

that a writer could have seriously envisaged the Epidaurians giving it up.[13] The story that P. seems to point to is one in which the Romans understood the oracle to mean that they were meant to take the statue, found it impossible, but instead were able to take the snake, which was a *signum* in another sense. Cf. Ov., *Met.* 15.644–62, which does not explicitly mention the statue, but implies a similar story when he says that the Epidaurians were reluctant to 'hand over their god' at the Romans' request; cf. also *Vir. Ill.* 22.2, where the Romans 'marvel at the huge image', though it is not directly said that they were planning to take it.

deportaverunt: Livy's standard word for transferring a foreign god to Rome: see 5.22.4, 29.11.7 and cf. *TLL* V.1 588.41–62.

⟨**et**⟩ **in quo:** The asyndeton of the transmitted text is awkward with the relative clauses in this order: it would be less problematic were the order reversed, such that the relative clause defining the general nature of the snake appeared first and the description of its specific action here second (see K-S 2.325–7; H-S 565). Rather than reverse the clauses, however, or attribute it merely to the (sometimes overstated) clumsiness of P.'s Latin, it is simplest to assume that a conjunction has dropped out.

numen esse: Snakes were closely associated with the Epidaurian cult of Asclepius, and he was regularly assumed to be present in them: see Edelstein and Edelstein (1945), vol. 2, 226–31. For iconographic depictions of gods (including Asclepius) as snakes see Mitropoulou (1977).

constabat: Livy uses this word a number of times in the context of allegedly supernatural events (27.11.4, 37.3.3, 41.21.13). The usual interpretation (e.g. by Levene (1993), 19–20) is that by employing this and other such phrases Livy sceptically distances the authorial voice from any endorsement of the existence and/or the supernatural nature of the event. This has been challenged by Davies (2004), 28–61, who argues that the tendency of these phrases is not to undermine the supernatural, but rather to insist on the historical process of its verification, and this at times amounts more to Livy's validation than rejection of the events. Davies's reasoning is often methodologically problematic (see Levene (2006b)), but his case is strong when it comes to *constabat*, which (unlike e.g. *nuntiare*) is never used by Livy of matters which turn out to be untrue or even questionable, and which accordingly is hard to see as marking scepticism.

P. thus effectively affirms the presence of the deity in the snake, which presumably mirrors Livy, but is also is important given the polemically sceptical reading of the episode among Christians from the third century onwards. Other late antique epitomizers offer not merely an affirmation of the divine but an account of the features of the snake which allowed people to draw that conclusion. *Vir. Ill.* 22.2

---

[13] Oros. 3.22.5 says that the Romans brought back not only a snake but also 'the very stone of Aesculapius' (*ipso Aesculapi lapide*); but this appears to be a conflation with the story of the Magna Mater (Torelli, *Fontes* 36).

refers to the snake as *venerabilis non horribilis*, which seems to be a deliberate response to the image relayed by Arnobius of the *horrentis...animalis* (*Nat.* 7.45; cf. also Orosius' *horrendum...illum Epidaurium colubrum*). The loose summary of Val. Max. 1.8.2 by Julius Paris, despite its brevity, is equally forceful, repeatedly alluding to the divine nature of the snake in terms which do not reflect Valerius' original text.[14]

This might imply that all three writers were pagan; but since Valerius certainly treated the snake as divine, and Livy probably did also, it may say nothing about the individual epitomizers' religious views, but simply reflect the way that the post-Livian tradition coalesced around a narrative which accepted that certain key stories showed the divine at work in Roman history. It is also worth noting that even a Christian polemicist like Lactantius accepted that there was a supernatural power at work in the episode, but attributed it to a diabolic rather than a heavenly presence.

in insulam Tiberis: For a similar story of a site being determined by a snake from Epidaurus see Paus. 3.23.6–7.

eodem loco: For the location see Besnier (1902), 185–9, D. Degrassi in *LTUR* vol. 1, 21–2, P. Carafa and P. Pacchiaronni in Carandini, *Atlas* 1.552–3. The temple is depicted on a coin from 87 BC (*RRC* no. 348.6: see Zehnacker (1964)).

aedis Aesculapio constituta est: The dedication was on 1 January, according to the *Fast. Praen.*, the *Fast. Antiat. Mai.*, and Ov., *Fast.* 1.289–94. Hence, on the assumption that the mission to Epidaurus took place in the consular year 292 (see above), the earliest possible date would be 1 January of the calendar year corresponding to the Julian year 291, which was probably the same consular year as that of the expedition to Epidaurus, since it is likely that new consuls took up office at this period on 1 May.[15] However, it is also altogether possible that the temple was dedicated a year or more after that, in 290 or even 289.

11.3 *Condemnation of Postumius*. For the historical background see FF 1–2nn. The most striking point about P., compared with the surviving Livian fragments and the version of Dionysius is that, for him, the sole grounds of Postumius' condemnation is his use of his soldiers on his estate. Dionysius has many other charges against him, related above all to his conduct in the Samnite War, and while we cannot tell whether all of these were in Livy, he certainly referred to Postumius' conflict with Q. Fabius Gurges; and it is at least plausible, if not certain, that Livy made it one of the grounds for his condemnation, as in Dionysius (Bravo and Griffin (1988), 517). But P. ignores all of this: unlike Livy (11.1n.), he gives Fabius Gurges the primary credit for the Samnite War and does not suggest that Postumius even took any part in the campaign.

---

[14] For Paris' adaptations of Valerius see Hansen and Bergquist (1998).
[15] Holzapfel (1885), 99–104; cf. Leuze (1909), 370–2.

L. Postumius consularis: L. Postumius Megellus, *cos.* 305, 294, and 291 (*RE* 55). Although the events for which he was condemned took place during his consulship in 291, the trial and condemnation was in the following year, 290, and P., focusing on that moment, accordingly refers to him as an ex-consul, not a consul.

in agro suo: Note that F 1 refers to Postumius sending his troops *in agrum suom*.

damnatus est: According to D.H., *AR* 17/18.5.4 he was fined '50,000 of silver', though our text of Dionysius, possibly because of compression by the excerptor, does not specify the denomination. Rome may have been beginning at this period to mint silver didrachms (see e.g. Crawford (1985), 28–30, *contra* Holloway (1992): cf. 15.5n.); but they do not appear to have been in general circulation, and it is more likely that Dionysius is anachronistically retrojecting the monetary system of a later period.

11.4 *First consulship of Curius Dentatus.* Other brief narratives of these events are found in Flor. 1.10, *Vir. Ill.* 33.1–3, Eutr. 2.9.3, Oros. 3.22.11. There is, however, an interesting division between them. It appears that in his consulship Dentatus fought against the Samnites and the Sabines and celebrated triumphs over them both (cf. below); this is the version in both P. and *Vir. Ill.* However, Eutropius has Dentatus as the ultimate victor in the Samnite Wars (cf. 11.1n.), but does not mention the Sabines, while Florus and Orosius have him fighting the Sabines alone, with no mention of the Samnites.[16] Indeed, the sequence of Florus' narrative implies that his victory over the Sabines had taken place more than a generation earlier, before the Samnite Wars even began.

The tendency to associate Dentatus' consulship with victories over either the Samnites or the Sabines (but not both) can be seen in the most famous anecdote from it: that he was offered a large sum of money by the enemy's ambassadors, but declined it on the ground that he preferred to rule over wealthy people than to be wealthy himself. The embassy in most versions comes from the Samnites (Cic., *Sen.* 56, *Rep.* 3.30a (Powell), *Parad.* 48, Val. Max. 4.3.5, Plu., *Reg. Imp. Apophthegm.* 194F, *Cat. Ma.* 2.2, Flor. 1.13.22, Ampel. 18.8, *Vir. Ill.* 3.7); but in two places the story is transferred to the Sabines (Ath. 419A, citing the otherwise unknown Megacles, *On Famous Men*; *Schol. Bob. Pro Sulla* 80.35 (Stangl)). Along similar lines, Frontinus' *Strategems* refers to Dentatus only in the context of the Sabines (1.8.4 and 4.3.12: cf. Colum. 1 pr.14), and ignores the Samnites; Plu., *Cat. Ma.* 2.1–2, on the other hand, mentions only the Samnites (along with Dentatus' later victory over Pyrrhus) and ignores the Sabines.

---

[16] Flor. 1.13.22 does refer in passing to the anecdote about Dentatus refusing Samnite gold, but does not give it any particular historical context, except to say that it happened 'in peace' (*in pace*), thus still maintaining the impression that Dentatus had nothing to do with the victory in the Samnite Wars.

It appears that the various strands of the tradition found it difficult to maintain the idea that Curius Dentatus achieved the almost unique feat of a double victory and triumph during his consulship (cf. Forni (1953), 193–6). As suggested above, a primary driver for the versions which removed him from the Samnites and confined his successes to the Sabines may have been the desire to tidy the complex history of the Samnite Wars into a more comprehensible sequence,[17] which in some cases (Florus, Orosius) involved seeing the true victory coming earlier. While P., unlike most writers, acknowledges both victories (which were presumably in Livy), he also, like Orosius, presents Fabius Gurges, and not Dentatus, as the chief victor in the wars (cf. 11.1n.). Maintaining these apparently contradictory readings of the history required some finely tuned phrasing: see below.

For many modern historians, Dentatus is accepted as the true victor of the Third Samnite War: see e.g. De Sanctis II 345–7 [363–5], Salmon (1967), 276–7; *contra* Bruno (1906), 107–13 and Forni (1953), 196, who (like P.) see the war as already effectively ended in the previous year.

Samnitibus: Omitted by the chief MSS, but a necessary insertion made in some later ones.

foedus quarto renovatum est: 'The treaty was renewed for the third time': *quarto* here means that it was 'renewed such that it existed for the fourth time', not that it was struck and then underwent four further renewals: cf. 20.6n. *iterum*.[18] Compare Livy 9.43.26 *cum Carthaginiensibus eodem anno foedus tertio renovatum*, and *Per.* 13.6 *cum Carthaginiensibus quarto foedus renouatum est*: the sequence of treaties between Rome and Carthage is notoriously controversial, but these passages are overwhelmingly likely to refer to the third and fourth in a series of four treaties in total (see e.g. Oakley (1998), 252–62 and 13.6n. below).

A treaty with the Samnites was struck in 354 (Livy 7.19.4, D.S. 16.45.8). It had previously been renewed twice: in 341 following the First Samnite War (Livy 8.2.1–4) and in 304 following the Second Samnite War (Livy 9.45.1–4, D.S. 20.101.5). For the probable terms of the original treaty see Salmon (1967), 187–93. Livy implies that the earlier renewals had been on the same terms, but there must have been some modifications each time given the Roman advances in the intervening period (Salmon (1967), 202–3, 252–4, Oakley (1998), 399, (2005a), 591). Likewise new conditions must have been added now such as would mark the defeat: the Samnite tribes certainly lost a great deal of territory

---

[17] This is more plausible than the suggestion that the historians could not distinguish Sabines from Samnites and simply confused the names (so Beloch, *RG* 426–9, who argues that Dentatus fought against the Sabines alone; but see *contra* Forni (1953), 195–6, Salmon (1967), 30–3).

[18] This Latin idiom is regularly misinterpreted: e.g. by Toynbee (1965), 1.519–20 (on Livy 9.43.26 and *Per.* 13.6), leading to an unfortunate attempt to identify the supposed missing treaty (Toynbee (1965), 541–3); similarly (on this passage) Cornell (2004), 122, who assumes that the peace agreement at Livy 9.20.2–3 was a further renewal; but Livy is explicit there that this was not a renewal of the treaty, but simply a temporary truce (cf. Oakley (2005a), 538–9).

and were formally subordinated to Rome as they had not been before (Salmon (1967), 277–8).

Most scholars (e.g. De Sanctis II 345–6 [363–4], Salmon (1967), 276) assume that the treaty was renewed after Curius Dentatus' victories in 290. This is plausible enough, but P., our only source for the treaty, leaves the matter open (see below). There is no reason in principle to think that the Romans could not have continued to fight on some pretext even after a formal treaty had been struck, especially given that the Samnites did not form a single political unit but (at most) a military confederation (Salmon (1967), 95–101, Tagliamonte (2000), 62–7, Senator (2006)); even more sceptical is Cornell (2004), 127–8, arguing that, even though the different Samnite tribes often acted in unison for military purposes, there is very little evidence for a stable 'Samnite League' with a fixed political authority, for all that ancient writers generally speak as if 'the Samnites' were a unitary entity on the analogy with 'the Romans'. Hence it is altogether possible that the Romans could find themselves campaigning against 'Samnites' even when 'the Samnites' had just concluded a treaty with them.[19]

Curius Dentatus cos.: M.' Curius Dentatus, consul in 290 (*RE* 9): his colleague was P. Cornelius Rufinus (14.4n.). He became a famous *exemplum* of the simple life: in addition to the anecdotes discussed above, see e.g. Cic., *Rep.* 3.5 (Powell) (quoting Enn., *Ann.* 456 Sk.), *Parad.* 12, 38, 50, Hor., *Carm.* 1.12.41–4, Val. Max. 4.4.11, Colum. 1.3.10, Sen., *Vit. Beat.* 21.3, Plu., *Comp. Arist. Cat.* 4.5, Juv. 11.78–9. For his career and reputation see Forni (1953), Beck (2005), 188–203.

For the form of the name given here see 4.4n.; according to Plin., *Nat.* 7.68 the reason for the *cognomen* was that he was born with teeth.

Samnitibus caesis et Sabinis, qui rebellaverant, victis: P., as often, constructs his sentence so as to focus attention on a single key moment—in this case the unprecedented double triumph—with the back-story generating it packed into subordinate clauses or phrases (cf. 2.2n.). In this case, however, his doing so leaves it open whether the battles for which Dentatus received the triumphs took place before or after the renewal of the treaty with the Samnites in the previous sentence, and hence similarly leaves open the degree to which he was responsible for the final victory. The fact that the Samnites, unlike the Sabines, are not explicitly said to have rebelled implies that this is a continuation of an unfinished war rather than the renewal of one that had been concluded; but on the other hand the textual order, with the treaty described before Dentatus has even been named, points in the opposite direction. P. orders his sentences in such a way as to leave the impression that the Samnite War had in some sense already been ended by Fabius Gurges even before Dentatus entered on the scene and was awarded a triumph for his actions.

---

[19] For the capacity and willingness of individual groups of Samnites to act independently of the others in international affairs see Scopacasa (2019), esp. 54–61, 66–71; also cf. Terrenato (2019), 136–7.

bis in eodem magistratu triumphavit: For the triumphs see Degrassi 545. The triumphal *Fasti* are missing for these years, but the surviving record for 275 has Dentatus' triumph in that year as his fourth, which is consistent with P.'s statement that he received two separate triumphs in his consulship in 290. Dentatus' triumphs over the Samnites and Sabines are likewise recorded in Cic., *Cato* 55, Apul., *Apol.* 17.8, *Vir. Ill.* 33.1-3, though with no indication that they took place in the same year.

For a consul to celebrate two separate triumphs in the same year was virtually a unique feat (though it was common to celebrate a single triumph over more than one enemy), which helps explain P.'s focus on it. The only Republican parallel is in 266, where (according to the *Fasti Capitolini*) both consuls, D. Junius Pera and N. Fabius Pictor, on different dates from each other celebrated separate triumphs over first the Sassinates and then the Sallentini and Messapi (see Degrassi 74–5 and 547; and cf. 15.6n.).

11.5 '*Annalistic*' notices. As often, P. includes a brief and far from comprehensive selection of Livy's 'annalistic' material. One major criterion for the selection (as here) is to focus on the factual material that shows the development and growth of the Roman state: the creation of new colonies and officials, as well as census data.

coloniae deductae sunt: See 1.B.1n. The general assumption among scholars is that Livy recorded all three of these colonies as being founded in the same year, and since on other grounds (see below) there is some reason to think that the first named colony, Castrum, was founded in 289, which is also a plausible date for the census mentioned shortly afterwards, that date is assigned to the other two colonies in the notice as well. But such an assignment is more arbitrary than is often appreciated. P. elsewhere (8.6, 39.7) unites under a single notice colonies founded in different years, in the first case following the notice with events which actually occurred prior to the foundation of the second colony. It would not be especially surprising if he did the same here. For the implications of that, see below.

Castrum: Vell. 1.14 gives what purports to be a complete list of all Roman colonies founded between the Gallic Sack and the Second Punic War. However, neither Sena nor Hadria appears on Velleius' list, while at 1.14.8 he lists the foundation of Castrum (along with Firmum) not in the period covered by Livy Book 11, but a generation later, at the start of the First Punic War in 264.

The simplest solution: Velleius, despite his pretensions to comprehensiveness, was clearly working from an incomplete source, and there were two separate colonies of this name, one founded, as in P., after the Samnite Wars, which Velleius overlooked, and one in 264. And indeed Pliny, in his survey of Italy, lists two towns called 'Castrum Novum', one in Region VII of Italy = Etruria (*Nat.* 3.51), and the other in Region V = Picenum (*Nat.* 3.110). The site of the former is certain: it is the modern Chiaruccia on the Tyrrhenian coast (*BarrAtl* Map 44 A1), and several inscriptions found there confirm the name (*CIL* XI 3576, 3579–80; for the archaeology see Gianfrotta (1972)). The one in Picenum is generally identified with the modern Giulianova, on the Adriatic coast (*BarrAtl* Map 42 F3). No inscriptions found at or near the site name the town (*CIL* IX 5143–54); but the location is reasonably well assured by the geographical sources (Plin. *Nat.* 3.110, Str. 5.4.2, Ptol., *Geog.* 3.1.21, along with *Itin. Anton.* 101, 308, 313).

However, although that is the simplest solution, various scholars have seen problems with it. Some (e.g. T. Mommsen, *CIL* IX, p. 491, Hülsen (1899), Sonnabend (1997)) claim that the notices in both P. and Velleius refer to the town in Picenum alone, and that the one in Etruria had some other (unspecified) foundation prior to its first being recorded by Livy at 36.3.6. Their reason is that the Picenum town is close to the other sites which both P. and Velleius record being founded with it (Hadria and Sena for P., Firmum for Velleius); but as Salmon (1963) 20 rightly notes, Livy and Velleius elsewhere list colonies from different regions side by side.

Conversely, Salmon (1969), 180 n. 119 (followed e.g. by Briscoe (1981), 223, and implicitly by Cornell (1989), 390–1) argues that both P. and Velleius are referring to the Etrurian town, which is called a colony in inscriptions, and that the town in Picenum was not a colony at all. His reasoning is that it is not a Latin colony, since it is not in the list at Livy 27.9–10; and it is also not a citizen colony, 'since its chief official was a praetor (*CIL* IX 5143 and perhaps 5073), and officials with that title are unknown in Citizen colonies before Gracchan times'.

The problem with the first argument is that Livy actually calls the colonies he lists 'colonies of the Roman people', not Latin colonies (27.9.7), though he later (29.15.2) calls the same colonies 'Latin'. In general the distinction between 'Roman' and 'Latin' colonies is less clear in later sources than Salmon's model claims, and it may well be that this reflects the reality that colonization in the middle Republic was more fluid and complex than is suggested by the neat binary division of Latin colonies and citizen colonies found in much twentieth-century scholarship.[20] Hence the *absence* of a colony from a Livian list does not prove it does not belong in that group.

As for Salmon's second argument, he appears to have been under some confusion. The key inscription he cites, *CIL* IX 5143 (= I^2 598), is indeed probably pre-Gracchan, but the praetors in it have nothing to do with the local government, since the most likely reconstruction of the text makes it a copy of a Roman *lex repetundarum* rather than a local document: see Crawford (1996), vol. 1, 343–4. Moreover, it was not found in the town but around 16 km away, near the modern

---

[20] See esp. Bispham (2006), 81–5; cf. Crawford (2014), 204–6; also Grelle (2011) for a sketch of how these fluidities may have developed into the more rigid definitions found in later antiquarian sources.

Guardia Vomano; Mommsen's assignment of it to Castrum Novum was only tentative.[21] Hence it is worthless for the argument Salmon needed it for.

In an earlier version of the same argument, on the other hand (Salmon (1963), 20–1), he cited not *CIL* IX 5143, but IX 5145: perhaps the later citation was a misprint? But the problem, if so, is that there is no particular reason to believe that IX 5145 (which is lost) was pre-Gracchan, although the fact that the praetors in it have no *cognomina* makes a republican rather than an imperial date more probable. But in any case Salmon's argument in 1963 was quite different from the one he made in 1969: then he made no mention of the inscription's date, but cited the praetors in the inscription *in favour of* the possibility that the town was a citizen colony, only then to reject the idea on the (inadequate) grounds that the Romans would be unlikely to have established two citizen colonies of the same name.

Hence, given the weakness of the case against it, we can conclude that Castrum Novum in Picenum was indeed a colony; but there is not adequate evidence to determine what type of colony it was. Accordingly, since there were two colonies of this name, Velleius and P. is each recording one of the foundations.

The question remains which is which. Of the five towns Velleius and P. mention between them, four are on or near the Adriatic coast, one (Etrurian Castrum Novum) on the Tyrrhenian coast. On balance it seems more likely that after the victory over the Samnites and Sabines the Romans would take advantage of the new-found expansion of their power to send out colonies to take control of the coast farthest from Rome (cf. Flor. 1.10), while the foundations at the start of the Punic War would seek to consolidate Roman positions by covering both coasts, including the coast nearest Africa. So the most likely solution is that P. here is referring to the Picenum Castrum Novum, and Velleius to the Etrurian one (e.g. Beloch, *RG* 603, 607, Harris (1971), 148–9, Gianfrotta (1972), 85).[22]

The date of the foundation is generally taken to be 289, on the assumption that the colonies would be sent out as soon as was practically possible following Dentatus' victory over the Sabines in 290: this also fits the chronology of the censorship reported by P. afterwards (cf. below).

Sena: Modern Senigallia (*BarrAtl* Map 42 E1). Plb. 2.19.12 dates the foundation to 284/3, after a Roman victory over the Gauls (see 12.1n.); however, on the assumption that P., and hence Livy, was dating it to 289, this is seen as an inconsistency, and 'Livy's date' is generally preferred (De Sanctis II 340 [358] n. 37, Ortolani and Alfieri (1953), 161, Walbank (1957), 189, Brennan (1994), 428,

---

[21] The site where it was found is in fact rather closer to Hadria—see below—though this does not of course mean that it originated there either.

[22] *Contra* De Sanctis II 349 [368] n. 67, who prefers it the other way round, since the 264 foundation would then follow the defeat of Picenum earlier in the 260s (cf. *Per.* 15.4n.). But the fact that the town fell within the region later called Picenum does not necessitate that the site belonged to the people of Picenum in the third century.

216   COMMENTARY

contra e.g. *MRR* I 189). The reasoning is that since Sena was the first Roman colony on Gallic territory, it must have appeared more natural to Polybius to associate it with a victory over Gauls, but the Romans had already defeated the Gauls at Sentinum in 295, and may well have acquired some Gallic territory then (De Sanctis II 340 [358] n. 37).[23] Lepore (2014), 227–8 seeks to reconcile the dates on the basis of an excavated sanctuary from the beginning of the third century, which appears to have been originally an extra-urban sanctuary, but which was then enclosed within the city walls: he hypothesizes that this reflects two stages of the colonial foundation, one when the settlers were originally sent out, and the second when the urban centre was built, and that P. reports the first date, Polybius the second.

However, the entire debate is based on a false premise: that P., following Livy, is dating the foundation to 289. Once it is recognized that it could have occurred later (see above), then there is no incompatibility between the date in Polybius and the date in P., since P.'s book is likely to have covered events as late as 283 (11.7n.), which means that the foundation could have occurred in exactly the same time-frame as Polybius reports for it. It is true that Polybius reports the foundation as occurring after the death of L. Caecilius, which P. does not record until Book 12, but the chronology of that campaign is so inconsistent between the different sources (see 12.1n.) that it is entirely possible that P. could have reported the colonial foundation before Caecilius' death but in the same year as Polybius did, in which case there would be no problem about having it in Book 11.

Hence we should not assume any inconsistency between the sources. Polybius reports the foundation in 284/3, and Livy may have done the same. Polybius' is the only firm date given, and we have no reason to reject it on the basis of P.'s report. As for the archaeological evidence adduced by Lepore, what it may show is not so much that there were two discrete and different dates under which the 'foundation' may have been recorded, as that third-century colonization was a far more fluid and less deterministic process than the reports in Livy and other writers imply (see also the discussion above).

P., like Polybius, calls the town 'Sena', as do most later literary sources; but some geographical and other writers (e.g. Plin., *Nat.* 3.113, *Itin. Ant.* 100, 316) call it by varieties of the name 'Senogallia' (whence the modern name). That it was a citizen colony is implied by its appearance in a list of 'maritime colonies' at Livy 27.38.4, a category which is generally argued to comprise citizen colonies alone (see Salmon (1963), (1969), 70–81), though the caveats about the definitions of colonies discussed above apply here also. Noteworthy in this regard is that, although 'citizen colonies' are generally assumed to have a small military

---

[23] Corbett (1971), 656–7 claims that the Romans would not have planted a small colony within Gallic territory while the Gauls still occupied the bulk of it. But Corbett exaggerates the danger (this was not the only colony east of the Apennines, contrary to what he says), and fails to appreciate the strategic considerations for locating a colony here: see Morgan (1972b), 314.

population, a very large area around Sena shows signs of having been assigned for colonial agricultural use, and the urban centre is also larger than one would have expected on the basis of other such colonies (Lepore (2014), 229–32), though it also appears that after the foundation of Ariminum, to its north (15.4n.), its importance seems to have greatly diminished (Lepore (2014), 233–5).

For a survey of its history see Ortolani and Alfieri (1953); for the recent excavations on the site see Lepore (2014); cf. also Lepore and Silani (2021).

Hadria: Modern Atri (*BarrAtl* Map 42 F3). That it was a Latin colony is implied by its appearance in Livy's list at 27.10.7–8. Some have claimed, on the basis of two necropolises that have been excavated nearby, that there was already a town on the site, but see *contra* the more cautious analysis of Azzena (1987), 6–8. The town's original name was 'Hatria', as appears from coins dating from immediately after or even (on the hypothesis of a pre-existing town) before the Roman settlement (see Azzena (1987), 10–13), as well as from an early amphora inscription (*CIL* IX 6389). However, the spelling 'Hadria' appears to have become dominant by the end of the Republic: it appears that way in other inscriptions from the town, as well as all literary sources.

triumviri capitales: Their introduction is also mentioned by Pompon., *Dig.* 1.2.2.30, who links it with the creation of a number of other minor official positions, but without providing an exact date. The *triumviri capitales* are often identified with the Republican-era officials called the *triumviri nocturni*, whose only attested function (Paul., *Dig.* 1.15.1) was to supervise the city's fire-brigade (so e.g. Mommsen *StR*^{3} II 594, Oakley (2005a), 620); but no ancient source makes that identification explicit, and it is implicitly contradicted by Licinius Macer (*FRHist* 27 F 24, cited by Livy 9.46.3), who claimed that Cn. Flavius held the office of *triumvir nocturnus* more than a decade before the creation here of *triumviri capitales*. This may be an anachronistic invention on Macer's part, but it is just as probable that when the *triumviri capitales* were created, with a wider range of responsibilities (see below), the *triumviri nocturni* became obsolete (so e.g. Cascione (1999), 1–24).

Like the *triumviri nocturni*, the *triumviri capitales* were involved in fire prevention, but they also had a number of judicial functions, including maintaining public order, the pursuit of suspected criminals and runaway slaves, supervising the prisons and the transfer of convicted offenders to execution. But the precise scope of their authority is not clear, and it may not have been clearly defined even in Roman eyes, since several of their functions overlapped with those of other official bodies. For the same reason, it is difficult to see what in particular might have prompted their introduction at this time, beyond the more general sense that the growth of Rome made it desirable to increase the numbers of officials to control public affairs.

For a full history of the office see esp. Cascione (1999); also Mommsen, *StR*^{3} II 594–601, *StrR* 298–9; Nippel (1995), esp. 22–6 considers their duties in light of the wider problems of maintaining public order in Rome.

tunc primum: *tunc* may indicate that Livy dated the introduction of the office to the same period as that in the previous notice, namely the foundation of the colonies, the first of which was probably in 289 (above); 289 is also a likely year for the census in the following notice (below). While P. frequently alters Livy's chronology, this is less true when he uses *tunc* or *tum*. This often explicitly relates the notice to the one directly before (4.2, 7.2, 8.7, 16.2, 20.9, 24.6); moreover, even when the link is not explicit, comparison with the surviving books shows that the pattern broadly holds: Livy likewise juxtaposed this notice with the preceding one (1.B.6, 5.1, 10.4). There are, it is true, a couple of partial exceptions,[24] but the pattern is sufficiently marked to indicate that it is not unreasonable to conclude that P. is following chronology here—or at the very least, that he wishes to give the impression that he is doing so.

Moreover, since *tunc* in most of these cases appears in the phrase *tum/tunc primum*, this indicates not only P.'s interest in 'firsts' and constitutional innovations, but his specific concern to date such innovations precisely: this strengthens the image he gives of the development of the Roman state.

censu acto: For the probable date of the census and identity of the censors see *MRR* I 184–5, which hypothesizes 289 (the previous censorship had been in 294, the next would be in 283), and suggests Sp. Carvilius Maximus for one censor, and (on rather weaker grounds) Q. Fabius Gurges for the other (cf. Degrassi 113).

lustrum conditum: *lustrum condere* was the formal phrase for the ceremony with which the censorial period was closed: it is common in Livy, as also in other writers (*TLL* IV 152.27–39). P. too, presumably reflecting Livy, regularly uses it. Its exact meaning is however controversial: see the discussion in Ogilvie (1961). For a description of the ceremony see Suolahti (1963), 45–6.

CCLXXII milia: The historicity of this number, along with other census figures for this period, is dubious: see Brunt (1971), 26–33, who notes that they probably depended on family records of censors rather than any official documents; also Hopkins (1978), 20–1, arguing that they give an impossibly high population density. There is a further problem in this case: the number seems suspiciously close to the figure of the previous census as recorded by P. (10.9n.). Overall, therefore, the figure cannot be trusted as an accurate record of the tradition, and it is unlikely to be reliable even if it had been an accurate record of the tradition.

---

[24] The only real anomalies are 4.10 and 34.5. The latter is placed after a 'round-up' passage which by definition cannot be related to it chronologically, while the notice prior to that refers to the settlement with Sparta at the end of the previous year. As for 4.10, P.'s notice links two events which in Livy are separated by eight years and nine chapters of text; in this case it appears that he is deliberately making a causal connection between them, albeit one which was not explicit in Livy (see *ad loc.*).

11.6 *Secession of the plebs*. None of the other epitomizing Latin historians mentions this episode, no doubt because they tend to focus more relentlessly on wars and less on domestic affairs than P. does. The one extended (though highly fragmentary) account is in Dio fr. 37.2, briefly summarized in Zonar. 8.2.1; there are also shorter mentions of it by Plin., *Nat.* 16.37 and Aug., *Civ.* 3.17. From various legal sources (Laelius Felix *ap.* Gell. 15.27.4, Gaius, *Inst.* 1.3, Pompon., *Dig.* 1.2.2.8, *Inst. Iust.* 1.2.4) we learn of the aftermath: that Hortensius passed a law giving plebiscites legal authority over all citizens. But the narratives in P., Augustine, and Dio/Zonaras do not mention this law, and the legal writers do not mention the secession.[25] Pliny is the only writer to make a connection between them, and that is merely in the context of a brief anecdote concerning the place where the law was passed.

Clearly the post-Livian historical tradition did not place much emphasis on the passing of the law; and this may even be because Livy himself did not. The scholarly tradition for a long time saw the *lex Hortensia* as a watershed, the resolution of the patrician–plebeian conflict that had torn Rome apart for so many generations, setting the stage for an extended period of greater social harmony while at the same time incorporating the plebeian office of the tribunate into the wider aristocratic political system (so e.g. Bleicken (1955), 18–26, Maddox (1983)). But there is no ancient source which actually says that, and indeed one—Dio, as summarized by Zonaras (see below)—which directly denies it. It is unlikely that Livy entirely ignored the law on plebiscites in the way that the later, briefer historical narratives did: for them law *per se* was of less concern than it was to legal writers,[26] and in any case the law here was of purely antiquarian interest, since plebiscites as a source of universally binding authority had by late antiquity become no more than an interesting theoretical possibility.

But even on the assumption that Livy included the law, he may well have seen it—and have been right to have done so—as no sort of watershed (Hölkeskamp (1988), 303 = (2004), 73). The effect of the *lex Hortensia* was less far-reaching

---

[25] Noted by Maddox (1983), 278–9, but he implausibly claims that it is because both the events and the law were so well known that each writer could take for granted the readers' knowledge of the material he omitted. In fact Pomponius does refer to secessions in the context of the *lex Hortensia*, but in a rather different narrative sequence: secessions led to the creation of plebiscites, but when the existence of plebiscites began to create social conflict, the *lex Hortensia* was passed in order to regularize their authority.

[26] Gran. Lic. Book 2, *ap.* Macr., *Sat.* 1.16.30, referred to a *lex Hortensia* which allowed courts to be open on market days; this may be a separate provision of the 'plebiscites' law, since Macrobius attributes it to a desire to give *rustici* access to the legal system; but in any case it is not of sufficient importance to P. for him to mention. In addition, both the *lex Maenia* (on comitial voting) and the *lex Aquilia de damno* (on damages) have tentatively been assigned by some scholars to the aftermath of this secession (see Torelli, *Fontes* 72–6). No surviving historian mentions them, but the *lex Aquilia* is assigned to the year of a secession in Theophilus' sixth-century Greek paraphrase of Justinian's *Institutes* (4.3.15): no other secession is plausible, and other aspects of the compilers' account of the law in the *Institutes* suggest independent information about it (Pugsley (1969), 72–3).

than one might have imagined it would be, since plebiscites could be passed only under certain conditions, and hence plebeian authority over the Senate remained in practice extremely limited: see von Ungern-Sternberg (2005), 319–23; Cornell (1995), 378–80; even more importantly, tribunes had been working less antagonistically with the Senate ever since the 360s (as emphasized by Hölkeskamp (1988)). Indeed, if one takes Livy's earlier narrative seriously, it even appears that plebiscites had been passed for decades earlier that were taken to be binding on the entire state (Mitchell (1984), Hölkeskamp (1988), 290-3 = (2004), 63–6).[27] Hence the consequences of Hortensius' dictatorship were far less radical a break than many suppose, and the selectivity of P. in omitting the law has not been applied inappropriately.

But Dio appears to reflect a different tradition from P.: it does not appear that the plebs actually secede in his account. It is true that the text is very fragmentary, and that the στάσις which is the ultimate consequence of the conflict in Zonaras' brief summary could in principle refer to a secession (cf. e.g. Zonar. 7.16.1). But if one compares the surviving text of Dio with Zonaras, the dynamic in Dio is of the plebs taking increasing control of matters even without seceding, and that is what Zonaras seems to be referring to. Indeed, if Zonaras' summary is to be believed, in Dio the conflict was not resolved internally at all, but had to wait for the people to unite as a consequence of the Tarentine War.[28] For other differences between Dio and P. see below.

By contrast P., like Augustine, centres the story on the secession; moreover, unlike Augustine, he includes a reason for it in a debt crisis, which both makes it the latest stage of a history of social conflict going back to Book 2, and suggests a possible justification for the plebs' actions. Similarly P. has nothing of the suggestion found in Augustine that the plebs plundered the city prior to their secession. Augustine's omission is of course driven by his theological purpose: he wants to suggest a series of random disasters striking Rome from which their gods are unable to protect them. P., despite his brevity, is more balanced and more interested in the underlying social and causal dynamic.

The events are usually uncritically assigned to 287 (e.g. *MRR* I 185–6, Torelli, *Fontes* 69–72), but for no good reason. The only evidence for the date is this very

---

[27] Note, however, Humbert (2012), who, more radically, argues that Livy's entire treatment of plebiscites as binding prior to the *lex Hortensia* is an anachronistic retrojection created by the annalistic tradition. A more limited account along similar lines is offered by Elster (1976), 74–119, who, without rejecting the historicity of the earlier laws altogether, argues that their validity should be construed more narrowly, not as decrees that literally bound the state as a whole. While one can hardly say that either of these reconstructions is impossible, both are subject to the same objection (cf. Mitchell (1984)): it is not obvious that one should be willing to reject so much of the broad outline of Livy's earlier narrative in order to maintain a sweeping and strong significance for the *lex Hortensia*, a law which is only reported briefly by later sources which give no real sense of the contours and conditions that surrounded it.

[28] The sequence of Zonaras' narrative makes it clear that he means the Tarentine war, not (as Maddox (1983), 278 claims) the war with the Lucanians.

passage, and even if P. is on the whole following chronological order (and he may not be), one cannot use the wars against Lucania and Vulsinii in 11.7 as a chronological marker, as *MRR* wants (see 11.7n.). The best that one can say is that the events may (*if* P. is broadly chronological) fall between the census in (perhaps) 289 and the earliest events recorded in Book 12, namely 283 (see 11.7 and 12.1n. below): seven possible years in total, all equally likely. Hence the probability of its actually having been in 287 is less than 15 per cent.[29]

aes alienum: Dio's version has much more detail—the tribunes proposed a law to cancel debt, but were opposed by the wealthy to whom the money was owed; a variety of compromises were then argued over. Some such account might conceivably underlie P., but we should not assume it does, since the ultimate result in Dio is quite different (cf. above). Moreover, Dio seems to assume not merely pressure on indebted people, but specifically debt-bondage—*nexum*—which in Livy 8.28 (followed by P.) had been abolished in 326. That episode does not appear in the surviving fragments of Dio or in Zonaras' summary, and it is likely that we simply have two different traditions of the process by which debt-bondage was abolished; in which case we cannot use Dio to illuminate the background to P.

post graves et longas seditiones: The chief MSS read *propter*, a corruption from *propter aes alienum* shortly before. *post* is restored in a couple of the Renaissance MSS, perhaps partly on the basis of Aug., *Civ.* 3.17, where the identical phrase appears.

The overlap between P. and Augustine goes beyond this phrase: P.'s *ad ultimum secessit in Ianiculum* is mirrored in Augustine's *ad ultimum plebs in Ianiculum… secesserat*, and P.'s *in ipso magistratu decessit* by Augustine's *in eodem magistratu exspiravit*. We may presume that Augustine is drawing on P. (see the Introduction); their implied moral and theological slants are quite different (see above), but the overall trajectory of their accounts (perhaps ultimately reflecting Livy's) is identical—a series of extreme actions by the plebs, Hortensius finally restoring the state to balance, but his death immediately following.

Ianiculum: Previous secessions of the plebs in Livy supposedly took them to the Mons Sacer or the Aventine (see Livy 2.32.2–3 citing Piso, *FRHist* 9 F 24, 3.52.1–4), though Flor. 1.17.25 and Ampel. 25.3 record what appears to be an alternative tradition: they list secessions without mentioning the one here, but they include a secession to the Janiculum at the time of the *lex Canuleia* in the mid-fifth century.

Whether or not the secession actually took place, the Janiculum in some respects would seem an obvious place for a secession to withdraw to (which

---

[29] Even if one were to want to label it *circa* a particular year—and that is itself misleading, when the range of possible dates extends over seven years—one should logically say 'c.286' (the central year of the range), not 'c.287'.

might of course have facilitated historical invention):³⁰ closer to the city than the Mons Sacer, but higher than the Aventine. Indeed, it to some degree functioned symbolically in opposition to the Capitoline across the river (see Liverani (1996)). Although legend spoke of it being inhabited from the earliest period (e.g. Virg., *Aen.* 8.355–8, D.H., *AR* 1.73.3, Plin., *Nat.* 3.68), and it is plausible that some early settlement on it existed, this cannot be confirmed given the lack of archaeological data, and it is in any case unlikely that the bulk of the hill was densely occupied in the Republic (Coarelli (1996)).

Q. Hortensio: *RE* 7. As far as we can tell, the Hortensii had held virtually no senior magistracies prior to this, which made Hortensius a surprising choice as dictator, but also an appropriate one to reconcile the people to the state (De Sanctis II 218–19 [231]; Forsythe (2005), 347–8).

11.7 Wars against Vulsinii and the Lucanians.

res praeterea...gestas continet: Cf. 2.16n.: it is invalid to assume that the material included under this heading will necessarily have occurred towards the end of Livy's book, as is done e.g. by *MRR* I 186–7, Torelli, *Fontes* 78–9.

Vulsinienses: Vulsinii (more commonly spelled Volsinii) was an Etruscan city (*BarrAtl* Map 42 C3), nowadays generally agreed to be the modern Orvieto (whose name derives from the Latin *Urbs Vetus*: see Oakley (1998), 80–1). It is not identical with the Roman city later called Volsinii, the modern Bolsena (*BarrAtl* Map 42 B3), which lies around 13 km south-west of it, and which was founded following the destruction of Etruscan Volsinii in 264 (see 16.6n.). See Buchicchio (1970).

There are occasional earlier references in Livy to Rome fighting against Vulsinii: see 5.31.5–6, 5.32.2–5, 9.41.6, 10.37.1–2. But Livy had made little of these campaigns, and P. does not mention them. The campaign here, which could have occurred at any point in Livy's book, is in no other source, and P. does not even say whether the Romans were victorious. However, as noted by Harris (1979a), 257, the gap between 291 and 282 in the triumphal *Fasti* is too large to be filled with victories mentioned in literary sources. This makes it moderately likely that the campaign against Vulsinii likewise resulted in a triumph, and that P. is simply omitting the victory from his notice of the campaign.

For a brief survey of the history of Volsinii and its relationship with Rome see Harris (1985).

Lucanos: An Oscan-speaking people of southern Italy; there is, however, considerable doubt, as with many other ancient Italian ethnicities, whether the clear and unequivocal identification of them as a group in ancient literary sources was

---

³⁰ *Contra* Forsythe (2005), 347, who regards the appearance of the Janiculum here as a sign of the story's authenticity.

matched by a clear ethnic self-perception as a unified group or culture. Certainly the archaeological record suggests something far more diffuse, with local identity counting for much of the time more than ethnic unity, but also broad interaction and exchange with neighbouring communities (Isayev (2007)), though this is not incompatible with the idea that they, like other Italian ethnic groups, may have acted in a more unified fashion for particular purposes, especially (but not only) under external military pressure (Bispham (2014)).

Up to this point in Livy's narrative they have appeared primarily as supporters of Rome: they formed treaties at 8.25.3 and 10.12.1–3, and were last seen as Roman allies at 10.33.1; though they were tricked into repudiating the initial alliance at 8.27.6–11, and there had also been suggestions of anti-Roman agitation at 10.18.8. None of this, however, had appeared in P.; in his account they emerge for the first time on the opposite side to Rome, where they will remain for the next three books.

auxilium...ferre: For P. here, as often in the Roman historical tradition, Rome is not the aggressor, but is drawn into wars through a desire to protect herself, to aid allies, or to obtain restitution for a wrong committed by the enemy. For general reasons to question this tradition see Harris (1979a). For specific reasons to suspect that Lucanians might have felt threatened by Rome see Oakley (2005b), 25, noting the foundation of the colony Venusia near Lucanian territory in 291 (D.H., *AR* 17/18.5.2, Vell. 1.14.6) and the admittedly controversial reference to subduing Lucania in the *elogium* for L. Cornelius Scipio Barbatus, *cos.* 298 (*ILS* 1 = *ILLRP* 309).[31] Neither of these possible provocations is mentioned by P.

Thurinis: The chief MSS have *Tyrrhenis*, but this makes neither linguistic nor historical sense, for three reasons. (1) Latin prose writers do not usually use the Greek name *Tyrrheni* of Etruscans. (2) It is unlikely (though not perhaps totally inconceivable) that the Etruscans in central Italy would come have into conflict with the Lucanians in southern Italy in a period where they were retrenching rather than expanding: the Latin implies that the Lucanians are the aggressors, and the Etruscans did not have a southern Italian presence at this time. (3) Even if such a conflict somehow arose, it is hard to imagine why the Romans would take the side of the Etruscans against their (then) Lucanian allies.

Hence the emendation to *Thurinis* found in some late MSS is overwhelmingly likely (even if it effectively introduces into the narrative a war that may otherwise be entirely unattested—but see the discussion below), since the Romans certainly were supporting Thurii against the Lucanians shortly after this.

---

[31] One might also note the ovation apparently given to Curius Dentatus for a victory over them in a war usually dated to 290–289 (*Vir. Ill.* 33.4: see Degrassi 545, Torelli, *Fontes* 58–9); however see *contra* Brennan (1994), 432–7, who more plausibly argues that it is to be dated to Dentatus' praetorship in 283: see also 12.3n.

Thurii (*BarrAtl* Map 46 D2) was a Greek colony founded on the east coast of Calabria in 444/3 on the site of the archaic colony Sybaris, which was proverbial for its luxury, but which had been destroyed more than sixty years earlier. Thurii was under pressure from its Italian neighbours at least since the early fourth century (D.S. 14.101.1–102.3, 16.15.2). According to one reading of a brief note in Livy 10.2.1–2, Rome had come to their aid a few years earlier when they had been attacked by Sparta, but both the text and the geography of that passage are dubious, and it is possible some other town was meant (Oakley (2005b), 55–7). In any case P. (unsurprisingly) has nothing of this; this is Thurii's first and last appearance in his narrative, as the *casus belli* against the Lucanians.

The usual interpretation of the sequence of events (e.g. De Sanctis II 356–7, 360 [375, 379], *MRR* I 187–9, Torelli, *Fontes* 79, 90–5) is that this war with the Lucanians in support of Thurii took place around 285. It was then followed in 282 by another (and better-known) war during the consulship of C. Fabricius Luscinus, where the Lucanians and Bruttians besieged Thurii only for Fabricius to raise the siege and liberate the city (see esp. D.H., *AR* 19.13.1, 20.4.2, Val. Max. 1.8.6, and cf. 12.3n.). On this version, the earlier war appears in no other source, except for a notice in Plin., *Nat.* 34.32. That notice records that the first public statue in Rome donated by foreigners was by the Thurians in honour of the tribune C. Aelius for passing a law against the Lucanian Sthennius Stallius 'who had twice assaulted the Thurians' (*qui Thurinos bis infestaverat*); Pliny then notes that 'afterwards' (*postea*) the Thurians donated a statue to Fabricius for raising their siege. Aelius' tribuneship is placed in 285, and the war likewise in that year.

Nothing in this is impossible, or even unlikely; but it involves an unnecessary duplication, as well as overlooking an important hint in P.'s language which seems to point to a different and rather neater sequence (see below). First, Pliny's *postea* does not entail two separate wars: it is perfectly compatible with there being a single war in which Aelius was honoured for his actions and then Fabricius shortly afterwards for his. Pliny's *bis* indicates more than one attack by Sthennius Stallius, it is true—but the attacks would not have to be in separate wars years apart: indeed, the first attack could have taken place prior to Rome's involvement altogether.[32]

---

[32] Cf. however Bleicken (1955), 45–6, claiming that Pliny's notice is problematic. He suggests that the declaration of war is meant, but that was not likely to have been done via a plebiscite; so he proposes one of two mistakes in Pliny. Either Aelius as tribune merely initiated the proposal to go to war rather than passing the law, or else *tr. pl.* is a mistake, and Pliny is actually referring to C. Aelius Paetus, the consul of 286, and the war is to be dated in that year.

  The problem that Bleicken identifies in Pliny is not, however, a significant one, since *lege perlata in Sthennium Stallium* is an unlikely way to refer to a declaration of war against the Lucanians. It is more likely that some sort of sanction against the individual is meant, despite the fact that he was non-Roman: we can compare the case of Vitruvius Vaccus at Livy 8.20.7–8 (cf. Cic., *Dom.* 101), an enemy general who owned property in Rome, and where a *senatus consultum* was passed which enjoined not only his execution, but also the destruction of his house and the dedication of his property to the god Semo Sancus. Something similar is likely to underlie Pliny's report here, and if so, we have no reason to doubt that Aelius acted as tribune. Bleicken's objection that it would be surprising

Second, the events described in P. could be taking place as late as 283, in other words just one year prior to Fabricius' raising of the siege of Thurii in 282. The earliest datable event in Book 12 as P. records it is 283 (see 12.1n.), and there is no reason to think that this year began with the new book: book-divisions in Livy rarely coincide with the beginnings and ends of years (see Levene (2010a), 35–6). The dating to 285 in *MRR* and elsewhere is entirely arbitrary, for all that it appears to have become canonical in much of the scholarship.

In which case what is being recorded at the end of *Per.* 11 could well be not a separate war in 285, but the opening of a war in 283 which will then continue into the consulship of Fabricius in the following year (similarly Hof (2002), 13–14).

placuerat: P. records going to war while focusing on the decision rather than the war, language which suggests that he is presenting it not as a self-contained action, but as the start of something longer: compare *Per.* 7.10, where he uses similar language to show how Rome was drawn for the first time into their long series of wars against the Samnites after receiving an appeal from the Campanians. This does not prove that Livy did the same—the interpretation could be purely P.'s; moreover, even if it does reflect something in Livy, it might be not a single war extending over two years but one war foreshadowing a separate but later one. But it would obviously be very natural for P. to treat the war here as a start of a longer sequence *if* it was closely connected chronologically with Fabricius' war in Livy's text; and this weights the argument slightly more strongly towards the suggestion above: that we have here not two wars, but one war which began in 283 and was continued by Fabricius in 282.

---

for a plebiscite to engage so directly in foreign affairs has less force if it were a sanction directed against an enemy in a war which the Romans were already fighting.

Bleicken is however correct to argue that if Aelius was indeed tribune, the tribuneship should be placed at the time of the Fabrician war, in 283 (or better still, 282), whenever one thinks the war described in P. happened (*contra MRR* I 187), since Pliny indicates that the tribuneship came after two Lucanian attacks on Thurii. This conclusion would be overwhelmingly likely if the Sthennius Stallus attacked by the tribune here were identical with the Statius Statilius whom Valerius Maximus 1.8.6 records as the leader of the assault on Thurii in 282: for the possible identification see Münzer (1929).

Book 12

12.1 *War against the Senonian Gauls.* A broadly similar version to P.'s appears in Aug., *Civ.* 3.17 and Oros. 3.22.12–15. Both, however, see the Gallic war as part of a larger anti-Roman movement including Lucanians, Bruttians, Samnites, and Etruscans, whereas P. treats those as separate (though cf. 12.3n.). Moreover, in Augustine and Orosius the legates are sent precisely because the Romans are responding to the uprising against them, whereas P. gives no reason for the legates being sent, and sees the war as triggered solely by their killing.

Plb. 2.19.7–20.5, however, has an entirely different account. Here the trigger for the war is an attack by the Senonian Gauls on Arretium, and Caecilius Metellus is killed when attempting to relieve the town; Curius Dentatus takes command in his place, and it is he who sends legates to the Gauls. Those legates are killed: in order to avenge them the Romans attack and defeat the Gauls. It is subsequent to this that the Boian Gauls form an alliance with the Etruscans, but here too they are defeated. Hence Polybius' version focuses on a series of Roman successes rather than the initial defeat, and the killing of the legates is the trigger for Roman victory rather than the beginning of disaster.

Yet another version appears in App., *Samn.* 6 (*Gall.* 11 is similar). Here, as in Augustine and Orosius, the alliance between the Senonian Gauls and the Etruscans comes first; it is in response to this that the Romans send legates to complain and the legates are killed. However, then the stories diverge: in Appian the Romans immediately avenge the killing under the leadership of P. Cornelius Dolabella and then Cn. Domitius Calvinus (coss. 283), attacking and massacring the Gauls. Here there is no Roman defeat at all, simply an effective Roman response to Gallic treachery. A variation on this cuts out the killing of the legates, and simply has Dolabella defeating the Senonian Gauls either alone or in alliance with another group: so Flor. 1.8 and Eutr. 2.10 (cf. also D.H., *AR* 19.13.1, though this is a brief summary of Dolabella's career, and so naturally omits events unconnected with him).

There is thus no consistent feature in the tradition: not the order of events, not the killing of legates, not the reason for sending legates, not the identity of the enemy, not the leaders on the Roman side, not even whether the Romans are defeated or victorious. Most historical reconstructions, taking their lead from Mommsen (1879), 365–77, have accepted the broad outline from Polybius (our earliest source, and probably drawing on Fabius Pictor, who wrote when the events were within living memory), and fit the other sources around his account (so e.g. De Sanctis II 357–9 [375–8], Forni (1953), 204–14, *MRR* I 188–9, Torelli, *Fontes* 80–9, Corbett (1971), Harris (1971), 79–82, Cornell (1989), 381, Brennan (1994); *contra* Beloch, *RG* 452–5, Salmon (1935), Morgan (1972b)). Controversy has centred primarily on the accuracy of Polybius' chronology and the position of Curius Dentatus (cf. below).

P.'s version is among the most negative: as in Augustine and Orosius, the Romans are betrayed and defeated, and there is no compensatory victory. It is conceivable that he treats it this way because Livy himself did so; however, it would run against the moral structure that Livy usually applies to history to have the Romans engage unsuccessfully in a just war (cf. Levene (2010a), esp. 339–53, 375–6),[33] and it is after all clear that the Senones were defeated in the end. More probably Livy presented the Romans as ultimately victorious (cf. 12.3n.), but P.—and other writers also—read Livy in such a way as to ignore the aftermath and understand the story as unmitigated disaster. This strand of tradition dovetailed neatly with Christians' interpretations, whether or not it originated with them. Augustine and Orosius are primarily interested in the weakness and failure of Roman power; both explicitly make the Gallic war part of a wider uprising, both emphasize the number of soldiers and officers killed with Caecilius Metellus, and Orosius concludes by making a connection to the Gothic invasions of his own day. It is likely that P. was Christian (cf. the Introduction), and his presentation of the Gallic war falls within the same broad tradition, though his focus is more narrowly on the treachery of the Gauls and on the fact (rather than the scale) of the defeat. It is however worth noting that his account closely parallels the next event in his sequence, namely the opening of hostilities with Tarentum, where maltreatment of ambassadors likewise triggers a war (see 12.2n.). In the run-up to Pyrrhus' invasion of Italy, the Romans are being forced by their neighbours' treachery into a sequence of difficult wars which appear to be left unconcluded.

Gallis Senonibus: A Gallic tribe which apparently migrated into central Italy around the fourth century BC, settling primarily in the northern coastal area of Marche: they are identified in the archaeological record by the appearance in that region of the distinctive material culture of Transalpine Gaul known as La Tène: for the archaeology see Grassi (1991), 65–80. According to Livy 5.35.3, followed by P. (5.7), they were the tribe who had sacked Rome in the early fourth century, but see Wolski (1956), 30–5, who argues that this tradition was invented retrospectively following the Romans' conquest of the Senones. In P. (as in Livy) the Senones' sack of Rome had been precipitated by the misdeeds of Roman ambassadors, so there is a certain appropriateness to their reappearance here with an unrequited attack on Roman ambassadors, the more so since this is the last time that the tribe is mentioned by him. According to Plb. 2.19.11 they were expelled from their land following the Roman victory in this war, but P. naturally has nothing of this, as he has nothing of the victory.

---

[33] Cf. more broadly Clark (2014) on the way in which Romans of the Republic typically constructed defeats as stages on the road to ultimate victory.

bello ob id... indicto: As noted above, the order of events in P., by which the killing of the envoys becomes a *casus belli*, is not in all sources and is likely not to be correct. However, it does allow P., despite the brevity of his account, to confirm the justice of the war (cf. 11.7n.), since killing envoys was a clear-cut violation of ancient interstate norms: see e.g. Caes., *Gall.* 3.9.3, Livy 30.25.10. The more unusual side to the story in P. is that the justice of the war does not appear to lead to success in it: cf. above.

L. Caecilius praetor: L. Caecilius Metellus Denter, cos. 284 (*RE* 92, *MRR* I 188). P. is clear that his defeat and death was during his praetorship, which is presumably to be ascribed to 283, not his consulship in the previous year. This fits the explicit chronology in Orosius, who dates the entire war to 283, and also the chronology implicit in the Appianic version. However, Polybius' chronology implies a longer war beginning in 284, and he refers to Metellus as στρατηγός, a term he chiefly uses of consuls, even though in Roman-period Greek it is usually reserved for praetors (Walbank (1957), 188). But in that case we would expect to find a *consul suffectus* for that year, which is not supported by the *Fasti Capitolini* (Degrassi 112, *MRR* I 188-9), and P.'s dating is therefore to be preferred.[34] Curius Dentatus' immediate rescue of the campaign, which appears in no source but Polybius, may be an invention to mitigate the Roman defeat (so Salmon (1935), Morgan (1972b), 313-16), or (more likely) it is genuine, in which case he probably acted as *praetor suffectus* (*MRR* I 188, Brennan (1994), 432-7).

cum legionibus: Augustine and Orosius give the losses as 13,000 Roman soldiers. If this is taken literally, it implies a loss of three-quarters of the entire Roman force under arms, which in a normal year (unless a particular emergency led to extra troops being levied) comprised just four legions of around 4,500 Roman citizens apiece (Livy 9.30.4; cf. Plb. 1.16.1-2, 6.20.8-9). Augustine's and Orosius' number may well go back to Livy, since P.'s *legionibus* implies losses of something of the same order; but if so, Livy's figure is likely to be exaggerated. It is unlikely that so high a proportion of the citizen army would have been in the hands of a single praetor in the first place, since this was not the only war that the Romans were currently involved in. It is possible that (as certainly happened at later periods) Metellus had kept under arms the troops who had served with him during his consulship,[35] while new armies were levied for the new consuls; but even so the number seems too high to be plausible. Unless it is pure fiction (which is not impossible), the most likely explanation is that losses of allied troops serving in the same force, whose numbers were greater than those of citizen soldiers (Plb. 2.24.3-4, 6.26.7, and cf. Walbank (1957) *ad locc.*), have been conflated with the legions.

---

[34] Morgan (1972b), 320-4 accepts the date of 283, but argues Metellus was proconsul rather than praetor, his command having been prorogued. See however *contra* Brennan (1994), 429-32.

[35] Cf. Brennan (1994) 429-32 for the suggestion that Metellus stayed in the field with his army and was elected praetor *in absentia*.

12.2 *Opening of the war against Tarentum.* The story of the attack on the Roman fleet by the Tarentines, and the subsequent abuse of the embassy sent by the Romans to seek restitution, is found in a number of other sources. App., *Samn.* 7.1–2 and Dio fr. 39 (cf. Zonar. 8.2.2–3) have the most detailed accounts; there are briefer versions in Flor. 1.13.2–5 and Oros. 4.1.1–2. Dionysius' account of the attack on the fleet is lost, but a full description survives of the insult to the embassy (*AR* 19.5.2–5), which is also relayed as an independent anecdote in Val. Max. 2.2.5 and is alluded to briefly by Plb. 1.6.5 and Eutr. 2.11.1.

The basic outline of events does not vary much between these sources, although there are some differences in the details (see also below under *direpta esset*). The chief discrepancy comes in the implied reason for the Tarentines' actions. P. gives no reason, thus suggesting that it was a spontaneous and entirely unprovoked assault: cf. Oros. 4.1.1, where the Tarentines simply happened to see the Roman fleet from their theatre, put to sea, and attacked it. Flor. 1.13.4, while telling the same story, gives an explanation that reflects less unfavourably on the Tarentines: the Romans were rowing to shore and the Tarentines mistook them for an attacking enemy. Dio fr. 39.5 likewise suggests that the Tarentines thought the Romans were attacking them, but in his version the mistake arises because they are drunk, and he stresses that the Romans had done nothing to justify so violent a response. He also indicates that the Tarentines had already been plotting war against Rome, which is why the Roman fleet was sent there in the first place (fr. 39.3; cf. Zonar. 8.2.2).

An altogether different explanation, however, comes in App., *Samn.* 7.1: in this version the Tarentines attack the fleet because the Romans are in violation of an 'ancient treaty' (παλαιῶν … συνθηκῶν) which prevented them from sailing further into the bay of Tarentum than the promontory of Lacinium. The general scholarly opinion accepts Appian's account, and sees the suppression of any mention of this treaty in other sources as the consequence of patriotic rewriting. Such a treaty provides the most plausible explanation for the actions on both sides, since it suggests why the Tarentines reacted so violently to the Roman presence, but also why the Romans, given the conquests of the previous decades, might well have seen such a treaty as obsolete and no longer binding them (cf. De Sanctis II 361–2 [380–1]), especially if it was indeed an 'ancient' one.[36]

The chief controversy concerns the treaty's date. Most scholars have associated it with the Spartan prince Cleonymus' expedition to Italy in 303/2 (cf. Livy

---

[36] *Contra* Barnes (2005), 88–97, who, in an elaborate argument, claims that the treaty is a fabrication by Appian, and indeed meant to be seen as such by the reader, since the reference to it is put into the mouth of the demagogue Thais. But Appian speaks of Thais 'reminding' (ἀνεμίμνησκε) the audience of the treaty, which is not the word an author would use of a fabrication, and Barnes's other arguments against the existence of the treaty (such as the similarity between Appian's language and Polybius' description of the first treaty between Rome and Carthage at 3.22.5) are not at all persuasive.

10.2).³⁷ This is possible, but, while the Romans' rapid expansion through the Italian peninsula would doubtless have made such a restriction on their activity seem more urgent to the peoples of southern Italy in 303/2 than it had earlier, the Romans would have had correspondingly less incentive to assent to it; moreover this would make the treaty barely twenty years old, so hardly 'ancient'. While it is true that Appian's language may misrepresent the case, on balance it seems better to assume that the treaty dates from an earlier period, such as the invasion of Alexander of Epirus in the late 330s (so e.g. Cary (1920), 165–70, Mitchell (1971), 638, Oakley (1998), 681 n. 1, Forsythe (2005), 350–1, Steinby (2007), 57–8).

Appian also indicates that the attack on the Romans was initiated by a democratic grouping within Tarentum rather than by the upper classes; cf. Plu., *Pyrrh.* 13.2, and the fragmentary comments in D.H., *AR* 19.4.2. This connection between the war and internal Tarentine politics is widely accepted (e.g. De Sanctis II 363 [382], Thiel (1954), 24, Lévêque (1957), 247–9, Brauer (1986), 125, Cornell (1995), 363, De Juliis (2000), 31), though perhaps rashly so, given the tendency in the Roman historical tradition to associate pro-Roman attitudes with the upper classes and anti-Roman with the lower classes, even when the actual course of events did not warrant such an interpretation (see e.g. Reid (1915), Ungern-Sternberg (1975), 63–76). Lomas (1993), 15–16, 51 is more sensibly cautious, accepting the evidence for internal divisions, but questioning the mapping of class conflict onto support of or opposition to Rome.

Orosius dates the attack of the Tarentines to 282,³⁸ which is supported by D.H., *AR* 19.5.5 (who says that the Roman embassy complaining about it returned home shortly after the beginning of the consulship of L. Aemilius Barbula (*cos.* 281)), and also by wider synchronicities in the story, since our fuller sources link the Tarentine war to other conflicts in south Italy that the Romans were engaged in. Appian has the Tarentines place the prime blame on the people of Thurii, whom the Romans were supporting in 282 against the Lucanians (see 11.7n. and 12.3n.); they accordingly attack Thurii and send the Roman garrison away; the Roman embassy's demands, in his version, include restitution for the people of Thurii as well as for the Romans themselves.³⁹ Dio claims that the Tarentines were allied to other groups in Italy then fighting Rome, including the Gauls

---

³⁷ Thiel (1954), 20–3 makes a full case for the date; see also e.g. De Sanctis II 329–30, 361–2 [346–7, 380–1], Beloch, *RG* 435, Wuilleumier (1939), 87, 94–5, Schmitt (1969), 60–1, Bayer (1972), 338, Torelli, *Fontes* 99, Brauer (1986), 122, Cornell (1995), 363, De Juliis (2000), 30–1.

³⁸ His date is AUC 464, which on the face of things might be taken to mean 290 BC; but Orosius' AUC dates often need adjusting (cf. F 38n.), and at 3.22.12 he explicitly identified AUC 463 with 283 BC.

³⁹ Various historians have plausibly suggested that it was the need to support Thurii which brought the Roman ships to the bay of Tarentum in the first place: so e.g. Thiel (1954), 24–6, Raaflaub *et al.* (1992), 20–1, Hof (2002), 15–17, Forsythe (2005), 350–1, Barnes (2005), 144–5. Others (e.g. Wuilleumier (1939), 102, Lévêque (1957), 247, Kienast (1963), 128) somewhat less plausibly argue that it was an attempt to intervene directly in internal Tarentine politics. Ferone (2001) interprets it as routine coastal defence, but this too seems unlikely given that Rome's fleet was small (see below under *classis Romana*) and she had then little territory to defend in that region.

(fr. 39.1; cf. Zonar. 8.2.1); so too Plu., *Pyrrh.* 13.5–6. D.H., *AR* 19.6.2 (cf. App., *Samn.* 7.3), while not suggesting any connection between the wars, synchronizes the conflict with Tarentum with the others being fought against Samnites, Lucanians, and Bruttians. P., as often, does not make any direct link between this war and others, treating the Tarentine War as a free-standing episode, albeit one with important ramifications later (see 12.4n.); however, the order in which he treats his material does hint at some of these connections (see 12.3n.)

For a general study of the representation of these events in the historical tradition see Hoffmann (1936), esp. 12–15, and above all Barnes (2005).

Tarentinis: Tarentum (Greek Taras, the modern Taranto: *BarrAtl* Map 45 F4), originally a Spartan colony, with a traditional date of foundation of 706; by this time it had become the leading Greek power in south Italy. In Livy's history the Tarentines had appeared first at 8.25–7, where they were concerned by Roman support for their neighbours; they reappeared at 9.14.1–5, attempting to mediate between the Samnites and Romans. Neither of these episodes, however, is mentioned by P.: this is Tarentum's first appearance in his text.

The standard study of Tarentum is still Wuilleumier (1939); for a more recent account of the archaeology of the site see De Juliis (2000), and of the history and coinage see Brauer (1986).

classis Romana: Although there is a single mention of a warship in early Roman history (in the story of the captured expedition to Delphi told at Livy 5.28.2–4 and Plu., *Cam.* 8.4–5), and occasional evidence that implies the possession of ships (such as the restrictions on their use in the early treaties with Carthage recorded at Plb. 3.22–4), the Romans are first attested as formally organizing a fleet as late as 311 (Livy 9.30.4), and the current episode is only the second time it is recorded as being used, the first being a disastrous raid on Campania shortly after the fleet was established (Livy 9.38.2–3). This history of occasional—and ineffectual—naval usage strongly supports the explicit (if somewhat exaggerated) testimony in our sources (e.g. Plb. 1.20.7–9, D.S. 23.2, Sen., *Brev. Vit.* 13.4; cf. Livy 7.26.13) that the Romans showed little interest in naval warfare until the First Punic War; it is certainly the case that no one received a triumph for a naval victory before C. Duilius did in the course of that war (17.2n.). See Thiel (1954), 3–59; also Oakley (2005a), 394–5; *contra* e.g. Staveley (1959), 419–23, Mitchell (1971), 639–41, Starr (1980), 62–4, Steinby (2007), 29–77.

According to App., *Samn.* 7.1 the fleet here consisted of ten ships: this accords with testimony from the early second century (Livy 40.18.7–8, 41.1.2–3: see also below) that the total fleet under the *duumvirs* consisted of twenty ships, ten under the command of each (*contra* Steinby (2007), 60–2, who implausibly imagines a much larger fleet being created at the rate of ten new ships per year).

direpta esset: *classis direpta* is an unusual phrase, only otherwise found in Oros. 6.15.28. As to its meaning, *diripio* could conceivably mean 'tear apart'

(*TLL* V.1 1261.7–38). But, especially with an inanimate object, that is a far less common sense than 'plunder', with the direct object referring either to the thing from which plunder is taken (*TLL* V.1 1261.68–1262.31), or the plunder itself that is taken (*TLL* V.1 1262.32–1263.10). In other places where similar phrases are used of ships it appears to refer to their looting rather than their destruction or capture: see esp. Just. 25.2.6 and Caes., *Civ.* 3.112.3 (which makes explicit the connotations of piracy); that is likely to be the implication here also. In that case, P. is offering a different version from that found in App., *Samn.* 7.1 where, of the fleet of ten ships, four are sunk and one captured (Dio fr. 39.5 similarly focuses on the sinking, but is less precise about the numbers); conversely Flor. 1.13.4 is (cf. above) less hostile to the Tarentines, suggesting that they boarded the Roman ships, but says nothing about their sinking or plundering. P.'s version appears closer to the one in Orosius, where, while five ships escape as in Appian, none is sunk: the rest are taken, their captains executed, and their crews killed or enslaved.

duumviro, qui praeerat classi: Other sources speak more vaguely about the 'commander' of the fleet (Dio fr. 39.4: ναυαρχῶν; Oros. 4.1.1 uses the plural *praefecti*), but the more technical term in P. is certainly accurate. The naval duumvirate was created in 311 to supervise the fitting out of ships, according to Livy 9.30.4, but the duumvirs also appear to have commanded the fleet (possibly as subordinates of the consuls). Subsequent to the events here the office appears to have fallen into desuetude only to be revived in the early second century. Livy 40.18.7–8 and 41.1.2–3 implies that at that point it was not annually elected, but people were appointed as and when necessary and held it for as long as needed; this may have been the case from the start, though there is no direct evidence for it. See Mommsen, *StR*³ II 579–81, Thiel (1946), 421–9, (1954), 26–8, 48, Suolahti (1956), 188–97, Dart (2012).

According to App., *Samn.* 7.1, the name of the *duumvir* was Cornelius; Dio fr. 39.4 gives it as L. Valerius. *MRR* I 190 is properly agnostic; Wuilleumier (1939), 102 n. 5 prefers Cornelius, Suolahti (1956), 190 Valerius, while Thiel (1954), 23 n. 60 doubts both names.

legati: According to D.H., *AR* 19.5.1–6.1, App., *Samn.* 7.2, Dio fr. 39.8, and Zonar. 8.2.3, the embassy was headed by Postumius: Zonaras gives his *praenomen* as Lucius. He is generally identified with L. Postumius Megellus (11.3n.): e.g. *MRR* I 189–90. The identification is by far the most likely one, even though other figures called 'L. Postumius' are attested at the time (two are mentioned at Plin., *Nat.* 11.186, for example), and despite Postumius' disgrace following his last consulship. It was normal to entrust the leadership of such an embassy to a senior consular, and Megellus is the only L. Postumius in that category.

missi: The postponement of *missi*, with the result that it is juxtaposed with *pulsati*, is clumsy, and might be suspected as corrupt in a more classical writer; but P.'s style can accommodate it.

pulsati sunt: *pulsare* implies that the ambassadors were physically assaulted with blows by the Tarentines (*TLL* X.2 2606.25–2607.2);[40] the same term in a similarly phrased passage (cf. Introduction) is used in Oros. 4.1.2. D.H., *AR* 19.5 gives a rather different and more memorable version: not an assault in the sense of physical violence, but he recounts how Postumius was not only mocked for his poor Greek, but also was defecated on by a drunken Tarentine, only to respond with dignity that the Tarentines would wash out the stain with their blood. Much the same story is in App., *Samn.* 7.2 and Dio fr. 39.6–8, who add that the Romans' clothing was also the subject of mockery; cf. the euphemistic version of Flor. 1.13.5: *foede per obscenam turpemque dictu contumeliam violant*—'they foully violated them with an insult obscene and shameful to mention'. Val. Max. 2.2.5 is broadly similar, but the offending substance is urine, and the Romans' dignified response consists of their refusing to make a response. But in the later writers this entire motif disappears: P. (like Orosius, and cf. the even more minimal account of Eutr. 2.11.1) avoids any sense of cultural conflict, let alone grotesqueness, and presents the outrage in the minimum terms that would justify the Roman declaration of war.

ob id: Another clumsy locution (cf. under *missi* above). The juxtaposition of *id* and *bellum* misdirects the reader into assuming that they agree. P. may have unconsciously repeated the phrasing of *bello ob id...indicto* from a few lines earlier, without appreciating the ambiguity created once it becomes a main clause. Classical writers generally avoid such ambiguities, though cf. e.g. Val. Max. 6.1.7 *ob id tribunicium auxilium implorante*.

bellum his indictum est: D.H., *AR* 19.6 dates the declaration of war against Tarentum to early 281; cf. App., *Samn.* 7.2–3.

12.3 *Wars against other Italian tribes.* P. here, as often (see 2.16n.), lists in summary a number of other wars that Livy covered in the book. Unusually, however, he does not list them at the end, but rather in the middle, between the opening of the war with Tarentum and the arrival of Pyrrhus, and this invites the reader to consider some sort of unspecified connection between them, similar to those in other historians. Aug., *Civ.* 3.17 and Oros. 3.22.12 both suggest that the same four groups mentioned here were in alliance with the Senonian Gauls, who are likewise allied to the Etruscans in App., *Samn.* 6, and Eutr. 2.10 (who adds the Samnites), while Plb. 2.19.7–20.5 has them allied to the Boii: see 12.1n. The Tarentines are said by Zonar. 8.2.1 to start their war in concert with the Gauls, Etruscans, and Samnites,[41] while Just. 18.1.1 says that the Lucanians and Samnites joined the

---

[40] *Contra* Barnes (2005), 70–1, who translates the word as 'expelled', and so concludes that the *Periochae* reflects a version of the story in which the ambassadors were not even allowed into the city to present their case.

[41] Cf. Dio fr. 39.1, who however oddly appears to substitute Umbrians for Samnites: the text may be corrupt.

Tarentines in summoning Pyrrhus, Plu., *Pyrrh.* 13.6 lists these (along with the Messapi) as allies of Tarentum, and App., *Samn.* 7.1 suggests that the Tarentines were angered by the Roman defence of Thurii against the Lucanians (see 12.2n.). P. does not offer anything so explicit, but the implicit narrative sequence suggests at the very least that the wars are being fought simultaneously with the Tarentine one, as in D.H., *AR* 19.6.2 (cf. 19.13.1) and App., *Samn.* 7.3, although *aliquot proeliis a compluribus ducibus* discourages the reader from interpreting them as all part of a single campaign.

Samnites defecerunt: P. had recorded Roman victory in the Samnite Wars in the previous book, with triumphs awarded to Fabius Gurges and Curius Dentatus (11.1n., 11.4n.). From that point the post-Livian historical tradition no longer seems to have regarded the Samnites as an independent entity campaigning against Rome, but rather a rebellious group which sometimes allied themselves with external enemies. P. accordingly mentions it only as part of a general list of successful Roman campaigns; the same is true in Books 13 and 14, after which the Samnites disappear from his narrative altogether until the Social War in Book 72 (cf. 15.4n.). In this he (like other authors) diverges from Livy himself, who appears to have constructed the history rather differently and to have seen the fighting here as a continuation of the main series of Samnite Wars (see 11.1n.).

No ancient source describes the campaign in any detail, though (as noted above) the Samnites are associated with the Gallic war by Eutropius, Augustine, and Orosius, and with the Tarentine War by Plutarch and Zonaras; the Samnite rebellion is also referred to in passing by D.H., *AR* 19.6.2, 19.13.1, and 19.16.3. According to the last two of these passages, C. Fabricius Luscinus defeated them as consul in 282, a date that appears to be supported by the *Fasti Capitolini*, where the names of the peoples triumphed over are lost, but the length of the space leads us to expect three names, the other two being the Lucanians and Bruttians, who are also mentioned by Dionysius (cf. below). Eutropius on the other hand explicitly states that Cornelius Dolabella was victorious against the Samnites as well as the Gauls during his consulship in 283 (cf. Oros. 3.22.12), while Dionysius had earlier indicated (19.6.2) that the Samnite rebellion was still continuing at the beginning of the consulship of L. Aemilius Barbula in 281, who is recorded as fighting against them in App., *Samn.* 7.3 before leaving to attack Tarentum; cf. also Plu., *Pyrrh.* 13.6. This is supported by the *Fasti Capitolini*, which record a triumph for Aemilius over the Samnites (along with the Tarentines and Sallentini). Admittedly the triumph was in the following year (280), when Aemilius was proconsul, but it was nevertheless presumably awarded because of his victory during his consulship (De Sanctis II 364 [383]). This is shown by the fact that the triumph was also over the Tarentines, who by 280 were allied with Pyrrhus, against whom Aemilius did not fight; moreover the triumph took place on 10 July, leaving insufficient time for Aemilius to win a new victory, have a triumph voted to him, and return to Rome to celebrate it, all within the same consular year.

Our sources taken together thus record fighting against Samnites in three consecutive years; however, the most secure evidence appears to be that inferred from the *Fasti* and stated explicitly in Dionysius: that Fabricius campaigned successfully against the Samnites in 282, but that the war continued through the consulship of his successor.[42] The backdating of the Samnite rebellion to 283 so as to link it to the Gallic war is not in Polybius, our best source for that war (see 12.1n.), and is likely to be an invention, showing Rome's enemies unifying against her even before Pyrrhus' arrival (so e.g. Torelli, *Fontes* 89, *contra* e.g. De Sanctis II 357–8 [376–7], Wuilleumier (1939), 101, Salmon (1967), 284), though the error may already have been in Livy, and hence be part of what P. is summarizing here.

Lucanos et Brittios: The war against the Lucanians and Bruttians is better documented than the Samnite one. Fabricius' fight as consul in 282 to support Thurii when it was besieged by them is described in some detail by Val. Max. 1.8.6, the chief point of whose anecdote is that Mars was thought to have fought on the Romans' side (the story is also mentioned in passing by Amm. 24.4.24). In addition Fabricius' victory in 282 is here too (cf. above) mentioned by D.H., *AR* 19.13.1, 19.16.3, 20.4.2, and (probably) supported by the *Fasti Capitolini*. Fabricius' defence of Thurii is referred to by Plin., *Nat.* 34.32; likewise Str. 6.1.13, who only mentions the Lucanians among the attackers, but who also, like App., *Samn.* 7.1–2, links the Roman support for Thurii to the outbreak of the Tarentine War (see 12.2n.).

As with the Samnites, there are indications that the fighting was not confined to 282, but extended both earlier and later. D.H., *AR* 19.6.2 says that this war too continued into 281. More importantly, the evidence suggests that the Lucanians were at war with Rome already in 283. It is true that, as with the Samnites, we should probably discount the suggestion in Orosius and Augustine that they were in league with the Gauls in that year. But the note in *Vir. Ill.* 33.4 that M.' Curius Dentatus was awarded an ovation for a victory over the Lucanians needs to be taken seriously historically,[43] and is probably to be assigned to Dentatus' campaigns as *praetor suffectus* in 283: so Brennan (1994), 432–7, Hof (2002), 14–15; *contra* e.g. Degrassi 545, Torelli, *Fontes* 58–9. If so, however, it is more likely that Dentatus' victory was recorded by Livy in Book 11 than in Book 12, since, as I argued at 11.7n., the war with the Lucanians referred to there was probably the campaign in 283.

Hence the campaign which P. is referring to here is likely to be that of Fabricius in 282, with a possible aftermath in 281.

Brittios: The Bruttians were an Oscan-speaking people inhabiting modern Calabria; their territory bordered on both the Lucanians and Tarentum and other

---

[42] *Contra* Beloch, *RG* 463–4, who argues that the *Fasti* are mistaken, and that the Samnite rebellion was not until 281. However, Beloch's argument depends on the assumption that P. is following strict chronology, which cannot be assumed, especially with summary passages like this.

[43] An ovation rather than a triumph is an arcane detail less likely to have been invented, and it is supported by the record of the *Fasti Capitolini* for 275 that Dentatus triumphed for the fourth time in that year: see Brennan (1994), 433.

Greek cities, with whom they had often been in conflict. According to ancient sources (D.S. 16.15, Str. 6.1.4; but cf. the rather different version in Just. 23.1), they emerged as a separate people in the mid-fourth century after revolting from the Lucanians. Their alliance with their neighbours here is likely to have been governed primarily by fear of the growing and aggressive power of Rome, since their territory was distant and their prior contact with the Romans had been limited: this is their first mention in P., and in Livy's surviving text they had appeared only once, as opponents of Alexander of Epirus at 8.24.4–5. For the archaeology of the region and the development of the society in relation to its neighbours see the essays in De Sensi Sestito and Mancuso (2011).

The spelling *Brittii* is less common than *Bruttii* in literary texts, but it is often attested in epigraphy (e.g. *CIL* VI 1699 (= *ILS* 2946), IX 2213 (= *ILS* 1164), X 4, X 517 (= *ILS* 708)), and is certainly correct here. It may represent P.'s spelling rather than Livy's, since the epigraphical sources show it in regular use in the fourth century.

Etruscos: That the Romans fought against Etruscans in these years is securely founded: Plb. 2.20.1–5 records that, subsequent to the Roman victory over the Senones (see 12.1n.), the Etruscans formed an alliance with the Boii and fought against the Romans in two consecutive years, presumably 283–282. This is supported by the fact that Roman victories over Etruscans in 283 by the consul P. Cornelius Dolabella are described by App., *Samn.* 6 (cf. *Gall.* 11, Flor. 1.8.21, Eutr. 2.10), while a campaign in 282 by the consul Q. Aemilius Papus is mentioned by D.H., *AR* 19.13.1 and (probably) Frontin., *Strat.* 1.2.7 (who however refers to the consul in question as 'Aemilius Paulus': see Beloch, *RG* 454–5, Salmon (1935), 26).[44] Fighting against Etruscans appears to have continued even beyond this, according to the *Fasti Capitolini*, which record a triumph against them by Q. Marcius Philippus during his consulship in 281 and one by Ti. Coruncanius in 280 against the Etruscan towns Volsinii and Vulci (though this last should probably rather be associated with the fighting described in Book 13: see 13.8 below and cf. App., *Samn.* 10.3 and Zonar. 8.4.1–2). However, it is less likely that the Etruscans were already in alliance with the Senones in 284/3, as claimed by Aug., *Civ.* 3.17 and Oros. 3.22.12–13: that too (cf. above) is probably a backdating of the anti-Roman alliance that fought with Pyrrhus (cf. Dio fr. 39.1 and Zonar. 8.2.1, who suggest that it was under the prompting of the Tarentines that both the Gauls and the Etruscans broke with Rome).[45] P.'s brief notice could be referring to all or any of these.

---

[44] For a similar error see Plin., *Nat.* 3.138, who calls L. Aemilius Papus (*cos.* 225) 'L. Aemilius Paulus'.

[45] So Mommsen (1879), 370–1. *Contra* De Sanctis II 357 [376] (also e.g. Beloch, *RG* 451–4, Salmon (1935)), who relates the Etruscan alliance to the war against Volsinii mentioned in *Per.* 11 (see 11.7n.); but as noted above, Polybius gives reason to question the reliability of the late sources on these alliances. Morgan (1972b), 318–20 seeks to reconcile the versions by suggesting that the Etruscans were allied with the Gauls from the start, but did not take part in the actual fighting until they joined the Boii in 283.

aliquot proeliis: A phrase regularly used by P. when summarizing the results of several battles: see 18.1, 20.9, 21.3, 29.11, 76.4, 78.2; cf. also related phrases like *(com)pluribus proeliis* (30.1, 75.7, 83.3, 91.3, 98.5) and *expugnare aliquot urbes* (50.11, 53.3, 91.2, 93.1, 115.4). The locution is rare elsewhere in Latin literature[46]—except in Livy himself, who uses it three times in his surviving text (29.28.8, 39.32.4, 44.10.5; cf. also 21.12.2, 35.7.7, 39.2.1, 40.16.8, 40.34.1). P.'s use of Livian language here underlines the extent to which his own project is continuous with Livy's, since even Livy's giant canvas did not allow him to record every battle in detail, and even he was compelled to employ the language of summary.

compluribus ducibus: The phrase (or the related *pluribus ducibus*) recurs at 19.9, 40.3, 41.6. *complures* is a word favoured by P.: it appears more times in his brief text than in the entire surviving work of Livy.

bene pugnatum est: A variation on P.'s favourite *prospere* (cf. 2.6n., 13.1n.); he uses it twice more in the second decade (16.2, 18.1), but never otherwise. Livy too uses it, but infrequently rather than routinely: see 2.16.1, 4.29.5, 38.51.5; cf. 44.35.19.

12.4 *Arrival of Pyrrhus*. P. presents the events somewhat differently from most other sources. He states that the purpose of Pyrrhus' entry into Italy was to support the Tarentines; he does not make it clear that the initiative for this came from the Tarentines (so Plb. 1.6.5, 8.24.1, Plu., *Pyrrh.* 13.2–6, D.H., *AR* 19.8, Just. 18.1.1, App., *Samn.* 7.3, Paus. 1.12.1, Eutr. 2.11.1, Zonar. 8.2.5). Nor does he say that the invitation was prompted by the Romans bringing armies into their territory (App., *Samn.* 7.3, cf. Paus. 1.12.1, Oros. 4.1.4). Nor does he mention that it was part of a fifty-year pattern in Tarentine foreign policy, under which they invited generals and armies from the Greek mainland (known to modern scholars as the *condottieri*) to aid them against their enemies (Archidamus III of Sparta in the late 340s, Alexander of Epirus in the late 330s, Cleonymus in the late 300s): see Str. 6.3.4, and esp. Urso (1998); also e.g. Lévêque (1957), 266–9, Brauer (1986), 61–86.

Instead P. writes as if the initiative was Pyrrhus' own. This in some respects does dovetail with other historians for whom, even though Pyrrhus is not the initiator, he enthusiastically accepts the task (Plu., *Pyrrh.* 13.1, 14.2–8, Just. 18.1.1–2, Dio fr. 40.4–5; cf. Zonar. 8.2.7–8), but those sources see Pyrrhus as using the Tarentine War as a jumping-off point for a far more ambitious sequence of conquests that would leave him dominant in the whole Mediterranean. P. has nothing of these grand plans either: Pyrrhus is not, for him, a failed Alexander.[47]

---

[46] Outside Livy and the *Periochae* it appears only in Caes., *Gall.* 3.1.4 and Flor. 1.33.9.

[47] On the pervasive image in Plutarch of Pyrrhus as a failed Alexander see Mossman (1992), though note also the reservations of Schepens (2000b), 430–1. The truth of this account of Pyrrhus' ambitions for conquest is accepted by e.g. Wuilleumier (1939), 106–7, Lévêque (1957), 250–1, 262–4, Garoufalias (1979), 63–5; others (e.g. Bickerman (1947), 145, Scardigli (1991), 183, Lomas (1993), 52) are justly sceptical.

The particular balance P. adopts is, however, close to that in Flor. 1.13.6 and Oros. 4.1.5–6, who likewise imply (without stating directly) that Pyrrhus himself took the lead in coming to aid the struggling Tarentines, but do not indicate any grand scheme of conquest on his part: his motive is simply to assist his fellow Greeks. On the reading of history shared by these later Latin writers it is Pyrrhus himself who is at the heart of the narrative, not the Tarentines, but he matters as a foe of Rome, not as a potential rival as they begin to rise to world conquest.

The implication of Appian and Zonaras is that the Tarentines summoned Pyrrhus while the consul Aemilius Barbula was campaigning against them, in other words in 281 (cf. Lévêque (1957), 248–9). He sent advance troops immediately, according to Plu., *Pyrrh.* 15.1 and Zonar. 8.2.8–11: the latter explicitly states that these arrived during the same year, though Aemilius sought to avoid battle with them and withdrew for the winter. Pyrrhus' own arrival in Italy is to be dated to the spring of the Julian year 280: we can reasonably assume that it took a significant amount of time after receiving the invitation for him to prepare his resources for so substantial an expedition,[48] and Plu., *Pyrrh.* 15.1 indicates that the storm which dispersed his fleet (see below) was unseasonable ($\pi\alpha\rho'$ $\H{\omega}\rho\alpha\nu$), implying a spring crossing. It is true that Dio fr. 40.6 (cf. Zonar. 8.2.12) says that on the contrary 'he did not wait until spring', but this is probably an invention to suit their depiction of Pyrrhus' impatient character (Kienast (1963), 129).[49]

We do not know the precise correspondence between the Julian and the Roman calendar at this time; however, both Zonar. 8.6.8 and Oros. 4.2.7 refer to Pyrrhus' departure from Italy in 275 as being in the fifth year after his arrival, which suggests that they (or their sources) saw him as arriving after the consuls of 280 had taken office on 1 May (Holzapfel (1885), 103). Even allowing for the preparations that he and the consul Laevinus must have made before setting off for battle (Plu., *Pyrrh.* 16.1–2, App., *Samn.* 8, Zonar. 8.2.13–15, 8.3.1), this is not problematic,

---

[48] According to Just. 17.2.13–14 he received ships from Antigonus Gonatas, money from the Seleucid ruler Antiochus I, and above all substantial forces from Ptolemy Ceraunus. The precise numbers in Justin are questionable, since they do not wholly accord with the figures given by Plu., *Pyrrh.* 15.1 for the entire expeditionary force, but it seems relatively plausible that Pyrrhus acquired resources from other kings. See esp. Manni (1949b), setting Pyrrhus' expedition against the background of the interstate dynamic in the Eastern Mediterranean at that time, and arguing that the Tarentines' appeal arrived at a moment of unusual stability between the different Greek kingdoms; cf. also Evans (1889), 148–52, arguing that Macedonian and Seleucid motifs on Tarentine coins at this period are in tribute to the support of those powers for Pyrrhus' expedition.

[49] For a detailed attempt to calculate the precise date of Pyrrhus' expedition see De Sanctis II 370 [390] n. 21, basing himself not only on the passages mentioned here but also on various synchronisms offered by Polybius (1.6.5, 2.20.6, 2.41.11). He gives more credence than I do to Dio's claim of a premature crossing, but nevertheless reaches a similar conclusion: that the most likely date is March/April 280 (Julian), late March being the earliest safe date for putting to sea warships (as opposed to merchant ships, whose sailing season was far more extensive: see Beresford (2013), esp. 134–72). Beloch, *GG* IV.2 107–8 and Lévêque (1957), 286–8 place it slightly later, in May 280.

since their encounter at Heraclea did not take place until well into the summer (13.1n.).

Pyrrhus: Pyrrhus, son of Aeacides, king of the Molossians (319/18–272 BC). He is the best-documented figure in Roman history of this period, thanks especially to Plutarch's detailed biography, which, though of course the product of a later period, drew in part on contemporary sources, not least Hieronymus of Cardia, whom Plutarch cites three times (*Pyrrh.* 17.4, 21.8, 27.4). Before intervening in Italy Pyrrhus had already had an extensive military career, substantially expanding his kingdom through a mixture of conquests and dynastic alliances, though directly prior to his expedition to Italy he had been forced to retrench and withdraw from his Macedonian acquisitions. He was the author of a work on military tactics (Ael., *Tact.* 1.2, Cic., *Fam.* 9.25.1, Plu., *Pyrrh.* 8.2) as well as (probably) a volume of memoirs,[50] and was widely celebrated as one of the greatest military figures of antiquity (see e.g. Ter., *Eun.* 783, Livy 35.14.8–11 with *Per.* 35.1n., Plu., *Sert.* 23.2, Luc., *Hipp.* 1; cf. Lévêque (1957), 652–60). For his career see esp. Nenci (1953), Lévêque (1957), Kienast (1963), Garoufalias (1979).

Epirotarum rex: Epirus was a territory comprising a substantial part of northwestern Greece, extending into modern Albania: Hammond (1967) is a large-scale study of its archaeology and history.

Whether Pyrrhus can correctly be spoken of as the Epirotes' 'king' has been a controversial scholarly question. Literary texts, as P. does here, regularly speak of Pyrrhus as 'king of the Epirotes' (e.g. D.H., *AR* 19.9.1 (purporting to be a letter from Pyrrhus himself), Frontin., *Strat.* 2.4.13, 2.6.9, 3.6.3, 4.1.14, 4.1.18, 4.4.2, *Vir. Ill.* 35.1), or as 'king of Epirus' (e.g. Just. 16.2.2, 17.2.11, Plin., *Nat.* 3.101, App., *Samn.* 8.1, 10.1, Dio fr. 40.3–4). But this title is never found on the (admittedly scanty) contemporary epigraphy, nor on his coins, both of which refer to him as Βασιλεὺς Πύρρος, but with no descriptive genitive of a people or territory over which he ruled; the Epirotes at this period formed a *symmachia*, a military confederacy, with the Molossians, of whom Pyrrhus was certainly the king, the dominant force within the confederacy. Despite this, some scholars have argued that the description of Pyrrhus as 'king of the Epirotes' is an accurate one (e.g. Lévêque (1957), 207–16, Garoufalias (1979), 165–85; cf. Cabanes (1976), 180–1),[51] while

---

[50] D.H., *AR* 20.10.2 and Plu., *Pyrrh.* 21.8 both refer to Pyrrhus' ὑπομνήματα. Jacoby on *FGrH* 229 notes that these appear to be tralatician references taken respectively from the contemporary historians Proxenos (*FGrH* 703 F 9) and Hieronymus of Cardia (*FGrH* 154 F 12), and argues that they are more likely to represent documents from the royal archive than a memoir composed for a wider readership. However, the content of the Dionysius passage, referring to the anger of Persephone following Pyrrhus' sacrilege in Locri, more plausibly originates in a narrative for a general readership than in archival documents, though we need not believe that copies were widely distributed, since there is no evidence of its being in circulation after Pyrrhus' own day.

[51] Cabanes is formally agnostic on whether the actual title 'king of the Epirotes' was used, but insists that, regardless of the title, the constitutional position of Pyrrhus was that of king of the entire *symmachia*.

others have insisted that it is mistaken (e.g. Bickerman (1947), 144, Nenci (1953), 84–6, Franke (1954), 47–67, Kienast (1963), 117–19, Hammond (1967), 561–2; also Meyer (2013), 73–4, but see below).

One point seems easy to resolve, since there is extensive epigraphic evidence from both the classical and the early Hellenistic periods for Greek kings being called 'king of' a people, but very little for their being 'king of' a territory (Aymard (1948), 235–8):[52] we can therefore exclude 'king of Epirus' from consideration. A stronger case has been made that Pyrrhus used the title 'king of the Epirotes', although admittedly the literary sources are not adequate to prove this (the fact that most of them use the clearly anachronistic 'king of Epirus' does not inspire confidence in the tradition). The key evidence is an inscription from the time of Neoptolemus II (Pyrrhus' second cousin and—briefly—co-ruler): a grant of tax-exemption issued by the allies for the whole of Epirus, and dated ἐπὶ βασιλέος Νεοπτολέμου Ἀλεξάνδρου, ἐπὶ προστά(τα) Δέρκα Μολοσσῶν (SGDI 1336).[53] This has been understood as meaning that Neoptolemus was king and Derkas the *prostates* for the confederacy in whose name the grant was issued (so esp. Cabanes (1976), 179; *contra* Hammond (1967), 566–7), rather than that Neoptolemus and Derkas held their offices for the Molossians alone; indeed, Cabanes, like other scholars, went further on the basis of this and other inscriptions, and claimed that Epirus, despite being formally a *symmachia*, its structures were that of a single federal state (Cabanes (1976), 172–85; also Larsen (1968), 273–81, Funke (2000); *contra* Hammond (1967), 557–71).

However, this entire reconstruction has been strongly challenged by Elizabeth Meyer, who, partly by a systematic redating of much of the Molossian epigraphy, has (*inter alia*) rejected the idea of a federal Epirote state at this period, and, with specific reference to SGDI 1336, argues that it is mistaken to assume that the grant of a tax-exemption presupposes a state-like organization, and that there is, accordingly, no reason to interpret Neoptolemus' kingship as extending beyond the Molossians (Meyer (2013), 67–9). Hence Pyrrhus was not 'king of the Epirotes'— but Meyer also argues that the title is not for that reason anachronistic, but that it marks a development in contemporary Epirote ideas of their own identity, and that it represents the way his position was understood by outsiders such as the Romans in his own day, and that it entered the historical tradition from there (Meyer (2013), 72–9). In that respect P's formulation here, even if not constitutionally correct, is not an unreasonable one.

---

[52] The chief exception is SIG 185 = Rhodes-Osborne no. 21, an Athenian decree from the fourth century BC, where Straton of Sidon is called interchangeably 'king of the Sidonians' and 'king of Sidon'. Aymard (1948), 236–7 plausibly explains this partly as literary *variatio*, but more importantly that Straton's title was assimilated to non-Greek usage, since oriental kings were regularly referred to, both by themselves and by Greeks, as 'king of' a land.

[53] Cf. the wording of Pyrrhus' victory dedication at Dodona (SIG 392 = SGDI 1368: Βασιλεὺς Πύρρος καὶ Ἀπειρῶται καὶ Ταραντῖνοι), which is at least compatible with his holding the title 'king of the Epirotes', even if it does not necessarily require that interpretation.

in Italiam venit: According to Plu., *Pyrrh.* 15 and Zonar. 8.2.12 (cf. App., *Samn.* 8), the fleet encountered a heavy storm on the crossing, and many of the ships were either lost or scattered: it took some time for the force to be reassembled in Tarentum. P. has nothing of this, nor of the stories of the harsh measures that Pyrrhus took in Tarentum to prepare the city for war following his arrival there (Plu., *Pyrrh.* 16.2, App., *Samn.* 8, Zonar. 8.2.13-15; cf. Plb. 8.24.1, D.H., *AR* 19.8, Plu., *Pyrrh.* 13.2-5).

It is likely that Livy himself contained some account of Pyrrhus' (alleged) mistreatment of the Tarentines, to judge by his later citation of the story as part of a warning to the Capuans by Decius Magius against Hannibal: 'the arrogant domination of Pyrrhus and the wretched servitude of the Tarentines' (23.7.4: *Pyrrhi superbam dominationem miserabilemque Tarentinorum servitutem*). If one takes this at face value, Livy presented the story in the harshest light, much as Appian and Zonaras do, rather than the offering the mitigating version of Plutarch, for whom Pyrrhus was taking necessary military measures when faced with a recalcitrant population.[54] The fact that Decius Magius' warnings about Hannibal being a second Pyrrhus are soon proved correct (cf. 23.10.1-9) might be thought to make it likely that Livy showed Pyrrhus, like Hannibal, acting tyrannically towards his allies. But Livy regularly reworks *exempla* to suit his speakers' current rhetorical needs, even when his original narrative handled them differently (see esp. Chaplin (2000)), and we can hardly exclude the possibility that he did the same here.

But P. in any case omits the story altogether: although the Tarentines were the *casus belli*, he ceases to be interested in them or in Pyrrhus' relationship to them once he has arrived. His focus will be entirely on the conflict between Pyrrhus and Rome.

12.5 *Occupation of Rhegium.* The fullest surviving account of this story is in D.H., *AR* 20.4-5; it is also narrated in Plb. 1.7.6-13, D.S. 22.1.2-3, App., *Samn.* 9, Dio fr. 40.7-12, and Oros. 4.3.3-5. It is noticeable, however, that the interest in it is skewed. The most detailed accounts are in Greek historians (which then survive primarily because of the equal interest shown by Byzantine excerptors): it was a story with various resonant implications for them, especially with regard to the relationship between the Romans and their allies, as well as the brutality of armies when given the opportunity. Within the Latin tradition it is far more the latter than the former theme which dominates, as is shown not least by the way that Livy in his surviving text has speakers cite it as an *exemplum*. First, at 28.28.2-7

---

[54] Lévêque (1957), 299-303 and Garoufalias (1979), 67-8 both share Plutarch's perspective, but are over-reliant on the stereotype of the Tarentines as luxury-loving and unwarlike; cf. Hoffmann (1936) for an examination of how that stereotype has infected the historical accounts of their relationship with Pyrrhus.

Scipio uses it as a precedent with which to rebuke his mutinous troops (the focus there is on the potential for soldiers to 'go rogue'); secondly at 31.29.10 it is cited in passing by the Macedonians as an example of Roman perfidy towards their allies, only for the Romans to explain at greater length (31.31.6–7) that the garrison was intended to defend Rhegium, and that the Roman state was in no way responsible, as they proved by ultimately punishing the garrison and freeing the city; the Romans' punishment of the troops, rather than the original crime, is likewise the point at issue in Val. Max. 2.7.15f and Frontin., *Strat.* 4.1.38 (cf. 15.2n.). But the story then largely disappears from Latin writings: most of the epitomizers of Roman history ignore it, apart from P. himself and Orosius.

One factor underlying this disappearance may be the very resonance that gave it potency to the Greek historians: the tale of moral disasters of Roman imperialism, which was less attractive to the post-Livian Latin writers looking back to the Republican past. When cited out of historical context as an *exemplum*, as Livy does himself, it was possible to see it as a celebration of the reassertion of authority over criminals, but that was harder for a sequential narrative—even an abbreviated one—to handle without giving equal prominence to the crime. This was less of a problem for Orosius, whose distinctive approach to Republican history allowed him to turn the story into one of Roman self-destruction; it is unlikely to have been a problem at all for Livy, for whom the agonizing moral complexities engendered by Roman expansion were a central theme. But for P. another approach was needed, since he may have found the story hard to ignore completely, especially if (as is entirely possible, though of course not demonstrable) Livy gave over a generous proportion of his book to recounting it.

P.'s focus on the killing of the people and seizure of the city, with no explanation given, indicates it unequivocally as a crime, as in other sources. But unlike many, he focuses the criminality entirely away from Rome, by identifying the perpetrators as a 'Campanian legion'; for while two of the longer narratives of the episode describe the troops as Campanian (D.S. 22.1.2–3, D.H., *AR* 20.4.2; also the passing reference in Str. 6.1.6), other accounts generally do not. App., *Samn.* 9.1, Plb. 1.6.8 and 1.8.1, and Oros. 4.3.5 explicitly call them 'Romans';[55] Dio fr. 40.7–12 and the other shorter accounts, including Livy's own in his later citations,[56] leave their ethnicity undetermined, but the reader by default would always assume them

---

[55] In the case of Appian the word Ῥωμαίων admittedly appears only at the very start of the excerpt, and may represent a misleading summary by the excerptor, but Polybius clearly identifies the troops as Roman, though he refers to Decius himself as a Campanian (1.7.7). Orosius not only calls them 'Romans', but refers to their force as *octava legio*, as if it were a regularly constituted citizen legion, and indeed draws a moral from the story which is premised on their being fully Roman (4.3.6).

[56] At 28.28.2–7 Scipio has an interest in making the garrison at Rhegium appear as 'Roman' as possible, since he is emphasizing the contrast with his own mutinous troops, who followed non-Roman leaders (cf. Levene (2010a), 227 n. 175); but the same is not true at 31.31.6–7, where one might have thought it an effective argument for the Romans to point out the non-Romanness of the troops.

to be Roman (see further below). The fact that P. mentions their foreignness is therefore pointed, indicating their moral distance from Rome (especially given the widespread stereotype of the corrupt Campanians: see e.g. Levene (2010a), 216–18, 224–5, 359–67): this is clearly presented as a renegade force.

The sources differ also on the date and the purpose for which the garrison was sent. According to D.H., *AR* 20.4.2, the original request from Rhegium for a garrison came at the same time as Fabricius' defence of Thurii against the Lucanians and Bruttians—in other words in 282; however the troops did not take over the city until after Pyrrhus had reached Italy (20.4.4). Other sources (Plb. 1.7.6, D.S. 22.1.2) attribute the garrisoning of the city, as well as the take-over, to the time of Pyrrhus' crossing. The fact that P. places the whole episode after Pyrrhus' arrival suggests the latter reading; it is not impossible that his (typical) 'background' clause represents an event which Livy had narrated earlier in the book (cf. 11.2n. for P. distorting Livy's chronology in this way), but the fact that Livy, too, later refers to the garrison having been sent during the Pyrrhic War (31.31.6), suggests that P.'s sequence may be a fair representation of the original order.

However, Dionysius' account is preferable: it seems more likely that the Rhegians would originally have sought Roman protection against Italians who were attacking another Greek city than against Pyrrhus, whose expedition was premised on the protection of the Greeks (De Sanctis II 375 [395], Beloch, *GG* IV.2 480–2, Walbank (1957), 52). Indeed, Dionysius suggests that the troops were prompted by fear that the town would betray the Romans to Pyrrhus (*AR* 20.4.4–6; similarly App., *Samn.* 9.1, Dio fr. 40.9–10), offering two versions of the story: in one this fear is only the result of a ploy by Decius, but in the other—which Dionysius says that he finds no less plausible—Decius is warned of the Rhegians' impending betrayal by a letter from Fabricius. Many scholars have accordingly taken the threat as a serious one, and as a likely explanation of the troops' actions against the town they supposedly protected, as well as the failure of the Romans to act against them for so long.[57] The alternative chronology, apparently followed by P., anachronistically assimilates Rhegium's interests to that of Rome, treating it as an Italian city under threat from outside Italy.

For an exhaustive study of the historiography of the episode, and a speculative attempt to reconstruct the detailed history from it, see La Bua (1971); also Bleckmann (1999), Hof (2002), 73–87, Santagati (2018). Cristofani (1968) tentatively attempts to relate the story to archaeological discoveries in the town from that period.

---

[57] So Beloch, *GG* IV.2 482–4, arguing that the 'mutiny' was actually sanctioned by the Roman government, who only belatedly turned against the 'mutineers'. Beloch's analysis is followed by e.g. Lévêque (1957), 330–1, Cassola (1962), 172–7, La Bua (1971), 92–6, Garoufalias (1979), 348–9, Santagati (2018), 253–5. We can compare the similar case of Locri, which a brief note in Justin (18.1.9) suggests had received a Roman garrison which it then betrayed to Pyrrhus; cf. Antias, *FRHist* 25 F 25 and Plu., *Pyrrh.* 17.5 for former Roman allies joining Pyrrhus.

in praesidium: *in praesidium mittere*, meaning 'sent in order to be a garrison' (W-M *ad* 27.3.9), is rare in other authors (though cf. Val. Max. 3.7.10a), but is a regular Livian phrase: 23.39.8, 27.3.9, 31.16.7, 36.9.3, and esp. 28.28.2 and 31.31.6, where he describes the occupation of Rhegium in similar language to that here. This may mean that P. is reflecting the language of Livy's text, though it is also possible that, as often, he is employing typically Livian language even when Livy did not use that particular phrase in the passage being summarized.

Reginorum: Greek *Rhegion*, Latin *Regium*; but usually in English spelled 'Rhegium' (*BarrAtl* Map 46 C5); modern Reggio Calabria. It had been founded as a Chalcidian colony around 720 BC in a strategic location on the Straits of Messina; it was sacked by the Syracusans in the early fourth century, but was then restored by Dionysius II around 350. No contact with Rome prior to this is recorded; it was the rapid expansion of Roman power in southern Italy which compelled the different states either to ally themselves to the Romans (as also with Thurii: see 11.7n.) or to take a stand against them. For a survey of its history through the Hellenistic and Republican period see Castrizio (1995).

legio Campana: As noted above, P. is unusual in referring to the troops as Campanian: most other sources, including Polybius, who is by far the earliest and would generally be thought the most reliable, describe them explicitly or implicitly as Roman. Most scholars pay no attention to this variation, and simply assume that 'Campanian' is correct.[58] This is surprising, since transferring the identity of the perpetrators from the Romans to the proverbially corrupt Campanians would have an obvious patriotic motive within the tradition, and would be made easier by the Campanian identity of their leader, Decius Vibellius, which seems secure given his name (cf. below), as well as the fact that Polybius refers to him as such. A second possible reason for the troops being thought of as Campanian is assimilation from the remarkably similar story of the Mamertine seizure of Messana (cf. 16.2n.): for the Mamertines were themselves of Campanian origin, and all the Greek sources claim a direct link between this event and the capture of Rhegium on the other side of the strait (Plb. 1.7.1–8.1, D.S. 22.1.2–3, cf. 21.18.1, 3; D.H., *AR* 20.4.4, 20.4.8, App., *Samn.* 9.1, Dio fr. 40.8, 11; cf. Livy 28.28.6).

Indeed, the idea that these troops were fully Roman rather than Campanian may be inferred even from Dionysius, the longest account and one of the few which identifies them 'Campanian' in the first place. Following the capture of the renegades by the Roman government, he refers to a second takeover by the new garrison (comprised, he says of 'Romans and allies' (20.16.1)), followed by their own capture and execution. This is surely a doublet: Dionysius or his source has mistakenly treated two separate versions of the same event as if they were two

---

[58] La Bua (1971), 82 notes the discrepancy, but dismisses it as either an error by Timaeus, whom he believes to be Polybius' source here, or as a simple consequence of the Campanians' holding Roman citizenship (on which see further below).

separate events (see 15.2n.). But in that case it is worth observing that only the first of those versions had the villains as Campanian: Dionysius (or his source) had a second version in front of him in which they were Romans.

It is true that it does not seem plausible that a regular legion would be under the command of a Campanian, however distinguished he was: there is no parallel at this period for such a thing.[59] However, *legio* in P. (and also Livy 28.28.3 and Orosius; cf. 15.2n.) need not be interpreted literally, and the number 4,000 in Plb. 1.7.7, Livy 28.28.3, and Frontin., *Strat.* 4.1.38 (cf. the 4,500 in D.H., *AR* 20.16.2) presumably derives from the assumption that this was the size of a legion. It is highly unlikely that so large a force would be sent to garrison a single relatively remote location; it is preferable to assume that the term *legio* was being used to designate a force of no set size (cf. *OLD s.v. legio* 2: note esp. Juv. 2.155, speaking of the 300 Fabii at the Cremera), but that this was misunderstood by the historians (Beloch, *GG* IV.2 484–5, Heurgon (1942), 204–5): D.H., *AR* 20.4.2 gives the number as 1,200 (though this too could be an invention).

Yet even if the force was a smaller division, one might feel on general principles that it is more likely that a Campanian would be commanding a force of Campanians than of Romans. Hence an alternative interpretation might seem preferable: that the troops were indeed Campanians, but that they are referred to as 'Romans' in Polybius and other sources in consequence of their possessing a version of Roman citizenship—*civitas sine suffragio*—as Campanians had done since the 330s (Livy 8.14.10, Vell. 1.14.3).[60] Indeed, possessors of *civitas sine suffragio* are sometimes explicitly described as having 'become Roman' (Enn., *Ann.* 157 Sk., Livy 8.17.12), and according to one antiquarian source (Paul., *Fest.* 117L) they were liable for military service. It is interesting in that case that whereas P. emphasizes their Campanian identity, Polybius and others suppress it so completely:[61] indeed, Polybius not only calls them Romans, but implicitly denies that they were Campanian at all, when he contrasts them with the Campanians at Messana (1.7.8; cf. 1.10.4). If we are to maintain this solution, therefore, we have to assume that Polybius was simply unaware of the Campanian background of the 'Roman' troops at Rhegium, but that the truth passed through the tradition to Dionysius, Livy, and thence to P.

---

[59] Münzer (1999 (1920)), 48–61 controversially argued that a number of leading Roman office-holders in the middle Republic were Campanian in origin, but that this has been generally suppressed in the historical tradition; see however *contra* e.g. Beloch, *RG* 338–9.

[60] The extent to which this form of citizenship conferred equal rights on its holders is controversial: Sherwin-White (1973), 39–58, 200–14 holds that it largely did, at least in its origins; Humbert (1978) and Oakley (1998), 544–59 argue that it did not. However, regardless of the precise nature of the legal status, it is uncontroversial that at least some of the time our literary sources treat its holders as 'Roman'.

[61] In his surviving text Livy himself is, as often, more ambivalent than either: with Campanians, as well as other Italians, his narrative veers between identifying them with the Romans and treating them as alien (Levene (2010a), 222–7).

This is far from impossible, but it should not automatically be assumed to be right. There are two reasons to question it. The first is that the status of this 'Campanian legion' is difficult to understand. It is clear that the Campanian cavalry served as separate units (Heurgon (1942), 206-9), but there is little evidence that the infantry did. D.H., AR 20.1.5 is the only hint at Campanian infantry units (apart from the passages under dispute here): he mentions Campanians and others with *civitas sine suffragio* as part of a longer list of non-Roman allies serving separately from the legions in the early third century (cf. 13.5n.), and this can hardly be regarded as unassailable—it is easy to see how such a list could have been mistakenly expanded. At a slightly later period it looks as if Campanians were integrated into the legions: Plb. 2.24.14, enumerating the total Roman forces in 225 BC (cf. 20.8n.), counts Romans and Campanians together, and the absence of explicit references to Campanian infantry before and during the Hannibalic War is best understood as meaning that they served alongside Romans (Brunt (1971), 17-21, Oakley (1998), 556), rather than that they served separately (Humbert (1978), 318-20)[62] or not at all (Frederiksen (1984), 224-5). Heurgon (1942), 201-6 (cf. *MRR* III 220), recognizing the problem, proposed that this *legio Campana* was a force of irregular mercenaries rather than regularly conscripted troops,[63] but there is no known parallel at this period at Rome for the employment of such a force.[64]

Secondly, we must admit that our knowledge of the internal workings of the Roman army at this period is not sufficiently detailed to be sure that an upper-class Campanian could not hold a military post that would allow him to command a division of Roman troops. Certainly at a slightly later period it seems well attested that the Campanian upper-classes intermarried with and had close relationships with their Roman counterparts (cf. e.g. Livy 23.2.6, 23.4.7, 26.33.3). One cannot readily exclude the possibility that there was a process by which such a person could serve in—or even be an officer in—a Roman unit.

In conclusion, therefore, P.'s 'Campanian legion' *may* have existed, but the possibility that the villains of Rhegium were in fact Romans under a Campanian officer should not be excluded.

---

[62] Humbert suggests that units of *cives sine suffragio* are recorded under the general heading of allies (*socii*), which is possible in theory, but has little positive evidence in its favour. His chief argument is that, according to Plb. 6.19-20, recruitment to the legions was by tribes, and *cives sine suffragio* were not members of tribes; but Polybius' description is over-simplified and anachronistic, and does not take account of the necessary variations in recruitment in different times and places (see esp. Brunt (1971), 625-34).

[63] Bleckmann (1999) draws on Heurgon's suggestion, but proposes a very different reconstruction, under which the force was not originally sanctioned by Rome, but was in the employ of the Rhegians themselves, and that it was only later that they made themselves a sufficient irritant to Rome to warrant capture and punishment. This is not impossible in itself, but if the problematic troops had no real connection to Rome, it is not readily apparent how this transmuted into a story which is premised on their official status.

[64] Livy 24.49.8 states directly that the Romans never employed mercenaries before doing so in Spain during the Second Punic War, though he is contradicted by Zonar. 8.16.8, who refers to the employment of former Carthaginian allies as mercenaries during the First Punic War. But both sources see this as a departure from Rome's traditional practice.

praefecto: According to Livy 28.28.4 he was *tribunus militum*; D.H., *AR* 20.4.8 (cf. App., *Samn.* 9.1, Dio fr. 40.11) refers to him as φρούραρχος, and D.S. 22.1.3 as χιλίαρχος. The correct title is hard to determine given the uncertainty over the unit under his command, especially since *praefectus* was a generic title covering different kinds of military officer, including those in charge of non-citizen units (Suolahti (1956), 198–210). If the unit was indeed a separate Campanian one, as in P., it is unlikely to have been under the command of a *tribunus militum*,[65] which was a specific position within the legions (Suolahti (1956), 43–51), and *praefectus* is more likely to be correct. Conversely, Livy's *tribunus militum* seems designed to indicate that this was a regular legion; that might be his adjustment to suit the rhetorical situation (cf. above), or may reflect an account where this was a Roman division rather than a Campanian one.

Decio Vibellio: Livy 28.28.4 calls him D. [sc. Decimus] Vibellius, but the name Decius is recorded in the Greek sources also, and is certainly correct here;[66] it is a version of the Oscan *Dekis* (La Bua (1971), 63). *Vibellio* is the reading of the oldest MSS; some later MSS give the name as *Iubelius*, versions of which are also found in the MSS of Val. Max. 2.7.15f, which has led some, including De Sanctis II 375 [395] and *MRR* I 189 (corrected in III 219–20), to give the name as Iubellius or Vibullius. However, the Vibellii were a distinguished Capuan family, as appears from Cic., *Leg. Agr.* 2.93: the best-known member was the Vibellius Taurea who heroically sacrificed himself after the fall of Capua during the Second Punic War (Livy 26.15.11–15; cf. 23.46.12–47.8 and Cic., *Pis.* 24: see Levene (2010a), 73–4); the transmitted text is thus to be preferred.

D.H., *AR* 20.5.2–5 gives a circumstantial and detailed account of his eventual fate: he was blinded as the result of taking an eye-ointment prescribed to him by a Rhegian doctor; he was then handed over to Rome by his own men, but evaded execution through suicide; the story is also recounted more briefly by D.S. 22.1.2–3 and App., *Samn.* 9.2–3 (Val. Max. 2.7.15f. offers an alternative version in which he died before the city's capture). The story has the romanticized neatness which made it attractive in antiquity and suspect to modern scholars, and of course much of the historical record of this period cannot be relied on; but neatness alone is not sufficient reason for impugning it as fiction.

---

[65] It is true that Diodorus, one of the few sources to identify the troops as Campanian, refers to Decius as χιλίαρχος, the usual Greek term for *tribunus militum* (cf. e.g. Plb. 6.12.6); but this may reflect only his position as garrison commander, and hence be little different in meaning from φρούραρχος in the other Greek sources (cf. LSJ s.v. χιλίαρχος I).

[66] It is not the only place where Livy gives different forms of a person's name, only one of which can be right: note the case of L. Marcius, emergency commander in Spain during the Second Punic War, who is variously called by him L. Marcius son of Septimus (25.37.2), Septimus Marcius (28.28.13), and L. Marcius Septimus (32.2.5); cf. Levene (2010a), 73.

Book 13

13.1 *Battle of Heraclea*. This battle, the Romans' first against Pyrrhus, was famous not least for the sequel, where numerous anecdotes circulated in which the Romans demonstrated their irrepressibility in the face of disaster (see 13.2–3n.). For the battle itself the longest surviving account is in Plu., *Pyrrh.* 16.4–17.5; the detailed version of D.H., *AR* 19.11–12 survives only in fragments, as does that of Dio (fr. 40.18–19, 21–4; cf. also Zonar. 8.3.7–12). There are also abridged narratives in Flor. 1.13.7–8, Just. 18.l.4–7, Eutr. 2.11.2–3, *Vir. Ill.* 35, Oros. 4.1.8–15, and many briefer allusions, including two in Livy (22.59.8, 25.6.3; also e.g. Frontin., *Strat.* 2.4.9. 4.1.24, 4.7.7, Fest. 214L, Paus. 1.12.3–4, Gell. 3.8.1, Aug., *Civ.* 3.17).

Most of the battle narratives focus less on the tactics or manoeuvres of the armies than on a series of anecdotes concerning Pyrrhus' conduct. According to Plutarch, Pyrrhus was initially surprised by the effectiveness of the Romans, and so led his army in person, until his horse was killed under him. Pyrrhus then exchanged armour with his friend Megacles, a ploy which itself backfired when Megacles was killed, leading the soldiers to assume that Pyrrhus was dead, until he removed his helmet and rallied his troops in person. In the end the Romans were disrupted by Pyrrhus' elephants, which he had apparently kept in reserve, and Pyrrhus won a narrow victory. Plutarch gives two versions of the losses on each side—in one, Hieronymus of Cardia (*FGrH* 154 F 11) had Pyrrhus losing fewer than 4,000 to the Romans' 7,000, while on Dionysius' account (which does not survive independently) Pyrrhus lost 13,000, the Romans 15,000[67]—but concludes by noting that the troops Pyrrhus lost were in any case his best.

These three elements—the story of Pyrrhus' narrow escape and exchange of armour, the decisive role of the elephants, and Pyrrhus' slender victory—form the core around which most of the surviving accounts and anecdotes revolve; however, they are often cited selectively and slanted in ways that change the significance of the narrative. A clear example of a slanted narrative is Florus, where the attack on Pyrrhus in person forces him ignominiously from the field, with only the elephants to rescue the day; still more striking is Frontin., *Strat.* 2.4.9, who ignores the elephants altogether and instead uses a version of the Megacles story alone to imply that the Romans, and not Pyrrhus, were victorious; that Pyrrhus was defeated at Heraclea is also implicit in Claud., *Bell. Goth.* 128–32, referring to three defeats that Pyrrhus suffered (Claudian also appears to assume a version in which Fabricius was the commander at the battle, instead of merely the ambassador after it). Whereas Plutarch quotes, apparently approvingly, Fabricius' comment that Laevinus was primarily to blame for the defeat (*Pyrrh.* 18.1; cf. *Reg.*

---

[67] A similar figure for the Roman losses is given with implausible precision by Oros. 4.1.11, who speaks of 14,880 infantry and 246 cavalry killed.

Imp. Apophth. 194F), in certain other accounts he is exculpated by a story that, shortly after the battle, he confronted Pyrrhus with a new army almost immediately and forced him to retreat without a fight, so negating the disaster; Pyrrhus supposedly remarked that the Romans were growing new heads as each was cut off, like the Hydra in the Hercules story (App., *Samn.* 10.3, Dio fr. 40.28; cf. Zonar. 8.4.3, *Vir. Ill.* 35.7).[68] A completely different slant is offered by Oros. 4.1.10–11, who damns the Roman soldiers as cowards and attributes the loss more to their cowardice than to the elephants: this might be thought to be the consequence only of his Christian interpretation, but the same version is found, remarkably, in Livy himself, when at 22.59.8 the survivors of Cannae employ it as an *exemplum*— albeit unsuccessfully—to show why they themselves are more virtuous and deserving than their predecessors had been; similarly the cowardice of the Roman troops is assumed in the anecdote about the punishment of the prisoners freed by Pyrrhus in Val. Max. 2.7.15, Frontin., *Strat.* 4.1.24, and Eutr. 2.13.2.

Part of the complications in assessing the after-image of Heraclea is that it was often conflated or confused with the battle of Ausculum in the following year (Wuilleumier (1939), 124–5, Lefkowitz (1959), 154, 164–5). The conflation is most obvious in Festus, who defines an *Osculana pugna* as one in which 'the defeated are victorious', explaining it with reference to the fact that 'the Roman commander Valerius Laevinus had been defeated by Pyrrhus, and soon had overcome the same king' (*Valerius Laevinus imperator Romanus a Pyrrho erat victus, et brevi eundem regem devicerat*)—Laevinus was in command at Heraclea, not Ausculum. Just. 18.1.7 speaks of Pyrrhus being seriously wounded at Heraclea; in other sources (Plu., *Pyrrh.* 21.8,[69] Flor. 1.13.10, Oros. 4.1.20, Zonar. 8.5.6) this happened at Ausculum. In Flor. 1.13.10 night brings the battle at Ausculum to an end, in Eutr. 2.11.2 and Oros. 4.1.10 it is Heraclea. An anecdote of a Roman soldier wounding an elephant and so showing his companions how to turn them away is associated with Ausculum by Flor. 1.13.9–10, but with Heraclea by Oros. 4.1.10 and Zonar. 8.3.11. Even the famous statement by Pyrrhus that any more such victories would destroy him—the source of the proverbial 'Pyrrhic victory'—floats between Heraclea and Ausculum. Zonar. 8.3.12 (cf. Dio fr. 40.19), *Vir. Ill.* 35.5, and Oros. 4.1.14–15[70] associate it with the former, Plu., *Pyrrh.* 21.9–10 and *Reg. Imp. Apophth.* 184C with the latter.[71] (Admittedly, Zonaras and Orosius could

---

[68] Appian also has a version in which this is said not by Pyrrhus, but by Cineas after his embassy to Rome; also Plu., *Pyrrh.* 19.5. Flor. 1.13.19 has the anecdote, but does not indicate when Pyrrhus said it.

[69] Plutarch cites Dionysius as his source, but it is not in the fairly extensive surviving excerpts of Dionysius' narrative of Ausculum (*AR* 20.1–3).

[70] Orosius also quotes some Latin hexameters to the same effect, allegedly representing an inscription that Pyrrhus erected after Heraclea on the Pyrrhic victory. These cannot be genuinely Pyrrhus' own—he would hardly have admitted his own failure (cf. *SIG* 392 for Pyrrhus' actual victory inscription), and are generally argued to be from Ennius (*Ann.* 180–2 Sk.: see Skutsch (1985), 343–6).

[71] A different conflation—between the battles with Pyrrhus at Ausculum and the final battle at (perhaps) Beneventum (but see 14.3n.)—seems also to have infected the tradition. *Vir. Ill.* (so also Augustine) has only two battles, with Pyrrhus victorious in the first, the Romans in the second. *Vir. Ill.*

hardly have done otherwise, since they regard Ausculum as a Roman victory (13.5n.), and *Vir. Ill.* does not mention Ausculum at all.)

P.'s account, unlike many, does not minimize the Roman defeat in itself. He does not suggest that Pyrrhus' victory was only narrow—there is no hint here at the 'Pyrrhic victory' anecdote—nor does he have anything of Pyrrhus' brush with death or his exchanging armour, which are in other sources readily interpreted to the Romans' advantage. Indeed, he makes Pyrrhus' victory appear even more decisive than it may really have been (cf. below): unlike most accounts, there is nothing in his version to suggest a close fight. But he does, like Plutarch, slant the primary blame away from the Roman soldiers and towards the commander. The defeat is announced as Laevinus' in the opening phrase (cf. Eutropius' laconic notice that 'Laevinus fled'—*Laevinus...fugit*), while the Romans do not retreat, but are said to have died facing the enemy. This prepares the way for the subsequent negotiations with Pyrrhus, in which the Romans stand steadfast, and more generally allows a clear and simple structure to the entire Pyrrhic War, where initial disaster gradually turns to victory. That broad pattern is not unexpected or unfamiliar, but most other sources do not work it through in precisely the same way—in most Pyrrhus is already struggling from the start, or the reverse in favour of Rome happens more swiftly or (as in Augustine) suddenly.

P.'s patterning *may* in part derive from Livy, but, even if so, it is likely to be a distilled and simplified version of him. Certainly Livy 22.59.8, as noted above, suggests a different picture. Admittedly that citation appears as part of a slanted argument and not in the narrative voice; moreover, those troops who died in the battle may well have been presented by Livy rather differently from those who survived (cf. below). But it is possible that Orosius' not dissimilar slant derives ultimately from Livy's narrative of the battle, and Orosius too is distilling it, albeit in a different way from P.

As for the actual history of Heraclea, the layers of anecdote and confusion are hard to strip away. Pyrrhus' victory is not in doubt (despite the various efforts within the tradition to rehabilitate Laevinus). His victory dedication (*SIG* 392) shows that he himself represented it as such, and his subsequent movements and the various accounts of his negotiations with Rome make sense only on that hypothesis (though cf. 13.2–3n.); also, Hieronymus (quoted by Plutarch) is a contemporary witness for the losses on each side, which give Pyrrhus a clear but not overwhelming advantage, though these figures should not be taken unquestioningly, since they may well depend on Pyrrhus' own memoirs, and as such may have been skewed in his favour (cf. 13.5n.). The significant role allotted to the elephants in that victory seems moderately secure (*contra* Beloch, *GG* IV.2

---

dates the second battle at the time of Ausculum, prior to Pyrrhus' move to Sicily, but has the commanders as those of Beneventum, namely Fabricius (but see 14.3n.) and Curius Dentatus (cf. Flor. 1.13.9–11, who correctly has three battles, but wrongly makes Curius and Fabricius the commanders at both of the last two).

474–5); they would after all genuinely have been unfamiliar to the Romans (cf. below), and it may be relevant that the Tarentines began around this point to mint coins with images of elephants on them, perhaps in celebration of the victory (Brauer (1986), 144–5; *contra* Holloway (1992), 229–30). But the other anecdotes of Pyrrhus' actions and words during and after the battle cannot readily be assessed. All of the accounts are coloured by the recognition of Pyrrhus' ultimate retreat and the Romans' ultimate success, and several of the anecdotes are likely to have been developed purely with hindsight, whether initially attached to Heraclea or to Ausculum. Others may depend on contemporary sources and be historical in some form, but which ones, and how far historical, cannot be determined.

Plu., *Pyrrh.* 16.4–6 locates the battle at the river Siris. Pyrrhus had encamped between Heraclea and Pandonia, the Romans on the far side of the river; the battle took place at the point where the Romans crossed (*BarrAtl* Map 45 E4). It is argued by Beloch, *GG* IV.2 273–5 (followed by e.g. Wuilleumier (1939), 114, Lévèque (1957), 328–9, Urso (1998), 127) to have occurred in the second half of July (Julian). He fixes the earliest date as mid-July, not only by the need for both Pyrrhus and Laevinus to assemble their troops and prepare to take the field, but also by Aemilius Barbula's recorded triumph on 10 July (12.3n.: Beloch claims it equates to late July in the Julian calendar): this would not, he suggests, have taken place had the news of the defeat reached Rome (*contra* Judeich (1926), 6–7). The latest date is, he calculates, governed by the three months which he reckons Pyrrhus required for his march on Rome before the campaigning season ended at the end of October.

However, this last assumes an unnecessarily slow rate of progress by Pyrrhus. The road distance between the gulf of Tarentum and Rome is around 600 km, so at an average marching speed of 24 km a day (typical for a Hellenistic army, especially given the existence of relatively good roads for much of the route: see Roth (2007), 391–3), Pyrrhus could have marched on Rome from Heraclea and then returned to Tarentum in little more than a month and a half. Hence there is no reason why the battle should not have occurred much later in the summer than Beloch allows.

Detailed studies of the battle include Lévèque (1957), 317–34, Garoufalias (1979), 69–77.

Valerius Laevinus cos.: P. Valerius Laevinus, consul in 280 (*RE* 213, *MRR* I 190). Nothing is recorded of his career apart from this battle (along with its preliminaries and aftermath). For the form of the name used by P. here see 4.4n.

parum prospere: A favourite phrase in P. to summarize an unsuccessful battle, especially in conjunction with the alliterative *pugnavit* (47.8, 73.4, 92.2, 98.7; also 47.10, 48.12, 97.3, 103.8, 105.5, 112.6). No other author uses it so assiduously, although it occurs once in Livy 29.2.9, from whom P. may have derived it, and occasionally in other authors (Val. Max. 3.2.8, Quint., *Inst.* 6.5.7, Oros. 7.29.6), sometimes in non-military contexts (Plin., *Epist.* 8.10.2, Suet., *Jul.* 79.1; also Colum. 4.30.6 according to some MSS). Slightly more common is the related *parum* *prosperus*, which is likewise in Livy (7.4.6), and various other prose writers (Sall., *Hist.* 4.69.3M, Val. Max. 1.6.4, 7.5 pr., Sen., *Tranq. An.* 2.7, *Epist.* 92.19, *Nat.* 5.16.4 [= C 50], Curt. 9.5.25, Fronto, *Amic.* 2.7.15, Ampel. 11.3, 33.1).

elephantorum...territis militibus: P.'s typical sentence constructs an event by placing a temporal or causal clause at the start (2.2n.). Here, by contrast, he has the main clause first, and then has an explanatory ablative absolute. Such 'appendix' sentences are found in Livy, but are especially typical of Tacitus, and focus the interest on the explanation that the historian sees lying behind the outcome (Martin (1981), 221–3).

elephantorum: Pyrrhus' elephants were part of a herd of Indian elephants originally acquired by Alexander the Great, and then brought to Macedon by Antipater (Arr., *FGrH* 156 F 11.43). The herd remained in Macedon through its many changes of ruler over the next forty years (see Scullard (1974), 81–100). There are two versions of how they came into Pyrrhus' hands: according to Paus. 1.12.3 he had captured them from Demetrius Poliorcetes (presumably when he and Lysimachus defeated Demetrius and took Macedon from him in 288), while according to Just. 17.2.14 he was lent them by Ptolemy Ceraunus, who took the throne of Macedon after Lysimachus' death in 281. Either is possible, but either way they came from the Macedonian herd (Scullard (1974), 100). Justin gives the number as fifty, but Plu., *Pyrrh.* 15.1, Oros. 4.1.6, and Zonar. 8.2.12 more plausibly have twenty. In the wars of the previous decades the Hellenistic generals on all sides had made extensive use of elephants, but this was the first time that they had been seen in Italy.

maxime: For *maxime* used to form a superlative see *TLL* VIII 72.43–73.34.

inusitata facie: A phrase otherwise found only in writers of the late fourth and early fifth centuries: e.g. Aug., *Civ.* 1.7, *Epist.* 128.3, *Gen. ad Litt.* 4.18, Paul. Nol., *Carm.* 24.97. In classical writers other phrases are used, such as *inusitata species*: cf. e.g. Hyg., *Fab.* 138.2, Plin., *Epist.* 6.16.4, and esp. Caes., *Gall.* 2.31.1, 4.25.1–2, both of which illustrate the same theme as P., of being terrified by the sight of an unfamiliar weapon wielded by an enemy. Livy 5.35.4 in a similar context has *invisitata...forma*, as do Just. 18.1.6 and 25.1.6 in some MSS, though others read *inusitata...forma* in both passages (cf. Cic., *Div.* 2.138, where the MSS likewise vary between *invisitata* and *inusitata*).

Pyrrhus inspiceret: The victorious general surveying the bodies on battlefield was a Roman literary commonplace: see esp. Sen., *De Ira* 2.5.4, Lucan 7.786–99, Sil., 10.449–523, Tac., *Hist.* 2.70, Suet., *Vit.* 10.3, Dio 64(65).1.3. In these other cases, however, it invariably reflects badly on the general, who appears to gloat sadistically over the carnage.[72] The force of the scene in P., as in the other Latin

---

[72] Ash (2007), 271; more generally cf. Pagán (2000), 425–34 on 'aftermath narratives' of battles in Latin literature, though her typology does not specifically distinguish those where the general is the one viewing the scene.

historians who describe it (see below), is quite different: after his first encounter with the Romans, Pyrrhus appreciates the courage of his enemy.

The idea that Pyrrhus recognized the heroic qualities of Rome that would ultimately prevail against him is ubiquitous in the historical tradition, and appears in many other contexts: not only the 'hydra heads' and 'Pyrrhic victory' anecdotes (above), but also (e.g.) Pyrrhus' admission that he was wrong to fight so virtuous a nation as Rome (D.H., *AR* 20.6.1), the impression made on him by Laevinus' camp (Plu., *Pyrrh.* 16.4–5), and his admiration of Fabricius (e.g. D.H., *AR* 19.18.8, Plu., *Pyrrh.* 20, App., *Samn.* 10.5, Eutr. 2.12.3–4). It was of course developed with hindsight and flattered the Romans' own sense of their invincible qualities,[73] but it also led to a portrait of Pyrrhus as a generous and chivalrous foe which itself came to dominate the traditions about him, Greek as well as Roman: cf. e.g. Cic., *Lael.* 28, *Off.* 1.38–9 (quoting Enn., *Ann.* 183–90 Sk.), 3.86.[74] In P., however, this characterization is muted by the fact that although Pyrrhus sees the dead Romans, he does not, as in all the other epitomizers, explicitly draw the conclusion himself: P. is more interested in the courage of the Romans than Pyrrhus' response to that courage.

omnia versa in hostem: This anecdote is found only in the Latin epitomizers (Flor. 1.13.17–18, Eutr. 2.11.3, *Vir. Ill.* 35.4; though cf. Dio fr. 40.19),[75] who emphasize it as the key demonstration of the exemplary courage of the Roman troops. In all of these, however, it is specified not merely that the corpses were facing the enemy, but that they had their wounds in front. This is a commonplace of courage going back at least to Tyrt. 11.17–24 and 12.25–6 (West) (cf. Leigh (1997), 210–15), but in the context of viewing the bodies of a defeated army it directly recalls Sallust, *Catil.* 61.3. By not mentioning the wounds P. to some degree suppresses any allusion to Sallust, which is more immediately apparent in the other epitomizers. However, it is worth noting also Tac., *Hist.* 3.84.3, itself alluding to Sallust: <u>cecidere omnes</u> contrariis volneribus <u>versi in hostem</u> ('all fell with wounds in front facing the enemy'). P.'s close linguistic overlap here points the reader to Tacitus, and thence indirectly to Sallust, even in the absence of wounds. But Livy himself needs to be part of the discussion: it is reasonably likely that the wounds mentioned by Florus, Eutropius, and *Vir. Ill.* were present in Livy's original text also, that he was himself alluding to Sallust, but that he also included a phrase such as *versi/versa in hostem* which P. reproduces. If so, Tacitus reflects Livy as much as Sallust, while P. draws on Livy's language in such a way as to privilege the later Tacitean echo over Livy's own Sallustian one.

---

[73] Cf. Schepens (2000a) on the way in which Plutarch's *Pyrrhus*, through the perspective of its ostensible protagonist, provides an idealized portrait of Rome; though cf. Mossman (2005), arguing for a more double-edged image of the *Life* which gives weight to a Greek sense of their own cultural pre-eminence over Rome.

[74] Frank (1926), 314–16 (*contra* Lévèque (1957), 46) less plausibly proposes that the 'chivalrous Pyrrhus' traditions are a creation of Ennius, and were a consequence of his awareness (as a Messapian) that his own ancestors had sided with Pyrrhus.

[75] It also appears in John of Antioch fr. 107 (Roberto), who derives it from a Greek translation of Eutropius.

It is in any case significant that this is barely present in the Greek sources: it is part of a specifically Latin historical tradition which celebrates the overriding courage of Roman troops, even those who, like Catiline's in Sallust or Vitellius' in Tacitus, fought in a dubious cause. That general celebration is even more prominent in P. than allusions to particular events or predecessors.

populabundusque: So also Ampel. 28.3, 45.2, Eutr. 2.12.1 (both specifying that the plundering was aimed at Campania: cf. Zonar. 8.4.2–3), Flor. 1.13.24 (plundering the Liris and Fregellae), and Plu., *Pyrrh.* 17.5. App., *Samn.* 10.3, also refers to plundering by Pyrrhus on his march to Rome, but dates it after the peace negotiations. Dio fr. 40.25–6 claims that the Epirotes in their plundering made no distinction between Roman territory and that of Pyrrhus' own allies, which undermined his attempt to alienate the Italians from Rome. P. does not suggest any such self-defeating actions: the ravaging, like the march on the city, is there to demonstrate the threat that Pyrrhus posed, and hence the steadfastness of the Romans in resisting it.

The adjectival ending *-abundus* has a vivid and dramatic effect, and is typically, as here, used with verbs of motion: see Woodman (2014), 280.

ad urbem Romanam processit: *ad urbem* = 'towards the city' (sc. without reaching it): cf. e.g. Caes., *Gall.* 7.76.5 *ad Alesiam profiscuntur*. According to Plu., *Pyrrh.* 17.5, Pyrrhus reached a point around 300 stades from the city, around 35–40 Roman miles (depending on the length of the stade, which could vary dramatically, even in a single author: see *OCD*[4], 917, and cf. Bauslaugh (1979)); App., *Samn.* 10.3, while dating the march later in the sequence of events, agrees on the distance, describing him as reaching Anagnia, which is 60 km from Rome, around 40 Roman miles. On the other hand, Flor. 1.13.24 refers to him at Praeneste (37 km = 25 Roman miles from the city), and indeed even closer—the 20th milestone from Rome (also Ampel. 28.3, 45.2, *Vir. Ill.* 35.6; Eutr. 2.12.1 gives the distance as 18 miles); this perhaps derives ultimately from Livy, who later refers to Pyrrhus coming 'almost to the city itself' (31.7.10: *prope ad ipsam urbem*). However, this closer approach may be nothing more than an invention to accentuate the danger the Romans found themselves in (Beloch, *GG* IV.1 549; *contra* Wuilleumier (1939), 118, Lévèque (1957), 338). Florus, consistently with this, appears to imply that Pyrrhus' aim was to capture Rome (so also Zonar. 8.4.2), but that seems implausible given his failure to move any further forward and his apparent willingness to treat with the Romans (Plu., *Pyrrh.* 18.2 more plausibly suggests that he had calculated that it was beyond his forces to take the city at that point). The march on Rome was perhaps designed only to pressurize the Romans into accepting terms, and also to induce their allies to abandon them.[76] P. leaves

---

[76] Brauer (1986), 147, De Sanctis II 377 [397] less plausibly suggests that his plan was to join the rebellious Etruscans, but that he found it more difficult than he had expected to reach them by that route. Lévèque (1957), 337–9 proposes that he had all three ends in mind.

Pyrrhus' motives open: the general sense of threat to the city matters to him more than the precise nature of that threat.

urbs Romana is less common than *urbs Roma*, but is nevertheless found quite widely, not least in Livy, who uses both phrases equally. The effect appears to be to amplify the impressiveness of the city as the centre of imperial power (Krebs-Schmalz II 697, Kuijper (1968), 50 n. 9): here too P.'s phrasing, perhaps derived from Livy, is emphasizing the drama of the occasion.

13.2–3 *Negotiations after Heraclea*. The negotiations supposedly conducted between Pyrrhus and the Romans are a notorious historical crux. There is broad agreement between the sources that there were (at least) two embassies, as in P. One was to Pyrrhus headed by Fabricius, which (in most versions) successfully sought the restoration of captives, and involved an unsuccessful attempt by Pyrrhus to bribe Fabricius. The other was to Rome by Pyrrhus' envoy Cineas, seeking a broad peace agreement, which was derailed by the intervention of Ap. Claudius Caecus, who forcefully advised against coming to any sort of terms. Apart from the continuous historical narratives, almost all of which[77] describe both embassies (Plu., *Pyrrh.* 18–21, App., *Samn.* 10, Flor. 1.13.15–20, Just. 18.2.6–10, Eutr. 2.12.2–13.3, Zonar. 8.4.4–5.9 (cf. Dio fr. 40.29–40)), the steadfastness of Appius Claudius and the incorruptibility of Fabricius were staples of the Roman exemplary tradition, and appear as independent anecdotes in dozens of places.[78]

However, this superficial unanimity masks major differences on the timing and the terms of the negotiations. Appian and Zonaras have not one, but two sets, one after Heraclea and one after Ausculum; Plutarch appears to have a similar version, but his chronology is confused, since he explicitly dates the second round of negotiations before Ausculum in 279, but also says it took place in Fabricius' consulship in 278. On the other hand, P. and Eutropius mention negotiations after Heraclea, but nothing after Ausculum.[79] Conversely, in Justin there are no negotiations at all after Heraclea, though Pyrrhus frees the captives spontaneously at that point (18.1.10); they begin only after Ausculum the following year, with

---

[77] There are two exceptions. Dionysius' fragments describe Fabricius' embassy in detail, dating it after Heraclea (19.13–18), but there is no explicit mention of Cineas': this is presumably an accident of survival, since the isolated fragments 20.6 appear to relate to peace overtures by Pyrrhus. Oros. 4.1 uniquely mentions neither embassy, which is consistent with his general denigration of Roman achievement in the Pyrrhic war: cf. 13.1n.

[78] For a full list see Torelli, *Fontes* 137–63.

[79] It is true that both have the anecdote about Fabricius and the traitor after Ausculum, which in Plutarch, Appian, and Zonaras is bound up with the second round of negotiations, since it is what prompts Pyrrhus to free prisoners once again and send his second embassy to Rome (cf. Frontin., *Strat.* 4.4.2). But there is no necessary association between this anecdote and the embassies: it appears from Gell. 3.8.5 that Valerius Antias (*FRHist* 25 F 25) may have had a version which did not involve the release of prisoners by Pyrrhus, since Gellius mentions this only as part of the incompatible account of Claudius Quadrigarius (*FRHist* 24 F 41). See 13.7n.

Fabricius seeking not the return of captives but a broader peace, which Cineas was unsuccessfully sent to have ratified by the Senate. That Pyrrhus did not negotiate at all until after Ausculum appears to be supported by Ennius, *Ann.* 183–90 Sk. (Skutsch (1985), 347–9).[80]

Even if we focus on the negotiations after Heraclea alone, the sources diverge. P., like Eutropius and Zonaras, places Fabricius' mission first and Cineas' second, while Plutarch, Appian, and (implicitly) Florus have Fabricius negotiating over the captives only after Cineas has returned empty-handed from Rome. Consistent with this timing, Plutarch and Appian date the release to the time of the Saturnalia and make it conditional on the Senate ratifying peace, with the prisoners compelled to return to Pyrrhus after the festival when the ratification does not take place; but in all other sources (including those who mention it as an independent anecdote) Pyrrhus releases the captives unconditionally out of admiration for Fabricius. Most sources, like P., appear to assume that the negotiations with Pyrrhus are taking place in the vicinity of the city, but in some he has already retreated to Campania (Eutropius)[81] or Tarentum (Zonaras)[82] before they begin. Most strikingly, while in most versions Pyrrhus' peace offer to Rome is moderate and requires only limited concessions by them (albeit still ones that Appius Claudius warns them not to accept), in two—Appian and the so-called *Ineditum Vaticanum* (*FGrH* 839 F 1.2)—Pyrrhus effectively demands total Roman withdrawal from most of their Italian conquests: the *Ineditum Vaticanum* indeed says that Pyrrhus wanted Roman territory to be limited to Latium.

Scholars have, unsurprisingly, interpreted this divergent evidence in divergent ways. On the dating, some accept that (as in Appian and Zonaras) there were negotiations after both Heraclea and Ausculum (e.g. Judeich (1926), 11–17, *MRR* I 192–3, Lévèque (1957), 341–70, 404–9, Garoufalias (1979), 79–88, 94–6, Hof (2002), 21–59); others regard this as a doublet, and believe that there was only one set of negotiations. Some of this second group follow P. and Eutropius, and place them after Heraclea (e.g. Kienast (1963), 139–43), others (as in Justin and—probably—Ennius) after Ausculum (e.g. Niese (1896), 485–97, Beloch, *GG* IV.1

---

[80] In addition, Cic., *Cato* 16 dates Appius' intervention against Pyrrhus 'in the seventeenth year after his second consulship' (*septimo decimo anno post alterum consulatum*). Niese (1896), 489–91 takes this to provide further support for Justin's date: Appius' second consulship was in 296 and hence the 'seventeenth year' would be 279. Lévèque (1957), 362–3 objects that under the 'inclusive' counting that the Romans usually used for dates, the seventeenth year after 296 is 280, not 279: hence (he argues) Cicero is evidence against Justin's date, not for it. See, however, Powell (1988), 139, 288, showing that the reference is to 279 and so supporting Niese's interpretation of Cicero against Lévèque's—but then noting that, since Ausculum took place *during* the consular year 279, Cicero's date is equally compatible with an embassy before the battle as one after it, providing that it was in the spring rather than the winter.

[81] App., *Samn.* 10.3 places Pyrrhus' march on Rome and his return to Campania between the two embassies.

[82] Livy 22.59.7 similarly refers to Fabricius' embassy being sent to Tarentum, but does not mention Cineas'.

550–1, De Sanctis II 382–3 [403–4], Passerini (1943), 93–5).[83] Of those who accept that at least some negotiations took place after Heraclea, some believe the circumstantial account of the conditional release of prisoners for the Saturnalia given in Plutarch and Appian, and place Fabricius' embassy during the winter, whether before or after Cineas' (e.g. Wuilleumier (1939), 128–9, Garoufalias (1979), 85–8, Hof (2002), 27–8, 49–50); others, arguing that negotiations concerning prisoners would typically occur soon after a battle, have those taking place first, and regard the story of a conditional release as an invention, founded on the more famous story of Regulus' conditional release from Carthage (see 18.5n.), to set Pyrrhus in a slightly worse light (so e.g. Lévèque (1957), 366–8, Lefkowitz (1959), 154–5, Kienast (1963), 140).

There is, however, more consensus on the content of Pyrrhus' offer. Given that Pyrrhus achieved a significant if not decisive victory at Heraclea (13.1n.), almost all scholars[84] have found it implausible that he would sue for peace in conciliatory terms, and have concluded instead that (as in the *Ineditum Vaticanum* and Appian) his offer, at least at that point, was much harsher, though some of those who believe in two embassies to Rome regard the less harsh terms as being those offered after the Romans had achieved greater success at Ausculum (e.g. Judeich (1926), 15–16, Hof (2002), 56–8).

The truth is hard to determine, but a few points of probability may be raised. We can accept that Pyrrhus in reality was not unlikely to have sent embassies to Rome after both Heraclea and Ausculum: he may well have assumed on each occasion that he had achieved sufficient military success to be able to obtain favourable concessions without further warfare. But this does not mean that the second embassy in the historians derives ultimately from authentic records. Historically plausible fictions are likely to have entered the tradition as least as often as historically implausible ones, and in this case the details of the two embassies look suspiciously close to one another (both have the same personnel and the same outcome, both are linked with the release of prisoners to Fabricius; the supposed attempt by Cineas to bribe the Roman women—a story which probably appeared in Livy, to judge by his later reference to it at 34.4.6–10—is attached to the first embassy by Plutarch and Zonaras, to the second by Appian). This, combined with the general tendency to confuse the circumstances of Heraclea with those of Ausculum (13.1n.), makes it not improbable—though hardly provable—that somewhere in the tradition two narratives, which described one set of events but dated them differently, were combined together. In which case, if a real second embassy occurred, it either originally went unrecorded or was completely superseded in the tradition by the displaced version of the first.

---

[83] Wuilleumier (1939), 128–30 splits the difference, and has Fabricius' embassy after Heraclea, Cineas' after Ausculum.

[84] Exceptions include Passerini (1943), 109–10, who regards its terms as an invention to discredit those Romans who were initially ready to treat with Pyrrhus.

Second, almost all sources, apart from Justin and (probably) Ennius, date the best-known set of negotiations—the one involving the embassy of Fabricius and the famous rejection by Appius Claudius—after Heraclea, and there is no good reason to object to this, at least if we accept (as we should) the harsher version of the terms offered, and see the more moderate offers as an invention in the 'generous Pyrrhus' tradition (13.1n.), designed to emphasize the invincible implacability of the Romans. It is true that Ennius' account, apparently placing the negotiations solely after Ausculum, is the earliest that survives; it is nevertheless more than a century later and moreover an epic poem, whose commitment to accurate chronology can hardly be relied on. The consensus in the Greek historians is that negotiations took place after Heraclea, and at least some of those historians had access to contemporary narratives such as Hieronymus and Proxenus; it is hard to see that under those circumstances so ubiquitous a chronological displacement would have taken hold throughout the tradition. Indeed, it may reasonably be conjectured that Ennius was the original source of the post-Ausculum version, that this version was then picked up (directly or indirectly) by Justin's source Pompeius Trogus and assumed to be historical,[85] and was elsewhere combined with the post-Heraclea version so as to create a double set of embassies.[86]

As for the order of Cineas' and Fabricius' embassies, Lefkowitz's argument that under normal procedure the discussions over prisoners would be earlier rather than later seems plausible, though we should naturally allow that the details of the alleged attempt to bribe Fabricius may well have been invented.

P., as noted above, has only the first set of embassies; this may be because of his compression of a Livian original in which both appeared, but their similar absence from the slightly fuller narrative of Eutropius makes it more probable that Livy himself had embassies only after Heraclea, or at most the later ones were mentioned only in passing, as in Plutarch. In any case, P., as one might expect given the prominence of these stories in the exemplary tradition,[87] is interested more in the virtues exhibited by the Roman heroes than in the details of the diplomacy (cf. below).

13.2 C. Fabricius: C. Fabricius Luscinus (*RE* 9). He had been consul in 282, fighting successfully in defence of Thurii against the Lucanians and Bruttians, as well as against the Samnites (12.3n.); he went on to hold a further consulship in 278

---

[85] Compare the way that Cicero regularly treats Ennius as an authoritative historical source: see Elliott (2013), 152–95, and more broadly Elliott (2015) for the way in which Ennius' claims to truth allowed him to meld into—or indeed often generate—historical tradition.

[86] Those who place all the embassies after Ausculum typically relate them to the treaty between Rome and Carthage that may have been signed around that time (though see 13.6n.), and suggest that the Romans' willingness to reject Pyrrhus' overtures was bolstered by that treaty (so e.g. Niese (1896), 494–7, Beloch, *GG* IV.1 551–2, De Sanctis II 384–5 [404–5]). But while it is true that, *if* the peace negotiations are dated so as to coincide with the Roman-Carthaginian treaty, one can construct the history in such a way as to connect the two neatly, that does not provide any reason to date the negotiations then in the first place.

[87] Cf. Schettino (2009) for the centrality of diplomacy in the historical traditions of the Pyrrhic War.

(13.7n.) and a censorship in 275 (14.4n.). His partner in all three offices was Q. Aemilius Papus (cf. Cic., *Lael.* 39), who also (according to D.H., *AR* 19.13.1) joined him on this embassy, along with P. Cornelius Dolabella (*cos.* 283). Otherwise he is primarily known from a handful of anecdotes, most relating to his proverbial status as an archetype of frugality and archaic virtue, but some of which seem to hint at rivalry with certain of his contemporaries (cf. 14.4n.): on this fragile basis some scholars have attempted to reconstruct his role in Roman politics of the period (e.g. Münzer (1909c)). In particular, he is often argued to have supported a more conciliatory approach to Pyrrhus in opposition to Appius Claudius (e.g. Münzer (1909c), 1933, Passerini (1943), 100–12, Cassola (1962), 163–8: see 13.3n.), but this depends entirely on the brief notice in Just. 18.2.6 that Fabricius negotiated a peace-treaty with Pyrrhus after Ausculum which the Senate refused to ratify, and requires that we give Justin's account more credence than it probably deserves (cf. 13.2–3n.). For his career more broadly see Beck (2005), 204–16.

P., like every other source except Dionysius, ignores the other ambassadors. Nor has he mentioned anything of Fabricius' earlier career; he referred in passing to the battles where Livy (presumably) had him leading, but did not attribute the successes to Fabricius by name. Like most other writers, his interest in Fabricius is not as a military hero, but as a major *exemplum* of Roman incorruptibility and honour, and all three of his appearances in his text are in that context.

redimendis captivis: *captivos redimere* is found a number of times in Livy, including a reference to the mission to Pyrrhus (22.59.7; also 22.57.12, 22.61.3, 22.61.7, 38.47.12, 44.24.7). P.'s language here may accordingly reflect Livy's original; but it is worth noting the close similarity of this whole passage with Eutr. 2.12.2: *legati ad Pyrrum de redimendis captivis missi ab eo honorifice suscepti sunt. captivos sine pretio Romam misit.* This may result from both P. and Eutropius drawing on Livy or some other intermediate source, but the clustering of similar phrases despite each text containing material not present in the other makes it more plausible that one is partially drawing on and alluding to the other, albeit perhaps also with an awareness of Livy's text in the background (cf. Introduction).

patriam desereret: *patriam deserere* is Livian (9.4.14, 38.53.10); it can, as in the second of these, mean literally 'abandon one's country' by going elsewhere (*TLL* V.1 679.59–680.17), or it can, as in the first, mean 'betray one's country' with no particular sense of physical abandonment (*TLL* V.1 675.42–65). P.'s language allows both readings: in many versions Pyrrhus proposes that Fabricius come with him and join his court (so e.g. D.H., *AR* 19.14.6, Plu., *Pyrrh.* 20.4, App., *Samn.* 10.4, Dio fr. 40.33), and this is certainly alluded to here, but the broader connotations of betrayal are relevant too (cf. Lucan 3.160: *te Fabricius regi non vendidit auro*)—there is no indication, as in the Greek historians, that, at least in Pyrrhus' eyes, Fabricius could join him honourably once a mutually agreeable peace had been concluded. Moreover, most other sources give far more detail about what Fabricius was offered—often money, but also anything up to and including a share in Pyrrhus' rule (Flor. 1.13.21, Plu., *Reg. Imp. Apophth.* 195A, Aug., *Civ.* 5.8); there is nothing of this in P. P. thus does not seek to characterize Pyrrhus' offer as generous or Pyrrhus himself as magnanimous; similarly, while he goes on to say that the prisoners were freely released, he does not connect this with Fabricius' refusal of the offer, or indeed give any explanation of why Pyrrhus did this. As before, he mutes the portrait of Pyrrhus as a generous foe which is so prominent elsewhere; at most he allows the reader to use any prior knowledge of this famous story to inform the interpretation of his laconic and open summary.

13.3 **Cineas:** Pyrrhus' chief diplomat, who is recorded as his envoy not only to Rome, but also to other cities (Plu., *Pyrrh.* 14.1–2, 22.3), and as the leader of the troops that Pyrrhus had sent ahead of him to Tarentum (Plu., *Pyrrh.* 15.1, Zonar. 8.2.8; cf. 12.4n.). According to Plutarch (*Pyrrh.* 14.1) and Appian (*Samn.* 10.1; cf. Cic., *Cato* 43) he was Thessalian, and had learned oratory from Demosthenes, which is not impossible, though suspiciously neat. In a famous anecdote, he is recorded as expounding Epicureanism to the Romans (Cic., *Cato* 43, Val. Max. 4.3.6, Plu., *Pyrrh.* 20.3–4), suggesting that he might have studied with Epicurus too (who was still alive in 280); but the story is suspect, since in its current form it is clearly designed to flatter the Romans, who are said to have scoffed at the Epicurean doctrine of pleasure. Along the same lines, Plutarch describes him as giving a philosophically inflected warning to Pyrrhus not to invade Italy (*Pyrrh.* 14.2–7; cf. Dio fr. 40.5, Them., *Or.* 140c–d (Harduin), Stob. 3.10.50), but this is likely to owe more to the 'tragic warner' tradition in Greek historiography going back to Herodotus' Artabanus than to historical reality.[88] More securely, he is attested as having written an epitome of Aeneas Tacticus (Ael., *Tact.* 1.2, cf. Cic., *Fam.* 9.25.1), and (probably) some sort of history (*FGrH* 603).[89]

ad senatum missus: The immediate repetition of the language of Fabricius' embassy (*missus ad eum a senatu*) emphasizes the parallels between the two stories implicit in other narratives also. Fabricius' successful mission to Pyrrhus is mirrored in Cineas' unsuccessful one to Rome, with the result in both cases determined by the king's failure to understand how to deal with the incorruptible virtue of the Romans.

---

[88] *Contra* Canfora (1993), who accepts the basic historicity of Cineas' Epicurean inclinations, and uses the conversation recorded by Plutarch to argue that Pyrrhus, too, was able to argue in philosophical terms.

[89] The identification of the historian with Pyrrhus' envoy is accepted by Jacoby and others. It is doubted by Stähelin (1921), 476 on the grounds that the name was common in Thessaly, but this overlooks not only our Cineas' known literary interests, but also the congruity of the few surviving fragments with the career of Pyrrhus, notably the account of Dodona, the major oracle in Pyrrhus' territory (*FGrH* 603 F 2).

rex in urbem reciperetur: This is unique to P.: Appius Claudius does not, as in every other source, merely advise the rejection of Pyrrhus' more or less moderate terms, but refuses Pyrrhus even the right of entry to the city for the purpose of setting out what those terms are. There is hence no question—even implicitly— that Pyrrhus' offer might have attracted some of the Senate, since he has not made an offer; and P. makes it clearer than does any other version that Appius' objection was to the very idea of a negotiated settlement even after a defeat, not to the specifics of what was on offer. This may derive from Livy, but it is unlikely that Livy contained no indications of Pyrrhus' intended offer. More plausible is that Livy separated the description of the offer from the request to enter Rome; if so, P.'s summary omits the former and so, without misrepresenting Livy, focuses him in such a way as to accentuate what all see as the key point: Appius' steadfastness.

de qua re: sc. whether Pyrrhus should be allowed into the city.

ad frequentiorem senatum referri: *frequentior senatus* could mean nothing more than 'a fuller Senate' (sc. with more senators present than at the prior meeting: cf. *TLL* VI.1 1297.75–9); however, it is likely to have a more technical sense here. There was a quorum for at least some categories of senatorial business to be validly conducted (Ryan (1998), 13–51; cf. Mommsen, *StR*^{3} III 989). Summoning a meeting of a *frequens senatus* meant that senators were alerted that the quorum would be enforced (e.g. Cic., *Catil.* 3.7, *Fam.* 1.9.8, *Phil.* 1.8, 3.19, Livy 26.10.2, 28.9.5; cf. Balsdon (1957), 19–20). It is true that Ryan (1998), 36–41 argues that *frequentissimus senatus*, unlike *frequens senatus*, did not have a technical sense of the Senate being quorate, but simply meant colloquially 'a crowded Senate'; but this still leaves open whether the comparative was used in the technical or the colloquial sense. Ryan does not discuss the question, claiming ((1998), 40) that this passage is the only example of the phrase; but he overlooks Livy 35.7.1 *ad frequentiores consultatio dilata est.* The context of the latter passage is an unexpected dispute over a consul's dispatches—when formally receiving them, the Senate learned that he had been accused by his *legatus* of misconduct despite achieving a victory: in other words, an apparently routine meeting was about to turn into one where a major and contentious decision was needed. It is reasonable to assume that the problem was that such a decision should not be taken by an inquorate meeting, and that the word has a technical sense, and, accordingly, that the same is true in the *Periochae*.

No source other than P. mentions it here: the information presumably came from Livy, but P. highlights the procedural detail to explain Appius' last-minute intervention, whereas other sources add to the drama by a more personal and circumstantial account of the old, blind man being carried to the Senate on a litter and/or supported by his sons (Val. Max. 8.13.5, Plu., *Pyrrh.* 18.5–6, App., *Samn.* 10.2, *Vir. Ill.* 34., Zonar. 8.4.11; cf. Cic., *Phil.* 1.11).

Appius Claudius: Appius Claudius Caecus[90] (*RE* 91): the best-known Roman political figure of the period, and the one whose political programme has engendered the most extensive scholarly debate. He was most famous for his censorship in 312 (his one prior appearance in P.'s narrative (9.4)), during which he built the *Via Appia* and the *Aqua Appia*, reformed certain religious cults, and revised the rolls of the Senate and the tribes in order (it appears) to give a place to the descendants of freedmen in the former and to enhance the power of the lower classes in the latter. He had also held many other offices, including consulships in 307 and 296; among his recorded actions outside his censorship are defences of patrician rights against the encroachment of plebeians into priesthoods and the consulship (Livy 10.7.1, 10.15.7–12), which do not seem at first sight in accord with the populist actions associated with his censorship. Much of this has manifestly been coloured by later historical stereotypes and political assumptions about the behaviour of Claudian aristocrats and/or demagogues; but which parts and how far is highly controversial.

For attempts to interpret Appius' political career see e.g. Mommsen (1864), 301–13, Lejay (1920), Garzetti (1947), Staveley (1959), Ferenczy (1970), Raaflaub *et al.* (1992), Beck (2005), 159–87, Humm (2005), Oakley (2005a), 350–72, 669–77.

propter valetudinem oculorum: *valetudo oculorum* is Livian (26.22.5, 32.34.3), and is found in other authors also (e.g. Cic., *Fam.* 14.4.6, Cels. 6.6.27). In these places, however, it suggests only a weakness or infection of the eyes: P. alone uses it of total blindness. Nevertheless the reading should be accepted (cf. *OLD s.v. valetudo* 3), rather than the *invaletudinem* of one late MS and the *editio princeps*: *invaletudo* is used only by Tertullian prior to the fifth century, and never appears with a genitive of the affected part until even later.

Appius' blinding was allegedly divine punishment for his reorganization of the *Ara Maxima* cult of Hercules during his censorship: so Livy 9.29.9–11, a story which became popular later in antiquity (cf. Val. Max. 1.1.17, Lact., *Inst.* 2.7.15, *Vir. Ill.* 34.2, Serv. *Aen.* 8.179), although P. does not mention it (cf. 9.4n.). An alternative version in D.S. 20.36.6 made it a pretence on Appius' part in order to avoid senatorial resentment, but the general assumption of the tradition was that his blindness was genuine. The suggestion that it had kept him out of politics (cf. e.g. Plu., *Pyrrh.* 18.5, Zonar. 8.4.11) assumes that it came on him only after he had held most or all of his political posts: this is not incompatible with the story that it was punishment for his activities in his censorship, since Livy specifies that the punishment came several years after the crime (9.29.11: *post aliquot annos*; cf. App., *Samn.* 10.2)—certainly it is hard to imagine that one could command an army, as Appius did as praetor in 295, while blind. For blindness precluding a person from engaging in political affairs see Ulp., *Dig.* 3.1.1.5 (cf. Mommsen, *StR*³

---

[90] Frontin., *Aq.* 1.5 suggests that his *cognomen* was originally Crassus, but this may be a scribal interpolation: see Rodgers (2004), 144.

I 493–4); the only counterexample he offers is Appius himself, and his overall conclusion is that while a blind man may act as senator, and may continue to hold an office he was elected to prior to his blindness, he could not stand for a new one.

diu: Appius' last securely dated appearance on the political stage had been as praetor in 295, when he apparently took over Decius' army against the Samnites after Sentinum (Livy 10.31.3–7), but it is recorded on his *elogium* in the Forum Augustum (*CIL* I p. 287 = XI 1827 = *ILS* 54) that he held a dictatorship, presumably between 292 and 285, when we have neither Livy nor the *Fasti Capitolini* intact (*MRR* I 187).

sententia sua: The numerous ancient sources for Appius' speech treat it as an act of disinterested and far-sighted patriotism, and modern attempts to claim otherwise largely depend on more or less fragile reconstructions of Appius' earlier career and of early third-century Roman politics in general (cf. above). So e.g. Passerini (1943), 109–12 (*contra* Garzetti (1947), 219–22) sees Appius as a defender of the 'aristocratic' party, who sought expansion in southern Italy, against the 'democrats' headed by Fabricius who preferred to seek territory in the north; Staveley (1959), 431, along related lines, suggests that it might have been connected with the protection of Roman economic interests in southern Italy (which he regards as the key to Appius' entire programme: *contra* Oakley (2005a), 675–7). Humm (2009) wants to link Appius' speech to the gradual growth at Rome of the idea that 'Italy' should be conceived as a natural political unity, with Rome defining her own sphere of hegemony around it, while Ferenczy (1970), 98–102 links it to his supposed long-standing policy of allying Rome with Carthage against their mutual enemies. None of these can be accepted with any degree of probability: if Appius had a narrow political end in view when he spoke against Pyrrhus, all knowledge of that end has vanished.

The speech is explicitly said by Cicero (*Brut.* 61; cf. *Cato* 16) to have survived to his own day. This, if true, would be by far the earliest piece of 'literary' Latin prose of which we have direct record (cf. Varro, *De Gener. Litterar.* fr. 319 (Funaioli) *ap.* Isid., *Orig.* 1.38.2). It cannot merely be dismissed as an obvious fabrication of Cicero's own day (as do e.g. Niese (1896), 493, Lévèque (1957), 352, Hof (2002), 30–1): there is no apparent motive for the alleged forger, and the speech's language and manner had to be plausibly archaic to convince Cicero of its authenticity (cf. Cicero's dismissive comment at *Brut.* 61 about its unattractiveness by comparison with later oratory). Moreover, *Brut.* 61–2 also indicates a likely medium of its preservation, namely alongside the funeral speeches which families apparently kept in an archive in order to retain a memory of their ancestors' deeds (Cicero, it is true, suggests that the deeds so 'recorded' were often fictional, but not that the speeches were not real ones).

Nevertheless, the speech of Appius read by Cicero is unlikely to have been genuine. If he was indeed blind, as almost every source indicates, he would not have had any sort of text or notes to assist him in speaking, so there would have been no existing document to archive; there is also no known institutional mechanism for recording verbatim a speech in the Senate at so early a period, nor an existing cultural practice of publishing or distributing such speeches.[91] Nor, in the absence of such a practice, is there any obvious reason why Appius himself would have produced after the event a text of this speech and only this speech, especially since, with the outcome of the Pyrrhic War still unknown, his intervention could not have achieved the iconic status that it subsequently came to do once Pyrrhus had left Italy.

The most likely way of reconciling these considerations is to suggest that, once Appius' steadfastness against Pyrrhus had begun to be viewed as archetypical, some Claudius composed for the family archive an imagined record of his ancestor's words, and this was later circulated (perhaps in good faith) as genuine. As for the date of the composition, it must have been relatively early for the language to retain its archaic flavour. Cic., *Cato* 16 quotes from Ennius' version of the speech (*Ann.* 199–200 Sk.), and then refers to the speech of Appius as if it presented a comparable account. This is reasonably taken (e.g. by Powell (1988), 138–9) to mean that the speech Cicero read was relatively close to Ennius', in which case one is likely to have drawn on the other. Given the breadth of circulation of Ennius, and the absence of any reference before the late 50s to Appius' speech being in the public domain, it is more likely that our hypothetical Claudian composer based it on Ennius than *vice versa*:[92] this would point to a composition in the second quarter of the second century BC. If so, Cicero could indeed have read an early work of oratory denouncing peace with Pyrrhus, albeit not the one that Appius actually delivered.[93]

Livy could in theory have done the same, but on balance it seems unlikely. If he had read it, he probably would not have composed a speech of his own, but simply inserted a note to the effect that the speech was extant and could be read

---

[91] *Contra* e.g. Lejay (1920), 139–41, who anachronistically assumes such a practice; Humm (2005), 72–3 seeks to deflect the charge of anachronism by offering a series of parallels, none of which do more than show the occasional publication of texts of a quite different character.

[92] So Luiselli (1960), 26 (who, however, dates it implausibly late: see above); *contra* Suerbaum (1995), 256, who suggests the reverse; but cf. n. 85 above for another example of Ennius' central role in solidifying historical traditions. Humm (2005), 65–72, 511–12 rightly notes that the similarity of the speeches in Ennius, Plutarch, Appian, and the *Ineditum Vaticanum* points to at least one common source. However, his argument that all of these are directly dependent on an historian of Appius' own time such as Timaeus is much weaker; and the further suggestion that this single source was based on the speech read by Cicero appears to have no evidence at all. The far more likely possibility, as Luiselli (1960) argues, is that the ultimate source was simply Ennius himself, a possibility which Humm mentions only to exclude on the basis of a narrow and implausible *Quellenforschung* (Humm (2005), 71).

[93] If this hypothesis is accepted, then it is tempting to speculate further on the occasion when it left the family archives and circulated more widely. The absence of any mention of it in *De Oratore*, which Niese and others mistakenly take as a proof of late composition (cf. above), suggests that Cicero may first have encountered it in the late 50s or early 40s; hence the obvious person to have drawn it to his attention was Ap. Claudius Pulcher, with whom he had a lot of dealings at this very time (not least because he had been Cicero's predecessor as proconsul of Cilicia: cf. Cic., *Fam.* 3.1–13), and who dedicated to Cicero a work on augury (Cic., *Fam.* 3.4.1). However, this scenario, though attractive, has no direct evidence to support it.

elsewhere, as he does at 38.54.11 and 45.25.3.[94] And if P. had read of the existence of the speech in Livy, he might well have included a reference to the fact, as at 39.5, 41.5, 49.13, 49.15, and 59.6. We cannot, it is true, prove that this was P.'s uniform practice, but we at least know of no instance where he refers to an extant speech without noting the fact: he omits Livy's comments on the extant speeches in Books 38 and 45, but in those cases he makes no reference to the speech at all. It is, accordingly, fair to deduce from P.'s account of Appius' speech that Livy either did not know the version read by Cicero or doubted its authenticity.

tenuit: 'Won his point' (*OLD s.v. teneo* 16b).

13.4 *Census.* The date of the censors' election was 280, according to the *Fasti Capitolini*; the previous censorship in 283 had (also according to the *Fasti*) been aborted when one of the censors abdicated before completing the *lustrum*, which is presumably one reason why P. did not mention it. The *lustrum* will have taken place in the following year, 279: Livy's usual practice, on those occasions he mentions the *lustrum*, is to record it at the end of that second annalistic year (3.24.10, 10.9.14, 10.47.2, 27.36.6, 35.9.2, 42.10.1). There are, however, exceptions: 38.36.10, where it is in the second year but not at the end, and the same must have been true for the census P. records at 41.4 (see *ad loc.*); also 29.37.5-6, where the *lustrum* appears, exceptionally, to take place in the year of the election.[95] Livy may have followed his usual practice here also, in which case he placed it after Ausculum and P. has displaced it. But we should note that (a) Livy's practice is an artificial construct, as the *lustrum* generally must have taken place well before the end of the year, and he is often flexible in his annalistic arrangement, so we cannot exclude the possibility that he preferred in this case to introduce it at the start of the year; and (b) even if he did not, and P. did indeed displace it, then—doubtless coincidentally—his arrangement probably reflects the true historical sequence more closely that Livy's did. See Mommsen, *StR*³ II 352-4.

Cn. Domitius censor: Cn. Domitius Calvinus Maximus (*RE* 45, *MRR* I 191). He had been consul in 283, according to Appian (*Samn.* 6 and *Gall.* 11) defeating the Gauls after they attacked his army (but cf. 12.1n.). Prior to that he is attested as curule aedile in 299 (having previously lost the election in 304, according to Plin.,

---

[94] In this he follows the usual practice of ancient historians: it was rare to provide a version of an extant speech, except when there was reason to doubt that the audience would have access to the original (Brock (1995)). Livy does give an extended summary of an extant speech of Cato at 39.42.6-12, but that is in the context of a refutation of Valerius Antias, who gave an entirely different version of it (39.43).

[95] The censorship, according to the *Fasti Capitolini*, was in 204, which is also the year under which Livy records the *lustrum*—though paradoxically he claims that it was later than usual (29.37.6; cf. Mommsen, *StR*³ II 352-3). Presumably Livy, despite this claim, has in fact displaced the *lustrum* to a year earlier than it actually took place, perhaps in order to fill out the anomalously short Book 29, at the end of which the account of the censors appears (cf. Levene (2010a), 30), and also to keep the focus of Book 30 on the conclusion of the Second Punic War.

Nat. 33.17), but this is controversial: according to Livy 10.9.10–13 he was named as aedile by Piso (*FRHist* 9 F 30), but not by Licinius Macer (*FRHist* 27 F 25) and Tubero (*FRHist* 38 F 9). Piso's evidence should probably be accepted, though the aedileship may be better placed in 300 or 298: see Oakley (2005b), 139–44. In the current year the *Fasti* record him as being appointed dictator to hold elections as well as censor (see Degrassi 113).

His colleague as censor is not recorded, though it may have been L. Cornelius Scipio Barbatus, whose *elogium* (*ILS* 1 = *ILLRP* 309) mentions an otherwise unattested censorship (so e.g. Degrassi 113, *MRR* I 191, Suolahti (1963), 253).

primus ex plebe: As often, P. highlights constitutional innovations (cf. 11.5n.): in this case the fact that it was the plebeian censor, and not his patrician colleague, who performed the formal ceremony to complete the censorial period. By this point very few positions and duties were completely closed to plebeians, and this new right accordingly represented merely a minor additional move towards practical equality with their patrician colleagues. See Oakley (2005b), 11–12.

lustrum condidit: See 11.5n.

CCLXXXVII milia CCXXII: As before (cf. 11.5n.) this number cannot be regarded as reliable. In itself it represents a significant (though perhaps not implausible) increase from the 272,000 citizens recorded a decade or so earlier, but that figure is itself likely to reflect manuscript corruption, and in any case no data from this period, even if uncorrupted in the manuscripts, can be presumed accurate. Some later MSS provide slightly different figures from those of the main tradition, but these are merely the result of further corruption.

13.5 *Battle of Ausculum.* The second battle against Pyrrhus took place in 279; the Romans were commanded by the two consuls, P. Sulpicius Saverrio and P. Decius Mus. By far the longest surviving account is in Dionysius (*Rom. Ant.* 20.1–3); other narratives include Plu., *Pyrrh.* 21.5–10, Zonar. 8.5.1–6 (cf. Dio fr. 40.43), Flor. 1.13.9–10, and Oros. 4.1.19–22, while there are briefer mentions in (e.g.) Cic., *Fin.* 2.61, Frontin., *Strat.* 2.3.21, Just. 18.1.11, and Eutr. 2.13.4.

What happened at Ausculum is even less easy to determine than at Heraclea. Dionysius' account makes reasonable tactical sense, with circumstantial details about the battle order of the two armies, and describing how a detachment of Roman allies was able to destroy Pyrrhus' camp, which was poorly guarded (20.3.1–3); Dionysius also describes in some detail the Romans' tactics for dealing with the elephants (20.1.6–7, 20.2.5, 20.3.6; cf. Zonar. 8.5.5). Plutarch's version, however, while briefer and less detailed, is quite different, and also makes reasonable sense: he spreads the battle over two days, the first indecisive, but with the elephants giving Pyrrhus a clear victory on the second.

An entirely different narrative tradition centres on the role of Decius. Cicero (*Fin.* 2.61, *Tusc.* 1.89) claims that, like his father and grandfather,[96] he 'devoted' himself at Ausculum;[97] Dio and Zonaras appear to reflect the same tradition, but say that while it was thought that Decius might do so, he was thwarted by Pyrrhus, who said that he would foil the plan by capturing him alive, should he see him in the ceremonial regalia. Skutsch (1985), 353–5 suggests that Enn., *Ann.* 191–4 Sk. is similarly drawn from an account of a *devotio* by Decius at Ausculum, and that this was suppressed in the main historical tradition because the consul survived and the battle was lost. Cornell (1986), 248–9 agrees that a failed *devotio* underlies the accounts of Ausculum in Cicero and Dio, but denies that this fragment of Ennius refers to it, because it seems unlikely that Ennius would have described a failed *devotio*: he suggests instead that it comes from Ennius' account of Sentinum.

However, Skutsch and Cornell both overlook a far more likely way in which a *devotio* at Ausculum would have entered the tradition: that it was invented (on the model of Decius' supposed father and grandfather), and included in Ennius, in the context of a narrative of Ausculum in which the Romans won, and the *devotio* could accordingly be presented as successful. That the Romans were straightforwardly victorious at Ausculum is commonly stated by ancient sources: Zonar. 8.5.6 refers directly to a Roman victory (cf. Flor. 1.13.9–10, Claud., *Bell. Goth.* 129–30), and several authors (Frontin., *Strat.* 2.3.21, Eutr. 2.13.4, Oros. 4.1.22) support this with lopsided casualty figures in the Romans' favour (they lost only 5,000 troops to Pyrrhus' 20,000).

While this version is firmly ingrained in the historical tradition, it is far from the only one, and is unlikely to be true. Plutarch, as noted above, indicates that Pyrrhus came out on top: he cites casualty figures very similar to those he gave for Heraclea, with the Romans losing 6,000 to Pyrrhus' 3,500; and this version is implicit also in Gell. 3.8.1, Just. 18.1.11 (cf. 18.1.7; also cf. 38.4.5), and Aug., *Civ.* 3.17, all of whom regard Pyrrhus as victorious. Plutarch's casualty figures come from Hieronymus of Cardia (*FGrH* 154 F 12), who took them from Pyrrhus' own memoirs (cf. above, n. 50). Pyrrhus had an interest in presenting the battle as a

---

[96] However, Cavallaro (1976), 271–6, shows that the *Fasti Capitolini* for 279 read not 'P. Decius P.f. P.n.', but 'P. Decius P.f. D.n.': on this account, the consul of 279 was not the son of the consul of 295 who devoted himself at Sentinum at all, but from a different branch of the family. This strongly suggests that Cicero's version is a secondary construction based on the similarity of names: see further below.

[97] Beloch, *RG* 440–2 argued that the *devotio* at Ausculum was the only genuine one, and the earlier accounts were invented on its model; but this was in part based on a misreading of the *Fasti Capitolini*, from which he concluded that Decius died at Ausculum. See Degrassi (1939), 22–5, showing that the *Fasti* have no record of Decius' death (though cf. *contra* Fraccaro (1947), 245–7, arguing that one cannot exclude the possibility that such a notice appeared in a margin of the stone that has been lost); moreover, Cavallaro's demonstration (n. 96 above) that this Decius was not the descendant of the earlier ones makes it more probable that the *devotio*, like the filiation, was an invention to make the tradition neater.

success: we should not assume his reliability.⁹⁸ However, he did at least convince his contemporary, Hieronymus, and is unlikely to have done so had he distorted the figures so massively as to turn a lopsided defeat into a victory: the casualty figures in the Latin sources should accordingly be rejected as crude pro-Roman inventions.

Plutarch (*Pyrrh.* 21.9), however, also acknowledges Dionysius' version, which left the outcome indecisive: he gives Dionysius' casualty figures (which do not appear in the extant text) as 15,000 on each side. These figures too look exaggerated—even if Pyrrhus may have changed the proportionate losses, he is unlikely to have diminished them by more than half on both sides—but, unlike the versions that point to a Roman victory, they may derive from accurate historical considerations: a sense that Pyrrhus' success was not decisive. The discrepancy in casualty figures aligns with the different narratives of the battle (above): Plutarch's account is premised on an eventual victory for Pyrrhus, Dionysius' on a broad equality of outcome. The latter is also suggested by P., when he refers to the battle as *dubio eventu* (cf. also Plb. 18.28.10–11, who refers to the outcome, not only here but at Heraclea, as ἀμφίδοξα). There do not appear to be any strong considerations favouring one of these over the other (so e.g. Salmon (1932), 48–9; *contra* e.g. Beloch, *GG* IV.2 465, De Sanctis II 380 [400] n. 44, Lévèque (1957), 379–80, who argue for Plutarch, and Engerbeaud (2013), who prefers Dionysius' account). Both versions may well go back to contemporary or near-contemporary sources, and, unlike at Heraclea, we do not have enough of a picture of Pyrrhus' subsequent actions to be able to determine whether he behaved more like a victor or someone who had been fought to a standstill—indeed the line between 'clear but narrow victory for Pyrrhus' and 'outcome unclear' can be a very fine one (especially in a complex action in which neither side was completely routed, as is the case even in Plutarch's version), and people may have had different perceptions even at the time.

P.'s version once again (cf. 13.1n.) reflects the pattern which he gives to the Pyrrhic War: an initial defeat at Heraclea is followed here by a virtual draw at Ausculum, to be followed by a final Roman victory (14.3n.). P.'s version of Ausculum may be distilled from Livy—like his Augustan contemporary Dionysius, Livy may well have presented the battle in terms of a balance between Roman success and failure—but how that balance was constructed in Livy's narrative is of course unknown.

Ausculum, near which the battle was fought, is the modern Ascoli Satriano, in northern Apulia (*BarrAtl* Map 45 C2). The precise location of the battle is controversial. D.H., *AR* 20.3.7, Plu., *Pyrrh.* 21.5, and Zonar. 8.5.4, despite their other

---

⁹⁸ Cf. Engerbeaud (2013), 70–2, arguing that the similarity of the casualty figures to those at Heraclea makes them suspicious: Pyrrhus may have used a formulaic ratio of deaths on each side to give the impression of a close but nevertheless clear victory.

discrepancies, agree that it was fought near a river, but there are two significant rivers in the neighbourhood of Ausculum, and both have been supported: in particular Beloch, *GG* IV.2 466–70 (followed by e.g. Judeich (1926), 8, Lévêque (1957), 380–4) argues for it being the Aufidus (the modern Ofanto), but Salmon (1932) makes a much stronger case for the Carapelle, which flows very close to the town.

The time of year when it was fought is even more problematic. Salmon (1932), 49 favours May or June, Beloch, *GG* IV.2 275 claims that it was no earlier than the end of June (Julian); but the arguments on all sides are weak, since Pyrrhus' and the Romans' activities before and after the battle are too little documented to lead to any moderately firm conclusions about how much time would be needed for them.

Discussions of the battle include Wuilleumier (1939), 119–25, Lévêque (1957), 375–400.

dubio eventu: Used several other times by P. (74.2, 92.1, 128.1), but never by Livy, whose preferred phrase is *incertus eventus* (1.17.9, 7.23.4, 9.38.8, 10.34.2, 28.22.7, 33.20.9, 35.1.5, 37.37.9, 37.45.13, 42.14.4, 42.17.6, 42.49.4; cf. 34.37.7), which P. conversely never uses. The first attested example of *dubius eventus* is Cic., *Part.* 96, but it is otherwise found mainly in the later historians (Curt. 4.16.28, Tac., *Ann.* 2.18.1, Amm. 27.10.7, Oros. 2.4.9, 4.20.20, Sulp. Sev., *Chron.* 1.17.2, 1.41.6; also Sil. 1.597, Paul., *Dig.* 10.2.23, Claud., *In Ruf.* 2.199–200), though no other author uses it as often as P.

In P. it invariably refers to a battle that has already taken place (as opposed to prospects for the future, as in some other writers), and its primary meaning is 'doubtful success' (sc. neither side could claim a clear victory: cf. *TLL* V.2 1018.53–70). But it could also mean 'doubtful outcome' (cf. *TLL* V.2.1018.71–1019.40): in other words, that the outcome of the battle was actually unknown. That ambiguity is especially pertinent in the case of Ausculum, where, as we have seen, the sources veer between awarding a clear victory to Pyrrhus and an overwhelming one to the Romans. It is not improbable that Livy, like Plutarch later, noted the discrepancy in the historical record, and P. uses phrasing that allows, even while not requiring, a similar interpretation.

13.6 *Treaty with Carthage*. The terms of the treaty mentioned by P. here are given in detail by Plb. 3.25.1–5,[99] though the Greek text is in some respects difficult to interpret (Schmitt (1969), 102 has a convenient summary of the different possibilities). According to Polybius, the treaty maintained the terms of the earlier

---

[99] Note in particular 3.25.3–4: ἐὰν συμμαχίαν ποιῶνται πρὸς Πύρρον ἔγγραπτον, ποιείσθωσαν ἀμφότεροι, ἵνα ἐξῇ βοηθεῖν ἀλλήλοις ἐν τῇ τῶν πολεμουμένων χώρᾳ· ὁπότεροι δ' ἂν χρείαν ἔχωσι τῆς βοηθείας, τὰ πλοῖα παρεχέτωσαν Καρχηδόνιοι καὶ εἰς τὴν ὁδὸν καὶ εἰς τὴν ἄφοδον, τὰ δὲ ὀψώνια τοῖς αὑτῶν ἑκάτεροι.

treaties between Rome and Carthage which delineated their respective spheres of influence and the permitted activities outside them, but added new clauses concerning Pyrrhus.

Three interpretations in particular can be highlighted: (i) According to Walbank (1957), 350–1, Rome and Carthage agreed that if either made a treaty with[100] him, its terms must expressly allow both states to come to each other's aid in the event of an attack on one of them. This reading, however, requires that one reads the ἵνα clause as consecutive rather than final, which is unusual, even if not entirely impossible in Polybius' Greek; it also requires that ἀμφότεροι be read as meaning 'either of two', rather than 'both', as one would usually expect. (ii) Beloch, GG IV.2 476–9 avoids these problems by repunctuating so as to have a full stop after ἀμφότεροι: the requirement is now that neither can make a treaty with Pyrrhus without the participation of the other. The repunctuation necessitates transferring δέ after ἵνα, so that the ἵνα clause depends on the clause that follows and simply explains the reasons for the condition about Carthage providing transport. But such an emendation seems an even more desperate expedient. (iii) Hoyos (1984a), 424–30 proposes to read ἀμφότεροι as Beloch does and the ἵνα clause as final, while maintaining the transmitted text: he translates 'If they make a written alliance with Pyrrhus, both parties shall make it, in order that it shall be permissible to bring aid to each other &c.'. This does the least violence to the Greek, and is probably to be preferred, although it is not straightforward to explicate a treaty which appears to envisage the formation of a multi-side alliance with a mutual enemy, nor is it obvious why mutual aid between Rome and Carthage should be named as the central aim of such an alliance, since the need for aid would appear to be diminished by both sides allying themselves with Pyrrhus in the first place.

On all interpretations, however, the context appears to be a concern that Rome would come to an agreement with Pyrrhus, and that Pyrrhus would then (as indeed he was soon to do) threaten Carthaginian interests in Sicily, but with his position in Italy secured by a treaty with Rome (so e.g. Walbank (1957), 350–1, Hoyos (1984a), 407, Scardigli (1991), 169–73).

The date of the treaty in Polybius is 'at the time of the crossing of Pyrrhus [sc. into Italy] and before the Carthaginians engaged in the war for Sicily' (3.25.1: κατὰ τὴν Πύρρου διάβασιν πρὸ τοῦ συστήσασθαι τοὺς Καρχηδονίους τὸν περὶ Σικελίας πόλεμον). This suggests that it dated from Pyrrhus' invasion in early 280,[101] in contradiction to the implied chronology in P., which lists it after

---

[100] Not 'against' him, as in e.g. Kienast (1963), 146–7, Mitchell (1971), 651–3: this would be an anomalous meaning for συμμαχία...πρός. For the proper interpretation, see Walbank (1957), 350, Hoyos (1984a), 420–4.

[101] ἡ Πύρρου διάβασις is used elsewhere by Polybius (2.20.6, 2.41.11) as a specific chronological marker for the year of Pyrrhus' invasion, which makes it hard to read it here as merely meaning 'during the Pyrrhic War' (see esp. Hoyos (1984a), 405; contra e.g. Flach (1978), 616–17).

Ausculum in 279. Admittedly P. often records events out of chronological sequence, and it is altogether possible that Livy recorded the treaty earlier in the book. A stronger reason for rejecting Polybius' date is that the treaty is plausibly to be associated with a mission sent to the Romans by the Carthaginians under the command of Mago (Just. 18.2.1-5; cf. Val. Max. 3.7.10): this too is dated after Ausculum by Justin, though once again it is not unassailable evidence, since Justin does not actually mention the treaty, and moreover he makes Mago's mission contemporaneous with the negotiations between Pyrrhus and Rome (18.2.6-10), which he has probably postdated by a year (above, 13.2-3n.). But this textual evidence, while weak, is considerably strengthened by the content of the treaty, which would appear to make most sense as a response to Pyrrhus' successes in Italy rather than to his initial invasion:[102] these successes might well have made the Carthaginians concerned that the Romans would come to terms with him and support him (actively or tacitly) in an invasion of Sicily.

A possible reconciliation of these different considerations is offered by Hof (2002), 40-8. She rightly notes that (contrary to what is usually assumed) it is far more likely that Mago's mission, which supposedly involved bringing a fleet of more than 100 ships to Italy to assist the Romans, occurred after the treaty than before it (Hof (2002), 46): even given the existence of earlier accords between Rome and Carthage, so substantial a force would hardly be sent on the off-chance that the Romans were looking for help, even though that is what Justin and Valerius Maximus imply. She also argues that Polybius' dating to 'the time of Pyrrhus' crossing' requires no more than that the treaty occurred in the *year* in which Pyrrhus came to Italy, and that—given the difficulties of converting Olympiads to Roman consular years—Polybius could have associated this with the consular year 280, which did not end until spring of the Julian year 279. Hence, she argues, the treaty was formed in early 279 (Julian), following (and as a response to) Pyrrhus' success at Heraclea, and that the Carthaginians then followed it up by sending support to the Romans after Ausculum. This still assumes that P. displaced the treaty from before to after Ausculum, but so minor a displacement is altogether unsurprising. This reconstruction also allows her to relate, as others do, the Carthaginian treaty to the Romans' famous rejection of Pyrrhus, without requiring that the latter took place in the following year (cf. 13.2-3n.).

Hof's argument is ingenious; it may even be correct. Its weakest link, however, is the attempt to preserve Polybius' accuracy by arguing that, because the end of the Olympiadic year in which Pyrrhus came to Italy overlapped with the *beginning* of the consular year 280, Polybius could have referred to a treaty formed at

---

[102] *Contra* Nenci (1958) (cf. (1953), 154-64), who supports Polybius' date. But his argument depends not only on strained source-analysis, but also on his broader but implausible theory that Pyrrhus' primary aim from the very beginning was an attack on Carthage. See the detailed refutation by Hoyos (1984a), 404-10.

the *end* of that consular year as being 'at the time of Pyrrhus' crossing'. It is preferable to assume that Polybius, who is introducing the treaty in a digression rather than in a chronologically sequential narrative, simply misdated it. In that case the treaty could still have been between Heraclea and Ausculum, as Hof has it, but it could equally have occurred after Ausculum, as in the sequence of P., not long before Mago's mission—indeed, both could have taken place in 278, prior to Pyrrhus' departure for Sicily (14.1n.: so e.g. Beloch, *GG* IV.1 551–2 and IV.2 275–6, followed by e.g. Wuilleumier (1939), 130–1, Garoufalias (1979) 98).

Detailed discussions of the treaty include Beloch, *GG* IV.2 476–9, Nenci (1953), 154–64, Lévèque (1957), 409–18, Nenci (1958), Schmitt (1969), 101–6, Mitchell (1971), 644–55, Flach (1978), Hoyos (1984a), Scardigli (1991), 163–203, Hof (2002), 33–48.

quarto ... renovatum est: For the meaning of the phrase see 11.4n. P. had mentioned only one of the three previous treaties, at 7.9 (see *ad loc.*), which is also his only previous reference to Carthage, corresponding to Livy 7.27.2. That appears to be what Livy regarded as the second treaty between Rome and Carthage (although he did not mention the first); he explicitly refers to the further treaty struck in 306 as the third (9.43.26), and this is accordingly the fourth. There is a well-known discrepancy with Plb. 3.22–6, who argues at some length that prior to the First Punic War there had only been three treaties between Rome and Carthage in total—but also (3.26) refers to a fourth treaty mentioned by the historian Philinus (*FGrH* 174 F 1), demarcating broad spheres of influence for Rome and Carthage, but which Polybius regards as spurious. Since the treaty at 7.27.2 appears to correspond to Polybius' second treaty (3.24: so Walbank (1957), 345–6, Oakley (1998), 257), an obvious conclusion would appear to be that Livy's 'third treaty', not in Polybius, is the one recorded by Philinus (so e.g. Mitchell (1971), 634–44, Scardigli (1991), 129–62, Serrati (2006), 120–1), but see *contra* e.g. Oakley (1998), 258–9, 261–2. The question cannot be considered in isolation from the historicity of Philinus' treaty, which is immensely controversial, but which (fortunately) largely lies outside the discussion here (but see 14.7n.). The one point of relevance is that some have argued that Philinus' treaty was somehow related to that struck at the time of the Pyrrhic War, perhaps a secret annex to it (but see *contra* Oakley (1998), 261, noting that this does not fit Polybius' description of the treaty in Philinus), or a garbled version of it (so De Sanctis III.1 97 [100], Walbank (1957), 354, Hoyos (1985), 108–9, Eckstein (2010), 424–5).

In favour of the latter is that P., presumably following Livy, later (14.7) records that the Carthaginians violated a treaty by intervening at Tarentum in 272. One reasonable conclusion from this is that Livy recorded a treaty whose terms the Carthaginians violated then, which can only be the one here. Admittedly, it is not impossible that Livy was merely inconsistent, and claimed that the Carthaginians violated a treaty without having previously discussed the treaty in question; alternatively, he may have narrated the Tarentum episode in such a way as to suggest that the Carthaginians were in violation of some other treaty terms, not the ones in the treaty of Philinus—certainly Orosius' version of the Tarentum story would seem to leave the Carthaginians vulnerable to such an accusation (see 14.7n.), and Livy's may have done the same. But on balance it is most likely that Livy (mis)represented the treaty here as including a Philinus-like clause, with a general ban on the Carthaginians intervening in Italy.

P.'s language is almost identical to that with which Livy recorded the third treaty (9.43.10), and it is accordingly very likely to be taken more or less verbatim from Livy (Nenci (1958), 282). P.'s mention of a fourth treaty, without having referred to the first or the third, makes this one of the very few places (cf. Introduction) where his narrative is not internally complete. This is an incompleteness he shares with Livy himself, since, as we have seen, Livy speaks of the 'third treaty' despite having only recorded one previously; but the length of Livy's text makes the omission vastly less obvious.

P.'s interest is nevertheless merely in the fact of the treaty, rather than in its content or the historical circumstances that prompted it. It is unlikely that this was true of Livy, since (unlike the third treaty, which Livy did describe in a similarly laconic way) this treaty was, on any reading of the history, formed at a moment of acute crisis for Rome, when the intervention of Carthage could hardly be regarded as unrelated to the war with Pyrrhus. For P., however, the existence of the treaty as a stage in the onward march of Roman history, looking back to the earlier treaty in Book 7 and (more importantly) forward to the First Punic War that would begin in Book 16, is a far more relevant consideration.

13.7 *Fabricius and the traitor.* This episode appears in most of the surviving narratives of the Pyrrhic War: e.g. Claudius Quadrigarius, *FRHist* 24 F 41, Valerius Antias, *FRHist* 25 F 25 (both *ap.* Gell. 3.8), App., *Samn.* 11.1, Plu., *Pyrrh.* 21.1–3, Flor. 1.13.21, Eutr. 2.14.1–2, Zonar. 8.5.8; cf. D.H., *AR* 20.6.1–2. It also, like the earlier account of Fabricius' dealings with Pyrrhus (13.2n.), was widely relayed as an *exemplum* of honesty and virtue (see Torelli, *Fontes* 182–9). Its historicity is highly doubtful, not least because its surviving versions are so clearly driven by the desire to convert it into an ethical lesson; but it cannot be directly disproved. Lévêque (1957), 404–6 (cf. Wuilleumier (1939), 129) claims that invention is shown by the similarity to other stories, notably that of Camillus and the Faliscan schoolmaster (below) and the poisoning of Alexander recounted in Just. 12.14, but the latter is not especially similar, and in any case history genuinely repeats itself often enough that one should be wary of using repetition as evidence for unhistoricity (cf. 11.1n.). Lévêque also argues that the assumption of the story is that Fabricius and Pyrrhus were encamped relatively close to one another, yet Pyrrhus did not campaign in Italy in 278. But while it is clear that Pyrrhus fought no battles with Rome that year, our evidence is too scanty to conclude that he never kept his army in the field without joining combat.

The basic narrative pattern is found elsewhere, most notably in the story of Camillus and the Faliscan schoolteacher (cf. 5.4n.), to which it is directly compared by Livy himself (24.45.3; so also Jer., *Epist.* 87.3 and esp. Zonar. 8.5.8, who suggests that Fabricius was attempting to emulate Camillus' achievement); cf. also the (apocryphal) story of Aristides' rejection of Themistocles' plan to burn the enemy fleet (Cic., *Off.* 3.49, Val. Max. 6.5 ext. 2, Plu., *Them.* 20.1–2, *Arist.* 22.2). In all of these a dishonourable route to victory is proposed, but then heroically rejected: the key lesson is that an unethical victory must be repudiated. These stories are especially prominent among later Romans looking back to an idealized Republic which grew to power while maintaining traditional moral values; the contrast with the slippery treachery of the foreigner also reinforced the Romans' sense of their ancestors' uprightness. This example is particularly useful for that purpose, in as much as the Romans were, in Pyrrhus, faced with the possibility of actual defeat, not merely the failure to win, as they were at Falerii; yet Fabricius even so refused victory by such means. Its popularity was of course aided by the fact that in the end the Romans won, so ethics and expediency went comfortably hand-in-hand: Fabricius never had to pay a price for his honesty.

The episode is generally associated with Fabricius' consulship in 278, though Cic., *Fin.* 5.64 dates it to Pyrrhus' advance to Rome in 280, and Plutarch mistakenly places it, and hence the consulship, before rather than after Ausculum: see 13.2–3n.[103] Several sources (Claudius Quadrigarius, Plutarch, Appian, Zonaras, also probably Dionysius; cf. Frontin., *Strat.* 4.4.2) relate it directly to Pyrrhus' freeing of prisoners and attempting to negotiate with the Romans once again; but that is not true in Eutropius or P., or (probably) Valerius Antias, who have nothing of the second round of negotiations (above, n. 79).

A no less important difference between Antias and Quadrigarius is in the story's implicit ethics. In Antias Fabricius does not reject the traitor outright, but merely sends him on to the Senate, and it is they who make the decision to warn Pyrrhus. In Quadrigarius it is Fabricius and his colleague who take the initiative to return him to Pyrrhus, and he quotes in full the letter which they (allegedly) sent warning him. Antias' version is obviously much less complimentary to Fabricius, in as much as he appears, at least in principle, willing to entertain the traitor's plan, while leaving the final decision to the Senate; moreover, even the Senate is prepared, while warning Pyrrhus of treachery, to keep faith with the traitor by suppressing his name. Antias is followed by Val. Max. 6.5.1, but most other sources prefer Quadrigarius' version, which allows Fabricius to play his heroic exemplary role.

It seems plausible that Antias' version is the original one, and Quadrigarius' a secondary development (Münzer (1909c), 1935–6, *contra* Mommsen (1866),

---

[103] A different confusion appears in Flor. 1.13.21, who makes the hero of the story Curius Dentatus rather than Fabricius.

210 = (1879), 499–500, Rich in *FRHist* 3.342), since it seems more likely that a story where Fabricius behaves more dubiously would be converted into one honouring his incorruptibility than the converse (cf. 12.5n. for another episode showing Fabricius in a more ethically nuanced light which appears in only a minority of sources).

P. does not provide enough detail to make it clear which version he is using (cf. below); nor, accordingly, is it possible to learn from him which version appeared in Livy. Livy does, however, use the story as an *exemplum* three times in his later books (24.45.3, 39.51.11, 42.47.6). The first and third of these are clearly following Quadrigarius, but it has been argued that the second, referring to *horum patres* who warned Pyrrhus of the traitor, reflects Antias' version, in which the warning came from the Senate as a whole, rather than Fabricius alone (so W-M *ad loc.*, Briscoe and Rich in *FRHist* 3.313); it might appear to follow that Livy recorded both versions in Book 13. However, *horum patres* is vague enough to be compatible with Quadrigarius' account, where the letter comes jointly from the consuls (so, rightly, Briscoe (2012a), 315); moreover, Livy's reference at 24.45.3 not only follows Quadrigarius, but is implicitly denying Antias' version, since the point of the *exemplum* there is that the traitor is handed over to Pyrrhus (cf. below), whereas in Antias the Senate refuses to do so. It is rare (though admittedly not unheard of: see Chaplin (2000), 39–41) for Livy to use a different version when referring back to an earlier event in his narrative; we should, accordingly, assume that Livy followed Quadrigarius. He may have presented Antias' version as a variant, but the likelihood is that, if he did so, he strongly signalled that it was not his preferred version.

As to the manner in which Livy handled it, it is noticeable that his later citations represent a rare departure from the use of the story for national self-flattery. Although in Book 13 he may well have treated this episode purely as a celebration of Roman values (though this is inevitably uncertain), when he uses it as an *exemplum* he does so in a way that emphasizes ethical complexity. In 39.51.11 it is the enemy Hannibal who compares the Romans of his day unfavourably with the uprightness of Fabricius, while at 42.47.6 it is adduced in the failed attempt by a minority of the Senate to instil proper values into their colleagues (cf. Chaplin (2000), 106–7). Most interesting is 24.45.3, where the ethics are even more intricate: the Romans are approached by a traitor from Arpi, and initially propose to punish him as Fabricius did, but are deterred by Fabius Maximus, who notes the differences from Fabricius' circumstances and the practical implications of such actions (24.45.4–8).[104] Instead they treat him well while keeping him under restrictions, and it is Hannibal who ultimately takes vengeance on the traitor— but out of avarice rather than ethical concerns (24.45.13–14). For Livy, it is more

---

[104] Cf. Levene (2010a), 202–3, 209–10, 229–31 for other places where Fabius is the locus of ethical complexity in Livy.

the limitations of Fabricius' example than its ability to inspire that are to the fore. Needless to say, nothing in P. suggests that the *exemplum* could be so double-edged: instead he, like other writers of later antiquity, has taken Livy's story and distilled from it a straightforward moral.

cum: See 2.2n. for this common sentence pattern in P. The resulting sentence in this case is inelegant, with the subject of the main clause buried away as a pronoun within the subordinate clause, but such inelegance is not uncharacteristic of P., and there is no reason to doubt the text (cf. below).

C. Fabricio consuli: His partner in the consulship was once again Q. Aemilius Papus (*MRR* I 194; cf. 13.2n.).

is: Sources differ on the identity of the traitor. Antias (here too followed by Valerius Maximus) calls him Timochares, and (according to Gellius) describes him as an Ambracian and a friend (*amicus*) of the king; he adds that his sons were in charge of Pyrrhus' drinks. This is not implausible, given that in Hellenistic courts a 'friend' (φίλος) of the king was not merely someone more or less intimate with him, but a person who held a specific place in the court hierarchy (see esp. Savalli-Lestrade (1998); also Weber (1997), 42–52), and boys from elite families formed a corps of pages, among whose functions included waiting at the royal table (Hammond (1990), esp. 263). Quadrigarius calls him Nicias, and refers to him as *familiaris*, which could likewise mean 'friend' (*OLD s.v. familiaris* 4a), but offers a broader range of possibilities, including even slaves (*OLD s.v. familiaris* 1b). The later sources dependent (directly or indirectly) on Quadrigarius provide another detail (which may well have been in Quadrigarius' original text but omitted from Gellius' summary), referring to him as a doctor (e.g. Livy 42.47.6, Sen., *Epist.* 120.6, Frontin., *Strat.* 4.4.2, Plu., *Pyrrh.* 21.1, *Reg. Imp. Apophth.* 195A–B, Eutr. 2.14.2, Jer., *Epist.* 87.3); this is transferred into Julius Paris' epitome of Valerius Maximus, which melds Valerius' version with the more common one—he still calls the traitor Timochares, but now identifies him as a doctor, and also has Fabricius, not the Senate, providing the warning. There are also occasional confusions: Ael., *VH* 12.33 identifies the treacherous doctor as Cineas, while Amm. 30.1.22, noting the discrepancy of versions, gives one name as Demochares rather than Timochares, and identifies him as Pyrrhus' 'attendant' (*ministrum*: cf. Suid. Φ5 (Adler) 'either a doctor or one of those arrayed at the king's table'—εἴτε ἰατρὸς εἴτε ἕτερος τῶν περὶ τὴν τράπεζαν τοῦ βασιλέως τεταγμένων).

P. neither names him nor identifies his position: this, combined with the awkwardness of the sentence (above), led Jahn to emend *is* to *Nicias*; but unnecessarily: it is altogether characteristic of P. to leave minor characters unidentified (cf. 5.4n.). Rossbach *ad loc.* suggests that it is the discrepancy of the names in the sources that led P. to prefer anonymity here. While that is possible, it is less likely, since Quadrigarius' version, which named him as Nicias, was probably the one preferred by Livy (cf. above).

polliceretur venenum se regi daturum: The version of the story in Cic., *Off.* 1.40 uses almost identical phrasing. It is conceivable that this is because Livy alluded to him, or because they drew their language from a shared source, but far more likely is that P. took his phrasing directly from Cicero, since *De Officiis* was widely read, and probably a school text, in the fourth century (Dyck (1996), 41–2), and P. will soon closely follow the language of Cicero's previous paragraph when summarizing the story of Regulus (18.5n.).

13.8 *Wars against Italian tribes.* P.'s usual end-of-book round-up mentions four groups: Lucanians, Bruttians, Samnites, and Etruscans. Little of this is attested in other sources. Prior to Heraclea the consul Laevinus is said to have taken control of positions in Lucania (Zonar. 8.3.3), while, according to Eutr. 2.12, Pyrrhus on his march to Rome was accompanied by Lucanians, Bruttians, and Samnites, and, at least in some sources (App., *Samn.* 10.3, Dio fr. 40.28; cf. Zonar. 8.4.3, *Vir. Ill.* 35.7; cf. 13.1n.) his army was confronted by Laevinus: it is possible that Livy had something similar, and that this is part of what is included under this heading by P. The same three groups are listed by D.H., *AR* 20.1.1–3 among Pyrrhus' forces at Ausculum, though P. has mentioned that battle earlier, and did not treat it as an unequivocal success for the Romans (13.5n.).

In addition, Fabricius is recorded by the *Fasti Capitolini* as having triumphed over Lucanians, Bruttians, Tarentines, and Samnites during his consulship in 278 (also Eutr. 2.14.4, which mentions only the Lucanians and Samnites).[105] In theory that fighting could have been described by Livy either in Book 13 or Book 14, since Fabricius' consulship spanned both. Zonar. 8.5.9 (cf. Dio fr. 40.45), explaining Pyrrhus' decision to leave Italy (cf. 14.1n.), lists among the reasons that the Romans were 'overrunning and capturing the cities allied to him': it is possible that this is referring to the campaigns for which Fabricius was awarded his triumph, and, whether or not that is the case, it is likely to include the peoples mentioned by P., and Livy may have included them in Book 13. But no other source indicates direct Roman action against Pyrrhus' allies between Ausculum and his departure for Sicily, which makes it less likely that Livy did so; the fact that Fabricius' triumph included the Tarentines, whom he could hardly have defeated while Pyrrhus was around, weights the argument in the opposite direction (cf. Niese (1896), 499, Judeich (1926), 14–15): note that Eutropius records Fabricius' victory only after Pyrrhus' departure for Sicily. See further 14.8n.

---

[105] *Contra* Beloch, *RG* 464–5, who regards the report in the *Fasti* as a mere doublet of the success achieved by Fabricius in his first consulship, four years earlier; since he argues that there was insufficient time for him to obtain these victories after Pyrrhus' departure. But this depends on too narrow a view of the chronological window he had available. Even on Beloch's chronology, on which Pyrrhus left Italy in early September (see 14.1n.), that still left nearly two months for Fabricius to fight and win these battles—far from impossible, assuming that he was already in the field in southern Italy at that point.

None of this, however, is very firmly founded: it may be that Livy presented some of these events differently from the way they appear elsewhere, or P. may be treating equivocal outcomes in Livy as unequivocal successes. Alternatively, it is entirely possible that Livy in this book recounted some battles for which there is no other surviving source.

As for the Etruscans, the consul of 280, Ti. Coruncanius, is recorded as obtaining a triumph over the Etruscan cities Volsinii and Vulci in the *Fasti Capitolini*, while he is mentioned by App., *Samn.* 10.3 and Zonar. 8.4.1–2 as campaigning in Etruria at the time of the defeat of Heraclea, and Zonaras suggests that he made them come to terms. It seems reasonable to assume that these all relate to the same campaign, and that this is also the one referred to here (*contra* Degrassi 545, followed by Torelli, *Fontes* 115, who strangely relates Coruncanius' victory to the wars mentioned at 11.7, which is hardly possible, since Book 11 ends before the Gallic war in 283: see 11.7n.). Harris (1971), 82–3 argues that Coruncanius' victories were recounted in Book 12, and hence that what P. is referring to in Book 13 was further fighting after them. But this is based on the assumption that Coruncanius was withdrawn from Etruria to face Pyrrhus around the time of his arrival in Italy, which contradicts Appian and Zonaras, both of which have him leaving Etruria only after Heraclea.

res praeterea...gestas continet: See 2.16n.

res...prospere gestas: See 3.10n.

Lucanos [et] Bruttios Samnites Etruscos: When listing the peoples over whom the Romans were victorious, P. does not generally favour asyndeton: he instead connects each name with *et*, even when the list extends to as many as seven (see e.g. 7.13 or 9.5). Here, however, the mediaeval MSS have only one *et*, after the first name, in a position where it could hardly stand alone, and it is hard to imagine that *et* would have dropped out twice in such quick succession. In some Renaissance MSS *et* is added before *Etruscos*, creating two balanced pairs of names, but elegant balance is not characteristic of P.'s style, and while the Lucanians and Bruttians form a natural pair, the Samnites and the Etruscans do not, since the evidence suggests that the campaign against the latter was separate from fighting with the other three (see above). It is accordingly preferable to remove the first *et*, leaving a list in asyndeton which, even if not P.'s regular practice, can be paralleled from elsewhere in his text (see 10.7).

Bruttios: Cf. 12.3n.: if the manuscripts are to be trusted, then P. here reverts to the more common spelling.

Book 14

14.1 *Departure of Pyrrhus.* Pyrrhus' departure for Sicily, according to the ancient sources, was prompted by both 'push' and 'pull' factors. Among the former was that his campaign in Italy appeared to have stalled, the Romans showed no willingness to come to terms (Plu., *Pyrrh.* 21.10, Zonar. 8.5.9, cf. Oros. 4.1.23; see 13.2–3n.), and indeed (according to Zonaras: cf. Dio fr. 40.45) were attacking Pyrrhus' allies (but see 13.8n.). Among the latter was that he had been directly appealed to by Sicilian cities to take over their leadership and aid them against Carthage. Plu., *Pyrrh.* 22.1 lists the cities as Agrigentum, Syracuse, and Leontini, though Zonar. 8.5.9 and Oros. 4.1.23 mention Syracuse alone; D.S. 22.8 (cf. 22.6.3) suggests that the initial invitation came from Syracuse, but that once he had achieved visible success there he was approached by Leontini and other cities also. Justin more extravagantly (and implausibly) has the Sicilians offering Pyrrhus 'command over the whole island' (18.2.11: *totius insulae imperium*), although much of the island was not currently theirs to offer.

Both of these considerations appear relevant: while Pyrrhus would obviously not have taken on a campaign that he thought he would lose, it may plausibly be reckoned that his decision was influenced as much by his failure to achieve a rapid victory in Italy as by the opportunities offered in Sicily. With success against Rome denied to him, an entirely new campaign looked all the more attractive, even though this involved abandoning his Italian allies.[106] According to Plu., *Pyrrh.* 22.3 he promised to return and left a garrison in Tarentum (Zonar. 8.5.10 mentions other towns also), but even so the Tarentines were complaining about his leaving; the garrisons appear to have been only of limited effectiveness, since the Romans were certainly claiming victories against Tarentum and others of Pyrrhus' allies almost immediately (13.8 and 14.8nn.), though they did not move directly against Tarentum itself at this point.

D.S. 22.8.1 dates Pyrrhus' departure from Italy two years and four months after his arrival. If we assume (cf. 12.4n.) that he arrived in late March or April 280 (Julian), then this means that he departed in the high summer of 278, late July or August (Julian). Beloch, *GG* IV.2 276, who dated the arrival in Italy to May 280

---

[106] *Contra* Lévêque (1957), 421 (cf. also e.g. Niese (1896), 498–9, Beloch, *GG* IV.1 552, De Sanctis II 386–7 [406–7], Garoufalias (1979), 100–1), who sees in Pyrrhus' plan a brilliant strategic decision to conquer Sicily precisely so as to give him a base from which he could wage war on Rome with new resources. It can hardly be proved that Pyrrhus did not intend this, but, if so, it appears more shortsighted than Lévêque would have it. Victory in war is rarely achieved by opening up a new front against powerful new enemies.

(n. 49 above), correspondingly dates the move to Sicily to the first half of September (Julian).

P. records the bare fact of Pyrrhus' departure, with no indication either of the reasons for it or of what he did once he reached Sicily. It is unlikely that Livy completely excluded Pyrrhus' Sicilian campaign from his narrative, even if he did not recount it in great detail, since its successes and failures were not unrelated to Pyrrhus' return later in the book (cf. 14.3n.), and Pyrrhus, like Hannibal later, was a resonant figure in Roman history even when not strictly speaking on the Roman stage (cf. 14.8n.). P.'s methods do not require so detailed a recounting of causes, and he is uninterested in Pyrrhus as a figure in his own right: he matters only in as much as he is a challenge to Rome (see esp. 12.4n.).

14.2 *Prodigies*. This is one of very few examples of prodigies in P.: it does not seem to have been a topic in which he had much interest (cf. 32.1n.). In this case, the same incident is described in Cic., *Div.* 1.16 (cf. 2.45), who offers more detail: it was a statue of Summanus on the roof of the temple (but see further below on the identity of the statue), was made of clay, and the missing head was found in the Tiber, at the spot which the *haruspices* identified.

P. gives no date, except in as much as his implicit narrative sequence places it between Pyrrhus' departure from Italy in 278 and the consulship of Curius Dentatus in 275. Some scholars (e.g. Torelli, *Fontes* 196–7) suggest 276, on the basis of the reference to 'other prodigies' in P., which they relate to a description in Oros. 4.2.1–2 of a plague in that year (cf. Aug., *Civ.* 3.17: see below).[107] But this, while possible, is hardly a secure inference, since prodigies and related events were typically recorded every year at Rome, and are common in Livy's narrative, certainly from the end of the second pentad onwards.

It is plausibly suggested that this prodigy led to the foundation of the temple of Summanus in the Circus Maximus, since Ov., *Fast.* 6.731–2 refers to that temple being founded at the time of Pyrrhus (so e.g. Torelli, *Fontes* 197, Ziolkowski (1992), 154–5, F. Coarelli in *LTUR* vol. 4, 385).

cum: See 2.2n.

inter alia prodigia: The phrase is found once in Livy (3.10.6), but otherwise only in P., who uses it again at 35.2.

fulmine: 'Thunderbolt'; we nowadays speak of things being 'struck by lightning', but the ancients were not clear that the flash in the sky and the destruction on the ground were simply two manifestations of the same phenomenon. See esp. Sen., *Nat.* 2.12–21, who surveys different views on them, ultimately concluding (2.21) that they are related phenomena, but nevertheless distinct.

---

[107] MacBain (1982), 46–7 assigns it to 278, but this appears entirely arbitrary.

deiectum esse in Capitolio Iovis signum: The natural translation of *in Capitolio Iovis signum* is 'the statue of Jupiter on the Capitol', contradicting Cicero, according to whom the statue was of Summanus. In theory one might translate 'the statue on Jupiter's Capitol', so maintaining consistency, but, while *Capitolium* regularly means the temple of Jupiter Optimus Maximus (*TLL, Onomasticon* II 160.56–161.68), 'Jupiter's Capitol' is an unparalleled phrase (though note Ov., *Ars* 3.115–16). It is possible that P. misread Livy; it is also possible that Livy's version was different from Cicero's. The issue is complicated by the fact that the sky-god Summanus, although a separate deity (e.g. Plin., *Nat.* 2.138), was sometimes syncretized with Jupiter (*CIL* V 3256, 5660 = *ILS* 3057–8; cf. Wissowa (1912), 53, 135), so a third possibility is that P. (or, less probably, Livy), while correctly understanding the reference to be to Summanus, transmitted the information on the assumption that Summanus and Jupiter were different names for the same god.

caput eius... inventum est: This parallels the famous story of the original finding of a head at the time of the Capitol being built (Livy 1.55.5–6 *et al.*), which was interpreted as meaning that the Capitol would be 'head of the world' (*caput rerum*).[108] Here too the finding of the missing head is likely to have given the prodigy a more optimistic cast (*contra* e.g. Garoufalias (1979), 117–18) than one would have expected from the thunderbolt striking a temple, which is generally listed among prodigies expressing divine anger (e.g. Livy 24.10.9, 27.4.11, 27.37.2, 27.37.7, 33.26.8, 37.3.2, 39.22.4). It is presumably relevant that it was the haruspices who found the head (see further below): unlike other forms of 'official' divination prevalent in the Republic, their interpretations were not purely premised on the assumption that prodigies were a manifestation of divine anger, but could include more detailed and indeed optimistic understandings (cf. Bouché-Leclercq (1882), 47–9, Thulin (1906–9, vol. 1, 89–90, vol. 3, 77–81, MacBain (1982), 121–6).

In accord with this, Livy, as he does elsewhere,[109] may well have written the prodigies in such a way as to 'convert' their apparently negative impact into a sign that the final victory over Pyrrhus was at hand; in accordance with this P., too, transmits it precisely because it marks a stage in the Romans' march to success. Certainly the impression left by P. is entirely unlike Orosius, for whom the period between Pyrrhus' departure and his return is one of divinely sent gloom and disaster in the form of a plague (4.2.1–2: see above). If Livy recorded the plague in the same year as the thunderbolt, then he is likely to have used one to negate the effect of the other.

---

[108] It is indeed possible that both stories were developed at the same time: Ogilvie (1965), 211–12 (followed by MacBain (1982), 53–4) argues that the interpretation of the head found on the Capitol as presaging Roman success was a product of the third century BC.

[109] e.g. 30.38.11–12, 31.5.2–7, 36.1.1–3, 42.20.1–4; cf. Levene (1993), 76, 78–9, 86–7, 109.

haruspices: Cf. F 18n. This is not the first time that *haruspices* are recorded as being consulted by the Romans, but is the first that appears even moderately reliable (MacBain (1982), 45). As MacBain (1982), 46–9 argues, it is surely relevant that Rome had defeated the Etruscans and come to terms with them only a couple of years earlier (13.8n.): the importation of Etruscan religious experts was part of the process of consolidation of relations with the local elite population in Etruria. The opening of the official processes of Roman divination to foreign experts is moreover interestingly analogous to the importation of foreign cults to the city, a phenomenon which was likewise increasingly prominent around this time (11.2n.): both are likely to be connected with the Romans' increasing awareness of and openness to the practices of foreign communities as their empire expanded. MacBain (1982), 50–3 suggests that the specific impetus in this case was that the prodigy involved a thunderbolt, a subject on which the haruspices claimed particular expertise (cf. Bouché-Leclercq (1882), 32–57, Thulin (1906–9), 1.13–128, esp. 117).

inventum est: If it was indeed found in the Tiber, as Cicero says, then it is hardly surprising that it needed special expertise to discover, since the Tiber flows no closer than 300 m to the Capitoline temple, with the Forum Holitorium lying between. Even granted the height of the temple, it is a remarkable distance for an object to be displaced by a lightning strike.

14.3 Curius Dentatus' second consulship and defeat of Pyrrhus.

Curius Dentatus cos.: For Dentatus see 11.4n.; this consulship was in 275, and his colleague was L. Cornelius Lentulus Caudinus (*MRR* I 195). *cos.* is the necessary correction in some later MSS for the *is* of the main MSS.

cum dilectum haberet: This story is also found in Val. Max. 6.3.4, who supplies further details (cf. also Varro, *Men.* 195). According to Valerius, Dentatus announced the levy at short notice, and no one responded. So he selected a tribe by lot, then a person by lot from that tribe. When the person in question still failed to respond to the call, he ordered his property to be confiscated and put up for sale; and when the young man appealed to the tribunes, Dentatus not only sold off the property, but had him sold as well.

Dentatus' difficulty with the conscription is attributed by various scholars (e.g. Wuilleumier (1939), 134, Forsythe (2005), 357) to the plague recorded by Orosius in the previous year (14.2n.). While that is not impossible, it should be noted that the plague is specifically said by Orosius (also Aug., *Civ.* 3.17) to have affected women more than men. If true, this would be less likely to hinder military readiness, and in any case those are not the terms in which Valerius presents the problem. Valerius talks of the suddenness with which the levy was announced, and that may well have been the most salient factor if we are to give the story any credence at all. It is, after all, unlikely that even a substantial drop in manpower because of a plague would lead to literally no recruits responding, unless it was associated with a wider insurrection, which no source mentions; yet the story in Valerius is precisely premised on the levy initially receiving no response at all. See also F 4n.

On the face of things, P. softens Dentatus' harshness: there is no indication that the man as well as his property was to be sold, although that is the focus of Varro's version as well as of Valerius'. However, the transmitted text is plainly corrupt (see further below), and it may be that the corrected version should include a reference to the sale of the individual as well. Either way, however, the chief effect, as with the anecdotes associated with Fabricius and Appius Claudius, is to highlight the extent to which the iconic figures at the time of Pyrrhus exemplified morals of a sort that would later be regarded as extreme or quixotic (though see also the discussion below).

primus: The transmitted text *bona primus vendidit* identifies Dentatus as the 'first' to sell off the property of someone who did not respond to a levy. That reading would fit P.'s regular interest in constitutional and other innovations (11.5n.); nevertheless it is unlikely to be correct. Harsh penalties of various sorts against those who evaded a levy were assumed to exist from the earliest days of the Republic: see e.g. Livy 2.28.5–29.4, 2.56.1–5, 7.4.2. It is true that none of these passages in Livy refers specifically to confiscation of goods or indeed to enslavement as a punishment, but they do not exclude them either, and such punishments are mentioned in other sources (e.g. D.H., *AR* 8.81.3, 8.87.5). It seems highly implausible that Livy, or indeed P., could have seen the penalty employed by Dentatus as innovative.

There is an additional problem. Although by modern standards confiscating goods—and still more enslavement—as a penalty for refusing conscription is extremely harsh, it was not regarded as abnormal in the late Republic and Empire (cf. Mommsen, *StrR* 43–5, Brunt (1971), 391–2). Cic., *Caec.* 99 describes this as one of the circumstances under which enslavement was clearly acceptable, and Suet., *Aug.* 24.1 refers to Augustus confiscating the property of and enslaving a man who had mutilated his sons to spare them from conscription (cf. also Val. Max. 6.3.3, Dio 56.23.2–3). It is true that Suetonius mentions this after referring to Augustus' restoration of 'old-fashioned customs'; it is also true that Menenius, *Dig.* 49.16.4.10 describes enslaving one who refused conscription as something that used to happen in the past, rather than a penalty current in his own day. But his explanation is that such a penalty was superfluous in the days of a mainly volunteer army, rather than that it was archaic *per se*; and he does not offer any such qualification to the similarly harsh penalties laid down against people who (as in the anecdote about Augustus) enabled their sons to avoid the draft (*Dig.* 49.16.4.11–12).

So the text clearly needs emending: it also needs emending in such a way as to indicate why P. regarded Dentatus' actions as worth highlighting, rather than being an acceptable legal norm. The key point emerges from the fuller account of Valerius: that it was not so much the penalty as the randomness of its application that was distinctive—the young man punished in this way was merely chosen as a name drawn out of a hat, and was not even present at the time (presumably because, as Valerius indicates, the levy was called 'suddenly'). Moreover, Dentatus' response to his understandable attempt to appeal was simply to increase the penalty. While P. cannot have told this story in detail, something of it needs to survive into his phrasing in order to make sense of its inclusion.

For this reason, Lipsius' emendation of *bona primus* to *bona primum mox eum* is inadequate: it still places the focus only on the penalty, which was not, as noted above, exceptional.[110] Better is Rossbach's tentative proposal to transfer *primus* into the *qui* clause, which goes some way towards marking that the arbitrariness of the choice of victim, as much as the specific punishment he suffers, is central to the anecdote. It nevertheless still looks relatively lame, even if we grant that P.'s language is not always efficiently focused, and it may well be that something further has dropped out of the text—perhaps a reference to the appeal followed by the increase of the penalty in the space occupied by *primus* in the MSS, or perhaps a word such as *subito* in the first clause, as in Valerius. But any proposed emendation must be increasingly speculative the further we remove ourselves from the transmitted text.

citatus non responderat: The terminology is technical (cf. Brunt (1971), 628–9). *citari* refers to the reading out of the names of those selected for the army, *respondere* is when the person whose name was called identifies himself.

iterum: *iterum* might appear otiose, since *reversum* already indicates that Pyrrhus is coming to Italy for the second time; but it is commonplace to use it with verbs of returning *vel sim.*: cf. *TLL* VII.2 556.66–557.33.

in Italiam reversum: According to Plu., *Pyrrh.* 23.5–24.3 (cf. D.H., *AR* 20.8.1, App., *Samn.* 12.1, Zonar. 8.6.5; Just. 23.3.5–10 is slightly different), Pyrrhus' primary reason for returning was his disastrous failure in Sicily, where his rule had alienated many of his erstwhile allies, though he used as an excuse the appeals he had received from Tarentum[111] and the Samnites, who were under pressure from Rome yet again (cf. 14.8n.). Plutarch also describes how his returning forces came

---

[110] Admittedly the fragment of Varro recording the same event (*Men.* 195) likewise appears to focus solely on the penalty; but without further context of how Varro uses it in the satire it is hard to conclude that this is as anomalous as it seems in P.

[111] Beloch, *RG* 466 (followed by e.g. Hof (2002), 65) doubts that the Tarentines made such an appeal, as they are not recorded as fighting the Romans during Pyrrhus' absence; but that depends on Beloch's dubious argument against Fabricius' probable victory over them immediately after Pyrrhus' departure (13.8n.), and, more importantly, our evidence for events in Italy in those years is so scanty that it is rash to reject Plutarch on those grounds alone.

under attack from both the Carthaginians and the Mamertines before arriving in Tarentum. For P., however, who is largely uninterested in Pyrrhus beyond his being an opponent to Rome (12.4n., 14.1n.), the reason for his return is irrelevant.

App., *Samn.* 12.1 says that Pyrrhus returned in the third year after leaving for Sicily; accordingly Beloch, *GG* IV.2 276, who dated his departure to September 278 (Julian), suggests that he returned in 'autumn 276, or at the latest in the following spring'. But this depends not only upon accepting Appian as reliable here, but also in being able to use the date derived from Diodorus for his departure as a reliable baseline (14.1n.); it may well be that such calculations are merely adding inaccuracies to inaccuracies.

vicit: The Romans' third battle against Pyrrhus is the least documented of the three. The fullest account is once again Plutarch's (*Pyrrh.* 25.2–5; cf. D.H., *AR* 20.11–12), according to whom Dentatus held off attacking because of bad omens and the imminent arrival of his colleague; Pyrrhus led a detachment to attack his camp, but they were routed; Dentatus then engaged and defeated Pyrrhus' full army, despite some temporary setbacks caused by Pyrrhus' elephants. Oros. 4.2.3–6 is similar, with less strategic detail, but more information about the tactics used against the elephants: he gives Pyrrhus' losses as 33,000 killed[112] and 1,300 captured out of a total force of 80,000 infantry and 6,000 cavalry, but all of these numbers appear to be exaggerated (Plu., *Pyrrh.* 24.4 gives Pyrrhus' own forces, excluding his Italian allies, as 20,000 infantry and 3,000 cavalry), as does the insistence in D.H., *AR* 20.10.1 that Pyrrhus' army was three times as large as Dentatus'. There are also briefer and less informative accounts in (e.g.) Flor. 1.13.11–13, Zonar. 8.6.6.

That the battle was a victory for the Romans is assumed by almost all sources. It has been doubted (e.g. by Beloch, *GG* IV.1 557, Garoufalias (1979), 120–1, 419–20), on the grounds that Plb. 18.28.11 and Just. 25.5.5[113] imply that Pyrrhus was never defeated by Rome. But both of these are very loose summaries of his career, as can be seen by the fact that Polybius regards not even Heraclea as a victory for him, while Justin did earlier refer to this battle as 'foul' for Pyrrhus (23.3.12: *foedam*) and also says that he was not defeated by the Carthaginians, despite having said exactly the opposite shortly before (25.3.1) (Lévèque (1957), 525–6). To set against that is not only the consensus of the narrative sources, but also the well-documented fact of Dentatus' triumph (below), at which, according to several authors (Sen., *Brev. Vit.* 13.3, Plin., *Nat.* 8.16, Flor. 1.13.28, Eutr. 2.14.5; cf. D.H., *AR* 20.12.3, Zonar. 8.6.6, Polyaen. 6.6.1, Syncellus p. 515 (Dindorf)),[114]

---

[112] In Eutr. 2.14.5 it is 23,000: presumably this derives from the same source as Orosius (or Orosius derives it from Eutropius), but one or other figure has been corrupted either in the source or in the later MS tradition.

[113] Also Just. 38.4.5, but that is in an anti-Roman speech of Mithridates, and its commitment to factual accuracy cannot be assumed.

[114] This too is doubted by Beloch, *GG* IV.1 557 (also *RG* 469; cf. Lévèque (1957), 526–7), because Pliny elsewhere (*Nat.* 7.139) speaks of elephants first being led in triumph during the First Punic War; but that is likely to be Pliny's error (Schilling (2003), 204; cf. 19.1n.).

Pyrrhus' captured elephants were displayed: it seems unlikely that anything short of victory would have brought these into the Romans' hands.

P., like Plutarch, gives the full credit for the victory to Dentatus, which is the view of the main tradition, and likely to be correct. Certainly he alone was credited with the triumph, according to the *Fasti Capitolini*, and likewise most of the later tradition regards him as the commander (Cic., *Mur.* 31, *Cato* 55, Livy 45.38.11, Sen., *Brev. Vit.* 13.3, Plu., *Cat. Ma.* 2.1, Apul., *Apol.* 17, Eutr. 2.14.4–5, Claud., *Bell. Goth.* 124–32, Oros. 4.2.3). A minority tradition (Sen., *Contr.* 7.2.7, Flor. 1.13.9–11, Ampel. 28.3, *Vir. Ill.* 35.6, Serv., *Aen.* 6.839; cf. above, n. 71) has Dentatus and Fabricius as joint commanders, but this derives merely from an understandable failure to appreciate that one of the chief heroes of the Pyrrhic War never actually engaged Pyrrhus in combat: cf. Claud., *Bell. Goth.* 130–1 for a different—and no less unhistorical—way of crediting Fabricius with a victory (13.1n.). Syncellus p. 515 (Dindorf) uniquely—but equally mistakenly[115]—attributes the victory to the other consul of the year, L. Cornelius Lentulus.

Plu., *Pyrrh.* 25.2 locates the battle near the town of Beneventum in Samnium, though he should strictly have called it Maleventum, which was then its name, prior to the founding of the Roman colony in 268 (15.4n.). On the other hand, a Latin historical tradition (Flor. 1.13.11, Oros. 4.2.3) describes the location as the Arusinian plains, in Lucania:[116] the site is not otherwise known, but Lucania is at its closest hardly less than 100 km from Beneventum.

There is no easy way of resolving this: the repeated confusions of these later Latin historians in the Pyrrhic War make Plutarch's testimony intrinsically more credible, as does the fact that Dentatus' victory is described in the *Fasti Capitolini* as being over the Samnites as well as over Pyrrhus (cf. Plu., *Pyrrh.* 25.1). But on the other hand Plutarch himself is not always free from confusion (cf. e.g. 13.2–3n.), and even if some Samnites joined Pyrrhus' army, it seems more likely on the face of things that the battle would take place in Lucania, closer to Pyrrhus' base in southern Italy, than in Samnium. Beloch, *GG* IV.2 476 prefers the Lucanian location, on the grounds that it is more likely that the site would be transferred by the tradition to a well-known site from an obscure one; but that is a weak argument, since it may be that the Arusinian plains were in fact in Samnium, and the error of the Latin tradition was merely to locate this obscure site in Lucania instead (so Forni (1953), 217–21, Lévêque (1957),

---

[115] *Contra* Beloch, *RG* 467, who argues that Lentulus shared the credit for the victory with Dentatus. However, that is based on a mistaken belief that the *Fasti Capitolini* recorded him also as triumphing over Pyrrhus: see Degrassi 546.

[116] Frontin., *Strat.* 4.1.14 appears to combine the two versions, referring to 'the Arusinian plains around the city of Maleventum' (*campis Arusinis circa urbem Malventum*), but that passage is not in all manuscripts, and is probably to be deleted as an interpolation (see Ireland (1990) *ad loc.*).

519–20).¹¹⁷ Conversely De Sanctis II 394 [414] n. 73 argues that the fact that Lentulus, and not Dentatus, is recorded in the *Fasti Capitolini* as triumphing over the Lucanians proves that Dentatus' battle did not take place in Lucania, but there is no reason why Pyrrhus could not fight a battle in Lucania without the Lucanians participating. Still less satisfactory is Wuilleumier (1939), 134–5. He notes that (according to Plu., *Pyrrh.* 25.1) Pyrrhus broke his army in two and sent the other part to Lucania to stop Lentulus joining Dentatus, and concludes that there were two battles, one against Lentulus in Lucania, and one against Dentatus at Beneventum, with each source recording one. But the sources which refer to the battle in Lucania are clear that Dentatus was the commander there; it is moreover hard to see, on this theory, why Lentulus was not credited with a victory over Pyrrhus, if he fought part of his army (Lévêque (1957), 518–19). The arguments on all sides are weakly founded, but the balance of the evidence is weighted slightly towards Plutarch's version, which is *a priori* more likely to be reliable and which there is no compelling argument against.

The date of the battle is also hard to determine, given that we have so little other information about events of that year. Even Beloch (*GG* IV.2 276) does not try to pin it down more closely than 'summer 275'.

Italia expulit: Most sources suggest that Pyrrhus' departure from Italy followed immediately after his defeat; but there are a few indications that it might have been more carefully managed. Polyaen. 6.6.1, Paus. 1.13.1, and Just. 25.3.1–3 tell of an attempt to form an alliance against Rome with Antigonus Gonatas of Macedon, which was refused (though Pausanias and Justin imply that the request, and possibly the refusal as well, took place before the battle). Pyrrhus, however, concealed the refusal from his allies and/or the Romans in order to give himself space to leave safely. Just. 25.3.4 and Zonar. 8.6.7 record that he left behind a garrison in Tarentum, implying that he intended to return. For P., however, as for the bulk of the sources, Pyrrhus himself has little or no agency in his departure: Dentatus compels him to leave.

14.4 *Censorship of Fabricius.* Fabricius' expulsion of Rufinus from the Senate for possessing an excessive amount of silver was another popular anecdote illustrating the old-fashioned simplicity of the heroes of the earlier Republic. It formed an especially poignant contrast with later periods, in which senators were more liable to be expelled for possessing too little wealth than too much of it (see esp. Val. Max. 2.9.4, Plin., *Nat.* 33.153).

Fabricius censor: For Fabricius see 13.2n. His censorship was in 275; his colleague yet again was Q. Aemilius Papus (*MRR* I 196). On his third appearance in P.'s text, he is sufficiently familiar that his *praenomen* is no longer needed.

---

¹¹⁷ Forni (1953), 220 pertinently observes that both Flor. 1.18.7 and Oros. 4.1.8, describing the battle of Heraclea, mistakenly locate Heraclea in Campania rather than Lucania. Beloch, *RG* 466–8 subsequently added further arguments, based on the contamination of names in Frontinus, but that passage is likely to be spurious (n. 116 above).

P. Cornelium Rufinum: *RE* 302. He had been consul in 290 (when his colleague was Curius Dentatus: see 11.4n.) and again in 277; according to several sources (D.H., *AR* 20.13.1, Val. Max. 2.9.4, Gell. 4.8.7, 17.21.39) he had also held a dictatorship, presumably between 292 and 285, when our records from Livy and the *Fasti* are incomplete (*MRR* I 187). Plin., *Nat.* 18.39, 33.142 refers to him (albeit not by name) as a *triumphator*; if this is true, and not simply Pliny's loose phrasing, then the triumph is probably best dated to his first consulship in 290 (so Degrassi 545, *MRR* I 183–4) rather than to his dictatorship (Beloch, *RG* 430).

According to an anecdote relayed by a number of sources (Cic., *De Orat.* 2.268, Quint., *Inst.* 12.1.43, Gell. 4.8.1–6, Dio fr. 36.33, fr. 40.1–2), Fabricius had earlier supported Rufinus for the consulship on the grounds of his military suitability in a time of crisis, despite his being a personal enemy as well as (in Fabricius' view) excessively avaricious. However, little or no historical weight can be placed on this. The most likely mode of the story's preservation, from a period where there was no contemporary historiographical record, was via popular memory of the witty *mot* supposedly uttered by Fabricius to explain his actions (that he preferred to be looted by his fellow citizen than enslaved by his enemy). But such stories centring on *ben trovato* comments are notoriously liable to be developed independently and then 'attached' to the most appropriate person—in this case to Fabricius precisely because of his actions against Rufinus during his censorship. Hence it gives no strong reason to deduce either Fabricius' prior enmity with or his prior support for Rufinus (*contra* e.g. Münzer (1909c), 1933, Beck (2005), 212–13).

consularem: This is the first recorded instance of a consular being expelled from the Senate: the next is in 184 (39.5: see Astin (1988), 28–9). So unusual and dramatic a gesture against luxury strongly suggests that it was intended to serve an exemplary function (Astin (1988), 29–30; cf. below).

movit: Here used in the technical sense of expulsion by the censors: see *TLL* VIII 1539.59–70.

X pondo argenti facti: For *argentum factum* = 'silver plate' see *TLL* II 522.56–64, 522.74–523.6, VI.1 125.71–9; according to other sources (e.g. D.H., *AR* 20.13.1, Val. Max. 2.9.4, Gell. 17.21.39), it was some sort of tableware.

Rufinus' offence is described slightly differently in different places. Most, like P., simply say that he was expelled for possessing ten pounds of silver. Plin., *Nat.* 33.153 says that Fabricius forbade senators to have more than a dish and a salt-cellar made out of silver, which seems to come from conflation of the Rufinus story with a separate anecdote told of Fabricius, that this was the total silver that he himself possessed (Val. Max. 4.4.3). According to Plu., *Sull.* 1.1 and *Schol. ad Juv.* 9.142, the problem was that Rufinus had one extra piece over ten pounds, as if there was a ten-pound limit which he had exceeded, but it seems unlikely that there was such bureaucratic precision to the rule, or that Rufinus would have been caught in so narrow a violation of it if there were. It is far more probable that Rufinus violated a vague sense of propriety than that the precise amount of silver permitted had already been specified: he was condemned under the censors' power to regulate morals under a wide variety of headings, which gave them virtually total discretion to determine the acceptable limits of behaviour (Mommsen, *StR*³ II 375–84, esp. 376; Astin (1988), Baltrusch (1989), 5–30).

Regardless of any personal hostility between Fabricius and Rufinus, for which the evidence is highly doubtful (above), the expulsion was presumably related to anxieties consequent on the accelerating expansion of Roman power and resources around this time. Such concerns (as later Roman history amply illustrates) are typical at times of rapid change brought about by the influx of wealth, which is seen as a threat to traditional values; it is plausible that Fabricius either shared or exploited these anxieties. The concern may often be that material goods subvert existing distinctions of rank by allowing new marks of status to members further down the hierarchy (see esp. Wallace-Hadrill (2008), 315–55); but it may also, as here, reflect a concern about excessive differentiation even within the existing social structure, when luxury goods allow individuals to set themselves apart from their peers. The role of the censors in the Republic was in part to maintain social cohesion by discouraging such breaches of existing norms (Astin (1988), 32–4, Baltrusch (1989), 28), and their powers in this regard, though in theory extending to the whole of Roman society, were in practice overwhelmingly employed, as here, against men of high status (Baltrusch (1989), 22–5).

lustro...condito: See 11.4n.

CCLXXI milia CCXXIIII: This appears to represent a significant fall in citizen numbers—around 6 per cent—from the last recorded figure in 280/79, at the time of the battle of Ausculum (13.4n.). This has variously been attributed to losses in the Pyrrhic War, or to the plague recorded by Oros. 4.2.1–2 for 276 (so e.g. Forsythe (2005), 357); but all such speculation is unwise, since neither this nor the preceding figure can be presumed accurate (11.4n.).

14.5 *Diplomacy with Egypt.* In most other sources the focus of this episode is not on any agreement (which usually goes unmentioned), but rather on the moral conduct of the Roman ambassadors. In D.H., *AR* 20.14.1–2, Val. Max. 4.3.9, and Dio fr. 41 (cf. Zonar. 8.6.11) the ambassadors are given substantial gifts by Ptolemy; they properly turn these over to the Senate on their return to Rome, but the Senate allow them to keep them as a reward for their service. Just. 18.2.8–9 has a different version, in which the ambassadors place the gifts on the king's statue rather than keeping them. Only in Eutr. 2.15 is the interest in the forming of the agreement, as it is in P.

P. is not, of course, averse to narrating morally improving stories, but in this case the story, at least as told in Dionysius *et al.* (and perhaps also in Livy), would need a certain amount of explanatory finessing if it was not to contradict the implications of the one immediately preceding it, in which the mere possession of a small amount of wealth by a senator was the object of censure. Instead it is omitted, and the focus placed on the agreement itself, which marks a further expansion of Roman influence.

No source gives any indication of actual terms of the agreement (cf. below). It is dated by Eutropius to 273, who says that it was initiated by envoys sent by Ptolemy to Rome; Zonaras agrees, and adds, plausibly enough, that he was prompted by the defeat of Pyrrhus, which made him aware of the growth of Roman power. Ptolemy had a good relationship with Pyrrhus, but this appears to have begun to cool around the time of Pyrrhus' campaign in Sicily against Carthage, with whom Egypt likewise was on good terms (Adams (2008)). He may also have been prompted to look for new friends because his territory had recently come under attack from the Seleucids in the so-called 'First Syrian War' (Gruen (1984a), 674). It is less obvious what Rome had to gain, though various possibilities have been canvassed (see below); Gruen (1984a), 673–5 plausibly suggests that they were doing little more than extending a diplomatic courtesy towards a flattering approach from afar.

Ptolemaeo, Aegypti rege: Ptolemy II Philadelphus (308–246 BC), king of Egypt 282–246 BC. For his reign see McKechnie and Guillaume (2008).

societas: Strictly speaking this would imply a formal alliance, which is hardly likely (Gruen (1984a), 62–3); P. may be using the word loosely. Eutropius speaks of *amicitia* (the equivalent of the Greek φιλία: cf. App., *Sic.* 1), which need suggest nothing more than a general statement of mutual good will; it is altogether possible that there were no terms to the agreement beyond that (so Gruen (1984a), 673–5). Some (e.g. Neatby (1950), Heinen (1972b), 633–7), on the basis of a striking coincidence—a series of early Roman coins with controlmarks derived from near-contemporary Alexandrian ones—have argued for some sort of trade accord (cf. Manni (1949a), 83–7). But the Roman coins probably date from a decade or more after the embassies (*RRC* I 39–40), and, even if they were earlier, it is not obvious what sort of accord between such distant powers there would be, nor why it would manifest itself in such a form.

14.6 'Annalistic' notices. Cf. 11.5n.

virgo Vestalis: The Vestal Virgins were thought of by the Romans as central to their religious system. There were six at any time, all chosen from upper-class families before puberty; they lived as a community under the ultimate authority of the *pontifex maximus*, and served for a period of thirty years. Their primary ritual role was to tend the sacred fire in the shrine of Vesta (cf. 41.1n.), but they performed many other functions, and were vowed to virginity for the term of their appointment.

P., like many other authors (cf. Münzer (1937), 56, Beard (1995), 172–3), is interested in Vestals only when they transgress (mostly for unchastity) and are punished (2.13, 8.5, 20.5, 22.11, 28.3, 63.3), though he does not record all of the known instances. This particular example is also recorded by Oros. 4.2.8, and it appears in the chronicles of Syncellus p. 522 (Dindorf) and Jerome p. 130 (Helm), who lists it under the year 276. This is the only explicit indication of date in any source; and Jerome's Roman chronology is clearly awry at this point, since under the following year (275) he records the capture of Tarentum, which certainly took place in 272 (15.1n.). If (as is not implausible) the whole sequence in Jerome has been displaced by three years, then this would place the Vestal's execution in 273, which would fit the implicit sequence in both P. and Orosius also, for all that neither is especially rigorous when it comes to chronology (so *MRR* I 197, Torelli, *Fontes* 215).[118]

Orosius' language is almost identical to P.'s (*Sextilia virgo Vestalis convicta damnataque incesti ad portam Collinam viva defossa est*), suggesting either a common source or (more probably: see Introduction) that he has used P. directly. If the latter, his additional comment that the burial took place at the *porta Collina* may come from a second source, or alternatively is simply his own expansion based on general knowledge, since that was the standard place for it to be carried out (e.g. Plu., *Num.* 10.4; cf. Livy 8.15.8).

Important studies of the Vestals include Münzer (1937), Koch (1958), 1732–53, Beard (1980), (1995), Staples (1998), 129–56, Parker (2004).

damnata incesti: Cf. 8.5n. It was held to be central to Rome's safety and prosperity that Vestal Virgins should continue to perform their functions diligently, and thus their sexual corruption was felt to pollute the entire city (see esp. Fraschetti (1984)); moreover, an unchaste Vestal at Rome was not simply a violator of a religious rule that might bring down the gods' wrath, but was regularly treated as a prodigy, and hence a sign, as well as a cause, of divine hostility endangering the state. How—or indeed whether—those two apparently contradictory interpretations were reconciled is controversial,[119] but, either way, the divine breach needed expiating by her death—since, unlike other religious offences, her loss of chastity was assumed to be both deliberate and irrevocable (Cornell (1981), 35). Unlike the prodigy recorded earlier in the book (14.2n.), P. offers nothing to mitigate the sense of future disaster: he (like Orosius) records it directly prior to Carthage's

---

[118] *Contra* Münzer (1923), followed by Rüpke, *FS* 895, who for no apparent reason dates it to 274; Cornell (1981), 28 and Parker (2004), 593 no less arbitrarily propose 275.

[119] Wissowa (1923–4), focusing on the uniqueness of the punishment in a judicial context, argues that it is only explicable if the unchaste Vestal was seen as a prodigy which needed to be removed if it was to be expiated; conversely Koch (1958), 1747–52, along with Cornell (1981) (cf. also Staples (1998), 133–5), claims that the Vestal's crime was not in any strict sense viewed as a prodigy at all, but only as a danger to the state to be dealt with through specific legal processes. But see Parker (2004), esp. 583–8, who argues persuasively that both accounts operate simultaneously.

(alleged) breach of their treaty (14.7n.), an event which sets Rome on the road to the First Punic War. Livy may well have used it to similar effect, though in his far longer text it is less likely that the juxtaposition was so stark.

Staples (1988), 134–8 (following a suggestion in Cornell (1981), 27–8) argues that executions of Vestals for loss of chastity were associated with political crisis and instability in Rome, and were accordingly used to restore hope in the future of the state, since the person assumed to be responsible for the crisis had been discovered and punished (cf. 63.3n.). However, she does not discuss this instance, where the pattern appears not to hold (at least if it is dated to 273, as argued above); for, while later historians like P. (and Livy) may with hindsight be using it to foreshadow future events, there is no known crisis in 273 with which it can be directly associated.

viva defossa est: Burial alive (along with a small portion of food) was the standard punishment for unchaste Vestals. The intention appears to have been to carry out the execution while avoiding formal bloodguilt (Plu., *Num.* 10.5, *Quaest. Rom.* 286F; cf. Parker (2004), 586, though see Staples (1998), 151–2 for an alternative interpretation); Fraschetti (1984), 121–8 also plausibly argues that burial alive, accompanied as it was by the accoutrements of a funeral, effectively consigned the guilty woman—and hence the guilt of the city as a whole—to the world of the dead.

coloniae deductae sunt: See 1.B.1n. These two foundations are also recorded by Velleius 1.14.7. He dates them to 'the consulship of Fabius Dorso and Claudius Canina', which must refer to 273, though the *Fasti Capitolini* give Fabius' *cognomen* as Licinus. Loreto (2007), 48–9, 79–80 suggests that there was a broad strategic aim in this dual foundation, specifically to provide a coastal presence for Rome at opposite ends of the eastern coastline of Italy under her control; but against that, there is no suggestion anywhere of these colonies having a specifically naval function, and in general see 15.4n. for doubts about analysing colonial foundations in terms of large-scale military strategy.

Posidonia: *BarrAtl* Map 44 H5 = Map 45 B4. It was founded as a Greek city, apparently around 600; it was then captured by the Lucanians in the late fifth century, who used an Oscan version of the name, calling it Paistom. Accordingly, the colony established on the site by Rome went under the name Paestum, which is what it is called in Velleius, and is also the modern name of the site.

Why P. uses the original Greek name is puzzling. Livy in his surviving text invariably refers to it as Paestum, even when referring to the time before the colony was founded (8.17.9, 22.36.9, 26.39.5, 27.10.8). Moreover, while Greeks continued to call it Poseidonia, this is not otherwise found in Latin sources except when attention is drawn to its being the original name of the town (Plin., *Nat.* 3.71, Gell. 14.6.4). Even more noteworthy is that Aristoxenus (fr. 124 (Wehrli) *ap.* Ath. 632A) early on singled out the town as one that had almost entirely lost its Greek identity. Admittedly there is extensive archaeological evidence for Greek culture through the period of Lucanian rule (Pedley (1990), 97–112, Crawford (2006), 60–4), and the Greek language remained in use (Torelli (1988), 95–6, (1999), 77–8)—in particular, the pottery produced then was painted in the Greek manner by people with Greek names and sometimes inscribed in Greek (Pedley (1990), 109–12). Aristoxenus may have been distorting the case for rhetorical ends,[120] or he may be pointing to a sense that the Lucanian conquerors of the town were already beginning to take on cultural elements of Roman identity (so Humm (2018)). Certainly, while the archaeology indicates a measure of continuity between the Greek and Roman periods (Crawford (2006), 64–7; cf. Bradley (2006), 172–3), in contrast to many cities of Magna Graecia there are no Greek inscriptions surviving from the Roman period, though there are a large number in Latin (Mello and Voza (1968–9): see Lomas (1995), esp. 109–11; cf. Crawford (2006), 64).

Given this, the only likely explanation for the appearance of the Greek name here is that Livy, when describing the foundation of the colony, offered a brief historical excursus in which the change of name was noted, and that P., summarizing him, misleadingly records only the original name and not the version actually used for the colony.

Its appearance in Livy's list of colonies at 27.10.7–8 indicates that it was a Latin colony. Its foundation is to be connected with Rome's recent successes in Lucania (13.8n., 14.8n.), which extended her authority over a broader territory than ever before. More specifically, Torelli has proposed that both Paestum and Cosa (see below) were founded as coastal sites with the intention of providing ships for Rome, something directly attested for Paestum (Livy 26.39.5), though the connection with Cosa is much more tenuous, depending on the prosopographical connections of the officials mentioned on one of the rams found at the Aegates Islands (below, 19.9n.; also 15.7n.).[121]

For the history and archaeology of the town see Greco (1988), Stazio and Ceccoli (1988), Pedley (1990), Torelli (1999), 43–88.

Cosa: Modern Ansedonia (*BarrAtl* Map 42 A4). The name appears to derive from Etruscan, and there were Etruscan settlements in the vicinity (Brown (1951), 13–16); but this colony is the first known town on the site. This too is named at

---

[120] See esp. Fraschetti (1981): he focuses in particular on the oddity that Aristoxenus identifies as the agents of 'barbarization' not the Lucanians who had actually captured the town, but the Etruscans and Romans. This makes no literal sense in the fourth century, but (he argues) reflects their cultural image in Greek eyes. Torelli, more controversially, argues that Aristoxenos was writing not in the fourth century BC, but after the foundation of the Roman colony, and so rightly reflected a sense that by then the town's affiliations were no longer Greek (Torelli (1988), 96–8, (1999), 77–8), but see *contra* Humm (2018), 356–8.

[121] Torelli (2019), but see the cautious scepticism of Prag (2020), 99–100, 105. Torelli's theory is possibly supported in a general way by the fact that two of the Aegates Islands rams have Etruscan numerals on them which appear to represent information for the metalworkers casting the rams (Royal (2020b), 225–9, (2020c), 287), pointing to manufacture in Etruria or Latium; but the rams in question are not those naming the individuals whom Torelli identified as being of Cosan origin.

27.10.7–8, which implies that it was a Latin colony (but cf. above). The foundation follows Ti. Coruncanius' successes in Etruria in 280 (13.8n.): the territory belonged to Vulci, which lies just 30 km away (Plin., *Nat.* 3.51), and over which Coruncanius celebrated his triumph. Presumably it was ceded to Rome as part of the settlement following his victory (13.8n.): almost all earlier habitations on the site appear to have been destroyed (Fentress (2000), 12–13), and the archaeological evidence points to the existing inhabitants being forcibly moved to the margins of the territory associated with the colony (Roselaar (2011), 537–9).[122] Now with the departure of Pyrrhus Rome was able to consolidate her control of the territory (Brown (1951), 17): it was Rome's first colony in Etruria, if the hypothesis is accepted that Etrurian Castrum Novum was not founded until 264 (11.5n.).

The site was considerably smaller than that of Paestum (Salmon (1969), 63), but that was probably due to topographical considerations rather than being an indication of the importance attached to it or the number of colonists, since Cosa is on a hilltop, and most of the colonists lived outside the town proper (Salmon (1969), 38). The total territory appears to have comprised around 500 km^2, with something under a third of it suitable for farming: traces of its original centuriation have been argued to be detectable archaeologically (Rathbone (1981), 16–17), but note the scepticism of Pelgrom (2008), 358–67.

For the history and topography see Brown (1951) (cf. Salmon (1969), 29–39); but see also Fentress (2000) and Bispham (2006), 95–105, who challenge various aspects of Brown's interpretative model.

14.7 *Carthaginians in Tarentum*. A Carthaginian intervention in support of Tarentum is mentioned in a number of sources, albeit only briefly. It is narrated by Oros. 4.3.1–2 (cf. 4.5.2) and Zonar. 8.6.12–13, both of whom date it after the death of Pyrrhus. Since the final fall of Tarentum was in 272 (15.1n.), that implies that—if these events are historical (see below)—either Pyrrhus died in the previous year, or the Tarentines' appeal to Carthage in fact predated his death (see 14.8n. for discussion); but, either way, 272 is the most probable date for the events here. According to Zonaras, the Tarentines' appeal was not for support against Rome, but against Pyrrhus' lieutenant Milo, whom he had left behind in the city, and he describes the Carthaginians and the Romans fighting jointly against Milo. However, Orosius has a different version, whereby the Tarentines appealed for help against Rome, and the consequence was that the Romans directly fought (and defeated) the Carthaginians. In addition, these events are cited as one of the causes of (or excuses for) the First Punic War by Livy 21.10.8, Ampel. 46.2, and Dio fr. 43.1 (cf. Zonar. 8.8.3).

---

[122] Despite the expulsion, there is significant evidence of continued interaction between Cosa and Vulci, at least on the level of material culture; but at the same time Vulci appears to have been largely superseded by Cosa, both economically and culturally: see Scott (2019).

There is a double historical controversy here: first, whether the Carthaginians did in fact intervene in Tarentum, and second, whether or not they did, if there was indeed a treaty that would have been violated by such an intervention.

To begin with the second (and more complicated) question: it is clear that the treaty that would allegedly have been violated by Carthage's support for Tarentum is the one recorded by the historian Philinus (*FGrH* 174 F 1; cf. 13.6.n.), which, according to Plb. 3.26, established spheres of hegemony for Carthage and Rome: the Carthaginians were not allowed to operate in Italy, nor the Romans in Sicily. However, Polybius is adamant that the treaty was not historical: he had thoroughly checked the records kept in Rome, and no such treaty was ever struck. Scholarly controversy on this topic has been immense. Various scholars have endorsed the historicity of Philinus' treaty against Polybius (e.g. Thiel (1954), 12–20, Cassola (1962), 87–8, Toynbee (1965), 1.543–55, Mitchell (1971), 634–44, Scullard (1989), 532–6, Scardigli (1991), 129–62, Serrati (2006), 120–9, Steinby (2007), 78–84); others have insisted that Polybius was right to reject it (e.g. Badian (1980), Hoyos (1985), Oakley (1998), 258–61, Eckstein (2010)).

Arguments that have been adduced in favour of Philinus' treaty include the following.

(i) Polybius may not have had as complete an access to records as he thought (Toynbee (1965), 1.552–3, Mitchell (1971), 634, Scullard (1989), 533–4, Serrati (2006), 120–4)—in particular, the Romans might have suppressed the treaty in the light of their subsequent actions in Sicily in violation of it (Thiel (1954), 14, Cassola (1962), 88, Mitchell (1971), 635, Scardigli (1991), 142–3, Serrati (2006), 123). But the problem with the argument is noted by Badian (1980), 169 and Eckstein (2010), 409–15: that precisely because the Romans claimed that the original violation was by Carthage over Tarentum, they would have had no reason to suppress a treaty which supported this case. (This of course assumes that the story about Carthage's intervention in Tarentum predated Polybius: Eckstein sets out the case for that in detail.)

(ii) The treaty of 279/8, as recorded by Plb. 3.25.1–5, refers to 'maintaining *all* the terms of the existing treaties' (cf. 13.6.n.). This must, it is argued, relate to a treaty made more recently than the previous one recorded by Polybius (dating from 348), which spoke of Carthage potentially engaging in activities in Latium, and was effectively obsolete by 278 (Toynbee (1965), 1.543–5, Mitchell (1971), 635–6, Serrati (2006), 128, Steinby (2007), 81). It is true that no more than minor changes would be needed to bring the treaty of 348 up to date, which Polybius might have overlooked or regarded as insignificant (Badian (1980), 167–8, Hoyos (1985), 103–7); nevertheless, Polybius claims that there were *no* changes, and we can only reject Philinus' treaty if we assume some degree of inaccuracy in Polybius' sweeping statement.

(iii) The treaty of 279/8 also gave permission to Rome and Carthage to engage in each other's territory under certain circumstances; it is suggested that this assumes the existence of spheres of influence such as those in Philinus' treaty (Cassola (1962), 88, Toynbee (1965), 1.545–9, Scullard (1989), 535, Serrati (2006), 128). However, that is by no means the most obvious reading of the passage, which may mean nothing more than the territory under the actual control of each power, rather than the broader spheres of influence described by Philinus (cf. Hoyos (1985), 96, Eckstein (2010), 422–3).

(iv) The very passages under discussion here (cf. also Serv. auct, *Aen.* 4.628) attest to a record at Rome of a treaty such as Philinus' which the Carthaginians could be deemed to have violated by their (alleged) support of Tarentum (Thiel (1954), 14–15, Cassola (1962), 87–8, Toynbee (1965), 1.549–50, Mitchell (1971), 636, Scullard (1989), 534–5, Scardigli (1991), 145–8, Serrati (2006), 125–6). However, these passages are likely simply to depend directly or indirectly on Philinus, rather than deriving from independent knowledge of such a treaty at Rome (Hoyos (1985), 98–103).

Arguments against Philinus' treaty include the following.

(v) If Philinus' treaty is presumed to predate the treaty of 279/8, as is generally assumed, then its designation of the whole of Italy as a sphere of Roman hegemony is anachronistic, since Rome was far from in control of much of Italy prior to the Pyrrhic War. Against this, however, it is rightly noted that a state does not need to be in actual control of an area for it to be designated as within its sphere of influence which other powers should stay away from, and Rome was clearly looking to expand her powers throughout the peninsula (Mitchell (1971), 636–43, Serrati (2006), 124, 127–8).

(vi) A stronger argument looks at the same question from Carthage's point of view. There was little incentive for Carthage to assent to such a treaty, which would have appeared to tie her hands in a sphere where she might well find vital interests, in return for a Roman promise not to engage in a place where at that point she had neither shown any signs of or capacity to intervene. Some more specific concerns and conditions might conceivably have been relevant to her, but not a sweeping designation of spheres in this way (Hoyos (1985), 96–7, Eckstein (2010), 421).[123]

(vii) If there was no suppression by the Romans of the treaties in the archives (cf. under (i)), then the very fact that Polybius was able to find such an extensive set of *other* treaties demonstrates that the archives were sufficiently comprehensive and well-ordered to make it unlikely that such a key one would accidentally have gone missing (Eckstein (2010), 417–19).

(viii) From the Carthaginian point of view Philinus' treaty is 'too good to be true' (Hoyos (1985), 107), obviating as it does any need to weigh up finely

---

[123] *Contra* Steinby (2007), 79–81, who relies on some highly speculative leaps of imagination to describe a situation in which in the late fourth century Carthage was far more on the defensive in Sicily and far less involved in Italy, while the Romans already had a large and expanding navy which could threaten them. None of these seems a reasonable interpretation of the evidence (cf. 12.2n.).

balanced considerations of right and wrong in assessing responsibility for the First Punic War—especially as it appears to be the *only* treaty that Philinus included in his history, even though the treaty of 279/8 would surely have been relevant to any consideration of the case (Hoyos (1985), 108). But even if the existence of Philinus' treaty is assumed, the real history would be messy and problematic, with potential violations on both sides (Serrati (2006), 128-9; cf. below).

(ix) Polybius implicitly attests to the fact that the treaty of 279/8 rules out there being a treaty such as Philinus', since it transferred terms over from the earlier treaties (cf. (ii)), and the ones Philinus describes manifestly did not appear in the text Polybius saw (Badian (1980), 165-6, Eckstein (2010), 419-20). It might be objected that the treaty in 279/8 did not spell out in detail the earlier clauses that it was maintaining, but that is highly improbable: cf. Badian (1980), 165, Hoyos (1985), 105-6.

(x) The Romans appear not to have treated the Carthaginian intervention in Tarentum as a *casus belli*, as one might have expected them to, had a treaty forbidding it truly been in existence. However, this assumes that the intervention did indeed occur, and moreover, even if it did, that it took a form that was clearly in violation of the treaty. Both of these propositions (especially the second) are questionable: cf. below.

(xi) Most immediately relevant to us, Eckstein (2010), 424-5 argues that the text of the *Periochae* shows that P. saw the violation by the Carthaginians as being not of the treaty of Philinus, but that of 279/8—the one he has mentioned not long before (13.6). However, this relies on P. showing a type of narrative consistency that cannot reasonably be assumed for him; and in any case, even if (as is not unlikely) he intended the reader to connect his mention of the treaty at 13.6 with his account of the violation at 14.7, it does not mean that he saw the violation as being of the terms of that treaty in particular, since he explicitly said in 13.6 that it was a renewal of earlier treaties.

The strongest point in favour of Philinus' treaty is (ii); but that is overwhelmingly outweighed by the arguments against it, the most solid of which are (vi), (vii), and (ix). It is reasonable to conclude that Polybius was right, and that Philinus' treaty did not exist.

If that is accepted, then it still leaves open the question of the Carthaginian intervention at Tarentum: whether it genuinely occurred (and then was subsequently parlayed by the Romans into a violation of a supposed treaty), or whether it was entirely an invention in the light of the (supposed) treaty (so e.g. Beloch, *GG* IV.2 276-8, Wuilleumier (1939), 138-9, Thiel (1954), 14-15); if it was an invention, that would explain its absence from Philinus (as implied by Plb. 3.26.3: cf. Beloch, *GG* IV.2 277-8).

The weight of the evidence is in the former direction. The version of the story in Zonaras has the Carthaginians arguably intervening on the same side as Rome, rather than against her:[124] Rome was besieging Tarentum, which was however garrisoned by Pyrrhus' lieutenant Milo; the Carthaginians joined in the siege against Milo, though at the request of the besieged Tarentines, who had turned against him, rather than of Rome. That might have been a technical violation of a supposed treaty demarcating Italy as a Roman sphere of influence, and (according to Dio/Zonaras) was regarded by the Romans as such, but how far and what sort of violation depends partly on the ambiguous question of whether the Romans, in besieging a Tarentum unwillingly under the control of Milo, were regarded as attacking the Tarentines, in which case the Carthaginians were on the opposite side to them, or as attacking Milo, in which case the Carthaginians were helping them (which is implied by the description of the fighting in Zonaras). The Romans may well have believed the former, as is indicated by the triumphs celebrated after the capture of Tarentum (cf. 15.1n.), but one can easily see how the opposite view could be taken. It is hard to see why a messy and legally ambiguous story like this should have been invented in order to bolster Rome's case; conversely it is easy to see why, even if it occurred, Philinus might have ignored it as irrelevant to the outbreak of the Punic War.

The version in Orosius, on the other hand, shows the Carthaginians in clear violation not only of the treaty in Philinus, but also of other agreements with Rome, and that is highly likely to be invented: it is hard to see why Carthage would do anything as provocative as fighting Rome in defence of the ally of their recent mutual enemy Pyrrhus. But it is more plausible that it was adapted from the version found in Zonaras, rather than being created independently in defence of Rome and then softened by Dio (or his source) into a version where Rome was less clearly in the right (Hoyos (1984a), 435, Hof (2002), 69–70).

Accordingly, the most likely way that the story developed is that (a) Carthage did indeed briefly intervene in support of the Tarentines against Milo; (b) once Philinus' text began to circulate, with its account of a treaty that the Romans had violated, the incident at Tarentum in 272 was dredged up in order to 'prove' that the Carthaginians had violated the same treaty first; and (c) the story of the incident at Tarentum was 'improved' in order to make it clearer that what the Carthaginians did *was* actually in violation of their treaty obligations.

As for P., his interest is of course above all in the (supposed) violation of the treaty, which proves Carthaginian responsibility for the Punic Wars which will begin a little more than a book later (that he drew this from Livy is indicated by 21.10.5 and 21.10.8, which make the same connection). The explanation for or outcome of Carthage's actions goes unmentioned. It is accordingly unclear whether Livy's version was that of Dio/Zonaras or the one found in Orosius; the

---

[124] Hoyos (1984a), 434–7 misinterprets this key point, and so finds it hard to speculate why the Carthaginian fleet might have come at all: see Hof (2002), 70, suggesting that it was aimed at separating Milo from the Tarentines and ensuring that they could not threaten Carthaginian interests in Sicily.

weight must be slightly in favour of the latter, both because that is the version with a clearer violation of the treaty, and because P. and Orosius work in the same tradition more often than P. and Dio do, but neither argument is close to being conclusive.

quo facto: The phrase is awkward, since it cannot, as one would usually expect, be read as a participial ablative absolute in a temporal sense (cf. K-S 1.774–5): that would be meaningless in this context. Instead we must understand *facto* as a noun rather than a participle, and *quo facto* (= 'through this action') as explaining the manner in which the violation came about (cf. 5.7 *hoc facto*).

14.8 Wars against Italian tribes and death of Pyrrhus.

res praeterea...gestas...continet: See 2.16n.

Lucanos et Bruttios et Samnites: Book 14 covered five full campaigning seasons (277–273), as well as the end of 278 and at least part of 272 (cf. 13.8n. and 14.7n.). In that time the *Fasti Capitolini* record triumphs over the Lucanians every year except 274, over the Bruttians every year except 275 and 274, and over the Samnites every year except 277 and 274. There are occasional notices of these campaigns in other sources. Fabricius' victory in 278 over the Lucanians and Samnites is referred to by Eutr. 2.14, who implicitly dates it after Pyrrhus' departure (13.8n.); Zonar. 8.6.5 briefly alludes to fighting with the Bruttians and in Samnium and Lucania in 276; L. Cornelius Lentulus' victory over the Samnites in 275 is mentioned in Plin., *Nat.* 33.38, while Plin., *Nat.* 34.43 refers to a victory over the Samnites by Sp. Carvilius, *cos.* 272—though it is unclear whether that notice belongs to this consulship (so e.g. Torelli, *Fontes* 224) or his previous consulship in 293, when he likewise triumphed over the Samnites (e.g. MRR I 180). In addition, the *Fasti* include the Samnites when recording Curius Dentatus' victory over Pyrrhus in 275 (14.3n.), which is supported by Plu., *Pyrrh.* 25.1 and Zonar. 8.6.6. In 277 Zonar. 8.6.2 describes a successful campaign by the consul P. Cornelius Rufinus (cf. 14.4n.) against the Lucanians and Bruttians (cf. Frontin., *Strat.* 3.6.4)—but the *Fasti* for that year credit the triumph to his colleague C. Junius Bubulcus Brutus, who in Zonaras is described only as being defeated by the Samnites. Finally, victories over various Italian tribes between 278 and 276 are assumed in the accounts of Pyrrhus' return which have them appealing to him for help (14.3n.).

All and any of these might have appeared in Livy and be referred to here by P.

feliciter: P. regularly uses this as a variation on his favourite *prospere* (3.10n.). Similar phrases are often found in other writers (*TLL* VI.1 451.14–47), including Livy (esp. 9.42.2, 10.44.1, 27.7.4, 31.20.2, 34.10.3, 39.4.2), though he uses it less commonly than P.

Pyrrhi regis mortem: There are various versions of the death of Pyrrhus during an attack on Argos. Plu., *Pyrrh.* 34.1–3 gives the most circumstantial and detailed account: he was fighting in the street against an ordinary soldier, whose mother then threw down a roof-tile on him, badly injuring him: he was then recognized by another soldier, who cut off his head. Paus. 1.13.7–8 (cf. also Polyaen. 8.68) gives less detail, but similarly has a woman throwing a tile on him, with the extra twist that the Argives themselves claimed that the woman was Demeter.[125] An alternative version in Zonar. 8.6.8 has the woman herself falling off the roof onto him, not out of hostility, but simply losing her footing in her eagerness to see him. Str. 8.6.18, while agreeing that he died when a woman threw a tile on his head, is adamant that this happened outside the walls, not inside the city (cf. Just. 25.5.1, Vir. Ill. 35.10).

That Pyrrhus' death came as a result of a tile (or rock) thrown by a woman is almost universal in the tradition (cf. also Quint., Inst. 5.11.10, Syncellus p. 515 (Dindorf)), and is probably true: it seems too individual to be the result of invention. It is not implausible in itself—when an enemy army was inside a city or close to the walls, it was not uncommon for women to participate in the city's defence by hurling down roof-tiles or other missiles—but this is a unique instance of its bringing down the enemy's commander (Schaps (1982), 195–6). But with the other matters, such as whether he was killed inside or outside the town, as well as the circumstantial details offered by Plutarch, there is no obvious way to decide. On balance one would probably prefer Plutarch, as the writer most likely to be employing reliable sources (so e.g. Beloch, GG IV.1 577, Kienast (1963), 161, Garoufalias (1979), 460–1), but to set against this, it seems uncomfortably neat that (as Plutarch would have it) the woman who struck him from above was the mother of the very man Pyrrhus was fighting at that moment.

Livy himself seems in general (if not necessarily in detail) to have followed the tradition represented by Plutarch and Pausanias rather than that of Strabo and Justin, to judge from 29.18.6, which refers to Pyrrhus being killed after entering the city (cf. 13.7n.).

As for the date, Plu., Pyrrh. 30.1 indicates that Pyrrhus' attack on Argos took place not long before he was planning to move to winter quarters, while his death is said in Zonar. 8.6.8 and Oros. 4.3.2 to predate the Carthaginian intervention at Tarentum, and indeed to prompt that intervention (14.7n.). If both of those are true, then it would require that Pyrrhus died in autumn 273 (so e.g. Kienast (1963), 161–2, Hof (2002), 70). But that seems unlikely, since it makes the timing very difficult for the extensive series of campaigns which Pyrrhus engaged in after his return to Greece in late 275.[126] It is far more plausible that the connection

---

[125] Paus. 1.13.9 notes that Hieronymus of Cardia (FGrH 154 F 15) gave a different version—but unfortunately does not provide enough information for us to know which, if any, of the other known versions is Hieronymus'.

[126] Plutarch describes a major campaign in Macedon, in which Pyrrhus drove Antigonus Gonatas off the throne (Pyrrh. 26.2–7), followed by another campaign against Sparta, culminating with his fatal attack on Argos (Pyrrh. 27.8–34.6). In theory the first of these could have been in 274 and the second in 273, with his death at the end of the latter year; but Plutarch's description of the process of

between Pyrrhus' death and the specific events in the siege of Tarentum is a fabrication of the Roman historians, based on imaginative reconstruction about the Carthaginians' plans and motivation rather than evidence, and that Pyrrhus died in autumn 272 (Julian), around the same time as the fall of Tarentum (15.1n.).

This is one of relatively few occasions where Livy seems to have stepped outside his Romanocentric narrative to record events which are only marginally related to Roman history, though any sense of digression was presumably muted, first by the fact that Pyrrhus had been so prominent a figure over the previous two books, and, second, by the reasonable likelihood that Livy too, like Orosius and Zonaras, linked the death of Pyrrhus with the fighting at Tarentum. P. himself does not make that connection, however, but removes Pyrrhus' death from any narrative sequence, even implicit, by rolling it into the general summary of 'other things' at the end of the book.

---

taking control of Macedon, though abbreviated, includes more events than could easily be fitted within a single year: Pyrrhus moved his army to Macedon, captured a large number of cities, then defeated Antigonus in battle and occupied the country. This is doubly true if one accepts (as almost all do: e.g. Beloch, GG IV.1 573–4, Lévèque (1957), 570, Kienast (1963), 157) the evidence of Just. 25.3.7–8, that Antigonus then acquired a mercenary army and sought to regain the throne, only to be defeated once again by Pyrrhus' son Ptolemy; also note that Pyrrhus had enough time, while in charge of Macedon, to have a series of coins minted (Lévèque (1957), 564–5). Only by spreading the Macedonian campaign over two years can one make reasonable sense of the timing (cf. Lévèque (1957), 632–5).

Book 15

15.1 *Capture of Tarentum*. The Romans' final victory over Tarentum is recounted in slightly more detail by Frontin., *Strat.* 3.3.1 and Zonar. 8.6.13 (cf. also Syncellus p. 514 (Dindorf) and Jer., *Chron.* p. 130 (Helm), who however mistakenly dates it to 275: see 14.6n.). According to Zonaras, Milo, who had been left in charge by Pyrrhus, but who was under pressure not only from Rome but also from the Carthaginians and hostile Tarentines (14.7n.), decided to surrender to the Romans on condition of safe conduct for himself and the other Epirotes; once he had left, the Tarentines gave over the town to Papirius. Frontinus is slightly different, slanting the story in terms of treachery by Milo: he is induced by Papirius' promise of safe conduct to have himself sent to the Romans as ambassador, and brings back a sufficiently optimistic report that the Tarentines leave the town unguarded, enabling Papirius to take it.

Zonaras' version appears to make more sense, especially since it takes account of the role of the Carthaginians, which is probably historical (14.7n.), but who are hard to fit into the story as told by Frontinus;[127] it also is not clear that Milo, who was in control of the garrison in the citadel rather than of the entire town (as is clear in Zonaras: cf. also Just. 25.3.4), was actually in a position to betray Tarentum as a whole to the Romans (Hof (2002), 71).[128] Frontinus' version may arise in part from contamination from Hannibal's capture or the Romans' recapture of Tarentum during the Second Punic War (25.2, 27.3), both of which were the result of treachery by people within the town.

The capture is firmly dated to 272 not only by the *Fasti Capitolini*, which record triumphs over the Tarentines, Lucanians, Bruttians, and Samnites by both of the consuls of that year, L. Papirius Cursor and Sp. Carvilius Maximus, but also by Frontinus and Zonaras, who, however, mention Papirius alone in this context. The contradiction is less stark than it appears, since the *Fasti* list the Tarentines first for Papirius but last for Carvilius, implying that, although both received credit for the victory and hence were in some sense involved, Papirius was its prime mover (Degrassi 546). It is, however, not impossible that the surrender by the Tarentines did not follow immediately on Milo's departure, but came after further fighting with Rome, which might help explain why Carvilius, as well as Papirius, was able to be present and receive some credit for the victory (so Hof (2002), 71–2).

---

[127] *Contra* De Sanctis II 397–8 [418–19], but his reconciliation of the two narratives is strained.

[128] Certainly by the time of the Second Punic War the citadel at Tarentum was independently fortified and separated from the main town (Plb. 8.32.3, Livy 25.11.1; cf. Wuilleumier (1939), 239–41). Wuilleumier (1939), 138–9 prefers Frontinus' version of the capture (though arguing that it is more likely that Milo was negotiating in good faith as the Tarentines' agent rather than with the intent to betray them); but this is because he is unreasonably sceptical about Zonaras' account of the role of the Carthaginians (14.7n.).

victis: P. gives no account of the messy complexities with which Tarentum was taken, but presents it as a straightforward victory. This fits the general slant with which he summarizes this book of Livy, listing the Romans' conquests as they serially take full control of the Italian peninsula prior to their first great overseas adventure with the First Punic War: cf. Flor. 1.14–16 for a similar summary of the period between Pyrrhus and the Punic Wars, explicitly speaking of it as the final pacification of Italy (1.14.1, 1.18.1). Oros. 4.4–5 treats it very differently, focusing on a series of prodigies and other disasters. It is possible that both of these readings of history are distillations of aspects of Livy, but filtered in very different ways: cf. esp. Oros. 4.5.10–13, reflecting on his selection of signs of disaster from sources whose own slant was more patriotic.

pax et libertas: The pairing of these words in the context of a postwar settlement is Livian: see 31.31.15 and 33.34.3.

The precise terms offered to the Tarentines, according to Zonaras, were that they should hand over their weapons and ships, destroy their walls, and pay the Romans tribute. Moreover, the Romans in the run-up to the Second Punic War maintained troops (e.g. Plb. 2.24.13, 3.75.4) and a fleet (Livy 23.38.7–12) in Tarentum; and they took hostages from the city at the same time (Livy 25.7.11–13). This is not incompatible with what Rome might have regarded as 'peace and liberty',[129] especially since the Tarentines retained some degree of formal independence: they continued, for example, to mint their own coins and to have the status of an allied power rather than being under the direct control of Rome (Wuilleumier (1939), 139, Brauer (1986), 172–8); according to Str. 6.3.4, it was only after their support of Hannibal during the Second Punic War that they lost their 'liberty'. However, 'liberty' was a flexible term, and from the perspective of the subordinate city the same situation might be presented as domination rather than freedom. Hannibal, according to Plb. 8.25.2 (cf. Livy 25.8.8), promised to 'free' (ἐλευθερώσειν) the Tarentines from Rome, while Livy has Hannibal speaking of the Romans' 'arrogant domination' (25.10.9: *dominationem superbam*), and subsequently imagines the Tarentines, after Hannibal took over, thinking that

---

[129] Gruen (1984a), 132–57 demonstrates that appeals to 'liberty' by powerful states were commonplace in Greece in the century or so after Alexander; they typically took the form of promises to 'liberate' a small state from the hegemony of one power—even while the 'liberator' simultaneously exercised a comparable hegemony (esp. Gruen (1984a), 135–8, 152–3). Gruen also argues ((1984a), 143–5) that this use of 'freedom' was alien to Rome before she adopted it in the context of 'freeing' Greece from Philip V during the Second Macedonian War, but his attempts to explain away apparent counterexamples look like special pleading, and he does not discuss the passage here, which appears to fit very well the Hellenistic use of the term 'as polite terminology to indicate the suzerainty of greater over lesser powers' (Gruen (1984a), 156). Admittedly, however, we have no assurance that the language here derives from contemporary perceptions, as opposed to being applied later in the historical tradition, and Gruen argues rightly that, whatever the meaning applied to the term, there is no evidence that Rome in the third century, unlike contemporary Hellenistic states, used 'liberty' as a slogan of interstate propaganda against powerful rivals.

they had 'recovered their city from the Romans after almost 100 years' (26.39.10: *reciperata urbe ab Romanis post centesimum prope annum*).

However, even if the terms recorded by Zonaras could have been compatible with 'liberty', their historicity is problematic. The Tarentines appear to have had ships shortly after 272: according to Plb. 1.20.14 they provided them to the Romans to assist in their invasion of Sicily at the start of the First Punic War. As for weapons and walls, Tarentum was manifestly in possession of both during the Second Punic War.

There appear to be three possibilities. One widely canvassed one is that Zonaras has confused the terms of the settlement in 272 with those imposed after the Second Punic War (so e.g. Wuilleumier (1939), 139–40, 167, Lomas (1993), 207 n. 13). However, it is far from clear that these terms were imposed then either. The Tarentines lost territory after the Second Punic War, since a substantial amount of Roman *ager publicus* appears in the region, which must have been confiscated from the city (cf. Kahrstedt (1959), 205–6), but the confiscation of territory does not appear on Zonaras' list for 272. Tarentum's walls do not appear to have been destroyed even after Hannibal (*contra* Wuilleumier (1939), 167, Brauer (1986), 203): Str. 6.3.1 refers to the 'ancient wall' as still existing in his own day, though commenting that the city no longer occupied the entire space circumscribed by it; and significant remnants of it still survive (De Juliis (2000), 54–8, though see further below). We admittedly do not have evidence for the Tarentines possessing ships and armies after the Second Punic War, but there is no reason to believe that this is the result of punishment, as opposed to being the consequence of gaps in our evidence for the region: we have no evidence for most southern Italian cities possessing these, including some that certainly were not punished (Lomas (1993), 83–4).

One item from Zonaras appears to be confirmed from other evidence: at some point the Tarentines began to pay tribute to Rome. In a debate between the Romans and the Seleucids in Livy 35.16, the speakers refer to a *stipendium* paid by the Tarentines (35.16.3), which dates from the time 'when they came under our [Roman] power' (35.16.8: *ex quo in nostram venerunt potentiam*). This might be assumed to be the same point at which Strabo says that they 'lost liberty', in other words the Second Punic War. But Livy's own account here is certainly confused (or, less plausibly, he is representing the speakers as being confused), since he associates Tarentum with Naples and Rhegium, which came under Roman control in a different way and with different terms (Briscoe (1981), 169), and, as noted above, Livy could in other contexts speak of Roman control over Tarentum beginning already in 272. It is entirely in accord with his evidence that the payment of *stipendium* began then, in which case it would confirm (part of) Zonaras rather than being evidence against him.[130]

---

[130] When Hannibal in Plb. 8.25.2 negotiates the betrayal of Tarentum, part of what he agrees is that the Tarentines should pay no tribute to Carthage. In context this appears to be making a contrast with

So the suggestion that Zonaras' list arises from confusion with the Second Punic War is weakly founded. A second possibility is that his list is accurate, but that some of the terms initially imposed were softened. In support of this, part of a roughly constructed late Hellenistic wall has been excavated inside the line of the old fortifications: it has been suggested that this might represent a new defensive system that had to be created when the old one was destroyed after 272 (De Juliis (2000), 60). In that case the survival of much of the old wall (above), combined with the limited evidence so far discovered for the new one, might indicate that only part of the old wall was in the end destroyed (ibid.); perhaps the Tarentines were also ultimately allowed to retain some of their ships and weapons. The third possibility is that these items on Zonaras' list are not transferred from the terms imposed at a later period, but are nothing more than imaginative reconstruction somewhere earlier in the tradition. There is no easy way of deciding between these last two options: whether the apparent incompatibility between Zonaras' statement and our other evidence is the result of mere invention in the former or of otherwise unattested events which allow the two to be compatible after all.

The one thing that we can reasonably say is that Tarentine hostility to Rome remained, as is clear from the willingness of at least a substantial portion of the city to go over to Hannibal during the Second Punic War, and also from the Romans' taking hostages from them in a (vain) attempt to ensure their loyalty (cf. Lomas (1993), 60–2, 71–2). This suggests continuing resentment over the terms imposed in 272—however heavy or light they may have been—or at least a feeling that they represented a humiliating subordination of a once-powerful state.

15.2 *Capture and punishment of the renegades at Rhegium.* For the beginning of this story see 12.5n., with the sources given there. P.'s conclusion is simple and straightforward: those who had seized Rhegium after the arrival of Pyrrhus in Italy are now captured and executed. This matches the sequence of events in Polybius (who likewise dates the Roman recapture of Rhegium after the departure of Pyrrhus: 1.6.8, 1.7.9–10), Zonar. 8.6.14, and Oros. 4.3.5 (who attributes it to C. Genucius, *cos.* 270: cf. D.H., *AR* 20.16.1, but see the discussion below). It also matches the *Fasti Capitolini*, which record a triumph over Rhegium for the other consul of 270, Cn. Cornelius Blasio (though referring to the defeated enemy as *Regini*, as if they were the inhabitants of the town, not its occupiers—presumably a shorthand to conceal the messy reality).[131]

---

their treatment under Rome, and *may* indicate that tribute was part of what had been imposed by the Romans. Ciaceri (1932), 184 less plausibly relates the *stipendium* to the confiscation of land for *ager publicus*, and suggests that the Tarentines were compelled to pay rent in order to retain a portion of it.

[131] Hof (2002), 83–7 proposes that Blasio's triumph in 270 was really over the people of Rhegium, not the mutineers, who had been (on her account) taken and executed by Genucius in his earlier consulship in 276. But this gives insufficient weight to the chronology in Polybius and Livy, which is not only incompatible with the mutineers being captured in 276, but also closely fits their being taken

However, App., *Samn.* 9.3 attributes the capture of Rhegium not to the consuls of 270, but to Fabricius (cf. D.S. 22.7.5, who records an attack on Rhegium by the Carthaginians and Romans shortly after the alliance of 279/8: cf. 13.6n.). The significance of the discrepancy emerges from the fuller account of Dionysius, who records not one, but two separate captures of Rhegium by the Romans. First, the Romans responded immediately to the atrocity by sending out an army under Fabricius against the renegade troops (*AR* 20.5.1); the garrison in the city then surrendered and handed over to Fabricius the (now blinded) Decius, but the troops were nevertheless taken to Rome and executed (*AR* 20.5.4–5). However, the new Roman garrison that was left there attempted once again to take over the city and killed or exiled the inhabitants, in response to which the consul Genucius captured the city, took the criminals to Rome and executed them.

This sequence in Dionysius, however, looks like a doublet (Niese (1896), 487, Torelli, *Fontes* 181, Cassola (1962), 176, Bleckmann (1999), 127–8, Hof (2002), 78). At some point in the tradition the recapture of Rhegium was backdated, possibly in an attempt to defend the Romans against the charge of having neglected their renegade troops for an entire decade (La Bua (1971), 67–8): the ascription of the restoration of order to the proverbially moral Fabricius (cf. 13.2n.) gave plausible colour to the invention—and was perhaps also designed to protect him from the charge of having prompted the rebellion in the first place (La Bua (1971), 68–70, and cf. 12.5n.). Either Dionysius or his source combined this with the other version, failing to appreciate that they were different accounts of the same story. The backdated and/or doubled version is perhaps also assumed by a number of other sources also, even those who record only a single execution, since not all put a date or a name to the recapture of Rhegium, and it is possible that some of them either date it early or else are drawing on some longer account such as Dionysius', under which there was another set of troops who took over the city but were executed.

But the account of an early recapture by Fabricius is in any case directly contradicted by Polybius, who explicitly says that the Romans did not address the situation in Rhegium until Pyrrhus departed, as well as Livy 28.28.2, who states that the troops under Decius held the city for ten years. This more historically reliable version presumably likewise stood in the original narrative in Livy's second decade, and P. is reflecting that here.

legio Campana, quae Regium occupaverat: P. reuses the phrasing of 12.5, linking the two halves of the story.

securi percussa est: For the phrase see 2.2n. The fuller sources (Plb. 1.6.12, D.H., *AR* 20.5.5, 20.16.2, Val. Max. 2.7.15f., App., *Samn.* 9.3, Oros. 4.3.5) specify that

in 270. That the Romans defeated Rhegium in an entirely separate war which just happened to fall in the same year to which Polybius and Livy mistakenly attributed the suppression of the Rhegian mutiny is an implausible coincidence.

they were flogged and then beheaded, the traditional mode of execution at Rome (Mommsen, *StrR* 916–18). Dionysius and Orosius refer to a trial before the people; while according to Valerius Maximus the tribune M. Furius Flaccus sought to intervene on their behalf, but the execution continued regardless. Valerius' account is confused, leaving the legal basis for the tribune's intervention unclear, but it may reflect an appeal against summary execution, followed by an affirmation of the penalty in the trial mentioned in Dionysius and Orosius (so e.g. Lintott (1972), 240–1, Humbert (1988), 492–5). It appears in any case that they were subjected to the strict legal procedure for Roman citizens, which would be expected whether the troops were Roman or Campanian (12.5n.): cf. Livy 26.33.10–14 for Campanians as *cives sine suffragio* possessing the same protection against punishment that full citizens did (see Humbert (1978), 280–1).

15.3 *Apolloniate embassy to Rome.* The story is told in more detail in Val. Max. 6.6.5 and Dio fr. 42 (cf. Zonar. 8.7.3). According to Valerius, the Senate not only handed over the offenders to the Apolloniates, but also ensured that the foreign ambassadors were accompanied by a quaestor to protect them from any attacks by the Romans' aggrieved relatives. Dio adds that when they reached Apollonia the Apolloniates released the offender (only one in his version) unharmed. No source gives a date, but Zonaras places it immediately prior to his account of events in 265, suggesting that perhaps in Dio's original narrative it stood in 267 or 266. P., on the other hand, places it earlier in the sequence, between the capture of Rhegium in 270 and the victory over Picenum in 268 (15.2 and 15.4nn.). It is more likely that P. has reworked the chronological sequence than that Dio or Zonaras has; accordingly the later date is preferable (so e.g. De Sanctis II 407 [428], *MRR* I 201–2, Torelli, *Fontes* 253–4, *contra* Beloch, *GG* IV.2 382, who prefers 270). The historicity of the story is doubted by Münzer (1909a), but on very weak grounds: while we naturally cannot rule out that it is invented, nothing in it directly signals that conclusion.

For P. neither the details of the hand-over nor the ultimate outcome is important; he treats it simply as a vignette of Roman virtue, showing how carefully they observed the proprieties due to ambassadors (cf. Livy 38.42.7, Val. Max. 6.6.3, and Dio fr. 61 for a very similar instance). For P. to mention that the offenders in this case were ultimately not harmed would if anything diminish that sense of virtue, since the key moral lesson to be drawn requires that the Romans are handed over even at their peril.

cum: See 2.2n.

Apolloniatium: Apollonia (modern Pojan: *BarrAtl* Map 49 B3), a Greek city in Illyria, founded in the late seventh or early sixth century (Beaumont (1936), 168–9). Various sources (Str. 7.5.8, Paus. 5.22.4, ps.-Scymn. 439–40) refer to it, perhaps correctly, as a joint colony of Corinth and Corcyra (the latter itself a Corinthian colony), though Th. 1.26.2 says that it was founded by the Corinthians alone, and Plu., *Ser. Num. Vin.* 552E–F attributes it to the Corinthian tyrant Periander.

A reference in Appian (*Ill.* 7) suggests that it had been under the rule of Pyrrhus; it appears to have passed into the hands of his son Alexander, who inherited his kingdom (Cabanes (1976), 81–3). But there is no indication of its political status at the time of this embassy, at least if we are right to prefer a later date for it (cf. above). Alexander, according to Just. 26.2.9–3.1, at some point attacked Antigonus Gonatas of Macedon, but instead lost his own kingdom for a time when the Macedonians counterattacked. But even the dates of these wars are unknown, though they probably fell in the 260s (Heinen (1972a), 175–7, Cabanes (1976), 85–8); still less do we know their impact on a city like Apollonia, on the periphery of Alexander's kingdom. For that reason the political context of the embassy is unclear. But it is probably relevant that around now Rome took control of Brundisium, directly across the Adriatic from Apollonia (15.6n.). This, along with the destabilizing effect of the wars on the Greek mainland, might well have prompted the Apolloniates to open up friendly channels with Rome (Cabanes (1976), 85).

For the archaeology of Apollonia, along with a full collection of documents and sources relating to the town, see Dimo *et al.* (2007).

missos...pulsassent: The same vocabulary is used to describe the insult offered to the Roman embassy to Tarentum prior to the Pyrrhic War (12.2n.): the parallel of course points up all the more forcibly the moral difference between Rome and Tarentum.

quidam iuvenes: According to Valerius Maximus, the offenders were two ex-aediles, Q. Fabius and Cn. Apronius; Dio mentions only Fabius, referring to him as a senator.

Assuming that Valerius' identification of their position is correct, their actual youthfulness cannot be determined precisely, since there does not appear to be any set age for holding offices at this period (Mommsen, *StR*^{3} I 563–4). Plb. 6.19.4 indicates that in his day there was a rule that ten years of military service were required before holding any political office, though it is not clear that this was applicable in earlier periods (Mommsen, *StR*^{3} I 505, *contra* Develin (1979a), 58–9). During the Second Punic War the twenty-two-year-old Scipio Africanus was apparently challenged for attempting to gain the aedileship too young (25.1; cf. Livy 25.2.6–7); even though the challenge was unsuccessful, it suggests that by then, at least, there was some sort of expectation that would normally preclude holding the aedileship at this age. Develin's survey of all deducible ages for office-holders in the middle Republic indicates that few people would reach the aedileship before thirty, and fewer still by twenty-five.[132]

---

[132] Develin (1979a), 58–80, though admittedly his data-set is heavily skewed towards the later part of the period, and it is possible that practices were different earlier.

Hence it seems plausible that the ex-aediles here would have been at least in their mid-twenties, and very possibly in their thirties. P.'s treating them not as senators but as anonymous youths, while not perhaps formally misrepresenting the case,[133] gives a misleading impression, and one which makes their acts appear less scandalous, since violence by young men is part of their stereotypical behaviour (cf. Néraudau (1979), 249–56), whereas it is more shocking for senators—even relatively young senators—to engage in it.[134]

15.4 Conquest of Picenum and foundation of colonies.

Picentibus: A people of central Italy east of the Apennines, occupying approximately modern Marche. This is their first appearance in P.; in Livy they had been mentioned only briefly, first in passing at 9.19.4, then as forming an alliance with Rome in 299 (10.10.12; cf. 10.11.7–8). What led to their fighting Rome now is nowhere recorded.[135]

victis: The defeat of Picenum is dated to 268 by the *Fasti Capitolini*, which record triumphs for both consuls, P. Sempronius Sophus and Ap. Claudius Russus; Eutr. 2.16 agrees, adding that the war began the previous year and was completed in 268. The other (brief) narrative sources (Frontin., *Strat.* 1.12.3, Flor. 1.14.2, Oros. 4.4.5–7) mention only Sempronius, presumably because he was involved in the one recorded anecdote about the war—that an earthquake disrupted the battle, but Sempronius turned this to victory either by rallying the troops (Frontinus) or by placating the goddess Tellus with a promise of a temple (Florus).[136] According to Str. 5.4.13 (cf. Plin., *Nat.* 3.70) the Romans expelled part of the population from Picenum to an area near Paestum; here too it is unclear what prompted so drastic an action.[137]

coloniae deductae: See 1.B.1n. The foundations are also mentioned by Vell. 1.14.7 and Eutr. 2.16, who date them to 268.

---

[133] In some contexts the Romans could speak of people even up to the age of forty-five or fifty as *iuvenes*, although there was no consistency, and in practice *iuvenes* were often conceived as being considerably younger. But one should not regard the question simply as a chronological one: the term often had as much to do with the cultural role of the person to whom it was applied as his literal age. See Néraudau (1979), 93–5, 126–43.

[134] Cf. Johner (1996), 71–9 for Livy's often critical treatment of the violence of young men who fail to be restrained by their elders.

[135] De Sanctis II 401–2 [422] suggests that it was the proposal to found the colony of Ariminum (below) that led to the revolt. This is chronologically difficult; more importantly, it is hard to see why the Picentes should have been provoked by a foundation which did not in any way encroach on their own territory, when they had accepted colonies being founded much closer to them at Hadria, Sena, and (probably) Castrum Novum two decades earlier (11.5n.).

[136] This is presumably the temple in the former house of Sp. Cassius (D.H., *AR* 8.79.3, Val. Max. 6.3.1): see Ziolkowski (1992), 155–62, F. Coarelli in *LTUR* vol. 5, 24–5.

[137] For the historicity of this episode, which had been challenged by e.g. Beloch, *RG* 475, see Silva Reneses (2015), proposing that it was aimed at controlling the populations on both coasts by placing the displaced Picentines between two potentially hostile groups.

Ariminum: Modern Rimini (*BarrAtl* Map 40 D4). Although P. identifies it as being in Picenum, thus connecting it directly with the defeat of the Picentes mentioned immediately before, this is an error. Cato, *Orig.* (*FRHist* 5 F 46, *ap.* Varro, *Rust.* 1.2.7) explicitly describes that region as Gallic as opposed to being part of Picenum, and Livy 28.38.13 (cf. 24.44.3, 30.1.9) says that 'Ariminum' was the name used for Gaul at the time of the Second Punic War. Hence the close connection that P. implicitly makes with the conquest of Picenum is probably unhistorical, and is more likely to be his own mistake than Livy's. His error may in part be one of anachronism, since the region was subsequently assimilated to Picenum in popular usage: see esp. Colum. 3.3.2, quoting and updating that same passage of Cato in Varro; also Plb. 2.21.7, where the entire region is referred to as Picenum (cf. Walbank (1957), 192).[138]

Although it was thought of as being in Gallic territory, according to Plb. 2.19.11 the Gauls had been expelled from the region following their defeat in 283 (see 12.1n.), and Str. 5.1.11 reports that Ariminum itself was an Umbrian town, and indeed part of the population remained Umbrian even after the colony was founded. Strabo's ethnography should not necessarily be taken at face value, but it is likely to be generated by an awareness of some sort of Umbrian ethnic tradition in his own day,[139] even though it is hard to identify specifically 'Umbrian' elements in the archaeology or epigraphy of the region.[140] There is certainly archaeological evidence of cultural continuity, notably a sanctuary just outside the city which remained in use from well before to well after the foundation (Zuffa (1970), 312–13); rather than being the result of something specific to this colony,[141] it appears to be part of a wider pattern in many Roman colonies to integrate the Roman arrivals with elements of the existing population.[142] But at the same time elements of its pottery production are unusually close stylistically to contemporary Roman pottery (Morel (1988), 52–3), which indicates that members of the colony were advertising their affinities to Rome especially strongly, perhaps wanting to do so precisely because of the prominent presence of non-Roman inhabitants, as well as the physical remoteness from Rome. Also unusual (it is only otherwise found at Beneventum: see below), and also perhaps the result of the

---

[138] To complicate matters further, under Augustus' administrative reforms—admittedly after the probable date when Livy wrote Book 15—Ariminum was not even close to Picenum: it formed part of the administrative region of Aemilia (Plin., *Nat.* 3.115).

[139] See esp. the analysis of Strabo's ethnography in this section of his work by Raviola (2006).

[140] This is hardly surprising, given that 'Umbrians' are notoriously hard to identify archaeologically at all: see the sceptical survey by Stoddart and Redhouse (2014).

[141] As argued by e.g. Brunt (1971), 540, who suggests that the Umbrian population was allowed to remain as a defence against the Gauls.

[142] So Bradley (2006), 172–6; cf. also Terrenato (2019), 221–4. Harris (1971), 3 is sceptical about Umbrians in Ariminum and other coastal cities, treating Strabo's statement as arising 'because of some real or supposed early stage of their history'. But Strabo refers to the Umbrian presence as a current reality, and it is altogether plausible that, given the generally diffuse nature of 'Umbrian' identity (or self-identification; see above), Umbrians and Gauls were not neatly separated by regions (cf. Bradley (2000), 20–2, 27–8; see 15.6n.).

same pressures, is that the chief magistrates were originally called 'consuls' (*ILLRP* 77; cf. Bispham (2006), 88).

It appears that some form of less formal Roman settlement may have been begun on the site after the conquest of the region in 283 and prior to the formal foundation of the colony (Ortalli (2006)). There is likely to have been a desire for a Roman presence to protect Italy against future incursions from Cisalpine Gaul, since it is located precisely at the point where the plain of the Po Valley narrows to a small strip of coast between the Apennines and the sea (Brizzi (1995); cf. Salmon (1969), 63–4, 88–9). As for the foundation of the colony itself, it was perhaps impelled by the Picentes' revolt, and the consequent sense that more strength was needed in that part of Italy: the powerful fortifications dating from an early phase of the foundation (on which see Curina (2015)) suggest that it was seen as a Roman outpost in hostile territory. Similarly Purcell (1990), 10–12, persuasively arguing that the simultaneous foundations of Ariminum and Beneventum at opposite ends of the territory under Roman control are part of a series of policies that suggest that the Romans are acting on a wider strategic and geographic awareness than they had previously. But there may have been other considerations at work as well: see below.

That Ariminum was a Latin colony is implied by its appearance in Livy's list at 27.10.7–8. Cic., *Caec.* 102 mentions it as one of a group of twelve colonies with a specific set of rights; he does not name the other eleven, but it is widely argued that they were the eleven Latin colonies founded after Ariminum—that henceforward new Latin colonies were given a new set of rights (*contra* e.g. Salmon (1936), 58–61, Antonelli (2006)). Cicero, however, does not say what those rights were, and it is even controversial whether they represented a diminution of the rights enjoyed by colonies founded earlier (so e.g. Mommsen, StR^3 III 623–5), or an enhancement of those rights (e.g. Bernardi (1948), Salmon (1969), 92–4).

For a general study of the town's history and archaeology, see Mansuelli (1941); also the essays in Calbi and Susini (1995) and Lenzi (2006).

Beneventum: Modern Benevento (*BarrAtl* Map 44 G3). The site had been settled from prehistoric times; in Greek and Roman legend the city was founded by Diomedes. It enters history as a Samnite town in the territory of the Hirpini under the name Maleventum: Livy 9.25.14 mentions it as a place of refuge for the Samnites after they were defeated by the Romans in 314, though the historicity of this episode is doubtful (Oakley (2005a), 299–301). A further battle against the Samnites was apparently fought there in 297 (Livy 10.15.1), and it may have been the site of the Romans' final victory over Pyrrhus in 275 (14.3n.).

The Romans appear to have finally defeated the Samnites in 272 (14.8n.), since they do not appear subsequently in the triumphal record. Nor is any fighting against them mentioned in historical sources, apart from a reference to a brief rebellion in 269 in D.H., *AR* 20.17) and Zonar. 8.7.1: Dionysius suggests a full-scale war, but Zonaras treats it as a mere episode of brigandage, albeit one that required the consuls' army to put it down. Zonaras is more likely to be correct in this regard, since no triumph was awarded for the victory;[143] it is possible that the event's relative insignificance explains its absence from P. also, though the brevity of his summary of Book 15 means that we certainly cannot be sure that he does not omit events that Livy treated as significant. This final military suppression of the Samnites is presumably connected with Rome's decision now to consolidate control over the territory with the foundation of the colony—apparently a Latin colony, since it appears on Livy's list at 27.10.8.

The choice of location may have been strategic, in as much as the town later commanded many key routes through south-central Italy; in addition the intention may have been to separate the Hirpini from other Samnites (so Salmon (1989), 227). But Salmon's general tendency to ascribe 'strategic' criteria to the location of Roman colonies[144] has been subjected to an acute and detailed critique by Pelgrom and Stek (2014), 18–22, who note that the criteria he used to identify 'strategic' locations were in some cases arbitrary and even circular. This is particularly obvious in the case of Beneventum: the roads that made it so central at a later period (the Via Appia was eventually extended to connect it to Rome via Capua, and in the other direction to Tarentum and Brundisium), were not yet built when the colony was founded, and their full extent can hardly even have been planned then.[145] And the pre-existence of a Samnite town, as noted above, suggests that there may have been wider cultural considerations in placing a colony there, especially since there is no evidence that the existing inhabitants were expelled. As with Ariminum and other colonies (cf. above), it appears likely that at least some of them were incorporated into the newly founded colony, whose layout appears to have been designed to include parts of the existing city,[146] whose funerary practices continue without break, and where in later periods Oscan names appear among the leading citizens (Scopacasa (2015), 248–9);[147] but to set against that, this, along with Ariminum, is the only Latin colony whose chief magistrates were 'consuls' (*ILLRP* 169, 553; cf. Bispham (2006), 88), emphasizing its connections with Rome. That complex mix of local practices and emphatically Roman affinities may itself have been part of the point of the foundation, integrating Rome into the local community.

---

[143] *Contra* Salmon (1967), 288, who claims that no triumph was awarded because the consuls were not adding to Roman power; but triumphs were regularly awarded even when that was the case: for example Claudius Nero and Livius Salinator against Hasdrubal during the Second Punic War.

[144] Even more emphatic and systematic than Salmon in this interpretation of colonies is Loreto (2007), 75–97.

[145] See esp. Bradley (2014), 66–9 on the danger of arguing from hindsight when claiming that colonial foundations and the Roman road network were linked together in a single grand strategy.

[146] See Giampaola (2000), 39.

[147] Note, however, the cautious reservations of Roselaar (2011), 531–2 about the danger of using onomastic evidence as demonstration of the incorporation of the original population, since they may either still be the result of immigration from other parts of Italy, or may derive from a time when those names had ceased to reflect local origins.

Although the name probably was etymologically unconnected with the Latin *malus* (Battisti (1959), 33–4), the Romans saw an ill omen in it, so changed it to Beneventum on the foundation of the colony (Plin., *Nat.* 3.105, Fest. 458L, Paul., *Fest.* 31L; cf. Oakley (2005a), 328–9). For the history of the town see Torelli (2002).

The *editio princeps* balances the phrase describing Ariminum by adding *in Samnio* after Beneventum. This is accepted by most modern editors, but unnecessarily: it is entirely in accord with P.'s style to have one town qualified by a location, the other not (cf. e.g. 19.5). Placing the town with a locator first and the one with a bare name second admittedly reads awkwardly, but not so much so as to appear anomalous: it is explained by the connection with the previous sentence, which implicitly (though misleadingly) explains how the colony came to be founded at this point (cf. above).

15.5 *Beginning of silver coinage at Rome.* This is mentioned also in Plin., *Nat.* 33.44, Zonar. 8.7.2, and the chronicles of Syncellus p. 523 (Dindorf) and Jerome p. 130 (Helm). Pliny explicitly dates it to 269; Jerome lists it under 271, but his Roman chronology for this period cannot be relied on (14.6n.). P. dates it by *tunc*, which is often (though not always) a marker that he is following Livy's chronology (11.5n.), and if so, he placed it around the same time or shortly after the foundation of the colonies in the previous note, namely 268.

How far, if at all, this approximate date is reliable is controversial. Pliny speaks as if the silver coinage that was introduced now was the denarius; but the numismatic evidence shows that the denarius was not minted until c.211 BC, during the Second Punic War (*RRC* I 28–35). A slightly better case for his timing can be made if we consider the minting of silver at Rome. The first distinctively Roman silver coins are the didrachms marked ROMANO, probably to be dated to the late fourth century BC;[148] but these do not appear to have been minted at Rome, nor to have been in general circulation (Crawford (1985), 28–30). Later issues of silver coins seem to begin with the Pyrrhic War; it is not clear which of these is struck at Rome, but it is not out of the question that c.269 did indeed represent the moment when this first happened.[149] Alternatively, Pliny may have garbled something (much else in his account of early Roman coinage is garbled), and the actual significance of c.269 may have been quite different.[150]

---

[148] *Contra* Holloway (1992), who dates the earliest didrachm series to the time of the First Punic War.

[149] Crawford (1985), 31–2 is sceptical, but formally agnostic about the possibility; *contra* Burnett (1978), 125–31, who would prefer to see all the coins, including those earlier than 269, minted at Rome.

[150] Alternative views for the significance of 269: that the denarius was introduced then, not as a coin, but as an accounting unit (Lo Cascio (1980–81), 337–41, *contra* Burnett (1989), 35), or that it was the first time coined money was distributed to the people (Burnett (1978), 124–5, citing D.H., *AR* 20.17.2). Any of these are possible, but they necessarily rest on a flimsy evidential basis.

The impulse for Romans' minting of coins is argued by Burnett (1989), 48–57 to have been cultural rather than economic: the issues are on a small scale before the First Punic War, and not substantial even during the war, certainly too small for systematic military purposes, or indeed for any other large-scale use. He suggests that it is primarily begun from a desire to imitate their Greek neighbours, which also explains why the motifs on the coins largely derive from Greek models. Hence there is no particular reason to tie the introduction of coinage to any particular crisis or event.

argento uti coepit: Taken literally this is clearly false: the Romans had been 'using' silver—and even silver coinage—for a long time. Zonaras presents it the same way, as the 'use' of coins; but in other sources it is slightly different. Pliny makes two separate statements on the subject: first he says (*Nat.* 34.42) that the Romans did not begin to 'use' (*usus est*) silver coins before the time of Pyrrhus; then later in his discussion (*Nat.* 34.44) he says that silver was first 'struck' (*signatum*) in 269. It is possible that he means these to represent the same thing, telescoping the decade between the arrival of Pyrrhus and 269 into a single instant; alternatively, he may intend this to represent two stages in the introduction of coinage, one moment when the Romans began to use coins, the other when they struck them for themselves. Syncellus and Jerome talk in terms of coins being struck for the first time 'in Rome', allowing the possibility that they had previously been struck by the Romans but outside the city, which may be closer to the truth.

P.—perhaps because it stood that way in Livy—chooses the least accurate version, but the one which makes this the clearest watershed in the development of Rome, albeit one that would have negative connotations to many Roman moralists (cf. 14.4n.). Even if this is indeed derived from Livy, P.'s selection of it and his handling it in this way is typical of his interest in key innovations as Rome expands and develops her empire (11.5n.).

15.6 *Victory over the Umbri and Sallentini.* Victories over the Sallentini (and the nearby Messapi)[151] are attributed in the *Fasti Capitolini* to both of the consuls of 267, M. Atilius Regulus and L. Julius Libo, and to both of the consuls of 266, N. Fabius Pictor and D. Junius Pera. The *Fasti* also record triumphs to both of the consuls of 266 over the people of Sassina (= Sarsina), a town in northern Umbria.[152] Since P. focuses in both cases on the final surrender rather than on the battles, presumably it is the campaigns of 266 that he primarily has in mind.

---

[151] This notice is complicated by the fact that the Sallentini and the Messapi were ethnically related, and indeed the terms were applied to them differently by different authors: see Lamboley (1996), 304–12.

[152] Beloch, *RG* 89 (cf. De Sanctis II 403 [424] n. 101) rejects the historicity of the double triumph by each of the consuls, largely on logistical grounds: he believes that each consul triumphed over only one of the people. But the triumphs are recorded as taking place on different dates, and Beloch does not explain how these could have entered the record if the triumphs were mere doublets; his logistical objections are in any case questionable (see Rosenstein (2004), 205–6).

Elsewhere in the historical tradition, however, the focus is on 267 rather than on 266. This is partly because Regulus was in command, someone who would later be celebrated in other contexts (so Cic., *Fin.* 2.65, *Vir. Ill.* 40.1; cf. 17.6n., 18.1–2n., 18.5n.), partly because in the course of the campaign the strategic port of Brundisium was captured (Flor. 1.15, Eutr. 2.17, Zonar. 8.7.3). It is unsurprising that P. shows no interest in the former, since he is often ruthlessly selective when it comes to naming specific individuals, even those who are elsewhere important to him (a quality he shares with Livy himself). It is more surprising that he would not mention Brundisium, since he does appear to be interested in the expansion of Roman power at this point. It is perhaps that his focus on legal and constitutional developments, which is greater than that of most other of the historical summarizers, leads him to regard the capture of the town as less significant than the eventual foundation of the colony, which he duly records at 19.5, but which Florus, Eutropius, and Zonaras all ignore. It is, however, also true that, for whatever reason, he is unusually terse throughout the summary of Book 15, and it may be idle to seek to interpret specific omissions.

Umbri: Umbria roughly covered a large portion of central Italy on either side of the Apennines. It was not in any sense a political unity, though the people may sometimes have come together collectively in times of emergency (cf. Bradley (2000), 118–28), and even to think of it as a cultural unity is not unproblematic: archaeology shows a great deal of cultural diversity across the region, and parts have more affinities with neighbouring cultures outside Umbria than with each other within it (Bradley (2000), 83–100; also Stoddart and Redhouse (2014)).

This lack of unity is at least partly implicit in Livy's own narrative. The Umbrians appeared there at 9.36.7–8, where the town of Camerinum assisted the Romans against the Etruscans in 310/9; although within a short time some Umbrians are up in arms against Rome. (9.37.1). The Umbrians then are said to fight against Rome *en masse* in 308, only to be easily defeated (9.41.8–20). Umbrians are said to have joined the anti-Roman coalition in 296–295, though in that campaign Livy veers between suggesting that only some Umbrians were part of the coalition (10.18.2) and implying that the whole of Umbria was involved (10.27.3; cf. 10.21.2, 10.21.12); elsewhere he has the Romans campaigning against small groups of Umbrians or particular Umbrian towns (10.1.4–6, 10.9.7–9, 10.10.1–5). But most of Umbria is not recorded as being conquered militarily: Roman control probably came as much through diplomatic alliances as military victories (Bradley (2000), 107–28), and accordingly was achieved piecemeal over a number of decades. The notice in the *Fasti* that the consuls' campaign in 266 was against the Sassinates alone fits that picture.

P., by contrast, has nowhere mentioned the taking over of individual parts of Umbria, and his two previous references to the Umbrians (9.5, 10.7) have treated them as a single unit. Now he closes that sequence by suggesting the submission of Umbria as a whole, once again showing the Romans completing their conquest over Italy (cf. 15.1n.). This is misleading; however, what does appear to be true is that Sassina, the northenmost Umbrian town, represented the final part of Umbria to hold out against Rome, and its defeat in 266 accordingly represented the moment where Umbria as a whole could finally be said to be under Roman control. In that respect, P.'s expansion of the victory from the Sassinates to the Umbrians in general does not excessively misrepresent the case.

Sallentini: The name is restored by Frobenius on the basis of the *Fasti Capitolini*; they were a people occupying the 'heel' of Italy. They were not previously mentioned by P.; in Livy they first appear at 9.42.4–5, which notes a supposed campaign against them in 307 by the consul L. Volumnius; but the historicity of this has been questioned, since it is not clear why Volumnius would have been campaigning so far afield (Oakley (2005a), 550–1). They reappear in 302/1, when the territory is invaded by the Spartan prince Cleonymus and the Romans have to drive him from it (Livy 10.2.1–3); but that notice too is problematic (Oakley (2005b), 48–51, 55–7). The campaigns of 267–266 represent their final submission to Roman power; according to Zonar. 8.7.3, the Romans deliberately provoked the war out of a desire to capture Brundisium, though they gave as their excuse that the Sallentini had supported Pyrrhus.

15.7 *Enlargement of the quaestorship*. This passage raises difficult historical and textual issues, especially since P. does not give a date, and the number of quaestors has dropped from the MS tradition. The other sources for the quaestorship's being enlarged at this period are Tac., *Ann.* 11.22.5 and Lyd., *Mag.* 1.27. Tacitus says (without offering a date) that the number of quaestors was doubled (sc. from four to eight), and that the reason was the funds accruing from tribute from Italy and the provinces. Lydus dates it specifically to 267, and says (in the transmitted text) that twelve new quaestors were added, which he refers to as *quaestores classici*: he explains them as being naval commanders (ναύαρχαι), and the reason for their introduction was so that the Romans could make war on the allies of Pyrrhus. Lydus' number is clearly impossible, and the relationship to the Pyrrhic War appears to be problematic, in as much as by 267 few allies of Pyrrhus remained, and no source suggests that the Romans used a fleet against any of them; nor is there any other source that has quaestors commanding a fleet at any period.

The commonest reconstruction (esp. Mommsen, *StR*³ II 570–3) put the information about the number of these new quaestors from Tacitus together with the information about their date, title, and purpose derived from Lydus (with the support of P.); the conclusion was that after 267 four *quaestores classici* were chosen. Admittedly the name is not attested outside Lydus, but the fact that Tacitus connects them with tribute from Italy and the provinces encouraged people to identify two of them with the quaestors otherwise attested as having functions outside Rome: the *quaestor Ostiensis* (Cic., *Mur.* 18, *Sest.* 39, Suet., *Claud.* 24.2), and the *quaestor Gallicus* (Suet., *Claud.* 24.2, Plu., *Sert.* 4.1).¹⁵³ As for their naval role, Thiel (1954), 31–4 suggested that their appointment related to the organization of a new auxiliary navy, with ships supplied by naval allies, and that Lydus is misleading in his description of them as 'naval commanders'. This is sometimes suggested to relate to the coming war with Carthage, for which Rome, on this view, is already thought to be preparing (so e.g. Meiggs (1973), 24–5; Hoyos (1998), 19 is rightly sceptical).

In accordance with this, the missing figure in P. is usually supplied as VIII.

However, Mattingly (1969), 509–11 (cf. also Harris (1976)) argued that this construction is extremely problematic. As he rightly notes, Tacitus does not say outright (though he admittedly implies) that the doubling of the quaestorship took place all at once, nor that it happened as early as 267: his reference to 'provinces' in fact implies a date after the First Punic War. Hence it is likely that only two were added in 267, and the other two later, perhaps in 227, when the number of praetors was increased (see 20.7n.).¹⁵⁴

As for Lydus, Mattingly proposed a slight textual emendation, changing δυοικαίδεκα to δυοί καὶ δέκα, with the first number referring to the *quaestores classici*, whom Lydus has mentioned just before, and that this was in fact an error by Lydus for the *duumviri navales* (cf. 12.2n.), who (Mattingly suggests) were appointed in 267 for the campaign against the Sallentini. Lydus' second number then describes the (new) total number of quaestors dealing with financial matters, which he describes in the following clause, though it should in fact have been six, not ten. However, this argument is weak. First, there is no evidence for *duumviri navales* being appointed this year against the Sallentini, nor for a fleet being used in that or any other campaign then. Second, even if there were, it would be exceedingly strange for Lydus to have inserted a reference to them in the middle of his discussion of the quaestorship, especially since he is describing innovations, and the appointment of *duumviri navales* would not have been innovative in 267. Moreover, while Lydus is a late author who is hardly free from error, it is not clear that it is methodologically justifiable to correct an error in him by emending the text in such a way as to produce two further errors. A better solution, therefore, is proposed by Smith (1978) (*contra* Harris (1979b)): reading the number in Lydus simply as δυοί, with the 'ten' coming from dittography of iota in an MS where the number was abbreviated as figures. This number, as in the traditional view, refers to the introduction of *quaestores classici*; the following clause is parenthetical, describing the normal function of the quaestors in general.

---

¹⁵³ Mommsen, *StR*³ II 571 suggested that a third was based in Cales in Campania; but this is based on an erroneous emendation of Tacitus, *Ann.* 4.27.2: see Koestermann (1965), 102–3, Harris (1976), 99.

¹⁵⁴ Any expansion of the quaestorship is likely to have been in even increments, in accordance with Rome's usual practice (Harris (1976), 94–5; *contra* Loreto (1993), 496–7).

This still leaves their role in the fleet open. Here Thiel's suggestion seems plausible (above): the *classici*, at least in the first instance, organized the procurement of ships from Rome's allies—it is reasonably clear from the opening phases of the First Punic War that Rome was in the process of setting up a new naval system, centring on ships provided by allies.[155] This would still have Lydus wrongly treating them as actual commanders, but that is a minor error that could easily have come from overinterpreting the word *classici*. This function of the quaestors would not have outlasted the First Punic War, by the end of which Rome's naval power primarily rested on her own resources, not her allies, and it is likely that even prior to that point they took on other roles also, since the procurement of a fleet, while a significant task, could not have been enough to have occupied two officials permanently. But Thiel's basic picture has recently received some support from the Latin inscriptions on the naval rams recovered from the site of the battle of the Aegates Islands at the end of that war (see 19.9n.): these record the procurement of each ram under the authority of one or two named quaestors, thus showing that, at the very least, the quaestors in the mid-third century did indeed perform something of the functions which Thiel had long ago hypothesized for Lydus' *classici*.[156] If so, it is noteworthy that officials with this function were appointed as early as 267: it suggests that, contrary to the impression given by Polybius (e.g. 1.20.8–9), the Romans, even before the First Punic War brought them into naval conflict with the Carthaginians, saw a need to project their power on the sea as well as on land, to the point that they designated specific officials to ensure it.[157]

Of course, it remains possible that Lydus, aside from providing a date for some sort of innovation in the quaestorship, is garbled through and through, and that the quaestors' epigraphically attested role in the procurement of naval rams is a

---

[155] *Contra* Harris (2017), 40, but his grounds are largely *a priori*: that it is unlikely that the Romans would have put such trust in unreliable foreign allies. But this is partly circular (it assumes that the Romans in the 270s and 260s placed great stress on the importance of naval power, such that they would need a reliable source of it—but that is what Harris is seeking to prove), and also, as Harris himself acknowledges, contradicted by Polybius' report (1.20.14) that the Romans did indeed trust those foreign allies to transport them to Sicily in 264.

[156] So Coarelli (2014), though he more controversially (and not altogether plausibly) interprets the text of one of the rams as suggesting that there were six quaestors involved each year in the procurement, and hence that, as Tacitus suggests, there were eight quaestors at that time in total, including the two involved in city administration. The reading is strained in itself, and if it is hard to imagine two quaestors involved solely in fleet procurement, it is trebly hard to imagine six *quaestores classici* performing this function.

Prag (2014), 199–201, (2020), 100–2 denies that the ram inscriptions lend any support to the thesis that *quaestores classici* were appointed at this period with a specific naval role, arguing that the quaestors in question could be urban or consular quaestors. But Prag's reasoning is methodologically flawed (cf. Gnoli (2020), 108–9): he confuses the question of whether the inscriptions *require* quaestors with a specifically naval role (they do not) with the question of whether their discovery *makes more probable* the existence of quaestors with a specifically naval role that had been hypothesized on other grounds (which they unquestionably do).

[157] So, rightly, Pina Polo and Díaz Fernández (2019), 35–41, though they perhaps overstate the case when they argue that the Romans were specifically preparing for war with Carthage at this point.

mere coincidence, deriving from their general administrative functions rather than implying a new role. But it is methodologically preferable to regard the overlap of information of Lydus and the ram inscriptions as mutually supporting rather than merely coincidental. And at all events we can reasonably rely on P.'s statement that new quaestors were added in the 260s, combined with Tacitus' clear indication that at least some new quaestorships postdated 241, and that the resulting total was eight: hence two added in 267 and two more in (possibly) 227.

The remaining question is the text of P. He, too, is not error-free, but, when reconstructing his text, it is better to assume in the first instance that he is accurate; hence the missing figure should be supplied as VI.

ampliatus est: See 1.B.2n.

Book 16

16.1 *The history of Carthage.* Although he rarely indicates a structural feature of Livy's original text (but cf. 104.1n.), a likely inference from P.'s opening words (cf. also 16.3n. and 16.6n.) is that Livy began Book 16 with a digression on the history of Carthage, introducing the Punic Wars which will be the focus of the next fifteen books. Such digressions were fairly common in ancient historiography, where the historian began a new war by going back in time to give not just an ethnography but also a history of the new enemy. Herodotus constantly offers them, most famously in Book 2 when Cambyses attacks Egypt, and 4.1–82, as Darius prepares his invasion of Scythia; among Roman historians Pompeius Trogus likewise repeatedly loops back in time, as new peoples enter his history and are given an historical back-story. But the practice is in some ways more noteworthy with historians, like Livy, whose narrative is structured more chronologically than Herodotus' or Trogus' in the first place: note e.g. Tac., *Hist.* 5.2–10 on the Jews, or Amm. 23.6 on the Persians.

What is less common is to use such a digression as a structural marker to set off a new section of the work. The central precedent here is Thucydides, who opens his narrative of the Sicilian Expedition, which will occupy the whole of Books 6–7, with an account of the earlier history of Sicily (6.2–5).[158] The complication in the case of Thucydides is that it is far from clear that he himself even intended the passage to stand at the beginning of a book, since our eight-book division of Thucydides is not his own, and indeed was only one of the versions circulating in antiquity: divisions into nine and thirteen books are also attested (Bonner (1920)). It is nevertheless likely that Livy had the eight-book version available to him, which appears to have been used by his contemporary Dionysius of Halicarnassus (esp. *Thuc.* 16), and which was later the most popular (Marcellin., *Vit. Thuc.* 58). It is, however, also the case that Livy was probably innovative in his careful structuring of his history into groups of books (Vasaly (2002)), and such introductory passages—beginning, as in this case, not only a book, but a pentad—are one key mode by which that structure is articulated. That the passage served a structural role is clear from the fact that this was not by any means the Carthaginians' first appearance on Livy's stage; but he reserves the descriptive digression for now, when Carthage emerges as an existential opponent of Rome.

For the content of Livy's Carthaginian history, see also F 5n.

primordia urbis: P. never uses *primordium* apart from here; Livy does so only twice in his surviving work—both in the *Preface* (one, indeed, in the very first

---

[158] For the key structural positioning of 6.2–5 see Rawlings (1981), 65–7, though his broader argument about its place in the overall structure of the work, with Book 6 introducing the second half of an uncompleted ten-book whole, is less persuasive.

line of the entire history), both, as here, qualifying *urbis* or *urbium*, and both with reference to the beginnings of Rome herself (*Praef.* 1, *Praef.* 7). The phrase here accordingly looks pointed, as if a parallel is being drawn between the beginnings of Rome and the beginnings of Carthage (the idea of Carthage as a counter-Rome is common in Latin literature, and indeed in Livy himself).[159] It is, however, unclear whether the parallelism is Livy's—if he himself repeated here the language of the *Preface*. Whether or not he did, P. either takes it over or introduces it himself, so either creating or reproducing an allusion to the opening of Livy's history as a signal to the reader who might be familiar with it. Compare 22.12 for P. offering a signal that would be comprehensible only to readers who were familiar with the unabridged work, though in this case the fact that we have lost the opening of the summary of Book 1 means that we cannot be certain that this phrase of the *Preface* was not in some way reproduced there.

referuntur: For the phrasing cf. esp. 38.3. P. regularly uses *referri* to allude explicitly to the fact that he is summarizing Livy's text (cf. 2.16n. for the not dissimilar *res...continet*); most interestingly, it is often used, as here, when drawing attention to Livy's digressions, interpretations, or comments (31.1, 38.3, 39.2, 48.2, 51.7, 109.1); similarly it is used of the activities of non-Romans, which might be thought extraneous to Livy's narrative (38.3, 40.2, 48.19, 52.7, 59.9, 60.10, 82.5).

16.2 Beginning of First Punic War; fighting against Syracuse.

Hieronem, regem Syracusanorum: Hiero II of Syracuse, lived c.306–215. He was son of Hierocles, perhaps—though not certainly—himself of royal descent (Berve (1959), 7). Hiero took power in Syracuse as general in 275/4 (Paus. 6.12.2; cf. Plb. 1.8.3), and subsequently took the title of king after his victory over the Mamertines (Plb. 1.9.8: see below). Subsequent to the events here, he remained a loyal supporter of Rome for almost fifty years. Livy mentions him several times in the context of his pro-Roman activities in the early years of the Second Punic War (21.49.3–6, 21.50.7–51.1, 22.37, 22.56.6–8, 23.21.5, 23.30.10, 23.38.12–13), but in P. he never appears again until his death at 24.1 (cf. Livy 24.4.1–5).

For his career see Berve (1959), De Sensi Sestito (1977).

auxilium...ferendum: P. heavily abridges (and to some degree distorts: see below) his account of the Romans assisting the Mamertines. There are three key—and connected—questions concerning this: (i) the sequence of events by which the Romans came to intervene; (ii) the Romans' intention in doing so; (iii) whether, by doing so, they bore (a) legal and/or (b) moral responsibility for the war which followed.

(i) The best-known account of the events is Polybius'. According to him, Hiero decided to attack the Mamertines in Messana, who had been threatening Syracuse

---

[159] See Miles (2003); for a broader account of how Rome and Carthage developed their perceptions of themselves and each other in parallel cf. Purcell (2017). For Livy see Levene (2010a), 235–6.

for several years, and inflicted a major defeat on them (1.8.1, 1.9.3–10). The Mamertines appealed both to Carthage and to Rome for help against him (1.10.1); the Carthaginians took control of the citadel, but the Mamertines removed them when the Romans came (1.11.4). Hiero and the Carthaginians then formed an alliance against Rome (1.11.6–7).[160]

However, D.S. 22.13–23.1 is entirely different. His narrative is not complete, but one crucial detail is clear: in this version, the fight with Hiero, the Mamertines' appeal to the Carthaginians, and the Carthaginian occupation of the town took place earlier—perhaps as much as five years earlier (though the chronology is controversial),[161] but certainly well before any appeal was made to Rome. On this account, the Mamertines' appeal to the Romans could only be against the Carthaginians, and Rome, in responding to it, did so in full knowledge that war with Carthage would be likely to result.

The essential facts do not greatly differ between the sources, and as a consequence, we are not limited to simply choosing one version: it may well be that more than one has something of the truth to it, and that we need to meld details from one into the narrative framework of another. But the crucial respect in which a choice needs to be made is in the timings of (a) the Mamertines' appeal to Carthage; (b) the Mamertines' appeal to Rome; (c) the Carthaginian alliance with Hiero; (d) the Roman intervention. Depending on the order in which these occur, our judgements on the actions of the participants will vary dramatically.

The central issue is the credibility of Polybius. He was writing a century later, but on his own account was drawing on sources written close to the time, comparing partisan versions on both sides and reaching a conclusion of his own. This does not make him even close to infallible: his assessment of the relative likelihood of competing versions is at least as likely to be flawed as anyone else's, especially since he is by no means an impartial observer, but draws his conclusions in the light of his own prejudices and presuppositions. But it does give him the priority *a priori*: his account, at least in its basic outline, should be seen as the 'default'—the one that is the most probable on balance in the absence of compelling objections to it. And nothing in it appears fundamentally objectionable. The most surprising feature is the Mamertines' simultaneous appeal to Rome and Carthage (e.g. Hampl (1972), 414–15), but Rome and Carthage were at this point

---

[160] Zonar. 8.8.4–6 is similar in outline, but changes the timing of the alliances: the Mamertines originally appealed to Rome alone, Rome agreed to an alliance, then delayed sending help, so the Mamertines had recourse to Carthage instead; the Carthaginians gave help, and had already made peace with Hiero by the time the Romans arrived to help the Mamertines, who by now had wearied of Carthaginian control. This has little historical credibility: it looks like a secondary elaboration to clarify the Romans' innocence of provoking a Carthaginian war (so e.g. Thiel (1954), 147).

[161] Dating the Mamertines' battle with Hiero primarily depends on interpreting various synchronicities in Polybius which appear to point in different directions. Many scholars, broadly accepting Diodorus' sequence of events, also argue that the balance of evidence favours 269/8, five years before the Romans' intervention (so e.g. Thiel (1954), 145–8, Berve (1959), 14–15, Hampl (1972), 416–17, Molthagen (1975), 93–6, De Sensi Sestito (1977), 45, 52–3, 223–32, Huss (1985), 217); some prefer 265/4, as Polybius' main narrative indicates (so e.g. Beloch, *GG* IV.1 644, IV.2 280–1, Heuss (1949), 465, Lazenby (1996), 36, Hoyos (1998), 33–40).

still governed by friendly relations with each other (cf. 13.6n., 14.7n.), and the Mamertines may well have expected themselves to be able to forge working relationships of different sorts with each of them (so Hoyos (1998), 43–6).

The objection that many scholars have to Polybius lies less in any intrinsic implausibility of his narrative, but rather in the degree to which his account appears to exculpate the Romans of aggressive intent against Carthage: this smacks to many of pro-Roman propaganda (e.g. Thiel (1954), 144–53). But that question needs to be considered separately: for even if we grant in principle that Rome often conducted foreign policy to expansionist and aggressive ends, this does not preclude that in a particular case they may have been making a limited response to particular events rather than pursuing grand imperial aims. It is unreasonable to object to Polybius' version of the origins of the First Punic War because it might constitute an exception to a wider pattern of Roman strategy.

(ii) Moving, therefore, to consider the Romans' motives: on the face of things—at least if Polybius' narrative sequence is accepted—they were simply helping the Mamertines against Hiero, and had no aggressive aims against Carthage at all. Polybius does suggest, however, that this was not primarily altruistic, nor were thoughts of Carthage out of their mind: they feared that if Carthage took over Messana, they might gain control of Sicily and threaten Italy (1.10.5–9); they were also prompted by the possibility of plunder (1.11.2; see also below). For that reason, even on his account, they envisaged that war with Carthage might result from their intervention. Still, on this view, Rome's aims were defensive rather than expansionist, and they were reacting to the immediate crisis generated by the Mamertines' war rather than pursuing a long-term strategy. Polybius' version is accepted as a reasonable (if not necessarily complete) account of the Romans' motivations by (e.g.) Walbank (1957), 57–8, Scullard (1989), 540, Lazenby (1996), 37–42, Loreto (2007), 11–15.

However, even in antiquity, other views were put forward, including by people who saw Rome as intervening against Hiero rather than the Carthaginians. Dio (fr. 43.1–4; cf. Zonar. 8.8.1–5) argues that the primary motivations on both sides were aggressive and defensive in virtually equal measure: both Rome and Carthage were acquisitive and expanding empires, but both also feared the expansionist tendencies of the other. The Mamertine crisis was the trigger which brought them into conflict, but, Dio suggests, if it had not been that, something else would have prompted it. Flor. 1.18.2–4 goes further, and directly states that the Romans' intervention was against Carthage; and even though, like Dio, he places the responsibility on the aggressive tendencies of both sides, he has a greater focus on Rome, emphasizing her greed for plunder, and does not mention any sort of defensive aim.[162] And of course Diodorus' account, as noted above,

---

[162] It is also worth noting that Florus, unlike Dio, appears to regard this as entirely to the Romans' credit—a sign of their irrepressible ambition to achieve their imperial destiny (cf. esp. Brunt (1978) for the Romans' celebration of their own imperial expansion).

appears to be premised on the Romans deliberately starting a war against Carthage, which presupposes some degree of aggressive intent on their part; and as for their notional support of the Mamertines, he argues—albeit in the mouth of Hiero—that it was so egregiously immoral that it could only be explained by an aggressive desire to gain control of Sicily (23.1.4).

Hence, even if we grant, as we should (cf. above), that Polybius' narrative sequence is on balance to be preferred, this still allows considerable variation in (a) how far we see the Romans deliberately seeking a *casus belli* that would or could bring them into conflict with Carthage, and (b) how far they were motivated by fear of Carthaginian expansion and how far by their own desires for power and conquest.

On (a), there is, of course, a danger of hindsight: the fact that war with Carthage did result from the Roman intervention does not mean that was the intention with which they intervened. Accordingly, some argue that the Romans' concern was with Hiero alone, and all references in our sources to fears of the Carthaginians are anachronistic (e.g. Heuss (1949), 468–79, Eckstein (1987), 79–80, Hoyos (1998), 51–7). One objection is noted by Walbank (1957), 58, 62–3: that the consul's willingness to fight Carthage when he had the opportunity (Plb. 1.12.1–2) implies that he had at least conditional authorization to do so, even though (*contra* Walbank) there is unlikely to have been a 'conditional declaration of war' in a formal sense (see Eckstein (1987), 84–9; cf. Rich (1976), 120–1). More importantly, while avoiding hindsight is important, it above all means that we need to recognize that the Romans were working within a range of possible outcomes visible to them rather than with the outcome that actually occurred. The proximity of the Carthaginians to Messana, and the corresponding potential for conflict with them, was a brute fact that could hardly be overlooked (cf. Welwei (1978), 577, Bleckmann (2002), 78).[163]

This does not, however, mean that the Romans in 264 'intended' to fight Carthage, and still less that at this point they anticipated a full-scale war of conquest against them: if Polybius' sequence of events is accepted, then helping the Mamertines would be a very roundabout and unlikely way for the Romans to set about deliberately provoking a Carthaginian war.[164] All it means is that such a war must have stood somewhere in the range of possibilities they were considering.

---

[163] *Pace* Eckstein (1987), 79–80 (cf. also (2006), 165), who argues that the Romans would have assumed that the Carthaginians would support their taking action against Hiero, since Carthage and Rome had friendly relations, while Carthage and Hiero were long-standing enemies. This suggests that the Romans had demonstrably too narrow and arguably an unrealistic picture of Carthage's policy and interests in Sicily. This is not impossible, since misconceptions of that sort do occur, especially when people wrongly assume that their own (self-described) benign intentions will be instantly apparent to others. But it is far less likely in an international system such as Eckstein himself elsewhere argues for (esp. Eckstein (2006)), where every state was aggressively jockeying for power and looking suspiciously at every potential rival.

[164] Loreto (2007), 34 discusses the logistical inadequacy of the initial Roman expedition to engage the full Carthaginian power.

But they may well have regarded it as standing on the lower end of likelihood—a risk they were prepared to take rather than an outcome they were directly seeking.[165]

How much of a risk this represented for them, and how enthusiastic they were for such a war (should it occur), is a more difficult question, and one which can hardly be determined except by a far wider consideration of Roman strategic aims and her willingness to adopt aggressive policies in the middle Republic. This is a hugely controversial question which cannot be resolved here.[166] Polybius himself, though not suggesting it as a primary cause of the First Punic War in particular, regularly refers to Rome as prompted by expansionist aims (e.g. 1.3.6, 1.6.6, 9.10.11).[167] Certainly the fact that the Romans, after their victory over Syracuse, expanded the fight into western Sicily, attacking the Carthaginian stronghold at Agrigentum (Plb. 1.17.6–19.15), suggests at the very least an opportunistic willingness to seize the initiative even at the cost of escalating the war, a choice which a more militarily cautious state might not have made.

As for (b), on the other hand, the debate as to whether the Romans' motivation in this particular case was 'defensive'—prompted by fear of Carthage, as Polybius claimed—or whether it was 'aggressive'—prompted by desire for power and resources, as in Florus—is somewhat sterile and unnecessary. It is not clear that in many instances these can or should be separated: the fact that Messana stood in a vital strategic position meant that the desire to hold it oneself and the desire to prevent it from being held by others went closely in tandem. And elaborate attempts to show that Carthage was not in fact a threat to Rome[168] are irrelevant:

---

[165] So e.g. Loreto (2007), 32–6, who however argues for an implausibly broad range of rational and strategic considerations on the Romans' part in making their decision.

[166] The key work is Harris (1979a), arguing forcefully—and against the grain of much earlier scholarship—that the high degree of militarization of Roman society went hand in hand with an unashamedly aggressive form of imperialism, and that the great majority of the wars in the Republic can be attributed to this. Harris's basic thesis has been widely accepted: it is supported with at most limited reservations by (e.g.) North (1981), Gabba (1984), Cornell (1989), 383–91. More serious qualifications are offered by Rich (1993), who notes that Roman aggressiveness appears to have varied across time, that social pressures sometimes could push against war as well as promoting it, and that decisions to go to war regularly involved weighing up different sorts of arguments on both sides of the case; and esp. Eckstein (1987), arguing that the uninformed, haphazard, and *ad hoc* nature of decision-making at Rome often led Romans away from aggressive and provocatively 'imperialist' policies, and that in as much as there was a broad move towards expanding Roman interests through diplomacy or conquest, it was the consequence of an international system where every other state was doing the same, rather than something specific to Roman militarism. The latter point is expanded on in Eckstein (2006), analysing the rise of Rome and her contests with other (equally aggressive and militarized) Mediterranean powers in terms of modern theories of international relations.

[167] Walbank (1963), 5–6 suggests that Polybius sometimes contradicts himself, since he elsewhere appears to suggest that Roman expansionism was in large part a consequence, rather than a cause, of their victories over Carthage (3.2.6, cf. 1.20.1–2, 1.63.9); but Derow (1979), 2–6 = (2015), 127–34, shows that Polybius' statements are consistent with his seeing Rome as an expansionist power from the start, but being prompted by each victory to set her sights higher. Walbank (1963), 6–13 also suggests that Polybius' general statements on imperialism are to some degree contradicted by the details of his narrative; but see *contra* Derow (1979), 6–15 = (2015), 134–49, Harris (1979a), 107–17.

[168] As offered by (e.g.) Heuss (1949), 470–3, Huss (1985), 220.

the key thing is that the Romans might have perceived her as such (Scullard (1989), 540–1, Lazenby (1996), 38–9; cf. Rich (1993), 63–4). In the early twenty-first century, a significant majority of the citizens of the United States, the greatest military power in world history, became convinced that the security of their country was seriously threatened by an impoverished Middle Eastern state six thousand miles away.[169] This offers a salutary corrective to the idea that a wildly exaggerated fear of the power and intentions of a rival must be the invention of some later propagandist rather than a true account of what was thought at the time.

This does not show that the Romans *did* act (in part) out of fear of Carthage. Polybius' account of the Romans' deliberations over the war is in various ways untrustworthy (see below), and may be in this respect also: our evidence is inadequate to decide. But it does show that such fears can exist alongside aggressive and expansionist aims, and that they need not be closely correlated to the actual level of threat.

(iii) (a) On the legal front, much depends on the so-called 'Treaty of Philinus'. If that treaty existed, then Rome clearly violated it by crossing to fight in Sicily—unless the treaty had been violated first by Carthage. But this is a moot point, since Philinus' treaty is unlikely to have existed (14.7n.); and no other treaty explicitly barred the Romans from intervening in Sicily. It is possible that aspects of the earlier Roman–Carthaginian treaties could have been held to assume that there were spheres of influence for each party from which the other would stay clear, but there was no explicit statement to that effect, and no system by which such disputes could be arbitrated. The fact that the Romans fought the Carthaginians at Messana would appear to involve a violation of the friendly relations established in the earlier treaties—but even there, who was in violation depends on the order of events. On Polybius' version, it was the Carthaginians who chose to join Hiero against Rome, whereas on Diodorus', the Romans deliberately chose to support the Mamertines against Carthage; as before, Polybius here is to be preferred.

(b) Polybius thus acquits the Romans of legal guilt (cf. 3.26.7)—but he is less forgiving of them morally. Since the Mamertines were brutal renegades, he argues, the Romans had no business aiding them, especially given that they had recently acted in exactly the opposite fashion towards the renegades in Rhegium, whose behaviour had been virtually identical (1.11.1, 3.26.6; cf. 12.5n., 15.2n.). Dio's account also fails to clear the Romans of moral guilt, since he regards the war as the consequence of their aggressive and acquisitive tendencies (although in Dio's version the guilt is equally shared with Carthage). D.S. 23.1.4 describes a speech by Hiero which combines both of these motifs: not only was it outrageous that

---

[169] See e.g. https://www.latimes.com/world/la-na-iraqpoll17dec17-480pa1an-story.html (site last accessed 23 February 2022).

the Romans supported the Mamertines, but it was also a mere cover for their ambitions in Sicily.

Modern historians tend to be more sparing with their moral judgements. Let us simply observe that on the one hand no state in history, even less powerful and more pacific ones than Rome, has ever observed moral purity and consistency in forming its alliances; but on the other, it is not unrealistic to require that states as far as possible refrain from pursuing their interests at the cost of provoking hugely destructive wars.

As for P., he straightforwardly clears the Romans of war-guilt, even though he appears to accept the Treaty of Philinus: like other writers, he explicitly states that the Carthaginians were the ones who violated the treaty by intervening at Tarentum in 272 (14.7n.), and, accordingly, he comfortably ignores any question of a violation by the Romans here, since on his account the Carthaginians' own actions had made that treaty (and presumably any prior treaties also) defunct. Nor does he directly suggest any other moral problems with their behaviour: he neither says, as Polybius does, that the Mamertines were unworthy recipients of Rome's help, nor does he point to any motives on the Romans' part other than altruism. His account contains no hint of the double game that the Mamertines were playing by seeking support from both Carthage and Rome, with the resulting complications for assessing Rome's motives: in his presentation, the Carthaginians were simply the Mamertines' enemies, exactly as Hiero was. This is a neat simplification that he shares with others in the Latin historical tradition: see Flor. 1.18.3, Oros. 4.7.1. Livy can hardly have been so simplistic,[170] but he may have presented the matter in such a way as to make it easy to distil simplistic readings from him. However, the fact that P.—unlike Florus and Orosius—indicates dissension at Rome over the decision to intervene (see below) draws to the reader's attention that it was controversial, and may induce the reader to recall from other sources— perhaps indeed from Livy himself—possible points of controversy, some of which raise issues that might reflect less well on Rome. That teasing ambiguity also appears in his narrative sequence: for while his account opens with the Mamertines appealing for help equally against Carthage and Hiero, in the immediate sequel the war appears to be against Hiero alone, undercutting any sense that Rome formally began the fighting with Carthage.

Mamertinis: A group of Campanian mercenaries, who for some years had been in control of Messana. According to Plb. 1.7.2–4 (cf. D.S. 21.18.3, Dio fr. 40.8), they had originally served under Agathocles of Syracuse; they had been welcomed

---

[170] *Contra* Rich (1976), 122–3, who attributes this reading of the history to Livy himself, comparing Livy 30.31.4, where Scipio describes the First Punic War as a time when the Romans took up 'loyal and righteous weapons' (*pia ac iusta...arma*) against Carthage in support of their Mamertine allies. However, Livy's Scipio here is expanding on a similar (though vaguer) description of the war given by Scipio in Plb. 15.8.1. Polybius' own presentation of the war was in quite different terms, as we have seen; Livy's may well have been also.

into Messana, and then had treacherously taken control of the town; they had subsequently taken the name 'Mamertines' (1.8.1). In an alternative version cited by Fest. 150L from the otherwise unknown historian Alfius (*FRHist* 69 F 1), they were Samnite rather than Campanian, and their incorporation into Messana occurred through mutual consent rather than violence, but this is questionable.[171] According to Festus, the name derived from Mamers (the Oscan name for Mars), but Campanile (1993), 601–4 suggests on linguistic grounds that it is more likely to come from the town of Mamertium in Bruttium (Str. 6.1.9), indicating that the mercenary force at some point had passed through that region, and perhaps included people from there.

senatus censuit: In Polybius, unlike P., the Senate does not vote in favour of helping the Mamertines: the decision is taken by the popular assembly (1.11.1–3; cf. D.S. 23.1.4).[172] It is true that, while under Roman constitutional procedures such matters were regularly brought to a popular vote, it was usually only when ratifying a prior senatorial decision (Mommsen, *StR*³ III 345, 1170–3). The one known exception, apart from the case here, is the proposal to go to war with Rhodes at Livy 45.21, and there the objection is made that to do so without prior consultation of the Senate and notification of the consuls was unprecedented (Livy 45.21.4–5). But the fact remains that the proposal over Rhodes was brought to the assembly, and the point made then about lack of precedent does not conflict with the scenario described by Polybius, where the Senate had already debated the matter, and the initiative to bring it to the people is the consuls' own; hence Polybius' version of the Punic War debate is still to be preferred to P.'s.[173] It is altogether possible, indeed, that Livy, like Polybius, reported a popular vote, but that it was elided in P., so as to place the whole decision on the Senate. It might be that Livy said that the people's decision was ultimately ratified by the Senate, and

---

[171] Crawford (2007), 276–8 suggests reasons for giving credence to Alfius' version, which includes circumstantial details of names and places which various documentary sources connect to the Mamertines. But there is considerably more evidence for Campanian mercenaries in Sicily than for Samnites (though cf. D.S. 20.11.1, 20.64.2), and the story of a violent capture of the town is sufficiently widespread and early that it is uncomfortable to reject it on the basis of a brief summary in a source of doubtful provenance and unknown motives (cf. Thiel (1954), 135, hypothesizing that Alfius' version originated in an attempt to exculpate the Romans of immorality for intervening on the Mamertines' behalf).

[172] Some have argued that this is a misinterpretation of Polybius: that οἱ πολλοί at 1.11.3 refers to 'the majority of the Senate', not the people, and hence that Polybius, like P., is reporting a Senatorial decision that is merely rubber-stamped by the Assembly (so e.g. Eckstein (1980a)); but see *contra* e.g. Hoyos (1984b), Bleckmann (2002), 71–6. Still less plausible is the claim by Bellomo (2013) that it refers to a *contio*, and that the following sentence in Polybius conflates an assembly decree ratifying an earlier senatorial decision to support the Mamertines with an entirely separate senatorial decree to send military support to them; this solves the constitutional question at the cost of an impossibly convoluted reading of Polybius' text.

[173] *Contra* e.g. De Sanctis III.1 97 [99], Welwei (1978), 576; but as Harris (1979a), 188 rightly argues, it is more likely that a popular decision would be transferred to the Senate in the later tradition (to regularize the declaration of war), rather than *vice versa*. See also Tan (2017), 101–8, arguing that the state's heavy reliance on taxation at this period made it more probable that a decision with potentially vast expenditure at stake would require the active support of the wider citizen body.

this is what P. is reporting (so Walbank (1957), 60–1), but P. could easily have simplified the narrative in a misleading way even in the absence of that (Hoyos (1984b), 91–3, rightly comparing 31.3: see *ad loc.*).

cum: Concessive: 'although'.

contentio: Plb. 1.10.2–11.3 presents the initial conflict as being within the Senate, who were on the one hand afraid of Carthage, but on the other concerned about the immorality and inconsistency of aiding the Mamertines (above). But when the Senate ultimately refused to take action, the consuls took a vote of the people, and persuaded them to go to war, with additional arguments about the plunder that they could obtain.

This account, however, seems implausibly neat and sanitized (*contra* Walbank (1957), 58, Scullard (1989), 540). It seems highly unlikely that a debate on war would break down so readily and philosophically into a conflict between ethics and expediency, nor that these would align so neatly with decisions made by Senate and people respectively (cf. Gabba (1977), 64–5). Certainly one would expect that opponents of war would point to the dangers at least as much as the immorality of helping the Mamertines, or might regard the threat from Carthage as exaggerated. It is also altogether possible—even if one does not accept that the primary motivations were aggressive (cf. above)—that arguments were put forward about the advantages of expanding Roman influence in Sicily. Conversely, if ethical arguments came up at all, it is likely that they were made on the other side also, notably the one which Polybius reports the Mamertines making in their appeal—that Rome should help them on grounds of ethnic solidarity (1.10.2; cf. Zonar. 8.8.4). This all, of course, is speculative—there is no direct evidence that any of these arguments actually were used[174]—but it would be unwise in this respect to trust Polybius' summary of the debate.

transgressisque tunc primum exercitibus: *exercitibus* is Weissenborn's correction to the MSS *equitibus*, which makes little sense in context. While the Roman army probably included cavalry (cf. Zonar. 8.9.5), it was only one part of their force, and there was no apparent significance to its employment here that would lead either Livy or P. to highlight it. The significance lay in the fact that a Roman army was for the first time brought to fight outside Italy, something highlighted as being of monumental importance by many writers (e.g. Plb. 1.5.1, 1.12.5, Vell. 2.38.2, Sen., *Brev. Vit.* 13.4, Suet., *Tib.* 2.1, Eutr. 2.18.1, Zonar. 8.8.1). Given P.'s regular interest in 'first times' (cf. 11.5n.) it is hardly surprising that he, too, would emphasize the point.

---

[174] However, cf. Rich (1993), 60–4 for the range of considerations that the Romans typically took into account when making decisions to go to war or forming judgements about the wars they had undertaken.

Polybius dates the crossing to the 129th Olympiad (1.5.1), which began during the consular year 264.[175] It was led, according to all sources, by the consul of that year, Ap. Claudius Caudex.

adversus Hieronem: In Polybius the battle is initially against the Syracusans, but the war quickly transfers itself to the Carthaginians (1.11.12–12.1); this too was the perception of Philinus, though he claimed that the Romans were defeated rather than victorious in both encounters (*FGrH* 174 F 2, cited in Plb. 1.15.1–5: see also below). P. removes the Carthaginians from the equation, to be swept into the 'other things' at the end of the book (16.6n.), and focuses on Hiero alone, where the Romans move seamlessly from attack to victories to a peace-agreement.

saepius bene pugnatum: Polybius records only one actual fight with the Syracusans: an initial victory over Hiero at 1.11.12–14, after which Hiero retreated to Syracuse and Appius followed him and placed the city under siege (1.12.4). In the following year, 263, the Romans sent the two new consuls to Sicily, but they did not appear actually to join combat: instead Hiero sued for peace, seeing the extent of the Romans' power (1.16.1–5). Philinus' version (*FGrH* 174 F 2), according to Plb. 1.15.1–5, was similar, but with the Romans defeated rather than victorious in the initial encounter—Polybius is scathing about this, noting that Hiero's retreat and the Roman siege of Syracuse, both of which Philinus apparently accepted, are unmotivated under this scenario (1.15.6–11).[176] The fragmentary account of Diodorus offers no further Roman victories against Hiero, though he mentions a successful attack on the Syracusan colony Adranon (23.4.1). Zonar. 8.9.8 sketchily refers to numerous battles during Appius' siege of Syracuse, but

---

[175] Hoyos (1998), 64–6 dates the crossing to the second half of August, but does not make it clear whether this is a Julian date or a Roman consular date (or if he believes they coincided at this period): his *terminus post* appears to be governed by the Roman consular calendar (the time needed for debate and recruitment after the beginning of the consular year), the *terminus ante* by the Julian calendar (the time needed for Appius' campaigns prior to winter). For reasons to doubt the correspondence of the consular and Julian calendars see Morgan (1977), 92–5, arguing that two years later, in 262, they were more than a month apart.

[176] One widespread solution to the dilemma Polybius sets Philinus is to accept Philinus' account of Appius' defeats, but to argue that Appius did not go on to besiege Syracuse: it was Valerius Messalla the following year who not only won a victory at Messana, but successfully besieged Syracuse, which is why he received a *cognomen* from the city he rescued (*Fasti Capitolini*: cf. Degrassi 115, Sen., *Brev. Vit.* 13.5), and why he, not Appius, was given the triumph (so e.g. Beloch, *GG* IV.2 533–6, De Sanctis III.1 107 [109] n. 29). This requires that either Polybius misinterpreted (or misrepresented) Philinus, or Philinus himself did not realize that he was describing campaigns by separate consuls in different years: neither is especially plausible. Far preferable is to assume that the outcomes of Appius' battles were more equivocal, and could be described as either defeat or victory depending on the perspective of the narrator (so Berve (1959), 30, Molthagen (1975), 109–10, Eckstein (1987), 342, Lazenby (1996), 49–50, and esp. Hoyos (1998), 96–9, showing well how the precise wording of Polybius' summary of Philinus supports such an interpretation). Hence the decision to deny Appius a triumph could well have been the result of political resentment rather than the result of his having no case for one (so Bleckmann (2002), 82–4); though it is also possible that at the time the unfinished war with Syracuse and the presence of the Carthaginians in the wings simply carried more weight than Appius' ability to present himself as successful on the battlefield. Loreto (2007), 41–2 suggests, far less plausibly, that Appius was unequivocally victorious but was even so denied a triumph because the senators were upset by his escalation of the war.

with successes on both sides; Eutr. 2.18–19 (falsely) awards a triumph to Appius (cf. Sil. 6.660–2, *Vir. Ill.* 37.5),[177] then (equally falsely) extends the fighting against Syracuse to 262, but does not refer to any more actual victories. Other historians in the later Latin tradition appear to suggest a quick victory by Appius, followed by Hiero immediately coming to terms (Flor. 1.18.6, Oros. 4.7.2–3).

Hence no source other than P. has the Romans racking up a consistent run of multiple victories against Syracuse. This may well be because Livy recorded victories absent from other accounts. Certainly the fact that, according to the *Fasti Capitolini*, one of the consuls of 263, M'. Valerius Messalla—but not his colleague M'. Otacilius Crassus—was awarded a triumph over both the Carthaginians and Hiero, and the report in Plin., *Nat.* 35.22 that Valerius had this victory depicted in a painting on the *Curia Hostilia*, together strongly imply that there was some fighting which goes unmentioned in the surviving historical narratives, which never directly show Valerius fighting without his colleague (though Zonar. 8.9.10 cursorily mentions that they worked separately to win over Sicilian allies).[178]

saepius: Not otherwise used by P., though it is not uncommon in Livy. The force of the comparative is, as often, largely lost: it is little different from the positive *saepe* (K-S 2.476), which P. uses rather more.

bene pugnatum: Cf. 12.3n. P. regularly describes Roman battles with the impersonal *pugnatum est*, but this is the sole place where *est* is omitted, a common stylistic feature of Latin which P. employs only rarely. Here it gives a livelier movement to a (for P.) relatively long and complex narrative sentence.

pax data est: According to Plb. 1.16.9, the terms were that Hiero had to return all Roman prisoners and pay tribute of 100 talents. D.S. 23.4.1 records the tribute as 150,000 drachmas (= 25 talents), while in Eutr. 2.19.2 and Oros. 4.7.3 it is 200 talents. Polybius' version, as before, is to be preferred, though it is plausibly suggested that Diodorus' figure represents a down-payment, with the rest to be paid by instalments: this is supported by Diodorus' additional statement that the treaty was to continue for fifteen years, combined with the notice in Zonar. 8.16.2 that in

---

[177] Bleckmann (2002), 83–4 suggests that Eutropius' report is because Appius may have unofficially triumphed without senatorial approval, as is reported as happening in other cases; but Eutropius is genuinely mistaken sufficiently often that it is methodologically unsound to postulate an unattested event in order to save his credit.

[178] That Valerius conducted some of the campaign alone is also indicated by Naev., *Carm.* 3 (Strzelecki), Varro *ap.* Plin., *Nat.* 7.214 (Hoyos (1998), 110 suggests that the former refers to the campaign in western Sicily after the fall of Syracuse, but on very weak grounds). Molthagen (1975), 113–15 argues that the reason that he alone received a triumph was because of his superior social status compared to Otacilius, but that seems unlikely, given that Otacilius had sufficient status to achieve the consulship and conduct the campaign. Still less likely is Molthagen's further idea that the *Fasti* and Pliny are simply wrong to attribute to him a victory over Carthage (he claims that Zonaras' account (8.9.11–12) of Valerius fighting against Carthage after the defeat of Syracuse is misdated and belongs to the next year's consuls: Molthagen (1975) 117–19). This pays no attention to P., who implies that Livy recorded some fighting during the Syracusan campaign absent from other accounts, some of which could well have involved Carthage (cf. also 16.6n.).

248 (i.e. fifteen years later) the tribute was discontinued (Berve (1959), 36).[179] Diodorus adds that Hiero's sovereignty over Syracuse and a number of specified subject cities was explicitly recognized, with the implication that he lost control of other cities, which had gone over to Rome (Beloch, *GG* IV.1 650–1): this is not unlikely. Contrary to what is often stated (e.g. Walbank (1957), 68–9), there appears to have been no formal alliance between Rome and Syracuse, but only a looser agreement of friendship (De Sensi Sestito (1977), 102–12, Eckstein (1980b), 184–92, Gruen (1984a), 67–8).

16.3 *Censorship.* The censors were Cn. Cornelius Blasio and C. Marcius Rutilus. Marcius, uniquely in the history of the Republic, was holding the censorship for the second time, having been first elected to it in 294, and therefore (according to the *Fasti Capitolini*) acquired the *cognomen* Censorinus; he apparently had a law passed barring future iterations of the office (Plu., *Cor.* 1.1; cf. Val. Max. 4.1.3): see Mommsen, *StR*³ I 520–1.

P. pays no attention to this, despite his usual interest in 'firsts' and constitutional innovations. It is possible (but unlikely) that it is because it did not appear in Livy; far more likely is that it is a consequence of Livy's chronological arrangement. The censors, according to the *Fasti*, were elected in 265, but the *lustrum*, as usual, must have taken place the following year, in 264. Livy in his surviving text almost invariably reports the *lustrum* in that second year (cf. 13.4n.), and presumably did so here also. However, the unique position of Marcius related to his election in 265 rather than to the completion of the *lustrum* in 264, and would have been recorded by Livy under that year.[180] But, as suggested above (16.1n.), it is likely that Book 16 began with Carthage and, accordingly, moved directly into the Mamertines' appeal to Rome and the opening of the First Punic War in 264.[181] If so, Livy recorded material for 265, including the election of the censors, in Book 15 (though nothing from that year is mentioned by P. in that book). P. is exceptionally laconic in Book 15 in general (15.6n.), and is unlikely in any case to have recorded the same censorship twice in separate books; so he focuses his attention on the *lustrum*, giving the census figures, as he often does in this part of his summary.

lustrum ... conditum: See 11.5n.

---

[179] De Sanctis III.1 114 [117] suggests that Diodorus and Polybius are referring to different things, and imagines an initial indemnity of 100 talents, followed by an annual payment of 25 talents for fifteen years: a total payment of 475 talents. This does not accord sufficiently with either text to be plausible, though the total sum is not out of line with those that Rome would exact in the next century from her conquered enemies (see Gruen (1984b), 62).

[180] Similarly in 209/8, Livy records an innovation in the choice of censors at their initial election (27.11.7), but still describes the *lustrum* at the end of their office in the following year (27.36.6–7).

[181] Compare the way in Book 21 Livy's narrative begins by going back in time to give a short biography of Hannibal, then moves into his attack on Saguntum and the Saguntines' appeal to Rome in (on his chronology) 218, at that point joining his main annalistic sequence of Roman history (cf. Levene (2010a), 13–14).

CCLXXXXII milia CCXXXIIII: The MSS of P. give the figure as 382,234 or 382,734. This is entirely out of line with all other recorded census numbers from the third century, none of which go above 300,000; moreover, it contradicts the report of the same figures in Eutr. 2.18.2; according to the MS tradition of Eutropius, the number is 292,334. That something of this order stood in Eutropius' original text is confirmed by Paeanius' Greek translation, in which the figure is 292,234.

These are clearly all derived from the same original number, which has however undergone corruption in some MS traditions. The coincidence of Paeanius and P. shows that 234 must be correct for the 'hundreds' figure, and that it has been corrupted in Eutropius. As for the 'thousands' figure, Eutropius is far more likely to be right, both because the same figure is in Paeanius, showing that it was already in Eutropius' text in late antiquity, and because of the general implausibility of so high a number in P. This still leaves open the question of whether the difference between Eutropius and P. is because P. was drawing on a different (perhaps corrupt) text of Livy (in which case his text should be left intact), or whether P. originally had the same figure as Eutropius, but it has been corrupted in the later MSS (and so his text should be emended to conform with Eutropius' figure). The latter is more likely, not least because Eutropius may well have been drawing on P. rather than on Livy directly (see Introduction).

If we accept, therefore, that 292,234 was the figure that originally stood in both Eutropius and P., the question remains whether it is reliable. It represents an increase of around 8 per cent over the previous figure a decade earlier; if both of these figures are genuine, it is most likely to reflect some form of large-scale enfranchisement, for which there is no other evidence.[182] But the earlier figure may well be erroneous or corrupt (14.4n.); and as for this one, it is worth noting that it looks problematic when compared with the next recorded figure, but for the opposite reason: it appears not too high, but too low (see 18.4n.). The bottom line is that it cannot be relied on, for all that it is closer to the period where census data may begin to be more trustworthy (Brunt (1971), 31–3).

16.4 *First gladiatorial show at Rome*. For P.'s regular interest in innovations cf. 11.5n.;[183] it is similarly identified as the first show by Val. Max. 2.4.7, who dates it to 264, and says that it took place in the Forum Boarium; Auson., *Griphus* 36–7 adds that it comprised three pairs of Thracians. The number of gladiators may well be authentic, since the point of Ausonius' poem is to identify things that

---

[182] Vell. 1.14.7 reports that the Sabines were enfranchised in 268 (cf. 19.11n.), but he also notes (1.14.6) that they had previously received *civitas sine suffragio* in 290; they would therefore have been included in the census from that point (Brunt (1971), 17–21, *contra* De Sanctis II 404 [425] n. 106).

[183] That this was the first appearance of gladiators at Rome is denied by De Sanctis II 512–13 [534], who, however, offers no reasons; also Futrell (1997), 20–1, who finds various possible hints of earlier shows, but none of her examples are at all persuasive.

happened in sets of three, but the type of gladiator is probably a product of his imagination. The occasion is also described by Servius auct., *Aen.* 3.67.

Gladiatorial contests are widely assumed to have been an import from neighbouring Italian peoples, though it is disputed which: both the Etruscans and the Campanians have been proposed. Nicolaus of Damascus (*FGrH* 90 F 78 *ap.* Ath. 153F) attributed it to the Etruscans (cf. Isid., *Orig.* 10.159), but this may well derive from a moralizing attempt to associate gladiators with supposed Etruscan decadence (Wiedemann (1992), 30–3). The first unambiguous iconographic representations of gladiators appear at Paestum (then a Lucanian town: see 14.6n.) in the fourth century BC, and it is more likely that the practice reached Rome from Lucania and Campania (Ville (1981), 1–8, 19–42),[184] though, since the Etruscans themselves had colonies in Campania in the fifth century, it is not out of the question that they too had some hand in its transmission (so Oakley (2005a), 526). Livy himself describes gladiators performing at banquets in Capua in 310/9 (9.40.17), though this is only weak support for Campanian origins, as it may be his own elaboration rather than derived from his sources (Ville (1981), 24): that gladiators fought at banquets is a regular part of the stereotype of Campanian decadence (Str. 5.4.13, Sil. 11.51–4, Ath. 153E).

Decimus Iunius Brutus: This is presumably the consul of 266 (*RE* 124, *MRR* I 201; cf. 15.6n.), whom the *Fasti Capitolini*, however, refer to as 'D. Iunius Pera', not 'Brutus'; while according to Valerius Maximus, the father's name (not given by P.) was Brutus Pera. The most probable explanation is that the father's name was D. Junius Brutus Pera, as in Valerius, but the son's was D. Junius Pera, and that P. (or, less likely, Livy) misinterpreted (Münzer (1918a)). According to Valerius Maximus and Ausonius, Decimus laid the show on jointly with his brother Marcus, who however goes unmentioned in P.

in honorem defuncti patris: The association of gladiatorial shows with the commemoration of the dead continued into the Empire, though from the last decades of the Republic shows were increasingly presented on other occasions also. This association was held by some in antiquity to be the result of its derivation from rites of human sacrifice (so Tert., *Spect.* 12.1–3, Serv. auct., *Aen.* 3.67, Serv., *Aen.* 10.519); along related lines, Auson., *Ecl.* 16.33–6 suggested that the gladiatorial shows during the Saturnalia were a form of sacrifice to Saturn. This is debunked by many (e.g. Ville (1981), 9–19, Wiedemann (1992), 33–4, Edwards (2007), 59–60), but Versnel (1993), 210–27 puts together various pieces of evidence which suggest that the death of gladiators and others in the arena was held by at least some in antiquity to have propitiatory or magical properties—though he

---

[184] Those who prefer Etruscan origins (e.g. Futrell (1997), 11–19) regard the 'Phersu pictures' as evidence for Etruscan gladiators: these are sixth-century tomb-paintings from Tarquinia, depicting (*inter alia*) a man with a dog attacking another, hooded, man. But whatever this is meant to signify (which is highly doubtful), it is not related to any form of gladiatorial combat familiar at Rome (Ville (1981), 4–6); at most it recalls other events later associated with gladiators, such as the *venatio*.

also argues that such interpretations may have arisen spontaneously later rather being than a survival from the funerary origins of gladiatorial combat.

16.5 *Foundation of colony of Aesernia.*

colonia...deducta est: Cf. 1.B.1n.

Aesernia: Modern Isernia (*BarrAtl* Map 44 F2). The foundation of the colony is also reported by Vell. 1.14.8, who dates it a year after the beginning of the First Punic War (sc. 263). The location of the town, in what appears a strongly defensible site in Samnium, has suggested to some scholars that the reason for its foundation was strategic. But it is surprising, in that case, that there is no archaeological evidence for its settlement prior to the foundation of the colony (cf. De Benedittis *et al.* (1999), 60), though there were various other Samnite forts in the vicinity (Oakley (1995), 26–8). It is noteworthy in this context that even after the formal foundation of the colony, archaeological evidence suggests that the urban centre of Aesernia was surprisingly small, and the bulk of the population was widely scattered through the colonial territory (Stek (2017)): it does not appear that the Romans were seeking to consolidate the community around a central position of strength, whether military or economic.

It was a Latin colony, to judge from its appearance in Livy's list at 27.10.8. There does not appear to be any clear reason for its foundation at this point: no fighting in Samnium appears in our records for nearly a decade prior to this (cf. 14.8n.).[185] It may be that some low-level disaffection has gone unrecorded: cf. Zonar. 8.11.8–9 for a slightly later (alleged) Samnite conspiracy against Rome. Alternatively, the colony may have been planted out of fear that the Samnites would once again rise when Rome was distracted in Sicily (cf. Salmon (1969), 63–4): for while with hindsight we can see that by now the Samnites had been essentially suppressed, that cannot have been obvious at the time. More broadly, however, the pattern of colony foundation at this period and for some years after (cf. 15.4n., 19.5n., 20.2n.) suggests a determination to plant loyal communities throughout Italy, and it may well be a mistake to seek to tie their foundation to specific concerns about particular groups of locals (cf. 15.4n. for the danger of overemphasizing military strategy in explaining the location of colonies). It may be relevant in this context to note that there is some evidence that, despite the lack of prior urban settlement, there are indications of Samnite influence, notably a painted tomb in the Samnite style (Morel (1991), 133), suggesting that local Samnites formed part of the colonial population (Roselaar (2011), 541); in the following century a dedication by 'Samnite inhabitants' (*CIL* I² 3201: *Samnites*

---

[185] The region had been mentioned in passing by Livy at 10.31.2 in terms that imply that it had already fallen into Roman hands at that point (295), though the very fact that the colony was not founded until later may indicate that this is an anachronism (so Beloch, *RG* 450–1), or that the Samnites had subsequently resumed control (Oakley (2005b), 335).

inquolae) similarly indicates a distinctive Samnite element within the colony that possibly went back to its foundation.[186]

For the archaeology of the colony see De Benedittis *et al.* (1999).

16.6 *Fighting with Carthage and Volsinii.*

res praeterea...gestas continet: See 2.16n.

Poenos: As noted above (16.2n.), P. unexpectedly focuses his attention in the initial stages of the First Punic War on Rome's battles with Hiero, sweeping all the fighting with Carthage in the opening years of the war into his end-of-book summary. Only in Book 17 does he turn his attention to the battles with the Carthaginians, and the earliest episode he records there dates from 260 (17.1n.), while the latest datable events in Book 16 date from 263 (16.2n., 16.5n.). We may presume that the fighting with Carthage in 264 and 263 is covered by the general statement here: according to Polybius Ap. Claudius fought them successfully not long after his arrival in Sicily (1.12.1–3; cf. Dio fr. 43.12 and Zonar. 8.9.7, Oros. 4.7.2),[187] while in the following year M'. Valerius Messalla must have fought the Carthaginians, since he was awarded a triumph over them (16.2n.), and Zonar. 8.9.11–12 refers sketchily to him and his colleague M'. Otacilius Crassus campaigning against them.

The problem comes with the campaigns of 262–261: whether Livy included them in Book 16 (and hence they might be covered by P.'s report here), or whether they were in Book 17, in which case P. omits them altogether. The first of those years was especially significant, since the Romans besieged and captured Agrigentum (Plb. 1.17.6–19.15, D.S. 23.7–9, Oros. 4.7.4–6, Zonar. 8.10.2–5), though in the second relatively little fighting is reported, and that not to the Romans' credit: only an unsuccessful siege of Mytistraton by the Romans (D.S. 23.9.3), and a destructive attack on the Romans by Carthage's disaffected Gallic mercenaries, deliberately set up by the Carthaginian commander to kill as many as possible on both sides (D.S. 23.8.3, Frontin., *Strat.* 3.16.3, Zonar. 8.10.7).

On balance it seems most plausible to assume that the siege of Agrigentum in 262 was included in Book 16 and hence is covered here—it is more likely that P. would have referred to so major a Roman victory in a summary than that he would have failed to refer to it at all. But with the fighting in 261, it is impossible to say whether Livy included it in Book 16 or Book 17, and if the former, whether P. simply fails to mention it, or whether Livy, unlike other surviving historians, described it as an unequivocal Roman success, in which case it too is included in the general statement of Roman victories against Carthage.

---

[186] La Regina (1970–1), 452–3. For the legal status of such *incolae* (not citizens of the colony, but under its jurisdiction) see Gagliardi (2006); cf. Gagliardi (2015), 358–64.

[187] Philinus appears to have recorded the same battle, but regarded it as a Roman defeat rather than victory (*FGrH* 174 F 2 *ap.* Plb. 1.15.1–15: see 16.2n.).

However Livy divided his books, the overall effect of P.'s version is to elide the escalation of the war (and hence also the question of responsibility for its escalation). The fact that the war is fundamentally against Carthage is clear from his description at the start of Book 16, so there is no thematic surprise when he launches into Book 17 with the Romans engaged in full-scale war against the Carthaginians; but in terms of narrative logic, how that full-scale war developed out of fighting which appears to be primarily against Syracuse is left undetermined. The First Punic War, for him, is founded in the existential rivalry between two fundamentally opposed powers. This may well have been an aspect of Livy's treatment also—certainly his account of the Second Punic War draws on that motif (Levene (2010a), 235–6)—but Livy is naturally unlikely to have omitted the more mundane details of the war's development in the way that P. does.

Vulsinios: See 11.7n. The war is described in various sources, all in broadly similar terms (Val. Max. 9.1 ext. 2, Flor. 1.16, *Vir. Ill.* 36, Oros. 4.5.3–5, John of Antioch fr. 115 (Roberto), Zonar. 8.7.4–8; cf. Metrodorus of Scepsis *ap.* Plin., *Nat.* 34.34).[188] According to these, it began in 265 as a result of internal dissension: the Volsinians had manumitted and enfranchised their slaves, who had then seized political power at the expense of their former masters. The old aristocracy appealed for help to Rome, but when the ex-slaves discovered they had done so, they murdered them; at which point the Romans sent an army against Volsinii under the consul Q. Fabius Maximus Gurges. Fabius was, however, killed in battle, and the war was not completed until 264, under the consul M. Fulvius Flaccus, whose victory is recorded in a contemporary dedicatory inscription discovered in the Forum Boarium (Torelli (1968)), and who (according to the *Fasti Capitolini*) received a triumph; he destroyed the city, punished the offenders, and resettled the surviving inhabitants. The popularity of the story lay less in the fighting itself, and more in the moral of the dangers of aristocratic decadence and excessive leniency towards one's social inferiors: virtually all accounts focus on this aspect of it.[189]

---

[188] The only significant variation is in the name of the victor: Florus attributes the victory to Fabius Gurges himself, while in *Vir. Ill.* the victor is Decius Mus. But the epigraphic evidence proves that these are simply in error. Some have thought that a Decius Mus was sent out to command after Fabius was killed (e.g. Beloch, *RG* 459), but the *Fasti* do not appear to record a suffect consul that year (Degrassi 115), which in turn suggests that Fabius' death, if it really happened, occurred close to the end of the year, and that Fulvius took over the following year. The attribution to Decius is best explained by confusion with an earlier Decius' war against Volsinii in 308 (Livy 9.41.6: see Harris (1971), 83–4); less plausibly, Wiseman (1986), 95–9 = (1994), 44–7, suggests that it was the invention of an annalist hostile to the Fulvii Flaccones, and was partly enabled by the destruction of Fulvius' victory monument in a fire a generation later.

[189] Capozza (1997) suggests that the story developed in part out of anxieties over the increasingly prominent role of imperial freedmen under the Empire. While imperial authors may have seen the story in that light, her argument relies heavily on the fact that Valerius Maximus, the oldest surviving source, speaks only of slaves, and does not specifically refer to their being manumitted. This is likely to be the consequence of Valerius' abridgement rather than reflecting a transformation in the narrative, since Romans regularly spoke of freedmen as 'slaves', especially in disparaging contexts (Treggiari (1969), 265–6; cf. Plin., *Epist.* 8.6.4).

P. makes no mention of this, nor of the initial Roman failures, and this too (cf. 16.3n.) may be the consequence of how a war spreading between 265 and 264 relates to Livy's book-division. In all likelihood Livy narrated the opening of the war in 265, along with the death of Fabius Gurges, in Book 15, leaving its conclusion to Book 16: only thus could he fit it into a chronological narrative in which Book 16 began with Carthage, leading into the preliminaries of the Punic War. So P. could in theory have described the Volsinian crisis and Fabius' death in Book 15; but, even apart from his heavy abridgement of the book, that would not have fit so well the general pattern he was adopting there, which focuses on the consolidation of Roman power in Italy (15.1n.). Instead he ignores the first part of the story altogether, and here merely alerts the reader in passing to the Roman victory over Volsinii.

Book 17

17.1 *Capture of Cn. Cornelius*. Polybius tells the story rather differently (1.21.5–7): in his version Cornelius' capture was the consequence of (failed) deceit on his part rather than on the part of the Carthaginians. He was hoping to gain Lipara through treachery, but when he arrived there, he was bottled up in the harbour by the Carthaginian fleet and was forced to surrender to them. However, at 8.35.9 Polybius appears to hint at a different version, in which Cornelius was somehow betrayed by the Carthaginians. Probably this is the same as P.'s account of his being captured after being invited to negotiate, which is the version uniformly relayed through the rest of the historiographical tradition (e.g. Val. Max. 6.6.2, Flor. 1.18.11, App., *Pun.* 63, Polyaen. 6.16.5, Oros. 4.7.9, Zonar. 8.10.8–9). It is told with little variation, though occasionally with extra details added (so Appian, Polyaenus, and Zonaras relate that in order to lure Cornelius into the trap, the general feigned illness).[190]

Reconciling these versions is not difficult in principle: it is possible that Polybius was right to see the initial move as being Cornelius', and that he hoped to win Lipara through treachery, but that the other parts of the tradition rightly record that he was in his turn treacherously captured at the parlay. That is indeed how both Polyaenus and Zonaras tell the story (though with the additional twist—not in Polybius—that the supposed betrayal of Lipara was itself a Carthaginian trick), and Livy may have done the same. It is true that the claim of Carthaginian treachery looks like Roman propaganda, especially given that it accords so neatly with the hostile stereotype of them (cf. below), but it is also possible that Polybius' account derives from Carthaginian propaganda relayed to him through Philinus (so e.g. Walbank (1957), 76–7).[191] While we might regard Polybius as intrinsically

---

[190] There are a few other points where the sources differ. In Zonar. 8.10.8 Cornelius is not commander of the fleet, as in Polybius, but of the legions—but he decides to use the ships that transported him to Sicily in order to secure Lipara. Almost all scholars endorse Polybius; Bleckmann (2002), 129–31 prefers Zonaras' version, as it is supported by the Duilius inscription (below), which claims that Duilius was the first to outfit a fleet, implying that he was in charge of it from the start. But even if the inscription is genuine, little weight can be placed on so obviously self-promoting a claim, produced at a time when Duilius' colleague may well not have been around to object; and the consuls may in any case have shared in the work (Walbank (1957), 78, not contradicted by Polybius' text, *contra* Bleckmann (2002), 130).

The number of ships also varies slightly between the sources: Plb. 1.21.4 has seventeen, Appian twenty-two, Orosius sixteen—these are close enough that it is impossible to decide on grounds of plausibility, but here too it is certainly best to follow Polybius, as the earliest source, since numbers are so often corrupted in textual traditions.

[191] Less plausible is that it is pro-Scipionic propaganda from Polybius' sources in that family, aimed at minimizing his responsibility for the defeat, as argued by Bleckmann (2002), 134–8. This underestimates how far within the Roman tradition reliance on treachery was frowned on as a means of warfare (cf. Levene (2010a), 228–34), and, correspondingly, how willing the Romans might be in propagandistic contexts to show a commander defeated through falling into a treacherous trap.

more believable (cf. 16.2n.), that methodological principle cannot be readily applied to a case such as this, where Polybius tells both versions at different times.

Nevertheless, it is still preferable to reject the idea that Cornelius was captured through treachery—while both versions may be propagandistic, the one which appears to be constructed to fit a stereotype must be considered more dubious. But this conclusion is based on little more than a balance of probabilities, and cannot be seen as strongly founded.

As for P., he treats it simply as an instance of Carthaginian betrayal. If (as is not improbable) Livy narrated it as a case where the consul's own attempt at treachery was turned against him by Carthaginians who were more skilled in betrayal,[192] P., like others in the Latin tradition, selects only those parts of the story which make the Roman into a mere victim of perfidious Carthage.

Cn. Cornelius consul: Cn. Cornelius Scipio Asina,[193] consul in 260 (*RE* 341, *MRR* I 205). Nothing of his earlier career is known. Subsequent to the events here he must have been released by the Carthaginians (though Oros. 4.7.9 mistakenly claims he was killed), since he held the consulship again in 254, and received a triumph the following year (18.3n.), but this is his only appearance in P.

a classe: *a(b)* of agency is regularly used by Livy, like other writers, with nouns showing military units, such as *classis* (22.11.6, 23.34.3, 30.19.5) and *exercitus* (4.50.5, 6.33.11, 22.59.5, 32.22.10, 39.6.7): see W-M *ad* 27.31.3 for the implied personalization of the collective unit; P. employs it not only here, but also e.g. 4.10, 39.2, 54.5, 75.1, 83.5, 83.8.

et: The parataxis is contrary to P.'s usual manner of sentence construction (cf. 2.2n.). It creates a stronger sense of narrative movement, with two separate points of interest, rather than focusing attention on a single moment and providing the background. In general, the summary of this book has a clearer narrative line than most: it is one of the few which overtly follows chronological order throughout.

---

[192] Compare, for example, 22.16–17, where Fabius' attempt to outmanoeuvre Hannibal using Hannibal-like methods fails when Hannibal shows his superiority in that form of warfare; more generally see Levene (2010a), 300–10 for Livy's interest in showing military commanders' plans backfiring against them.

[193] The only ancient explanation for his *cognomen* is an anecdote of dubious historicity about a financial guarantee relayed in Macr., *Sat.* 1.6.29. In a highly speculative article in *Archiv für lateinische Lexicographie und Grammatik* VII (1892), 279–80, Eduard Wölfflin proposed that it in fact was given to him after his actions here, and was an insult derived from the idea that female asses avoid water, a myth relayed by Plin., *Nat.* 8.169. Wölfflin was cited approvingly by De Sanctis III.1 123 [126] n. 63, who misprinted the volume of the journal as VI; then by Thiel (1954), 181, who however placed the Pliny reference first as the source, and retained the misprint of the volume of Wölfflin from De Sanctis. Thiel's order seems to have misled later scholars: in citations by (e.g.) Walbank (1957), 76, Lazenby (1996), 67, Rankov (2011), 153, Beck (2013), 135 all reference to Wölfflin disappears, and 'Pliny, *Nat.* 8.169' is offered without comment, as if Pliny described the source of Asina's *cognomen*. No one reading that passage of Pliny could possibly relate it to Cn. Cornelius Scipio Asina in the absence of Wölfflin's speculative argument; but it does at least provide a useful object-lesson about the dangers of tralatician references, even when supplied by highly distinguished scholars.

per fraudem: A standard phrase (*TLL* VI 1276.14–38), used a few times by Livy (albeit only in his later books: 24.37.1, 33.29.3, 34.32.4, 35.7.4, 36.31.10), but only once elsewhere by P. (55.7). It is suggestive that *fraus* appears on the very first occasion when P. gives a description of fighting between Carthage and Rome, since it was viewed as an archetypal Carthaginian quality: see Burck (1943), Prandi (1979), Waldherr (2000), though cf. the more nuanced account of Gruen (2011), 115–40. Livy too regularly draws on that stereotype, referring a number of times to *Punica fraus* (22.48.1, 26.17.15, 27.33.9, 30.22.6; cf. e.g. 21.34.1, 31.11.13, 43.3.6), a phrase used in Orosius' account of Cornelius' capture (4.7.9; similarly Flor. 1.18.11 refers to *perfidia Punica*). At Levene (2010a), 216–21, 228–35 I argued that Livy is far more ambivalent and complex in his application of it than appears at first sight (cf. Gruen (2011), 113–14), but nothing of that ambivalence or complexity is apparent in P. (or indeed Florus or Orosius), who merely relays the stereotype.

veluti: For *velut* attached to a phrase to indicate deception cf. *OLD s.v. velut* 5c.

in conloquium evocatus: For *evocare* used with connotations of deception see *TLL* V.2 1055.51–68.

in conloquium evocare is found once in Livy (37.48.2), but *ad conloquium evocare* is far more common (1.1.7, 4.10.1, 21.25.7, 23.43.9, 25.28.3, 30.12.8, 31.27.3). The latter is also found occasionally in other writers (Caes., *Civ.* 3.16.3, and esp. Oros. 4.7.9, describing the same episode as here), but there is no other example of *in conloquium evocare* outside P. (though the related *in conloquium vocare* appears at Curt. 9.1.23 and Just. 6.1.3), who uses it once more (106.4), but never has *ad conloquium*. The distinction is that *ad conloquium* indicates the purpose for which the people were invited, leaving it open whether or not it took place, while *in conloquium* assumes that it did (cf. its common use, in Livy and elsewhere, with verbs of motion such as *ire* and *venire*): P. stresses that Claudius actually fell into the trap.

17.2 Victory of C. Duilius at Mylae. The fullest account of the battle is in Plb. 1.22–3; there are briefer versions in Flor. 1.18.7–9, Eutr. 2.20.1–2, *Vir. Ill.* 38.1, Oros. 4.7.7–10, Zonar. 8.11.1–3; cf. Frontin., *Strat.* 2.3.24. There are virtually no substantial differences between them: after the capture of Cornelius (17.1n.), Duilius took command of the fleet, and prepared his ships for battle, compensating for their sluggishness relative to those of the Carthaginians by constructing a device called a 'raven': a swinging spiked gangway attached to the front of the Roman ship, which enabled the Romans to immobilize and board the enemy ships.[194] He used these to devastating effect when he encountered the Carthaginians at Mylae,

---

[194] For the construction and logistics of the device: see e.g. Saint-Denis (1946), Thiel (1946), 432–47, (1954), 101–28, Poznanski (1979). Its historicity is questioned by Tarn (1907), 51; but see *contra* Thiel (1946), 437–43.

on the north-eastern coast of Sicily: according to Plb. 1.23.7–10, of the 130 ships in the Punic fleet, fifty were captured or destroyed, thirty (or thirty-one, depending on the interpretation of the text) being taken at the initial assault.[195]

Apart from the exploits of Regulus (17.6n., 18.1–2n., 18.5n.), no other episode in the First Punic War caught the imagination of later Romans as much as this victory. This was less because of the battle itself, and more because of what it signified, as the Romans, at least on their own account,[196] for the first time showed their mastery in a sphere that had hitherto been largely alien to them, and set themselves on the road to their overseas empire. This balance of interest is shared by P., who has nothing of the detail of the fighting, nor of the tactics through which Duilius achieved his victory. Instead he records the victory in a passing phrase and, like most others, focuses his attention instead on the honours that Duilius received in consequence (see below), which were a concrete demonstration of his remarkable significance in Roman history.

C. Duillius consul: Consul in 260 (*RE* 3, *MRR* I 205). His name is spelled 'Duilius' in the *Fasti*, which is probably correct. Most literary sources call him 'Duillius' (as P. does here) or 'Duellius', but those probably arise from a false etymology which connected the name with *duellum* = *bellum* (Münzer (1905)). Nothing is known of his prior career; subsequent to his consulship, he was censor in 258 and dictator for holding elections in 231, but this is his only appearance in P.

adversus classem...prospere pugnavit: See 2.6n.

primusque omnium Romanorum ducum: P. is, as often, interested in 'firsts' (11.5n.), but *omnium Romanorum ducum* lays unusual stress on the point. This is doubtless because, even among those less focused on the unprecedented than P. is, the fact that Duilius' victory marked Rome's first naval success was the single thing that was best known about him. The point is made repeatedly within the Latin tradition: it appears on the inscription on his *columna rostrata*, and as such may even go back to the creation of his image in his own lifetime (see below);[197] it is mentioned in the record of his triumph in the *Fasti Capitolini*, his *elogium* in the Forum Augustum (*CIL* I² p. 193 no. XI = VI 31611 = *ILS* 55), also Cic., *Cato*

---

[195] Other sources have slightly different numbers: D.S. 23.10.1 suggests that the Carthaginians had 200 ships; Oros. 4.7.10, far more implausibly, that Duilius' fleet was only thirty ships. For the Carthaginian losses, Orosius and Eutr. 2.20.2 agree that thirty-one ships were captured; Orosius has thirteen sunk, Eutropius fourteen.

[196] Various scholars have suggested that this image of Duilius as breaking new ground for Roman naval success is a construct of the Romans' own ideology, and that in fact they entered the Punic War far more adept and experienced at naval warfare than this image implies: so esp. Steinby (2007), esp. 29–77, 87–94; Ladewig (2014), esp. 94–103, Harris (2017). Nevertheless, as Ladewig acknowledges, even on this view the victory of Duilius was ground-breaking, in as much as for the first time a consul had an intimate connection with the creation and command of the Roman fleet (Ladewig (2014), 100); one may also add that, for all Steinby and Ladewig's arguments about the earlier development of the navy, there is no recorded (and probably no unrecorded) prior occasion when a Roman fleet was victorious in a major naval battle.

[197] See esp. Biggs (2017), 359–60, setting the inscription more broadly within Roman tradition, with the First Punic War as the moment when Romans wholeheartedly adopted the rhetoric of 'firstness'.

44, Val. Max. 3.6.4, Sen., *Brev. Vit.* 13.3, Plin., *Nat.* 34.20, Sil. 6.665–6, Tac., *Ann.* 2.49.1, Flor. 1.18.9, Jer., *Adv. Jovin.* 1.46. No surviving Greek writer, by contrast, mentions this: their interest is in Duilius' tactical acumen rather than his symbolic significance in the rise of Roman power.

navalis victoriae: For the genitive cf. Livy 33.37.10 (with W-M *ad loc.*), 38.49.4; and see *OLD s.v. triumphus* 2b. More common, however, is an adjectival expression: thus a triumph for a naval victory is usually a *navalis triumphus* (*OLD s.v. triumphus* 2e). It appears that a naval triumph was seen as distinct from other triumphs, but it is not clear how (if at all) this distinction was manifested in the ceremony, save that the beaks of the enemy's ships were presumably displayed: see Östenberg (2009), 46–50, Ladewig (2014), 251–62.

duxit triumphum: The usual phrase is *triumphum agere* (cf. *OLD s.v. triumphus* 2d), or else the verb *triumphare* is used: Livy invariably employs one or other of these. P., too, most commonly uses *triumphare*, and has *triumphum agere* at 19.1, 30.6, 116.1, 133.2; but he uses *triumphum ducere* both here and 105.1 (cf. 37.8n. for the even rarer *triumphum deducere*). This usage, apparently constructed on the analogy of phrases like *pompam ducere* (cf. *TLL* V.1 2142.7–19), was especially favoured by writers of the first century AD, notably Valerius Maximus (2.8.6, 2.8.7, 5.5.2, 6.9.9, 8.1 damn. 1, 8.15.8) and Lucan (3.20, 9.598–9, 10.63, 10.152); also e.g. Sen., *Cons. Polyb.* 13.2, Plin., *Nat.* 7.98, 34.14, Sil. 3.615, 6.662, Mart. 9.101.19. It is occasionally found in later antiquity (e.g. Claud., *Rapt. Pros.* 3.329, Petr. Chrys., *Serm.* 154.2), but it seems likely that, while not (on the available evidence) being Livian, for P. it had the general flavour of early imperial Latin.

ei perpetuus quoque honos habitus est: The honour cited here by P. is widely recorded: it is mentioned on the *elogium* in the Forum Augustum (above), Cic., *Cato* 44, Val. Max. 3.6.4, Sil. 6.667–9, Flor. 1.18.10, *Vir. Ill.* 38.4, Amm. 26.3.5. However, the reason for it and the interpretation vary. Cicero, Valerius Maximus, Florus, and Ammianus all indicate that it was Duilius' own decision to do this, not an honour granted to him by the state, whereas the *elogium* and *Vir. Ill.* say the opposite: that it was an official honour. The latter is also implied by P.'s use of the passive, as well as (perhaps) by Silius' reference to it as an *honos*. On balance it is perhaps more likely to have been Duilius' own initiative (so Powell (1988), 193, *contra* Kondratieff (2004), 6), although the fact that he was not prevented from acting in this way constituted at least tacit official endorsement.

As for the interpretation, Florus explains its significance as being 'as if he triumphed daily' (*quasi cotidie triumpharet*), but being accompanied by a torch and flute-players was an honour given to magistrates in general (Mommsen, *StR* I³ 367, 423–4), not the *triumphator* in particular:[198] this is implicit in Cicero, who

---

[198] Florus' interpretation may have been influenced by the practice (sporadic in the Republic but increasingly used by Roman emperors) of the *triumphator* wearing triumphal dress on subsequent occasions (cf. Beard (2007), 272–7).

indicates that what was distinctive was the fact that Duilius continued with it even after he became a *privatus*. Likewise *quoque* in P. contradicts Florus' version: this was an extra honour independently commemorating the victory, not a reminiscence of the victory at second hand via a recreation of the triumph (Roller (2009), 223).

An additional honour not mentioned by P. was that Duilius had a *columna rostrata* (sc. a column decorated with the beaks of the enemy ships) set up in the Forum (Plin., *Nat.* 34.20, Sil. 6.663–4, Quint., *Inst.* 1.7.12, Serv., *Georg.* 3.29; cf. Livy 42.20.1).[199] Substantial fragments from the inscription on this column survive (*CIL* I² p. 384 = VI 1300 = *ILS* 65 = *ILLRP* 319). The inscription is in archaic Latin, but the surviving stone dates from the early imperial period: it is disputed whether what survives is a reinscription of an original composed in the third or early second century (so e.g. Wölfflin (1890), Frank (1919), Niedermann (1936), Degrassi (1937), 47–8, Bleckmann (2002), 116–25, Kondratieff (2004), 11–14), or an archaizing forgery of the early first century AD (so e.g. Mommsen, *CIL* 12 p. 386, Fay (1920), Wachter (1987), 359–61). Much of the argument turns on technicalities of early Latin which I am unqualified to judge. From a narrative point of view, the inscription, like much of the literary tradition (cf. above), lays great stress on the fact that Duilius was the first to succeed at naval warfare. This implies that it may have been written later, since it was only in retrospect that its full significance can have become apparent (Degrassi (1937), 47; *contra* Kondratieff (2004), 12); but that is still compatible with its having been set up before the mid-second century, perhaps even in Duilius' lifetime, since he seems to have lived for a good forty years or so after his victory (Cic., *Cato* 44).

Whenever the inscription was written, it remained as a public point of reference for Duilius' victory throughout the imperial period, reinforcing his foundational role in Roman military success: the monument on which it appeared was directly imitated by others, including one set up by Augustus to a naval victory of his own not far from Mylae (Hölkeskamp (2001), 112–13, Roller (2009), 221–3, (2013), 120–6). However, while the inscription's narrative broadly matches the historians', the existence of the monument, despite its visibility within the Forum, is not something that P. or any other surviving historian felt it necessary to mention: it did not carry the resonance of the unique procession that followed Duilius' daily activities for the rest of his life.

revertenti a cena tibicine canente: Val. Max. 3.6.4 adds a lyre-player to the performers, but this is probably merely an error. The phrase in P. is elegantly constructed, with the interlocking treble assonance *revertenti...canente*, *revertenti...tibicine* and *cena tibicine canente*, which together provide an onomatopoeic representation of Duilius' musical accompaniers, as well as a play on the common ancient etymology which derived *tibicen* from *canere* (Maltby (1991), 611).

---

[199] It was probably also mentioned on the Forum Augustum *elogium* (above): see Degrassi (1937), 20.

funale: 'A torch of wax- or tallow-soaked rope' (*OLD*). The word is corrupted in the earliest MSS, but corrected in the later.

17.3 *Victory of L. Scipio in Sardinia and Corsica*. No detailed account of these events survives. The only one with even moderate pretensions to a full narrative is Zonar. 8.11.7. On his account, Scipio began his campaign by attacking Corsica and capturing Aleria. He then sailed to Sardinia; *en route* he encountered a Carthaginian fleet, which however fled without fighting him. Scipio proceeded to Sardinia, and reached Olbia, but there the Carthaginian ships once again appeared, and it was Scipio's turn to flee back to Italy, since he felt that he had insufficient infantry to fight them.

Zonaras thus differs from P. on a number of counts: he has no indication that Scipio achieved any sort of victory in Sardinia, let alone that he was successful against the Carthaginians there (quite the contrary). Zonaras' version is supported (at least implicitly) by the earliest reference to these events, namely Scipio's *elogium* (*ILS* 3 = *CIL* VI 1287 = *ILLRP* 311), which mentions only his victory in Corsica and at Aleria, and refers to neither Sardinia nor the Carthaginians. P.'s account, on the other hand, appears to be confirmed by the *Fasti*, which record a triumph for Scipio over Sardinians and Carthaginians as well as Corsicans. It is also the version found elsewhere in the Latin tradition, which consistently talks about his victories in Corsica and Sardinia side by side with one another (so Flor. 1.18.15–16, Eutr. 2.20.3, Oros. 4.8.11), or even highlights his victories in Sardinia over those in Corsica: so e.g. Val. Max. 5.1.2 (describing his generous treatment of Hanno's corpse after the latter had fallen in battle in Sardinia), Sil. 6.671-2, Frontin., *Strat.* 3.9.4 (mistakenly calling him Rufinus), 3.10.2. Frontinus moreover offers a point of contact between the more common tradition and that of Zonaras, since he refers to Scipio fleeing, but only as a feint to mislead the enemy; but that may well merely be a secondary elaboration by someone who noted the discrepancy between the two versions.

There does not appear to be any ready way of reconciling these. It seems reasonably certain that the Carthaginian fleet in Zonaras, before which Scipio withdrew, was that of Hannibal, who, according to Plb. 1.24.5–7, came to Sardinia after his defeat at Mylae, only to be defeated by the Romans in 258 (e.g. Eliæson (1906), 53–5, De Sanctis III.1 128–9 [132], Thiel (1954), 195, Walbank (1957), 80–1; cf. 17.5n.). The commander of the defeated Carthaginians in P. is Hanno (also Valerius Maximus, Orosius: see below), so it is theoretically possible that this represents a different army altogether, and that Scipio defeated Hanno but then withdrew before Hannibal (so e.g. Leuze (1910), 418–19). However, this still leaves unresolved the discrepancy between the *elogium* and the *Fasti*, as well as Zonaras' clear statement that the reason Scipio withdrew was because his forces were insufficient for a land battle, which is incompatible with his obtaining any sort of victory in Sardinia as described in the Latin sources (Bleckmann (2002), 149).

Either the *elogium* or the *Fasti* would usually be considered good evidence for the events of the war: it is uncomfortable when they disagree. It is possible that the *elogium* simply omitted the part of Scipio's victory that covered the fighting in Sardinia and against Carthage, perhaps because it was the Corsican victory alone which prompted the dedication of a temple to the Tempestates described in its next line (cf. Ov., *Fast.* 6.193-4), or perhaps because the Sardinian victory seemed with hindsight less decisive to those who erected the inscription after Scipio's death (Leuze (1910), 420-3; *contra* Bleckmann (2002), 149-50). But even given these considerations, it seems implausible that Scipio's victory over a strategically less significant enemy would be highlighted to the exclusion of the Carthaginians themselves. It may also be noteworthy that Polybius pays no attention to any of the campaigns of 259. He says that nothing of note happened in Sicily (1.24.8), and ignores the island campaign altogether: the more that Scipio accomplished, the more unlikely it is that Polybius would have omitted it so completely.

So in this case it is more likely that it is the *Fasti* which is in error (e.g. Eliæson (1906), 48-9, Debergh (1989), 46-55; *contra* Leuze (1910), 407-19): that the compilers of the triumphal record, perhaps precisely on the basis of the historical tradition, expanded a genuine triumph over the Corsicans into one which encompassed the Sardinians and Carthaginians also, although they were not in fact defeated until the following year. On this account, the circumstantial versions of Scipio's activities in Sardinia in the Latin historians are false (Bleckmann (2002), 148-9). In part (especially the part concerning the death of Hanno, who is more likely to have survived: see below) it is probably the product of invention within Scipio's family tradition (so Eliæson (1906), 46). But it is likely that it is also in part because some of the victories achieved by the obscure C. Sulpicius Paterculus in the following year (cf. 17.5n.) have been transferred to a better-known figure. Zonar. 8.12.4-6 (rightly) ascribed the Roman success in Sardinia to Sulpicius (though Zonaras has the success as only a temporary one: cf. below), as did Plb. 1.24.6-7, albeit only implicitly; the bulk of the historical tradition (wrongly) ascribed it solely to Scipio. Only P. and Orosius (4.7.11 and 4.8.4) have both victories in Sardinia (and even they focus on the defeated Hannibal rather than the victor, and do not mention Sulpicius by name); presumably both likewise stood in Livy.[200] This is therefore probably a doublet in Livy:[201] faced with sources offering a victory for Sulpicius in 258, and ones which (wrongly) transferred it to Scipio in 259, he incorporated both into his narrative.

If this sequence of events is accepted, the question remains as to what brought the Romans to campaign in Corsica and Sardinia in the first place. Zonar. 8.10.1 says that the Carthaginians had sent reinforcements there in 262 to use as a base

---

[200] Cf. Lippold (1954), 264-5.

[201] Far more plausible than the converse suggestion of Meltzer (1896), 566: that the omission of Scipio's campaign from Polybius is because he mistakenly believed it a doublet of the later one. This accounts for neither the representation of the events in the *elogium* nor the discrepancy with Zonaras.

for attacking Italy: Plb. 1.20.7 suggests that such coastal raids on Italy did indeed take place. If so, then it would have seemed a natural move to the Romans, after achieving relative success in Sicily, to challenge the Carthaginians there also, the more so if they could begin by establishing a base of their own in Corsica.[202] Call., *Del.* 4.19 and Plb. 1.10.5 show that Corsica was under Carthaginian control at this time,[203] but the occupation may have been limited in extent then (Eliæson (1906), 40–1, Debergh (1989), 44–5), leaving it a relatively easy target. Certainly little archaeological evidence has been found for Carthaginian occupation, apart from coins (perhaps used to pay mercenaries), although at Aleria itself there is evidence that it was destroyed during the third century, which may be the result of the sack by Rome (Debergh (1989), 42–4).

L. Cornelius consul: L. Cornelius Scipio (*RE* 323, *MRR* I 206); he was son of L. Cornelius Scipio Barbatus, and brother of the unfortunate consul of the previous year (17.1n.). His *elogium* (*ILS* 2–3 = *ILLRP* 311 = *CIL* VI 1286–7) records that he held the censorship and aedileship, the former in the year following his consulship, according to the *Fasti Capitolini*; but this is his sole appearance in P.

Sardos et Corsos: See 20.4n.

Hannonem: Hanno was a relatively common Carthaginian name (cf. Levene (2010a), 63, 67), which makes it hard to identify this one, and to rule definitively on his identity or otherwise with other Hannos at the time. Twelve Hannos are recorded in the twenty-five-year span of the First Punic War and its immediate aftermath: (1) The commander of the Carthaginian garrison in Messana, who was crucified after being forced to abandon the city (Zonar. 8.8.6, 8.9.1–4; cf. Plb. 1.11.5); (2) The commander who sought to relieve Agrigentum from the Roman siege in 262 (Plb. 1.18.7–19.7, Oros. 4.7.5, Zonar. 8.10.2–6), and was defeated by the Romans at Ecnomus in 256 (Plb. 1.27–8; cf. Oros. 4.8.5, cf. 17.6n.). Diodorus appears implicitly to identify him with the commander who fought Ap. Claudius at Messana, whom he describes as the son of Hannibal (23.1.2–4, cf. 23.8.1); he further states that after his failure at Agrigentum he was fined and disgraced by the Carthaginians (23.9.2). (3) Our commander here, who was (allegedly) defeated and killed by the Romans in Sardinia in 259 (cf. Val. Max. 5.1.2, Oros. 4.7.11). (4) According to Zonar. 8.12.6, in 258 a Hanno ultimately defeated Sulpicius after the latter's earlier successes in Sardinia. (5) According to D.S. 23.12 (cf. Zonar. 8.12.9), Hanno son of Hamilcar led the embassy to Regulus after his invasion of Africa (cf. 18.1–2n.). (6) The commander who defended Carthage at the time of Regulus' invasion (Zonar. 8.12.10). (7), (8) According to Oros. 4.9.7

---

[202] Cf. Loreto (2007), 56–7, 102–4.

[203] Walbank (1957), 59–60 claims that Polybius was mistaken, and that the Carthaginians did not have a presence in Corsica; but he appears to have missed the support offered by Callimachus, whose hymn is probably to be dated between 275 and 261, perhaps earlier rather than later in that period, but still barely a decade before the beginning of the First Punic War (Mineur (1984), 16–18).

(cf. 18.3n.), the Romans fought two Hannos in Africa in 255. (9) According to Zonar. 8.15.13, a commander captured at Lilybaeum by P. Claudius Pulcher in 249 (cf. 19.2n.). (10) The commander of the Carthaginians at their defeat at the Aegates Islands in 242 (Plb. 1.60, D.S. 24.11.1): cf. 19.9n. (11) The commander in Africa at the time of the Mercenary War (Plb. 1.67, D.S. 24.10; cf. Plb. 1.73.1), who shared the command against the Mercenaries (Plb. 1.73-74, 1.81.1, 1.82.1, 1.87, 1.88.4). (12) The commander sent to Sardinia to fight the Mercenaries there, who was betrayed and crucified by his own troops (Plb. 1.79.3-4).

It is possible that all of these are different people, but various attempts have been made to suggest that some of them are identical. Most plausible is that (3) and (4) are the same man, and that there is simply a variance between the sources as to whether he was killed, as in the circumstantial (but probably fictional) account supplied by the Latin historians, or whether he survived and was ultimately victorious, as in Zonaras (so e.g. Eliæson (1906), 77, De Sanctis III.1 129, 132 [132, 135]; *contra* Meltzer (1896), 284, Lenschau (1912b)).

All other identifications, however, are more or less arbitrary: given how common the name was, and the lack of prosopographical information from which to construct Carthaginian careers, there are rarely strong reasons to assume any particular identities in the absence of clear indications in the ancient sources. So, for example, Hanno (4) is widely assumed to be the same as (2) (so e.g. Lenschau (1912a), Walbank (1957), 144, but see *contra* Eliæson (1906), 77-80, De Sanctis III.1 132 [135]), which implies that either he recovered from his disgrace after Agrigentum very quickly, or Diodorus' report of his punishment is false. De Sanctis III.1 386 [397] proposed an identification between (4) and (12); this was rejected by Walbank (1957), 144, but Walbank failed to note that his grounds for rejecting it depended on his own no less arbitrary claim that (4) and (2) were the same man (which De Sanctis had denied). De Sanctis III.1 183 [186], on no better evidence, identified (2) and (10) (cf. Lenschau (1912a); *contra* Walbank (1957), 125).

17.4 *Heroic deed of M. Calpurnius.* According to the brief narratives of the Romans' Sicilian campaign in 258 found in Plb. 1.24.9-13, D.S. 23.9.4-5, Flor. 1.18.12, *Vir. Ill.* 39.1-2, and Zonar. 8.11.10-12.3, they fought at a number of cities, capturing several of them (though the precise details vary between the sources). P., however, ignores this entirely, singling out instead a well-known exemplary anecdote about a heroic military tribune who rescued the Romans from a disastrous situation. This story is first found in Cato, *Orig.* (*FRHist* 5 F 76, *ap.* Gell. 3.7.1-20),[204] and it is cited as an *exemplum* by Livy himself at 22.60.11; also Claudius Quadrigarius (*FRHist* 24 F 42-3, *ap.* Gell. 3.7.21, 1.7.9), Sen., *Epist.*

---

[204] Cf. Cic., *Cato* 75 and *Tusc.* 1.101, citing Cato's *Origines* (*FRHist* 5 F 114) on Roman legions being willing to go to their deaths. Cornell, *FRHist* III 143 (cf. Powell (1988), 251) argues that this is an unrelated fragment of Cato; but Cicero's wording is closely mirrored by Seneca, who, although he

82.22–3, Plin., *Nat.* 22.11, Frontin., *Strat.* 1.5.15 (= 4.5.10), Flor. 1.18.13–14, Ampel. 20.5, *Vir. Ill.* 39.3–4, Oros. 4.8.1–5, Zonar. 8.12.1–3.

The story is told with only minor variants (cf. also below); when the Romans were caught in a trap during an attempt to attack Camarina (*Vir. Ill.* mistakenly has Catina), the tribune came to the commander and proposed a sally with a small detachment to draw the enemy away from the main army. All were killed, except for the tribune himself, who was left for dead, but survived.[205] The attraction of the story was the key lesson on how individual interests must be sacrificed to protect the collective, and the illustration of a past in which such self-sacrifice appeared to be the norm (cf. P.'s highlighting of a similar story at 7.11n.). That lesson mattered to P., as to other writers, far more than temporary Roman successes or failures in battles and sieges; he moreover emphasizes this as a key moral by eliding the fact (presumably present in Livy, as in most other sources) that Calpurnius survived, which would be at best irrelevant to and at worst could undermine the impression made by his heroic willingness to die for his country.[206]

Orosius' version, though fuller than P.'s, has a number of linguistic overlaps with it: *temere... deduxit exercitum, virtute et opera,* and *in se... convertit,* and also a clause (*qui lecta trecentorum manu insessum ab hostibus tumulum occupavit* taken verbatim from Florus): the most probable explanation is that Orosius constructed his account out of both (see Introduction).

Atilius Calatinus cos.: Consul in 258 (*RE* 36, *MRR* I 206). His name is invariably given in the *Fasti* as A. Atilius Caiatinus (Degrassi 115–16), but in literary sources 'Calatinus' is generally used. Both names are derived from Campanian towns, Caiatia and Calatia; for this reason it seems more likely that Caiatinus is correct, since Calatia was later better known, so it is more likely that the name would be 'corrected' to that (Münzer (1999 (1920), 401, *MRR* I 207). The MSS of P. in fact give the name here as Calasinus, and as Calanus at 19.3, but in both places it is best corrected to the form in which it most commonly appears in the literary tradition.

Nothing of his earlier career is known. Subsequent to his consulship here, he retained command in Sicily in the following year (probably as praetor: so *MRR* I 208, Brennan (2000), 80–3, *contra* Thiel (1954), 201–2, Develin (1975), 720, who argue that he was proconsul), in which capacity he received a triumph. He held

---

does not give the name, can in context hardly be talking about anything else. This makes it highly likely that Cicero's citation of Cato, though generalized, is a further reference to the story here.

[205] Its historicity is doubted by Lazenby (1996), 75–6, and like almost anything else recorded at this period, it could indeed be a fiction. But Lazenby's argument is partly that the 300 troops are suspiciously close to Thermopylae: that number is demonstrably a later development in the story (see below), and gives no reason to question the core account.

[206] Ampelius explicitly—and revealingly—states that he did die, which indicates the 'natural' form one might expect for the story, and perhaps also is driven by the comparison with Leonidas at Thermopylae, which Ampelius, like others, makes explicitly (see below). Florus, while acknowledging that Calpurnius, unlike Leonidas, survived, claims that this was to his credit, though it is not clear why he thinks this follows.

a further consulship in 254, in which he captured Panormus, a dictatorship in 249 (see 19.3n.: Florus wrongly attributes his activities here to his dictatorship),[207] and the censorship in 247 (19.5n.). Although he is not now a name to conjure with, Cicero appears to have admired him greatly, and repeatedly refers to him as an exemplary figure of the Roman past (esp. *Cato* 61, *Fin.* 2.116–17; also e.g. *Pis.* 14, *Planc.* 60, *Rep.* 1.1, *Tusc.* 1.110, *Nat. Deor.* 2.165).

cum: See 2.2n.

temere: *temere* is one of Livy's favourite descriptive adverbs. P., by contrast, uses it far less often, only here and in 48.10 and 49.9. These last two are the most expansive of P.'s summaries and, accordingly, may be argued to be the most likely to reproduce Livy's phrasing. This makes it moderately likely that P. here too is reflecting Livy's own vocabulary.

M. Calpurni: His name is given in almost all sources as M. Calpurnius Flamma (*RE* 42). The exception is the two earliest to survive, namely Cato and Claudius Quadrigarius, the former of whom, it appears from Gellius, called him Q. Caedicius (*RE* 7),[208] the latter Laberius (*RE* 1: Frontinus records all three variants). The most likely reason for the variation is that it floated as a popular story of heroism independently of the name of the hero, and various families claimed it for their own ancestors. The name Calpurnius may have entered the historical tradition through Piso Frugi (Calboli (1996), 1); the reason that Livy preferred it may be because of that family's greater prominence at the time he was writing. It is doubtless because of Livy that this version prevailed in the subsequent tradition.

CCC militibus: In Cato the number of troops is 400; all later sources have 300. The change is likely to have been contamination from the story of the 300 Spartans at Thermopylae. Cato himself explicitly compares the two (see esp. Krebs (2006), Popov-Reynolds (2010), 173–81), and later both Florus and Ampelius do the same, while Seneca implicitly links the two stories by citing them side by side (cf. also Cic., *Tusc.* 1.101). Indeed, it may have been Cato's own (rather sour)

---

[207] See Leuze (1911), 555–6 for an intriguing and ingenious explanation of Florus' error: he is structuring the narrative around the geographical expansion of Roman power, and wants a discrete sequence of heroes with whom to associate each moment of conquest, so he prefers to associate the victories here with Caiatinus' ground-breaking dictatorship.

[208] The name does not appear in the fairly extensive quotation and summary of Cato's narrative, but only in Gellius' opening and closing notes. From this, most conclude (e.g. Astin (1978), 232–3, Cornell, *FRHist* III 121–2, Popov-Reynolds (2010), 181–2; *contra* Calboli (1996), 5–12) that the name was avoided by Cato, in line with his practice of excluding the names of Roman leaders from his history (Nep., *Cato* 3.4, Plin., *Nat.* 8.11). But Gellius seems clear that Cato specifically offered this name, since he goes on to comment (3.7.21) that Claudius Quadrigarius used a different one; and Nepos and Pliny attest only that Cato excluded the names of *commanders* (*duces* in Nepos, *imperatores* in Pliny)—but Caedicius was not a commander. For that reason it seems likely that Caedicius' name appeared in Cato, even if not in the surviving extract. It should be noted that Gellius indicates that only the second half of the extract is taken verbatim from Cato (even though the first half is likely to follow his wording to a considerable degree: see Astin (1978), 238, Cornell, *FRHist* III 121–2): the omission of Caedicius' name in that part of the story could therefore even be because Gellius decided to omit it (he had, after all, already mentioned it in his introduction, so it was superfluous to him, as it might not have been to Cato himself).

citation of the two in parallel which influenced later writers to accentuate the parallel by changing the numbers, since the stories are not especially close in terms of the military circumstances (cf. Calboli (1996), 12, *contra* T. J. Cornell, *FRHist* III 121): the link consists largely in the moral they illustrate, since both show an elite band of soldiers deliberately facing death for the greater good.

17.5 *Defeat and crucifixion of Hannibal.* No source has more than a summary account of this story: apart from P., it is found in Plb. 1.24.5-6, Oros. 4.8.4, and Zonar. 8.12.4-5 (cf. Dio fr. 43.32b). Only Zonaras names the victorious Roman commander, C. Sulpicius Paterculus, though his victory is confirmed by the *Fasti Capitolini*.[209] According to Zonaras, Sulpicius, after successfully campaigning in Sardinia as consul in 258, sought to attack Africa. Hannibal launched his own fleet in defence, but both were turned back to Sardinia by the weather. Sulpicius then lured Hannibal into a trap by feigning another crossing to Africa,[210] and defeated his fleet, capturing those ships that reached land. Hannibal abandoned his ships and escaped to Sulci, where he was killed by his own men. The other sources mention only Hannibal's defeat and execution by his troops, though Polybius notes that it was after he was 'blockaded by the Romans in a harbour' (1.24.6: συγκλεισθεὶς ὑπὸ τῶν Ῥωμαίων ἔν τινι λιμένι), which is not hard to reconcile with Zonaras' slightly more detailed account.

P.'s interest in the Carthaginian commander rather than his Roman conqueror is thus of a piece with the general effacing of Sulpicius in the Roman tradition. It is nevertheless slightly surprising that he should have chosen to focus on the death of an enemy, rather than omitting the matter altogether. This may be because it was highlighted in Livy, but P. changes Livy's emphases so often that this can hardly be an adequate explanation. More important may be that it illustrated a common Roman 'proof' of Carthaginian cruelty:[211] their unforgiving attitudes towards their defeated commanders (for the stereotype cf. Livy 22.61.15):[212] that image, with the implicit contrast with and self-flattery for

---

[209] Plb. 1.24.9-13 seems mistakenly to place Sulpicius' campaign entirely in Sicily; this is in part a consequence of his chronological arrangement, since he brings the story of Hannibal to a close before returning to the consuls of the previous year, so never relates his defeat and death to any specific Roman campaign (cf. Leuze (1910), 423-9).

[210] Zonaras actually names the other consul, Caiatinus, at this point; this is generally assumed to be an error (e.g. Debergh (1989), 55, Lazenby (1996), 77), but Bleckmann (2002), 154-6 defends the idea that Caiatinus was involved in the purported crossing, though Sulpicius achieved the victory. On the assumption that Zonaras meant Sulpicius, it has been widely doubted that he can have planned two crossings to Africa, one genuine, one fake: for attempts to construct the story in such a way as to preserve its main features while only having the Romans and Carthaginians put to sea once, see e.g. Thiel (1954), 197-8, Lazenby (1996), 77.

[211] On the Greco-Roman image of the Carthaginians as a barbarically cruel people see e.g. Waldherr (2000), 206-7, 215-16, though he does not discuss this specific aspect of it.

[212] At 38.48.13 Livy goes further, and claims that even victorious commanders might be executed by the Carthaginians if they were felt to have acted imprudently (cf. Val. Max. 2.7 ext. 1). This seems highly implausible, and no actual examples are known, but it does show how extreme the Romans assumed Carthaginian practices to be.

Rome, did not lose its impact even though the Carthaginian empire had long vanished.

Hannibal: *RE* 3: according to Zonar. 8.10.2, he was son of Gisgo. He had commanded the garrison in Agrigentum at the time of the Roman siege (16.6n.), but escaped the city (Plb. 1.18.7–19.12); subsequently he was also the commander who trapped Cornelius Scipio Asina (Plb. 1.21.6–8: cf. 17.1n.) and then was defeated at Mylae by Duilius (Plb. 1.23.4–7: cf. 17.2n.). In the Roman exemplary tradition he was best known for the story of how he (allegedly) avoided punishment after Mylae by informing the Carthaginian senate of the position before the battle and asking their permission to fight, only revealing the result once they had agreed with his decision (D.S. 23.10.1, Val. Max. 7.3 ext. 7, Dio fr. 43.18, cf. Zonar. 8.11.4, *Vir. Ill.* 38.2–3 [calling him Himilco]).

a militibus suis: Lazenby (1996), 26, 76 suggests that it was his officers who did this. This is compatible with Polybius, who speaks of him being 'seized' (συλληφθείς), a word which he often—but not invariably (cf. e.g. 38.17.2)—employs in the context of an official or quasi-official arrest (*Polybios-Lexikon* III.1 193). But it is less compatible with the other sources, all of whom imply a more general mutiny. Given how vague even Polybius is here, it is methodologically unsound to reject the later sources on the basis of his wording, though of course they too might well be in error.

in crucem sublatus: The phrase is standard (*TLL* IV 1256.76–84): it is used by Livy at 22.13.9, 30.43.13, 38.48.13. Polybius has the same method of killing; in Orosius the troops stone him to death, while Zonaras does not specify it. Crucifixion was a sufficiently common punishment at Carthage (not least for defeated generals) to make it likely that it was used here, though it is naturally also possible that this very fact is what influenced the Greek and Roman historians to assume its use even without actual evidence.

17.6 *Regulus' invasion of Africa.* A textual oddity with this notice is that the MSS place it in different books: N, along with some of the Renaissance MSS, puts it at the end of Book 17, P and others of the Renaissance MSS at the beginning of Book 18. The overwhelming probability is that N is correct: it would not fit the author's usual practice to repeat a character's full name in consecutive notices in the same book.

Assuming that the notice does indeed belong here, P.'s narrative sequence here involves some misdirection—perhaps deliberate misdirection—of his better-informed readers. So far the book has listed in order the events of 260, 259, and 258, identifying each year by at least one consul; one might naturally expect that we would now reach 257, when indeed Atilius Regulus was consul, and achieved a naval victory at Tyndaris and a triumph (Plb. 1.25.1–4; also *Fasti Capitolini*; cf. *MRR* I 207). However, the Atilius Regulus who was consul in 257 was not the famous M. Atilius Regulus, but his less-famous relative[213] C. Atilius Regulus; and it cannot be the latter that P. is referring to, as is made clear by the words *in Africam traiecit*. P. thus at the end of the sentence corrects the mistake readers might have made on reading its opening: he has skipped over 257 completely, and instead has moved to the following year.

P. thus still retains the strictly chronological movement of the book (cf. 17.1n.), but ends it—as Livy too must have done—on an unresolved note: the outcome of Regulus' expedition will await the following book.

Atilius Regulus cos.: For Regulus see F 9n. P. introduces him for the first time here, at the start of his famous (if ultimately disastrous) expedition against Carthage, which will be his focus in his summary of Book 18. For the form of name used here see 4.4n.

victis navali proelio Poenis: The battle took place at Ecnomus, on the southern coast of Sicily. By far the fullest account is in Polybius (1.26–8); briefer versions include Zonar. 8.12.8–9 (cf. Dio fr. 43.19). As Polybius describes it, the Romans, commanded by both consuls, Regulus and his colleague L. Manlius Vulso Longus, were seeking to cross to attack Africa, but they were intercepted by the Carthaginians. The Carthaginians drew out the Roman ships in front away from the rest, and fought them separately, while the other Roman ships were attacked from the wings and behind. The front group eventually overcame the Carthaginians, once again using the 'ravens' (17.2n.), and were able to come to the aid of the others and between them defeat the enemy. According to Polybius, the Carthaginians lost more than thirty ships, with sixty-four captured, while the Romans lost twenty-four with none captured.[214]

On Polybius' account (1.25.7–26.9), 680 ships and nearly 300,000 men were involved. Various people have argued that these figures are exaggerated estimates, and the true numbers were probably around two-thirds of these (so e.g. Tarn (1907), 52–4, De Sanctis III.1 134–6 [137–9], Thiel (1954), 209–12, 215–17, Walbank (1957), 82–6; but see *contra* Tipps (1985), 433–45, Lazenby (1996), 82–7). Nevertheless, even the lesser figure puts the battle on an epic scale, one of the largest ancient battles known. Despite this, P., like most other writers (e.g. Flor. 1.18.17–19, Eutr. 2.21.1, Oros. 4.8.6–7), is less interested in it in its own right, and treats it only as a prelude to the adventuresome crossing to Africa.

Detailed studies of the battle include Thiel (1954), 116–20, 209–23, Tipps (1985), Lazenby (1996), 81–96. Scholarly controversy has focused particularly on the wedge-formation which Polybius describes the Romans adopting prior to the battle, which has been claimed to be unfeasible (e.g. De Sanctis III.1 136–7

---

[213] Zonar. 8.15.8 describes them as brothers, but this appears to be an error, since their grandfathers in the *Fasti* have different *praenomina*.

[214] Eutr. 2.21.1 has the total Carthaginian losses as sixty-four ships (perhaps through misunderstanding a source), and the Roman as twenty-two ships; Oros. 4.8.6 similarly speaks of sixty-four Carthaginian ships lost.

[140], Thiel (1954), 119–20); but see *contra* e.g. Tipps (1985), 446–52, Lazenby (1996), 87–9.

in Africam traiecit: The crossing and initial landing are described in detail by Plb. 1.29 (cf. also e.g. D.S. 23.11, Flor. 1.18.17–19, Zonar. 8.12.11): the Romans landed at Aspis (called Clupea in Latin), capturing it and using it as a base to ravage the country. Messages from the Senate then recalled Manlius to Rome, where (according to the *Fasti Capitolini*) he celebrated a triumph. Manlius' departure was at the beginning of winter (so Zonar. 8.13.1; but see further 18.1n.); Regulus remained in Africa.

Book 18

18.1–2 *Regulus in Africa*. Regulus dominates P.'s account of Book 18, as he may well also have done in Livy's original book. P. opens and closes the book (cf. 18.5n.) with unusually elaborate sentences in which he summarizes the key features of the story, and offers explicit and implicit judgements on the moral that the reader might draw from it.

Two features of P.'s account of Regulus' campaign and capture are especially noteworthy. First, by comparison with other sources, P. offers virtually no military detail: nothing more is said about the initial Roman successes over the Carthaginians than that they occurred, nor is there any indication of the tactical acumen and leadership shown by Xanthippus which enabled him to achieve victory.

Second, while Regulus is explicitly treated as an *exemplum* of the vicissitudes of fortune, and hence as a potentially ambivalent figure in that respect, there is no hint in P. that he himself illustrated severe moral failings in his campaign, although those form a major part of the historical tradition. These failings are especially associated with his negotiations with Carthage following his victories. The sources dispute whether the initiative for those negotiations came from the Carthaginians or from Regulus himself, but it is universally accepted that Regulus badly mishandled them, and did so out of misplaced arrogance and self-confidence:[215] although the Carthaginians were receptive to a deal, he offered them such harsh terms that they balked and instead returned to fight, thus opening the door to Regulus' own defeat and capture, not to mention prolonging the war for another fourteen years.

Livy himself appears, not surprisingly, to have shared this widespread ambivalence towards Regulus. Regulus is cited three times in his surviving history as an *exemplum*. He is introduced on both sides of the Fabius–Scipio debate in Book 28 over Scipio's proposed invasion of Africa, in the context of Regulus' initial success but ultimate failure: this is a similar point to the one P. makes about the fragility of fortune, and will be discussed further in that context (see 18.2n.). But the third

---

[215] Dio fr. 43.22–3 (cf. Zonar. 8.13.4) gives a full list of what Regulus (allegedly) demanded: that the Carthaginians give up Sicily and Sardinia; that they release all Roman captives without ransom but pay ransom for their own prisoners; that they pay to the Romans all war expenses and tribute in addition; that all decisions about war or treaties would be in the Romans' hands; that Carthage should retain only one warship for her own use but should supply fifty for the Romans. The historicity of these terms is, however, dubious: some (e.g. De Sanctis III.1 147 [149], Walbank (1957), 90, Lazenby (1996), 101–2) reject them outright, while others (e.g. Eliæson (1906), 88–91, Hoyos (1998), 116–17, Bleckmann (2002), 166–7) are rightly less sure, and suggest that at least some could be authentic. Other sources (Plb. 1.31.5–8, D.S. 23.12, Eutr. 2.21.4, Aug., *Civ.* 3.18, Oros. 4.9.1) simply say that the demands were so extreme as to be unacceptable; they differ only in as much as the Greek historians (esp. D.S. 23.15.1–4 and Zonar. 8.13.5) criticize Regulus far more extensively for taking such a line, and draw out in detail the unfortunate consequences for him and Rome.

is more revealing: Hannibal refers to Regulus in his negotiations with Scipio directly before Zama (30.30.23):

> inter pauca felicitatis virtutisque exempla M. Atilius quondam in hac eadem terra fuisset, si victor pacem petentibus dedisset patribus nostris; sed non statuendo felicitati modum nec cohibendo efferentem se fortunam, quanto altius elatus erat, eo foedius corruit.
>
> M. Atilius would have once been one of the few models of success and courage in this same country, if in his victory he had granted peace when our senators were looking for it; but instead, because he did not set a limit to his success nor contain the fortune that was elevating him, the higher he was elevated, the more horribly he collapsed.

This explicitly alludes to the story of Regulus' refusal to offer the Carthaginians reasonable peace terms, making it virtually certain (though cf. 13.7n.) that Livy included that story in his narrative in Book 18, something that is also implied by its presence in Eutropius and Orosius, who work within a broadly Livian tradition. The inclusion of the story in Livy does not necessarily prove that it was treated by him to Regulus' detriment, but it is likely that it was, not so much because that is how Hannibal uses it here (it is not unusual for Livy to have a character use a story as an *exemplum* in a manner at variance with the way it was originally narrated: see Chaplin (2000) *passim*), but because that is the slant that is uniformly put on it elsewhere, and indeed is a slant which might seem very natural when it is added to the perception (explicit in both P. and Livy) that Regulus' campaign veered between extremes of fortune: Regulus had the opportunity to avoid the worst, but failed to take it.

Yet P. has nothing of this, and the omission looks studied, especially when the relative fullness with which he does narrate the events of Regulus' time in Africa is taken into consideration. As often, a character whom Livy treated with regard to his moral failings is flattened by P. into an uncomplicated hero, and his defeat and capture are seen as the consequence of the vicissitudes of fortune (cf. the story of the serpent foreshadowing his failure: 18.1n.) rather than of any personal weakness, whether moral or strategic. Any sense of moral weakness or complacency is deflected from Regulus himself onto the senators who, out of misguided trust in his success, refuse his request to be replaced (cf. 18.1n.). This reading of Regulus is far from standard in the post-Livian period, but it is also not unique to P.: it rather seems to represent one distinctive strand of tradition. Both Flor. 1.18.19–23 and *Vir. Ill.* 40 likewise present a Regulus who is morally flawless, though both, unlike P., have at least some indication that he was defeated because Xanthippus was the superior general (cf. 18.2n.).

18.1 serpentem...occidit: For Livy's original version of this story see F 9n. P., like various other writers, implicitly treats it as a portent of the ultimate outcome of

Regulus' African campaign (cf. below): snakes are a regular feature of Roman prodigy literature, and in particular appear as harbingers of death. At the start of Regulus' war in Africa, its outcome is already apparent.

portentosae: The sole occurrence of the word in P., who also never uses the related *portentum* or *portendere*. *portentosus* is not found at all in Livy, although the cognate terms are common in his surviving text.

P. in general includes prodigies only intermittently in his history, and when he does have them, his implicit interpretations do not necessarily reproduce the significance that Livy originally attached to them (32.1n.). In this case, however, his wording makes explicit the ominous nature of the event, which accords with the general sense of his account that Regulus' failing is due to some wider cosmic plan rather than any personal failings. It seems plausible that Livy, too, while not evading Regulus' moral weaknesses (cf. 18.1–2n.), saw his fight with the serpent as foreshadowing his downfall. Certainly Valerius Maximus, who explicitly cites Livy here, speaks of it as something miraculous that 'went beyond normal rationality' (1.8 ext. 19 *supra usitatam rationem excedentia*); more explicitly, Florus refers to the snake as 'born as if for the defence of Africa' (1.18.20: *quasi in vindictam Africae nata*), and Sil. 6.287–93 states that in killing the snake Regulus committed a sacrilege, which he then paid for with his defeat.

cum magna clade: The phrase recurs at 22.7 and 111.4. It occurs nowhere else in extant Latin in precisely this form, but slightly different versions appear several times in Livy (42.55.3 *magna sua cum clade*; also 24.20.9 *cum maxima omnium... clade*, 28.41.16 *cum maximis cladibus suis*, 31.31.10 *cum magnis nostris cladibus*), and in several other authors, mostly from the late Republic and early Empire (Cic, *Div.* 1.77, Vell. 2.107.3, 2.115.2, Val. Max. 8.6.4, Mela 1.38; also Tac., *Ann.* 2.46.1, Oros. 4.22.9): P. may well have seen it as distinctive to that period. In the majority of these cases, as here, the *clades* is inflicted on the supporters of the subject of the verb: it accordingly implies 'loss received' rather than 'destruction inflicted'.

cum...pugnasset: P.'s common sentence-pattern of a 'background' temporal or causal clause followed by the central point of the anecdote (cf. 2.2n.) is here developed into a much more complex syntactic structure. It remains the core of the sentence, but the *cum* clause has two parts linked by *-que*, and the main clause is then followed by an explanatory relative clause giving the content of the letter that Regulus wrote to the Senate.

aliquot proeliis: The fullest account of Regulus' campaigns after the departure of Manlius (cf. 17.6n.) is in Plb. 1.30.4–15, which refers to him first capturing Adys, then defeating the Carthaginian army which had sought to confront him. After this he had, according to Polybius, free rein to plunder the country and attack other towns, though the only one which Polybius names is Tunis, which then became his base.

Polybius, therefore, in contrast to P., speaks only of a single actual battle (cf. D.S. 23.15.7, Zonar. 8.13.3). Moreover, no other source speaks of further fighting in the field, though they all mention large numbers—indeed, implausibly large numbers[216]—of towns that Regulus captured. The most likely explanation is that P., in summarizing Livy, has misleadingly conflated the capture of towns with fighting between armies, although *proelia* strictly should refer only to the latter (*OLD s.v. proelium* 1; Val. Max. 4.4.6 more accurately talks about *crebris victoriis*, without specifying what sort of victories). Cf. 30.1n.

Since Regulus' final battle and capture appear to have been in May 255 (Julian), shortly after the start of the new consular year (18.2n.), this battle, the capture of Tunis, and the subsequent negotiations with Carthage, all must have occurred in the consular year 256 (*MRR* I 209). Hence Regulus continued actively campaigning even after Manlius left at the start of the winter (17.6n.), something entirely feasible in northern Tunisia, where winters are typically mild and rainfall low (a point surprisingly overlooked by e.g. De Sanctis III.1 146, 252 [148, 260], Morgan (1977), 99–100).

bene...pugnasset: Cf. 12.3n.

successorque...non mitteretur: The assumption is that Regulus learned that the Senate was planning to prorogue his command, so that he would remain with the army until the end of the summer of 255 (cf. Brennan (2000), 81). However, not only does Polybius have nothing of this proposal, but he directly implies the opposite: that Regulus assumed that a successor would shortly arrive (1.31.4: see below)—indeed, far from complaining about being left in command, he was resentful about the fact that someone else might take over and deny him the credit for victory (which is why he entered on his ill-fated attempt to negotiate with Carthage: see 18.1–2n.). This last may simply be an inference by Polybius (or his source), based on (not unreasonable) assumptions about the attitudes of ambitious generals faced with the imminent end of their command (so Walbank (1957), 90); but it does at least show that Polybius knew nothing of any proposal to prorogue Regulus' command for a further year (Develin (1975), 721; *contra MRR* I 209–10, followed by e.g. Kloft (1977), 97–8, Tipps (2003), 375, which mistakenly deduces that prorogation was not merely proposed, but actually took place).[217]

---

[216] Seventy-four in Eutr. 2.21.3; 200 in App., *Pun.* 3, *Vir. Ill.* 42, 300 in Flor. 1.18.19. Orosius has 300 forts captured before Manlius' departure (4.8.8), and a further eighty-two towns following Regulus' victory in battle (4.8.16).

[217] Bleckmann (2002), 163–4 relates the proposal to extend Regulus' command in P. *et al.* to Plb. 1.29.8, referring to the order given to Regulus to remain in Africa at the start of the winter (17.6n.). But P. is talking about something entirely different from Polybius, since his version assumes not merely that Regulus was being asked to remain in the field, but that the Senate decided to send no successor to relieve him. Kloft (1977), 98 not only makes the same false connection, but directly misinterprets Polybius as describing the legal prorogation of Regulus' command: the only issue in Polybius is whether the winter of Regulus' consular year should be spent in Rome or in Africa.

The story here (also found in Val. Max. 4.4.6 and Frontin., *Strat.* 4.3.3) accordingly is unhistorical: an attempt to construct Regulus along the familiar lines of early Republican frugality and modesty most obviously exemplified in the figure of Cincinnatus in Books 3 and 4. It is mirrored in a piece of homespun agricultural wisdom attributed to him (Colum. 1.4.2, Plin., *Nat.* 18.27), which is once again part of his image of a farmer who happened to be a military hero.

inter causas...erat, quod...: 'Among the reasons...were that...': for the construction cf. Sen., *Epist.* 123.6, Suet., *Claud.* 40.2.

erat: Omitted in the MSS, but restored later: the ellipse of the verb in the relative clause would be abnormal for P.

agellus: The only occurrence of this word in P.; nor does Livy use it in his surviving text; diminutives of any sort are rare in them, as they are in other historians (though cf. 49.18n.). However, Val. Max. 4.4.6, Frontin., *Strat.* 4.3.3, and Apul., *Apol.* 18.11 all use the same term to describe Regulus' farm, which may suggest that all of them derived it from Livy, or at the very least that the smallness of Regulus' land-holding was so central to the post-Livian historical tradition that it regularly overrode normal stylistic limitations on the use of diminutives.

According to Valerius, the farm was 7 *iugera*. This appears to be the size that the Romans conventionally regarded as the norm in the early period of their history (cf. Plin., *Nat.* 18.18), and perhaps should not be taken literally, as it is not clear that a 7-*iugera* farm worked by hand could produce enough to feed a family,[218] although that is the premise of the story here (cf. below).

eius: One might have expected *suus*; however, that logic is regularly violated in later Latin (cf. 8.2n.). Moreover, in contexts like this, where the contents of a message are being summarized in a relative clause, *eius* is quite often found even in the classical period: P. is effectively summarizing the letter in his own words (cf. K-S 1.610, H-S 175; also Heubner (1968), 46 on Tac., *Hist.* 2.9.2, and Woodman (2018), 304 on Tac., *Ann.* 4.67.1).

a mercennariis desertus esset: The context is filled in by Val. Max. 4.4.6 (cf. Sen., *Cons. Helv.* 12.7, *Vir. Ill.* 40.2): Regulus' bailiff (*vilicus*) had died, and the *mercennarius*—hired labourer—who worked the land under him had left,

---

[218] Brunt (1971), 193–5, Hopkins (1978), 21, suggest it could not; Garnsey (1980), 37–8 cites a range of possible minimum sizes (6 to 20 *iugera*) for a subsistence farm, but also notes that the issue is complicated by the possibility that a peasant farmer might supplement his resources by using common land for grazing animals, or his income by working outside his farm during slack agricultural periods. So also Brunt (1971), 194, Frayn (1979), 90–3 (who also (57–72) discusses the use of wild plants for supplying extra nutrition), and especially Evans (1980), esp. 137–9 and 159–63, who adds hunting as a further possibility, but also points to the dramatically different yields of different soils. Evans further notes that the fact that Roman colonists were sometimes assigned as little as 5 *iugera* apiece (e.g. Livy 39.55.7, 40.29.2) makes it probable that a farm of that size, at least in the context of the other resources mentioned above, was considered sufficient to support a household. See more generally Rosenstein (2004), 66–81 for hypothetical models of a subsistence farm's agricultural yield, the labour required to produce it, and the family's nutritional needs.

taking with him the farming equipment; his wife and children were therefore starving.

If this story is true, it gives a remarkably precise and revealing description of Regulus' financial circumstances. He relies on his farm to feed his wife, his children (number and ages unspecified), the bailiff, and presumably himself when he is present. He has sufficient money to own the bailiff, who is presumably a slave (Guthrie (1949), 45–6); but any surplus money is inadequate to purchase a second slave, or even to replace the bailiff when he dies; instead he hires a day-labourer to do extra work on the farm. This is typical of the way in which peasant farmers manage the fluctuations of their farm's needs and output (Halstead (1987), 85), and is plausible given the economics of ancient farming, where labour needs were variable, and hence a capital outlay on a slave would rarely be economically preferable to hiring labour *ad hoc*, at least on a small farm (Hopkins (1978), 110–11, Rathbone (1981), 14–15). Without the produce of the farm, there is also insufficient money to purchase food for the family. This is not utter impoverishment, but it is barely a step above it; it also is coherent and plausible economically.

Unfortunately, though economically plausible, the story is unlikely to be true, as noted above. It accordingly cannot be used as valid evidence for senatorial wealth or land-holdings at the time of the First Punic War. In general, like the exemplary stories told of figures like Cincinnatus, Curius Dentatus, or Fabricius (cf. 14.4n.), it expresses the later Romans' sense of the virtuous rustic simplicity in which their ancestors had lived, and from which they themselves had declined.[219] More specifically, however, it appears to reflect the conditions—or rather the assumed conditions—of Rome in the later second century BC, when there was supposedly a crisis of depopulation owing to Roman smallholders having to abandon their farms in order to serve overseas for extended periods (e.g. Sall., *Jug.* 41.8, Flor. 2.3.3; cf. 58.1n.). That picture has been vigorously challenged in much modern scholarship, and is likely to be false;[220] but this story appears to

---

[219] However, Garnsey (1980), 36–7 overstates the case when he asserts dogmatically that 'if M. Atilius Regulus owned merely seven *iugera* of land...he would never have risen to the consulship and led an army against the Carthaginians'. While the story is doubtless invented, as noted above, our evidence for the socio-economic structure of mid-third century Rome is too scanty to be able to claim it as impossible.

[220] A major problem is the apparent mismatch between (a) the archaeological evidence, which appears to show a broad continuation of peasant-sized smallholdings, and (b) the picture we get from much of the literary evidence, apparently supported by the logistical practicalities of maintaining the Roman army, which indicates mass displacement of the rural population from their farms and the amalgamation of the land into large estates. The general picture of rural depopulation is accepted by (e.g.) Hopkins (1978), 4–8, 24–37 (cf. the reservations of Witcher (2008), 274–80 about the possibility of disproving such a scenario via archaeological data); a very different picture derived largely from the archaeology is suggested by (e.g.) Frederiksen (1970–71), Garnsey (1980), 35–6, Rathbone (1981), while the important work of Rosenstein (2004) gives strong reason to doubt the underlying assumptions that long-term military service began only in the second century BC, or that it was usually incompatible with peasant-scale agriculture. It is important to remember that the two positions are not in all respects mutually exclusive: a continuation of peasant smallholding is certainly compatible

have been invented at a time when it was seen as plausible. The plight of Regulus, the first Roman to campaign outside the Greco-Roman world for an extended period, foreshadows the circumstances that would (supposedly) affect many of his fellow-countrymen later (cf. Brunt (1971), 642–3, Hopkins (1978), 4–5).

According to Valerius (also Apul., *Apol.* 18.11, *Vir. Ill.* 40.2), the Senate's response was to have the land farmed, his family fed, and his property replaced, all at public expense. This may have been in Livy too, but P. omits that side to the story: his interest is in the crassness of the Senate in wanting to have Regulus replaced at all, not their sympathetic response to his plight.

18.2 quaerente…fortuna, ut magnum utriusque casus exemplum proderetur: This image of Fortune as an active agent showing her powers by generating an exceptional outcome is unusual for P. It is, however, a common image in Livy, in whom, as in other Roman writers, the dominant picture of *fortuna* is of something intrinsically divine, but which (from a human perspective) may appear wilful or unexpected, and which is especially associated with the capacity to cause reverses between success and failure (see e.g. 5.49.5, 45.41.9).[221]

This fact alone does not necessarily imply that P. is reproducing the slant that Livy gave to his account of Regulus (cf. 39.6, a passage with a similar account of *fortuna* which owes surprisingly little to Livy himself: see *ad loc.*). However, that P. here is reflecting Livy's own reading of Regulus is supported by the way in which Livy has Fabius and Scipio cite the story in Book 28, especially Fabius' introduction of Regulus as a warning to Scipio, in language remarkably similar to P.'s here: *insigne utriusque fortunae exemplum* (28.42.1: 'a distinguished model of both extremes of fortune').[222] This strongly indicates either that (a) Livy in Book 28 is alluding to his own language earlier, having Fabius reflect the moral that he himself had drawn from Regulus, or that (b) P., in summarizing the story, did so using not the language of Livy's original account of it in Book 18, but that of his later reference to it ten books later.

Although the second of these is perhaps more interesting, the first is nevertheless more likely. While such cross-book allusions are common in P.'s work (see the Introduction, xxiii–xxiv), a self-allusion by Livy here reinforces a point that is already implicit in the way Fabius and Scipio use Regulus in Book 28—namely

---

with a gradual decline exacerbated in some individual cases by military service, since large estates certainly increased in number in the late Republic and early Empire (cf. Rich (1983), 296–9). It is understandable that ancient sources might well focus on the plight of the dispossessed, even if they formed only a minority of the rural population.

[221] On *fortuna* in Livy see above all Davies (2004), 116–23, completely superseding Levene (1993), 30–3.

[222] Regulus appears elsewhere as a model of the reversal of fortune: above all in Plb. 1.35, who has an extended reflection on the subject (see Walbank (1957), 92–3), and from whom Livy may well have derived his own thoughts. See also Flor. 1.18.22 (for whom, unlike Polybius, Livy, and P., the key effect of fortune's changes is to give the Romans a new opportunity to demonstrate their outstanding virtue).

that it is Fabius who has the better arguments in this part of their exchange.²²³ Fabius, as noted, cites Regulus as a warning; he goes on to note how Africa, unlike Spain, would not provide a ready haven for Roman troops (28.42.2-7); Scipio replies that the lesson is irrelevant, since Regulus had no difficulty landing, and was in fact undefeated by the Carthaginian generals he faced (28.43.17). This response misses Fabius' point. Fabius never denied that Regulus was able to land and win his initial victories—indeed, *insigne utriusque fortunae exemplum* assumes as much. Fabius had cited Regulus more generally as an example of someone who was betrayed by fortune and whose ambitions failed him: Scipio disingenuously conflates the argument with the separate one Fabius had made immediately afterwards, and replies as if Fabius had claimed that Regulus had failed to find a safe landing in Africa. That disingenuousness would be even more apparent were Fabius' reading of Regulus validated by its use of the narrator's own language, which provides some grounds for concluding that what P. says here reflects both the wording and the sentiment of Livy's original in Book 18.

quaerere ut meaning 'seeking to bring about' is Livian (2.57.3: cf. *OLD* s.v. *quaero* 6a). The specific combination *fortuna quaerit* appears originally to have had a poetic register: it first appears in Manil. 2.591, then in ps.-Sen., *Herc. O.* 697-8. But from the second century onwards it is found only (though still rarely) in prose: see Flor. 1.40.21, 2.13.54, *Paneg.* 2.15.3). If the argument above is accepted that the phrase probably derives from Livy, then it is a (not uncommon) example of a poeticism in his work; however, by the time it reaches P., that sense of poetry has been muted.

deinde: P. uses *deinde* above all to link his pieces of information into a coherent narrative sequence, especially in passages where his summary is more detailed; it appears in this sense in the next sentence (18.3), and also in (e.g.) 5.9, 22.4, 22.7, 37.4, 49.10, 49.18, 58.3, 68.2, 71.2, 116.4, 119.3.

Xanthippo, Lacedaemoniorum duce: Nothing is known of him beyond what we are told in the various accounts of his fighting for the Carthaginians in this year.²²⁴ Diodorus (23.14.1-2, 23.15.7) describes him as a Spartiate (sc. one of the Spartan elite trained to warfare), which is possible, though Plb. 1.32.1 says only that he had undergone the Spartan education system (cf. Veg., *Mil.* 3 pr.5), which could mean that he was a *mothax*—a product of an irregular union who had

---

²²³ Cf. Chaplin (2000), 93-6, who also discusses a further key point: that despite the superiority of Fabius' arguments, and their apparent endorsement by the author and the internal audience, Regulus is not the right model for Scipio, since the latter's attack on Africa will prove successful.

²²⁴ A Xanthippus is recorded by Jer., *In Dan.* 11.7-9 as being a *dux* whom Ptolemy III Euergetes, following his invasion of the Seleucid empire in 246/5, made governor of the provinces beyond the Euphrates. The identity with our Xanthippus is accepted by e.g. De Sanctis III.1 152 [154], but scepticism is warranted: even if Jerome's information is accurate (and it may not be), it would represent a remarkable ascension for a man who a decade earlier had been an *ad hoc* mercenary leader. It is probably preferable to assume that Jerome is referring to another general of the same name.

nevertheless been brought up through the elite military training.²²⁵ On Polybius' account (1.32.1–5; cf. D.S. 23.15.7, *Vir. Ill.* 40.3), he was brought to Carthage as a mercenary, but was given effective command over the army because he impressed the Carthaginian generals with his military acumen. Other sources, however, seem to imply that he held a position of leadership in Sparta, and came as part of an allied force to support Carthage (App., *Pun.* 3, Flor. 1.18.23, Eutr. 2.21.4, Zonar. 8.13.6), and that seems to be the implication of P.'s *Lacedaemoniorum duce* (Oros. 4.9.2 calls him the Spartans' king). Polybius' version is overwhelmingly more likely: the Carthaginians' reliance on mercenaries is exceptionally well documented, whereas an alliance with Sparta such as would lead the latter to send a force to fight the Romans in Africa is not. The story of the alliance is more flattering to Rome, in as much as it suggests that Regulus was defeated by the leader of a force with a great military tradition, not a mere mercenary unexpectedly elevated to command.

According to Plb. 1.36.2–3 (also Oros. 4.9.4), Xanthippus after his victory returned rapidly to Greece, in order not to provoke resentment among the Carthaginians. Polybius does refer to another version (1.36.4): this does not appear in his surviving text, but is perhaps that found in Val. Max. 9.6 ext. 1, according to whom the Carthaginians deliberately sank the ship he was sailing on (though Xanthippus survived), presumably so that he should not share the credit for the victory. The same story appears in D.S. 23.16, Sil. 6.680–3, App., *Pun.* 4 (in all of which Xanthippus fails to escape), and Zonar. 8.13.9–10, though Zonaras offers an alternative version that he knew the danger and sailed on a different ship. These, however, all appear to be constructed around a stereotype of intrinsic Carthaginian treachery (cf. De Sanctis III.1 151 [153]), since their alleged motives for the attempt to kill Xanthippus are so flimsy (as Valerius himself appears to acknowledge); a more concrete reason to doubt the story (as well as the related one in Zonar. 8.13.9, that the Carthaginians sought to cheat the mercenaries of their pay) is that an issue of Carthaginian gold coinage is plausibly argued to have been minted specifically in honour of his victory (Baldus (1988), 171–6). At all events P. has nothing of it: he has no interest in Xanthippus beyond the fact that he was the agent of Regulus' defeat.

victus proelio: The fullest source for the battle is once again Polybius (1.32.7–34.12), according to whom Xanthippus rapidly restored the morale of the army, then set out to face the Romans. Xanthippus placed elephants in his front line to face the Roman infantry, while both sides had their cavalry on the wings. The Carthaginian cavalry outnumbered and forced back the Romans, and so were able to surround the main body of the army. Regulus himself escaped with a small number of troops, but was soon captured.

---

²²⁵ So Lazenby (1996), 102–3, though his description of the *mothax* as 'a man of poor family who had been patronized by someone wealthier' is probably erroneous: see Ogden (1996), 217–24.

However, other sources are quite different. In App., *Pun.* 3 the prime reason for the Romans' defeat is that they are fighting in the heat, and exhausted after a long day's march, and fall victim to a sudden Carthaginian attack. Zonar. 8.13.7 is entirely different again: the Romans are overconfident and despise Xanthippus as a mere Greek; but when they face him, the elephants rout the cavalry. Still another version is in Frontin., *Strat.* 2.3.10, who mentions neither cavalry nor elephants, but has Xanthippus winning through intelligent deployment of his light-armed infantry and auxiliaries; while Cic., *Off.* 3.99 (cf. Val. Max. 1.1.14) seems to assume yet another version: where Regulus is caught in an ambush. While any of these might have been accepted in the absence of contrary information, the circumstantial details in Polybius are most likely to go back to a reliable source, and hence to be preferred.[226]

The best indication of the date of the battle comes from the rescue of the remnants of Regulus' army, which Plb. 1.36.10 puts at the beginning of the summer of 255,[227] with the fleet setting out after the news of the defeat had already reached Rome (Plb. 1.36.5-8); the fleet was wrecked on its return 'between the rising of Orion and Sirius' (Plb. 1.37.4): i.e. July (Walbank (1957), 96-7: cf. 18.3n.). This suggests a battle in the spring, perhaps later rather than earlier, since time has to be allowed not only for an eventful campaign, but also for Xanthippus to take command and reinvigorate the army: De Sanctis III.1 252 [260] suggests May 255 (Julian), though with March and April as possibilities. Polybius' narrative implies that it was shortly after the beginning of the new consular year (which probably began on 1 May at this period: see Mommsen (1859), 101-2, Holzapfel (1885), 99-104, De Sanctis III.1 241 [248]),[228] and if the later date is accepted for the battle, then that indicates that the consular and the Julian years more or less coincided at this time (so Morgan (1977), 98-102).[229]

---

[226] Cicero's and Zonaras' versions look especially suspicious: the former simply assumes, perhaps without any source to back him up (cf. Dyck (1996), 622-3), that Regulus was defeated in much the manner of various later Romans during the Second Punic War; while Dio may well have favoured the version found in Zonaras because of the opportunity it gave to challenge Roman anti-Greek prejudices.

[227] Not 254, as has sometimes been argued (e.g. Beloch, *GG* IV.2 288): this depends not only on accepting the prorogation of Regulus' command, which is very unlikely (cf. 18.1n.), but also on assuming that the Romans cut Regulus loose in Africa without supplies or reinforcements for a full year, which is even less so (De Sanctis III.1 249-50 [257]).

[228] This is not incompatible with Polybius' earlier suggestion that Regulus' command was not prorogued (18.1n.): no formal prorogation was needed to allow Regulus to retain command of the army until the new consul arrived to take over from him (Mommsen, *StR*³ III 1089-91).

[229] Morgan does, however, overstate the case: it is still possible (if less likely) that the battle took place in March or April (Julian), and that this coincided with 1 May (consular). Morgan's reason for excluding that possibility is that the campaigning season in 255 could not have begun before mid-March (Julian); but this does not take account of the mild local climate (cf. 18.1n.). If one removes that premise, there is no reason in principle why 1 May (consular) should not (e.g.) have occurred on 1 April (Julian).

18.3 *Success and shipwrecks*. P. here rolls into a single notice what appears to be several years of Roman successes and failures. Two shipwrecks are recorded in this period of the Punic War, one in 255, when the fleet which had rescued the remnants of Regulus' army was caught in a storm off the coast of Sicily and almost entirely destroyed (Plb. 1.37; cf. D.S. 23.18.1, Eutr. 2.22.3, Oros. 4.9.8), and one in 253, when the fleet returning from Sicily to Rome was caught in another storm and again substantially destroyed (Plb. 1.39.5–6, D.S. 23.19, Eutr. 2.23.1, Sol. 27.40, Oros. 4.9.11). The intervening successes were, however, also numerous—or at least could be presented as such: in 255 the Romans defeated a Carthaginian fleet on their way to Africa to pick up Regulus' troops (Plb. 1.36.11, D.S. 23.18.1, Eutr. 2.22.2: Oros. 4.9.5–7, and Zonar. 8.14.3 add a (probably invented)[230] land victory to the success); the *Fasti Capitolini* record a triumph for the consuls,[231] and it appears that one of them, M. Aemilius Paullus, erected a *columna rostrata* on the model of Duilius' (Livy 42.20.1: cf. 17.2n.). In 254 the Romans captured Panormus (Plb. 1.38.7–10) and (according to D.S. 23.18.3–5) other towns also; the consul P. Cornelius Scipio Asina celebrated a triumph, though as proconsul in the following year (*Fasti Capitolini*). In 253 Eutr. 2.23.1 and Oros. 4.9.10 say that towns in Africa were captured; this is likely, since the *Fasti Capitolini* have one of the consuls, C. Sempronius Blaesus, triumphing in that year for a Carthaginian victory, although Polybius claims that the consuls' landings achieved 'nothing noteworthy' (1.39.2: οὐδὲν ἀξιόλογον).[232] In the following year, 252, the consuls captured Lipara and Thermae (Plb. 1.39.13, D.S. 23.20; for the date see Zonar. 8.14.7 (below)), and one, C. Aurelius Cotta, likewise had a triumph (*Fasti Capitolini*: Polybius again damns the victory with faint praise). All of these years will have been covered in Livy (this book includes events down to at least 252: see 18.4–5nn. and 19.1n.), and hence included in P.'s notice; it seems plausible that Livy included most if not all of these victories.

However, other sources—notably Zonar. 8.14.1–7—narrate this period rather differently, with at least as many military failures as successes. Zonaras lists the victories mentioned by Polybius, but adds more equivocal episodes. According to him, in 255 the fleet captured the island of Cossura halfway between Sicily and Carthage (cf. *Fasti Capitolini*)—but the Carthaginians recaptured it soon after. In 254 the Romans tried but failed to take Lilybaeum, and they lost ships to the Carthaginians after the capture of Panormus (cf. Dio fr. 43.29a); in 252 the capture of Lipara was marred by a disastrous interlude where a military tribune was left in charge (cf. Val. Max. 2.7.4, Frontin., *Strat.* 4.1.31). The surviving fragments

---

[230] So e.g. Lazenby (1996), 109, *contra* Thiel (1954), 234–5.
[231] Because of the shipwreck they could not celebrate it until in the following year, so they did so as proconsuls (Develin (1975), 720, Brennan (2000), 279, correcting De Sanctis III.1 157 [160] n. 32).
[232] The triumph is overlooked by Walbank (1957), 99–100, who accordingly concludes that Eutropius and Orosius are exaggerating; it is more likely that Polybius here is downplaying a real success (Thiel (1954), 248–9, Lazenby (1996), 117).

of Diodorus offer more failures: the Carthaginian recapture of Agrigentum in 255 (23.18.2), an unsuccessful Roman attempt to capture Drepana in 254 (23.18.3), failure in 252 at a large-scale attempt on Hercte (23.20), and a bizarre episode at Thermae where the Romans think the town will be betrayed to them, only to be betrayed in their turn when out of greed they enter unprotected (23.19).

Was anything of this in Livy? There is no firm indication that it was: this material is almost all absent not only from P., but from other sources which might plausibly be thought to derive from the Livian tradition. Livy, despite his broadly patriotic orientation, does not systematically omit Roman defeats and failures, but that in this case he at least played them down, even if he did not pass over them altogether, may be inferred from the shared slant of the sources. Polybius constructs the events of the years after Regulus' disaster through a systematic contrast: the Romans' success in warfare is undermined by their inability to come to terms with the operation of a navy, where the elements are as much of a threat as the enemy is (1.37.4–10, 1.39.3–6); in consequence, the Romans for the time being abandoned the seas to the Carthaginians (1.39.7). The same basic position is shared by P. here, who has only military successes undermined by naval disasters; it is also that of Eutr. 2.22–23 and Oros. 4.9.5–12. While we should never exclude the likelihood that the late antique historians are reading and citing one another (see Introduction), the coincidence of the pattern of omissions and interpretation with Polybius is more likely to have reached them via Livy than from a direct reading of Polybius or of any other source; accordingly, it is moderately likely that Livy, too, passed lightly over the failures described in Diodorus and Zonaras, if he included them at all.[233]

res...prospere gestas: See 3.10n.

deformaverunt: 'Disfigured': a vivid word, which appears only here in P. Livy, however, uses it several times, four times, as here, of a victory being undermined by other events (3.71.1, 8.32.15, 33.36.15, 37.54.9). The image is rare in other historians: it is otherwise found only in Amm. 25.3.14. This suggests that P. is either reproducing Livy's wording here, or else using a phrase that appeared to him distinctively Livian.

naufragia classium: The storm in 255 wrecked all but eighty ships, all sources agree, though they differ on the original size of the fleet: 364 ships according to Plb. 1.37.2, 464 in Eutr. 2.22.2, 300 in Oros. 4.9.8. Diodorus does not give the number of ships that survived, but has 340 warships plus 300 transport ships lost (23.18.1). That in 253 apparently destroyed 150 ships (Plb. 1.39.6, D.S. 23.19,

---

[233] The omission of the military failures from Orosius is particularly noteworthy: in accordance with his overall project, he generalizes the point from the Romans being undermined by poor judgement on the sea to argue that the Romans never consistently succeeded at anything. More defeats would have reinforced that point for him; the likelihood is that he did not find them in his source-material for this chapter.

Oros. 4.9.11). For discussion of the problems raised by these numbers see e.g. Tarn (1907), 52–6, Thiel (1954), 84–9, Lazenby (1996), 107–8.

18.4 *'Annalistic' notices.* Cf. 11.5n.

Tib. Coruncanius: *RE* 3, *MRR* I 210. According to Cicero (*Planc.* 20; cf. *Sull.* 23), he was a native of Tusculum; Tac., *Ann.* 11.24.2, on the other hand, has the Emperor Claudius say that the Coruncanii came from Camerium. Since Camerium's last known historical appearance was when it was destroyed by Rome in 502 (D.H., *AR* 5.49.5), Cicero is more likely to be correct.[234] Coruncanius had previously been consul in 280, achieving a victory and a triumph over the Etruscans (13.8n.); he was subsequently dictator for holding elections in 246, according to the *Fasti Capitolini*. He was, however, far more famous as a *pontifex maximus* than as a consul or dictator: his consulship is barely noted outside the brief surviving historical narratives, and his dictatorship is mentioned nowhere except the *Fasti*, but Cicero repeatedly mentions him as an iconic *pontifex maximus* (*Dom.* 139, *De Orat.* 3.134, *Brut.* 55, *Nat. Deor.* 1.115, 3.5; cf. also *De Orat.* 3.56, *Cato* 15). Along similar lines, Vell. 2.128.1 not only places Coruncanius at the head of a list of distinguished *novi homines* from the 300 years before his own day, but he regards his being *pontifex maximus*, rather than his magistracies, as the crowning glory of his career (cf. Woodman (1977), 258). To be *pontifex maximus* was, after all, to join a far more exclusive club than to be consul: indeed, after Coruncanius, no other *novi homines* apart from Marius and Cicero are securely attested as holding any major priesthood at all until the 40s (Wiseman (1971), 169; cf. more broadly 169–73).

The fact that his sole appearance in P. is in the context of his pontificate rather than his consulship is therefore unsurprising. In theory the particular impetus for his inclusion is, as often, that he represents a 'first' (cf. 11.5n.), but that can hardly be a sufficient explanation, since P. had not thought it worth noting when plebeians obtained the right to the pontificate and other priesthoods in the first place, even though constitutionally that was the key barrier, after which it was presumably only a matter of time before one became head of the college. Instead P. merely recorded the expansion in the augurate without mentioning either the simultaneous expansion of the pontificate or its implication for the rights of plebeians (10.3n.). His interest here may have been piqued by the fact that the innovation could be tied to a single named person (several of his other 'firsts' fall under that heading: e.g. 6.4, 13.4, 16.4, 17.2, 19.3, 30.6, 37.1, 68.6), but it seems plausible that it was also relevant that the person in question was treated elsewhere as an exemplary

---

[234] It may be that Tacitus (or Claudius) had some evidence that Camerium was the origin of the family, which moved to Tusculum after Camerium's destruction (so Münzer (1901a)), but even if that was the case, he was misleading, since he speaks of the Coruncanii 'being summoned into the Senate' (*in senatum accitos*) from Camerium, and the evidence suggests that our Coruncanius was the first to hold office at Rome.

figure: he was regularly associated with Fabricius and Curius Dentatus as an exemplar of traditional Roman morality (Cic. *Cato* 15, 43, *Lael.* 18, 39, Sen., *Contr.* 2.1.18, Sen., *Vit. Beat.* 21.3, Gell. 1.10.1, *Paneg.* 2.9.5; cf. Cic., *Planc.* 20).[235] It would of course be especially relevant to P. if Livy himself had treated Coruncanius in such a way in Book 18, as he may have done, though he never refers to him in his surviving books.

Various rulings are attributed to Coruncanius: according to Cicero (*Leg.* 2.52), he ruled on the obligations of legatees to perform funeral rites, while Ateius Capito (*ap.* Gell. 4.6.10), says that he instituted the practice of *feriae praecidaneae* on an *ater dies* (it is uncertain what precisely this practice involved: see van Haeperen (2002), 232–4). He was also regarded as a distinguished jurisconsult, the first to give rulings in public (Pompon., *Dig.* 1.2.2.35, 1.2.2.38; cf. Cic., *Cato* 27, *De Orat.* 3.134): in the middle Republic religious and civil law, and hence the roles of jurist and *pontifex maximus*, substantially overlapped (Beard, North, and Price (1998), vol. 1, 24–6). Pomponius, however, implies that his rulings may have originally been transmitted orally (cf. Rawson (1985), 203–4).

It has also been argued (Rüpke, *FS* 24–38) that Coruncanius was the *pontifex maximus* who began the practice of publishing an official record of events, a record which was presumed (albeit perhaps mistakenly: see Frier (1999), esp. 255–84) to stand at the core of the so-called annalistic tradition at Rome, around which Livy and his predecessors constructed their narrative: no ancient source connects this directly with Coruncanius, but it is inferred from the fact that religious material begins to appear systematically in the historians only after his time.[236] That inference is, however, challenged by J. W. Rich (*FRHist* I 149–51), who notes that, though the quantity of such material increases in the third century, it appears in Livy's records earlier also, albeit more intermittently, and he suggests that there is no reason to doubt that this earlier material, too, went back to the pontifical record, which may not have been kept as systematically in the earlier period.

For an extensive (but wildly speculative) study of Coruncanius' career, see Bauman (1983), 71–92.

---

[235] Litchfield (1914), 50 notes that Coruncanius, while regularly cited as an *exemplum* by Cicero, appears much less often in later authors; he whimsically hypothesizes that this was because of the metrical intractability of his name. The falling off is clear, but there are better explanations. First, the apparent chronological change may be a product of Cicero's unusual degree of interest in him—if we exclude Cicero, citations are rarer but more steady, and Cicero may have latched onto Coruncanius as a fellow *novus homo* from small-town Italy (cf. Wiseman (1971), 107–8). And, second, it seems reasonable to suspect that the relative popularity of Fabricius and Dentatus by comparison with Coruncanius in the later tradition is above all due to the fact that the virtues of the former pair were tied to a series of memorable exemplary anecdotes, which appears not to have been the case for Coruncanius.

[236] That Coruncanius was responsible for this innovation had earlier been argued by Enmann (1902), 529–33, but on far weaker grounds: he claimed that various aspects of the earlier history of Rome suggested that it had been formulated by a plebeian *pontifex* of the mid-third century. The assumptions underlying this argument are many and dubious.

pontifex maximus: This is, as far as we can tell, P.'s first mention of either *pontifices* in general or the *pontifex maximus* in particular, although they had been intermittent presences throughout Livy's early books. It is, naturally, possible that P. included a mention of the original creation of the office under his account of Numa (cf. Livy 1.20.5–7), but nothing of that part of his summary survives (see Introduction to *Per.* 1).

The *pontifices* had wider-ranging functions than any other Roman priesthood, including supervision of the calendar, the laws of burial and sacrifices, and much else. The pontifical college, of which the *pontifex maximus* was the head, included not only the *pontifices*, but also the *rex sacrorum*, the *flamines*, and Vestal Virgins; the *pontifex maximus* thus had the most extensive religious authority of any figure at Rome, albeit not unlimited authority, since there were still many parts of Roman religious life which did not fall within his purview. Some (e.g. Mommsen, *StR*^{3} II 20–3) have argued that the *pontifex maximus* possessed powers which were effectively (if not formally) those of a magistrate, but see *contra* Bleicken (1957a).

For a general study of the pontifical college, see Wissowa (1912), 501–23, van Haeperen (2002).

creatus est: Later in the century the procedure for electing the *pontifex maximus* was that he was chosen from among the existing *pontifices* by an assembly consisting of seventeen of the thirty-five tribes (chosen by lot): see Mommsen, *StR*^{3} II 27–8. It is not certain that this procedure already existed in Coruncanius' day, but it is not unlikely; if (as some have thought) he was the first *pontifex maximus* chosen in this way, that may have been the reason that the office was for the first time entrusted to a plebeian.

No closer indication for the date of Coruncanius' election can be given than that deducible from his appearance in this book. The book begins in the last months of the consular year 256 (18.1n.). The last securely datable event is the census in 252 (see below); but it is altogether possible that some material from 251 was included here as well, and the book may even have extended into 250. The question turns on a double problem: whether Metellus' victory at Panormus was narrated by Livy in Book 18 or Book 19, and whether it was under the year 251 or 250 (see 18.5n., 19.1n.). Certainly if it appeared in Book 18, as I argue below is more likely, then the book may have included the beginning of 250, even if (as is also likely) the victory itself was placed by Livy under 251. But even if (as appears to be the case at first sight) the victory was narrated in Book 19, then the start of the year in question, whether it was 251 or 250, could certainly still have been in Book 18. Livy sometimes reports priestly elections at the end of the year (e.g. 40.42.12), sometimes at the start of the year (e.g. 39.46.1–2).

So Coruncanius may have been elected any time between 256 and 250 (*contra* MRR I 210, followed by Rüpke, *FS* 647, who limits it to 255–252).

Valerius Maximus Sempronius Sophus censores: Neither has appeared previously in P., although P. Sempronius Sophus (*RE* 86) had been one of the conquerors of Picenum as consul in 268 (15.4n.), while M'. Valerius Maximus Messalla (*RE* 247) had been consul in 263, capturing Messana (and hence receiving his cognomen) and compelling Hiero in Syracuse to come to terms (16.2n.). According to the *Fasti Capitolini*, D. Junius Pera and L. Postumius Megellus were the men originally chosen as censors (in 253), but Postumius died in office and Junius resigned; Valerius and Sempronius took their place, and completed the *lustrum* in 252.

Little else is known about either of these men, apart from an anecdote that Sempronius at some point divorced his wife because she had, without his knowledge, gone to watch funeral games (Val. Max. 6.3.12, Plu., *Quaest. Rom.* 267C: according to Plutarch he was only the third Roman to divorce). The story could conceivably be true, but, even if not, the fact that it attached itself to Sempronius indicates that he had attracted some sort of reputation for old-fashioned moral rigour. Nothing in surviving accounts of his career makes it clear what that would be based on, but it is most plausibly connected with his activities as censor: see below.

The names are confused in the MSS. P, and the Renaissance MSS, refer to Valerius as *M. Sempronius Valerius Maximus*, and Sempronius as *C. Sempronius Stofus*; N has conflated the two names into one, as *M. Sempronius Stofus*. The *nomina* and *cognomina* are properly corrected from the Fasti Capitolini; most editions also give the correct *praenomen* for both men from the same source, but it is more plausible that P. here, as often (4.4n.), omitted the *praenomina* altogether, and that in the confusion in the tradition mistaken attempts were made by later copyists to supply them.

XVI senatu moverunt: This information is in no other source. A separate anecdote in Val. Max. 2.9.7 and Frontin., *Strat.* 4.1.22 has them degrading 400 knights to the level of *aerarii* for refusing to help with military works in Sicily; P. is more interested in their striking action against their own senatorial colleagues (cf. 14.4n.). He does not indicate what the grounds for the expulsion were, but, given the surviving anecdote about Sempronius' divorce (above), as well as the tendency in later sources to construct Romans of this period as figures who made an exemplary moral stand against even the slightest hint of laxity, it is most likely that, as with the earlier anecdote about Fabricius (14.4n.), it was narrated by Livy as an attempt to hold a moral line which would later be readily transgressed. On this occasion, however, P. focuses on the general senatorial rigour represented by the numbers expelled, rather than drawing a specific moral lesson.

The two branches of the MS tradition give slightly different figures from one another: sixteen as against thirteen. I have printed the former, as the one supported by the older, and on the whole more reliable, manuscript, but it clearly cannot be ruled out that the latter is the correct reading.

For the technical sense of *moveo* here see 14.4n.

lustrum condiderunt: See 11.5n.

CCXCVII milia DCCXCVII: This is a modest (slightly more than 1.5%) increase over P.'s last recorded figure a decade earlier, at the start of the First Punic War (16.3n.). In peacetime that might be unexceptionable, but it seems extremely improbable in wartime, where the Romans had recently recorded substantial losses at sea, and presumably suffered other casualties also—even if those losses were not all of citizens, a fair number must have been. There is no known source of additional citizenry in this decade.

It accordingly seems fairly clear that there has been corruption either in the pre-Livian tradition or in post-Livian textual transmission: at the very minimum, either the previous figure was too low, or this one is too high. The problem with postulating that the earlier figure was too low is that it actually looked anomalously high when compared with the figure directly before it (16.3n.). This gives a slight reason for preferring to regard this figure as the one that is corrupt (so e.g. Thiel (1954), 95); but it is more likely still that the figures from the First Punic War are suspect through and through, as the ones from the previous half-century certainly were (11.5n.: cf. Brunt (1971), 32).

18.5 *Embassy and death of Regulus.* This is not only the most famous episode from the First Punic War, but one of the most-cited anecdotes in Roman history, alluded to in surviving literature dozens of times. It is, accordingly, unsurprising that P., too, narrates it relatively fully; it is also unsurprising that his focus is on what was universally agreed to be the key features of the story: Regulus' coming to Rome on parole in the hope that he will persuade the Romans to the Carthaginians' terms, his speaking instead against the proposed terms, his keeping his oath and returning to Carthage, and his death by torture. The precise details vary in the different accounts (see further below), but all share these basic narrative elements.

The popularity of the story rested partly on its value as a moral lesson (see esp. Langlands (2018), 272–87). Cicero and Seneca both repeatedly refer to Regulus as the ideal *exemplum* for proper conduct, especially in Stoic terms:[237] a lesson in patriotism, in endurance, in being able to overcome misfortune, and above all in preferring strict moral rectitude over (apparent) expediency. But the story was sufficiently protean to allow other sorts of lessons also. Cic., *Off.* 3.100–10 raises and responds to various possible objections to Regulus' conduct, and it is plausible to think that these objections were not purely hypothetical, but formed part of a tradition of debate about the proper response to Regulus' situation (cf. Langlands (2011), 105–6). We can also see some of the alternative readings of

---

[237] Cicero: see esp. *Off.* 3.99–115; also e.g. *Fin.* 2.65, 5.82, *Tusc.* 5.14, *Cato* 75, *Parad.* 16, *Off.* 1.39. Seneca: e.g. *Tranq.* 16.4, *Benef.* 5.3.2, *Epist.* 67.7, 98.12, *Prov.* 3.9.

Regulus elsewhere: for example, it appears from Cic., *Sest.* 127 that the prosecutor at Sestius' trial had interpreted Regulus' return as being a refusal to abandon his fellow captives in Carthaginian hands.[238] In Hor., *Carm.* 3.5 the key lesson relates to the refusal to ransom prisoners (hence forming an exemplary parallel to the possible return of Roman captives from Parthia, with which the poem begins); while Polyaen. 8.12 treats Regulus' actions as a self-sacrificing military stratagem: he deceives his Carthaginian captors into thinking that he will support them, only to do the opposite once he arrives in Rome. Moreover, Regulus became an exemplary figure of a slightly different sort within the Christian tradition: a model— albeit often an explicitly inferior model—of Christian martyrdom (so e.g. Tert., *Mart.* 4.6, Lact., *Inst.* 5.13.13, Aug., *Civ.* 1.15, 1.24, 2.23, 3.18, *Epist.* 125.3; cf. Mix (1970), 44–8, Felmy (2001), 170–85).

P. narrates the story without explicitly evaluative language, but he too is likely to have had some of these lessons in mind: this is clear not least because his account, with its focus on the oath, appears to allude to Cicero's Stoicizing version in *Off.* 1.39, but also contains a nod to the interpretation of Regulus in terms of Christian martyrdom by employing distinctively Christian theological language (see below).

But what he omits is also noteworthy. The story's interest to Romans rested not only on its morality, but on its spectacular and dramatic qualities: surviving accounts—even brief ones—often describe the pathos of Regulus' rejection of his family on his mission, and the lurid tortures with which he was killed. On this, however, P. is entirely silent: he says nothing of Regulus' actions in Rome beyond his address to the Senate, and gives no details of the manner of his death. The story also had legal implications: it is cited by Pompon., *Dig.* 49.15.5.3 in the context of *postliminium* (i.e. the loss of civic rights by someone captured by the enemy and the regaining of them on his return), arguing that it did not apply to Regulus, since his oath to Carthage kept him from exercising civil rights at Rome; and the question is then addressed implicitly by many authors who show Regulus refusing to wear a toga or take on the role of a Roman senator while on his embassy (e.g. Cic., *Off.* 3.100, Sil. 6.392–400, App., *Sic.* 2, Dio fr. 43.27 (cf. Zonar. 8.15.2), Eutr. 2.25; cf. Hor., *Carm.* 3.5.42).[239] This question, too, is irrelevant to P. The implicit focus is entirely on Regulus' ethical position, and everything that might distract from that is discarded: in this he is likely to have been true to the spirit of Livy's conception of history (cf. Levene (2006a)), even though Livy does not in practice eschew drama or pathos, and may well have had many of the details found elsewhere.

---

[238] *Contra* Kaster (2006), 361, who prefers to emend Cicero's text in order to have the anecdote conform with the main tradition. But the emendation is violent, and yields awkward sense: it is better to accept that the Regulus legend was more protean than Kaster allows.

[239] On the relevance of *postliminium* to the Regulus story see Kornhardt (1954), esp. 101–6.

As is typical of P.—in this, however, unlike Livy—he also omits morally complicating elements of the story.[240] Most notably, he has nothing of the aftermath narrated by Tuditanus, *FRHist* 10 F 8 (*ap.* Gell. 7.4.4), D.S. 24.12, and Zonar. 8.15.7: that in revenge Regulus' family tortured Carthaginian prisoners to death in a similar fashion. In Tuditanus and Zonaras the impetus for this comes from the Senate, whereas in Diodorus the Senate disapproves when it learns of it, and rescues one of the Carthaginians before he dies; but either way it gives the anecdote troubling overtones, since it ceases to be an uncomplicated celebration of Roman heroism faced with Carthaginian brutality. The omission may merely be because it was absent from Livy, but that cannot be assumed, given his regular tendency to reveal darker moral overtones to the Roman past.

Although the story is thoroughly ingrained in Roman tradition, its historicity is problematic. The key evidence is its absence from Polybius, which for most scholars is decisive against it (e.g. Klebs (1896), 2089, De Sanctis III.1 152 [155] n. 20, Walbank (1957), 93–4, Lazenby (1996), 106; *contra* e.g. Frank (1926), 311–14, Kornhardt (1954), 101, Wardle (1998), 111, Minunno (2005), 218–22). Some argue that we cannot be sure that Polybius would have narrated such a story even if he knew of it (so e.g. Frank (1926), 312, Kornhardt (1954), 121); but, as is often noted, it is hard to imagine that Polybius would have omitted to make some comment on it when he digresses on the lessons to be learned from the fate of Regulus at 1.35.

As for the motive for invention: some have proposed that it could be in response to the cruelty inflicted by his family on Carthaginian prisoners (above: so e.g. Klebs (1896), 2090–1, De Sanctis III 152 [154], Blättler (1945), 27–8): D.S. 24.12, in narrating that, has Regulus' wife avenging herself not for his torture, but for his death by (as she thought) neglect, which in turn seems to imply his dependence on a version without the embassy, since execution is always assumed to be the inevitable consequence of his return from the embassy to Carthage (*contra* Frank (1926), 313).[241] That is inevitably speculative, but invention of some sort looks likely: most obviously, Regulus' warning not to accept any peace short of Roman victory looks like a positively slanted version of his earlier attempt to impose an unequal peace on Carthage (18.1–2n.), and the reported manner of his death clearly owes a great deal to Roman stereotypes of Carthaginian cruelty.

---

[240] In certain respects, however, moral complexity is intrinsic to the story, in as much as the very fact of Regulus being a prisoner of war might have been thought to compromise his heroic status: see Langlands (2018), 277–80.

[241] Diodorus does apparently narrate Regulus' death by torture at 23.16.1, but there is no mention of the embassy there, and that fragment of Diodorus is preserved only in a summary by Tzetzes which appears in other respects to have been garbled (cf. below). Even if Tzetzes has reported him accurately, it may be that Diodorus narrated the torture but not the embassy (which is why, on his account, Regulus' wife did not know the manner of his death); alternatively Diodorus may have (not for the only time) inadvertently contradicted himself through switching sources.

Regulus' embassy is dated by Eutr. 2.24.2, Oros. 4.10.1, and Zonar. 8.15.1 immediately after Metellus' victory at Panormus in 251 or 250 (19.1n.).[242] P. apparently dates it earlier, since he, following Livy, puts it in Book 18, whereas he does not mention the Panormus victory until Book 19. But this is not as straightforward as it might appear, since his notice in Book 19 focuses on Metellus' triumph; it is hence possible that Livy described the victory itself in Book 18 and the triumph in Book 19, but that P. delayed any mention of the victory until the latter occasion (except in as much as it presumably counted as one of the Roman successes in 18.3).[243] In favour of that interpretation is that one would expect the peace mission to have been narrated by Livy as a response to a spectacular Roman victory, and Panormus is the next that is presented in surviving sources as a grand set-piece success (though cf. 18.3n. for other Roman achievements in the intervening period), and the one that is chosen for the setting elsewhere in the tradition. It would admittedly be idiosyncratic for P. to have delayed his report of the victory to Book 19, if Livy indeed narrated it in Book 18, but such idiosyncrasies are not out of line with his general approach to summarizing Livy: cf. esp. 11.2n., 38.7n., 41.2n. for a similar displacements of an event into a different book; also e.g. 2.2n., 2.11n. for even clearer (albeit less dramatic) examples of P. reversing Livy's narrative order as a result of his only reporting an event when describing its final outcome.

missus: Here too, as in the first sentence of the book (18.1n.), P. adapts his typical sentence-structure (2.2n.) to accommodate a fuller and more complex narrative. Here, instead of a single sentence being expanded, effectively two separate sentences of the form 'background clause + main clause' are joined into one with *et*. This creates two focal points of interest within the sentence, one being Regulus' heroic stand when on his embassy, the second his death. Variation is achieved by the 'background' clauses governed by the first main verb being participial (*missus...adstrictus*), while the clause governed by the second main verb is temporal (*cum...reversus esset*); the first half is moreover expanded further by the fact that there are two participles, with additional clauses dependent on each.

de pace: That the Carthaginians wanted above all to strike a broader peace-treaty, and that the idea of exchanging prisoners was at best a secondary consideration, is standard in those versions of Regulus' embassy which embed it into a broader historical narrative, especially those which explicitly date it after the Carthaginian defeat at Panormus (see above: cf. e.g. Sil. 6.346–9, App., *Pun.* 4, Flor. 1.18.24, Dio fr. 43.26 with Zonar. 8.15.1, Eutr. 2.24.2): it helps reinforce the impression of

---

[242] App., *Sic.* 2 dates it to the final peace-negotiations in 241, but appears to contradict this at *Pun.* 4, where he places it not long after Regulus' capture.

[243] Blättler (1945), 44 rightly observes that it is probable that Livy, like Eutropius, Orosius, and Zonaras, narrated Regulus' embassy after the victory at Panormus; but he less plausibly seems to suggest that the *Periochae* has transferred the embassy from Book 19 into Book 18 in order to create a pattern of Roman failures in the first book and successes in the second.

Roman military superiority to have the Carthaginians sue for peace, only for the Romans to see it in their interests to prosecute the war further. When the story is told as a free-standing anecdote, however, it is usual to present it as if only a prisoner-exchange were at issue (e.g. Cic., *Off.* 1.39, 3.99–100, Hor., *Carm.* 3.5, with ps.-Acro, *Carm.* 1.12.35, 3.5.13,[244] Val. Max. 1.1.14, Gell. 7.4.1,[245] Tert., *Mart.* 4.6, *Vir. Ill.* 40.4, Aug., *Civ.* 1.15): that way it is clear that Regulus himself would be the primary beneficiary of the proposed deal, and accentuates his heroism in rejecting it. That point is further reinforced in those versions which suggest that Regulus alone was to be exchanged for all of the Carthaginian prisoners in Roman hands (e.g. Val. Max. 1.1.14, Sil. 6.348–9, 463–5, Tert., *Mart.* 4.6).

de commutandis captivis: *captivos commutare* is used nowhere except here and Cic., *Off.* 1.39, likewise talking about Regulus (though the related *commutatio captivorum* appears at 19.4—see *ad loc.*—Flor. 1.18.24, ps.-Acro, *Carm.* 1.12.35, 3.5.13).[246] The similarity between P. and Cicero extends beyond this phrase: compare Cicero's *cum de captivis commutandis Romam missus esset iurassetque se rediturum* with P.'s *missus a Carthaginiensibus ad senatum ut de pace et, si eam non posset impetrare, de commutandis captivis ageret, et iureiurando adstrictus, rediturum se Carthaginem*. This is likely to be because P. is constructing his account with Cicero's version in mind: cf. below, and also 13.7n., where P. uses Cicero's next paragraph when retelling the story of Fabricius.

Prisoner exchanges were not uncommon in antiquity: cf. 19.4 for a later example. A prisoner exchange may also have been the medium for Scipio Asina's return to Rome following his capture (17.1n.).

iureiurando adstrictus: The same phrase is found at 2.1 and 22.8, but is relatively rare (cf. *TLL* II 963.41–7): it is found at Suet., *Caes.* 84.2, Apul., *Met.* 10.8, ps.-Quint., *Decl.* 16 pr., Serv. auct., *Ecl.* 5.20, Dares 40; cf. Sen., *Contr.* 1.6.12. Most importantly, however, it appears in Cic., *Off.* 1.40 (cf. the slightly different 3.111), directly after Cicero's account of Regulus, in relation to the ten Roman prisoners released on parole by Hannibal after Cannae. That passage does not appear in all MSS of *De Officiis*, and has been argued to be an interpolation, but its authenticity is strongly defended by Dyck (1996), 150–3. It looks likely that, at the very least, it stood in the text of Cicero that P. was using, and that as well as drawing

---

[244] Horace seems to assume the ransom rather than exchange of prisoners: this provides a closer parallel to the proposed return of prisoners from Parthia which is the political impetus for the ode, though it may also have been influenced by accounts of the later proposals to ransom Roman prisoners after Cannae (cf. 22.9: see Nisbet and Rudd (2004), 81–2; more generally Kornhardt (1954), 106–8).

[245] Gellius is here citing Tuditanus (*FRHist* 10 F 8), but in summary form and not verbatim: it is accordingly a mistake to deduce that Tuditanus knew nothing of the broader peace-proposal, or that the latter must be a later accretion into the tradition (*contra* Klebs (1896), 2091, De Sanctis III.1 152 [155] n. 20).

[246] More common is *captivos permutare*, used at Livy 22.23.6, Val. Max. 2.9.8, 5.2 ext. 2, Gell. 6.18.3 (cf. 6.18.6), Tuditanus, *FRHist* 10 F 8 (*ap.* Gell. 7.4.1), *Vir. Ill.* 40.4 (the last two with reference to Regulus).

directly on *De Officiis*' account of Regulus, he incorporated a distinctive phrase from Cicero's next anecdote.

auctor senatui: *senatui* is a correction by a late MSS; earlier MSS read *senatus*. The body advised to act is normally in the dative (cf. Woodman and Martin (1996), 193), but the copyist has mistakenly attracted it into the case of the gerund.

fide custodita: Another unusual phrase. It is employed by Cic., *Leg.* 3.11, but in a very different sense; it appears in no other pagan source, but it is extremely common in Christian writers in theological contexts. P. is describing Regulus in the language of contemporary Christianity.

supplicio...sumpto: That Regulus was tortured to death is universally agreed in all versions of the anecdote; the manner of torture used varies, though it usually involves some version of sleep deprivation. One version has the Carthaginians cutting off or sewing back his eyelids and then placing him to look at the sun (though this alone would presumably blind him rather than killing him): so Tubero, *FRHist* 38 F 12 (*ap.* Gell. 7.4.2), ps.-Acro, *Carm.* 1.12.35. A more popular version has him placed standing in a spiked box so that he could not lie down or support himself (Sen., *Tranq.* 16.4, *Epist.* 67.7, Sil. 6.539–44, App., *Pun.* 4, Sic. 2, Tert., *Mart.* 4.6, *Vir. Ill.* 40.4, Aug., *Civ.* 1.15), while some versions combine both of these: e.g. Cic., *Pis.* 43 (copied verbatim by Oros. 4.10.1), Val. Max. 9.2 ext. 1, Sen., *Prov.* 3.9, Zonar. 8.15.7. Cic., *Fin.* 2.65 and 5.82 adds starvation to the mix, while D.S. 23.16.1 (from Tzetzes) has a unique version where, after having his eyelids cut off, he is trampled by an elephant—but this last probably comes from conflation by Tzetzes with the story in Zonar. 8.13.8 that the Carthaginians sought to frighten Regulus with an elephant immediately after his capture (Mix (1970), 19). Alternatively, some authors suggest that he was crucified (Sen., *Epist.* 98.12, Sil. 2.343–4, Flor. 1.18.25)—a traditional Carthaginian punishment (cf. 17.5n.), which for the Romans carried connotations of humiliation as well.

It is impossible to say which is the original version, especially since the story is unlikely to be historical (cf. above), and may have been transmitted in varying oral versions prior to its first being recorded; it draws on various stereotypes of Carthaginian cruelty, perhaps mixed with some memory of some such tortures actually being carried out on someone (not necessarily Regulus). For a detailed analysis of the different elements of the tradition and their possible origins see Minunno (2005), 222–32.

periit: P. often produces closure to his book-summaries by ending with a death: cf. e.g. 14.8, 30.7, 48.19, 55.7, 60.10, 71.3, 83.8, 88.3, 91.3, 92.4, 116.8, 121.2, 124.3, 133.3. Sometimes Livy may have done the same, but that is not true in the one case where Livy's original survives (30.7: see *ad loc.*), and it may be that many of these closural effects are constructed by P. himself.

Book 19

19.1 *Triumph of Metellus.* This victory, achieved at Panormus, was one of the greatest Roman successes of the war. P., however, focuses his attention not on the victory itself, but on the triumph that followed it, which was unusually spectacular. This is not the only time that he gives precedence to a famous and distinctive triumph over the actual battle which led to it (cf. e.g. 11.4n.): the additional twist here is that in doing so he (misleadingly) implies that the battle, as well as the triumph, was in Book 19, whereas it is more likely that it was in Book 18, prior to Regulus' embassy towards the end of that book (18.5n.).

Caecilius Metellus: L. Caecilius Metellus (*RE* 72); he was once again consul in 247, here too, according to Zonar. 8.16.5, successfully campaigning in Sicily. According to the *Fasti Capitolini*, he was *magister equitum* in 249 (cf. Zonar. 8.15.14) and dictator for holding elections in 224; Plin., *Nat.* 7.139–40, summarizing the funeral oration given by his son, adds to his honours that he was *quindecimvir agris dandis*. Apart from his victory here, he was best known for two anecdotes relating to his time as *pontifex maximus*, both of which are described by P. later in the book (see 19.8, 19.10nn.): Cic., *Cato* 30 gives the dates when he held the post as 243–221. Cicero refers to him as an example of someone who retained his strength into old age, a noteworthy feat, given that, according to Val. Max. 8.13.2 and Plin., *Nat.* 7.157, he lived to the age of 100. This would make him around seventy-one at the time of his victory at Panormus: not impossible in itself, even though Polybius describes him as taking a relatively active role in the battle, but it does suggest a remarkably late flourishing of his career, since he is not attested as having held any senior office at Rome prior to this, and it is preferable to assume that his longevity was exaggerated.

For the form of name used here see 4.4n.

rebus...prospere gestis: For the phrase see 3.10n. This was the last major land-battle of the First Punic War: a relatively full account is found in Plb. 1.40 (cf. Frontin., *Strat.* 2.5.4). According to him, the Carthaginian commander Hasdrubal marched against the Roman forces occupying Panormus (modern Palermo) under the command of Metellus; Metellus kept his forces in the city in order to tempt Hasdrubal to overconfidence. Hasdrubal brought his whole force up to the walls, whereupon Metellus had his light-armed troops and his allies in the city attack the elephants with missiles. The elephants turned on the Carthaginian soldiers and trampled them down, at which point Metellus sallied and cut down the army.

Other sources describe the battle rather differently. In Zonar. 8.14.9–10, while the opening phase of the battle is not dissimilar to Polybius, Metellus, rather than getting the elephants to turn on their own troops, traps the Carthaginians in a narrow place where the elephants are unable to manoeuvre. The key reason for the victory, however, is that the Carthaginian fleet (which played no role in Polybius) seeks to land to evacuate the army, but this causes chaos when the soldiers rush to the ships. D.S. 23.21 is still more different (though it too depends on the motif of Hasdrubal's overconfidence): Metellus' victory has nothing to do with the elephants, but instead comes because Hasdrubal failed to fortify his camp, and his Gallic mercenaries were drunk and so were unable to defend the camp when Metellus attacked.

Diodorus' version looks the least plausible: it offers little detail, and what is there is nothing more than a stereotypical summary of a battle that turned on an assumed ethnic trait.[247] There is less to choose between Polybius and Zonaras; on balance, as often, we probably should conclude that Polybius' account is closer to the time and more likely to depend on reliable sources, but we cannot rule out that Dio had authentic material available to him that Polybius did not.

It is likely, as argued above (18.5n.), that Livy narrated the victory itself not in Book 19, but in Book 18. As to the date, the majority of sources explicitly date it to Metellus' consulship in 251 (D.S. 23.21, Frontin., *Strat.* 2.5.4, Flor. 1.18.27, Eutr. 2.24.1, Oros. 4.9.14), and Livy probably did the same, since several of these sources are likely to have derived the date directly or indirectly from his history (De Sanctis III.1 254–5 [262–3]).

However, that date appears problematic. Metellus' triumph was certainly as proconsul in (consular) September 250, as confirmed by the *Fasti Capitolini*. Moreover, the narrative sequence in Plb. 1.39.7–41.4, while admittedly complex, is most naturally to be interpreted as meaning that the battle did not take place until after the consuls for 250 had been elected (cf. Morgan (1972a), 123–9); Polybius moreover dates the battle to 'the peak of the harvest' (1.40.2: ἀκμαζούσης τῆς συγκομιδῆς: cf. 1.40.5),[248] which in Sicily is June (Julian) (Beloch, *GG* IV.2 285). Putting those considerations together, Polybius may be seen to have dated the battle to June 250 (Julian): and this seems likely to be correct, not only because Polybius is to be regarded as broadly reliable *a priori*, but his version makes good logistical sense, since it explains why Metellus was fighting without his colleague (who must have returned to Rome to conduct the elections), and it removes an otherwise problematic gap in the narrative, since, were the battle to be dated to June 251, it is odd that the Romans did nothing to follow up the victory until 250 (cf. Leuze (1907), 137–9).

This may mean that the sources who date the victory to Metellus' consulship are merely in error (so e.g. Morgan (1972a), 121–2), but the two versions could be reconciled if the battle took place towards the end of Metellus' consulship, after

---

[247] For the (alleged) Gallic susceptibility to alcohol see e.g. Cic., *Font.* fr. 10 (*ap.* Amm. 15.12.4), D.S. 5.26.3, Livy 5.33.2–3.

[248] *Contra* Leuze (1907), 145–6, who elaborately but implausibly interprets the phrase to mean 'when the harvest would soon be at hand', and so dates the battle a couple of months earlier.

the new consuls were elected but before they took office on (probably) 1 May: this is entirely compatible with Polybius, and would simply imply that the Roman calendar was running a month or two behind the seasons at this point, such that May 1 (consular) corresponded with mid-June (Julian) or later (so Beloch, *GG* IV.2 264–5).[249] On balance one should perhaps prefer this reconstruction, which saves the credit of all sources, but it cannot be ruled out that the battle after all took place in (consular) 250, and that it was misdated to Metellus' consulship by the later writers.

speciosum: The only use of this word in P; it appears several times in L., but never of a triumph. *speciosissimus triumphus* was, however, a favourite phrase of Valerius Maximus (2.7.1, 5.3.2c, 6.3.1b, 6.9.1, 7.1.1, 8.1 damn. 1), it is rare elsewhere (though cf. Flor. 1.13.26, *Hist. Aug. Aurelian.* 33.1); the phrase for P. may have evoked the historical tradition of the early empire, if not Livy in particular.

egit triumphum: Cf. 17.2n.

XIII ducibus hostium: No other source speaks of these; since Metellus won only a single battle, these *duces* presumably represent not leaders of entire armies, but subordinate commanders (cf. *TLL* V 2322.39–74, *OLD s.v. dux* 4a). P.'s inclusion of them adds to the sense that the triumph was on an unprecedented scale.

CXX elephantis: All sources agree that the centre-piece of Metellus' triumph was the captured elephants he displayed; the number, however, varies between them. Sen., *Brev. Vit.* 13.8 and Zonar. 8.14.11 agree with P. In Plb. 1.38.2 Hasdrubal began with 140 elephants, and he implies (1.40.15) that the Romans captured them all (though this may be an overstatement), while in D.H., *AR* 2.66.4 it is 138; Plin., *Nat.* 8.16–17 offers as alternatives 142 and 140. Frontin., *Strat.* 2.5.4 reduces the number to 130 elephants, as does Eutr. 2.24.1. Oros. 4.9.14–15 has 130 in the battle, but 26 are killed and only 104 captured; similarly in Flor. 1.18.28 it is 'around 100'. The outlier is D.S. 23.21, where the number is 60. Any of these could be true.

Plin., *Nat.* 8.17 cites Verrius Flaccus as recording that after the triumph they were compelled to fight in the circus, where they were killed, but then notes an alternative version by Piso (*FRHist* 9 F 32), according to which they were merely driven around the circus; this latter version is supported by Fenestella, who claimed that no elephants fought at Rome (as opposed to being merely displayed) before 90 BC (Plin., *Nat.* 8.19 = Fenestella *FRHist* 70 F 15). Piso's and Fenestella's version is supported by A. Drummond in *FRHist* 3.580; but Pliny himself notes an objection, when he remarks, slightly caustically, that no source which denies that they were killed explains what was then done with them (*Nat.* 8.17): since we

---

[249] Morgan (1977), 103–4 rejects this possibility, and argues for an exact correspondence of the consular and Julian calendar in these years, but his argument depends on a highly speculative reconstruction of the Carthaginians' strategy in 251/0, and little weight can be placed on it.

do not hear of elephants at Rome in subsequent years, we would have to assume that they were slaughtered privately, rather than for display.

An anecdote in Plin., *Nat.* 8.16, Frontin., *Strat.* 1.7.1, and Zonar. 8.14.12 tells how the captured elephants were transported from Sicily to Italy on rafts made of earthen jars tied together and covered with planks: a remarkable feat, if true, given the breadth of the Straits of Messana. According to Plin., *Nat.* 7.139, Metellus was the first to lead elephants in a triumph, but that is almost certainly an error, since Curius Dentatus is attested as having done so after the defeat of Pyrrhus in 275 (14.3n.); it is possible that the error was not simply the result of Pliny's carelessness, but derives from an exaggeration in the funeral speech by Metellus' son, which Pliny is summarizing here (cf. above). Certainly Metellus' elephants became a point of pride in his family: they were depicted by his descendants on coin issues in 128, 127, 125, 81, and 47–46 (*RRC* nos. 262, 263, 269, 374, 459), as well as a Cretan coin from the period in the 60s when Q. Caecilius Metellus (*cos.* 69) controlled the island (Scullard (1974), 274–5).

19.2 *Defeat and disgrace of Claudius Pulcher.* A further well-known episode in the war, narrated or referred to in numerous sources. Livy's version is summarized not only in P., but also in Serv., *Aen* 6.198 (F 12), though Servius' account of Livy is very confused (see commentary *ad loc.*).

P., like almost all Latin sources,[250] concentrates less on the battle itself, and more on the sacrilege: this was not necessarily the balance in Livy, but reflects the way the story developed as an *exemplum* of arrogant irreligiosity leading to disaster. The sequel in P., however, is more distinctive: most discuss Claudius Pulcher's trial following the battle, but P. ignores that, as well as the related story of Claudius' consular colleague L. Junius Pullus (see F 12n.): he focuses instead on a less commonly told story, of Claudius' attempt to impose an unqualified subordinate on the state as dictator.

Claudius Pulcher cos.: P. Claudius Pulcher, consul in 249 (*RE* 304, *MRR* I 214). He was the son of Ap. Claudius Caecus (13.3n.); given that Appius held the censorship in 312, more than sixty years earlier, either Claudius Pulcher ascended to the consulship at a relatively advanced age, or he was born to Appius very late in life.[251] Little is known of him apart from his activities in this year, but an inscription on a milestone on the Via Appia indicates that he had at some point been

---

[250] The exception is Orosius, who has no interest in showing the Roman gods effectively punishing sacrilege.

[251] Walbank (1957), 113, following a suggestion of De Sanctis III.1 167 [169] n. 62, resolved the difficulty by proposing that he was in fact the son of Ap. Claudius Caudex, *cos.* 264. However, De Sanctis himself noted the problem: that Pulcher's identification as a son of Caecus is already present in Cic., *Div.* 1.29, and is likely to reflect the family traditions of the patrician Claudii. It is far more plausible that either Appius was an elderly father or Pulcher an elderly consul than that the Claudii would be in error concerning so prominent a sequence of their own ancestors.

curule aedile (*CIL* X 6838 (with Mommsen's correction on p. 1095) = *ILS* 5801 = *ILLRP* 448). Although he survived his disgrace here (see below), he was apparently dead by 246 (but see 19.6n.).

For the form of name used here see 4.4n.

contra auspicia profectus: For the implications of *profectus* cf. F 12n. The phrase *contra auspicia profectus* is repeated at 22.2 (see *ad loc.*), but occurs nowhere else in surviving Latin.

mergi pullos, qui cibari nolebant: For the use of chickens to provide auspices prior to (and on) campaigns, see Mommsen, *StR*³ I 83–5, Valeton (1890), 211–15. They were kept in cages (and deliberately starved, according to the cynical comment by Cic., *Div.* 2.73); they were then released in front of food, and it was considered a good omen if, while they ate, some food fell from their mouths. In Claudius' case, the problem was apparently that they refused to eat at all (Cic., *Nat. Deor.* 2.7), or even to leave the cage (Julius Paris, summarizing Val. Max. 1.4.3): Servius' account is closer to Cicero's (see commentary on F 12), suggesting that this was Livy's version also.

Cic., *Nat. Deor.* 2.7 is wittier than P.: Claudius says 'that they should drink, since they were unwilling to eat' (*ut biberent, quoniam esse nollent*); Servius' account seems to reflect the same version, although Claudius' quoted words there are simply *vel bibant* (see commentary on F 12). P.'s contrast between *mergi* and *cibari*, while still pointed, is less sharply worded. It is most probable that here it is Servius who is closer to Livy's original: the vivid sarcasm in direct speech can be paralleled in a similar context at 22.3.13, and it is not unlike P. to have reworded Livy into more pedestrian language.

infeliciter...pugnavit: The battle was at Drepana (modern Trapani), on the western point of Sicily. The only detailed account is in Plb. 1.49.5–51.12: according to him, Claudius, attacking the town, found his ships caught in a narrow position at one entrance to the harbour while the Carthaginians escaped to open sea at the other. When battle was joined the Carthaginians had the advantage of more manoeuvrable ships and a superior position, whereas the Romans were too close to land and unskilled to be able to reposition their ships when under attack. Other sources (e.g. D.S. 24.1.5, Flor. 1.18.29, Eutr. 2.26.1) add nothing to this, telling no more than the bare fact of the defeat; Zonar. 8.15.13–14 ignores the battle entirely. For a detailed study of the battle see esp. Thiel (1954), 275–81.

According to Plb. 1.51.11–12, Claudius escaped with thirty ships, but the remaining ninety-three were captured; he refers in addition to numerous ships being sunk in the battle (1.51.7). D.S. 24.1.5 has the losses as 117 ships and 20,000 men, though with the total fleet as 210 ships: this may depend on the same basic source as Polybius, since the number 210 is equal to his own claimed losses of 117 ships added to the ninety-three which Polybius says were captured (De Sanctis III.1 168 [170] n. 65, *contra* Walbank (1957), 114–15). A similar order of losses is found in Eutr. 2.26.1: a fleet of 220 ships, with 100 sunk, ninety captured, and thirty escaped.[252]

However, as Thiel (1954), 279–80 notes, it is highly unlikely that a battle fought so close to shore would have involved so many ships being sunk. Accordingly, it is better to assume that these sources all depend on a version which has mistakenly counted the Roman losses twice, at one point treating the lost ships as all sunk, at another point as all captured. In that case there were around 120 ships in total, which is the version found in Oros. 4.10.3, who, like Polybius, has thirty escaping, but explicitly says that the other ninety were captured *or* sunk (he adds that 8,000 Romans were killed, 20,000 captured). Although Orosius is late, and not generally the most reliable source, in this case his figures make the most sense, and are most likely to go back to authentic information (so Thiel (1954), 279–80, *contra* De Sanctis III.1 168–9 [170–2]).

revocatus: This presents an historical problem. Claudius can only have been recalled in order to punish him for his defeat. It makes sense that, as P. implies, it was followed directly by the nomination of a dictator, if the object of both was to remove Claudius from his command following his misconduct (cf. Rosenstein (1990), 35–6). This would then explain why Claudius' response was to select so unlikely a candidate (see below): Glicia may well even have been his own client, or at the very least someone whose lower social status placed him under obligation to Claudius and would allow the latter to maintain some measure of power behind the scenes. This scenario also makes sense given the anger against Claudius that is indicated by his trial and conviction shortly afterwards (see below).

However, according to Plb. 1.52.5, the other consul, Junius, did not leave for Sicily until after Claudius' defeat was known at Rome. Admittedly, Polybius has certainly garbled something in his sources, since he mistakenly makes Junius consul in the following year; but this does not preclude the broad sequence of his narrative from being accurate. But in that case, the naming of a dictator is unlikely to have been immediately connected with Claudius' recall, since one would not expect Junius to have been sent out at all if the appointment of a dictator was imminent: indeed, he could have been asked to nominate the dictator himself. On this account, it can only have been later in the year, after Junius' own disaster, that it was decided to nominate a dictator; in which case it was a response to the generally poor military situation (cf. Zonar. 8.15.14), rather than a move against Claudius in particular.[253]

---

[252] Frontin., *Strat.* 2.13.9 has an anecdote about Claudius escaping with twenty ships through a stratagem whereby he arrayed them as though they had been victorious. This has been thought implausible, but cf. Konrad (2015), who shows that Frontinus' language suggests that he is not describing Claudius' escape from the battle itself, but rather his evasion of Carthaginian naval defences on his way back to Rome (which explains the lower number of ships in his fleet than the survivors reported by Polybius).

[253] So e.g. De Sanctis III.1 170–4, 255–6 [173–7, 263–4], Thiel (1954), 283–4, 291, Morgan (1977), 105–8; also Bleckmann (2002), 189–90, who goes further and even rejects the idea that Claudius was recalled prematurely from his command.

The problem with the latter reconstruction, however, is that it makes Claudius' anomalous choice of dictator less readily explicable, and if he was allowed to continue acting as consul for several months after his defeat, it is more surprising that he was—unusually (cf. above)—put on trial and convicted soon afterwards.

The solution is, however, to hand: if Polybius was wrong about the sequence, and if Junius in fact set out on his campaign before news had come in of Claudius' defeat,[254] then Claudius could have been recalled and compelled to name a dictator immediately, even while Junius was still campaigning and perhaps even prior to his disaster[255]—a consul in the field could continue in his command even after a dictator had been appointed (Mommsen, StR³ II 155-6). This hypothesis is indeed supported by one detail in Polybius: at 1.53.1 he has the Carthaginian commander Adherbal sending the ships and troops captured at Drepana to Carthage directly before the Carthaginians encountered Junius. This makes most sense if the two consuls were campaigning in Sicily simultaneously.

On balance, therefore, P.'s account, though heavily abridged, is likely to reflect the real sequence of events.

According to Plb. 1.52.2-3, Claudius was put on trial, convicted, and fined (cf. Cic., Nat. Deor. 2.7, Div. 2.71). A circumstantial account of his trial is given in Schol. Bob. p. 90.3-8 (Stangl) (cf. Val. Max. 8.1.absol.4): he was originally tried by two tribunes for *perduellio* (sc. acting against the interests of the state) before the centuriate assembly, but the trial was disrupted by a storm, which was held to constitute a religious flaw. When the tribunes sought to resume the trial, their colleagues vetoed the proceedings, arguing that it was not legal for the same people to prosecute the same person for *perduellio* twice in the same magistracy; instead the charge was changed to a non-capital one, and Claudius was convicted and fined. See Linderski (1986), 2176-7.

P. says nothing about Claudius' trial, but implies only that he was deliberately recalled so as to remove him from his command (see below). Instead, P.'s interest is in his choice of substitute, which not only provided a further vivid illustration of Claudius' outrageous conduct, but also provided a rare instance of a lower-class person ascending to the highest office—P., as often, highlights the extension

---

[254] This is rejected by Morgan (1977), 106, on the grounds that Junius' route along the southern coast of Sicily suggests a desire to avoid the victorious Carthaginian fleet on the northern coast. But while it is *compatible* with such a desire, it does not *indicate* it, since it is equally compatible with the desire to control the southern coast of Sicily at a time when his colleague (as he thought) controlled the northern. Moreover, as Lazenby (1996), 137 notes, Junius sent out transport ships with only a limited force to protect them, according to Plb. 1.52.7: this would be odd, if the Romans had recently suffered a major defeat and the Carthaginian fleet was known to be roaming the Sicilian coast unchallenged.

[255] Walbank (1957), 115-16 accepts that Junius left early from Rome, but oddly denies the corollary, and, like De Sanctis *et al.*, has the dictator appointed only after his defeat. Lazenby (1996), 137-41, even more oddly, seems to veer between both versions, at one point (137) dating the appointment of the dictator immediately after Claudius' defeat, but then (141) describing it as happening only after the failure of Junius' final campaign.

of Roman constitutional practice, even if, as here, in a direction he clearly regarded as deleterious.

iussusque dictatorem dicere: This is not the only time when the historical tradition records a dispute between the Senate and the consul over the appointment of a dictator, with the latter giving way only reluctantly: see e.g. Livy 4.26.5–11, 8.12.11–13, 9.38.9–14, 27.5.14–19. Mommsen argued that in such cases the Senate did not ultimately have the authority to enforce that decision: it was the consul who made the final determination, both to make the appointment at all and to choose a specific candidate (Mommsen, *StR*³ II 146–51). However, as Jahn (1970), 39–42 argues, this very episode demonstrates that the consul was not seen as having the ultimate authority in these matters. Claudius had an obvious interest in refusing to make the appointment, since the likely purpose of appointing a dictator was to remove him from office (see above), yet he saw no way to resist the Senate's authority directly, and the most he was able to do was try to sabotage it by selecting an unsuitable candidate.

Claudium Gliciam: The name is corrupted in the MSS, but was corrected by Sigonius from the *Fasti Capitolini*, which give his full name as M. Claudius Glicia (*RE* 166, *MRR* I 215); for the version of the name used here cf. 4.4n. Suet., *Tib.* 2.2 calls him simply Glycias, with no clan name, perhaps to emphasize his lowly background (cf. below). According to the *Fasti*, he had no *magister equitum*: this is probably because he was forced to resign before he could name one, rather than a deliberate violation of constitutional precedent (Mommsen, *StR*³ II 159 n. 2).

sortis ultimae hominem: According to Suet., *Tib.* 2.2 he was Claudius' *viator*, but in the *Fasti Capitolini* he is a scribe. Both of these were *apparitores*, attendants on magistrates, with the scribe having a somewhat higher social status (cf. Purcell (1983), esp. 152–61, Badian (1989), 598–603). Suetonius' version suits his interpretation of Claudius' actions (that he made the choice out of deliberate mockery), but the version of the *Fasti* is vastly more plausible. No *viator* is known to have achieved political office at any time under the Republic (though under the Empire several became equestrians: see Purcell (1983), 152–4), but at least one scribe had reached the Senate in the previous century, namely Cn. Flavius, who had been curule aedile in 304 (cf. 9.6), and in the next century another, C. Cicereius, would hold a praetorship in 173. Hence Claudius' choice, while unusual, was not completely outside social norms. It was nevertheless likely to generate controversy. Flavius' reaching the aedileship is described as having caused considerable conflict, and the dictatorship was even more exclusive. Glicia is one of only a handful of dictators in the middle Republic who had not previously held the consulship (Mommsen, *StR*³ II 146; cf. 11.6n.), and the others are likely to have held at least some lower magistracies.

However, even if Glicia was indeed a scribe, P.'s description of him as from the lowest background, while certainly exaggerated, may not be completely misplaced (*contra* Lindsay (1995), 60): it seems likely that his family had risen relatively recently from humble origins. The key evidence is that the *Fasti*, in recording his dictatorship, provide his father's name, but not his grandfather's. This is unusual, though not unique: the most likely interpretation is that the grandfather was not a Roman citizen, and in Glicia's case it is not impossible that he was even a slave (Mommsen, *StR*³ I 488 n. 2, Degrassi 21-2).

More generally, scribes as a class were sometimes also the object of social scorn not unlike P.'s here. We cannot, of course, attest this securely for the middle Republic, given the lack of contemporary documentation, but it is not implausible; it is certainly the case in the late Republic and early Empire (cf. Purcell (2001)), and P.'s language may well reflect Livy's attitude, even if not his wording. This may partly be because the post, held by freedmen and freeborn side by side, provided an opportunity for social advancement for people of lower backgrounds, and so undermined existing structures of privilege; it was perhaps partly also because the scribe's access to writing and documents gave them a potential power which was hard to regulate. Paradoxically, this power could best be controlled by insisting on the scribe's lowly status, and so discouraging him from exploiting his position in the way an aristocrat might (see esp. Purcell (2001), 662-71).

P., however, does not himself specifically identify Glicia as a scribe. This may be because by the fourth century AD scribes were more respected as a group (cf. Purcell (1983), 136-7), so naming the office would have, for P.'s readers, undermined the impression of the utter inappropriateness of Claudius Pulcher's choice.

praetextatus: The higher Roman magistrates wore a purple-bordered toga, the *toga praetexta* (Mommsen, *StR*³ I 418-20); they moreover continued to wear it on public occasions for the rest of their lives (Mommsen, *StR*³ I 437). Glicia's doing so was, accordingly, legally proper, but it also implies the compounding of the original offence (in P.'s eyes) of taking on such a post despite his lowly status.

19.3 *Dictatorship of Caiatinus.*

A. Atilius Calatinus: For Calatinus—or, better, Caiatinus—see 17.4n. Apart from P., his dictatorship is recorded in the *Fasti Capitolini* and Zonar. 8.15.14 (cf. Dio 36.34.3); it is also mentioned by Flor. 1.18.12, but in a context which indicates that he has confused it with his consulship in 258 (17.4n.). It appears from the *Fasti* that Caiatinus was the substitute chosen in 249 after Glicia was compelled to resign (19.2n.), but P. does not make the connection: his interest in Caiatinus is only in the constitutional innovation that he represents (below).

primus: As often, P. draws attention to a 'first' (cf. 11.5n.). Caiatinus was indeed the first dictator to campaign outside Italy. He was also the last, at least until the extraordinary rule of Julius Caesar in the early 40s; the limitation of a dictatorship to a maximum of six months made it less effective for leading an army overseas (so Mommsen, *StR*³ II 169). P. does not mention anything he achieved on his campaign; this might be thought to be because his interest was solely in the innovation, but in this particular instance his omission is more plausibly explained by the fact that Caiatinus achieved nothing at all, as Dio 36.34.2 and Zonar. 8.15.14 say directly: the constitutional innovation is the only thing that this dictatorship was remarkable for.

19.4 *Exchange of captives*. For prisoner exchanges see 18.5n. Zonar. 8.16.6 mentions one, which he appears to date to 247: this is likely to be the one P. is referring to here. According to Zonaras, there were more Carthaginian prisoners than Roman, and so the surplus were ransomed by the Carthaginians for money: cf. Livy 22.23.6–8, apparently alluding to the exchange described by Zonaras.

De Sanctis III.1 173–4 [176] (followed by e.g. Thiel (1954), 290–2, Lazenby (1996), 141) suggests that one of the Roman prisoners returned in the exchange was L. Junius Pullus, the consular colleague of Claudius Pulcher in 249, since Zonar. 8.15.14 records that he was captured towards the end of his year of office, but a separate notice (Cic., *Nat. Deor.* 2.7, *Div.* 2.71, Val. Max. 1.4.4 (Paris' epitome)) indicates that he must have been in Rome, since he committed suicide rather than face trial. However, the latter notice appears historically dubious (Münzer (1918b), 1081; cf. Linderski (1986), 2176), not least because Polybius does not indicate that Junius, unlike Claudius, faced any charges—the suicide story may simply have been an inference from his supposed sacrilege (19.2n.), combined with the absence of any account of proceedings against him; moreover Münzer even questions the capture, though perhaps over-sceptically. One needs to be reasonably sure of both the capture and the suicide if one is to relate Junius to the exchange described here: as it is, the connection goes beyond what can be confidently asserted from the evidence.

What precise role the episode of the prisoner exchange played in Livy's narrative is unknown. In P., the pointed phrasing (cf. below) implicitly links it to the failed attempt to exchange captives that the Carthaginians made with Regulus at the end of the previous book: with the quixotic heroism of Regulus no longer at issue, the Romans and Carthaginians can proceed to negotiate on normal terms. This connection is probably an artefact of P.'s presentation rather than a reflection of the way Livy handled it: the language is more likely to be P.'s than Livy's (18.5n.), and for P. the two passages are only a few lines apart, whereas for Livy they stood in separate books.

commutatio captivorum: For the phrase cf. 18.5n.

19.5 *'Annalistic' notices*. Cf. 11.5n.

coloniae deductae sunt: See 1.B.1n.

Fregenae: *BarrAtl* Map 43 A2. *Itin. Ant.* 300–1 locates it on the coast, halfway between Ostia and Alsium (cf. Str. 5.2.8, Plin., *Nat.* 3.51); however, the precise location is uncertain, since no excavations have uncovered the site. A colony is mentioned in a fragmentary inscription found in Maccarese (*CIL* XI 3727), around 2.5 km north of modern Fregene, which may indicate that it was in that vicinity: see also *Via Aurelia*, 42–3 for other archaeological remnants in the area which may be related to the colony.

According to Vell. 1.14.8, the colony was founded in 245, two years after the foundation of Alsium, around 11 km up the coast. Both were 'maritime colonies' of Roman citizens (Fregenae: Livy 36.3.6; Alsium: Livy 27.38.4; but cf. 11.5n.). It is likely that the foundation of two colonies in such close proximity to one another around the same time was in order to defend the coastline near Rome at a time when the Carthaginians had, under the command of Hamilcar, concentrated their efforts on raiding Italy (Plb. 1.56.2–3, 1.56.10).

Brundisium: Modern Brindisi (*BarrAtl* Map 45 G3). It was originally a Messapian town: according to Str. 6.3.6 the name derived from 'stag's head' in Messapian, an allusion to the shape of the harbour. It had been captured by Regulus during the war on the Sallentini in 267, though P. had not mentioned the fact at that point (15.6n.).

Vell. 1.14.8 dates the colony's foundation to 244; Cic., *Sest.* 131 and *Att.* 4.1.4 records that the official foundation day was 5 August. That it was a Latin colony is implied by its appearance in Livy's list at 27.10.7–8. Like Fregenae (above), the immediate impetus for its foundation may have been Hamilcar's raids, but wider strategic and commercial considerations are likely to have operated also: it commands the shortest crossing point to Greece on the Adriatic, with an excellent natural harbour; it was later directly connected to Rome when the Via Appia was extended there.

For studies of the history and archaeology of the town and the surrounding region, see Lombardo and Marangio (1998).

lustrum...conditum est: For the phrase see 11.5n. The censors are recorded in the *Fasti Capitolini* as being A. Atilius Caiatinus (17.4n.) and A. Manlius Torquatus Atticus. The censorship was in 247, with the *lustrum* performed in the following year; so P. is (as often) reordering Livy's sequence of events, since the censorship predated the foundations of the colonies mentioned directly before.

CCXLI milia DCCXII: This figure is substantially less than the one recorded for the previous census (18.4n.)—a drop of 19 per cent. This may reflect military losses, but since the previous figure already looked suspiciously high, it is more likely that the apparent reduction in citizen numbers is a consequence of the unreliability of the figures: indeed, it is doubtful whether the figure here should be regarded as any more robust than its predecessors: see Brunt (1971), 32.

19.6 *Prosecution of Claudia.* Gell. 10.6 tells the story at greater length, with a much fuller version of Claudia's offensive comment, but does not differ in any significant detail; briefer accounts are also found in Val. Max. 8.1 damn. 4 and Suet., *Tib.* 2.3. Gellius, citing the Augustan legal writer Ateius Capito, dates the episode to 246; he identifies those who imposed the fine as the plebeian aediles C. Fundanius and Ti. Sempronius, presumably the consuls of 243 and 238 respectively (*MRR* I 216–17). It may be relevant to note that Livy 24.16.19 mentions that the latter built the temple of Liberty on the Aventine out of money collected in fines.

The historicity of this episode, however, must be regarded as questionable, for all of the circumstantial details of date and prosecutors: it is part of a pattern of stories about the arrogance of the patrician Claudii which are intrinsically suspicious, and hardly any of which can be attested before 50 BC (F 12n.). For that reason, one should be cautious about making any historical inferences from it, although we should not necessarily question one essential premise of the story, namely that Claudius was dead by 246 (19.2n.), since the story may have been generated in part in light of that information.

The alleged prosecution and charges provide additional grounds for doubt. Prosecutions by the aediles are widely attested in the middle Republic, though they appear to have become controversial later (Bauman (1974), Garofalo (1989)). The specific charge against Claudia is more problematic. Suetonius says that *novo more iudicium maiestatis ad populum mulier subiit* ('under a new procedure the woman was subjected to a court of *maiestas* before the people'), and while this does not necessarily entail that the charge of *maiestas* was something new, as opposed to this particular way of handling it (Bauman (1974), 258), it remains the case that this is the first time that a charge of *maiestas* is explicitly referred to—the next is nearly twenty-five years later—and the only one ever to be supposedly conducted by the aediles. It may well be that all of these early charges of *maiestas* were in fact cases of *perduellio*, anachronistically labelled as *maiestas* by later writers (so e.g. Garnsey (1969), 283, Sherwin-White (1969), 289, *contra* Bauman (1967), 28–32).

Still worse, even as a case of *perduellio*, problems remain. There is, once again, no parallel for prosecutions by aediles under this charge, and it is in any case hard to see how Claudia's alleged words fell under any of the usual categories of either *perduellio* or *maiestas* (see e.g. Mommsen, *StrR* 537–94). It may be true that *maiestas* was a 'vague, default category for offenses that are otherwise difficult to prosecute' (Riggsby (1999), 81; though Bauman (1967), 88–90 suggests greater definition to the concept); nevertheless, this extends the boundaries of these types of offence further than any other known case in the Republic. This is presumably why Valerius Maximus treats it as a case of manifest injustice: he lists it under the heading of 'people whom matters extraneous to the trial harmed more than their innocence helped' (8.1 damn. 1: *eos quibus...magis quae extra quaestionem erant nocuerunt quam sua innocentia opem tulit*), and describes Claudia herself as 'innocent of the charge of which she was accused' (8.1 damn. 4: *insontem crimine quo accusabatur*).[256]

---

[256] Briscoe (2019), 90–1 takes this to mean that Valerius thought that Claudia was not on trial because of her words, but for a different offence altogether, and hence argues that there is a discrepancy from P.'s account. But Valerius' wording is compatible with her being convicted in a (supposed)

Suolahti (1977) sought to solve the problem by arguing that Valerius and Suetonius were mistaken in saying that Claudia was actually put on trial: he proposed that the aediles issued her with a summary fine for resisting their authority, which she then appealed to the people.[257] This is clearly not impossible, but not only does it contradict the sources, it seems an unlikely and extreme response to the situation: Suohlati has to hypothesize an entire sequence not mentioned in our narratives, where the aediles were summoned to the scene to preserve public order and then engaged in an altercation with Claudia. He also presumes a political vendetta on their part against Claudia's family, which is perhaps less implausible (cf. below), but which again is unsupported in the sources.

None of these anomalies would be sufficient to demonstrate the unhistoricity of the episode in the absence of other considerations against it, but given that the historicity is highly dubious on other grounds, they add extra support for the notion that both the offence and the prosecution are late inventions, with the procedure and the charge constructed according to later ideas how prosecutions were conducted in the time of the First Punic War. The date, and the identification of Fundanius as one of the prosecutors, may derive from the information that as tribune he had been one of the prosecutors of Claudia's brother (*Schol. Bob.* p. 90.4 (Stangl); cf. *MRR* I 215), so the trial of Claudia could naturally be assigned to his aedileship.

P., unlike the other sources, pays no attention to the legal procedure. Nor does he show any sign, unlike Valerius, of regarding Claudia as unjustly punished. Instead, he ties her actions closely to the offence given by her brother, which he reminds the reader of despite having described it only a few lines back—none of the other sources makes explicit reference to Claudius' sacrilege in this context.

Claudia: *RE* 382. Since nothing is known of her apart from this anecdote, and since this anecdote may well be fictional (above), it is not improbable that she is likewise invented, although naturally it cannot be ruled out that Claudius Pulcher had a sister and Ap. Claudius Caecus a daughter.

P. Claudi: See 19.2n.

contemptis auspiciis: *auspicia contemnere* is an uncommon phrase, used only in the context of Claudius Pulcher (Flor. 1.18.29), Flaminius (Oros. 4.13.14), or both (Min. Fel. 7.4). Livy never uses it in his surviving work: it is possible that he did so of Claudius, and that this is the reason it is picked up in that context by later writers, but that can be little more than speculation.

a ludis revertens: Valerius and Gellius likewise mention that Claudia was coming home from the games, perhaps to explain how it came about that an upper-class woman in the middle Republic was out in a crowd at all—the usual (patriarchal)

---

trial for *maiestas* based on her words, which Valerius regarded as unjust since her words did not constitute *maiestas* as he understood it.

[257] For the process, cf. Mommsen, *StR*³ II 492–5.

assumption of the historians is that women typically remained at home. Suetonius answers the implicit question in a different way, by having her not on foot, but riding in a *carpentum*, the two-wheeled carriage which women, according to Livy 5.25.9, had been granted the special privilege of using.

viveret ⟨et⟩ iterum classem duceret: Both verbs are subjunctives of present counterfactual wishes. The first is explicitly marked as a wish with *utinam*; the second, according to the chief MSS, is not, which is not the standard prose usage (K-S 1.184–5). It is possible that this is the consequence of P.'s compression, but it is more likely that P. originally wrote *et* (cf. Suet., *Tib.* 2.3, Gell. 10.6.2),[258] and it has dropped out by haplography with *viveret* and *iterum*.

multa... dicta est: Gellius gives the fine as 25,000 *aes grave* (sc. the coins of heavy bronze used at this period).

19.7 *Enlargement of the praetorship*. This is reported in two other sources: Lyd, *Mag.* 1.38, 1.45, and Pompon., *Dig.* 1.2.2.28, both of whom (anachronistically)[259] record the title of the new praetor as the *praetor peregrinus*, supplementing the existing praetor, later called the *praetor urbanus*. Pomponius suggests that his role was to hear legal cases between foreigners, and this is widely accepted as the main purpose of the creation of the office (esp. Daube (1951)). Against this, however, the evidence for his activities in this early period indicates that a major part of his role was to take command outside Rome (Gilbert (1939), Brennan (2000), 85–97, 106–7; see further below); the need for some such official is likely to have been the primary reason for the creation of the office.

But at the same time, it is likely that some sort of legal function concerning non-Romans fell under his jurisdiction (cf. Livy 22.35.5: see below), even if not as dominant a part of his role as it later became. It seems highly probable that the increasing economic integration of Italians and Romans (Roselaar (2019), esp. 61–120) vastly increased the number of legal disputes involving non-Romans but which Rome needed to be seen to judge fairly (*contra* Brennan (2000), 86). But, as Roselaar observes, it seems improbable that the praetor would only oversee cases in which no Roman citizen was involved[260]—many of those could and would have been resolved locally, without requiring recourse to Rome, which a Roman citizen is more likely to have insisted upon, though it may have also been useful

---

[258] Presumably following similar reasoning, two late MSS, along with the *editio princeps*, read *iterumque*, accepted in all early editions; but that corruption is a little less probable.

[259] This title is not found before the early Empire (the earliest attestation is in *AE* 1991, 307, from AD 18): in the Republic he was described by phrases like *praetor qui inter peregrinos ius dicit* (Mommsen, *StR*³ II 196–7: see also the next note).

[260] Roselaar (2019), 124–5: note that Livy 22.35.5 explicitly describes the function of the praetor in 216 as *iuri dicundo...inter civis Romanos et peregrinos* ('giving legal rulings between Roman citizens and foreigners'). *Contra* Daube (1951), 124–5, who relies on Pomponius' phrase *inter peregrinos ius dicebat* ('gave law between foreigners'). But *inter* here is more likely to mean 'among' or 'in the case of' (Briscoe (2012b), 998).

for disputes between foreigners of different states to have a Roman official available as an ostensibly impartial judge (Briscoe (2012b), 998).

tunc primum: Once again (cf. 11.5n.), P. lays particular stress on a constitutional innovation. Some (e.g. Gilbert (1939), 51–2, Thiel (1954), 83, Lazenby (1996), 151–2), have suggested that the creation of the new praetorship was connected with the ban on the consul Postumius taking command of the army in 242, which P. records immediately afterwards (19.8n.). The chronological indications are, however, against this. *tunc* appears to relate this chronologically to the previous episode (11.5n.), the alleged trial of Claudia, which elsewhere is dated to 246: Livy is, accordingly, likely to have recorded it then or soon after. This date approximately fits the evidence from Lydus, who dates it to the 263rd year after the establishment of the consulship: this can be calculated in more than one way, but it appears to come to either 247 or 244 (Brennan (2000), 85–6). Most probably, therefore, the creation of the office was prompted by the Carthaginian coastal raids that Italy was suffering at this time (19.5n.; cf. Brennan (2000), 86–7).

19.8 *Ban on Postumius leaving Rome.* This episode is alluded to later by Livy at 37.51.1–2, in the context of a similar ban enforced in 189 by the *pontifex maximus* against the *flamen Quirinalis*. It is also described in Val. Max. 1.1.2, and Tac., *Ann.* 3.71.3, the latter once again in the context of a ban on a different *flamen*: Tiberius in AD 20 prevented the *flamen Dialis* taking up the governorship of Asia. A number of other similar bans are known: Livy 40.42.8–10 recounts how in 180 L. Cornelius Dolabella was prevented by the *pontifex maximus* from taking up the post of *rex sacrorum* while holding the office of naval duumvir; in 131 the consul P. Licinius Crassus, who was *pontifex maximus*, prevented his colleague, the *flamen Martialis*, from going on campaign (Cic., *Phil.* 11.18: for further discussion cf. 59.3n.); while at Livy 24.8.10 the impossibility of sending the *flamen Quirinalis* on campaign is used as an argument against his election to the consulship. *Per.* 47.1 is sometimes claimed to refer to a similar incident (e.g. Briscoe (1981), 369, Wardle (1998), 87), but P.'s wording there suggests a different scenario: it is not clear that the person fined by the *pontifex maximus* there was a priest at all (see *ad loc.*). For discussion of these episodes, with particular focus on of the legal and political significance, cf. Bleicken (1957b), 450–68; also Richard (1968).

Valerius indicates that Metellus imposed a fine on Postumius; a fine is also mentioned with respect to the incidents of 189, 180, and 131, as well as the perhaps different case (cf. above) of *Per.* 47.1. In those other three cases the priest appealed to the people, who remitted the fine, but concurred with the restriction on leaving the city. Some (e.g. Bleicken (1957b), 450, Richard (1968), 787, Wardle (1998), 87) suggest that the same must have happened here, but that goes beyond the evidence: while it may have happened that way, it is also possible that the punishment against Postumius was fully exacted. At all events, P. does not mention it: he is more interested in the ban than in the mechanism whereby it was enforced.

Caecilius Metellus: See 19.1n.

A. Postumium consulem: A. Postumius Albinus, *cos*. 242 (*RE* 30, *MRR* I 218). Subsequently he was censor in 234, but nothing else is recorded of his career. Because he was unable to join his colleague Lutatius on campaign in Sicily, the praetor Q. Valerius Falto took his place (cf. 19.9n.).

flamen Martialis: One of the fifteen *flamines* who were designated to serve a particular named god—in this case Mars.[261] Like the *flamen Dialis* and the *flamen Quirinalis*, the *flamen Martialis* was regarded as one of the 'major *flamines*' (Gaius, *Inst.* 1.112), and the position could be held only by patricians (Paul., *Fest.* 137L): the *flamen Martialis* was regarded as second in rank to the *flamen Dialis* (Fest. 198L; cf. Vanggaard (1988), 27). He was a member of the pontifical college, which is why the *pontifex maximus* exercised authority over him.

For the history and roles of the *flamines* see Vanggaard (1988).

a sacris recedere: According to Serv. auct., *Aen.* 8.552, neither the *flamen Martialis* nor the *flamen Quirinalis* were banned from leaving Italy: that ban applied to the *flamen Dialis* alone, since, unlike the other *flamines*, he was required to perform daily sacrifices. This appears to conflict with the evidence set out above for such bans being regularly enforced against both the *Martialis* and the *Quirinalis*. In support of Servius, however, in the early empire at least one *flamen Martialis* is known to have held a governorship (Woodman and Martin (1996), 423);[262] we may compare Tac., *Ann.* 3.58.1, where the *flamen Dialis* Servius Maluginensis, as part of his argument for being allowed to take up a governorship, notes that the *flamen Martialis* and the *flamen Quirinalis* were not restricted in the way the *flamen Dialis* was—in fact, according to him, none of them should have been formally restricted at all.

With regard to the last point, it is clear that Maluginensis' argument is disingenuous, in as much as the broad restriction on the movement of the *flamen Dialis* is regularly attested even outside the specific debates over individual *flamines* attempting to take up offices. That restriction is alluded to even prior to the time when Tiberius confirmed the rule by banning Maluginensis from his province (Livy 1.20.2, 5.52.13), and there is no certain case of its being violated.[263] This still

---

[261] The exclusive relationship of the *flamines* to a single god is questioned by Vanggaard (1988), 105–15, who notes that they are sometimes involved in rituals of other gods also. Nevertheless, the Romans themselves took them to be priests devoted to the god for whom they were named, even if in practice they recognized their involvement in other rites also.

[262] C. Junius Silanus: his proconsulship is mentioned in Tac., *Ann.* 3.66.1, while the fact that he was already *flamen Martialis* at that point is recorded in the *Fasti Capitolini*.

[263] A possible exception appears in the early third century AD: Terentius Gentianus is recorded as *flamen Dialis* (*CIL* VI 2144 = *ILS* 4927), and he has been argued to have been the governor of Arabia as well, on the basis of Waddington 2460 = *IGRRP* III 1149. But the name in the latter inscription is fragmentary and its reconstruction dubious (Groag (1934), 656), and even if the identity with

leaves two possibilities (cf. Woodman and Martin (1996), 422-3): that the restrictions on the movement of the *flamen Martialis* and the *flamen Quirinalis* were once similar to those on the *flamen Dialis*, but had been relaxed by the time of Tiberius, or that those two priests were never formally restricted, but the *pontifices* raised tendentious bans against them for political reasons.

The latter is what Maluginensis himself claims (Tac., *Ann.* 3.58.3), but, even if one leaves aside the dubious context in which he makes this argument (above), it seems unlikely that such a ban would be so regularly cited and enforced if no religious rule was recognized as underlying it. The most likely conclusion, therefore, is that while the *flamen Martialis* and the *flamen Quirinalis* were originally required to be present in Rome to perform certain rites, some sort of work-around was devised over time that would allow them to be away from the city for some or all of the year (Vanggaard (1988), 64; *contra* Richard (1968), 794-7).[264] This seems more plausible than the idea that Postumius was the victim of an anti-patrician conspiracy to keep him from the command, as proposed by Münzer ((1953); cf. (1999 (1920)), 241-2, expanded on by Richard (1968)), or that Metellus objected to Postumius as an inferior commander (De Sanctis III.1 181 [185], Thiel (1954), 82, 305-6).[265] While it cannot be ruled out that some form of political animosity or strategic calculation underlay Metellus' decision, we do not need to frame it in those terms.

If that is accepted, the question is why Postumius would have been elected consul at all, if his priesthood precluded him from performing many of the duties of the office. It may be that the issue had never arisen previously, either because no major *flamen* had ever been elected consul, or (more plausibly) because none had sought to lead troops on an extended campaign far from the city before—the First Punic War was the first time when consuls held commands outside Italy—and so it had never been realized to be a potential problem. But it is also noteworthy that, subsequent to this episode, *flamines* were periodically elected to the consulship despite the apparent precedent set here, only to have their offices challenged. This suggests that there may have been broader doubts about the nature of the ban and the authority behind it, and, even if enforced, what precise limits it would impose on the *flamen* in question, and also how far the decision in one case imposed a precedent for all later cases (cf. Lundgreen (2011), 171-7).

Gentianus is accepted, it is not clear that he was already *flamen* at the time of his governorship (Vanggaard (1988), 66-7).

[264] We can compare the case of the *pontifex maximus* himself: at Livy 28.38.12 the *pontifex maximus* refuses on religious grounds to take a province outside Italy, but manifestly this was not perceived as a problem later, when (to mention only the most obvious example) the *pontifex maximus* Julius Caesar commanded armies outside Italy for several years. See further 59.3n.

[265] As Lazenby (1996), 151 rightly observes, there is no evidence for any prior campaign by either Postumius or Valerius that could have led Metellus to assume that the latter would perform better than the former.

a sacris recedere is otherwise found only in Quint., *Decl.* 252.19; elsewhere the phrase used is *a sacris discedere* (Cic., *Phil.* 11.18, Val. Max. 1.1.2) or *sacra deserere* (Livy 1.20.2, 22.56.5). For the meaning cf. *OLD s.v. recedo* 7a.

19.9 *Battle of Aegates Islands: Roman victory in the First Punic War.*

rebus...a pluribus ducibus prospere gestis: The last battle mentioned by P. had been Claudius Pulcher's defeat at Drepana in 249 (19.2n.). He now builds up to the final defeat of Carthage with a summary which implies that it was the culmination of numerous Roman successes in the intervening period. This is not the impression given by the narrative of Plb. 1.56-8. According to him, after Drepana and the shipwreck of Junius in the same year, the Romans withdrew from the sea, leaving the Carthaginians in control there. The Carthaginian general Hamilcar made his base at Hercte, and sent his fleets from there to raid the Italian coastline (1.56.1-10); the Romans, meanwhile, were based nearby at Panormus, and the two armies spent the next years in constant skirmishing without achieving a decisive victory on either side (1.56.11-57.8). Hamilcar also besieged the Roman forces on Eryx, but here, once again, no decisive result emerged (1.58.1-6, citing Fabius Pictor, *FRHist* 1 F 19; cf. D.S. 24.9.2-3). Only then, after things had come to a standstill in Sicily, did the Romans in 242 rebuild their fleet and achieve the final victory (1.59.1-8). For Polybius, therefore, the final Roman victory represented a final reversal after seven years in which no successes were achieved on land and the Carthaginians ruled the sea unchallenged.

However, an entirely different account is given by Zonar. 8.16.1-7. At least for the first part of the period, he suggests that the Romans achieved successes not only on land, but even at sea. On land the consuls of 248 and 247 kept the Carthaginians off-balance by attacking their bases at Lilybaeum and Drepana, and in the latter year they captured the island of Pelias. As for the sea, although no fleet sailed under an official command, in 247 they used privateers to sack Hippo in Africa and defeat the Carthaginians at Panormus. Only after that, Zonaras suggests, were matters reduced to a stalemate. An additional victory is recorded by Flor. 1.18.30-2, according to whom Fabius Buteo, the consul of 245, intercepted and defeated the Carthaginian fleet at Aegimurus, but lost his own fleet in a storm.

The historicity of Fabius Buteo's naval victory must be regarded as dubious: it runs counter to Polybius' clear statement that the Romans were not contesting the sea at this point, while the pattern of victory undermined by the wreck of the fleet is sufficiently close to some of the earlier episodes in the war (cf. 18.3n.) to suggest the basis on which it might have been invented.[266] The events recorded by Zonaras, on the other hand, should be taken more seriously, even if Polybius'

---

[266] See esp. Leuze (1911), 557-8, suggesting that Florus has transferred the earlier episode here in order to fit his overall scheme of the expansion of Roman power in the war; also more generally cf. De Sanctis III.1 181 [184-5], Thiel (1954), 300-1.

account is regarded as reliable overall (cf. Beck (2013), 137–8). It is easy to see that Polybius might have passed over unofficial Roman naval actions as irrelevant to the pattern of warfare he describes, or that Zonaras (following Dio) might have selected out of the back-and-forth land fighting described by Polybius a few episodes to highlight which suggest greater Roman success.[267] This is not sufficient to show that these must have happened the way Zonaras relates them, but there is no fundamental objection to them (*contra* Thiel (1954), 298, who is sceptical about the capture of Pelias).

On the face of things, one might assume that some or all of these Roman successes were found in Livy also, and that this forms the basis for P.'s statement here. However, at Livy 23.13.3–4 Hanno recalls the battle of the Aegates Islands as a defeat that immediately followed a period where *numquam terra marique magis prosperae res nostrae visae sunt* ('never had our affairs seemed more successful on land and sea'). In other words, far from relating a sequence like Zonaras or Florus, Livy here is constructing the history rather like Polybius did, with a sudden final reversal in favour of Rome rather than a sequence of victories leading up to the ultimate Roman success. If that was the way Livy handled it in Book 19, then P. here has recast the history very substantially.

Admittedly, we cannot be sure that Hanno in Book 23 represents Livy's account in Book 19 fairly. He is certainly a sympathetic figure, and someone whose case Livy is presenting as powerful and cogent, since his warnings to Carthage are ultimately vindicated (cf. Chaplin (2000), 78–9). But it would not be uncharacteristic of Livy to have even a sympathetic figure adjust the history in order to press his arguments, and his language here looks exaggerated. Even Polybius did not go so far as to claim, as Hanno does, that the last years of the First Punic War represented the apogee of Carthaginian success. On balance, however, it is most likely that, even if exaggerated, Hanno's construction of the history is a recognizable version of Livy's own, which P. has, accordingly, misrepresented. It may be that the reason for P. presenting the history in this way is to explain why the Carthaginians sued for peace after this particular defeat: this is something which the Polybian narrative leaves surprisingly underdetermined (see below). It is easier to see why a run of Roman successes culminating in a major defeat would leave Carthage unwilling to continue the war (Livy, as we shall see below, seems to have explained the Carthaginian surrender quite differently).

None of this, of course, means that Livy described no Roman victories: P. may be pulling out a handful of Roman successes from a Livian narrative whose overall tenor was entirely different. It should be noted in particular that *pluribus ducibus* would not be a fair representation even if Livy had narrated the history much as Zonaras later would, since the most important victories in Zonaras' version

---

[267] Cf. Rawlings (2016) for the general importance, both militarily and psychologically, of 'irregular' warfare during the Punic Wars, even though it is generally downplayed by the ancient narrators by comparison with the set-piece battles on which they focus their attention.

were not achieved by *duces* in the usual sense, but privateers. It is, however, naturally also possible that Livy's narrative, though not pointing overall to Roman success, included individual Roman victories (real or invented) that are not mentioned in any other surviving source.

summam victoriae...imposuit: *summam victoriae imponere* is unique to P., who repeats the phrase at 98.8. Since *summa victoriae* (sc. 'decisive victory': lit. 'crowning point of victory') is a phrase that appears in Caesar (*Gall.* 7.21.3, *Civ.* 1.82.3), and later in various fourth-century authors (e.g. Veg., *Mil.* 3.1.2, ps.-Heges. 3.13), it might be thought that *victoriae* here is a genitive. However, that leaves *imposuit* hanging awkwardly without its usual dative or prepositional phrase, and while that is not impossible (cf. W-M *ad* Livy 26.51.12), it makes it more likely that a Roman reader would understand *victoriae* as a dative: 'put the finishing touch on victory' after the successes mentioned in the previous clause (cf. Val. Max. 4.3.3 and *OLD s.v. summa* 8a).

C. Lutatius cos.: C. Lutatius Catulus, cos. 242 (*RE* 4, *MRR* I 218).

Nothing is known of his career apart from the events of his consulship and its immediate aftermath. According to several sources (Varro, *De Vit. Pop. Rom.* fr. 100 (Riposati) = Non. p. 887L, Val. Max. 2.8.2, Eutr. 2.27.2, Oros. 4.10.5, Zonar. 8.17.1), he was wounded prior to the battle, apparently while attempting an assault on Drepana (Orosius, Zonaras); this necessitated the active command being taken by the praetor, Q. Valerius Falto (cf. 19.8n.). Although Polybius, like P., has nothing of this, that something of the sort occurred is indicated by the fact that not only Lutatius, but also Valerius, was awarded a triumph the following year, according to the *Fasti Capitolini*, although Valerius' was two days later and only *ex Sicilia*, not *de Poenis ex Sicilia*, as Lutatius' had been, indicating that it was the consul who formally retained the command and took the credit for the victory (Brennan (2000), 280). Val. Max. 2.8.2 has a circumstantial and detailed account of Valerius suing in order to share Lutatius' triumph. On the face of things this unlikely to be historical, not least because the entire story is designed to lead up to the conclusion that Valerius lost his case and was denied the triumph, which is contradicted by the *Fasti*; but it is possible that the story, which is elaborated with some legal detail, is compatible with his being denied a share of Lutatius' triumph but awarded his own lesser one (see Mancinelli (2015)).

victa...classe Poenorum: The fullest account of the battle is in Plb. 1.59.6–61.8. Lutatius took command of a new Roman fleet of 200 ships, and sailed with them to Sicily, where he took control of the harbour at Drepana and laid siege to the town. In response, the Carthaginians sent under the command of Hanno a fleet laden with supplies for their troops in Sicily; Lutatius intercepted them. The Carthaginian fleet was encumbered and hence less manoeuvrable; the ships were also manned by inexperienced crewmen and soldiers. The Romans, on the other hand, had lightened their ships and also trained their troops effectively.

Accordingly, the Carthaginians were quickly routed: fifty ships were sunk, seventy captured, and nearly 10,000 troops were taken prisoner.

This basic picture of the battle is virtually uniform throughout the historical tradition. In particular, the image of the Carthaginians losing because they had over-encumbered their own fleet clearly caught the imagination of many writers (Livy 22.14.13, Flor. 1.18.34–37, *Vir. Ill.* 41.1, Zonar. 8.17.2; cf. Eutr. 2.27.3), perhaps because it dovetailed so neatly with the stereotype of material success (especially of an Oriental empire) leading to downfall: several writers elaborate on the ships' cargo, claiming that it included not merely food supplies, but also vast amounts of money (Eutropius, Zonaras) or military equipment (Florus). P., however, does not mention any reason for the victory, perhaps because he is less interested in the stereotype, but, more significantly, because he, unlike these other sources, presents the victory as a culmination of a series of Roman successes, so it is less necessary for him to explain what factors mattered here in particular.

The only significant variation is in the numbers. D.S. 24.11, Eutr. 2.27.1, *Vir. Ill.* 41.1, and Oros. 4.10.5 all give the Romans not 200, but 300 ships (and Diodorus adds a further 700 transports); there is no particular reason to prefer these to Polybius, though there is nothing intrinsically implausible about the higher number. The numbers of Carthaginian ships vary even more, from 250 (Diodorus) to 400 (Eutropius, Orosius) to 600 (*Vir. Ill.*). The Carthaginian losses are recorded as 117 ships in Diodorus (who also has the Romans losing eighty), which is fairly close to the number in Polybius, and 4,040 or 6,000 men taken prisoner. In Eutropius and Orosius 125 ships are sunk and sixty-three captured, with 32,000 Carthaginians captured, 13,000 killed. The numbers for Carthaginian ships and losses in Diodorus may go back to a pro-Carthaginian source: he explicitly cites Philinus (*FGrH* 174 F 5) as the source for one estimate of prisoners. This does not, of course, mean that they are accurate, but it is less plausible that the Romans won so decisively despite being dramatically outnumbered, as the later Roman sources would have it.

Eutr. 2.27.3 dates the battle to 10 March, in other words, close to the end of the consular year 242; this is supported by Zonar. 8.17.3, who specifically notes that the battle was close to the end of Lutatius' term of office. If so—and there is no particular reason to doubt it—this implies that the Roman calendar was running at least a month behind the Julian, so that 10 March corresponded to a Julian date in April 241, since it would be surprising if the Carthaginians, after waiting several months to set sail, then suddenly risked their entire fleet on the crossing to Sicily before spring had set in properly.[268]

---

[268] Beloch, *GG* IV.2 261–2 argues for a displacement of at least two months, placing the battle in May; but this is based on his claim that the whole sequence from Lutatius departing Italy to the battle took no more than a couple of months, which is dubious: see De Sanctis III.1 256–8 [264–7]. De Sanctis himself regards it as possible that the Roman and Julian calendars coincided here, but the

The battle-site has recently been identified and the sea-floor is being progressively surveyed and excavated—the first such excavation of any major sea-battle from antiquity. Preliminary results of the excavations were published in Tusa and Royal (2012), and a much fuller account in Royal and Tusa (2020); among the finds to date are twenty-five rams from warships, at least eighteen inscribed (two in Punic, sixteen in Latin),[269] seven helmets of a familiar Celto-Italian style known as Montefortino, which was standard in the Roman army at this period, along with a further fragmentary helmet of unknown type that may be Carthaginian (Goldman and Rose (2020)).[270] Also found (to date) are 557 amphoras, around 10 per cent Punic, but 90 per cent Greco-Italic (Royal (2020a)). But the latter is of a type that was produced more widely, from Gaul to Spain to Carthage itself, and at least one of the twenty-one Greco-Roman amphoras that have so far been raised had Punic graffiti (Royal (2020a), 193-7). This last fits—though does not require—the picture in Polybius and other sources of the Carthaginian fleet being laden with supplies for Sicily (Tusa and Royal (2012), 37). Moreover, Murray (2020), 40-1 argues that Polybius' narrative of the battle is supported by the

---

parallel he offers for a sea-battle in early March is based on a problematic interpretation of Xen., *HG* 1.2.4 (cf. the arguments of Beresford (2013), 134-72 that ancient warships would not usually sail prior to mid-March). Moreover, De Sanctis's suggestion (followed by Thiel (1954), 308-9, Morgan (1977), 110) that the Carthaginians were relying on their superior naval prowess to sail when the Romans would not is oddly self-contradictory: if they really believed in their naval superiority, one might feel they had less reason to fear a naval battle, and less reason, rather than more, to leave their fleet vulnerable to destruction by the elements with no Roman intervention. While it cannot be ruled out that the Carthaginians were reasoning inconsistently, or that they estimated themselves as superior in navigation but inferior in combat, it is unsatisfactory to conclude that the calendars coincided if the sole basis for doing so is to assume such precise (mis)calculations: a calendar displacement is far more probable. The argument for a coincidence of calendars in Morgan (1977), 109-12 is even weaker: he claims the flooding of the Tiber in Oros. 4.11.5-7, which *praevenit triumphum* ('anticipated the triumph'), is to be dated to the first months of (Julian) 241, which fits a battle in March 241 (Julian). This not only assumes that Orosius is a reliable source for both the prodigy and its chronological relationship with the battle, which is dubious, but ignores Orosius' actual date for the flood—Orosius dates it to the consular year *after* the battle, as is clear not only from his narrative sequence but also from his note that it 'followed hard on' (4.11.5: *superveniens*) the joy of the victory. The *triumphus* that the flood (allegedly) anticipated is, accordingly, Lutatius' triumphal celebration in October 241, not the victory several months earlier. Thiel (1954), 307-12 assumes, rather than arguing for, the coincidence of the calendars, accordingly claiming that the Carthaginians did indeed make the crossing in the winter. His primary puzzle is why they waited so long to send the ships, where he canvasses various possibilities, but does not consider the obvious solution: that the Roman and Julian calendars diverged, and the delay was because they were waiting for spring.

[269] See Prag (2017) and (2020) for details: the seven remaining rams may have been inscribed as well, but two are fragmentary and five are still unread. Since the Romans undoubtedly won the battle, it is surprising that so many more Roman than Punic rams have been found. Murray (2020), 37-8 plausibly argues that some of them were from ships built earlier in the war, which had been captured by the Carthaginians and pressed into service for their fleet. As he notes, this is supported by the fact that the sunk rams were found scattered among dense groupings of amphoras (see the plans in Tusa and Royal (2020), 27-8), and Polybius indicates that the Carthaginian ships were heavily laden with supplies (above).

[270] Here too (cf. above) it is at first sight surprising that the helmets found are overwhelmingly of the style used by the Roman army. Possible explanations are that they are the result of the Carthaginians' use of Italian mercenaries (Tusa and Royal (2012), 27), or that they were captured Roman weapons being sent as supplies to Hamilcar (Goldman and Rose (2020), 164-5).

condition of the rams, some of which show evidence of having been in head-on collisions, both in the severe damage to the rams and the presence of wood fragments trapped in them (cf. also Royal (2020c), 289–93), and the proximity of the rams to the amphorae, suggesting the ships were sunk very rapidly and while largely intact.

More difficult to fit with the literary evidence is the small size of the rams, which suggests that all the ships were triremes (1.59.6–8), whereas Polybius refers only to quinqueremes in the battle (for detailed calculations demonstrating this see Murray (2020), 31–6). However, Polybius specifically describes only the Roman ships in these terms, and the rams discovered are more likely to come from the Carthaginian fleet (cf. n. 269 above). It is true that Polybius sometimes speaks as if all the fleets of the First Punic War overall were composed solely of quinqueremes: see esp. 1.63.5–8—but that passage is clearly an overgeneralization designed to show the magnitude of the war compared with those earlier. In any case Polybius sometimes uses the word πεντήρης (sc. 'quinquereme') as a generic term for all kinds of warships (cf. Tarn (1907), 59–60), and even more often does not specify type of ship at all (Murray (2020), 38–9). But the detailed accounts both in Polybius (e.g. 1.20.9) and on Duilius' victory inscription (*CIL* I^2 p. 384 = VI 1300 = *ILS* 65 = *ILLRP* 319; cf. 17.2n.) point to triremes being used at various points in the war. A mixed force at this battle is also implied by D.S. 24.11.1, and the ratio (*c*.140:1) of Carthaginian prisoners to ship losses on Polybius' figures is unfeasibly low for a fleet composed entirely of quinqueremes, whose manpower was much higher (cf. Tusa and Royal (2012), 39–42).

ad Aegates insulas: The modern Egadi Islands (*BarrAtl* Map 47 A3).

petentibus Carthaginiensibus: That the Carthaginians took the initiative to sue for peace following Lutatius' victory is generally accepted in the sources (e.g. Plb. 1.62.1–7, Nep., *Ham.* 1.3–4, *Vir. Ill.* 41.2, Zonar. 8.17.3), and is doubtless true: the ultimate terms were largely in the Romans' favour (see below), which implies that they were in the much stronger position if the war were to continue, and accordingly had less incentive to come to an agreement.

It is less obvious from the sources what led the Carthaginians to conclude that they needed a peace agreement. It is true that they had recently been defeated, but both sides had suffered many defeats over the decades of war, and the battle of the Aegates Islands appears not to have been on a substantially larger scale than its predecessors. Polybius' explanation (1.62.1–2) is that the Carthaginians, even though their morale remained strong, were concerned about their inability to supply their forces in Sicily, and were short of additional men and commanders to send out. Since the Carthaginian forces were substantially composed of mercenaries, and Sicily itself had resources to maintain troops, this appears inadequate as an explanation, the more since, on Polybius' account (1.62.7), the Romans themselves were exhausted by the war.

P., as noted above, explains the Carthaginian surrender after the Aegates Islands by presenting the battle as merely the culmination of a long sequence of Roman victories. Flor. 1.18.33–37 solves the problem a different way from P., making the size of the Carthaginian fleet, and the amount it was carrying, of such magnitude that the whole of Carthage was effectively wiped out by the defeat. But neither P.'s version nor Florus' is mirrored elsewhere in the tradition, and neither is likely to be accurate. Livy himself appears to have handled the issue quite differently: he depicts Hamilcar as later anguished by the fact that 'Sicily had been surrendered out of *excessively swift* desperation concerning their circumstances' (21.1.5: *Siciliam* nimis celeri *desperatione rerum concessam*)—even though Hamilcar himself, in most of the tradition, had been the one who negotiated the surrender of Sicily. Along similar lines, at 22.54.11 Livy in his own voice contrasts the Carthaginian collapse after their defeat here with the Romans' steadfastness after a no less disastrous defeat at Cannae: the difference, he concludes was that the Carthaginians met disaster *minore animo* ('with less spirit'). It appears that Livy recognized that the narrative of the final surrender in Polybius was under-motivated, and had effectively reversed Polybius' explanation: whereas Polybius had the Carthaginians strong in morale but in practice unable to continue, Livy showed them as weak-mindedly conceding even though they could have pursued the war further.[271] It is not surprising, if so, that P. ignores this, and prefers to see the Romans as decisive victors in all respects.

As to the actual history, the brief summary of Nep., *Ham.* 1.3, referring to Carthage being *exhaustam sumptibus* ('worn out through expense') may have more truth to it than any of the accounts so far mentioned, since it indicates that the key problem may have been the lack of financial means to support the war, something unmentioned in Polybius.[272] It is also likely that the Carthaginian position in Sicily had been completely eroded over the years of war: even though Polybius implies a stalemate in which Hamilcar even had the advantage, in practice there is no record of them having occupied anything but the far west of the island for several years prior to the final defeat.

pax data est: The terms of the treaty are recorded in a number of sources, and with relatively little variation. According to most sources, the treaty was effectively struck twice: first Lutatius negotiated a provisional treaty with Hamilcar, but when it came to be ratified in Rome, the Romans rejected the proposed terms, and insisted on some modifications.

The earliest, fullest, and (as often) most reliable source is Polybius. According to his initial account (1.62.8–63.3), the original terms negotiated by Lutatius were as follows: (i) The Carthaginians were to evacuate Sicily and not to make war

---

[271] Lazenby (1996), 157 reaches a similar conclusion about the reason for the Carthaginian surrender, although he surprisingly does not acknowledge that Livy anticipated him.

[272] For an analysis of the Carthaginians' financial weaknesses that led them to sue for peace see esp. Loreto (2001), 96–101; also cf. Bleckmann (2002), 218–19.

on Hiero or his allies. (ii) Roman prisoners were to be returned without ransom. (iii) Carthage was to pay an indemnity of 2,200 Euboean talents over twenty years by instalments. However, the treaty explicitly stated that it required ratification by Rome, and when it was sent there, the Romans refused: instead, they sent a commission to investigate, and the commission proposed some slight modifications. Under these, the indemnity was increased to 3,200 talents, to be paid over ten years, and not only Sicily, but the islands between Italy and Sicily were to be ceded.

These are the only terms Polybius mentions at this point; but he gives a fuller account of the final treaty later (3.27.1–6), where he adds more: (i) The allies of both sides were to be immune from attack; (ii) Neither side could, in the territory of the other, take money for public construction or enrol mercenaries, nor could they ally themselves to the other's allies. It is unclear whether any of these clauses were in Lutatius' original draft, or if they were added on later; but the failure to mention Hiero specifically here seems to imply that the clauses in the original treaty protecting him from Carthaginian interference were expanded in the final treaty into a general protection for allies on both sides.[273] If so, this was a significant concession by the Romans to the Carthaginians, perhaps as a compensation for the increased indemnity that was being imposed on them (Walbank (1957), 359), and also suggesting that despite the defeat at the Aegates Islands, the Carthaginians were perceived by the Romans as retaining some leverage in the negotiations.[274] This clause then became a major point of contention in 219, when Hannibal initiated the Second Punic War with an attack on Saguntum in Spain, then allied to Rome (Plb. 3.21.3–5, 3.29.4–10, Livy 21.18.8, 21.19.4–5): the question arose whether it covered only those allies who existed at the time when the treaty was struck (as the Carthaginians claimed), or if it also included those taken on later (so the Romans). Clearly the wording offered some measure of ambiguity on this crucial question.

---

[273] Derow (2015), 181–4 argues that this provision, and indeed the whole account of the treaty in Plb. 3.27.1–6, is a later Roman invention, designed with hindsight to bolster her case following the Carthaginian attack on Saguntum at the beginning of the Second Punic War. However, he never addresses the question why the Romans should invent treaty terms which were relatively favourable to Carthage, nor the fact that there are a number of other terms reported by Polybius only in the later account (concerning the levying of troops and the raising of money), but which serve no obvious propagandist purpose, nor why the treaty contains a loophole (when did the allies have to be acquired to be covered by the clause?) which gave Carthage an arguable, if not necessarily a compelling case (see Plb. 3.29.4–10). It is far more likely that the version in 3.27.1–6 (which after all purports to be verbatim) is historical, and the omission of these terms from the account in Book 1 is solely a function of the brevity of Polybius' summary there.

[274] Loreto (2007), 252–3; though he goes further, and, in line with his overall interpretation of the war as leading to a poor outcome to Rome, sees this as not merely showing limited leverage by Carthage, but the extent to which the Romans were anxious to end the war on any good-seeming terms. But this pays too little to the severe financial penalty imposed on Carthage (the annual tribute levied was greater than that after the Second Punic War, where the Roman dominance is undeniable, though the total to be paid with the latter was more, since the terms of payment were over fifty years, not ten); the pressure this put Carthage under was immediately apparent in the Mercenary War, which was itself caused by Carthage's inability to provide compensation to her own troops.

Other sources for the treaty (e.g. App., *Sic.* 2, *Vir. Ill.* 41.2, Oros. 4.11.2, Zonar. 8.17.4–6) broadly agree with Polybius' account. On one point there is a major difference, albeit clearly the result of error. *Vir. Ill.* and Orosius (cf. Ampel. 46.2, Eutr. 3.2.2) mistakenly conflate into this treaty the Carthaginian cession of Sardinia, which Plb. 1.88.8–12 (cf. 3.27.7–8) shows did not occur until several years later, and *Vir. Ill.* adds the Ebro treaty struck with Hasdrubal. Livy is extremely unlikely to have made this error in Book 19, since he describes the sequence of treaties correctly at 21.1.5 and 21.2.8,[275] but it is likely to have been a popular misreading of the history already in his day, since at 21.40.5 and 22.54.11 he loosely summarizes the aftermath of the battle of the Aegates Islands as involving the cession of Sardinia as well as Sicily.[276] The prevalence of the error in the Latin sources doubtless reflects the moral problems raised by the way Sardinia was actually seized from Carthage:[277] the Romans threatened her with a renewal of fighting at a time when she was unable to resist owing to the Mercenary War. This provided a significant justification for the Carthaginians resuming war against Rome a generation later (cf. Plb. 3.10.1–4, 3.15.10, 3.30.4). It showed Rome in a better light if Sardinia, like Sicily, were the legitimate prize of their victory at the Aegates Islands.

Interestingly, the same misreading of history is visible in P.'s version,[278] since he later reports a rebellion by the Sardinians against Rome without having mentioned when the island came under Roman control (20.4n.), and Hannibal's crossing the Ebro *contra foedus* (21.1: 'against the treaty') without having recounted the treaty in question (cf. 21.1n.). This does not require that P. himself misunderstood the actual terms of the treaty, any more than Livy did, but at the very least his sequence dovetails with the same popular history visible in other sources, and could easily have generated or reinforced confusion in others. A less-informed reader of P. might naturally assume that the treaty that ended the First Punic War both ceded Sardinia to Rome and banned the Carthaginians from crossing the Ebro.

On three further points the other sources add provisions absent from Polybius. First is the question of Carthaginian prisoners in Roman hands. Livy is likely to have included some discussion of this, since at 21.41.6 he refers to the Romans requiring that Hamilcar's troops in Eryx pay a ransom in return for their release. This precise provision is admittedly not mentioned elsewhere, but Zonar. 8.17.4

---

[275] See the detailed discussion in Eliæson (1906), 100–19.

[276] On the development of this version in the Roman historical tradition see Ameling (2001), 121–3.

[277] Carey (1996) argues that the Romans might well have seen her seizure of Sardinia as justified according to the presuppositions of Roman civil law, which allowed property to be taken over once it was abandoned by its previous owner, as Sardinia arguably had been. But even if that is so, it was not a justification which carried any weight with Polybius, nor, as Carey acknowledges (Carey (1996), 221–2), would it have had much appeal in the later historical tradition, which preferred justifications that were not based in a parochial legalism.

[278] Rightly observed by Eliæson (1906), 103–7; however, his explanation is that P. is drawing not on Livy, but on the 'lost Epitome', a theory which is dubious on other grounds (see Introduction).

says more generally that Carthaginian prisoners of war were to be ransomed, which is not explicitly mentioned by Polybius, but is the natural corollary of the clause which required no ransom for the Romans. According to Eutr. 2.27.4-5 (cf. Val. Max. 5.1.1a), the Senate waived the ransom, paying it themselves in the case of prisoners held in private hands. But although Eutr. relates this to the treaty of Lutatius, it is more probably a version of the story told in Plb. 1.83.8, that the Romans released the prisoners from the Punic War in their hands as part of later diplomatic negotiations over Italian traders captured by the Carthaginians during the Mercenary War.

Second, Zonar. 8.17.6 claims that among the terms of the revised treaty was that Carthaginian warships were banned from Italian waters. This is not implausible in itself, but one might have expected Polybius to have mentioned it, were that genuinely a condition placed on them: it is, accordingly, more likely that this was invented by a later source, on the assumption that it was the natural corollary of the clauses restricting other sorts of activity on Italian territory.[279]

Third, D.S. 24.13 and Nep., *Ham.* 1.5 both claim that Lutatius' initial demand to Hamilcar included that his troops should surrender their weapons, but that he withdrew the demand when Hamilcar was outraged and refused (Zonar. 8.17.5, less plausibly, has Lutatius demanding that Hamilcar lead his troops under the yoke as formal indication of their surrender). This could possibly be true, but is more likely to be the product of hindsight, as Hamilcar's continuing resentment of Rome, which was seen as the ultimate trigger for the Second Punic War, in the historiographical tradition was thought to be partly generated by the sense that he personally had never been defeated (e.g. Plb. 3.9.7), and this could well have been the seed of a story about his refusing to surrender his arms.

According to Livy 30.44.1, the treaty was ratified in the consulship of Q. Lutatius Cerco and A. Manlius Torquatus: i.e. in 241.[280] This fits the evidence that the battle took place close to the end of the consular year 242 (above): several weeks—or, more probably, months—have to be allowed for the Carthaginians to hear of the outcome and delegate authority to Hamilcar to negotiate peace, then for the draft to be sent to Rome, and for the Roman commissioners to arrive and for the final treaty to be negotiated and ratified. It accords with this that the triumphs of Lutatius and Valerius took place in October 241, as recorded in the *Fasti Capitolini*; it also accords with it that, more than a century later, the victory was commemorated on a coin of 109 or 108 (*RRC* no. 305)—but the moneyer who celebrated it was not a descendant of the actual victor, C. Lutatius Catulus, but of

---

[279] *Contra* Scardigli (1991), 230; her explanation for its omission from Polybius is that it was part of the original negotiations which disappeared from the revised treaty. This, however, directly contradicts Zonaras, our only source for the clause, who specifically relates it to the revised treaty; and if he is presumed wrong on this point, it is hard to see why his account of it should be given any credence at all.

[280] This may be in part the source of the confusion in Val. Max. 1.3.2, who, according to the epitomes of Paris and Nepotianus, identified Lutatius Cerco rather than Lutatius Catulus as the victor of the Aegates Islands: see Wardle (1998), 146.

his brother Q. Lutatius Cerco, during whose consulship Carthage finally conceded defeat.

Detailed discussions of the treaty include De Sanctis III.1 184–9 [188–92], Schmitt (1969), 173–81, Scardigli (1991), 205–43.

19.10 *Fire in the temple of Vesta*. A popular anecdote, reported in many other sources also.[281] Dionysius refers to the honours that Metellus received from the city in consequence, which he saw recorded on an inscription on his statue on the Capitol; Pliny refers specifically to his being granted the right to ride in a chariot to meetings of the Senate. Even though the statue seen by Dionysius need not have dated to Metellus' own time, it is reasonably likely that it reflected an authentic record of the rewards given to Metellus for his heroism during the fire, and that the basic story is, accordingly, historical (cf. Leuze (1905), 96–9; *contra* Brelich (1939), who sees it as essentially mythical, but does not consider the implications of the statue).

According to several sources (Seneca, Pliny, ps.-Plutarch, Ampelius; also Sen., *Prov.* 1.5.2, Juv. 6.265), Metellus was blinded by the fire, though in ps.-Plutarch's account his sight was miraculously restored later. The blinding, however, seems overwhelmingly improbable (see esp. Leuze (1905), 102–15). No one mentions it prior to Seneca, despite the fullness of several of the earlier accounts, and Metellus is recorded as having held a dictatorship several years later, in 224, which is unlikely to have been granted to him if he were blind (cf. 13.3n.). Moreover, Seneca introduces it as part of a declamatory thesis centring on a (supposed) rule requiring a priest to be unblemished (cf. below): the declaimers offered arguments for and against depriving him of his office. The likelihood is, accordingly, that it was merely an early imperial invention for the purpose of declamatory exercise,[282] which was then mistakenly assumed to be historical. Hence it is unlikely to have appeared in Livy.

There is an alternative version, recorded by Oros. 4.11.9 (cf. Aug., *Civ.* 3.18), in which Metellus' injury was not to his eyes but to his arm, and it is possible that this was the original story, and indeed may have been found in Livy, for all that P. does not refer to it (so Leuze (1905), 103). Since such an injury was less severely debilitating than blindness, it is less surprising that Cicero or Ovid (or indeed P.) might have omitted to mention it, or indeed that it would have been superseded in much of the tradition by the more dramatic version; it is also a less likely candidate for invention in the first place, although invention naturally cannot be ruled

---

[281] See esp. Cic., *Scaur.* 48, D.H., *AR* 2.66.3–4, Ov., *Fast.* 6.437–54, Val. Max. 1.4.5 (in epitomes by Paris and Nepotianus), Sen., *Contr.* 4.2, Plin., *Nat.* 7.141, Juv. 3.138–9 (also scholia), Ampel. 20.11, Aug., *Civ.* 3.18, Oros. 4.11.9; also ps.-Plu., *Par. Min.* 309F–310A, citing as his source the *Italika* of Aristeides of Miletus (*FGrH* 286 F 15), though identifying the protagonist of ps.-Plutarch's anecdote with Metellus requires textual emendation.

[282] The origin of the invention may rest in the idea that Metellus rescued the Palladium (see below), which men were not supposed to see (so Brelich (1939), 35).

out. It is true that Metellus appears to have continued to hold his priesthood subsequent to this (cf. Cic., *Cato* 30), and it might be objected that this would not have been possible had he suffered a permanent injury of any sort, since (it is claimed) one could not hold a priesthood if mutilated (cf. Wissowa (1912), 491, Beagon (2002), 114–15). However this alleged rule is poorly founded (see Morgan (1974)): it is attested only in Sen., *Contr.* 7.2, where it is part of a fiction for declamatory purposes (see above)—declaimers regularly invented the laws on which their cases rested. A couple of related rules are recorded, but these refer to (a) a priest with an ulcer being banned from watching for an omen (Plu., *Quaest. Rom.* 281C), the specificity of which seems to imply that other priestly functions could be validly performed by such a priest; and (b) a rule (paralleled elsewhere in the ancient world: see Garland (1995), 63–5) that certain categories of priest must be unblemished at the time of appointment (D.H., *AR* 2.21.3), which leaves it open that such a priest, like a senator (cf. 13.3n.), could continue in office if the injury was received subsequently. Hence there is no reason to question Metellus' injury on these grounds.

The episode is dated by Orosius to 241, which fits the implicit sequence in P., who places it after the peace agreement with Carthage, but before the revolt of the Faliscans, both of which were in that year (see 19.9, 20.1nn.); D.H., *AR* 2.66.3 says more vaguely that it took place 'at the time of' (κατά) the First Punic War.

templum Vestae: The temple stood in the Forum, as part of a complex adjacent to the *Regia* that included the house of the Vestals. It was a round building, whose origins, according to the Romans, dated to early in the regal period (e.g. D.H., *AR* 2.64.5–65.4, Plu., *Num.* 11.1); however, the earliest surviving remnants on the site date from the late sixth century BC, and the round structure is not apparent in the remains until a rebuilding in the early fourth century, perhaps subsequent to the Gallic sack (Arvanitis (2010), 54–7). It was damaged and reconstructed several times, but the reconstructions do not appear to have involved any fundamental alterations to the design of the building. One of those reconstructions dates from the late third or early second BC, which supports (but does not require) the account of its damage by fire here (R. T. Scott in *LTUR* vol. 5, 126; Scott (2009), 19–21).

Properly speaking it was not a *templum*, but an *aedis*, since a *templum* needed to be consecrated as one by the augurs, which the shrine of Vesta was not (Varro *ap.* Gell. 14.7.7, Serv., *Aen.* 7.153). Admittedly, the term was used loosely, and writers of all periods speak of it as a *templum*, as P. does here. Livy himself, however, is stricter in his terminology, and consistently speaks of *aedis Vestae* (5.30.5, 5.32.6, 26.27.4, 26.27.14, 28.11.6; cf. P. at 28.3, 41.1, and 86.5), or of *delubra Vestae* (7.20.4); only at 5.52.7 does he use the word *templum* of it in a looser rhetorical context. This makes it probable that the phrase here is P.'s rather than Livy's.

Much of the interpretation of the archaeology and history of the building is controversial: for discussion see e.g. Scott (1993), R. T. Scott in *LTUR* vol. 5, 125-8, Scott (2009), Arvanitis (2010).

Caecilius Metellus: See 19.1, 19.8nn.

sacra: According to many of the sources (Cicero, Ovid, Valerius Maximus, Seneca, Pliny, ps.-Plutarch, Juvenal, Ampelius), the object that Metellus rescued was the Palladium, supposedly brought by Aeneas from Troy. However, this story is unlikely to go back to an authoritative source (cf. Leuze (1905), 99-100): D.H., *AR* 2.66.5-6 not only questions the rescue of the Palladium, but even expresses uncertainty whether the Palladium was present in the temple in the first place (cf. Plu., *Cam.* 20.5-6 for alternative views about the identity of the sacred objects in the temple). The fact that P. uses the vague plural *sacra* may indicate that Livy, likewise, was cautious about identifying what was rescued with a single iconic object, although he does elsewhere (5.52.7, 26.27.14) speak of the temple as containing a 'pledge of empire' (*pignus imperii*): the Palladium is not explicitly named, but the phrase strongly implies it (cf. Ogilvie (1965), 745-6). Orosius, similarly to P., speaks of 'gods about to burn' (*arsuros deos*), suggesting a rescue of cult objects in general rather than the Palladium in particular. Cf. also F 21n.

19.11 *Addition of new tribes.* For P.'s interest in the addition of new tribes see 2.7n. The date is generally assumed to be 241, following on from the two previous notices, which are to be dated to that year (19.9, 19.10nn.) and preceding the rebellion of the Faliscans at the start of the next book, which likewise took place in 241 (see 20.1n.). The *Fasti Capitolini* record censors for that year: it appears that the laws which created tribes were typically passed during the censorial period, and the censors would then formally institute them by adding them to the registers (Taylor (2013 (1960)), 17).

One potential problem is that in 10.9.14 Livy records the addition of the new tribes under the completion of the *lustrum*, an event which he there, as he usually does elsewhere (13.4, 16.3nn.), places in the year after the censors' election (the *Fasti Capitolini* register the censorship under 300, Livy records the *lustrum* and the addition of tribes in 299). If he followed that pattern here, then he would have recorded the *lustrum* for the censorship of 241 in 240, a year which certainly fell in Book 20, not Book 19. So one might suspect that Livy recorded the addition of the tribes under the previous censorship in the book, in 247/6 (see 19.5n.), and P. has transferred the notice here. But, even if we leave aside the relative unlikelihood of P. splitting the events of a single censorship in this way, there is a different consideration against that conclusion. In 20.11 P. records the number of *lustra* in that book; the number is unfortunately corrupt (see *ad loc.*), but probably should read three, possibly four. But, even without the censorship of 241/0, there are likely to have been four *lustra* in the period covered by that book: the problem of identifying the number is compounded were we to transfer this *lustrum* to Book 20. If we combine that information with P.'s implicit sequence of events here, the most likely scenario is that Livy, with a slight measure of anachronism, compressed the entire censorship of 241 into Book 19, as he would later compress the censorship of 204 into Book 29 (see 13.4n.). He accordingly recorded the foundation of the tribes under the year 241, although strictly speaking he should, following his usual practice, have placed it—and the accompanying *lustrum*—in 240.

tribus: The tribes were one of the primary administrative and political divisions at Rome. All male citizens were assigned a tribe, primarily according to their geographic location. Their functions developed through the Republic, but at least by the late fourth century they were used as the basis for the census and for military levies, and the tribal assemblies were used to pass legislation and to vote for various elected officials.

In the early Republic there were four urban and seventeen rural tribes. From 387 onwards an additional fourteen rural tribes were created; but the episode here is the final time that tribes were added, despite the considerable expansion of the citizen body in later centuries. Henceforward all new citizens were added to the existing tribes, which loosened the link between tribes and geography, since newly enfranchised communities were assigned a tribe, even though their territory might have no geographic contiguity with the areas previously allotted to that tribe (cf. Taylor (2013 (1960), 79–100). The link was also diminished in many other ways: for example, by the fact that new citizens might take the tribe of their patron, that a successful prosecutor might sometimes take the tribe of the person convicted, and that for much of Roman history all freedmen, regardless of their location, were placed in the four urban tribes (Taylor (2013 (1960), 17–24, 132–49: see also 20.11n.).

For the history and function of tribes see esp. Taylor (2013 (1960)); also Silvestrini (2010).

adiectae sunt: Livy's usual formula for the addition of tribes is *additae* (which may have been the formula used in the official records also: see Oakley (1997), 440). P. invariably changes Livy's *additae* to *adiectae* (see 1.B.3n.); the same pattern was probably followed here.

Velina: Taylor (2013 (1960)), 63 associates the name with the Lacus Velinus near Reate, which leads to a problem, since this was nowhere near the territory associated with the tribe, which primarily covered Picenum (Antolini and Marengo (2010)). However, it is more likely to be derived from a Lacus Velinus in Picenum referred to by Plin., *Nat.* 2.226 (a suggestion Taylor peremptorily but groundlessly rejects).

Quirina: According to Fest. 304L, the name Quirina derived from the city Cures Sabini. This has been considered odd, since the territory allotted to the tribe covered part of the Sabine land, but not (it is claimed) Cures. Accordingly, other possibilities have been canvassed. Mommsen, *StR*³ III 172-3 proposed that the name was intended to signify the entire Roman people—the *Quirites*—since this was the last tribe to be created. Taylor (2013 (1960)), 63-4, in an elaborate but highly implausible reconstruction, suggested that the tribes were originally proposed by Curius Dentatus (the conqueror of the territory) a generation earlier, but the hostility of the nobles to his political programme led to a delay in their establishment: the name, in her view, was meant to honour Dentatus himself as well as referring to Cures. Wiseman (2009), 43-4, without following Taylor's reconstruction in its entirety, likewise suggests a connection with Curius Dentatus. The name Quirina, he argues, evokes a complex of word-associations: not only the Roman people's citizenship, but specifically the Sabine origins to many Roman practices and institutions, and also the Sabine *curis* ('spear'); all of these, he claims, are tied together by Curius Dentatus' radical policies of equality, as he (allegedly) divided the land into 7-*iugera* portions and refused any more for himself (e.g. Plin., *Nat.* 18.18; cf. 18.1n.).

While none of these can be ruled out in principle, the premise on which Festus' information is rejected—that the tribe's territory did not include Cures Sabini—is weakly founded. Taylor (2013 (1960)), 59-63 argues that the Sabines whom Vell. 1.14.7 records as being enfranchised in 268 were specifically the people of Cures, in which case they must have been assigned to another tribe than the Quirina, but her arguments are based on indirect evidence (that the Romans regularly spoke of the people of Cures as if they were 'the' Sabines, so Velleius may be doing the same here) and are hardly secure. There are only ten inhabitants of Cures Sabini whose tribe is known, and only two of these are of the tribe of Quirina—but they appear in the oldest two inscriptions, and no other tribe has more than three (Buonocore (2010), 36, 40). Certainly there is no particular epigraphic support for the assignment of the town to the Sergia, where Taylor places it: that tribe is mentioned only in two early imperial inscriptions (Buonocore (2010), 36). Even if Velleius is right that some of the Sabines were enfranchised in 268, it was clearly not all of them, since the weight of epigraphic evidence shows several Sabine towns unmistakably within the Quirina tribe (cf. Buonocore (2010), 40).

This does not prove that Festus is correct—his phrase 'seems to have been derived' (*videtur traxisse*) is tentative, and may be based on mere speculation: one of the other proposals may after all be closer to the truth. But his evidence cannot merely be dismissed on the grounds of geography.

Book 20

20.1 *Revolt of the Faliscans.* The episode is noted in a number of other places (Plb. 1.65.2, Val. Max. 6.5.1, Eutr. 2.28, Oros. 4.11.10, Zonar. 8.18.1), but none gives more than minimal detail. The main emphasis of several of the sources, as in P., is the speed of the Roman victory: Eutropius, like P., specifically says that it took place in six days, while Polybius refers more vaguely to 'a few days' (ὀλίγαις ἡμέραις). This interpretation is likely to have been reflected in Livy also: P. simply distils it down. Eutropius and Orosius both give the enemy losses as 15,000, which is no more likely to be plausible than any other battle casualties that appear only in late sources (De Sanctis III.1 271 [279]: 'ridicola esagerazione'; *contra* Di Stefano Manzella (1990), 342).

This version is, however, contradicted (at least implicitly) by Zonaras, who does not give a time-frame, but describes the campaign in terms that indicate something longer and more difficult. He speaks of two battles (Orosius, the only other source to refer specifically to a battle, mentions just one), one with an equivocal outcome (the Roman infantry were defeated, their cavalry victorious), followed by an outright victory. While it is not impossible that these battles should have taken place in quick enough succession to be compatible with total victory in six days, it is more likely that Zonaras depends on an alternative tradition which elaborated the war into a more significant drama; he also attributes the campaign to only one of the consuls, A. Manlius Torquatus, whereas the *Fasti Capitolini* have both consuls awarded triumphs (cf. also Eutropius). Since our earliest source, Polybius, is one of those who speaks of a swift victory, and we cannot detect any earlier traces of Zonaras' version, the former should be preferred.

Plu., *CG* 3.3, purportedly citing speeches by Gaius Gracchus (= *ORF*³ fr. 31), refers to a war with the Faliscans being provoked by an insult to a tribune named Genucius. Münzer (1910) (followed by e.g. *MRR* I 219), argued that it must be this war, since the earlier wars with the Faliscans are described in the surviving books of Livy, who gives no indication of any such motive behind them. However, Plutarch's information may well not genuinely go back to Gracchus or any other reliable source; even if it does, it does not seem to match very closely the other accounts of this war, where the clear indication is that it was a broad revolt; even if an insult to a magistrate were seen as tantamount to revolt, it is unlikely that the Romans would send two consular armies to avenge it. Accordingly, it represents at best a minority historical tradition, in which case it is at least as likely to be a story relating to one of the earlier wars as to this one.[283]

---

[283] At Livy 5.18.7–8 a consular tribune named Cn. Genucius is trapped and killed while fighting the Faliscans; Gracchus (or Plutarch) may be reflecting an alternative version of this episode (so Loreto (1989), 730).

The campaign is dated to the consular year 241 by an inscription found on a cuirass (presumably from the spoils of the campaign: see Zimmermann (1986), Flower (1998)), by the *Fasti Capitolini*, Eutropius, and (implicitly) Polybius, and Livy probably did the same, though Orosius misdates it to 238. Livy, unlike Orosius, was writing a detailed year-by-year narrative, and the broad chronological framework of the period was reasonably well established: it is unlikely that he (or his source) would have misdated the victory by three years. However, no more precise date can be given, since the triumphs took place at the very end of that year (on 1 and 4 March: March 240 in the Julian calendar).

For full discussion of the Faliscan revolt see esp. Loreto (1989).

Falisci: A tribe inhabiting a region of southern Etruria; their chief city was Falerii (*BarrAtl* Map 42 C4), the modern Civita Castellana, occupying a large plateau to the west of the river Treia, with natural defences on three sides from the steep surrounding river valleys. Livy (esp. 5.8.4) treats them as essentially indistinguishable from the Etruscans, but the relationship between the two groups appears more complex. On the one hand, the epigraphic evidence shows that their language was an Italic one (cf. Str. 5.2.9), and their artefacts and funerary practices differ from those of their Etruscan neighbours (Potter (1979), 56–8; cf. 74). But, on the other hand, recent scholarship has emphasized the archaeological and historical evidence for links with the Etruscan city of Veii in particular: it may be that it was primarily after the fall of Veii in the early fourth century that the Faliscans stressed their distinctness from the Etruscans around them (Cifani (2013)).

The Faliscans appeared in P. once previously, in the context of their being subdued by Camillus at the time of the famous episode of the Faliscan schoolteacher (5.4n.). In Livy they had previously appeared as part of a broader Etruscan alliance against Rome (4.17.11); he also briefly referred to their involvement in subsequent uprisings in 357 (7.16.2–17.9; cf. 7.22.4–5, 7.38.1) and 293 (10.45.6), after which they swiftly came to terms with Rome (10.46.12), but these do not rate a mention in P.

The town of Falerii was inhabited from prehistoric times; even after the destruction of the original city (see below), the well-known shrine of Juno, which was outside the walls, continued to be in active use at least into the early imperial period (Ov., *Am.* 3.13; cf. Comella (1986), 185–7), and some form of later occupation is indicated by a cemetery from the second century AD (Frederiksen and Ward Perkins (1957), 131–2). Although much of the original town is now under the modern city, substantial archaeological remains survive from its vicinity: see e.g. Andrén (1940), 80–148, Frederiksen and Ward Perkins (1957), 128–33, Scullard (1967), 113–15, Comella (1986), Moscati (1990), De Lucia Brolli (1991), 28–39.

in deditionem venerunt: Cf. 8.4n. According to both Eutropius and Zonaras, the Faliscans were deprived of half their territory; Zonaras adds that they had to hand over their weapons, horses, goods, and slaves. Since other aspects of Zonaras' account of the campaign appear to reflect later elaborations rather than going back to an original source (see above), these terms cannot be assumed to be authentic, and they would be unusual for a punishment of a rebellious state at this period, though it is not impossible that they were indeed imposed on the Faliscans at this time (Loreto (1989), 723).

A further point in Zonaras, however, can be authenticated (cf. Moscati (1990), 167–71): that the original city was destroyed, and a new one built in a different location. This is generally taken to be another punishment for the revolt; however, this interpretation has been questioned by Terrenato (2004), on the grounds that the move from the old Falerii to the new town is more plausibly explained in terms of a general pattern in Italy at this time of shifts from defensive sites to ones on communication routes; he also queries why the new town would be placed commanding a key road, if its foundation was a punishment. Terrenato's case (though he appears not to have realized this) is supported by Zonaras' wording, since Zonaras does not in fact relate the move to Roman punishment for the revolt: he says that it happened 'later' (ὕστερον), and indicates that the reason was the convenient access of the new city (εὐέφοδος) compared to the old one built on a steep mountain.

The move in population at this time was not limited to Falerii alone: almost all of the existing Faliscan towns seem to have been abandoned in the mid-third century (Moscati (1990), 170–1), and the evidence suggests that a substantial proportion of the farms ceased to be worked then (De Lucia Brolli (1991), 14–15). This too has been related to Roman punishment (e.g. Potter (1979), 100–1), but the process seems to have begun earlier in the century: it accordingly seems likely that the depopulation of the region was in part the consequence of broader economic pressures as a result of trading competition from Rome, which predated the revolt and could even conceivably have been a cause of it (so Cambi (2004), 78–9).

The new town—Falerii Novi—was built around 6 km to the west, on the Via Amerina, a major route to the north which seems to have been constructed around the same time. Much of the circuit of the walls survives above ground, and the buried structures inside the town have been systematically surveyed, though still only partially excavated (Keay *et al.* (2000)). On the town's foundation, status, and population see Di Stefano Manzella (1990), esp. 345–50; for the archaeological remains see also De Lucia Brolli (1991), 48–63.

According to Valerius Maximus, the surrender was written by a certain Papirius; Hanslik (1949), 1062 (followed by *MRR* I 220) identifies him with C. Papirius Maso, *cos.* 231, on the basis that that he was *pontifex* at his death in 213 (Livy 25.2.1); Rüpke, *FS* 826 prefers his father, whose *cursus honorum* is entirely unknown. But both of these identifications rest on a slender thread of inferences: first, that Valerius' information is authentic; second, that the drafter of the surrender terms acted in his capacity as a *pontifex*; third, that no other member of the *gens Papiria* was *pontifex* in 241. All of these could be true, but any one could be false, and, if so, the entire reconstruction fails.

20.2 *Foundation of colony.*

Spoletium: Modern Spoleto (*BarrAtl* Map 42 D3). It is described as a Latin colony in Cic., *Balb.* 48, and likewise appears on the list of such colonies at Livy 27.10.8. It was founded on a naturally fortified location in Umbria in the western foothills of the Appennines, and controlling one of the major routes that connect the eastern and western sides of the mountains. Although four necropolises, dating from the seventh century BC, have been excavated in and around the town (Di Marco (1975), 16–17, 37–8), it is hard to determine whether there was an actual city on the site prior to the foundation of the Roman colony: no historical text mentions one, and the archaeological evidence leaves the question unclear. In particular, it is disputed whether the oldest strata of the city's walls can be dated to pre-Roman times (see Di Marco (1975), 21–31, cautiously concluding that they probably should be, though Bradley (2000), 135 disagrees).

The colony's foundation is dated to 241 by Vell. 1.14.8, which, on the assumption that Livy described the Faliscan revolt also in that year (20.1n.), would appear to fit the order of events in P. However, there is a complication. Velleius also says that this was the year when the Floralia was instituted, and according to Plin., *Nat.* 18.286 (citing Varro), that took place in 238.

All scholars, even while acknowledging that the discrepancy over the date of the Floralia is unresolvable, accept Velleius' date for the foundation of Spoletium. But this overlooks a key piece of evidence. P. refers to the next event, the war with the Ligurians, as happening *tunc primum*; and this phrase usually implies that in Livy that event took place at the same time as the one directly before (see 11.5n.). Since the Ligurian war in Livy probably was recounted under 238 (20.3n.), and certainly not in 241, this implies that Livy placed the foundation of Spoletium, too, in 238. This weights the evidence strongly in favour of 238 for both the institution of the Floralia and the foundation of the colony: the coincidence between Livy's and Pliny's date allows us to exclude that the latter is merely the result of textual corruption (as suggested in *MRR* I 219–20), while Varro and Livy are far more likely to be reliable on the chronology than Velleius is. Velleius was right to synchronize the Floralia and Spoletium (presumably a synchronism he found in his sources), but he misdated them by three years.

Salmon (1969), 65 argues for a close connection between the foundation of Spoletium and the Faliscan revolt, either because the Faliscans were provoked into revolt by the foundation, or the colony was founded in response to their rebellion. Revising the chronology for the foundation, as proposed above, makes the first of these impossible; but even if it were after all to be dated to 241, both of Salmon's connections are implausible (cf. Loreto (2007), 95–6): Spoletium was not on Faliscan territory, and indeed is more than 60 km distant from Falerii, separated from it by a substantial range of high ground. Nor is there evidence for any recent unrest in Umbria that might explain the foundation at this time. As with previous colonies like Ariminum and Beneventum (15.4n.), Aesernia (16.4n.), and Brundisium (19.5n.), the decision to found it is more likely to have been governed by a broad aim to place a loyal community in a new area of Italy rather than specific conditions of local disaffection: cf. also 15.4n.

For the history and archaeology of Spoletium see Di Marco (1975); cf. also Syme (1970–1).

colonia deducta est: See 1.B.1n.

20.3 *War against the Ligurians*. Fighting with the Ligurians at this period is recorded in several places, but only briefly and not always consistently. Eutr. 3.2 mentions a Roman victory and triumph over them by L. Cornelius Lentulus and Q. Fulvius Flaccus, the consuls of 237; however, the *Fasti* record no triumph for 237, but instead have one awarded to Lentulus' brother P. Cornelius Lentulus during his consulship in 236 (Eutropius—or his source—presumably was misled by the similar names of the consuls of 237 and 236 into predating the triumph by a year). Flor. 1.19 does not give the year when fighting began, but implies that it was well before 237: they fought for a long time (*diu*) before Fulvius 'at last hemmed in their hiding places with fire' (1.19.5 *tandem latebras eorum igni saepsit*), with subsequent victories by 'Baebius' (presumably an error for C. Atilius Bulbus, *cos.* 235), and Postumius (L. Postumius Albinus, *cos.* 234). Zonar. 8.18.2 has a victory by Ti. Sempronius Gracchus, *cos.* 238, which he links to a campaign of his colleague Valerius against the Cisalpine Gauls, in which he was first defeated and then was subsequently victorious; he then records further fighting with the Ligurians every year from 236 to 233.

That the Ligurian war concluded in 233 is certain: the commander that year was Q. Fabius Maximus, the hero of the Second Punic War, then in his first consulship, and his victory and triumph are recorded not only in the *Fasti Capitolini*, but in several other places.[284] When it began—which is what P. here is describing— is more difficult to determine. On the face of things there does not seem any reason to doubt Zonaras' claim (implicitly supported by Florus) that it was as early as 238, for all that Eutropius does not mention it until 237, and certainly no triumph was received until 236. The problem is that Zonaras directly links the war with a campaign in the same year against the Cisalpine Gauls by Valerius, a campaign described also in Oros. 4.12.1.[285] The existence of such a war is,

---

[284] They are mentioned on his *elogium* in the Forum Augustum (*CIL* XI 1828 = *ILS* 56); also Plu., *Fab.* 2.1, *Vir. Ill.* 43.1; cf. Cic., *Nat. Deor.* 2.61.

[285] Orosius dates this to the same year as the Faliscan revolt (20.1n.): Loreto (2007), 147 argues that this is correct, and that the war against the Ligurians and the associated war with the Gauls in fact took place in the immediate wake of that revolt, in 240. But the fact that both Orosius and Zonaras associate the campaign with the consuls of 238 and never mention those of 240 (or 239) makes that improbable.

however, contradicted by Plb. 2.21.1-5, who explicitly states that the Romans did not fight the Gauls between the war in 283-282 (12.1n.) and an abortive Gallic attack on Ariminum in 237 (misdated by Zonaras to 236: cf. 20.8n.).[286] If Polybius is correct, and the tradition represented by Zonaras and Orosius placed the Gallic war a year too early, then they may have done the same with the Ligurian war, and Eutropius was right to record that war only in 237 (so e.g. Weiss (1926), 533).

On balance, however, it seems more probable that Polybius was unaware of the fighting in 238, given that he is skating very sketchily over his material at this point, rather than following a source which systematically narrated events in chronological sequence; hence it is preferable to accept that fighting against both Gauls and Ligurians took place in 238, and that P., following Livy, is referring to that year.

No source has any account either of the causes of the war or of the fighting itself, except for a vague comment by Florus that the Ligurians were protected by forests, that 'it was somewhat harder work to find them than defeat them' (1.19.4: *maior aliquanto labor erat invenire quam vincere*), and that they fought more through brigandage (*latrocinia*) than open warfare (cf. Plu., *Fab.* 2.1). It has been proposed (Feig Vishnia (1996), 15-17) that the war originated as part of a plan by the Romans to control the routes to the Po Valley as a prelude to conquering the region; but that seems to attribute more long-range strategic planning by the Romans than is plausible, for all that the war can hardly be seen as the product of anything except Roman aggression: even on Feig Vishnia's account, it is a further fourteen years before the Romans made any attempt to launch a major invasion of the Po Valley by this route (see 20.9n.). It is sufficient to hypothesize that the Romans may, especially in the course of taking over Sardinia and Corsica (below), have noticed the general strategic advantages of control of the north-western coast of the Italian peninsula.

Liguras: The collective name for a group of tribes inhabiting the coastal region between Provence and north-western Italy. Ancient sources (e.g. D.H., *AR* 1.10.3; cf. Str. 2.5.28) generally claimed that they were the original inhabitants of the region, distinct from the neighbouring Gauls, who supposedly arrived later; moreover, there are traces of pre-Indo-European elements in certain toponyms in the region which led some scholars to conclude that these belonged to the Ligurian language. However, these toponyms do not correlate closely with the regions traditionally associated with the Ligurians, and it is also hard to discover any archaeological distinction between Ligurians and Gauls: indeed, even in antiquity the boundary between 'Gallic' tribes and 'Ligurian' ones was uncertain (for examples see Peyre (1979), 26-7), and Gauls and Ligurians were sometimes

---

[286] For the dating see Walbank (1957), 191.

seen to have melded with one another (see esp. Str. 4.6.3, Plu., *Aem.* 6.1). Accordingly, it is preferable to regard the 'Ligurians', not as the remnants of a pre-Celtic culture, but rather as a group of Celtic tribes who were constructed as a distinct nation by ancient ethnography. See esp. Arnaud (2001), Haeussler (2013), 87–91, Garcia (2014), 20–37.

This is the Ligurians' first known encounter with Rome; but they resisted Roman power over several generations, and it took rather more than a century before they were ultimately subdued: the final victory over them recorded in the *Fasti* is in 117 (cf. 62.1n.).[287] For a comprehensive set of essays on the archaeology of the region, see De Marinis and Spadea (2004).

tunc primum: For the implications of this phrase for the chronology see 20.2n. In addition, it implies that what was here initiated was something significant and long-lasting: P. most commonly uses it of innovations in Roman practice or in the constitutional order; he also uses it to mark stages in the extension of Roman power, as when they first campaigned overseas (16.2) and beyond the Po (20.9). Its application here to the Ligurians is, accordingly, slightly unexpected, for, while the Ligurians would be a persistent thorn in the Romans' side for several decades after this, few nowadays would think of the fight against them as a major stage in the development of Rome. It is likely that P. highlights it largely because Livy himself did (where Livy's text survives, almost all examples of the phrase fall into that category), and Livy appears to have regarded the Ligurians as symbolically important in a way that went beyond the actual scale of the fighting against them. At 39.1.2–8 he has an extended discussion of the significance of the Ligurian wars to Rome: he describes the Ligurians as 'an enemy born, so to speak, to maintain military discipline for the Romans in the periods between major wars' (39.1.2: *hostis velut natus ad continendam inter magnorum intervalla bellorum Romanis militarem disciplinam*), and refers to the difficulty of ever completely subjugating them. P.'s phrase here appears to confirm that Livy's broader interest in the Ligurians as an enemy was present from the very first campaign against them.

exercitus promotus est: *promovere* to describe the movement of troops is found in Livy (see esp. 35.23.5), and is reasonably common in other military contexts (*TLL* X.2 1895.13–32). The specific phrase *exercitum promovere*, however, is found only in later antiquity: it first appears in Just. 14.1.6 (cf. also Amm. 16.12.19). Accordingly, it is more likely to derive from P. than from Livy.

20.4 *Rebellion of Sardinians and Corsicans.* The only sustained narrative of the Roman campaigns against the Sardinians and Corsicans at this time is in Zonar. 8.18.7–14: he records a sequence of campaigns in the period 236–231, with repeated Roman victories followed by renewed fighting. First, in 236, the Romans

---

[287] It appears that one group of Ligurians held out for a century even beyond that: see Dio 54.24.3 for Augustus' reduction of the 'long-haired Ligurians' in the Maritime Alps.

attacked Corsica; Zonaras does not explain the grounds,[288] and the degree of Roman control over it at this point is not clear from the sources. The Romans had successfully campaigned there and driven out the Carthaginians more than twenty years earlier, in 259 (cf. 17.3n.); but it is not certain at what point they began to claim authority there. According to the antiquarian writer Sinnius Capito (*ap.* Fest. 430L), they had taken it over at the same time as Sardinia, in 238 (see below). However, Sinnius' reliability is dubious, since he also speaks of an active campaign rather than a cession by the Carthaginians, something implausible in itself (no triumph was awarded for the 'conquest'), and contradicted by all other sources. Polybius, when describing the cession of Sardinia, does not mention Corsica, a surprising omission if he knew of it, given the significance that he attached to the loss of Sardinia as a primary cause of the Second Punic War (cf. 19.9n.): the loss of Corsica would have strengthened the Carthaginians' sense of grievance, as Polybius saw it. Accordingly, it is more probable that the invasion in 236 was the first systematic attempt to conquer the island rather than the response to a rebellion, although it is highly probable that it was preceded by some form of diplomatic engagement, perhaps in the aftermath of the campaign in the First Punic War, that led the Romans to conceive of themselves as having certain rights which the Corsicans were resisting.

That the Romans did not conceive of the Corsicans as under direct Roman control is supported by the one anecdote concerning the campaign described in a number of other sources (Val. Max. 6.3.3, Dio fr. 45; cf. Amm. 14.11.32): the initial attack was made by an advance force under a legate, M. Claudius Clineas, who came to terms with the Corsicans. The commander, C. Licinius Varus, despite this prosecuted the war in violation of those terms and defeated the Corsicans. His rationale was that Claudius did not have the authority to make an agreement; in accordance with this, the Senate decided to surrender Claudius to the Corsicans, but they refused to take him, so instead he was executed (Valerius Maximus) or exiled (Dio/Zonaras). This story, if there is any truth to it, implies that the Romans were treating with the Corsicans as if they were formally independent rather than rebellious vassals.

Zonaras refers to the Romans around the same time as campaigning successfully against the Sardinians, 'who were not obeying them' (8.18.9 μὴ πειθομένους αὐτοῖς)—Sardinia had been ceded to Rome by the Carthaginians in 238 (Plb. 1.88.8–12, Sinnius Capito *ap.* Fest. 430L, Zonar. 8.18.3; cf. Eutr. 3.2).[289] This was

---

[288] Prag (2013), 58–9 suggests that it is related to the Ligurian war (20.3n.), and was aimed at controlling the westward sea-routes in that part of the Mediterranean, although the connection is slightly looser if, as I argue, the attack on Corsica is to be dated to 236 rather than 238/7, as Prag prefers.

[289] Eutropius describes the cession of Sardinia only after the Ligurian war in 237 (above, 20.3n.). This apparent discrepancy has caused unnecessary confusion in some scholars, who construct elaborate scenarios in order to reconcile the sources (e.g. Walbank (1957), 149–50, Carey (1996), 206). A careful reading of Eutropius shows that he is only dating the later Sardinian rebellion to that time (see below), not the original cession.

followed by a further rebellion of the Sardinians and Corsicans, the former covertly inspired by the Carthaginians (cf. Eutr. 3.2, Oros. 4.12.2). Zonaras does not indicate any Roman victory at this time, but it seems certain that they achieved one in Sardinia, since the consul of 235, T. Manlius Torquatus, was awarded a triumph against them, according to the *Fasti Capitolini*, Livy 23.34.15, and several other sources (Vell. 2.38.2, Eutr. 3.3, Oros. 4.12.2); Velleius indeed treats this as the point when Sardinia came under effective Roman rule.

Nevertheless, again according to Zonar. 8.18.10, fighting continued in 234 in both Corsica and Sardinia: the consul Sp. Carvilius Maximus fought in Sardinia, the praetor P. Cornelius in Corsica; Cornelius died of a disease which struck his army, so Carvilius transferred his forces to Sardinia, won, and (according to the *Fasti Capitolini*) received a triumph. Yet the Sardinians rebelled again on his departure; in 233 the consul M'. Pomponius Matho campaigned there, and (according to the *Fasti Capitolini*) was awarded a further triumph. The following year (232) saw another Sardinian rebellion; the consuls M. Aemilius Lepidus and M. Publicius Malleolus defeated them, but then were defeated in their turn when they arrived on Corsica. Only in 231 was the success more durable: one consul, M. Pomponius Matho, was in Sardinia, and it appears did not need to fight a pitched battle (he used dogs to track down the Sardinian rebels); the other, C. Papirius Maso, fought successfully in Corsica, though with significant casualties through the enemy's guerrilla tactics. Then at last the Corsicans submitted.[290] According to various sources Maso sought a triumph, but was denied it (probably— at least ostensibly—because of his losses during the campaign: see Brennan (1996): 320). He instead held an informal triumph on the Alban Mount,[291] the first to do so (*Fasti Capitolini*, Piso *FRHist*, 9 F 33 (*ap.* Plin., *Nat.* 15.126), Val. Max. 3.6.5; cf. Paul., *Fest.* 131L).

No further wars in either Corsica or Sardinia are recorded in the period covered by Book 20, apart from a brief reference to an uprising in Sardinia some time prior to 225 (Zonar. 8.19.10; cf. 20.7n.); it may be connected with this that the consul of 225, C. Atilius Regulus, is recorded by Plb. 2.23.6 as having an army there, though Polybius mentions no actual fighting.

All of this could well have appeared in Livy. If, as argued above, 236 was the point at which the Romans first sought to acquire military control over Corsica, it

---

[290] Meloni (1990), 47–51 (following a passing suggestion by De Sanctis III.1 274 [282]) proposed that the campaigns of 232 and 231 (which are linked in Zonaras) were not against Corsica, but against a Sardinian tribe called the Corsi, which is mentioned by a few ancient sources (Plin., *Nat.* 3.85, Paus. 10.17.8, Ptol., *Geog.* 3.3.6); he suggests that it would have made no sense for the Romans to have diverted their forces to Corsica in 232 following their victory in Sardinia. However, on balance this seems less likely. While it is true that Paul., *Fest.* 131L has the victory of 231 over the Sardinians, Cic., *Nat. Deor.* 3.52 refers to it as being over the island of Corsica, and it is more likely that Paulus' version has been garbled than that Cicero's has. Meloni's objection to the standard reconstruction of events is very weak (one could hypothesize many reasons why the Romans might have diverted north after leaving Sardinia).

[291] For this (occasional) practice in the middle Republic see esp. Brennan (1996).

would appear to follow that the campaigns of that year are not covered by P.'s statement here, unless (as seems unlikely) Livy shared Sinnius Capito's misapprehension that there had been fighting there in 238. As for the rest, the whole of the repeated cycle of rebellions and suppressions could presumably be covered by P.'s statement, but to a reader unaware of the sequence of events his phrasing would appear to suggest a single rebellion followed by a Roman victory. This might not be an unreasonable representation of events in Corsica, since no source records a decisive victory there before Papirius' in 231. It is less obvious for Sardinia, but a single rebellion and victory in Sardinia is also implicit in Eutropius and Orosius, both of whom describe nothing except the events of 235, when Torquatus defeated the Sardinians. As noted above, Velleius explicitly refers to that as the point of Roman conquest, and Livy's own later reference to that victory (23.34.15), while not incompatible with subsequent rebellions and fighting, uses similar phrasing to P. to imply a decisive outcome: 'he subdued...the Sardinians (*subegerat...Sardos*). Orosius, too, describes the victory in these terms: *mox Sardi subacti et oppressi sunt* (4.12.2: 'soon the Sardinians were subdued and crushed').

This suggests that P. is reflecting a wider post-Livian tradition which reduced the messy Sardinian wars of the 230s to a single key year, and it seems not unlikely that this reading of history was given some warrant by Livy's own narrative, highlighting the victory of 235 even if not necessarily failing to mention the subsequent fighting. One plausible way that might have been framed, though not mentioned by P., is via the tradition that, following Torquatus' victory, the temple of Janus was closed, indicating that Rome had concluded all fighting and pacified all territory round her (Vell. 2.38.2–3, Plu., *Num.* 20.2; Eutr. 3.3, Oros. 4.12.4).[292] If Livy placed substantial weight on this point, it would have been easy to transmute his account into a single decisive pacification of Sardinia that took place in that year.

A further noteworthy aspect of P.'s account is his failure to mention when the islands came under Roman control in the first place, thus misleadingly implying that it was part of the treaty that ended the First Punic War. As discussed above (19.9n.), this is a misapprehension that is explicit in other sources, and which helps occlude the extent to which the Romans' own actions may have provoked the Second Punic War. P. may not have shared the misapprehension, but he does not appear interested in assigning the Romans any blame for subsequent events.

---

[292] A different version, found in Livy 1.19.3 (also Varro, *Ling.* 5.165, Plu., *Fort. Rom.* 322B), relates the closure of the temple to the end of the First Punic War rather than the victory in Sardinia, though still giving T. Manlius Torquatus as the consul under whom it occurred. This is presumably an error, albeit an understandable one, given the key significance of the former victory by comparison with the latter, facilitated by the fact that A. Manlius Torquatus was consul when the First Punic War ended, and also (as suggested by Ameling (2001), 121–2) that an 'alternative' version of the First Punic War had the Carthaginians cede Sardinia on their defeat (19.9n.). It is at all events unlikely to have been repeated when Livy came to narrate the history of the period in detail: the fact that it is dated to 235 in Orosius and Eutropius strongly indicates that it stood this way in Livy also.

Sardi: Sardinia had been colonized by both the Phoenicians and the Carthaginians, the latter having progressively taken control from the mid-sixth century onwards; however, their settlements were disproportionately in the south-western segment of the island, and many sites show considerable archaeological continuity from earlier periods, suggesting that the indigenous culture was maintained right up to the time of the Roman conquest. Nevertheless the people whom P. calls 'Sardinian' certainly had mingled in both ethnicity and culture with the settlers (cf. Dyson and Rowland (2007), 112–26). The archaeological remains on the parts of Sardinia most heavily colonized by the Carthaginians not only are clearly Punic in the period prior to the Romans' arrival, but continue to be so for the remainder of the Republican period (van Dommelen (1998), Dyson and Rowland (2007), 137–43); but there is also considerable variety between different sites, and even heavily 'Punic' regions sometimes incorporate material remains associated with pre-Carthaginian societies, suggesting a cultural complexity that is not easily reducible to a simple picture of 'indigenous' societies being colonized and superseded (see esp. van Dommelen (2002)). Nevertheless, the strength of Carthaginian influence allowed Sardinia to be perceived as primarily 'Punic' even as late as the 50s BC: Cic., *Scaur.* 42–3, in an admittedly partial and prejudiced discussion, claims that the Sardinians exhibited the ethnic traits of their Phoenician and Carthaginians forebears, but with additional degeneration as the result of the race mixing with other populations.

D.S. 15.27.4 says that the Romans sought to send colonists to Sardinia in the early fourth century, but this is highly unlikely to be true: Rome was hardly in a position then to challenge Carthaginian hegemony so far from her own territory (Meloni (1990), 20–1; *contra* Dyson and Rowland (2007), 127–8). Otherwise there is no indication that they showed any interest in the island before their campaigns during the First Punic War (17.3n.). After the events here, in 227, Sardinia was turned (with Corsica: see below) into a Roman province: see 20.7n.

For a detailed study of the conquest of Sardinia and its subsequent history under Roman rule see Meloni (1990); more broadly on the archaeology and history of the island see Dyson and Rowland (2007).

Corsi: At the time of the Roman conquest, the Corsicans, like the Sardinians, were not an unmixed 'indigenous' community: the island had already seen numerous waves of settlement, including Greeks and Etruscans. In the early third century the Carthaginians had control there, although probably not an extensive presence (17.3n.). The Romans are recorded as taking an interest in the island as early as the late fourth or early third century, when they apparently made an abortive attempt to found a city on it (Thphr., *HP* 5.8.2), but no serious campaign was conducted by them before the First Punic War, when they sought to dislodge the Carthaginians based there (17.3n.).

20.5 *Condemnation of Vestal Virgin*. Cf. 14.6n. This episode is controversial. Several other sources (D.H., *AR* 2.69.1–3, Val. Max. 8.1 absol. 5, Plin., *Nat.* 28.12)[293] refer to a Vestal named Tuccia, who was accused of unchastity, but vindicated herself by a miracle (she was able to carry water in a sieve). Münzer (1937), 203–9 (followed by e.g. *MRR* I 227–8, Rüpke, *FS* 923) argues that this is the same person, and that these are simply alternative versions of the story; indeed, he suggests that Livy himself may have recorded both versions,[294] and P., as usual, confines himself to one of them, perhaps the one that Livy appeared to lay more stress on.

This conclusion, however, is problematic. First, the most reliable MSS of P. read the Vestal's name not as Tuccia, but as Lucia or Luccia. It is true that the *editio princeps* reads Tucia, while Sigonius preferred Tuccia, and this has remained through subsequent printed editions. But the *editio princeps*' readings frequently show an unreliable editorial hand at work: it may indeed be that its text, like that of Sigonius, was influenced by the anecdote in Valerius and Pliny.

Second, the only explicit reference to the date of Tuccia's acquittal is in Pliny. Unfortunately, the oldest MS tradition of Pliny is not consistent: the manuscripts read either the Varronian year DXVIIII (sc. 235 BC), or DCVIIII (145 BC), or DCVIII (146 BC). There is no ready way to decide between these. The versions which place the event later are more widespread in the MS tradition, but that can be given relatively little weight, given that the tradition is diffuse and no surviving MSS of this part of the text carry much authority (see the succinct and trenchant account of Reynolds (1983)). The reading DXVIIII, on the other hand, places it within the time-period of Livy Book 20, albeit earlier in the period than is implied by P.'s order (cf. below). The earlier date is perhaps supported by the fact that Tuccia's trial does not appear in *Per.* 52, *EpOxy.* 52, or Obsequens, whose surviving text covers 146/5 but not 235 (Münzer (1937), 206, Eckstein (1982), 83). But *Per.* 52 is relatively brief, and much Livian material must be omitted from it; *EpOxy.* 52 is even briefer; and Obsequens, despite his religious focus, in practice excludes most religious material from the surviving part of Livy's text. It is thus problematic to draw any strong inferences about dating from the absence of the Tuccia trial from these texts.

Hence neither (probably) the name of the Vestal in question nor (certainly) the recorded outcome of her trial in P. match those in the Tuccia story. The only real

---

[293] Also alluded to in Tert., *Apol.* 22.12, Aug., *Civ.* 10.16, 22.11 (citing Varro as the source), but these do not mention the Vestal's name.

[294] Münzer (1937), 207, supported by Eckstein (1982), 84–5, Rüpke, *FS* 923. Rüpke's reasoning is, however, flawed. He claims that P., like Livy, 'consistently gives the method of death...as well as the sentence (*damnatio*) when reporting Vestal trials. If the former information is lacking here, we may assume that the outcome was more complicated.' This is simply false. Of the five other Vestal trials reported by P., he records the method of death in just two (2.13—Livy himself does not supply it here: see *ad loc.*—and 14.6), but refers to the condemnation alone in three, as here (8.5, 22.11, 63.3—with the first two the corresponding passage of Livy uncomplicatedly describes the manner of execution, and P. has omitted it).

link is the possible coincidence of date, and even that depends on a doubtful textual reading.[295] In light of this, it is more probable that we have two separate stories than two versions of a single one (Cichorius (1922), 20–1); accordingly, we should accept the reading *Luccia* in P., and allow that the story has no connection with the anecdote about Tuccia found in other authors. Admittedly, no other members of the *gens Luccia*[296] are recorded in the middle Republic (Eckstein (1982), 85), but our knowledge of the prosopography of the period is sufficiently patchy that this cannot be a strong objection: after all, the *gens Tuccia* is barely attested at this time either (Münzer (1937), 203–4).

The question remains when this condemnation took place. If P. is recording events in chronological sequence, this would place it between the defeat of the Corsicans in 231 and the beginning of the First Illyrian War in 229. However, P. records events out of sequence sufficiently often that this cannot be strongly relied upon, though with a book covering so many years it is less probable that he would have displaced this episode very substantially. One possible suggestion is that the Vestal trial occurred in conjunction with the human sacrifice of Gauls and Greeks that took place for the first time in 228 (Oros. 4.13.3–4, Plu., *Marc.* 3.4; cf. Zonar. 8.19.9: for the date see Cichorius (1922), 15–16). P. does not record this sacrifice, as he does not record similar sacrifices in 216 and 114: P., unlike Livy (see 22.57.6; cf. Levene (1993), 49–50), has little interest in focusing on episodes that illustrate the moral complexity of the Romans' position. But both of the later sacrifices were associated with Vestal trials, which P. does record (22.11, 63.3), and it could be that the pattern held here also, and that the crisis which led to the sacrifice in 228 also led to the Vestal's execution recorded by P. (Cichorius (1922), 16–20, *contra* Eckstein (1982), 75–7).[297]

incesti damnata est: Cf. 8.5n.

20.6 *First Illyrian War*. The fullest account of this war, the first to bring Roman troops east of the Adriatic, is in Plb. 2.8, 2.11–12. The ruler of Illyria, Teuta, as part of a broad policy of aggression towards their neighbours, had authorized privateers to plunder merchant vessels (2.4.8); a number of Italian ships were attacked. The Romans sent two envoys to Illyria to complain, only to be met with

---

[295] Doubly doubtful if, like Münzer (1937), 206 and Eckstein (1982), 83–4, we argue that the date in Pliny needs to be emended to DXXIIII (sc. 230 BC) in order to align the anecdote more precisely with the implied chronology in P. However, P.'s chronology is not sufficiently robust to require such an emendation (cf. also below).

[296] More usually spelled *Lucceia*, but wrongly: see Shackleton Bailey (1976), 48.

[297] Eckstein's reasoning depends on taking an excessively narrow view of the limits within which P. is willing to vary chronology (cf. above). He is, however, on much stronger ground in his broader argument (Eckstein (1982), 69–82) that the coincidence of Vestal trials with human sacrifice should not be taken to mean that the human sacrifice was an attempt to expiate the Vestals' unchastity, as Cichorius had argued. It is more likely that the human sacrifice and the execution of Vestals were separate (but linked) manifestations of the general atmosphere of crisis in those years (Eckstein (1982), 71–5).

an arrogant refusal by Teuta. When one of them remonstrated with her, she arranged for him to be murdered on the way home. In response, the Romans sent both a fleet and a land army across the Adriatic; they took control of Corcyra (where Demetrius of Pharus, the commander of the Illyrian garrison, defected to them) and Epidamnus, and captured some Illyrian cities while receiving the surrender of a number of their subject peoples. The Romans then handed control of most of Illyria to Demetrius, and returned to Italy, but left a portion of their fleet at Epidamnus for the winter, where Teuta ultimately sent an embassy to come to terms with them. Polybius' account is broadly supported by Flor. 1.21 (Cavallaro (2004), 122–3), who similarly has Teuta as the recipient of the embassy, and attributes it to the Illyrians' 'raids' (1.21.4 *populationibus*), though he is far briefer and vaguer; he also exaggerates the atrocity, saying that the ambassadors were both killed (cf. below), 'like sacrificial victims with an axe' (1.21.3 *ut victimas securi*), and that the captains of the Roman ships were burned alive.

A rather different version appears in App., *Ill.* 7. His narrative of the war itself broadly (if not in all details) accords with Polybius', and he also agrees that the immediate *casus belli* was the killing of a Roman ambassador, but tentatively (he acknowledges doubt on the matter: *Ill.* 6) he gives quite a different account of the killing. In his version the embassy was prompted, not by attacks on Italian shipping, but by the Illyrian attack on the island of Issa; the Issans appealed to the Romans for support, and the Romans joined the Issans in an embassy to Illyria, but the ship carrying the ambassadors was attacked by the Illyrians *en route* and a Roman and Issan ambassador were killed. Appian also has the perpetrator not as Teuta, but her husband Agron, though Agron died prior to the Roman invasion and Teuta took over (as regent for her stepson Pinnes).[298] Dio (fr. 49; cf. Zonar. 8.19.3–5) combines Appian's version with that of Polybius: as in Appian, the ambassadors are sent in support of the Issans, but also to complain about attacks on Italian shipping. The atrocity against them was, as in Polybius, committed by Teuta when she felt insulted, though in Dio, unlike Polybius, the surviving ambassadors were imprisoned by her.

Which version is likely to be correct has been the subject of some controversy. Some (e.g. Badian (1952a), 73–5, Walbank (1957), 153, 158–9, Hammond (1968), 4–6, Harris (1979a), 195–7, Gruen (1984a), 361–2, Eckstein (2008), 35–6) argue that we should accept Polybius' (though not necessarily all the details of the

---

[298] In Polybius, by contrast, Teuta appears to rule in her own right (esp. 2.4.7); but that she acted as regent is accepted by almost all scholars, even those who prefer Polybius' account overall. Cavallaro (2004), 38–52 is an exception; but Polybius' limited knowledge of internal Illyrian politics is shown by his failure to mention Pinnes, who clearly existed, as Cavallaro acknowledges (Cavallaro (2004), 42), and her objections to Appian's version are not strong. She queries why, if there was a regency, it would be Teuta, rather than Pinnes' mother, who was chosen; but in a hierarchical polygamous court it is not especially surprising that a more powerful wife would be preferred as regent to an inferior one, even if the latter had produced the heir. Her second argument is that Teuta is described as acting in her own name rather than in Pinnes'; but she draws her examples of this from Polybius, who, as noted above, shows no awareness of Pinnes' existence. Hence this argument is effectively circular.

exchange between Teuta and the ambassadors), and see the account of Appian as later propaganda showing that Rome's intervention was in support of allies. Others (e.g. De Sanctis III.1 286-7 [295], Walser (1953-54), Petzold (1971), Derow (1973), Cavallaro (2004), 145-8, Zahrnt (2008)) prefer Appian, suggesting that Polybius or his source has suppressed the role of the Issans in order to avoid a complicated debate about responsibility, as was generated by the not dissimilar case of the Mamertines (cf. 16.2n.), and instead, by emphasizing Illyrian piracy, to make the Romans appear to be acting on behalf of civilized values. It is hard to decide between these: neither is intrinsically implausible, and either could go back to contemporary accounts. If it comes to a straight choice between Appian and Polybius, the latter should probably be preferred simply on the grounds that he is closer to the time and of greater general reliability.[299]

The question often becomes entangled with wider issues about how far Rome was adopting a deliberately aggressive and expansionist policy at this time, although in fact either version is compatible with a picture of Roman expansionism or the converse. For those who see Roman aggression behind the war, the Romans, on Polybius' account, launched a large-scale expedition in response to a relatively minor provocation (e.g. Hammond (1968), 20-1, Harris (1979a), 195-7), while on Appian's version, the Romans acted as (on one view) they had at the beginning of the First Punic War, deliberately affiliating themselves with a supposed victim of a larger power in order to provide an excuse for intervention against that power (e.g. Petzold (1971), 219-21). Conversely, those who see Rome's motives as more reactive emphasize the extent to which, as both Polybius and Appian suggest, the Illyrians were themselves engaging in a wide-ranging campaign against their neighbours which the Roman might well (rightly or wrongly) have seen as threatening their interests (e.g. Badian (1952a), 73-7, Gruen (1984a), 362-8, Eckstein (2008), 32-41). As acutely noted by Čašule (2012), Rome was not intervening in a vacuum, but against the background of a long history of economic and cultural integration between the different sides of the Adriatic, including the various Roman colonies on that seaboard, which is likely to have increased the sense of destabilization and threat that Illyrian activity represented.

As also with the First Punic War (cf. 16.2n.), these two versions of Roman policy are not altogether incompatible (cf. Eckstein (2008), esp. 15-21): the sheer scale of the expedition, involving not only a large proportion of the available armed forces but both consuls, suggests that Rome was acting aggressively (*contra* Hammond (1968), 6, Eckstein (2008), 35-6), but her aggression could well have

---

[299] Čašule (2012), 227-8 suggests tentatively that the incompatibility between Appian and Polybius may be overstated, in as much as Italian traders would be likely to be concerned for the safety of Issa, which lay in their own trading network (cf. below). That would not enable us to reconcile the radically different versions of the embassy in the two authors, but could at least help explain something of the origins of the divergent accounts.

been prompted by a desire to secure a key border area against an aggressive neighbour who, even if not an immediate threat, might well have been perceived as a potential one if left unchallenged.

P., however, does not come down on either side of either controversy. He records the killing of an ambassador (only one, as both Polybius and Appian agree), but shows no interest in the run-up to the embassy (Eutropius and Orosius are similarly non-committal).[300] It is more probable that Livy's narrative was closer to Polybius, since that is the one implied in Florus, for all that Florus implausibly elaborates the murder beyond anything that is likely to have stood in Livy; but the wider geopolitical context which is central to Polybius, and also (in a different way) to Dio and Appian, is of no interest to P., even though Livy can hardly have failed to give prominence to it in some form. Instead, P. distils the narrative down to a single moment of crime and retribution; this too doubtless stood in Livy, who typically organizes his narrative through such moral structures (see esp. Levene (2010a), 339–75), but P. abandons the ancillary details which could—and probably did—complicate the morality.

The war is securely dated to 229:[301] the fleet and army were, according to all sources (Plb. 2.11.1, Eutr. 3.4, Oros. 4.13.2; cf. Flor. 1.21.4), commanded by the two consuls of that year, Cn. Fulvius Centumalus and L. Postumius Albinus (cf. 20.3n.), while the *Fasti Capitolini* record a triumph for Fulvius as proconsul in 228. Plb. 2.44.2 synchronizes the beginning of the war with the death of Demetrius II of Macedon, which seems to have occurred in spring 229 (Holleaux (1930), 255–8; cf. Walbank (1967), 633–4).

Illyriis: The collective name for peoples inhabiting the area between Greece, the Alps, and the Danube. It is, however, unlikely that they saw themselves as a single group; it appears that it was the Greeks, and especially the Romans, who applied this generic name to the peoples of the region (see e.g Wilkes (1992), 86–94). In the context of this war, however, the reference is specifically to the Illyrian kingdom, which controlled the southern part of the Adriatic coast; its earlier history and political structure is disputed (cf. Cabanes (1988), 87–182), but by this period it was a coherent political unit under the control of kings who came from the tribe of the Ardiaeans. Livy had mentioned them in passing in 10.2.4, but this is their first appearance in P.

For the archaeology and history of ancient Illyria see Wilkes (1992); also Cabanes (1988) for the history of the Illyrian kingdom, and Dzino (2010) for Illyria's relations with Rome in the Republic and early Empire.

---

[300] Hence it is a mistake to assimilate, as various scholars do (e.g. Beloch, *GG* IV.1 664, Walbank (1957), 158–9), the versions of P., Florus, Eutropius, and Orosius to those of Appian and Dio, and to regard them all as products of 'the annalistic tradition': cf. Derow (1973), 123–4 = (2015), 156–8.

[301] Beloch, *GG* IV.2 262–3 (cf. 531–2) argued that the Roman attack was launched towards the end of the consular year 229, hence in spring 228 (Julian)—in his view, the Roman calendar was running more than two months behind the seasons in this period (cf. *GG* IV.2 271), which makes this feasible (similarly Walser (1953–4), 311–12, Cavallaro (2004), 170–5). See, however, the comprehensive reply by Holleaux (1930), showing that the evidence far better fits an attack in 229 (Julian).

propter unum ex legatis...occisum: According to Plb. 2.8.3, the two ambassadors were C. and L. Coruncanius; the younger of them (2.8.9) was the one killed, presumably Lucius, the one named second (De Sanctis III.1 287 [295]). Appian agrees that a Coruncanius was the ambassador killed, adding that (according to his version) the Issan ambassador Cleemporus was as well. Plin., *NH* 24.34 gives the names of the ambassadors as Ti. Coruncanius and P. Junius, the former perhaps arising from confusion with the only famous member of the *gens Coruncania*, namely the *pontifex maximus* (18.4n.), who may have been the father (Münzer (1901b)) or (more probably) grandfather of the ambassadors here.[302]

P., like Polybius and Appian, is clear that only one Roman ambassador was killed; however, a strong strand of the later tradition (Plin., *Nat.* 34.24, Flor. 1.21, Oros. 4.13.2) speaks of it being both.[303] P.'s version presumably reflects Livy's, and the other is a secondary exaggeration, though it is possible that Livy contained both versions as alternatives (Cavallaro (2004), 127–8). Either way, P.'s phrase *unum ex legatis* looks pointed, perhaps indicating awareness of and correcting the alternative version: cf. 39.5, where a similar phrase appears in a context where, unusually, P. explicitly offers more than one version of a story (see *ad loc.*).

qui subacti: The transmitted text reads *subactique*, but if *subacti* here is a participle, as it is elsewhere in P., then the omission of the subject is abrupt and anomalous: it is common to omit the subject of participles in oblique cases, especially in ablative absolutes (cf. K-S 1.773–4), but not with a new subject in the nominative. Taking *subacti* as a noun (= 'the defeated people') would solve this, but that is itself a virtually unparalleled locution.[304] Better is to read *qui subacti*: the corruption by transposition to *subacti qui* and thence to *subactique* is an easy one. Admittedly, the separation of the relative clause from the antecedent is itself difficult and unparalleled in P., especially with another relative (with a different antecedent) appearing in the interim, but on balance it appears the better solution.

in deditionem venerunt: Cf. 8.4n. Plb. 2.12.3 (cf. also App., *Ill.* 7–8) details the terms: Teuta agreed to pay the Romans any indemnity they chose, to establish a limit at Lissus beyond which not more than two unarmed Illyrian ships could sail (cf. 20.10n.), and to surrender most of Illyria. The precise meaning of the last is controversial, since Appian indicates that Pinnes remained as formal ruler of much of the kingdom, with only a limited number of places independent of Illyrian hegemony, and this picture seems in accord with the subsequent course of events. The role of Demetrius of Pharus is also problematic. Polybius had earlier (2.11.17) stated that Demetrius had been given substantial power by the Romans

---

[302] Cavallaro (2004), 124 supports Pliny's account of the ambassadors' names, but on weak grounds.

[303] Pliny adds that statues were erected in their honour, though it appears that these did not survive to his day.

[304] Cic., *Font.* 36 uses *subacti* as a noun, but in a general statement about 'subdued peoples', rather than referring to one specific set of people subdued. This makes it only of limited value as a parallel.

even before the treaty, Appian, conversely, that the Romans, mistrusting him, had restricted him to a few holdings. Appian's claim about Demetrius is almost certainly the product of reconstruction with hindsight, but that still leaves it unclear who controlled what in Illyria.

The most likely explanation (Badian (1952a), 78–81)[305] derives from Zonar. 8.19.7 (cf. Dio frr. 49.7, 53): that Demetrius took over from Teuta as regent. Hence Teuta surrendered the regency, but was given suzerainty over a small region, while Demetrius took control of much of the kingdom, but not in his own right.

20.7 *Enlargement of the praetorship*. Other sources (Pompon., *Dig.* 1.2.2.32, Sol. 5.1; cf. Zonar. 8.19.10) sketch out a little more fully the rationale for this change: Sicily and Sardinia (the latter presumably including Corsica) were now formally designated as provinces, with the two new praetors assigned to control them.

No source gives a precise date to the enlargement. P.'s implicit sequence puts it between the Illyrian War in 229 (20.6n.) and the Gallic war in 225 (20.8n.); this matches the implication of Zonar. 8.19.10, who mentions an (otherwise unrecorded) Sardinian revolt in response to their being placed under the control of a praetor (cf. 20.4n.), and his sequence seems to date it between 228 and 225. Most scholars (e.g. Mommsen, *StR*³ II 198, *MRR* I 229) tentatively split the difference and assign it to 227. This is mere guesswork, but has been put on a firmer footing by Brennan (2000), 92–3, who plausibly connects the enlargement with the immediate aftermath of the Illyrian War, where the decision to send both consuls across the Adriatic (20.6n.) made the Romans aware of the potential vulnerability of their newly acquired holdings in the west if left without troops under a designated commander. Accordingly, as Brennan argues, the most likely chronology is that the Romans made the decision to enlarge the praetorship in 228, with the first of the new praetors taking office in 227 (cf. 20.11n.).

ampliatus est: See 1.B.2n.

20.8 *Gallic invasion of Italy*. By far the fullest account is in Plb. 2.21.1–31.6. He places the origins of the war in the 230s: first in an abortive Gallic invasion of

---

[305] Eckstein (2008), 58–9 objects to Badian's reconstruction: on his account, Teuta retained the regency, but in a kingdom reduced under the treaty, with some of the rest given to Demetrius; Demetrius subsequently took advantage of Roman inattention to marry Pinnes' mother, taking over the regency and hence reconstituting the kingdom by combining it with his own holdings. However, Eckstein's grounds for this are weak. He objects, first, that no source mentions Teuta surrendering the regency, which is an error (see Zonar. 8.19.6); and, second, that Polybius has Teuta swearing the treaty as regent—but this is not incompatible with the idea that one of the treaty's terms was that she should henceforward be removed from the regency. In addition, Eckstein misreads Dio fr. 53 and Zonar. 8.20.11: they do not indicate, as he implies, that Demetrius took the regency prior to the treaty, but Dio fr. 53 does suggest that Demetrius was already regent prior to his marriage, supporting Badian's reconstruction over Eckstein's.

Italy in 237,[306] where an army reached Ariminum, only to be fought off by their fellow Gauls in the region (cf. 20.3n.); but more directly in the Roman decision in 232, under a proposal from the then-tribune C. Flaminius (see 20.11n.), to distribute among the populace the *ager Gallicus* north of Picenum (cf. 15.4n.).[307] This was taken by the Gauls as an existential threat; they sent a large force to invade Italy in 225, which reached as far as the Etruscan town of Clusium before encountering a Roman army. In the first encounter the Romans (under the command of a praetor) were badly defeated, but they were then reinforced by the army of the consul L. Aemilius Papus. The Gauls retreated without a fight, but as they marched up the coast they encountered the other consular army, led by C. Atilius Regulus, near the town of Telamon. Caught between the two armies, they fought vigorously, killing Regulus himself, but were ultimately defeated. Aemilius led his army to plunder the land of the Boii, then returned to Rome for a triumph (the last is confirmed by the *Fasti Capitolini*, which dates it to the end of his consular year, on 5 March).

No other source adds anything more than minimal detail. The main variation is in the sequence of the battles. D.S. 25.13 separates the battle of Telamon into two, with Regulus killed in the first, Aemilius victorious in the second; he also has Aemilius' triumph as proconsul rather than consul. Zonar. 8.20.1–2, too, separates Telamon into two halves, and fills out the events in a rather different order: the Gauls' retreat after their initial victory was prompted not by the arrival of Aemilius, but by a thunderstorm; it was Regulus, not Aemilius, who pursued them, though he was then killed, and it was not until several days later that Aemilius decided to join battle and was victorious. The same version seems to be implied by Oros. 4.13.8–9, who enlarges on Regulus' defeat, with Aemilius' victory in a subsequent fight reduced to a brief appendage. Even aside from Polybius' broad credibility on events which are relatively close to his own time, the solid logistical detail that he gives of the original deployment of the various armies and their subsequent movements and encounters makes his version vastly more likely. The only other significant—and no less implausible—addition is the neat anecdote in Flor. 1.20.3 (cf. Dio fr. 50.4, Zon. 8.20.2) that the Gauls had sworn not to

---

[306] Itself presumably a response to fighting between the Romans and the Gauls in the previous year, which Polybius does not mention: see 20.3n.

[307] Various scholars (e.g. De Sanctis III.1 296 [304–5]; cf. Erdkamp (2009), 495–503) have suggested that this claim by Polybius is implausible, deriving from the widespread hostility to Flaminius in the historical tradition (cf. 20.11n.): they note that the Gallic invasion took place seven years after his bill. Ungern-Sternberg (2005), 316–17 suggests in addition that the land-distribution from the Gallic point of view would have been inconsequential, given that colonies on Gallic territory had been founded at Sena and Ariminum decades earlier (11.5, 15.4nn.). However, the new distribution of land presumably went in hand with renewed expulsions of the existing inhabitants, so the Gauls had an immediate cause of resentment, and it is likely to have been the progressive implementation of the policy over subsequent years, rather than the initial bill, which generated Gallic hostility (so Gelzer (1933), 150–1, Eckstein (1987), 11–12).

take off their belts until they reached the Capitol—an oath which was ironically fulfilled when they were disarmed at the end of Aemilius' triumph.

P., by contrast with these, mentions neither the death of one consul nor the triumph of the other. His focus instead is on the significance of the invasion as a prelude to the events of the subsequent years, when the Romans turned the tables and attacked Gallic territory: his sequence and wording has the effect of strongly connecting them, and it is the fact of the Roman counter-invasion that is, for him, an important stage in the development of the empire (cf. 20.9n.). The tendency to play down the fighting is, interestingly, mirrored in Livy himself, when he later refers to all the wars with the Gauls in these years as 'really an uprising rather than warfare' (21.16.4: *tumultuatum verius quam belligeratum*); while it is true that this is in the mouths of senators rather than in the authorial voice, and that the senators may be downplaying the Gallic threat in order to emphasize the Carthaginian one,[308] it does at least indicate that P.'s perspective is shared by one of Livy's internal audiences, even if not necessarily Livy himself.

On the other hand, P. (like all other historians apart from Polybius) does not try to explain the reason for the Gallic invasion: he treats it as an unprovoked assault which then receives its just deserts. Livy may have done the same, but it is more likely that he, like Polybius, made at least some attempt to give the Gauls' own perspective, since he later shows some interest in Gallic grievances in the opening years of the Second Punic War (e.g. 21.20.5-6, 21.25.2, 22.6.3-4; cf. Levene (2010a), 291). This is yet another example of the ethical flattening of Livy which P. shares with most of the post-Livian tradition: a recognizable version of Livy is distilled into something less morally challenging and more flattering to the Roman self-image.

The other emphasis in P.—this too shared by much of the tradition—is an interest in the numbers of troops involved: see further below.

Galli transalpini: Plb. 2.22.1-23.4 describes an alliance between the Boii in northern Italy, the Insubrians north of the Po (cf. 20.9n.), and the Gaesatae, whose territory extended beyond the Alps. Other sources tend to focus on only one of these: thus Flor. 1.20.1 and Zonar. 8.20.1 (cf. Dio fr. 50.4) talk only about the Insubrians (though Zonaras does speak of them allying with other Gauls across the Alps); similarly, Plu., *Marc.* 3.1 has the Insubrians taking the initiative, though

---

[308] That Livy may well not have shared the senators' perspective is indicated by the fact that his language hints at the concept of the *tumultus Gallicus*, an official state of emergency that might be declared at the time of a Gallic uprising: see Cic., *Phil.* 8.3, Fest. 406L, 486L, Serv., *Aen.* 7.614. Livy himself regularly refers to *tumultus Gallicus* in such contexts (e.g. 7.9.6, 7.11.4, 7.25.11, 8.20.2, 9.29.2, 10.10.12, 10.26.13, 31.10.1, 31.11.2, 31.48.7, 41.19.3); cf. Plin., *Nat.* 3.138, who specifically uses the phrase of the invasion in 225. The tenor of most of these suggests that it was seen as more, rather than less, threatening than a 'regular' war, since the normal exemptions from conscription were suspended for the period of the emergency. Hence the very terms in which Livy has the senators dismiss the Gallic war by comparison with the Carthaginian suggests that it was more serious than they imply. On the Roman sense of danger that led to the declaration of the *tumultus Gallicus* in 225, and the mass mobilization of military and diplomatic forces that it entailed, see Bellen (1985), 9-19.

with an alliance with the Gaesatae (see below). On the other hand, Eutr. 3.5 and Oros. 4.13.5, like P., concentrate on the Transalpine element: Orosius mentions the Gaesatae by name, while indicating that the invasion coincided with an uprising in Cisalpine Gaul: this may suggest that Livy, too, focused primarily on the Transalpines' role in the invasion. Emphasizing the Insubrians, as Florus and Dio/Zonaras do, tightens the connection with the subsequent fighting against them, but on the other hand speaking of the Gaesatae shows the extent to which the expansion of Roman power is resonating further and further abroad, which corresponds to one of P.'s key themes.

The complication is that Polybius, Plutarch, and Orosius say that 'Gaesatae' was not the name of a tribe *per se*, but a name applied to these Gauls because they served as mercenaries. This claim may go back to Fabius Pictor, whom both Eutropius and Orosius cite shortly after (*FRHist* 1 F 21 = fr. 23P; cf. below); it has been widely challenged (see esp. Heuberger (1938), arguing that it was a term meaning 'warrior' that was used of certain Transalpine tribes). Whether or not it is true, the basic fact that the invasion included significant numbers who came from beyond the Alps seems clear.

Latinique nominis: This refers to those allies with the legal status of Latins (cf. Mommsen, *StR*^{3} III 660–1, Sherwin-White (1973), 96–118); hence this is, strictly speaking, an error by P., since it is clear from all the other sources for this figure (see the next note) that it refers to all troops supplied by the Romans and their allies in Italy, not solely allies 'of the Latin name': the standard phrase, in Livy and elsewhere, for the Italian allies collectively was *socii Latinique nominis* ('allies and those of the Latin name': for the phrase see esp. Wegner (1969), 95–104, Ilari (1974), 1–3). However, already by Livy's day the distinction had become obsolete, and he sometimes uses the phrase *Latini nominis* to imply all of the Italian allies as opposed to Roman citizens (e.g. 22.7.5, 22.37.7, 22.50.6, 30.23.13, 37.39.13, 39.20.1; cf. Wegner (1969), 103–4). Accordingly, it may be that P. is reproducing Livy's language here.

DCCC milia armatorum: The chief MSS of P. read ACCC, with no mark for the 'thousands', but the correction (by Mommsen (1879), 385) is overwhelmingly probable, since both Eutr. 3.5 and Oros. 4.13.6–7 give the number as 800,000. Both of these, like (probably: see below) P., cite Fabius Pictor (*FRHist* 1 F 21 = fr. 23P), underpinning his authority by stating that he was a participant in the war himself. The number broadly corresponds to a far more detailed accounting of the Roman forces by Plb. 2.24, who probably himself derived it from Fabius, and similar figures appear also in D.S. 25.13 (700,000 infantry and 70,000 cavalry) and Plin., *Nat.* 3.138 (700,000 infantry and 80,000 cavalry).

Polybius makes it clear that these figures include not only troops under arms, but also a far larger number of men who were capable of bearing arms but not actually enlisted in the forces. Diodorus and Orosius distort this into a nonsensical claim that this represented the size of the Roman army fighting the Gauls.

P., like Pliny and Eutropius, is more circumspect. He still misleadingly gives this as the number under arms, but does not state outright that they were actually engaged in conflict: his language allows, but does not require, the latter interpretation.

The reason for P.'s handling it circumspectly may be connected with the question of why he includes this point at all. It is on the face of things surprising that so many authors would be so fascinated by the number of Roman troops at this particular point in time. In Polybius' case the reason is explicit (2.24.1, 2.24.16–17): he is less interested in the troops the Romans had for the Gallic wars *per se*, but rather in showing the size of the Roman power that Hannibal would be confronting a few years later, when he boldly invaded Italy with an army consisting of less than 5 per cent of the troops the Romans potentially had available. But this is not true of most of the later tradition. There, the interest is in the sheer size of the battle, with hundreds of thousands of troops supposedly involved on the Roman side: it is the factual distortion that makes it worth transmitting the information at all. P. transmits the number, thus implicitly acknowledging that this is the key point of the story for his readership, but keeps the implausibility within bounds by not suggesting that these troops were all actually fighting.

If we grant that the figure of 800,000 refers to the men available for military service rather than the troops serving under arms, the question remains whether it is accurate. The raw data on which it is based may well be, since, according to Plb. 2.23.9, the allies were asked to supply an official record of the number of people they had available for combat, and this is presumably the source of those figures, while the troops serving in the field were calculated from the size of the separate units serving with the different commanders. However, the total figure of 800,000 is more problematic. One issue is that Polybius—presumably here too following Fabius—reaches it by adding up the number of troops in the field to the figures supplied by the Romans and allies for the men available. But it seems extremely unlikely that the latter figure included only those people available but who were not currently serving: it is much more likely that the returns counted everyone available, including those currently under arms (Brunt (1971), 44–7, *contra* Mommsen (1879), 390–3, De Ligt (2012), 55), in which case the total figure involves a large measure of double counting. A second problem is that Polybius' number of Roman citizens appears to reflect the census returns,[309] and hence probably counted all adult males,[310] whereas, according to Plb. 2.23.9, the

---

[309] Rejected by Hin (2008), 197–201 and De Ligt (2012), 52–5; but the similarity of the figure supplied by Polybius for the Romans and Campanians on the registers and the census figure in P. makes it far too coincidental that they could have, as Hin and De Ligt want to argue (on different grounds), have been calculated on entirely different bases (cf. 20.11n.).

[310] Hin (2008), 198–200 proposes that neither Polybius' figure nor the census returns counted the entire population, but different subsets of the population: she argues that Polybius was counting men of military age, while the census was counting those who were *sui iuris* and hence eligible to be taxed, and those just happened to be the same size. This can hardly be ruled out in principle, but here too the

allies were only asked to count those of an age to bear arms: so combining the two either seriously undercounts the number of men or risks overcounting the number of potential soldiers (Brunt (1971), 52–7).[311] There are a large number of other problems in detail (see the discussion in Brunt (1971), 44–60; cf. also Walbank (1957), 196–203); in short, while it *may* be possible to use the breakdown of the figures for different groups in Polybius as a basis for calculating the Italian population, the grand total relayed by P. and others is essentially meaningless.

habuisse ⟨Fabius⟩ dicit: While it is not uncommon for P. to refer self-consciously to the fact that he is summarizing another book by mentioning that that book contains certain things (cf. e.g. 2.16n., 16.1n.), it is far rarer for him to use an active verb of speaking to describe information that it—or, more likely, Livy—is transmitting: the only parallels are 9.7 *mentionem habet…colligit* and 21.1 *belli…ortum narrat* (see both *ad loc.*). Mommsen (1879), 383, accordingly, proposed that the word *Fabius* has dropped out (perhaps owing to haplography with *habuisse* directly before, which shares most of its letters: cf. E. H. Bispham and T. J. Cornell in *FRHist* III 36–7), and that P., like Eutropius and Orosius, directly mentioned Fabius Pictor as the source of the information. This would itself be a rare occurrence in P.—there are only two other places where he refers by name to one of Livy's sources in summarizing Livy's text (67.2n., 70.1n.; though see 53.4n.), which tells against so drastic an emendation. In Mommsen's support, however, is that it is hardly any less unusual for Eutropius to refer to a source in this way (Orosius does so rather more often): the explanation could be either that they all depend on a single lost source which is in turn dependent on Livy or (more probably) that Eutropius drew the information from P. and Orosius from Eutropius (cf. Introduction).[312]

20.9 *Roman invasion of Transpadine Gaul: Marcellus wins the* spolia opima. The fullest source for this is once again Polybius (2.31.8–35.1), who describes the Roman campaigns in Cisalpine Gaul over three successive years, 224–222 (see further below). Other narrative sources (e.g. Flor. 1.20.4–5, Eutr. 3.6, Oros. 4.13.11–15, Zonar. 8.20.3–9) are far briefer, apart from Plu., *Marc.* 6–8 (cf. also *Marc.* 4), who has a relatively detailed account of the final year, in which Marcellus was the commander. That final year supplied the best-known episode of the campaign, Marcellus' winning of the *spolia opima*. This is not mentioned by Polybius,

---

coincidence of figures makes it uncomfortable to postulate two different counting systems that happened to lead to near-identical results.

[311] *Contra* De Ligt (2012), 55–63, who believes that allies and Romans alike recorded all men between seventeen and sixty: he shows that Polybius' wording *could* in some contexts indicate that, but it remains unlikely that in this context it did so.

[312] Orosius cannot have taken it directly from P. independently of Eutropius, since his phrase *Fabius historicus, qui eidem bello interfuit* is almost identical to Eutropius, but corresponds to nothing in P.

but forms the centre of Plutarch's narrative, and became a staple anecdote to illustrate the traditions of Roman heroism.

tunc primum trans Padum ductis: For *tunc primum*, as well as P.'s general interest in 'firsts', cf. 11.5n. Here, as with the opening of the First Punic War (16.2n.) and the first campaign against the Ligurians (20.3n.), he uses the phrase to mark a key moment in the expansion of Roman power. It also, as often, specifically implies a chronological relationship with the previous notice—the Romans took the fight across the Po directly following the defeat of the invading Gauls in 225. This fits the evidence of Oros. 4.13.11, who describes the crossing as occurring under the consuls of 224, T. Manlius Torquatus and Q. Fulvius Flaccus, and he too marks it as a 'first', as does Zonar. 8.20.3; both indicate that the Romans at this time fought against the Insubrians, which is also what is implied by P.—Orosius refers to a substantial victory, with 23,000 Insubrians killed and 5,000 captured.

Plb. 2.31.8–10, on the other hand, presents a rather different picture. He has the consuls of 224 fighting only against the Boii, with the war not extended to the Insubrians until 223 (see below). He does not specify when in this process the Po was first crossed, but the Boii are generally accepted to have had their territory south of the Po (cf. e.g. Plb. 2.17.7, Livy 5.35.2), which would suggest that the Po was not crossed until the following year. Nor does the triumphal record indicate a major victory in 224 of the sort Orosius relays.

It is, accordingly, likely that the fighting against the Insubrians in 224 described by Orosius was a pure invention, albeit an invention which was probably already in Livy. The more difficult question is whether the Romans might nevertheless have crossed the Po in 224 in the course of the Boian campaign. The widely accepted view is that they did not (so e.g. De Sanctis III.1 304 [313] n. 114, Walbank (1957), 207; *contra* MRR I 231): the first crossing, like the initial victory over the Insubrians, was in 223, but it was backdated by a year, perhaps out of hostility to Flaminius, the victorious general in 223, whose image was widely blackened in the tradition: he was not the best person to associate with a significant advance in Roman power.[313]

An alternative possibility is that the Roman army did after all cross the river in 224 while fighting the Boii; for although Boian territory was conventionally thought to end south of the Po, as noted above, it is unlikely that such territorial boundaries were starkly marked or strictly observed either by the Gauls or the Romans. The Boii may well have had some holdings north of the river (cf. Plin., *Nat.* 3.124 for the Boii as the founders of the Transpadine town later known as Laus Pompeia)—and whether they did or did not, the Roman commanders may have felt it worth taking some or all of their troops across to perform some

---

[313] Note that Sil. 4.704, 5.107, 5.645–50 mistakenly has Flaminius' victory over the Boii rather than the Insubrians. This may simply be because the Gallic tribes were easily confused, but it may also reflect a tradition which diminished Flaminius' campaign by keeping it south of the Po.

exemplary destruction there. If that were the case, it would readily explain the invention of a victory over the Insubrians: precisely because the Boii were generally associated with the region on the Roman side of the Po, the Insubrians would need to be introduced as a plausible explanation for bringing the army over. The crossing of the Po was of much less interest to Polybius than to the later historians; he would presumably have ignored it even if it occurred. Polybius was focusing on the Roman conquest of the Mediterranean, and treated the Gallic wars as a mere sideshow to that (cf. 2.35). Livy and other later authors, on the other hand, were writing after the Romans had expanded their rule right through Celtic territory to the North Sea and beyond, while Transpadania itself was legally incorporated into Italy in the late first century, something of particular relevance to Livy, as a native of the region.

Which (if any) of these scenarios is correct is not provable; both appear plausible routes of invention within the practices of ancient historiography, though the second is perhaps slightly preferable, given the historians' interest in 'first times'. It is more likely that they were right in the attribution of the 'first crossing' but wrong in the circumstances, than that their account was an invention through and through.

Galli Insubres: The best-known of the Gallic tribes of the region between the Alps and the Po; their chief town was Mediolanum (modern Milan). There are, however, serious complications about identifying them. According to various ancient sources (e.g. D.S. 14.113.1-3, App., *Gall.* 2), the Gauls migrated *en masse* to Italy in the late fifth or early fourth century. Yet, in contrast to other parts of northern Italy (cf. 12.1n.), there is no marked introduction of the most distinctive material culture of Transalpine Gaul, the so-called La Tène culture, into the archaeological record of the Insubrian region at this period. It is, accordingly, often argued (e.g. De Marinis (1988), esp. 169-75, 237-44) that the Insubrian culture was a continuation of the previous culture of the region, that known as the western Golasecca, which existed there from the eighth century, though with roots going back several centuries earlier (for analysis see esp. Pauli (1971)); this is apparently supported by Livy 5.34.9, who not only dates the Gallic influx much earlier, in the late seventh or early sixth century, but also seems to indicate that there was already an existing group called the Insubrians whom the Gallic invaders found in the region.

This model has in turn been challenged by Williams (2001), 187-207, who notes that Golaseccan material remains themselves largely disappear from the archaeological record after the late fifth century: indeed, material culture from the fourth and third centuries is altogether harder to find in the region, not least because the society seems to have revolved far less around nucleated centres than it had previously; accordingly, the material remains do not support a picture of cultural continuity any more strongly than they support one of invasion. Nor, as Williams notes, is it clear that the earlier Golaseccan culture would have been identified as Gallic, either by themselves or others, for all that there are occasional hints of Gallic presence such as brief Celtic graffiti. Williams finally argues that it is unlikely that the Insubrians even existed in this period as a coherent tribal unit: his suggestion is that at most it was a loose agglomeration of separate groups linked by relations among their elites, and it was the Romans who constructed their Gallic enemies in terms of discrete and coherent tribes. This extreme conclusion, however, probably goes too far: see the sympathetic but sceptical response by Eckstein (2002), 627–8.

The passage of Livy cited above is his only previous mention of the Insubrians in his surviving text; their first entry in the historical record comes when they joined the Boii and the Gaesatae in the invasion of Italy in 225 (20.8n.). For the archaeology of the region see also Grassi (1991), 111–25; cf. Peyre (1979).

aliquot proeliis: For the phrase see 12.3n. One of the battles is presumably the invented one in 224 found in Orosius (cf. above). In the following year, according to Plb. 2.32–3, the consuls C. Flaminius and P. Furius Philus invaded the Insubrians' territory and defeated them thanks to clever tactics by the military tribunes, and despite some strategic mismanagement by Flaminius, who drew up his troops with their backs to the river and hence with no room to manoeuvre backwards; according to Livy 22.6.3–4, Flaminius also cut a swathe of destruction through Insubrian territory that ultimately was to lead to his death at the hands of an outraged Insubrian. However, most of the later historical tradition (e.g. Plu., *Marc.* 4.2–3, *Fab.* 2.4, Oros. 4.13.14, Zonar. 8.20.4–7), including Livy himself in his other references to this year (21.63.2, 21.63.7, 21.63.12, 22.3.3, 22.3.13), was less interested in Flaminius' conduct in the war, and rather more with his alleged irreligion and conflict with the Senate prior to it, which prefigured the events surrounding his disastrous defeat at Lake Trasimene six years later; nevertheless both Flaminius and his colleague were, according to the *Fasti Capitolini* (cf. also Livy 21.63.3, 23.14.4, Sil. 5.653–4, Plu., *Marc.* 4.3, Zonar. 8.20.7), awarded a triumph. P. ignores Flaminius' misconduct, however, despite his interest in it in Book 22 (cf. 22.2n.): cf. his treatment of Flaminius' censorship below (20.11n.). This entire period between the Punic Wars appears for him to be one of uninterrupted Roman growth and success.

The Romans resumed their onslaught across the Po in 222, and the consuls Marcellus (below) and Cn. Cornelius Scipio Calvus were faced with the forces not only of the Insubrians, but also of the Gaesatae (20.8n.), to whom the Insubrians had appealed for help (Plb. 2.34.1–2).[314] The Romans besieged the Insubrian town of Acerrae; the Insubrians, unable to raise the siege, counterattacked across the Po, and besieged Clastidium; Marcellus took a relatively small force to relieve the town and defeated the Gauls (Plb. 2.34.3–9, Plu., *Marc.* 6.2–3, Zonar. 8.20.8–9: see also below for the events of this battle). Scipio captured

---

[314] Cf. Plu., *Marc.* 6.2, where, however, the Gaesatae are the ones who take the initiative.

Acerrae, pursued the Gauls to Milan, and defeated them after a hard-fought battle, subsequently capturing the town, after which the Insubrians surrendered (Plb. 2.34.10–35.1, Plu., *Marc*. 7.4–5, Eutr. 3.6, Oros. 4.13.15, Zon. 8.20.9). Marcellus was awarded a triumph, according to the *Fasti Capitolini* (cf. also Plu., *Marc*. 8.1–2, Eutr. 3.6.2).

All of this is likely to have appeared in Livy, and hence to be covered by P.'s phrase here.

in deditionem venerunt: Cf. 8.4n.

M. Claudius Marcellus cos.: *RE* 220. The first appearance in P. (cf. 23.3, 23.10, 24.3, 25.9, 27.2, 27.4) of one of the best-known Roman figures of the late third century. Following this consulship in 222, he was elected to a further four, in 215 (when, however, he was compelled to resign before taking office), 214, 210, and 208, as well as a praetorship in 216. He was the first commander to successfully challenge Hannibal after Cannae, and subsequently held commands either as praetor, consul, or proconsul every year between 216 and 208, in the course of which he captured Syracuse and returned Sicily to Roman rule; but in his last consulship he was trapped and killed by Hannibal. Little is known of his career prior to 222: he had apparently fought in Sicily during the First Punic War (Plu., *Marc.* 2.1), and had been curule aedile, perhaps in 226 (so *MRR* I 229), during which he is said to have denounced his colleague to the Senate for attempting to seduce his son (Val. Max. 6.1.7, Plu., *Marc.* 2.3–4); he also became an augur around this time (Plu., *Marc.* 2.2; cf. Cic., *Div.* 2.77). In addition, Livy 22.35.6–7 indicates that his praetorship in 216 was his second; the date of his first is unknown, but may itself have predated 222 (so e.g. *MRR* I 231).

His combination of exceptional heroic achievement and dubious moral flexibility makes him a key figure in Livy's construction of his narrative of the Second Punic War (see esp. Levene (2010a), 197–215; also Carawan (1984–5), Mensching (1996)); in Plutarch's life he is ambivalent in a rather different way, owing to his inadequate relationship to Hellenic culture (Pelling (1989), 199–208, Swain (1990), 140–2).[315] P. overall retains no vestiges of that ambivalence (see 25.9n., 27.4n.), and if Livy prefigured it in his account of Marcellus here, P. removes it completely. For him, as for the rest of the Roman exemplary tradition, Marcellus in 222 was simply the performer of a remarkable deed to be remembered and celebrated.

occiso Gallorum Insubrium duce: Polybius has no account of this, perhaps because of his (or his source's) hostility to Marcellus (so e.g. De Sanctis III.1 308 [317], Flower (2003), 46–7); but the case for its historicity is overwhelmingly strong; it is mentioned in the *Fasti Capitolini* as well as many other sources. The

---

[315] See more generally Flower (2003) for the historical traditions that grew up around Marcellus during the Republican period, and especially for the way in which his heroic achievements were regularly undercut by more critical assessments of him.

most detailed account is in Plu., *Marc.* 6.5–7.3: Marcellus, leading his cavalry on horseback against a far larger force, vowed to dedicate the finest armour among the enemy to Jupiter Feretrius (see below). He was then challenged by the Gallic ruler, who himself rode in front of his line wearing (as it happened) an exceptional array of armour. Marcellus rode against him, struck him off his horse with a single spear-blow, and then rapidly killed him on the ground (Plu., *Marc.* 2.1 had already noted Marcellus' especial enthusiasm for single combat, though this may be plausible reconstruction in light of later events rather than based on specific evidence).

Plu., *Marc.* 6.2–3, 7.5 implies that the king killed by Marcellus was not the ruler of the Insubrians, but of the Gaesatae (the dominant group in his version of the story: see n. 314 above). P.'s version (shared by Flor. 1.20.5) is slightly neater, since he makes a direct link between the tribe attacked by Rome and the identity of the leader killed, which might suggest that it is a secondary tidying up of the tradition and Plutarch's is the original; but on the other hand the account of Marcellus' triumph in the *Fasti Capitolini* refers to the Insubrians and not the Gaesatae—though they do add the 'Germans', which might be a reference to the latter, whether in error (e.g. De Sanctis III.1 309 [318] n. 129), or, more probably, because the people in question genuinely were (or could reasonably be described as) German.[316] Neither conclusion can be asserted to be even moderately more probable than the other.

Vertomaro: The *Fasti Capitolini* give the name as Virdumarus, Plutarch as Britomartos (*Marc.* 6.2, *Rom.* 16.7). Most Latin writers have Viridomarus (Fest. 204L, Flor. 1.20.5, Ampel. 21, Eutr. 3.6.1, *Vir. Ill.* 45.1, Serv., *Aen.* 6.855), while Propertius 4.10.41 (presumably for metrical reasons) and Oros. 4.13.14 have Virdomarus. P.'s version looks anomalous in the light of these, but it appears in all of the main MSS and probably should not be emended: it may be that P. is reflecting the reading of Livy that he found in his copy, whether or not that was how Livy originally wrote it. All of these spellings are recognizably transcriptions of a single original name, and one which seems to have been relatively common among Celtic peoples—several others are attested either in literature or epigraphically (see Bannert (1978)).

Nothing further about this particular Vertomarus/Viridomarus is known: in the Roman historical tradition he exists only to be killed.

---

[316] So e.g. Degrassi 550, basing himself partly on the view that 'Gaesatae' did not denote a tribe, but was only an appellation used of mercenaries (20.8n.). Even if that specific point is not correct, however, the view that the *Fasti* were not merely in error is supported by the fact that the division Romans often made between Germans and Gauls is likely to have been an artificial one. It is not held uniformly in the literary tradition, nor is it readily discovered in the archaeology; its most common formulations appear to have originated with Caesar, and owe a great deal to his desire to claim a complete conquest of the Gauls, marking a clear distinction between them and those who remained outside his control (see Riggsby (2006), 59–71).

opima spolia: For the *spolia opima* see F 14n. Marcellus' dedication of them is widely mentioned in the Roman historical tradition, usually as part of the canonical list of three dedicators (e.g. Prop. 4.10.39–44, Val. Max. 3.2.5, Plu., *Rom.* 16.7, Ampel. 21; cf. Plu., *Marc.* 7.3, 8.3, Flor. 1.20.5), less often as a free-standing image of an exceptional Roman hero, as at Virg., *Aen.* 6.855–9, Sil. It. 1.132–3, 3.587, 12.279–80, Frontin., *Strat.* 4.5.4, *Vir. Ill.* 45.2: even with this latter class there is often a nod to his position as 'third'. P. does not refer to that: as in Eutr. 3.6 and Oros. 4.13.15, Marcellus' deed is described as a key moment of the events of this war, rather than being slotted directly into an exemplary canon. However, he does employ almost identical phrasing to that which he had used in the case of Cossus (4.6: *Cossus Cornelius tribunus militum occiso Tolumnio, Veientum rege, opima spolia secunda rettulit*; see further *ad loc.*), thus implicitly linking Marcellus to his predecessors.

20.10 *Istrian War; Second Illyrian War.* These two wars, although taking place a couple of years apart (and separated by the censorship of Flaminius, which P. does not mention until 20.11—see *ad loc.*), are juxtaposed by P., perhaps because Livy presented them as intertwined, as App., *Ill.* 8 does: according to him, the Istrian War came about because Demetrius in Illyria persuaded the Istrians to engage in piracy; the Romans, having defeated the Istrians, took the fight to the Illyrians. P. does not make that explicit, but the order of his narrative hints at the link. Gruen (1984a), 371–2 suggests that Appian (and, presumably, Livy) was right to link the wars, but since he (probably rightly)[317] rejects Appian's suggestion that Demetrius was behind the Istrians' piracy, he is vague on what the connection between them was: it is better to regard the two wars as independent.

Histri: A people inhabiting the Istra peninsula in modern Croatia; they are described by App., *Ill.* 8 as an Illyrian tribe—presumably one of the many such tribes which did not form part of the Illyrian kingdom (see 20.6n.)—but scholarship has thrown various doubts upon that, noting the cultural links with the Veneti bordering them in Italy as well as those to their south in the Balkans (Vedaldi Iasbez (1994), 263–4). Livy had mentioned them in passing in 10.2.4, but this is their first appearance in P. This war is recorded by Eutr. 3.7.1, Oros. 4.13.16, and Zonar. 8.20.10 as taking place in 221, under the consuls M. Minucius Rufus and P. Cornelius Scipio Asina, but nothing of the events which led up to the Roman victory are recorded, apart from the fact that the Romans were responding to piracy by the Istrians (Eutr. 3.7.1, App., *Ill.* 8; cf. above), Zonaras' comment

---

[317] *Contra* Dell (1970), but the key evidence here is the silence of Polybius. His failure to mention the Istrian War is explicable in itself, given that it was a relatively minor event in a period he was treating cursorily, but it is much less likely if Demetrius had been involved and it had formed a *casus belli* for the Second Illyrian War, matters in which he was more keenly interested. Dell confuses the strong case for the historicity of the Istrian War with the much weaker case for Demetrius' involvement in it. The same argument tells against the suggestion by Cavallaro (2004), 202–3 that the accusation, even if false, was one that went back to the Romans at the time rather than being a later construction.

that many nations were subdued 'some by war, some by agreement', and Orosius' (perhaps tendentious) claim that the Roman losses were considerable. The last is implicitly contradicted by Livy 21.16.4, which links the Istrians with the Sardinians, Corsicans, and Illyrians, as enemies who *lacessisse magis quam exercuisse Romana arma* ('troubled rather than tried Roman forces'), though this is not in the authorial voice, but spoken by the senators panicking over the imminent war with Hannibal, and it may well not fully reflect the way Livy narrated the Istrian War in Book 20.

The Romans are not recorded as fighting the Istrians again until 182 BC, when they once again responded to allegations of a wave of piracy originating there (Livy 40.18.4, 40.26.2–3); they then conducted an extended campaign in 178–177 (Livy 41.1–5, 10–11; cf. *Per*. 41.6), at the end of which the Istrians were conquered and placed under direct Roman rule. Under Augustus the Istra peninsula was incorporated into Italy.

iterum...rebellassent: 'Renewed the war again'—in other words, this was a second war, not the second renewal and hence a third war (cf. 11.4 *quarto renovatum* and *ad loc*.).

The only extended account of the war is in Plb. 3.16, 18–19; there is a briefer version in Zonar. 8.20.11–13 (cf. Dio fr. 53) and a still briefer one in App., *Ill*. 8. Unlike Appian and (probably) Livy, Polybius does not connect it with the Istrian War, which he does not mention. Instead, he, like Zonaras, sees its origins in the activities of Demetrius of Pharus, who was then ruling Illyria (20.6n.): Demetrius was attacking his neighbours, including towns which were under the hegemony of Rome, and (according to Plb. 3.16.3) had directly violated the treaty at the end of the First Illyrian War (20.6n.) by taking a fleet beyond Lissus and attacking the Cyclades (cf. 4.16.6–9). All of this was something the Romans wished to respond to, but the timing, according to Polybius, was determined by other considerations. This was partly a wish to contain Macedon, with whom Demetrius had allied himself (3.16.3–4), by taking control of a territory that could potentially fall within the sphere of interest of either power. An additional aim was to secure Illyria before turning to Spain and the Carthaginians (3.16.1)—Polybius (rightly) synchronizes the war with Hannibal's capture of Saguntum, which began the Second Punic War. Livy's chronology of the first phases of the Second Punic War is not internally consistent (see Levene (2010a), 55–61), but its opening section dates the capture of Saguntum to 218 (esp. 21.6.3), and one likely reason is precisely that he wished to keep the Hannibalic War clearly separate from the Illyrian War: he brought the latter to a conclusion before bringing the Carthaginians into play (Levene (2010a), 59). Accordingly, he must have given a different explanation for the war from Polybius', perhaps focusing solely on Demetrius' behaviour, and probably linking it to the Istrian War (above).

Even on Polybius' version, however, this renewed campaign in Illyria was essentially reactive rather than aggressive on the part of the Romans; however, many modern historians have queried this picture. In particular, the king of Macedon for whom Demetrius had fought, Antigonus Doson, had recently died, and the new king, Philip V, was an adolescent who was barely secure on his throne; hence it seems doubtful that, as Plb. 3.16.2-3 has it, Demetrius could have been deliberately challenging Rome in the hope of Macedonian support. The problem is, in that case, that it is hard to make sense of his reported actions. Rome had shown her power in her wars with the Gauls, and was not yet sufficiently involved against the Carthaginians in Spain for Demetrius to be able to hope that this would distract them from him (Badian (1952a), 83-5).

One possibility is that Demetrius (who had, after all, depended largely on Rome for his rise) was at most engaging in some minor jockeying for influence, and the descriptions in the historians of his aggressive campaign is at the least severely exaggerated. In which case the necessary corollary is that, if Demetrius was not acting aggressively, Rome herself was doing so (cf. 16.2, 20.6nn.)—perhaps seeking to secure her influence over the Adriatic by corralling a local client whom she could well have seen as unreliable in the light of his recent willingness to fight for Macedon. This does not mean that one needs to give a maximalist account of her expansive aims: certainly there is little to suggest that this was a conflict with the Macedonians by proxy (Eckstein (2008), 63-6; contra e.g. Hammond (1968), 9-12), and Rome could have extended her control of the eastern Adriatic coast further and cut off Macedonia more completely, had she wanted to (Badian (1952a), 87-8; cf. Eckstein (2008), 70-2). But the absence of maximalist expansive aims does not entail the absence of any expansive aims.

There is an alternative possibility: the reason that it is hard to make sense of Demetrius' reported actions may be that he was in fact acting irrationally (Eckstein (1994); also (2008), 58-73), that he was recklessly seeking to enhance his own power even at the cost of provoking Rome, perhaps indeed out of exaggerated expectations of a Macedonian intervention. Attributing irrational behaviour to a ruler is, it is true, an interpretation that one should not adopt lightly; nevertheless, one does not have to look far to find parallels,[318] and in this case, as Eckstein notes, it is an interpretation which is supported by Polybius, who consistently—and not only in the context of the Second Illyrian War—characterizes Demetrius as irrationally reckless. The best one can say for Demetrius' actions, on this view, is that he might have overlooked the extent of his provocations (Eckstein (2008), 61-2): it is clear from Polybius 4.16.6-9 that when he sailed south of Lissus he was not attacking Roman interests, and he was probably using his personal holding of ships rather than the Illyrian state fleet (Badian (1952a), 84-5). But even if that is so, a sensible ruler would not have depended on so narrow a

---

[318] An instructive contemporary example is the former President of Georgia, Mikhael Saakashvili, who, in August 2008, engaged in aggressive military actions which (inevitably and predictably) provoked a war with Russia, a war which Georgia (inevitably and predictably) lost humiliatingly in a matter of days.

legalism to assume that the treaty did not apply, given that he had now effectively taken on responsibility for the Illyrian kingdom (Petzold (1971), 212, Eckstein (1994), 57–8).

Eckstein's view has the advantage of fitting Polybius' interpretation more closely, and, as he argues, it is likely that Polybius based his view of Demetrius' character on a range of sources. Nevertheless, as he has to admit, Polybius has misrepresented some of Demetrius' actions—it is highly unlikely that he in fact attacked cities subject to Rome (Eckstein (1994), 58; cf. Badian (1958), 85–6, Gruen (1984a), 371). Another problem is that Polybius insists that not only Demetrius, but also Rome, was reacting to the supposed resurgence of Macedon (cf. Eckstein (1994), 49). Even if Demetrius was irrationally misreading the situation, it seems less likely that the Romans were (cf. Badian (1952a), 86): it is more likely that with both of these, Polybius was interpreting with hindsight. A further point against Eckstein is that Demetrius, in sailing beyond the Lissus, acted in consort with another Illyrian dynast, Scerdilaidas (Plb. 4.16.6–10). Positing two irrationally aggressive Illyrian leaders is more of a stretch than one, and in fact the Romans did not punish Scerdilaidas. This suggests that neither he nor they saw the expedition as unacceptably provocative, in which case it is hard to conclude that Demetrius' participation was obviously reckless (Badian (1958), 84–8, Gruen (1984a), 370–1, Cavallaro (2004), 204–6).

All of this seems more compatible with Roman decision-makers deliberately looking to expand Roman influence in the Adriatic by taking an excuse to cut Demetrius down to size than with a picture of Demetrius irrationally provoking Rome into conflict—for all that Demetrius may indeed have been incautious in various aspects of his dealings with Rome, and insufficiently careful to keep within the Romans' implicit parameters.

Polybius' and Zonaras' accounts of the campaign itself diverge significantly. In Polybius, the Romans began with an attack on Dimale, which Demetrius had strongly fortified, and rapidly captured it (3.18.1–6). They then took the fight to Pharus, where Demetrius was waiting with a large force; the Romans lured him out through a stratagem, concealing the bulk of their army at night, and then feigning an attack with a small number of ships. They routed Demetrius' troops, and Demetrius himself fled to Macedon; the Romans captured Pharus and rapidly subdued the rest of Illyria. Zonaras, on the other hand, has the initial Roman attack taking place against Issa (cf. Dio fr. 53), and it is there that the Romans employed a similar (though not identical) stratagem to the one Polybius describes at Pharus, luring the enemy with a small number of ships and thus giving themselves an opportunity to attack with their full force. Demetrius then fled to Pharus, which the Romans took 'by treachery', but Demetrius had already escaped to Macedon. There is no ready way of reconciling these: Dimale and Issa are not easily confused with one another (the former is a mainland town several kilometres from the sea, the latter an island off a quite different part of the coastline).

As often, Polybius is probably to be preferred on the grounds of his being closer to the time and more broadly reliable: Issa may have entered the tradition, as De Sanctis III.1 316 [325] n. 150 suggests, as a duplication of its role in the First Illyrian War (cf. Plb. 2.11.12 and 20.6n.).

Plb. 3.16.7 and Zonar. 8.20.11–13 date the entire war to 219, under the consuls L. Aemilius Paullus and M. Livius Salinator, although Appian places it in the year after the Istrian War, and hence has it beginning in 220. The former version, which is given by both Polybius and Zonaras with circumstantial detail, is more likely to be correct than Appian's rough summary which fails to name the consuls involved.

Illyrii: See 20.6n.

in deditionem venerunt: Cf. 8.4n. No source has any account of the settlement the Romans imposed on Illyria, apart from a brief comment in App., *Ill.* 8 that they spared the country at the request of Pinnes, the legitimate king (cf. 20.6n.). Livy 22.33.5 refers to a *stipendium* which Pinnes owed to them but which was overdue—but it is not clear whether this was simply an instalment of the indemnity already imposed after the First Illyrian War (20.6n.), or included an additional imposition after the second war.

20.11 *Censorships.* P. here rolls into a single notice three separate censorships, each presumably described by Livy in its own place: cf. 3.3, where two censuses that are separated in Livy are placed together by P. It is unusual for him to summarize thematically rather than in a (presumed) narrative order, though this bears a slight similarity to his regular way of sweeping up events not individually summarized under the general heading of *res praeterea gestas continet* (2.16n.). The reason for his doing so now is unclear, though it may be in order to include the key information about the censorships in question, while not overwhelming with repetitive events a book which covered twenty-two years and hence was already somewhat piecemeal. As often, the matters he is most interested in are the ones which mark the growth of Rome, with notices about the size of the citizen body and the tribes; but he also introduces a key character from Livy's narrative of the period.

lustrum...conditum est: See 11.5n.

ter: The older MSS reading here is *per*; though in some of the *recentiores* it appears as *bis*. Clearly some number is concealed; the question is what number that is. The *Fasti Capitolini* lists no fewer than five sets of censors in the period covered by this book: in 236, 234, 231, 230, and 225, while the censorship of 241 would have had its *lustrum* in 240, a year which likewise fell within Book 20, and we can add the censorship of C. Flaminius and L. Aemilius Papus in 220, which is not in the surviving portions of the *Fasti*, but is mentioned by various literary sources, including P. (see below). However, the evidence of the *Fasti* allows us to cut down the number somewhat: the censors elected in 231 (T. Manlius Torquatus and Q. Fulvius Flaccus) certainly did not complete the *lustrum*, since they were forced to resign owing to flaws in their election; the censors of 230, Q. Fabius Maximus and M. Sempronius Tuditanus, were elected to replace them. The censors of 236, L. Cornelius Lentulus and Q. Lutatius Cerco, likewise cannot have completed the *lustrum*, since Lutatius died in office, and suffect censors were not permitted (Mommsen, *StR*³ I 215-16; cf. 13.4n.); this explains why the next censorship (of C. Atilius Bulbus and A. Postumius Albinus) followed only two years later. The *lustrum* of 241/0 was probably, contrary to Livy's usual practice, recorded by him under the year 241 in Book 19 (see 19.11n.).

This leaves four possible *lustra*; hence we might emend to read *quater*. However, even if we exclude the more jejune narratives of the early books, Livy does not invariably record *lustra* when describing the activities of censors: he does not mention the *lustrum* of the censorship of 199 (32.7.1-3), nor, more surprisingly, that of the censorship of 184—the famous censorship of M. Porcius Cato and L. Valerius Flaccus, which he describes at considerable length (39.40.1-41.4, 39.42.5-44.9). Accordingly, Madvig proposed to read *ter*, which is palaeographically the easiest emendation, although *quater* obviously cannot be excluded: were it written iiii, the loss of one digit would be unexceptional, though this still requires a double corruption rather than a single one. We have to balance an easy emendation that makes historical reconstruction a little more difficult, against a harder emendation where the reconstruction is slightly easier: the first option is probably preferable.

This, then, leaves the question of which *lustrum* Livy may have failed to include. It is unlikely to be that of the censorship of C. Flaminius and L. Aemilius Papus in 220 (cf. below): P.'s notice here, which juxtaposes Flaminius' activities as censor with the report of the three *lustra*, is more likely to have been triggered by Livy's text if Flaminius' censorship was itself one of the three. Hence it is most likely that Livy did not narrate the *lustrum* of either 234/233, 231/230, or 225/224. On the face of things there is no basis for deciding which, since nothing is known of any of these censorships beyond the notices in the *Fasti* and P.'s brief description here: however, there is one extra consideration which should lead us to conclude that the *lustrum* of 234/233 is likely to have been omitted: see the next note.

primo lustro: On the argument above, this must be the *lustrum* of either 233 or 230. Brunt (1971), 46-7 assumes the former, but has no apparent reason for doing so, since he proceeds to argue that in fact the census in 230, which he believes to be the basis of the figures for Roman manpower supplied by Polybius for 225 (20.8n.), gave a total citizen body very close to the one offered by P. here (cf. Brunt (1971), 61. Indeed, since Polybius' figure has probably been rounded (cf. Brunt (1971), 46), then its rough congruence with P.'s here confirms both that the latter is more likely to relate to 230 than to 233 (and hence that Livy's 'missing' *lustrum* was that of 234/3), and that Brunt's broad hypothesis about the way in which Polybius' data should be interpreted was correct.

CCLXX milia DCCXIII: This figure, unlike those from earlier in the decade (cf. 11.5, 19.5nn.), is the first which has some claims to be reliable, at least in regard to reflecting the number of citizens recorded by the state at this time (Brunt (1971), 32-3). Nevertheless, the procedures for registration are likely to have resulted in undercounting the actual number of the citizen body (Brunt (1971), 33-5): it is controversial how extensive this was (cf. De Ligt (2012), 79-134), but undercounting must have existed to some degree.

libertini in quattuor tribus redacti sunt: Cf. 9.6n.: it is likely that the phrase here also is P.'s rather than Livy's.

This is the first clear historical occasion recording[319] an issue that continued to be controversial throughout the Republic (cf. 77.1n., 84.5n.; also e.g. Livy 45.15.1-6, Dio 36.42.2, Cic., *Mil.* 87 and 89 with Ascon. 44C), namely the form in which freedmen should be registered in the tribal assembly: whether they should be confined to the four urban tribes, or to just one of those tribes, or whether they were potentially eligible, like other citizens, to register for the thirty-one rural tribes. Allowing the last would increase their political influence, since each tribe's votes had equal weight, and confining all freedmen to just four populous tribes would mean that the vote of any individual freedman would count for less.

It is often suggested (e.g. Mouritsen (2001), 34) that those who would limit the rights of freedmen were those who would want power to be disproportionately in the hands of aristocrats. However, that is not necessarily so. The Roman system of patronage might lead aristocrats to expect to exercise some control over the votes of their own freedmen,[320] at least prior to the institution of the secret ballot in the 130s;[321] it would, accordingly, be in their interests to maximize their voting power. Conversely, those whose influence might be most immediately threatened by increased power for freedmen were the free population enrolled in the rural tribes, and not only (or primarily) its wealthiest members.[322] It is also possible

---

[319] The question may have originally arisen with the censorship of Ap. Claudius Caecus in 312: the reports are difficult and in some respects contradictory, but one possible interpretation is that he sought to extend to freedmen membership of the rural tribes (so e.g. Taylor (2013 (1960)), 132-8, Oakley (2005a), 629-34; *contra* e.g. Treggiari (1969), 38-42, Bernard (2018), 138-40). Even if this was the case, his reforms were reversed by the censors of 304 (Livy 9.46.14-15).

[320] In a fundamental essay, Brunt (1988), 382-442 demonstrated that patronage in the Republic was far more fluid and less prescriptive than previous scholars had assumed, that most freeborn Romans did not have exclusive or absolute obligations to particular members of the upper classes, and that, accordingly, patronage was not an effective tool of control by the latter. However, Brunt's essay is almost entirely concerned with the freeborn; unlike them, freedmen were one group for whom we can assume a strong relationship of obligation to their former masters (cf. Treggiari (1969), 68-81). Hence his argument supports rather than undermines the position here: for if the aristocracy had little control over the freeborn poor, it would benefit them all the more to increase the voting power of those over whom they did have a degree of control.

[321] For the idea that the introduction of the secret ballot substantially diminished the power of the aristocracy, see the extended discussion in Cic., *Leg.* 3.33-39 (cf. *Sest.* 103); cf. Yakobson (1995).

[322] It is worth noting, for example, that although at the time of the Gracchi the voting of freedmen had been even more severely restricted—they were confined to just one urban tribe—no source suggests that the Gracchi showed any concern about this. Support for the freeborn poor was not obviously congruent with increasing the voting rights of freedmen.

that individuals may have been moved by concern for justice on the one hand or tradition on the other, even without direct motives of self-interest. For all of these reasons, it is hard to identify which censors were responsible for the reform here: we know too little about the political programmes and allegiances at this time.[323] In the light of the argument sketched here, it would be not be unreasonable to imagine Flaminius (cf. below) as the author of this proposal (so *MRR* I 235)—he might well have seen restricting the rights of freedmen as a way of reducing the influence of the aristocracy and increasing that of the freeborn poor—but it should be emphasized that this is nothing more than theoretical speculation.

cum: This is concessive: 'although'.

Esquilinam, Palatinam, Suburanam, Collinam: The four urban tribes of Rome; according to Livy 1.43.13 (cf. D.H., *AR* 4.14.1-2), they were originally created by Servius Tullius, and corresponded, as their names suggest, to different regions of the city (cf. Taylor (2013 (1960), 4-5). The order here presumably reflects Livy's, but does not appear to have any broader significance: there was an official order of tribes, but that began with the Suburana, not the Esquilina (Taylor (2013 (1960)), 69-72).

⟨**C. Flaminius censor viam Flaminiam**⟩: Supplied by Sigonius to fill the obvious lacuna. The supplement is clearly close to what P. wrote, since Flaminius must be introduced in order to form the subject of *extruxit* later in the sentence, and no other construction than the *via Flaminia* is a likely object of *muniit*. *censor* is slightly more problematic, since there is only one other place, namely Cassiod., *Chron*. 337M, where this building programme is dated to 220, and Paul., *Fest*. 79L in fact attributes it to his consulship (see also below). However, P.'s order, juxtaposing the building with other censorial activity, is more likely to mean that this too appeared under the heading of the censorship, and Cassiodorus' listings for the middle Republic almost invariably agree with Livy's, albeit probably drawn from an intermediate source rather than from Livy himself (Mommsen (1861), 551-8). Hence Livy—and thus P.—almost certainly attributed the building to the censorship.

What is unknown is whether P. indeed treated Flaminius' actions as neutrally as this supplement implies, or whether he might have introduced some more negative characterization to reflect the likely negative characterization in Livy (cf. n. 325 below). The former is more probable, given P.'s relatively flat handling of Livy's characters, but the latter is not impossible, since there are certainly other places—including with Flaminius himself at his reappearance at 22.2 (see *ad loc.*)—where P. does offer a brief note to slant his narrative (cf. Levene (2015b), 315-16). However, in the absence of any direct evidence, Sigonius' supplement must stand as the most likely placeholder.

---

[323] Taylor (2013 (1960)), 138 proposed Q. Fabius Maximus in 230 as the censor responsible, but the only reason she offered was that his ancestor had been responsible for a possibly analogous move more than seventy years earlier.

C. Flaminius: *RE* 2; *MRR* I 235–6. Perhaps the most controversial figure of the period, despite regularly holding high offices: as well as the censorship in 220, he held a tribuneship in 232,[324] a praetorship in 227 (the first praetor to govern Sicily: cf. 20.7n.), and consulships in 223 (20.9n.) and 217; he also was selected as *magister equitum* in 221. He is, however, almost universally blackened by the historians as a reckless demagogue and incompetent commander.[325] The one recorded event of his tribuneship was his distribution to citizens of public land in the *ager Gallicus*. This was blamed by Polybius for the Gallic invasion several years later—possibly rightly (cf. 20.8n.), but Polybius' hostility to Flaminius' programme goes beyond this, since he claims his land reform 'for the Romans…was the beginning of the people's turn to the worse' (2.21.8: ʽΡωμαίοις…ἀρχηγὸν μὲν γενέσθαι τῆς ἐπὶ τὸ χεῖρον τοῦ δήμου διαστροφῆς); along similar lines, other sources treat it primarily in the context of the opposition it received from the Senate (e.g. Cic., *Inv.* 2.52, *Cato* 11, *Ac.* 2.13, Val. Max. 5.4.5). His first consulship in 223 was marked by accusations of military incompetence, irreligion, and unconstitutional conflict with the Senate (20.9n.); the same themes, with (perhaps) more justification, recur in his consulship in 217, where he was trapped, defeated, and killed by Hannibal at Lake Trasimene. Modern scholars have assessed his career far more positively, emphasizing his willingness to challenge vested interests in support of the broader Roman populace, and the reciprocal support he received from them (e.g. Fraccaro (1919), Yavetz (1962); *contra* Develin (1979b), who, though sympathetic to Flaminius, argues for much less consistency in his policies; similarly Beck (2005), 244–68). One should not, however, fail to remark that his support for the Roman people came at the direct expense of the Gauls, towards whom his policy appears to have been consistently violent and exploitative (20.8, 20.9nn.).

His censorship, unlike his activities in his tribuneship and two consulships, is hardly remarked upon in ancient sources, perhaps precisely because it lent itself less obviously to hostile characterization. P.'s interest in it presumably relates to his general tendency to record key moments in the growth of Rome: it is less usual for him to note monuments *per se*, but both of Flaminius' major building projects remained iconic parts of the landscape for centuries. But apart from the notice here, and a few passing references later in Livy to the censors' review of the Senate (23.22.3, 23.23.3–5, 24.11.7), the only reference to these censors is Plin.,

---

[324] Plb. 2.21.7 dates the tribunate to 232; Cic., *Cato* 11, on the other hand, speaks of Fabius Maximus' opposition to Flaminius' land law as consul in 228. It may be that Cicero simply made a mistake (so e.g. *MRR* I 225); but Powell (1988), 276–7 ingeniously argues that Cicero is better understood as referring to Fabius' subsequent opposition to the actual distribution of land, not the original passing of the law.

[325] The hostility of the historical tradition to Flaminius is likely to have begun with his contemporary Fabius Pictor (Gelzer (1933), 152–3); for its further development see Caltabiano (1976), (1995). Note, however, Feig Vishnia (2012), arguing that while aspects of the hostility go back to Fabius, other elements were introduced by the later historians, not least Polybius, who had reasons of his own for disliking Flaminius' policies.

Nat. 35.197, who describes their sponsorship of the *lex Metilia de Fullonibus* (a law regulating fullers). Flaminius' foundation of the *via Flaminia* and the *circus Flaminius* are mentioned by Plu., *Quaest. Rom.* 279F–280A and Paul., *Fest.* 79L, but neither specifically relates it to his censorship: indeed Paulus—probably mistakenly (cf. below)—dates it to his consulship. Conversely, Cassiod., *Chron.* 337M dates these two foundations to the consular year 220 (thus incidentally confirming the date of the censorship, which is missing from the *Fasti*, as noted above), but does not mention either the censorship or Flaminius explicitly. In addition, the foundation of the colonies Placentia and Cremona is quite likely to be associated with this censorship (cf. 20.12n.), but no ancient source makes the connection.

viam Flaminiam: The major Roman road north of the city, probably incorporating existing routes in many places (Ashby and Fell (1921), 126). It ran along the western Tiber valley as far as Ocriculum (modern Otricoli), then turned into the hills, crossing the Apennines via Narnia (Narni), Mevania (Bevagna), Fulginiae (Foligno), and Forum Flaminii (S. Giovanni Profiamma: it was presumably founded by Flaminius at the same time as the route was laid out). It reached the Adriatic coast at the later town of Fanum Fortunae (Fano); finally it turned and followed the coast north-west to Ariminum (15.4n.). After the building of the Aurelian Wall at Rome in the late third century AD, the portion within the wall was renamed the *via Lata*; it remained (and remains) a major axis of the city of Rome, now (since the fifteenth century) called the Via del Corso. The road's construction, like that of the Circus Flaminius (below), is dated to Flaminius' consulship by Paul., *Fest.* 79L, but this is probably simply an error, perhaps as a result of careless compression in the course of epitomizing (so Coarelli (1997), 363).[326] Given that Flaminius spent a large portion of his consulship far from the city, campaigning in Transpadania, it is less likely that he commissioned major public works then (Wiseman (1970), 125).

According to Plu., *Quaest. Rom.* 279F–280A, the road was virtually an afterthought: Flaminius gave land to the state, the sale of which paid for the Circus Flaminius (below), but since there was some money left over it was decided to build a road with it. This story, however, is highly improbable. The road had a clear military value for the swift and efficient movement of troops to Cisalpine Gaul, something which the Gallic wars of the previous years—in which Flaminius himself had played a major part (20.9n.)—had presumably shown to be desirable;

---

[326] *Contra* Radke (1967), 233–4, who prefers to assign it to the consulship on the dubious grounds that Flaminius as censor would not have had authority to build a road that took up land in Latin colonies. A more patent error is in Str. 5.1.11, who attributes the building of the road to Flaminius' son during his consulship in 187. The likelihood is that Strabo has been misled by the fact that Flaminius' son did apparently build a road himself (Livy 39.2.6), and moreover that his colleague, M. Aemilius Lepidus, built in that year the *via Aemilia*, which ran from Placentia to Ariminum, where it connected with the *via Flaminia* (J. R. Patterson in *LTUR* vol. 5, 135; cf. 39.1n.). A similar error may appear in *EpOxy* 39 col.2.4: see *ad loc.*

it also connected Rome with the *ager Gallicus* which Flaminius had controversially distributed to the populace during his tribuneship (above).[327] It can thus easily be seen as part of his wider programme, and an ambitious one: it was only the second (after the Via Appia: see 9.4n.) major Roman road to be constructed, and as such established an important pattern for the unprecedented manner in which Rome exercised control over its territory (see Purcell (1990), 12–14).

For detailed studies of the route and the surviving remains of the road see Ashby and Fell (1921), Pineschi (1997), Luni (2002).

muniit: For *viam munire* ('build a road') see *TLL* VIII 1658.44–54; also Oakley (2005a), 373. The phrase is Livian (9.29.6, 34.28.2, 37.7.13, 39.28.8, 44.9.11); cf. also 9.4n.

circum Flaminium: In the south-eastern portion of the Campus Martius: its site, obscure for many years, was definitively identified in the early 1960s (Gatti (1960), (1961)), although its precise limits are still subject to debate. On the reconstruction of Coarelli (1997), 364, it was oriented NW–SE: extending from a little west of the modern Largo Arenula to the east of the site now occupied by the Rome Synagogue, the upper boundary following the line of the modern Via del Portico d'Ottavia. Coarelli's reconstruction assumes that it was an elongated rectangle with rounded ends, the 'circus' shape familiar from the Circus Maximus and many other hippodromes around the empire. Against this, Wiseman (1974) (also Wiseman (1976), 44–5) argues that this entire picture is mistaken: that the Circus Flaminius was not a constructed building, but something closer to a piazza, laid out as a circular open space, with other buildings over time constructed in and around it; he assembles extensive evidence to demonstrate that those other buildings are described as if the Circus itself was an open space rather than a structure; moreover he argues that it was not, despite its name, primarily used for entertainment.

Wiseman's final point is relatively strong: it is true that the primary attested functions of the Circus Flaminius are more similar to those of a forum than a place of entertainment (Wiseman (1974), 4). It was used for assemblies (Cic., *Att.* 1.14.1, *P. Red. In Sen.* 13, 17, *Sest.* 33, Livy 27.21.1, Plu., *Marc.* 27.3) or for business (Cic., *Att.* 1.14.1, Mart. 12.74.2, *CIL* VI 9713 = *ILS* 7511); the army appears to have assembled there prior to entering the city for a triumph (Livy 39.5.17, 45.39.14, Plu., *Luc.* 37.2). The evidence for games taking place there is much scantier: the only regular ones attested are the quinquennial *ludi Taurii* mentioned by Varro, *Ling.* 5.154, whose language implies that no others took place there in his day (Wiseman (1976), 44–5); but on the other hand we do hear of one-off entertainments (Dio 55.10.8), and there is evidence that at some point

---

[327] Wiseman (1970), 138 emphasizes the former purpose and denies the latter; but it is hard to see why the road should not have served both functions.

there was some sort of fixed seating structure for spectacles (Val. Max. 4.4.8),[328] which presumably in turn entails that there were enough spectacles to make one worth erecting.

This last tells also against Wiseman's first theory, that the Circus Flaminius was not an actual structure, and further evidence against it is the very language of P. here, since *exstruxit* certainly implies the erection of a building (*TLL* V.2 1939.40–1940.28), as does *aedificatus* in Varro, *Ling.* 5.154; indeed, were there not a building of some sort, it is hard to see why Livy—and hence P.—would have focused on the Circus Flaminius as one of the achievements of Flaminius' censorship. Wiseman (1974), 7 suggests that some sort of exterior wall is meant (albeit one broken down in subsequent years as other buildings encroached on the area), but that hardly seems sufficient to account for the notice. The best way of reconciling these considerations might be to posit that the original structure was in fact more extensive, and was perhaps indeed constructed on the analogy of the Circus Maximus for entertainment, but that, as other uses for the space were found across time, subsequent builders had little compunction about removing sections of it in order to accommodate their own monuments.

According to Varro, *Ling.* 5.154, the Circus Flaminius took its name not from its builder, but the *campus Flaminius* on which it was situated; similarly Livy 3.54.15 (cf. 3.63.7) refers to the *prata Flaminia* as the name of the site at the time of the Decemvirate. It may be that the *prata Flaminia* / *campus Flaminius* in fact only acquired this name once the Circus was built, and was mistakenly retrojected by Varro and Livy as the original name. Alternatively, there may be some connection with the story in Plutarch (above) that Flaminius funded the building by donating land to the city, the sale of which paid for the structure: it is possible that Flaminius erected the Circus on part of a parcel of land that he owned, though even in this case Livy appears anachronistic, since it seems unlikely that Flaminius' family, none of whom is known to have achieved public office prior to him, could have already been in ownership of so large a property so close to the city in the mid-fifth century.[329]

For general discussions of the Circus Flaminius and its functions, see A. Viscogliosi in *LTUR* vol. 1, 269–72; Coarelli (1997), 363–74.

---

[328] The key phrase is dismissed as a gloss by Wiseman (1976), 45, but see *contra* Briscoe (2008), 549–50.

[329] Coarelli (1997), 363–5, 371 less plausibly suggests that the site was chosen by Flaminius precisely because of the coincidence of name. M. T. D'Alessio (in Carandini, *Atlas* 1.496; cf. 1.500), along similar lines, proposes that the *prata Flaminia* took its name not from the *gens Flaminia*, but because it was land that had been given to the *flamines*; however, her only basis is Orosius' reference to priests (not only *flamines*) having been granted land 'in the circuit of the Capitol' (5.18.27: *in circuitu Capitolio*), but Orosius does not identify the site more closely, and the *circus Flaminius* is hardly 'in the circuit of the Capitol'; she does also want to maintain a connection with Flaminius, suggesting that the Flaminii were among those priests, but this appears entirely arbitrary. Still less plausible is the suggestion of Wiseman (1974), 5, that the true reason for the name is the pre-existing fields on the site, and the entire association with the censor of 220 is an invention.

20.12 *Foundation of colonies.* The foundation of Placentia and Cremona is reported in several other sources. Plb. 3.40.3–5 and Livy 21.25.2 both refer to it in the context of the attack on the newly founded colonies by the Boii at the start of the Second Punic War. Vell. 1.14.8 similarly dates the foundation to shortly before Hannibal's arrival in Italy, as does Tac., *Hist.* 3.34.1, who gives the consular date of 218, while Ascon. 3C dates it even more precisely: '29 December' (*pridie Kal. Ian.*) of 218, the consulship of P. Cornelius Scipio and Ti. Sempronius Longus, which he describes as the first year of the Second Punic War.

This last is, however, chronologically strange. Asconius' date places the foundation at the very end of 218. But by the end of 218 Hannibal was in Italy and had begun his run of early successes against Rome. All of the other sources are clear that Placentia and Cremona had already been founded by that point (the defeated Roman troops retreated there after the disaster of the Trebia in late 218: see Plb. 3.74.6–8, Livy 21.56.3–5, 21.56.9); it is anyway implausible that the Romans would have sought to establish new colonies once Hannibal's army was in the vicinity. Moreover, the middle of winter would under any circumstances be an exceptionally bad time to found colonies in the Po Valley, since the entire site could well be under deep snow (Crawford (1995), 189 = (2014), 204).

The problem was partially solved by Madvig (1828), 20–1 (cf. Eckstein (1983), 258–65), who plausibly argued that Asconius' text should be emended to '31 May' (*pridie Kal. Iun.*). This is readily compatible with Polybius, Livy, Velleius, and Tacitus, since Hannibal cannot have crossed the Alps by that point; however, it is less easy to reconcile it with P. While Livy presumably reported the consular elections for 218 in Book 20, and in principle might have narrated some events from the start of that year in that book (Madvig (1828), 21), in practice it seems highly unlikely he would have recorded formal domestic material such as the foundation of colonies there, since 21.6.6–8 (cf. 21.17) assumes that the assignment of provinces, which would normally be a central part of that domestic material, has not yet taken place (Eckstein (1983), 263, Levene (2010a), 57–60). Hence Fronda (2011), 429–31 argues that the simplest solution is to conclude that P. is referring not to the actual foundation of the colonies, but to the decision to found them, which could easily have been made some time earlier:[330] he shows that the phrase *coloniae deductae sunt*, which strictly speaking should refer to the formal moment at which the colonies were founded (cf. 1.B.1n.), can be used by P. to mark earlier stages of the foundation process (8.6n.).[331]

---

[330] A similar interpretation had been suggested more briefly by (e.g.) Madvig (1828), 21, Eckstein (1983), 264; *contra* Gargola (1990), 469–70, who uses the apparent discrepancy between Asconius and P. to construct an unlikely story in which Placentia and Cremona each have two separate formal foundations.

[331] Fronda is, however, wrong to draw a similar conclusion from the phrase *coloniae plures deductae sunt* at 34.6 (see *ad loc.*). As he notes, there are several stages of several different colonial foundations mentioned by Livy in Book 34, but it does not follow from this that P.'s notice refers to all of those colonies, rather than only those which are *deductae* in the strict sense in that book.

But once we have reached that conclusion, it follows that the decision to found the colonies need not have happened at the very end of the period covered by Book 20, namely at the end of the consular year 219 (as assumed by Fronda (2011), 432). The previous notice in P. has already moved a little back in time from the one prior to it, moving from the Second Illyrian War in 219 via a general notice of censorships in the book to describe the censorship of Flaminius in 220/19 (20.11n.). Accordingly, even if we accept that P.'s notice is broadly in chronological position, the decision to found the colonies could have been taken any time in the years 220–219. It would not be unreasonable to hypothesize that Livy could have linked it with Flaminius' censorship (described in P.'s previous notice), and indeed that he might have been right to do so (so e.g. *MRR* I 236, Yavetz (1962), 339–40, Salmon (1969), 66). P., presumably following Livy, links the foundations to his previous account of the Gallic wars (20.9n.), emphasizing that the colonies were allocated territory recently captured from the Gauls; other sources note that the colonies were specifically intended to provide an outpost against the Gauls (Livy 31.48.7, Ascon. 3C, Tac., *Hist.* 3.34.1). Flaminius both was closely associated with the conquest of that territory and had a history of settling Romans on Gallic land.

Placentia: Modern Piacenza (*BarrAtl* Map 39 F3), on the south bank of the Po near the confluence with the Trebia; Ascon. 3C states that it was a Latin colony, something also indicated by its appearance in Livy's list of colonies at 27.10.7–8; there is a little archaeological evidence that suggests that it was founded on the site of an earlier settlement (Marini Calvani (1990), 774–5). Its early history as a colony was chequered. It came under attack from the Gauls immediately on its foundation (Plb. 3.40.8, Livy 21.25.3), and was unsuccessfully besieged by Hasdrubal after his crossing the Alps in 207 (Livy 27.39.10–14). It survived those attacks, but was destroyed by the Gauls in 200, not long after the end of the Second Punic War (Livy 31.10.2–3); the town was then rebuilt in 195 (34.22.3). The colony, however, continued to struggle: in 190 it, along with Cremona (below), appealed to the Senate for supplementary colonists to be sent, and a further 6,000 were dispatched to the two towns (Livy 37.46.9–47.2). Thereafter it appears to have prospered, remaining an important regional centre throughout antiquity.

For the history and archaeology of Placentia see Ghizzoni (1990).

Cremona: Still called by the same name (*BarrAtl* Map 39 G3), the first Roman colony on the north bank of the Po; archaeological evidence indicates that there had previously been a Gallic town on the site (Gualazzini (1985), 23–4; cf. more generally 21–9). Like Placentia on the other side of the river (cf. above), it is listed by Livy at 27.10.7–8, and so is assumed to have been founded as a Latin colony; also like Placentia, it was attacked by the Gauls on its foundation (Plb. 3.40.8, Livy 21.25.3). It survived not only that, but—unlike Placentia—the subsequent Gallic attack in 200, when it was besieged (31.10.3), but the siege was relieved by the

Romans in the same year (Livy 31.21); also like Placentia, it was reinforced with extra settlers in 190. Its fortunes diverged substantially from that of its neighbour, however, when it was sacked by the Flavian troops under Antonius Primus in the civil war of AD 69 (Tac., *Hist.* 3.27-34); although refounded, it never fully recovered from the disaster.

For the history and archaeology of Cremona see Pontiroli (1985).

[in Italia]: In the MSS the phrase *in Italia* is attached to the beginning of *Per.* 21, where it makes no sense. Sigonius proposed emending it to *initia* (sc. the beginning of the *belli Punici*); Gronovius preferred to transfer it to the end of Book 20, where it belongs more naturally. Even there, however, it looks out of place, and Rossbach argued plausibly that it should be deleted as a gloss. Even though by Livy's (and P.'s) day the official boundaries of Italy had been expanded to include Placentia and Cremona, neither is likely to have made a point of asserting that anachronistic identification here, especially since P. has already explained that the towns were on Gallic land (though cf. 31.6n.). It is more probably to be attributed to a later copyist who wrote *in Italia* in order to explain that the towns which P. identifies as being on Gallic land were not so in his own time.

Book 21

21.1 *The beginning of the Second Punic War*. Corresponds to Livy 21.1–15 and 21.23.1. From Livy's multifaceted narrative of the opening of the war, P. selects just two points: the crossing of the Ebro, and the capture of Saguntum. Of those, Livy himself makes a great deal of the latter, but very little of the former. The reason that it is highlighted by P., however, is clear: he can use it to demonstrate Hannibal's fundamental war-guilt. This is something that Livy himself likewise presses, but, for the reasons I shall explain, he is unable to make the case quite as clear-cut.

While drawing out those two points, P. omits many others. He has nothing of Hannibal's predecessors as commanders in Spain, his father Hamilcar and his brother-in-law Hasdrubal (Livy 21.2), nor anything of the process by which Hannibal himself came to command there despite the prescient warnings of Hanno in Carthage (21.3–4), nor Hannibal's opening campaigns (21.5). Nor does he have the ineffectual response of the Romans when approached by Saguntum for help, with their embassies to Hannibal and to Carthage (21.6, 21.9.3–11.2); he also omits the popular anecdote of Hannibal's oath of hatred to Rome (Livy 21.1.4).

This particular balance sets P. apart from the other Latin summarizing historians. Nep., *Hann*. 2.3–3.3, Flor. 1.22.3–6, Eutr. 3.7.2–3, *Vir. Ill*. 42.1–2, and Oros. 4.14.1–3 all record the attack on Saguntum, but not the crossing of the Ebro; the same is true of the first two books of Silius Italicus. Of these, all but Nepos and *Vir. Ill*. also mention the Roman embassies, and all but Eutropius add the oath of Hannibal (which is also recorded as a free-standing anecdote by Val. Max. 9.3 ext. 3[1] and Mart. 9.43.9). In the case of Nepos, Eutropius, *Vir. Ill*., and Orosius, the difference appears in part to be that they are less concerned than P. to highlight Carthaginian guilt; Florus, by contrast, is certainly concerned with it, but addresses it in a different way, by emphasizing the treaty that (allegedly) kept Saguntum immune from attack, stressing the brutality of Hannibal's assault, and treating the Roman resort to embassies as scrupulousness rather than (as in Livy; cf. Levene (2010a), 59–60) culpable procrastination.

Surprisingly, P. is in this respect closer to the Greek tradition represented by Polybius, Appian, and Dio/Zonaras. These are, it is true, longer and more detailed than those in the Latin summarizers, and so they all include the oath of Hannibal (Plb. 3.11.5–7, App., *Hisp*. 9, *Hann*. 3, Zonar. 8.21.2), Hannibal's succession to the Spanish command (Plb. 3.13.3–4, App., *Hisp*. 8, *Hann*. 3, Zonar. 8.21.3), and the Roman embassies (Plb. 3.15, App., *Hisp*. 11, Zonar. 8.21.7–10). More significant, however, is that they all lay some stress—more, indeed, than Livy had—on the

---

[1] Interestingly, though, not in Paris' epitome, which includes a less famous anecdote about Hannibal's hatred of Rome which Valerius had included under the same heading, but not the oath story.

crossing of the Ebro as well as the siege of Saguntum (App., *Hisp.* 10, *Hann.* 3, Zonar. 8.22.9), perhaps in part because of a certain geographical vagueness. P. acknowledges this tradition, but also appears to be aware of the geographical problems: see further below.

belli... ortum: *ortum* is a correction in some Renaissance MSS of *actum* found in the chief MSS; it is almost certainly the true reading, even though the resulting phrase is striking and unparalleled. *ortus* can, as here, sometimes mean the 'beginning' of a period of time (*TLL* IX.2 1068.39–70), but the metaphorical overtones of 'rising' are still present: P. treats the Second Punic War as if it were the dawn of an age for the Romans (cf. Woodman (2014), 83, discussing Tac., *Agr.* 3.1 *primo statim beatissimi saeculi ortu*).

narrat: sc. *Livius*: it would be extremely unusual for a book, rather than an author, to be the subject of *narrare*. This is one of only a handful of places where P. makes Livy himself the subject of the sentence (see 9.7n.; also cf. 20.8n.).

contra foedus per Hiberum flumen: That a treaty between the Romans and the Carthaginians forbade the latter from crossing the Ebro is stated explicitly by Livy (21.2.7), and is confirmed by Polybius in his detailed survey of the Roman–Carthaginian treaties (3.27.9; cf. 2.13.7).[2] The problem, as Livy knew (e.g. 21.5.3, 21.5.17, 21.7.2), is that Saguntum lay to the south of the Ebro, and so an attack on it was not covered by the treaty. Hence, although the Romans treated the attack on Saguntum as the true *casus belli*, and declared war with Carthage as a result, it is not clear that they were justified in doing so. Livy nevertheless argues that the Saguntines were protected from attack, partly because, on his account, the same treaty as made the Ebro a boundary guaranteed Saguntine independence (21.2.7), and partly because he claims that an earlier treaty, made at the end of the First Punic War, and which protected the allies of Rome from attack, covered the Saguntines, even though they did not become allies until later (21.19.4–5: for full discussion of the latter treaty, including this provision, see 19.9n.).

The second argument had previously been made at greater length by Plb. 3.29.4–10, whom Livy is following here. However, it depended on a narrow legalistic question about the precise wording of the earlier treaty, and was thus less compelling than the simple claim that Hannibal had attacked a Roman ally whose independence had been explicitly guaranteed. But Livy's claim that Saguntum was mentioned in the treaty is directly contradicted by Plb. 2.13.7, who says that the treaty made no other provision concerning Spain (cf. 3.27.9, which once again says nothing of a clause concerning Saguntum). Instead, Polybius indicates that the Ebro treaty was violated by Hannibal's attack on Saguntum in a different way: he appears to think that Saguntum was north, rather than south, of the Ebro (esp.

---

[2] The Ebro treaty has occasionally been claimed as a pro-Roman fabrication (so e.g. Seibert (1993), 129–35); but see *contra* e.g. Hoyos (1998), 154–6.

3.30.3, also implicitly 3.21.1-2, 4.28.1;[3] though contrast 3.14.9, 3.97.6, 3.98.6-7, where Polybius' geography is correct). Polybius is followed in his error by Appian (*Hisp.* 10, *Hann.* 3).[4]

P. appears to make the same mistake as Polybius had and which Livy himself avoided: he refers to the crossing of the Ebro before mentioning the attack on Saguntum, and thus indicates that both of these were equally causes of the war. It is true that, at least taken in isolation (but see 21.2n.), his account is compatible both with Livy and with the real geography. The reference to the crossing of the Ebro comes as part of his general summary of how Livy narrated the opening of the war; the siege of Saguntum is then mentioned as a specific element. However, whether or not P. knew that Saguntum stood to the south of the Ebro, only a careful reader, and probably only one who knew Livy's text well, would appreciate that as a possible interpretation of his wording: most readers would naturally take him to mean that the crossing of the Ebro came first. P. draws on Livy, but

---

[3] Polybius' accuracy is defended by Cuff (1973) and Rich (1996), 10-12, but their arguments involve a strained and unlikely reading of Polybius' text. They claim that the reference at 3.30.3 to the attack on Saguntum as violating the Ebro treaty is an ellipse for both attacking Saguntum and crossing the Ebro, referring back to 3.6.1-2. But the immediate context of his argument is entirely about Saguntum, and it strains credulity that a reader should be expected to add in the Ebro on the basis of an argument Polybius had referred to many pages earlier. Moreover, Cuff does not discuss, and Rich has only the vaguest refutation of, those who read 3.21.1-2 as indicating that Saguntum was north of the Ebro: Rich's claim is that earlier writers had introduced the Ebro treaty into the debate over Saguntum, and Polybius 'failed to notice its relevance' (12). As to 4.28.1, Cuff's argument is circular (168: '*when taken against the background that Polybius knew where the town was*', it is merely 'a piece of loose thinking'); Rich does not mention the passage at all. It is worth observing in this context that ancient writers were in general often vague and inconsistent when it came to geography (cf. esp. Horsfall (1985)); Polybius, while on the face of things more intensely interested in geography than most others, was far from immune to these problems (see Walbank (1947), 162-8 = (2002), 36-41).

An alternative defence of Polybius is offered by Baron (2018), 205-12: he argues that Polybius at 3.30.3 is presenting only a false Roman perspective which he does not himself accept. Polybius says that *if* one took the attack on Saguntum to be the cause of the war, then the Carthaginians should be blamed for violating the treaty of Hasdrubal, but since it was *not* the cause of the war (in his view, the Roman seizure of Sardinia was), the Carthaginians should not be blamed. But this violates the entire logic of Polybius' argument: the Roman case is based (in his view) on ignoring the prior offence over Sardinia, but he says here that if one does ignore it, then the Romans are correct to see an attack on Saguntum as violating Hasdrubal's treaty—which can only be the case if Saguntum was south of the Ebro. Baron also ignores 4.28.1, and mentions 3.21.1-2 only in passing and without explaining the aspect of it that suggests Polybius has the wrong geography in mind.

On the other hand, Cuff is right (168) to note that 3.15.5, which is sometimes cited as another example of the error (e.g. by Walbank (1957), 172), does not require that reading. At this point, Hannibal has neither attacked Saguntum nor crossed the Ebro, and Polybius suggests only that the Romans were warning him against both: he does not imply that Hannibal would have to cross the Ebro to attack Saguntum.

[4] It has been argued that Polybius and Appian were correct: that the *Iber* in the treaty referred to by Polybius was not the Ebro, but a different river to the south of Saguntum (for various proposals see Carcopino (1953), Sumner (1968), 219-32, Vollmer (1990), 123-35, Barceló (1996), 52-3); but see *contra* e.g. Bringmann (2001). A slightly different version of the same idea is that of Derow (2015), 188: that while the treaty of Hasdrubal in reality referred to the Ebro, Polybius in Book 3 reflects a pro-Roman fabrication in which it referred to some fictional river south of Saguntum. This, however, strains Polybius' language beyond plausibility, and also saves him from one inconsistency at the cost of another, because he now offers incompatible versions of the same treaty.

effectively 'corrects' him, even without explicitly contradicting him, offering a reading which suggests the false geography and chronology over Livy's more accurate version. In this way he is able to give the Romans a stronger argument against Hannibal than Livy himself did.

Moreover, P. has certainly distorted Livy's chronology in a different respect: for he is explicit that the crossing of the Ebro preceded (and was a reason for) the Roman declaration of war, instead of, as in Livy, following it: see 21.2n.

A further respect in which P. appears tacitly to give space for a misreading of history here is that the most recent *foedus* between Rome and Carthage that he has mentioned was the treaty of Lutatius (19.9), and so the less-informed reader might well assume that the ban on crossing the Ebro was a provision of that treaty, rather than of a later one. This appears to be a version of history accepted elsewhere (cf. *Vir. Ill.* 41.2: see 19.9n.). P.'s language does not require this interpretation, but it would be a natural reading, especially if one was aware of the alternative tradition.

transitum: Rossbach's correction of the MSS *transitus*; the plural makes little sense in this context. An alternative would be to take *transitus* as a nominative singular and to read the verb as *narratur*, as in the *editio princeps*. That would have the advantage of removing the anomalous reference to the author (cf. above), but would require a further change of *ortum* to *ortus*; Rossbach's emendation does the least violence to the readings found in the chief MSS.

civitas socia: Some word for 'ally' is required by the context. The *editio princeps* offers *sociorum*, and this reading is accepted by Rossbach and Jal. *sociorum civitas* is used once in the surviving text of Livy, albeit not in this book (26.20.1); it also appears in Cicero (*Verr.* 2.3.79, *Leg. Man.* 38, *Balb.* 22). It is rarer later, though it is used by Justin (18.2.12, 22.3.4). But while this reading is possible, a better correction is offered by two late MSS, since *civitas socia* is a very common Livian phrase: see 23.21.5, 26.20.1, 28.42.6, 29.10.8, 32.40.9, 33.20.11, 34.22.6, 34.35.6 (*sociis populi Romani civitatibus*), 37.46.4, 39.30.7, 41.6.12, 42.26.8, 43.17.8, F 23.9. It is used elsewhere by P. (31.3, 42.5), and it is far more likely that he adopted it here also, since he often employs Livian phrasing.

octavo mense capta est: Cf. Livy 21.15.3: *octavo mense quam coeptum oppugnari captum Saguntum*. Livy, however, reports this only as the views of 'some people' (*quidam*): he then goes on to note the incompatibility of this time-frame with his narrative to date, which has assumed a much shorter siege (see Levene (2010a), 56–61). P. simply gives the 'long' chronology, which not only goes back to Polybius (3.17.9), but became the dominant version in the post-Livian tradition also: see Oros. 4.14.1, Drac., *Laud. Dei* 3.446, Zonar. 8.21.10, also Flor. 1.22.6 (nine months), and *Vir. Ill.* 42.2 (six months).

capta: Agrees with *civitas* (the noun in apposition) rather than *Saguntum* (Pinkster 1.1259–60).

21.2 *Roman embassy declares war on Carthage.* Corresponds to Livy 21.18; the declaration of war is also recorded by Plb. 3.20.6–21.8 and 3.33.1–4, Sil. 2.270–390, App., *Hisp.* 13, Flor. 1.22.7, Dio fr. 55.9–10 (cf. Zonar. 8.22.7), Eutr. 2.8.1; cf. Frontin., *Strat.* 1.11.4. Most of these, however, unlike P., focus on the moment when the Roman ambassador dramatically (if metaphorically) told the Carthaginians that war and peace were in the fold of his toga, and they could choose which to take (the exceptions are Eutropius and Frontinus, who record the bare fact of the declaration). P. is concerned with the declaration itself, but, unlike Eutropius, he emphasizes in particular that it was generated by Roman complaints which he has shown to be justifiable (21.1n.).

de quibus iniuriis: The plural clearly shows that it was both the crossing of the Ebro and the attack on Saguntum which formed the substance of the Roman ambassadors' complaints. This is a distortion of Livy, for whom the crossing of the Ebro does not take place until after the embassy (21.23.1; cf. 21.1n.). Livy does, however, have the Carthaginians make a passing reference to the Ebro in terms that imply that it might have formed part of the Roman case against them (21.18.12). Moreover, P.'s narrative appears at least at times to be supported by Polybius, who, in recounting the debate with the ambassadors in Carthage, implies that it took place in the light of the crossing (3.21.1–2, 3.30.3; see 21.1n.). Interestingly, it is also supported by certain modern scholars, who hold that the real *casus belli* was not the siege of Saguntum but the crossing of the Ebro, and that the embassy took place only after the latter (so esp. Hoffmann (1951); cf. Scullard (1952)); however, see *contra* (e.g.) Dorey (1959–60), 7–8, Astin (1967b), Eckstein (1983).

21.3 *Hannibal's march to Italy, his crossing of the Alps; battle of Ticinus.* Corresponds to Livy 21.24.1–5, 21.26.3–46.10. P. crams into a single sentence the whole of the central portion of the book, including the highly dramatic episodes of the crossing of the Alps and the battle of Ticinus. Needless to say, his account is extremely sketchy, but he touches on most of the main points in Livy. The most surprising aspect of his narrative is that he speaks of Hannibal crossing the Pyrenees, which are a very minor part of Livy (though see further below), but not of the crossing of the Rhone, which Livy makes rather more of—instead of the river itself, he speaks about the routing of the Gauls who sought to block him. Another surprise is his failure to mention the thing which for many was the most remarkable feature of Hannibal's march, namely that he was accompanied by elephants; a further feature is that he pays a great deal of attention to something which Livy mentions only in passing, namely Scipio Africanus' (alleged) rescue of his father at the Ticinus: see further below.

When we consider how these events are represented elsewhere, the balance in P. appears less extraordinary.[5] Oros. 4.14.3–6 is remarkably similar to P. in his

---

[5] Cf. Horster (2017), 41.

patterns of inclusions and exclusions. He too has the crossing of the Pyrenees, and substitutes the fighting with the Gauls for the crossing of the Rhone; he also fails to mention elephants, but includes Scipio's rescue of his father. This makes it not unlikely that either he is drawing on P. or (less probably: see Introduction) *vice versa*. However, neither Orosius nor P. can depend solely on the other, since each includes information that the other does not have—Orosius records the timing of the invasion, and the number of troops with which Hannibal crossed the Alps, the youth of Scipio; P. has the name of the tribe Hannibal fought against at the Rhone, and the fact that the Ticinus was a cavalry battle.

The other Latin summarizers are more distant from P., but still show some measure of overlap with him. Both Nep., *Hann*. 3.3–4.1 and Eutr. 3.8.2–9.1, like P., mention the Pyrenees, but ignore the Rhone. However, both refer to elephants; and Eutropius, unlike P., also does not mention the battle with the Gauls at the Rhone; he instead spends some time recounting the Romans' deployment, and also mentions the number of troops that Hannibal brought into Italy; he says nothing, on the other hand, of the fighting in the Alps, or of Scipio's rescue of his father. Nepos, too, does not mention the younger Scipio at this point, but does speak of Hannibal having to fight his way through the Alps, and with regard to the Rhone, refers to the skirmish with Scipio's troops there, but not to the actual crossing of the river.

Vir. Ill. 42.2–3 has a bare notice of the crossing of the Alps and the battle at the Ticinus. Florus' rather more heightened and poetic narrative (1.22.9–11) presents the crossing solely from the perspective of the Romans receiving Hannibal in Italy—he is metaphorically described as a thunderbolt flying through the Alps against them. He has nothing else of Hannibal's march, and has no mention of elephants, but puts all his attention on the Ticinus, where Scipio's rescue of his father has a substantial role. The Greek sources are mostly longer and more detailed, and as such less easily comparable with P.; but it is worth noting that App., *Hann*. 4–5, like P., Nepos, Orosius, and Eutropius, has Hannibal crossing the Pyrenees but does not refer to him crossing the Rhone.

In short, therefore, P. is broadly within the mainstream of post-Livian writers in his selection of episodes to bring forward, even though none apart from Orosius matches him in great detail. For a detailed explanation of his omissions and inclusions, see below. The omission of the elephants may be in part because they now could no longer be characterized as a novelty to the Romans (contrast 13.1, 19.1, and see *ad loc.*), and also in part because he is paying less attention to the more spectacular side of Hannibal's achievement; but the fact that Florus and Orosius likewise show no interest in them may suggest that they simply did not loom quite as large in the Roman image of Hannibal as they do for modern writers (though there are exceptions, such as Juv. 10.150, 158).

superato Pyrenaeo saltu: The emphasis on the Pyrenees appears odd to a reader approaching the history from the perspective of Livy (or indeed Polybius), but it is possible to make sense of it, even in terms of a text summarizing Livy. First, as noted above, P. is far from unusual in his decision to highlight this episode: the same is true of Nepos, Appian, Eutropius, and Orosius; in addition, it is worth remarking that Silius Italicus, though not ignoring the crossing of the Rhone (3.442–65), is quite unlike Livy in giving equal time to the Pyrenees (3.415–41); we may also compare Ampel. 28.4 and Aug., *Civ.* 3.19, both of whom say nothing of the Rhone, but who refer to both the Pyrenees and the Alps in summarizing Hannibal's march. Livy is the one who is anomalous in making the crossing appear unproblematic (21.23.4, 21.24.1);[6] although Polybius had done much the same (3.35.7, 3.40.1), he at least referred in the latter passage to 'the impregnability of the places' (τὰς ὀχυρότητας τῶν τόπων). The reality of the Pyrenees is that they represent a formidable obstacle to an army, even if not one on the level of the Alps:[7] it is, accordingly, not especially surprising that a sense should have crept into the tradition that crossing them was a noteworthy feat, even if (as is highly probable) most—perhaps all—of the later writers had no personal acquaintance with the mountains.

In the case of Livy, the reason he made so little of the crossing of the Pyrenees may be connected with his complex treatment of the crossing of the Alps (on which see Levene (2010a), 149–53). As part of a critique of Polybius' claims for Hannibal's supreme rationality, Livy shows Hannibal carefully planning in order to cross the Alps—only for his plans to go awry when the Alps prove far vaster than he had ever anticipated. One of the arguments that Hannibal uses with his troops, in order to reassure them that the Alps may readily be crossed, is to compare them to the Pyrenees, which they had already crossed with relative ease (21.30.5; cf. 21.30.7). It thus suits Livy's purposes that the Pyrenees should have appeared only a minor obstacle, in order to show how Hannibal may have erred in inferring that the Alps would present little more difficulty. If this is so, it is interesting to note that P.'s language here comes not from Livy's account of the crossing of the Pyrenees, but from Hannibal's reference back to the crossing in his speech to his troops (21.30.5: *Pyrenaeum saltum…superatum*). When P. uses the same phrase in the context of an abridged narrative which attaches some importance to the Pyrenees, he alludes to but also implicitly corrects Livy's dismissal of them.

ei: The necessary correction is made for the *et* of the main MSS by one late copyist. The substitution of *is* for the reflexive in a relative clause is common in historiography: see H-S 175, and cf. 18.1n.

ad Alpes venit: Cf. Livy 21.32.6 *ad Alpes pervenit*.

laborioso…transitu: A unique phrase. *laboriosus* is found in Livy only at 5.19.10 and 39.1.6; it is more characteristic of Cicero. P. uses the word also at 107.6 and

---

[6] However, contrast 23.45.3, where in retrospect Livy has Hannibal treat the two crossings as equal proofs of his troops' achievements.

[7] See the survey of possible routes by Seibert (1993), 191–3.

112.6: Briscoe (2008), 212 hypothesizes that the former is taken from Livy, but that is on balance not likely: see *ad loc.*

montanos... Gallos: The phrase appears also in the corresponding passage of Orosius (4.14.4), but nowhere else in surviving Latin. This supports the hypothesis of a close relationship between P. and Orosius in this section: see above.

quoque: sc. as well as the Volcae mentioned earlier in the sentence.

aliquot proeliis: See 12.3n.

descendit in Italiam: See Livy 21.44.3 *descendimus in Italiam*; cf. Flor. 1.22.9 *in Italiam... descendit.*

protexit filius: P. shows an intense interest in Scipio Africanus: he records every moment he appears in Livy prior to his taking up his command in Spain in Book 26 (see 22.8, 25.1), and numerous other incidents concerning him, even relatively minor ones (cf. Introduction, xliii). It is in accordance with this that he focuses on him here, even though Livy himself mentions the rescue only in passing (21.46.8), and even notes (while not endorsing) a query concerning it (21.46.10)—namely that Coelius Antipater attributed the action to a slave, not to Scipio at all. This focus on Scipio also has a further effect, as Horster (2017), 41–2 observes: the war in the *Periochae* begins not only with Roman defeats, but an immediate gesture to the ultimate Roman victory.[8]

21.4 Battle of Trebia; Hannibal in the Apennines. Corresponds to Livy 21.52–6 and 21.58. P. omits the Roman and Carthaginian manoeuvres prior to the arrival at the Trebia (21.47–8) and the Roman naval victories in Sicily (21.49–51), as well as the response to the defeat in Rome (21.57.1–4) and Hannibal's subsequent attacks on Placentia and Victumulae (21.57.5–14). Instead he has just two points: the battle of the Trebia and the crossing of the Apennines. Surprisingly, he not only subordinates the former to the latter, which is far from the emphasis in Livy, but with the Apennines, he substantially alters Livy, turning an unsuccessful crossing into a successful one (see further below).

Once again, a close analogue to P. is Oros. 4.14.7–8, suggesting some relationship between the texts (cf. 21.3n. and Introduction); Orosius, too, follows the Trebia with the crossing of the Apennines (cf. also 4.pr.8), though he includes many details that P. omits and, most importantly, does not make it clear whether the crossing was successful. However, in some respects P. is closer to Nep., *Hann.* 4.2: not only are they similarly laconic when it comes to the details, but there is some linguistic overlap at the crucial point where P. and Livy disagree, namely the success of the crossing (see below).

---

[8] Livy, too, though with more allusions over a longer set of episodes, repeatedly foreshadows the ultimate Roman victory in Book 21: see Levene (2010a), 14–15.

Most other Latin sources are further from P.: neither Flor. 1.22.12 nor Eutr. 3.9.1 mentions the crossing of the Apennines at all, nor does any Greek source. The one other source which speaks of Hannibal crossing the Apennines after the Trebia is Sil. 4.739–48, who, like P., indicates that he was successful. It is possible that P. derived his account here from Silius, but it is more probable that both took it from Nepos or some other non-Livian source. It is also worth observing that, as I show below, Livy's account is historically problematic in ways that one would not necessarily require an alternative source to discern: P. and Silius both may be seeking to make a correction.

Apenninum quoque…transiit: Livy gives an account of an unsuccessful attempt by Hannibal to cross the Apennines in Book 21 (21.58). In Book 22, he then gives what is often described as a successful crossing of the Apennines (22.2). However, that passage does not actually mention mountains, but rather represents Hannibal as crossing into Etruria through the Arno marshes (the same is true of his source, Plb. 3.78.6–79.12). An examination of the real geography of Italy shows that the Carthaginians could not have reached the Arno marshes without first passing over the Apennines. But a plain reading of Livy without prior knowledge of the geography—and neither Livy himself nor his readers can be assumed to have known the geography—suggests a different picture: Hannibal attempted but failed to cross the Apennines in Book 21, so took a different route—one marshy, but non-mountainous—into Etruria a few weeks later (cf. Levene (2010a), 346–7).

An ancient reader of Livy who did happen to know the geography thus had a problem: should he assume that Livy has omitted a crossing from Book 22, or that he was in error when he described the Book 21 crossing as unsuccessful? Modern historians usually (and rightly) assume the former (especially given that Polybius does not mention a failed crossing): they assume that the crossing of the Apennines took place immediately prior to the crossing of the marshes in Book 22, and that the failed crossing in Book 21 was a mere invention. But it is easy to see that a Roman might well have concluded otherwise, and that P., like Silius, could be seeking to correct Livy by having Hannibal succeed in crossing the Apennines in Book 21.

If P. was drawing on an alternative source, one possibility is Nep., *Hann.* 4.2, who employs similar phrasing (*inde per Ligures Appenninum transiit*: cf. 22.2n.). However, it is worth noting that Livy 21.58.3 himself begins his account of the failed crossing with the words *transeuntem Appenninum*: P. alludes back to Livy's version while at the same time marking the difference by changing the form of the verb to the perfect. Certainly his use of *quoque* points to P.'s change being more than careless phrasing: it draws explicit attention to the fact that this is the third successful mountain crossing in the book.

permagna vexatione: Jahn's emendation of the less idiomatic *per magnam vexationem* of the MSS. *permagnus* is used only once in the surviving text of Livy (32.34.4), but is extremely common in Cicero. It is rarer later, even though it never completely disappears: for P. it presumably had general overtones of late Republican Latin. *permagna vexatio*, however, is found nowhere but here.

21.5 *Gnaeus Scipio in Spain.* Corresponds to Livy 21.60–1. Cn. Scipio's initial campaigns, and his capture of the Carthaginian commander, are also recorded in Plb. 3.76, Zonar. 8.25.1, and Oros. 4.14.9 (App., *Hisp.* 15, by contrast, suggests that Scipio did nothing of note at this time). However, both Polybius and Livy, and to some extent Zonaras also, suggest that the Roman victory was not total. Polybius and Livy refer to a successful counterattack by Hasdrubal against the Roman sailors when they were off guard; Livy and Zonaras both mention also Hasdrubal's attack on Spaniards who had supported Scipio. P. omits those, turning the episode into a report of unequivocal Roman success.[9]

prospere pugnavit: Cf. 2.6n.

Magone: According to Livy 21.60.5–7, as well as Plb. 3.76.5 and Zonar. 8.25.1, the general captured by Scipio was not named Mago, but Hanno; P.'s version is found also in Oros. 4.14.9, who may be deriving his information from him (cf. 21.3n.). The error may arise from a careless confusion of common Carthaginian names attached to relatively unmemorable figures (cf. Levene (2010a), 63, 67), or more specifically from the conflation of the commander captured here with the Mago captured more famously but in not dissimilar circumstances by Scipio Africanus at New Carthage (Livy 26.46.8–9). In either case the error did not necessarily originate with him; he may have derived it from an earlier source, now lost, which may have appeared to him to represent a superior tradition.

---

[9] Cf. Horster (2017), 42, suggesting that this points at the ultimate Roman victory at the hands of another Scipio.

Book 22

22.1 *Hannibal in the Arno Marshes.* Corresponds to Livy 22.2; P. omits the material at the very opening of the book, namely (i) the devices Hannibal used to protect himself from the Gauls (22.1.1–4), and (ii) the opening of the new year in Rome, with a lengthy account of a set of prodigies and their expiation (22.1.4–20). His primary interest here is in Hannibal's feat of endurance, illustrated above all by the length of time it took him to cross the marshes without taking rest, and, secondarily by the loss of his eye. Other aspects of the hardship that Livy recounts (largely following Plb. 3.78.6–79.12) are ignored; notably, P.'s focus is entirely on Hannibal himself, and he does not mention the losses and sufferings endured by the rest of his army. This exclusive focus on Hannibal is a long way from either Livy or Polybius; indeed, even among the more abridged sources P. is unusual in describing the crossing of the marshes without mentioning the Carthaginian army—contrast Oros. 4.15.2–3 and Zonar. 8.25.2.

The one author who is similarly focused on Hannibal is Nep., *Hann.* 4.2–3, although he does not mention the crossing of the marshes *per se*, conflating it with the crossing of the Apennines (21.4n.), and having Hannibal lose his eye there. It is unsurprising that Nepos, writing a biography, would focus on Hannibal to the exclusion of his soldiers; it is more noteworthy in P., but it fits a wider pattern in his account of the Second Punic War: that he subordinates the experience of the Carthaginian army to Hannibal to the point that one often loses sight of the former altogether.

per continuas vigilias: The phrase, though readily comprehensible, appears nowhere else in extant Latin. *per vigilias* is found in Sallust, but with an entirely different meaning (*Jug.* 99.1: cf. Koestermann (1971), 351). *continua vigilia* is used twice by Celsus in the singular (4.14.1, 7.26.5); in the plural it is found only in writings of the early fifth century AD: Rufin., *Orig. in Rom.* 7.15.2, Aug., *Civ.* 22.23, Macr., *Sat.* 7.3.19. The closest analogy to the entire phrase comes in the Vulgate (Psalms 62:7: *per singulas vigilias*); P. reflects the literary language of his own day.

per quas paludes ... iter fecit: Cf. Livy 22.2.2: *propiorem viam per paludes petit.* There is a certain redundancy to P.'s writing here, since the material in the relative clause adds little to the main clause; but the closeness of the language of the clause to Livy's own phrasing makes it unlikely that this can be a copyist's gloss; P. does occasionally, despite his general brevity, become more expansive.

quadriduo et tribus noctibus: Cf. Livy 22.2.7: *per quadriduum ... et tres noctes.*

22.2 *Battle of Lake Trasimene.* Corresponds to Livy 22.3.1–7.5. P. has little detail about the battle, focusing on two basic elements: namely the death of Flaminius and the fact that the defeat arose because Hannibal set a trap. However, he sandwiches this simple narrative between two points about which he has a little more to say, first, that Flaminius ignored omens prior to the battle, and second, that Hannibal revoked the agreement made with a group of troops who surrendered to the Carthaginians.

The stress on Flaminius' ignoring of omens prior to the battle, and indeed highlighting that over the events of the battle, had not been uncommon within the earlier Latin tradition. Indeed, Livy's own account to some extent gives warrant to that reading of the battle, partly because he structures the period prior to it around an escalating series of prodigies and omens to which Flaminius fails to respond appropriately (Levene (1993), 38–43), but also partly because he has Fabius explicitly draw the moral that this, rather than his failings as a commander, was the primary reason for Flaminius' defeat (22.9.7). The omens neglected by Flaminius are likewise emphasized by Cic., *Div.* 1.77 (cf. 2.21, 2.67, 2.71, *Nat. Deor.* 2.8),[10] Ov., *Fast.* 6.765–8, Val. Max. 1.6.6 (also the epitomes by Paris and Nepotianus), Sil. 5.59–129, Plu., *Fab.* 2.3 and 3.1, Flor. 1.22.14, Min. Fel. 7.4, 26.2, Serv. auct., *Aen.* 11.19. However, they are generally ignored by the Latin historians of later antiquity and almost all Greek sources (there is nothing of it in Plb. 3.81.1–85.6, App., *Hann.* 9–10, Eutr. 3.9.2, *Vir. Ill.* 42.3, Oros. 4.15.4–6, Zonar. 8.25.5).[11] P's distillation of Livy in this respect maintains a stream of tradition which appears to have been less important to his contemporaries' understanding of the history. Even in the earlier Latin authors, however, the actual content of the omens varied significantly from author to author:[12] there was more agreement on the fact of Flaminius' impiety than on the specifics of what he failed to respond to.

One element of the battle present in Livy but omitted by P. highlights this point. According to Livy 22.5.8, there was an earthquake during it. This could naturally have been treated as another omen, and that is the way it appears in Cic., *Div.* 1.78 (presumably reflecting the way Coelius handled it: *FRHist* 15 F 14b) and Flor. 1.22.14; but most of the authors who report it do not explicitly treat it in that way (Plin., *Nat.* 2.200, Sil. 5.611–26, Plu., *Fab.* 3.2, Zonar. 8.25.7, Oros. 4.15.6); Livy, like several of these, is more interested in the curious fact that the fighting was so intense that the earthquake went unnoticed. Since the earthquake is unrelated to the theme of omens ignored, P. omits it.

As for the agreement with the surrendering Romans, this appears regularly in the Greek tradition: see Plb. 3.84.14–85.4, App., *Hann.* 10, Zonar. 8.25.8. It is

---

[10] Cicero cites Coelius Antipater, *FRHist* 15 F 14b = fr. 20P, who is presumably Livy's source also, although it is naturally impossible to be sure precisely what balance Coelius drew between the omens and the conduct of the battle itself.

[11] The prodigies in Dio fr. 57.7 are generally assumed to be from the time of Flaminius, but that is far from certain, and even if they are, no explicit connection is made with his impiety or his defeat. Cf. Oros. 4.15.1, who mentions prodigies only prior to Flaminius' election.

[12] Several authors mention omens which are absent from Livy and P.: the sacred chickens refusing to eat (Coelius Antipater *FRHist* 15 F 14b = Cic., *Div.* 1.77, Sil. 5.59–62, Min. Fel. 26.2), an omen of birds (Ov., *Fast.* 6.765–6: possibly another reference to the chicken omen), fire burning the lake (Sil. 5.70–4; cf. Plin., *Nat.* 2.241), bees settling on the standards (Flor. 1.22).

ignored by Latin writers, apart from Livy and P. Those who report it vary in their evaluation of Hannibal's actions. For Polybius, the agreement was to spare the lives of those who surrendered, and so Hannibal, while insisting that his lieutenant made the agreement without his authority, nevertheless abides by it. In the later writers, however, the agreement was to release them, and so Hannibal's refusal to release the Romans (even while releasing the Italians), was in violation of that. Yet even on that premise, the violation could be handled in different ways. Appian, like Polybius, has Hannibal stressing that the agreement was made without his authority, an excuse which at least carries enough plausibility to explain why his refusal to act on it might be reasonable. In Livy, as in Zonaras, no excuse is given, and it is merely treated as a perfidious action; and this version, which casts Hannibal in the worst light, is explicitly followed by P. also.

C. Flaminius cos.: See 20.11n. for P.'s original introduction of him.

temerarius: The rashness of Flaminius was a standard part of the tradition of the defeat of Trasimene: see e.g. Plb. 3.80.3–4, App., *Hann.* 10, Flor. 1.22.14 *temerario duci*. Livy attributes *temeritas* to him at 22.3.4; cf. 22.44.5. See also 22.9.7, where Fabius denies that the defeat was the result of Flaminius' *temeritas* or *inscitia*, but rather to his religious neglect; but, as P.'s language implies, Fabius is making a misleading division, since it was at least in part his *temeritas* that led him to ignore the divine signs he received.

contra auspicia profectus: See 19.2n. When Flaminius in Livy left Rome he did not strictly speaking do so *contra auspicia*; rather he failed to take any *auspicia* at all (21.63.5–9, 22.1.6–7). However, that is not the primary referent in P.: the participial phrase here is followed by two further participial phrases joined by *et*, the first in the ablative absolute, which appear to qualify the earlier phrase, explaining that the *auspicia* in question were the omens of the standards and of Flaminius' fall. Hence *profectus* is being used of his march to the battlefield from Arretium, where he had joined his army, not the initial departure from Rome.

signis militaribus effossis, quae tolli non poterant: P.'s account differs in certain respects from Livy. Most obviously, he reverses the order of the omens, so that the immovable standards appear prior to Flaminius' fall from his horse: the sequence in P. does not culminate in something that should prevent the entire army from moving, as in Livy, but rather in an omen that focuses on the commander alone. This may simply be an idiosyncratic alteration, but it is worth noting that in Livy 22.3.11–13 Flaminius gives the order to pull up the standards before falling from his horse, although it is not until afterwards that he discovers that the standard-bearers were unable to do so. P.'s sequence, though not identical to Livy's, appears to derive from the way the events were represented in his text.

Second, the idea that the standards were dug up is not explicit in Livy: it is Flaminius who sarcastically orders the standard-bearers to do so (22.3.13: *effodiant signum*), but it is never made clear that this is the expedient that was ultimately adopted. P. flattens the pointed sacrilege of Flaminius' words in Livy into a crassly literal statement.

ab equo quem conscenderat per caput devolutus: *ab equo...devolutus* is unparalleled in surviving Latin. *per caput* = 'head-first', an all but unique meaning of the phrase; the only parallel is Catull. 17.9 *per caputque pedesque* (Livy 22.3.11 has *super caput*). *equum conscendere* is found once in Livy (42.7.6); it became relatively common in early imperial Latin, but is rare after the second century AD. P. combines choice and poetic phrasing to create language with an archaic flavour.

insidiis ab Hannibale circumventus ad Thrasymennum lacum cum exercitu caesus est: P.'s language does not derive from Livy, but is adapted from Nep., *Hann.* 4.3: *C. Flaminium consulem apud Trasumenum cum exercitu insidiis circumventum occidit*; cf. 21.4n. for another instance of P. following Nepos rather than Livy. *cum exercitu caesus est*, used first by P. here, is a phrase that he subsequently comes especially to favour: see 23.6n.

Thrasymennum: Modern editions of Livy typically spell the name *Trasumennus*, but it is not at all clear that this was in fact how Livy spelled it: the orthography in the archetype varies hugely (see the list in Briscoe (2016), 378–9), and the spelling here is indeed one of those attested. Whether or not it was the spelling in Livy, it may be that this was the form in the MS that P. used; it is also possible that it was a deliberate choice on P.'s part. Sil. 5.7–23 tells an aetiological story which relates it to the Greek θρασύς (see esp. Cowan (2009)); it may be awareness of that etymology that led P. to prefer that form of the name as the site of the defeat of Flaminius, whom he pointedly described as *temerarius* (above: so also Flor. 1.22.14).

sex milia quae eruperant: Cf. Livy 22.6.8: *sex milia...eruptione impigre facta*.

fide ab Atherbale data: Cf. Livy 22.6.11: *fidem dante Maharbale*. Some later MSS record the name in P. as Maharbal, but those are presumably secondary corrections based on Livy's text. It may be that, once again (cf. 21.5n.), P. confuses familiar Carthaginian names; but Wölfflin (1900b) notes that some of the major MSS of Flor. 1.22.19 call the same Maharbal 'Adherbal', shortly afterwards. This could be coincidence, but Wölfflin hypothesizes that the original error was in the 'lost epitome' on which both Florus and P. drew (see the Introduction); it does, at any rate, appear to suggest that 'Maharbal' may have become 'Adherbal' more broadly in the historical tradition. The only Atherbal/Adherbal recorded in the Second Punic War is a minor commander in Livy 28.30.4–12, but a far more famous figure was the grandson of Masinissa who was Jugurtha's rival for the Numidian throne (cf. 62.2n.), and the fame of Sallust's *Jugurtha*, and the consequent familiarity of the names in it, may be the original source of the error.

22.3 Response at Rome to the defeat at Trasimene. Corresponds to Livy 22.7.6–8.7, 9.7–10.10. Out of Livy's account of the trauma at Rome and the measures taken in response to the defeat, P. selects just two: the Sacred Spring, which is the single aspect to which Livy pays the most attention, and the anecdote of the mothers who perished from joy at their sons' survival; neither of these appears in other versions, apart from Val. Max. 9.12.2, who recounts the story of the mothers (Gell. 3.15.4 tells the same story, but attaches it to Cannae rather than Trasimene); there is also a brief mention of the *ver sacrum* in Plu., *Fab.* 4.4. P. omits other aspects of Livy; notably, he has nothing of the defeat of Centenius (22.8.1), nor Hannibal's subsequent movements (22.9.1–6), while the selection of Fabius Maximus as dictator, which in Livy is recorded prior to the vowing of the *ver sacrum*, is reserved by P. for the next point in his narrative.

cum: Cf. 2.2n.

ad nuntium cladis Romae: Cf. Livy 22.7.6 *Romae ad primum nuntium cladis*.

ex insperato: A common Livian phrase (cf. Oakley (2005a), 112); it is occasionally found elsewhere in early imperial Latin, but then falls into desuetude until the fourth century. P., as often, employs Livian language even when it is not specifically the language of the passage he is abridging.

mortuae sunt: After this phrase, N adds *quod subito et nimio quis gaudio moriatur*: manifestly a gloss.

22.4 *Dictatorship of Fabius Maximus; conflict with M. Minucius.* The dictatorship of Fabius in Livy runs from 22.8.6 to 22.31.11; and P.'s narrative here covers that broad period. In it he describes in some detail the main narrative line of the dictatorship, namely the new tactics adopted by Fabius and his consequent rivalry and ultimate reconciliation with Minucius. However, he reserves three episodes for separate treatment, the second and third of which accordingly appear out of chronological order: namely the aftermath of the battle of Trasimene at Rome (22.3n.), the stratagem by which Hannibal evaded Fabius (Livy 22.15.1–18.4: see 22.5n.), and Hannibal's attempt to compromise Fabius by sparing his farm from destruction (22.23.4–8: see 22.6n.). Leaving these aside reduces the dictatorship to a simple narrative arc (cf. Bingham 229–30): Fabius' tactics, Minucius' opposition to them, and Fabius' vindication. The complication when Fabius is outmanoeuvred by Hannibal is separated from this, while Minucius' own (apparent) vindication when he claims a victory against Hannibal is ignored completely, even though it is that, and not (as P. implies) merely Minucius' slanders, which prompts the Romans to give him equal command (Livy 22.24.1–25.11). The intervening section on the war in Spain (22.19–22) is likewise passed over (though see 22.11n.). As so often, the difficult morals of Livy are turned by P. into simple stories of black and white.

Of other sources, Plb. 3.87.6–94.7 and 3.100–5 mirrors Livy's narrative quite closely (no doubt because Livy used him directly; but cf. 22.3n., 22.6n. for exceptions), apart from the final submission of Minucius to Fabius, of which he has nothing. Sil. 6.590–7.750, himself dependent on Livy (though with the expected poetic elaborations), is also close, as is Plu., *Fab.* 3.4–13.5 and Zonar. 8.25.12–26.11 (cf. Dio fr. 57.8–9, 15–17, 19–20). The briefer account of App., *Hann.* 12–15 is closer to P. in the pattern of inclusions and omissions, though adding in the 'victory' of Minucius as part of the explanation for his promotion to equality with Fabius; interestingly, he too reserves the story of Hannibal's stratagem for later (cf. 22.5n.).

Other summarizing historians in the Latin tradition largely reduce the entire episode to a laudatory description of the Fabian strategy (so esp. Flor. 1.22.27–8, Eutr. 3.9.3; cf. Ampel. 18.6, 46.6). Oros. 4.15.7 is less effusive, treating it as a brief interlude between Hannibal's victories; *Vir. Ill.* 43.2–4 (cf. 14.5) adds a comment about Fabius' willingness to assist Minucius even after he had his authority reduced in favour of the latter. Fabius' strategy of delay is the central point of the story in most other sources also, while the conflict with Minucius is more often sidelined (but see Val. Max. 5.2.4, Frontin., *Strat.* 2.5.22).[13] The famous line of Ennius (*Ann.* 363 Sk.), which Livy will later cite himself in his obituary of Fabius (30.26.9), perhaps contributed to that,[14] but it is also referred to by (e.g.) Val. Max. 3.8.2, Frontin., *Strat.* 1.3.3, Polyaen. 8.14, Claud., *Bell. Goth.* 138–9. Most of these indicate it to be a major component of Hannibal's ultimate defeat: the phrase *fregit Hannibalem* ('broke Hannibal') cycles through several authors (Ampelius, *Vir. Ill.*, Eutropius). P., in line with Livy's nuanced picture of the different factors that led to the ultimate Roman victory, is more measured.

cum...impediret: Cf. 2.2n. The sentence is more elaborate than usual; the 'background' information in the *cum* clause is set out in two distinct parts, separated by an explanatory final clause.

deinde: P. usually leaves chronology implicit in his sequencing; but in this book it is given more explicit emphasis, providing a clearer sense of narrative development. Fabius' dictatorship succeeds the defeat at Trasimene and in turn (cf. 22.7n.) is followed by the defeat at Cannae.

dictator adversus Hannibalem missus: P.'s phrasing comes from Livy 22.31.8 *omnium prope annales Fabium dictatorem adversus Hannibalem rem gessisse tradunt*. The oddity is that this is a passage (22.31.8–11) where Livy is challenging (on dubious grounds: see Mommsen, *StR*³ 2.147) the generally accepted view—which his earlier narrative apparently endorsed—that Fabius fought Hannibal as dictator, arguing instead that he was only acting dictator (*pro dictatore*). P., as he does on other occasions (see e.g. 4.6n.), overtly endorses the commonly accepted version of the story, while tacitly indicating awareness of the problem for the small minority of readers who know Livy's original.

---

[13] More distinctive is Nep., *Hann.* 5.1–3, presenting the story from Hannibal's viewpoint, who does not mention Fabius' strategy of delay; instead he focuses on Hannibal's successes—his stratagem to escape Fabius, and his defeat of Minucius.

[14] No line of archaic Latin poetry was more widely cited: see the list in Skutsch (1985), 529–30.

contra...hostem adversis proeliis ⟨territos⟩ milites pugnae committeret: The reading of the chief MSS is *contra...hostem adversus proeliis milites pugnare committeret*, which is impossible. Rossbach deletes *contra*, arguing that it was an addition by a scribe who did not understand that *adversus* was postponed after the noun it governed. But as Bingham 289 rightly observes, P. never elsewhere postpones *adversus* in this fashion, although he is fond of the word; it is preferable to retain *contra* and correct *adversus* to *adversis*, as in the *editio princeps*.

However, even with this correction, the MS reading is problematic. First, *adversis proeliis* in the transmitted sentence would have to mean not, as it usually does, 'lost battles', but 'battles which would probably turn out to be unfavourable', which is extremely awkward. Possibly the phrase should be excised as a gloss, but on balance it is preferable to assume that a word which governed it has dropped out of the MS tradition. Following Madvig (but in a different point in the phrase), I have offered *territos* merely *exempli gratia* (another possibility would be e.g. *fractos*), but it receives some slight measure of support from the Aldine edition, which adds *territum* at this point, though it is unclear what (if any) MS authority it had for the addition.

Second, the infinitive after *committere* is unparalleled. It might be related to the use of infinitives after verbs of giving, a construction that became increasingly common in post-classical prose (K-S 1.681), but it is far more likely that P. wrote *pugnae*, as in the *editio princeps*, since *pugnae committere* is found in Livy (3.4.7, 5.32.4), and P. often employs Livian phrasing (for *contra* dependent on *pugna* cf. *TLL* X.2 2547.1–2).

ferocem tot victoriis: *ferox victoriā* is a Livian phrase (1.25.11, 25.39.9, 27.2.2, 29.9.5, possibly 39.31.2),[15] albeit not one he uses in Book 22; it is rarely used outside Livy—P., as often, summarizes Livy in Livian phrasing taken from elsewhere in the work. The only place Livy applies the phrase to Hannibal is 27.2.2, where it refers to Marcellus' first victory over him after Cannae. Fabius and Marcellus were regularly treated, in Livy and elsewhere, as complementary but contrasting figures (Levene (2010a), 198): it is possibly significant that P. applies a phrase which Livy connects with Marcellus' willingness to fight Hannibal to Fabius' unwillingness to do the same.

opponendo se tantum: A clumsy phrase. *opponere* can mean 'blockade' (*TLL* IX.2 766.73–767.12), but in the context of military deployment *opponendo se* would naturally be taken to mean 'arraying himself against' the enemy, with no implication of the avoidance of conflict (cf. *TLL* IX.2 769.70–770.11). Hence P., in order to make sense of Fabius' strategy while using this word, is compelled to add *tantum* (= 'only'), restricting the scope of the verb to its narrowest sense.

---

[15] The MSS of 39.31.2 vary between *ferocibus* and *inflatis*; the latter is usually printed, but either could be correct (Briscoe (2008), 326).

ferox et temerarius: Both of these qualities are repeatedly ascribed to Minucius by Livy: *ferocitas* at 22.12.11, 22.14.15, 22.15.5 (cf. 22.24.3, 22.28.9), *temeritas* at 22.23.3, 22.27.8, 22.28.2, 22.29.1. In addition, *temerarius* links Minucius to Flaminius, of whom the same word was used shortly before (22.2n.):[16] outside this book, P. only uses the adjective on one other occasion (73.6). The linkage reflects one implicit in Livy: both men are part of a sequence of 'rash commanders' in the opening years of the war.[17]

tamquam: 'on the grounds of being' (*OLD s.v. tamquam* 7b).

segnem et timidum: Both words are used of Fabius by Minucius (22.12.12; cf. 22.44.5). Livy uses them to reflect on the way Minucius distorts Fabius' virtues into closely related vices; that complexity is, unsurprisingly, removed by P.

populi iussu aequaretur ei cum dictatore imperium: Livy does not employ this precise phrasing, but the different components come from his narrative: see e.g. 22.25.10 *aequando magistri equitum et dictatoris iure*; 22.26.7 *de aequato imperio*; 22.27.3 *dictatorem magistro equitum...iussu populi aequatum*.

castra cum eo iunxit: Cf. Livy 22.29.10 *castra cum Fabio iungamus*.

patrem eum salutavit: Cf. Livy 22.30.2 *patrem Fabium appellasset*.

idemque facere milites iussit: This is a distortion of Livy, for whom Minucius does not order his troops to hail Fabius as their parent, but rather to hail Fabius' troops as their patrons (22.29.11; cf. 22.30.2). This may simply be the consequence of P.'s compression, but Valerius Maximus 5.2.4 has the troops hailing Fabius alone as *patronus*, while in Sil. 7.735 Minucius and his troops alike call Fabius *parens*: P.'s version reflects a broader development of the tradition: see also 27.3n.

22.5 Hannibal's tricking of Fabius. Corresponds to Livy 22.15.1–18.4. P. includes the basic elements of Livy's narrative: Hannibal ravaging land, then being shut in by Fabius, but escaping by the device of binding straw to the horns of oxen and setting them on fire, and thus dislodging one of the garrisons blocking him. The same story appears in other writers who are narrating these events relatively fully: Plb. 3.92.8–94.7, Sil. 7.282–376, Plu., *Fab.* 6.2–7.1 (cf. *Comp. Per. Fab.* 2.2), App., *Hann.* 14–15, Zonar. 8.26.1–2; it is also highlighted by Nep., *Hann.* 5.2, who focuses his account on Hannibal's successes against Fabius and Minucius rather than the reverse. In addition, it appears as a brief self-standing anecdote in Frontin., *Strat.* 1.5.28 and Quint., *Inst.* 2.17.19. It is not, however, mentioned by any of the other post-Livian Latin historians; their abridged narratives are more Romanocentric even than P.'s, and have no interest in a temporary success by Hannibal, however spectacular.

---

[16] Horster (2017), 44.
[17] On the 'rash commander'/'cautious commander' antithesis in Livy's Third Decade see Catin (1944), 42–53, Will (1983), Bernard (2000), 211, 261–4, Levene (2010a), 165, 170–2, 186–208.

Unlike others who narrate the stratagem, P. does not specify why the sight frightened the Roman soldiers. This may be because he assumes prior knowledge of the story, but that would be an uncharacteristic narrative strategy on his part; it is more likely that it simply appears sufficiently obvious to him that such a sight would cause fear and/or confusion among those who observed it.

P. narrates the episode after concluding the Fabius–Minucius conflict; this is part of a process of simplifying the narrative arc, but the same order appears in Appian, whose narrative choices in this part of the war are relatively close to P.'s in other respects also (22.4n.). While it is highly unlikely that P. is using Appian directly, the similarity between them may indicate that his ordering reflects a version of the story current elsewhere. This is supported by the fact that Nep., *Hann.* 5.1–2 displaces it further still, stating that it took place after Cannae and was part of the Romans' attempt to prevent Hannibal from marching on the city after his victory. Along similar lines, *Vir. Ill.* 43.4, while not mentioning the stratagem, refers to Fabius trapping Hannibal in Falernia between his rescue of Minucius and his rewarding of certain soldiers whose loyalty appeared to be wavering, something which Plu., *Fab.* 20 records after Cannae.[18] *Vir. Ill.* is thus compatible with either the version in Nepos or that in Appian, but not the order of events in Livy. Flor. 1.22.28, likewise, does not mention the stratagem, but implies that Fabius' campaign in Falernia took place after Cannae; similarly Ampel. 46.6 suggests that Fabius' successful adoption of a strategy of delay began after Cannae.

Earlier discussions of this issue are vitiated by their excessively rigid accounts of how ancient historical writers employed sources, either trying to find a single post-Livian source which might have been used by P., Appian, and *Vir. Ill.* alike, or attributing the similarities between them to mere coincidence (see the discussion in Bingham 228–30). Neither seems plausible, especially in the light of Nepos, whose evidence is usually ignored in this context, but who demonstrates that even before Livy the timing of this part of the campaign was not firmly fixed. It is far better to see P., here as elsewhere, working within a fluid tradition, whereby he shaped and adapted Livy in the light of other historical narratives familiar to him. See further the Introduction.

vastata Campania: In Livy it is not Campania which Hannibal ravages, but Falernia (22.13.9, 22.14.2–4); he carefully distinguishes the two regions as being on opposite sides of the river Volturnus (22.15.3–4). However, other writers regard the Falernian plain as part of Campania (e.g. Str. 5.4.3, Plin., *Nat.* 3.60–1); hence P.'s phrasing, though a slight misrepresentation of Livy's version of the geography, is not unreasonable. Zonar. 8.25.13 similarly refers to Campania as the area ravaged by the Carthaginians.

---

[18] Cf. *Vir. Ill.* 42.6, which appears to date the whole of Fabius' challenge to Hannibal after the latter's march on Rome, which in turn was after Cannae (cf. 26.1n.).

a Fabio clusus sarmentis ad cornua boum alligatis et incensis: The language here may ultimately derive from Livy 22.16.7–8: *aridi sarmenti praeligantur cornibus boum…Hasdrubalique negotium datum ut nocte id armentum accensis cornibus ad montis ageret*; but the phrase in its entirety is far closer to Quint., *Inst.* 2.17.19: *inclusus a Fabio, sarmentis circa cornua boum deligatis incensisque*. P., as often, filters his abridgement of Livy through another post-Livian writer who had described the event equally succinctly.

22.6 *Hannibal's attempt to discredit Fabius*. Corresponds to Livy 22.23.4. In Livy, however, Hannibal's trick to discredit Fabius by sparing his land is only one part of a double problem that Fabius has at this point—the other is that the Senate refused to ratify the payment of money Fabius promised the Carthaginians as part of an exchange of captives. Fabius solves both problems at a stroke by selling off the land Hannibal had spared and using the money to pay the debt (22.23.5–8). Of this neatly constructed episode, P. tells only the first part, which focuses on Hannibal's deceit rather than Fabius' problems with the Senate or the solution he finds for both of these: it forms a pair with Hannibal's stratagem to escape Fabius earlier (22.5n.). Moreover, as noted above (22.4n.), he tells the story out of chronological sequence, separating Hannibal's successes from the main narrative arc of Fabius' dictatorship.

Relatively few other sources refer to the episode: it is not, for example, in Polybius, Nepos, or Appian; nor does it appear in any of the Latin historians of later antiquity. Plu., *Fab.* 7.2–5 reports the sequence in much the same terms as Livy did, as does Dio fr. 57.15–16, with the important difference that in Dio the selflessness of Fabius' actions is recognized, and leads to the people deciding not to depose him outright, but to instead make Minucius his equal; in Livy, by contrast, the entire episode is part of showing the increase in resentment against him. Zonar. 8.26.8 is in this respect closer to Livy; and also, like P., focuses on the sparing of the fields. The only other writer to treat the episode is Val. Max. 4.8.1 (also Paris' summary: cf. 3.8.2), but he makes the opposite selection to P., describing the debate over the ransoming of the hostages, along with Fabius' payment of the debt with his own farm, but does not mention that Hannibal spared the farm in the first place.

circumposita: 'The surrounding area': a unique use of the neuter plural of *circumpono* as a substantive (*TLL* III 1157.83–1158.1).

agro pepercit: The phrase is Livian, though not used in this passage (see 32.15.5); it is otherwise found only in Tert., *Adv. Marc.* 2.17 in an entirely different sense.

22.7 *Battle of Cannae*. Corresponds to Livy 22.35.1–52.6. The surprising thing about P.'s treatment of Cannae is that not only does he not give any sense of the factors in the battle which led to defeat or victory (something far from unusual in his notices of battles), he does not even hint at the aspect which for Livy, as for many other writers, is central, namely the conflict between the two consuls over the appropriate strategy and the consequent responsibility of Varro for the defeat, when he rashly engages in battle over his colleague's opposition. Instead, P.'s only interest is in the magnitude of the defeat: he carefully records not only the total Roman losses (along with the death of Paulus), but also the number of distinguished Romans who perished.

This may be connected with the fact that there was a surprisingly broad tradition, going at least back to the early Empire, of exculpating Varro for his role in the defeat (see e.g. Manil. 4.37-8; also esp. Frontin., *Strat.* 4.5.6, Flor. 1.22.17, Lact., *Inst.* 2.17.6, Schol. ad Juv. 11.201; cf. Levene (2015b), 321-2). It is true that P.'s omission of any criticism of Varro would not of itself carry a direct implication that he is aligning himself with that tradition, as opposed to the criticism disappearing in consequence of the extreme abridgement of P.'s narrative. However, with the reappearance of Varro at the end of the book, there is a stronger hint that P.'s removal of blame for him over Cannae is deliberate: see 22.12n. Criticism of Varro is likewise softened, if not entirely removed, by Eutr. 3.10 and Oros. 4.16.1.

Aemilio...Paulo et Terentio Varrone coss.: For the forms of the names used see 4.4n.

deinde: As earlier (22.4n.), P. gives a clear sense of the sequence of the narrative in this book: Cannae follows the interlude of Fabius' dictatorship.

Romanorum XLV milia cum Paulo cos.: Livy 22.49.15 gives slightly different figures: 45,500 infantry and 2,700 cavalry fell on the Roman side, and he appears to suggest (though the text is corrupt: see Briscoe *ad loc.*) that around half of those were allies rather than citizens. P.'s total figure is very close to that given by Eutr. 3.10.4 and Oros. 4.16.2-3, both of whom (in almost identical wording) give the numbers as 40,000 infantry and 3,500 cavalry; Orosius rounds it up into a total loss of 44,000. Certainly there were various estimates of the Roman losses at Cannae, and Livy's numbers, though very possibly the most reliable (Lazenby (1978), 84-5), did not dominate the tradition. Plu., *Fab.* 16.8 and App., *Hann.* 25 both give a round number of 50,000 dead, which is much the same as Livy; but Quint., *Inst.* 8.6.26 and Flor. 1.22.15 have it as 60,000 (Plb. 3.117.4 had 70,000, which is less probable, not least because they do not fit Polybius' other indications of the numbers in the field: see Lazenby (1978), 84; also Walbank (1957), 439-40 for a broader discussion).

It is thus possible that P. substituted for Livy's numbers those he was familiar with from elsewhere; however, since his figures for the losses among officeholders (below) are closer to Livy's (without being identical) than to those of Eutropius and Orosius, the balance of likelihood is weighted towards his having derived the figures for total troop losses from Livy, rather than from the alternative tradition that those other writers used. Unless (as is not impossible) P.'s text of Livy had a different number in it from those in the surviving archetype, he presumably reached 45,000 by dint of ignoring the cavalry and rounding down the infantry numbers (cf. Bingham 233).

P. also varies from Livy in treating all of the losses as Romans; this is true of most other post-Livian writers also, who either directly describe to the dead troops as Roman (Plutarch, Orosius), or at most do not refer explicitly to the fact that allied troops died as well (Florus, Eutropius). The distinction between Romans and their Italian allies was far less meaningful in P.'s time than it was for Livy, writing when the extension of citizenship across the Italian peninsula was still within living memory.

senatoribus XC et consularibus aut praetoriis aut aediliciis XXX: Here too P.'s figures differ slightly from Livy's. Livy 22.49.16–17 speaks of *undetriginta tribuni militum, consulares quidam praetoriique et aedilicii...octoginta praeterea aut senatores aut qui eos magistratus gessissent unde in senatum legi deberent* ('twenty-nine military tribunes, some of whom were ex-consuls, ex-praetors and ex-aediles... moreover eighty who were either senators or who had held offices from which senators should be selected'). The only other source to supply figures for upper-class losses is Eutr. 3.10.4 (along with Oros. 4.16.3 in almost identical wording): *periit enim in eo consul Aemilius Paulus, consulares aut praetorii XX, senatores capti aut occisi XXX, nobiles viri CCC.*

In this case Eutropius and Orosius are clearly drawing their information from a non-Livian source, while P. is relatively close to Livy, even though not identical with him. It is most plausible to think that P. derived his figures for the losses of ex-office-holders from Livy, assuming (in contradiction to the implications of Livy's *quidam*) that all of the *tribuni militum* fell into that category, and then rounding the figure up to thirty. It is harder to see how P. arrived at ninety senators; he (perhaps not unreasonably) conflated those who had held offices but were not in the Senate with actual senators, but that still does not explain the rise from eighty to ninety. It may be that the text used by P. had that figure, in variance from the surviving archetype: if so, it is impossible to tell which reading stood in Livy's original text.

22.8 *Scipio prevents his colleagues from abandoning Italy.* After brushing relatively swiftly over Cannae itself (22.7n.), P. gives rather more attention to a short story that Livy tells in its aftermath (22.53): that some of the Roman survivors who had escaped to Canusium considered abandoning Italy altogether, but were stopped by the young Scipio, who, with sword theatrically brandished, compelled them to join him in an oath to support the state. P.'s interest in this story is part of his insistent focus on Scipio (see 21.3n.); it looms far less large in other writers—most accounts of Cannae either omit it altogether (e.g. Polybius, Nepos, Plutarch, Appian, Florus, Eutropius) or allude to it cursorily (*Vir. Ill.* 49.5). The only authors who allot it a comparably large role to that in P. are Val. Max. 5.6.7 (also Paris' epitome), Sil. 10.415–48, Dio fr. 57.28 (but, interestingly, not Zonar. 9.2.1), and

Oros. 4.16.6 (cf. 4.16.19), all of whom have the same essential elements of the story.

post quae: Once again (cf. 22.4n.) P. is especially concerned in this book to mark the chronological sequence of events.

propter desperationem consilium de relinquenda Italia iniretur: The phrasing is not taken from Livy; it is, however, not dissimilar to Oros. 4.16.6 (*ultima desperatio...fuit, ut senatores de reliquenda Italia...consilium ineundum putarint*), suggesting either that one (probably Orosius) is dependent on the other, or that they are drawing from a common source; if the former, it should be noted that both have information which is not in the other, so at least one further source must be at issue (see also the Introduction, pp. xx–xxii): it is, of course, wholly possible that both of them have independent access to Livy himself.

P. Cornelius Scipio tribunus militum, qui Africanus postea vocatus est: P. identified Scipio in similar language at 21.3. Livy had referred to his later adoption of the name Africanus in Book 21 (21.46.8), but does not do so here, instead describing him as *fatalis dux huiusce belli* (22.53.6). Oros. 4.16.6 once again (cf. above) is close to P.: *Cornelius Scipio tribunus tunc militum, idem qui post Africanus*.

stricto supra capita deliberantium ferro: Cf. Livy 22.53.9: *stricto super capita consultantium gladio*.

iureiurando adstringerentur: Cf. 2.1n., 18.5n. As I argued at 18.5, the phrase, which is rare, appears there to be drawn from Cicero's account of the Roman prisoners sent on an embassy after Cannae (*Off.* 1.40); it is presumably no coincidence that that story will be told by P. immediately after his account of Scipio (22.9n.). In constructing his account from Livy, P. once again draws his vocabulary from a related section of Cicero.

22.9 Roman responses to Cannae. Livy spends the last section of Book 22 describing the responses to Cannae at Rome: measures taken to get accurate information of the scale of the defeat and to restrict mourning (22.55.1–56.5), followed by news of the Carthaginian threat in Sicily (22.56.6–8); a number of religious measures (22.57.2–6: the punishment of unchaste Vestals, the despatching of Q. Fabius Pictor to Delphi, human sacrifices); the redeployment of existing troops and levying of new ones, including the arming of slaves (22.57.5–11). He culminates (22.58.1–61.10) with a long account of the debate over whether Roman prisoners in Hannibal's hands should be ransomed (a proposal rejected after a speech by T. Manlius Torquatus), along with different accounts of what happened to the prisoners who had come to Rome to appeal for the ransom to be paid. Finally, Livy concludes with a survey of the allies who now defected from Rome, along with an account of Varro's reception in the city (22.61.10–15).

P. makes a patchy selection from all this material: he mentions the arming of slaves, but not the other military provisions; he alludes to the refusal to ransom prisoners, but includes none of the anecdotes connected with that. Both of these, in different ways, reflect the extreme behaviour of the Romans in response to crisis. Of the religious material, he mentions—out of chronological order—only the punishment of the Vestals (22.11n.); but he concludes, as Livy had, with Varro's return to Rome (22.12n.).

P.'s selection becomes more explicable if one compares it to other writers who describe the same period. The only historian who includes much the same elements as Livy is App., *Hann.* 27–8, who covers the sending of Fabius to Delphi and a lot of detail of the redeployment and enlisting of soldiers, including the slaves, and also gives an account of the debate over ransoming the captives. Most other writers focus their attention on the re-arming of Rome after Cannae: so Sil. 10.640–9, Flor. 1.22.23–6, Aug., *Civ.* 3.19, Oros. 4.16.7–8, Zonar. 9.2.2–3; and all of these report (in Orosius' case at rather greater length than P.) the enlisting of slaves as a key element of that the re-arming. The refusal to ransom the prisoners is the other most popular element, treated by Sil. 10.650–8, Eutr. 3.11.1, and Zonar. 9.2.4–5: Eutropius, unlike P., gives some idea of the arguments the Romans used, and also refers to the defection of the allies; different versions of the story of the captives' embassy and the refusal of ransom appear as free-standing anecdotes in Plb. 6.58, Cic., *Off.* 1.40 and 3.113–15 (the latter passage citing both Polybius and Acilius *FRHist* 7 F 2 = fr. 3P = *FGrH* 813 F 4), Val. Max. 2.7.15e, 2.9.8 (the second also in Paris' epitome), and Gell. 6.18 (citing Nep., *Exempla* fr. 12 Marshall). P. is manifestly aware of the first Cicero passage, since he had employed the passage immediately preceding it when narrating the not dissimilar story of Regulus; moreover, both with Regulus and the story of Scipio directly prior to this one he employs the otherwise rare phrase *iureiurando adstringere*, which Cicero had used in his account (see 18.5n., 22.8n.).

P.'s selection is thus not completely arbitrary, but aligns to some extent with the rest of the tradition: it stands apart primarily in its failure to give a broader sense of why the ransom of prisoners was refused.

cum potestas esset redimendi: Cf. Livy 22.57.12: *cum…redimendi captivos copia fieret* (cf. 22.58.4).

22.10 *Panic in the city; successes in Spain.* For his regular 'round-up' of other events in the book, P. singles out two things: the panic that struck Rome after Cannae, and the Roman successes in Spain. The oddity is that the first of these is tied very closely to the specific context that P. is narrating in the passages immediately surrounding, but the second returns to an episode far earlier in the book— the only fighting in Spain described in Book 22 is at 22.19–22 (cf. 22.4n.), as an interlude in the dictatorship of Fabius in the year prior to Cannae. P. is not formally deviating from Livy here, since it is normal in his work for these 'round-up' passages to draw material from all parts of the book. Nevertheless the procedure is surprising, not only because the Spanish material is attached to the more immediately relevant post-Cannae material, but also because this comes not at the very end of the book, as is most usual, but in the middle of a sequence of other passages recounting what happened after Cannae, with P.'s *meliore* making a direct comparison between them. The upshot is that P. gives the misleading impression that Livy presented Roman successes in Spain in the wake of Cannae, thus offering immediate compensation for the disaster.

praeterea ... res ... gestas continet: Cf. 2.16n.

meliore eventu: The expression is not common, but used once in the surviving books of Livy (28.8.5), and occasionally elsewhere. P. is more fond of it than is any other writer: it recurs at 27.2 and 73.3; cf. 13.5n. on the related expression *dubio eventu*, which P. likewise favours.

22.11 *Condemnation of Vestals*. Corresponds to Livy 22.57.2–4. As often (cf. 2.13n.), P. shows a particular interest in Vestal trials. In this case, unlike Livy, he does not connect it to the stresses that Rome found herself under after Cannae—he treats such trials rather as a self-contained phenomenon (cf. 2.13n.).

Opimia et Florentia: The main MSS refer to them as Opima and Florentia; Livy 22.57.2, however, calls them Opimia and Floronia. The first name is easily corrected on the basis of Livy's text, since Opima is not a Latin name, and hence is unlikely to have been written by P., but represents a later scribal error. With the second, however, the name has been corrupted from a rare one to a more common one, and there is no way of telling whether the corruption had already occurred in the MS of Livy that P. was using, or if it represents his own mistake, or if it is a scribal error within the later MS tradition. In the first two cases the MS reading should be retained, as here.

incesti damnatae sunt: Cf. 8.5n.

22.12 *Varro's return to the city*. Corresponds to Livy 22.61.13–15. P. ends the book, as Livy had, with Varro's return to the city and his being greeted and thanked by the Roman population. Livy brings up the story again at 25.6.7; it is found also in Val. Max. 3.4.4, Sil. 10.605–39, Plu., *Fab.* 18.4–5, Oros. 5.5.8–9. In all of these, however, the central feature is the pointed contrast between Varro's responsibility for the defeat and the generosity with which he was treated by his fellow countrymen. P. is unusual in including the story despite not explicitly blaming Varro for the defeat (cf. 22.7n.); this combination is otherwise found only in Frontin., *Strat.* 4.5.6, who uses it for a rather different end—namely to praise Varro for his acceptance of responsibility over the remainder of his life.

P.'s account thus appears odd, in that the story of giving thanks to Varro appears pointed, yet he does not supply the information which allows the reader to understand the point. He follows Livy's language exceptionally closely (see below), yet he neither gives the story a Livian cast nor explains its presence in any other terms. The most likely explanation is that he is drawing on the widespread pro-Varro tradition (22.7n.) in refusing to blame him, but introduces this episode in Livy's own words, in order to give a nod to the small minority of readers who were aware that Livy had handled the story entirely differently. See Levene (2015b), 318–22.

obviam itum et gratiae actae, quod de re publica non desperasset: Cf. Livy 22.61.14: *obviam itum... et gratiae actae quod de re publica non desperasset.*

Book 23

23.1 *Defection of the Campanians.* Corresponds to Livy 23.1–10. P. reduces Livy's complex narrative to a bare notice of the defection, not even referring to the prime role played by the Capuans (though cf. 26.2). The lack of interest showed by P. is, however, not surprising: apart from Sil 11.28–368, who gives a highly elaborated version, no other surviving writer pays the story anything like the attention Livy does, and most omit it altogether. A number of Greek historians included it, but their accounts survive only in fragments or summaries (Plb. 7.1.2 [from Athenaeus], D.S. 26.10, Zonar. 9.2.7–9), and, given the distribution of material across their books, it is unlikely that even when complete they offered a narrative as full as Livy's. It is not mentioned at all by Eutropius, it is at most implicit in Appian and Florus (both of whom record the city's recapture, but not the defection that led to its needing to be recaptured). There are passing references in Val. Max. 3.8.1 and Oros. 4.16.10, both of whom offer little more detail than P. does. It was a story that appears, despite Livy, to have had little resonance among later writers.

23.2 *News of Cannae reaches Carthage.* Corresponds to Livy 23.11.7–13.8. For P., as for Livy, the story falls into two clear halves: the spectacular demonstration of victory, in the form of the rings which Mago brought to Carthage, and Hanno's sceptical response, challenging whether the victory was indeed as comprehensive as Hannibal claimed. The balance of Hanno's argument in Livy is, however, rather different from that in P. While Livy's Hanno does indeed advise suing for peace, the bulk of what he says is addressed to a different (albeit related) point: that the Romans are far from defeated, and that fortune may well come back to favour them. This ties into wider themes in Livy—and many other ancient writers also—about the mutability of fortune. Such arguments are not alien to P. (see 18.2n.), but it is relatively rare for him to offer such perspectives.

Among other writers, the first half—the bringing of the rings to Carthage, with its concrete demonstration of the scale of the Roman defeat—is far more popular than the second. Most other summary historians have the rings story alone, without Hanno's intervention (Flor. 1.22.18, Eutr. 3.11.2, Oros. 4.16.5); in addition, it appears as an independent anecdote in Plin., *Nat.* 33.20, Fronto, *Bell. Parth.* 8, Luc., *DMort.* 25, Tert., *Apol.* 40.8, Aug., *Civ.* 3.19. Only in Val. Max. 7.2 ext. 16,[19] Sil. 11.483–611, and Zonar. 9.2.6 are the stories combined, as in Livy and P. All three of those, like P., give more emphasis than Livy had to the peace proposal, and rather less to the argument about the possibility of a Roman revival; P.'s interpretation thus fits into a broader tradition. The passage as a whole provides a

---

[19] In addition, Julius Paris' summary of Valerius, uniquely, tells the objections of Hanno without reporting the spectacular anecdote of the rings.

good example of the distinctive way in which P.'s dependency on Livy requires an interpretation that does not reduce the narrative to a single author's perspective: P.'s account of the episode both is and is not Livy's (cf. Introduction), since it filters the Livian story through a popular understanding of the episode which, without material alteration to the narrative, reworks its emphasis.

nuntius Cannensis victoriae, Mago, Carthaginem missus: Cf. Livy 23.11.7: *nuntius victoriae ad Cannas Carthaginem venerat Mago*.

anulos aureos...in vestibulo curiae effudit: Cf. Livy 23.12.1: *effundi in vestibulo curiae iussit anulos aureos*.

corporibus occisorum detractos: Livy does not spell out precisely how the Carthaginians took the rings, but Mago clarifies later in his explanation that only the leading *equites* wore such rings (23.12.2). Most other writers, like P., feel it necessary to explain that they were taken from the corpses (although Livy in fact does not specify that all of the rings' owners were killed: some could have been prisoners): so Valerius Maximus, Silius Italicus, Fronto, Tertullian, Augustine, Orosius. P. does not, however, explain that *equites* wore these rings; in this, too, he aligns with most other sources (only Florus, Fronto, and Orosius mention the point).[20]

corpora occisorum is not a Livian phrase. It is found once in Sallust (*Jug.* 94.6), but not again until the late fourth century, appearing in the Vulgate (Tob. 2:9), Augustine (*Cur. Mort.* 2.4, 8.10, *Civ.* 1.12), and Oros. 3.2.3. P. here falls into the idiom of his literary contemporaries.

quos excessisse modii mensuram traditur: Livy 23.12.1–2 offers two versions of this. One, vouched for by *quidam auctores*, is that the pile 'filled more than three *modii* for those measuring it' (*metientibus supra tris modios explesse*); the second, vouched for by *fama*, and which Livy explicitly says is more likely to be true,[21] is that 'it was scarcely more than one *modius*' (*haud plus fuisse modio*). P. on the face of things endorses Livy's preferred version, but subtly changes its emphasis: it is true that Livy suggests that the measure may have been more than a *modius*, but only slightly so, whereas P. removes that qualification. Since three *modii* are certainly more than one, P.'s language allows the possibility that Livy's first version was after all the correct one; this may be because it is the version which was endorsed by most other writers (Valerius Maximus, Pliny, Fronto, Eutropius, Augustine, Orosius); only Tertullian has the single *modius*, while Florus, relaying (as often) an anomalous version, has two *modii*.[22]

---

[20] Eutropius misleadingly states that they came from *equitum Romanorum, senatorum et militum*; he was possibly misled by Valerius Maximus, who speaks vaguely of *nostris civibus*.

[21] Livy often, as here, indicates that *fama* is a reliable source of information: see Doblhofer (1983), 143–4; Levene (2006a), 77–87, (2010a), 149–55, (2012), 228.

[22] Ay (1894), 11, proposes that Florus' number is a scribal error; more speculatively (and implausibly), he suggests that P.'s *modii* could itself be another scribal error for *mod. iii* (following a suggestion by Zangemeister (1882), 105, who wants to read *mod. ii*).

post quem nuntium: The repetition of the noun with a connecting relative is not a common construction in P., but cf. 48.19 *inter quos motus*. Even with other relatives it is comparatively rare in post-Ciceronian literary Latin, though it is common in writers of all registers up to Cicero; in later Latin (including Livy) it is chiefly associated with formal legal language. Cf. K-S 2.283–4, Oakley (1997), 396–7. P.'s adoption of it here gives his language a formal and archaic flavour.

Hanno: The MSS spell the name here *Hannon*; the archetype of Livy spells the name *Hanno*, as do the MSS of P. later in the book (23.12). *Hannon* is a Greek form which is extremely rare in Latin, except in Silius, who uses it constantly. While it is not impossible that P. may be influenced by Silius or another Greek-flavoured author, or else that he was using a text of Livy that spelled the name in this fashion, the inconsistency between 23.2 and 23.12 in the MSS makes it more likely that the spelling in this passage is the result of scribal corruption.

peteret: So the primary MSS; later MSS and the *editio princeps* read *peterent*, which is preferred by Rossbach, but the singular is unexceptional and should be retained.

nec tenuit: 'Nor did he win his argument' (*OLD s.v. teneo* 16b).

23.3 *Marcellus' success at Nola*. Corresponds to Livy 23.16.2–16. P. passes over the narrative of how Marcellus came to be at Nola in the first place and his treatment of the Nolans (23.14.5–16.1, 23.17.1–3). Instead, he focuses on the battle alone: Marcellus' sally from Nola against Hannibal. Livy is relatively equivocal on the question of how great a victory this was in numerical terms: the true measure of Marcellus' achievement was that he was not defeated, which Livy accounts as more significant than achieving actual victories against Hannibal later in the war (23.16.15–16). P. reduces this to his standard language of Roman success.

According to Livy, Marcellus fought successfully three times against Hannibal at Nola in successive years, the battle here in 216, then again in 215 and 214 (cf. 23.10n.; also Livy 24.17); P., like Plu., *Marc.* 10–12, includes the first two of these and ignores the third. All other sources (Cic., *Brut.* 12, Val. Max. 1.6.9 (also the epitomes by Paris and Nepotianus), Sil. 12.158–294, Flor. 1.22.29, Ampel. 46.6 (cf. 18.10), Eutr. 3.12.1, *Vir. Ill.* 45.4, Jer., *Ep.* 7.1, Oros. 4.16.12, Zonar. 9.2.12) mention only one battle. Most of these do not indicate which of Livy's three battles it is: the exceptions are Eutropius and Orosius, who date it to 214 and 215 respectively, and Zonaras, the sequence of whose narrative allows us to place it in 216.[23] The general scholarly tendency (e.g. Münzer (1899c), 2741, *MRR* 1.248, Wardle (1998), 201) is to assume that all of these are referring to the first battle: indeed, both Münzer and *MRR* include even Orosius under this heading, despite the fact that he explicitly gives a date which corresponds to the second battle. The

---

[23] Zonar. 9.3.5 refers to another setback that Hannibal suffered near Nola in the following year, but does not explicitly attribute the victory to Marcellus.

reason, presumably, is that they consider only the first battle historical; Livy's detailed account of a victory in the following year is at best an exaggerated account of a minor skirmish (Münzer (1899c), 2740–3; cf. Lazenby (1978), 97). However, even if that is correct, it is methodologically inappropriate to assume that all of the post-Livian sources who describe one battle are thinking of a battle in 216: it is at least as likely that many of them are drawing, directly or indirectly, on Livy's account of the battle in 215, which is the one on which he places the greatest emphasis. For example, some of the details in Silius' version appear to derive from the battle in 215 (cf. Nesselrath (1986), 218–19): it takes place after the corruption of the Carthaginians at Capua (12.15–26), and Hannibal's speeches are based on those that he gives then in Livy. That the battles could be conflated in the tradition is evident, indeed, from P. himself, whose account of the second battle appears to some extent to draw on elements of the first (see 23.10n.).

Whichever battle they are referring to, most writers give little more information than P. does: the fact of Marcellus achieving a victory after Cannae mattered far more than any details of how the victory was obtained.[24]

Claudius Marcellus: His second appearance in P., following his winning of the *spolia opima* in Book 20 (see 20.9n.). For the form of the name, see 4.4n.

prospere pugnavit: See 2.6n.

23.4 *Siege of Casilinum.* Corresponds to Livy 23.17.7–18.9 and 23.19.1–20.3. The siege of Casilinum in Livy falls into two clear sections, separated by the account of the Carthaginians' winter in Capua and the consequent moral decline they suffer. P. postpones this interlude until the end of the book (cf. 23.13n.); but even leaving that aside, his account of the siege is very different from Livy's. He ignores the whole of the first section of the siege, with the Roman successes in warding off the Carthaginians; nor does he describe the end of the story, with Hannibal agreeing to a negotiated surrender. His interest is solely in the extremity that starvation reduced the defenders to, but also the ingenious device used to supply the town. Moreover, he reverses the order of Livy's narrative, so as to make it appear that the nuts were used to rectify the problem of starvation. The consequence is that he converts the account of a Roman defeat into a celebration of successful Roman endurance and ingenuity; this is obviously a misrepresentation of Livy, though it does to a certain extent reflect the way that Livy treats the final outcome, Hannibal's negotiation of a conditional surrender (rather than storming the town or forcing it to unconditional terms), as a setback for him (23.19.14–15).

In this, P. is in accord with various other tellings of the story. None of the other Latin epitomizers include it; but it is referred to by other writers, most of whom

---

[24] An exception is Frontin., *Strat.* 2.4.8, who picks up one detail of Livy's first battle: the loud noise made by camp-followers, which gave the impression of a larger army (23.16.14).

focus on the endurance of the defenders: indeed, it appears from Cic., *Inv.* 2.171 that their willingness to endure famine rather than surrender was proverbial. The precise selection of stories, however, varied. One anecdote not told by Livy, but relayed in Str. 5.4.10, Val. Max. 7.6.3 (also Paris' epitome), and Plin., *Nat.* 8.222, was of a mouse sold at a high price, where the buyer survived but the seller died; Val. Max. 7.6.2 (also Paris' epitome), like P., tells of the eating of leather. Strabo, Frontin., *Strat.* 3.15.3, and Zonar. 9.2.15, like Livy but not P., add the story of the defenders sowing turnips and so impressing Hannibal with their confidence in holding out; Frontin., *Strat.* 3.14.2 and Zonaras, like P., relay the expedient used to supply the city, though focusing on the first stage, where grain was sent, rather than the final stage, when it was nuts, as in P. (see further below) and also Fest. 176L. But Strabo, Valerius, Pliny, Frontinus, and Festus do not mention that the town was eventually taken, any more than P. does; only Zonaras includes this point (along with Sil. 12.426-8, who has nothing more than a brief and vague notice of the capture), though it is implicit in the dilemma set out by Cicero that Hannibal came into control of it in some way.

lora et pelles scutis detractas: Cf. Livy 23.19.13 *lora detractasque scutis pelles*.

inclusi essent: A surprising phrase, since one might take *mures inclusi essent* to mean 'mice had been shut in'; but that would fit neither the context nor the accusatives earlier in the clause; the latter show that *mures* likewise is accusative, but *inclusi* is nominative ('the besieged', a Livian usage: 25.26.2, 38.4.6, 38.15.4; and cf. *TLL* VII.1 951.67–71), with *essent* being the imperfect subjunctive of *edo*. Since the potential ambiguity could easily have been avoided by substituting *ederent* for *essent*, one can suspect some sly humour on P.'s part.

nucibus... missis vixerunt: In Livy, the nuts represent a last-ditch effort by the Romans, after Hannibal discovers the jars of grain they originally sent down the river (23.19.7–11). P. ignores the former in favour of the latter: his interest is less the Roman expedient in itself than the desperate straits that the defenders found themselves in.

a Romanis: The chief MSS of P. read *a Roma*, which is geographically impossible: the Volturno never comes closer than 130 km to Rome; the later Italian MSS correct this to *Romanis*, perhaps based on Livy himself, who has *ab Romanis castris* (23.19.12), or perhaps because of a copyist's awareness of the actual geography. The question is whether P. could have been so vague on Italian geography as to have distorted the story in such a way, or whether it is a scribal error. While the former is not impossible, the latter is on balance more likely.

23.5 Replenishing of the Senate. Corresponds to Livy 23.22–3. Livy records in some detail a highly contentious debate, centring on a proposal to replenish the Senate from Latins as well as Romans; P. ignores all of the problematic detail, and instead simply records the final outcome.

ex equestri ordine: Livy 23.23.5–6 describes the new senators as coming from a number of categories: those who had held curule magistracies since the previous censorship but had not yet been chosen for the Senate, those who had been aediles, tribunes, or quaestors, and finally certain men who had enemy spoils displayed in their home or who had been awarded the *corona civica*.

P. claims that all of those added were equestrians. Whether he is correct to do so largely depends on what text is read for Livy's final category (cf. Mommsen, *StR*³ I 20). The archetype of 23.23.6 refers to those who had spoils or the *corona civica* among those *qui magistratus cepissent*. Since Livy has already discussed raising to the Senate those who had held the higher magistracies, this presumably would refer to lesser ones, such as the *triumviri capitales* (cf. Livy 39.16.13, and 11.5n.), though that interpretation would be more straightforward if Stroth's addition of *minores* after *magistratus* is accepted.

Most editors, however, prefer to follow Sigonius in adding *non* to the clause. On Sigonius' reading, *all* men who had earned the *corona civica* or the right to display spoils were eligible for adlection to the Senate, and it seems all but certain that these would include non-equestrians. On the MS reading, however, only those who had *both* held (minor) magistracies *and* had received those military honours would be eligible. This is more plausible, given the hierarchical nature of Roman society;[25] and it is given some measure of support by P. here, whose interpretation of Livy makes it more likely that *qui magistratus cepissent* (with or without the addition of *minores*) was already the reading in the fourth century.

hominibus CXCVII: Livy 23.23.7 has *centum septuaginta septem...hominum*. Either P. was using a text which (rightly or wrongly) read 197, or he misread the text, or there was a corruption by a later copyist. Only in the last case should P.'s text be emended to conform with Livy's; since there is no way of telling which is correct, the MS reading must stand.

23.6 *Defeat and death of Postumius.* Corresponds to Livy 23.24.6–13. Livy describes the disaster in some detail, along with the response to it at Rome (23.25.1–6); P. reduces it to a bare notice, as do Plb. 3.118.6 and Oros. 4.16.11; Zonar. 9.3.3 has slightly more detail, and Frontin., *Strat.* 1.6.4 more still, but none of these suggest that the story carried much resonance for them, any more than it did for P.

L. Postumius praetor a Gallis cum exercitu caesus est: Oros. 4.16.11 has very similar wording: *L. Postumius praetor adversus Gallos pugnare missus cum*

---

[25] See esp. Barber (2020), arguing that prior election to a public office was a *sine qua non* for senatorial membership at this period; even if that point is not accepted, he shows in addition that there would have been sufficient prior holders of minor magistracies to fill the gaps in the Senate, and that Buteo would have had no reason to look further.

exercitu caesus est: the language, very typical of P., strongly indicates that Orosius took it from him (see further the Introduction).

P. refers to Postumius as praetor. This was indeed his official position at the time of his death; however, he had been elected consul for 215 (though he had not yet taken up the office), as is clear from the *Fasti Capitolini*; cf. *MRR* I 249, 253. Accordingly, Livy describes him as *consul designatus* (23.24.6). The only time Livy had mentioned that he was in Gaul as praetor was when he was originally assigned the command in Book 22 (22.35.6). P. often shows a knowledge of Livy's text beyond the particular passage that he is summarizing; nevertheless in this case, when the relevant information is mentioned by Livy only briefly and in a different book, it seems likely that P. is drawing his information at least in part from a different source.

23.7 *Victory of the Scipios in Spain*. Livy in Book 23 describes two victories that the Scipios achieved over Hasdrubal in Spain: the first in 23.26–9, reporting events of the year 216, and the second at the very end of the book (23.49.5–14), reporting events of 215. On the face of things, the passage here refers to the first of those, since it occurs at the same point in the narrative sequence; the second is covered by P.'s second report of Spanish events (23.12), which is itself at the end of P.'s book.

However, there are complications. First, the passage here describes the total conquest of Spain. It is true that both of Livy's Spanish narratives conclude on a point that could embrace such an interpretation, with the first campaign ending *ea pugna si qua dubia in Hispania erant Romanis adiunxit* (23.29.16: 'That battle brought over to the Roman side waverers in in any part of Spain'), the second ending on the words *tum vero omnes prope Hispaniae populi ad Romanos defecerunt* (23.49.14: 'Then indeed almost all the peoples of Spain defected to the Romans'). But, while this is slightly awkward, there is no formal inconsistency, since Livy has described how, in the intervening period, Mago is sent to Spain with reinforcements for Hasdrubal, presumably allowing him to renew the war (23.32.5–12: cf. 23.49.5, where Mago joins Hasdrubal in his attack on Iliturgi). P., however, does not mention the arrival of reinforcements, and so it might seem more natural to associate so decisive an outcome with the second rather than the first campaign, and to refer 23.12, which signals itself as a 'round-up' passage, and which accordingly is not expected to be in chronological sequence, to the earlier campaign.

Second, while there are few other accounts of fighting in Spain in this period,[26] Eutr. 3.11.3–5 mentions the defeat of Hasdrubal in 216, with losses (not taken from Livy) of 35,000 of Hasdrubal's troops killed or captured, followed by the

---

[26] One source who does describe it is Zonar. 9.3, whose account is much as Livy's, at least in outline: a defeat of Hasdrubal, followed by the arrival of reinforcements, followed by a further Roman victory. Zonaras, unlike Livy, indicates that the second victory was more decisive than the first.

arrival of reinforcements (with numbers given which, while not identical with Livy's at 23.32.5, seem to derive from him); however, he does not describe any fighting in Spain in 215. Oros. 4.16.13, conversely, does not describe any battle in 216, but applies Eutropius' figures to a battle which he explicitly dates to 215. P. is, in other words, writing against a background where the chronology of the Spanish campaign in these years is fluid and uncertain, and he reflects that fluidity by including two notices of the campaign, but leaving sufficient ambiguity that either notice could refer to the campaign of either year.

23.8 *Survivors of Cannae sent to Sicily*. Corresponds to Livy 23.25.7 and 23.31.4. The decision to send survivors of Cannae to Sicily is reported by Livy twice, once at the end of 216, once at the beginning of 215. This is presumably a doublet, although the fact that Livy identifies the troops slightly differently in the two passages (in the first, it is those serving with Marcellus at Nola, in the second, it is troops in the *castra Claudiana*) means that the duplication may not have been apparent to him. P.'s notice seems to derive more from the first than the second passage in Livy, since that is where the condition is recorded that the troops were to remain in Sicily for the remainder of the war. Hence he is a strict sense changing Livy's order, since the first notice occurs before Livy has offered any account of the fighting in Spain, but the duplication of the notice in Livy makes any dislocation more formal than real, especially since P.'s language in any case draws on a reference to the punishment of the troops later in Livy, rather than on either mention in Book 23 (see below). It should be noted, however, that the vagueness with which P. treats Livy's chronology of the campaigns in Spain, where his notice in 22.7 could refer to events of 216 or 215 (22.7n.), is reinforced by his immediately introducing an episode which itself could belong to either year.

reliquiae Cannensis exercitus in Siciliam relegatae sunt: P.'s language derives not from Book 23, but from Livy 25.5.10, where the troops appeal against their punishment, and where Livy explicitly refers back to his earlier notices: *Cannensis reliquiae cladis hic exercitus erat, relegatus in Siciliam, sicut ante dictum est.*

nisi finito bello: This represents a material if slight change to what Livy says at 23.25.7 (*donec in Italia bellum esset*; cf. 24.18.9, 26.2.14): it was, after all, the case that fighting ended in Italy before the end of the war as a whole. However, as noted above, P. appears to be drawing more on Livy's account of the troops' punishment at 25.5.10, where the condition is characterized much as it is here: *ne ante Punici belli finem in Italiam reportarentur.*

23.9 *Victory over the Campanians*. Corresponds to Livy 23.35.5–16. Livy's account of the opening of the year 215 interweaves a number of episodes, the most notable of which are the treaty between Hannibal and Philip V of Macedon (23.33.1–34.9, 23.38.1–39.4), the campaign in Sardinia (23.34.10–17, 23.40.1–41.7), and Gracchus' battles in Campania (33.35.1–37.9). P. includes all of these (see 23.11n., 23.12n.), but separates them out so as to treat them sequentially; the order he adopts is the order in which Livy concludes each episode, rather than the order in which he introduces them; moreover, he inserts between them the account of Marcellus' second victory at Nola (23.10n.), which takes place still later in Livy. All of this adds to the dislocation of Livy's narrative sequence that was already apparent in P.'s ambiguous treatment of the two episodes prior to this (23.7n., 23.8n.)

As for the account of Gracchus, he has nothing more than a brief notice of his victory over the Campanians, ignoring the important role played by Cumae, in whose support Gracchus is first drawn into battle, and where he is subsequently besieged by Hannibal.

Sempronius Gracchus cos.: For the form of name see 4.4n.

23.10 *Marcellus' second success at Nola.* Corresponds to Livy 23.41.13–46.7. As noted above (23.3n.), this is the second victory of Marcellus over Hannibal at Nola that P. describes. However, his comment that this for the first time gave hope to the Romans after the series of defeats that Hannibal inflicted on them would more naturally relate to the first battle than the second: Livy, while framing it rather differently, likewise refers to the first battle as a landmark in the war (23.16.16; cf. 23.30.19). (P. also has Marcellus as praetor rather than proconsul, but cf. below.) The most likely reason is that P. is drawing not only on Livy, but on an existing exemplary tradition which spoke only of a single battle (see below), and he attached those comments to the second battle, since it is the one on which Livy himself places by far the greatest emphasis.

praetor: Marcellus in 215 was proconsul; he was praetor at the time of his victory at Nola in 216. P. may possibly be drawing in part on a non-Livian source which was describing Marcellus' status at the time of the first battle; but it is in fact not unusual, in Livy and elsewhere, to use *praetor* of a promagistrate (Mommsen, *StR*[3] II 240 n. 5), and indeed Livy himself at one point does so of Marcellus at the time of the second battle of Nola (23.43.12).

Hannibalis exercitum ad Nolam proelio fudit: Cf. Oros. 4.16.12 *Hannibalis exercitum proelio fudit*: Orosius is probably dependent on P. here: cf. below.

primusque tot cladibus fessis Romanis meliorem spem belli dedit: Livy himself does not describe either battle of Nola in Book 23 in this way: the closest he comes is 23.30.19 *post Cannensem cladem unus Romanorum imperatorum in Italia prospere rem gessisset* ('after the disaster at Cannae he alone of Roman commanders had campaigned successfully in Italy'). Interestingly, however, Plu., *Marc*. 11.4 quotes Livy in remarkably similar terms to this (see C 53n.). Since P. is extremely unlikely to have read Plutarch, the shared misreading of Livy is likely to derive from a common source: this accordingly stands as one of the strongest pieces of evidence for P.'s partial dependence on an earlier epitome, which Plutarch too used (see further the Introduction), although it would be a mistake to see them as deriving their account from this alone, since Plutarch applies the comment to the first battle of Nola, P. to the second. There was in addition a prominent exemplary tradition, going back at least to Cicero, which knew of only one battle of Nola (cf. 23.3n.), and which spoke of Marcellus as the first Roman to resist Hannibal successfully (Cic., *Brut.* 12, Val. Max. 1.6.9 (cf. 4.1.7), Ampel. 46.6 (cf. 18.10), *Vir. Ill.* 45.4, Jer., *Epist.* 7.1, Claud., *Bell. Goth.* 139–40); it is likely that this too will have had an effect on P.'s willingness to read Livy in those terms (cf. Bingham 245–6).

It is interesting to note that Oros. 4.16.12, while not using P.'s language, phrases his thought in a very similar way to P. (*primusque post tantas reipublicae ruinas spem fecit Hannibalem posse superari*): it may well be that he is in part dependent on P. here (cf. Introduction), which would help explain why Orosius explicitly dates his one battle of Nola to 215, the date of the second battle in Livy and P. (cf. 23.3n.).

meliorem spem belli, while readily comprehensible, is a slightly stilted phrase: *spes melior* is found in various authors, including Livy (1.9.14, 1.50.6, 44.5.12), and *spes* + objective genitive is commonplace (cf. *OLD s.v. spes* 1b, 3b); but the combination is only paralleled in Claud. Don., *Aen.* 10.250 p. 236 *futurorum tamen meliore spe sublevatus* (though cf. Cass. ap. Cic., *Fam.* 12.13.1 *optimam spem patriae*; also Hil., *In Psalm.* 1.22 *bona est spes aeternitatis*, ps.-Cic., *Epist. ad Oct.* 2 *bona spe posteritatis me consolatur*).

23.11 *Treaty between Hannibal and Philip V of Macedon*. Corresponds to Livy 23.33.1–34.9 and 23.38.1–39.4. In Livy, the focus is as much on the Roman discovery of the treaty as on the treaty itself; P. is interested only in the bare fact of the treaty, which serves as a suitable introduction to his other references to the First Macedonian War during the Third Decade (24.4, 26.4, 27.8. 28.1, 29.5). Flor. 1.23.4 likewise has a bare reference to Hannibal's Macedonian treaty, albeit as an introduction to the Second Macedonian War rather than the first; App., *Mac.* 1, Eutr. 3.12.3–4, and Zonar. 9.4.2–3, by contrast, both offer more detail about the content of the treaty and give a brief account of the Romans' learning of it; Justin. 29.4.1–4 has the latter, not the former. Oros. 4.16.20 refers in passing to the First Macedonian War, but not the treaty that generated it, while the surviving text of Plb. 7.9 gives nothing more than the text of the treaty. P.'s mildly anomalous treatment is explicable not only by his brevity, but also by the tightness of his abridged narrative.

23.12 *Roman victories in Spain and Sardinia*. For his 'round-up' of previously unmentioned events at the end of the book, P. refers to the victories of the Scipios in Spain and of Manlius in Sardinia. With regard to the former, this is his second notice of a Spanish campaign, and it is ambiguous as to whether it covers the first or the second of the two campaigns in Livy: for full discussion see 23.7n.

Livy describes the fighting in Sardinia in 23.34.10–17 and 23.40.1–41.7; P., as often, ignores all of the detail of the battles and focuses solely on the outcome; in this case his lack of interest in the fighting is shared by the only other historical sources for the campaign, Flor. 1.22.35 (mistakenly attributing the victory to Gracchus), Eutr. 3.13.1–2 (slightly fuller than P.), and Zonar. 9.4.1 (slightly less full). The exception is Sil. 12.342–419, who considerably elaborates the fighting, centring his account on the Sardinians Hampsagoras and his son Hostus on the one side (cf. Livy 23.40.3–4, who calls the former *Hampsicora*), and the poet Ennius on the other.

praeterea...res gestas continet: See 2.16n.

feliciter: See 14.8n.

a Publio et ⟨Cn. Scipionibus, in Sardinia a T.⟩ Manlio praetore: On the reading of the MSS, the campaign in Spain was led by 'Publius' and 'Manlius', and in it, three Carthaginian leaders were captured. However, this does not represent Livy's narrative in any way: in Livy, Manlius campaigned in Sardinia, not Spain; the commanders in Spain throughout the book were the two Scipios, but it was in Sardinia where the Carthaginian leaders were captured (Livy 23.41.1). Jahn provided the necessary supplement.

The MSS read the commander's name as *Manlio*. P. does not usually identify Romans on their first appearance by *nomen* alone, so either the *praenomen* or the *cognomen* must have been omitted: the former is far easier palaeographically, especially since the effective homoeoteleuton (ET...AT) helps explain the corruption.

a quo: The correction of the Aldine edition to the MSS *quibus*, which is erroneous, since these Carthaginians were captured by Manlius in Sardinia. It is possible that P.'s keenness to compress multiple events into a single compact sentence has led him to misrepresent the events, but more probably *quibus* is a correction of a later scribe faced with the lacunose text, who assumed that the campaign needed to be ascribed equally to the two commanders mentioned; similarly in the previous clause the chief MSS read *praetoribus*, which various later MSS correct to *praetore*.

Hasdrubal dux et Mago et Hanno capti: Cf. Livy 23.41.1 *Hasdrubal imperator captus est et Hanno et Mago.*

23.13 *Corruption of Hannibal's army.* Corresponds to Livy 23.18.10–16. The story that Hannibal's army was corrupted by its stay in Capua is important thematically in Livy's narrative: he has Marcellus allude back to it at the time of the second battle of Nola (23.45.2–4), with the memorable phrase that 'Capua was Hannibal's Cannae' (23.45.4 *Capuam Hannibali Cannas fuisse*), and endorsed by Hannibal himself (23.45.6; cf. also 23.35.1, 27.3.2). Prior to Livy it is found in Cic., *Leg. Agr.* 1.20, 2.95, and later it is especially prominent in Silius Italicus (11.385–483,

12.15–26, 12.83–4); also Str. 5.4.13, Val. Max. 9.1 ext. 1 (with Paris' epitome), Flor. 1.22.21–2, *Vir. Ill.* 43.5, Auson., *Ord. Urb.* 54–9, Zonar. 9.3.4.

P.'s version, however, has certain oddities. One is that it is introduced so late: not only does it appear nowhere near the point in the narrative sequence where Livy had placed it, but it is tacked onto the end of the book, appearing after the 'round-up' passage of other events that Livy had recounted (23.12n.). That positioning, however, may suggest not so much an afterthought on P.'s part, but rather an acute reading of Livy (cf. 9.7n.): for Livy is extremely unclear where exactly in the chronology of Book 23 one should understand the moral decline of the Carthaginians in Capua to have occurred (see Levene (2010a), 363–5). The retirement into winter quarters appears to take place out of season, well before the end of an impossibly extended year, and the alleged decline of the Carthaginians during that winter does not in fact appear to affect their fighting ability until they encounter Marcellus at Nola at the end of the book, although they have had an earlier failure against Marcellus prior to their winter in Capua (but after their initial welcome there). P.'s detachment of the Carthaginians' decline from any precise point in the narrative sequence is a fair reflection of the way in which Livy is more assured about the fact of corruption than the time when it actually occurred.

Second, and perhaps more surprising, is that P. does not associate the corruption with Capua or Campania. This may be because the stereotype of Campanian luxury had less salience in his day than it had in earlier times:[27] it is noticeable that the story of the corruption of the Carthaginians there goes entirely unmentioned by both Eutropius and Orosius. Auson., *Ord. Urb.* 46–63 is especially relevant in this context: his account of Capua draws on the stories of its luxury and wealth, including the corruption of Hannibal, but explicitly describes this as representing a past prosperity which the current city no longer exhibits (contrast Str. 5.4.13). There was also the complication of a separate tradition, represented by App., *Hann.* 43, where the Carthaginian decline through luxury occurs in Lucania rather than Campania (and several years later): while P. is unlikely to have known Appian's text, it may be that this version of the story was still current in his day. In any case, for P. it appears to be unimportant where the Carthaginian decline took place; it is presumably relevant that he considerably downplays the story of the Capuan defection also (cf. 23.1n.), which in Livy provides the essential backdrop for the theme of corruption through luxury which ultimately implicates the Carthaginians (Levene (2010a), 354–75).

per hiberna: 'During the time spent in winter quarters'. The phrase only occurs with this meaning in one other place in Latin—but that one other place is in this

---

[27] It is alluded to by Symm., *Epist.* 1.37.1; but that is because his addressee, Praetextatus, was at his Campanian estate, and Symmachus draws a direct comparison with the charms of the locality that attracted Hannibal.

very book of Livy (23.46.9). The context is different, but the passage in which it is used comes directly after the second battle of Nola, where Livy had referred back to the Carthaginians' corruption. It appears as if P. is here constructing his partial pastiche of Livy out of language that was directly in front of him at the time he is making the summary.

luxuriatus: Rossbach adds *est*; but the omission is paralleled elsewhere in P. (see 16.2n, and compare e.g. 3.6 *translatum*, 7.4 *expleta*, 7.6 *adiectae*, 22.3 *votum*, 22.12 *obviam itum et gratiae actae*, 42.4 *datus*, 43.4 *facta*, 44.5 *missus*). The deponent *luxurior* is nowhere found in Livy; P., by contrast, uses only the deponent (also 29.9, 130.1: cf. *TLL* VII.2 1926.34–5).

corporis animique viribus enervaretur: Cf. Livy 23.18.12: *enervaverunt corpora animosque*.

Book 24

24.1 *Defection and assassination of Hieronymus.* Corresponds to Livy 24.4.1–7.9. P. omits Livy's brief narrative of Carthaginian successes in southern Italy at 24.1–3, and moves directly to his account of the Syracusan defection from Rome. Livy had recounted this in considerable detail, beginning here with the account of Hieronymus' accession to the throne, his move to align with Carthage, and his assassination, but continuing in 24.21.1–32.9 with a detailed account of the political instability in Syracuse between Hieronymus' death and the beginning of the Roman attack, with pro-Roman and pro-Carthaginian forces each jockeying for power; moreover, the causal sequence that leads from Hieronymus' break from Rome to war with Rome is complex and not chronologically transparent (Levene (2010a), 321–5). P. omits all of this, but moves directly from Hieronymus' death to Marcellus' arrival in Sicily, substituting a very simple and straightforward narrative for Livy's difficult and convoluted account: Hieronymus leads Syracuse to defect, he is assassinated because of his brutality, then the Romans attack.

Other accounts of Hieronymus' accession, reign, and death are largely fragmentary. Plb. 7.7 has a digression on his reign, in which he criticizes other historians for representing the man's cruelty in lurid terms; two of the historians whom Polybius may have had in mind are Bato of Sinope (*FGrH* 268 F 4 = Athenaeus 6.241e–f) and Eumachus of Neapolis (*FGrH* 178 F 1 = Ath. 13.577a). It appears to have been their image of Hieronymus rather than Polybius' which prevailed in the tradition; Hieronymus' brutality is likewise the focus of the brief accounts in D.S. 26.15, Val. Max. 3.3 ext. 5 (also Paris' epitome), and Sil. 14.85–109. It is, accordingly, unsurprising that P., too, places that at the centre of his summary.

One anecdote from the civil strife that followed Hieronymus' death appears in Valerius Maximus 3.2 ext. 9 (also Paris' epitome); but otherwise the entire account of the internal politics of Syracuse in the build-up to the Roman attack on the city disappears from the tradition: there is, for example, nothing of it in Florus, Eutropius, Orosius, or Zonaras. Silius offers the only other continuous narrative apart from Livy and P. himself; and he is relatively close to P., in as much as Silius, too, elides the period between Hieronymus' death and Marcellus' arrival into a short compass, although he does give at least a cursory indication of the internal chaos that Syracuse was in at that point, and also refers to the divisions between supporters of Rome and those of Carthage. P.'s reduction offers just enough to reflect the fact that Livy has some measure of focus on Syracuse, but his vast omissions also reflect the general lack of interest of the post-Livian tradition in these events.

pater Hiero: Hiero was Hieronymus' grandfather, not his father. P.'s error is not in Livy, nor in other sources: it presumably results from careless reading, but this too may speak to his lack of interest in the Sicilian narrative.

amicus populi Romani fuerat: Hiero had last been mentioned making peace with the Romans, at the start of the First Punic War (16.2); P. says just enough to connect up the narrative.

propter crudelitatem superbiamque: Both qualities are ascribed to Hieronymus by Livy (24.4.5: *tam superbum apparatum habitumque…superbae aures…inhumana crudelitas*); but more important is that they are regularly paired, in Livy and elsewhere, in discussions of actual or potential tyrants (e.g. Livy 3.56.7, 8.33.11, 8.33.13, 42.23.5; also e.g. Cic., *Mur.* 8, *Prov.* 11, *Phil.* 3.34, Sall., *Catil.* 51.14, Sen., *Epist.* 83.20, Tac., *Ann.* 2.15.3; cf. Dunkle (1967), Oakley (1997), 519. P. compresses Livy into a familiar mould.

24.2 *Gracchus' victory at Beneventum.* Corresponds to Livy 24.14–16. Prior to this, P. omits the contentious elections for 214 (Livy 24.7.10–9.9), and various aspects of Hannibal's campaign in southern Italy, including the prelude to the defection of Tarentum which will play a significant role in the next book (Livy 24.12–13; cf. 24.20.9–16); he likewise omits various points subsequent to it, notably Marcellus' third battle at Nola (24.17), the activities of the censors (24.18), and Fabius' and Marcellus' recapture of Casilinum (24.19). The reason that P. focuses on Gracchus alone is presumably because of the most unusual feature of his campaign, namely his use of slave volunteers, whom he ultimately frees, though P. presents the decision as more straightforward than it proves in Livy, where Gracchus repeatedly changes his mind about the reward (cf. Levene (2010a), 282–3).

There are few other surviving accounts of these episodes, but Flor. 1.22.30, like P., singles out Gracchus' slave army to illustrate the extremity of the situation faced by Rome; Gracchus' freeing of the slaves is discussed briefly in Frontin., *Strat.* 4.7.24, who provides more detail than P.; while Zonar. 9.4.5 mentions the battle at Beneventum (but says nothing of Gracchus' unconventional army). P.'s selection, while not widespread in the tradition, is thus not especially surprising. Hardly any of the other events in this part of Livy find any place in the tradition at all, apart from Val. Max. 5.6.8, who also speaks of Gracchus freeing the slaves, but in the context of the censorship—he is primarily interested in the selflessness of the slave-owners, as of other Romans at that time, in temporarily forgoing compensation (cf. Livy 24.18.10–15); likewise Val. Max. 2.9.8 (with Paris' epitome) also recounts the censors' punishment of those who thought of deserting Rome in the wake of Cannae and the captives who violated their oaths to the Carthaginians (Livy 24.18.3–9).

prospere adversus Poenos et Hannonem ducem…pugnavit: Cf. 2.6n.

quos liberos esse iussit: Cf. Livy 24.16.9 *omnes eos liberos esse iubere*.

24.3 *The Roman siege of Syracuse.* Corresponds to Livy 24.33–9. P. once again (cf. 24.1n.) shows little interest in Livy's narrative of the war in Sicily. He reduces

Livy's account of the opening of Marcellus' campaign in Sicily to a bare notice of the siege of Syracuse and the defection of the island. Nothing is said of the campaign itself, even of the role played by Archimedes in defending Syracuse against the Romans, which for most other writers is the most memorable feature of the siege (see esp. Jaeger (2008), 101–22): so e.g. Plb. 8.3–7, D.S. 26.18, Sil. 14.177–579, Plu., *Marc.* 14–17, Flor. 1.22.33, Firm., *Math.* 6.30.26, Oros. 4.17.1, Zonar. 9.4.7–8; cf. Val. Max. 8.7 ext. 7. Eutropius and *Vir. Ill.* are closer to P., but go even further: they do not have even a minimal reference to the events of the siege, referring only to the fact of the city's capture (cf. 25.9n.). In the absence of Archimedes, the details of the siege had no traction in the later tradition.

But even more striking than this omission is P.'s reworking of the causal sequence in Livy's narrative. On P.'s chronology, the all but total defection of Sicily preceded (and implicitly was part of the reason for) Marcellus' attack on Syracuse. Livy, however, presents it quite differently; Marcellus even after the start of the siege has some success in preventing mass defections of the Sicilians to Carthage (24.36.2),[28] but the defection of Murgantia encourages still more defections (24.37.1), and then the Roman massacre of potential defectors at Henna has the effect of bringing even those who were hesitating onto the side of Carthage (24.39.9): the defection of Sicily is in part the Romans' own fault (Levene (2010a), 341–3). P.'s effective reversal of Livy's sequence turns it into a far simpler and less morally problematic story.

24.4 Beginning of First Macedonian War. Corresponds to Livy 24.40. P. spends as much time summarizing the single chapter in which Livy recounted the opening of hostilities with Philip of Macedon as he does on the Syracusan narrative which occupied more than half of Livy's book. His relative lack of interest in Syracuse is clear; it is less obvious why he should be invested in this episode (which is not referred to in any other ancient source apart from passing references in Plu., *Arat.* 51.1–2 and Eutr. 3.12.4 (cf. 3.13.1, 3.13.3), and a slightly fuller account in Zonar. 9.4.4). The likely explanation is that he is already looking ahead to the events of the Second Macedonian War, which he carefully notes as a resumption of previous hostilities rather than something entirely new (cf. 31.1n.). From this perspective, the initial engagement of the Romans in Greece appears noteworthy.

P. represents the basic military situation much as Livy does: the Romans defeat Philip in a night battle at Apollonia, driving him into an ignominious flight back to Macedonia. However, the politics of the initiation of war in Livy are less straightforward than P. implies: see below.

---

[28] Similarly to Livy, Sil. 14.192–257 indicates that a large portion of Sicily remained on the Romans' side at the start of the siege.

bellum indictum est: In Livy, no formal declaration of war is noted; in the previous book, after the discovery of Philip's treaty with Hannibal, Laevinus had already been entrusted with a mission to confront him (23.38.9–12, 23.48.3; cf. 24.10.4), and is then drawn into battle at the request of the Apollonians. The question is whether P.'s reference to a declaration might have any historical basis behind it. Rich (1976), 14–15 (implicitly) and Gruen (1984a), 377 (explicitly) assume that the absence of any such declaration from Livy means that none took place. This perhaps places more weight on the completeness and transparency of Livy's narrative than is warranted; but the *ad hoc* nature of Laevinus' action here, fighting Philip in response to the appeals by the Apollonians but then not pursuing the campaign further, is probably best understood as him acting on his own initiative, though on the basis of the general mandate he had received to ensure that Philip did not threaten Italy (Livy 23.38.11, 23.48.3). P. is reworking Livy's messy narrative into a sequence which makes the justice of the Romans' intervention more obvious.

Macedoniam cum prope inermi exercitu profugit: Cf. Livy 24.40.17 *Macedoniam petit magna ex parte inermi exercitu spoliatoque.*

24.5–6 *Events in Spain: Syphax and Masinissa; the Celtiberi.* To set against his massive abridgement of Livy's Syracusan narrative, P. spends around a third of the book's summary on Spanish material which in Livy occupies only the final two chapters (24.48–9): namely the fighting with Syphax and Masinissa (24.48.1–49.6), and the Scipios' employment of Celtiberian mercenaries (24.49.7–8). Formally the generic reference to fighting in Spain includes the battles which Livy had recorded in the previous year (24.41–2), but the specific details given relate entirely to material from 24.48–9. Everything else that Livy records in the last part of the book about the campaigns in Italy in 213 (24.43–7) disappears. That is largely unsurprising, since little of it was consequential, though the failure to mention one well-known anecdote about Fabius Maximus as legate deferring to his son as consul is more noteworthy (though cf. 27.3n.): see Livy 24.44.9–10; also Quadrig. *FRHist* 24 F 57 = Gell. 2.2.13, Plu., *Fab.* 24.1–2, *Reg. Imp. Apophth.* 196A; cf. Val. Max. 2.2.4 (also Paris' epitome), who ascribes the story to Q. Fabius Maximus Rullianus (cf. 11.1n., 27.3n.).

However, the focus on the material here is striking. None of it is found in any other source,[29] apart from a brief mention in App., *Hisp.* 15 to the Carthaginians defeating Syphax at this time, and a passing reference to the Celtiberian mercenaries at Oros. 4.16.14; nor is it sufficiently prominent in Livy's narrative to explain it as a 'natural' reflection of Livy by the summarizer. The better explanation is that P. is once again engaging in narrative foreshadowing (cf. 24.4n.).

---

[29] Eutr. 3.13.3 mentions the victories of the Scipios that Livy describes in 24.41–2; Zonar. 9.3.9 describes the recovery of Saguntum (cf. Livy 24.42.9–11). Neither has the material here.

Syphax and Masinissa's stories will intertwine closely with Scipio Africanus' in Book 28–30, and P. will be covering that in some detail. He has a particular interest in Africanus (21.3n.), and here he extends that to two ancillary but nevertheless important characters in Africanus' story (and, in Masinissa's case, in the ultimate victory over Carthage in the Third Punic War). Something of that foreshadowing is of course already present in Livy himself (cf. Levene (2010a), 247–8); but P. makes it a far more prominent feature of his own narrative than it had been in Livy's. The fact that he uses a 'round-up' formula to introduce these foreshadowing elements is interesting in this context: in general it speaks to the creative ways in which he uses such formulae (cf. e.g. 2.16n., 3.10n., 6.1n., 14.8n.), but more specifically here it mirrors the way in which Livy himself had tacked this thematically significant material onto the end of the book as a brief final comment.

P.'s reference to the Celtiberian mercenaries, on the other hand, is not to be explained in terms of foreshadowing, although it played something of that role in Livy, since they betray the Scipio brothers to their deaths in Book 25. P. does not mention this point. Instead, his interest appears to be in the supposed fact (noted by Livy himself) that this was the first occasion mercenaries were used by the Romans: P., as usual, is particularly interested in 'firsts' (cf. 1.B.7n., 11.5n.).

24.5 res praeterea…gestas continet: Cf. 2.16n.

in amicitiam adscitus: A rare phrase, not attested before the fourth century AD (Ambr., *Off.* 3.12.80, Amm. 14.6.13), but the related *in societatem adscisco* is Livian (27.7.2; cf. e.g. Curt. 4.13.28, Tac., *Hist.* 4.24.1).

Massyliorum rege: In the MSS of Livy, Masinissa's people is called the *Maesuli* (24.48.13). However, the form of the name used by P. is standard in Greek, and more common in Latin writers: see e.g. Virg., *Aen.* 4.132, 6.60, Plin., *Nat.* 5.30, Stat., *Theb.* 8.124. More important is that Masinissa, according to Livy, was not king at this point: the king was his father Gala (cf. 29.11n.). P.'s summary combines material apparently taken directly from Livy (see below) with an account of Masinissa's status that presupposes his later elevation to the throne.

in Hispaniam ad Scipiones cum magna manu transiit contra Gades, ubi angusto freto Africa et Hispania dirimuntur. Once again (cf. above) P. is at error here: Syphax did not, according to Livy, cross over to Spain at this (or any other) time. However, in this case the error appears to derive from a misreading of Livy. Livy, speaking of Syphax's flight following his defeat by Masinissa, writes of his arriving among the Numidians who lived *prope Oceanum adversus Gades* (24.49.5: 'near the Ocean opposite Gades'), where he gathered a large force, *cum quibus in Hispaniam angusto diremptam freto traiceret* (24.49.6: 'with whom he might cross into Spain, separated by a narrow strait'). The subjunctive shows Syphax's intention; it does not explicitly preclude that the intention was carried out, and P. may have been misled into believing that it was by the following words in Livy: 'And

Masinissa arrived with his victorious army, and he *there* waged war with Syphax' (24.49.6: *et Masinissa cum victore exercitu advenit; isque ibi cum Syphace...gessit bellum*). In the context, *ibi* must refer to the point in North Africa opposite Gades; but a superficial reading might mislead one into thinking that it referred to *Hispania*, the last place to be named directly.

The MSS have *Scipionem*, but Livy (24.48) does not show the Scipio brothers acting separately. It is possible that P. is simply in error here, as he is in other parts of this notice, perhaps as a result of unconsciously connecting (or consciously recalling) Scipio Africanus' later dealings with Syphax; however, it is at least as likely that the error was by a copyist, and the text should be emended, as tentatively proposed by Jal.

24.6 Celtiberi...habuerunt: In the MSS this sentence precedes the section about Syphax and Masinissa; it was first moved to the end by the Aldine edition, and this order has been generally accepted by editors. The transmitted order in the MSS is unproblematic in itself, since the 'round-up' formula in 24.5 means that P. is not expected to be following Livy's order at that point. However, *quoque* makes little sense at that point in the text; it has to follow, rather than precede, the account of Syphax's alliance with Rome.

in amicitiam recepti sunt: Cf. 1.B.2n. Strictly speaking this was not the point when the Celtiberi first came into friendship with Rome: Livy had referred to them coming to terms with the Romans and attacking Carthaginian territory on the Romans' behalf at 22.21.7–8. However, it is an understandable interpretation on P.'s part, since Livy refers to the troops employed by the Romans as mercenaries here as having previously fought for the Carthaginians.

auxiliis adscitis: *auxiliis* is a late but necessary correction for the *auspiciis* of the chief MSS. *auxilia adsciscere* is not common, but it is found at Livy 45.25.13; cf. Briscoe (2012a), 685.

tunc primum mercennarium militem Romana castra habuerunt: For *tunc primum* cf. 11.5n. Cf. Livy 24.49.8 *mercennarium militem in castris neminem antequam tum Celtiberos Romani habuerunt*. Briscoe, following Geyer, deletes the entire sentence in Livy, but appears not to have recognized that the phrase in P. strongly supports the authenticity of the received text.

Book 25

25.1 *Aedileship of Scipio*. Corresponds to Livy 25.2.6–7; P. omits the events described briefly by Livy prior to this, notably the defeat of T. Pomponius Veientanus (25.1.2–5) and the influx of superstition into Rome (25.1.6–12).

No other source reports this episode, apart from Plb. 10.4–5, who has a different story concerning Scipio's aedileship, extremely circumstantial and detailed but highly improbable, which he appears to date to a different year. The reason for P.'s inclusion of a story which occupies so little space in Livy and is ignored by other writers is clear: it relates to his keen interest in Scipio Africanus (21.3n.).

ante annos: 'Before the proper age'. The phrase with this meaning is unusual. It appears once in Virgil (*Aen.* 9.311; cf. also Ov., *Ars* 3.18 *ante annos…suos*, Stat., *Silv.* 2.7.74); and it is used by Sil. 13.508, of Scipio's taking the Spanish command. Either of these may have influenced P. here, but there are other data which lead in a slightly different direction. It is used twice by *Vir. Ill.* (49.12, 58.5), respectively of the consulships of Scipio Africanus and Aemilianus, and also by Porphyrio and ps.-Acro in their explanations of *praecanum* at Hor., *Epist.* 1.20.24. It is, accordingly more likely that P. is using a usefully succinct phrase that later commentators had taken over from the poets than that it had specifically poetic connotations. However, the fact that three of the occasions it was used relate specifically to different moments in the career of Scipio Africanus is noteworthy: it suggests that his precocity was so familiar that a formulaic language developed around it.

25.2 *Hannibal captures Tarentum*. Corresponds to Livy 25.7.10–11.20. P. has omitted prior to this Livy's account of the fraud perpetrated by the *publicani* (25.3.8–5.1) and the account of the Cannae survivors appealing for the remittance of the penalty imposed on them (25.5.10–7.4). The absence of the first is unsurprising—it finds no place in the tradition apart from Livy itself. The second omission is slightly more surprising, since the story is transmitted in a few later places (Val. Max. 2.7.15, Frontin., *Str.* 4.1.44, Plu., *Marc.* 13). However, it does not appear in any late antique source except Paris' epitome of Valerius; P. has shown his awareness of the episode by drawing on its language in the context of discussing the troops' original punishment (23.8n.), but does not describe it now.

As for the Tarentine capture itself, it is mostly ignored in the later Latin tradition, apart from passing mentions of the fact of the capture at Sil. 12.434–5, Flor. 1.22.21, 1.22.42, Oros. 4.18.5 (also Zonar. 9.5.1). However, Polybius' detailed account survives (8.24–34), which was probably Livy's source; there are also briefer but relatively full versions in Frontin., *Strat.* 3.3.6, App., *Hann.* 32–3. All of these emphasize the pretended nocturnal hunt and the retention of the citadel; the latter is also referred to by Silius, and assumed in a famous anecdote about Tarentum's recapture (see 27.3n.). It is, accordingly, unsurprising that those are the two elements that P. singles out from Livy's narrative, and that, in accordance with his usual practice, he omits the morally complicating fact that the revolt was precipitated by the brutality with which the Romans executed some Tarentine hostages who had sought to escape (Livy 25.8.1–2).

Tarenton: So the spelling in the MSS; but the usual Latin form was *Tarentum* (though other variants were found: cf. *BTCGI* 21.115), and that is the way it appears in Livy's archetype. *Tarentos/on* appears otherwise to be unattested, apart from in certain MSS of Flor. 1.13.2 and 1.14.1. The question therefore is whether P. could have written *Tarenton* here. On the one hand the rarity of the spelling suggests it should not be, but against that, the MSS offer Greek forms in *-on* not only here but with several other place-names (52.2–3, 52.8, 59.9, 99.1): it seems improbable that they can all be scribal errors, and they are more likely to reflect the habits of the author.

praesidium Romanorum fugerat: The main MSS place this phrase after *simulabant*, which is an impossible word-order. One fifteenth-century MS restored it to its proper place.

cepit: The main MSS read *petit*, but it is corrected to *cepit* in various of the later ones.

25.3 *Introduction of the Ludi Apollinares.* Corresponds to Livy 25.12.2–15. The introduction of the games under the influence of the prophecies of Marcius is also mentioned in Sinnius Capito *GRF* fr. 23 (*ap.* Fest. 438L), and described in detail in Macr., *Sat.* 1.17.27–30 (in language that appears to depend closely on Livy); but is in no other source. P.'s interest may, as often, have been in the introduction of institutions that mark the growth and development of Rome.

Cannensis clades praedicta fuerat: Cf. Livy 25.12.5 *Cannensis praedicta clades...erat*. The substitution of *fuerat* may be part of P.'s tendency to create a pastiche of Livy's language, since Livy especially favours the construction of the pluperfect passive with *fuerat* (K-S 1.166); cf. 29.14, 38.4, 52.8.

25.4 *Defeat of Hanno.* Corresponds to Livy 25.13–14. The only other surviving account of this battle is in App., *Hann.* 37 (though there is an oblique mention in Sil. 12.480–1). In Livy, as also in Appian and Silius, the importance of the episode relates to Capua, which the Romans are preparing to besiege and at whose request Hannibal sends Hanno to support the city. P., however, consistently downplays Capua in his narrative of the war (23.1n., 23.13n.), and one effect of that is that a battle, which in Livy and elsewhere is the prelude to the Roman campaign to recover Campania, is turned into a self-contained victory over a Carthaginian general.

Q. Fulvio et Ap. Claudio coss.: According to Livy, only Fulvius commanded the army that defeated Hanno, although Claudius joined him not long after (25.14.12). However, the campaign is in general treated by Livy as the joint effort of the two commanders, and P.'s distortion is from that point of view relatively minor.

adversus Hannonem, Poenorum ducem, prospere pugnatum est: Cf. 2.6n.

25.5 *Killing of Gracchus.* Corresponds to Livy 25.16–17; P. omits prior to it Livy's account of the defections of Metapontum and Thurii, episodes which appear to have been of little interest elsewhere in the tradition also. By contrast, the death of Gracchus is recorded in a number of sources: there are relatively detailed accounts in Val. Max. 1.6.8 (also the epitomes by Paris and Nepotianus: cf. 5.1 ext. 6 with Paris), and App., *Hann.* 35; a briefer one in Sil. 12.473–8, and short references in Plb. 8.35.1, Cic., *Tusc.* 1.89, Nep., *Hann.* 5.3, Ampel. 28.4, Polyaen. 6.38.1, Oros. 4.16.15, Zonar. 9.5.1. The most commonly observed point, as here, is that Gracchus died as a result of treachery by his Lucanian host (Valerius, Silius, Appian, Orosius); it is also regularly noted that Hannibal gave him an honourable burial, as in what Livy describes as the most widespread version of the story (25.18.4–5: cf. Valerius, Silius, Appian, Polyaenus), but this P. ignores—he has little interest in showing Hannibal as anything but brutal and treacherous (cf. e.g. 22.2n.). He also, less surprisingly, does not mention the prodigies which Livy describes prior to his death, which are the centre of the account in Val. Max. 1.6.8 and his epitomizers, but which otherwise find no place in the later versions.

Orosius' notice of the episode (*Sempronius Gracchus proconsule ab hospite suo Lucano in insidias inductus occisus est*) is almost identical to P.'s, apart from the fact that P. identifies Mago as the Carthaginian general: Orosius is almost certainly deriving it directly from P. (see Introduction).

deductus: Cf. 2.2n.

25.6 *Defeat of Centenius Paenula.* Corresponds to Livy 25.19.8–17. Prior to this, Livy has told of the duel between the Campanian Badius and the Roman Crispinus (25.18), a story that is symbolically important in its illustration of the nature of the Capuan break with Rome, but apparently self-contained and inconsequential, were it not that Livy himself explains that it had a far greater effect, by altering the respective morales of the two forces, and so counteracting the effect of an earlier Capuan defeat of Rome (25.18.1–3); the same episode appears in Val. Max. 5.1.3 (and Paris' epitome). P. is relatively uninterested in Livy's Capuan narrative, however (cf. 23.1n., 25.4n.), and ignores the story. He pays much more attention to an episode to which Livy devotes less time, namely the disaster that befell the centurion M. Centenius Paenula when he persuaded the Senate to grant him an army. The story appears in no other source, apart from Oros. 4.16.16, who may derive from P. himself (cf. below);[30] but P. singles it out as another illustration of the desperate straits to which the Romans were reduced at this time (cf. 24.2n., 25.8n.). Hence he, like Livy, emphasizes Centenius' relatively lowly

---

[30] Note, however, App., *Hann.* 9–11, who describes a battle fought by an apparently different Centenius five years earlier (Livy 22.8.1; cf. *MRR* 1.245) in terms that suggest that the two stories grew from a single source: cf. Münzer (1899a), (1899b).

status and the extent of the disaster, though eschewing Livy's scathing comments on both Centenius' and the Senate's rashness and folly in expecting that this could succeed against Hannibal.

Orosius describes the episode in language extremely close to P.'s: *Centenius Paenula centurio decerni sibi ultro bellum aduersum Hannibalem petiit: a quo cum octo milibus militum, quos in aciem eduxerat, caesus est*. Here, too (cf. 25.5n., also the Introduction) Orosius is almost certainly depending on P.

centurio militaverat: *militare* with a nominative of rank meaning 'serve as' is found once in Livy (35.26.4), but is primarily a usage of later antiquity (see *TLL* VIII 966.70-9); it is especially common on funerary inscriptions recounting soldiers' careers (e.g. *CIL* VI 32974, *AE* 1936, 31, 1968, 497, 1995, 1710), and something of those overtones may be present here.

cum exercitu caesus est: Cf. 23.6n.

25.7 Roman siege of Capua. In Book 25 Livy recounts the siege of Capua in several parts: an initial reference to the plans to do so at 25.13.1 (cf. 25.4n.), the consuls' entry into Campania *en route* to the siege at 25.15.18–19, a sally made by the Capuans against the Romans with the victory of the former at 25.18.1–3 (cf. 25.6n.), and then a more sustained resumption of the siege at 25.20.1, with the full investment of the city at 25.22.6–16. P. reduces this to a bare notice of the siege; he is far less interested in Capua than Livy had been (cf. 23.1n., 25.4n., 25.6n.), and offers just enough to form a narrative connection between the account of the original Capuan defection (23.1) and its recapture in the next book (26.2n.).

Other sources are similarly laconic; there is something more of this episode in Sil. 12.449–57, 12.479–86, App., *Hann*. 37, and Zonar. 9.5.1–2 (though the sequence of his narrative is confused). But Eutropius and Orosius ignore this portion of the siege altogether, though Orosius has a reference to the ultimate Roman victory (4.17.12). Not only P., but the whole later Latin tradition tended to downplay the role of Capua in the war (cf. 23.13n.).

25.8 Defeat of Cn. Fulvius. Corresponds to Livy 25.20.5–21.10. Fulvius' defeat is also described briefly in Sil. 12.469–72 and Oros. 4.16.17, both, like P., offering it, along with the death of Gracchus and the defeat of Centenius (25.5–6nn.), as one of a series that the Romans suffered in Italy at this time. The pattern that P. presents here is thus not unique to him; but it is striking that here too he spends much more time on a relatively minor and self-contained defeat that the Romans suffered than he does on the steady advances that they make in the siege of Capua; indeed, the three episodes together loom much larger in his version of the war than Marcellus' capture of Syracuse does, something which for Livy is far more significant (24.3n., 25.9n.). The overall tenor of Book 25 in P's reading is, if not an unmitigated series of disasters that the Romans suffer, at any rate one in which the balance between defeat and victory sways more towards the former than Livy's narrative might have led one to expect, and the division between Book 25 and the more consistent successes of Book 26 far starker for him than Livy had made it.

male adversus...pugnavit: Cf. 11.1n.

XX milia hominum ceciderunt: This is a discrepancy from the transmitted text of Livy, which reads (25.21.9) *ex duodeviginti milibus hominum duo milia haud amplius evaserint*. The most likely explanation for the discrepancy is that P. was using a text of Livy which read not *duodeviginti* (or IIXX) but *duobus et viginti* (or XXII).

ipse cum equitibus CC effugit: Cf. Livy 25.21.9 *cum ducentis ferme equitibus effugit*.

25.9 *Capture of Syracuse.* Corresponds to Livy 25.23.1–31.11. In the historical tradition, the capture of Syracuse was one of the major moments in the Second Punic War; P. could hardly omit it, but nevertheless it looms relatively less large in his account than one might expect from the attention devoted to it by Livy (cf. 24.1, 24.3nn.). Among the many references to and descriptions of Marcellus' victory, four elements are overwhelmingly prominent, all of which find a place in Livy. First is the killing of Archimedes; Livy presents it as an afterthought to his account of the siege (25.31.9–10), but elsewhere it is the single most recorded element of it (Cic., *II Verr.* 4.131, *Fin.* 5.50, D.S. 26.18, Val. Max. 8.7 ext. 7 (also Paris' epitome), Plin., *Nat.* 7.125, Sil. 14.676–8, Plu., *Marc.* 19.4–6, Zonar. 9.5.5; cf. Firm., *Math.* 6.30.26), and it is, accordingly, unsurprising that P., too, focuses on that point. Nor is it surprising that he reduces the death of Archimedes to a brief description of his being killed while sketching a plan in the dust—that is at the centre of most accounts—nor that he omits any other reference to the circumstances of his death, to the point of not even identifying his killer. As Mary Jaeger has shown (Jaeger (2008), 77–100), a major feature of the later accounts of Archimedes' death is to displace the responsibility away from the Romans in general and from Marcellus in particular, and it is in accordance with that pattern that P. vaguely refers the death to nothing more than something that happened in the chaos of the city's capture.

Far more important to Livy is the actual process by which the city was taken (25.23.1–24.10, 25.25.1–26.6, 25.30.1–31.8), along with the story of the tears of Marcellus as he surveyed the city before its capture (25.24.11–14). Of those, versions of the former appear in various places, including Polybius' surviving fragment of the capture (8.37; cf. Frontin., *Strat.* 3.3.2, Plu., *Marc.* 18, Polyaen. 8.11, Zonar. 9.5.3–4); the latter is described in Val. Max. 5.1.4 (also Paris' epitome), Sil. 14.665–73, Plu., *Marc.* 19.1, Aug., *Civ.* 1.6, 3.14. Both disappear in P.'s abridgement; the latter in particular makes Syracuse into a central moment of symbolic importance in Roman history (cf. Rossi (2000)), which is not the tenor of P.'s account.

The fourth major element in Livy is the plunder taken from Syracuse; on the face of things this too goes unmentioned by P., but cf. further below.

Claudius Marcellus: Cf. 23.3n.

Syracusas expugnavit tertio anno: The chronology reflects an explicit statement in Livy (25.31.5: *se quidem tertium annum circumsedere Syracusas*); it is almost certainly correct. It is true that Livy's actual narrative has pointed to a longer sequence, with Marcellus originally arriving in Sicily in 214 and completing the conquest in 211, so the fourth year, not the third; but it is manifest that he has predated the beginning of Marcellus' campaign by a year (see De Sanctis III.2 318–20 [330–2]). Cf. *Vir. Ill.* 54.5 *Syracusas per tres annos expugnavit*; the language is sufficiently close to P.'s to suggest that one may be dependent on the other.

†ingentem virum gessit†: The transmitted reading has generally been accepted unquestioningly; it is, however, very unlikely to be correct. *ingens vir* = 'great man' is found elsewhere, including in Livy 9.17.9 (see Oakley (2005a), 214 and cf. *TLL* VII.1 1540.24–7), as is *gerere* + accusative = 'play a role' (*TLL* VI 1940.75–1941.25). However, the phrase is vague and lame in a way which is entirely unlike P.'s usual manner. P. provides direct evaluative comments on individuals only rarely, and when he does, they usually involve the addition of specific and pointed descriptive terms to qualify an action, and his judgements usually reflect something in Livy's original account (cf. Levene (2015b), 315–18). There is no parallel in his text for his devoting an entire syntactic unit merely to inform us that someone was a great man, especially when no comparable idea appears in Livy.

What one could have expected, and what I believe to be concealed beneath the text here, is a reference to the booty captured at Syracuse: it plays a major role in Livy's account of the siege and its implications for Rome (e.g. 25.30.12, 25.31.8, 25.31.11, 25.40.1–2, 26.21.7–9, 26.30.9–10, 26.32.4), and among other authors is discussed by (e.g.) Plb. 9.10, D.S. 26.20.1, Plu., *Marc.* 21, Eutr. 3.14.3 *praeda ingens Romam perlata est*.[31] My suspicion is that *virum* is corrupted from the last letters of *thesaurum*, and the first syllable of *gessit* from *regis*; and that the original phrase was along the lines of *ingentem thesaurum regis cepit*; but it is also possible that some longer phrase has dropped from the text. Certainly there is likely to have been more than one stage to the corruption, and any attempt to reconstruct the process can only be speculative. The safest course is to obelize.

in eo tumultu captae urbis Archimedes intentus formis quas in pulvere descripserat interfectus est: Livy 25.31.9 reads (following Briscoe's text) *in tanto*

---

[31] Sil. 14.641–65 describes the opulence of Syracuse at some length, but then praises Marcellus for sparing the city from plunder (14.665–88).

tumultu, quantum †captae urbis† in discursu diripientium militum ciere poterat, intentum formis quas in pulvere descripserat...interfectum. Various options have been canvassed to emend the MS *captae urbis*; Briscoe, preferring not to choose between them, leaves the words obelized. Oddly, no editor mentioned in Briscoe's apparatus appears to have considered transferring the phrase before *quantum* (with a subject introduced for *ciere poterat*, perhaps along the lines of *furor* or *pavor*, which the transposed phrase will have replaced), though P.'s text makes it at least reasonably probable that this was the reading that stood in the manuscript he was using.

25.10–11 *Events in Spain: deaths of the Scipios and the victory of Marcius.* Corresponds to Livy 25.32–9. Once again P., having given relatively cursory attention to events in Capua and Syracuse (and continuing to do so: he ignores the account of Marcellus' final actions in Sicily with which Livy ends the book (25.40.1–41.7)), shows himself much more keenly interested in Spain, perhaps because the defeat and partial recovery here forms the prelude to Scipio Africanus' taking up the command in the next book (cf. 24.5–6n.). It is noteworthy that, while in Cicero the Scipio brothers are regularly cited in their own right as examples of patriotic self-sacrifice (*Rep.* 1.1, *Parad.* 1.12, *Cato* 75, *Tusc.* 1.89; cf. *Nat. Deor.* 3.80), in the post-Livian tradition they appear largely in order to provide the context either for Africanus' appointment in Spain (so Val. Max. 3.7.1 (also Paris' epitome), Sil. 13.381–4, 650–95, Flor. 1.22.36–7, Eutr. 3.14.2, 3.15.1, Oros. 4.17.12–13; cf. App., *Hisp.* 16–17),[32] or for Marcius' extraordinary command, a matter in which later authors are rather more interested (so Val. Max. 1.6.2 (also Paris' and Nepotianus' epitome), 2.7.15 (also Paris' epitome), 8.15.11, Plin., *Nat.* 2.241 = Antias, *FRHist* 25 F 27b, 35.14, Frontin., *Strat.* 2.6.2, 2.10.2; cf. Cic., *Balb.* 34, Sil. 13.698–702).

As for what P. highlights from Livy's account, it is in accordance with the balance of interest set out above that he does not give any detail of what led to the Scipios' defeat—he mentions neither the treachery of the Celtiberi nor the commanders' strategic errors nor even the fact that their deaths were in separate engagements. Most other writers do the same, although slightly more information is provided by some of those for whom this is not an isolated anecdote but part of a longer narrative: Polybius' surviving account consists of nothing more than a single isolated fragment (8.38), but it is clear from the later references in his narrative that he described, as Livy did, both the role of the Celtiberi and the separation of the two Roman armies from one another (10.6.2, 10.7.1), and Sil. 13.679–93, Flor. 1.22.36, and App., *Hisp.* 16 briefly outline the nature of the two battles. With Marcius, on the other hand, P. offers more detail: as noted above,

---

[32] Appian's version eccentrically has Marcellus being sent from Sicily to take the command in Spain after the Scipios' death; this is presumably a garbled version of Marcius' name and story.

Marcius was of more interest to the post-Livian writers than the Scipios were, especially because of the unusual way in which he received his *ad hoc* command. Livy himself focuses on that point, but even more on his forcefulness in rousing the army and the boldness of his attack on the camps of the victorious Carthaginians, and P.'s account reflects this.

25.10 rerum feliciter gestarum: This is virtually a formulaic phrase of P.'s (cf. 14.8n.), but in this case is made more pointed by being placed in antithesis to *tristem exitum*.

tristem exitum tulerunt: *tristis exitus*, never a common phrase, appears intermittently at all periods of Latin, including once in the surviving text of Livy, namely F 62 (see *ad loc.*). For *exitum ferre* (= 'endure an outcome') cf. e.g. Cic., *Flacc*. 105, Sen., *Phaedr*. 138.

prope cum totis exercitibus: Livy does not give the precise extent of the Roman losses, but indicates that they were to much the same degree as P. suggests here: see 25.37.1 *deleti exercitus...viderentur* ('the armies seemed to have been destroyed'); cf. 25.35.2 (on the victory over Publius) *imperatore tanto cum omni exercitu deleto* ('with so great a general having been destroyed along with his entire army'), 25.36.14, 25.37.16, 26.37.8. Some later writers soften the degree of the disaster (e.g. Val. Max. 3.7.1 *cum maiore parte exercitus*; Eutr. 3.14.2 *exercitus tamen integer mansit*), perhaps in order to explain how the Romans were able to recover from their losses so quickly, but P., like Livy, does not appear especially concerned by those logistical questions.

anno octavo quam in Hispaniam ierunt: Cf. Livy 25.36.14 *anno octavo postquam in Hispaniam venerat, Cn. Scipio...est interfectus*. The precise chronology of the Scipios' campaign is problematic, since Livy narrates their deaths as occurring in 212, but the passage here assumes that it was in 211, which is probably correct (see De Sanctis III.2 432–3 [445–6]). But P.'s version is inaccurate on any chronology, since Gnaeus Scipio arrived in Spain a year before his brother did, something that Livy implicitly notes when he comments immediately afterwards that Gnaeus had commanded in Spain longer than Publius had, and so was more deeply mourned (25.36.16). P. appears to have overlooked the point when redeploying Livy's phrasing to construct his summary; his interest is less in the chronology *per se* than in the contrast between the Scipios' long and successful service and its abruptly disastrous conclusion.

For *quam* replacing Livy's *postquam* see *OLD s.v. quam* 12b.

25.11 amissaque eius provinciae possessio foret: As often, P. takes his phrasing not from the passage of Livy which he is summarizing, but from a later reference back to the events: 26.41.5 *amissam tanta clade provinciae possessionem*. Moreover, as at certain other times (cf. e.g. 4.6n.), drawing on the later passage carries a pointed charge, albeit one visible only to the small minority of readers who knew Livy's original text. It comes from a speech of Scipio Africanus, in which he praises his troops for the *virtus* by which they salvaged the Roman position after the earlier defeats, but in which he does not make a single mention of Marcius.[33] P., using the same language, restores to Marcius the credit which Scipio had denied him, with the quality of *virtus* now applied to him rather than to the army as a whole.

L. Marci, equitis Romani: Cf. Livy 25.37.2 *L. Marcius Septimi filius, eques Romanus*.

virtute et industria: This pairing appears only once in the surviving text of Livy (38.23.11), but it is frequent in Cicero, almost always in the same order (e.g. *II Verr.* 5.39, 5.181, *Mur.* 16, *Sest.* 137, *Rep.* 1.2, *Phil.* 13.24, *Att.* 8.11b.1, *Fam.* 3.12.1, *ad Brut.* 2.5.2; cf. *Rhet. Her.* 4.13, Vell. 2.43.4). It is relatively uncommon later (but see e.g. Gell. 9.3.1, Ambr., *Hex.* 3.7.28, Cassian., *Conl.* 3.10, 12.8, Oros. 3.1.16); it seems likely that for P. it did not have the flavour of Livy in particular, but rather conveyed a sense of ideal Republican virtue (cf. Woodman (1983a), 62).

bina castra hostium expugnata essent. ad XXVII milia caesa, †ex† mille octingentos, praeda ingens capta: Cf. Livy 25.39.11–13 *bina castra hostium oppugnata ductu L. Marcii. ad triginta septem milia hostium caesa auctor est Claudius, qui annales Acilianos ex Graeco in Latinum sermonem vertit; captos ad mille octingentos triginta, praedam ingentem partam.* P. takes this portion of his account largely verbatim from Livy. However, there is a slight oddity. A version of (see below) the figures that P. presents are ascribed by Livy to Claudius Quadrigarius (*FRHist* 24 F 58 = Acilius *FRHist* 7 F 3); he then goes on to present alternative, lower figures from Valerius Antias (*FRHist* 25 F 27a) and Piso (*FRHist* 9 F 34). This is not the only time when P. narrates something that Livy had presented only as a variant (cf. e.g. 8.1n.), but in this case it is not unjustified, since Livy's main narrative has implicitly endorsed Claudius' version: neither Antias nor Piso had the victory arising from an attack on two separate Carthaginian camps (cf. Klotz (1940), 169–70).

XXVII milia: The archetype of Livy reads 37,000. The discrepancy must be due to manuscript corruption, but it is unclear whether Livy originally wrote 27,000, and the Livian archetype is in error, or if he wrote 37,000; if the latter, it is equally unsure whether the error was already present in the text P. was using, or if it arises from a later corruption of the manuscript tradition. In the face of this uncertainty, the MS reading should be retained.

†ex† mille octingentos: The chief MSS read either *ex mille octingentos* or *ex mille octingentis*; neither is acceptable Latin. Clearly the text originally read something

---

[33] Cf. also 26.20.3, where Scipio, on his arrival in Spain, *Marcium secum habebat cum tanto honore ut facile appareret nihil minus vereri quam ne quis obstaret gloriae suae*. Livy's comment is double-edged: Scipio is assumed to place his own glory first, and to honour his predecessor in as much as he is confident that Marcius will not overshadow him.

along the same lines as Livy's *captos ad mille octingentos triginta*; the question is what might account best for the MS reading. N's *octingentos* must be correct, not only because it corresponds to Livy's original, but because the alternative *octingentis* is manifestly a secondary correction in the light of *ex*. But it is problematic simply to add *capti* in the nominative, as Sigonius does, because there is no obvious way of seeing how to account for the *ex*, and the repetition of *capere* is awkward. Rossbach proposed *circa mille octingentos et praeda ingens capta*, but the application of *capta* to both an unqualified number (*hominum* or *hostium* being understood) and to *praeda* is itself awkward Latin—perhaps not too awkward for P., but certainly too awkward to be introduced by conjecture. Reluctantly, I follow Jahn in obelizing.

dux Marcius appellatus est: An odd statement. Livy shows the soldiers electing Marcius as *dux* after the Scipios' deaths (25.37.5-6), and in the next book the question of Marcius' title comes up when the Senate objects to him calling himself *propraetor* (26.2.1-4); but neither of these seems adequate to explain P. The most likely explanation is that P. has misinterpreted Livy 25.39.16 *apud omnes magnum nomen Marcii ducis est* ('the name of Marcius, the general, was magnified on everyone's lips'); he might easily have taken this to mean something along the lines of 'everyone gave him the great name of 'Marcius *dux*'.

Book 26

26.1 *Hannibal's march on Rome.* Corresponds to Livy 26.7-11. In Livy, the story of Hannibal's march on Rome is intimately bound up with the Roman siege of Capua. He describes the progress of the siege and Hannibal's attempts to defend the city at 26.4-6; Hannibal's explicit aim when he attacks Rome is to draw the Roman armies away from Capua, and Livy's account of the Roman response to Hannibal's attack centres on the debate of how whether they should do so—they ultimately decide to leave Claudius and his troops at Capua, but to bring Fulvius to Rome to fight Hannibal. Livy furthermore gives a vivid account of the chaos and panic in the city that is generated by Hannibal's proximity to it.

All of this context disappears from P.: no connection is made to Capua; Hannibal is described as being at Rome, but nothing is said of his march to or from it, matters of some importance in Livy, nor is Fulvius identified as the commander who defended the city. Indeed, the events are not seen from the Roman perspective at all, but describe only the activities of Hannibal himself, and his battle is as much with the gods as with the Romans, given the remarkable miracle which prevents the armies from meeting. That last point does indeed reflect something very important in Livy, for whom the gods are the key defenders of the city (cf. Levene (1993), 58-60), but P. nevertheless leaves the story as a self-contained anecdote, illustrating Hannibal's personal failure rather than the Romans' successful piety.

P.'s approach, however, is not altogether out of line with the way that the accounts of Hannibal's march on Rome developed in the historical tradition. It was all but unavoidable[34] that those narrating the Hannibalic war would treat this as a central moment: the one time when Hannibal literally came to the gates of the city. There are, accordingly, extended accounts in Plb. 9.4.6-7.6, Sil. 12.489-752, App., *Hann.* 38-40, Flor. 1.22.42-8, and Zonar. 9.6.2-4; all of these provide the context that P. lacks. In all of them, Hannibal's decision to march on Rome is explicitly connected with his being stalled at Capua, and the reaction of the Romans is depicted, including (in almost every source)[35] the recall of Fulvius. But these accounts must be set beside those which, like P., detach Hannibal's march from a specific context in the war. It is unsurprising, admittedly, that passing references to it, such as those in Plin., *Nat.* 15.76, Frontin., *Strat.* 3.18.1-2, Juv. 6.290-1, and Paul., *Fest.* 355L, would say nothing of what precisely brought Hannibal to Rome; it is of greater interest that Val. Max. 3.7.10 describes it as

---

[34] But not entirely so: Nepos, *Hannibal* makes no mention of the episode.
[35] The exception is Polybius, who—presumably depending on a different tradition—does not mention Fulvius' coming to Rome, but comments on the fact that Appius Claudius did not leave the siege as Hannibal had hoped. Polybius' version is almost certainly historically correct (De Sanctis III.2, 325-6 [338], Salmon (1957), 158): thus P., by omitting this detail from Livy, has (presumably unknowingly) increased his accuracy.

being at a time when 'the strength of the Roman empire was exhausted because of the disaster at Cannae' (*Cannensi clade exhaustis Romani imperii viribus*), implying, without actually stating, that it occurred rather earlier in the war than was in fact the case; similarly *Vir. Ill.* 46.6 tells of it immediately after describing the corruption of Hannibal's army in the winter after Cannae, but before the stratagems of Fabius Maximus. Most notable, however, is that the other summary historians of later antiquity—even Orosius, who devotes a great deal of attention to the moment—remove the Capuan context just as P. does (Eutr. 3.14.1, *Vir. Ill.* 46.6, Oros. 4.17.2–7),[36] and present the narrative in an almost entirely Hannibal-centred way. This tendency to detach the episode from its context in the war may perhaps be connected with the fact that the idea of 'Hannibal at the gates' was proverbial at Rome (see Otto (1890), 158–9, citing Cic., *Fin.* 4.22, *Phil.* 1.11).

Within that abstracted context, P.'s choices are relatively normal. He omits two anecdotes which were popular in later authors, but which were mentioned by Livy only in passing (26.11.5–7): that the Romans sent reinforcements to Spain even while he was besieging the city, and that the land on which he was encamped was sold at auction without any reduction in price (cf. Val. Max. 3.7.10, Frontin., *Strat.* 3.18.1–2, Sil. 12.686–90, Flor. 1.22.47, Zonar. 9.6.4). But the two points he highlights were even more central to the tradition. First, he emphasizes how close Hannibal came to Rome, with specific reference to the camp on the Anio at the third milestone from the city (cf. Plin., *Nat.* 15.76, App., *Hann.* 38, Flor. 1.22.44, *Vir. Ill.* 46.6, Oros. 4.17.2; cf. Sil. 12.538–44; also the slightly different versions of Plb. 9.5.9 (cf. Walbank (1967), 124), Eutr. 3.14.1 *ad quartum miliarium urbis accessit*) and his approach to the gates of the city (Cic., *Fin.* 4.22, Val. Max. 3.7.10, Plin., *Nat.* 15.76, 34.32, Sil. 12.563–8, Juv. 6.290–1, App., *Hann.* 40, Eutr. 3.14.1, Oros. 4.17.4, Fest. 354L). Second, he speaks of the miraculous dispelling of the battle by the weather, which he, like Livy, implies to be divinely instigated (see above, and cf. Sil. 12.602–67, Flor. 1.22.44–5,[37] *Vir. Ill.* 42.6, Oros. 4.17.5–7, Zonar. 9.6.3–4).

Hannibal ad tertium lapidem ab urbe Roma super Anienem castra posuit: Cf. Livy 26.10.3 *Hannibal ad Anienem fluvium tria milia passuum ab urbe castra admovit.* P.'s language is, however, closer to *Vir. Ill.* 46.6 *ad tertium ab urbe lapidem castra posuisset*, suggesting that one (probably *Vir. Ill.*: cf. Introduction) is dependent on the other, or that both go back to a shared source.

---

[36] Oros. 4.17.2 mentions that Hannibal came to Rome *ex Campania*, but does not explain what he was doing in Campania in the first place.

[37] Florus' version is slightly different, in as much as it is Hannibal's advance to the city from his camp, not his projected battle with Fulvius, which is prevented by the weather. The precise nature of the gods' assistance to Rome appears in any case to have been fluid within the tradition: there are remnants of noticeably different versions in Varro, *Men.* frr. 213–14 (Astbury), Fest. 354L (cf. Paul., *Fest.* 355L), and also at Prop. 3.3.11 (which, if *cecinit* rather than *cecini* is read at 3.3.7, he attributes to Ennius).

ipse cum duobus milibus equitum usque ad ipsam Capenam portam, ut situm urbis exploraret, obequitavit: Cf. Livy 26.11.3 *ipse cum duobus milibus equitum ad portam Collinam usque ad Herculis templum est progressus, atque unde proxime poterat moenia situmque urbis obequitans contemplabatur*. The substitution of the *porta Capena* for Livy's *porta Collina* is striking. There was an alternative version, represented by Val. Max. 3.7.10 and Fest. 354L (cf. Paul., *Fest.* 355L), in which the *porta Capena* was indeed the part of the city that Hannibal approached,[38] and P.'s *usque ad ipsam* looks pointed, as if he was drawing the attention of anyone who happened to know Livy's original to the substitution. It is possible that he was seduced by the etymological 'proof' in the version recorded by Paulus/Festus, who use Hannibal's retreat as an aetiological explanation for the existence of a shrine of Rediculus outside the Porta Capena (*Hannibal ex eo loco redierit*: for the location cf. Plin., *Nat.* 10.122): see Meyer (1915).

As to the question of whether Livy's or P.'s version is historically accurate, the weight of evidence is strongly with the former. The route Hannibal took to Rome was debated in antiquity, with Livy and Polybius offering significantly different versions, and Livy recording also a variant account by Coelius Antipater (26.11.10–13 = *FRHist* 15 F 25);[39] but the consensus was that he encamped close to the river Anio (Plb. 9.5.9, Livy 26.10.3), which implies that he is far more likely to have approached the city at the *porta Collina* to the north-east, rather than the *porta Capena* to the south-east (De Sanctis III.2 328 [341]).

per triduum: Livy has this happening only on two days (26.11.1–3); no other surviving version of the story suggests it took place across three. P. may simply be at error, or he may, as with the *porta Capena* (above), be reflecting an alternative version of the story. In favour of the latter is that Silius Italicus, too, has Hannibal making three attempts on the city (12.602–732). In the third he is not deterred by a miraculous storm which then disappears, but by the vision of Juno, but Silius' account of the last attempt uses the image of a storm—one created by Hannibal himself (12.685 *imitatur murmura caeli*; 12.700 *parat accensis imitari fulmina flammis*; cf. also Juno's presentation of Jupiter defending Rome at 12.719–24)[40]— and his final retreat is marked by the heavens growing brighter (12.731–2: *redditur extemplo flagrantior aethere lampas, / et tremula infuso resplendent caerula Phoebo*). This may be nothing more than Silius' imaginative expansion of the

---

[38] Bessone (2015), 431–2 argues that the similarity between P. and Valerius is the result of both of them drawing on the 'Lost Epitome' (cf. Introduction, xii–xiii), which in turn had mixed up its summary of Livy 26.10.1, where, shortly before Hannibal's approach, Fulvius Flaccus entered Rome by the Porta Capena before camping near the *Porta Collina*. But Bessone's theory takes no account of Festus, which can hardly be derived from a lost epitome of Livy.

[39] For comparisons of the different accounts, and discussion of which is more likely to be accurate, see e.g. De Sanctis III.2 324–9 [336–42], Salmon (1957), Davis (1959).

[40] Cf. Stocks (2014), 224–7 for Silius' presentation of Hannibal as an (inadequate) imitator of Jupiter in this passage.

story, but it may also reflect a version in which Hannibal made three attacks and was driven back by three storms, as in P.

in aciem...descendisset: Cf. 7.5n.

certamen tempestas diremit; nam cum in castra redisset, statim serenitas erat: Cf. Livy 26.11.3 (of the second abortive battle): *acies instructas eadem tempestas diremit; ubi recepissent se in castra, mira serenitas cum tranquillitate oriebatur*. *diremit* derives directly from Livy, but *certamen diremit* is ambiguous in a way that Livy's *acies instructas diremit* is not. *certamen diremit* could mean that the storm prevented the battle from taking place (*TLL* V.1 1260.25–55, esp. 50–3), which appears to reflect the situation in Livy, who appears to envisage the armies drawn up for battle but never coming to blows; but it could also imply the halting of a battle that has already begun (*TLL* V.1 1259.79–1260.24), which is the version in Zonar. 9.6.3, who refers to the fighters ἀκροβολιζομένων ἤδη ('already hurling their weapons'). P. adjusts Livy's language so as to accommodate both.

Crevier argued for a lacuna before *nam*; Hertz proposed (on the basis of Livy 26.11.4) *ea res in religionem vertit*. But *nam* here is being used adversatively, as often in later Latin (Löfstedt (1950), 55–60).

26.2 *Capture of Capua*. Corresponds to Livy 26.12.1–16.4. At the capture of the city P. for the first time gives sustained attention to Capua (cf. 23.1n., 25.4n., 25.6–7nn.); but even here his account is as notable for what it omits as for what it includes. He has ignored the narrative of the siege of Capua prior to Hannibal's march on Rome (26.1n.); with the capture itself, he notes the suicide of the Capuan leaders and the device used by Fulvius Flaccus to evade the Senate's orders to spare the surviving Capuans, but has nothing of the feigned defectors who sought to get a message through to Hannibal, and whose brutal punishment prompted the Capuans' suicide and surrender (Livy 26.12); nor does he consider the wider question of how Capua should be treated after its defection, which Livy considers at some length (26.16.5–13, 26.27.1–15, 26.33–34). The account of the Capuans' punishment ignores the anecdote which stands at its heart in Livy, namely the heroic self-sacrifice of Vibellius Taurea.

Once again, however, P.'s distillation of Livy makes sense in the light of the way the capture of Capua developed through the historical tradition. The Greek accounts of App., *Hann*. 43 and Zonar. 9.6.5–7 offer different but broader versions of the story more comparable to Livy's: Appian focuses primarily on the longer-term question of the Capuans' punishment, while Zonar. gives an abbreviated version which touches on many of the points in Livy (although not the story of Fulvius' evading of the Senate's orders or the heroism of Vibellius); the earlier Latin tradition likewise extracts from the story a number of key elements, including Vibellius Taurea (Val. Max. 3.2 ext. 1, Sil. 13.369–80), or the Capuan women who assisted the Romans (Val. Max. 5.2.1). But in the later Latin tradition, perhaps in consequence of the loss of a sense of the distinctive stereotypes concerning Capua (cf. 23.13n.), much of this disappears. Julius Paris' summary of Valerius Maximus omits the Vibellius Taurea anecdote (though he includes the story of the Capuan women). Eutropius does not even mention the capture of Capua; Flor. 1.22.42 has only a bare notice.

The other later Latin author who gives the fall of Capua some attention is Oros. 4.17.12, and he focuses on the same two points as P. does (possibly because he is partly drawing on him: cf. below), namely the Capuans' suicide and Fulvius Flaccus' evasion of the Senate's orders; the former is also found in Sil. 13.261–78, the latter in Val. Max. 3.8.1 (also Paris' epitome). Valerius, unexpectedly, treated the episode as entirely to Fulvius' credit; Livy, however, was far more ambivalent, with a complex mass of alternative versions and possible justifications (cf. Levene (2010a), 366–70). P. (like Orosius, and indeed Paris) removes all of the complexity, but presents the episode relatively neutrally, not (for example) mentioning the opposition of Claudius to Fulvius' actions, but also not offering any direct justification in terms of the Capuans' (alleged) crimes, or presenting the punishment as after all authorized by the Senate, as in one of Livy's versions.

Q. Fulvio et Appio Claudio coss.: A clear error: Fulvius and Appius were consuls when they began the siege of Capua in 212, but by the time of its capture in 211 were proconsuls. However, P.'s error was not unique to him, but appears to have been deeply ingrained in the tradition: it had earlier appeared in Sil. 13.206, Plu., *Comp. Per. Fab.* 2.1, and Flor. 1.22.43, and may have arisen from confusion, not only over the length of the siege, but from the fact that another Fulvius, Cn. Fulvius Centumalus, was indeed consul in 211.

principes Campanorum veneno sibi mortem consciverunt: Oros. 4.17.12 is almost identical (*principes Campanorum veneno mortem sibi consciverunt*), suggesting either that he was dependent on P. or *vice versa*, or that they drew on a shared source. The fact that Orosius, unlike P., correctly identifies Fulvius as proconsul rather than consul at the time of the capture (see above) weights the argument slightly in favour of the shared source, though it is also possible that Orosius has used other sources to correct the error that he found in P.: at 4.17.4, a passage clearly independent of P. (cf. 26.1n.), he had accurately described Fulvius as proconsul at the time of Hannibal's march on Rome.

senatus Campanorum deligatus esset ad palos: Cf. Livy 26.15.8 *productique Campani deligarentur ad palum*.

securi feriretur: Cf. 2.2n.

quibus iubebatur parcere: *parcere* = 'to be merciful' (*TLL* X.1 338.21–57).

lege agi iussit: Cf. Livy 26.15.9 *lictorem lege agi iuberet*.

26.3 Scipio Africanus takes command in Spain and captures New Carthage. P.'s fascination with the figure of Scipio Africanus is once again apparent here (cf. 21.3n.), but exhibits itself in an unexpected way. Livy has an extensive account of events in Spain in this book, climaxing in an extended account of Scipio's capture of New Carthage and his settlement in Spain in the aftermath of his victory (26.41–51), but also including an account of what brought Scipio to Spain in the first place: first the abortive campaign of C. Claudius Nero (21.17), then the choice of Scipio to take the command, with a detailed sketch of his unusual personal qualities (26.18.1–19.9), and then a description of his move to Spain and his taking over the army there (21.19.10–20.6). P. reduces the capture of New Carthage to a single brief phrase, but embeds it into a longer description of the decision to entrust the command to Scipio and his exceptional personal background. The astonishing victory that Scipio achieved is massively downplayed by comparison with Livy (and indeed is removed from Livy's narrative sequence), and instead the focus is almost entirely on his dramatic elevation to the command, combined with an account of his all but superhuman status.

This combination sets P. apart from other narratives of the Second Punic War. Scipio's taking of command and his first Spanish campaign are, naturally, key moments in any narrative of the war, but it is highly unusual for the second to be so completely subordinated to the first. Most other narrative sources (notably Plb. 10.2–20,[41] App., *Hisp.* 18–24, Flor. 1.22.36–40, Eutr. 3.15, Oros. 4.18) all give considerably more space to the taking of New Carthage than to Scipio's being sent to the Spanish command. The partial exceptions are Sil. 15.1–285, and *Vir. Ill.* 49.1–2 and 7–8, both of whom are more balanced in their treatment (though in Silius' case that is because he devotes a substantial portion of his account of Scipio's making the decision to go to Spain to a Hercules-style debate between Virtue and Pleasure); but even they pay more attention to New Carthage than P. does. Most of these also include some version of the famous story of Scipio's kindly treatment of a noble Spanish prisoner, whom he returned to her parents and fiancé (Livy 26.50; cf. Plb. 10.19.3–6, Sil. 15.270–82, Flor. 1.22.40, Dio fr. 57.43 (cf. Zonar. 9.8.5), *Vir. Ill.* 49.8; cf. also Val. Max. 4.3.1 (with Paris' epitome), Frontin., *Strat.* 2.11.5, Gell. 7.8.3, Polyaen. 8.16.6, Amm. 24.4.27).[42] Admittedly, the absence of this from P. is less remarkable, since not only Appian, but also Orosius omits it, while Eutropius at most alludes to it obliquely when he refers to Scipio returning 'hostages' to their parents (3.15.3)—it appears to have been less central to the image of Scipio in the late antique summary tradition than it had been earlier. But altogether, P.'s reworking of Livy creates a highly idiosyncratic balance in Scipio's story.

---

[41] In Polybius' case this can only be an inference, since his account of Scipio's accession to the command is lost; but it seems a relatively secure one, given that he not only narrates the siege of New Carthage and its aftermath at considerable length, but prefaces it with an account of Scipio's character and background of the sort which in most other writers is introduced, if at all, when Scipio volunteers to go to Spain.

[42] Gell. 7.8.6 also quotes a contradictory version from Valerius Antias (*FRHist* 25 F 29), according to which Scipio did not return the woman but kept her as his mistress.

The other remarkable part of P.'s treatment is his handling of Scipio's claims to divine status. Livy describes these, but in coolly sceptical terms (26.19.3–9: cf. Levene (1993), 18–19); Florus and Orosius omit them altogether, though they are present in different forms in Plb. 10.5.4–7, Val. Max. 1.2.2 (in the epitomes of Paris and Nepotianus), Sil. 13.628–47, Quint., *Inst.* 2.4.19, App., *Hisp.* 23, Gell. 6.1.1–6, Dio fr. 57.39 (though not Zonar.), *Vir. Ill.* 49.1–2, Eutr. 3.20.1. But no other narrative source apart from *Vir. Ill.* gives them such prominence relative to the length of the narrative; and of those who do relay them, most either do not mention the story of the snake (Polybius, Valerius Maximus *ap.* Paris and Nepotianus,[43] Appian), or present it only as a report by others (Quintilian, Gellius,[44] Dio). If we exclude Silius, who as an epic poet is clearly an outlier on these matters,[45] only *Vir. Ill.* and P. tell the story as something uncomplicatedly true.[46]

All of these factors show the extent to which, more than in most sections of the summary, Livy's original text is being summarized in a very distinctive fashion. For P., Scipio is a great general, but his greatness resides in his unique personal qualities even more than in his generalship.

P. Scipio, P. filius eius qui in Hispania ciderat, professus est se iturum: Cf. Livy 26.18.7 *P. Cornelius, P. Corneli qui in Hispania ciderat filius…professus se petere* [*sc. imperium*].

videreturque divina stirpe: Cf. Livy 26.19.6 *stirpis eum divinae virum esse*. The ablative is surprising (hence Drakenborch reverted to Livy's genitive, and the *editio princeps* inserts *creatus*). It is true that the uses of the ablative and genitive in descriptive clauses are often more or less interchangeable (cf. Woodcock 64–8); but in later antiquity the movement is far more in the other direction, with genitives used where classical authors might have preferred the ablative (Pinkster 1.1025–6). P.'s substitution of the ablative is part of his archaizing mode of writing, preferring what may have appeared to him an 'ancient' usage to the language of Livy himself.

togam acceperat: *togam accipere*, never used in Latin of the classical period (the usual classical phrase is *togam sumere*, which Livy uses in the parallel passage at 26.19.5), is distinctive to late antiquity, found primarily in the *Historia Augusta*

---

[43] It is possible that Valerius' original text referred to the snake story, but it was omitted by the epitomizers; however, even if that is the case, the fact that the entire episode appears under the heading of 'feigned religion' (*de simulata religione* or *qui religionem simulaverunt*) makes it unlikely that Valerius would have been anything but sceptical.

[44] Gellius cites as his sources Oppius, *FRHist* 40 F 1–2 and Hyginus, *FRHist* 63 F 3–4; he narrates the story in *oratio obliqua* as coming from them, but leaves it unclear whether or not they themselves told it in their own voice.

[45] In Silius the episode is narrated to Scipio by the ghost of his mother, whom he meets during his visit to the underworld.

[46] See Felmy (2001), 205–7 for a discussion of the relative unpopularity of this aspect of the Scipionic legend in later antiquity, though he overlooks P. as a place where it is present.

(*Ver.* 3.1, *Comm.* 12.3, *Sept. Sev.* 1.7, *Alex.* 40.8); also Porph., *Hor. Carm.* 1.36.9, Eutr. 1.17.2. Strictly speaking P. should have written *togam virilem*, as Livy does at 26.19.5; for the omission of *virilem* in this context cf. Plin., *Epist.* 2.14.6, Suet., *Cal.* 10.1, *Hist. Aug., Comm.* 2.1.

in cubiculo matris eius anguis saepe videbatur: Cf. Livy 26.19.7 *in cubiculo matris eius visam persaepe prodigii eius speciem.*

26.4 *Events in Sicily and Greece.* For his regular 'round-up' of other events in the book, P. primarily focuses on the First Macedonian War, which Livy had narrated in 26.24.1–26.4. As with his previous reference to Macedonian events (24.4n., cf. 23.11n.), he pays it a surprising amount of attention relative to its prominence in Livy, giving somewhat more detail than the bare fact that fighting took place, which is his more usual manner: once again, his interest is perhaps explicable on the assumption that he is already looking forward to the Second Macedonian War, and treating this as a prelude to it. No other source describes these events in Greece, apart from a brief mention in Zonar. 9.6.12, and a vague account in Eutr. 3.14.4, who seems to imply that the war came to an end at this point.

For the rest, a substantial portion of the book has remained untouched by the summary thus far: not only the aftermath of the victory in Capua (26.2n.), but also the continuation of the campaign to retake Tarentum (26.20.7–11, 26.39), the Roman recovery of Salapia (26.38.6–14), the election in which Manlius Torquatus refused to accept the consulship (21.22), and the debate over funding the fleet which culminates in the Romans' voluntary donations of their wealth to the state (26.35–6). The last two of these in particular represent the sort of story that might have attracted P.'s attention for the exemplary moral lessons they embody (cf. Val. Max. 6.4.1 (with Paris' epitome) and Flor. 1.22.26 for the first;[47] Val. Max. 5.6.8, Flor. 1.22.25, Fest. 500L, Oros. 4.17.14 for the second); nevertheless he passes over them completely, and mentions nothing except 'events in Sicily'. Livy in fact described very little going on in Sicily in this book (26.21.14–17, 26.40), but conceivably P. saw the lengthy account of the aftermath of Marcellus' capture of Syracuse, including the question of his triumph (26.21.1–13), and his extended dispute with the Sicilians concerning his treatment of them (26.26.5–9, 26.29–32), as falling under this heading.

res praeterea gestas... continet: Cf. 2.16n.

---

[47] Cf. Dio fr. 35.9 and *Vir. Ill.* 28.5, who tell a similar story about an earlier Manlius Torquatus, presumably a mistaken conflation of the two figures.

Book 27

27.1 *Defeat of Cn. Fulvius.* Corresponds to Livy 27.1.3–15. The story, though given relatively little emphasis in Livy, is commonly included even in relatively brief narratives of the war, perhaps because the seriousness of the defeat was underscored by the death of the commander: see Frontin., *Strat.* 2.5.21, Plu., *Marc.* 24.3, App., *Hann.* 48, Eutr. 3.14.5, Oros. 4.18.3; cf. Sil. 17.303–4. Accordingly it finds its place in P. also, although he tells nothing of the defeat apart from Fulvius' death and the location where it took place. All other sources apart from Silius give some sense of the scale of the Roman losses, but for P. it is enough to refer to Fulvius' death alone and vaguely gesture at the numbers by noting that his army died with him.

cum exercitu…caesus est: See 23.6n.

ad Herdoniam: The chief MSS read *adhieroniam*; some later ones read *ad Herioneam*. Sigonius corrected it to *ad Herdoneam*, which is the spelling in all MSS of Livy. There is considerable variation in the orthography of the town's name in literary sources, but the most common spelling (and the only one attested epigraphically: *CIL* IX 1156, in the plural) has an *i* rather than an *e* (cf. *BTCGI* 12.494–5). While it is entirely possible that P. wrote *Herdoneam*, the fact that the *i* both is more widely attested elsewhere and is present in the oldest MSS weights the evidence in favour of retaining it here. It may be that it was the reading in the MS of Livy that P. used, or else he himself may have changed the name to a more familiar form.

27.2 *Marcellus twice confronts Hannibal.* Livy shows Marcellus and Hannibal coming into conflict on two separate occasions in the first third of Book 27: once in 210 at Numistro and Venusia, during Marcellus' consulship (27.2), and then again in the following year at Canusium (27.12.7–14.15). P.'s notice clearly reflects the first of these: the location, the fact that Marcellus is described as being consul, and Hannibal's retreat following the first battle, with Marcellus pursuing him and renewing the fight, all belong to the events of 210. But the outcome of the battles described by P.—two battles, in the first of which Hannibal is victorious, with Marcellus winning the second—derives from Livy's account of the battles at Canusium in 209, not those of 210. In 210 the first battle is explicitly said by Livy to have an equivocal outcome rather than a victory for either side (27.2.8 *incerta victoria*), and Marcellus, after catching up with Hannibal, does not engage in a full-scale battle at all, but rather in minor skirmishes, though admittedly ones in which the Romans are largely successful (27.2.11: *mixta equitum peditumque tumultuosa magis proelia quam magna, et ferme omnia Romanis secunda fuere*; cf. 27.2.12 *sine ullo memorando certamine*).

Hence P. has conflated the events of two separate years into one; he is perhaps assisted in this by the fact that this part of the war was of very little interest to the later tradition, and some of those who do report it conflate the events of 210 and 209 just as P. does (Plu., *Marc.* 24.4-6, 25.4-26.4 keeps the battles separate, but Frontin., *Strat.* 2.2.6 treats the battle at Numistro as a victory for Hannibal, while Oros. 4.18.4 believes Marcellus to have been consul at the time of the battles at Canusium). The conflation in P. also may relate to the fact that he passes without comment over everything that Livy records between the two sets of battles, including the aftermath of the Capuan settlement (27.3.1-7), a controversial election of priests (27.8.1-10), and especially the dispute with the allies over conscription (27.9.1-10.10); everything in this part of the book is run into a single notice.

meliore eventu: Cf. 22.10n.

Claudio Marcello: Cf. 23.3n.

27.3 *Fabius Maximus retakes Tarentum.* Corresponds to Livy 27.15.4-16.10. The recapture of Tarentum was a key moment in the Second Punic War; in addition, it offered a number of widely reported anecdotes, all of which appear in Livy. First is the way in which Fabius engineered the capture, via a Bruttian soldier serving with the Carthaginians who was in love with the sister of one of Fabius' soldiers (Livy 25.15.9-19; also Sil. 15.320-33, Plu., *Fab.* 21.1-22.3, App., *Hann.* 49, Polyaen. 8.14.3). The second is Fabius' handling of the spoils, where the emphases—and the facts—vary between the sources: Livy 27.16.7-8, while emphasizing the quantity of spoils taken, has Fabius refusing to take some images of the gods, and he contrasts him favourably with Marcellus at Syracuse—a similar story (and contrast) appears in Plu., *Marc.* 21.3 and Aug., *Civ.* 1.6. By contrast, another strand of the tradition focuses on a colossal statue of Hercules that Fabius did take from Tarentum and installed on the Capitol (Str. 6.3.1, Plin., *Nat.* 34.40, *Vir. Ill.* 43.6); while Plu., *Fab.* 22.4-6 has both, and hence (unlike in the *Marcellus*) makes a comparison far less in Fabius' favour. Eutr. 3.16.1 and Oros. 4.18.5 offer neither anecdote, but still emphasize the quantity of what was captured. The third famous anecdote was Fabius' put-down of Livius, the Roman commander who held the citadel in Tarentum (Livy 27.25.5; also Cic., *De Orat.* 2.273, *Cato* 11, Plu., *Fab.* 23.3, *Reg Imp. Apophth.* 195F). Other authors mention the capture in passing in other contexts: that Cato the Censor participated in it as a young soldier in Fabius' army (Cic., *Cato* 10, Plu., *Cat. Ma.* 2.3), or that the poet Livius Andronicus was supposedly captured there (Accius *ap.* Cic., *Brut.* 72; but note the reservations of Douglas (1966), 63-4 concerning the text).

Surprisingly, P. offers virtually none of this: he refers to the fact that the capture came about through betrayal, but gives no sense of what form that betrayal took; and he says nothing whatever about the plunder of the city. Few other sources are so laconic: the only real parallel is Flor. 1.22.42, who says even less than P., and does not even mention Fabius as the author of the capture.[48] This

---

[48] Appian, more remarkably given the greater length of his account, also does not mention Fabius by name.

is another example of the way in which P. can rework the priorities of other authors in the historical tradition: he was more forthcoming when it came to Hannibal's capture of the city which Fabius is here reversing, and in that, too, he goes against the grain of the Latin summary tradition (25.2n.). It may suggest a relative lack of interest in Fabius: the salvation he offered to Rome after Trasimene was told at some length (22.4–6nn.), but he subsequently is mentioned only twice, both briefly—here, and with his opposition to Scipio's invasion of Africa (28.9). Unlike Scipio himself, or even Marcellus, Fabius has just one iconic moment for P. (though cf. also below). Once it is over, he has only a minor role, which is far from the tenor of his portrayal in Livy, who places him at the centre of many other episodes, especially ethically contentious ones.

Fabius Maximus cos. pater: For the form of name cf. 4.4n. That he is called *pater* is unexpected. It is true that Fabius had a son, who was himself consul a few years earlier, and who had moreover made a brief appearance in Livy's Book 27, when his father sent him on a mission to Sicily (27.8.13). Nevertheless, that son has not appeared in P., who even failed to mention the one famous anecdote involving him, when as consul he insisted that his father, who was acting as his *legatus*, show him appropriate respect (cf. 24.5–6n.).

Hence we need to look elsewhere for an explanation, and in the context of P.'s narrative, calling Fabius *pater* sets up two particular resonances. The first is the fact that Fabius was called *pater* by Minucius' troops at the time of their rescue by him, an idea that P. had developed beyond the version in Livy (22.4n.). The second, and more striking one, is that the language recalls an earlier Fabius Maximus whom P. had described as *pater*: namely Rullianus, the father of Fabius Gurges (11.1n.). That Fabius, too, had served as *legatus* to his son; the situations of the two were directly compared by Plu., *Fab.* 24.3, while other sources appear to conflate them (Val. Max. 2.2.4, 4.1.5, Polyaen. 8.15; cf. Ampel. 18.6, who places them in parallel). P. did not mention Fabius' son, but his language here, with its gesture back to Rullianus and Gurges, at least reminds his readers of the relationship, and perhaps even of the story that he declined to include explicitly—it may be relevant that Plutarch tells that story not in its chronological place, but directly after the fall of Tarentum, perhaps because the son's consulship might be 'naturally' thought to occur after his father's last one, much as Gurges' consulship had.

27.4 *Death of Marcellus*. Corresponds to Livy 27.26.1–28.2. P. focuses narrowly on the episode that culminated in Marcellus' death; prior to it he omits various relatively minor episodes in Italy, notably the suppression of a purported defection in Arretium, and Marcellus' and Crispinus' activities before coming to face Hannibal (27.24, 27.25.6–14). No less noteworthy is that he also omits what happened after it, including Hannibal's honourable treatment of Marcellus' body (27.28.2), Crispinus' death from the wounds he suffered at this time (27.33.6–7), and also

Hannibal's failed attempt to forge a letter from Marcellus to enable him to capture Salapia, and his successful raising of the siege of Locri (27.28.3–17).

The death of Marcellus was another central moment in the Second Punic War that one would have thought could hardly be omitted (were it not that Florus does in fact omit it…); but there is little discernible pattern to what aspects of it writers choose to include and what they omit—Livy himself notes how variable the accounts of his death were (27.27.12–14), and something of that variability persisted in the later tradition. Most writers, like P., mention that he was killed while on a scouting expedition—but that point is omitted in the other Latin summarizers (Eutr. 3.16.2, *Vir. Ill.* 45.7–8, Oros. 4.18.6–8), as well as App., *Hann.* 50, Zonar. 9.9.1, and Paris' abridgement of Val. Max. 5.1 ext. 6 (it appeared in Valerius himself), and Livy 27.27.14 implies it was not the version found in all of his sources. Nep., *Hann.* 5.3, Plu., *Marc.* 29.3–4, *Fab.* 19.5, *Vir. Ill.*, and Orosius, like P., explain that he fell into a trap set by Hannibal, but Val. Max. 1.6.9 and 5.1 ext. 6 and Eutropius do not mention the point—it may be relevant that Plb. 10.32.3–4 and App., *Hann.* 50 appear to conceive of the ambush on Marcellus as having been made *ad hoc* by troops who happened to be around, rather than by troops deliberately placed in concealment by Hannibal. Hannibal's noble treatment of Marcellus' body is omitted not only by P., but also Eutropius and Orosius, but is present (albeit in very different versions) in Cic., *Cato* 75, *Vir. Ill.*, Val. Max. 5.1 ext. 6 (with Paris' epitome), Sil. 15.381–96, Plu., *Marc.* 30.1–3 (who cites as sources not only Valerius and Livy himself (see C 61n.), but also Cornelius Nepos and Augustus), and App., *Hann.* 50. In one respect, however, P.'s choice clearly reflects his time: the bad omens received by Marcellus prior to his death are a significant part of the story in Livy (27.23.1–4), and also in Val. Max. 1.6.9, Plin. *Nat.* 11.189, and Plu., *Marc.* 28.1–2 and 29.4–5, but in no later writers except Paris' and Nepotianus' epitomes of Valerius.

There is another respect in which P.'s version is altogether unique. Most writers do not mention Crispinus' presence in the battle (exceptions are Sil. 15.345–98 and Plu., *Marc.* 25.5–9); but every other writer who mentions his presence refers to the fact that he perished of the wounds he received. P.'s reference to Crispinus' flight, while not incompatible with Livy's, has a markedly different character, with overtones of cowardice rather than disaster. Combining it with a reference to the trap set by Hannibal sets up an implicit contrast between two Romans: Hannibal outwitted them both, but Marcellus stayed and died a hero, Crispinus did not. It is of a piece with this that P. also says nothing to endorse the criticisms of Marcellus' rashness that are prominent in Livy (esp. 27.27.11; also Plb. 10.32.7–12, Val. Max. 1.6.9, Plu., *Marc.* 28.2–3, *Comp. Pelop. Marc.* 3.3; cf. App., *Hann.* 50); while it is true that other late writers also avoid criticisms of that sort,[49] the

---

[49] Nepotianus' epitome of Valerius removes that aspect altogether, though Paris' retains something of it.

implicit contrast P. makes with Crispinus leaves a stronger impression of Marcellus as courageous rather than rash.

Claudius Marcellus: For the form of the name, see 4.4n.

speculandi causa progressi e castris insidiis ab Hannibale circumventi sunt: Cf. Livy 27.27.14 *plerique loci speculandi causa castris egressum, omnes insidiis circumventum tradant*. P. takes his language from Livy's explanation of the variability of the story in his sources, although his addition changes a point on which Livy said there was no disagreement to one in which there was indeed disagreement: while all versions accept that Marcellus fell into a trap, not all had Hannibal as the author of that trap (cf. above).

For the sentence structure cf. 2.2n.

27.5 *Census*. Corresponds to Livy 27.36.6-7. After the death of Marcellus and its aftermath (27.4n.), Livy's chief focus for the remainder of the consular year is on the First Macedonian War (27.29.9-33.5), which P. ignores here (but cf. 27.8n.). More noteworthy is that he also ignores Livy's striking account of the contentious choice of C. Claudius Nero and M. Livius Salinator as consuls (27.33.9-34.15, cf. 27.35.5-9): they will appear only when it comes to their defeat of Hasdrubal later in the book (27.7n.); contrast *Vir. Ill.* 50.2, which at least hints at the problem; also Val. Max. 7.2.6, cf. 9.3.1 (both with Paris' epitome). However, he pauses to take note of the census, a minor episode in Livy, but a topic in which P. is keenly interested (cf. 1.B.3n., 3.3n.).

lustrum a censoribus conditum est: Cf. Livy 27.36.6 *lustrum conditum est a censoribus*; also 11.5n.

censa sunt civium capita: Cf. Livy 27.36.7 *censa civium capita*; also 3.3n.

CXXXVII milia CVIII: The MSS of Livy have the same figure. Drakenborch and Walsh both emend Livy's text, respectively to read 187,118 and 177,118; Beloch (1886), 349-50 proposes 237,108. This is partly because of the dramatic drop in numbers since the last census (20.11n.), on which both Livy and P. explicitly comment (below), but also because of the substantial rise at the time of the next, which occurred just five years later, and where 214,000 citizens are recorded (29.15n.). However, the coincidence of the figures between the MSS of P. and those of Livy show that it is the correct reading in P., and thus should be retained here.

As for its historical accuracy, the issue of whether this is the number that the censors actually recorded in 208 is a separate question from whether it was the number that originally stood in Livy. With the second question, the evidence strongly suggests that it did stand there, for two reasons. First, the fact that the same figure appears in P. ensures at the very least that the MS reading was in Livy's text by late antiquity; but since we have no reason to think that the text of Livy that P. used was part of the same tradition that produced our surviving mediaeval MSS of Livy 26–30, we can reasonably postulate that the reading goes back much further than that, indeed to Livy's own time (cf. Feraco (2017), 397). Second, the fact that Livy, like P., goes out of his way to comment on the drop in numbers, strongly implies that it was considerably lower than the last figure he offered, and so the fact the figure is surprisingly low is an argument for retaining it in his text, not for emending it. If, as is possible, the figure is corrupt, and the real figure was much larger,[50] then the corruption was already present in the source that Livy was using.

ex quo numero apparuit quantum hominum tot proeliorum adversa fortuna populo Romano abstulisset: Livy 27.36.7 comments that 'the number was less by some degree than the one before the war' (*minor aliquanto numerus quam qui ante bellum fuerat*). P.'s transformation of this remark is, however, noteworthy. First, he does not, unlike Livy, say explicitly that the number was lower than the previous one: he presumably expects the reader to glance back to *Per.* 20 in his text and understand that point for himself (something that Livy could not reasonably expect, given his far greater length). But against that, he is more explicit that the primary reason for the dramatic fall was military losses. Livy formally left that matter open, although the fact that he offers such a note at all while failing to offer any other explanation (such as that certain categories of citizens were not counted on this occasion: cf. n. 50 above) makes it probable that he intended the reader to deduce what P. states directly.

fortuna...abstulisset: The phrase is not Livian, and is rare in Republican texts (but cf. Catull. 101.5, Cic., *Fam.* 5.18.1), but became very common in early imperial prose and poetry, before slipping out of fashion again in later Latin (though cf. Aug., *C. Acad.* 3.2). P. here falls into what may have seemed to him a general archaizing mode, even if not specifically a Livian one.

27.6 *Scipio's victory at Baecula.* Corresponds to Livy 27.18–19. P.'s handling of the Spanish narrative in Book 27 is noteworthy. His notice here focuses on the victory Scipio achieves at Baecula, with the subsequent approach to Masinissa via the release of his nephew. The preliminaries to the battle, including the negotiations with Mandonius and Indibilis which culminate in their defection to the Roman side (27.17), might be thought, in accordance with P.'s usual practice, to be elided by him into the battle itself—were it not that his final 'round-up' passage refers to other activities of Scipio in Spain, which can only be the events of 27.17, unless P. is considering events that Livy either did not include or placed in another book (cf. 27.8n.).

---

[50] Toynbee (1965), 1.473–4 argues for the authenticity of the number in Livy, suggesting that the drop in 208 was the result of the failure to count citizens under arms and also large numbers of people displaced from their homes; Brunt (1971), 62–4 regards corruption as possible, but on balance prefers a version of Toynbee's argument, though criticizing him on the specifics of who was omitted.

The events after the battle, where Scipio makes a decision not to pursue Hasdrubal, thus allowing him to march into Italy to join Hannibal (27.20.1-8), appear to go unmentioned by P., perhaps in part because it might be thought to reflect less well on Scipio that his inaction placed Italy in potential danger—but the connection between Scipio's victory in Spain and Hasdrubal's arrival in Italy is marked by P. in a different way, since he reorders Livy's account such that Scipio's victory at Baecula is placed after Marcellus' death and the census (27.4-5), and directly before Hasdrubal's arrival in Italy (27.7). This reordering implies a different chronology from Livy's, since it places an event which Livy records in 209 subsequent to one that occurred in 208. P.'s chronology is certainly correct (De Sanctis III.2 453 [468] n. 38, Seibert (1993), 258-9), which might be a coincidence; but it is also possible that he was dependent on a source which ordered events in this way (the longer account of Scipio's victory in Oros. 4.18.7 likewise appears to date it to 208, though Orosius may have drawn the order from P.). Moreover, this is not the only time when P. appears to show awareness that Livy's chronology of Spanish events is problematic (cf. 22.7n., 23.8n.), and in this case it would not be especially hard to see the difficulty with Livy's version even in the absence of other sources, since it seems highly improbable that, as Livy would have it, Hasdrubal took more than a year to accomplish his march from Spain to Italy.

The battle of Baecula and its aftermath were recounted at considerable length by Polybius (10.38.7-40.12), although he does not, at least in his surviving text, include the story of Massiva. There is also an extended version in Sil. 15.410-92, and briefer accounts in App., *Hisp.* 24-28 (conflating it with the later battle of Ilipa), and Zonar. 9.8.6. Eutr. 3.15.3, and Oros. 4.18.7, too, have brief references to it, with Orosius giving more detail than either P. or Eutropius about the extent of the victory. But none of these includes the story of Massiva, which appears in no other source except Val. Max. 5.1.7—it is even omitted from Paris' summary. P.'s interest in that is part of his wider exploration of the role of Scipio in the war, which earlier expanded to encompass Masinissa (24.5-6n.).

cum Hasdrubale Hamilcaris: The MSS read *cum Hasdrubale et Hamilcare*, but there is no other record of a Hamilcar as a Carthaginian commander in this battle. It is true that P. elsewhere confuses Carthaginian names (21.5n., 22.2n.). But the degree of error here goes beyond that confusion: there is a considerable difference between getting Livy's version of a name wrong, and introducing a commander from a non-Livian version of the history *and* getting the name wrong. It is possible that P. is dependent on a non-Livian source in which some Hamilcar did play such a role;[51] but it is far more likely that the text is corrupt. Livy elsewhere refers to this Hasdrubal as *Hasdrubal Hamilcaris* (25.35.1, 26.17.4), and

---

[51] At a much earlier point in the war a Hamilcar is recorded as commanding troops under Hasdrubal (Plb. 3.95.2: Livy 22.19.3 calls him *Himilco*).

P. often employs phrases taken from other parts of Livy; hence the Aldine edition corrected to the genitive, followed by most subsequent editors (though not Rossbach or Jal). The corruption from *Hasdrubale Hamilcaris* to *Hasdrubale et Hamilcare* is not a difficult one: presumably the ending of *Hamilcaris* was assimilated to that of *Hasdrubale*, and then *et* was inserted to clarify the meaning.

inter alia: The neuter is slightly unexpected: it presumably takes into account the booty as well as the people captured.

puerum eximiae formae: Livy 27.19.8 has *puerum adultum...forma insigni*. *eximia forma* is a relatively common phrase, used by Livy among others (26.50.1, 38.24.2, 44.28.15), but in this case P. may have derived his phrasing not from Livy, but from Valerius Maximus 5.1.7 *puer eximiae formae*.

27.7 Battle of Metaurus. Corresponds to Livy 27.39–49. The battle of the Metaurus is treated by Livy as the major dramatic climax of the book, and indeed one of the key episodes of the entire decade. P. manages within a single sentence to incorporate—albeit not in chronological sequence—the chief contributions of the three main characters: first Hasdrubal, who crosses the Alps in order to join up with his brother, only to fall into defeat; second Livius, who commands the army that achieves the victory, but finally Claudius Nero, who evades Hannibal and performs a remarkable march to join his colleague in confronting Hasdrubal. This summary inevitably misses a great deal of Livy: important omissions include not only the details of the fighting, which Livy recounts at great length, but the entire aftermath of the battle, with the description of the ecstasy at Rome at the news of the victory, and Claudius Nero's reappearance in front of Hannibal's army (27.50-1); also omitted is the vivid account of the panic in the city prior to the battle (27.40.1-7, 27.44), the difficult relationship of the two consuls (cf. 27.5n.), and the fighting between Hannibal's army and Claudius' prior to the latter's abrupt departure (27.41-2).

It is hardly surprising that these events were regarded as a central moment in Roman history, recounted or alluded to by many authors, although at least some of that may be the result of Livy's own influence, since the battle appears to have been of considerably less interest in the Republican period (Cicero mentions it only once, in a passing reference to Livius Salinator whom he is discussing in a different context: *Brut.* 73); it presumably assisted its later visibility that one of the victors was the ancestor of the emperor Tiberius. Most narrative accounts contain the same basic information as P.: that Hasdrubal crossed into Italy, seeking to join Hannibal, but was foiled by Nero and Livius, who combined their armies to face him (so e.g. Val. Max. 7.4.4 (also Paris' summary), Sil. 15.493–823, App., *Hann.* 52-3, Flor. 1.22.49–53, Eutr. 3.18.2, *Vir. Ill.* 48.1–4, Porph., *Hor. Carm.* 4.4.37, Oros. 4.18.9–16, Zonar. 9.9.5–11); a minority of authors tells the same basic story, but focus on only one of the consuls, usually Nero (so Hor., *Carm.* 4.4.37–76, Suet., *Tib.* 2.1, Ampel. 18.12, 36.3, 46.6), less often Livius (Manil. 1.790–1, Sidon., *Carm.* 7.555–6).

A number of anecdotes that Livy tells concerning the battle were highlighted in the later tradition: of these, one surprisingly omitted by P. is the popular story of Claudius Nero returning to face Hannibal and flinging his brother's head into his camp, along with Hannibal's despairing response (Livy 27.51.11–12: cf. Frontin., *Strat.* 2.9.2, Sil. 15.813–21, Flor. 1.22.53, *Vir. Ill.* 48.3–4, Oros. 4.18.15, Zonar. 9.9.12). Most authors, including Livy, use the episode not only to wind up their account of the battle in a dramatic fashion, but to foreshadow the ultimate Carthaginian defeat, implying that Hannibal has now lost any chance of victory. P. shows no interest in shaping his account of the war in that way: we may compare his abstracted treatment of Hannibal's march on Rome (26.1n.). Conversely, P. shows rather more interest in the casualty figures; this is something he has included irregularly during the Hannibalic war from Cannae onwards (22.7, 25.6, 25.8, 25.11); but after this battle he again appears less interested in such figures, with occasional exceptions, notably Marius' campaigns against the Cimbri and the war against Spartacus (67.2, 68.2, 68.4, 96.1, 97.1, 97.1–2; also 31.6, 55.5, 97.5, 104.5). The only other authors who include them with the Metaurus, apart from Livy himself (27.49.5–7) are Oros. 4.18.14, as well as Plb. 11.3.3 and Porph., *Hor. Carm.* 4.4.37, whose numbers are rather different.

One respect, however, in which P. conforms more closely to the mainstream of the post-Livian tradition is in his handling of Claudius Nero's march to join Livius, which he explains as a trick that Nero played on Hannibal. That idea is present in Livy, but not prominently—it is not described in those terms when Nero leaves, but only in retrospect through the perspectives of others (27.44.3, 27.46.9, 27.47.6, 28.9.12). But in the later tradition it becomes a more central feature of the story, as here: see Val. Max. 7.4.4 (also Paris' epitome), Frontin., *Strat.* 1.1.9, Flor. 1.22.52, Oros. 4.18.9, Zonar. 9.9.7.

cum exercitu novo: That Hasdrubal recruited new troops for his march into Italy is stated by Livy (27.20.7, 27.36.1–4); P. highlights it here in order to make the connection with the notice of his defeat at Baecula, which he has recounted just before (27.6n.), and so to explain how, despite that defeat, he still posed a serious threat.

Claudi Neronis: Cf. 4.4n.

electa manu: *electus* used adjectivally in military contexts is not uncommon (*TLL* V.2 386.35–56), but the specific phrase here is rare, and not Livian: it appears only in a couple of texts of the early Empire (Sil. 11.64, Tac., *Hist.* 4.77.2). P. highlights Nero's achievement with choice language.

Hasdrubalem circumvenerat: This is misleading (no doubt in consequence of P.'s compression). It is true that, according to Livy, the victory at the Metaurus was achieved when Nero led his troops around Hasdrubal's army to attack from behind (27.48.14); but P.'s language leaves the false impression that the outflanking was something he accomplished directly on his march, rather than after uniting his army with Livius'.

27.8 *Roman successes in Spain and Greece*. For his typical 'round-up' passage P. selects two spheres of action: events in Spain, and the fighting in the First Macedonian War.

The second of these is relatively unproblematic: Livy had described events in Greece in some detail at 27.29.9–33.5. It is true that it hardly counts as a fair summary to treat this merely as 'Roman successes against Philip and the Achaeans': while one segment of it describes a victory on the part of Sulpicius (27.31.9–32.6), Philip himself achieves a number of victories both before and after that point, and while the one afterward was not against the Romans (27.32.7–8), two earlier ones were (31.30.1–2, 31.31.2–3). But this is not the only place where P.'s end-of-book summary converts equivocal fighting into Roman victories (cf. 7.13n., 9.5n.): it is characteristic of him in general to make Livy appear more celebratory of Roman success than he actually was.

More puzzling is his reference to Scipio's successes in Spain. There is only one part of the book where Livy describes Scipio's campaign, namely his account of the events culminating in the battle of Baecula, and P. would seem to have covered that as fully as one might have expected at 27.6. The two possibilities are that he was thinking of the preliminaries to that battle, where Scipio obtains the defection of Mandonius and Indibilis (27.6n.), or else that he is referring to material that Livy did not actually include in this book. In favour of the latter is that Eutr. 3.16.2 describes what appears to be a further season of campaigning by Scipio after Baecula but prior to the death of Marcellus, in which he brought seventy states onto the Roman side. It may be that this is itself merely a (misdated) account of the successes of Scipio in obtaining allies prior to Baecula: note that Oros. 4.18.7 describes what appears to be something similar, but clearly relates it to Baecula itself. But Eutropius also refers to the participation of Lucius Scipio in that action, who in Livy does not campaign in Spain until Book 28 (cf. 28.1n.). There was clearly some fluidity in the tradition of Spanish fighting in these years, possibly in part because of Livy's own chronological imprecision, and just as P. tacitly corrects Livy's chronology (27.6n.), he may have felt it proper to supplement him by hinting at a further campaign which Livy did not include.

Whatever the explanation, the effect of P.'s narrative is to accentuate the role of Scipio. Book 27 is the only book in the second half of the decade in which Scipio has a relatively minor role; in keeping with his general promotion of Scipio's significance, P. uses his final gesture at the 'other material' absent from his sequential account in order to imply—without actually stating—that Scipio's part in Book 27 was more substantial than was in fact the case.

res praeterea feliciter…gestas continet: Cf. 2.16n., 14.8n. *gestas* is omitted from the main MSS, but the necessary restoration is made in some later ones.

Book 28

28.1 *Events in Spain and Greece.* The first notice of Book 28 is a mirror of the last of Book 27, recording events in Spain and Greece using a formula which resembles the 'round-up of other things in the book' employed there. However, there is a difference: the word *praeterea*, signalling that the events are being recorded out of chronological sequence, does not appear here, and indeed this notice does follow Livy's narrative sequence, since Livy begins the book with victories by Marcus Silanus and Lucius Scipio in Spain (28.1.1–4.4), and follows it with the campaign conducted by Sulpicius and Attalus against Philip (28.5–8). With the latter, it is once again the case (cf. 27.8n.) that P.'s version of Livy suggests a more straightforward series of successes than Livy himself had: in Livy, Sulpicius and Attalus capture Oreum and Opus, but fail to take Chalcis; they then withdraw, and Philip reasserts his control, including retaking both cities.

res...prospere gestae: Cf. 3.10n.

Silano, Scipionis legato: Silanus was not Scipio's *legatus*, but propraetor (26.19.10; cf. 27.7.17, 27.22.7): see *MRR* 1.280 (with 1.284 n. 4). There is, however, a question whether his *imperium* equalled Scipio's. In a speech, Livy has Scipio imply that it did (28.28.14), and some have argued that this is accurate and that Silanus had been raised to proconsular status (esp. Vervaet (2014), 206–11; also Jashemski (1950), 25–6, Sumner (1970), 88, Develin (1980), 359–60). But this argument places a weight on the rhetoric of an invented Livian speech that it can hardly bear: in that speech Scipio has a clear interest in enhancing Silanus' authority, since he is seeking to show his mutinous troops that nothing would be materially changed by his own death. To set against that are Livy's plain statements in his narrative voice: he had earlier referred to Silanus as Scipio's 'assistant' (26.19.10: *adiutor*), and later says that the victories in Spain were under the latter's auspices (28.38.1), as well as the simple fact that Livy says that Scipio was directly given proconsular *imperium*, and says nothing comparable about Silanus. Extraordinary grants of proconsular authority such as Scipio received were extremely rare at this time, and it would be still less likely to find two such grants (so esp. Brennan (2000), 159; also e.g. De Sanctis III.2 441 [455] n. 19, Scullard (1970), 251, Richardson (1986), 46, Seibert (1993), 268). Certainly in terms of Livy's narrative Silanus is very obviously inferior to Scipio,[52] and it is hardly surprising that P. carelessly inferred that he was nothing more than Scipio's direct subordinate.

a Sulpicio: The chief MSS read *L*., but this is an error. Rossbach reads *P.*, as at Livy 28.5.1 (cf. *MRR* 1.252), but unnecessarily: P. has mentioned the proconsul

---

[52] Acknowledged by Vervaet (2014), 211; but he regards this as merely the consequence of a 'gentleman's agreement' between Scipio and Silanus that the latter should cede the supreme command to the former.

with his *praenomen* in the previous sentence (27.8), and he often omits the *praenomen* on the second occasion when he refers to the same figure twice in rapid succession, and it is better to omit it, as in one late MS.

socio Attalo: One might have expected *cum*, explaining that Attalus joined Sulpicius on the campaign; but we should rather see this as a description of the circumstances under which Sulpicius conducted the campaign, with the noun phrase shading into an ablative absolute (Pinkster 1.854–6; cf. H-S 138–9).

referuntur: Cf. 16.1n. From this point onwards P. uses this formula increasingly often to refer explicitly to the fact that he is summarizing aspects of Livy's narrative, including 'round-up' summaries for which he has previously used the *res...continet* formula (see 2.16n.).

28.2 *Triumph of Livius and Nero*. Corresponds to Livy 28.9. P. allots a substantial amount of space to this episode, explaining it in some detail. Livy does not highlight it to the same degree, and moreover its significance in his overall narrative is quite different, since it is the final act (until their conflict is resumed in Book 29: see 29.14n.) in the trajectory through their consulship that brought Livius and Nero from hostile political adversaries at the start to true partnership at the end. P. has had nothing of the original hostility (27.5n.), and hence the story of the triumph is, for him, simply an exceptional demonstration of modesty on the part of a commander from whom nothing else might be expected. The same is true in Val. Max. 4.1.9 (with Paris' epitome), although the one other[53] account of the triumph, *Vir. Ill.* 50.2, does refer to the change from enmity to friendship, albeit in a different section from that in which Nero's taking a lesser role was recounted (48.5).

More interesting is that P.'s compression of Livy significantly alters the grounds on which Nero gave way to Livius. The key point in Livy is that the two were awarded triumphs for their part in the victory, but they did not want to celebrate them separately (28.9.9). Given that wish, one had to cede to the other, and it was fairly obvious that Nero needed to be the one to give way, both because the victory was in Livius' province, but also because only Livius' army was present (something that was decided on before the triumph was even agreed: 28.9.3, 28.9.10).[54] So Nero giving way to Livius was as much the consequence of their shared harmonious relationship as expressive of a particular virtue on his part, although, as Livy notes at some length, Nero's willingness to take a secondary role

---

[53] There is also a reference to it in Enn., *Ann.* 299 Sk., but the lack of context for that fragment makes it impossible to say how Ennius treated the relationship of Livius and Nero in the episode.

[54] Auliard (2001), 104–12 (cf. Beard (2007), 206–10) is rightly sceptical about the existence of a 'rule' that prevented a general from triumphing without his army: she adduces several cases where such a triumph was granted. But even though there was no 'rule' to this effect, it was sufficiently enshrined in practice that generals triumphed with their armies to make it natural that a commander with his army present would take precedence over one whose army was not present.

in the triumph was highly ironic given the far more substantial role he played in the victory.

P., however, reworks this into something very different. The decision to hold their triumph together is unmentioned; the fact that the victory occurred in Livius' province is cited as a reason for his taking the chief role, but not the even more salient point that only Livius had his army available. Exactly the same pattern of reasons stated and omitted is visible in Valerius Maximus (Paris' epitome, by contrast, offers no reasons at all, any more than does *Vir. Ill.* 48.5).[55] The result is that P., like Valerius, turns a story which is primarily about the consuls' shared harmony into one which places the emphasis on Nero's personal virtue and modesty; and it can hardly be overlooked that the latter might well appear more salient than the former to writers living under an autocratic political system.

cum: Cf. 2.2n.

Claudio Neroni: The MSS read *L. Neroni*; Rossbach made the obvious correction.

in provincia sua rem gesserat: Cf. Livy 22.9.10 *in provincia M. Livi res gesta esset*; also Val. Max. 4.1.9 *res in provincia Salinatoris gesta erat*.

gloriae reverentiaeque: A choice combination of words: apart from P., this pairing is found only in *Consult. Zacch.* 3.3.8, which may well postdate him.

28.3 *Extinguishing of fire in the temple of Vesta*. Corresponds to Livy 28.11.6–7. For P.'s interest in the transgressions and punishments of Vestals cf. 2.13n., 14.6n. It is noteworthy that he does not mention that people took it as a portent from the gods, and responded with appropriate ceremonies; he treats the episode, as Livy himself implies it should have been treated, as nothing more than a question of human negligence (see below). The episode is also recorded in Val. Max. 1.1.6 (also the epitomes by Paris and Nepotianus), for whom, similarly, the question of its being a divine portent does not come up.

ignis in aede Vestae…extinctus est; caesa est flagro: Cf. Livy 28.11.6 *ignis in aede Vestae extinctus: ob quam causam caesa flagro est Vestalis*.

neglegentia virginis: Livy refers to the *neglegentia* in order to explain why the extinguishing of the fire was not a divine portent (28.11.7); P. takes that point to heart, not mentioning that it was treated as a portent at all. As often, the punishment of Vestals is a topic of interest to him in its own right.

28.4 *Scipio Africanus drives the Carthaginians from Spain and concludes an alliance with Syphax*. Corresponds to Livy 28.12.10–18.12. P. ignores all of the details of the final battle at Ilipa that led to Carthage abandoning Spain; it is only the outcome in which he is interested, summarizing the extent of the Roman victory.

---

[55] Briscoe proposes a lacuna in Valerius after the explanation about the province: if that is correct, then it is possible that Valerius included other reasons also.

Just as important to him, however, is a matter which might appear largely anecdotal, namely the alliance that Scipio formed with Syphax, and the fact that when visiting Syphax to conclude that alliance, he dined on the same couch as Hasdrubal, who was visiting at the same time.

That combination of inclusion and omission, however, is far from surprising, both in the light of the post-Livian tradition and P.'s own interests. Syphax and Masinissa appear to have been of considerable importance to him, not least because of the contentious part they played in Scipio's ultimate victory, and he has already spent a certain amount of time giving the background of their relationship with Rome (24.4, 27.6; see *ad loc.*). Moreover, P. is in the mainstream of post-Livian writers in his lack of attention to the details of Ilipa (although Sil. 16.23–114 describes the battle, and Frontin., *Strat.* 2.1.1, 2.3.4 and Polyaen. 8.16.1 note aspects of it). Zonar. 9.8.9–10 is very brief; Oros. 4.18.17 says even less than P., doing nothing more than marking the Roman conquest of Spain; Appian, Eutropius, and *Vir. Ill.* appear to ignore Ilipa altogether in their recounting of Scipio's victories. But Sil. 16.170–276, App., *Hisp.* 29–30 (also *Pun.* 10), *Vir. Ill.* 49.10, and Zonar. 9.10.1 all pay rather more attention to the meeting with Syphax, which is also discussed by Val. Max. 9.8.1 (also Paris' epitome), albeit only to draw attention to Scipio's supposed rashness in going to it with so little protection. The Greek writers also all refer to Hasdrubal's presence at the meeting, an anecdote which appears to have been of less interest to the Latin authors: apart from P., it is mentioned only by Silius. It is conceivable that P. was aware of the Greek tradition, but more likely that he was influenced by Silius: see below.

debellavit: Frobenius' obvious correction of the MSS *bellavit*.

XIIII anno eius belli, quinto post anno quam ierat: Cf. Livy 28.16.14 *pulsi Hispania Carthaginienses sunt quarto decimo anno post bellum initum, quinto quam P. Scipio provinciam et exercitum accepit.*

praeclusisque in totum possessione provinciae eius hostibus: An unexpected phrase: 'with the enemy totally excluded from occupying that province'. Livy uses *praecludere* only once in his surviving text (33.13.5), though P. does often employ non-Livian phrases. More problematic is the construction of the verb here: *praecludere* constructs with a personal object extremely rarely (*TLL* X.1 493.63–6), and nowhere else is it used with an ablative of separation. Possibly the text is corrupt, and we should read *praeclusaque* (*hostibus* then being dative, a far more regular construction), but the fact that P. uses *praecludere* with a personal object on one other occasion (119.6) weights the evidence toward maintaining the text here: P. expands on Livy with an imaginative use of language.

The adverbial *in totum* is likewise not Livian; it is first found in the early imperial period, when it rapidly became very popular.

regem Massyliorum: This is an error: Livy refers to Syphax as king of the Masaesuli (28.17.5), not the Massylii; the latter nation in Livy is in fact Masinissa's, as P. recorded at 24.5. It is noteworthy, indeed, that whereas in Book 24 P.'s ethnic designations for Syphax and Masinissa followed Livy's, listing Syphax as from Numidia and Masinissa from the Massylii, in Book 28 he reverses them, and refers to Syphax as king of the Massylii and Masinissa as king of the Numidians (though the latter has warrant in Livy's text: see 28.8n.). This may be nothing more than carelessness—the similarity of the names made it easy for the Masaesulae and the Massylii/Maesuli (24.5n.) to be confused. But it is worth noting that exactly the same ethnic designations appear in Silius Italicus (16.116, 154, 170, 183, 234, 252); the overall narrative trajectory for this episode in P. is closer to Silius than to other post-Livian Latin writers (above), and he may have taken the names from there.

28.5 *Gladiatorial show at New Carthage*. Corresponds to Livy 28.21. P. passes over Scipio's capture of Iliturgi and Castulo (Livy 28.19–20), an episode ignored by most of the post-Livian tradition apart from App., *Hisp.* 32 and Zonar. 9.10.2; however, he pauses to describe Scipio's gladiatorial show. His interest was presumably generated in part by its unusual nature, since the competitors were volunteers, and in one case even used the fight to settle a dispute over a chieftainship; but he may also once again (cf. 28.4n.) have been influenced by Silius Italicus, who not only described the duel in question (16.527–56), but took the opportunity to expand a passing reference in Livy (28.21.10) into an epic account of funeral games along the lines of Homer, *Iliad* Book 23 or Virgil, *Aeneid* Book 5.

There are few other accounts of the show, but cf. Zonar. 9.10.3 and esp. Val. Max. 9.11 ext. 1 (also Paris' epitome), both of whom, like P. and Silius, are interested in the duel for the chieftainship. The one surprising omission by P. is that he gives no account of the outcome: but Paris' abridgement of Valerius does likewise. Livy and Valerius, with their intensely ethical focus, both are interested in the justice of the result, but for their summarizers the mere fact that such a duel took place at all is the chief point.

munus gladiatorium in honorem patris patruique Carthagini Nova edidit: *Carthagini* is locative; this was misunderstood in the MS tradition, which assumed it was dative, reading *Carthagini Novae dedit*; Drakenborch made the correction. For the phrase, cf. Livy 28.21.1: *Scipio Carthaginem…munusque gladiatorium, quod mortis causa patris patruique paraverat, edendum rediit*.

non ex gladiatoribus: The repetition makes for awkward logic, since it seems odd to say that a gladiatorial show did not use gladiators. Livy himself avoided the problem with more circuitous phrasing (28.21.2 *non ex eo genere hominum ex quo lanistis comparare mos est, servorum de castata ac liberorum qui venalem sanguinem habent*), but P.'s abridgement leads him to substitute the single word.

ex his qui aut in honorem ducis aut ex provocatione descendebant: Cf. Livy 28.21.4: *alii ipsi professe se pugnaturos in gratiam ducis, alios aemulatio et* *certamen ut provocarent provocatique haud abnuerent traxit.* P. omits Livy's first category of contestants: those sent by their princes to display the courage of the people (28.21.3); he focuses on those who made the decision entirely by themselves.

reguli fratres de regno ferro contenderunt: This represents a change to Livy. The lesser point is that Livy does not describe them as fighting *de regno* (nor does he call the men *reguli*), but rather *de principatu civitatis* (28.21.6; 28.21.7). More important is that Livy refers to them as cousins (28.21.6 *patrueles fratres*), not brothers. However, all other writers refer to them as brothers fighting over a kingdom (in Silius they are even twin brothers), and P. substitutes that more memorable version for Livy's.

28.6 *Mass suicide by Spaniards.* Corresponds to Livy 28.22.2–23.5. The story did not have a significant place in the later tradition—apart from P., it is found nowhere except App., *Hisp.* 33, along with a passing reference in Zonar. 9.10.2. P.'s inclusion of it is nevertheless not remarkable, given that it is a strikingly narrated episode in Livy; but as often, he eschews Livy's moralizing, reporting nothing but the bare fact of the suicide, without providing any context as to what brought the people to such an extremity and how the Romans responded to it.

cum: Cf. 2.2n.

Gisia urbs: Livy, like Appian, calls the town Astapa, although in later sources it is referred to as Ostippo (Plin., *Nat.* 3.12, *Itin. Anton.* 411.3; cf. *CIL* II 1438). On the face of things P.'s text appears impossible: there is no reasonable way that *Gisia* could be a corruption of *Astapa* or *Ostippo*; nor is there any other Spanish town of a similar name in the vicinity. However, W-M *ad* 21.60.7 plausibly hypothesize that P. is referring to the city which Livy calls *Kissis*, but which in other literary sources is called *Kissa* (Plb. 3.76.5) or *Gissa* (Plin., *Nat.* 3.140; there are also coins with the legend CE-S-E or CE-E-S-E or CE-E-S-S-E (Tovar (1989), 435)). The obvious problem is that this city was hundreds of kilometres away from Astapa, on the Mediterranean coast (so Jal (1984), 111); nevertheless, there is no reason to suppose either that P. was sufficiently aware of Spanish geography to know this, or that an alternative tradition would have to relate to a Spanish town near to Astapa.

P.'s version, however, even if representing a legitimate tradition, must be regarded as being of dubious historicity: there is no reason to prefer an account found only in one late summarizer to that of Livy and Appian. As to how such a tradition might have started, it is presumably relevant that Cissa/Cissis appears to have been in the immediate vicinity of Tarraco, a city that was, apparently, founded by the Scipios, and which later became a Roman colony (Plin., *Nat.* 3.21: cf. Schulten (1932), 2399). There is an attractive neatness to the idea a town associated with Scipio's family succeeded to and replaced a site that was the scene of such horrific self-destruction by the Spaniards; the same neatness, however, is an additional reason to doubt the historicity of the tradition.

28.7 *Mutiny of Scipio's troops; Spaniards surrender to Scipio.* Corresponds to Livy 28.24–9 and 28.31.5–34.12, omitting Livy's brief account of victories the Romans obtained over the Carthaginians who were attempting to retain a foothold in Spain. The events mentioned here are found in the narrative sources which give the Spanish campaign in some detail (Plb. 11.25–33, App., *Hisp.* 34–6, Zonar. 9.10.4–8), but are referred to nowhere else—the other late Latin summarizers ignore them completely. The reason P. pays attention to them is presumably in part because of their significance to Livy, who spends a good deal of time on them, but also in part because of his own interest in Scipio, and his general unwillingness to omit any of his achievements. As usual, he does not reproduce Livy's detailed exploration of the roots of the mutiny and the Spanish rebellion, or the moral significance either of them or of the manner in which they were suppressed; instead he allows the reader to assume that it was merely the result of the gap in leadership left by Scipio's illness, which is a reasonable if partial reflection of Livy's initial introduction to the episode (28.24.1–2).

ipse Scipio, dum gravi morbo implicitus est: Cf. Livy 28.24.1 *Scipio ipse gravi morbo implicitus*.

confirmatus: 'Recovered'; the usage is relatively rare, and not found in Livy, but appears in a number of texts from the late Republic and early Empire (*TLL* IV 220.5–16).

coegit in deditionem venire: Cf. 8.4n.

28.8 *Scipio makes alliances with Masinissa and Gades, then returns to Rome.* Corresponds to Livy 28.35.1–38.11. P.'s focus on Masinissa is of a piece with his earlier handling of both him and Syphax: as before, he provides some narrative detail, in this case not only prefiguring the role that Masinissa will play as an ally of Scipio in the next two books, but also for the first time referring to Scipio's invasion of Africa. The handling of Gades is more unexpected. Livy himself has Gades brought onto the Roman side almost as an afterthought (28.37.10); the bulk of his attention is on Mago's campaign and movements, as he first attempts and fails to recapture New Carthage, then crosses to the Balearic Islands. P. reverses those priorities: he places the acquisition of Gades as an ally in parallel to that of Masinissa; as far as Mago goes, the important thing is his proposed crossing to Italy, which P. presents as a mirror image of Scipio's plan to attack Africa (see below, and also 28.10n.).

Both App., *Hisp.* 37 and Zonar. 9.10 have slightly more on Mago's movements than P. does; but Appian, like P., makes relatively more of the acquisition of Gades, which was for a long time a wealthy and powerful centre of Roman Spain (though apparently derelict by the fourth century: see Avien., *Ora* 271–2), and focuses far less than Livy had on Mago's campaign, which would have little lasting effect even on the Second Punic War.

rege Numidarum: Cf. 24.5n., 28.4n.

si in Africam traiecisset: P. uses very similar language of Mago shortly afterwards (*in Italiam traiceret*). That language draws directly on Livy (28.36.1 *ut classem... in Italiam traiceret*), but Livy does not use a comparable phrase of Scipio at the point when Masinissa speaks of the possible crossing into Africa. *traicere* is admittedly P.'s favourite word when referring to sea-crossings, but it is not the only such word in his repertory: others include *transgredi* (16.2), *transvehi* (28.5), *transire* (38.2, 42.3, 49.8), *transportare* (48.16), or indeed *venire* (13.4, 78.3). P. harmonizes the language so as to point up the parallel between Scipio and Mago: on his presentation, the Romans and the Carthaginians engage in movements which mirror each other, but the latter campaign, with no Scipio at its helm, is aborted and unsuccessful (cf. 28.10n., 30.7n.).

⟨**cum**⟩ **Gaditanis quoque:** According to Livy 28.37.10, the people of Gades surrendered to the Romans; there is no mention of *amicitia*. It is true that *amicitia* is a very loose term, in Livy and elsewhere (cf. 7.9n., 14.5n.), but one would not naturally use it of a surrender, unless some other agreement accompanied it (cf. 10.2n.). It is, however, likely that such an agreement was made: according to Cicero, Gades made a treaty with Marcius, albeit one which was not ratified at Rome (Cic., *Balb.* 34, cf. 39), something that Livy alludes to indirectly in a later book (32.2.5). Briscoe (1973), 170–1 argues that this treaty probably accompanied or immediately preceded the surrender, *contra* Dahlheim (1968), 58–9, who suggests that it was concluded the following year, after Scipio's departure. P.'s account, which may simply be his own deduction from Livy, but may also derive from an independent tradition, provides some modest support for Briscoe's position (cf. Heuss (1933), 82–3, also Flurl (1969), 192–5).

cum is omitted in the MSS; it is restored in the Aldine edition.

post discessum inde Magonis: Cf. Livy 28.37.10 *post Magonis ab Oceani ora discessum*.

cui: A correction by one late MS for the *cum* of the main manuscript tradition.

28.9 Scipio given permission to invade Africa. Corresponds to Livy 28.40.1–45.11; prior to it, P. omits the embassy of the Saguntines giving thanks to the Senate (28.39). In Livy this episode has strong symbolic resonance, given that Saguntum had been the original *casus belli*, and its capture by Hannibal had been dramatically narrated; P., however, has had nothing of Saguntum beyond the bare fact that Hannibal attacked it (cf. 21.1n.), though it will make a surprising reappearance in his narrative in Book 31 (31.5n.).

As for the decision to send Scipio to Africa, this was a necessary part of any account of the war; the question is how far it is treated as a foregone conclusion, and how far the narrator acknowledges the level of opposition to Scipio's plans. Livy himself not only includes the speech of Fabius articulating reasons why Scipio's proposal should not be accepted, and suggests that it swayed at least part of the Senate, but also recounts a dispute over jurisdiction as to who had the right to make the decision in the first place. In addition, a number of the Greek sources (Plu., *Fab.* 25.4–26.2, App., *Pun.* 7–8, Zonar. 9.11.6) emphasize that the Romans did not give him the necessary resources for the invasion, leaving him to collect them himself, a point played down in Livy, who presents it rather as Scipio's own decision to conduct the campaign without creating a burden for the state (28.45.13–14). Conversely, the Latin summary tradition outside P. presented the decision to send Scipio to Africa as entirely uncontentious (Flor. 1.22.55, Eutr. 3.20.1, *Vir. Ill.* 49.11, Oros. 4.18.17). P., like Sil. 16.592–700, crafts a course between these, acknowledging the opposition of Fabius, but not suggesting that it extended beyond Fabius alone. Unlike the other summarizers, and indeed unlike Silius, he notes that the primary province given to Scipio was not Africa but Sicily, but he also quotes from Livy the permission given to Scipio to transfer the war to Africa, suggesting that he carried the day in every material way.

permissumque ut in Africam traiceret, si id e republica esse censeret: Cf. Livy 28.45.8 *permissumque ut in Africam, si id e re publica esse censeret, traiceret.*

28.10 *Mago crosses to Italy.* Corresponds to Livy 28.46.7–13. P. describes Mago's arrival in Italy, though nothing of what he did while he was there, or indeed about the Romans' response to his arrival. Nevertheless, it is remarkable that he included it at all: it is an episode on which Livy himself places relatively little stress, and which appears in no other source apart from a passing mention in Zonar. 9.11.7. Part of the reason is presumably, as before (28.8n.), to note the parallel between Scipio's invasion of Africa and Mago's of Italy; but it also may be relevant to note that, as usual, he not only follows Mago's story through to its conclusion (29.3, 30.7), but ultimately makes a dramatic alteration to the sequence of Livy's narrative in order to round off the Second Punic War with Mago's defeat (30.7n.).

Mago, Hamilcaris filius, a minore Baleari insula, ubi hiemaverat, in Italiam traiecit: Cf. Livy 28.46.7–8 *Mago Hamilcaris filius ex minore Baliarum insula, ubi hibernarat...in Italiam...traiecit.* P. substitutes *hiemare* for Livy's *hibernare*. Both are classical, but *hiemare* is the more popular term in Latin generally (P. uses it again at 130.2), whereas *hibernare* is far more common in Livy, who uses *hiemare* only twice (5.2.1, 40.17.7). P. removes a characteristically Livian word in favour of a less distinctive one: this is unusual for him, given his tendency to pastiche Livy's language, and may simply arise from a desire not to reproduce Livy's wording too exactly.

Book 29

29.1 *Laelius brings Scipio a message from Masinissa.* Corresponds to Livy 29.1.15, 29.3.7, 29.4.7–5.1. The opening chapters of Livy's book (29.1–5) intertwine a number of separate episodes, including Scipio's recruitment of troops in Sicily (29.1–18), a revolt in Spain (29.2n.), Laelius' expedition to Africa and his meeting with Masinissa, and the Carthaginians' response to the threat of Scipio, including sending reinforcements to Mago (29.3n.). P. omits the first altogether, perhaps surprisingly: one story Livy told, concerning the nervousness of the Sicilians to serve with the Roman forces, and Scipio's offer to allow them each to provide arms and horse for a Roman instead, was distinctive and memorable, told also in D.S. 27.2a (*ap.* Eust., *Comm. Il.* 23 p. 1302), Val. Max. 7.3.3 (with Paris' epitome), App., *Pun.* 8. P.'s omission may have been because in Book 28 he also omitted the prelude to the story, namely Scipio having to supply his own troops for his campaign (28.9n.).

With the rest of the episodes, he untangles them into discrete stories by uniting the various references to Laelius' expedition into a single notice, which he places first in the book. That positioning is slightly surprising: on some other occasions where P. has combined different parts of a story, he has placed it at the last point it appears in Livy's narrative, an approach that is formally justified by his practice of putting the first part of the story into a 'background' participial or *cum* clause (2.2n., 2.11n., 11.2n., 38.7n.; cf. 18.5n.). Here he uses similar grammar, but inserts the entire story at the place where in Livy's narrative it begins. This may be in part to keep Scipio's invasion of Africa in a prominent position—certainly one can see why P. highlights the ongoing negotiations with Masinissa over the self-contained episode of the Spanish revolt, which had no further consequences within the war, especially when Livy makes it clear that the two took place simultaneously (29.1.19 *eadem aestate*). The positioning also enables P. to reproduce something of Livy's causal sequence, since the support sent to Mago by the Carthaginians was prompted when they discovered that Laelius' raid was not the full-scale invasion they had feared, and was an attempt to keep Scipio in Italy (29.4.5).

Laelius: The chief MSS read *Caecilius*; the correction is easy.

praedam reportavit: An unusual phrase. The only direct parallel is in two other late writers: Cypr. Gall., *Num.* 760 and Greg. Ilib., *Tract.* 8.9; but Manil. 5.188 has *praedas…reportavit*; cf. also Cic., *Rep.* 2.15.2 *nihil ex praeda…reportaret*.

mandata Masinissae Scipioni exposuit querentis quod nondum exercitum in Africam traiecisset: Cf. Livy 29.5.1 *mandata Masinissae Scipioni exposuit*; 29.4.8 *questus, quod iam non exercitum in Africam traiecisset*. The word-order, with *querentis* separated from *Masinissae* by a verb, is an example of 'verbal hyperbaton', a stylistic device which became increasingly popular in literary prose in the

Augustan period and later (see Adams (1971)). In imperial authors the noun usually appears last (Adams (1971), 13); but the particular version here, with a participle and associated dependent clause postponed until after the verb, became common in historians, even those (like Sallust and Tacitus) who usually avoid other forms of verbal hyperbaton (Schlicher (1933), 297–9, Adams (1971), 8–9). P. artfully combines material from two separate sentences in Livy into a single sentence of a manner distinctive to historiographical prose.

29.2 *Revolt in Spain*. Corresponds to Livy 29.1.19–3.6. P. provides no details of the fighting, but only the fact that Indibilis began the war and was killed in battle, after which Mandonius was surrendered to the Romans also. The oddity from the point of view of P.'s narrative is that this is the first and only time that Indibilis and Mandonius have been mentioned by him, whereas in Livy they were regular but intermittent presences from 22.21.3 onwards (cf. Levene (2010a), 67). Having ignored them up to this point, P. suddenly highlights them. The reader is not required to know Livy in order to comprehend the events, but the presence of the names draws attention to the fact that they have an importance that is not limited to their role in the final throes of Spanish resistance, and invites recognition by the minority of readers who do happen to be familiar with Livy.

bellum in Hispania finitum victore Romano, quod Indebilis excitaverat: For *bellum excitare* (a Livian phrase) cf. Woodman (1983a), 105; the word-order here is unusual, with *victore Romano* apparently introducing a new idea, only for P. to return to an explanation of the war in the relative clause. For the collective *victore Romano*, cf. Livy 6.29.5, 9.36.13, 28.4.7; also Petron. 119.1, Flor. 1.38.9.

Livy usually spells the name *Indibilis*; but as Rossbach rightly points out *ad loc.*, the Puteanus MS reads *Indebilis* at 29.2.14, which makes it more probable that P. is preserving a spelling which he found in his own copy of Livy.

Mandonius: The chief MSS read *Madonius*, but the MSS of Livy spell it *Mandonius*, which should accordingly be restored.

29.3 *Mago in Liguria receives reinforcements*. Corresponds to Livy 29.4.5–6 and 29.5.2–9. For the placement of this notice, cf. 29.1n. P. here continues the story of Mago's campaign in Italy that he began at the end of Book 28 (28.8n., 28.10n.). However, he says nothing about Mago's attempt to assemble local allies, which is the centre of Livy's account, but instead focuses solely on the resources he received from Carthage. This is perhaps best explained by Livy's subtle account of the way the Gauls and Ligurians put Mago off rather than supplying troops immediately, and indeed his presence among them has little long-term effect on the war, to judge by Livy's narrative. The Carthaginians' arrival in Italy at this point in the war is important to P., as a counterbalance to Scipio's plans to attack Africa (cf. 28.10n., 30.7n.), but he, more straightforwardly than Livy, does not allow any suggestion that he has any success in attracting local allies.

qui Albingauni in Liguribus erat: According to Livy, the Carthaginian ships 'landed between the Ligurian Albingauni and Genoa; Mago happened at that time to have his fleet in that neighbourhood' (29.5.2–3: *inter Albingaunos Ligures Genuamque accesserunt. in iis locis tum forte Mago tenebat classem*). Since nearly 100 km of coastline separate Albingaunum (modern Albenga) and Genoa, P.'s claim that Mago was at Albingaunum itself seems incompatible with Livy. It is possible that this is P.'s own deduction, arrived at by combining Livy's text with an inexact sense of the geography, but the fact that P. specifically refers to the town by an accepted form of its name (cf. e.g. *CIL* VI 2529), whereas Livy only speaks of the people, suggests that at the very least he had some sort of knowledge independent of Livy (cf. 39.3n.), and very probably a non-Livian source as well.

There is, however, no way of assessing the reliability of P.'s version, except on the general consideration that Livy is on the whole more likely to have had access to sources with authentic information about Mago's movements than he was.

ampla manus: An unusual phrase: P. uses it once more later in this book (29.11) and then at 49.10, but outside P. it is found only in Char. 5 p. 404.11–12 (Barwick), where it appears as part of a list of idiomatic Latin phrases, and at *AE* 1903, 368. For other uses of *amplus* to indicate numbers of people cf. *TLL* I 2007.53–60.

pecuniae, quibus auxilia conduceret: Cf. Livy 29.4.6 *magna pecunia ad conducenda auxilia*. The plural *pecuniae* is a reasonably common idiom in Livy, but is also used, especially in later antiquity, to emphasize the amount of money at issue, which fits the context here (*TLL* X.1 942.71–943.9).

ut se Hannibali coniungeret: Cf. Livy 29.4.6 *coniungeretque se Hannibali*.

29.4 *Scipio recaptures Locri.* Corresponds to Livy 29.6.2–8.4. P. passes over the situation in Locri prior to Scipio's arrival, where neither Carthaginians nor Romans were able to get the upper hand, and focuses instead on the time when Scipio arrived and secured the Roman victory, though in terms that would appear to suggest victory in a pitched battle (*pulso, fugato*), instead of what Livy indicates to be a strategic withdrawal by the Carthaginians before a superior force (29.7.9–10), albeit one which, at least as regards the Carthaginian garrison, was 'with a speed similar to flight' (29.7.10 *fugae simili cursu*). A messy and anticlimactic battle (cf. Levene (2010a), 306–7) is turned by him into an unequivocal Scipionic victory; a similar effect is created by the brief notice of the fight at Locri by App., *Hann.* 55 (the summary version of Zonar. 9.11, on the other hand, is closer to Livy).

Scipio…Locros…recepit: As often, P. takes his phrasing not from Livy's primary narrative, but from a later reference to the events, in this case the speech of the Locrians to the Senate complaining about Pleminius (29.17.4 *P. Scipione, qui Locros recepit*); see also below.

a Syracusis: Livy 29.7.2 describes Scipio crossing 'from Messana' (*a Messana*); but he was at Syracuse a little earlier, at the time when he first planned the retaking of Locri (29.6.10). P. presumably inferred that he was based at Syracuse, and that Messana was merely the point from which he embarked for Locri. This inference may have been correct, but against it is that, according to Livy, Scipio left his brother to garrison Messana rather than Syracuse (29.7.2), and was still at Messana when the problems with Pleminius came up, although he returned to Syracuse not long after (29.9.8); this suggests that he may have had a longer-term base there.

in Bruttios traiecit: Livy does not speak of Scipio sailing to the country of the Bruttii, but to Locri itself; the country of the Bruttii began inland from there (Str. 6.1.9). However, Bruttium was sometimes treated as equivalent to the entire peninsula (e.g. Sall., *Hist.* 4.23M, Plin., *Nat.* 3.5; cf. Mela 2.115), and it is more probable that P. is depending on this understanding of the geography than that he was offering an alternative version of Scipio's route.

For the spelling of *Bruttios* see 12.3n., 13.8n.

pulso Punico praesidio: Here too (cf. above), the language is taken from the Locrians' speech to the Senate: 29.17.1 *pulso Hannibalis praesidio*.

29.5 *Peace of Phoenice: end of First Macedonian War.* Corresponds to Livy 29.12. P. has been relatively assiduous at providing notices of Livy's occasional references to the progress of the First Macedonian War (cf. esp. 23.11n., 24.4n., 26.4n.); but he now brings it to a conclusion with surprising abruptness, offering no more than the barest fact of the peace, with no reference to the complex diplomatic dance between the different states that preceded it. The explanation for the abrupt ending may be similar to that for the fuller treatment earlier: that P. is looking ahead to the Second Macedonian War, which will begin less than two books later, and, given the abbreviated scale of his narrative, the peace forms no more than a brief interlude in the developing hostilities between Rome and Philip (cf. 31.1n.).

Prior to reporting the peace treaty, Livy has described the beginnings of the stories of Pleminius in Locri and of the Magna Mater coming to Rome; P., however, reserves both of those for a later point: see 29.6–7n. and 29.8n.

29.6–7 *Bringing the Magna Mater to Rome.* Corresponds to Livy 29.10.4–11.8 and 29.14.5–14. On the face of things, the amount of space that P. devotes to this episode may appear surprising—it occupies a greater portion of his text than a large number of events that might on the face of things appear more consequential both in Livy's narrative and in the Second Punic War. However, that surprise is lessened once one considers the overwhelming popularity of this story—it is one of the most famous episodes in Roman history, retold or alluded to in a vast number of places.⁵⁶ It is nevertheless interesting that, despite its fame, neither Florus nor Eutropius nor Orosius includes it in their narratives; it suggests that the story primarily existed as a free-standing anecdote rather than as an integral part of the narrative of the war (but cf. below), and it also shows the difference between them and an author like P., who is overtly summarizing a predecessor.

To some extent, P.'s narrative follows Livy's closely: he reports the oracle that led to the decision to bring the goddess to Rome, the approach to Attalus, the nature of the image, and the reception at Rome by Scipio Nasica, all of which are told in Livy. At the same time, the entire episode becomes an excellent example of how the process of summary, without changing Livy in any material way, distils from his narrative a significance which is only partially related to the original. Some of the distinctive features of Livy's version not only remain, but are enhanced. For example, Livy is unusual in the close link he makes between the arrival of the Magna Mater and the ultimate victory in the Punic War: that idea is absent from all other Republican and early imperial sources apart from Silius (Levene (1993), 70), though it reappears in Arnobius and Julian, who are likely to have derived it from Livy himself. P., however, reproduces it, and indeed it forms a more significant part of his inevitably shorter narrative than it did of Livy's: as in Livy, a story with no necessary connection to the war is locked into it far more tightly. Related to this is the role of Attalus; here too Livy is unique in explicitly making the point that Attalus' willingness to aid Rome over the Magna Mater was the consequence of the Romans' having formed an alliance with him in the First Macedonian War (29.11.2-3, 29.11.7);⁵⁷ P. does not say this explicitly, but his description of Attalus as *regem Asiae*, language not taken from Livy here, alludes back to his use of the same phrase at 28.1 in the context of that alliance.

On the other hand, P.'s summary also mutes some of the more distinctive features of Livy. For most authors, the story centres on Scipio Nasica, Claudia Quinta, or both; Livy is highly unusual in undercutting the importance of both of them, instead focusing on the collective part played by the Roman citizen body, especially the women (Levene (1993), 71–2). P.'s version removes any sense of collective action, and instead draws on Livy's statements about Nasica so as effectively to turn him into the one person who receives the goddess at Rome, exactly

---

⁵⁶ e.g. Cic., *Har. Resp.* 27, *Cael.* 34, *Fin.* 5.64, *Cato* 45; Varro, *Ling.* 6.15, D.S. 34/35.33.1–2, *Fast. Praenest., Apr.* 4, Prop. 4.11.51–2, Ov., *Fast.* 4.247–348, *Pont.* 1.2.141–2, Str. 12.5.3, Val. Max. 7.5.2, 8.15.3 (both with Paris' epitome), Plin., *Nat.* 7.120, Sil. 17.1–43, Stat., *Silv.* 1.2.245–6, Suet., *Tib.* 2.3, App., *Hann.* 56, Juv. 3.137–8 (also Scholia), Dio fr. 57.61, Hdn. 1.11, Sol. 1.115 (Mommsen), Fest. 268L, Arnob., *Nat.* 7.49–51, Min. Fel. 7.3, Lact., *Inst.* 2.7.12, Jul. *Or.* 5, 159C–161B, Amm. 22.9.5–6, *Vir. Ill.* 44.1, 46, Jer., *Adv. Jovin.* 1.26 = Sen., *De Matr.* fr. 80, Claud., *Laus Seren.* 17, 28–30, Aug., *Civ.* 2.5, 10.16, Sidon., *Carm.* 24.41–3; cf. Livy 35.10.9. The centrality of the story in Roman cultural memory may be shown by the fact that Cic., *Brut.* 79 can casually identify a later Scipio Nasica by saying that he was 'son of the man who received the sacred objects' (*illius qui sacra acceperit filium*; cf. Vell. 2.3.1).

⁵⁷ Most other sources do not mention Attalus at all; one of the few who does is Ovid, whose narrative has exactly the opposite dynamic—Attalus does not want to help the Romans, until he is ordered to do so by Cybele herself.

as many other sources do (e.g. Cic., *Fin.*, Valerius, Dio, Solinus, Ammianus, Aug., *Civ.* 2.5): indeed, he even supplements Livy to enhance Nasica's role beyond that in any other surviving source (see below).

Noteworthy in a different way is P.'s treatment of the nature of the image that is brought to Rome: he indicates that it was not an anthropomorphic image, but a stone. This too is taken from Livy almost verbatim, but in the context of P.'s shorter narrative, in conjunction with the changed historical and religious context under which he was writing, the effect is entirely different from what it had been in Livy. Most other sources either do not describe the image, or else they directly indicate that it was anthropomorphic;[58] but Arnobius takes the idea of the stone and turns it into the centre of his polemic, mocking at great length the idea that a mere stone could have driven out Hannibal and won a war for the Romans (cf. Prud., *Perist.* 10.154–60 for Christian mockery of the worship of a stone in the Magna Mater cult). P.'s inclusion of this detail does not necessarily mean that he shared Arnobius' perspective, but it does suggest that he was highlighting rather than suppressing a point that had been seized upon as a topic of polemical religious debate, a narrative strategy that is perhaps more likely in a sceptic than in someone who accepted the claims that bringing the Magna Mater to Rome was instrumental in Hannibal's defeat.

29.6 mater Idaea deportata est Romam a Pessinunte...carmine in libris Sibyllinis invento, pelli Italia alienigenam hostem posse, si mater Idaea deportata Romam esset: P. takes his phrasing from Livy's account of the Sibylline oracle (29.10.5 *quandoque hostis alienigena terrae Italiae bellum intulisset, eum pelli Italia vinciquae posse si mater Idaea a Pessinunte Romam advecta foret*); but he repeats the wording, first in order to summarize the event, then when offering the oracle in explanation (both times substituting *deportare* for *advehi*, perhaps because Livy uses that verb a little afterwards in a passage P. will also be drawing on closely: 29.11.7—see below). This close repetition appears clumsy, but it has the effect of reinforcing one of Livy's major points (cf. above): that the oracle promised victory if the goddess was brought, and the Romans followed its prescription exactly.

The sentence structure reverses the more common pattern in P., the main clause appears first, with the ablative absolute then taking the sentence in a new direction (a typically Tacitean structure: see Kohl (1959), esp. 31–5, 99–103).

oppido Phrygiae: P. takes this information not from Livy's account of when the oracle was received, but slightly later, when the Roman ambassadors are led *Pessinuntem in Phrygiam* (29.11.7).

---

[58] Cf. e.g. Ov., *Fast.* 4.345 *sedens plaustro*; note also the representation of the legend of Claudia Quinta in an early imperial relief in the Capitoline Museum (reproduced at Beard, North, and Price (1998), vol. 2, 46), where the goddess's image is clearly anthropomorphic.

lapis erat, quem matrem deum incolae dicebant: Cf. Livy 29.11.7 *lapidem quam matrem deum esse incolae dicebant*; however, Livy's MSS vary between *quam* and *quem*. Both are grammatical—on one reading the gender of the relative is attracted to that of the complement, in the other it is retained in the masculine— though the first is by far the more common in classical Latin (Pinkster 1278–81). The presence of *quem* in P. might be taken to support that reading in Livy (so Bingham 275); but any such support would be very weak. The corruption from *quam* to *quem* in this context is so easy that it might well have arisen several times independently, and even if the MS of Livy that P. was using read *quam*, he could easily have changed it to *quem* himself.

29.7 **excepit:** The object is understood from the previous sentence (cf. Pinkster 756–8).

P. Scipio Nasica: Livy does not provide Scipio's *cognomen* when describing the arrival of the goddess, but it was so widely reported within the tradition that P. could easily supplement the information from other sources.

Cn. filius eius qui in Hispania perierat, vir optimus a senatu iudicatus, adulescens nondum quaestorius: Cf. Livy 29.14.8: *patres conscripti P. Scipionem Cn. filium eius qui in Hispania ceciderat, adulescentem nondum quaestorium, iudicaverunt… virum bonorum optimum esse.*

ita responsum iubebat: In Livy, the oracle that prescribed that the *vir optimus* should welcome the Magna Mater to Rome was not the original Sibylline oracle, but one that the Roman ambassadors subsequently received at Delphi (29.11.5–6). P., without directly contradicting Livy, allows the reader to infer that only one oracle was at issue, as in other versions of the story (e.g. Diodorus, Silius, Appian, Solinus, Ammianus; Val. Max. 8.15.3 has the oracle from Delphi, as in Livy, but makes no reference to the Sibylline oracle; cf. also Dio).

exciperetur consecrareturque: In Livy, the oracle prescribes that the *vir optimus* should 'receive' the goddess into the city (29.11.6 *exciperet*), but says nothing about his 'consecrating' her; nor is this element found in any other surviving version of the story. However, P.'s notice here fits his account of the eventual dedication of the temple in Book 36, where he explicitly ascribes the dedication to Scipio Nasica, in whose consulship it took place, in contradiction to Livy 36.36.4, who names the dedicator as the praetor, M. Junius Brutus. It is most likely that P. is here depending on an alternative ancient version of the dedication (see 36.2n.). If that is accepted, then the remaining question is whether the notice here, insisting that Nasica's dedication of the temple was not just coincidental, but was demanded from the start by the oracle, was similarly derived from an earlier source, or merely reflects P.'s own rewriting of Livy in order to tidy the story; but there does not appear to be any decisive consideration that would weight the argument in one direction or the other: either is possible (but see the introductory note to Book 36).

For the final *-que* cf. 2.12n.; it is especially noteworthy that P. here introduces this typically Livian linguistic device while offering information which does not derive from Livy.

29.8 Locrians complain about Pleminius. Corresponds to Livy 29.8.6–9.12 and 29.16.4–19.9, 29.21.1–12, 29.22.7–9.[59] P. here introduces Pleminius' story for the first time, although in Livy the problems were set out much earlier (cf. 29.6n.); prior to introducing it, P. omits the aftermath of the story of the colonies who had refused military service (29.15), which is unsurprising, given that he had also omitted the opening of that story in Book 27 (27.2n.).

In Livy, the story of Pleminius is closely bound up with that of Scipio, and the complaints, both at Locri and at Rome, that are directed against Pleminius' abuses of power, are also complaints—at least partially justified, on Livy's account—against Scipio for failing to keep him under proper control and even directly condoning those abuses. P. carefully unweaves the story, treating Pleminius and Scipio as entirely separate; he acknowledges charges against Scipio, but only related to his conduct in Syracuse (29.9n.), which in Livy is more of a supplementary charge than a major part of the indictment (29.19.11–13), for all that Scipio's eventual ability to clear himself of the charges relates far more to the question of Syracuse than that of Pleminius (29.22.1–6).

This way of handling the story is clearly related to P.'s general partiality for Scipio (cf. e.g. 21.3n., 26.3n., 27.6n., 27.8n., 29.4n.), which repeatedly leads him to accentuate his successes and play down the more ambivalent aspects of his character in Livy (see 29.9n.). It has, however, some parallels in the way in which the accusations against Pleminius and Scipio were handled in other ancient sources. The claims that Scipio 'Hellenized' in Syracuse are usually self-contained and unrelated to Pleminius: see Val. Max. 3.6.1 (with Paris' epitome), Plu., *Cat. Ma.* 3.5–8, Tac., *Ann.* 2.59.1, Symm., *Or.* 1.16. Conversely, Pleminius, even if identified as Scipio's lieutenant, is seen as acting entirely independently of him, and 'Hellenizing' is not mentioned in this context (Val. Max. 1.1.21 (with Paris' epitome), App., *Hann.* 55)—indeed, Scipio, if he appears, only does so in order to act promptly to punish him (as in the minority version cited by Livy at 29.21.2: cf. D.S. 27.4, Nepotianus' epitome of Val. Max. 1.1.21). Among surviving sources, only Dio fr. 57.62 directly puts the different accusations against Scipio together, though not enough of that fragment remains to be sure how Dio handled it.

It is of a piece with this that P. cuts down substantially the charges against Pleminius: he highlights his maltreatment of the Locrians and his sacrilege against Proserpina, but does not mention the episode on which Livy himself places the most emphasis, namely his brutal treatment of the Roman military

---

[59] Assuming that 29.22.10, giving Clodius Licinus' version of Pleminius' story, is a later gloss: see Oakley (1992).

tribunes who tried to prevent Pleminius' troops from plunder (29.9.1–10). These are mentioned in Diodorus,[60] but in no other source: as in P., it was the sacrilege and after that, the mistreatment of the Locrians, which attracted the most attention. Similarly, whereas in Livy it is repeatedly made clear that the Roman troops under Pleminius' command have followed his lead (esp. 29.9.1–4, 29.16.7, 29.17.14–15, 29.21.4–6, 29.21.12), P. treats Pleminius' crimes as particular to him, as do Valerius and his epitomizers: Diodorus and Appian do refer to Pleminius' partners in crime, but the point is still muted by comparison with Livy.

A more surprising omission is the Senate's restitution of Pleminius' sacrilegious plunder, which is a prominent part of every other source, even the brief epitomes of Paris and Nepotianus, but which finds no place in P. It is relatively rare for P. to fail to follow the expected ethical patterning of the story in this way, and to show the ways in which justice was accomplished and recompense made; nevertheless, it is not a unique example in his text (cf. e.g. 12.1n., 28.5n.); in this case, the fact that the perpetrator was punished appears to have mattered to him more than the restitution to the god.

impudentia: So the MSS: Frobenius, followed by Rossbach, read *impotentia*, on the basis of Livy 29.8.8 *nihil omnium quae inopi invisas opes potentioris faciunt praetermissum in oppidanos est*; but that passage is too distant from P.'s phrasing to support an emendation when the MS reading is perfectly acceptable in context.

in catenis Romam perductus: Cf. Livy 29.21.12 *in catenis Romam miserunt*.

29.9 Accusations against Scipio dismissed; he invades Africa. Corresponds to Livy 29.19.10–20.11, 29.21.13–22.6, 29.22.11–12, 29.24.8–27.15. As noted above (29.8n.), P. separates out the charges against Scipio from the question of Pleminius, which is of a piece with the handling of the story in most other ancient sources. What is more distinctive is the manner in which he treats those charges. Unlike every other version, he does not provide any detail as to what Scipio's offence consisted in. Livy summarizes them (29.19.11–13): walking in the gymnasium dressed in Greek costume, occupying himself in books and exercise, and giving licence to his troops to indulge themselves. The claims of Hellenizing in costume and activities are similarly raised by Valerius Maximus (though Paris' epitome reduces it to a bare reference to his spending time in the gymnasium), Plutarch, Tacitus, Dio, and Symmachus; while Plutarch makes even greater play with the corruption of the army. P. has nothing more than a vague allegation of luxury. Moreover, Livy is explicit that there is a significant degree of truth to the charges: he refers to them as 'partly true, partly mixed, and to that extent similar to the truth' (29.20.1: *partim vera partim mixta eoque similia veris*), and every other source likewise indicates that the charges against Scipio were well founded.

---

[60] However, Diodorus handles the matter very differently from Livy: the tribunes in his version are merely trying to get their own share of the plunder, and are indignant at being deprived of it.

For P., the charges are simply false (*falsus rumor*): the shadow that constantly rests over Livy's Scipio is removed (cf. Levene (2015b), 323–4).

To set against that, however, is that P. pays so much attention to the charges at all. The fact that Scipio is accused, even if falsely, forms the bulk of his notice, whereas the crossing into Africa, despite forming the main clause, becomes a brief pendant. That crossing was a key point in the narrative, and one that no account of the war could omit; nevertheless by comparison with Livy, who recounts it in considerable and elaborate detail, P.'s willingness to treat it merely as the sequel to the attack on Scipio seems out of proportion. His manifest interest in Scipio is as much in the controversy that surrounded his image as in the conduct of his military campaign.

cum: Cf. 2.2n.

luxuriaretur: Cf. 23.13n.

29.10 *Syphax repudiates his alliance with Rome.* Corresponds to Livy 29.23.1–24.3. Livy reports this before Scipio's crossing to Africa, and indeed it is closely connected to his narrative of that crossing, since Syphax uses his new alliance with the Carthaginians as a reason to deter Scipio from coming to Africa, and Scipio not only conceals this but actively lies to his soldiers about the reason for the presence of African envoys. As he did earlier in the book, P. unweaves Livy's intricate narrative into discrete units; but he also alters the implicit narrative sequence, since Syphax's change of allegiance is implied to take place after Scipio's arrival. In contrast, both Frontin., *Strat.* 2.7.4 and Zonar. 9.12.2, like Livy, tell of Syphax's approach and warning to Scipio following his defection, a defection which Zonar. 9.11.2, like App., *Pun.* 10, dated to the period when Scipio was still in Spain. P.'s ordering, however, closely mirrors Sil. 17.59–75, who does not describe Syphax's defection until after Scipio's arrival in Africa, and moreover implies that Scipio did not learn of it until that point, although Silius, unlike P., makes it clear by his tenses (17.61 *paraverat*, 17.70 *ruperat, pararat*) that it had in fact taken place earlier. P. may have been influenced by Silius' order, or they may have reached the same point independently: both authors simplify the moral position of Scipio, who now not only does not act deceptively, but has no reason for deception on this account; and in P.'s case it may also be relevant that this sequence allows him to juxtapose directly Syphax's treachery with Masinissa's demonstration of loyalty, thus bringing to the fore a contrast which is prominent (though more complex: see Levene (2010a), 247–59) in Livy also.

29.11 *Masinissa loses his kingdom, but joins Scipio and defeats Hanno.* Corresponds to Livy 29.29.4–35.2. P. tidies up Livy's complex narrative in a variety of ways. Livy introduces his account of Masinissa's loss of his kingdom in a lengthy digression following his arrival at Scipio's camp; P. treats the events in chronological order, although he carefully (unlike with Syphax: see 29.10n.) indicates that

Masinissa had lost his kingdom earlier. Moreover, the complexities of the internal politics of the Massylii are simplified to the point of being misleading. A reader of P., combining the reference to Masinissa as king with the statement that he lost his kingdom after his father's death and that he sought to regain it through war, would naturally assume that Masinissa was the heir to the kingdom, who would have inherited from his father had he not been absent in Spain, and was attempting to recover what was rightfully his own. In Livy, however, Masinissa's uncle initially succeeded to the throne 'by Numidian custom' (29.29.6: *ita mos apud Numidas est*), followed by first his elder son, then his younger (the latter, however, being the puppet of an older relative); Masinissa then took the kingdom by force, only to have it taken from him in turn by Syphax with the support of the Carthaginians; Masinissa took the kingdom a second time, but Syphax once again deposed him. P. gives a vague pointer to the multiplicity of conflicts recorded by Livy with the phrases *saepe repetito* and *aliquod proeliis*, but the overall situation he describes is still a long way removed from Livy's, although the essential endpoint is the same—Masinissa, when he joins Scipio, may be formally a 'king', but he is not in possession of a kingdom.

All of this may simply derive from P.'s desire to keep the story to an easily summarized minimum, but one should note that the result is that the version of the story which he records is not unlike that of App., *Pun.* 10–12: Masinissa's father dies while he is in Spain, but he is prevented by Syphax and the Carthaginians from inheriting the throne, and instead he engages in constant fighting against them. This similarity may arise because Appian (or Appian's source) and P. were independently adopting similar techniques of simplification; but it may also be that both are drawing on a post-Livian tradition which had reduced the story (which is, after all, largely tangential from a Roman perspective) to these manageable proportions.

rex Massyliorum: P. had used the same phrase (inaccurately) at Masinissa's original introduction: cf. 24.5n.

dum pro Carthaginiensibus in Hispania militat: Cf. Livy 29.29.6 *militanti pro Carthaginiensibus in Hispania*.

de regno exciderat: For *excidere* = 'to be deprived of', cf. *TLL* V.2 1236.73–1237.16. The construction with *de* is not found prior to late antiquity; earlier authors either employ the ablative alone, or else *ab* or *ex*.

quo...saepe repetito: Cf. Livy 29.33.9 *saepe repetiti regni paterni*.

aliquod proeliis: Cf. 12.3n. *aliquod = aliquot*.

in totum: Cf. 28.4n.

privatus est: *privo* generally takes an ablative, and is almost never found absolutely (though cf. *TLL* X.2 1409.44–55); hence the verb here must govern *quo* [sc. *regno*]. This reads awkwardly: on first reading *quo...repetito* appears to be an ablative absolute, a construction often used by P., and its separation from the verb by a further participial phrase makes it doubly uncomfortable now to construct them together. This may simply be the result of clumsy writing, but it also means that the reader, reaching *privatus*, will initially read it adjectivally, which is highly appropriate in the context—Masinissa is indeed helping Scipio as a *privatus*—and that connotation remains, even when *est* shows that *privatus est* must be taken as a verb.

cum CC equitibus exul: At the start of his account of Masinissa joining Scipio, Livy noted that the majority of his sources recorded that he had 2,000 cavalry, and that 200 was a minority view (29.29.4). At the end of the digression, he concludes that, since Masinissa was an exile, the lower figure is more likely to be correct (29.33.10). P. not only correctly reports Livy's conclusion, but introduces the word which Livy had offered in support of that conclusion, which looks pointed.

primo...bello: For *primum bellum* = 'the first part of the war', see e.g. Caes., *Gall.* 3.9.9 *Venetiam, ubi Caesarem primum esse bellum gesturum constabat*; cf. Sil. 7.105, with Littlewood (2010), 73-4. In Livy this is not in fact the first battle of Scipio's African campaign: prior to Masinissa's arrival his troops defeat the Carthaginian cavalry and kill their commander, also called Hanno (29.29.1). However, Livy himself notes that the existence of two battles in which a Hanno was killed was not accepted by all of his sources (29.35.2). In the two sources he names—Coelius Antipater (*FRHist* 15 F 39) and Valerius Antias (*FRHist* 25 F 31)—this Hanno was captured rather than killed (as indeed he is in App., *Pun.* 14 and Dio fr. 57.65-7 (cf. Zonar. 9.12.3-5)).[61] But an alternative solution, which Livy indicates was the version he found in other sources, would be to dismiss one battle altogether as a doublet (similarly, Appian, Dio, and Oros. 4.18.17, do not mention the first battle at all):[62] various modern scholars argue that in fact only one battle took place (e.g. De Sanctis III.2 566-7 [583], *contra* e.g. Lazenby (1978), 205). P., by failing to mention the first battle, implicitly aligns himself with those sceptics, and in this context the phrase *primo bello* appears pointed, marking that he is convinced by the query that Livy appended to his narrative rather than by the narrative itself.

---

[61] Whether Coelius and Valerius reported this version in the context of a single battle, or as a way of distinguishing the first battle from the second, unfortunately depends on a textual crux. One MS tradition of Livy 29.35.2 reads *Coelius quidem et Valerius captum etiam Hannonem tradunt*; however, other MSS omit *etiam*; and it is unclear which version is correct. On the former reading, which is preferred by most modern editors, Coelius and Valerius, as Appian and Dio would later do, not only reported just one battle, but said that Hanno was captured in it. As for the latter reading, J. Briscoe *ap.* *FRHist* III 257 claims that 'if [Livy] did not write *etiam*, he is saying nothing about the number of Hannos and battles in Coelius and Antias'. But in context, if *etiam* were not present, the introduction of Coelius and Antias with *quidem* would appear to suggest that Livy saw Coelius and Valerius offering an alternative solution to the one presented by the authors who reported only one battle, and hence that they were among those who included two.

[62] Eutr. 3.20.2 refers to two battles, but solves the 'doublet' question in a different way, since on his account the same Hanno was involved in both, and he does not mention his death.

ampla manu: Cf. 29.3n.

29.12 *Scipio fails to capture Utica.* Corresponds to Livy 29.35.3–15. P., like Livy, shows Scipio's initial campaign in Africa ending on a note of failure: the attempted siege of Utica is aborted by the arrival of Hasdrubal and Syphax. P.'s willingness to include a minor setback goes against his broadly eulogistic treatment of Scipio; it may be related to the fact that he is far more expansive in Book 29, the shortest of Livy's Third Decade, than he is elsewhere—relatively little in the book goes entirely unnoticed. But more broadly, it shows the extent to which P.'s agenda is not entirely his own, but is in part governed by the overall tenor of Livy's narrative (cf. Introduction).

prope cum centum milibus armatorum: A reasonable summary of Livy's numbers: Livy recorded Hasdrubal arriving with 30,000 infantry and 3,000 cavalry, and Syphax with 50,000 infantry and 10,000 cavalry (29.35.10–11): 93,000 troops in total.

hiberna communiit: Cf. Livy 29.35.12 *castra hiberna… communit.*

29.13 *Sempronius defeats Hannibal.* Corresponds to Livy 29.35.4–9. In Livy, the result of the initial engagement was a victory for Hannibal; only when Sempronius' army is combined with that of the proconsul Licinius are the Romans victorious. The more equivocal narrative slant in Livy is more obviously reflected in Dio fr. 57.70, who briefly refers to the defeat then victory; Oros. 4.18.18 is more idiosyncratic still, having only the defeat, followed by Sempronius fleeing to Rome. P.'s treating it as an unequivocal success makes him an outlier in the tradition, although one thing he shares with both Dio and Orosius is that all three focus on Sempronius alone and ignore Licinius' significant contribution.

prospere adversus Hannibalem pugnavit: Cf. 2.6n.

29.14–15 *Censorship of Livius Salinator and Claudius Nero.* Corresponds to Livy 29.37. P., as usual, includes Livy's census figures (1.B.3n., 3.3n.), and indeed highlights them by extracting them from the narrative of the censorship and presenting them as a notice in their own right at the conclusion of the book. However, he spends even more time on the censorship itself, focusing on three particular aspects: Nero's demotion of Livius, Livius' reciprocal demotion of Nero, and Livius' culminating act of demoting all but one of the tribes. He omits a number of other of the censors' actions that Livy records, not only those that were relatively uncontentious, like their building plans, or their inclusion of the Latin colonies in the census, but also Livius' introduction of a salt tax (which provided him with his *cognomen*), itself apparently out of resentment against the citizen body. He also does not mention the abortive attempt by the tribune Baebius to prosecute Livius and Nero for their conduct.

P.'s selection is at least in part explicable, partly by his own interests, but also partly by the treatment of the story elsewhere in the post-Livian tradition. The omission of the census of the Latin colonies is presumably related to the fact that he has earlier omitted the account of their refusal of conscription, which forms a prelude to the notice here (27.2n., 29.8n.). The focus on the reciprocal demotions by the censors, and Livius' culminating demotion of virtually the entire citizen body, closely mirrors Val. Max. 2.9.6: both P. and Valerius draw on the same phrases of Livy (cf. below); and the brief biography of Livius in *Vir. Ill.* 50.3 includes the demotion of the citizens, though not the conflict with Nero, as also does Suet., *Tib.* 3.2. On the other hand, a separate notice in Valerius (7.2.6; also Paris' epitome) describes the attempted prosecution of the censors, which P. omits, and the surviving fragments of Dio (fr. 57.70–1) focus more on the registration of the Latins and the salt-tax. P. appears to reflect one strand of tradition, but the story was not a popular one, and never appears to have coalesced around a single theme (it is notable that the epitomators of Valerius omit 2.9.6 altogether).

29.14 notabilis: Livy never uses this word, nor indeed is it found anywhere in Republican or Augustan writing apart from Cic., *Fam.* 5.12.5 and Ov., *Met.* 1.169; but it became popular subsequently.

Claudius collegae ecum ademit, quod a populo damnatus actusque in exilium fuerat: Cf. Livy 29.37.9 *M. Livium quia populi iudicio esset damnatus equum vendere iussit*; also Val. Max. 2.9.6 *et citari collegam et equum vendere iussit, quia populi iudicio damnatus esset*. Neither Livy nor Valerius, however, lists among Nero's reasons that Livius had been driven into exile, and Livy has in fact said directly that Livius' withdrawal from Rome was voluntary, not a punishment (27.34.4), contrary to what P. implies when he has Nero cite it as a reason for Livius' demotion. It is unlikely that P. is recording an alternative tradition; more probably he is elaborating Livy on the basis of his memory, but does so misleadingly. It may be noted that Val. Max. 4.2.2, in a different context, does say that Livius 'set off for exile' (4.2.2 *in exilium profectus fuerat*): nothing in Valerius suggests that Livius was compelled to do so, but it is easy to see how P., reading this or some other similar passage, might have wrongly deduced that exile was part of the penalty.[63]

For the spelling *ecum* see *TLL* V.2 731.47–9; for *fuerat* cf. 25.3n.

quod falsum in se testimonium dixisset et quod non bona fide secum in gratiam redisset: Cf. Livy 29.37.10 *unius quod falsum adversus se testimonium dixisset, alterius quod non sincera fide secum in gratia redisset*; also Val. Max. 2.9.6

---

[63] Bingham 280 less plausibly suggests that P. was misled by the comparison Livy made in Book 27 between Livius' return from exile and Camillus' (27.34.14): he suggests that P. deduced from this comparison that the circumstances of Livius' withdrawal must have been like those of Camillus.

(who, however, omits the first reason) *quod non sincera fide secum in gratia redisset.*

idem omnes tribus extra unam aerarias reliquit, quod et innocentem se damnassent et posthac consulem censoremque fecissent: Cf. Livy 29.37.13–14 *praeter Maeciam tribum...populum Romanum omnem...aerarios reliquit, quod et innocentem se condemnassent et condemnatum consulem et censorem fecissent*; also Val. Max. 2.9.6 *cum se damnassent, postea consulem et censorem fecissent.*

29.15 lustrum a censoribus conditum est: Cf. 11.5n.

censa sunt civium capita: Cf. 3.3n.

Book 30

30.1 *Scipio defeats Syphax and Hasdrubal and captures their camps; Syphax is captured.* Corresponds to Livy 30.3.3–9.2 and 30.11.1–12.4. In describing the Romans' fighting against Syphax and Hasdrubal, P. makes some significant alterations to Livy. Most obvious—and least surprising—is that he omits altogether the successful Carthaginian counterattack against the Roman forces at Utica (30.9.3–10.21); it is not uncharacteristic of him to overlook minor Roman defeats, the more so in this case because Scipio was the Roman commander. More interesting is that he changes the entire dynamic of the campaign. P. suggests that Scipio was victorious in 'numerous battles' prior to his capturing the two camps. In Livy, however, the assault on the camps takes place first; it is only subsequent to this that the Romans encounter Syphax and Hasdrubal on the battlefield—and there are not 'several' battles, but just two (though the first is preceded by some minor skirmishing): 30.8 and 30.11.4–12.4 (cf. 18.1n.). The alteration may simply be because it might appear more 'natural' to have the capture of the camps as a consequence of rather than a prelude to the battles; but it may also reflect a desire to occlude (but cf. below) the fact that the actual way, according to Livy, that the camps were captured, was because Scipio eschewed fighting but deceptively engaged in negotiations (albeit formally breaking them off just prior to attacking the camps), thus putting the enemy off their guard.

P.'s account appears less idiosyncratic, however, in the light of other parts of the post-Livian tradition. The longer narratives, it is true, are relatively similar to Livy in the basic sequence of events, although they vary in many details (App., *Pun.* 18–26, Zonar. 9.12.7–13.1): they have first the capture of the camps, then the battles (including the Carthaginian counterattack at Utica), and finally the capture of Syphax; similarly Oros. 4.18.18–21, despite overlapping linguistically with P. in one phrase (see below), does not share his narrative approach (though Orosius' narrative itself varies substantially from Livy's, only having a single battle against Hasdrubal and Syphax after the destruction of the camps, with Syphax captured in flight following the battle). However, both Florus and Eutropius show closer similarities with P. Florus writes 'What forces, good gods, of Hasdrubal, what cavalry of Syphax, the Numidian king, did he [Scipio] rout! What and how great were the camps of them both, which he destroyed in a single night after bringing in torches' (1.22.56: *quas ille, dii boni, Hasdrubalis copias fudit, quos Syphacis Numidici regis equitatus! quae quantaque utriusque castra facibus inlatis una nocte delevit!*). It is possible that Florus' order is purely for rhetorical effect rather than intended to represent the chronological sequence of events, but it is also possible that he is reflecting an existing interpretation of the African campaign—or else that his rhetoric was misunderstood by later writers as representing the chronology, and that he is thus the ultimate source of P.'s version.

As for Eutropius, he is unlike P. (and indeed any other surviving source) in having Syphax himself captured prior to the capture of his camp, but this version likewise seems to presuppose that fighting came first, and the camps were taken afterwards (3.20.2: 'He captured Syphax, the king of Numidia, who had joined himself to the Africans, and attacked his camp'—*Syphacem, Numidiae regem, qui se Afris coniunxerat, capit et castra eius invadit*). P.'s account is not Livy's, nor is it entirely identical to that of any other ancient source, but it represents the filtering of Livy through an interpretation of the campaign that is found more broadly in the tradition.

⟨...⟩ **in Africa Carthaginienses et eundem Syphacem...vicit:** In the chief MSS, *vicit* lacks a subject; since the subject is obviously Scipio, his name was inserted in various places by the later MSS: after *Hasdrubalemque*, or after *vicit*, or after *Africa*, or as the first word of the book. Jahn, noting P.'s regular practice (in around 65 per cent of the books whose openings survive) of starting a book with the name of an individual, preferred the last, and this reading has been accepted by subsequent editors.

However, *eundem* suggests a different reconstruction. P. almost invariably employs *idem* of a person (or people) who played a role in the previous sentence or clause; the one exception (69.4: *idem Apuleius Saturninus*) still is of someone who was a major figure slightly further back in the same book. Nowhere else does P. use *idem* of a person whose last appearance was in the previous book, let alone someone who was last referred to several sentences back in that book. This makes it far more likely that an entire sentence has dropped out, a sentence of which Scipio was the subject, and which also referred to Syphax: and that sentence can only have been a summary of the negotiations that took place between them (Livy 30.3.4–4.9). It remains the case that P., as argued above, is covering up the connection between those negotiations and the capture of the camps, by inserting a number of battles between them; but he has not overlooked that side of the story completely.

Numidiae regem: P. used the same phrase of Syphax on his first introduction (24.5); its repetition here closes off the arc of his career.

pluribus proeliis: Cf. 12.3n.

adiuvante Masinissa: Livy uses the same phrase, but of the help Masinissa gave to Laelius in subduing the rest of Numidia after Syphax's capture (30.12.22). This reinforces the sense that P. is knowingly rewriting the campaign so as to place the fighting at the start: it also alerts the small number of readers with a good knowledge of Livy to the fact that he is doing so (cf. 22.12n.).

XL milia hominum ferro ignique consumpta sunt: Cf. Livy 30.6.8 *caesa aut hausta flammis ad quadraginta milia hominum sunt*; also cf. 30.6.9 (of the elephants in the camps) *octo ferro flammaque absumpti*. Oros. 4.18.19 has almost exactly the same phrase as P. (*quadraginta milia hominum igni ferroque consumpta sunt*): one is clearly drawing it from the other, or else both derive it from a prior source. Since Orosius provides more information than P. (for example, he includes Livy's figures for the number of captives), one might assume that it is more likely that P. depends on him than *vice versa*; however, the fact that the entire narrative sequence in P. is different (cf. above), suggests that he cannot depend directly on Orosius either, nor, for the same reason, is it likely to go back to a single common source. Far more likely is that Orosius is incorporating this phrase from P. into an account which he is constructing in part from other sources (cf. Introduction).

Syphacem per C. Laelium et Masinissam cepit: It is, of course, the case that Laelius and Masinissa were ultimately under Scipio's direction when they captured Syphax (cf. Livy 30.9.1); nevertheless, it is a striking illustration of the Scipio-centricity of P.'s narrative that he makes him the subject of the sentence.

30.2 *Masinissa and Sophoniba.* Corresponds to Livy 30.12.11–15.8. P. is unique in the post-Livian Latin tradition of telling this story at all: while it is a significant part of the longer Greek accounts (D.S. 27.7, App., *Pun.* 27–8, Zonar. 9.13.2–6), it does not appear in any other Latin source apart from P. and Livy himself. His interest in including it no doubt stems from its very prominence in Livy; but his distillation of it is unlike those found in the Greek tradition. Not only do they present the episode as a continuation of an earlier relationship between Masinissa and Sophoniba (cf. App., *Pun.* 10, Zonar. 9.11.1–2 (with Dio fr. 57.51)), but they also, like Livy, give a prominent role in the story to Syphax, who warns Scipio against Sophoniba. P. removes Syphax from the equation.

What P. does share with the Greek authors is the diminution of Sophoniba herself as an active agent. In Livy, she extracts from Masinissa at the very start the promise that he will kill her rather than hand her over to the Romans (30.12.14–16), and his sending her poison is simply a fulfilment of that promise. For the Greek writers, and likewise for P., she is only a passive recipient (indeed, Diodorus suggests that she even took the poison involuntarily). In this case it is unlikely that the similarity between P. and the Greeks is the result of direct or even indirect influence; it is more likely that it is Livy himself who is the outlier, in being willing to offer so heroic a role to a foreign woman (esp. Toppani (1977–8), 573–8; also cf. Johner (1996), 86–7, Kowalewski (2002), 238–9).

Sophonibam, uxorem Syphacis, filiam Hasdrubalis: Cf. Livy 30.12.11 *Sophoniba, uxor Syphacis filia Hasdrubalis Poeni.* P., like Livy, introduces Sophoniba in terms of her male relationships, but it is necessarily more central to his account, given the degree of abridgement. Given that her father is not obviously as relevant to the narrative as was her marriage to Syphax, P.'s description reinforces the general sense of passivity that he invests her with (cf. above).

captam: The idea comes from Livy, who, however, invests Masinissa's love for Sophoniba with a greater sense of paradox (30.12.18 *amore captivae victor captus*).

adamavit: Livy never uses *adamo* in his surviving work; and the word, though common in Cicero, is not used of sexual passion before Ovid (*Ars* 2.109).[64] Thereafter this sense becomes a regular part of its usage: cf. *TLL* I 567.51–70.

nuptiis factis: Cf. Livy 30.12.21 *factis nuptiis*.

castigatus: Livy uses this verb, not of Scipio's speech blaming Masinissa for his marriage, but rather of the mild rebuke he makes to him after Sophoniba's suicide (30.15.10). P. transfers it here.

30.3 *Hannibal recalled to Africa; battle of Zama.* Corresponds to Livy 3.19.12–20.9, 3.25.11–12, 3.29–35. P.'s account of the final campaign of the war may appear surprising in its selectivity. Most obviously, Scipio's victory at Zama, which Livy recounted in considerable detail, is reduced to three words: while it is not unusual for P. to restrict a battle to a bare notice (cf. 22.7n.), it is more surprising in a case that was so central historically (though cf. 44.3n.), and still more surprising that he does not at least make it the focus of the sentence, but instead has it as an appendage to events which he describes more fully: the Carthaginian decision to recall Hannibal to Africa, and Hannibal's attempt to negotiate with Scipio. Moreover, P. entirely passes over the embassies sent by the Carthaginians, first to Scipio, then to Rome, which sought to negotiate peace terms, as well as the violation of the armistice by the Carthaginians. His focus here is on Hannibal himself, to the point that he does not even explicitly name Scipio as the general by whom the victory at Zama was won.

In this, however, P. is not altogether an outlier in the tradition. The other Latin summary historians likewise largely reduce the victory at Zama to the bare fact (though Orosius offers some sense of its scale by providing casualty figures), and spend more time on the preliminaries (Flor. 1.22.57–61, Eutr. 3.20.3–23.1, Oros. 4.19.1–3; cf. also *Vir. Ill.* 49.14 *revocatum ex Italia Hannibalem superavit*). They vary on the details of those preliminaries—for example, Eutr. spends considerable time on the Carthaginian embassies, and places the meeting between Scipio and Hannibal much earlier in the sequence of events; Orosius includes Hannibal's massacre of Italians prior to departing Italy, and the bad omen he received on his journey. But Florus, though not overlapping in language, is close to P. in his inclusions and omissions, to the point that he, too, does not explicitly name Scipio as the victor. It is true that this was far from inevitable—not only do the Greek

---

[64] *Contra OLD s.v. adamo* 1a, which amusingly interprets this passage as an example of intellectual admiration.

historians narrate the story in vastly more detail (Plb. 15.1–16, App., *Pun.* 31–47, Zonar. 9.13.8–14.9), but Frontin., *Strat.* 2.3.16 uncharacteristically offers a detailed account of the entire battle, while Sil. 17.149–617 counterbalances a full description of Hannibal's return with an equally full (if highly fictionalized) account of the battle (but has nothing of Scipio and Hannibal meeting prior to it).

It appears that for P., as for others in the later Latin tradition, the sole relevant thing about Zama was the fact that it was when the Romans achieved their final victory in the war; the manner in which that victory was won was irrelevant. The effect is to provide a sense of inevitability: the fact of Hannibal's ultimate defeat was, of course, well known,[65] and P. has, like Livy, arguably been foreshadowing it from the time he has introduced Scipio in Book 21. His narrative places Hannibal at its centre and takes him back from Italy to Africa to meet that defeat. That alone appears to be enough.

effectumque multis Scipionis victoriis: It is relatively rare for P. to create narrative connection by beginning a new notice with *-que* or *et* (though cf. 5.8, 21.4, 28.8, 41.2, 60.7, 80.7, 85.2, 86.4, 106.3, 109.2, 111.5, 113.2, 115.4); but here he not only does so, but begins the next sentence in the same way (*isque*).[66] This increases the impression of a sequence of events driving forward from Scipio's victories in Africa earlier in the book to Hannibal's defeat (cf. above). The reference to *multis Scipionis victoriis* reinforces the continuity: in Livy's narrative Scipio achieves no further victories between the death of Sophoniba and the Carthaginian decision to recall Hannibal, and, while P.'s language leaves it open whether he is introducing new victories not in Livy, or referring only to victories already mentioned (cf. 30.1n.), it is at least capable of being interpreted in the latter way, especially since *multis victoriis* picks up *pluribus proeliis vicit* from earlier.

in desperationem acti: The phrase is unparalleled in surviving Latin, although *ad* or *in desperationem* is found with various other verbs to similar effect (*TLL* V.1 738.78–739.3).

in auxilium publicae salutis Hannibalem evocarent: For *evocare* used of summoning troops cf. *TLL* V.2 1057.68–1058.8; for *evocare in auxilium* cf. Suet., *Aug.* 16.4; for *auxilium publicae salutis* cf. Caes., *Gall.* 5.48.1 *unum communis salutis auxilium in celeritate ponebat*. The phrase as a whole, however, reads awkwardly; it may be that P. is influenced by the not infrequent use of the phrase *auxilium salutis* in Christian theological contexts (e.g. Ambr., *In Luc.* 5.44 *ad propagandum auxilium salutis humanae*), leading him to expand the military language beyond what would be natural in a classical historian.

anno XVI Italia decedens: Cf. Livy 30.28.1 *post sextum decimum annum ex Italia decedentem*; also 30.21.9 *sexto decimo...anno*; 30.32.6.

---

[65] Among the many passing references to it in Latin writers, see e.g. Cic., *Fin.* 5.24, Val. Max. 5.3.2, 6.9.2, Quint., *Inst.* 5.10.48, Juv. 6.170, Ampel. 24.1, Jer., *In Dan.* 3.11.17b–19.

[66] Jahn accordingly emended to *itaque*, but that itself is only used once in P. (89.8).

30.4 *Peace treaty between Rome and Carthage.* Corresponds to Livy 30.36.1–38.5, 42.11–44.11. In Livy, the peace agreement after Zama is set out in two separate places: first, where the Carthaginians sue for peace and Scipio offers a set of provisional terms, which are debated and ultimately accepted in Carthage; the second, where the Carthaginian ambassadors are received by the Senate in Rome, and the Senate gives Scipio the authority to determine the terms of peace. In both parts, Hannibal plays a substantial role: in the first, violently challenging an opponent of Scipio's terms, in the second, upbraiding the citizens for being more concerned by the private losses than by those of the state, and prophetically warning of the danger a weakened Carthage will now face.

P. conflates the two stages of the peace agreement into one, and, of Hannibal's two interventions, he describes only the first. He further omits a large number of other points, including the last-ditch attempt by the son of Syphax to renew the war (30.36.7–8), the sinking of the fleet commanded by Claudius Nero (30.39.1–4), the consul Lentulus' failed attempt to have Scipio's command transferred to himself (30.40.7–16), and the embassy from Macedon with regard to their alleged violations of the treaty with Rome (30.42.1–10). The reason that the last of these disappears is presumably that, unlike Livy, P. is keeping a strict division between the Punic War and the Second Macedonian War, confining all of the preliminaries of the latter to Book 31; none of the others, with their indications of continued strife both internal and external even after Zama, is allowed by P. to break the narrative of Scipio's victory. As for the conflation of the stages of the peace treaty and the reduction of Hannibal's role, this too is relatively unsurprising; while the longer Greek narratives, like Livy, present a two-stage process (App., *Pun.* 49–65, Zonar. 9.14.10–12 with Dio fr. 57.82–3; cf. Plb. 15.17–19), the Latin authors generally compress them in much the same way as P. (Nep., *Hann.* 7.1, Sil. 17.618–24, Eutr. 3.23.2, Oros. 4.19.4–5; cf. *Vir. Ill.* 49.16); and if Hannibal plays any part at all, it is in his recommendation of peace (Plb. 15.19, App., *Pun.* 55, Oros. 4.19.4). That P. focuses so heavily on the attack on Gisgo, however, is more surprising: the story appears nowhere outside Polybius and Livy himself; it is of interest to P. that Hannibal not only endorsed the peace, but that he was prepared to take a transgressively active step to promote it. Symbolically resonant moments such as Hannibal's warning to Carthage, or indeed the burning of the Carthaginian ships (cf. Sil. 17.622–4, Oros. 4.19.5), are of less importance to him.

Hannibal Gisgonem pacem dissuadentem manu sua detraxit: Cf. Livy 30.37.7–8: *cum...Gisgo ad dissuadendam pacem processisset,...Hannibal...arreptum Gisgonem manu sua ex superiore loco detraxit.* P.'s language comes entirely from Livy, but Livy's lengthy sentence is distilled selectively into a succinct statement.

excusata deinde temeritate facti ipse pacem suasit: Cf. Livy 30.37.10: *excusata imprudentia de pace multis verbis disseruit. excusata...temeritas* is an unparalleled phrase (but cf. ps.-Quint. *Decl.* 8.9 *excusationem temeritatis*).

30.5 *Masinissa is granted his kingdom.* In terms of the sequence of Livy's narrative, this appears to correspond to Livy 30.44.12, where, after the peace with Carthage has been concluded, Scipio 'in addition to his father's kingdom, granted Masinissa the town of Cirta and other cities and territories which had passed from the kingdom of Syphax into the power of the Roman people' (*Masinissam ad regnum paternum Cirta oppido et ceteris urbibus agrisque quae ex regno Syphacis in populi Romani potestatem venissent adiectis donavit*). However, there are two earlier occasions in the book when Masinissa appears to be 'granted his kingdom'. At 30.15.11–14 Scipio gives Masinissa the title of 'king'; nothing is said about his receiving a kingdom at that point, but only that Masinissa was led by this to 'the imminent hope of obtaining all of Numidia with Syphax removed' (30.15.14 *spem propinquam sublato Syphace omnis Numidiae potiundae*). But shortly afterwards his envoys are received by the Senate (30.17.7–14), and they refer to Scipio having 'not only called Masinissa king, but had made him so by restoring him to his father's kingdom' (30.17.8 *Masinissam non appellasset modo regem, sed fecisset restituendo in paternum regnum*). The Senate then ratify Scipio's actions in the following terms: 'Scipio seemed to them to have acted rightly and properly in calling him king, and the senators approved and praised whatever else he did that was pleasing to Masinissa' (30.17.12 *Scipionem recte atque ordine videri fecisse quod eum regem appellaverit, et quicquid aliud fecerit quod cordi foret Masinissae id patres comprobare et laudare*).

One possible way of reading this would be that Livy carelessly neglected to mention the restoration of the kingdom at the time when Scipio honoured Masinissa with the title, but now refers to it; and that the Senate ratified it along with all of Scipio's other acts to honour him. On that reading, 30.44.12 must either be a doublet, or else is referring only to the grant of additional territory previously belonging to Syphax, as Masinissa had hoped at 30.15.14, the grant of Masinissa's ancestral kingdom having been given earlier.

However, there is a better interpretation, which takes Livy's precise words more seriously (see Saumagne (1966), 44–7). The reason he mentioned nothing of the kingdom before the ambassadors came to the Senate was that Scipio said nothing: he granted Masinissa the title, but made no specific promise as to what territory was to be associated with it.[67] His envoys then deceptively implied to the Senate that Scipio had promised him a precise territory as well as the title[68]—a

---

[67] It is even possible—though hardly provable—that this was historical. Certainly the grant of the title of 'king' to an ally is unparalleled at this period, and there can have been no automatic assumption as to what accompanied the title (cf. Badian (1958), 295, who uses this as a reason to doubt the historicity of the entire story, but see *contra* Rawson (1975), 155 = Rawson (1991), 181–2).

[68] *non appellasset modo regem* appears pointed: it draws attention to the possibility that the grant of the title might have been a mere form without substance—as indeed it looks to be on Livy's actual account of Scipio's grant to Masinissa.

style of deception that Masinissa has been regularly practising on Scipio, on Livy's account (Levene (2010a), 252–8). But the Senate, whether or not recognizing the deception, did not explicitly endorse that grant, but rather threw the decision back to Scipio, who eventually—and only at the very end, after Masinissa proved himself at Zama—gave him what he was hoping for.

On that reading of Livy, the fact that P. refers to the restoration of Masinissa's kingdom now, rather than when Scipio first (and, in Livy's narrative, at greater length) called him 'king', suggests at the very least that P. recognized this, rather than the earlier honours, as the key moment in Livy—but at the same time, he shows those of his readers who know Livy's original text his awareness of the discrepancy, by drawing his language from the earlier rather than the later passage (cf. below). He gives no hint of deception on Masinissa's part, any more than he had earlier.

The passage makes the necessary narrative connection between Masinissa's earlier loss of territory (29.11), and his much later presence as a ruler, which will be essential to P.'s account of the Third Punic War (see esp. 47.7, 48.3). This interest in having sufficient elements in place to make sense of his long-term narrative is characteristic of P.; and explains why he alone among the Latin summarizers mentions Masinissa's restoration (though it is referred to in a handful of other places, notably Plb. 15.18.5; cf. Sall., *Jug.* 5.4, App., *Pun.* 48, Dio fr. 57.82, Ampel. 37).

Masinissae regnum restitutum est: Cf. Livy 30.17.8 *restituendo in paternum regnum.*

30.6 *The triumph of Scipio.* Corresponds to Livy 30.45. Scipio's triumph after his victory was regularly treated as the culmination of the narrative of the Second Punic War; it is, admittedly, not mentioned explicitly by either Florus or Zonar., but it is described by Plb. 16.23, Sil. 17.626–54, App., *Pun.* 65–66, Ampel. 37, Eutr. 3.23.2, Oros. 4.19.6; there are also later references by Livy himself (38.46.10, 38.51.14) and other authors (e.g. Cic., *Fin.* 4.22, Val. Max. 5.2.5 (with Paris' epitome), 6.2.3). The most common elements to be referred to, all mentioned by Livy, are the appearance of Syphax in the procession (Polybius, Val. Max. 6.2.3, Silius, Ampelius), the presence of the freed captive Q. Terentius Culleo (Val. Max. 5.2.5; also Orosius, who confuses him with the playwright Terence), and the receiving of the name Africanus (Silius, Eutropius, Orosius; cf. Sall., *Jug.* 5.4, Zonar. 9.14.13). P. includes the last two, but not the first, the historicity of which Livy himself indicates was controversial (30.45.4–5). Overall, an episode which in Livy stands out for its position at the end of the book, but certainly not for its length or detail, is given relatively more emphasis by P. in terms of length, but surprisingly displaced from the book's conclusion (see 30.7n.).

amplissimum nobilissimumque egit triumphum: This is the only place where P. employs two superlatives in conjunction, presumably reflecting the fact that Livy himself refers to the triumph as 'the most distinguished of all' (30.45.2 *omnium clarissimo*). *amplissimum nobilissimumque* is Ciceronian (*Clu.* 197 *homines amplissimi nobilissimique*; cf. *II Verr.* 2.106). For *egit triumphum* cf. 17.2n.

Q. Terentius Culleo senator pilleatus secutus est: Cf. Livy 30.45.5 *secutus Scipionem triumphantem est pilleo capiti imposito Q. Terentius Culleo*. However, the closest parallel to P.'s language here is in Julius Paris' epitome of Val. Max. 5.2.5 (*Q. Terentius Culleo...currum eius pilleatus secutus est*); Valerius himself is closer to Livy in wording (*Q. Terentius Culleo...Africani superioris currum triumphantis, pilleum capite gerens secutus est*). It is possible that P. and Paris arrived at similar phrasing through independent processes of compression of their separate authors, but it is also possible that one drew on the other—most probably P. on Paris (cf. 37.3n.; also Introduction).

P. takes the information that Terentius was a senator not from this passage, but from Livy's account of his release (30.43.11).

Scipio Africanus incertum militari prius favore an populari aura ita cognominatus sit: Cf. Livy 30.45.6 *Africani cognomen militaris prius favor an popularis aura celebraverit...parum compertum habeo*. P., unusually, faced with a passage where Livy is agnostic, maintains the dilemma rather than choosing a preferred version. However, he omits Livy's third option, the one which reflects least well on Scipio: that the name originated out of private flattery.

primus certe hic imperator victae nomine a se gentis nobilitatus est: Cf. Livy 30.45.7 *primus certe hic imperator nomine victae a se gentis est nobilitatus*. As usual, even when P. stays close to Livy's phrase, he maintains a measure of distance by reordering the words.

30.7 *Defeat and death of Mago*. Corresponds to Livy 30.18.1–19.6. For the end of the book—and the end of his account of the Second Punic War—P. returns to an earlier moment in Livy, the defeat and death of Mago, which on Livy's account had taken place two years earlier, and which he had recounted prior to the return of Hannibal from Africa. It clearly matters to P. to complete the story of Mago, to which he had earlier given a surprising amount of attention, and which he had treated as, in effect, the Carthaginian parallel to Scipio's invasion of Africa (28.10n.; cf. 28.8, 29.3). Even given that, however, it is unexpected that it appears here, rather than in its chronological place.

One possible reason is P.'s regular interest in using a death to provide closure (cf. 18.5n.); but that alone does not seem adequate to explain so dramatic a displacement. One additional possibility is suggested by a comparison with Appian, who dates the recall of Mago after the battle of Zama (*Pun.* 49; cf. 54, 59): while it is unlikely that P. can have used Appian, his ordering may reflect an awareness of a version in which Mago's retreat from Italy took place later. A third reason, perhaps the most pertinent of all, is to provide a sense of continuity; for on Livy's account, reflected in P., conflict with the Carthaginians in northern Italy did not end here, but was to resume in the following book (31.6n.). Even the decisive victory of the Second Punic War, from the perspective of P.'s sweeping account of Roman history, left the Romans still with work to do (cf. 11.1n.).

quo: The chief MSS read *qui*, but *quo*, found in various later ones, is more idiomatic.

in agro Insubrum: Livy identifies the location of the battle in identical wording (30.18.1).

ex vulnere mortuus est: Cf. Livy 30.19.5 *ex volnere moritur*.

Book 31

31.1–3 *The causes of the Second Macedonian War.* Livy's account of the outbreak of the Second Macedonian War is notoriously convoluted and controversial. Much of the controversy relates to the Romans' motives for engaging in the war, which I will not be considering here; but even understanding the sequence of events as Livy presents them is extremely difficult (and, naturally, different reconstructions of the sequence may offer better or worse support for particular accounts of the Romans' motives, and be chosen accordingly).[1]

Livy presents the events as follows. (1) Rome received envoys from Athens complaining about Philip attacking their land; envoys from Pergamum and Rhodes also came (31.1.10–2.1). (2) The Romans sent ambassadors to Egypt, appealing for neutrality in any war against Philip (31.2.3–4). (3) The Romans sent a fleet to Macedonia, where they meet a Roman legate who recommends war (31.3). (4) A second embassy from Athens warns that their city is under threat from Philip (31.5). (5) The consul puts a bill to the assembly proposing war, but the assembly votes against it (31.6); (6) the consul then reintroduces the bill and it passes (31.7.1–8.4). (7) Envoys from Egypt report an appeal to them by the Athenians; Ptolemy promises the Romans that he will offer whatever help they want against Philip (31.9.1–5). (8) The consul goes to Brundisium, where he is met by another Athenian embassy, saying that they are under siege and requesting help; he sends troops, though Philip is not present, but at Abydus (31.14.1–5).

Livy then explains the background to the Athenian quarrel with Philip. (9) Two Acarnanians inadvertently violated the Eleusinian Mysteries and were put to death; the Acarnanians appealed to Philip, who allowed them to attack Athens (31.14.6–10). (10) Attalus of Pergamum came to Athens, along with the Rhodians, who were then fighting Philip. With their encouragement, the Athenians declared war on Philip (31.14.11–15.11). (11) Philip sends his officer Philocles to attack Athenian territory, while he himself attacks a number of other cities, including Abydus (31.16–17). (12) Philip, then besieging Abydus, received a warning from the Roman ambassadors who had been sent to Egypt in (2); he concludes the siege (31.18).

Livy's account is extremely hard to understand. Part of the problem is that the fragments of Polybius show that Livy has suppressed the presence of a Roman embassy in Athens when the Athenians declare war on Philip in (10), as well as an earlier warning given by that embassy to the Macedonians (Plb. 16.25–7); but, even leaving that aside, it is hard to dovetail the sequence of events in Greece set

---

[1] The bibliography is immense: a short list of relevant discussions includes Holleaux (1920), De Sanctis IV.1 15–42 [16–43], McDonald and Walbank (1937), Bickerman (1945), Balsdon (1954), Badian (1958), 62–9, Ferro (1960), Luce (1977), 53–73, Rich (1976), 73–87, Harris (1979a), 212–18, Warrior (1996), Eckstein (2006), 259–89, Eckstein (2008), 230–70.

out in (9)–(12) into the account of the various political and diplomatic movements at Rome in (1)–(8). The fixed point is that (8) coincides with (11), but that still leads to problems. There is a dispute over the two Athenian embassies in (1) and (4): were there really two such embassies, or is one or both of them a fiction?[2] If either took place, what prompted them? They refer to a direct attack by Philip (31.5.6), but none had taken place: at most it can only have been Philocles' raids in (11) (so Briscoe (1973), 43–4); but that appears to be what the Athenians in (8) were complaining about as well: on that interpretation the chronology is extremely hard to follow. Other scholars suggest that the Athenian embassy in (4) (if it occurred at all) must have been provoked by something earlier (so e.g. Balsdon (1954), 35–7, Ferro (1960), 75,[3] Warrior (1996), 37–81); alternatively, it may have been misdated, and really took place after the war-vote (McDonald and Walbank (1937), 199–200, Bickerman (1945), 141). There are many other subsidiary questions, which is why so many reconstructions are possible which vary from one another in details: people have, for example, questioned whether a Roman fleet was in fact sent to Macedonia prior to the war debate (3),[4] or whether the two votes for war (5)–(6) were as close in time to one another as Livy implies.[5]

P. clearly saw something of the problem, because he drastically reworks Livy's narrative to present a more comprehensible chronological sequence. He begins with the violation of the Mysteries, followed by the attack on Athens by the Acarnanians. He then has one Athenian embassy to Rome in response to it; P.'s next notice also records an Athenian embassy at Rome, which is now responding to what he refers to as the siege of Athens by Philip (*a Philippo obsidebantur*); and it is this embassy which leads to the war vote at Rome. P.'s language does not require that this is the same embassy as he mentioned previously, but the repetition of the phrase *auxilium petere* implies that it is, and the same conclusion would naturally be drawn from a comparison with Livy's sequence, where no other embassy can be at issue. He specifically dates it to a period 'a few months' after the peace with Carthage, echoing Livy's language at 31.5.1: this must, accordingly, be the embassy in (4), which Livy reports immediately afterward.

However, even on Livy's account, no siege of Athens is reported to Rome at this point—the Athenians say only that Philip is approaching their borders (31.5.6). Nothing corresponding to an actual siege is mentioned until the later Athenian

---

[2] The historicity of the first is rejected by e.g. Holleaux (1920), 82, Ferro (1960), 88–9, Briscoe (1973), 43, 55; *contra* e.g. Bickerman (1945), 141–2; Warrior (1996), 26, 97–9 believes that Livy in (1) is referring in summary form to the embassy in (4) which he will later recount in more detail; but, as Briscoe notes, that interpretation is incompatible with Livy's language. The second embassy is considered unhistorical by Holleaux (1920); *contra* e.g De Sanctis IV.1 31–2 [32–3], Ferro (1960), 88–90.

[3] Ferro justifies this reconstruction with the ingenious but grammatically implausible claim that *suis* (31.5.6) refers to Philip, not the Athenians, and that he is said to be returning to his own country.

[4] e.g. De Sanctis IV.1 21 [21], Bickerman (1945), 143, *MRR* 1.322; *contra* e.g. Ferro (1960), 94–6, Briscoe (1973), 60, Warrior (1996), 53–8.

[5] That the second vote took place much later than the first is argued by e.g. McDonald and Walbank (1937), 192–7, Briscoe (1973), 44–5; *contra* e.g. Balsdon (1954), 38–9, Warrior (1996), 64–5.

embassy reaches the consul in (8) (31.14.3-4), and even that does not fit very closely the narrative of the attack on Athens, where no direct assault on the city occurs until later, after the Roman arrival in Greece (31.24.1-25.2, 31.26). P. thus reworks the embassy in such a way to make it respond to the different stages of the attack on Athens; this on one interpretation (cf. above) is not incompatible with Livy's chronology, if indeed the 'siege of Athens' reported to the consul in (8) is identical to the raid which prompted the embassy in (4), but it also hints at an alternative version, under which the entire attack on Athens by Philip took place prior to the embassy, even though that is literally impossible on Livy's chronology of the war. For the reader of P. who did not know Livy's text, this is the only place where P. records a direct attack on Athens by Philip, and, as far as that reader is concerned, it took place before the Romans voted to go to war. Only the reader of P. who did know Livy would appreciate that the real attack on Athens was still to come at that point.

Moreover, while the reader of Livy can deduce that the two embassies mentioned by P. are one and the same, this would not be apparent to the majority of readers of P., who did not have Livy's text in front of them. For them, the possibility remains that we have here two embassies, one following the initial Acarnanian attack, and a second after Philip's siege—thus echoing, without directly endorsing, Livy's own apparent allusion to two embassies, although, here too, only the small number of readers who knew Livy would appreciate what lies behind the ambiguity.

This focus on Athens comes at the expense of the remainder of Livy's account: the Roman ambassadors to Egypt and Philip disappear, while the siege of Abydus and the role of Attalus and Rhodes are separated out (31.5n., 31.7n.), as indeed is the fighting against the Gauls and Carthaginians, which in Livy is interspersed with the narrative of the Macedonian War (31.6n.). But the chief point is not that P.'s limited and partial reconstruction is correct, but rather that he is responding critically and constructively to the same problems in Livy that baffle modern scholars. That he chose this particular reconstruction is not surprising: Livy highlights the Roman desire to defend Athens at the very start (31.1.10; cf. 45.22.6), and it was, according to Livy, Philip's aggression against Roman allies which forms the substance of the case against him in the war vote (31.6.1). P.'s account dovetails with other ancient sources, which likewise emphasize that Rome was prompted to go to war by Philip's attack on Athens (App., *Mac.* 4, Paus. 1.36.5-6, Flor. 1.23.4, Ruf. Fest. 7.2; cf. Zonar. 9.15.1-3, though Just. 30.2.8-3.6 presents a rather different version, in which Athens plays no role); the cultural fame of Athens presumably was a major reason why it became so central to the tradition. But no other post-Livian source provides such detail—indeed, the other late Latin summarizers pass over these events altogether, beginning their accounts of the Macedonian War with Flamininus' arrival in Greece (Eutr. 4.1, Oros. 4.20.1). P. is doing something unique: trying to reconstruct Livy's confusing narrative as coherently as he can within the outlines provided by the historical tradition, and doing so in such a way that simplifies the narrative while showing to the reader who knew Livy his awareness of some of the complexities.

31.1 belli…repetiti: The hyperbaton is striking, emphasizing the new war as the chief topic of the book. *repetere bellum* = 'renew a war' is not Livian, but is found in Stat., *Theb.* 10.790, Pomp. Trog., *Prol.* 14, Ambr., *Off.* 1.24.109; cf. *OLD s.v. repeto* 3.

Philippum, Macedoniae regem: P. used the same phrase to identify him at 23.11 and 26.4; cf. also 24.4 and 28.1.

quod intermissum erat: That the Second Macedonian War was effectively a resumption of the first is implied by Livy 31.1.8 *coeptum bellum adversus Philippum decem ferme ante annis triennio prius depositum erat* and 31.1.10 *ad renovandum bellum*. P. treats it here in the same manner, which is of a piece with the surprising attention he paid to the first war, and the curtness with which he recorded the peace that ended it (24.4n., 29.5n.).

causae referuntur hae: Cf. 16.1n. The word-order is striking, partly because of the verbal hyperbaton (29.1n.), but also because of the postponement of *hae* (for which see *TLL* VI 2739.33–41); since *hic* usually precedes its noun, and since in all cases nouns usually precede adjectives in cases of verbal hyperbaton (Adams (1971), 13), this throws exceptional emphasis on *hae*.

tempore initiorum duo iuvenes Acarnanes, qui non erant initiati, Athenas venerunt et in sacrarium Cereris cum aliis popularibus suis intraverunt: Cf. Livy 31.14.7 *Acarnanes duo iuvenes per initiorum dies non initiati templum Cereris imprudentes religionis cum cetera turba ingressi sunt*. Livy does not specify that the young Acarnanians were with their fellow-countrymen; it may be that P. is dependent on another tradition, but it is more likely to be his own inference.

tamquam summum nefas commisissent, ab Atheniensibus occisi sunt: Cf. Livy 31.14.8 *tamquam ob infandum scelus interfecti sunt*; P., as often, carefully varies Livy's phrasing; but with *tamquam* he retains something of Livy's moral judgement that the young men were unjustly punished for an inadvertent error.

31.2 Acarnanes…auxilia a Philippo petierunt…Athenienses auxilium a Romanis petierunt: The phrasing makes the Acarnanian appeal exactly parallel to the Athenian one: on P.'s account, the Romans and Macedonians are drawn into war with one another at the request of less powerful allies. This is not the impression that is left by Livy's narrative, in which the Acarnanians play a much more subsidiary role, and it is the direct hostilities between Athens and Macedon which is at the centre.

31.3 post pacem Carthaginiensibus datam paucis mensibus, quingentesimo quadragensimo anno ab urbe condita coeptum est bellum: The chief MSS of

P. at this point read *post pacem Carthaginiensibus datam quadragintesimo anno ab urbe condita paucis mensibus. coeptum est autem anno quingentesimo quinto.* This is clearly impossible: the double dating, with neither date corresponding to Livy's text, the odd position of *paucis mensibus*, and the lack of any subject to *coeptum est*, all point to serious corruption having taken place. Jahn read *post pacem Carthaginiensibus datam quadragesimo anno paucis mensibus*, altering the date to refer to the end of the First Punic War, and claiming the remainder as a gloss; Rossbach went further, excising everything except *post pacem Carthaginiensibus datam paucis mensibus*.

However, such radical excisions are unacceptable. This is first, because the transmitted text clearly derives from Livy's own wording at 31.5.1 (from one branch of the chief Livian MSS):[6] *anno quingentesimo quadragesimo ab urbe condita...bellum cum rege Philippo initum est, paucis mensibus post pacem Carthaginiensibus datam.* It is far more likely that P. would have a text of Livy in front of him than that a scribe would be supplementing the text of P. from a text of Livy. Second, Jahn's and Rossbach's versions require that the date is attached to the Athenian embassy, rather than to the war, as in Livy, which seems perverse. Far more likely is that P. wrote the same date as Livy (or, rather, as these MSS of Livy), and that *quingentesimo quadragesimo* was conflated into *quadragintesimo*; the number at some point prior to that was duplicated by a scribe, with the second version itself corrupted. Transpositions such as that of *paucis mensibus* are commonplace; while *bellum* was corrupted to *autem*, presumably in an attempt to make sense of the double dating once the duplication of the number had occurred.

cum: Cf. 2.2n.

legati auxilium a senatu petissent: The phrasing is repeated from 31.2: cf. 31.1–3n.

et id senatus ferendum censuisset: Livy differs from P. on this point (cf. Hoyos (1998), 59). For Livy, the Senate carefully does not vote on giving aid to Athens, saying that they will wait to answer the Athenians until the people can be consulted on the war (31.5.9). P. perhaps mistook Livy's account of the unanimous support of the Senate for war (31.6.5) for an actual vote on the topic.

quod tot bellorum continuus labor gravis erat: Livy does not express the reason for the opposition of the people to the war in precisely these terms—he refers to the length of time, but not to the number of wars (31.6.3). The tribune Baebius, in his harangue against the Senate, accuses them of arranging for 'wars to be sown out of wars' (31.6.4 *bella ex bellis seri*), which is closer to P.; but P. does not mention Baebius; more importantly, whereas Livy never endorses his accusation, and

---

[6] Another branch of the MSS adds *uno* after *quadragesimo*, emended to *primo* by Voss; in addition, Glareanus corrected the chronology by emending *quadragesimo* to *quinquagesimo*. Both of these emendations are generally accepted in modern editions; however, I give here the readings which are likely to underlie P.'s text.

indeed criticizes his reviving of anti-senatorial rhetoric, P. places the clause in the indicative, indicating that he saw it as a plain fact.

continuus labor is Livian (5.19.11, 6.4.10); *labor bellorum* is not, but *labor belli* is used by a number of other late Republican and early imperial writers (e.g. Caes., *Gall.* 6.31.5, Cic., *Font.* 43, Colum. 12 *praef.* 4, Lucan 7.93, 9.1016, Sil. 15.652-3). But the closest parallel to P.'s phrasing here is Amm. 28.5.1 *dux diuturno bellorum labore compertus.*

tenuit auctoritas patrum ut: An unusual phrase. For *tenere ut* = 'accomplish one's point that' see *OLD s.v. teneo* 16c; it is used by Livy (esp. 2.42.2), but never with an abstract subject. It is possible that P. arrived at the phrase from combining this idiom with the separate (and extremely common) Livian phrase *auctoritas patrum*; it is also possible that he was influenced by the Christian use of *auctoritas tenere* (or, more often, *auctoritate teneri*) in theological contexts (e.g. Aug., *C. Epist. Fund.* 4, *C. Faust.* 18.7).

sociae civitati ferri opem: Cf. 21.1n. In Livy, the primary motivation for going to war is less to aid Athens than to protect Rome against an expansionist Macedon: that is the primary focus of the consul's speech advocating war, in which the need to defend allies is mentioned only in passing (31.7). P., in accordance with the general tenor of his account, and also the centrality of Athens to later traditions about the war (cf. above), ignores the question of self-defence altogether.

31.4 *Roman attack on Philip*. Corresponds to Livy 31.33.4-38.10. P. continues his account of the Macedonian War with a notice of the direct fighting between the first commander, P. Sulpicius Galba, and Philip; the other fighting in the war, both before and after, is reserved for later (cf. 31.7n.).

Livy describes an inconclusive cavalry skirmish (31.33.4-11), followed by a battle in which the Romans were successful (31.35), then a further battle two days later, in which Philip unsuccessfully sought to ambush the Romans (31.36.1-3). Finally, on the following day, there was a more substantial fight, which began with Philip successfully attacking Roman foragers, but when Sulpicius brought out his main forces the Macedonians were defeated (31.37-8). Livy makes it clear that the battles in 31.35-8 involved more than just cavalry: he refers many times to light-armed troops on both sides (so also Dio fr. 58; cf. Zonar. 9.15.5-6), and indeed to Sulpicius bringing his legions into the fight (31.37.1). But Livy himself speaks of them in retrospect as 'two cavalry battles' (31.38.9 *duas...equestres pugnas*), and the only casualties referred to are cavalry (31.37.12; cf. 31.38.9), so it is not unreasonable that P. treats the fighting in those terms.

prospere...pugnavit: Cf. 2.6n.

31.5 *Mass suicide at Abydus.* Corresponds to Livy 31.16.6-18.9. After beginning his account of the war with the opening battles between Rome and Philip, P. moves back to an earlier point: the siege of Abydus. In Livy this was directly connected with the move to war: Philip is already at Abydus when the Roman forces are preparing to cross to Greece, and it is at Abydus that he receives the final ultimatum (31.1–3n.). P., however, treats it as something entirely self-contained, and, implicitly, subsequent to the beginning of the war. His interest is above all in the dramatic story of the mass suicide, not unlike the one from Spain he recounted in Book 28 (28.6n.), but cf. also below.

Aboedeni: Livy, like every other Latin writer, spells the town *Abydus*, and the people *Abydeni*; but *Aboedos* is the spelling of the homonymous Egyptian city in Sol. 32.41 (Mommsen), and should probably be retained here: it is at least as likely that P. read this in his MS of Livy (or introduced the spelling himself) as that it is the fault of a later copyist.

ad exemplum Saguntinorum: Livy twice makes an explicit comparison between Abydus and Saguntum: 31.17.5 *ad Saguntinam rabiem versi* ('turning to the Saguntine madness'), 31.18.9 *velut Sagunti excidium Hannibali, sic Philippo Abydenorum clades ad Romanum bellum animos fecisset* ('Just as the fall of Saguntum stimulated Hannibal to war with Rome, so did the disaster of the Abydenes do with Philip'). P. reproduces the first of those here, with the additional implication that the Abydenes deliberately followed the Saguntine example, an idea that nothing in Livy supports. His introduction of the comparison, however, may have been in part influenced by the second, which establishes a parallel between the two stories in the opening phases of their respective wars (cf. Livy 31.7.3, 31.7.7). This stands out all the more because P. did not in fact mention the mass suicide when describing the fall of Saguntum (21.1), so the reader of P. who did not know Livy might associate Saguntum only with its role at the beginning of the Second Punic War.

31.6 *Defeat of Gauls and Hamilcar.* Corresponds to Livy 31.10.1–11.3, 31.21.1–22.3. Livy interweaves the story of the Gallic uprising with the opening phases of the Macedonian War; P. separates it out, and indeed places it clearly out of sequence, just as he had done with the siege of Abydus (31.1–3n., 31.5n.). His account of the battle, as often, reduces it to a bare notice that it took place and to its outcome; subsidiary details, such as the Gauls' sack of Placentia and attack on Cremona, and the Romans' complaint to the Carthaginians about Hamilcar (31.11.4–6, 31.19.1), are ignored. The rather different account of Zonar. 9.15.7–8, by contrast, does mention the sack of Placentia, though it suggests that it was accomplished by Hamilcar after Furius' victory; this presumably depends on a different version of the story, in which Hamilcar survives for a longer period in Italy—there are two separate versions of this in Livy, in one of which he is killed in battle later (32.30.12), in one of which he is captured alive (33.23.5); similarly Oros. 4.20.4, who mentions the attacks on the colonies, dates the war to several years later (and calls the Roman commander Fulvius).

566 COMMENTARY

Gallos Insubres rebellantes: In Livy there are several other tribes involved: the Cenomani, the Boii, and several tribes of Ligurians (31.10.2). Orosius mentions the Cenomani and the Boii, and Dio fr. 58 (cf. Zonar. 9.15.7) makes a point of separating out the Ligurians, suggesting that they alone were successful in obtaining peace terms after the war. However, the opening phrase of the Dio fragment appears to imply that he, too, focused on the Insubrians, which suggests that there were versions of the story in which they were the main opponents, which P. may be following. Certainly Livy himself in the later phases of the war places the Insubrians at the centre of the fighting (cf. 32.7, 33.6, 34.4), and it is clear that, at the very least, there was a tendency in the tradition for the different stages of the Gallic campaign to be confused with one another (see above, and cf. Briscoe (1973), 82). It may also be relevant for P. that his notice of the death of Mago, with which he ended his account of the Second Punic War, had him defeated *in agro Insubrum*, and he has displaced that notice in such a way as to stress the continuity between Mago's presence in Italy and Hamilcar's continuing to fight now (30.7n.).

The chief MSS read *Insubras*, a form not otherwise found; the *editio princeps* corrected the text.

in ea parte Italiae: The region inhabited by the Insubrians was legally incorporated into Italy far later than this time; hence P.'s phrase is technically anachronistic. However, it is an anachronism which may well have had some basis in contemporary perceptions: Cato included the peoples of Cisalpine Gaul in his recounting of the history of Italy in the *Origines*, which probably (though not certainly) implies that he saw *Italia* as encompassing the entire peninsula (see Cornell in *FRHist* I 212). Moreover, even if P. is being anachronistic, he has some licence from Livy himself, who intermittently engages in the same anachronism in his history, albeit not here (see esp. Mahé-Simon (2003)).

Hamilcar eo bello occisus est: Cf. Livy 31.21.18 *Hamilcar dux Poenus eo proelio cecidit.*

et milia hominum XXXV: Cf. Livy 31.21.17 *caesa aut capta supra quinque et triginta.* The figure clearly derives from Livy, but P. in summarizing ignores both the fact that it was 'above' that figure,[7] and that the figure included captives as well as casualties.

31.7 *Campaigns and sieges conducted by Philip and Sulpicius.* In his usual 'round-up' passage, P., having already mentioned the direct conflicts between Philip and the Romans (31.4), includes all the places where Livy describes their military

---

[7] It is, however, worth noting that, while XXXV is the reading of N, the other branch of the MS tradition reads XXXVI. The possibility should not be excluded that the latter was the original reading, and that P., as he does elsewhere (cf. e.g. 23.2n.), is adjusting the figure precisely because he notes Livy's qualification about 35,000 being the lower limit.

activities against others: 31.16.3-6 (Philip takes various towns and fortresses), 31.23 (the Romans sack Chalcis, then retreat), 31.40.1-6 (the Romans attack a number of towns), 31.40.7-43.7 (the Macedonians fight against the Dardanians, Aetolians, and Athamanians, achieving a number of victories), 31.45-6 (the Romans attack various towns by sea). The major question comes with Philip's attack on Athens (31.24.1-25.2, 31.26). Strictly speaking, it should be included under this heading as well, since it is a city attacked by Philip where the attack has not been described in P.'s main narrative. But, as argued above, P. has effectively treated it as part of his account of the opening of the war, alluding (anachronistically, at least on Livy's chronology) to a siege of Athens prior to the Romans' voting for war. See 31.1-3n.

P. also notes here the role of Attalus and the Rhodians helping Sulpicius in the war. Their direct military assistance only appears in the naval campaigns of 31.23 and 31.45-6, but on Livy's account they played a substantial role in encouraging both Rome and Athens to move to war in the first place. P. suppressed that in his narrative of the opening of the war (31.1-3n.), giving them a far less ambivalent role: allies of Rome, rather than enemies of Philip with independent interests that led them to promote the war; they play a similar part in Flor. 1.23.8.

The primary aspect of the book which P. fails to mention either here or elsewhere is the debate that took place at the meeting of the Aetolian League (31.29-32); he focuses on the military campaigns rather than the diplomatic debates that in Livy's presentation underpinned them. Similarly, the narrative of these years in Zonar. 9.15.3-6 does not mention any negotiations, but refers only to the military actions, and refers to Attalus and the Rhodians solely as supporters of Rome in the naval campaign.

praeterea expeditiones...expugnationesque urbium ab utroque factas continet: P. here varies his standard *res gestas continet* formula (cf. 2.16n.), giving more detail about the specific activities involved. This may be because he is here reporting not just the Roman campaigns, but also those of Philip: similarly when, in Books 62-81, P. changes his practice to use the 'round-up' formula only of non-Roman activities (cf. 62.6n.; also 68.8, 70.9, 74.8, 76.8, 78.4, 81.3), he also employs a wider variety of objects of *continet*, and that variation continues, at least at times, when he resumes using the formula for Roman events after Book 84 (e.g. 84.6, 86.6, 103.11, 109.2, 117.6, 128.4).

For the combination of *expeditiones* and *expugnationes* cf. 72.4; also 115.3.

Sulpicius cos. bellum gerebat adiuvantibus rege Attalo et Rhodiis: Cf. Livy 31.47.3 *haec ea aestate...ab consule et legato Romanis adiuvantibus rege Attalo et Rhodiis gesta.*

31.8 *Triumph of Furius over the Gauls.* Corresponds to Livy 31.47.4-49.3; cf. 31.49.8-11. In Livy Furius' triumph is strongly contested by the consul C. Aurelius Cotta and other senior members of the Senate; the dispute is also recorded by Dio fr. 57.81. P. ignores that debate; the fact that he repeats that Furius was praetor might be thought to hint at it, since part of the debate turned on whether, as praetor commanding the consul's army, Furius had the authority to conduct the campaign at all: as Livy notes, his triumph was not accompanied by his captives and soldiers, because they were held to belong to the consul (31.49.3). But P. often repeats a person's office when they appear in a new notice, and in this case, the reference to his praetorship is additionally explained by the fact that he is following Livy's wording (see below).

This is one of a minority of cases where P. places a final notice after his 'round-up' notice; in this case, the most likely reason is that the episode took place close to the end of the book, after the fighting summarized in the previous notice (cf. 9.5n.). Unlike at the start of the book, P. is to some extent here following the sequence of Livy's narrative.

triumphavit de Gallis L. Furius praetor: Cf. Livy 31.49.2 *triumphavit de Gallis in magistratu L. Furius praetor*.

Book 32

32.1 *Prodigies.* Corresponds to Livy 32.1.10–14. P. rarely introduces prodigies: almost all of the exceptions are cases, as here, where the prodigy has an apparent bearing on current events, and in at least two of them, as also here (32.1.14), Livy indicates that exceptional assistance was sought from the *haruspices* (14.2, 35.2n.; cf. 55.5n., 117.1n.). It may be noted that Florus, too, singles out this prodigy, and treats it as a clear sign of future victory (1.23.7). Livy himself does not offer any such interpretation, but it is likely that P., like Florus, saw that as its implication, which explains why he mentions the prodigy at all.

It is possible that P.'s usual reticence on prodigies is connected with a Christian-inspired scepticism about the Roman gods (note that both here and at 35.2 he distances himself from them by explicitly attributing them to Livy, rather than describing them in his own voice), but see 11.2n. and 55.5n.: the very fact that P. is prepared to introduce prodigies at all indicates that, at the very least, he saw some significance in a small number of highly charged instances.

ex diversis regionibus: *diversae regiones* is a Livian phrase (9.44.6, 26.41.20, 26.42.2, 28.9.4, 29.37.1, 41.18.9), but it is typically used not to mean 'various regions', as here, but more specifically to refer to commanders operating in two (or occasionally three) separated areas. P. employs the phrase in a manner that is common in other authors: he is employing Livian phraseology without Livy's distinctive usage.

referuntur: Cf. 16.1n.

in puppe longae navis lauream esse natam: Cf. Livy 32.1.12 *lauream in puppi navis longae enatam.*

32.2 *Flamininus defeats Philip in Epirus.* Corresponds to Livy 32.9.6–13.9. P. passes entirely over the military campaign of 199 under the command of P. Villius Tappulus (Livy 32.3–6), and moves instead to the arrival of Flamininus in Greece as the consul of 198. This is hardly surprising, given that Livy himself comments on the failure of Villius to accomplish anything during his year of office (32.6.8), dismissing the alternative version of Valerius Antias, who had recorded an outstanding victory on Villius' part (31.6.5–8 = *FRHist* 25 F 35). Almost all other surviving sources, like P., ignore Villius altogether, the exceptions being Plu., *Flam.* 3.1–4 and Zonar. 9.16.1, who note that he encamped opposite Philip when the latter was blockading the pass into Macedonia.

As for the content of Flamininus' campaign, P., as often, gives few details, mentioning only its location (cf. below) and the fact that the Romans were victorious. He fails to mention even those aspects that received more attention in other sources: the negotiations between Philip and Flamininus prior to the battle (Livy

32.10.1-8; cf. D.S. 28.11, App., *Mac.* 5), and the fact that a shepherd (or shepherds) guided Flamininus' troops into a position where they could trap the enemy (Livy 32.11; cf. Plu., *Flam.* 4.2-3, App., *Mac.* 6, *Vir. Ill.* 51.1, Zonar. 9.16.1). However, Flor. 1.23.10, though far more rhetorically expansive, is no more forthcoming than P. on the details of the campaign.

feliciter pugnavit: Cf. 14.8n.

in faucibus Epiri: Livy does not describe the location in this fashion at the time of the battle itself, but he uses the phrase several times (31.16.1 *in Epiri faucibus*; cf. 32.21.14, 33.4.2, 33.8.4). P. may have been deriving this from his broader knowledge of the tradition (note that Zonar. 9.16.1 similarly speaks of τὰ τῆς Ἠπείρου...στενά; cf. Livy 32.5.9, referring to the Greek name as *Stena*), but it is more probable that, as often, he draws his language from a passage where Livy refers back to the incident in question, rather than from the main narrative.

32.3 *Campaigns of the Flamininus brothers.* Corresponds to Livy 32.13.10-18.9, 32.23.4-24.9. Livy presents Titus' and Lucius' campaigns in Book 32 in two distinct sections, separated from one another by the decision of the Achaeans to come over to Rome (32.4n.). P. has just one notice, which could in principle refer to only the first, but could equally well encompass the second: if one compares his text with Livy's, the fact that he describes the campaign before the Achaean alliance might favour the first interpretation, especially since the Achaeans actually join the Romans in the siege of Corinth in the second section. On the other hand, the fact that P. has no other account of the Roman campaigns in Greece in this book might suggest the second, given that the actual point at which the Achaean alliance is formed is less clear in Livy than might appear at first sight (32.4n.): certainly the reader who did not know Livy would naturally assume that this notice covered the whole campaign.

The only other references to these events are Plu., *Flam.* 5.3 (who suggests, unlike Livy and P., that Thessaly came over to Titus without fighting), Paus. 7.8.1 (Lucius' capture of Eretria), and Zonar. 9.16.2 (who refers briefly to both brothers' campaigns). P. presents the campaign as one of harassment, rather than conquest, which allows him to elide the fact that Livy's narrative includes a lengthy account of a failure by Titus, as he attempts unsuccessfully to capture Atrax (32.17.4-18.2), and another by Lucius, who fails to capture Corinth (32.23.4-14); moreover, Livy appends to his account of the Roman campaign the exploits of Philip's lieutenant Philocles, who both raises the siege of Corinth and succeeds in winning over Argos (32.25).

The distinctive feature of P. is his emphasis on the support given to Titus by the Aetolians and Athamanians, and to Lucius by Attalus and the Rhodians— the latter is mentioned also by Zonaras. Livy treats this very differently: with the Aetolians and the Athamanians, he describes at considerable length how they took advantage of the Romans' victory to make gains for themselves (33.13.10–14.4); the idea that they assisted Titus is mentioned only in passing (33.14.7–8), and Livy makes a point of saying that he wanted them only as guides, not as soldiers. Similarly, with Attalus and the Rhodians, they are initially shown as campaigning independently against Philip (33.16.6–8), and only after that do they join up with the Romans. As before (cf. 31.7n.), P. sees this as simply a war between Macedon and Rome, with other participants shown not as independent actors, but as supporters of one side or the other. At the same time, the stress on the Romans' Hellenic allies underscores P.'s essential picture of the war (31.1–3n.): that the Romans are fighting Macedon on behalf of the Greeks, not of themselves.

quae est vicina Macedoniae: Livy does not explicitly locate Thessaly, but its proximity to Macedonia is implicit throughout his account of the campaign. P. provides the information, thus helping to clarify how Flamininus' activities are part of a broader strategy following Philip's retreat, something that would not otherwise be apparent from his abridged narrative.

L. Quintius Flamininus, frater consulis...Euboeam et maritimam oram ⟨...⟩: Cf. Livy 32.16.2 *L. Quinctius frater consulis*. On the reading of the chief MSS, *vexavit* needs to be understood from the previous clause, but the omission is abrupt, and it is not surprising that certain later MSS sought to supplement the sentence: a significant number read *cepit*, which is then accepted by the early editors. Jahn, however, proposed a lacuna, which is probably the safest course to follow.

navali proelio: For *proelium* used of an entire campaign, rather than a single conflict, see *TLL* X.2 1650.75–1651.6; it is primarily a usage of later antiquity.

Attalo rege et Rhodiis adiuvantibus: P. repeats almost verbatim his phrasing from 31.7: see *ad loc.*

32.4 *The Achaeans join the Romans.* Corresponds to Livy 32.19.1–23.3. Livy recounts in detail the meeting of the Achaean League which culminated in their decision to join Rome, centring on a speech by Aristaenus in favour of the alliance, but also emphasizing how contentious the issue was among the Achaeans, who heard speeches by various of the participants. The heated dispute is also referred to in the briefer accounts of App., *Mac.* 7, Paus. 7.8.1–2, and Zonar. 9.16.3; but P., like Plu., *Flam.* 5.3, has only the bare fact of the alliance, which suits his broader picture of the support the Romans received in their war from the Greeks (31.1–3n., 31.7n., 32.3n.).

In Livy, while the Achaeans decide to join Rome now, they do not form an alliance until later, waiting until they can send an embassy to Rome (32.23.2–3). The actual moment when the alliance happens is nowhere described by Livy, but he indicates that the treaty was concluded before the end of his Macedonian narrative for the year 198 (32.25.11 *post pactam inter Achaeos ac Romanos societatem*).⁸ P.'s reference on the face of things suggests that he was referring only to that final conclusion, which would suit the idea advanced above (32.3n.), that his account of the campaigns of the Flamininus brothers would include those that they conducted after the meeting of the Achaean League. On the other hand, it may be relevant that P., unlike Livy, speaks of *amicitia*, not *societas*, the former being a rather looser term, which could certainly cover the agreement reached between the Achaeans and Rome prior to the formal treaty (cf. 7.9n., 14.5n.).

in amicitiam recepti sunt: Cf. 1 B.2n.

32.5 *Enlargement of the praetorship*. Corresponds to Livy 32.27.6. P., as often, is interested in constitutional innovations attesting to the growth of Rome, even those, such as this, to which Livy himself gave little emphasis (cf. 11.5n.). He narrates it out of order, before the slave rebellion which in Livy takes place immediately beforehand (cf. 32.6n.); there is no obvious explanation for the reversal.

ampliatus est: Cf. 1 B.2n.

seni: Livy has *sex praetores*; see 10.2n.

32.6 *Slave conspiracy*. Corresponds to Livy 32.26.4–18. Comparison between Livy and P. is complicated by the fact that there are two certain lacunas in Livy's text, at 32.26.8 and 32.26.13, and almost certainly a third at 32.26.7 (Briscoe (1973), 216, *contra* McDonald in the OCT). In the transmitted text of Livy, it is not clear that the conspiracy was initiated by the slaves, as P. suggests, nor that the object was to release the Carthaginian hostages, nor that 2,500 of them were killed. McDonald, accordingly, supplements Livy from P., proposing to add *ut obsides captivosque Carthaginiensium custodia solverent et sibi adiungerent ea quae cum iis erant* at 32.26.8, and *fugitivos...ipse praetor quaestionem exercuit...de duobus ferme milibus hominum supplicium sumpsit* at 32.26.13 (the other 500 executed are referred to at 32.26.16).

There is more dispute about how to supplement the lacuna at 32.26.7: whether it should have the slaves or the hostages initiating the conspiracy. However, if the principle of supplementing Livy on the basis of P. is accepted (see below), it follows that one should also emend 32.26.7 so that it is clearly the slaves (Capozza (1966), 106–7): Madvig's *ea*, referring to *mancipia* in the previous sentence, would be the simplest. That the slaves initiated the conspiracy is also implied by

---

⁸ This passage is surprisingly overlooked by Badian (1952b), who, in attempting to determine when the treaty between Rome and Achaea was actually formed, claims that the earliest evidence points to 196 (based on App., *Mac.* 9.4: Badian himself rejects this, and canvasses a number of dates between then and the late 180s, ultimately preferring a date of 192/1). This does not mean that Livy is reliable on this topic—as Badian notes, Plb. 18.42.6–7 provides strong evidence that the treaty was not concluded until later—but he states the point clearly (cf. also 33.2.9), and P. would have had no reason not to take it seriously.

Livy 32.26.16—the Romans' fear that the hostages were responsible would be strange and anticlimactic if Livy had told us so from the start (so Bosworth (1968), 273–4). Briscoe (1973), 218 argues against this, claiming that Livy is here talking only about the attempted revolt in Praeneste, and that it might, accordingly, be possible that Livy thought the hostages initiated the original attempt in Setia. But one would have expected Livy to say *quoque* (*vel sim.*) were that the case; moreover, while P. is not always a reliable guide to Livy (this is true even when it comes to numbers—see e.g. 22.7n., 23.5n., 29.12n.), when, as here, P.'s narrative supports one interpretation of Livy (sc. that the Romans' reaction was generated by the conspiracy in Setia) over another (sc. that they were responding to Praeneste alone), it offers strong evidence that the first interpretation is correct.

The same principle argues that it is indeed appropriate to emend Livy in order to make his account conform with P.'s. P., for all his independence, reflects Livy's narrative considerably more often than he fails to do so. Hence Madvig's supplement to 32.26.7 and McDonald's to 32.26.8 and 32.26.13 (or others along the same lines) should be accepted, provided it is recognized that they are based only on a (reasonably strong) balance of probability.[9] Certainly it is wrong to ignore P.'s evidence altogether, and state that the object of the conspiracy was something other than to free hostages (as does e.g. Toynbee (1965) 2.318–19).

coniuratio servorum...oppressa est: P. had used the same phrase at 4.9.

32.7 *Cethegus defeats the Gauls.* Corresponds to Livy 32.30. Livy describes campaigns against the Gauls by both consuls: Cethegus defeats the Insubrians (the Boii having withdrawn just before the battle and the Cenomani going over to Rome just prior to it), while Minucius ravages the lands of the Boii and the Ligurian Ilvates, who are demoralized and refuse to fight (32.31). P., understandably, focuses solely on the victory in battle, and also ignores the presence of Hamilcar, whom Livy (inconsistently) says was killed at this time (31.6n.; cf. Zonar. 9.16.7–8).

Cornelius Cethegus cos.: For the form of name used here see 4.4n.

32.8 *Agreement with Sparta.* Corresponds to Livy 32.39–40. The last part of Livy's book consists of a series of diplomatic manoeuvres. There is an extensive description of negotiations between Flamininus and Philip, along with their respective supporters, at the end of which embassies are sent to Rome, but no terms are agreed (32.32.5–37.6). Following that, Philip agrees with Nabis of Sparta that the latter should take control of Argos from him (32.38); however, after doing so,

---

[9] No help comes from the only other author to describe these events, Zonar. 9.16.6, since he gives no information on the numbers or the object of the conspiracy. He does indicate, unlike P., that the hostages and not the slaves were primarily responsible, but, as noted above, that is not compatible with other parts of Livy's narrative in any case.

Nabis double-crosses Philip by approaching Flamininus and Attalus; the upshot is that he agrees to send troops to support the Romans and to a temporary truce with Achaea, but Argos remains in his hands.

This messy series of events, with Argos left under oppressive Spartan rule, is reduced by P. to a bare notice of *amicitia* between Rome and Nabis' Sparta. From the point of view of P.'s narrative this serves a double function; it continues the impression he has constantly sought to convey, of Rome fighting Philip with and on behalf of the Greeks (31.1–3n., 32.3n.), but at the same time, with its reference to Nabis as a tyrant, it prepares the ground for Rome's later war against him (34.3; cf. 35.3).

32.9 *Attacks on Macedonian cities.* P.'s 'round-up' notice in this book is odd: while the book does contain numerous references to attacks on cities (32.15.1–4, 32.16.10–18.2, 32.18.6–9, 32.23–4), none of those cities is in Macedonia—they are explicitly identified by Livy as being in Thessaly, Euboea, or Phocis—and they arguably all formed parts of the campaigns covered earlier (32.2, 32.3), with the possible exception of the attacks on Corinth and Elatia at 32.23–24 (cf. 32.3n.).

One simple answer might be to delete *in Macedonia* as a gloss, in which case this would presumably be referring only to Corinth and Elatia; but it seems unlikely that P. would simply speak of 'attacks on cities' without offering additional information about either the attackers or the cities. Alternatively, P. may have erroneously thought that these cities were in Macedonia; but the fame of Corinth, and the fact that Livy explicitly says that Elatia is in Phocis, makes that, too, highly unlikely. More possible is that P., as often, was supplementing Livy from an alternative source, in which Macedonia was indeed directly attacked at this time: no such source survives, but the very different narrative of this period in Plu., *Flam.* 5 shows at the very least that there was no single accepted version of Flamininus' campaigns before Cynoscephalae in the post-Livian tradition.

A completely different possibility is that P., as he sometimes does elsewhere (cf. 27.8n.), is duplicating in the 'round-up' notice events that he has mentioned earlier. He may well have conceived of 'Macedonia' more expansively than Livy did: the Roman province of Macedonia at some point in the early Empire was expanded so as to incorporate Thessaly (Papazoglou (1979), 329–30), and even after the province was divided as a result of the reforms of Diocletian, the southern division retained the name (Bechert (1999), 76); hence P. could have seen Flamininus' attacks on Thessalian cities as being attacks 'in Macedonia'. If so, this speaks to a certain disingenuousness on his part, since in his account of Flamininus' campaign in Thessaly (32.3n.), he had explicitly distinguished it from Macedonia, which is correct from the standpoint of the geography of the time, though not the geographic boundaries of P.'s own day. On that reading, P. is exploiting the ambiguity to increase the impression of Roman successes, implying a direct assault on Philip's territory. At all events, either this reading, or the hypothetical alternative source, seems more likely than textual corruption or crude error.

praeterea...referuntur: P. again (cf. 31.7n.) introduces a new version of his 'summary' formula. He began to use *referuntur* in 28.1 (see *ad loc.*), but now he combines it with *praeterea*, conveying, as before, that the notice is not necessarily in chronological sequence (2.16n.). Henceforward P. employs this new formula intermittently, as an alternative to his more common *res gestas...continet* (34.4, 36.4, 48.19, 52.7, 82.5, 85.4; cf. 60.10).

Book 33

33.1 *Battle of Cynoscephalae.* Corresponds to Livy 33.7–10. P. focuses solely on the moment of the battle, which was (as he observes) decisive in the war, and ignores all of the prior campaign: the Boeotians' decision to join Flamininus (33.1–2), the mustering of troops on both sides (33.3–4), and the manoeuvring of the Romans and Macedonians before coming into conflict (33.5–6). No other surviving source handles it in precisely this way, but Flor. 1.23.11 moves directly from Flamininus' victory in Epirus to Cynoscephalae, while Eutr. 4.2.1 reduces the entire war to the single point of victory; Orosius' account is confused, since he turns the war into two separate wars, but with both of them only the final outcome is recorded (4.20.1, 4.20.5–6). Only in the Greek tradition is attention paid to the preliminaries: the Boeotian alliance is mentioned in both Plu., *Flam.* 6 and Zonar. 9.16.9.

cum Philippo ad Cynoscephalas in Thessalia acie victo debellavit: An unparalleled phrase. *cum Philippo debellavit* means 'brought the war with Philip to an end' (cf. Livy 9.16.1 *cum Frentanis uno secundo proelio debellavit*; also *TLL* V.1 84.30–5). However, there is a slight awkwardness in the combination with *victo*: presumably the sense is that by defeating Philip in the battle at Cynoscephalae, Flamininus was able to bring the entire war to its conclusion.

33.2 *Lucius Quinctius Flamininus defeats the Acarnanians.* Corresponds to Livy 33.16–17. P. reserves for later the peace negotiations which began in the immediate aftermath of Cynoscephalae (33.11–13: see 33.3n.), and ignores altogether victories of the Achaeans (33.14–15) and the Rhodians (33.18) over the Macedonians, and the confrontation of the Rhodians with Antiochus when he initiated attacks in Asia Minor (33.19.8–20.13). The omissions are most easily explained by P.'s general (if not invariable) tendency to pass over events in which Rome was not directly involved. As for the reordering of the episode here, it is noteworthy that it is given some justification by Livy himself, who has Lucius' campaign beginning before Cynoscephalae (33.16.1) and finishing when news of the battle reached the region (33.17.15).

In Livy, the attack on Leucas takes place after an account of a dispute among the Acarnanians themselves over whether they should transfer their allegiance from Macedon to Rome: it is only after the Roman side is rejected that Lucius begins his attack, and the final surrender of Acarnania is caused more by the news of Cynoscephalae than of the capture of the city (so also Zonar. 9.16.11). P. turns this into a more conventional account of a military victory: his emphasis that Leucas was the capital, while drawn from Livy (see below), gives the misleading impression that the loss of this city was the reason that Acarnania as a whole surrendered.

ille frater procos.: *ille* reminds the reader of the relationship that P. had already noted in 32.3. The information is all but superfluous, since it could hardly have been forgotten; hence it reinforces the picture of the two brothers campaigning in tandem.

quod caput est Acarnanum: Cf. Livy 33.17.1 *id caput Acarnaniae erat*.

33.3 Peace agreement with Philip: liberation of Greece. Corresponds to Livy 33.11–13, 33.24.3–7, 33.30–3, 33.34.5–35.12. P. unites into a single short notice matters which in Livy formed distinct episodes: first, the moves to peace immediately following the battle, and, second, the settlement that is agreed after the matter has been referred to the Senate. The surprising thing at first sight about P.'s account is that he ignores not only the details of the peace settlement, but the iconic moment when, at the Isthmian Games, there was a public proclamation that freedom was being granted to the Greeks. However, that omission is less surprising once one compares other accounts; for while the Isthmian Games scene was given a central role in some post-Livian writers (Val. Max. 4.8.5 (with Paris' epitome), Plu., *Flam.* 10.3–11.2, App., *Mac.* 9.4; also Flor. 1.23.13–15),[10] in later sources it largely vanishes, apart from Paris' epitome of Valerius and (probably—the text is corrupt) *Vir. Ill.* 51.4. It is not mentioned in Eutr. 4.2.1 or Oros. 4.20.1–6, nor in Zonar. 9.16.12—indeed, in the first two of these 'Greek freedom', which for P. is reduced to a passing ablative absolute, disappears altogether. It is possible that the rapid sweep of the narrative in these later sources made the idea of 'Greek freedom' seem less pertinent or even to introduce a dangerous note of irony, since it was, after all, due to disappear very soon with the Roman conquest (cf. the Introduction, lxviii).

33.4 Death of Attalus. Corresponds to Livy 33.21.1–5 (cf. also 33.2.2–3). On the face of things, P.'s inclusion of this notice is unexpected; it is relatively rare for him to take over from Livy events in which the Romans were not directly involved, and this was not even an especially prominent example: it is also referred to by Plb. 18.41, Plu., *Flam.* 6.3, and Zonar. 9.16.9, but in no other source. The reason is presumably because of the attention that P. paid to Attalus earlier (28.1, 29.6, 31.7, 32.3), making it more pertinent to complete his story.

Attalus ab Thebis…Pergamum translatus decessit: Cf. Livy 33.21.1 *Attalus rex…ab Thebis Pergamum advectus, moritur*. As often, P. derives his phrase from Livy while slightly altering the wording, in this case substituting synonyms.

subitam valetudinem: *subita valetudo* is not Livian; it appears in Quint., *Decl.* 268.22, three times in Suetonius (*Jul.* 72.1, *Nero* 3.2, *Galba* 7.1), and Paul, *Sent.* 2.15.1, but nowhere else in extant Latin.

---

[10] Florus assigns it to the Nemean Games, presumably confusing it with the announcement of the freedom of Argos there in the following year (Livy 34.41.3; cf. Plu., *Flam.* 12.2).

33.5 *Defeat of Sempronius Tuditanus in Spain.* Corresponds to Livy 33.25.8–9. It is unexpected that P. includes this notice at all, which casts a spotlight on a defeat to which Livy himself paid little attention. Possibly relevant is that Oros. 4.20.10 also includes this defeat, directly after discussing how the Roman historical tradition tended to downplay Roman failures. In this instance it appears unlikely that either P. or Orosius is directly dependent on the other, since Orosius does not include P.'s information about Tuditanus' title and opponents (below); but it is possible that P. is similarly activated by a wish to give a less one-sided account of Roman success.

praetor: Livy here refers to him as proconsul (33.25.9). P. may have simply drawn his information from the later reference to the defeat at 33.42.5, where Livy does speak of him as praetor; either title was acceptable, since praetors at this time were being sent to Spain with proconsular *imperium* (Mommsen, StR^3 II 647, Jashemski (1950), 40–8). It is worth noting that P.'s notice, as well as the second reference in Livy, implies that Tuditanus' defeat was in consular year 197, the year of his praetorship, even though the news of his defeat, according to Livy, did not reach Rome until the consuls of 196 had taken office (so, rightly, Briscoe (1973), 298; *contra* MRR 1.337).

ab Celtiberis: This information does not derive from Livy, who refers only to the defeat taking place in Nearer Spain: P. must have taken it from another source (cf. Bingham 306). P.'s information may be accurate: certainly it is not implausible or incompatible with Livy, since the Celtiberi inhabited a region of central Spain that apparently fell within the purview of the praetor for Nearer Spain (cf. 41.2n.).[11]

cum exercitu caesus est: Cf. 23.6n.

33.6 *Victory over the Gauls.* Corresponds to Livy 33.36.4–37.12. P. moves forward in Livy's book to the Gallic war, passing over the violent disputes in Boeotia narrated in 33.27.5–29.12, perhaps partly because the Romans are only marginally involved. Livy's account of the Gallic war involved victories on both sides: Marcellus is defeated by the Boii and is then victorious over the Insubrians and Comenses—but Livy acknowledges that the victory might in fact have preceded the defeat (33.36.15). He is then joined by his colleague, and together they defeat the Boii and the Ligurians; Marcellus celebrates a triumph over the Insubrians and Comenses, but not the Boii, because of his initial defeat before his colleague

---

[11] See Livy 34.10.1–5, where M. Helvius, who held command in Further Spain, wins a victory over the Celtiberi, but is denied a triumph on the grounds that he was not fighting in his own province (so, rightly, Richardson (1986), 182, rejected on weak grounds by Brennan (2000), 166–7, who then struggles to understand why Helvius' triumph was refused). P.'s information is overlooked by Sumner (1970), 93–5, who (on flimsy grounds: see Develin (1980), 365, Brennan (2000), 165–6) wants to reject Livy, and argue that Spain was not yet divided between the praetors, and that Tuditanus' defeat was in the part later regarded as Further Spain.

arrived. P.'s account removes every element of controversy, and turns it into nothing more than a Roman victory followed by a triumph, a triumph which he misleadingly implies was over the Boii as well as the Insubrians (that aspect of Livy's account is confirmed by the *Fasti Capitolini*, which has no reference to the Boii). The only other source for this war, Oros. 4.20.11, goes in the opposite direction to P., highlighting Marcellus' defeat by the Boii before he and Furius take revenge on them: he also implies that both the defeat and the victory were much more destructive than Livy had suggested.

Claudius Marcellus: For the form of name see 4.4n.

33.7 *Hannibal flees Carthage and joins Antiochus.* Corresponds to Livy 33.45.6–49.7. Prior to this, the longest notice in his book, P. omits a number of episodes from Livy. One is the introduction of *tresviri epulones*, a matter to which Livy himself paid little attention (33.42.1), but which is nevertheless surprising for P. to overlook, given his regular interest in 'firsts' (1.B.7n.). More prominent in Livy are the activities of Antiochus III, in particular his jockeying for position against Ptolemy, and the attempt by the Romans to settle affairs between them (33.38–41). P.'s omission may be in part, as before, because the narrative is primarily concerned with non-Roman matters; but in this case the Romans do play a role. It is more relevant to observe that passing over Antiochus' actions without comment increases the prominence of Hannibal, since now the first time we learn about Antiochus' aggression is when Hannibal comes to join him, even though, like Livy (e.g. 33.19.6 *iam Antiocho ex Syria moliente bellum*), P. does indicate that Antiochus was already preparing war on his own account. Moreover, the allegation that Hannibal was planning war in Africa, which P. presents as straightforwardly true, Livy strongly implies to be nothing more than a slander promoted by his antagonists in Carthage who opposed his civic reforms, reforms which P. ignores completely, though that is less surprising, given his usual lack of interest in purely non-Roman matters. P. treats Hannibal as the iconic and unrelenting opponent of Rome; Antiochus is merely following in his wake.

The episode is told in a number of other sources (Nep., *Hann.* 7.5–7, App., *Syr.* 4, Just. 31.1.7–2.8, *Vir. Ill.* 42.6, Oros. 4.20.13, Zonar. 9.18.11; cf. Val. Max. 4.1.6, Eutr. 4.3.2). All of these share P.'s uninterest in internal Carthaginian affairs; nevertheless in all of them, as in Livy, it is either explicit (esp. Just. 31.1.9 *falsa nuntiata*, Zonar. 9.18.11 διεβλήθη) or implicit that the accusations against Hannibal are false, for all that they are ultimately validated by Hannibal's support of Antiochus' war. P. removes that sense that the Romans' actions were wrong-headed and self-defeating, and presents instead an image of the Antiochan War as effectively the renewal of the Hannibalic one. While this makes him an outlier in the historical tradition, it is paralleled by both Flor. 1.24.6 and *Vir. Ill.* 42.6; the former not only shows Antiochus as prompted to war by Hannibal, but misleadingly implies that Hannibal's presence in Syria was simply the result of his implacable hostility to

Rome, while the latter states outright that Hannibal 'made Antiochus an enemy of the Romans' (*eumque hostem Romanis fecit*).

molitus...delatus: Cf. 2.2n.

Romanis per epistulas ab adversae factionis principibus delatus: Cf. Livy 33.45.6 *adversae Hannibali factionis principibus Romanis...identidem scribebant*. *defero* in the sense of 'accuse' with a personal object is not found in Livy, though it became increasingly common in the early Empire.

de eo: Cf. 21.3n.

profugus ad Antiochum, Syriae regem, se contulit bellum...parantem: P.'s language here is closer to the later reference to Hannibal's flight at 34.60.2: *Hannibal patria profugus pervenerat ad Antiochum*. For the verbal hyperbaton cf. 29.1n.

Book 34

34.1 *Repeal of the lex Oppia*. Corresponds to Livy 34.1.1–8.3. Livy spends the bulk of his account on the speeches given by Cato and the tribune L. Valerius for and against the law; he also describes the protests conducted by the women themselves. P., as he does elsewhere (cf. 30.2n.), ignores the agency of women, though it is present not only in Livy but also in Val. Max. 9.1.3 (who deplores the outcome: cf. also Tac., *Ann.* 3.33.4) and Zonar. 9.17.1–4; P. merely notes that there was controversy over the repeal. Nor does he bother detailing any of the law's provisions (unlike both Valerius and Oros. 4.20.14), but focuses on Cato as the primary opponent of repeal, as he is also in Zonaras and *Vir. Ill.* 47.6.

de finiendis matronarum cultibus: The law, according to Livy 34.1.3, limited the owning of gold, the wearing of coloured clothing, and the use of a carriage. *cultus* is a fairly generic term, but in the context of women would most naturally connote adornments such as clothing and jewellery (*TLL* IV 1337.59–1338.25); when the word is used in this fashion, the plural is primarily poetic (*TLL* IV 1338.12–25).

cum: Concessive; the construction implies that P. expects Cato to be familiar to his readership—even his opposition was not adequate to prevent repeal.

Porcius Cato: For the form of name see 4.4n.

ea lex aboleretur: *abolere* is not used of repealing laws before the early empire: the earliest use is Val. Max. 9.1.3 *ius* (*sc.* the *lex Oppia*)...*aboleretur*. It then appears to become technical terminology (Woodman and Martin (1996), 392), and was widely used in the fourth and fifth centuries in theological contexts. The common term in Livy is *abrogare*, but P. has already used that in this sentence, so he achieves variation by substituting a familiar term from his own time.

34.2 *Cato's victory in Spain*. Corresponds to Livy 34.8.4–9.13, 34.11–21. P. reduces Cato's entire campaign in Spain to a single brief notice, although it not only occupies a substantial amount of space in Livy, but was narrated by other authors also (App., *Hisp.* 39–41, Zonar. 9.17.5–7), and moreover generated a certain number of shorter anecdotes: there are, for example, no fewer than six in Frontinus' *Stratagems* (1.1.1, 1.2.5, 3.1.2, 3.10.1, 4.7.31, 4.7.35); also Cic., *Div. in Caec.* 66, Val. Max. 4.3.11 (with Paris' epitome), Plin., *Nat.* 14.91, and esp. Plu., *Cat. Ma.* 10.1–11.3. But the campaign—and, to some extent, Cato himself—appear to have fallen from prominence in later antiquity. It is mentioned only briefly by Flor. 1.33.9 and by *Vir. Ill.* 47.2–3, but not at all by either Eutropius or Orosius: indeed, neither Eutropius nor Orosius ever mentions Cato at all, except once in a dating formula (Oros. 4.20.12), and in Florus he only appears one other time, in the run-up to the Third Punic War (1.31.4–5). To some extent there is a precedent for this in the brevity of Nepos, *Cato* 2.1; but in general, P.'s reduction of the war is typical of the later Latin tradition.

The one slight surprise is that the single specific detail about the campaign that P. offers is that Cato began it from Emporiae. It is possible that this reflects some geographic awareness on P.'s part, since Emporiae stood on the north-east corner of the province, and would be a natural starting-point for a systematic attempt at pacification—he starts with Cato's travelling to Spain, and then notes his point of arrival. But it is also possible that the focus on Emporiae results from the unusual prominence given by Livy to the town, since he starts with a detailed description of its unusual topography and ethnic composition (34.9.1–9).

citeriorem Hispaniam: Livy does not say that Cato's province was 'Nearer Spain' in his narrative in Book 34, but he had done so when Cato was allocated his province in Book 33 (33.43.2).

pacavit: Cf. Livy 34.21.7 *pacata provincia*. P.'s narrative, unlike Livy's, reinforces the impression of a decisive victory on Cato's part by having no further fighting in Spain until Book 40.

34.3 *Flamininus defeats Nabis of Sparta.* Corresponds to Livy 34.22.4–41.10. As with Cato's campaign in Spain, P. compresses into a single notice an episode which occupies a large portion—in this case around a third—of Livy's book. In this case, however, P. is only doing what virtually every other source does. Apart from Zonar. 9.18.1–4, who gives a number of details about the campaign, every other writer, like P., gives a bare notice of the victory, followed in some cases by a brief version of the settlement that was imposed (Plu., *Flam.* 13.1–3, Just. 31.3.1, Eutr. 4.2.2; cf. also Flor. 1.23.12, *Vir. Ill.* 51.3, Oros. 4.20.2). The fact that Flamininus, despite the objections of his Greek allies, allowed Nabis to remain in charge of Sparta is central to some of these accounts (Plutarch, Justin); P. focuses instead on a less morally complex issue, namely the liberation of Argos, although he hints at the controversy that Flamininus' decisions caused (see below), and the fact that Nabis remained in control is in any case apparent from his return in the following book (35.3). See also 34.8n.

bellum...finiit: P.'s notice unexpectedly focuses on Flamininus' putting the war to an end, rather than the fact that it was fought at all; the postponement of the verb adds to the sense that the author is drawing the reader's attention to the aftermath more than to the war itself: cf. below.

prospere gestum: Cf. 3.10n.

qualem ipse volebat: A surprising phrase, because it appears to be superfluous: in the absence of any information to the contrary, one would naturally assume that Flamininus organized the peace settlement in the way that he wanted. Its presence alerts the reader—or at least the well-informed reader—to the fact that Flamininus' settlement with Sparta met with hostility among various of the Greeks: cf. 22.12n. for another example of P. using an apparently superfluous phrase so as to hint at a story which he does not introduce explicitly.

Eutr. 4.2.2 has a similar phrase: *quibus voluit condicionibus in fidem accepit*. Although there is no linguistic overlap with P., the parallel suggests that one is drawing on the other, or else that they depend on a common source, since it seems intrinsically unlikely that they would independently insert a phrase of this sort that nothing in the story required. More probably one drew on the other: see further the Introduction.

34.4 *Victories in Spain and Gaul.* P., unusually (but cf. 9.5n., 22.10n.), inserts his 'round-up' notice not at the end of the book, but in the middle. There is no obvious reason for the particular placement, although it does allow him to end this book, like the last, on the exceptional figure of Hannibal (cf. 33.7n., 34.9n.). Livy records fighting against the Boii and Insubrians at 34.22.1–3, 34.46.1, and especially 34.46.4–48.1. The last of these campaigns is less decisive than P. here makes it sound: although the Gauls, according to Livy, lost more than twice as many troops as the Romans did, they succeeded in driving the Romans back to their camp; P. turns equivocal success into a firm victory.

More puzzling is the reference to Spain. P. already included Cato's successful campaign there (34.2); the only other fighting in Spain in this book is a brief mention of a victory by M. Helvius shortly after Cato's arrival (34.10.1–2). While this is formally enough to account for the notice, it is so insignificant an episode in the context of the book as to suggest a measure of arbitrariness to P.'s inclusion of particular items in these notices (cf. 2.16n., 3.10n., 4.11n.).

res praeterea...feliciter gestae: Cf. 3.10n., 14.8n.

referuntur: Cf. 32.9n.

34.5 *Segregation of seating at games.* Corresponds to Livy 34.44.5 and 34.54.4–8; P. introduces his notice at a point appropriate to the first of these, between the Spartan settlement imposed by Flamininus (34.3) and the foundation of colonies (34.6). However, there is a complexity. Livy appears to introduce two distinct versions of the story in the two passages. The first, which comes from Valerius Antias, *FRHist* 25 F 41 (*ap.* Ascon. 69–70C), has the censors responsible for the innovation; the second, which appears in Cic., *Corn.* fr. 27 (Crawford)[12] and *Har. Resp.* 24, attributes it to Scipio Africanus, the consul that year.[13] P., however, conflates Livy's versions: the censors' names come from Livy's first passage, but the language, and also the observation that the people resented being separated from the Senate, comes from the second. P. maintains the impression of class conflict, while carefully excluding the suggestion that Africanus himself was in any way involved.

---

[12] Ascon. 70C argues that in this passage Cicero is following Antias, but see *contra* Fleck (1993), 209–13.
[13] Also Val. Max. 2.4.3 (with Paris' epitome); however, Valerius mistakenly attributes it to Scipio Aemilianus.

senatus tunc primum secretus a populo ludos spectavit: Cf. Livy 34.54.4 *ludos Romanos primum senatus a populo secretus spectavit*. *tunc primum* usually indicates that the events took place at the same time as those of the previous notice, but in this case the previous notice was only a 'round-up' summary, which makes any chronological connection clearly impossible (see 11.5n.); the notice prior to that, the Spartan settlement, refers to an event of the previous year.

34.6 *Foundations of colonies*. Livy refers to a number of colonial foundations in this book: Puteoli, Volturnum, Liternum, Salernum, Buxentum, Tempsa, and Croton (34.45.1–5). He also describes the vote to establish two further colonies, in Bruttii and Thurii (34.53.1–2), although the foundations themselves do not take place until the following book (respectively 35.40.5–6 and 35.9.7–8). Technically P.'s phrase *coloniae deductae* describes only the actual foundations, not the vote; it is true that at 8.6 P. uses it of an earlier stage in the process, but that does not mean that he is doing so here (*contra* Fronda (2011), 430: see 20.12n.).

coloniae plures deductae sunt: Cf. 1.B.1n.

34.7 *Triumph of Cato*. Corresponds to Livy 34.46.2–3. P. does not record all triumphs, but includes a good number of them, especially when, as here, the person celebrating it could be regarded as an iconic figure (though cf. 34.1n.), even though Livy himself does not describe it in great detail. In the case of Cato, it may be noted that Pliny repeatedly lists his triumph as one of his central achievements (*Nat. Praef.* 30, 14.44, 14.91, 29.13).

M. Porcius Cato ex Hispania triumphavit: Cf. Livy 34.46.2 *M. Porcius Cato ex Hispania triumphavit*.

34.8 *Triumph of Flamininus*. Corresponds to Livy 34.52.4–12. P. passes over Livy's account of Flamininus' final settlement in Greece and return to Italy (34.48.2–52.3; though see below), and moves directly to his triumph. Unlike Cato's, Flamininus' triumph was widely regarded as a memorable event (Cic., *Mur.* 31, *Pis.* 61, Val. Max. 5.2.6 (with Paris' epitome), Plu., *Flam.* 13.6–14.2,[14] Eutr. 4.2, Oros. 4.20.2–3). P. does not offer any details of the triumph, not even the fact that the sons of both Philip and Nabis were displayed at it, which both Eutropius and Orosius highlight (cf. also *Vir. Ill.* 51.2–3); he mentions only the (apparently) unprecedented length of the triumph as a sign of the magnitude of the affair.

---

[14] Plu., *Flam.* 14.1 cites his source; unfortunately, identifying that source is hindered by textual corruption. The MSS read τὸν ἰτανὸν or τουϊτανὸν; most scholars, following an early conjecture, read Τουδιτανὸν, referring it to Sempronius Tuditanus (*FRHist* 10 F 9); Cichorius (1902), 591–3 proposed τὸν Ἀντίαν (Valerius Antias *FRHist* 25 F 71), while Peter (cciii n. 4) suggested τὸν Τίτον—in other words, Livy himself, whom Plutarch refers to as 'Titus' in one other place (*Sull.* 6.10 = F 17; see *ad loc.*). But, as Cichorius rightly points out, that is not the way Plutarch usually refers to Livy, and least of all would he have done so in this Life, where 'Titus' is the name he uses for the protagonist. Cichorius' own proposal is more plausible, but Tuditanus is palaeographically easier, and probably correct.

Philippum, Macedoniae regem, et Nabidem, Lacedaemoniorum tyrannum: On the repetition of the rulers' titles here see Introduction, xxxiii–xxxiv. Philip and Nabis have their titles at the moment of Flamininus' triumph over them, giving the notice a formal resonance. Moreover, in the case of Nabis the superfluous description underlines the impression given by the remainder of the notice: that while the Romans showed moral virtue in defeating him, his survival as ruler of Sparta was at the very least in tension with the Romans' claims to be liberators. See further the next note.

Graeciamque omnem liberaverat: That Flamininus 'had freed all of Greece' is something that Livy (drawing on Plb. 18.46.15) stated at the Isthmian Games scene (33.33.7 *liberatas omnes Graeciae atque Asiae urbes*; cf. 33.31.8), and the claim is repeated in this book by Flamininus himself (34.32.4 *liberantibus omnem Graeciam*).[15] However, Livy has also recorded the Greeks' objection that the survival of Nabis as tyrant of Sparta stands in opposition to that (34.48.5–6). Technically Flamininus had a case: as used in the Hellenistic world, the common slogan of *libertas* was primarily an offer of autonomy to individual cities, and said nothing about the form of government within those cities (see Gruen (1984a), 132–57, esp. 146–8). But *libertas* at Rome had more the sense of freedom from tyranny domestically than of independence from foreign rule (cf. Wirszubski (1950), Arena (2012)), and the very fact that Livy's Greeks make the complaint they do shows how, even in this context, he saw the concept as encompassing both senses (cf. 34.41.5, 34.49.3).

From this perspective, and especially in light of P.'s hint at the controversy over Flamininus' Spartan settlement a few lines earlier (34.3n.), one may reasonably suspect that his statement that Flamininus received the triumph because he had freed *all* of Greece is similarly pointed. It does not derive from anything Livy says at the time of the triumph itself, but the minority of readers who knew Livy's text might remember the qualifications Livy had offered: how complete was the freedom that Flamininus offered to Greece?

ob hoc triduo triumphavit: Cf. Livy 34.52.4 *triduum triumphavit*. After *hoc* the chief MSS add *rerum factarum multitudinem*, with *hoc* corrected to *hanc* in some later MSS. However, even with the grammatical correction, the phrase is both pleonastic and unlike P. in manner; Rossbach rightly deleted it as a gloss.

34.9 *Hannibal conspires to make war.* Corresponds to Livy 34.60–1. For his final and longest notice in the book, as also of the previous book (33.7n.), P. returns to the iconic figure of Hannibal, who, accordingly, looms far larger in this section of his narrative than he had in Livy's (cf. 35.1n.). In Livy, the account of Hannibal's attempt to seduce the Carthaginians into war is surrounded by the debate in the

---

[15] Sanders (1904), 236–7 mistakenly takes P. to be referring here to a second proclamation by Flamininus, rather than the one at the Isthmian Games in Book 33: see *contra* Bingham 312–15.

Senate between Antiochus' ambassadors and Flamininus (34.57–9), and the border dispute between the Carthaginians and Masinissa (34.62); Livy connects both of these to the story of Hannibal, but P. nevertheless ignores them and focuses on Hannibal alone.

More or less the same story as Livy's is told by App., *Syr.* 7–8 and Just. 31.3.5–4.3 (who, however, changes the precise nature of Ariston's deception of Hannibal's enemies in Carthage); Nep., *Hann.* 8.1 has a rather different version, in which Hannibal himself returns to Carthage to urge war. All three, like Livy, state explicitly that the planned war involved a direct attack on Italy; P. (like Zonar. 9.18.12) speaks more vaguely about Hannibal's plans for war. Moreover, P. mentions that Ariston had nothing in writing from Hannibal, but does not give any further explanation. Livy's own account of that is typically subtle: Hannibal was afraid of his plans being disclosed if the letters were intercepted (34.61.1), but in the event the Carthaginians are all swiftly aware of what Ariston is doing on Hannibal's behalf, with or without letters (34.61.4). The lack of written instructions do, however, enable Ariston to maintain a measure of deniability long enough to escape (34.61.10). P. refers to the absence of letters and merely allows the reader to infer from this distinctive feature of the story that Hannibal was acting deceptively, without saying what the plan was or whether it worked (cf. Chaplin (2010), 459–60). Only the reader who knew Livy would appreciate exactly what ensued.

But the mention of letters may serve another purpose for P. In his narrative, unlike Livy's, the account of Hannibal's attempt to suborn rebellion at Carthage at the end of Book 34 is closely juxtaposed to the narrative of his flight to Antiochus at the end of Book 33—and that flight was prompted by the letters written by his enemies warning the Romans about him. The implication in P., therefore, is not only that Hannibal is devious, but also that he has learned from his experiences of the dangers of having a written record of his conspiracies, and the reader is assisted in making that connection by the very fact that P. is vague about the specifics of why Hannibal avoids letters here.

legati Carthaginiensium nuntiaverunt Hannibalem, qui ad Antiochum confugerat, bellum cum eo moliri: Cf. Livy 34.60.1 *a Carthagine legati bellum haud dubie parare Hannibale ministro attulerunt.* P., like Livy, introduces the story of Hannibal's plans for war by describing an embassy from Carthage, only then going on to set out the events that led to that embassy being sent. However, it is worth observing one subtle change that P. makes to Livy: whereas Livy speaks about Antiochus planning war and Hannibal as his assistant, P., turns Hannibal into the primary agent, here too placing him in a far more central position than Livy had (cf. above).

qui ad Antiochum confugerat: Similar phrasing is used in *Vir. Ill.* 42.6 *ad Antiochum regem Syriae confugit.*

ad bellandum: Cf. 8.8n.

Book 35

35.1 *Meeting of Scipio and Hannibal.* Corresponds to Livy 35.14.5–12. With his opening notice in the book, P. for the first time offers a detailed reproduction of an entire anecdote, namely the story of the meeting of Hannibal and Livy at the court of Antiochus. His focus on this moment is in a certain respect surprising. It was not by any means popular within the post-Livian Latin tradition: apart from P., and a passing reference in Orosius to Scipio 'having a friendly conversation with Hannibal' (4.20.18 *cum Hannibale conloquium familiare habuit*), it is transmitted solely in Greek sources: Plu., *Flam.* 21.3–4, *Pyrrh.* 8.2 (citing his lost life of Scipio), App., *Syr.* 10; Lucian, *DMort* 25, a debate between Alexander, Hannibal, and Scipio in the underworld, is an oblique version of the same story (cf. also *VH* 2.9, where Alexander is judged superior to Hannibal, but Scipio plays no role).

Indeed, Livy himself presents it outside his main account, naming his source as 'Claudius, following the Greek books of Acilius' (35.14.5 *Claudius, secutus Graecos Acilianos libros*):[16] this may suggest that even in his own day the story had a primarily Greek orientation. The reason for that may be seen if one considers the meaning of the story. It is often misunderstood by modern scholars as a celebration of Scipio's military genius, when it is in fact closer to the opposite: the implication of Hannibal's paradoxical comment is that Scipio's victory over him had been the result of something other than military genius.[17] That idea suits well Livy's image of the Second Punic War, in which military commanders, including Scipio, often win in spite of rather than because of their tactical decisions (Levene (2010a), 300–16); but the backhanded dig at one of the greatest Roman generals also may have satisfied Greek vanity, and may explain why the story is mainly transmitted among the Greeks. For the same reason, it is less obviously appropriate to P., who shows no sign of sharing Livy's complex attitude to military victory. It is

---

[16] Acilius *FRHist* 7 F 4 = Claudius Quadrigarius *FRHist* 24 F 66.

[17] That this point is often overlooked is at least in part the consequence of Livy's subtle language. He concludes the anecdote with the comment that Scipio was flattered, 'because he had separated him from the mass of commanders as if he were incomparable' (35.14.12 *quod e grege se imperatorum velut inaestimabilem secrevisset*). Scipio took Hannibal to be asserting that Scipio was so great as to be incommensurate with Alexander *et al.*, and hence implicitly the best of all. But Livy presents this as Scipio's view, not his own. Grammatically it is unclear whether Livy endorses this interpretation of Hannibal's words—the reader cannot tell whether the subjunctive results from the entire anecdote being in *oratio obliqua*, or whether it is because Livy is directly declining to vouch for Scipio's understanding—but in terms of logic, the interpretation makes little sense: Hannibal's failure to list Scipio as a great general shows that Hannibal did not regard Scipio as a great general, not that he regarded him as an incomparably good one. This is not the only time that Livy shows Scipio being misled by the cunningly ambiguous speech of an African (cf. Levene (2010a), 255–8, and note 35.14.12 *perplexum Punico astu responsum*).

possible that he, too, failed to understand the paradox;[18] alternatively, it may be that he recognized it, but that the neatness as a summary of the careers of two characters in whom he had invested a considerable amount of interest made it overwhelmingly attractive in spite of the potential complications. Certainly it is for him the culmination of his story of Hannibal: he has devoted an unusual amount of attention to his role in the run-up to the war with Antiochus—proportionately far more than Livy did (33.7n., 34.9n.)—but he says nothing of the relatively small part he played in the fighting; the next and last time he will appear will be at his death (39.6). It also allows Scipio to play a dominant part in a section of the work in which Livy makes him nothing more than a minor character (cf. Chaplin (2010), 461).

One textual oddity should be mentioned. In all the chief MSS, the *titulus* marking the beginning of Book 35 appears not before, but after the episode, which thus appears to belong to Book 34 rather than to this book. The Aldine edition corrected it, and that correction has been accepted by all subsequent editors. It is conceivable that the MS tradition is correct, and that P. wrongly inserted the meeting of Scipio and Hannibal to follow directly on the attempt of Hannibal to enlist the Carthaginians in Book 34; but it is far more likely that the *titulus* has been displaced, perhaps as a result of an early MS having written it in the margin (compare 17.6, which the Paris MS transfers to Book 18: see *ad loc.*). While P. does occasionally place material in the wrong book (cf. esp. 11.2n., 38.7n., 44.3n., and cf. 18.5n.), those occasions only cover parts of his notices, and are largely explicable in terms of his summarizing practice. There is no known parallel to his displacing an entire notice into the wrong book.

Assuming that this is correct, then we may observe that the anecdote in P. is highlighted not only by its length and detail, but also by its appearance at the start of the summary of Book 35. The opening chapters of Livy's book include accounts of fighting in Spain (35.1, 35.7.6–8) and Liguria and Gaul (35.3–5, 35.11); they include an account of the Aetolians' (35.12) and Nabis' (35.13.1–3) diplomatic manoeuvres against Rome, the movements of Antiochus (35.13.4–5), and Roman negotiations with Eumenes of Pergamum, who was keen that the Romans go to war with Antiochus (35.13.6–10). They also include references to certain matters in which P. habitually takes an interest, namely the census (35.9.1–2) and the foundation of a colony (35.9.7–9). Much of this material P. ignores altogether—the entire run of the narrative is subordinated to this one anecdote; the rest is displaced, with the 'round-up' passage at the end of the book covering the Ligurian fighting and Antiochus' war-plans (35.6n.), while the activities of Nabis and the

---

[18] As indeed Lucian may have done, when he allows Minos to conclude straightforwardly that because Scipio beat Hannibal, he was Hannibal's superior as a general; but in Lucian's case it is more probable that he is parodying such crass rankings than that he endorsed them (cf. Baldwin (1990), esp. 55–6).

Aetolians are encompassed by the notices concerning them later in the book (35.3n., 35.4n.).

ut, si fieri posset, metum ei, quem ex populo Romano conceperat, eximeret: Cf. Livy 35.14.3 *ut...si qua posset, metum demeret periculi quicquam ei ab Romanis esse*. Livy is here talking not about Scipio, but P. Villius Tappulus, the envoy who meets Hannibal in the main version of the narrative. P. transfers that to Scipio himself, in order to provide some context for the meeting. However, in P., it is even more obvious than it is in Livy that any such reassurance would be disingenuous, since the narrative in Book 33 made it very clear that Hannibal was right to fear Rome, and the repetition of *metus* in P. from that narrative, less than a page before, accentuates the point. Livy himself did not use *metus* of Hannibal in Book 33.

For *concipere metum ex* = 'conceive fear because of', cf. Frontin., *Strat*. 1. *Praef. metu, quem milites ex adversis conceperint ominibus*.

cum quaereret quem fuisse maximum imperatorem Hannibal crederet, respondit Alexandrum, Macedonum regem, quod parva manu innumerabiles exercitus fudisset quodque ultimas oras, quas visere supra spem humanam esset, peragrasset: This, unusually, repeats the whole of Livy 35.15.6-7 almost word for word: *quaerenti Africano quem fuisse maximum imperatorem Hannibal crederet, respondisse Alexandrum Macedonum regem, quod parva manu innumerabiles exercitus fudisset, quod ultimas oras, quas visere supra spem humanam esset, peragrasset*. Only Livy's asyndeton is removed, with *quodque* replacing *quod*.

quaerenti deinde quem secundum poneret, Pyrrhum, inquit, castra metari primum docuisse, ad hoc neminem loca elegantius cepisse, praesidia disposuisse: This too repeats Livy very closely: 35.15.8-9: *quaerenti deinde quem secundum poneret, Pyrrhum dixisse: castra metari primum docuisse, ad hoc neminem elegantius loca cepisse praesidia disposuisse*. P. omits Livy's third explanation for Pyrrhus' ranking: his success in winning over the Italians, perhaps because it was the least flattering to Roman power—it may be relevant that his narrative of the Pyrrhic War in Books 13-14 completely overlooked the existence of Pyrrhus' Italian allies.

exsequenti quem tertium diceret, semet ipsum dixit. ridens Scipio 'quidnam tu diceres', inquit, 'si me vicisses?' 'tunc vero me', inquit, 'et ante Alexandrum et ante Pyrrhum et ante alios posuissem': Cf. Livy 35.14.10-11: *exsequenti quem tertium diceret, haud dubium semet ipsum dixisse. tum risum obortum Scipioni et subiecisse 'quidnam tu diceres, si me vicisses?' 'tunc vero me', inquit, 'et ante Alexandrum et ante Pyrrhum et ante alios omnes imperatores esse'.*

35.2 Prodigies. Corresponds to Livy 35.21.2-6. For the second time in the decade (cf. 32.1n.), P. does something which he does only rarely elsewhere: he focuses on a prodigy from one of Livy's lists, in this case, as before, a prodigy whose interpretation appears relatively straightforward, with a direct bearing on the forthcoming war. Prior to that, he passes over the negotiations with Antiochus, along with the debates on either side (35.15–19); these are, however, covered, at least in general terms, by his final round-up of 'other things' at the end (35.6n.).

The same prodigy is found in Val. Max. 1.6.5, who, however, misdates it to the Second Punic War; it appears also in the epitomes of Valerius by Paris and Nepotianus, who retain the misdating. It is especially noteworthy that in Paris it is the only example that he transmits from Valerius' long list, suggesting that for him, as for P., it carried a particularly strong resonance. In the case of Valerius and his epitomators, the association with the Punic War, in which the threat to Rome is obvious, explains that resonance, and indeed may explain why the anecdote was transferred to that war in the first place. For P. it is less obvious: the interpretation of the prodigy is not hard, as noted above, but precisely for that reason it is not apparent why P. would highlight it in the context of an upcoming war which posed little real threat to Rome. In Livy's case the introduction of this prodigy is likely to be explicable simply as a gesture to tradition, which is the main way in which he employs prodigy lists in this decade,[19] but that explanation does not work for P., who does not have the regularity of Livy's annalistic material. Possibly it is merely an arbitrary inclusion—certainly such arbitrariness is found elsewhere in P.'s selections of material—but it is also possible that it is a function of the abridgement of P.'s narrative: it will not be long before (for example) he will show *luxuria* entering Rome from Asia (39.2n.), something that in terms of Roman morals could be seen as a threat as great as Hannibal.

inter alia prodigia: Cf. 14.2n.

quae plurima fuisse: Livy at various times suggests that a considerable number of prodigies were announced in a particular year, usually a year of crisis (e.g. 5.15.1, 10.23.1, 21.62.1, 24.10.6, 28.11.1, 40.19.1). This year happens not to be one of those times; and indeed the list, if anything, is on the short side. This comment by P. may be a justification for his introduction of a prodigy, contrary to his usual practice; it may also offer a sense that the prodigies did indeed have something significant to tell (cf. 32.1n.).

traduntur: Cf. 32.1n.

bovem Cn. Domitii cos. locutam 'Roma cave tibi': Cf. Livy 35.21.4 *consulis Cn. Domiti bovem locutum 'Roma, cave tibi'*.

refertur: P. has regularly been using *referuntur* with a plural subject to indicate aspects of Livy's text that he is summarizing (cf. 16.1n.). Here, less commonly (but cf. 68.7) he uses the impersonal *refertur* with an accusative and infinitive.

---

[19] Cf. Levene (1993), 78–102. At Levene (1993), 85–6, I tentatively suggested that the emphasis given to this prodigy might be connected with the presence of Hannibal in the war, but also noted the problem with that explanation: that although Hannibal's presence on Antiochus' side has been built up considerably by Livy, in the event he is 'largely ineffective'.

35.3 *Defection and death of Nabis.* Corresponds to Livy 35.13.1-2, 35.25-30, 35.34.4-37.3. Faced with the complexities of the run-up to the war with Antiochus, with its multiplicity of interlocking actors, P. to a large extent unweaves them. First comes the story of Nabis: his decision to engage in war despite the settlement he had struck with the Romans not long before, his war against the Achaeans under Philopoemen, and finally his death after he was betrayed by his Aetolian allies. That story is told by Livy in three sections, but P. combines them into one. Even doing it this way necessitates a foray into internal Greek politics, but to some extent P. mutes that. The bulk of his notice concerns the campaign against Rome, and the intra-Greek war centres on the report of Nabis' death, which is an effective conclusion to his defection as well. That the story is more involved than P. acknowledges explicitly is revealed by the role of the Aetolians, who are shown first inciting Nabis and others against Rome, then killing Nabis, and then, in the next notice, defecting from Rome themselves. That is not especially accurate in terms of its implied sequence of events (cf. 35.4n.), but does at least alert the reader that the Aetolians are playing a complex game, seeking their own advantage.

In simplifying the story, P. also makes one major change to it: he shows Nabis explicitly breaking his treaty with Rome, whereas Livy depicts a careful set of manoeuvres on his part, such that he fights his Greek enemies without directly challenging Rome (De Sanctis IV.1 134–5 [138], Gruen (1984a), 462–5). It is possible that this derives from P.'s misreading of Livy: it would not be hard to conclude on a superficial reading of 35.13.1 (where Nabis has pro-Romans executed) or 35.22.2 (where the Achaeans claim that he is acting *contra foedus* and a Roman fleet is sent to assist them), that he has openly broken with Rome, even though a careful reading of Livy's text would show otherwise. But it may also derive from an alternative version: certainly both Plu., *Phil.* 14.1 and Paus. 8.50.6 refer to Philopoemen joining the Romans in their war against Nabis in terms that appear to suggest that Rome and Sparta were openly in conflict at this point.

The role of Philopoemen is also noteworthy. This is the only time he appears in P., apart from his death (39.6), but his unusual status is revealed by the oddity of his introduction: Nabis is said to wage war against him, rather than against the Achaeans as a whole. This hardly reflects the way Livy describes Nabis undertaking the war, but it does make clear how central Philopoemen is to his account.

⟨**cum**⟩...**descivisset, bello...gesto:** Jahn proposed *cum...descivisisset* as a correction of the MSS *descivisse et bellum...gesto*; *descivisset bello* was already offered by a second hand in the oldest MS. Rossbach preferred *descivit sed bello*, but the *cum*-clause is far more characteristic of P.'s manner (cf. 2.2n.). Jahn, however, placed the *cum* after *sollicitabant*; I put it at the beginning of the sentence, which is less stylish, but more typical of P.

Nabis, Lacedaemoniorum tyrannus: As at 34.8 (see *ad loc.*), P. identifies Nabis formulaically as 'tyrant of the Spartans'; once again it appears to be a form of shorthand, setting him in opposition to the liberty the Romans purported to bring to Greece, and implicitly justifying his antagonists.

35.4 *Defection of the Aetolians.* Corresponds to Livy 35.12, 35.32–4. Once again (cf. 35.3n.), P. separates out the defection of the Aetolians from the rest of the narrative, although in this case there is an obvious overlap with the events of the previous notice: even the reader who does not know Livy's text can see that either the notices are out of chronological order, or else the Aetolians' anti-Roman activities predated their defection—and as it happens, both of these are true. In Livy the Aetolians take the decision to break from Rome at 35.12; but that does not turn into an open breach until the time of Flamininus' embassy to them at 35.33. Both of these, however, predate the Aetolian betrayal of Nabis, contrary to what P.'s sequence indicated.

35.5 *Antiochus and the Aetolians attack Greece.* Corresponds to Livy 35.43.2–46.13, 35.50.6–51.10. P. depicts Antiochus' move into Greece more straightforwardly than Livy did; whereas for Livy the attempt to take Chalcis, first by the Aetolians alone and then by Antiochus, meets a number of setbacks before it is finally accomplished, P. focuses only on the final moments of the book, when Chalcis and Euboea are finally in Antiochus' hands. Likewise the alliance with the Aetolians (cf. below) in Livy takes place only after extensive negotiations, of which P. says nothing; he likewise passes over completely the other negotiations Livy reports around this time (35.47–9), including the debate in Achaea between Flamininus and the ambassadors of Antiochus and the Aetolians. Here, as elsewhere in these books, the intricate diplomatic and military complexities found in Livy are cut down into a few discrete and simple moments. It is, however, interesting to observe that Zonar. 9.19.4–5 reduces the story to much the same elements, although he includes a brief reference to Flamininus' embassy, and it is possible that this is because Cassius Dio, Zonaras' source, constructed the narrative in a broadly similar fashion. If so, the way that P. collapses the story into a few simple elements may not be his own invention, but may reflect how the period was narrated in later antiquity.

cum: Cf. 2.2n.

societate iuncta: P. does not set out directly with whom Antiochus formed his alliance, but allows the reader to infer, correctly, that it was the Aetolians, whose defection he had just recorded.

Syriae rex: For the formal repetition of Antiochus' title as he begins his war with Rome, cf. 34.8n.

complures: Cf. 12.3n.

35.6 *Ligurian war; Antiochus' preparations for war.* For the 'other things' in this final notice, P. singles out two; first, the fighting in Liguria that continued intermittently through the book (35.3, 35.11, 35.21.7-11, 35.40.4), and second, the preliminaries to the war with Antiochus, in the form of the king's plans. The first of these is relatively unsurprising: minor (and sometimes less minor) wars are the commonest thing for P. to include in these notices; it is true that the fighting against the Gauls is equally prominent in the book (35.4-5, 35.22.4), and there is also a reference to fighting in Spain (35.22.5-8); but P. is frequently arbitrary in his choice of wars to include in these notices. The inclusion of Antiochus' preparations for war is more of a surprise, but it enables P. to wrap into a single notice some small but intricate episodes (35.13.4-5, 35.15, 35.17.3-19.7, 35.42.1-43.1), none of which might have warranted a notice in its own right, but which he might have been hesitant to overlook altogether. Handling it this way has the consequence of wiping Hannibal out of the war; in Livy he has a substantial role in Antiochus' preparations (35.18.8-19.7, 35.41.2-43.1), but, as noted above (35.1n.), the actual influence he had on the war was minimal, not least because ultimately Antiochus sidelined him (35.43.1: Livy regards this as the worst of his decisions), and P. does not now mention him again until his death (39.6n.).

res praeterea...gestas...continet: Cf. 2.16n.

Book 36

36.1 *Victory over Antiochus and the Aetolians.* Corresponds to Livy 36.15–19, 36.21.1, 36.22–30, 36.34.1–35.6. P. covers what are arguably the major points of Glabrio's campaign: his victories at Thermopylae and over the Aetolians. However, he has nothing of the campaigns and planning of Antiochus or the Romans that occupy the first part of Livy's book, nor the morally resonant account of Antiochus' decline into luxury over the winter (36.11.1–6: found also in Flor. 1.24.9–10, Just. 31.6.3, Zonar. 9.19.5), nor the independent campaigns of Philip. Conversely, he highlights the departure of Antiochus from Greece as the central outcome, something which Livy mentions only in passing in this book (36.21.1; but cf. below), and he says that Philip assisted at the battle, whereas Livy makes a point of his absence (36.25.1). None of this requires a non-Livian provenance to P.'s account—one can certainly parallel such misleading summaries elsewhere in his text, even in those parts which are more likely to depend on Livy. But, although it does not require it, when one combines this with the considerations set out above about the general level of imprecision and inaccuracy in the summary of this book, it is most easily explicable by the hypothesis that P. here did not have a copy of Livy's original text available to him (see the Introduction, lviii–lix). When it comes to the role of Philip, P. may possibly depend on a version of Thermopylae where Philip did indeed participate in the battle. But no such version is visible in surviving sources, and it is far more likely that P., without access to Livy's original text, is drawing on an earlier summary account of the war, but is misreading it in such a way as to misinterpret Philip's contribution to the war.

P.'s account of Thermopylae also ignores the role played by Cato, but this is less surprising: Cato is, admittedly, at the centre of many other versions (Cic., *Sen.* 32, Frontin., *Strat.* 2.4.4, Plu., *Cat. Ma.* 13–14, App., *Syr.* 18–19, *Vir. Ill.* 47.3, Zonar. 9.19.9–10), but Livy himself gives him only a passing mention in the course of the battle (36.18.8), and the diminution of Cato is not unusual in a late antique Latin writer (cf. 34.2n.).

Acilius Glabrio cos.: For the form of name cf. 4.4n.

Graecia expulit: Livy does not describe Antiochus' departure from Greece in such terms in Book 36; but he uses a similar phrase in Book 37 in a retrospective reference to Antiochus' campaign (37.3.9: *M'. Acilius consul Antiochum regem Graecia expulisset*). It is altogether characteristic of P. to draw on a later passage of Livy in this way when constructing his narrative; this is, accordingly, not a demonstration that he had access to Book 37 and not to Book 36, but it would be natural for him to employ the same technique if, as argued above, he was attempting to reconstruct Book 36 without possessing a copy of it.

36.2 *Dedication of the temple of Magna Mater.* Corresponds to Livy 36.36.3–5. In Livy, the dedicator is not Scipio Nasica, but the praetor M. Junius Brutus. While this is far from the only place where P. has a non-Livian version of a story, in this case the most likely explanation for the variation is that he did not possess an intact copy of Book 36, and was compelled to construct his narrative from other sources (see the Introduction). It could be that whatever P.'s source was may have itself been dependent on Livy, and misread Livy's introduction to his account of the dedication (36.36.3), where he notes the coincidence that Nasica was both the consul under whom it took place and the man who had received the goddess thirteen years earlier. However, it is far more likely that this is an alternative version of the story. The temple was subsequently twice destroyed and rebuilt (in 111 BC and AD 3: see Val. Max. 1.8.11, and cf. Obs. 39n.), and Ov., *Fast.* 4.347 remarks that the original dedicator was no longer known for certain. Ovid's statement makes little sense if Brutus were universally accepted to be the dedicator; it is far more understandable on the hypothesis that, once the original dedicatory inscription was destroyed, different stories about the dedication had arisen, including (as one would expect) a version that ascribed it to Nasica, given his canonical association with the goddess's introduction to Rome (29.6–7n.).

It is even possible that the ascription to Nasica is historical, and the one to Brutus is erroneous (certainly it is on the face of things surprising that Brutus and not Nasica performed the dedication, since Nasica, on Livy's own account (36.37.1; cf. 36.3.14), was present in Rome at the time: see Briscoe (1981), 274–5). However, precisely because of the strength of Nasica's association with the Magna Mater cult, it is unlikely that Brutus' name would have entered the tradition at all, had Nasica genuinely been the dedicator; it is far more likely that Livy's version is correct, and P.'s represents a secondary adaptation.

vir optimus a senatu iudicatus: P. repeats verbatim his description of Nasica from 29.7.

36.3 *Defeat of the Boii; triumph of Nasica.* Corresponds to Livy 36.38.5–8, 36.39.3–40.14. Livy sketches in the victory only very lightly; the bulk of his account centres on the triumph, and in particular the debate over whether Nasica should be awarded it. P. ignores the controversy, and has nothing more than a bare notice of the victory and triumph. In this case, however, the lack of detail is less surprising, since the other two surviving sources for the war, Oros. 4.20.21 and Zonar. 9.19.6, have only the victory and do not mention the triumph at all. The question might be why P. cared to introduce it at all; it is likely that some mention of Nasica's campaign was preserved in the source he used, precisely because his role in the Magna Mater episode led to his being perceived as an iconic figure (29.6–7n.).

36.4 *Naval victories over Antiochus.* Corresponds to Livy 36.42.1–45.8. Although this is formally a 'round-up' summary in P.'s characteristic manner, it is, unlike most such summaries, strictly in its proper place in Livy's narrative, since the naval victories in question, under the prefect C. Livius Salinator, occupy the final section of Livy's book. Since chronologically Livius' campaign overlapped with that of Glabrio (Briscoe (1981), 28–9), we cannot assume that all sources would have followed this sequence (although in practice the only two other surviving sources, App., *Syr.* 22 and Just. 31.6.7–8, have the same order as Livy did). It is possible that here too P. was following an existing summary or contents-list, and retained the order while making it appear that he was, as usual, creating the notice out of Livian material from different parts of the book.

praeterea... referuntur: Cf. 32.9n.

prospera: *prospere* is one of P.'s favourite words, but he employs the adjectival form far less commonly: apart from here, he uses it only at 94.1 and 117.1, and only the first of these is in the context of a battle. It may not be coincidental that Book 94 is a book whose summary, like that of Book 36, is extremely skimpy: in both cases P. may be reflecting the language of a pre-existing epitome.

Book 37

37.1 L. Scipio, with his brother as legate, crosses to Asia to confront Antiochus. Corresponds to Livy 37.1.7–10, 37.33. P. drastically reworks the narrative of Book 37 so as to focus the largest portion of his attention on the activities of the Scipio brothers. After the account of L. Scipio's appointment to the command against Antiochus (Africanus acting as his legate), described by Livy in the opening lines of the book, this first notice leaps to the moment when the Romans cross into Asia, which takes place more than halfway into the book. Part of the intervening material is reserved for the next notice (see 37.2n.), but a far larger proportion is omitted altogether: the fighting against the Aetolians (37.4.6–5.6), followed by the arrival of the Scipios, who negotiate with the Aetolians and others (37.6–7), the conflicts and machinations by the various parties in Asia, including the campaign of the Roman fleet first under C. Livius Salinator, then under L. Aemilius Regillus (37.8–24). This degree of omission is, however, not out of the ordinary in terms of the representation of this campaign by other post-Livian Latin writers: they similarly move directly from L. Scipio's appointment to his crossing into Asia, and ignore the intervening events (Flor. 1.24.14, Just. 31.7.2–3, Eutr. 4.4.1–2).

P.'s interest in the Scipios may also be seen in the content of the notice, where he first explains how Africanus arranged for his brother to be given the command, by promising to act as his legate, and, second, notes that L. Scipio was the first Roman commander to cross into Asia. The first of these is a story found elsewhere (but cf. below); the second observation is unique to P., and is arguably historically incorrect, since Salinator, as praetor in command of the Roman fleet, had brought his troops to land in Asia at the end of Book 36 (36.45.8). P. presumably based himself on Livy's more carefully phrased statement: that 'a Roman army had then for the first time pitched camp in Asia' (37.47.4 *exercitus Romanus tum primum in Asia posuisset castra*), but he reworks the idea into a Scipionic achievement.

With Book 37, we are for the first time able to compare P.'s account with that of the Oxyrhynchus epitome. Since *EpOxy* does not survive for the opening sections of the book, we cannot say how it handled the Scipios' selection and campaign; but it is apparent from the portions that do survive that its overall balance cannot have had nearly so intense a focus upon them, since it reports, albeit briefly, many more episodes than P. does, but does not once touch on the Scipios—it appears, for example, to omit Asiaticus' triumph and acquisition of his *cognomen*, and ignores the Scipios when recording the peace with Antiochus (37.4n., 37.5n.).

se legatum fratris futurum dixerat, si ei Graecia provincia decerneretur: Cf. Livy 37.1.9 *P. Scipio Africanus dixit si L. Scipioni fratri suo provinciam Graeciam decrevissent, se legatum iturum.*

598 COMMENTARY

C. Laelio...ea provincia dari videretur: This goes well beyond Livy, who does not state that the province was on the verge of being given to Laelius prior to Africanus' intervention; his comment about Laelius' influence in the Senate might seem to point in that direction (37.1.7: cf. below), but to set against that is his statement that the Senate was excited by the impending contest over the allocation, which implies that it was far from a foregone conclusion (37.1.9). It is, however, much closer to the versions in other sources (cf. Bingham 325-7). Cic., *Phil.* 11.17 has the decision being made initially by lottery for the province to go to L. Scipio, but the Senate planned to transfer it to Laelius because of concerns about L. Scipio's competence, until Africanus quieted those concerns with his offer; the same version appears in Val. Max. 5.5.1 (also Paris' epitome);[20] similarly App., *Syr.* 21, while not mentioning the possibility of transferring the province to Laelius, has the appointment of Africanus as legate being the consequence of the Senate's doubts about L. Scipio's abilities.[21] Cicero's account is likely to be correct, though the dispute was more probably generated by political rivalry than genuine concerns about L. Scipio as commander (Briscoe (1981), 291; for L. Scipio's experience and competence see Balsdon (1972), esp. 224-6). P., without overtly contradicting Livy, reworks the story so as to align it with Cicero and Valerius.

qui multum in senatu poterat: Cf. Livy 37.1.7 *multum Laelius in senatu poterat.*

primus: Strictly speaking this is not true: cf. above. The distortion in part presumably arises from P.'s interest in magnifying the Scipios, but he also has a broader interest in 'firsts' (1.B.7n.), which may have led him to construct this one even at the cost of some exaggeration.

37.2 *Naval victory at Myonnesus*. Corresponds to Livy 37.27-30. P., as often, says little about the battle beyond the outcome, but he does note the support of the Rhodians. This is a fair reflection of Livy, who notes that the Rhodians comprised more than a quarter of the fleet (37.30.1), and emphasizes their role in the battle (so also the only other account of the episode, in App., *Syr.* 27), but it more broadly fits the impression that P. has consistently been giving since the start of the Second Macedonian War (31.1-3n.): that the successive Roman interventions in Greece have been supported by the Greeks themselves.

Regillus: It is extremely unusual for P. to introduce a new Roman character by his cognomen alone without an indication of the office he was holding. The only real parallels are 127.1, 129.1, and possibly 138.1 (see *ad loc.*); other examples are 80.6,

---

[20] Briscoe (1981), 291 wrongly claims that Valerius' version is compatible with either Cicero's or Livy's. Valerius has Africanus pleading *ne provinciae sors fratri suo erepta ad eum* [sc. *Laelium*] *transferretur*; in other words, the initial decision was made by lot in L. Scipio's favour, and the proposal was to remove it from him, exactly as in Cicero.

[21] Just. 31.7.1 is rather different: the choice of Africanus there is because of the Senate's determination to have a rematch between him and Hannibal; cf. Oros. 4.20.22, who does not mention L. Scipio, but instead refers to a victory in a naval battle by Africanus over Hannibal.

102.4, 105.2, 107.3, 114.6, but none of those is a formal record of a victorious commander on campaign.

feliciter: Cf. 14.8n.

37.3 Antiochus releases Africanus' son. Corresponds to Livy 37.37.6–8; cf. 36.34, 36.36. The oddity about P.'s account is that it is given virtually no context. In Livy, it is done by Antiochus in order to encourage Scipio to accept a peace offer; Scipio is properly grateful to Antiochus, but refuses to be swayed in any material way, and the two sides proceed to battle. It is contextualized in a similar fashion in almost every other source: Plb. 21.15, D.S. 29.8, App., *Syr.* 29–30, Just. 31.7.4–7, Zonar. 9.20.4 (cf. Dio fr. 62.2). Even the strangely garbled account of Oros. 4.20.22 (who appears to date it after Antiochus' defeat at Magnesia) relates it to Antiochus' efforts to have his peace proposal accepted. This is, however, absent from P.: a reader might conceivably hypothesize reasons for Antiochus' generosity and guess at the response that it received, especially since P., unusually, makes a point of connecting the story chronologically to Antiochus' defeat (37.4n.). Nevertheless, P. does not set it out explicitly.

However, there was an alternative way of handling the story within the Latin tradition. It appears as a free-standing anecdote in Val. Max. 2.10.2 (with Paris' and Nepotianus' epitomes; it is also alluded to in passing by both Valerius and Paris at 3.5.1), and likewise in *Vir. Ill.* 49.16. Valerius directly treats it not as a diplomatic ploy, but rather as a disinterested tribute paid by Antiochus to Scipio's greatness. P., with his intense interest in Scipio, prefers to highlight that aspect than the muddy diplomacy of the Antiochan War.

filius Africani captus ab Antiocho patri remissus est: P.'s phrasing here reflects nothing in Livy, but is surprisingly close to Julius Paris' summary of Val. Max. 2.10.2: *filium Africani Scipionis a militibus suis interceptum ultro patri remisit*. Paris himself distilled his phrase from the much longer version of Valerius himself: *filium eius a militibus suis interceptum honoratissime excepit, regiisque muneribus donatum ultro et celeriter patri remisit*. It is possible that P. and Paris independently arrived at similar phrases, perhaps both abridging Valerius; but it is more likely that one is dependent on the other, presumably P. on Paris, who provides additional information taken from Valerius which P. omits.

37.4 Defeat of Antiochus; peace terms agreed. Corresponds to Livy 37.38–45; cf. 37.55.1–3. P.'s interest is less in the battle itself—he does not even provide its location—but rather in the moment of victory and the peace terms that followed it. As usual, he names the victor, and, as he has repeatedly been doing in this decade, identifies a key local ally of the Romans; he finally mentions the central territorial provision of the peace terms imposed on Antiochus, while ignoring the others—the vast indemnity he was required to pay, and also the demand that he surrender Hannibal (the territorial gains of Eumenes and the Rhodians he reserves for later: see 37.7n.). Of the many other writers who relay all or part of this sequence, the closest is probably Eutr. 4.4.2–3, who likewise focuses more on the aftermath than on the battle itself, and also provides several of the same details, notably the assistance of Eumenes, and the identification of the Taurus as the new boundary of Antiochus' kingdom. However, Eutropius offers much more than P. does: he names the site of the battle, he provides casualty figures, he describes the other peace terms; he also mistakenly identifies Eumenes as the brother, rather than the son, of King Attalus, an error that may ultimately go back to a misreading of Livy by Eutropius or his source, since Livy does refer to Eumenes' brother Attalus participating in the battle of Magnesia (37.43.5).

EpOxy says nothing more than that 'peace was given to King Antiochus' (37 col. 1.6: *Antiocho regi pax data*). This may be because the epitomizer omitted the detailed conditions (so Funari 71), but it is far more likely that something of this information was given in the lost earlier part of the epitome (see *ad loc.*).

deinde: Cf. 18.2n. P. tightens the narrative sequence, by indicating (rightly) that the battle of Magnesia followed shortly after the release of Scipio's son (cf. 37.3n.).

Eumene, rege Pergami, Attali filio: Attalus had repeatedly appeared in P.'s narrative as an ally of Rome; P. concluded that story with his death (33.4n.), but he now continues it anew by explicitly identifying Eumenes as his son and heir.

ut omnibus provinciis citra Taurum montem cederet: Cf. Livy 37.35.10 *cis Taurum montem possessione Asiae Antiochus cedat*. This passage comes not from the agreement struck after Magnesia, but from the Romans' peace proposals prior to it: as often, P. draws his phrasing from a Livian passage other than the chief one which he is summarizing. In this case the procedure is clearly justified by Livy's emphasis that the conditions offered prior to the battle were the same as those imposed after it (37.45.13–14).

P. substitutes a reference to 'provinces' for Livy's vaguer 'possession'. It is questionable whether the territory from which Antiochus was required to withdraw comprised a discrete set of provinces, as his language implies. Bergtson (1944), 13–16 suggests that it did, arguing that the list of territories handed over to Eumenes and the Rhodians at Livy 37.56.2–6 (cf. also 38.39.13–17) represents the satrapies in that part of the Seleucid kingdom; but see the cautious reservations of Ma (1999), 123–5. It should be noted in this context that the Taurus mountain range was not an especially well-defined boundary, which led to some dispute as the detailed treaty was negotiated (cf. McDonald 1967). Possibly P. is basing himself on a non-Livian source which formulated the treaty-terms in this fashion, which might give some (very limited) support to Bergtson's case, but it is at least as probable that he is offering his own clarification via a paraphrase of Livy, and that it has no independent historical value.

37.5 Lucius Scipio receives the name Asiaticus. Corresponds to Livy 37.58.6. Instead of summarizing the book in sequence, P. moves forward to complete the story of the victory over Antiochus, with a report on L. Scipio's acquiring a *cognomen* in consequence. This episode is recorded in a number of places, and most of those who mention it draw the same parallel with Africanus as P. does (Cic., *Mur.* 31, Val. Max. 3.5.1, 5.5.1, 8.1 damn. 1, Eutr. 4.4.3, Zonar. 9.20.11; also cf. *Vir. Ill.* 53.1). The oddity is that P. makes no mention of the triumph which in Livy immediately follows (37.59), and which was regarded as being of remarkable grandeur (Livy 38.59.3, Val. Max. 3.5.1, 5.3.2c, 8.1 damn. 1 (also Paris' epitome), Plin., *Nat.* 33.148, 37.12; cf. Livy 37.59.2); indeed, he omits Scipio's triumph, even though he includes those of Glabrio and Regillus, which are far less celebrated within the tradition (37.8n.).

The reasons why P. omitted the triumph are unclear, but there are a few points that may be relevant to note. First, Livy himself is somewhat dismissive of the triumph, comparing it unfavourably to Africanus', which may have been less grand, but was of far greater significance (37.59.2). Second, for Pliny, Asiaticus' spectacular triumph represented a stage in the decline of Rome into luxury; if P. knew of that tradition, he may have regarded it as less appropriate as a culmination of the story of the Scipios' victory in Asia. Third, and perhaps not unconnected with the last two, is that *Vir. Ill.* likewise, while including Asiaticus' gaining his *cognomen*, omitted the triumph. (Both are also omitted in the *Oxyrhynchus Epitome*; see commentary on *EpOxy* 37.) All of these points suggest that, for P., L. Scipio's *cognomen* may have appeared a grander and less problematic achievement.

37.6 *Foundation of colony*. Corresponds to Livy 37.57.7–8. After completing the story of the Scipios' victory, P. inserts a number of other episodes from the last quarter of the book; however, the arbitrariness of his selection may be seen from a comparison with *EpOxy* 37, which makes a very different choice of episodes from Livy. The fragmentary state of the papyrus epitome makes it hard to determine its pattern of inclusions and exclusions, but it certainly mentions the Roman defeat in Spain (37.46.7–9), the dispute over the provincial appointment of the *flamen Quirinalis* (37.51.1–6; cf. 19.8n.), the defeat of the Lusitanians (37.57.5–6), and the contentious censorial election (37.57.9–58.2); it also appears to refer (inaccurately: see *EpOxy* 37 col. 1.3n., *EpOxy* 37 col. 1.7n.) to the Aetolian embassy to Rome (37.49) and the dispute between Antiochus and the Rhodians over the city of Soli (37.56.7–8). None of these is mentioned by P.; instead, he focuses his attention on the Asian settlement, two triumphs, and a colonial foundation. P. is in general far more interested in documenting colonies and triumphs than *EpOxy* is (cf. Funari 73); and the Asian settlement is a dominant feature in this part of Livy's narrative (37.7n.), so it is more surprising that *EpOxy* omits it than that P. includes it. It is less obvious why P. omits the material found in *EpOxy*; it is true that none of these episodes looms especially large in Livy's narrative, but P. regularly includes similar matters of no greater significance, and the selection here is more likely to reflect arbitrariness than design.

colonia deducta est: Cf. 1.B.1n.

37.7 *Territory given to Eumenes and the Rhodians*. Corresponds to Livy 37.55.4–56.6, where the details of the territorial concessions are given; but cf. also 37.52–4, where first Eumenes and then the Rhodians address the Senate. P.'s account is once again (cf. 37.4n.) mirrored most closely in Eutr. 4.4.3, who likewise identifies Eumenes and the Rhodians as the beneficiaries, without giving any precise details of what territory was involved; the other post-Livian Latin source, Just. 31.8.9, says only that the Romans' allies received territory, without explaining which allies (Just. also adds a moral, that the Romans did well to keep their hands off such luxurious possessions). The allies are, however, largely ignored by the rest of the post-Livian tradition: there is nothing of this in Zonaras, and virtually nothing in Appian (there is a vague mention of Eumenes having formerly Pergamene territory returned to him at *Syr.* 38); and *EpOxy*, as noted above (37.6n.), eschews any mention of gains by the allies but instead concentrates on the city that the Rhodians wanted but did not ultimately get. P.'s interest is presumably generated not only by the prominence of the episode in Livy, but more by his attention to the Roman allies throughout this decade (cf. e.g. 31.1–3n., 32.3n.); for the same reason, he prefers to emphasize what they were given over what they were denied.

quo iuvante Antiochus victus erat: P. alludes back to 37.4 (*victo deinde Antiocho…adiuvante Eumene*), tying his narrative together.

regnum ampliatum: For *ampliare* = 'enlarge' cf. 1.B.2n.

37.8 *Triumphs of Regillus and Glabrio*. Corresponds to Livy 37.58.3–4 and 37.46.2–6. Neither triumph is recorded in any other post-Livian writer, except for the grammarian Caesius Bassus, who quotes lines from the triumphal *tabulae* that each of them erected (*GL* 6.265; cf. Livy 40.52.4–5); but P. often (though far from always) makes a point of recording triumphs. Two aspects are unexpected. One is that he records these triumphs, but not the more significant one of Asiaticus (see 37.5n.). The other is that he presents them in the opposite order to Livy; indeed, according to Livy, Glabrio's triumph took place the year before Regillus'.[22] The reason for the latter is presumably that Glabrio's triumph arguably represented a more substantial victory, over the king himself and the Aetolians, rather than (as P. makes a point of noting) over the king's *praefecti*, and so provides a more suitable climax for the book.

Aemilius Regillus: For the form of name see 4.4n.

qui praefectos Antiochi navali proelio devicerat: Cf. Livy 37.58.3 *qui classe praefectum Antiochi regis devicerat*; but also Livy 40.52.4 *L. Aemilius Regillus navali proelio adversus praefectos regis Antiochi*. P. combines the language of Livy's two

---

[22] The surviving portions of the *Fasti Capitolini* do not mention Glabrio's triumph, but there is a gap of three lines above that of Regillus into which it would fit, thus indirectly supporting Livy's chronology (Degrassi 553).

passages; in accordance with the second version in Livy, he has Regillus' victory being over multiple prefects rather than a single prefect. The version in Book 37 matches Livy's actual narrative more closely, since Livy refers to only a single prefect, Polyxenidas, who is a relatively significant character,[23] but P. prefers the version that makes the victory seem more impressive.

navalem triumphum deduxit: *triumphum deducere* is an extremely rare phrase (for the more common *triumphum ducere* see 17.2n.). P. is using choice language; apart from this passage, the phrase is found only in mythological contexts: Val. Max. 3.6.6 uses it of the return of Bacchus from India, and *Ilias Latina* 541 of Menelaus' capture of Adrastus (but cf. Isid. *Diff.* 1.156, who (implausibly) explains the difference between *triumphos ducere* and *triumphos deducere* as being that in the latter, not horses, but oxen were used in the parade).

quem Graecia expulerat: P. used a similar phrase of Glabrio's victory at 36.1: see *ad loc.*

---

[23] W-M *ad* 40.52.4 propose, possibly rightly, that Livy is there thinking of the subordinate commanders serving under Polyxenidas.

Book 38

38.1 *Campaign of M. Fulvius.* Corresponds to Livy 38.3.9–11.9, 38.28.5–29.11. P. begins his narrative of Book 38 by collecting together the activities of M. Fulvius Nobilior, although in Livy those are spread through the first half of the book. Moreover, he does not narrate the events in chronological order: he places the last, the conquest of Cephallenia, in the centre, presumably in order that the notice can follow a 'natural' progression from warfare to a peace agreement; P. also, unsurprisingly, ignores the narrative of intra-Greek warfare which Livy intertwines with the material involving Rome. Other post-Livian sources (notably Flor. 1.25 and Zonar. 9.21.1–4) likewise treat Fulvius' campaign as a single unit, but retain the chronology; *Vir. Ill.* 52.2 only has the Aetolian episode, and ignores Cephallenia. *EpOxy*, as often less interested than P. in presenting a coherent narrative, has nothing but an (inaccurate) reference to the siege of Ambracia, without even a mention of Fulvius (see Funari 74–5; also *EpOxy* 38 col. 1.1n.).

Cephalloniam: Most Greek sources call it *Cephallenia*; Livy (probably following Polybius: see Nissen (1863), 137) calls it *Cephallania*, but *Cephallonia* is the spelling found in various sources in later antiquity, both Greek and Latin, and should be retained here.

Aetolis perdomitis: Cf. Livy 38.28.5 *perdomitis Aetolis*. P., as often, uses phrasing taken from a later passage of Livy, albeit in this instance still a passage covered by this notice: a retrospective reminder of the defeat of the Aetolians at the time when Fulvius attacked Cephallenia.

38.2–4 *Campaign of Cn. Manlius.* Corresponds to Livy 38.12–27. P.'s account of Manlius' campaign against the Gallogrecians has nothing of the fighting beyond the bare fact of Manlius' victory. He pays more attention to two other aspects: first, the arrival of Gauls in Asia Minor—although his account is both inaccurate (see 38.2n.) and lacunose, explaining that Livy provided the background, without giving any indication of the manner in which he did so—and, second, the exemplary story of the revenge taken by a Gallogrecian princess on the Roman centurion who had raped her.

Among other writers, Flor. 1.27 is by far the closest to P.; he too privileges the origins of the Gallogrecians and the rape story over the details of the campaign; so too *Vir. Ill.* 55, while having nothing to say about the arrival of the Gallogrecians in Asia Minor, devotes the bulk of a notice which is ostensibly about Manlius and his campaign to the story of the rape, as does the summary of Livy in *EpOxy*; the rape is also told in some detail by Val. Max. 6.1 ext. 2 (also Paris' epitome) and Plu., *Mul. Virt.* 258D–E (= Plb. 21.38). Zonar. 9.20.14–15, who does not have the rape story, is similar to P. in as much as he too is more interested in the Gallogrecians themselves than in Manlius' campaign. Very different is App.,

Syr. 42, who concentrates on the actual fighting, as does Oros. 4.20.25, though mistakenly identifying Fulvius rather than Manlius as the commander.

38.2 Tolostobogios et Tectosagos et Trocmos: The same three tribes are listed by Livy 38.16.11–12 (in a different order) and 38.19.1–2 (in P.'s order). Other sources who mention all three are Memn., *FGrH* 434 F 1.11.6, Str. 12.5.1–2, and App., *Syr.* 42.

qui Brenno duce in Asiam transierant: This misrepresents Livy; he refers to Brennus as the leader of the Gauls when they migrated to the land of the *Dardani* (38.16.1), but the crossing into Asia was by a group who had left Brennus' army after a schism. No other source makes the same error as P.; however, both Flor. 1.27.3 and Zonar. 9.20.14 describe the crossing into Asia in terms which, while they do not require that Brennus was the leader, could easily be misinterpreted as having that meaning (both speak of the Gauls' attack of Greece under Brennus before noting, in the same sentence and naming no other leader, that they went on to Asia). It seems plausible that P. had a similar text in front of him when he was composing this notice; he was presumably assisted in making the error by the fame of Brennus, the archetypal Gallic leader who led the attack on Delphi, and whose name was (probably unhistorically: see Ogilvie (1965), 719) attached by Livy to the leader of the Gallic attack on Rome in Book 5.

cum soli citra Taurum montem non apparerent: Livy does not describe the Gallogrecians in these terms. It is at various points implicit in his narrative of the campaign that the Gallogrecians had not submitted to Rome after Antiochus' defeat, but it is nowhere stated that they are the only ones in their part of Asia to have held out (though note 38.12.5, where Manlius speaks of the ease of fighting the Gauls alone). By putting it in this way, P. provides an implicit justification for Manlius' attack, which in Livy proves highly controversial, when the commissioners challenge his right to a triumph (see 38.7n.), partly on the grounds that he had provoked an unnecessary war without senatorial authorization. P.'s language, repeating *citra Taurum montem* from 37.4, emphasizes the continuity between the Gallogrecian war and the Antiochan War that had been concluded in the previous book. *Vir. Ill.* 55.1, though no longer than P., is in this regard closer to Livy, saying that Manlius launched the war out of desire for a triumph, something suggested also by Flor. 1.27.2.

apparerent = 'obey': a rare sense of the word, but it is found in Cic., *Leg.* 2.21,[24] and occasionally in patristic writings (*TLL* II 268.10–13). P. is adopting a more elevated style than usual.

38.3 refertur: See 16.1n.

---

[24] But not in Sen., *Clem.* 1.26.1 (*contra OLD s.v. appareo* 6): see Braund (2009), 375.

38.4 exemplum quoque virtutis et pudicitiae: It is rare for P. to remark in his own voice on an *exemplum* (though cf. 2.5n.). One possible reason he does so here is that, while Livy does not explicitly cite this passage as such, both Val. Max. 6.1 ext. 2 and Flor. 1.27.6 do so; Valerius indeed refers to it as an *exemplum pudicitiae*, as P. does here.

traditur: This word does a double service for P. Like *refertur* in the previous sentence, it is a direct allusion to the fact that the episode is transmitted in Livy; but it also marks it as a traditional story (although it has a relatively secure provenance, since Polybius apparently met the woman herself: 21.38.7), highlighting its exemplary value.

cum…fuisset capta: Rossbach and Jal punctuate after *fuisset*, but that both makes the *cum*-clause difficult to comprehend and leaves *capta* hanging awkwardly in the sentence. Far more likely is that P., as elsewhere (cf. 25.3n.), is adopting the Livian idiom of forming the pluperfect passive out of the pluperfect of *sum* combined with the participle, with *uxor* in apposition ('when she, the king's wife, was captured'). The resulting sentence is not free from ambiguity, since it could in theory refer to one woman who avenged the rape of another, but it is a much less stilted understanding of the Latin. For the inversion of the participle see e.g. Livy 24.3.8 *per dolum fuerat capta*; 31.46.6 *quia ante fuerat temptata*; 33.26.5 *fuerat finitum*.

regis Gallograecorum uxor: Livy refers to her husband as *regulus*, not *rex* (38.24.2); P., like Florus and *Vir. Ill.*, increases his (and hence her) status, suggesting that he was the ruler of the Gallogrecians as a whole, not just one of their component tribes.

ei: Cf. 21.3n.

occidit: Livy, like Plutarch/Polybius and Valerius/Paris, depicts the woman ordering the centurion's death at the hands of her servant (*Vir. Ill.* 55.2 places the responsibility on the husband). A reader of P. who knew nothing of the story would naturally take *occidit* to mean that she personally killed the rapist, especially given that not only her *pudicitia*, but also her *virtus* are praised—the latter word does not, especially in later periods, necessarily imply physical courage, but it certainly can have that connotation. *EpOxy*, despite its other differences from P. (see *ad loc.*), phrases the killing in a similar way, which may indicate that both reflect a version in which the woman did indeed kill the centurion with her own hands.

38.5 *Census.* Corresponds to Livy 38.36.10. P., as usual (1.B.3n., 3.3n.), is interested in Livy's census figures, but ignores the account of intra-Greek conflicts, centring on Philopoemen, which Livy recounts in 38.30–4; he also, again as usual, has nothing of the various notices which Livy includes in his 'annalistic' sections at the end and beginning of the new year (38.35.1–36.9). *EpOxy*, by contrast, includes brief references to both of these, including from the annalistic material a reference to the decision to permit marriages between Campanians and Romans (38.36.5–6), but does not mention the census.

lustrum a censoribus conditum est: Cf. 11.5n.

censa sunt civium capita: Cf. 3.3n.

CCLVIII milia CCCX: The MSS of Livy give the number as 258,318. Either P. was using a MS with a different figure, or the figure in P. has been corrupted in transmission. Since there is no way of determining which of these is more likely, the transmitted figure should be retained.

38.6 *Agreement with Cappadocia*. Corresponds to Livy 38.37.5–6 and 38.39.6. From the continuation of Manlius' activities in Asia and subsequently in Thrace, which Livy records at 38.37–41, P. selects one minor notice for separate treatment, namely the agreement with Cappadocia. The battle with the Thracians, which occupies a far greater portion of Livy's text (cf. also App., *Syr.* 43), is overlooked entirely, while the finalizing of the peace with Antiochus is rolled into the next notice, concerning the conflict over Manlius' triumph (cf. 38.7n.). *EpOxy* 38 col. 1.20–3 appears to have a broader account of Manlius' activities, although the fragmentary text makes it hard to see its precise focus (see *ad loc.*), and adds a reference to the story of the Romans who attacked the Carthaginian ambassadors (Livy 38.42.7), which goes unmentioned in P.

The reason for P.'s interest in the Cappadocia agreement is unclear (it is otherwise referred to only in Greek sources: Plb. 21.45, Str. 12.2.11, App., *Syr.* 42, Zonar. 9.20.15). But it may be relevant that later he occasionally shows an interest in the Cappadocian royal family and its relationship with Rome (46.8, 47.6; cf. 70.4, 74.5, 76.7); this notice establishes the start of that relationship.

38.7 *Triumph of Cn. Manlius Vulso*. Corresponds to Livy 38.44.9–50.3; cf. 38.37–8. P. passes over the dispute over the activities of Fulvius Nobilior (Livy 38.43.1–44.6), and moves instead to the one to which Livy devotes considerably more of his narrative, namely the debate over Manlius' right to a triumph. No other author records this debate, except for Flor. 1.27.3, who claims that the triumph was refused; however, the triumph itself was cited by other authors as a key moment in the decline of Rome into luxury. Livy himself treats it in those terms in his description at 39.6.3–7.5, and it is also mentioned by Plin., *Nat.* 34.14 (citing Piso *FRHist* 9 F 36, who may well have been Livy's source also), 37.12, and Aug., *Civ.* 3.21. P.'s version makes an unexpected change to this: he refers misleadingly to the triumph as if it occurred in this book, whereas in Livy only the decision to permit the triumph takes place at this point, and the triumph itself is delayed until Book 39. P. does have a notice in Book 39 of the introduction of luxury, but he refers it vaguely to the *exercitus Asiaticus* (see 39.2n.), thus distancing it from both Manlius and the occasion of the triumph. As with the account of Manlius' campaign (38.2n.), P. suppresses any sense that it might have been morally problematic.

P.'s notice thus bundles into the account of the debate an event which in Livy's narrative only occurred much later; he also bundles into it an earlier event, namely the finalizing of the treaty with Antiochus by the Roman commissioners, which he mentions in passing in order to explain who was objecting to Manlius' being awarded a triumph. What he does not do is offer any of the grounds on which the commissioners objected; in this respect also he mutes the problems which Livy himself had highlighted.

contradicentibus X legatis: Cf. Livy 38.44.11 *contradixerunt pars maior decem legatorum...et ante alios L. Furius Purpureo et L. Aemilius Paullus.* P. simplifies Livy, making the opposition between all ten commissioners and Manlius, rather than only a subset of them.

ex quorum consilio foedus cum Antiocho conscripserat: Cf. Livy 38.38.1 *ex decem legatorum sententia foedus...cum Antiocho conscriptum est.* As often, P. bases himself on Livy's language while making minor alterations to it.

38.8–10 *Trials of the Scipios.* Corresponds to Livy 38.50.4–60.10. It is of little surprise, given his intense interest in the Scipios, that P. devotes over half his summary of Book 38 to their trials, which in Livy occupied less than a fifth of the book. Nor is it surprising that, faced with Livy's notoriously confusing narrative, he drastically reorganizes and simplifies it into something relatively comprehensible. Of the complexities and competing versions that Livy records, he reduces the points at dispute merely to the identity of Africanus' prosecutor and to the place of his death. For the rest, he separates out the story into three distinct acts: first, the trial of Africanus, which is specifically said to be on the charge of defrauding the Roman treasury (unlike in Livy, who is as ambiguous about what Africanus was charged with as he is about virtually every other aspect of the story), and which culminates with Africanus' leading the people to the Capitol, and then his exile. Then he has the conviction of Asiaticus on the same charge, combined with the intervention of Gracchus, and finally the confiscation of Asiaticus' property. All of these are derived from Livy, albeit from particular aspects of Livy.

P.'s approach matches the general way in which the trials of the Scipios were handled in the ancient tradition: it was usually the case that they were reduced to a series of more or less discrete popular anecdotes (an approach that goes back to Plb. 23.14). Moreover, the choice of anecdotes does not vary much between different writers: of the three that P. selects, the first two are common within the tradition, albeit not in tandem. Versions of the first (although not always the same version as in P.: see the detailed notes below) appear in Val. Max. 3.7.1 (cf. 5.3.2), Plu., *Reg. Imp. Apophth.* 196F–197A, App., *Syr.* 40, Gell. 4.18.3–6, *Vir. Ill.* 49.17–18; cf. Dio fr. 63 (with Zonar. 9.20.13) and Oros. 4.20.19; and of the second in Cic.,

Prov. 18, Val. Max. 4.1.8 (cf. 4.2.3 with Paris' epitome), Plin., *Nat. Praef.* 10, Plu., *Cat. Ma.* 15.1–2, Gell. 6.19, Dio fr. 65, *Vir. Ill.* 53.2, 57.1. Moreover, *EpOxy* 38 col. 1.25–7, though far more concise than P., includes a brief notice of Africanus' exile, though it apparently introduces Gracchus only to record his protection of Africanus (cf. Livy 38.52.9–53.6), not his support of Asiaticus (see *ad loc.*). P.'s third story, however, of Asiaticus' inability to pay the fine imposed upon him, is found in no other source except Dio fr. 63 and Zonar. 9.20.13.

There are two other anecdotes found in Livy which P. ignores but which were also popular in the tradition: Africanus ripping up the account books rather than providing the proof from them that had been demanded of him (Livy 38.55.10–12; cf. Plb. 23.14.7–11, D.S. 29.21, Val. Max. 3.7.1, Gell. 4.18.7–12, *Vir. Ill.* 49.17) and the story of his opening the treasury when the quaestors refused to take money from it (Livy 38.55.13; cf. Plb. 23.14.5–6, D.S. 29.21, Val. Max. 3.7.1, Plu., *Reg. Imp. Apophth.* 196F). There is no obvious reason why P. omitted these and preferred the story of Asiaticus: it is true that the episodes he passes over do not loom very large in Livy, but that is rarely a consideration in P.'s selection of anecdotes, especially ones concerning Africanus. In this case, however, it may be that the very complexity of Livy's narrative led him to highlight the episodes which play a substantial part in it, either by length, in the case of the first two, or by position, which is the case with the final story of Asiaticus, with which Livy closes his book and P. his summary.

38.8 *Trial and exile of Africanus.* Like Livy, but unlike virtually every other source (except *Vir. Ill.*), P. presents as the end of the story not Africanus' triumphant vindication, but his exile and death. More distinctive still is his account of Scipio's ascent to the Capitol, where he offers no explanation as to why Scipio went there accompanied by the people; in every other source it is explicit that it was to give thanks for what the gods had done for him, including the victory whose anniversary he has just mentioned. The very fact that every other source feels the need to spell the point out implies that it would not have been intuitively obvious to a Roman reader. This may be an instance where P. is relying on the reader's knowledge of the story, whether derived from Livy or from elsewhere; but there is another possibility also: that he is inviting the reader to recall his note about Scipio's daily visits to the Capitol (26.3), and to see Scipio's journey there now as part of that habit. In Livy those episodes are so widely spaced that the recall would be far from automatic, but in the narrow compass of P. the connection can easily be made. P.'s account does not contradict Livy's, but his omission of the explanation found in Livy and others leaves it open to another reading, one which returns the reader at the end of Scipio's life to his account of his (supposed) divine origins.

A third distinctive feature of P. is his alteration of the charge on which Africanus was tried. Livy himself is ambiguous about the charges: he mentions that other charges concerning Africanus' behaviour in Locri and Syracuse at the time of the Second Punic War were added, but that the main accusation concerned receiving bribes from Antiochus (38.51.1–2). However, Livy then goes on to record a law passed demanding that an account be given of money taken from Antiochus (38.54.2–4), and to the prosecution of Asiaticus under that law (38.55, 38.58.1–2)—and he associates the response to that prosecution with the anecdote concerning Africanus ripping up the account books (above: confusingly, Livy had earlier said that Africanus died before the law was passed under which the prosecution was taking place). This story clearly implies that the charge of misappropriating funds was associated with Africanus as much as with Asiaticus (38.55.10–12), and that also is the implication of the versions of that anecdote in Polybius, Diodorus, Gellius, and *Vir. Ill.* (although not Val. Max., where Africanus is acting in support of his brother rather than in indignation at being accused himself).

It is in accordance with this that P. tidies up the story by explicitly (cf. 38.9) having Africanus and Asiaticus prosecuted on the same charge, namely the misappropriation of money from the Antiochan War. This is, if not the only possible conclusion that might be drawn from Livy, at least a reasonable way of making sense of his confusing and self-contradictory narrative: it is even possible that P. knew of a non-Livian source that narrated the story along those lines. Of other sources, Gell. 4.18.3 and Zonar. 9.20.12 follow a different part of Livy, with Africanus prosecuted for accepting bribes from Antiochus. Appian appears to be working from a similar version, since he lists the charges as being corruption and treason, though he does not specify the form that took. However, *Vir. Ill.* has the charge against Africanus being *repetundae*—in other words, misappropriation of funds (though the term is anachronistic, since there was no specific law *de repetundis* at this period)—which, though vaguer, is not unlike P.'s version, and indeed probably based on it (see 38.9n.). Scholars have generally argued that Africanus, unlike Asiaticus, was prosecuted for bribery rather than embezzlement (so e.g. Mommsen (1866), 192–3 = (1879), 466–7, Fraccaro (1911), 331–2, 396–7 = (1956), 337–8, 381, Scullard (1973), 301–2, Briscoe (2008), 175–6),[25] and it is true that this is the most straightforward interpretation of Livy's narrative of the prosecution itself. But P.'s (and *Vir. Ill.*'s) version should not be dismissed (or ignored) as readily as it often is: Polybius' disjointed account (23.14.7–11) suggests that Africanus, as well as Asiaticus, was held accountable for the money taken in the Antiochan War, and hence could be liable for prosecution for its misappropriation (*contra* Scullard (1973), 301–2). While it can hardly be asserted that P. is correct, his version, whether taken from another source or only deduced from Livy,

---

[25] Gruen (1995), 80–6, reviving a suggestion by De Sanctis IV.1 581 [597] n. 276, argues that the entire trial of Africanus is a fiction, but he acknowledges (p. 85) that Plb. 23.14.2 attests at least to an attempt at a trial. As Briscoe (2008), 176 drily notes, 'it is indeed the case that all that happened was an *attempt* to try Africanus; it remains the case that it was also an attempt to *try* him'.

should be regarded as being as probable as the more widely accepted one, given the pervasive uncertainties of the entire affair.

die ei dicta...postquam is dies venit... 'hac die', inquit: That *dies* can be masculine or feminine is well known; it is unusual to have the gender switch twice in a single sentence. Since P. did not need to mark the second *dies* by its gender at all, and he anyway is reversing his Livian models, where the second was feminine and the third masculine rather than *vice versa* (see below), the choice to vary the gender in this way looks like a pointed joke at the expense of the grammatical vagaries of Latin.

ut quidam tradunt a Q. Petilio tribuno plebis, ut quidam a Naevio: Livy noted a similar discrepancy at 38.56.2: *alii M. Naevium, alii Petillios diem dixisse scribunt*; he also indicated earlier (38.50.5-6) that the Petillii both had the *praenomen* Quintus and were both *tribuni plebis* (they were presumably cousins: see Briscoe (2008), 179-80). However, P. has only one Petillius, which appears to have been a common version in later antiquity: see Plu., *Cat. Ma.* 15.1 (cf. *Reg. Imp. Apophth.* 196E-197A, referring to the prosecutors as 'Petillius and Quintus'), *Vir. Ill.* 49.17. Of other sources, Val. Max. 3.7.1 is close to Livy, with two Petillii (and also noting Naevius as an alternative); Gell. 4.18.3 has Naevius alone. *EpOxy* 38 col. 1.25 refers to the prosecutors as the *Quinti Metelli*, but that is presumably a scribal error (see *ad loc.*).

praeda ex Antiocho capta aerarium fraudasset: Gell. 4.18.7 uses a similar phrase (*pecuniae Antiochinae praedaeque in eo bello captae*), albeit in the context of the story of Scipio tearing up accounts rather than his prosecution, which Gellius indicates to be because of bribery (cf. above). It is usually argued that this is misleading, since the general was perfectly entitled to keep booty from the campaign and had no need to account for it (esp. Shatzman (1972); *contra* Churchill (1999)), while Plb. 23.14.7 suggests that a key point at issue was what happened to the money initially received from Antiochus which was due to Rome, but which the Scipios had given to their troops (so Shatzman (1972), 192-4, Scullard (1973), 293, Walbank (1979), 245-6). However, other complaints are reported around this time about generals misappropriating booty: Cato is recorded as having made speeches *Uti praeda in publicum referatur* (*ORF*[3] 98) and *De praeda militibus dividenda* (*ORF*[3] 224-6), and the most natural interpretation of the longest fragment of the latter suggests that he regarded those who took such booty as *fures publici*—'public thieves' (*ORF*[3] 224, quoted in Gellius 11.18.18). The case of Glabrio, whom Livy 37.57.12-14 records as being prosecuted on the grounds that he had not turned booty over to the treasury, is (if Livy's account is accurate) a concrete demonstration that similar objections to Cato's could rise to the level of legal proceedings.[26] It is highly likely, as Gruen (1995), 70-5 argues, that these

---

[26] Shatzman (1972), 191-2 wishes to dismiss this, but his grounds are circular (192: 'This is a strange accusation. Certainly Roman generals...were not obliged to give all the booty to the treasury'—which is the point that he is seeking to prove).

long-standing practices were under attack at this time,[27] as the Senate sought to rein in commanders who were perceived as over-powerful. Nor is the idea that booty was at issue with the Scipios incompatible with Polybius, who does not (*contra* Shatzman, Scullard, Walbank) say that the complaint was that the Scipios were wrong to use the money from Antiochus for their troops; his narrative is equally compatible with their being accused of diverting into that account money that they had acquired from other sources.

Accordingly, while one can hardly state firmly on the basis of P. (or Gellius) that the funds that Africanus (and Asiaticus) was accused of misappropriating included booty, one cannot dismiss the idea *a priori* either.

postquam is dies venit: Cf. Livy 38.51.5 *predicta dies est. ubi ea venit*; as noted above, P. pointedly changes the gender, instead of either retaining Livy's feminine or declining to offer a gender at all (cf. Livy 38.52.3 *ubi dies venit*).

evocatus in rostra: *evocare* is regularly used of summoning to court (*TLL* V.2 1057.40–67), but this phrase is unparalleled: the closest is Claud., *Pan. VI. Hon.* 592–3 *nunc ad rostra Quirites / evocat*, but the context there is somewhat different. P. keeps Livy's scenario, having Africanus arraigned at the *rostra*, but is accentuating the judicial overtones of the narrative.

'hac die', inquit, 'Quirites, Carthaginem vici': Livy 38.51.7 gives a far longer version of Scipio's statement: *'hoc' inquit 'die, tribuni plebis vosque, Quirites, cum Hannibale et Carthaginiensibus signis conlatis in Africa bene et feliciter pugnavi'*. It is, however, almost identical to the formulation in *Vir. Ill.* 49.17: *hac die, inquit, Carthaginem vici*: given that P. and *Vir. Ill.* also have Scipio facing similar charges in his trial (cf. above), it is reasonably likely that one is partially dependent on the other (although each has information that the other does not, so they must have used other sources as well), or else that they have a source in common; of these alternatives, by far the most likely is that *Vir. Ill.* is dependent on P. (see 38.9n.)

Capitolium escendit: Cf. Livy 38.51.12 *in Capitolium escendit*. P., as often, slightly varies Livy's phrasing, in this case employing the transitive form of the verb rather than *in* (cf. *OLD s.v. escendo* 1c).

tribuniciis iniuriis vexaretur: *iniuriis vexari* appears once in Cicero (*II Verr.* 3.52), but is otherwise primarily a usage of later antiquity. The implication of the phrase—which is also Livy's understanding, and is commonplace in other accounts of Africanus' trial—is that Africanus was unjustly accused.

in voluntarium exilium Liternum concessit: Cf. Livy 38.52.1 *in Literninum concessit*. Livy does not use the phrase *voluntarium exilium* of Africanus (in his surviving text, it appears only at 24.26.1), but here too P. is close to *Vir. Ill.* 49.18 *inde*

---

[27] Indeed, this point is accepted even by Shatzman (1972), 189, 202. His argument is that while there were attempts to create legal restrictions over the generals' rights to booty, those attempts all failed; but the case of Glabrio (above) suggests otherwise. Shatzman's mistake may be that he assumes that Roman law at this period was more consistent and less *ad hoc* than was in fact the case.

in voluntarium exilium concessit, who is probably drawing on him (38.9n.); cf. also Val. Max. 5.3.2, Sen., *Epist*. 86.3.

incertum ibi an Romae defunctus sit: Livy notes a discrepancy not only over the place of Africanus' death, but also over the date. P. does not explicitly refer to that discrepancy, and hence the immediate assumption of the reader would be that Africanus died now, with the prosecution of Asiaticus occurring afterwards, as in one version of Livy, and P. carefully phrases his account of the prosecution so as to be compatible with that, even if not requiring it (cf. 38.9n.). However, in 39.6 P. announces the death of Africanus—and at that point, the reader who does not know Livy can return to 38.8 and realize that P. did not actually say in so many words that Africanus died now. Indeed the small minority of readers who do know Livy, and were aware that he had drawn attention to the problems created by the date of Africanus' death, would be able to recognize from the start the artfulness of P.'s summary, allowing for both of Livy's versions at once.

monumentum eius utrobique fuit: Cf. Livy 38.56.3 *utrobique monumenta ostenduntur et statuae.*

38.9 *Gracchus defends Scipio Asiaticus.* Livy approaches the story of Gracchus and Asiaticus in an oddly oblique fashion: having adduced the speech of Gracchus as evidence against the version of the trials that he has been narrating prior to that point, he attempts to present a version compatible with that speech, according to which Africanus attempted to intercede on Asiaticus' behalf, but was criticized by Gracchus for doing so; and in the course of that criticism Gracchus then alludes to his own intercession on behalf of Asiaticus, a story which Livy then proceeds to give in more detail, culminating with Africanus' decision to betroth Gracchus to his daughter (38.56.8–57.8). As Livy notes, one problem with this is that it assumes that Africanus was alive at the time of Asiaticus' trial, whereas his earlier narrative had had Asiaticus prosecuted only after Africanus' death. He subsequently gives a different version of Gracchus' intervention, one which is indeed set after Africanus' death and makes no mention of the marriage (38.60.1–7). P. effectively combines the two: he tells the story, which, even apart from its prominence in Livy, was very famous (cf. 38.8–10n.), and maintains the account of Gracchus marrying Africanus' daughter, but does so in a way which allows him to maintain the (apparent) chronological sequence of his narrative, since he says nothing about whether Africanus himself was the one who made the arrangements.

It is in accord with this that he also omits the entire element of Scipio's attempted intervention and Gracchus' objection to it, although it is also true that this element is generally omitted in other accounts also (Gell. 6.19 is the one exception): the overwhelming majority of sources focus on the praiseworthy act of Gracchus being prepared to intercede on behalf of his enemy (Cic., *Prov.* 18, Val. Max. 4.1.8, Plin., *Nat. Praef.* 10, Gell. 6.19, Dio fr. 65, Ampel. 19.3, *Vir. Ill.*

53.2, 57.1);²⁸ only Dio joins P. in adding the marriage, though he, like Livy, attributes the initiative to Africanus.²⁹ Most sources follow Livy also in providing Gracchus' own justification for his act (Cicero, Valerius Maximus, Pliny, Gellius, Ampelius); P. allows it to speak for itself.

peculatus accusatus damnatusque: Cf. Livy 38.56.8 *et accusatus et damnatus sit pecuniae captae*. Livy nowhere directly uses *peculatus* of the charge against Asiaticus, although it is implicit in his reference to others being tried as co-conspirators on that charge (38.55.5). That is, however, explicitly stated to be the charge by Gell. 6.19.8 = Valerius Antias *FRHist* 25 F 52, and it is possible that P. drew the information from there.

cum in vincula et carcerem duceretur: Cf. Livy 38.57.3 *cum L. Scipio in vincula duceretur*. Livy does not directly refer here to Asiaticus being taken to the *carcer*, but it is implicit in Gracchus' statement that he would not allow Africanus' brother to be taken to the *carcer* into which Africanus himself had sent enemy leaders (38.57.4). It is also possible, however, that there is a nod to a different version of Asiaticus' conviction in Livy, where his cousin Scipio Nasica appeals on his behalf, referring to him as *L. Scipionis, qui in carcerem duceretur* (38.58.4). For the rare reader who might know the text of Livy, P. offers a discreet reminder of some of the complexities he has brushed over.

Here too *Vir. Ill.* 53.2 aligns closely with P.: *ne in carcerem duceretur*: see further below.

Tib. Sempronius Gracchus tribunus plebis, qui antea Scipionibus inimicus fuerat, intercessit: Livy does not describe Gracchus' defence of Asiaticus in these terms. However, he does use remarkably similar language a few chapters earlier of the enmity between Gracchus and Africanus: 38.52.9 *tribunus plebis eo tempore Ti. Sempronius Gracchus erat, cui inimicitiae cum P. Scipione intercedebant*. The use of the same verb is striking, not least because the meaning is so different: *intercedere* is a technical term for a tribunician veto (*TLL* VII.1 2155.52–2156.4), but here it is being used in a non-technical sense. It is possible that Livy is himself giving an advance hint at the moment when Gracchus will famously 'intercede'; but whether or not that is the case, it appears that P. slyly picked up the meaning, and announced Gracchus' use of his veto despite his enmity to the Scipios, in language which closely mirrored Livy's account of the earlier existence of that enmity.

Vir. Ill. 53.2 once again uses very similar language to P.'s (*Gracchus pater tribunus plebis, inimicus eius, intercessit*); but this time we have a strong reason to

---

²⁸ In addition, Plu., *Cat. Ma.* 15.2 refers to Asiaticus being released after appealing to the tribunes, but does not mention Gracchus, let alone his enmity to the Scipios.

²⁹ Cf. also Val. Max. 4.2.3 (with Paris' epitome), which has Africanus arranging his daughter's marriage to his enemy Gracchus, but does not connect it to the Scipios' trials; there are also passing references to Gracchus becoming Scipio's son-in-law after having been his enemy: e.g. Sen., *Contr.* 5.2.3, Plu., *TG* 1.2.

believe that *Vir. Ill.* is dependent on P. rather than *vice versa*. *Vir. Ill.*, despite its overall similarity to P., is much less close to Livy's specific phrasing, nor does he have *antea*, P.'s metatextual hint that he is referring back to an earlier passage. See further the Introduction.

38.10 *Confiscation of Asiaticus' property.* As noted above (38.8–10n.), P. is unusual in recording this story, which is not one of the popular anecdotes about the Scipios' trials. In Livy it forms the last episode of the book, and follows on directly from the second version of Gracchus' intervention: Livy explains that Gracchus refused to allow Asiaticus to be taken to prison, but regarded it as acceptable for him to be fined. P. does not explicitly connect it with the story of Gracchus, which would make less sense in terms of his narrative sequence, since his previous notice had ended with Gracchus reconciled to the Scipios, as in Livy's first version of the Gracchus story (cf. 38.9n.). In other respects he reproduces Livy's account very closely, but ignores his final comment, that it was the accusers who ultimately suffered for their persecution of Asiaticus. As with his Livy-derived picture of the trial of Africanus, which ends (unlike most other sources) with his exile and death (38.8n.), P. ends the story of Asiaticus on a sour note.

quaestores in bona eius publice possidenda missi essent: Cf. Livy 38.60.8 *in bona deinde L. Scipionis possessum publice quaestores misit*. P. substitutes the gerundive for the supine, which had largely fallen out of use in his time (H-S 381). He nevertheless retains Livy's *in*, despite the change of construction: surprising but not unparalleled Latin (for *in* instead of *ad* with the gerundive see K-S 1.750).

non modo in his ullum vestigium pecuniae regiae apparuit, sed ne quaquam tantum redactum quantae summae erat damnatus: Cf. Livy 38.60.8 *neque in iis non modo vestigium ullum comparuit pecuniae regiae, sed nequaquam tantum redactum est quantae summae damnatus fuerat*.

conlatam a cognatis et amicis innumerabilem pecuniam accipere noluit: Cf. Livy 38.60.9 *conlata ea pecunia ab cognatis amicisque et clientibus est L. Scipioni, ut si acciperet eam, locupletior aliquanto esset quam ante calamitatem fuerat. nihil accepit*. P. reduces Livy's explanation of the amount collected to the single word *innumerabilis*. The phrase *innumerabilis pecunia* is not used by Livy, and is hardly found elsewhere—apart from Cicero, who uses it repeatedly: hence for P. it presumably had the flavour of late Republican Latin.

quae necessaria ei erant ad cultum redempta: Cf. Livy 38.60.10 *quae necessaria ad cultum erant, redempta ei a proximis cognatis sunt*.

Book 39

39.1 *Building of the Via Aemilia*. Corresponds to Livy 39.1, 39.2.7–11. P. focuses the sentence on the building of the road, with Aemilius' victory over the Ligurians in a subordinate position (but see 39.3n.). This is surprising: no other source mentions the road being built at this time, apart from Str. 5.1.11 (who mistakenly associates it with the building of the Via Flaminia itself: see 20.11n.). P. has intermittently been interested in the building of roads (cf. 9.4, 20.11), though this is the last time he refers to one; it is presumably a by-product of his broader interest in marking the expansion of Roman institutions. It is also possible that the very fact of the Via Aemilia being an extension of the Via Flaminia roused his interest, since that was one of the previous roads he had recorded.

EpOxy 39 col. 2.1 likewise begins with a notice of the defeat of the Ligurians and the building of the road; like Livy, but unlike P., the author attributes the victory not only to Aemilius but to his colleague Flaminius, and adds Flaminius' road to Aemilius', apparently identifying it with the Via Flaminia built by the consul's father. See further *ad loc.*

Liguribus subactis viam Placentia usque Ariminum productam Flaminiae iunxit: Cf. Livy 39.2.10 *pacatis Liguribus…viamque a Placentia, ut Flaminiae committeret, Ariminum perduxit*. P. replaces Livy's unusual phrase *Flaminiae committeret* with the more straightforward *viam…Flaminiae iunxit* (for the language cf. esp. Ov., *Pont.* 1.8.44 *Flaminiae Clodia iuncta viae*; also e.g. Ov., *Fast.* 6.396, CIL XIV 375 = ILS 6147), and at the same time uses *producere* in place of Livy's *perducere*; the former makes it clearer that Aemilius was extending an existing road (cf. *TLL* X.2 1640.18–40). His phrasing suggests that he, like most modern scholars, understood Livy to be talking about Aemilius' road joining the Via Flaminia at Ariminum (and then extending it to Placentia), not joining the secondary road built by Aemilius' colleague Flaminius at Bononia (Livy 39.2.6), as proposed by Briscoe (2008), 214–15.

39.2 *The army from Asia sets Rome on the path of luxury*. Corresponds to Livy 39.6.3–7.5. As noted above (38.7n.), P. transfers the triumph of Manlius Vulso from Book 39 to Book 38, and one effect is to separate him from the question of the introduction of luxury to the city; P., unlike Livy, had treated the war he fought as entirely justified (38.2n., 38.7n.), and he also has nothing of the related question of the lax discipline that he allegedly permitted among his troops (Livy 39.6.5–6). Aug., *Civ.* 3.21, like Livy, connects Manlius' triumph to the introduction of luxury and hence the moral decline of Rome, but the only other source, Plin., *Nat.* 34.14, while recording the introduction of luxury goods at the time of Manlius' triumph (cf. *Nat.* 37.12), does not draw any explicit moral conclusions from this, although it is very possible that this had been done by Pliny's—and perhaps Livy's—source, Piso (*FRHist* 9 F 36: cf. *FRHist* 9 F 40 for Piso's moralizing along similar lines). P. is unique in retaining the moralizing while detaching it from Manlius' triumph.

Prior to this, P. omits the triumph of M. Fulvius Nobilior, as well as the controversy preceding it (Livy 39.4–5). The failure to mention even the fact of the triumph is surprising, since it is not only listed as a major triumph by Cic., *Mur.* 31, but is noticed by both Eutr. 4.5.1 and *Vir. Ill.* 52.2–3, authors who in general are paying much less attention to the Roman campaigns in the East at this period. P.'s omission is part of a pattern: he has consistently paid far less attention to Fulvius than to Manlius, whether with his campaign or the disputes in its aftermath (38.1n., 38.7n.), and shows no awareness of Fulvius' connection with Ennius, which *Vir. Ill.* comments on, and which perhaps explains the *Vir. Ill.*'s interest in him.

initia luxuriae in urbem introducta ab exercitu Asiatico referuntur: Cf. Livy 39.6.7 *luxuriae enim peregrinae origo ab exercitu Asiatico invecta in urbem est*. P.'s phrasing is an example of a participial phrase used to replace a noun-clause (Woodcock 75–6): 'The introduction into the city of the beginnings of luxury...is recorded'. For *referuntur* cf. 16.1n.

39.3 *Defeat of the Ligurians.* This notice is strangely placed. Livy described, in very similar language to P. here (see below), a defeat of the Ligurians *cis Appenninum* ('on this side of the Apennines') at 39.2.7–11—but P. had apparently already described that event in 39.1, as the background to the building of the *Via Aemilia*. Two other battles against the Ligurians appear later in the book, in the first of which the Romans lose, in the second of which they are victorious (39.20.5–10, 39.32.1–4), but neither is explicitly said by Livy to be against the Ligurians 'on this side of the Apennines'.

However, as it happens, the victory described in 39.32.1–4 was also on the south (Roman) side of the Apennines, even though Livy does not explicitly identify it as such: it is said to be against the Ligurian Apuani and Ingauni, both of whom lived on the north-western coast of the Italian peninsula, and the first campaign starts from Pisa and moves to the river Macra and the harbour of Luna, all of which are south of the mountains.[30] Hence P., as he does elsewhere, crafts his notice so that the (rare) reader who knew Livy's text may recognize that it alludes

---

[30] Briscoe (2008), 212–13 argues that by *cis Appenninum* and *trans Appenninum* Livy does not mean 'the Roman side' and 'the non-Roman side' of the mountains, but that the sides are defined in relation to the army then campaigning—so if the army began on the north side of the Apennines, then the north side would be *cis Appenninum*. But while Briscoe is right to note that phrases like *trans Appenninum abierunt* must be in relation to the campaigning army, that falls well short of proving that when a tribe is described as living *cis Appenninum* (39.2.9, 41.19.1), the phrase does not in that case refer to the side of the mountains in relation to Rome. Indeed, this very passage of P. shows that he interpreted Livy in that fashion, since his detached notice does not allow the reader any other possible orientation—the position of the army is not mentioned.

to two separate parts of that text. The positioning of the notice near the start of the book, as well as the explicit use of Livy's language, implies that he is referring to M. Aemilius' Lepidus' victory in 187; but the fact that Lepidus' victory has already been described, and that the notice comes after the account of the corruption brought to Rome by the army from Asia (39.2), point instead to the later victory in the same neighbourhood by the consuls of 185.

One may observe in passing that this is not the only place where P. writes a notice which appears to reflect geographic knowledge of north-western Italy that is not derived directly from Livy (see 21.4n., 29.3n.); one may speculate that this is the result of personal knowledge of that region. See further the Introduction.

Ligures quicumque citra Appenninum erant subacti sunt: Cf. Livy 39.2.9 *subactis cis Appenninum omnibus.*

39.4 *The Bacchanalia crisis.* Corresponds to Livy 39.8–19. This episode, which occupies nearly a fifth of Livy's book, is summarized by P. in a brief sentence. However, although the detailed narrative of the manner of the exposure of the alleged conspiracy is entirely omitted, P. does succeed in touching on many of the chief elements that on Livy's account made it appear threatening: its foreign provenance (39.8.3, 39.9.1, 39.15.3, 39.16.8–10), its night-time celebration (39.8.4, 39.10.1, 39.11.2, 39.12.4, 39.13.9, 39.14.4, 39.14.6, 39.14.10, 39.15.6, 39.15.12, 39.16.4), the connection with various crimes (39.8.6–8, 39.10.6–8, 39.11.7, 39.13.10–14, 39.15.3, 39.15.14–16.3, 39.18.3–4), the number of its adherents (39.8.5, 39.13.14, 39.15.8–10, 39.16.2–4), and the large-scale punishment (39.17.4–18.9). *EpOxy* 39 col. 2.9–14, by contrast, appears to contain none of these, but does include an outline narrative of the exposure of the conspiracy, naming the main characters (see *ad loc.*).

Apart from Livy and his epitomators, there are few literary accounts of the episode: it is mentioned in passing by Cic., *Leg.* 2.37 and briefly summarized in the scholia to Juv. 2.3; there is a rather longer account in Firm., *Err.* 6.9–10, setting out the process by which the conspiracy was exposed and punished. Most important for P. are the two notices in Val. Max.: a more general account in 1.3.1, which survives only in the epitomes of Paris and Nepotianus, and at 6.3.7 an account of the punishment of the women involved in the conspiracy (Paris' epitome changes Valerius so as to make those punished male rather than female). The first shows some revealing similarities with P.: Nepotianus, while not at all close to P. linguistically, refers to several of the same elements (foreignness, nocturnal rites, immorality, mass punishment[31]), while Paris, though mentioning only (implicitly) foreignness and immorality, structures his notice in a very similar fashion to

---

[31] Assuming that *multo colentium sanguine* in Nepotianus is to be taken with *abolita sunt*, as in the editions of Kempf, Briscoe, and Shackleton Bailey. Wardle (1998), 145 takes it with *furerentque*, but he offers no argument in support of his reading, and it seems less probable.

P.'s: *Bacchanalium sacrorum mos novus institutus, cum ad perniciosam vaesaniam iret, sublatus est.* Possibly the similarity points to P. being in part dependent on Paris' epitome (cf. 37.3n.).

sacrum Graecum et nocturnum: Livy describes the rites being introduced by a Greek, first to Etruria, and then spreading to Rome (39.8.3, 39.9.1). He does not explicitly say that the rites themselves came from Greece, but that is a reasonable deduction from his text. The phrase *sacrum nocturnum* derives directly from Livy (39.12.4, 39.13.9; cf. 39.8.4, 39.14.6).

omnium scelerum seminarium: A striking phrase, not derived from Livy. The closest parallel is perhaps Apul., *Apol.* 74 *omnium malorum seminarium*; it is possible that P. is alluding to it, but *seminarium* with the genitive of the crime was regularly used metaphorically by Christian writers in ethical contexts (e.g. Ambr., *In Psalm. 118* 11: *seminarium praevaricationis et sceleris*).

cum: Cf. 2.2n.

ad ingentis turbae coniurationem pervenisset: Another unusual phrase; neither *ad coniurationem pervenisset* (though cf. *TLL* X.1 1854.65–1855.23) nor *coniuratio turbae* is easily paralleled. The former phrase appears to be a medical metaphor: see Woodman (2010), 54 = (2012), 173–4.

multorum poena: One would usually expect *cum* with a noun describing an accompanying circumstance to an action, where the noun is not qualified by an adjective (Woodcock 33); nevertheless it is not unparalleled even in classical Latin (see the examples at Pinkster 1.900–1; also Woodman and Martin (1996), 386).

39.5 *L. Quinctius Flamininus is expelled from the Senate by Cato.* Corresponds to Livy 39.40, 39.42.5–43.5. P. passes without comment over the majority of Cato's activities as censor (39.44.1–9), and does not describe his contentious election (39.41.1–4). Instead he concentrates on the episode which Livy, too, allotted the most space to, namely the expulsion of L. Quinctius Flamininus from the Senate. The story was an immensely famous one in the early empire, as can be seen not least from the fact that it is recorded by Sen., *Contr.* 9.2, as a standard declamatory theme; versions of it also appear in Cic., *Cato* 42, Val. Max. 2.9.3 (with Paris' epitome; cf. also 4.5.1), Plu., *Cat. Ma.* 17.1–6, *Flam.* 18.3–5. However, like most other stories concerning Cato's political and military career (34.2n.), it appears to have been of less interest in later antiquity: it is mentioned only in *Vir. Ill.* 47.4 and Jer., *In Matth.* II, 14.11.

P. unusually retains a reference to Livy's variant version, taken from Valerius Antias, as well as the source by which Livy justified the version he preferred, namely Cato's own speech, which he claims Antias had overlooked: in Antias' version the request came from a female prostitute, and the victim was a condemned criminal whom Flamininus had executed, rather than a deserter killed by

Flamininus personally (*FRHist* 25 F 55). That P. kept Antias' alternative account in his notice may in part reflect the fact that there was no single accepted version of the story (cf. below). Virtually every other source follows Antias, apart from *EpOxy* 39 (col. 2.25–3.2), which records only Livy's main version, and Plu., who has a male prostitute, as in Livy,[32] but still makes the victim and the manner of his death the same as in Antias. Plutarch in both *Cat. Ma.* 17.5 and *Flam.* 18.4 notes the differences from Livy, and also provides (*Flam.* 18.5) his rationale for rejecting Livy's account (cf. C 75n.). His summary of Livy's version of the story reduces it to much the same core elements as P. does—a Gaul killed by Flamininus with his own hand, with Cato's own speech in support. This may perhaps suggest dependence by both on an earlier epitome (cf. 23.10n. for an even more striking overlap between Plutarch's and P.'s reading of Livy).

One change that P. makes to the story is noteworthy: in Livy's main version, the initiative for the killing comes from Flamininus himself, and his lover does not believe he is serious (39.42.11–12), but in every other source, including Valerius Antias as reported by Livy, and (probably) *EpOxy* 39 col. 2.25–27 (see *ad loc.*), the request originates with the lover. To that extent P. softens the perversity with which Livy invests the story as well as (slightly) shifting the moral focus away from Flamininus himself. Moreover he, like Cicero, Valerius/Paris, and *Vir. Ill.* (but unlike Seneca, Plutarch, and Jerome), does not give any explicit account of why the request was made; the fact that Flamininus complied with such a request would presumably be seen as damning enough.

et belli et pacis artibus maximo: The general sentiment comes from Livy 39.40.6; for the phrasing, see Livy 2.16.7 *princeps belli pacisque artibus*; cf. 1.21.6, 1.35.1. The fact that P. introduces this rather bland characterization of Cato is significant in a number of ways. First, it fits his general tendency to turn Livy's edgy moral ambiguities, which he explores over his lengthy character-sketch of Cato (39.40.4–12), into uncomplicated statements of virtue. Nevertheless, it is relatively rare for P. to include moral characterizations at all, even with figures he pays more attention to than he does to Cato. Doing so here acknowledges the fact that Livy had sketched in Cato's character at some length—something which is itself a rare exception within his work. But it also may suggest something of the faded position of Cato in the memory of later antiquity: he was recognized as a significant figure (it is possible that his role in Cicero, *De Senectute* had something to do with that), and he is repeatedly cited in decontextualized ethical anecdotes by writers like Augustine and Jerome, yet the specifics of his career were largely ignored (cf. 34.1–2nn.).

---

[32] As Briscoe (2008), 358, observes, Cicero and *Vir. Ill.* speak of a *scortum*, which could refer to a male or a female, but in the absence of any other indication would naturally be understood as the latter (*OLD s.v. scortum* 2a; *contra* Carawan (1989–90), 320, 325).

a Poeno Philippo, quem amabat, scorto nobili: Cf. Livy 39.42.8 *Philippum Poenum, carum ac nobile scortum*.

sive, ut quidam tradiderunt: Cf. Livy 39.43.4 *sive, ut Valerius tradit*. Livy does not indicate that anyone other than Antias relayed this version, but, as noted above, it was by far the more popular one, which explains P.'s change from singular to plural: it points to the fact that it is relayed outside Livy as well.

securi percusserat: Cf. Livy 39.43.3 *securi percussisse*.

meretrice Placentina, cuius amore deperibat: Cf. Livy 39.43.2 *Placentiae famosam mulierem, cuius amore deperiret*.

extat oratio M. Catonis in eum: Cf. Livy 39.42.6–7 *Catonis et aliae quidem acerbae orationes exstant...longe gravissima in L. Quinctium oratio*.

39.6 Deaths of Scipio, Hannibal, and Philopoemen. Corresponds to Livy 39.49–52. P. (like Oros. 4.20.29, whose language is very similar and may partly depend on P.) reverses the order in which Livy recounts the deaths: he starts with Scipio, the central focus of his account here as elsewhere, and then notes the coincidence with the death of Hannibal. Philopoemen, who is the least significant in terms of his narrative (he was previously mentioned only at 35.3: see *ad loc.*), is added on after that, without any explicit acknowledgement that he too died in the same year, although it is perhaps implicit in *quoque*, as well as the parallelisms that P. indicates between his death and Hannibal's (see below), but on the other hand P.'s introduction to the episode refers to two great men, not three, who died at that time, although he does then go on to refer to Philopoemen, like Scipio and Hannibal, as *vir maximus*.

The synchronization of the three deaths is explicit in certain other authors, notably Just. 32.4.8–9 (cf. 32.1.5–10) and Oros. 4.20.29, and probably in Diodorus also, although the surviving fragments (29.18–21) do not make it entirely clear; it is likely that Polybius was the ultimate source for both Livy and Diodorus in this respect, although his fragments mention only Philopoemen's death (23.12.3: see Walbank (1979), 235–6). Zonar. 9.21.7 links the deaths of Hannibal and Scipio, but does not mention Philopoemen. Other sources, however, confine themselves to one or other figure: thus Philopoemen's death is described in Plu., *Phil.* 18–21 and Paus. 8.51.5–8 (cf. 4.29.11–12), and Hannibal's in Nep., *Hann.* 12, Val. Max. 9.2 ext. 2, Plu., *Flam.* 20.2–6, App., *Syr.* 12, Paus. 8.11.11, *Vir. Ill.* 42.6 (cf. 51.5), Eutr. 4.5.2, Obseq. 4. For the sources on Scipio's death cf. 38.8n.

With Scipio's death, Livy once again registers the discrepancy over the date that he found in his sources (39.52.1–6); P. incorporates into his account an allusion to this discrepancy, since he mentions Scipio's death in two places, while at the same time he maintains the consistency of his own narrative, since he did not (even though that will not be apparent to the reader until now) explicitly state that Scipio died at the earlier point, and now affirms (via the synchronism with the death of Hannibal) that Scipio (contrary to what Livy, rejecting the synchronism, argues) actually died at this later point of the narrative. As for Hannibal, Livy gives a fairly detailed account of his suicide following Flamininus' embassy to Prusias; that Flamininus was the person who ultimately brought about the death is mentioned by almost every other source, even brief ones, as is the fact that poison was the means chosen,[33] and P. unsurprisingly includes both elements. P. reduces Philopoemen's death to the same two points—death by poison, and the people who brought it about—in such a way as to highlight the parallel with Hannibal.

tamquam iungente fortuna circa idem tempus duo funera maximorum virorum: *iungente* is the correction of a late MS for the transmitted *lugente*, but is overwhelmingly probable. P.'s emphasis on synchronism does not correspond to anything in Livy, not least because, as noted above, Livy rejects the synchronism of the death of Scipio with those of Hannibal and Philopoemen; even with the latter two, while the sequence of his narrative does indeed place their deaths in the same year, his final judgement plays down any significance in that coincidence, preferring instead to focus on the failure of all three deaths to match the men's remarkable lives (39.52.7–9). P., by contrast, draws attention to the simultaneity, which he regards as arising from the workings of an active Fortune, a very Livian concept, even if one that Livy does not employ here (cf. 18.2n.). It is not surprising that P. prefers the version of the story which provides a significant synchronism: cf. Feeney (2007), 43–4 for the attractions of such synchronisms to the ancient as well as to the modern mind (Livy's resistance to this one should, accordingly, receive more credit than it sometimes does).

However, P. ingeniously hints at Livy's construction of the comparison as well. The entire phrase is remarkably similar to an epigram attributed to Seneca (*Anth.* 438.1 (Riese) = 436.1 (Shackleton Bailey)):[34] *iunxit magnorum casus fortuna virorum*, and it is plausible that P. is alluding to that poem here (Breitenbach (2009), 409). The author is probably, as Shackleton Bailey suggests (*ad loc.*, comparing the very similar sentiments of *Anth.* 414 (Riese) = 411 (S-B)), thinking of Pompey and Cato, and the point is not the timing of their deaths, but their lack of a tomb equivalent to their achievements. P. takes a poem which, like Livy, is comparing great men who lacked in death what they had in life, but applies it to the coincidence of the time when they died.

---

[33] Neither of these elements is in the passing mention of his death in Valerius Maximus, nor in Zonaras; Justin and Obsequens mention poison, but do not refer to the role of Flamininus. Pausanias offers an alternative version of his death, in which Hannibal died of an accidental wound during his escape, and Plutarch also mentions other versions along with the Livian one.

[34] The authenticity of the 'Senecan' epigrams is persuasively denied by Holzberg (2004); but Holzberg also successfully demonstrates that the author is systematically adopting the persona of Seneca; cf. also Breitenbach (2010), 52–116, proposing that the collection dates from the first half of the second century AD.

a Prusia: Grammatically this belongs in the *cum*-clause ('when he was being surrendered by Prusias to the Romans'); but it may also hint at an alternative version of Hannibal's death, according to which he was poisoned by Prusias rather than committing suicide (so App., *Syr.* 11).

39.7 *Foundation of colonies.* Corresponds to Livy 39.44.10, 39.55.6–8. As usual, P. is interested in colonial foundations; he unites here in a single notice two separate groups of foundations in Livy: the second group is described by Livy near the end of the book, after the deaths of Philopoemen, Hannibal, and Scipio. He omits, however, the foundation of the citizen colony of Saturnia immediately following the second group (Livy 39.55.9).

coloniae...deductae sunt: Cf. 1.B.1n.

39.8 *Fighting in Spain: preliminaries to the Third Macedonian War.* For his end-of-book 'round-up', P. mentions two items: victories against the Celtiberi, and the 'beginnings and causes' of the Third Macedonian War. The fighting in Spain is not a major part of the narrative of Livy 39, but it is the only area where Livy describes significant Roman campaigns, which the summary of the book has not so far touched. Victories over the Celtiberi are explicitly referred to in 39.21 and 39.56.1; the longest Spanish narrative in the book (39.30–1) does not mention the Celtiberi by name, but in the context of the other Spanish material it is not hard to infer that they are the opponents there also (Briscoe (2008), 325).

As for the Third Macedonian War, P. gives a reasonable summary of Livy's account at 39.23.5–29.3, which both begins and ends by explaining that the origins of the Third Macedonian War lay in Philip's activities at this period, not, as generally thought, because of Perseus (cf. Plb. 23.18, which appears to lie behind Livy's analysis here); he summarizes Philip's various actions and the charges against him, along with the Romans' response to those charges: as P. says, Philip is compelled to reduce his kingdom to its earlier boundaries, and also to withdraw his garrisons from Thrace and elsewhere. There are also a number of references later in the book to Macedonian affairs (39.33.1–35.4, 39.46.6–48.4, 39.53), which P. does not summarize, although Livy inserts into them references to the imminent war which suggests that he saw this as part of the sequence leading up to it (e.g. 39.35.2, 39.53.2), as well as the Macedonian withdrawals which he had said to be the *casus belli* in Philip's eyes (39.33.3, 39.34.1, 39.46.9, 39.53.10). Moreover, P. says nothing at all about the debate over Achaean actions in Sparta, which Livy described at 39.35.5–37.21.

praeterea res adversus Celtiberos prospere gestas...continet: Cf. 2.16n., 3.10n.

initia causasque: A standard phrase, versions of which are used in Livy (2.51.6, 4.9.2) and at key moments by Tacitus (esp. *Hist.* 1.51.1, 2.1.1, 2.52.1, 4.48.1, *Ann.* 4.1.1); see Martin and Woodman (1989), 79–80. In this case the impetus to use the phrase may have been the fact that Livy uses both words in his introduction to the Macedonian episode (39.23.5), albeit not in the same phrase.

origo inde fluxit: A bold phrase: the metaphor is of a spring, but a spring which is itself flowing from some hidden source. The closest parallel in classical Latin is perhaps Quint., *Inst.* 8.4.22, where Quintilian illustrates *amplificatio* via a remarkable expansion of *Iliad* 3.161–5: he describes how Helen's beauty was the origin of the war with the words *faciem illam, ex qua tot lacrimarum origo fluxisset* ('That beauty, from which the spring of so many tears had flowed'), but in Quintilian the metaphor is anchored by the fact that tears do literally flow, which is not the case with P. More directly parallel is Prud., *Ham.* 203–4 *hinc natale caput uitiorum, principe ab illo / fluxit origo mali*; but it is unclear whether Prudentius or P. might have been inspired by the other, or if both independently draw on some lost original.[35]

regnum ... imminui: The phrase is unique. P.'s summary of the second half of this book shows a more imaginative use of Latin than usual (cf. 39.6n. and above).

cogeretur a Thracibus aliisque locis praesidia deducere: Cf. 39.53.10 *cogebatur decedere Thracia praesidiaque deducere*. As often, P. uses language taken from a later reference back to the events, rather than Livy's original description of them.

---

[35] A further parallel is *origo manabat*, used in various post-classical writers in the specific context of family origins (Sil. 10.175, Apul., *Plat.* 2.23, Just. 23.4.4, *Hist. Aug., Hadr.* 1.1).

Book 40

40.1 *Suicide of Theoxena.* Corresponds to Livy 40.3.3–4.15. P. reduces Livy's dramatic story to the essential element: Theoxena's proposal to her children and their resulting suicide. However, he substantially alters the underlying situation. In Livy 40.3.7 (itself following Plb. 23.10.8–10), Philip decides to imprison the children of the people whom he has killed. The idea that he might then go on to kill those children is implicit in Polybius (who cites a famous line from the *Cypria*) and explicit in Livy, who, however, also says that the killing would not be systematic, but would follow one at a time; nevertheless, the primary threat is imprisonment (hence Theoxena's fear of abuse when they were in Philip's hands: Livy 40.8.6). P., however, reverses this, describing the *execution* of the children of people *imprisoned* by Philip. This seems an unlikely scenario, unless perhaps it is envisaged that it was intended as a way of intimidating the prisoners; it is possible that P. has misread or misremembered Livy, or else that he is incorporating material from another version of the story.

cum: Cf. 2.2n.

nobilium hominum: Livy does not explicitly state that Philip's victims were from noble families, but Polybius does (23.10.11). It is unlikely that P. had read Polybius, but he may be dependent on a non-Livian source which ultimately derives from him, though it is also naturally possible that it is his own extrapolation of Livy.

conquiri ad mortem: 'To be sought out for execution', a phrase otherwise found only in Velleius 2.22.4.

admodum pueris: Cf. Livy 40.4.4 *parvis admodum*.

regis libidinem: Cf. Livy 40.4.6 *ludibrio futuros non regis modo sed custodum etiam libidinis ratus*. So the MSS: since Sigonius, most editors (including Briscoe in the Teubner) have read not *libidinis*, but *libidini*; but see *contra* Briscoe (2008), 420–1 in support of the MS reading. On either reading, there is a possible ambiguity, depending on whether *libidinis/i* is to be taken with *regis* as well as *custodum*, or only with the latter. Briscoe *loc. cit.* regards it as 'out of the question for *libidini* to go with *regis* as well as *custodum*: Theoxena cannot have thought that Philip was likely to rape the children he had imprisoned'. But that is far from obviously true (tyrants raping people under their power was a common ancient trope: cf. Dunkle (1967)), and this very passage of P. suggests that he understood Livy in that fashion.

P. does not refer here to *ludibrium* as a fear of Theoxena, but he introduces the word shortly afterwards, when Theoxena recommends suicide to her children as a way of avoiding this.

40.2 *Conflict between Perseus and Demetrius.* Corresponds to Livy 40.5.1–16.3, 40.20.3–24.8; cf. 40.57.1. P., as often, unites into a single notice a narrative which in Livy was treated in more than one place. Livy recounts Perseus' plot against Demetrius with intense drama and considerable detail, including a lengthy series of speeches which P. naturally ignores, but the outline is much as P. represents it (although he says nothing of the symbolically resonant scene where Philip leads his army up Mount Haemus in order to get a view of Italy, which forms the backdrop to Demetrius' final fall: 40.21–2). The major exception comes with the nature of the charges against Demetrius. P. presents these as coming in two stages: first, Demetrius is accused of attempting to kill Philip and take the throne, and only subsequent to that is his friendship for Rome adduced. In Livy Philip is alienated from Demetrius from the very start because of his Roman sympathies, and Perseus deliberately exploits that (40.5.5–14); he does insinuate that Demetrius is engaging in *fraude domestica* (40.5.11), but only later does he raise more specific charges of plotting, and even then the charges are bound up with the idea that Demetrius is acting on behalf of Rome. Moreover, the murder which, in Livy, Perseus accuses Demetrius of planning, is not of Philip, as one would naturally assume from reading P. (cf. below), but of Perseus himself: the idea that Philip too might be the object of Demetrius' plotting is insinuated in passing at 40.10.6, but is not stated outright. On Perseus' account, Demetrius' plan is to clear his brother out of the way so as to make himself, with Roman support, the unchallenged heir to the throne once Philip dies.

However, the manner in which P. tells the story partly mirrors the version found in other sources: both Oros. 4.20.28 and Zonar. 9.22.1 refer vaguely to Demetrius being accused of plots against Philip, with no suggestion that the specific accusation was of attempting to murder Perseus (though Just. 32.2.6–10, like Livy, does refer to this allegation). We cannot be certain that this was the understanding in earlier texts—both Orosius and Zonaras postdate P., and it is altogether possible that Dio, whom Zonaras is epitomizing here, presented a fuller account in which Perseus was the alleged victim, as in Livy; but at the very least we can see a parallel impulse among the epitomizers which simplified the story into a plot against Philip alone.

Conversely, P.'s separation of the allegations into two stages is not paralleled elsewhere, and does not, as noted above, accurately represent Livy's account of the role that Demetrius' Roman sympathies played in arousing Philip's suspicions of him. However, it does reflect a turning point that Livy himself marks in Perseus' campaign against Demetrius: for in the first section of Livy's story, Philip effectively clears Demetrius on the charge of attempted murder (40.16.1–3), but in the second, it is indeed solely his relationship with Rome that leads to his downfall, although it is not, as P. implies, only at that second stage that the charge was brought up against him, but was, for Livy, the primary reason that he was a target from first to last.

A further surprising aspect of P.'s notice is that it concludes with the death of Philip and Perseus' accession to the throne. In Livy this does not occur until close to the end of the book; P. has apparently elided the entire narrative of Philip and his sons, which spans the whole book, into one notice. However, that impression proves to be mistaken: the final notice in the book (40.6: see *ad loc.*) returns to Macedon, and recounts the final episode, in which Philip turns against Perseus, but then dies, after which Perseus takes the throne. The repetition is unexpected. P. introduces Perseus' succession to Philip proleptically, as the natural consequence of his plot against Demetrius, allowing the reader to believe that the succession is uncontested and he has successfully accomplished his aim of turning his father against his brother. But then P. provides the detail that undermines that initial impression: Philip has discovered Perseus' plot, but is unable to act against him, instead dying in the tragic knowledge that he had killed his innocent son.

But the repetition may at the same time derive in part from a close reading of Livy: for when describing the final days of Philip's life, Livy remarks (40.54.3) that Perseus, even before Philip's death, 'was unquestionably king both in his own opinion and in that of other people' (*haud dubie et sua et aliorum opinione rex*), and that 'some were waiting for his [Philip's] death, others were not even waiting for it' (*aliis expectantibus suam mortem, aliis ne expectantibus quidem*). P.'s proleptic reference to Philip's death and Perseus' accession will make sense to the reader who knows from Livy that Philip was effectively being treated as dead and Perseus as king from the moment Demetrius was taken off the scene. Few readers will have had such an awareness of Livy's text, yet P., as he not infrequently does elsewhere, includes elements that only they will be able to appreciate.

certamina inter filios: Cf. Livy 40.8.4 *expertes iuvenalium inter fratres certaminum*; but the closest parallel to P.'s phrasing is Pomp. Trog., *Prol.* 16 *ortisque inter filios eius certaminibus*, which describes the conflict for the throne of Macedon between two sons of a much earlier king—a conflict which was resolved when another Demetrius, the famous Poliorcetes, intervened and took the throne for himself. This may merely be coincidence, but it is at least possible that the prologue of Trogus reflects the phrasing of the original, and that P. is alluding to it here, showing how elements from Macedonian history are being partially replayed under Philip.

Macedoniae regis: Cf. 34.8n.

referuntur: Cf. 16.1n.

ut: = 'How'; the indicatives in the indirect question are not uncommon in late antique prose writers (H-S 538–9).

inter quae accusatione: For the 'adverbial' use of *inter quae* cf. *TLL* VII.1 2133.15–68.

parricidii: Livy uses this term several times to describe Demetrius' alleged attempt to murder his brother (40.8.7, 40.9.9, 40.12.15, 40.13.3, 40.13.4, 40.15.11);

this is normal Latin usage, but in the absence of any explanation, and especially when placed in conjunction with *adfectati regni*, the reader would naturally assume that the murder of Philip was meant: cf. above.

ad ultimum: Cf. 1.B.7n.

venit: 'Came to him' [sc. as a possession]: cf. *OLD s.v. uenio* 13.

40.3 *Wars in Liguria and Spain*. P. introduces his 'round-up' earlier than usual, but the positioning is easily explicable. In it, he focuses on the victories the Romans achieved over the Ligurians and over the Celtiberi in Spain, and these are indeed the major regions in which Roman campaigns take place in the book, as Livy signals at the very start (40.1.4–5). Victories over the Ligurians are described at 40.16.4, 40.25, 40.27–8, 40.41.1–5, and 40.53.1–2, and victories over the Celtiberi at 40.16.7–10, 40.30–3, 40.39–40, and 40.47–50. The first major battle against each group thus comes in the period directly after Livy's description of the death of Demetrius, and the account of the foundation of the colony of Aquileia (40.4); it is, accordingly, not surprising that P. chose this moment to mention that fighting, even if he includes under the same heading battles from other parts of the book.

item res...gestas continet: Cf. 2.16n. P., for the only time, substitutes *item* for his more usual *praeterea*.

compluribus ducibus: Cf. 12.3n.

feliciter: Cf. 14.8n.

40.4 *Foundation of the colony of Aquileia*. Corresponds to Livy 40.34.2–3; P., as usual, highlights a colonial foundation, although he has omitted one prior to this in the book, namely the foundation of Graviscae (40.29.1–2: see also 40.5n.).

colonia Aquileia deducta est: Cf. 1.B.1n.

40.5 *Discovery of the books of Numa*. Corresponds to Livy 40.29.3–14. Although the episode does not receive a great deal of prominence in Livy, it was sufficiently popular in other (mostly Latin) writers as to make it unsurprising that P., too, describes it in some detail: versions of the story appear in Val. Max. 1.1.12 (also Nepotianus' epitome), Plin., *Nat*. 13.84–7, Plu., *Numa* 22.4–5, Fest. 178L, Lact., *Inst*. 1.22.5–6, *Vir. Ill*. 3.2, Aug., *Civ*. 7.34; moreover, unusually, several of these writers (Livy, Pliny, Plutarch, Augustine) cite earlier sources who are now lost.[36] Although details vary (for example, the number of books discovered, or the name of the person who found them), the overall tenor of the story does not differ

---

[36] Pliny cites Cassius Hemina (*FRHist* 6 F 35), Piso (*FRHist* 9 F 14), Sempronius Tuditanus (*FRHist* 10 F 3), Valerius Antias (*FRHist* 25 F 9a, 25 F 58), and Varro (*Ant. Hum.* 6 fr. 3 Mirsch); Livy and Plutarch both cite Antias (respectively *FRHist* 25 F 9b and 25 F 57), and Augustine cites Varro, *De Cultu Deorum* fr. 3 (Cardauns).

among the sources: the books of Numa were discovered in a buried chest, they were taken to the praetor, and the Senate ordered them to be burned on the grounds of subverting religion. All of these elements are present in P.: he even notes the fact that the books were in both Greek and Latin (omitted only by *Vir. Ill.* and Augustine), and that the burning was public (not mentioned by Pliny, *Vir. Ill.*, Nepotianus, or Augustine). In one respect, however, Livy's own account is unusual: he strongly implies that the books were not genuine, whereas every other source assumes, and sometimes states directly, that they were. P. reworks Livy so as to align him with that common view: he refers to the books as *libri Numae Pompili*, which in Livy is what is said in the inscription on the chest (cf. below), but not what Livy himself appears to believe.

P. inserts this notice earlier than in Livy, who has it prior to the foundation of Aquileia (40.4). It is possible that the fact that Livy described the foundation of Graviscae directly before the account of the books of Numa (40.29.1–2) encouraged P. to narrate this episode after the foundation of another colony; but that is a tenuous thread on which to hang an explanation, since he does not mention the foundation of Graviscae at all, although he could easily have included it in the same notice as Aquileia. It may well be that P. was more influenced by aesthetic considerations: he places the 'formal' notices of minor wars and colonial foundations in the centre of the book, balanced by fuller stories of Rome and Macedon before and after them.

libri Numae Pompili: Cf. Livy 40.29.4 *libros Numae Pompili* (see also above).

in agro L. Petilli scribae sub Ianiculo: Cf. Livy 40.29.3 *in agro L. Petilli scribae sub Ianiculo*.

cum pleraque dissolvendarum religionum praetor... legisset: Cf. Livy 40.29.11 *cum animum advertisset pleraque dissolvendarum religionum*.

legerentur servarenturque: Cf. Livy 40.29.12 *legi servarique*.

40.6 *Death of Philip; succession of Perseus.* Corresponds to Livy 40.54.1–57.1. Apart from the summary notice of wars in Spain and Liguria (40.3n.), and the foundation of Aquileia (40.4n.), P. offers nothing at all from the second half of Livy's book, apart from the account here of Philip's unsuccessful attempt to punish Perseus for his treachery to Demetrius, along with Philip's death and Perseus' succession. This is largely unsurprising, however, since the second half of Livy's book contains little that was sufficiently memorable to find a place elsewhere in the tradition: the bulk of it consists either of the aforementioned wars, or accounts of relatively minor events in Rome. Only the censorship of Aemilius Lepidus and Fulvius Nobilior both occupied Livy more fully and was occasionally alluded to elsewhere (Livy 40.45.6–46.16, 51–2; cf. Cicero, *Prov.* 20, Val. Max. 4.2.1 (also Paris' epitome), Gell. 12.8.5–6); P. nevertheless passed over that as well, although he would later record the census data which Livy provides in the next book (41.4n.). He likewise ignores the account of the abortive migration of the

Bastarnae in the aftermath of Philip's death (Livy 40.57–8), an episode of symbolic significance to Livy (Levene (1993), 101–2), but significance which lies more in the fact that, miraculously, nothing resulted from it, than in any material consequences.

P. does not go into the detail of how Philip learned the truth about Perseus' plot, but, like almost every other author who reports the episode,[37] he takes it for granted that he did, and focuses instead on Philip's conscience-stricken awareness of his complicity in his son's death. Like Livy, he describes Philip's determination to hand the throne to Antigonus, though Antigonus plays a more significant role in Livy's version than one would guess from P., since he is the person who brings Philip to understand what he has done.

As discussed above, this notice in part duplicates the one from earlier in the book, since both report the death of Philip and the accession of Perseus. See 40.2n. for the suggestion that this represents a deliberate strategy on P.'s part, belatedly informing the reader that, contrary to what was implied earlier, Philip died in the tragic knowledge of his earlier mistake; it may also reflect Livy's description of how Perseus effectively took the throne even before Philip's death.

aegritudine animi confectus: A unique phrase, although *aegritudine...confectus* is found in Cic., *Tusc.* 3.27, and occasionally in late antique Christian writers (Ambr., *Epist.* 51.10, Rufin., *Hist.* 10.7); cf. esp. Pacuv. fr. 128 (Ribbeck), *non decet animum aegritudine...confici.*

de poena...cogitavit: Another rare phrase, but it is found once in Livy (38.14.7), as well as in Cic., *Flacc.* 97.

successorem regni sui relinquere: This phrase is not closely paralleled in Latin of the late Republic or early Empire (though cf. Vell. 1.6.2 *ita ut semper successor regni paterni foret filius*). Very similar, however, is Pomp. Trog., *Prol.* 36 *successoremque imperii Attalum Philometora reliquit*, which is probably a product of late antiquity: phrases of the form *successorem reliquit* become common in the fourth century and after (e.g. Eutr. 8.11.2, 8.19.3, 10.9.1, *Hist. Aug., Hadr.* 4.8, Aug., *Civ.* 8.2).

morte raptus est: Although *rapere* is often used in poetry in the context of death (Dahlmann (1975), 81–2), *morte raptus* is surprisingly rare; it is not found in Livy, or elsewhere in surviving Republican or Augustan Latin, but cf. Plin., *Epist.* 6.6.7 *doleo...illum immatura morte indignissime raptum*, and it appears occasionally in later writers (e.g. Aug., *Civ.* 1.28).

Throughout this notice (cf. also above) P., unusually, is employing neither Livy's phrasing nor phrasing that is distinctively Livian nor distinctively of his own time. Instead he crafts a sentence with affinities to choice literary Latin, but which extends its language in unexpected directions.

---

[37] D.S. 29.25, Plu., *Aem.* 8.9, Zonar. 9.22.2; the partial exception is Just. 32.3.1–5, who refers briefly to the torture of witnesses.

Book 41

41.1 *Fire in shrine of Vesta extinguished.* This passage does not appear in the surviving portions of Livy Book 41, but it is likely that in Livy, as in P., it stood relatively close to the start of the book. Book 40 ended with the election of the consuls for 178; it is highly probable that Livy began Book 41 with their taking up office, as he does on other occasions where the election of consuls stands at the end of a book (25–6, 29–30, 31–2, 36–7, 39–40, 41–2). That the event described in this notice was reported in 178 is guaranteed by Obsequens 8, who lists it under that year; it is furthermore reasonably likely that, according to Livy's usual (but not invariable) practice with prodigies (Levene (1993), 38–125), it appeared close to the start of the year, after the distribution of provinces among the magistrates but before the consuls left Rome. The events in Spain (41.2) would then have followed it.

Even if (as is far less probable) P. has reversed Livy's order, and Livy in fact introduced the Spanish narrative before the extinguishing of the fire, the latter must have appeared near the start of the pentad, since the total quantity of text missing is less than ten Teubner pages (Briscoe (2012a), 33). This breaks the pattern from Books 21, 26, 31, and 36, where prodigy lists, with their ominous implications for the narrative, are never placed in this position (Levene (1993), 104–5). This may be because, as he sometimes does, Livy rewrote the prodigy here in order to negate the ominous effect (cf. Levene (1993), 105): at 28.11.7 he explicitly states of an earlier extinguishing of the fire that it was not a sign from the gods, even though it was treated by the Romans as one (cf. 28.3n.). In addition, it may be that other aspects of the narrative context demanded the introduction of the prodigy here. Notably, it appears from Obsequens that it was described in the context of a fire in the forum which destroyed the temple; and that may have been tied by Livy to a particular point in the year.

It is surprising that P., having narrated the extinction of the fire, does not go on to describe the punishment of the Vestal involved, since that is a topic he is generally interested in (cf. 14.6n.). It is possible that the fact that her punishment involved being flogged for negligence rather than executed for unchastity reduced his interest, but he does record a comparable punishment at 28.3. Obsequens' narrative, presumably itself taken from Livy, suggests that the circumstances of the punishment here were less straightforward, since the extinction of the flame of Vesta was the consequence of external circumstances, namely the destruction of the temple in the fire. This makes it not improbable that Livy treated the punishment of the Vestal for negligence as unjust: Obsequens does not indicate that directly, but he does report that the Vestal promised that the flame would not go out again, a point that would hardly seem worth recording were this simply a question of an individual punished for transgression; and this in turn may be why P. was less keen to record it.

A legend recorded in D.H., *AR* 2.68.3–5, and more briefly in Val. Max. 1.1.7 (also Paris' epitome) and Prop. 4.11.53–4, about a chief Vestal called Aemilia, one of whose charges allowed the fire to be extinguished, but who was miraculously cleared of wrongdoing, is often thought to be related to this episode: see esp. Münzer (1999 (1920)), 161–4. However, Münzer's argument shows only that *if* one wishes to relate Dionysius' legend of Aemilia to the events of 178, one can make sense of it in terms of the politics of the day. It provides no reason to think that one should make that connection in the first place, and identify this Aemilia as the chief Vestal in 178 (as do e.g. Parker (2004), 581, 594, Rüpke, *FS* 513). It is true that a Vestal Aemilia appears on the coinage of the triumvir M. Aemilius Lepidus (*RRC* 419/3, 494/1), and it is likely that this is the Aemilia of the legend, but the family of the Aemilii Lepidi had been prominent since the early third century, and Aemilia could have held her office at any point subsequent to that. To set against Münzer's argument is the stark fact that Livy almost certainly did not relate Aemilia's story under the events of 178, since the outcome of the episode in his text appears from Obsequens to have been very different.

ignis: A fire was kept burning constantly in the shrine of Vesta, and one of the major roles of the priestesses was to ensure that it did not go out. On the most literal level, the centrality of fire to the cult is clearly connected with the role of Vesta as goddess of the hearth; but the symbolic significance of fire extends well beyond that. The fire of Vesta evoked both female chastity and male procreation, and fire has a double role (on which ancient writers explicitly comment: see e.g. Cic., *Nat. Deor.* 2.41) as creative and destructive, which arguably mirrors the ambiguous status of the Vestals themselves (see esp. Beard (1980), 24–5; cf. Staples (1998), 148–51). That paradoxical status of fire is especially apparent in the present episode, if (as Obsequens implies: see above) it was a fire in the Forum that caused the extinction of the flame.

in aede Vestae: See 19.10n.

extinctus est: For the significance of the extinction of the flame see D.H., *AR* 2.67.5. According to him, it was an omen threatening the destruction of Rome (something Livy himself denies: see above). Dionysius also adds that it was held to result from the unchastity of the Vestal in charge of maintaining the flame; however, even if some such connection were indeed assumed, it was clearly not deemed a proof of unchastity—if it were, the offending Vestal would presumably have been executed rather than flogged, and even the legend of the Vestal Aemilia that Dionysius then goes on to relate (*AR* 2.68.3–5: see above) has the extinction of the flame leading to a pontifical investigation of her chastity, not an automatic conviction (cf. Münzer (1937), 199–203).

41.2 *Roman victories in Spain.* The final part of this notice, namely the triumph, corresponds to Livy 41.7.1–3; the victories themselves are lost in the lacuna at the opening of the book, though they are referred to retrospectively at 41.6.4 and 41.26.1.

The only extended account of events in Spain in this year (178 BC) is given by App., *Hisp.* 43, who focuses solely on Gracchus and does not mention Albinus; after recounting Gracchus' victory (in fighting entirely unlike that in Livy), he goes into some detail about the settlement Gracchus imposed on the Spaniards: according to him, Gracchus established a series of treaties with the different Spanish tribes; he also allotted civic rights and land to the poorer classes. Subsequently (App., *Hisp.* 44), it emerges that the treaty with the Celtiberi had forbidden them to establish new cities, and had imposed on them a tribute and also a requirement to supply troops for the Roman army; also cf. Suid. *Π* 1109 (Adler) (argued to be a fragment of Polybius by Szádeczy-Kardoss (1976)), according to which Gracchus gave the Celtiberi the right to appeal to the Senate for relief from the impositions he was imposing on them. There are, moreover, indications from later complaints by the Spaniards (Livy 43.2) that the tribute applied not only to the Celtiberi, but to other Spanish communities also (Richardson (1986), 70–1). There is also a briefer reference to the peace treaty with Numantia in Plu., *TG* 5.3, to the foundation of Graccuris in Paul., *Fest.* 86L (see below), and other references to Gracchus' settlement in Plb. 35.2.15, App., *Hisp.* 48, and Oros. 4.20.32 (cf. D.S. 31.39, which refers to the treaties but does not mention Gracchus by name). As well as Graccuris, Gracchus is recorded as the founder of the city of Iliturgi by a later inscription (*AE* 1982, 545), albeit problematically.[38]

The tendency in the tradition to focus on Gracchus rather than Albinus, which P. to some degree shares (and which may well reflect the balance in Livy), may partly be because of his family connections with other iconic figures in Roman history (cf. below), but more importantly reflects the reality that he was the first commander in Spain to create a systematic network of treaties and obligations through which Roman control over the province might be exercised,[39] as well as intervening in the social dynamics of the community through the distribution of land to the disadvantaged;[40] it appears that he did this on his own initiative rather than as an instrument of a centralized Roman policy, but his arrangements appear

---

[38] The authenticity of this inscription has been questioned on epigraphic and linguistic grounds, and it is in addition certainly the case that the city is far to the south of the main areas in which Gracchus was campaigning, and indeed was technically part of Albinus' province of Further Spain, not Gracchus' own. For an exhaustive analysis of the question, including an extended discussion of the archaeological and historical context, see Wiegels (1982), who cautiously concludes that it is unlikely to be Republican or a genuine record of Gracchus' foundation, but probably is a patriotic invention from the imperial era; *contra* e.g. Knapp (1977), 109–10; cf. also Tovar and Blázquez Martínez (1982), 430–1.

[39] See Richardson (1986), 104–8, 112–23, (1996), 70–6; in both books he gives Albinus a share of the credit for the settlement. Possibly Richardson was influenced by the fact that, according to Livy (40.57.1), Gracchus and Albinus carefully coordinated their campaigning in the previous year; but while that fact makes similar coordination over the settlement not improbable, it remains the case that nothing in our sources directly supports it.

[40] Gracchus was not, however, the first commander to use land distribution as a tool of policy in Spain: see *ILS* 15 = *ILLRP* 514, an inscription of L. Aemilius Paullus dating from (probably) 189, freeing a community's slaves and allocating land to them (cf. Richardson (1986), 117–18).

to have become the basis for subsequent Roman activities in Spain over the next generation.

Tib. Sempronius Gracchus procos.: *RE* 53, *MRR* I 393. He was now in the third year of his command in Nearer Spain, having originally gone there as praetor in 180, and then having maintained his command as proconsul in the two subsequent years. Prior to that he had served on the staff of Scipio Asiaticus at the time of the war with Antiochus (Livy 37.7.11-14); then he had been tribune in either 187 or 184 (depending on the contested dating of the trials of the Scipios: see *MRR* I 378), and possibly one of an embassy sent in 185 to mediate in Greece between Philip and his enemies (Livy 39.24.13 and 39.33.1; but see *MRR* I 374); in 183 he had been one of the triumvirs for founding the colony of Saturnia, and had been curule aedile in 182. Subsequently he was twice consul, in 177 (when he commanded in Sardinia and won a triumph: see 41.6n.) and 163; he was also censor in 169 (cf. 43.6n., 45.5n.). His career was, by Roman standards, immensely distinguished; nevertheless a large portion of his place in popular memory depended on his iconic relatives, since he was son-in-law to Scipio Africanus and father to the Gracchi; the former relationship is central to his only other appearance in P. (38.9n.).

Celtiberos: See F 23.10n. As noted there, it is often unclear how restrictive the term is, but in this case the general context of Gracchus' comprehensive victory in the previous book implies that it is being used in its broadest sense, to mean the entire grouping of Celtiberian tribes.

victos: Gracchus had been recorded as defeating the Celtiberi in the previous book (40.47-50; cf. 40.3n.). Livy provides two versions of that victory, one in his own narrative voice, the other of which he attributes to *quidam auctores* (40.50.2) and reports in *oratio obliqua*. The first culminates with the victorious Gracchus ravaging Celtiberia and a large number of towns surrendering to him (40.49.1-50.1); the second adds that not all of these surrenders were made in good faith, and the towns revolted against Gracchus, who was required to defeat them again; following that defeat Livy says, still in *oratio obliqua*, 'from that point on the war came to an end and the Celtiberi made a true peace, with no wavering in their loyalty, as previously' (40.50.5 *inde debellatum, veramque pacem, non fluxa, ut ante, fide Celtiberos fecisse*). This indication of total victory is attributed to the *quidam auctores*, and the fact that Livy maintains *oratio obliqua* throughout this episode suggests that he himself has doubts about the historicity of the final battle (Briscoe (2008), 539). Nevertheless, the fact that the phrase explicitly describing the victory being complete is in *oratio obliqua* should not be taken to mean that Livy himself regarded the war as unfinished; rather this sentence completes the alternative story by noting that whereas before the final victory described in the second version the Celtiberi were disloyal even after their surrender, following that victory their loyalty was ensured. The implication is that the extra victory in the 'alternative' version brings the Celtiberi to the point that they had already reached in the version Livy tells in his own voice: of complete subjection to Rome.

This implies that, contrary to what one might have assumed from P.'s language, no victories by Gracchus are recorded by Livy in Book 41 itself: the defeat of the Celtiberi mentioned here is that in Book 40, and all we find in Book 41 is the settlement that Gracchus establishes in the wake of his victory. Cf. 18.5n. for another probable example of a victory which Livy reported in one book being delayed by P. until he records the aftermath in the following book.

monimentumque operum suorum: P. rarely refers to monuments, and the word *monumentum* appears only two other times in his text: 39.8 (of the double tomb of Scipio Africanus), and 140.2 (of the buildings erected by Augustus' sister Octavia). With first of these his interest, like Livy's, is in the paradoxical nature of a monument which fails to provide the information one would expect from it (cf. Jaeger (1997), 164–72); here too it is the unexpected nature of this 'monument' which is to the fore, since the naming of cities after prominent individuals is not the norm in the Republic—no previous example is known, and there would not be another for more than fifty years (Knapp (1977), 109).

Graccurim: Modern Alfaro (*BarrAtl* Map 25 D3). The foundation is also recorded by Paulus, *Fest.* 86L, who mentions that its original name was Ilurcis; however, this may be the result of confusion with the city of Iliturgi, which was itself probably a foundation by Gracchus (Tovar and Blázquez Martínez (1982), 431: see above). Coins from the time of Tiberius show that the town had by that point become a Latin *municipium*, but when founded it is likely to have been for settlement by Spaniards (Knapp (1977), 108–9). There are, however, remains of centuriation in the region which may go back to the time of Gracchus (Ariño Gil (1986); for the date see esp. 61), suggesting that the town was created on a Roman model, as is certainly true for other Spanish settlements in the second century BC (Richardson (1986), 172–3). The city occupies a strategic site near the confluence of two major rivers (the Ebro and the Aragón), presumably in order to consolidate Roman control over the territory (Burillo Mozota (1998), 236–7).

The MSS of P. spell it either *Gracchorum* or *Graccorum*; Frobenius, followed by most subsequent editors, corrected to *Gracchurim*. But the Tiberian coins spell the name *Graccurris*, and the version without *h* has no less MS support. While proof is naturally impossible, it is preferable to assume that P. used a spelling for which there is ancient textual warrant.

Postumio Albino procos.: L. Postumius Albinus (*RE* 41). Like Gracchus (above), he was sent to Spain in 180, as praetor of Further Spain, and had his command extended for 179 and 178; he subsequently became consul in 173.

Vaccaei: See F 23.13n.

Lusitani: A people inhabiting the central region of modern Portugal. Like the Celtiberi (above), they were not a single political unit, but appear to have consisted of loosely affiliated groups which fought together in the face of a common enemy. They fought extensively against the Romans both before and after this period; but this is the first time P. has mentioned them by name.

subacti sunt: Unlike with Gracchus (above), it looks plausible that Livy, as P. suggests, explicitly describes Postumius as achieving his victories in Book 41, since at 40.50.6–7 Livy rejects the accounts of the historians who claim that Postumius fought the Vaccaei in 179, arguing that he arrived in his province too late to do so.[41]

41.3 *Antiochus IV Epiphanes takes the Seleucid throne.* The surviving portions of Livy reflect the second half of P.'s notice, the character sketch of Antiochus (41.20); the description of his coming to the throne is lost, but presumably preceded the sketch.

Sources for Antiochus' accession are scanty, but sufficient survives to show that P.'s distilled account has radically simplified the process by which he took the throne. The two main (if brief) narrative sources are a contemporary honorific inscription from Athens for Eumenes of Pergamum (*OGIS* 248 = *IG* II^3 1 1323), and App., *Syr.* 45. From these it emerges that Seleucus, Antiochus' older brother and predecessor, was assassinated by his chief minister Heliodorus, who sought to rule himself, and that Antiochus was placed on the throne by Eumenes and his brother Attalus, despite the fact that Seleucus had two sons of his own. In addition, a Babylonian king-list (Sachs and Wiseman (1954)) shows that Antiochus IV initially had as co-ruler another Antiochus, his 'son', whom it says that he killed five years later. Mørkholm (1966), 42–9 demonstrated, partly on the basis of the coinage, partly on the basis of a fragment of John of Antioch (*FHG* IV, 558, fr. 58; cf. D.S. 30.7.2–3), and partly on the inherent unlikelihood of Antiochus' murder of his own son being overlooked in the hostile Greek historical tradition, that the boy who co-ruled with Antiochus was in fact his nephew, the younger son of Seleucus. Mørkholm suggested that the reason the Babylonian documents refer to him as Antiochus' son is that he adopted him, but a more economical explanation is that the Akkadian word translated by Sachs and Wiseman as 'son', *aplu*, primarily means 'heir', and is commonly used to refer to any form of successor, such as a crown prince, even if not the biological son (*CAD* A II, 173–7). P. has nothing of the assassination, nor of the role of Pergamum, nor of Antiochus' co-ruler.

Likewise, the image that P. provides, of Antiochus moving straight from Rome to his kingdom, is misleading. Antiochus was actually in Athens at the point when Seleucus was assassinated, having been replaced as a hostage in Rome by Demetrius, Seleucus' older son (see below). Furthermore, the Athenian

---

[41] So Briscoe (2008), 540, rejecting the suggestion that this is inconsistent with 40.39.3 and 40.47.1, where Postumius is present in Further Spain from the very start of the campaign: Briscoe argues that 'province' here refers only to the territory of the Vaccaei.

inscription indicates that he then went to Pergamum, where Eumenes and Attalus gave him military and financial resources and brought him to the Seleucid border. However, it is also possible that P.'s picture, of Antiochus taking the throne directly on leaving Rome, is intended to suggest that Rome played an active part in his accession, something that has been suspected by a number of scholars (so esp. Will (1982), 2.303–5; cf. Walbank (1979), 285; *contra* Gruen (1984a), 646). P. does not state this directly, but there is an oddity in his language which appears to hint at this interpretation: see below.

It is highly probable that much of this context stood in Livy, presumably derived from Polybius, who is also likely to be Appian's ultimate source. P., as often, cuts the story to what appeared to him the essential features: Antiochus' time in Rome, and his taking the kingdom after Seleucus' death. In the course of this he incidentally completes the story of Antiochus III, who had played a substantial role in the previous books, and whose death is now explicitly referred to. But the fact that he devotes so much attention to the accession and character of Antiochus IV at all, however, is interesting. It may be simply a reflection of the interest shown by Livy, but it is also likely that P. was influenced by the prominence of Antiochus in later Christian writings as a result of his activities in Judaea. P. says nothing of those, no doubt because Livy likewise said nothing; but the couple of pieces of information he selects about Antiochus' succession—his having been a hostage in Rome and the fact that he succeeded Seleucus—are surprisingly close to those offered in the Books of Maccabees (I Maccabees 1:10, II Maccabees 4:7); cf. also Sulp. Sev., *Chron.* 2.19.5. Moreover, P. maintains the central paradox from Livy's account of Antiochus' character, which could be seen to dovetail neatly into the Jewish-centred image of Antiochus—the worst of monarchs, but who nevertheless was an enthusiastic supporter of (pagan) religion.

Antiochus, Antiochi filius: Antiochus IV Epiphanes, son of Antiochus the Great; he ruled the Seleucid empire 175–164 BC. He was originally named Mithridates (after his maternal grandfather), as appears from *SEG* 37.859 (see Wörrle (1988), 451–4; cf. Livy 33.19.9),[42] but appears to have begun to use the name Antiochus after the death of his elder brother of that name in 193 (Mehl (1999), 18–26, Mittag (2006), 34–6). He is the only Seleucid monarch who is widely recognized outside circles frequented by ancient historians, thanks to his role as antagonist in the Maccabean revolt. His career and policies, both foreign and domestic, have been much debated, especially with regard to his relationships with Rome and Judaea: for discussion see e.g. Mørkholm (1966), Mittag (2006), Feyel and Graslin-Thomé (2014).

obses a patre Romanis datus: Antiochus was sent to Rome as a hostage after the battle of Magnesia in 189 (App., *Syr.* 39); he remained there until Seleucus' son

---

[42] Reading, with the MSS, *filiis duobus, Ardye ac Mithridate*, not *Ardyeque*, as was proposed by Holleaux and accepted by subsequent editors prior to the discovery of the inscription.

Demetrius came as a substitute. The date of his departure is not directly attested: however, an honorific inscription (*SEG* 32.131) shows that Antiochus was in Athens by 178/7, while Demetrius was born in 186, the year after Seleucus came to the throne (Plb. 31.2.5), and was unlikely to have been sent as a hostage in early infancy. Hence 178 is the most likely date.

Seleuco: Seleucus IV Philopator, who ruled the Seleucid empire 187–175 BC. He was the second son of Antiochus the Great, his older brother Antiochus having died in 193.

qui patri...egit: The MSS have the entire sequence at the end of the book; Drakenborch tentatively proposed the transposition (though declining to print it), and subsequent editors have followed this lead.

patri defuncto: Antiochus III had died more than a decade earlier, in 187, killed by the local inhabitants while attempting to plunder the temple of Zeus at Elymais (D.S. 28.3, 29.15, Str. 16.1.18, Just. 32.2.1–2).

in regnum Syriae ab urbe dimissus: *dimitto* is regularly used of releasing captives (*TLL* V.1 1212.74–1213.21); however, the prepositional phrase *in...* is hard to parallel when the verb is employed in this sense, although it is commonplace when the 'sending' is more literal. The consequence is that P.'s phrasing, effectively combining two different senses of the verb, implies that Antiochus was not only 'released' from being a hostage, but also was 'sent' to take his kingdom, and that in turn supports the hypothesis that the Romans played some role in the transfer of power (cf. above), or at least that Livy represented them as doing so. To that extent P.'s account, though misleading in literal terms, as noted above, may capture a significant truth about the affair.

praeter religionem: Livy 41.20.5 (following Plb. 26.1.10) states that there were two respects in which Antiochus behaved in a properly kingly manner: his benefactions to cities, and his worship of the gods. P., perhaps because of the Christian understanding of Antiochus as a promoter of pagan religion (cf. above), mentions only the latter.

multa templa magnifica multis locis: Cf. Livy 41.20.9 *magnificum templum*. The chief MSS read *multis sociis*, but that makes little sense: Livy does not refer to Antiochus specifically giving temples for his *socii*, and one of the two examples P. offers is of a temple in Antioch, his own capital. Far more plausible is the correction *locis* offered by one late MS and the *editio princeps*: Livy uses the phrase *alia multa in aliis locis* at 41.20.9—he is there referring to monuments that Antiochus promised but failed to build, but it is altogether characteristic of P. to retool Livy's phrasing in this way.

fecit: The chief MSS omit the verb. Rossbach proposed *fecit*; he acknowledged that *posuit* was also possible, but *fecit* is employed by P. on the other occasions he refers to temple foundations (1.B.3, 1.B.4), and so is on balance to be preferred.

Athenis Iovis Olympi: Cf. Livy 41.20.8 *Iovis Olympii templum Athenis*.

Antiochiae ⟨Capitolini⟩: *Capitolini* is omitted by the MSS, but was restored by Sigonius on the basis of Livy 41.20.9 *Antiochiae Iovis Capitolini*. It is possible that *Iovis* should be added as well, as in Livy; it would, admittedly, be redundant, but redundant repetitions of this sort are not alien to P.'s style.

vilissimum regem: A striking phrase, not found in the surviving portions of Livy. It is used in Florus 2.13.52 of Ptolemy XIII, the killer of Pompey, but a more notable parallel is the Vulgate of Daniel 11:20: *et stabit in loco eius vilissimus et indignus decore regio* ('and there will stand in his place a person most worthless and unworthy of kingly glory'). The verse in question is most naturally taken in context to be describing Seleucus, Antiochus' brother and predecessor, and was interpreted that way by Jer., *In Dan.* 3.11.20), but, given the oblique nature of the 'prophecies' in Daniel 11, it was applied to other royal claimants also, as Jerome himself attests. It is altogether possible that it was associated with Antiochus himself, who was (and is) widely assumed to be the subject of the following verses.

The phrasing of the Vulgate here does not correspond to either the Masoretic Hebrew text or the Septuagint, nor is it paralleled in the surviving Old Latin translations; it is, accordingly, hard to untangle the reason for its presence. It is at least plausible to suggest that P.'s using a related phrase in the context of a Seleucid monarch is more than coincidental: one possibility is that it was taken over by Jerome from an earlier Latin version which is now lost, in which case P. may equally have had access to that version. It provides an additional hint that P.'s image of Antiochus may have been filtered through the Jewish-Christian tradition concerning him (cf. above).

egit: 'Behaved like' (*OLD s.v. ago* 26a).

41.4 *Census*. As usual (cf. 3.3n.), P. includes the census numbers from Livy. This is the census conducted by M. Aemilius Lepidus and M. Fulvius Nobilior, elected in 179, whose election and whose activities during their censorship were described towards the end of Book 40 (40.45.6–46.16, 51–2). Livy's usual practice is to record the *lustrum* and the associated census at the end of the second year of the censors' office (13.4n.), but this year is an exception, since 41.1.1–8.3 contain the final events of 178; accordingly, the census data must have appeared earlier in Livy's narrative of the year. Moreover, the fact that P. inserts the notice after the account of the accession of Antiochus, which took place in 175 (41.3n.), shows that he is here not only changing Livy's narrative order, but placing events out of their chronological sequence.

lustrum a censoribus conditum est: Cf. 11.5n.

censa sunt civium capita: Cf. 3.3n.

CCLVIII milia DCCXCIIII: At 42.10.2 Livy remarks that the figure in the next census was *minor aliquanto* ('somewhat lower'). Toynbee took the view that this meant that the figure was lower than our census here, yet the transmitted figure is higher, and so at least one of the numbers must be corrupt (Toynbee (1966), 1.440, 443–4, followed by Brunt (1971), 72–3). See, however, Briscoe (2012a), 183, who correctly understands Livy's phrase to mean 'lower than expected'; hence there is no reason on those grounds to doubt the reliability of the number.

There are, however, other reasons to do so. The figure here is similar to that of the previous census, in 188 (38.5), something that happens disturbingly often with P. (cf. 10.9n.): it is likely, as Beloch (1877), 232 argues, that in P.'s text the figure from one census is transferred to the next. Hence all of these should be suspected as corrupt. Cf. also Brunt (1971), 73 for demographic reasons to doubt that the Roman population had remained as stable between 188 and 178 as the figure in P. would imply: he mentions the probable increase in the number of children born after the Second Punic War who would have reached maturity between 188 and 178, the low number of war casualties, the likely number of Latins immigrating to Rome in that period, and the manumission of slaves. All of these reasons support the intrinsic suspicion attaching to P.'s recorded figure.

41.5 *The lex Voconia*. This law, restricting the inheritance rights of women (see below), is explicitly dated by Cicero, *Sen.* 14 to 169; this is incompatible with Livy having reported it in Book 41, since that book covers the years 178–174. The explanation for the discrepancy was seen long ago (Lange (1879), 298):[43] Cicero, *II Verr.* 1.106 quotes a provision of the law, that it applied only after the censorship of Q. Fulvius Flaccus and A. Postumius Albinus, who became censors in 174. Livy's source (or that source's source) mistook this to mean that the law was passed in the year those censors took office. However, the reason the law referred to the censors of 174 was to clarify that it was not to take effect on the basis of the census they took during their term of office, but only once the next censors, C. Claudius Pulcher and Ti. Sempronius Gracchus, who took office in 169 (but may not have done so at the time that the law was promulgated), had completed the census.[44] This provision makes it overwhelmingly probable that Cicero's date is correct, since in 174 Flaccus and Albinus had not yet completed their own census, and it is hard to see why Voconius would have passed a law that would only take effect two censuses in the future. Accordingly Voconius, as Cicero states, proposed the law in 169.

---

[43] A far less plausible explanation (followed by e.g. Scullard (1973), 205–6, Weishaupt (1999), 32) is that the confusion arose from the fact that there were alternative traditions about the length of Cato's life, one of which made him five years older than the other. It is highly improbable that it was known (independently of the consular date of the year) how old Cato was when he spoke in support of the *lex Voconia*, or that an historian would use that information when constructing a sequential narrative even in the unlikely event that Cato's age was recorded.

[44] So, explicitly, Cicero, *II Verr.* 1.107: *sanxit in posterum, qui post eos censores census esset, ne quis heredem virginem neve mulierem faceret* ('He [Voconius] made provision for the future, that no one enrolled in the census after those censors should make a girl or woman his heir').

Livy must have narrated the law in 174, presumably in the lacuna between 41.20 and 41.21. Briscoe (2012a), 34–5 argues that the law might equally have been narrated in the lacuna at the beginning of the book, since it is unlikely that historians did not give an account of the *lex Voconia* before Cicero's speech in 70, or that Livy's source 'would have altered the date of the law on the basis of an obscure passage of Cicero'. But it is far more probable that the date was based on the text of the law itself, which Cicero is quoting verbatim, than on Cicero's speech; in which case it is not at all unlikely that whichever historian first included it in the chronological sequence slotted it into the narrative of 174 on that basis.

The law is discussed a number of times in Cicero in considerable detail (*II Verr.* 1.104–14, *Rep.* 3.17, *Fin.* 2.55; also *Balb.* 21, *Cato* 14, *Phil.* 3.16). The terms in which Cicero treats it suggest that it was seen in his day as an unjust imposition on women, since all three of his major discussions concern critiques of the law or accounts of attempts that were made to avoid it (see esp. Dixon (1985)). No ethical considerations of that sort emerge in P., although even the mention of a blanket restriction on female inheritance is likely to have appeared manifestly unjust to his contemporaries: certainly Augustine refers to it as an outstanding and obvious instance of the moral degeneracy of the Roman Republic (*Civ.* 3.21: 'I cannot think of anything which could be said or imagined more unfair than this law'— *qua lege quid iniquius dici aut cogitari possit, ignoro*). It is, however, extremely likely that Livy, given his usual intense interest in ethical questions, took the opportunity to explore the moral issues underlying the law, perhaps not solely in critical terms; cf. Gell. 20.1.23, where Caecilius refers to the law as something that at the time was useful, but which the vast expansion in Roman wealth rendered obsolete.[45]

The grounds on which the law was promulgated are nowhere explicitly stated; it seems, however, reasonable to extrapolate from Cato's support that it was of a piece with his wish, twenty-five years earlier, to maintain the *lex Oppia* (cf. 34.1). In both cases there appears to be a concern with women having free use of wealth and the products of wealth, and there may have been a sense that this represented a challenge to the patriarchal order, especially at a time when the fruits of Rome's conquests were massively increasing (Astin (1978), 114–17).[46] Astin (1978), 114–15 plausibly suggests that it was also a response to the increase in marriages without *manus* at this time (itself perhaps caused by the general increase of wealth at Rome, which could have encouraged fathers to prefer such marriages for their daughters so that they might inherit); women married without *manus* could maintain their own property independently of their husbands. The one substantial surviving fragment of Cato's speech (*ORF*³ fr. 158) is a satirical picture of the

---

[45] Cf. also Quint., *Decl.* 264, a declamation based around a supposed attempt to circumvent the law; but the specific provision on which the case revolves appears to be fictional: see Steinwenter (1925), 2423–4.
[46] Note that Gell. 20.1.23 links this law to Republican sumptuary laws; cf. Steinwenter (1925), 2426.

indignity a husband is subjected to whose wife is in control of her own fortune (cf. Astin (1978), 117, Weishaupt (1999), 132–4): this indicates that, at the very least, the proponents of the law wished to appeal to male resentment against the financial independence of a woman in a non-*manus* marriage (Vigneron (1983), 145–6).

As a way of limiting the wealth of women, the law was admittedly crudely designed: Cicero notes one obvious objection (*Rep.* 3.17)—that a woman could still receive half the estate (see below), and half of an extremely large estate might be more than the entire estate of most other people. This is taken by (e.g.) Pölönen (1999), 113 as a decisive objection against the idea that the aim of the law was to restrict women in this way; but this objection assumes far too mechanical a relationship between the intention of a law and its practical effects. It is far from unusual for the effect of a law in particular cases to be contrary to that law's rationale—especially with laws which appear to be activated as much by symbols and emotion as reason.

An alternative explanation that has been widely canvassed is that the law was not the result of animus against women's wealth, but arose from a purely practical desire not to dilute the wealth held by men, since only men were subject to *tributum* in wartime;[47] this would, it is argued, explain its promulgation in 169, during the Third Macedonian War. However, this explanation is highly improbable. Were it a response to a wartime crisis, then it would not have been limited to future estates, but would certainly have been designed so as to take effect immediately (and in fact the imposition of wartime *tributum* was shortly to be suspended, in 167, following the victory over Macedon and the vast extra wealth that accrued to Rome at that point). And the manifest growth in Roman wealth over the previous decades would have made it less rather than more urgent to concentrate it in the hands of men for taxation purposes, since even smaller estates in relative terms would now meet the higher property qualifications.

A similar point shows the weakness of Gardner's suggestion ((1986), 174–5) that object of the law was to give men property to use 'for social and political status in the increasingly competitive society of the period'. In absolute terms there was more property in circulation than ever before, and upper-class men could expect to receive much of it even if female inheritance were not restricted by the law; and in relative terms the potential 'dilution' of male property through female possession would apply to upper-class families across the board. It is in any case hard to see why Voconius or Cato should have believed that the state should take the lead in preventing women from becoming heirs, if the testator himself did not wish to protect his own family's status in this fashion.

In short, there is little reason to doubt that the law was primarily designed as a limitation on women.

---

[47] Originally proposed by Pomeroy (1976), 222; it has subsequently been accepted by (e.g.) Dixon (1985), 520, Tellegen-Couperus and Tellegen (1998), 71.

Detailed studies of the *lex Voconia* are numerous: they include Steinwenter (1925), Vigneron (1983), Dixon (1985), Gardner (1986), 170–8, Tellegen-Couperus and Tellegen (1998), van der Meer (1999), Pölönen (1999), Weishaupt (1999), Balestri Fumagalli (2008).

Q. Voconius Saxa tribunus plebis: Nothing is known of him apart from this episode: P. is the sole witness to record his *cognomen*.

nequis mulierem heredem institueret: This provision, preventing women from becoming heirs, is the most discussed aspect of the law. P. is, however, misleading, since it appears not to have applied to all estates, but only if the testator was enrolled in the census in the highest property class; those not enrolled at all, or those enrolled at a lower property classification, were not affected (Steinwenter (1925), 2419–20; Watson (1971), 29–31); and Vestal Virgins were also allowed to be made heirs (Cic., *Rep.* 3.17). P.'s mistake is understandable (note that Aug., *Civ.* 3.21 describes the law in similarly general terms: *ne quis heredem feminam faceret*): the law, though not formally repealed, had become to a large degree obsolete in his day, since the testator could leave the estate to a woman in a different way via a legally enforceable *fideicommissum* (Gaius, *Inst.* 2.274), and in addition Augustus had excluded certain classes of women from its provisions altogether (Dio 56.10.2).

Another provision prevented the testator from leaving a legacy larger than the amount left to the heir; it is unclear whether this, too, applied only to the highest class (so Cic., *II Verr.* 1.110), or whether it was more broadly based (as implied by Gaius, *Inst.* 2.225–6).[48] When combined with the first provision, it effectively prevented a woman from inheriting more than half of the affected estate.

M. Cato: M. Porcius Cato (*RE* 10), lived 234–149 BC. One of the best-known figures of the period, not least because his extensive political career (quaestor in 204, praetor in 198, consul in 195, censor in 184) was matched by his no less extensive literary career. His only complete surviving work is his handbook *De Agri Cultura*, but he was acclaimed as an orator and historian (though these works now known only through hundreds of fragments), and various other works in other genres are recorded also. He was famous (though also controversial) in antiquity for his ostentatious defence of what he saw (or claimed to see) as traditional values (cf. 48.5n.). He appears, however, to have been less of a name to conjure with in later antiquity (cf. 34.2n.); P. gives him a more prominent role than any other Latin writer of the period does, following his career from his opposition to the repeal of the *lex Oppia* during his consulship (34.1) to his campaigns in Spain (34.2, 34.7), his censorship (39.5), and culminating in a detailed picture of his advocacy of the

---

[48] See Watson (1971), 167–70, inclining slightly in favour of Cicero's opinion; also Steinwenter (1925), 2423. *Contra* Tellegen-Couperus and Tellegen (1998), 69–70; but their argument depends on a strained reading of Cicero's logic in such a way as to make him conform with Gaius. Weishaupt (1999), 88–9 proposes that the interpretation of the law changed over time: Gaius reflects the original understanding of its scope, Cicero a later view.

Third Punic War in opposition to Scipio Nasica, as well as other political stands he took at the time (48.2, 48.10, 48.16, 49.2, 49.7, 49.12–13, 50.3).

The best study of his career remains Astin (1978); Suerbaum (2004) offers a comprehensive bibliography.

extat oratio eius: Fragments of Cato's speech (= ORF³ frs. 158–60) are quoted by Gell. 6.13.3 and 17.6.1 (the second fragment also being quoted in Fest. 356L and Non. 76L), and by Serv. auct., *Aen.* 1.573. Livy presumably referred to the fact that the speech was extant, but, as usual with speeches that had survived to his day, did not offer a version of it himself (see 13.3n.).

41.6 *Wars; Perseus' preparations for war against Rome*. For the 'other things' round-up at the end of the book, P. lists victories against the Ligurians, Istrians, Sardinians, and Celtiberi, as well as the initial moves that Perseus was making towards war with Rome. Surprisingly, given the quantity of the book that has been lost, virtually all of this appears to correspond to material in Livy's surviving text. A war with the Istrians begins in the lacuna at the start of the book, but continues in the first surviving section (41.1.1–5.2), and in any case results in a defeat, so is not strictly speaking included in this list in any case; the Romans renew the war and win in 41.10.1–11.9. Roman victories in Sardinia are briefly described at 41.12.4–7 and 41.17.1–2, and over the Ligurians at 41.12.7–9, 41.16.7–9, and 41.18; the end of a further victory over the Ligurians in 175 appears at 41.19.1–2 following another lacuna. With the victory in 41.18, it is surprising that P. says nothing of the killing of the consul Q. Petillius Spurinus in the battle, since it is extensively foreshadowed by Livy (cf. Levene (1993), 105–7), is explicitly mentioned in Obsequens (see *ad loc.*), and also was relatively prominent in the exemplary tradition (Val. Max. 1.5.9 and 2.7.15, both with Paris' and Nepotianus' epitomes; also Frontin., *Strat.* 4.1.46).

As for the Celtiberi, apart from Gracchus' victory (41.2n.), Livy records a further victory at 41.26, in 174. Obsequens 10 also records a victory in 175 (see *ad loc.*). On the face of things this is an error, since Livy 41.26.1 confirms that no campaign took place between Gracchus' departure and the one reported here in 174, but his language appears to set the entire war shortly after the arrival of Ap. Claudius Centho as praetor in 175: 'they rebelled on the arrival of Appius Claudius, and began the war &c.' (41.26.1: *rebellarunt sub adventum Ap. Claudi, orsique bellum sunt &c.*). Hence Obsequens must have deduced that the war, although recorded by Livy in the year 174, actually took place in 175; and arguably he was right to do so (so W-M *ad loc.*, *contra* Briscoe (2012a), 134).

Perseus' diplomatic manoeuvres in Greece are described by Livy at 41.19.3–11 (though the end is lost in the lacuna between 41.19 and 41.20) and 41.22.4–24.20; his embassy to Carthage is referred to at 41.22.1–3 (it was presumably dispatched in one of the lacunae earlier in the book). P. relatively speaking makes more of the latter than the former, which is not the balance in Livy; but this presumably reflects the iconic status of Carthage as the opponent of Rome, as well as the fact that the longest episode in Livy is Perseus' attempt to curry favour with the Achaeans (41.23–4), which proves unsuccessful when they ultimately reaffirm their support of Rome (41.24.19–20). The essential point, however, is that P., like Livy (41.19.4; cf. 41.23.9–13), treats Perseus' actions as clearly aiming at war with Rome.

praeterea res adversus Liguras et Histros et Sardos et Celtiberos...prospere gestas...continet: Cf. 2.16n., 3.10n.

compluribus ducibus: Cf. 12.3n.

initia belli Macedonici: P. had already referred to the moves Philip (allegedly) made against Rome in Book 39 as the *initia...belli Macedonici* (39.8). His repetition of the phrase here may not be formally inconsistent (*initia* do not necessarily occur at a single moment), but in the absence of any further explanation of the relative weight to be attached to the activities of Perseus here and those of Philip a decade or so earlier, it gives the impression of clumsiness.

nocte: P. repeats this information from Livy (41.22.2 *noctu*): it is clearly meant to prove the sinister nature of the meeting, since the rule at Rome was that the Senate did not meet at night (cf. Mommsen, *StR*^{3} III 919–20).

et...audita erat: sc. *legatio*. The unexpressed change of subject after *et* would be unacceptable in the classical period; accordingly Jahn emended *et* to *ea*. However, the grammatical licence is not uncommon in later Latin (cf. H-S 733), and the MS reading should be retained.

sollicitabat: 'Was inciting to revolt' (*OLD s.v. sollicito* 5b).

Book 42

42.1 *Desecration of the temple of Juno Lacinia.* Corresponds to Livy 42.3. The episode appears also in Val. Max. 1.1.20 (also the epitomes of Paris and Nepotianus); Valerius incorporates the aftermath from later in the book (42.28.10–12), where Fulvius commits suicide from grief at the news that one of his sons had been killed and the other was seriously ill, which Livy explicitly connects with his actions here. P. has nothing of this, although he clearly was aware of the later passage when writing his note (see below): interestingly, Paris, too, ignores that aspect of the story, suggesting that for him, as for P., the story centred on the piety of the Senate in repairing Fulvius' wrongdoing, and the idea of divine retribution against Fulvius was less resonant.

templum Iunonis Laciniae...spoliavit: In his main narrative, Livy does not use the word *spolio*, and twice speaks of *aedes Iunonis Laciniae*, not *templum* (42.3.1–2; he uses *templum* later in the story, but without the name of the goddess). P. appears, as often, to have derived his language from Livy's later reference back to the story rather than from the main narrative: see 42.28.12 *Iunonis Laciniae iram ob spoliatum templum*. This may also serve to remind the rare reader who knew Livy's text of the sequel which P. ostensibly leaves aside.

aedificabat: The oldest MS reads *dedicabat*, which is accepted by all editors; its appearance in the Italian tradition as well shows that it was the reading of the archetype. However, the Parisinus reads *edificabat*, and this should be preferred, for all that it probably represents a scribal correction: the imperfect *dedicabat* reads a little oddly of a temple which was still incomplete and would not be dedicated until later, and also Livy's own account of Fulvius' desecration twice uses *aedifico* (42.3.2, 42.3.9) and never *dedico*.

tegulae...reportatae: Cf. Livy 42.3.10 *tegulae reportandae*.

42.2 *Anti-Roman actions of Perseus; Eumenes complains to the Senate.* Corresponds to Livy 42.11.1–18.5, 42.25–6 (cf. 42.6.3). P. explains the beginning of the Third Macedonian War in terms of wrongs committed by Perseus against Rome, combined with a complaint before the Senate against him by Eumenes of Pergamon. This is in a certain sense a reasonable representation of Livy, who gives a detailed description of Eumenes' address to the Senate at 42.11–13, and also explicitly refers to *iniuriae* which Perseus committed by violating the treaty between Rome and Macedon (42.25.7), and which, when Perseus refused to make restitution for them, led the Romans the following year to declare war against him (42.3n.). However, there is also a remarkable omission, namely Perseus' attempt to assassinate Eumenes at Delphi (42.15–16), along with the information that he was also plotting to murder various leading Romans (42.17). This is, for Livy, a key reason that the Romans determined on war (42.18.1), and it is presented as such also in most of the Greek sources: it is listed as a major charge against Perseus in the letter sent by the Romans to Delphi (*SIG* 643), as well as Plb. 22.18.5 (cf. 27.6.2) and App., *Mac.* 11.4, while it is described in anecdotes in D.S. 29.34.2, Plu., *Reg. Imp. Apophth.* 184A–B, *Frat. Am.* 489D–F. However, P.'s omission is less surprising in the light of the way the tradition about the war developed: the later historians of the war (Florus, Justin, Eutropius, Orosius, Zonaras) uniformly ignore the episode, despite its dramatic nature and the opportunity it gave to show Perseus in the worst light. In that regard, it is perhaps more noteworthy that P. included Eumenes' appeal, which is likewise unmentioned by those later historians (though it appears in App., *Mac.* 11.1–3); as with his account of the Second Macedonian War (cf. 31.1–3n.), the idea that Rome is acting in support of her allies matters more to him than the specifics of Perseus' violations.

Asiae rex…Macedoniae rege: Cf. 34.8n.

referuntur: Cf. 16.1n.

42.3 *Beginning of the Third Macedonian War.* The declaration of war, the Roman preparations for war, the negotiations between the two sides, and the Roman attack on Macedonia along with the initial fighting, occupies the last two-thirds of Livy's book (42.29–67). P. for his narrative of the war (but see 42.5n.) selects only the initial declaration of war (42.30.8–11), which he, like Livy, directly connects to the violations referred to in his previous notice; he then moves ahead to the activities of the consul P. Licinius Crassus, who in Livy does not leave for the war until 42.49, and whose campaigns are described in 42.55, 42.57–60, 42.62, and 42.64–7. Here, too, this is relatively unsurprising: Crassus, and the initial defeat that he received at the hands of Perseus, is likewise the focus of other later Latin writers (Just. 33.1.4–5, Eutr. 4.6.3, Oros. 4.20.37; also Plu., *Aem.* 9.2 and *Reg. Imp. Apophth* 197E–F), apart from Florus, who skips over the opening phases of the war altogether. Only in the Greek tradition does one find a fuller account: so the fragmentary remnants of Diodorus Siculus (30.1, 30.7.1) and Appian (*Mac.* 11.5–9) include the embassy sent by Perseus to Rome (Livy 42.36.1–7): in their versions they take place before the declaration of war, unlike in Livy, and in Diodorus' case the Roman deceit of Perseus as well (cf. Livy 42.47), while Zonaras' abridgement of Dio mentions not only Crassus as commander, but also the praetors Cn. Sicinius and C. Lucretius Gallus (9.22.5). It is more unexpected that P. does not mention Crassus' refusal after his defeat to accept Perseus' peace proposal, a story found in Just. and Eutr., as well as Plu., *Reg. Imp. Apophth.*

levibusque †expeditionibus† equestribus proeliis: The MSS reading is extremely improbable. The two phrases in apposition are uncharacteristic of P.'s style, and *levis expeditio* is in any case unparalleled and hard to comprehend in this context. Rossbach tentatively proposed deleting *equestribus proeliis* as a gloss, which would solve the first problem but not the second. My suspicion is that *expeditionibus* conceals a form of *expediti*, which was introduced as a gloss for *levibus*: Livy refers numerous times in the episode to the soldiers involved in the two battles being a mix of cavalry and light-armed troops, using *levis armatura* for the latter (42.57.6, 42.57.12, 42.58.2, 42.58.6, 42.58.11, 42.58.12, 42.59.1 42.64.5, 42.64.8, 42.65.12). One might, accordingly, consider deleting *expeditionibus*, replacing it with *et* or *atque*: *levia proelia* is a common phrase in Livy and other authors. However, the meaning of *levibusque et equestribus proeliis* would not be 'battles involving light-armed troops and cavalry', but 'minor battles and ones involving cavalry' (cf. *TLL* VII.2 1213.30–55). It is possible that P., in his compressed manner, might have used the phrase in the former sense, in which case it is very likely that a copyist would feel it necessary to gloss *levibus* with *expeditis*. But while this explains the transmitted text, one should not introduce by conjecture a phrase which requires a strained reading of the Latin; it may be that some other term has dropped out, or that a further corruption has occurred. Accordingly, I prefer to obelize.

dubio eventu: The chief MSS have *eventu* alone, with no word describing the nature of the outcome. Various later MSS attempted to supplement it so as to describe a victory or defeat, inserting (e.g.) *prospero* or *felici* on the one hand, or *improspero* or *parum felici* (so the *editio princeps*) on the other; along similar lines Rossbach tentatively offered *parum prospero*. But P. never uses *eventu* with these adjectives in the context of a victory or defeat, and *proeliis* in any case manifestly shows that P. has in mind both of Crassus' battles: his initial defeat followed by a narrow victory (Oros. 4.20.37 and Zonar. 9.22.5 likewise refer to both). Far more likely, therefore, is the supplement *dubio* found in one late MS: P. uses *dubio eventu* at 13.5, 74.2, 92.1, and 128.1, the last of these of a set of two battles, as here. Another possibility would be *vario eventu*, as at 46.9, 58.6, 124.1, and 129.1, but the first two of these appear in the context of general summaries of 'other things' in the books rather than specific battles; hence *dubio* in this context is marginally more probable.

42.4 *Dispute between Masinissa and the Carthaginians*. Corresponds to Livy 42.23–4. After giving a summary of the opening phases of the Macedonian War that extends to the end of Livy's book, P. returns to an episode from much earlier in the book, and indeed from the previous year, an episode which looms much less large in Livy's narrative—Livy in this book concentrates on the Macedonian War with an unusually intense focus. The reason for P.'s interest is likely to be that he has an eye to the longer-term implications of the dispute between Masinissa and Carthage: this will ultimately prove to be a trigger for the Third Punic War, and, as such, P. pays a great deal of attention to it in recounting the origins of that war (47.7, 47.12, 48.2–3; in those notices P. appears to allude back to his phrasing here—see *ad loc.*). In Livy the border tensions between Masinissa and the

Carthaginians have been marked in a series of minor notices (33.47.7–8. 34.62, 40.17.1–6), and the one here is the last and longest in his surviving text (unless the border question was alluded to in the lacuna after 43.3.5–7, the surviving part of which recounts an unrelated dispute between Carthage and Numidia). P., accordingly, takes this opportunity to prepare for his account of the Third Punic War, which he will turn into the single most prominent episode in his entire summary of Livy's 142 books.

P. unsurprisingly does not provide any of the details of the dispute. More noteworthy is that Livy clearly slants his account against Masinissa: he sets out in detail the Carthaginians' complaints of illegal encroachment on their territory; Gulussa, Masinissa's son, does not reply to the substance, but only impugns the motives underlying the complaint, and the Romans, while formally deferring a decision until the parties can each offer their case in full, couch the deferral in the form of a strong warning to Masinissa not to seek to expand his territory at the Carthaginians' expense (cf. also 42.29.8–10, where Livy gives a cynical account of Masinissa's calculations in supporting Rome during the Third Macedonian War). P., however, does not replicate that slant: he presents the dispute entirely neutrally. This has a bearing on possible differences between him and Livy with regard to their handling of the moral issues surrounding the Third Punic War, especially in Books 48 and 49: see further *ad locc.*

fuit lis. dies his: Jahn's correction of the incomprehensible *fuit dictis* of the chief MSS.

dies his a senatu ad disceptandum datus: Cf. Livy 42.24.6 *ut ad disceptandum veniant*. P.'s summary is misleading, in as much as he indicates that the Senate specified a particular date for the hearing, whereas in Livy it is couched much more vaguely: Masinissa was to send an embassy to defend his actions 'as soon as possible' (42.24.6 *quam primum*), and also to inform the Carthaginians when he did so, in order that they could state their case at that time as well. P. also omits the fact that the envoys from the two sides were to argue their case at Rome. The upshot is that he implies, without actually stating, that the hearing he mentions here was the one which took place in Book 47, when Roman ambassadors were sent to Africa to examine the border dispute—as noted above, he refers to that episode in language which appears to allude back to the notice here. In historical terms, that is impossible, since the embassy in question took place rather more than a decade later; but the compression of P.'s narrative obscures that time difference. In reality it is likely that Masinissa never followed through with what, according to Livy, he was instructed to do, and the Romans, occupied as they were with the Macedonian War, in which they were using Masinissa as an ally, never pressed him on it (so, implicitly, Walsh (1965), 158–9).

42.5 *Embassies to allies.* Corresponds to Livy 42.26.7–9, 42.37, 42.43.4–45.8. Livy has two separate accounts of Roman envoys in the run-up to the Third

Macedonian War to gain support from their allies: a brief one in 172, and then a much longer one in 171. In the first the Rhodians are described as wavering in their alliance with Rome, but by the time of the second (42.45.3-7), even before the envoys arrived, they had determined, under the influence of Agesilochus, to provide the Romans with extensive support, and had a fleet of forty ships ready at the time the Romans arrived; he adds that they were not swayed from this by the subsequent embassy sent to them by Perseus (42.46.1-6). It is sometimes argued, partly because of apparent overlap in their personnel, that the two separate embassies are a doublet (so esp. Schmitt (1957), 212-14, Walbank (1979), 294-5, *contra* Deininger (1971), 185-6): on this view, only one embassy was despatched to Rhodes, which was reported differently in two of Livy's sources—the second one clearly derives from Plb. 27.3, the first perhaps from an annalistic source. Whether or not that is the case, P. bases his account on the first rather than on the second (cf. below), presumably because its more sceptical attitude towards Rhodian support for Rome anticipates the detachment of Rhodes from the Roman side later in the war (see 44.2n.).

legati missi ad socias civitates regesque rogandos: Cf. Livy 42.26.7-8 *qui circa socios reges missi erant redierunt legati...et civitates socias adisse.*

in fide permanerent: Cf. Livy 42.26.8 *in fide permanere.*

dubitantibus Rhodiis: For the sentence-structure, with the appended ablative absolute offering a crucial qualification to the main notice, cf. 29.6n.

42.6 *Census.* Corresponds to Livy 42.10.1-4. As usual, P. presents Livy's census data; in this case he does so out of chronological sequence. In Livy it had appeared early in the book, not long after the account of the misbehaviour of the censor Q. Fulvius Flaccus (42.1n.); P. reserves it for the end, before his final 'round-up' of other events (42.7), thus diminishing any connection between the formal record of the census and the misdeeds of the particular censor.

lustrum a censoribus conditum est: Cf. 11.5n.

censa sunt civium capita: Cf. 3.3n.

CCLXVII milia CCXXXI: Livy 42.10.2 gives the figure as 269,015. It is more likely that the *Periochae* figure for the 'hundreds' is correct, especially given the corrupt state of the sole MS of Livy: it is easier to imagine CCXXXI being corrupted into XV than vice versa (Briscoe (2012a), 183).

The 'thousands' figure is more problematic, since the MSS of P. vary between CCLXVII and CCXLVII, neither of which is Livy's. Whichever we decide for P should not be corrected on the basis of Livy, since the corruption between each version and Livy's figure is easy in either direction (even if it is not what Livy wrote, it could well have been what P. read in his text of Livy), but it is unclear which should be preferred. On balance I decided to print the former, which is the version in N, which is on the whole more reliable than the tradition represented by the other MSS, but it could well be that the second version is the correct one.

42.7 *Wars in Corsica and Liguria.* As noted above (42.4n.), Livy in Book 42 has an unusually single-minded focus on the Macedonian War; the only other campaigns described in the course of the book are in the two areas which P. mentions here. The war in Corsica is only referred to very briefly (42.7.1–2); the actual fighting in Liguria also occupies very little of Livy's text (42.7.3–8.3, 42.21.2), but it looms much larger because of the controversy in the Senate, which objects to the mistreatment of the Ligurians by the consul M. Popillius Laenas, a controversy which continues into the following year, and which Livy, who in this book pays particular attention to Roman ethical lapses (Levene (1993), 108–13), narrates at far greater length (42.8.4–9.6, 42.10.9–12, 42.21.3–5, 42.21.8–22.8, 42.28.3). P., as usual lacking Livy's interest in nuanced moral questions, shows no interest in this.

res praeterea adversus Corsos et Liguras prospere gestas continet: Cf. 2.16n., 3.10n.

Book 43

43.1 *Prosecutions of Roman generals*. Livy records the prosecutions of Roman generals in two places in the surviving portions of Book 43: 43.2, where the prosecutions are of two governors of Spain, P. Furius Philus and M. Matienus (a third governor, M. Titinius, was also prosecuted but acquitted), and 43.7.5–8.10, where C. Lucretius Gallus is prosecuted for his behaviour in Greece (though cf. also 43.3n.). The position of P.'s notice at the start of the book suggests the first prosecution, but the language is more closely connected with the second. P.'s attention to this is interesting, in as much as it he tends to pay far less attention to Roman wrongdoing than Livy does: he moreover follows through the theme into the next two notices (see 43.3n.). With the first two, however, the focus is at least as much on the success of the Roman state in overcoming the misbehaviour of its representatives as on the misbehaviour itself: this is hardly the balance in Livy, as far as we can tell from the surviving portions of his text (cf. Luce (1977), 266–8, Levene (1993), 113–16).

No other prosecutions from the period covered by the book are known, apart from that of the consul P. Licinius Crassus, covered in P.'s next notice (43.2n.). At 43.5.6 the Senate offer the Gauls who had suffered under the consul C. Cassius Longinus the opportunity to accuse him in person after his return from Macedon, where he was serving as *tribunus militum*; but it appears from 44.31.15 that he had not yet returned at that point, and his censorship in 154 (48.1n.) makes it unlikely that he suffered any serious consequences for his actions.

praetores aliquot eo quod avare et crudeliter: Cf. Livy 43.7.8 *tum quae primo C. Lucretius in populares suos praetor Romanus superbe avare crudeliter fecisset.*

damnati sunt: Of the three prosecutions recorded by Livy, only Lucretius was actually convicted (43.8.10); Furius and Matienus both went into voluntary exile before their trial (43.2.10). P.'s plural *damnati* is accordingly misleading, but he may well have seen voluntary exile before trial as tantamount to condemnation (cf. e.g. Lact., *Inst.* 2.4.34 and *Vir. Ill.* 81.3 for Cicero's 'conviction' of Verres).

43.2 *Misdeeds of Crassus in Greece; restitution made by the Senate.* The aftermath of this is mentioned in passing by Livy at 43.4.5, and implicitly at 43.4.11 (see below), referring to atrocities that Crassus committed; the story itself must have appeared in the long lacuna between 43.3 and 43.4. The only other surviving narrative account is in Zonar. 9.22.6, who says little more than P.: according to him, Crassus attacked the Greek cities controlled by the Macedonians, failed to take most of them, but succeeded in capturing some; of those he captured, he destroyed some completely and sold the inhabitants into slavery. The Romans put Crassus on trial and fined him; the cities he had captured were set free, and the enslaved captives in Italy were repurchased and, presumably, set free.

One of the cities captured by Crassus was certainly Coroneia. Fragments of the senatorial decree concerning Coroneia survive (*SEG* 19.374 = *RDGE* no. 3), which mention him as the commander who took the city (cf. Livy 42.67.12, where the Thebans appeal to him for help against Coroneia). The surviving portions of the decree do not refer to the elements mentioned by P. or Zonar. (they rule that the pro-Roman inhabitants of the city should have their property restored to them); but at Livy 43.4.11 a senatorial ruling over the city of Abdera, which had been sacked and whose inhabitants had been enslaved by L. Hortensius, the praetor of 170 (see 43.3n.), is said to be the same as that which they had decreed with Coroneia. The similarity of the circumstances of Abdera to that of the cities referred to here in the *Periochae* and in Zonar. makes it probable either that the lost portion of the Coroneia decree included the provisions that P. and Zonar. describe, or, more plausibly, that those provisions, despite what P. says here (*ex S.C. …restituti sunt*), were not officially part of the decree itself, but were given as supplementary oral instructions for the magistrates to carry out.[49] However, there is a question about whether P.'s notice here did indeed cover Coroneia, or if it was dealing solely with other cities captured later: see below.

The entire episode reveals something of the tension surrounding Rome's relationship with Macedonian-aligned cities at the start of the war. Coroneia had a history of bad relations with Rome (Livy 33.29.6–12, 36.6.1, 36.20.1–4); it was one of the cities that had been induced to join Perseus (Plb. 27.5; cf. 27.1.8), and it was engaged in hostilities against a city which supported Rome (Livy 42.67.12). For those reasons alone it was, in Roman terms, a legitimate target for extreme measures (cf. Harris (1979a), 51–3), and a general like Crassus who on his own initiative took such measures might well have seen himself as acting within accepted norms.[50] Nevertheless, the wisdom, and indeed the morality, of acting in this way could readily be contested. That various individuals in the cities supported Rome was clearly one concern, as is apparent from the Coroneia decree (as also the near-contemporary decree concerning Thisbe, sacked by the praetor Lucretius in 171: *SIG* 646 = *RDGE* no. 2). But in the case of Coroneia and other cities, the Senate appears to have provided relief not only for the pro-Romans, but also for the mass of the enslaved, who presumably included many supporters of Macedon. It may have been felt, at a time when the Romans were competing for Greek support against Perseus, that a reputation for clemency would serve them better in the long run. In ethical terms, the representation of such debates in Livy and other historians shows that *crudelitas*, however ill-defined, was not seen as a desirable quality even towards defeated enemies: we should grant that the language is invented, but it at least shows that in the time of the historians ethical

---

[49] So Burton (2017), 207–9, noting that this appears to be what Livy describes as happening with Abdera at 43.4.12–13.
[50] See in general Eckstein (1987) for the personal initiative allowed to individual commanders in developing Roman policy towards conquered communities.

ideas could, in some circumstances, conflict with these norms of military behaviour and provide the guiding principles through which such behaviour was judged.[51] It is doubtless also the case that Crassus, in being prosecuted (if indeed he was, as Zonaras claims), fell victim to political rivalry at Rome, but his rivals could not have used his treatment of these cities against him were it simply an uncontested norm that it was appropriate for him to act in this way.

P. Licinius Crassus procos.: *RE* 60, *MRR* I 416. He was consul in 171, having previously been praetor in 176. Subsequent to this year, he is only heard of once more, when he was sent in 167 to mediate between Pergamum and the Galatians.

P.'s description of him as proconsul implies that the actions mentioned here took place in the consular year 170; however, Livy's reference at 43.4.11 to the decree over Coroneia having been in the previous year shows that he narrated it under 171, the year of Crassus' consulship. That the decree concerning Coroneia was, contrary to Livy's statement, promulgated in 170 has sometimes been argued, largely on the basis of there being insufficient time for it to occur in 171, but also partly on the basis of P.'s reference here to Crassus as proconsul (so esp. Schmidt (1881), Robert (1938), 290–2). The chronological argument is rightly rejected by Errington (1974); but his only comment on this passage of P. (84 n. 4) is unsatisfactory: he appears to assume that the notice does not cover Coroneia, but is confined to other cities that Crassus sacked and enslaved during his time as proconsul. It seems, however, highly unlikely that Livy both described in 171 the sacking of Coroneia and the subsequent senatorial decree, and then in his narrative of 170 described Crassus sacking a number of cities along with a further senatorial decree separate from the one for Coroneia. It is far more likely that Livy described the sack of Coroneia and the senatorial decree in 171, then added one or two cities assaulted by Crassus after the end of his consulship, and that P., summarizing this in accordance with his usual practice, attached the entire notice to the second year and referred to Crassus as if he were proconsul throughout (compare 11.1n., and cf. Mommsen (1872), 298). An alternative possibility is that P. is dependent on a different source, according to which Crassus did indeed sack Coroneia in 170 and the senatorial decree was likewise in that year. Even if that is so, it would still be the case that Livy's chronology should be preferred, since he is more likely than P. to have accurate information about the timing of Crassus' campaign (not least from Polybius). Either way, P.'s notice should be assumed to cover the sack of Coroneia.

corripuit: An all but unparalleled use of the verb. *moenia corripere* is occasionally found in early imperial poetry, used metonymically for the sack of a city (Lucan

---

[51] See Burton (2011), esp. 246–353 for a careful and nuanced examination of the ways in which Roman ethical commitments, and especially their prior relationships with the peoples in question, could temper the theoretical licence given to conquerors for brutality: in his words (Burton (2011), 248), the Romans were in part governed by 'the constraints of their discursive practices'.

2.99–100, Stat., *Theb.* 3.248), but *urbem corripere* appears nowhere but here. P. may be drawing the phrase from Livy, but whether or not that is the case, his heightened language emphasizes the level of Crassus' atrocity.

ab eo sub corona venierant: *sub corona venire* is a standard phrase for selling slaves at auction (*TLL* IV 984.84–985.18); Livy employs it at 43.4.10 for the parallel case of Abdera (cf. above). *ab* is not usually used of the enslaver, but cf. H-S 256 for the idiomatic use of *ab* with intransitive verbs.

For the practice of enslaving war captives see esp. Gaca (2010): she emphasizes the extent to which doing so was an accepted norm of warfare, as well as the degree of violence involved.

43.3 *Atrocities by fleet commanders.* Livy describes the aftermath of two atrocities against friendly states committed by the commanders of the fleet. First, the people of Abdera complain to the Senate about L. Hortensius' sack of the city, his execution of the leaders, and his selling the remainder of the population into slavery, all because they were unable to supply him with the money and supplies he had requisitioned: the Senate vote to rectify the situation in the same terms as they had with Coroneia (43.4.8–12; cf. 43.2n.). Shortly afterwards, the inhabitants of Chalcis make a longer complaint against Hortensius, and also against his predecessor C. Lucretius Gallus, whose policies Hortensius was apparently continuing: Lucretius had looted the city and enslaved some of its citizens. Lucretius—but not Hortensius—is prosecuted and convicted (43.7.5–8.10). In addition, Livy had referred earlier in more general terms to the cruelty and avarice of Lucretius in Greece (43.4.5). Presumably the attacks on Abdera and Chalcis by Lucretius and Hortensius had been described by Livy in the long lacuna between 43.3 and 43.4, and it is those that P. is referring to here.

The slight complication is that P. had already mentioned the prosecution of Lucretius over Chalcis under a different heading in 43.1 (see *ad loc.*). It is possible that this note is intended only to refer to Hortensius' actions and to other atrocities committed by Lucretius, excluding what he did at Chalcis; but to insist on that would be to assume a precision of reference that P. often does not show: this would not be the only time that he duplicated material between two different notices (cf. e.g. 27.8n., 31.7n., 32.9n.).

No other accounts of these events are known, apart from a brief anecdote about the sack of Abdera in D.S. 30.6, suggesting that it was engineered by Eumenes of Pergamum, who arranged for a traitor to admit his forces into the city. A fragmentary inscription (*SEG* 47.1646) has been argued to have been erected in the wake of the sack, and to describe the sufferings of the inhabitants (Marek (1997)); but note the cautious reservations of Eilers (2002), 118–19.

item: P. marks this as the third in his sequence of notices about the atrocities committed by Roman commanders (cf. 43.1n.).

socios: The envoys from Chalcis describe themselves as *socii populi Romani* at 43.7.10. The precise relationship between the Romans and Abdera at this time is not recorded, but the circumstances Livy sets out concerning its capture and from the Abderans' subsequent appeal the presumption is that they were seen at least as *amici*.

43.4 *Victories of Perseus*. P., exceptionally, uses his regular 'round-up' passage to record victories, not by Romans, but those by their chief antagonist in the book, albeit over non-Roman enemies. From time to time he has touched on non-Roman events in these passages (e.g. 14.8, 24.5, 31.7, 35.6, 39.8, 41.6; cf. 46.9), but this is the first time a non-Roman becomes the sole focus. After Book 45 this becomes a more regular part of his practice (48.19, 52.7–10, 60.10, 62.6, 68.8, 74.8, 76.8, 78.4, 81.3, 82.5, 100.5, 101.5), but the passage here is nevertheless unique in one respect: that he employs of a foreigner the entire *res...prospere gestas continet* formula, which he usually restricts to Roman victories. The result is that Perseus is established as an effective counterbalance to Rome, at a time when P. is showing the Romans descending to a low point (41.1–3nn.).

Perseus' victories over the Dardanians must have appeared in the lacuna between 43.3 and 43.4, as appears from 43.18.2 (cf. 43.20.1). Little more is known about them than P. records—there are passing mentions at Plb. 28.8.2 and Livy 45.5.3; Plu., *Aem.* 9.5 refers to 10,000 Dardanians killed in the battle, and it is possible that the fragment at D.S. 30.4, describing a victory over an otherwise unknown town called Chalestrum, where Perseus' troops massacred all the inhabitants (including some to whom he had promised safe conduct), was part of this campaign (so e.g. Hammond and Walbank (1988), 521, *contra* e.g. Papazoglou (1978), 169). Plutarch treats the campaign as a sign of Perseus' confidence: he was so contemptuous of the Romans after his victories that he could afford to conduct an extraneous campaign; but it is more probable that it is to be understood as an attempt to secure his northern frontier, of a piece with his attempted alliance with Illyria (below). It is worth noting that the consul of 171, C. Cassius Longinus, had apparently made an aborted attempt to attack Macedon from that direction (Livy 43.1.4–12; cf. 43.5.1–6): given the geography, it was unrealistic, but that may not have been apparent to either the Romans or the Macedonians. If, as is not improbable, some report of this had reached Perseus, he might well have wanted to secure his position in that region (cf. 43.18.3).

An account of Perseus' victories in Illyria, on the other hand, does survive in Livy (43.18.3–19.13), in a passage apparently derived from Polybius (cf. Plb. 28.8–9, and also D.S. 30.9, Plu., *Aem.* 9.6). P. does not, however, mention that he was unsuccessful in his chief aim, namely to pressure Gentius into an alliance with him (43.20.1–3; cf. 43.18.3, 43.23.8). This may be because at this point P. is interested only in an image of Macedonian success to set against the problems being faced by Rome; but it also alters the dynamic of the narrative involving Gentius when he reappears in Book 44, where P. will manipulate Livy's order in such a way as to imply a different relationship between the Romans, Perseus, and Gentius from the one Livy himself offers (44.5n., 44.7n.).

res…prospere gestas continet: Cf. 2.16n., 3.10n.

Dardanis: A people controlling an area corresponding approximately to the northern part of the modern Republic of North Macedonia, Kosovo, and the southern portion of Serbia; they are here mentioned for the first time in P., although they had been an intermittent presence in Livy's text since 26.25.3. At various times they had fallen under the sway of Macedon, but had been largely independent of them since the early third century BC, fighting numerous wars to maintain that independence, but also sometimes themselves attacking Macedon; they allied themselves with Rome against Macedon at the time of the Second Macedonian War (Livy 31.28.1–2). Ancient ethnographic writing saw the Dardanians as a subset of the Illyrians (so e.g. Str. 7.5.6–7, App., *Ill.* 2.5), but that reflects the fact that the 'Illyrians' themselves were not a single group, but a generic term used by the Greeks and the Romans for the peoples of the central and northern Balkans (see 20.6n.).

On the history of the Dardanians see Papazoglou (1978), 131–269.

cuius rex erat Gentius: P. introduces Gentius in a manner that implies that he will be significant—he would not usually mention the king of a defeated nation in a passage of this sort; the reader is prepared for his reappearance in Book 44.

43.5 *Suppression of uprising in Spain.* The passage immediately after the long lacuna in Livy's book, 43.4.1–4, describes the aftermath of a rebellion, where the heads of their leaders are brought into the enemy camp, after apparently having launched some sort of private attack. The panic that ensues leads to the rebels deciding to surrender, putting all of the blame on their two leaders; the Roman praetor pacifies the province without further fighting. Although neither Spain nor the name of any individual is mentioned, this must be the very end of the revolt of Olonicus mentioned by P. This is confirmed by the only other surviving account of the episode, by Flor. 1.33.13–14, who fills in some missing details: Olonicus was a charismatic Celtiberian, who claimed prophetic inspiration and had a silver spear that was supposedly given by the gods. He attempted to infiltrate the Roman camp and attack the commander, but was killed by a sentry. Florus' account is admittedly problematic, in as much as he refers to the Roman commander as a consul rather than a praetor, and he also differs on the name of the rebel leader (see below), but everything else is at least compatible with P., and there is no active reason to question it. The name of the other leader mentioned by Livy, and his role in the episode, is nowhere recorded: it is likely that Olonicus alone was the centre of Livy's attention, as he is in P. and Florus.

Olonico: His name is given in some MSS of Florus as Olyndicus, in others as Solondicus, but P. is more likely to reflect Livy than Florus is, and Livy, given Florus' overall unreliability, is likely to be closer to the original version of the name. An additional consideration is that a series of Celtiberian coins (*CNH* 278 nos. 1–3), minted at this period, include ones with the legend Oilaunicos, which appears to be a name of the people of a town, although the town in question is otherwise unknown (Untermann (1975), 85–6, 271–3). At the very least this demonstrates that the name transmitted by P. is authentically Celtiberian, and it may be more informative still: it suggests that Olonicus may have used a name reflecting his local community.

43.6 *Lepidus chosen as princeps senatus*. Corresponds to Livy 43.15.6. Livy's account of the censorship in this book is unusually extensive: he recounts the contentious levy they conducted, their conflict with the *publicani* over contracts, which escalated into a major dispute with a tribune who prosecuted them for *perduellio*. The last was a relatively well-known story, referred to in Cic., *Rep.* 6.2 (*ap.* Gell. 7.16.11), Val. Max. 6.5.3 (also Paris' epitome), and *Vir. Ill.* 57.3; nevertheless, P. passes over every aspect of the censorship except for the choosing of Lepidus as *princeps senatus*, something that Livy brushes aside in a sentence. The reason, however, is apparent from P.'s later handling of the story. This is, Livy notes, the third censorship in which Lepidus was chosen as *princeps senatus*—he had not made any similar comment on the previous two occasions, 40.51.1 and 41.27.1, which is presumably why P. was not alerted to its significance, but this notice begins a sequence in P.: he marks further selections of Lepidus as *princeps senatus* at 46.6 and 47.4, and finally, at 48.7, begins his account of Lepidus' exemplary instructions for his funeral (cf. *ad loc.*) by noting that he had been *princeps senatus* through six censorships. P. makes active use of the abridgement of his narrative to link passages whose connection would have been far less apparent in Livy's original text.

M. Aemilius Lepidus a censoribus princeps lectus: Cf. Livy 43.15.6 *M. Aemilius Lepidus princeps a tertiis iam censoribus lectus*. Some late MSS add *senatus* after *princeps*, and this reading is accepted by all editors. However, the fact that the same wording occurs in the MSS at 47.7 suggests that it is not simply a random scribal error, the more so since the passage of Livy that P. is imitating here does not itself include *senatus*. In this passage of Livy it is to be understood from the previous clause (*senatum deinde censores legerunt*), but even in the Republican period the *princeps senatus* was sometimes called *princeps* alone (Cic., *De Orat.* 1.211, *Brut.* 108, with Douglas (1966), 90). In any case the office was long obsolete in P.'s day (Mommsen, *StR*³ III 970–1), and there is no reason to believe that he had a clear picture of the nomenclature.

Book 44

44.1 *Q. Marcius Philippus invades Macedonia.* Corresponds to Livy 44.1–13. In Livy, the success of Philippus in managing his initial crossing over the mountains into Macedonia is partly undermined by the outcome; at first he has some success in driving Perseus away and capturing a number of cities, including Perseus' base at Dium, but Perseus almost immediately recaptures Dium (44.8.5), and subsequent attacks on other cities by the praetor C. Marcius Figulus and by Philippus himself are unsuccessful (44.10–13). P. thus—at least on the surface (see below)—gives a stronger impression of Roman success than Livy himself did. On the other hand, he also passes over the aspect of the campaign which attracted most attention from other ancient writers, namely Perseus' ignominious panic at Philippus' arrival, where he is caught unawares in the bath and orders his treasure to be thrown into the sea and his dockyards to be burned (Livy 44.6.1–2): see D.S. 30.10–11, App., *Mac.* 15–16, Flor. 1.28.5–6 (the last two 'improve' the story by substituting the fleet for the dockyards); cf. Ampel. 16.4. P. shows apparently untrammelled Roman successes against a worthy opponent, rather than the Romans making headway but failing to crush a coward.

Q. Marcius Philippus: Unusually, P. doesn't describe him as consul.

per invios saltus penetravit in Macedoniam: The phrasing does not derive from the language Livy used at the time of Philippus' invasion, but corresponds far more closely to 44.20.2 *exercitum per invios saltus in Macedoniam inductum*, where the senatorial envoys report on the state of the campaign in Macedonia.[52] It is not at all unusual for P. to draw his language from Livy's later reference back to the events rather than the main narrative of those events; in this case, however, it is noteworthy that the envoys' report is dismissive, indeed scathing, about Philippus' campaign, presenting it as a substantial failure. P. ostensibly, as noted above, presents a picture of complete success on Philippus' part, and the reader who did not know Livy would have no reason to take it any other way; but, as at other times (cf. e.g. 22.12n.), he points up the difference between Livy's presentation and his own for the small minority of readers who knew Livy's work.

complures: Cf. 12.3n.

44.2 *Rhodian attempt to reconcile Rome and Macedon.* Corresponds to Livy 44.14.5–15.8. P., however, changes the emphasis of Livy's account. In Livy the Rhodians say that they have sent a similar message to Perseus, insisting that he make peace with Rome, and they tell both sides that they will join forces against

---

[52] Note that *invius saltus* is a distinctively Livian phrase, used by him on five other occasions (9.14.10, 9.38.5, 21.25.13, 31.2.10, 40.27.11), but hardly ever found in other writers (though cf. Amm. 19.18.1, Salv., *Gub.* 6.2.10).

whichever one refuses peace; they also insist on peace between Macedon and Rome, but they do not demand *amicitia*. P. takes a proposal which Livy explicitly treats as outrageous, and makes it appear even more high-handed than Livy had done, as well as addressed directly against Roman interests. In this way he reinforces the doubts he introduced two books earlier about Rhodian support for Rome (42.5n.).

minantes ut Perseo auxilio essent: *minor* usually constructs with the infinitive; accordingly, one late MS rewrote the passage as *minantes se Perseo auxilio futuros*, while Perizonius, less radically, inserted *fore*. However, *ut* is paralleled in the Vulgate (Genesis 27:42), and in some MSS of Sen., *Epist.* 90.5 (though there too the MS reading has been doubted, probably correctly). It should probably be retained here in the absence of any clear explanation for how a corruption might have arisen.

pacem atque amicitiam: A pairing used several times in Livy (9.10.3, 9.45.18, 28.18.1, 34.57.8) and Caesar (*Gall.* 1.3.1, 4.18.3, 7.55.4; cf. *Bell. Alex.* 37.1). No other writer employs it as often, although it is found in texts of all periods.

indigne id latum: Livy, more strikingly, invites readers to consider their own indignation at the Rhodians' actions, and to imagine how much greater the Senate's would have been; he then gives two versions of the Senate's response, in one of which, attributed to Claudius Quadrigarius (*FRHist* 24 F 69), the Romans make no direct response to the Rhodians, but decree their subjects should be freed; in the other they reply in scornful terms. P. simply states the Senate's indignation as a fact, without specifying a particular version of it.

44.3–4 Aemilius Paullus chosen as consul: he defeats Perseus at the battle of Pydna. Corresponds to Livy 44.17–22, 33–42, 46. Much as he had with the battle of Zama at the climax of the Second Punic War (30.3n.), P. compresses the battle itself into a bare report of the fact of the victory, but pays rather more attention to certain material surrounding it. His omission of the details of the battle is less surprising in itself: Vell. 1.9.3–4 and Flor. 1.28.8–9 do much the same, though Eutr. 4.7.1 and Oros. 4.20.39 at least provide casualty figures, and all four refer to Perseus' flight. But none of these offers the other material from P.: the prediction of the eclipse and Aemilius' prayer, although versions of both of these are relatively common in other writers (cf. below). P., uniquely, gives what purports to be a narrative account of Pydna while focusing his entire attention on a couple of famous anecdotes which are tangential to the battle itself.

As with Zama, part of the reason for the removal of the details of battle may be to offer a sense of inevitability: Macedon comes to its familiar end at the hands of Rome's iconic victor. But the inclusion of Aemilius' prayer in particular displaces attention from the victory to a wider narrative issue: the question of Roman heroism combined with the potential costs of Roman success.

Astonishingly, however, P. transfers the prayer from Book 45, where Livy describes it (45.41.8–9), to Book 44. This is, admittedly, not the only time that he places material in the wrong book (see 11.2n., 38.7n, and cf. 18.5n.), but those other cases arise straightforwardly from his procedures of summary, where a story which in Livy spans two books is reported in its entirety by P. in just one of those books. What is happening here is far more radical. It is true that in Livy, as in most other writers who tell the story of Aemilius' prayer (D.S. 31.11.2–3, Val. Max. 5.10.2, Sen., *Cons. ad Marc.* 13.3, Plu., *Aem.* 36.7–9, App., *Mac.* 19; cf. Vell. 1.10.4–5, Ampel. 18.13, *Vir. Ill.* 56.4, Zonar. 9.24.4), it is described by Aemilius retrospectively: speaking after his sons' death, he explains that he had earlier prayed that any divine retribution for Rome's success should fall on him alone rather than on the city. But in Livy, as in those other writers, Aemilius represents himself as having made the prayer on his return to Italy following his victory. Only in P. does it take place before his departure.

One possibility is that P. is, as often, following an alternative version of the story, albeit one which is now lost; a second possibility is that he carelessly misread Livy in Book 45 and imagined Aemilius to be saying that he prayed in this way at the start of the campaign rather than the end, after which he transferred it to what he thought the 'proper' chronological position. Either of these could have happened; but no such version is reflected in any of the many surviving accounts, and the misreading of Livy would be far more obtuse than any other in P.

It is, accordingly, worth considering a further possibility: that P. deliberately transferred the material here because it made more sense to him in this position. It is essential to the story in Livy, as in other writers, that Aemilius' prayer occur after his outstanding victory, not prior to it: it is based on a widespread perception in Greece and Rome that excessive success was liable to meet with divine retribution. That story pattern is familiar in antiquity, going back in historiography to the famous legend of the ring of Polycrates in Hdt. 3.40–3; the best-known instance in Livy—and the closest parallel to the story here[53]—is Camillus' prayer following the capture of Veii, that any retribution for the success should be a minor one (5.21.14–16).[54] But such a story was far less resonant within the developed theology of Christianity, where the gulf separating God and man is too massive for the idea of divine jealousy over human success to appear sensible. One can, to be sure, find parallels in the conception of the 'evil eye', a popular belief shared by both pagans and Christians: that both human and superhuman powers (in the Christian version, demons) may envy human success and have the capacity magically to destroy it (Dickie (1995)); but that is usually addressed to overweening individuals, not to the state as a whole, which, if it met with success,

---

[53] The parallel is explicit in Zonar. 9.24.4.
[54] The version of the Camillus story in Val. Max. 1.5.2 (also Paris' and Nepotianus' epitomes) and Plu., *Cam.* 5.7–9 is even closer to the prayer of Aemilius: Camillus in those authors prays directly that disaster will strike him rather than the city. See Levene (1993), 184–6.

was assumed to have done so as part of a cosmological plan (cf. Segal (2014), 99–104).

Hence P. presents the story in a different form, one far more meaningful to a Christian: speaking *before* setting off on his campaign, with the outcome still uncertain, Aemilius effectively offers himself as a sacrifice, taking any disaster that might threaten Rome upon himself. That is itself not at all alien to traditional Roman ideas (it is closely comparable to the *devotio*), but the idea of a leader sacrificing himself for the community is a familiar one to Christians also. While, obviously, it would be a vast overstatement to refer to P.'s Aemilius as Christ-like, one can at least say that P.'s reordering of Livy's story slots Aemilius into a narrative pattern that a Christian would find familiar. It has, moreover, the effect of foreshadowing Aemilius' private tragedy (cf. 45.4n.) from the very beginning of his campaign, an approach to the story which is paralleled in Plutarch's *Aemilius*, but which Livy consistently eschews (Levene (1993), 120).

P.'s willingness to distort Livy to such a degree in the service of narrative meaning, if explicable, is nevertheless remarkable; it is not altogether unlike the way in which other historians will rework the facts of existing stories for appropriate rhetorical effect, but it is unexpected in a work which ostensibly ties itself so closely to its predecessor's structure.

The introduction of the eclipse is less remarkable; P. does so after he has already described Aemilius' victory, but he explicitly notes the correct chronology, that the episode took place prior to the battle. It was an extremely popular story (apart from Livy, it is found in Cic., *Rep.* 1.23, Val. Max. 8.11.1 (with Paris' epitome), Plin., *Nat.* 2.53, Quint., *Inst.* 1.10.47, Frontin., *Strat.* 1.12.8, Plu., *Aem.* 17.7–10, Zonar. 9.23.5).[55] Livy incorporates from Polybius the adverse interpretation of the eclipse in the Macedonian camp, and hence makes the story more than an illustration of scientific rationalism (cf. Levene (1993), 118–20), but P. follows the majority of non-Livian writers (Cicero, Valerius Maximus, Pliny, Frontinus, Quintilian) in ignoring that aspect: the supernatural overtones that Livy supplies are absent. More noteworthy is the striking change that P. makes to the original: the person who interprets the eclipse is not, as in Livy, C. Sulpicius Galus, but Aemilius himself. This is the version that appears in Zonaras, and also in Plutarch (who, however, does not have Aemilius announcing his interpretation to the army): as often, P. has introduced material from non-Livian sources.

44.3 cum: Cf. 2.2n.

sequentis anni cos.: P., unusually, connects this notice to the previous ones by observing that Aemilius took up his consulship in the following year. Aemilius' victory, as Livy presents it, is not only remarkable in itself, but sets Rome right

---

[55] In addition, the eclipse appears in Plb. 29.16.1–2 and Just. 33.1.7, but without the Romans offering a rationalizing explanation.

after the failures of the commanders that preceded him. It is true that the last such commander, Philippus, is not on the face of things presented by P. as having failed in the way that his predecessors had, but P. has hinted to the informed reader that his consulship, too, could be seen in those terms (cf. 44.1n.).

iterum: Cf. Livy 44.17.4 *consules creati L. Aemilius Paullus iterum, quarto decimo anno postquam primo consul fuerat, et C. Licinius Crassus*. P. mentions that Aemilius was in his second consulship, presumably because Livy commented on the gap in time since the first. P. did not mention the first consulship earlier—unsurprisingly, since Livy, too, made little of it (he referred to Aemilius' victory in Liguria that year in a single sentence without mentioning him by name: 40.16.4).

precatus ut quidquid diri populo Romano immineret in suam domum converteretur: P.'s language is taken not from Livy, but from Val. Max. 5.10.2: *precatus sum ut si quid adversi populo Romano immineret, totum in meam domum converteretur*.

in Macedoniam profectus: Cf. Livy 44.22.17 *consul et praetor Cn. Octavius in Macedoniam profecti sunt*.

44.4 praedixit exercitui ne miraretur: 'He warned the army not to be amazed' (*OLD s.v. praedico* 3c); however, *praedico* often means 'foretell' (*OLD s.v. praedico* 2), and it is used in that sense by Livy in this passage (44.37.6). P. plays on the double meaning of the word: Aemilius 'predicts' the eclipse, but the language of 'prediction' is applied to a different purpose.

luna proxima nocte defectura erat: Cf. Livy 44.37.5–6 *nocte proxima...lunam defecturam esse*.

44.5 *Defeat of Gentius*. Corresponds to Livy 44.30.1–32.5. After completing his account of Aemilius' victory over Macedon, P. returns to an earlier point in the narrative, namely the victory of Anicius in Illyria. The chronological displacement is not surprising; Anicius' victory occurs after Aemilius takes over the Macedonian army but prior to his campaign, but P. has compressed that story into a single notice (44.3); Flor. 1.29 and Zonar. 9.24.1 likewise delay their account of Anicius until after Pydna, even though they both describe the Macedonian victory at greater length than P. does. A secondary consideration may be that Livy emphasizes that the perceived chronology of the campaigns was distorted by the speed of Anicius' victory: he comments at 44.32.5 that Rome learned that there was a victory before they even knew that there had been a war, a paradox also mentioned by Flor. 1.29.2 and Eutr. 4.6.4 (for the paradox cf. Woodman (1977), 269–70); but to complicate that still further, at 45.3.1–2 he describes the news of the defeat of Gentius arriving after the news of Pydna (cf. Briscoe (2012a), 615, who—probably correctly—attributes this to Livy's having switched sources). P.'s ordering thus reflects Livy's account of the contemporary Roman perception of the campaign.

P. says little about the campaign itself: the one detail he focuses on is that Gentius was sent to Rome along with his wife and children, which is similarly highlighted by Plu., *Aem.* 13.2 and Eutr. 4.6.4 (also App., *Ill.* 9, though he only mentions Gentius' sons, not his wife): it was evidently the one feature that resonated in the broader tradition concerning the war.

quoque: As he does earlier in the book (44.3–4n.), P. connects his notices more closely than usual, drawing a parallel between the campaign against Gentius and that against Perseus; it may be relevant that Livy later refers to the former as an 'appendage' of the latter (45.7.2, 45.39.3 *accessio*).

cum uxore ac liberis et propinquis Romam missus: Cf. Livy 44.32.4 *nuntium victoriae Perpennam Romam misit et post dies paucos Gentium regem ipsum cum parente, coniuge ac liberis ac fratre aliisque principibus Illyriorum.*

44.6 *Egyptian embassy complains about Antiochus.* Corresponds to Livy 44.19.6–14. After completing his account of the Macedonian War, along with the related war against Gentius, P. moves back to an earlier point, the brief account of the Egyptian embassy seeking Rome's help against Antiochus Epiphanes, who had invaded Egypt. P.'s interest in the episode presumably relates in part to the cultural resonance of Antiochus in his day (41.3n.); he will later go on to record in some detail the Roman response to Antiochus' invasion (45.2).

legati Alexandrini a Cleopatra et Ptolemaeo regibus venerunt querentes: Cf. Livy 44.19.6 *legati ab Ptolemaeo et Cleopatra regibus*; 44.19.10 *ea legati querentes.*

Antiocho rege Syriae: Cf. Livy 44.19.8 *Antiochus Syriae rex.*

44.7 *Eumenes and Gentius abandon Perseus.* Corresponds to Livy 44.25.1–26.2 and 44.27.8–12; cf. 44.23.1–7. There are a few oddities about P.'s handling of this story. The first, and least significant, is that he focuses solely on Eumenes and Gentius, omitting the third time when, according to Livy, Perseus' miserliness deprived him of allies, namely his refusal to pay money to the Gauls in return for their alliance (44.26.2–27.7). This episode is narrated by Livy at greater length than either of the other two, but P. ignores it, perhaps because it was not readily attached to a single royal name who plays a role elsewhere in the narrative.

Second, P. suggests that in both cases Perseus had previously promised money to the king but reneged on the promise: that is indeed the way Livy tells the story of Gentius, but, with Eumenes, Perseus never makes such a promise, but instead offers money which he will only release to Eumenes at the end of the war, an offer which Eumenes declines. Conversely, Gentius does not abandon Perseus in Livy, but continues to campaign on his side, in accordance with the agreement he made with Perseus at an earlier point in the negotiations (44.23.3): it is only Eumenes who refuses to help Perseus once he does not receive the hoped-for payment. P. conflates the two episodes, taking material from each one; out of Livy's complex diplomatic dances he creates a simple story with a simple moral: Perseus breaks his promises and loses his allies.

Finally, and perhaps related to the last, P. entirely reworks Livy's narrative sequence. In Livy the negotiations with Eumenes and Gentius take place prior to Aemilius' arrival in Macedonia; P. does not mention them until after Perseus' ultimate defeat. On the face of things, this makes it appear part of an attempt by Perseus to rectify his position after Pydna; but that makes little sense even in terms of P.'s own narrative, since he has already described Gentius as not only defeated, but sent to Rome (44.5); clearly he was in no position either to help or abandon Perseus at that point. The reader is obliged to assume that this took place earlier, but is given no guidance as to exactly when. The reason for treating it in this way may be to avoid having to explain the complexity of Gentius' position: on the promise of money from Perseus, Gentius decisively breaks with Rome by mistreating Roman ambassadors, and it is this that decides Perseus not to pay him the bulk of what he promised, since Gentius has by now committed himself to war (44.27.11-12; cf. Plu., *Aem.* 13.1-3, App., *Mac.* 18.1; also Dio fr. 66.1).[56] Livy depicts an edgy relationship between Gentius and Perseus going back to Book 43: Perseus attacks Illyria, but he hopes to use that as a bargaining counter to form an alliance with Gentius against Rome. Gentius declines at that point; but in Book 44 does agree, only to be cheated by Perseus of the promised money—yet by that point has committed himself to fight Rome in any case. P. does not show the attempted alliance in Book 43 (cf. 43.4n.), or the one concluded in Book 44. His narrative suggests something different: Gentius is defeated by Perseus, but fights Rome anyway, presumably on his own account; at some unspecified point prior to his defeat and capture Perseus tries to gain his help, but loses the opportunity because of his miserliness.

sollicitatis in auxilium: A rare phrase: it is not found in Livy or any other writer of the classical period, but is paralleled in Flor. 2.19.4 and Just. 16.5.1.

---

[56] Flor. 1.29 untangles the confusion of the narrative in a different way: in his version, the Illyrians simply receive money from Perseus and fight on his side, with no idea that they are cheated. App., *Ill.* 9 on the face of things tells the story in that way also, but he has already explained the situation more precisely in *Mac.*

Book 45

45.1 *Capture of Perseus.* Corresponds to Livy 45.4.2–6.12. P. concludes his account of Aemilius' campaign with a bare reference to Perseus' capture in Samothrace. He says nothing of the two stories that Livy associated with that, although they were among the most famous anecdotes of the Third Macedonian War: the miraculous fashion in which the news of Pydna reached Rome (Livy 45.1: cf. Cic., *Nat. Deor.* 2.6, Val. Max. 1.8.1, with epitomes of Paris and Nepotianus, Plin., *Nat.* 7.86, Plu., *Aem.* 24.4–7, Flor. 1.28.14–15, Min. Fel. 7.3, Lact., *Inst.* 2.7.10, *Epist. Paul. ad Sen.* 7, Zonar. 9.24.2), and the meeting of Perseus and Aemilius (Livy 45.7–8; cf. Val. Max. 5.1.8 with Paris' epitome, Plu., *Aem.* 26.8–27.6, Flor. 1.28.10–11, Dio fr. 66.4 with Zonar. 9.23.12, Eutr. 4.7.2, *Vir. Ill.* 56.3). He does, however, mention the place of his capture: this was something of considerable interest to historians, because of Samothrace's well-known religious associations, something that plays a key role in Livy's account (esp. 45.5.3–11, 45.6.10), and which almost all writers refer to (Sall., *Hist.* fr. 4.69.7M, D.S. 29.25, Vell. 1.9.4, Plu., *Aem.* 23.11, 26.1, Flor. 1.28.9, *Vir. Ill.* 56.3; cf. Ampel. 16.4, Porph., *FGrH* 260 F 3, Just. 33.2.5); this presumably explains why it is the one detail about his capture which P., too, introduces, although he does not himself mention the religious side.

45.2 *Antiochus forced to abandon Egyptian invasion.* Corresponds to Livy 45.11.1–12.6. After brushing rapidly over the final defeat of Perseus, P. spends somewhat more time on an episode which Livy treats more cursorily, namely the Roman embassy that compelled Antiochus Epiphanes to abandon his invasion of Egypt. He was presumably influenced by the fame of the story, which is recorded in much the same form by many other writers (Plb. 29.27.1–8, Cic., *Phil.* 8.23, D.S. 31.2, Vell. 1.10.1–2, Val. Max. 6.4.3 (also Paris' epitome), Plin., *Nat.* 34.24, Plu., *Reg. Imp. Apophth.* 202F–203A, App., *Syr.* 66, Jer., *In Dan.* 11:30, Just. 32.3.1–4, Zonar. 9.25.1–3); but it is no less relevant to note that P. appears to have a particular interest in Antiochus, deriving from his role in Jewish history (cf. 41.3n.), and that his retreat from Egypt is mentioned in the Books of Maccabees as occurring directly prior to his institution of religious persecution in Judaea (esp. II Macc. 5:11–15; cf. I Macc. 1:16–20).

cum: Cf. 2.2n.

Syriae rex...Aegypti reges: Cf. 34.8n.

Ptolemaeum et Cleopatram: Livy does not say that Antiochus' attack was against 'Ptolemy and Cleopatra', and indeed P. appears to have misread the situation. There were in fact two Ptolemies who had competed for the throne: Ptolemy VI Philometor, and his younger brother Ptolemy VIII Euergetes; Antiochus had supported the former, while Euergetes was supported by his sister Cleopatra II.

At this point, however, the brothers had reconciled: hence Antiochus' attack that was now renewed was directed against both brothers alike (cf. Livy 45.11.8).

However, P.'s misreading is understandable. In the previous book Livy had described the embassy as coming from Ptolemy and Cleopatra—in this case Euergetes, who was seeking to defend his throne against his brother and Antiochus—and P. had correctly reported that (44.6); and moreover, more significantly, in the immediate aftermath of the episode here, an embassy of thanks from the Egyptian rulers to Rome is said by Livy—mistakenly (cf. Briscoe (2012a), 642)—to come 'in the name of the king and Cleopatra' (45.13.4 *nomine regis et Cleopatrae*; Plb. 30.16.1, more accurately, describes it as coming from 'the kings'— οἱ βασιλεῖς). It is easy to see how P. might have carelessly deduced that Antiochus had attacked the same pair of rulers as before. The result is that he reduces the complexities of Ptolemaic-Seleucid relations in these years to a simple and easily comprehensible narrative; Antiochus attacked 'Ptolemy and Cleopatra'; they sent to Rome for help; the Romans sent an embassy, which compelled Antiochus to withdraw.

qui iuberent...absisteret...iussitque...responsum daret: It is rare in classical Latin to construct *iubere* with the bare subjunctive; however, it becomes more common in later periods (*TLL* VII.2 579.73–580.7; cf. K-S 1.718, H-S 530).

ab obsidione socii regis: The chief MSS read *ab obsidione solo regis*, which is meaningless. Certain late MSS emended *solo* to *socii*, which was then accepted by subsequent editors. On this reading, as often, P. uses phrases garnished from Livy, who in a short passage in Book 44 both speaks of the Ptolemies as *socii reges* (44.19.11) and refers to Antiochus' initial attack on Alexandria as an *obsidio* (44.19.9; cf. 45.11.7): as noted above, P. is conflating the entire story in Books 44 and 45 into a single simple version, and it is characteristic of him to transfer language from one book to the next in this fashion (see Introduction, xxiii–xxiv). Moreover, *obsidione absistere* is a Livian phrase, used by him at 9.15.3 and nowhere else in surviving Latin literature.

Rossbach (followed by Jal) proposed instead retaining *solo* and deleting *obsidione* as a gloss ('From the territory of the king'), but, while in principle this could have happened, the resulting phrasing is unusual and poetic (cf. *OLD s.v. solum*[1] 5a). It is far more probable that P. engaged in his common practice of repurposing Livian phrases than that he employed poetic language that Livy himself did not use here.

editisque mandatis: A phrase used twice by Livy (33.35.3, 45.20.2), the second of which is a passage not long after the embassy here, albeit in an unrelated context; it is otherwise rare (but cf. Nep., *Con.* 3.3, and see *TLL* V.2 90.17–21, V.2 93.69–70). P. is not replicating Livy's language from the episode he is summarizing, but appears to be drawing on phrases he has picked up in his reading of the book.

consideraturum se quid faciendum esset respondisset...Popilius virga regem circumscripsit iussitque, ante quam circulo excederet, responsum daret:

Cf. Livy 45.12.5 *se consideraturum...quid faciendum sibi esset dixisset, Popillius...virga...circumscripsit regem, ac 'priusquam hoc circulo excedas' inquit 'redde responsum senatui'*.

asperitate: Livy likewise sees Popillius' actions as an example of *asperitas* (45.12.5).

45.3 *The Rhodians and the Senate*. Corresponds to Livy 45.19.1–25.10. Livy gives considerable emphasis to this episode—he composes for the Rhodians the longest speech in the Fifth Decade (45.22–4)—and for that reason alone it is unsurprising that P., too, includes a relatively lengthy notice concerning it. The embassies from other states are reduced to a passing mention, even that of Pergamum headed by Attalus, where Livy offers some detail (45.19.1–20.3). P. reproduces the same outcome as in Livy—that the Rhodians were considered neither allies nor enemies—unlike the only other narrative account of the episode, Zonar. 9.24.6, which suggests that the Rhodians were successful in becoming Rome's allies.

More notable is that P. fails to mention the speech of Cato, which Livy refers to at 45.25.3–4, and which he says he would have written a version of had Cato not included it in the *Origines*. The speech is well known, not least because of the extensive discussion and quotation of extracts in Gellius 6.3 (cf. also App., *Pun.* 65); awareness of Cato's intervention similarly lies behind Sallust's discussion of the episode (*Cat.* 51.5; cf. Levene (2000), 185–8). Nevertheless, it does not appear to have a strong presence in the later historical tradition—it is mentioned neither in Plutarch's *Cato Major* nor in the potted biography of Cato in *Vir. Ill.* 47 nor in Zonaras, an omission presumably connected with the relative invisibility of Cato among the historians of later antiquity (cf. 34.2, 36.1, 39.5nn.).

legationes gratulantium populorum atque regum: Cf. Livy 45.19.1 *inter multas regum gentiumque et populorum legationes*.

in senatu: The ablative with *in* is less common after *admitto* than the accusative; but cf. *TLL* I 750.44–9.

qui eo bello contra populum Romano faverant: For the 'absolute' use of *faveo* see *TLL* VI.1 373.47–374.13; for the phrasing here cf. esp. *Hist. Aug., Ver.* 6.2 *quod turpissime contra eos faveret*. On Livy's account, the Rhodians did not take sides against Rome, but merely declined to take their side against Perseus (a point made by the Rhodians themselves in their speech before the Senate: 45.23.1–4). They did threaten to join Perseus if he agreed to peace while the Romans did not, but they made an identical threat to Perseus; and in the event neither condition was met, so they joined neither side. However, P. has slanted his account so as to present them as anti-Roman rather than neutral (see 44.2n.), and he concludes the story now in accordance with that.

exclusa. postera die…: The surviving text of Livy does not indicate that the Rhodians were admitted to the Senate the day after they were initially excluded.

They are prevented from addressing the Senate at 45.20.7–8, and they speak to the Senate at 45.22, but 45.21 narrates a series of procedural moves at Rome which appear too extensive to have taken place in a single day. There is a lacuna between 45.21 and 45.22, which includes the beginning of the Rhodians' speech, and it is possible that Livy presented the events in such a way that would fit the account in P., for example having the Rhodians formally excluded a second time before finally being allowed to speak, or alternatively showing that, despite what one might think, the events of 45.21 did after all happen in one day. However, Plb. 30.4.6 is explicit that several days elapsed between the events which Livy describes in 45.21 and the Rhodians addressing the Senate. Livy combines Polybian material here with other sources (Briscoe (2012a), 668–9), but the general overlap between their accounts makes it more probable that he followed Polybius' chronology, and that the alteration is due to P., perhaps following some now lost version.

cum de eo quaereretur ut his bellum indiceretur: Cf. Livy 45.21.2 *rogationemque promulgaverunt ut Rhodiis bellum indiceretur*. *quaereretur* is unexpected; it is commonly used for judicial proceedings (*OLD s.v. quaero* 10), but not for proposing a bill, the usual term for which is *rogo* (*OLD s.v. rogo* 5a, 5b). It appears that P. has, as often (cf. Introduction), adapted Livy's language by substituting a synonym, but has overlooked the fact that, although *rogo* and *quaero* have similar meanings in informal contexts, their technical senses do not overlap.

nec tamquam socii nec tamquam hostes dimissi: Cf. Livy 45.25.4 *nec hostes fierent nec socii permanerent*; P.'s language may also be influenced by 45.23.6, where the Rhodians plead that they have not acted as enemies to Rome (*neque fecimus igitur quicquam tamquam hostes*).

45.4 Aemilius reorganizes Macedonia; he celebrates a triumph marred by the deaths of his sons. Corresponds to Livy 45.29.1–32.7, 45.33.1–7, 45.34.1–9, 45.35.1–42.1. P. has little to say about Aemilius' settlement in Macedonia, and what he does say is mistaken (cf. below): most other writers share P.'s lack of interest in those administrative details, though cf. D.S. 31.8.5–9, Str. 7 fr. 47, Plu., *Aem.* 28.6, Just. 33.2.7, Eutr. 4.7.3. He concentrates instead on the events after his return to Rome, in particular on the debate over his triumph, the fact that Perseus and his children were led in it, and the way it was marred by the deaths of Aemilius' sons. The triumph and Perseus' and his family's presence in it were frequently referred to as iconic moments in Roman history (cf. Cic., *Mur.* 31, *Catil.* 4.21, *Pis.* 61; D.S. 31.8.12, Vell. 1.9.5–6, Sen., *Cons. Marc.* 13.3, Plu., *Fort. Rom.* 318B, *Aem.* 32.4–34.8, Flor. 1.28.12–13, Ampel. 16.4, 18.13, Eutr. 4.8.1, *Vir. Ill.* 56.3, Zonar. 9.24.3), though P. (unlike not only Livy, but also Velleius, Plutarch, *Aemilius*, Florus, Ampelius, Eutropius, Zonaras) has nothing to say of the opulence with which it was conducted—the entire issue of the wealth of Macedon that was transferred to Rome at this time (cf. Cic., *Off.* 2.76, D.S. 31.8.10–12, Val. Max. 4.38

(with Paris' epitome), Plin., *Nat.* 33.56) is of little interest to him, at least for now (but cf. 46.10n.). The death of Aemilius' sons at the moment of his greatest success was likewise a staple part of the tradition, which P., unlike Livy, has prefigured since the previous book (44.3n.). The contentious debate is depicted at great length in Livy, and for that reason it is of little surprise that P. included it, although it was mentioned by few other writers (though cf. Vell. 1.9.6, Plu., *Aem.* 30.4–32.1): the one oddity is that he mentions the opposition to the triumph by Ser. Sulpicius Galba, but not the support offered to Aemilius by M. Servilius.

Macedonia in provinciae formam redacta: P. is mistaken: Macedonia did not become a province at this time, but, as Livy makes a point of observing, was divided politically, with the individual portions formally maintaining their independence (45.29.4–9; cf. 45.32.7, 45.34.2). Not until the early 140s BC was it placed under direct Roman rule (cf. 50.12n., 52.3n.). No other writer describes Aemilius' settlement in such terms.

It is easy to see the source of P.'s error. Aemilius, in his speech after his triumph, says that he 'reduced Macedonia into the power of the Roman people' (45.41.5: *Macedoniam in potestatem populi Romani redegi*). P. presumably misinterpreted this to mean that Macedonia came under direct Roman rule; he has based himself on Livy's wording but, as usual, has slightly altered it, in this case into a standard expression for the creation of a province (*OLD s.v. redigere* 10b); note that Zonar. 9.24.2, perhaps via a parallel process of compression from Cassius Dio, refers to the Romans 'having acquired Macedonia' (τὴν Μακεδονίαν κτησάμενοι). More generally, while P. has apparently failed to observe Livy's careful comments on the Macedonians' independence, he could fairly observe that the independence, even on Livy's account, was very circumscribed, since the inhabitants of the four states into which Macedonia was divided were prevented from purchasing property and even intermarrying outside their own borders (45.29.10)

repugnantibus militibus: An unusual phrase: the only parallel is in *Hist. Aug., Alex.* 2.4. Cf. 4.1n. on P.'s predilection for the even more unusual *patribus repugnantibus*.

ipsius: In Republican and Augustan Latin one would expect *suis*, but later writers it is not uncommon for *ipsius* to be substituted (K-S 1.631).

Persen cum tribus filiis duxit ante currum: The surviving portion of Livy's description of the triumph does not refer to Perseus' children, but Aemilius mentions them in his speech at 45.41.10, and the information presumably appeared in the lacuna between 45.39 and 45.40. Eutr. 4.8.1 refers to *duo filii*; but P. is presumably including Perseus' daughter in the count (D.S. 31.8.12, Plu., *Aem.* 33.7; cf. Zonar. 9.24.3).

cuius triumphi laetitia ne solida ei contingeret: *solida* is predicative: 'so that the joy of that triumph would not be granted to him as unmixed'. See *OLD s.v.*

contingo 8d; for the purpose clause used to mark something fated see esp. Nisbet (1923).

duorum filiorum funeribus insignita est: Livy regularly uses *insignis* in the context of an event marked by disaster; for the extension of Livy's idiom to *insignio* cf. Tac., *Agr.* 41.3 with Woodman (2014), 296.

praecessit: The verb is not used of the death of Aemilius' son in Livy, but is in Val. Max. 5.10.2.

45.5 *Census.* This is the census taken by the censors of 169, C. Claudius Pulcher and Ti. Sempronius Gracchus. Livy, in accordance with his usual practice (13.4n.), recorded the *lustrum* towards the end of the year 168, and the data here appeared in the lacuna between 45.14 and 45.15, since 45.15 recounts other activities of the censors. Hence P. records it out of chronological sequence.

lustrum a censoribus conditum est: Cf. 11.5n.

censa sunt civium capita: Cf. 3.3n.

CCCXII milia DCCCV: The figure is substantially more than that of the previous census (42.6), but Livy had noted that the latter was anomalously low, because of the exclusion from the count of Latins resident at Rome (42.10.2–3); that alone is sufficient to explain the increase here. Brunt (1971), 74 claims that 'there is no ground for supposing that the censors in 168 were particularly liberal towards Latins'; but the very fact that Livy treated the exclusion of Latins from the count in 173 as something exceptional and worthy of comment provides one such ground (Brunt was perhaps misled by his misinterpretation of Livy: see 41.4n.).

45.6 *Prusias in the Senate.* Corresponds to Livy 45.44.4–21. There is a major division between Greek and Latin writers on the subject of Prusias and his visit to Rome. The former, taking their lead from Plb. 30.18, describe him as a shameless and ludicrous flatterer who earned the contempt of the Romans (D.S. 31.15, Plu., *Fort. Alex.* 336E (mistakenly associating the anecdote with Prusias' son Nicomedes), App., *Mith.* 2, Dio fr. 69 with Zonar. 9.24.7). Most of the Latin sources, on the other hand, have nothing of this: in their version, Prusias behaves nobly, is treated honourably, and goes away a friend of the Romans. This latter version is found in Val. Max. 5.1.1 (also Paris' epitome) and Eutr. 4.8.2. but was also, apparently, the story Livy found in his Latin sources (45.44.19). Livy himself offers both variants, but the balance of his account is weighted toward the Latin one, which he recounts at considerably greater length.

P. follows Livy in reporting both, but unlike Livy, integrates them into a single account. He does not refer to the story of Prusias' flattery as a variant, and, no less importantly, removes from Livy every aspect of Prusias' visit which might appear incompatible with the obsequiousness that Polybius and the other Greek writers transmit: he does not mention anything of Prusias' dignified entry to Rome, his delaying his audience before the Senate in order to visit the temples and other parts of the city, nor his account of his services to Rome and his vows of sacrifice, nor his refusal of gifts, nor the favourable impression he made on leading Romans. He reworks Livy's story of Prusias into a seamless account of a shameless flatterer who humiliated himself in the hope of favours from Rome; in that respect his account, though derived from Livy, aligns itself more closely with the Greeks. It may be relevant in this context to note that P. thereby anticipates his later treatment of Prusias at the time of his death, which similarly focuses on his vices and unfitness as a king (50.2–4nn.).

Prusias, Bithyniae rex: Cf. 34.8n.

Nicomedem filium senatui commendavit: Cf. Livy 45.44.9 *filium... Nicomedem senatui commendavit*. Eutr. 4.8.2 has an almost identical phrase: *Prusias etiam filium suum Nicomedem senatui commendavit*.

libertum se populi Romani dicebat: Cf. Livy 45.44.19 *libertumque se populi Romani ferre*. P. implies that Prusias did this on his visit to Rome, whereas the Greek sources have it happening when Roman envoys came to him in Bithynia. However, Livy's abridged account of Polybius does not explicitly associate Prusias doing this with his behaviour towards Roman envoys, but implies that it was his usual practice; hence P.'s version is understandable.

Bibliography

Aberson, M., Biella, M. C., Di Fazio, M., and Wullschleger, M. (eds) (2014). *Entre archéologie et histoire: dialogues sur divers peuples de l'Italie préromaine*. Bern: Peter Lang.
Adams, G. W. (2008). 'The Unbalanced Relationship between Ptolemy II and Pyrrhus of Epirus', in McKechnie and Guillaume (2008), 91–102.
Adams, J. N. (1971). 'A Type of Hyperbaton in Latin Prose', *PCPhS* 17: 1–16.
Allen, Jr., W. (1953). 'Caesar's *Regnum* (Suet. *Iul.* 9.2)', *TAPhA* 84: 227–36.
Ameling, W. (2001). 'Polybios und die römische Annexion Sardiniens', *WJA* 25: 107–32.
Andrén, A. (1940). *Architectural Terracottas from Etrusco-Italic Temples*. Lund: C. W. K. Gleerup.
Antolini, S., and Marengo, S. M. (2010). '*Regio V (Picenum)* e versante adriatico della *Regio VI (Umbria)*', in Silvestrini (2010), 208–15.
Antonelli, L. (2006). 'Silla, *Ariminum* e lo *Ius duodecim coloniarum*', in *Ariminum, storia e archeologia*. Rome: L'Erma di Bretschneider, 241–8.
Arena, V. (2012). Libertas *and the Practice of Politics in the Late Roman Republic*. Cambridge: Cambridge University Press.
Ariño Gil, E. (1986). *Centuriaciones romanas en el valle medio del Ebro: Provincia de la Rioja*. Logroño: Instituto de Estudios Riojanos.
Arnaud, P. (2001). 'Les Ligures: la construction d'un concept géographique et ses étapes de l'époque archaïque à l'empire romain', in V. Fromentin and S. Gotteland (eds), *Origines Gentium*. Bordeaux: Ausonius, 327–46.
Arvanitis, N. (ed.) (2010). *Il santuario di Vesta: La casa delle Vestali e il tempio di Vesta VIII sec. a.c.–64 d.c.* Pisa: Fabrizio Serra.
Ascher, L. (1968–9). 'An Epitome of Livy in Martial's Day?', *CB* 45: 53–4.
Ash, R. (2007). *Tacitus: Histories Book II*. Cambridge: Cambridge University Press.
Ashby, T., and Fell, R. A. L. (1921). 'The Via Flaminia', *JRS* 11: 125–90.
Assmann, J. (2006). *Religion and Cultural Memory*. Tr. R. Livingstone. Stanford, CA: Stanford University Press.
—— (2011). *Cultural Memory and Early Civilization*. Cambridge: Cambridge University Press.
Astin, A. E. (1967a). *Scipio Aemilianus*. Oxford: Clarendon Press.
—— (1967b). 'Saguntum and the Origins of the Second Punic War', *Latomus* 26: 577–96.
—— (1978). *Cato the Censor*. Oxford: Clarendon Press.
—— (1988). '*Regimen Morum*', *JRS* 78: 14–34.
Auliard, C. (2001). *Victoires et triomphes à Rome*. Paris: Presses Universitaires Franc-Comtoises.
Ay, G. (1894). *De Livii Epitoma Deperdita*. Diss. Leipzig. M. Hoffmann.
Aymard, A. (1948). 'Le protocole royal grec et son évolution', *REA* 50: 232–63.
Azzena, G. (1987). *Atri: forma e urbanistica*. Rome: L'Erma di Bretschneider.
Badian, E. (1952a). 'Notes on Roman Policy in Illyria (230–201 B.C.)', *PBSR* 20: 72–93.
—— (1952b). 'The Treaty between Rome and the Achaean League', *JRS* 42: 76–80.
—— (1958). *Foreign Clientelae (264–70 B.C.)*. Oxford: Clarendon Press.
—— (1962). Review of Taylor (1960), *JRS* 52: 200–10.
—— (1980). 'Two Polybian Treaties', in Φιλίας χάριν: *Miscellanea di studi classici in onore di Eugenio Manni*. Vol. 1. Rome: Giorgio Bretschneider, 69–79.
—— (1989). 'The *Scribae* of the Roman Republic', *Klio* 71: 582–603.

Baldus, H. R. (1988). 'Zwei Deutungsvorschläge zur punischen Goldprägung im mittleren 3. Jahrhundert v. Chr.', *Chiron* 18: 171–9.
Baldwin, B. (1990). 'Alexander, Hannibal, and Scipio in Lucian', *Emerita* 58: 51–60.
Balestri Fumagalli, M. (2008). *Riflessioni sulla 'Lex Voconia'*. Milan: Edizioni Universitarie di Lettere Economia Diritto.
Balsdon, J. P. V. D. (1954). 'Rome and Macedon, 205–200 B.C.', *JRS* 44: 30–42.
—— (1957). 'Roman History, 58–56 B.C.: Three Ciceronian Problems', *JRS* 47: 15–20.
—— (1972). 'L. Cornelius Scipio: A Salvage Operation', *Historia* 21: 224–34.
Baltrusch, E. (1989). *Regimen Morum: Die Reglementierung des Privatlebens der Senatoren und Ritter in der römischen Republik und frühen Kaiserzeit*. Munich: C. H. Beck.
Bannert, H. (1978). 'Viridomarus', *RE* Supplementband XV: 917–29.
Barber, C. M. (2020). '*Quibus Patet Curia*: Livy 23.23.6 and the Mid-Republican Aristocracy of Office', *Historia* 69: 332–61.
Barceló, P. (1996). 'Rom und Hispanien vor Ausbruch des 2. punischen Krieges', *Hermes* 124: 45–57.
Barish, J. (1981). *The Antitheatrical Prejudice*. Berkeley: University of California Press.
Barnes, C. L. H. (2005). *Images and Insults: Ancient Historiography and the Outbreak of the Tarentine War*. Stuttgart: Franz Steiner.
Barnes, T. D. (1998). *Ammianus Marcellinus and the Representation of Historical Reality*. Ithaca, NY: Cornell University Press.
Baron, C. (2018). 'The Historian's Craft: Narrative Strategies and Historical Method in Polybius and Livy', in N. Miltsios and M. Tamiolaki (eds), *Polybius and His Legacy*. Berlin: De Gruyter, 203–21.
Barwick, K. (1936). 'Zwei antike Ausgaben der Pliniusbriefe?', *Philologus* 91: 423–48.
Battisti, C. (1959). *Sostrati e parastrati nell'Italia preistorica*. Florence: Felice le Monnier.
Bauman, R. A. (1966). 'The Abdication of "Collatinus"', *AClass* 9: 129–41.
—— (1967). *The Crimen Maiestatis in the Roman Republic and Augustan Principate*. Johannesburg: Witwatersrand University Press.
—— (1968). 'The Abrogation of *Imperium*: Some Cases and a Principle', *RhM* 111: 37–50.
—— (1974). 'Criminal Prosecutions by the Aediles', *Latomus* 33: 245–64.
—— (1983). *Lawyers in Roman Republican Politics*. Munich: C. H. Beck.
Bauslaugh, R. A. (1979). 'The Text of Thucydides IV 8.6 and the South Channel at Pylos', *JHS* 99: 1–6.
Bayer, E. (1972). 'Rom und die Westgriechen bis 280 v. Chr.', *ANRW* I 1: 305–40.
Beagon, M. (2002). 'Beyond Comparison: M. Sergius, Fortunae Victor', in G. Clark and T. Rajak (eds), *Philosophy and Power in the Graeco-Roman World: Essays in Honour of Miriam Griffin*. Oxford: Oxford University Press, 111–31.
Beard, M. (1980). 'The Sexual Status of Vestal Virgins', *JRS* 70: 12–27.
—— (1995). 'Re-reading (Vestal) Virginity', in R. Hawley and B. Levick (eds), *Women in Antiquity: New Assessments*. London: Routledge, 166–77.
—— (2007). *The Roman Triumph*. Cambridge, MA: Harvard University Press.
——, North, J., and Price, S. (1998). *Religions of Rome*. 2 vols. Cambridge: Cambridge University Press.
Beaumont, R. L. (1936). 'Greek Influence in the Adriatic Sea before the Fourth Century B.C.', *JHS* 56: 159–204.
Bechert, T. (1999). *Die Provinzen des Römischen Reiches*. Mainz: Philipp von Zabern.
Beck, H. (2005). *Karriere und Hierarchie*. Berlin: Akadamie Verlag.
—— (2013). 'Polybius' Roman *prokataskeuē*', in B. Gibson and T. Harrison (eds), *Polybius and His World: Essays in Memory of F. W. Walbank*. Oxford: Oxford University Press, 125–42.

Begbie, C. M. (1967). 'The Epitome of Livy', *CQ* 17: 332–8.
Bellen, H. (1985). *Metus Gallicus—Metus Punicus: Zum Furchtmotiv in der römischen Republik*. Wiesbaden: Franz Steiner.
Bellomo, M. (2013). 'Polybius and the Outbreak of the First Punic War: A Constitutional Issue', *SCO* 59: 71–90.
Beloch, K. J. (1877). 'Die römische Censusliste', *RhM* 32: 227–48.
—— (1886). *Die Bevölkerung der griechieschrömischen Welt*. Leipzig: Duncker and Humblot.
Beresford, J. (2013). *The Ancient Sailing Season*. Leiden: Brill.
Bergtson, H. (1944). *Die Strategie in der hellenistischen Zeit*. Vol. 2. Munich: C. H. Beck.
Bernard, J.-E. (2000). *Le portrait chez Tite-Live: Essai sur l'écriture de l'histoire romaine*. Brussels: Latomus.
Bernard, S. (2018). *Building Mid-Republican Rome*. New York: Oxford University Press.
Bernardi, A. (1948). 'Ius Ariminensium', in *Studi giuridici in memoria di Pietro Ciapessoni*. Pavia: Tipografia del Libro, 235–59.
Berry, D. H. (1996). *Cicero. Pro P. Sulla Oratio*. Cambridge: Cambridge University Press.
Berve, H. (1959). *König Hieron II*. Munich: Bayerische Akademie der Wissenschaften.
Besnier, M. (1902). *L'Ile Tibérine dans l'antiquité*. Paris: Libraire des Écoles Françaises d'Athénes et de Rome.
Bessone, L. (1977). *La tradizione liviana*. Bologna: Pàtron.
—— (1982). 'La tradizione epitomatoria liviana in età imperiale', *ANRW* II 30.2: 1230–63.
—— (1984). 'Le *Periochae* di Livio', *A&R* 29: 42–55.
—— (2015). 'The Periochae', in B. Mineo (ed.), *A Companion to Livy*. Malden, MA: Wiley-Blackwell, 425–36.
Bickerman, E. J. (1945). '*Bellum Philippicum*: Some Roman and Greek Views Concerning the Causes of the Second Macedonian War', *CPh* 40: 137–48.
—— (1947). 'Apocryphal Correspondence of Pyrrhus', *CPh* 42: 137–46.
Biggs, T. (2017). '*Primus Romanorum*: Origin Stories, Fictions of Primacy, and the First Punic War', *CPh* 112: 350–67.
Bispham, E. (2006). '*Coloniam ducere*: How Roman Was Roman Colonization during the Middle Republic?' in Bradley and Wilson (2006), 73–160.
—— (2014). 'The Lucanians: Historical Perspective', in Aberson *et al.* (2014), 311–30.
Blättler, P. P. (1945). *Studien zur Regulusgeschichte*. Diss. Freiburg in Schweiz.
Bleckmann, B. (1999). 'Rom und die Kampaner von Rhegion', *Chiron* 29: 123–46.
—— (2002). *Die römischen Nobilität im Ersten Punischen Krieg*. Berlin: Akademie Verlag.
Bleicken, J. (1955). *Das Volkstribunat der klassischen Republik*. Munich: C. H. Beck.
—— (1957a). 'Oberpontifex und Pontificalcollegium: Eine Studie zur römischen Sakralverfassung', *Hermes* 85: 345–66.
—— (1957b). 'Kollisionen zwischen Sacrum und Publicum: eine Studie zum Verfall der altrömischen Religion', *Hermes* 85: 446–80.
Bodel, J. (2015). 'The Publication of Pliny's Letters', in I. Marchesi (ed.), *Pliny the Book-Maker: Betting on Posterity in the Epistles*. Oxford: Oxford University Press, 13–108.
Bonner, R. J. (1920). 'The Book Divisions of Thucydides', *CPh* 15: 73–82.
Bosworth, A. B. (1968). Review of Capozza (1966), *JRS* 58: 272–4.
Bouché-Leclercq, A. (1882). *Histoire de la divination dans l'antiquité*. Vol. 4. Paris: Ernest Leroux.
Bradley, G. (2000). *Ancient Umbria: State, Culture, and Identity in Central Italy from the Iron Age to the Augustan Era*. Oxford: Oxford University Press.
—— (2006). 'Colonization and Identity in Republican Italy', in Bradley and Wilson (2006), 161–87.

Bradley, G. (2014). 'The Nature of Roman Strategy in Mid-Republican Colonization and Road Building', in Stek and Pelgrom (2014), 60–72.
―――, and Wilson, J.-P. (eds) (2006). *Greek and Roman Colonization: Origins, Ideologies and Interactions*. Swansea: Classical Press of Wales.
Bradley, K. R. (2001). 'Imagining Slavery: The Limits of the Plausible', *JRA* 14: 473–7.
Brauer, G. C., Jr. (1986). *Taras: Its History and Coinage*. New Rochelle, NY: Aristide D. Caratzas.
Braund, S. (2009). *Seneca. De Clementia*. Oxford: Oxford University Press.
Bravo, B., and Griffin, M. (1988). 'Un frammento del libro XI di Tito Livio', *Athenaeum* 66: 447–521.
Breitenbach, A. (2009). *Kommentar zu den Pseudo-Seneca-Epigrammen der Anthologia Vossiana*. Hildesheim: Weidmann.
――― (2010). *Der Pseudo-Seneca-Epigramma der Anthologia Vossiana*. Hildesheim: Georg Olms.
Brelich, A. (1939). 'Il mito nella storia di Cecilio Metello', *SMSR* 15: 30–41.
Brennan, T. C. (1994). 'M'. Curius Dentatus and the Praetor's Right to Triumph', *Historia* 43: 423–39.
――― (1996). 'Triumphus in Monte Albano', in R. W. Wallace and E. M. Harris (eds), *Transitions to Empire: Essays in Greco-Roman History 360–146 B.C., in Honor of E. Badian*. Norman: University of Oklahoma Press, 315–37.
――― (2000). *The Praetorship in the Roman Republic*. 2 vols. Oxford: Oxford University Press.
Bringmann, K. (2001). 'Der Ebrovertrag, Sagunt, und der Weg in den Zweiten Punischen Krieg', *Klio* 83: 369–76.
Briscoe, J. (1973). *A Commentary on Livy Books XXXI–XXXIII*. Oxford: Clarendon Press.
――― (1981). *A Commentary on Livy Books XXXIV–XXXVII*. Oxford: Clarendon Press.
――― (1985). Review of Jal (1984), *Gnomon* 57: 419–24.
――― (2008). *A Commentary on Livy: Books 38–40*. Oxford: Oxford University Press.
――― (2012a). *A Commentary on Livy: Books 41–45*. Oxford: Oxford University Press.
――― (2012b). 'Notes on the Functions of the Peregrine Praetor in the Republic', *Latomus* 71: 996–9.
――― (2016). *Titi Livi Ab Urbe Condita. Tomus III: Libri XXI–XXV*. Oxford: Clarendon Press.
――― (2019). *Valerius Maximus*, Facta et dicta memorabilia, *Book 8*. Berlin: De Gruyter.
Brizzi, G. (1995). 'Da Roma ad *Ariminum*: per un approccio strategico alle regioni nordo-rientali d'Italia', in Calbi and Susini (1995), 95–109.
Brock, R. (1995). 'Versions, "Inversions" and Evasions: Classical Historiography and the "Published" Speech', *PLLS* 8: 209–24.
Brown, F. E. (1951). 'Cosa I: History and Topography', *MAAR* 20: 6–113.
Bruno, B. (1906). *La terza guerra sannitica*. Rome: Ermanno Loescher & Co.
Brunt, P. A. (1971). *Italian Manpower 225 B.C.–A.D. 14*. Oxford: Clarendon Press.
――― (1978). 'Laus Imperii', in P. D. A. Garnsey and C. R. Whittaker (eds), *Imperialism in the Ancient World*. Cambridge: Cambridge University Press, 159–91 = Brunt (1990), 288–323.
――― (1980). 'On Historical Fragments and Epitomes', *CQ* 30: 477–94.
――― (1988). *The Fall of the Roman Republic and Related Essays*. Oxford: Clarendon Press.
――― (1990). *Roman Imperial Themes*. Oxford: Clarendon Press.
Buchicchio, F. T. (1970). 'Note di topografia antica sulla Volsinii romana', *MDAI(R)* 77: 19–45.

Buonocore, M. (2010). 'Per una *regio IV Augustea tributim descripta*: problemi, dubbi, certezze', in Silvestrini (2010), 29–42.
Burck, E. (1943). 'Das Bild der Karthager in der römischen Literatur', in J. Vogt (ed.), *Rom und Karthago*. Leipzig: Koehler & Amelung, 297–345.
—— (1962). *Einführung in die dritte Dekade des Livius*. 2nd edn. Heidelberg: F. H. Kerle.
Burger, Jr., C. P. (1898). *Der Kampf zwischen Rom und Samnium bis zum vollständigen Siege Roms, um 312 v. Chr.* Amsterdam: Johannes Müller.
Burillo Mozota, F. (1998). *Los Celtíberos: Etnias y estados*. Barcelona: Crítica.
Burke, P. (1989). 'History as Social Memory', in T. Butler (ed.), *Memory: History, Culture and the Mind*. Malden, MA: Blackwell, 97–110.
Burnett, A. M. (1978). 'The First Roman Silver Coins', *NAC* 7: 121–42.
—— (1989). 'The Beginnings of Roman Coinage', *AIIN* 36: 33–64.
Burton, P. J. (2011). *Friendship and Empire: Roman Imperialism and Diplomacy in the Middle Republic (353–146 BC)*. Cambridge: Cambridge University Press.
—— (2017). *Rome and the Third Macedonian War*. Cambridge: Cambridge University Press.
Butrica, J. L. (1983). 'Martial's Little Livy (14.190)', *CB* 59: 9–11.
Cabanes, P. (1976). *L'Épire de la mort de Pyrrhos à la conquête romaine (272–167 av. J.C.)*. Paris: Les Belles Lettres.
—— (1988). *Les Illyriens de Bardylis à Genthios (IVe–IIe siècles avant J.-C.)*. Paris: Sedes.
Cairns, F. (2012). 'Lentulus' Letter: Cicero *In Catilinam* 3.12; Sallust *Bellum Catilinae* 44.3–6', *Historia* 61: 78–82.
Calbi, A., and Susini, G. (eds) (1995). *Pro poplo Arimenese*. Faenza: Fratelli Lega.
Calboli, G. (1996). 'Die Episode des Tribunen Q. Caedicius (Cato, *Orig*. Frg. 7–43 Peter)', *Maia* 48: 1–32.
Caltabiano, M. (1976). 'Motivi polemici nella tradizione storica relativa a C. Flaminio', *CISA* 4: 102–17.
—— (1995). 'Gaio Flaminio: tra innovazione e tradizione', in Calbi and Susini (1995), 111–28.
Cambi, F. (2004). 'Le campagne di *Falerii* e di Capena dopo la romanizzazione', in Patterson (2004): 75–101.
Cameron, A. (1985). 'Polyonomy in the Late Roman Aristocracy: The Case of Petronius Probus', *JRS* 75: 164–82.
—— (2011). *The Last Pagans of Rome*. Oxford: Oxford University Press.
Campanile, E. (1993). 'Note sulle compagnie di ventura osche', *Athenaeum* 81: 601–11.
Canfora, D. (1993). 'Epicureismo alla corte di Pirro', *RAAN* 64: 135–42.
Capozza, M. (1966). *Movimenti servili nel mondo romano in età repubblicana. I: Dal 501 al 184 a.Cr*. Rome: L'Erma di Bretschneider.
—— (1997). 'La tradizione sui conflitti sociali a Volsini nel III secolo A.C.: dai *servi* agli *oiketai* attraverso i *liberti*', *Atene e Roma* 40: 28–41.
Carawan, E. M. (1984–5). 'The Tragic History of Marcellus and Livy's Characterization', *CJ* 80: 131–41.
—— (1989–90). 'Cato's Speech against L. Flamininus: Livy 39.42–3', *CJ* 85: 316–29.
Carcopino, J. (1953). 'Le traité d'Hasdrubal et la responsibilité de la deuxième guerre punique', *REA* 55: 258–93.
Carey, W. L. (1996). '*Nullus videtur dolo facere*: The Roman Seizure of Sardinia in 237 B.C.', *CPh* 91: 203–22.
Cary, M. (1920). 'The Early Roman Treaties with Tarentum and Rhodes', *Journal of Philology* 35: 165–73.

Cascione, C. (1999). *Tresviri Capitales*. Naples: Editoriale Scientifica.
Cassola, F. (1962). *I gruppi politici romani nel III secolo A.C.* Trieste: Istituto di Storia Antica.
Castrizio, D. (1995). *Reggio ellenistica*. Rome: Gangemi Editore.
Čašule, N. (2012). '"In Part a Roman Sea": Rome and the Adriatic in the Third Century BC', in C. Smith and L. M. Yarrow (eds), *Imperialism, Cultural Politics, and Polybius*. Oxford: Oxford University Press, 205–29.
Catin, L. *En lisant Tite-Live*. Paris: Les Belles Lettres.
Cavallaro, M. A. (1976). 'Duride, i *Fasti Cap.* e la tradizione storiografica sulle *devotiones* dei Decii', *ASAA* 54: 261–316.
——— (2004). *Da Teuta a Epulo: Interpretazione delle guerre illyriche e histriche tra 229 e 177 a.C.* Bonn: Rudolf Habelt.
Chaplin, J. D. (2000). *Livy's Exemplary History*. Oxford: Oxford University Press.
——— (2010). 'The Livian *Periochae* and the Last Republican Writer', in Horster and Reitz (2010), 451–67.
———, and Kraus, C. S. (eds) (2009). *Oxford Readings in Classical Studies: Livy*. Oxford: Oxford University Press.
Churchill, J. B. (1999). '*Ex qua quod vellent facerent*: Roman Magistrates' Authority over *praeda* and *manubiae*', *TAPhA* 129: 85–116.
Ciaceri, E. (1932). *Storia della Magna Grecia*. Vol. 3. Milan: Albrighi, Segati & C.
Cichorius, C. (1902). 'Das Geschichtswerk des Sempronius Tuditanus', *WS* 24: 588–95.
——— (1922). *Römischen Studien*. Leipzig: Teubner.
Cifani, G. (2013). 'Per una definizione storica dei Falisci, tra identità, cultura e territorio', in G. Cifani (ed.), *Tra Roma e l'Etruria: Cultura, identità e territorio dei Falisci*. Rome: Quasar, 1–53.
Clark, J. H. (2014). *Triumph in Disaster: Military Loss and the Roman Republic*. Oxford: Oxford University Press.
Clauss, J. J. (1997). '"*Domestici hostes*": The Nausicaa in Medea, the Catiline in Hannibal', *MD* 39: 165–85.
Coarelli, F. (1996). 'Il Gianicolo nell'antichità tra mito e storia', in Steinby (1996), 13–27.
——— (1997). *Il Campo Marzio: Dalle origini alla fine della Repubblica*. Rome: Quasar.
——— (2014). 'I *quaestores classici* e la battaglia delle Egadi', in M. Chiabà (ed.), *Hoc quoque laboris praemium: Scritti in onore di Gino Bandelli*. Trieste: Edizioni Università di Trieste, 99–114.
Comella, A. (1986). *I materiali votivi di Falerii*. Rome: Giorgio Bretschneider.
Confino, A. (1997). 'Collective Memory and Cultural History: Problems of Method', *American Historical Review* 102: 1386–1403.
Corbett, J. H. (1971). 'Rome and the Gauls 285–280 B.C.', *Historia* 20: 656–64.
Cornell, T. J. (1981). 'Some Observations on the "Crimen Incesti"', in *Le délit religieux dans la cité antique (Table ronde, Rome, 6–7 avril 1978)*. Rome: École Française de Rome, 27–37.
——— (1986). 'The *Annals* of Quintus Ennius', *JRS* 76: 244–50.
——— (1989). 'The Conquest of Italy', in *CAH*[2] VII. 2: 351–419.
——— (1995). *The Beginnings of Rome*. London: Routledge.
——— (2004). 'Deconstructing the Samnite Wars: An Essay in Historiography', in H. Jones (ed.), *Samnium: Settlement and Cultural Change*. Providence, RI: Brown University, 115–31.
Cowan, R. (2009). 'Thrasymennus' Wanton Wedding: Etymology, Genre, and *virtus* in Silius Italicus, *Punica*', *CQ* 59: 226–37.
Crawford, M. H. (1973). 'Foedus and Sponsio', *PBSR* 41: 1–7.
——— (1985). *Coinage and Money under the Roman Republic*. London: Methuen & Co.

—— (1995). 'La storia della colonizzazione romana secondo i Romani', in A. Storchi Marino (ed.), *L'incidenza dell'antico: Studi in memoria di Ettore Lepore*, vol. 1. Naples: Luciano Editore, 187–92.
—— (1996). *Roman Statutes*. 2 vols. London: Institute of Classical Studies.
—— (2006). 'From Poseidonia to Paestum via the Lucanians', in Bradley and Wilson (2006), 59–72.
—— (2007). 'The Mamertini, Alfius and Festus', in J. Dubouloz and S. Pittia (eds), *La Sicile de Cicéron: Lectures des* Verrines. Besançon: Presse Universitaires de Franche-Comté, 273–9.
—— (2014). 'The Roman History of Roman Colonization', in Richardson and Santangelo (2014), 201–6. Translated and revised version of Crawford (1995).
Cristofani, M. (1968). 'I Campani a Reggio', *SE* 36: 37–53.
Crosby, T. (1978). 'The Structure of Livy's History', *LCM* 3: 113–19.
Cubitt, G. (2007). *History and Memory*. Manchester: Manchester University Press.
Cuff, P. J. (1973). 'Polybius, III, 30, 3: A Note', *RSA* 3: 163–70.
Curina, R. (2015). 'Rimini: la città prima della colonia e la prima deduzione', in L. Malnati and V. Manzelli (eds), *Brixia: Roma e le genti del Po*. Florence: Giunti, 98.
Curschmann, J. (1900). *Zur Inversion der römischen Eigennamen*. Diss. Giessen. Büdingen: A. Heller.
Dahlheim, W. (1968). *Struktur und Entwicklung des römischen Völkerrechts im dritten und zweiten Jahrhundert v. Chr.* Munich: C. H. Beck.
Dahlmann, H. (1975). *Cornelius Severus*. Mainz: Akademie der Wissenschaften und der Literatur.
Damon, C. (2010). 'Déjà vu or déjà lu? History as Intertext', *PLLS* 14: 375–88.
Dart, C. (2012). '*Duumuiri Navales* and the Navy of the Roman Republic', *Latomus* 71: 1000–14.
Daube, D. (1951). 'The Peregrine Praetor', *JRS* 41: 66–70.
Davies, J. (2004). *Rome's Religious History: Livy, Tacitus and Ammianus on Their Gods*. Cambridge: Cambridge University Press.
Davis, E. W. (1959). 'Hannibal's Roman Campaign of 211 B.C.', *Phoenix* 13: 113–20.
De Benedittis, G., Matteini Chiari, M., and Terzani, C. (1999). *Aesernia: Il territorio e la città*. Campobasso: Palladino Editore.
De Caro, S. (1974). 'La necropoli di Pizzofalcone in Napoli', *RAAN* 49: 37–67.
D'Ippolito, F. (1988). 'Gli Ogulnii e il serpente di Esculapio', in G. Franciosi (ed.), *Ricerche sulla organizzazione gentilizia romana*. Vol. 2. Naples: Jovene: 155–65.
De Giorgi, A. U. (ed.) (2019). *Cosa and the Colonial Landscape of Republican Italy (Third and Second Centuries BCE)*. Ann Arbor: University of Michigan Press.
De Jonge, P. (1972). *Sprachlicher und historischer Kommentar zu Ammianus Marcellinus XIV, 2 Hälfte (c.7–11)*. Groningen: Bouma's Boekhuis.
De Juliis, E. M. (2000). *Taranto*. Bari: Edipuglia.
De Ligt, L. (2012). *Peasants, Citizens and Soldiers: Studies in the Demographic History of Roman Italy 225 BC–AD 100*. Cambridge: Cambridge University Press.
——, and Northwood, S. (eds) (2008). *People, Land, and Politics: Demographic Developments and the Transformation of Roman Italy 300 BC–AD 14*. Leiden: Brill.
De Lucia Brolli, M. A. (1991). *L'Agro Falisco*. Rome: Quasar.
De Marinis, R. (1988). 'Liguri e Celto-Liguri', in G. Pugliese Carratelli (ed.), *Italia: omnium terrarum alumna*. Milan: Libri Scheiwiller, 157–259.
——, and Spadea, G. (eds) (2004). *I Liguri: Un antico popolo europeo tra Alpi e Mediterraneo*. Genoa: Skira.

De Sensi Sestito, G. (1977). *Gerone II: Un monarca ellenistico in Sicilia*. Palermo: Editrice Sophia.

——, and Mancuso, S. (eds) (2011). *Enotri e Brettii in Magna Grecia*. Soveria Mannelli: Rubbettino.

Debergh, J. (1989). 'Autours des combats des années 259 et 258 en Corse et en Sardaigne', in H. Devijver and E. Lipiński (eds), *Studia Phoenicia X: Punic Wars*. Leuven: Peeters, 37–65.

Degrassi, A. (ed.) (1937). *Inscriptiones Italiae*. Vol. XIII, 3. Rome: La Libreria dello Stato.

—— (1939). 'Risultati della revisione del testo dei fasti capitolini', *Epigraphica* 1: 21–7.

Deininger, J. (1971). *Der politische Widerstand gegen Rom in Griechenland 217–86 v. Chr.* Berlin: De Gruyter.

Dell, H. J. (1970). 'Demetrius of Pharus and the Istrian War', *Historia* 19: 30–8.

Dench, E. (1995). *From Barbarians to New Men*. Oxford: Clarendon Press.

—— (2005). *Romulus' Asylum: Roman Identities from the Age of Alexander to the Age of Hadrian*. Oxford: Oxford University Press.

Derow, P. S. (1973). 'Kleemporos', *Phoenix* 27: 118–34 = Derow (2015), 151–67.

—— (1979). 'Polybius, Rome, and the East', *JRS* 69: 1–15 = Derow (2015), 125–49.

—— (2015). *Rome, Polybius, and the East*, ed. A. Erskine and J. C. Quinn. Oxford: Oxford University Press.

Develin, R. (1975). 'Prorogation of *imperium* before the Hannibalic War', *Latomus* 34: 716–22.

—— (1979a). *Patterns in Office-Holding: 366–49 B.C.* Brussels: Latomus.

—— (1979b). 'The Political Position of C. Flaminius', *RhM* 122: 268–77.

—— (1980). 'The Roman Command Structure and Spain 218–190 B.C.', *Klio* 62: 355–67.

—— (1985). *The Practice of Politics at Rome: 366–167 B.C.* Brussels: Latomus.

Di Marco, L. (1975). *Spoletium: Topografia e urbanistica*. Spoleto: Accademia Spoletina.

Di Stefano Manzella, I. (1990). 'Lo stato giuridico di Falerii Novi dalla fondazione al III secolo D.C.', in Maetzke et al. (1990), 341–68.

Dickie, M. W. (1995). 'The Fathers of the Church and the Evil Eye', in H. Maguire (ed.), *Byzantine Magic*. Washington, DC: Dumbarton Oaks, 9–34.

Dimo, V., Lenhardt, P., and Quantin, F. (eds) (2007). *Apollonia d'Illyrie. 1: Atlas archéologique et historique*. Rome: École Française de Rome.

Dipersia, G. (1975). 'Le polemiche sulla guerra sociale nell' ambasceria latina di Livio VIII, 4–6', *CISA* 3: 111–20.

Dixon, S. (1985). 'Breaking the Law to Do the Right Thing: The Gradual Erosion of the Voconian Law in Ancient Rome', *Adelaide Law Review* 9.4: 519–34.

Doblhofer, E. (1983). 'Livius und andere "Imperialisten"', in Lefèvre and Olshausen (1983), 133–62.

Dommelen, P. van (1998). 'Punic Persistence: Colonialism and Cultural Identities in Roman Sardinia', in R. Laurence and J. Berry (eds), *Cultural Identity in the Roman Empire*. London: Routledge, 25–48.

—— (2002). 'Ambiguous Matters: Colonialism and Local Identities in Punic Sardinia', in C. L. Lyons and J. K. Papadopoulos (eds), *The Archaeology of Colonialism*. Los Angeles: Getty Research Institute, 121–47.

Doody, A. (2009). 'Authority and Authorship in the *Medicina Plinii*', in L. Taub and A. Doody (eds), *Authorial Voices in Greco-Roman Technical Writing*. Trier: Wissenschaftlicher Verlag Trier, 93–105.

Dorey, T. A. (1959–60). 'The Treaty with Saguntum', *Humanitas (Coimbra)* 11–12: 1–10.

Douglas, A. E. (1966). *M. Tulli Ciceronis Brutus*. Oxford: Clarendon Press.

Dox, D. (2004). *The Idea of the Theatre in Latin Christian Thought: Augustine to the Fourteenth Century*. Ann Arbor: University of Michigan Press.
Drescher, F. (1900). *Beiträge zur Liviusepitome*. Diss. Erlangen.
Dubischar, M. (2010). 'Survival of the Most Condensed? Auxiliary Texts, Communications Theory, and Condensation of Knowledge', in Horster and Reitz (2010), 39–67.
Duhn, F. von (1886). 'Due bassirilievi del Palazzo Rondinini', *MDAI(R)* 1: 167–72.
Dunkle, J. R. (1967). 'The Greek Tyrant and Roman Political Invective of the Late Republic', *TAPhA* 98: 151–71.
Dyck, A. R. (1996). *A Commentary on Cicero, De Officiis*. Ann Arbor: University of Michigan Press.
Dyson, S. L, and Rowland, Jr., R. J. (2007). *Archaeology and History in Sardinia from the Stone Age to the Middle Ages: Shepherds, Sailors, and Conquerors*. Philadelphia: University of Pennsylvania Museum of Archaeology and Anthropology.
Dzino, D. (2010). *Illyricum in Roman Politics: 229 BC–AD 68*. Cambridge: Cambridge University Press.
Eckstein, A. M. (1980a). 'Polybius on the Rôle of the Senate in the Crisis of 264 B.C.', *GRBS* 21: 175–90.
—— (1980b). '*Unicum subsidium populi Romani*: Hiero II and Rome, 263 B.C.–215 B.C.', *Chiron* 10: 183–203.
—— (1982). 'Human Sacrifice and Fear of Military Disaster in Republican Rome', *AJAH* 7: 69–95.
—— (1983). 'Two Notes on the Chronology of the Outbreak of the Hannibalic War', *RhM* 126: 255–72.
—— (1987). *Senate and General: Individual Decision Making and Roman Foreign Relations, 264–194 B.C.* Berkeley: University of California Press.
—— (1994). 'Polybius, Demetrius of Pharus, and the Origins of the Second Illyrian War', *CPh* 89: 46–59.
—— (2002). Review of Williams (2001), *International History Review* 24: 625–8.
—— (2006). *Mediterranean Anarchy, Interstate War, and the Rise of Rome*. Berkeley: University of California Press.
—— (2008). *Rome Enters the Greek East*. Malden, MA: Blackwell.
—— (2010). 'Polybius, the "Treaty of Philinus", and Roman Accusations against Carthage', *CQ* 60: 406–26.
Edelstein, E. J. and Edelstein, L. (1945). *Asclepius: A Collection and Interpretation of the Testimonies*. 2 vols. Baltimore: Johns Hopkins University Press.
Eden, P. T. (1962). 'Caesar's Style: Inheritance versus Intelligence', *Glotta* 40: 74–117.
Edwards, C. (2007). *Death in Ancient Rome*. New Haven: Yale University Press.
Eilers, C. (2002). *Roman Patrons of Greek Cities*. Oxford: Oxford University Press.
Eliæson, Å (1906). *Beiträge zur Geschichte Sardiniens und Corsicas im Ersten Punischen Kriege: Quellenkritischgeschichtliche Untersuchungen*. Diss. Uppsala. Almquist & Wiksells.
Elliott, J. (2013). *Ennius and the Architecture of the Annales*. Cambridge: Cambridge University Press.
—— (2015). 'The Epic Vantage Point: Roman Historiographical Allusion Reconsidered', *Histos* 9: 277–311.
Elster, M. (1976). *Studien zur Gesetzgebung der frühen römischen Republik: Gesetzesanhäufungen und -wiederholungen*. Frankfurt am Main: Peter Lang.
Engerbeaud, M. (2013). 'La bataille d'Ausculum (279 av. J.-C.), une défaite romaine?', *RPh* 87: 61–80.
Enmann, A. (1902). 'Die älteste Redaction der Pontificalannalen', *RhM* XX: 517–33.

Erdkamp, P. (2009). 'Polybius, the Ebro Treaty, and the Gallic Invasion of 225 B.C.E.', *CPh* 104: 495–510.
Errington, R. M. (1974). '*Senatus Consultum de Coronaeis* and the Early Course of the Third Macedonian War', *RFIC* 104: 79–86.
Evans, A. J. (1889). 'The "Horsemen" of Tarentum', *Numismatic Chronicle* 3rd ser. 9: 1–228.
Evans, J. K. (1980). '*Plebs Rustica*: The Peasantry of Classical Italy', *AJAH* 5: 134–73.
Fay, E. W. (1920). 'The Elogium Duilianum', *CPh* 15: 176–83.
Fayer, C. (1962). 'Testimonianze di tribù Romane nelle legende delle monete, nei papiri e nelle fonti letterarie', *StudUrb* 36: 185–206.
Fear, A. T. (2010). *Orosius: Seven Books of History against the Pagans*. Liverpool: Liverpool University Press.
Feeney, D. C. (2007). *Caesar's Calendar: Ancient Time and the Beginnings of History*. Berkeley: University of California Press.
—— (2016). *Beyond Greek*. Cambridge, MA: Harvard University Press.
Feig Vishnia, R. (1996). *State, Society and Popular Leaders in Mid-Republican Rome 241–167 BC*. London: Routledge.
—— (2012). 'A Case of "Bad Press"? Gaius Flaminius in Ancient Historiography', *ZPE* 181: 27–45.
Felmy, A. (2001). *Die römische Republik im Geschichtsbild der Spätantike*. Berlin: dissertation.de—Verlag im Internet.
Fentress, E. (2000). 'Introduction: Frank Brown, Cosa, and the Idea of a Roman City', in E. Fentress (ed.), *Romanization and the City: Creation, Transformations, and Failures*. Portsmouth: Journal of Roman Archaeology, 11–24.
Feraco, F. (2017). *Titio Livio: Ab urbe condita liber XXVII*. Bari: Cacucci Editore.
Ferenczy (1970). 'The Career of Appius Claudius Caecus after the Censorship', *AAntHung* 18: 71–103.
Ferone, C. (2001). 'Appiano, Samn. 7,1. e la tutela dell'*ora maritima* a Roma nel III sec. a.C.', *Klio* 83: 377–87.
Ferro, B. (1960). *Le origini della II guerra macedonica*. Palermo: Accademia.
Feyel, Chr., and Graslin-Thomé, L. (eds) (2014). *Le projet politique d'Antiochus IV*. Nancy: Association pour la Diffusion de la Recherche sur l'Antiquité.
Firpo, G. (2002). 'Quale Sentino?', in D. Poli (ed.), *La battaglia del Sentino: Scontro fra nazioni e incontro in una nazione*. Rome: Il Calamo, 95–126.
Flach, D. (1978). 'Das römisch-karthagische Bündnisabkommen im Krieg gegen Pyrrhos', *Historia* 27: 615–17.
Fleck, M. (1993). *Cicero als Historiker*. Stuttgart: Teubner.
Flower, H. (1998). 'The Significance of an Inscribed Breastplate Captured at Falerii in 241 B.C.', *JRA* 11: 224–32.
—— (2000). 'The Tradition of the *Spolia Opima*: M. Claudius Marcellus and Augustus', *CA* 19: 34–64. Reprinted with additional appendix in Richardson and Santangelo (2014), 285–320.
—— (2003). '"Memories" of Marcellus: History and Memory in Roman Republican Culture', in U. Eigler, U. Gotter, N. Luraghi, and U. Walter (eds), *Formen römischen Geschichtsschreibung von den Anfängen bis Livius*. Darmstadt: Wissenschaftliche Buchgesellschaft, 39–52.
Flurl, W. (1969). *Deditio in Fidem: Untersuchungen zu Livius und Polybios*. Diss. Munich.
Formisano, M., and Sogno, C. (2010). '*Petite Poésie Portable*: The Latin *cento* in Its Late Antique Context', in Horster and Reitz (2010), 375–92.
Forni, G. (1953). 'Manio Curio Dentato uomo democratico', *Athenaeum* 31: 170–240.

Forsythe, G. (2005). *A Critical History of Early Rome: From Prehistory to the First Punic War*. Berkeley: University of California Press.
Fox. M. (1996). *Roman Historical Myths: The Regal Period in Augustan Literature*. Oxford: Clarendon Press.
Foxhall, L., Gehrke, H.-J., and Luraghi, N. (eds) (2010). *Intentional History: Spinning Time in Ancient Greece*. Stuttgart: Franz Steiner.
Fraccaro, P. (1911). 'I processi degli Scipioni', in E. Pais (ed.), *Studi storici per l'antichità classica*. Pisa: F. Mariotti, 217–414 = (1956), 263–392.
—— (1919). 'Lex Flaminia de agro Gallico et Piceno viritim dividundo', *Athenaeum* 7: 73–93 = (1957), 191–205.
—— (1947). Review of A. Degrassi, *Inscriptiones Italiae* XIII, 1, *Athenaeum* 25: 240–50.
—— (1956). *Opuscula* I. Pavia: Athenaeum, 1956.
—— (1957). *Opuscula* II. Pavia: Athenaeum, 1957.
Frank, T. (1919). 'The Columna Rostrata of C. Duillius', *CPh* 14: 78–84.
—— (1926). 'Two Historical Themes in Roman Literature', *CPh* 21: 311–16.
Franke, P. R. (1954). *Alt-Epirus und das Königtum der Molosser*. Diss. Erlangen.
Fraschetti, A. (1981). 'Aristosseno, i Romani e la "barbarizzazione" di Poseidonia', *AION(archeol)* 3: 97–115.
—— (1984). 'La sepoltura delle Vestali e la città', in *Du châtiment dans la cité: Supplices corporels et peine de mort dans le monde antique*. Rome: École Française de Rome, 97–129.
Frayn, J. M. (1979). *Subsistence Farming in Roman Italy*. London: Centaur Press.
Frederiksen, M. W. (1970–1). 'The Contribution of Archaeology to the Agrarian Problem in the Gracchan Period', *DialArch* 4–5: 330–57.
—— (1984). *Campania*. Rome: British School at Rome.
——, and Ward Perkins, J. B. (1957). 'The Ancient Road Systems of the Central and Northern Ager Faliscus (Notes on Southern Etruria 2)', *PBSR* 25: 67–203.
Frier, B. W. (1999). *Libri Annales Pontificum Maximorum: The Origins of the Annalistic Tradition*. 2nd edn. Ann Arbor: University of Michigan Press.
Fritz, K. von (1950). 'The Reorganisation of the Roman Government in 366 B.C. and the So-Called Licinio-Sextian Laws', *Historia* 1: 3–44.
Fronda, M. P. (2011). 'Polybius 3.40, the Foundation of Placentia, and the Roman Calendar (218–217 BC)', *Historia* 60: 425–57.
Funke, S. (2000). 'Ἄπειρος 317–272 BC: The Struggle of the Diadochi and the Political Structure of the Federation', in Mooren (2000), 107–21.
Futrell, A. (1997). *Blood in the Arena: The Spectacle of Roman Power*. Austin: University of Texas Press.
Gabba, E. (1977). 'Aspetti culturali dell' imperialismo romano', *Athenaeum* 55: 49–74.
—— (1984). 'Il consenso popolare alla politica espansionistica romana fra III e II sec. a.c.', in Harris (1984), 115–29.
Gabrici, E. (1948). 'Partenope e Palepoli', *RAL* 8.3: 167–76.
Gaca, K. (2010). 'The Andrapodizing of War Captives in Greek Historical Memory', *TAPhA* 140: 117–61.
Gagé, J. (1955). *Apollon Romain*. Paris: De Boccard.
Gagliardi, L. (2006). *Mobilità e integrazione delle persone nei centri cittadini romani. Aspetti giuridici. I: La classificazione degli incolae*. Milan: A. Guiffrè.
—— (2015). 'Fondazione di colonie romane ed espropriazioni di terre a danno degli indigeni', *MEFRA* 127: 353–70.
Galinsky, K. (ed.) (2014). *Memoria Romana: Memory in Rome and Rome in Memory*. Ann Arbor: University of Michigan Press.

Galinsky, K. (ed.) (2016). *Memory in Ancient Rome and Early Christianity*. Oxford: Oxford University Press.

——, and Lapatin, K. (eds) (2015). *Cultural Memories in the Roman Empire*. Los Angeles: J. Paul Getty Museum.

Gallia, A. B. (2012). *Remembering the Roman Republic*. Cambridge: Cambridge University Press.

Gamauf, R. (2007). '*Cum aliter nulla domus tuta esse possit*...': Fear of Slaves and Roman Law', in Serghidou (2007), 145–64.

Garcia, D. (2014). *La celtique Méditerranéenne*. 2nd edn. Arles: Éditions Errance.

Gardner, J. F. (1986). *Women in Roman Law and Society*. Bloomington: Indiana University Press.

Gargola, D. J. (1990). 'The Colonial Commissioners of 218 B.C. and the Foundation of Cremona and Placentia', *Athenaeum* 78: 465–73.

Garland, R. (1995). *The Eye of the Beholder: Deformity and Disability in the Graeco-Roman World*. London: Duckworth.

Garnsey, P. (1969). Review of Bauman (1967), *JRS* 59: 282–4.

—— (1980). 'Non-Slave Labour in the Roman World', in P. Garnsey (ed.), *Non-Slave Labour in the Greco-Roman World*. Cambridge: Cambridge Philological Society, 34–47.

Garofalo, L. (1989). *Il processo edilizio: Contributo allo studio dei iudicia populi*. Padua: Cedam.

Garoufalias, P. (1979). *Pyrrhus: King of Epirus*. 2nd edn. London: Stacey International.

Garzetti, A. (1947). 'Appio Claudio Cieco nella storia politica del suo tempo', *Athenaeum* 25: 175–224.

Gatti, G. (1960). 'Dove erano situati il Teatro di Balbo e il Circo Flaminio?', *Capitolium* 35.7: 3–12.

—— (1961). 'Ancora sulla vera posizione del Teatro di Balco e del Circo Flaminio', *Palatino* 5: 17–20.

Gehrke, H.-J. (2001). 'Myth, History, and Collective Identity: Uses of the Past in Ancient Greece and Beyond', in N. Luraghi (ed.), *The Historian's Craft in the Age of Herodotus*. Oxford: Oxford University Press, 286–313.

Gelzer, M. (1933). 'Römische Politik bei Fabius Pictor', *Hermes* 68: 129–66.

Ghizzone, F. (ed.) (1990). *Storia di Piacenza*. Vol. 1. Piacenza: Cassa di Risparmio di Piacenza e Vigevano.

Giampaola, D. (2000). 'Benevento: dal centra indigeno alia colonia latina', in *Studi sull'Italia dei Sanniti*. Milan: Electa, 36–46.

Gianfrotta, P. A. (1972). *Castrum Novum*. Rome: De Luca.

Gibson, R. (2014). 'Starting with the Index in Pliny', in L. Jansen (ed.), *The Roman Paratext*. Cambridge: Cambridge University Press, 33–55.

Gilbert, R. L. (1939). 'The Origin and History of the Peregrine Praetorship, 242–166 B.C.', *Res Judicatae* 50: 50–8.

Gnoli, T. (2020). 'The Rams from the Aegates Islands: Further Considerations', in Royal and Tusa (2020), 106–11.

Goldman, A. L., and Rose, A. (2020). 'Bronze Helmets from the Battle of the Aegates Islands', in Royal and Tusa (2020), 147–74.

Gordon, R. L. (1979). 'The Real and the Imaginary: Production and Religion in the Graeco-Roman World', *Art History* 2: 5–34.

Gowing, A. M. (2005). *Empire and Memory*. Cambridge: Cambridge University Press.

Graf, F. (1992). 'Heiligtum und Ritual: Das Beispiel der griechisch-römischen Asklepieia', in *Le sanctuaire grec*. Geneva: Fondation Hardt, 159–203.

Grassi, M. T. (1991). *I Celti in Italia*. Milan: Longanesi.

Greco, E. (1988). 'Archeologia della colonia latina di Paestum', *DialArch* 6: 79–86.
Grelle, F. (2011). 'Le colonie romane: definizioni, modelli, elenchi', in S. Cagnazzi et al. (eds), *Scritti di storia per Mario Pani*. Bari: Edipuglia, 193–205.
Griffin, M. (1976). *Seneca: A Philosopher in Politics*. Oxford: Clarendon Press.
Groag, E. (1934). 'Terentius Gentianus', *RE* V A. 1: 655–6.
Grossmann, L. (2009). *Roms Samnitenkriege*. Düsseldorf: Wellem Verlag.
Gruen, E. S. (1984a). *The Hellenistic World and the Coming of Rome*. Berkeley: University of California Press.
—— (1984b). 'Material Rewards and the Drive for Empire', in Harris (1984), 59–82.
—— (1995). 'The "Fall" of the Scipios', in I. Malkin and Z. W. Rubinsohn (eds), *Leaders and Masses in the Roman World*. Leiden: Brill, 59–90.
—— (2011). *Rethinking the Other in Antiquity*. Princeton: Princeton University Press.
Gualazzini, U. (1985). 'Aspetti meno noti della fondazione di Cremona', in Pontiroli (1985), 3–48.
Guthrie, P. C. F. (1949). *The Roman Vilicus*. Diss. Toronto.
Hackens, T., Holloway, N. D., Holloway, R. R., and Moucharte, G. (eds) (1992), *The Age of Pyrrhus*. Louvain: Collège Érasme.
Haeperen, F. van (2002). *Le collège pontifical (3ème s. a.C.–4ème s. p.C.)*. Brussels: Institute Historique Belge de Rome.
Haeussler, R. (2013). *Becoming Roman? Diverging Identities and Experiences in Ancient Northwest Italy*. Walnut Creek, CA: Left Coast Press.
Halbwachs, M. (1980). *The Collective Memory*. Tr. F. J. Ditter, Jr., and V. Y. Ditter. New York: Harper & Row.
Halstead, P. (1987). 'Traditional and Ancient Rural Economy in Mediterranean Europe: plus ça change?', *JHS* 107: 77–87.
Hammond, N. G. L. (1967). *Epirus*. Oxford: Clarendon Press.
—— (1968). 'Illyris, Rome and Macedon in 229–205 B.C.', *JRS* 58: 1–21.
—— (1990). 'Royal Pages, Personal Pages, and Boys Trained in the Macedonian Manner during the Period of the Temenid Monarchy', *Historia* 39: 261–90.
——, and Walbank, F. W. (1988). *A History of Macedonia*. Vol. III. Oxford: Clarendon Press.
Hampl, F. (1972). 'Zur Vorgeschichte des ersten und zweiten Punischen Krieges', *ANRW* I 1: 412–41.
Hansen, S. B., and Bergquist, S. (1998). 'Iulius Paris, An Epitomator at Work—or the Importance of an Epitome of Valerius Maximus' *Memorable Deeds and Words*', *C&M* 49: 237–74.
Hanslik, R. (1949). 'C. Papirius Maso', *RE* XVIII. 3: 1062–3.
Harnett, B. (2017). 'The Diffusion of the Codex', *CA* 36: 183–235.
Harris, W. V. (1971). *Rome in Etruria and Umbria*. Oxford: Clarendon Press.
—— (1976). 'The Development of the Quaestorship, 267–81 B.C.', *CQ* 26: 92–106.
—— (1979a). *War and Imperialism in Republican Rome 327–70 B.C.* Oxford: Clarendon Press.
—— (1979b). 'Lydus, *De Magistratibus* 1.27: A Reply', *BASP* 16: 199–200.
—— (ed.) (1984). *The Imperialism of Mid-Republican Rome*. Rome: American Academy in Rome.
—— (1985). 'Volsinii and Rome, 400–100 B.C.', *Annali della Fondazione per il Museo Claudio Faina* 2: 143–56.
—— (2017). 'Rome at Sea: The Beginnings of Roman Naval Power', *G&R* 64: 14–26.
Heinen, H. (1972a). *Untersuchungen zur hellenistischen Geschichte des 3. Jahrhunderts v. Chr.* Wiesbaden: Franz Steiner.

Heinen, H. (1972b). 'Die politischen Beziehungen zwischen Rom und dem Ptolemäerreich von ihren Anfängen bis zum Tag von Eleusis (273–168 v. Chr.)', *ANRW* I 1: 633–59.

Heuberger, R. (1938). 'Die Gaesaten', *Klio* 31: 60–80.

Heubner, H. (1968). *P. Cornelius Tacitus: Die Historien*. Vol. 2. Heidelberg: Carl Winter Universitätsverlag.

Heurgon, J. (1942). *Recherches sur l'histoire, la religion et la civilisation de Capoue préromaine des origines à la deuxième guerre punique*. Paris: De Boccard.

Heuss, A. (1933). *Die völkerrechtlichen Grundlagen der römischen Aussenpolitik in republikanischer Zeit*. Leipzig: Dieterich'sche Verlagsbuchhandlung.

—— (1949). 'Der erste punischen Krieg und das Problem des römischen Imperialismus (Zur politischen Beurteilung des Krieges)', *HZ* 169: 457–513.

Heyer, F. (1875). 'Die Periochae des Livius in ihrem Verhältnis zum livianischen Texte', *Jahrbücher für classische Philologie* 3: 645–52.

Hin, S. (2008). 'Counting Romans', in de Ligt and Northwood (2008), 187–238.

Hölkeskamp, K.-J. (1988). 'Die Entstehung der Nobilität und der Funktionswandel des Volkstribunats: Die historische Bedeutung der *lex Hortensia de plebiscitis*', *Archiv für Kulturgeschichte* 70: 271–312 = Hölkeskamp (2004), 49–83.

—— (1996). '*Exempla* und *mos maiorum*: Überlegungen zum kollektiven Gedächtnis der Nobilität', in H.-J. Gehrke and A. Möller (eds), *Vergangenheit und Lebenswelt: Soziale Kommunikationen, Traditionsbildung und historisches Bewusstsein*. Tübingen: Gunter Narr, 301–38 = Hölkeskamp (2004), 169–98.

—— (2001). 'Capitol, Comitium und Forum. Öffentliche Räume, sakrale Topographie und Erinnerungslandschaften der römischen Republik', in S. Faller (ed.), *Studien zu antiken Identitäten*. Würzburg: ERGON Verlag, 97–132 = Hölkeskamp (2004), 137–65.

—— (2004). *Senatus Populusque Romanus*. Stuttgart: Franz Steiner.

—— (2016). 'In the Web of (Hi-)Stories: Memoria, Monuments, and Their Myth-Historical "Interconnectedness"', in Galinsky (2016), 169–213.

—— (2018). '*Memoria* by Multiplication: The Cornelii Scipiones in Monumental Memory', in Sandberg and Smith (2018), 422–76.

Hof, A. (2002). *Die römische Außenpolitik vom Ausbruch des Krieges gegen Tarent bis zum Frieden mit Syrakus (281–263 v. Chr.)*. Hildesheim: Olms-Weidmann.

Hoffmann, W. (1936). 'Der Kampf zwischen Rom und Tarent im Urteil der antiken Überlieferung', *Hermes* 71: 11–24.

—— (1951). 'Die römische Kriegserklärung an Karthago im Jahre 218', *RhM* 94: 69–88.

Holleaux, M. (1920). 'Le prétendu recours des Athéniens aux Romains en 201/200', *REA* 22: 77–96.

—— (1930). 'Études d'histoire hellénistique. La date de la première guerre romaine d'Illyrie', *REG* 43: 243–61.

Holloway, R. R. (1992). 'The Romano-Campanian Coinage', in Hackens *et al.* (1992), 225–35.

Holzapfel, L. (1885). *Römische Chronologie*. Leipzig: Teubner.

Holzberg, N. (2004). 'Impersonating the Banished Philosopher: Pseudo-Seneca's *Liber Epigrammaton*', *HSCPh* 102, 423–44.

Hopkins, K. (1978). *Conquerors and Slaves*. Cambridge: Cambridge University Press.

Horsfall, N. M. (1985). 'Illusion and Reality in Latin Topographical Writing', *G&R* 32: 197–208.

—— (1987). 'From History to Legend: M. Manlius and the Geese', in J. N. Brenner and N. M. Horsfall, *Roman Myth and Mythography*. London: Institute of Classical Studies, 63–75.

Horster, M. (2017). 'Livius-Epitome: ein spätantiker Blick auf die (kurzgefasste) römische Republik', in S. Dusil, G. Schwedler, and R. Schwitter (eds), *Exzerpieren—Kompilieren—Tradieren*. Berlin: De Gruyter, 25–48.

———, and Reitz, C. (eds) (2010). *Condensing Texts—Condensed Texts*. Stuttgart: Franz Steiner.

Hoyos, B. D. (1984a). 'The Roman-Punic Pact of 279 B.C.: Its Problems and Its Purpose', *Historia* 33: 402–39.

——— (1984b). 'Polybius' Roman οἱ πολλοί in 264 B.C.', *LCM* 9: 88–93.

——— (1985). 'Treaties True and False: The Error of Philinus of Agrigentum', *CQ* 35: 92–109.

——— (1998). *Unplanned Wars: The Origins of the First and Second Punic Wars*. Berlin: De Gruyter.

Hülsen, C. (1899). 'Castrum Novum', *RE* III. 2: 1770.

Humbert, M. (1978). *Municipium et civitas sine suffragio: L'organisation de la conquête jusqu'à la guerre sociale*. Rome: École Française de Rome.

——— (1988). 'Le tribunat de la plèbe et le tribunal du peuple: remarques sur l'histoire de la *provocatio ad populum*', *MEFRA* 100: 431–503.

——— (2012). 'I "plebiscita" prima dell'equiparazione alle leggi (con la lex Hortensia del 287 ca.)', in J.-L. Ferrary (ed.), *Leges publicae: La legge nell'esperienza giuridica romana*. Pavia: IUSS Press, 307–37.

Humm, M. (1996). 'Appius Claudius Caecus et la construction de la *Via Appia*', *MEFRA* 108: 693–746.

——— (2005). *Appius Claudius Caecus: La république accomplie*. Rome: École Française de Rome.

——— (2009). 'Rome et l'Italie dans le discours d'Appius Claudius Caecus contre Pyrrhus', *Pallas* 79: 203–20.

——— (2018). 'La "barbarisation" di Poséidonia et la fin des cultes grecs à Paestum', *RHR* 235: 353–72.

Huss, W. (1985). *Geschichte der Karthager*. Munich: C. H. Beck.

Ilari, V. (1974). *Gli Italici nelle strutture militari romane*. Milan: A. Giuffrè.

Ireland, R. I. (ed.) (1990). *Iuli Frontini Strategemata*. Leipzig: Teubner.

Irigoin, J. (1997). 'Titres, sous-titres et sommaires dans les oeuvres des historiens grecs du Ier siècle avant J.-C. au Ve siècle après J.-C.', in J.-C. Fredouille, M.-O. Goulet-Cazé, P. Hoffmann, and P. Petitmengin (eds), *Titres et articulations du texte dans les oeuvres antiques*. Paris: Institut d'Études Augustiniennes, 127–34.

Isayev, E. (2007). *Inside Ancient Lucania: Dialogues in Archaeology and History*. London: Institute of Classical Studies.

Jaeger, M. (1997). *Livy's Written Rome*. Ann Arbor: University of Michigan Press.

——— (2008). *Archimedes and the Roman Imagination*. Ann Arbor: University of Michigan Press.

Jahn, J. (1970). *Interregnum und Wahldiktatur*. Kallmünz: Michael Lassleben.

Jahn, O. (1853). *T. Livi Ab Urbe Condita Librorum CXLII Periochae. Iulii Obsequentis Ab Anno Urbis Conditae DV Prodigiorum Liber*. Leipzig: Breitkopf and Hartel.

Jal, P. (1984). *Abrégés des livres de l'histoire romaine de Tite-Live*. Vol. 1. Paris: Les Belles Lettres.

Jashemski, W. F. (1950). *The Origins and History of the Proconsular and the Propraetorian Imperium to 27 B.C.* Chicago: University of Chicago Press.

Johner, A. (1996). *La violence chez Tite-Live: Mythographie et historiographie*. Strasbourg: AECR.

Jones, A. H. M. (1972). *The Criminal Courts of the Roman Republic and Principate*. Oxford: Basil Blackwell.

Joplin, P. K. (1990). 'Ritual Work on Human Flesh: Livy's Lucretia and the Rape of the Body Politic', *Helios* 17: 51–70.
Joshel, S. R. (1992). 'The Body Female and the Body Politic: Livy's Lucretia and Verginia', in A. Richlin (ed.), *Pornography and Representation in Greece and Rome*. Oxford: Oxford University Press, 112–30 = Chaplin and Kraus (2009), 380–408.
Judeich, W. (1926). 'König Pyrrhos' römische Politik', *Klio* 20: 1–18.
Kahrstedt, U. (1959). 'Ager Publicus und Selbstverwaltung in Lukanien und Bruttium', *Historia* 8: 174–206.
Kaster, R. A. (2006). *Cicero: Speech on Behalf of Publius Sestius*. Oxford: Clarendon Press.
Keay, S., Millett, M., Poppy, S., Robinson, J., Taylor, J., and Terrenato, N. (2000). 'Falerii Novi: A New Survey of the Walled Area', *PBSR* 68: 1–93.
Kelly, G. (2008). *Ammianus Marcellinus: The Allusive Historian*. Cambridge: Cambridge University Press.
Kienast, D. (1963). 'Pyrrhos von Epeiros', *RE* XXIV: 108–65.
—— (1966). *Untersuchungen zu den Kriegsflotten der römischen Kaiserzeit*. Bonn: Rudolf Habelt.
Klebs, E. (1896). 'M. Atilius Regulus', *RE* II: 2086–92.
Kloft, H. (1977). *Prorogation und außerordentliche Imperien 326–81 v. Chr*. Meisenheim am Glan: Anton Hain.
Klotz, A. (1913). 'Die Epitoma des Livius', *Hermes* 48: 542–57.
—— (1936). 'Zu den Periochae des Livius', *Philologus* 91: 67–88.
—— (1940). *Livius und seine Vorgänger*. Leipzig: Teubner.
Knapp, R. C. (1977). *Aspects of the Roman Experience in Iberia, 206–100 B.C.* Valladolid: Universidad de Valladolid.
Koch, C. (1958). 'Vesta', *RE* VIIIA: 1717–76.
Koestermann, E. (1965). *Cornelius Tacitus: Annalen. Band II: Buch 4–6*. Heidelberg: Carl Winter.
—— (1971). *C. Sallustius Crispus: Bellum Iugurthinum*. Heidelberg: Carl Winter.
Kohl, A. (1959). *Der Satznachtrag bei Tacitus*. Diss. Würzburg.
Kondratieff, E. (2004). 'The Column and Coinage of C. Duilius: Innovations in Iconography in Large and Small Media in the Middle Republic', *SCI* 23: 1–39.
Konrad, C. F. (2015). 'After Drepana', *CQ* 65: 192–203.
Kornemann, E. (1904). *Die neue Livius-Epitome aus Oxyrhynchus*. Leipzig: Dieterich'sche Verlagsbuchhandlung.
Kornhardt, H. (1954). 'Regulus und die Cannaegefangenen', *Hermes* 82: 85–123.
Kowalewski, B. (2002). *Frauengestalten im Geschichtswerk des T. Livius*. Munich: K. G. Saur.
Kraus, C. S. (1991). '*Initium turbandi omnia a femina ortum est*: Fabia Minor and the Election of 367 B.C.', *Phoenix* 45: 314–25.
—— (1992). 'How (Not?) to End a Sentence: The Problem of *-que*', *HSCPh* 94: 321–9.
—— (1994a). *Livy: Ab Urbe Condita Book VI*. Cambridge: Cambridge University Press.
—— (1994b). '"No Second Troy": Topoi and Refoundation in Livy, Book V', *TAPhA* 124: 267–89.
Krebs, C. (2006). '*Leonides Laco quidem simile apud Thermopylas fecit*: Cato and Herodotus', *BICS* 49: 93–103.
Kuijper, D. (1968). 'De honestate Plinii minoris', *Mnemosyne* 4th ser., 21: 40–70.
La Bua, V. (1971). 'Regio e Decio Vibellio', *MGR* 3: 63–141.
La Regina, A. (1970–1). 'I territori sabellici e sannitici', *DialArch* 4–5: 443–59.
Ladewig, M. (2014). *Rom—Die antike Seerepublik*. Stuttgart: Franz Steiner.
Lamboley, J.-L. (1996). *Recherches sur les Messapiens: IVe–IIe siècle avant J.-C*. Rome: École Française de Rome.

Lange, L. (1879). *Römische Alterthümer*. Vol. 2. 3rd edn. Berlin: Weidmann.
Langlands, R. (2011). 'Roman *Exempla* and Situation Ethics: Valerius Maximus and Cicero *de Officiis*', *JRS* 101: 100–22.
—— (2018). *Exemplary Ethics in Ancient Rome*. Cambridge: Cambridge University Press.
Laporte, J.-P. (1995). 'Notes sur les camps de *Tatilti* et d'*Aras* (Maurétanie Césarienne)', in Y. Le Bohec (ed.), *La hiérarchie (Rangordnung) de l'armée romaine sous le Haut-Empire*. Paris: De Boccard, 343–66.
Larsen, J. A. O. (1968). *Greek Federal States: Their Institutions and History*. Oxford: Clarendon Press.
Lazenby, J. L. (1978). *Hannibal's War*. Warminster: Aris & Phillips.
—— (1996). *The First Punic War: A Military History*. London: UCL Press.
Leary, T. J. (1996). *Martial Book XIV: The Apophoreta*. London: Duckworth.
Lefèvre, E., and Olshausen, E. (eds) (1983). *Livius: Werk und Rezeption: Festschrift für Erich Burck zum 80. Geburtstag*. Munich: C. H. Beck.
Lefkowitz, M. R. (1959). 'Pyrrhus' Negotiations with the Romans', *HSCPh* 64: 147–77.
Leigh, M. (1997). *Lucan: Spectacle and Engagement*. Oxford: Clarendon Press.
Lejay, P. (1920). 'Appius Claudius Caecus', *RPh* 44: 92–141.
Lenschau, T. (1912a). 'Hanno (7)', *RE* XIV: 2354–5.
—— (1912b). 'Hanno (8)', *RE* XIV: 2355.
Lenzi, F. (ed.) (2006). *Rimini e l'Adriatico nell'età delle guerre puniche*. Bologna: Ante Quem.
Lepore, G. (2014). 'La colonia di Sena Gallica: un progetto abbandonato?', in M. Chiabà (ed.), *Hoc quoque laboris praemium: Scritti in onore di Gino Bandelli*. Trieste: Edizioni Università di Trieste, 219–42.
——, and Silani, M. (2021). 'Lo sviluppo di una conquista. Dalla fondazione della colonia di *Sena Gallica* all'organizzazione dell'*ager*', in M. Tarpin (ed.), *Colonies, territoires et statuts: Nouvelles approches*. Besançon: Presses Universitaires de Franche-Comté, 179–212.
Leuze, O. (1905). 'Metellus Caecatus', *Philologus* 64: 95–115.
—— (1907). 'Die Schlacht bei Panormus', *Philologus* 66: 135–52.
—— (1909). *Die römische Jahrzählung: Ein Versuch, ihre geschichtliche Entwicklung zu ermitteln*. Tübingen: Mohr-Siebeck.
—— (1910). 'Die Kämpfe um Sardinien und Korsika im ersten punischen Krieg. (259 und 258 vor Chr.)', *Klio* 9: 406–44.
—— (1911). 'Die Darstellung des I. punischen Kriegs bei Florus', *Philologus* 70: 549–60.
Levene, D. S. (1993). *Religion in Livy*. Leiden: Brill.
—— (2000). 'Sallust's *Catiline* and Cato the Censor', *CQ* 50: 170–91.
—— (2006a). 'History, Metahistory, and Audience Response in Livy 45', *CA* 25: 73–108.
—— (2006b). Review of Davies (2004), *CPh* 101: 419–24.
—— (2010a). *Livy on the Hannibalic War*. Oxford: Oxford University Press.
—— (2010b). 'Pompeius Trogus in Tacitus' *Annals*', in C. S. Kraus, J. Marincola, and C. B. R. Pelling (eds), *Ancient Historiography and Its Contexts: Studies in Honor of A. J. Woodman*. Oxford: Oxford University Press, 294–311.
—— (2011). 'Historical Allusion and the Nature of the Historical Text', *Histos Working Papers* 2011.01 (https://histos.org/documents/WP2011.01LeveneHistoricalAllusion.pdf).
—— (2012). 'You Shall Blot Out the Memory of Amalek: Roman Historians on Remembering to Forget', in B. Dignas and R. R. R. Smith (eds), *Historical and Religious Memory in the Ancient World*. Oxford: Oxford University Press, 217–39.
—— (2015a). 'Allusions and Intertextuality in Livy's Third Decade', in B. Mineo (ed.), *A Companion to Livy*. Malden, MA: Wiley-Blackwell, 205–16.

Levene, D. S. (2015b). 'Three Readings of Characterization in the *Periochae* of Livy', in R. Ash, J. Mossman, and F. B. Titchener (eds), *Fame and Infamy? Essays for Christopher Pelling on Characterization in Greek and Roman Biography and History*. Oxford: Oxford University Press, 313–25.

——, and Nelis, D. P. (eds) (2002). *Clio and the Poets: Augustan Poetry and the Traditions of Ancient Historiography*. Leiden: Brill.

Lévêque, P. (1957). *Pyrrhos*. Paris: De Boccard.

Linderski, J. (1986). 'The Augural Law', *ANRW* II 16.3: 2146–312.

—— (1993). 'Roman Religion in Livy', in Schuller (1993), 53–70.

Lindsay, H. (1995). *Suetonius: Tiberius*. London: Bristol Classical Press.

Lintott, A. W. (1972). 'Provocatio: From the Struggle of the Orders to the Principate', *ANRW* I 2: 226–67.

Lippold, A. (1954). 'Die Darstellung des ersten punischen Krieges in den "Historiarum Adversum Paganos Libri VII" des Orosius', *RhM* 97: 254–86.

Litchfield, H. W. (1914). 'National *exempla virtutis* in Roman Literature', *HSCPh* 25: 1–71.

Littlewood, R. J. (2010). *A Commentary on Silius Italicus' Punica 7*. Oxford: Oxford University Press.

Liverani, P. (1996). 'Ianiculum da *Antipolis* al *Mons Ianiculensis*', in Steinby (1996), 3–12.

Lo Cascio, E. (1980–81). 'Il primo *denarius*', *AIIN* 27–28: 335–58.

Löfstedt, E. (1951). *Coniectanea: Untersuchungen auf dem Gebiete der Antike und Mittelalterlichen Latinität*. Uppsala: Almquist & Wiksells.

Lomas, K. (1993). *Rome and the Western Greeks 350 BC–AD 200: Conquest and Acculturation in Southern Italy*. London: Routledge.

—— (1995). 'Urban Elites and Cultural Definition: Romanization in Southern Italy', in T. J. Cornell and K. Lomas (eds), *Urban Society in Roman Italy*. London: UCL Press, 107–20.

Lombardo, M., and Marangio, C. (eds) (1998). *Il Territorio Brundisino dall' età messapica all'età romana: Atti del IV convegno di studi sulla Puglia romana*. Galatina: Mario Congedo Editore.

Loreto, L. (1989). 'Il conflitto romano-falisco del 241/40 A.C. e la politica romana degli anni successivi', *MEFRA* 101: 717–37.

—— (1989–90). 'Per una "Quellenforschung" della "Pax Caudina"', *BIDR* 92–93: 653–65.

—— (1993). 'Sull'introduzione a la competenza originaria dei secondo quattro questori (ca. 267–210 a.C.)', *Historia* 42: 494–502.

—— (2001). 'La convenienza di perdere una guerra: La continuità della grande strategia cartaginese, 290–237 a.C.', in Y. Le Bohec (ed.), *La première guerre punique*. Lyon: De Boccard, 39–105.

—— (2007). *La grande strategia di Roma nell'età della Prima guerra punica (ca. 273–ca. 229 a.C.)*. Naples: Jovene.

Love, R. L. (2019). *Writing after Livy: Historical Epitomes in the Livian Tradition*. Diss. Yale University.

Luce, T. J. (1971). 'Design and Structure in Livy: 5.32–55', *TAPhA* 102: 265–302 = Chaplin and Kraus (2009), 148–87.

—— (1977). *Livy: The Composition of His History*. Princeton: Princeton University Press.

Luiselli, B. (1960). 'Nota Enniana', *AFLC* 28: 21–6.

Lundgreen, C. (2011). *Regelkonflikte in der römischen Republik*. Stuttgart: Franz Steiner.

Luni, M. (ed.) (2002). *La via Flaminia nell' ager Gallicus*. Urbino: QuattroVenti.

Lushkov, A. H. (2015). *Magistracy and the Historiography of the Roman Republic*. Cambridge: Cambridge University Press.

Ma, J. (1999). *Antiochos III and the Cities of Western Asia Minor*. Oxford: Oxford University Press.
MacBain, B. (1982). *Prodigy and Expiation: A Study in Religion and Politics in Republican Rome*. Brussels: Latomus.
McDonald, A. H. (1967). 'The Treaty of Apamea (188 B.C.)', *JRS* 57: 1–8.
——, and Walbank, F. W. (1937). 'The Origins of the Second Macedonian War', *JRS* 27: 180–207.
McKechnie, P., and Guillaume, P. (eds) (2008). *Ptolemy II Philadelphus and His World*. Leiden: Brill.
McKeown, N. (2007). 'The Sound of John Henderson Laughing: Pliny 3.14 and Roman Slaveowners' Fear of their Slaves', in Serghidou (2007), 265–79.
Maddox, G. (1983). 'The Economic Causes of the *Lex Hortensia*', *Latomus* 42: 277–86.
Madvig, J. N. (1828). *Disputationis de Q. Asconii Pediani et aliorum in Ciceronis orationes commentariis appendix critica, locorum Ciceronianorum et Asconianorum emendationes et indices continens*. Copenhagen: H. F. Poppii.
Maetzke, G., Paoletti, O., and Tamagno Perna, L. (eds) (1990). *La civiltà dei Falisci: Atti del XV convegno di studi etruschi et italici*. Florence: Leo S. Olschki.
Mahé-Simon, M. (2003). 'L'Italie chez Tite-Live: l'ambiguité d'un concept', *RPh* 77: 235–58.
Mallan, C. T. (2016). 'The Book Indices in the Manuscripts of Cassius Dio', *CQ* 66: 705–23.
Malloch, S. J. V. (2013). *The Annals of Tacitus: Book 11*. Cambridge: Cambridge University Press.
Maltby, R. (1991). *A Lexicon of Ancient Latin Etymologies*. Leeds: Francis Cairns.
Mancinelli, A. (2015). 'Aspetti giuridici del trionfo in un processo del 241 a.C. L'*exemplum* di Val. Max. 2.8.2', *SDHI* 81: 221–62.
Manni, E. (1949a). 'L'Egitto tolemaico nei suoi rapporti politici con Roma. I—L' "Amicitia"', *Rivista di filologia classica* 27: 79–106.
—— (1949b). 'Pirro e gli stati greci nel 281/80 a.c.', *Athenaeum* 27: 102–21.
Mansuelli, G. A. (1941). *Ariminum (Rimini)*. Spoleto: Istituto di Studi Romani.
Marek, C. (1997). 'Teos und Abdera nach dem Dritten Makedonischen Krieg: Eine neue Ehreninschrift für den Demos von Teos', *Tyche* 12: 169–77.
Marini Calvini, M. (1990). 'Archeologia', in F. Ghizzone (ed.), *Storia di Piacenza*, vol. 1. Piacenza: Cassa di Risparmio di Piacenza e Vigevano, 765–906.
Martin, R. H. (1981). *Tacitus*. London: B. T. Batsford.
——, and Woodman, A. J. (1989). *Tacitus: Annals Book IV*. Cambridge: Cambridge University Press.
Matthaei, L. E. (1907). 'On the Classification of Roman Allies', *CQ* 1: 182–204.
Mattingly, H. B. (1969). 'Suetonius *Claud.* 24,2 and the "Italian Quaestors"', in J. Bibauw (ed.), *Hommages à Marcel Renard*. Vol. 2. Brussels: Latomus, 505–11.
Meer, T. van der (1999). 'The Voconian Law: Nova or Phoenix?', *RHD* 67: 115–23.
Mehl, A. (1999). 'Zwischen West und Ost / Jenseits von West und Ost: Das Reich der Seleukiden', in K. Brodersen (ed.), *Zwischen West und Ost: Studien zur Geschichte des Seleukidenreichs*. Hamburg: Verlag Dr. Kovač, 9–43.
Meiggs, R. (1973). *Roman Ostia*. 2nd edn. Oxford: Clarendon Press.
Mello, M., and Voza, G. (1968–9). *Le iscrizioni latine di Paestum*. 2 vols. Naples: Università degli Studi di Napoli.
Meloni, P. (1990). *La Sardegna romana*. 2nd edn. Sassari: Chiarella.
Meltzer, O. (1896). *Geschichte der Karthager*. Vol. 2. Berlin: Weidmann.
Mensching, E. (1996). 'Über Livius, den alten und den jungen Marcellus', in C. Klodt (ed.), *Satura Lanx: Festschrift für Werner A. Krenkel zum 70. Geburtstag*. Hildesheim: Georg Olms, 257–77.

Meyer, E. (1915). 'Die Götter Rediculus und Tutanus', *Hermes* 50: 151–4 = Meyer (1924), 457–61.
—— (1924). *Kleine Schriften* II. Halle: Max Niemeyer.
Meyer, E. A. (2013). *The Inscriptions of Dodona and a New History of Molossia*. Stuttgart: Franz Steiner.
Mignone, L. M. (2014). 'Remembering a Geography of Resistance: Plebeian Secessions, Then and Now', in Galinsky (2014), 137–50.
—— (2016). *The Republican Aventine and Rome's Social Order*. Ann Arbor: University of Michigan Press.
Miles, R. (2003). 'Rivalling Rome: Carthage', in C. Edwards and G. Woolf (eds), *Rome the Cosmopolis*. Cambridge: Cambridge University Press, 123–46.
Mineur, W. H. (1984). *Callimachus: Hymn to Delos. Introduction and Commentary*. Leiden: Brill.
Minieri, L. (1995). '"Mores" e "Decreta Gentilicia"', in G. Franciosi (ed.), *Ricerche sulla organizzazione gentilizia romana*. Vol. 3. Naples: Jovene, 121–68.
Minunno, G. (2005). 'Remarques sur le supplice de M. Atilius Régulus', *LEC* 73: 217–34.
Mitchell, R. E. (1971). 'Roman-Carthaginian Treaties: 306 and 279/8 B.C.', *Historia* 20: 633–55.
—— (1984). 'Historical Development in Livy', in D. F. Bright and E. S. Ramage (eds), *Classical Texts and Their Traditions: Studies in Honor of C. R. Traman*. New York: Scholars Press: 179–99.
Mitropoulou, E. (1977). *Deities and Heroes in the Form of Snakes*. Athens: Pyli Editions.
Mittag, P. F. (2006). *Antiochos IV. Epiphanes: Eine politische Biographie*. Berlin: Akademie Verlag.
Mix, E. R. (1970). *Marcus Atilius Regulus Exemplum Historicum*. The Hague: Mouton.
Molthagen, J. (1975). 'Der Weg in den Ersten Punischen Krieg', *Chiron* 5: 89–127.
Mommsen, T. (1857). 'Zu Festus', *RhM* 12: 467–70, 633–4.
—— (1859). *Die römische Chronologie bis auf Caesar*. Berlin: Weidmannsche Buchhandlung.
—— (ed.) (1861). 'Die Chronik des Cassiodorus Senator vom j. 519 n. Chr.', *Abhandlungen der königlich sächsischen Gesellschaft der Wissenschaften* 8: 547–696.
—— (1864). *Römische Forschungen*. Vol. 1. Berlin: Weidmann.
—— (1866). 'Die Scipionenprozesse', *Hermes* 1: 161–216 = Mommsen (1879), 417–510.
—— (1871). 'Sp. Cassius, M. Manlius, Sp. Maelius', *Hermes* 5: 228–71 = Mommsen (1879), 153–220.
—— (1872). 'Observationes epigraphicae XV: S. C. de Thisbaeis a.u.c. DLXXXIV', *Ephemeris Epigraphica* 1: 278–98.
—— (1879). *Römische Forschungen*. Vol. 2. Berlin: Weidmann.
Mooren, L. (ed.) (2000). *Politics, Administration and Society in the Hellenistic and Roman World*. Amsterdam: Peeters.
Morel, J.-P. (1988). 'Artisanat et colonisation dans l'Italie romaine aux IVe et IIIe siècles av. J.-C.', *DialArch* 6: 49–63.
—— (1991). 'La romanisation du Samnium et de la Lucanie aux IVe et IIIe siècles av. J.-C. d'après l'artisanat et le commerce', in J. Mertens and R. Lambrechts (eds), *Comunità indigene e problemi della romanizzazione nell'Italia centro-meridionale (IV°–III° sec. av. C.)*. Brussels: Institut Historique Belge de Rome—Belgisch Historisch Instituut te Rome, 125–44.
Morgan, M. G. (1972a). 'Polybius and the Date of the Battle of Panormus', *CQ* 22: 121–9.
—— (1972b). 'The Defeat of L. Metellus Denter at Arretium', *CQ* 22: 309–25.
—— (1974). 'Priests and Physical Fitness', *CQ* 24: 137–41.

―― (1977). 'Calendars and Chronology in the First Punic War', *Chiron* 7: 89–117.
Mørkholm, O. (1966). *Antiochus IV of Syria*. Copenhagen: Gyldendal.
Morstein-Marx, R. (2004). *Mass Oratory and Political Power in the Roman Republic*. Cambridge: Cambridge University Press.
Moscati, P. (1990). 'Nuove ricerche su Falerii Veteres', in Maetzke et al. (1990), 141–71.
Mossman, J. M. (1992). 'Plutarch, Pyrrhus, and Alexander', in P. A. Stadter (ed.), *Plutarch and the Historical Tradition*. London: Routledge, 90–108.
―― (2005). '*Taxis ou Barbaros*: Greek and Roman in Plutarch's *Pyrrhus*', *CQ* 55: 498–517.
Mouritsen, H. (2001). *Plebs and Politics in the Late Roman Republic*. Cambridge: Cambridge University Press.
Mülke, M. (2010). 'Die Epitome—das bessere Original?', in Horster and Reitz (2010), 69–89.
Münzer, F. (1899a). 'C. Centenius', *RE* III: 1927–8.
―― (1899b). 'M. Centenius Paenula', *RE* III: 1928.
―― (1899c). 'M. Claudius Marcellus', *RE* III: 2738–55.
―― (1901a). 'Coruncanius', *RE* IV: 1663.
―― (1901b). 'C. und L. Coruncanii', *RE* IV: 1663.
―― (1905). 'Duilius', *RE* V: 1776–7.
―― (1909a). 'Q. Fabius', *RE* VI: 1748–9.
―― (1909b). 'Q. Fabius Maximus Rullianus', *RE* VI: 1800–11.
―― (1909c). 'C. Fabricius Luscinus', *RE* VI: 1931–8.
―― (1910). 'Genucius', *RE* VII: 1207.
―― (1918a). 'D. Iunius Brutus Pera', *RE* X: 1026.
―― (1918b). 'L. Iunius Pullus', *RE* X: 1080–1.
―― (1923). 'Sextilia', *RE* II A. 2: 2038.
―― (1929). 'Sthennius Sthallus', *RE* III A. 2: 2140.
―― (1932). 'L. Minucius Esquilinus Augurinus', *RE* XV: 1949–55.
―― (1937). 'Die römischen Vestalinnen bis zur Kaiserzeit', *Philologus* 92: 47–67, 199–222.
―― (1953). 'A Postumius Albinus', *RE* XXII: 902.
―― (1999 (1920)). *Roman Aristocratic Parties and Families*. Tr. T. Ridley. Baltimore: Johns Hopkins University Press.
Murray, W. M. (2020). 'The Ship Class of the Egadi Rams and Polybius' Account of the First Punic War', in Royal and Tusa (2020), 31–41.
Neatby, L. H. (1950). 'Romano-Egyptian Relations during the Third Century B.C.', *TAPhA* 81: 89–98.
Nenci, G. (1953). *Pirro: Aspirazioni egemoniche ed equilibrio mediterraneo*. Turin: G. Giappichelli.
―― (1958). 'Il trattato romano-cartaginese κατὰ τὴν Πύρρου διάβασιν', *Historia* 7: 263–99.
Néraudau, J.-P. (1979). *La jeunesse dans la littérature et les institutions de la Rome républicaine*. Paris: Les Belles Lettres.
Nesselrath, H. G. (1986). 'Zu den Quellen des Silius Italicus', *Hermes* 114: 203–30.
Niebuhr, B. G. (1846). *Vorträge über römische Geschichte*. Berlin: G. Reimer.
Niedermann, M. (1936). 'L'inscription de la colonne rostrale de Duilius (*C. I. L.* I^2 25)', *REL* 14: 276–87.
Niese, B. (1896). 'Zur Geschichte des Pyrrhischen Krieges', *Hermes* 31: 481–507.
Nilsson. M. P. (1929). 'The Introduction of Hoplite Tactics at Rome: Its Date and Consequences', *JRS* 19: 1–11.

Nippel, W. (1995). *Public Order in Ancient Rome*. Cambridge: Cambridge University Press.
Nisbet, R. G. (1923). 'Voluntas fati in Latin Syntax', *AJPh* 44: 27–43.
Nisbet, R. G. M., and Rudd, N. (2004). *A Commentary on Horace, Odes, Book III*. Oxford: Oxford University Press.
Nissen, H. (1863). *Kritische Untersuchungen über die Quellen der vierten und fünften Dekade des Livius*. Berlin: Weidmann.
—— (1872). 'Das Geschichtswerk des Titus Livius', *RhM* 27: 539–61.
Norden, E. (1939). *Aus altrömischen Priesterbüchern*. Lund: C. W. K. Gleerup.
North, J. A. (1981). 'The Development of Roman Imperialism', *JRS* 71: 1–9.
O'Gorman, E. (2010). 'Intertextuality and Historiography', in A. Feldherr (ed.), *The Cambridge Companion to Roman Historiography*. Cambridge: Cambridge University Press, 231–42.
Oakley, S. P. (1992). 'Livy and Clodius Licinus', *CQ* 42: 547–51.
—— (1995). *The Hill-forts of the Samnites*. London: British School at Rome.
—— (1997). *A Commentary on Livy Books VI–X*. Vol. 1. Oxford: Clarendon Press.
—— (1998). *A Commentary on Livy Books VI–X*. Vol. 2. Oxford: Clarendon Press.
—— (2005a). *A Commentary on Livy Books VI–X*. Vol. 3. Oxford: Clarendon Press.
—— (2005b). *A Commentary on Livy Books VI–X*. Vol. 4. Oxford: Clarendon Press.
Östenberg, I. (2009). *Staging the World: Spoils, Captives, and Representations in the Roman Triumphal Procession*. Oxford: Oxford University Press.
Ogden, D. (1996). *Greek Bastardy in the Classical and the Hellenistic Periods*. Oxford: Clarendon Press.
Ogilvie, R. M. (1958). 'Livy, Licinius Macer, and the *libri lintei*', *JRS* 48: 40–6.
—— (1961). '"Lustrum Condere"', *JRS* 51: 31–9.
—— (1965). *A Commentary on Livy Books 1–5*. Oxford: Clarendon Press.
Olick, J. K., Vinitzky-Seroussi, V., and Levy, D. (eds). (2011). *The Collective Memory Reader*. New York: Oxford University Press.
Orlin, E. M. (1997). *Temples, Religion and Politics in the Roman Republic*. Leiden: Brill.
Ortalli, J. (2006). 'Ur-*Ariminum*', in Lenzi (2006), 285–311.
Ortolani, M., and Alfieri, N. (1953). 'Sena gallica', *RAL* 8: 152–80.
Otto, A. (1890). *Die Sprichwörter und sprichwörtlichen Redensarten der Römer*. Leipzig: Teubner.
Padilla Peralta, D.-E. (2020). *Divine Institutions: Religions and Community in the Middle Roman Republic*. Princeton: Princeton University Press.
Pagán, V. E. (2000). 'The Mourning After: Statius *Thebaid* 12', *AJPh* 121: 423–52.
—— (2004). *Conspiracy Narratives in Roman History*. Austin: University of Texas Press.
Palmer, R. E. A. (1965). 'The Censors of 312 B.C. and the State Religion', *Historia* 14: 293–324.
Panitschek, P. (1989). 'Sp. Cassius, Sp. Maelius, M. Manlius als Exempla Maiorum', *Philologus* 133: 231–45.
Papazoglou, F. (1978). *The Central Balkan Tribes in Pre-Roman Times*. Tr. M. Stansfield-Popović. Amsterdam: Adolf M. Hakkert.
—— (1979). 'Quelques aspects de l'histoire de la province de Macédoine', *ANRW* II 7.1: 302–69.
Parker, H. N. (2004). 'Why Were the Vestals Virgins? Or the Chastity of Women and the Safety of the Roman State', *AJPh* 125: 563–601.
Passerini, A. (1943). 'Sulle trattative dei Romani con Pirro', *Athenaeum* 21: 92–112.
Patterson, H. (ed.) (2004). *Bridging the Tiber: Approaches to Regional Archaeology in the Middle Tiber Valley*. London: British School at Rome.
Pauli, L. (1971). *Studien zur Golasecca-Kultur*. Heidelberg: F. H. Kerle.

Pease, A. S. (1920-3). *M. Tulli Ciceronis De Divinatione*. Urbana: University of Illinois Press.
Pedley, J. G. (1990). *Paestum: Greeks and Romans in Southern Italy*. London: Thames & Hudson.
Pelgrom, J. (2008). 'Settlement Organization and Land Distribution in Latin Colonies before the Second Punic War', in de Ligt and Northwood (2008): 333-72.
——, and Stek, T. D. (2014). 'Roman Colonization under the Republic: Historiographical Contextualization of a Paradigm', in Stek and Pelgrom (2014), 10-41.
Pelling, C. B. R. (1989). 'Plutarch: Roman Heroes and Greek Culture', in M. Griffin and J. Barnes (eds), *Philosophia Togata: Essays on Philosophy and Roman Society*. Oxford: Clarendon Press, 199-232.
Petzold, K.-E. (1971). 'Rom und Illyrien: Ein Beitrag zur römischen Außenpolitik im 3. Jahrhundert', *Historia* 20: 199-223.
Peyre, C. (1979). *La Cisalpine gauloise du IIIe au Ier siècle avant J.-C*. Paris: Presses de l'École Normale Supérieure.
Pina Polo, F. (2004). 'Die nützliche Erinnerung: Geschichtsschreibung, *mos maiorum*, und die römischen Identität', *Historia* 53: 147-72.
——, and Díaz Fernández, A. (2019). *The Quaestorship in the Roman Republic*. Berlin: De Gruyter.
Pineschi, I. (ed.) (1997). *L'antica via Flaminia in Umbria*. Rome: Editalia.
Pölönen, J. (1999). '*Lex Voconia* and Conflicting Ideologies of Succession: Privileging Agnate Obligation over Cognatic Family Feeling', *Arctos* 33: 111-31.
Pomeroy, S. B. (1976). 'The Relationship of the Married Woman to Her Blood Relatives at Rome', *Ancient Society* 7: 215-27.
Pontiroli, G. (ed.) (1985). *Cremona Romana*. Cremona: Biblioteca Statale e Libreria Civica di Cremona.
Popov-Reynolds, N. (2010). 'The Heroic Soldier as *Exemplum* in Cato and Livy', in W. Polleichtner (ed.), *Livy and Intertextuality*. Trier: Wissenschaftlicher Verlag Trier, 169-201.
Potter, T. W. (1979). *The Changing Landscape of South Etruria*. New York: St. Martin's Press.
Powell, J. G. F. (1988). *Cicero: Cato Maior De Senectute*. Cambridge: Cambridge University Press.
Poznanski, L. (1979). 'Encore le *corvus* de la terre à la mer', *Latomus* 38: 652-61.
Prag, J. R. W. (2013). 'Sicily and Sardinia-Corsica: The First Provinces', in D. Hoyos (ed.), *A Companion to Roman Imperialism*. Leiden: Brill, 53-65.
—— (2014). 'The Quaestorship in the Third and Second Centuries BC', in J. Dubouloz, S. Pittia, and G. Sabatini (eds), *L'imperium Romanum en perspective*. Besançon: Presses Universitaires de Franche-Comté, 193-209.
—— (2017). 'A Revised Edition of the Latin Inscription on the Egadi 11 Bronze *rostrum* from the Egadi Islands', *ZPE* 202: 287-92.
—— (2020). 'Bronze *rostra*: The Latin Inscriptions', in Royal and Tusa (2020), 77-105.
Prandi, L. (1979). 'La "fides punica" e il pregiudizio anticartaginese', *CISA* 6: 90-7.
Pugsley, D. (1969). 'The Origins of the Lex Aquilia', *Law Quarterly Review* 85: 50-73.
Purcell, N. (1983). 'The *apparitores*: A Study in Social Mobility', *PBSR* 51: 125-73.
—— (1990). 'The Creation of Provincial Landscape: The Roman Impact on Cisalpine Gaul', in T. Blagg and M. Millett (eds), *The Early Roman Empire in the West*. Oxford: Oxbow Books, 6-29.
—— (2001). 'The *ordo scribarum*: A Study in the Loss of Memory', *MEFRA* 113: 633-74.
—— (2017). 'The Non-Polis and the Game of Mirrors: Rome and Carthage in Ancient and Modern Comparison', *CPh* 112: 332-49.

Raaflaub, K. A., Richards, J. D., and Samons, L. J., II (1992). 'Rome, Italy, and Appius Claudius Caecus before the Pyrrhic Wars', in Hackens *et al.* (1992), 13–50.

Radke, G. (1967). 'Namen und Daten: Beobachtungen zur Geschichte des römischen Strassenbaus', *MH* 24: 221–35.

Rankov, B. (2011). 'A War of Phases: Strategies and Stalemates 264–241 BC', in D. Hoyos (ed.), *A Companion to the Punic Wars*. Malden, MA: Wiley-Blackwell, 149–66.

Rathbone, D. W. (1981). 'The Development of Agriculture in the "Ager Cosanus" during the Roman Republic: Problems of Evidence and Interpretation', *JRS* 71: 10–23.

Raviola, F. (2006). 'Rimini e gli Umbri di Strabone', in Lenzi (2006), 101–9.

Rawlings, H. R. (1981). *The Structure of Thucydides' History*. Princeton: Princeton University Press.

Rawlings, L. (2016). 'The Significance of Insignificant Engagements: Irregular Warfare during the Punic Wars', in J. Armstrong (ed.), *Circum Mare: Themes in Ancient Warfare*. Leiden: Brill, 204–34.

Rawson, E. (1975). 'Caesar's Heritage: Hellenistic Kings and their Roman Equals', *JRS* 65: 148–59 = Rawson (1991), 169–88.

—— (1985). *Intellectual Life in the Late Roman Republic*. London: Duckworth.

—— (1991). *Roman Culture and Society: Collected Papers*. Oxford: Clarendon Press.

Reeve, M. D. (1988). 'The Transmission of Florus' *Epitoma de Tito Livio* and the *Periochae*', *CQ* 38: 477–91.

—— (1991). 'The Transmission of Florus and the *Periochae* Again', *CQ* 41: 453–83.

Reid, J. S. (1915). 'Problems of the Second Punic War: III. Rome and Her Italian Allies', *JRS* 5: 87–124.

Reid, R. A. (1969). *The Manuscript Tradition of the Periochae of Livy*. Diss. Cambridge.

—— (1990). 'The α class of the Manuscripts of the *Periochae* of Livy', in E. Craik (ed.), *'Owls to Athens': Essays on Classical Subjects for Sir Kenneth Dover*. Oxford: Clarendon Press, 367–79.

Reynolds, L. D. (1983). 'The Elder Pliny', in L. D. Reynolds (ed.), *Texts and Transmission: A Survey of the Latin Classics*. Oxford: Clarendon Press, 307–16.

Rich, J. W. (1976). *Declaring War in the Roman Republic in the Period of Transmarine Expansion*. Brussels: Latomus.

—— (1983). 'The Supposed Roman Manpower Shortage of the Later Second Century B.C.', *Historia* 32: 287–331.

—— (1993). 'Fear, Greed and Glory: The Causes of Roman War-Making in the Middle Republic', in J. Rich and G. Shipley (eds), *War and Society in the Roman World*. London: Routledge, 38–68.

—— (1996). 'The Origins of the Second Punic War', in T. J. Cornell, B. Rankov, and P. Sabin (eds), *The Second Punic War: A Reappraisal*. London: Institute of Classical Studies, 1–37.

—— (2011). 'The *Fetiales* and Roman International Relations', in J. H. Richardson and F. Santangelo (eds), *Priests and State in the Roman World*. Stuttgart: Franz Steiner, 187–242.

Richard, J.-C. (1968). 'Sur quelques grands pontifes plébéiens', *Latomus* 27: 786–801.

—— (1979). 'Sur le plébiscite ut liceret consules ambos plebeios creari (*Tite-Live* VII, 42, 2)', *Historia* 28: 65–75.

Richardson, J. H., and Santangelo, F. (eds) (2014). *Oxford Readings in Classical Studies: The Roman Historical Tradition*. Oxford: Oxford University Press.

Richardson, J. S. (1986). *Hispaniae: Spain and the Development of Roman Imperialism, 218–82 B.C.* Cambridge: Cambridge University Press.

—— (1996). *The Romans in Spain*. Oxford: Blackwell.

Richardson, Jr., L. (1980). 'The Approach to the Temple of Saturn', *AJA* 84: 51–62.
Riggsby, A. M. (1997). '"Public" and "Private" in Roman Culture: The Case of the *cubiculum*', *JRA* 10: 36–56.
—— (1999). *Crime and Community in Ciceronian Rome*. Austin: University of Texas Press.
—— (2006). *Caesar in Gaul and Rome: War in Words*. Austin: University of Texas Press.
—— (2007). 'Guides to the Wor(l)d', in J. König and T. Whitmarsh (eds), *Ordering Knowledge in the Roman Empire*. Cambridge: Cambridge University Press, 88–107.
—— (2019). *Mosaics of Knowledge*. Oxford: Oxford University Press.
Robert, L. (1938). *Études épigraphiques et philologiques*. Paris: Champion.
Roberts, C. H., and Skeat, T. C. (1983). *The Birth of the Codex*. London: Oxford University Press.
Rodgers, R. H. (2004). *Frontinus: De Aquaeductu Urbis Romae*. Cambridge: Cambridge University Press.
Rohrbacher, D. (2016). *The Play of Allusion in the* Historia Augusta. Madison: University of Wisconsin Press.
Roller, M. B. (2004). 'Exemplarity in Roman Culture: The Cases of Horatius Cocles and Cloelia', *CPh* 99: 1–56.
—— (2009). 'The Exemplary Past in Roman Historiography and Culture', in A. Feldherr (ed.), *The Cambridge Companion to the Roman Historians*. Cambridge: Cambridge University Press, 214–30.
—— (2013). 'On the Intersignification of Monuments in Augustan Rome', *AJPh* 134: 119–31.
Roselaar, S. T. (2011). 'Colonies and Processes of Integration in the Roman Republic', *MEFRA* 123: 527–55.
—— (2019). *Italy's Economic Revolution*. Oxford: Oxford University Press.
Rosenstein, N. (1990). *Imperatores Victi: Imperial Defeats and Aristocratic Competition in the Middle and Late Republic*. Berkeley: University of California Press.
—— (2004). *Rome at War: Farms, Families, and Death in the Middle Republic*. Chapel Hill: University of North Carolina Press.
Rossbach, O. (1904). 'Die neuen Periochae des Livius aus Oxyrhynchus', *Berliner Philologischer Wochenschrift* 24: 1020–2.
Rossi, A. (2000). 'The Tears of Marcellus: History of a Literary Motif in Livy', *G&R* 47: 56–66.
Roth, J. P. (2007). 'War', in P. Sabin, H. van Wees, and M. Whitby (eds), *The Cambridge History of Greek and Roman Warfare*: Vol. I: *Greece, the Hellenistic World and the Rise of Rome*. Cambridge: Cambridge University Press, 368–98.
Royal, J. G. (2020a). 'Amphoras and Tablewares', in Royal and Tusa (2020), 185–200.
—— (2020b). 'Ram Manufacture and the Nature of Bronze Objects', in Royal and Tusa (2020), 219–38.
—— (2020c). 'The Warships: Construction and Tactics', in Royal and Tusa (2020), 257–96.
——, and Tusa, S. (eds) (2020). *The Site of the Battle of the Aegates Islands at the End of the First Punic War*. 2nd edn. Rome: L'Erma di Bretschneider.
Rüpke, J. (1990). *Domi militiae*. Stuttgart: Franz Steiner.
—— (2010). 'Representation or Presence? Picturing the Divine in Ancient Rome', *ARG* 12: 181–96.
Ryan, F. X. (1998). *Rank and Participation in the Republican Senate*. Stuttgart: Franz Steiner.
Sachs, A. J., and Wiseman, D. J. (1954). 'A Babylonian King List of the Hellenistic Period', *Iraq* 16: 202–12.

Saint-Denis, E. de (1946). 'Une machine de guerre maritime: le corbeau de Duilius', *Latomus* 5: 359–67.
Salmon, E. T. (1932). 'A Topographical Study of the Battle of Ausculum', *PBSR* 12: 44–51.
—— (1935). 'Rome's Battles with Etruscans and Gauls in 284–282 B.C.', *CPh* 30: 23–31.
—— (1936). 'Romanisation from the Second Punic War to the Gracchi', *JRS* 26: 47–67.
—— (1957). 'Hannibal's March on Rome', *Phoenix* 11: 153–63.
—— (1963). 'The *Coloniae Maritimae*', *Athenaeum* 41: 3–38.
—— (1967). *Samnium and the Samnites*. Cambridge: Cambridge University Press.
—— (1969). *Roman Colonization under the Republic*. London: Thames & Hudson.
—— (1989). 'The Hirpini: *ex Italia semper aliquid novi*', *Phoenix* 43: 225–35.
Salway, B. (1994). 'What's in a Name? A Survey of Roman Onomastic Practice from c. 700 B.C. to A.D. 700', *JRS* 84: 124–45.
Sandberg, K. (2018). '*Monumenta, Documenta, Memoria*: Remembering and Imagining the Past in Republican Rome', in Sandberg and Smith (2018), 351–89.
——, and Smith, C. (eds) (2018). *Omnium Annalium Monumenta: Historical Writing and Historical Evidence in Republican Rome*. Leiden: Brill.
Sanders, H. A. (1898). *Die Quellencontamination im 21. und 22. Buche des Livius*. Berlin: Mayer & Müller.
—— (1904). 'The Lost Epitome of Livy', *University of Michigan Studies: Humanistic Series* 1: 149–260.
Sansone, D. (1980–1). 'Totus Livius: Martial XIV 190', *CB* 57: 86–7.
Santagati, E. (2018). 'Reggio tra Pirro, Roma e Cartagine', *RSA* 48: 247–59.
Saumagne, C. (1966). *La Numidie et Rome*. Paris: Presses Universitaires de France.
Savalli-Lestrade, I. (1998). *Les philoi royaux dans l'Asie hellénistique*. Geneva: Librairie Droz.
Scardigli, B. (1991). *I trattati romano-cartaginesi*. Pisa: Scuola Normale Superiore.
Schaps, D. (1982). 'The Women of Greece in Wartime', *CPh* 77: 193–213.
Scheid, J. (1985). *Religion et piété à Rome*. Paris: Éditions La Découverte.
Scheidel, W. (2009). 'When Did Livy Write Books 1, 3, 28 and 59?', *CQ* 59: 653–8.
Schepens, G. (2000a). 'Plutarch's View of Ancient Rome: Some Remarks on the *Life of Pyrrhus*', in Mooren (2000), 349–64.
—— (2000b). 'Rhetoric in Plutarch's *Life of Pyrrhus*', in L. van der Stockt (ed.), *Rhetorical Theory and Praxis in Plutarch*. Leuven: Peeters, 413–41.
Schettino, M. T. (2009). 'Pyrrhos en Italie: la construction de l'image du premier ennemi venu de l'Orient grec', *Pallas* 79: 173–84.
Schilling, R. (2003). *Pline l'Ancien: Histoire naturelle livre VII*. Paris: Les Belles Lettres.
Schlicher, J. J. (1933). 'Non-Assertive Elements in the Language of the Roman Historians', *CPh* 28: 289–300.
Schmidt, E. (1909). *Kultübertragungen*. Giessen: Alfred Töpelmann.
Schmidt, J. (1881). 'Ein Fehler des Livius', *Hermes* 16: 155–9.
Schmidt, P. L. (1968). *Iulius Obsequens und das Problem der Livius-Epitome*. Wiesbaden: Akademie der Wissenschaften und der Literatur in Mainz.
Schmitt, H. H. (1957). *Rom und Rhodos*. Munich: C. H. Beck.
—— (1969). *Die Staatsverträge des Altertums*. Vol. 3. Munich: C. H. Beck.
Schudson, M. (1989). 'The Present in the Past versus the Past in the Present', *Communication* 11: 105–13.
Schuller, W. (ed.) (1993). *Livius: Aspekte seines Werkes*. Konstanz: Universitätsverlag Konstanz.
Schulten, A. (1932). 'Tarraco', *RE* IV A. 2: 2398–408.
Scopacasa, R. (2015). *Ancient Samnium*. Oxford: Oxford University Press.

—— (2019). 'Old Habits Die Hard: Samnites, Rome, and the Perception of International Relations in Republican Italy', *Historia* 68: 50–75.
Scott, R. T. (1993). 'Excavations in the *Area Sacra* of Vesta, 1987–1989', in R. T. Scott and A. R. Scott (eds), *Eius Virtutis Studiosi: Classical and Postclassical Studies in Memory of Frank Edwards Brown (1908–1988)*. Washington, DC: National Gallery of Art, 160–81.
—— (2009). 'The Excavations', in R. T. Scott (ed.), *Excavations in the Area Sacra of Vesta (1987–1996)*. Ann Arbor: University of Michigan Press.
—— (2019). 'Cosa: How Perfect! How Come?', in De Giorgi (2019), 21–9.
Scullard, H. H. (1952). 'Rome's Declaration of War on Carthage in 218 B.C.', *RhM* 95: 209–16.
—— (1967). *The Etruscan Cities and Rome*. Ithaca, NY: Cornell University Press.
—— (1970). *Scipio Africanus: Soldier and Politician*. London: Thames & Hudson.
—— (1973). *Roman Politics 220–150 B.C.* 2nd edn. Oxford: Clarendon Press.
—— (1974). *The Elephant in the Greek and Roman World*. Ithaca, NY: Cornell University Press.
—— (1989). 'Carthage and Rome', in *CAH*² VII. 2: 486–572.
Segal, E. (2014). *The Most Precious Possession: The Ring of Polycrates in Ancient Religious Narratives*. New York: Peter Lang.
Seibert, J. (1993). *Forschungen zu Hannibal*. Darmstadt: Wissenschaftliche Buchgesellschaft.
Senatore, F. (2006). *La lega sannitica*. Capri: Oebalus.
Serghidou, A. (ed.) (2007). *Fear of Slaves—Fear of Enslavement in the Ancient Mediterranean*. Besançon: Presses Universitaires de Franche-Comté.
Serrati, J. (2006). 'Neptune's Altars: The Treaties between Rome and Carthage (509–226 B.C.)', *CQ* 56: 113–34.
Shackleton Bailey, D. R. (1976). *Two Studies in Roman Nomenclature*. New York: American Philological Association.
Shatzman, I. (1972). 'The Roman General's Authority over Booty', *Historia* 21: 177–205.
Sherwin-White, A. N. (1969). Review of Bauman (1967), *Gnomon* 41: 288–93.
—— (1973). *The Roman Citizenship*. 2nd edn. Oxford: Clarendon Press.
Shils, E. (1981). *Tradition*. Chicago: University of Chicago Press.
Silva Reneses, L. (2015). 'Le déplacement de Picéniens dans le golfe de Paestum (Strab. 5,4,13): une analyse philologique et historique', *MH* 72: 190–206.
Silvestrini, M. (ed.) (2010). *Le tribù romane: Atti della XVIe rencontre sur l'épigraphie (Bari 8–10 ottobre 2009)*. Bari: Edipuglia.
Skutsch, O. (1968). *Studia Enniana*. London: Athlone Press.
—— (1978). 'The Fall of the Capitol Again: Tacitus, *Ann.* 11.23', *JRS* 68: 93–4.
—— (1985). *The* Annals *of Quintus Ennius*. Oxford: Clarendon Press.
Smith, C. J. (2006). *The Roman Clan*. Cambridge: Cambridge University Press.
Smith, M. (1978). 'Lydus, *De Magistratibus* 1.27 and the Quaestors of 267 B.C.', *BASP* 15: 125–6.
Sonnabend, H. (1997). 'Castrum', in *Der Neue Pauly*. Vol. 2. Stuttgart: J. B. Metzler, 1027–8.
Stadter, P. A. (1972). 'The Structure of Livy's History', *Historia* 21: 287–307 = Chaplin and Kraus (2009), 91–117.
Stähelin, F. (1921). 'Kineas', *RE* XI: 473–6.
Staples, A. (1998). *From Good Goddesses to Vestal Virgins: Sex and Category in Roman Religion*. London: Routledge.
Starr, C. G. (1941). *The Roman Imperial Navy 31 B.C.–A.D. 324*. Cambridge: W. Heffer & Sons.
Starr, C. G. (1980). *The Beginnings of Imperial Rome: Rome in the Mid-Republic*. Ann Arbor: University of Michigan Press.

Staveley, E. S. (1954). 'The Conduct of Elections during an *Interregnum*', *Historia* 4: 193-211.

—— (1959). 'The Political Aims of Appius Claudius Caecus', *Historia* 8: 410-33.

Stazio, A., and Ceccoli, S. (eds) (1988). *Poseidonia-Paestum. Atti del ventisettesimo convegno di studi sulla Magna Grecia: Taranto-Paestum, 9-15 Ottobre 1987*. Taranto: Istituto per la storia e l'archeologia della Magna Grecia.

Ste. Croix, G. E. M. de (1981). *The Class Struggle in the Ancient Greek World*. London: Duckworth.

Steinby, C. (2007). *The Roman Republican Navy: From the Sixth Century to 167 B.C.* Helsinki: Societas Scientarum Fennica.

Steinby, E. M. (ed.) (1996). *Ianiculum—Gianicolo: Storia, topografia, monumenti, leggende dall'antichità al rinascimento*. Rome: Institutum Romanum Finlandiae.

Steiner, D. T. (2001). *Images in Mind: Statues in Archaic and Classical Greek Literature and Thought*. Princeton: Princeton University Press.

Steinwenter, A. (1925). 'Lex Voconia', *RE* XII: 2418-30.

Stek, T. D. (2017). 'Motivazioni e forme alternative dell'espansionismo romano repubblicano: Il caso delle colonie latine nelle aree interne appenniniche', in G. Mastrocinque (ed.), *Paesaggi mediterranei di età romana*. Bari: Edipuglia, 135-46.

——, and Pelgrom, J. (eds) (2014). *Roman Republican Colonization: New Perspectives from Archaeology and Ancient History*. Rome: Palombi Editori.

Stocks, C. (2014). *The Roman Hannibal*. Liverpool: Liverpool University Press.

Stoddart, S., and Redhouse, D. (2014). 'The Umbrians: Archaeological Perspective', in Aberson *et al*. (2014), 107-25.

Strachan-Davidson, J. L. (1912). *Problems of the Roman Criminal Law*. 2 vols. Oxford: Clarendon Press.

Suerbaum, W. (1995). 'Rhetorik gegen Pyrrhos', in Ch. Schubert and K. Brodersen (eds), *Rom und der Griechische Osten*. Stuttgart: Franz Steiner, 251-65.

—— (2004). *Cato Censorius in der Forschung des 20. Jahrhunderts*. Hildesheim: Olds-Weidmann.

Sumner, G. V. (1968). 'Roman Policy in Spain before the Second Punic War', *HSCP* 72: 205-46.

—— (1970). 'Proconsuls and *Provinciae* in Spain, 218/7-196/5 B.C.', *Arethusa* 3: 85-102.

Suolahti, J. (1956). *The Junior Officers of the Roman Army in the Republican Period: A Study on Social Structure*. Helsinki: Suomalainen Tiedeakatemia.

—— (1963). *The Roman Censors: A Study on Social Structure*. Helsinki: Suomalainen Tiedeakatemia.

—— (1977). '*Claudia insons*: Why was a Fine Imposed on Claudia Ap. f. in 246 BC?', *Arctos* 11: 133-51.

Swain, S. C. R. (1990). 'Hellenic Culture and the Roman Heroes of Plutarch', *JHS* 110: 126-45.

Syme, R. (1959). 'Livy and Augustus', *HSCPh* 64: 27-87 = Syme (1979), 400-54.

—— (1970-1). 'Spoletium and the Via Flaminia', *DialArch* 4-5: 422-30 = Syme (1984), 885-91.

—— (1979). *Roman Papers I* (ed. E. Badian). Oxford: Clarendon Press.

—— (1984). *Roman Papers III* (ed. A. R. Birley). Oxford: Clarendon Press.

Szádeczky-Kardoss, S. (1976). 'Nouveau fragment de Polybe sur l'activité d'un proconsul romain, distributeur de terres en Hispanie', *Oikumene* 1: 99-107.

Tagliamonte, G. (2000). 'Ordinamenti politici e istituzioni nel Sannio preromano', in G. De Benedittis (ed.), *Cumae: Le conferenze del premio E. T. Salmon III*. Campobasso: Fondazione 'E. T. Salmon', 55-83.

Tan, J. (2017). *Power and Public Finance at Rome, 264–49 BCE*. Oxford: Oxford University Press.
Tarn, W. W. (1907). 'The Fleets of the First Punic War', *JHS* 27: 48–60.
Tarpin, M. (2021). '*Urbem condere / coloniam deducere*: la procédure de "fondation" coloniale', in M. Tarpin (ed.), *Colonies, territoires et statuts: nouvelles approches*. Besançon: Presses Universitaires de Franche-Comté, 13–94.
Taylor, L. R. (2013 (1960)). *The Voting Districts of the Roman Republic: The Thirty-Five Urban and Rural Tribes*. Reprinted with updated material by J. Linderski. Ann Arbor: University of Michigan Press.
Tellegen-Couperus, O. E., and Tellegen, J. W. (1998). 'La loi Voconia et ses sequelles', *RHD* 66: 65–95.
Terrenato, N. (2004). 'The Historical Significance of *Falerii Novi*', in Patterson (2004), 234–5.
Thiel, J. H. (1946). *Studies on the History of Roman Sea-Power in Republican Times*. Amsterdam: North-Holland.
—— (1954). *A History of Roman Sea-Power before the Second Punic War*. Amsterdam: North-Holland.
Thulin, C. O. (1906–9). *Die Etruskische Disclipin*. 3 vols. Göteborg: Wald Zachrissons Boktryckeri.
Tipps, G. K. (1985). 'The Battle of Ecnomus', *Historia* 34: 432–65.
—— (2003). 'The Defeat of Regulus', *CW* 96: 375–85.
Toppani, I. (1977–8). 'La regina da ritrovare: Sofonisba e il suo tragico destino', *AIV* 136: 561–78.
Torelli, M. (1968). 'Il donario di M. Fulvio Flacco nell' area di S. Omobono', *Quaderni dell' Istituto di Topografia Antica dell' Università di Roma* 5: 71–6.
—— (1988). 'Paestum Romana', in Stazio and Ceccoli (1988), 33–115.
—— (1999). *Tota Italia*. Oxford: Clarendon Press.
—— (2019). 'The *foedera navalia* of Paestum and Cosa and the Radical Switch in Roman Colonial Policy between 273 and 268 BCE', in De Giorgi (2019), 30–43.
Torelli, M. R. (2002). *Benevento Romana*. Rome: L'Erma di Bretschneider.
Tovar, A. (1989). *Iberische Landeskunde. Segunda Parte, Tome 3: Tarraconensis*. Baden-Baden: Valentin Koerner.
——, and Blázquez Martínez, J. M. (1975). 'Forschungsbericht zur Geschichte des römischen Hispanien', *ANRW* II. 3: 428–51.
Toynbee, A. J. (1965). *Hannibal's Legacy*. 2 vols. London: Oxford University Press.
Tränkle, H. (1977). *Livius und Polybios*. Basel: Schwabe.
Treggiari, S. (1969). *Roman Freedmen during the Late Republic*. Oxford: Clarendon Press.
Tullio, R. (1993). 'Gavio Ponzio e le Forche Caudine (commento al libro IX di Tito Livio)', *A&R* 38: 1–17.
Tusa, S., and Royal, J. G. (2012). 'The Landscape of the Naval Battle at the Egadi Islands (241 B.C.)', *JRA* 25: 7–48.
—— (2020). 'History of the Project and Overview of the Site', in Royal and Tusa (2020), 23–30.
Ungern-Sternberg, J. von (1975). *Capua im zweiten punischen Krieg: Untersuchungen zur römischen Annalistik*. Munich: C. H. Beck.
—— (2005). 'The End of the Conflict of the Orders', in K. A. Raaflaub (ed.), *Social Struggles in Archaic Rome: New Perspectives on the Conflict of the Orders*. 2nd edn. Malden, MA: Blackwell, 312–32.
Untermann, J. (1975). *Monumenta Linguarum Hispanicarum*. Vol. 1.1. Wiesbaden: Dr. Ludwig Reichert.

Urso, G. (1998). *Taranto e gli* xenikoì strategoí. Rome: Istituto Italiano per la Storia Antica.
Valeton, I. M. J. (1890). 'De modis auspicandi Romanorum: II', *Mnemosyne* 18: 208–63.
Van Nuffelen, P. (2012). *Orosius and the Rhetoric of History*. Oxford: Oxford University Press.
Vanggaard, J. H. (1988). *The Flamen: A Study in the History and Sociology of Roman Religion*. Copenhagen: Museum Tusculum Press.
Vasaly, A. (1987). 'Personality and Power: Livy's Depiction of the Appii Claudii in the First Pentad', *TAPhA* 117: 203–26.
—— (2002). 'The Structure of Livy's First Pentad and the Augustan Poetry Book', in Levene and Nelis (2002), 275–90.
Vedaldi Iasbez, V. (1994). *La* Venetia *orientale e l'*Histria. Rome: Quasar.
Versnel, H. S. (1981). 'Self-Sacrifice, Compensation, and the Anonymous Gods', in *Le sacrifice dans l'antiquité*. Geneva: Fondation Hardt, 135–85.
—— (1993). *Inconsistencies in Greek and Roman Religion II: Transition and Reversal in Myth and Ritual*. Leiden: Brill.
Vervaet, F. J. (2014). *The High Command in the Roman Republic*. Stuttgart: Franz Steiner.
Vigneron, R. (1983). 'L'antiféministe loi Voconia et les "Schleichwege des Lebens"', *Labeo* 29: 140–53.
Ville, G. (1981). *La gladiature en occident des origines à la mort de Domitien*. Rome: École Française de Rome.
Vollmer, D. (1990). *Symploker: Das Übergreifen der römischen Expansion auf den griechischen Osten*. Stuttgart: Franz Steiner.
Wachter, R. (1987). *Altlateinische Inschriften: Sprachliche und epigraphische Untersuchungen zu den Dokumenten bis etwa 150 v. Chr*. Bern: Peter Lang.
Walbank, F. W. (1947). 'The Geography of Polybius', *C&M* 9: 155–82 = Walbank (2002), 31–52.
—— (1957). *A Historical Commentary on Polybius*. Vol. 1. Oxford: Clarendon Press.
—— (1963). 'Polybius and Rome's Eastern Policy', *JRS* 53: 1–13 = Walbank (1985), 138–56.
—— (1967). *A Historical Commentary on Polybius*. Vol. 2. Oxford: Clarendon Press.
—— (1979). *A Historical Commentary on Polybius*. Vol. 3. Oxford: Clarendon Press.
—— (1985). *Selected Papers*. Cambridge: Cambridge University Press.
—— (2002). *Polybius, Rome and the Hellenistic World*. Cambridge: Cambridge University Press.
Waldherr, G. H. (2000). '"Punica Fides"—das Bild der Karthager in Rom', *Gymnasium* 107: 193–222.
Wallace-Hadrill, A. (2008). *Rome's Cultural Revolution*. Cambridge: Cambridge University Press.
Walser, G. (1953–4). 'Die Ursachen des ersten römisch-illyrischen Krieges', *Historia* 2: 308–18.
Walsh, P. G. (1961). *Livy: His Historical Aims and Methods*. Cambridge: Cambridge University Press.
—— (1965). 'Massinissa', *JRS* 55: 149–60.
Walter, U. (2004). Memoria *und* res publica. Frankfurt am Main: Verlag Antike.
Wardle, D. (1998). *Valerius Maximus*: Memorable Deeds and Sayings. Book 1. Oxford: Clarendon Press.
Warrior, V. M. (1996). *The Initiation of the Second Macedonian War*. Stuttgart: Franz Steiner.
Watson, A. (1971). *The Law of Succession in the Later Roman Republic*. Oxford: Clarendon Press.

Weber, G. (1997). 'Interaktion, Repräsentation und Herrschaft: Der Königshof im Hellenismus', in A. Winterling (ed.), *Zwischen 'Haus' und 'Staat': Antike Höfe im Vergleich*. Munich: Oldenbourg, 27–71.
Wegner, M. (1969). *Untersuchungen zu den lateinischen Begriffen socius und societas*. Göttingen: Vandenhoeck & Ruprecht.
Weishaupt, A. (1999). *Die Lex Voconia*. Cologne: Böhlau.
Weiss, J. (1926). 'Ligures', *RE* XIII: 525–34.
Welwei, K.-W. (1978). 'Hieron II. von Syrakus und der Ausbruch des ersten punischen Krieges', *Historia* 27: 573–87.
Wiedemann, T. (1986). 'The *Fetiales*: A Reconsideration', *CQ* 36: 478–90.
—— (1992). *Emperors and Gladiators*. London: Routledge.
Wiegels, R. (1982). 'Iliturgi und der "Deductor" Ti. Sempronius Gracchus', *MDAI(M)* 23: 152–221.
Wilkes, J. (1992). *The Illyrians*. Oxford: Blackwell.
Will, E. (1982). *Histoire politique du monde hellénistique*. 2nd edn. 2 vols. Nancy: Presses Universitaires de Nancy.
Will, W. (1983). 'Imperatores victi: zum Bild besiegter römischen Consuln bei Livius', *Historia* 32: 173–82.
Wille, G. (1973). *Der Aufbau des Livianischen Geschichtswerk*. Amsterdam: B. R. Grüner.
Williams, J. H. C. (2001). *Beyond the Rubicon: Romans and Gauls in Republican Italy*. Oxford: Oxford University Press.
Wills, J. (1996). *Repetition in Latin Poetry: Figures of Allusion*. Oxford: Clarendon Press.
Wirszubski, C. (1950). *Libertas as a Political Idea at Rome during the Late Republic and Early Principate*. Cambridge: Cambridge University Press.
Wiseman, T. P. (1970). 'Roman Republican Road-Building', *PBSR* 40: 122–52.
—— (1971). *New Men in the Roman Senate 139 B.C.–A.D. 14*. Oxford: Oxford University Press.
—— (1974). 'The Circus Flaminius', *PBSR* 42: 3–26.
—— (1976). 'Two Questions on the Circus Flaminius', *PBSR* 44: 44–7.
—— (1979). *Clio's Cosmetics: Three Studies in Greco-Roman Literature*. Leicester: Leicester University Press.
—— (1986). 'Monuments and the Roman Annalists', in I. S. Moxon, J. D. Smart, and A. J. Woodman (eds), *Past Perspectives: Studies in Greek and Roman Historical Writing*. Cambridge: Cambridge University Press, 87–101 = Wiseman (1994), 37–48.
—— (1987). '*Conspicui postes tectaque digna deo*: The Public Image of Aristocratic and Imperial Houses in the Late Republic and Early Empire', in *L'Urbs: Espace urbain et histoire (Ier siècle av. J.-C.–IIIe siècle ap. J.-C.)*. Rome: École Française de Rome, 393–413 = Wiseman (1994), 98–115.
—— (1994). *Historiography and Imagination: Eight Essays on Roman Culture*. Exeter: University of Exeter Press.
—— (1996). 'The Minucii and Their Monument', in J. Linderski (ed.), *Imperium sine fine: T. Robert S. Broughton and the Roman Republic*. Stuttgart: Franz Steiner, 57–74 = Wiseman (1998), 90–105.
—— (1998). *Roman Drama and Roman History*. Exeter: University of Exeter Press.
—— (2002). 'History, Poetry, and *Annales*', in Levene and Nelis (2002), 331–62 = Wiseman (2008), 243–70.
—— (2008). *Unwritten Rome*. Exeter: University of Exeter Press.
—— (2009). *Remembering the Roman People. Essays on Late-Republican Politics and Literature*. Oxford: Oxford University Press.

Wissowa, G. (1912). *Religion und Kultus der Römer*. 2nd edn. Munich: C. H. Beck.
—— (1923–4). 'Vestalinnenfrevel', *Archiv für Religionswissenschaft* 22: 201–14.
Witcher, R. (2008). 'Regional Field Survey and the Demography of Roman Italy', in de Ligt and Northwood (2008): 273–303.
Wölfflin, E. (1877). 'Die Periochae des Livius', in *Commentationes Philologicae in Honorem Theodori Mommseni*. Berlin: Weidmann, 337–50.
—— (1890). 'Die Inschrift der Columna rostrata', *SBAW* 1890.1: 293–321.
—— (1892). 'Cn. Cornelius Scipio Asina', *Archiv für lateinische Lexicographie und Grammatik* 7: 279–80.
—— (1900a). 'Die Latinität des verlorenen Epitoma Livii', *Archiv für lateinische Lexicographie und Grammatik* 11: 1–8.
—— (1900b). 'Zur Epitoma Livii', *Archiv für lateinische Lexicographie und Grammatik* 11: 212.
Wörrle, M. (1988). 'Inschriften von Herakleia am Latmos I: Antiochos III., Zeuxis und Herakleia', *Chiron* 18: 421–76.
Wolski, J. (1956). 'La prise de Rome par les Celtes et la formation de l'annalistique romaine', *Historia* 5: 24–52.
Woodman, A. J. (1977). *Velleius Paterculus: The Tiberian Narrative (2.94–131)*. Cambridge: Cambridge University Press.
—— (1983a). *Velleius Paterculus: The Caesarian and Augustan Narrative (2.41–93)*. Cambridge: Cambridge University Press.
—— (1983b). 'From Hitler to Hannibal: The Literature of War', *University of Leeds Review* 26: 107–24 = Woodman (1998), 1–20.
—— (1988). *Rhetoric in Classical Historiography*. London: Croom Helm.
—— (1998). *Tacitus Reviewed*. Oxford: Clarendon Press.
—— (2006). 'Mutiny and Madness: Tacitus *Annals* 1.16–49', *Arethusa* 39: 303–27 = Woodman (2012), 296–321.
—— (2009). 'Horace and Historians', *CCJ* 55: 157–67 = Woodman (2012), 112–20.
—— (2010). 'Community Health: Metaphors in Latin Historiography', *PLLS* 14: 43–61 = Woodman (2012), 162–80.
—— (2012). *From Poetry to History: Selected Papers*. Oxford: Oxford University Press.
—— (2014). *Tacitus: Agricola*. Cambridge: Cambridge University Press.
—— (2018). *The Annals of Tacitus: Book 4*. Cambridge: Cambridge University Press.
——, and Martin, R. H. (1996). *The Annals of Tacitus: Book 3*. Cambridge: Cambridge University Press.
Wuilleumier, P. (1939). *Tarente: Des origines à la conquête romaine*. Paris: De Boccard.
Yakobson, A. (1995). 'Secret Ballot and Its Effects in the Late Roman Republic', *Hermes* 123: 426–42.
Yardley, J. C. (2003). *Justin and Pompeius Trogus: A Study of the Language of Justin's Epitome of Trogus*. Toronto: University of Toronto Press.
Yavetz, Z. (1962). 'The Policy of C. Flaminius and the Plebiscitum Claudianum', *Athenaeum* 40: 325–44.
Zahrnt, M. (2008). 'Die Überlieferung über den Ersten Illyrischen Krieg', *Hermes* 136: 391–414.
Zangemeister, K. (1882). 'Die Periochae des Livius', in *Festschrift zur Begrüssung der in Karlsruhe vom 27.–30. September 1882 Tagenden XXXVI. Philologen-Versammlung verfasst von den philologischen Collegen an der Heidelberger Universität*. Freiburg: J. C. B. Mohr, 89–106.
Zehnacker, H. (1964). 'Le monnayage de L. Rubrius Dossenus', in M. Renard and R. Schilling (eds), *Hommages à Jean Bayet*. Brussels: Latomus, 739–48.

Zetzel, J. E. G. (2018). *Critics, Compilers, and Commentators: An Introduction to Roman Philology, 200 BCE–800 CE*. New York: Oxford University Press.

Zimmermann, J.-L. (1986). 'La fin de Falerii Veteres: Un témoignage archéologique', *GMusJ* 14: 37–42.

Ziolkowski, A. (1992). *The Temples of Mid-Republican Rome and Their Historical and Topographical Contexts*. Rome: L'Erma di Bretschneider.

Zuffa, M. (1970). 'Abitati e santuari suburbani di Rimini dalla protostoria alla romanità', in *Studi sulla città antica: Atti del convegno di studi sulla città etrusca e italica preromana*. Bologna: Istituto per la Storia di Bologna, 299–315.

General Index

Except in the case of Roman authors such as Sallust, Cicero, and Tacitus and emperors and other members of the imperial family, the index gives the full names of Roman citizens, as far as these are known. Roman officials are identified by the highest office held (all dates given as BC unless otherwise stated). Standard Roman abbreviations are used for the following personal names: Appius (abbreviated as Ap.), Aulus (A.), Decimus (D.), Gaius (C.), Gnaeus (Cn.), Lucius (L.), Mamercus (Mam.), Manius (M'.), Marcus (M.), Numerius (N.), Publius (P.), Quintus (Q.), Servius (Ser.), Spurius (Sp.), Tiberius (Ti.), Titus (T.). These names are ignored in alphabetization.

'A' *Periochae* xi, xxxiii
   authorship of 73–5
   narrative of 73–4
   sanitizes Romulus 76–7
   style of 73
ab urbe condita dating xlvi
Abdera 653, 655–6
Abydus 559, 561, 564–5
Acarnania, Acarnanians 559–62, 576
Acerrae 434–5
Achaea, Achaeans 524, 570–2, 574, 576, 591, 623, 645
Achaean League 571–2
Achaean War, origin of xxxix
M'. Acilius Glabrio (*cos.* 191) xxxv, 594, 596, 601–2, 611
Adherbal, Carthaginian commander 383
Adherbal, grandson of Masinissa 465
Adranon 330
Adys 357
Aeacides 239
aediles, prosecutions by 387–90
Aegates Islands, battle of 293, 318, 348, 394–402
Aegimurus 394
C. Aelius 224–5
Aemilia 632
L. Aemilius Barbula (*cos.* 281) 230, 234, 238, 251
M. Aemilius Lepidus (*cos.* 232) 417
M. Aemilius Lepidus (*cos.* 187, 175) xxxvi, 446, 616, 618, 629, 639, 658
M. Aemilius Lepidus (*cos.* 46, 42) 632
Mam. Aemilius Mamercinus (dictator 426) 130–2
L. Aemilius Papus (*cos.* 225) 236, 427, 441–2
Q. Aemilius Papus (*cos.* 282, 278) 236, 259, 276, 287
L. Aemilius Paullus (*cos.* 220, 216) 441, 472
L. Aemilius Paullus (*cos.* 182, 168) xxvi, xxxv, xxxviii, xliii, 633, 660–3, 666, 669–71

M. Aemilius Paullus (*cos.* 255) 365
L. Aemilius Regillus (*pr.* 190) xxiv, 597–9, 601–3
Aeneas 75–6, 406
Aequi 105, 109, 112–14, 114, 118, 122, 124, 132–3, 135, 139, 148, 187, 191
Aesculapius, temple of xli, 197, 205–9
Aesernia 335–6, 413
aetiology 157
Aetolia, Aetolians 567, 570–1, 588–9, 591–2, 594, 597, 601, 604
Aetolian League 567
aftermath narratives of battles 252–4
Agathocles 327
age for holding office 308–9
ager Gallicus 427, 445, 447, 450
Agesilochus 650
aggression by Rome 323–6, 414, 423–4, 438–40
agrarian legislation 109, 114, 148, 150–1, 153, 160–1
Agrigentum 279, 325, 336, 347–8, 352, 366
Agrippa *see* Menenius 105
Agron 422
Ahala *see* Servilius
Aius Locutius, temple of xli, li, 145–7
Alba Helviorum 76
Alba Longa 75–6, 79
Alban Lake 136–7
Alban Mount, triumphs on 417
Albans 170
Albingauni lvi
Albingaunum lvi, 536
L. Albinius 140
Albinus *see* Postumius
Aleria 345, 347
Alexander Balas xxxv
Alexander of Epirus 173–4, 230, 236–7
Alexander, son of Pyrrhus 308
Alexander the Great xxxix, 186, 189–90, 237, 252, 273, 587

Alexandria 667
Allia, battle of the 140, 142
allusion, in historiography lx–lxxiv
allusion, in late antiquity xxviii, lxiii
Alps lviii, 456–8
Alsium 386–7
ambassadors, violation of 129–31, 133, 233, 307–9, 421–4, 665
Ambracia 604
amicitia 162, 332
Ampelius, and *Periochae* 128, 161–2
Amulius 75
Anagnia 254
Ancus Marcius 73, 80, 83–6
L. Anicius Gallus (*cos.* 160) 663
Anio 508–9
L. Annius 167–9
T. Annius Milo (*tr.pl.* 57) xxi
L. Annius Setinus 1
Antiates 167
Antigonus 630
Antigonus Doson 439
Antigonus Gonatas 238, 287, 300–1, 308
Antioch 638
Antiochan War 579, 588–90, 592–4, 597–601, 605, 610, 634
Antiochus (nephew of Antiochus IV) 636
Antiochus I 238
Antiochus III xxvii, xxxv, xxxvii, xliii, lxviii, lxxiv, 576, 579–80, 586–8, 590, 592–4, 597, 599–602, 607–8, 610–11, 637–8
Antiochus IV Epiphanes lv, 636–9, 664, 666–7
Antiochus, eldest son of Antiochus III 637
Antipater 252
anti-Roman sentiment 230
M. Antonius Primus 451
M. Antonius (triumvir) 80
Anxur 134
Apennines lvi, 311, 315, 412, 459–60, 617
Apollonia 307–8, 493–4
L. Appuleius Saturninus (*tr.pl.* 100) xxxvi
Cn. Apronius (*aed.*) 308
Apuani 617
L. Apuleius (*tr.pl.* 391) 139
Apulians 183, 187
Aqua Appia 183–5, 262
Aquileia 628–9
Aquilonia, battle of xxxv, lxxv, 194, 196–7, 207
Ara Maxima 184, 262
archaism liv
Archidamus III 237
Archimedes 493, 501
Ardea, Ardeans 82, 92, 123–7, 142
Argos 299–300, 570, 573–4, 582
Aricia 102, 123–4

Ariminum 217, 309–13, 413–14, 427, 446, 616
see also *ius Ariminense*
Aristaenus 571
Aristides 'the Just' 274
Ariston 586
army, size of 245, 429–31
Arno marshes 460
Arpi, Arpinates 191, 275
Arretium 226, 464, 517
Arruns Tarquinius 98
Artabanus 260
Arusinian Plains 286–7
Asculum xxxv
Aspis 354
Astapa 530
Athamanians 567, 570–1
Athens, Athenians 559–64, 567, 636
C. Atilius Bulbus (*cos.* 245, 235) 413, 442
A. Atilius Caiatinus (*cos.* 258, 254) 349–51, 385–7
C. Atilius Regulus (*cos.* 257, 250) 352–3
C. Atilius Regulus (*cos.* 225) 417, 427
M. Atilius Regulus (*cos.* 267, 256) 342
  defeats Sallentini 387
  invades Africa 347, 352–8
  battles a serpent 356–7
  negotiates with Carthage 355–6
  extension of command 358–61
  defeated in Africa 361–6
  embassy and death 257, 314–15, 371–6, 386, 475
  as martyr lv
Atrax 570
Attalus I 525–6, 538, 559, 561, 567, 570–1, 574, 577, 600
Attalus II 636–7, 668
Attus Navius xxvi, 81, 85–7
augurs, augury 192, 367, 381, 405
Augustine, and *Periochae* xxxi, lvii, 95–6, 127, 221
Augustus, emperor lxxvi, lxxix, 80, 103, 116, 131, 151, 283, 319, 344, 415, 438, 635
Aurelian Wall 446
C. Aurelius Cotta (*cos.* 252, 248) 365
C. Aurelius Cotta (*cos.* 200) 567
Aurunci 105, 162, 166
Ausculum, battle of 255–9, 265–9, 271–2, 274, 277, 289
  conflated with Heraclea 249–50, 255–7
Ausones 172–3, 183, 187
authenticity, and literary copying lxvi–lxx
Aventine li, 83–4, 89, 106, 118–19, 123, 221–2, 388

Bacchanalia crisis 618–19
Badius 499

GENERAL INDEX   709

Cn. Baebius (*cos.* 182) 546
Q. Baebius (*tr.pl.* 200) 563–4
Baecula, battle of 520–4
Balearic Islands 531
Bastarnae 629–30
battle casualties, reliability of numbers 228, 248, 250, 267–8, 285, 342, 381–2, 397, 472–3
Beneventum 286, 310–13, 413, 492
  battle of 249–50, 285–7, 311
Bithynia 672
Boeotia, Boeotians 576, 578
Boii 226, 233, 236, 427, 432, 434, 449, 566, 573, 578–9, 583, 595
  see also Gauls
Bononia 616
Bovillae 185
Brennus 605
Brundisium 308, 312, 315–16, 387, 413, 559
Bruttium, Bruttians 224, 226, 231, 234–5, 243, 258, 277–8, 299, 302, 328, 537, 584
Brutus *see* Junius
Buxentum 584

L. Caecilius Metellus (*cos.* 251, 247) xxxviii, 369, 374, 377–80, 391–3, 404–6
Q. Caecilius Metellus Creticus (*cos.* 69) 380
L. Caecilius Metellus Denter (*cos.* 284) 216, 226–8
M. Caedicius 139
Q. Caedicius *see* M. Calpurnius Flamma
M. Caelius Rufus (*pr.* 48) xxi
Caere, Caerites 143, 161, 166
Caesar *see* Julius
Caiatinus *see* Atilius
calendar, publication of 187–8
Cales 173, 317
M. Calpurnius Flamma (*tr.mil.* 258) xxi, 106, 163–4, 348–51
Camarina 349
Cambyses 320
Camerinum 315
Camerium 367
Campania, Campanians 225, 231, 242–7, 254, 256, 287, 307, 327–8, 334, 470, 485–6, 489, 498–500, 607
  surrender to Rome 162–3
  defection of 167, 478
  stereotypes of 243
  see also Capua
campus Flaminius 448
Campus Martius 96–7, 447
Cannae, battle of xxiv, 249, 375, 400, 435, 466–8, 470–6, 478–9, 481, 485, 492, 497, 508
canon of historians xi
C. Canuleius (*tr.pl.* 445) xlii, 125
Canusium 473, 515–16

Capitol 140, 142–4, 167–8, 222, 428, 516, 608–9, 612
  seizure of 114–15
  see also Jupiter Capitolinus
Cappodocia 607
Capua xxi, xxix, xxxvii, xli, 164–7, 179, 183, 185, 241, 247, 312, 334, 478, 481, 488–90, 498–500, 503, 507, 510–11, 514, 516
Carsioli 191–2
Carthage, Carthaginians xlvii, xlix–l, 162, 279, 285, 290, 320–404 *passim*, 416, 418–19, 428, 438–9, 452–558 *passim*, 561, 572–3, 585–6, 588, 644–5, 648–9
  origins of xxxix, lxxiv, 320–1
  treaties with 162, 211, 231, 258, 269–73, 291–2, 295–9, 322–3, 326–7, 554
  in Tarentum 294–301
  as counter-Rome 320–1, 337, 644–5
  stereotypes of 339–41, 351–2, 373, 376, 587
  see also First Punic War, Second Punic War, Third Punic War
Sp. Carvilius Maximus (*cos.* 293, 272) 218, 299, 302
Sp. Carvilius Maximus (*cos.* 234, 228) 417
Casilinum 481–2, 492
Cassius Dio, contents-list in 74
Sp. Cassius 309
C. Cassius Longinus (*cos.* 171) 652, 656
Sp. Cassius Vicellinus (*cos.* 502, 493, 486) 109–10
Castrum Novum 213–15, 294, 309
Castulo 529
Catiline *see* Sergius 254
Caudine Forks, battle of xxv, 179–83, 198, 205
Celtiberia, Celtiberi li, 494–6, 503, 578, 623, 628, 633–5, 644, 657–8
Cenomani 566, 573
censors, regulating morals 288–9, 370
censorship 139
  establishment of 125–6
  reform of 132
census xlii, lii, 81, 88, 115–16, 173, 197, 218, 265–6, 441–3, 519–20
  problems with figures 197, 218, 266, 289, 333, 370, 387, 443, 519–20, 639–40, 650–1
M. Centenius Paenula 499–500
centos xxviii, liv
centuriae 78
Cephallenia 604
Cethegus *see* Cornelius
Chalcis 525, 567, 592, 655–6
Chalestrum 656
characterization, in *Periochae* xlv
Christian language lv–lvi, 107, 119, 376, 553, 564, 619, 639

Christians, Christianity xxxix, xlii, lv–lvi, 154–5, 170, 227, 372, 376, 539, 569, 637–8, 661–2
chronological markers 126, 137
C. Cicereius (*pr.* 173) 384
Cicero, and Catilinarian conspiracy xliv
  as *novus homo* 367
  exile of xliv
  death of xliv, li, lxxvi
Q. Cicero *see* Tullius
Cilicia 264
Cimbri 523
Cincinnatus *see* Quinctius
Cineas 255–8, 260, 276
Cinna *see* Cornelius
Circus Flaminius 445–8
Circus Maximus 85, 280, 447
Cirta 555
Cisalpine Gauls 413–15, 429, 431, 566
Cissa/Cissis 530
Civil War, origin of xxxix
civitas sine suffragio 245–6, 307, 333
Clastidium, siege of 434–5
Claudia, sister of P. Claudius Pulcher xxxv, 104, 387–91
Claudia Quinta 538–9
Claudian tribe xxxvii
Claudii, stereotype of xxxvii, 103–4, 262, 388
Claudius, emperor 367
Ap. Claudius (decemvir) 117–18, 122–3
Ap. Claudius Caecus (*cos.* 307, 296) 194, 283, 380, 389
  censorship of 132, 183–7, 443
  advises against peace with Pyrrhus 255–6, 258–9, 261–5
C. Claudius Canina (*cos.* 285, 273) 292
Ap. Claudius Caudex (*cos.* 264) 324, 329–30, 336, 347, 380
Ap. Claudius Centho (*pr.* 175) 644
M. Claudius Clineas 416
Ap. Claudius Crassinus Inregillensis Sabinus (*cos.* 471) li, 112–13
Ap. Claudius Crassus Inregillensis (*tr.mil.c.p.* 403) xxiv, 136–7
M. Claudius Glicia (dictator, 249) 382, 384–5
M. Claudius Marcellus (*cos.* 331) 174
M. Claudius Marcellus (*cos.* 222, 215, 214, 210, 208) xx, 200, 435
  wins *spolia opima* xxxv–xxxvi, 431–2, 434–7
  confronts Hannibal at Nola 480–1, 485–9, 492
  recaptures Casilinum 492
  in Sicily 491, 493
  besieges Syracuse 493
  captures Syracuse xlvii, 435, 500–2, 514, 516
  final campaigns in Sicily 503
  confronts Hannibal 435, 468, 515–16
  death of 435, 517–19, 521, 524
M. Claudius Marcellus (*cos.* 196) 578–9
C. Claudius Nero (*cos.* 207) xxvii, lviii, 312, 512, 522–3, 526–7, 546–7, 554
Ap. Claudius Pulcher (*cos.* 212) 498, 507, 511
Ap. Claudius Pulcher (*cos.* 54) 264
C. Claudius Pulcher (*cos.* 177) 640, 671
P. Claudius Pulcher (*cos.* 249) xxxv, 348, 380–6, 388–9, 394
Ap. Claudius Russus (*cos.* 268) 309
Ap. Claudius Sabinus Inregillensis (*cos.* 495) xxxvii, 102–4
Cleemporus 425
clemency 653–4
Cleonymus 191, 229–30, 237, 316
Cleopatra II 666–7
Cleopatra VII 80
Cloelia 99, 102
closure, and deaths xxxvi–xxxvii, 376, 557
Clusium 100, 140–1, 427
codex see scroll
coinage 210, 238, 290, 313–14
Collatinus *see* Tarquinius
collective memory lxx–lxxiv
Collina, tribe 444
colonies
  definition of 214–16, 311
  foundation of xl, lii, 84, 173, 183, 191, 194, 213–17, 292–4, 309–13, 335–6, 386–7, 412–13, 449–51, 584, 588, 623
columna rostrata 342, 344, 365
Comenses 578–9
Concord, Temple of 188
conscription 105, 117, 155, 282–4
consular tribunate
  establishment of 125–6
  plebeians in 132, 150–3
contents-lists 74–5
Cora 102
Corcyra 307–8, 422
Corinth 307–8, 570, 574
Coriolanus *see* Marcius
Corioli 105–6
Cornelia 613–14
P. Cornelius (*pr.* 234) 417
Cn. Cornelius Blasio (*cos.* 270, 257) 305, 332
C. Cornelius Cethegus (*cos.* 197) 573
L. Cornelius Cinna (*cos.* 87, 86, 85, 84) xxxiv, liii
A. Cornelius Cossus Arvina (*cos.* 343, 332) 164
A. Cornelius Cossus (*cos.* 428) xxxvi, 130–2, 437
L. Cornelius Dolabella 391
P. Cornelius Dolabella (*cos.* 283) 226, 234, 236, 259

Cn. Cornelius Lentulus (*cos.* 201) 554
L. Cornelius Lentulus Caudinus (*cos.* 275) 282, 285–7, 299
L. Cornelius Lentulus Caudinus (*cos.* 237) 413, 442
P. Cornelius Lentulus Caudinus (*cos.* 236) 413
Ser. Cornelius Lentulus Maluginensis (*cos.* AD 10) 391–3
P. Cornelius Rufinus (*cos.* 290, 277) 198, 212, 287–8, 299
L. Cornelius Scipio (*cos.* 259) 345–7
P. Cornelius Scipio (*cos.* 218) xxiv, 449, 456–7, 459, 484, 487–8, 494–6, 503–4, 506, 530
P. Cornelius Scipio Africanus Aemilianus (*cos.* 147, 134) xxxv, xliii–xliv, liii, lxxvi, 497, 583
P. Cornelius Scipio Africanus (*cos.* 205, 194) xxiv, xxvii, xxxi, xxxvi, lviii, lxxv, 108, 327, 495–6, 505, 525, 634
  in *Periochae* xliii, 524, 541
  claims divine ancestry 512–13
  protects father at Ticinus 456–7, 459
  rallies troops after Cannae 473–5
  aedileship xliii, 308, 497
  takes command in Spain 459, 497, 503, 505, 511–13
  captures New Carthage xxxv, 461, 511–12
  at New Carthage li, 529–30
  victorious at Baecula 520–1, 524
  suppresses mutiny 241–2
  drives Carthaginians from Spain 527–8, 531
  forms alliance with Syphax 528
  forms alliance with Masinissa 531–2
  elected consul 497
  plans invasion of Africa 531–4
  debate with Fabius 355, 361–2, 533
  recaptures Locri 536–7
  accusations against xlvii, 201–2, 541–3
  invades Africa 517, 543
  campaigns in Africa 546, 549–52
  meets Hannibal before Zama 355–6, 552
  defeats Hannibal at Zama lxiv, 552–4
  negotiates peace treaty 554
  makes Masinissa king 555–6
  triumph of 556–7
  second consulship 583
  meeting with Hannibal xliii, liii, lxviii, 587–9
  as brother's legate xliii, 202–3, 597–9, 601
  put on trial 608–15
  death of 609–10, 613, 621–3
L. Cornelius Scipio Asiaticus (*cos.* 190) xxxi–xxxii, xxxvii, 202–3, 524–5, 537, 597–8, 600–2, 608–15, 634
Cn. Cornelius Scipio Asina (*cos.* 260, 254) 339–41, 347, 352, 365
P. Cornelius Scipio Asina (*cos.* 221) 437

L. Cornelius Scipio Barbatus (*cos.* 298) 223, 266, 347
Cn. Cornelius Scipio Calvus (*cos.* 222) xxiv, 434–5, 461, 484, 487–8, 494–6, 503–4, 506, 530
P. Cornelius Scipio Nasica (*cos.* 191) xxxv, l, 538–40, 595, 614
P. Cornelius Scipio Nasica Corculum (*cos.* 162, 155) xlix–l, 538, 644
L. Cornelius Sulla Felix (dictator) xxi, lxxv–lxxviii, 103
Coroneia 653–5
Corsi 417
Corsica, Corsicans 345–7, 414–19, 421, 426, 438, 651
C. Coruncanius 425
L. Coruncanius 425
Ti. Coruncanius (*cos.* 280) 236, 278, 294, 367–9, 425
corvus *see* 'raven'
Cosa 293–4
Cossura 365
Cossus *see* Cornelius
counterfactual history 189
Crassus *see* Licinius
Cremera, battle of 111–12, 245
Cremona 446, 449–51, 565
Crispinus *see* Quinctius
Crixus xxxiii
Croton 584
crucifixion 351–2, 376
Cumae 486
Cures 407
Curia Hostilia 331
curiae 78
M'. Curius Dentatus (*cos.* 290, 275, 274) 274, 280, 288, 360, 368, 380, 407–8
  defeats Samnites and Sabines xxxv, lxxv, 198, 210–13, 215, 234
  defeats Lucanians 223
  defeats Gauls 226–8
  second consulship 282–7
  defeats Pyrrhus 250, 285–7, 299
  triumph of 285–6
M. Curtius 157–8
curule aedileship, creation of 154
Cybele *see* Magna Mater
Cyclades 438
Cynoscephalae, battle of lxxvii, 574, 576

Dardanians 567, 656–7
Darius I 320
De Viris Illustribus, and *Periochae* xxxi–xxxii, 98–9, 128, 150, 612–15
debt crises xxvi, 105, 149–51, 153, 161, 165, 176, 220–1

decades *see* pentads
decemvirs, decemvirate xxix, li, 117–23
decimation 112–13
Decius Magius 241
P. Decius Mus (*cos.* 340) xli, 163–4, 170–2, 194–6, 267
P. Decius Mus (*cos.* 312, 308, 297, 295) xli, 194–5, 198, 263, 267, 337
P. Decius Mus (*cos.* 279) 266–7
Decius Vibellius 242–7, 306
'defensive imperialism' 223, 323–6, 423–4, 438–9
Delphi, Delphic Oracle xli, 82, 91, 137–8, 231, 474–5, 540, 646–7
Demeter 300
Demetrius 626–7, 629–30
Demetrius I Soter xxxv, 636–8
Demetrius II of Macedon 424
Demetrius of Pharus 422, 425–6, 437–40
Demetrius Poliorcetes 252, 627
Demosthenes 260
Dentatus *see* Curius
Derkas 240
devotio xli, 170–1, 194–6, 267
Diana, temple of xli, li, 81, 88
dictatorship, creation of 102–3
Dimale 440
Diocletian, emperor 574
Dionysius II 244
Dium 659
divorce 370
Dodona 240, 260
Dolabella *see* Cornelius
Cn. Domitius Calvinus Maximus (*cos.* 283) 226, 265–6
doublets 244–5, 306, 346, 545, 555, 650
drama, founded at Rome xli–xlii, 154–5
Drepana 366, 394, 396
  battle of 381–3, 394
Drusus (Nero Claudius Drusus, *cos.* 9) lxxix
C. Duilius (*cos.* 260) 231, 339, 341–4, 352, 365, 399
duumviri navales 231–2, 317

earthquake 463
Ebro 402, 452–5, 635
  Ebro treaty 402, 452–5
eclipse 660, 662–3
Ecnomus, battle of 347, 353–4
Egypt, Egyptians 289–90, 320, 559, 561, 664, 666–7
Elatia 574
elephants 248, 250–2, 266, 285–6, 363–4, 376–80, 456–7
Eleusinian Mysteries 559–60

Emporiae 581
Ennius, as historical source 249, 253, 258, 264, 267
Epicurus 260
Epidamnus 422
Epidaurus xxxviii, 205–9
Epirus, Epirotes 239–40, 254, 302, 576
  see also Molossians
epitomizing, validity of lxv–lxvii
Eretria 570
Eryx 394, 402
Esquilina, tribe 444
Esquiline 88
Etruria, Etruscans xxv, 99–102, 142, 148, 161, 187, 191, 194–7, 213–15, 223, 226, 233, 236, 254, 277–8, 282, 293–4, 334, 410, 419, 427, 460, 619
Euboea 574, 592
Eumenes II 588, 599–600, 602, 636–7, 646–7, 655, 664–5
Eutropius, and *Periochae* xxx–xxxi, lv, lvii, 98, 259, 431, 583
execution at triumphs 205
exemplarity 99, 155

Fabii 111–12, 245
Q. Fabius (*aed.*) 308
M. Fabius Ambustus (*tr.mil.c.p.* 381, 369) 150–1
M. Fabius Buteo (*cos.* 245) 394
C. Fabius Dorsuo 142
C. Fabius Licinus (*cos.* 273) 292
Q. Fabius Maximus (*cos.* 213) 202, 494, 517
Q. Fabius Maximus Gurges (*cos.* 292, 276) xxx, xxxv, lxxv, 198–205, 207, 209, 211–12, 218, 234, 517
Q. Fabius Maximus Gurges (*cos.* 265) 337–8
Q. Fabius Maximus Rullianus (*cos.* 322, 310, 308, 297, 295) xxx, 169, 176–8, 188, 194–5, 199–204, 494, 517
Q. Fabius Maximus Verrucosus (Cunctator) (*cos.* 233, 228, 215, 214, 209) 275
  defeats Ligurians 413
  as censor 442, 444
  opposes Flaminius 445
  dictatorship of xxv, xxxvii, 466–71
  tries to outmanoeuvre Hannibal 340, 508, 517
  conflict with Minucius xxxvii, xlvii, 466–7, 469–71
  defers to his son 202, 494, 517
  recaptures Casilinum 492
  recaptures Tarentum 516–17
  debate with Scipio 355, 361–2, 517, 533
N. Fabius Pictor (*cos.* 266) 213, 314
Q. Fabius Pictor 474–5
Q. Fabius Vibulanus (*cos.* 467) 114

C. Fabricius Luscinus (*cos*. 282, 278) 248–50,
    253, 283, 286, 306, 360, 368, 370
  defeats Samnites 234–5, 299
  defends Thurii 224–5, 235, 243
  negotiates with Pyrrhus 255–60
  and the traitor 273–7
  defeats Lucanians 299
  censorship of 287–9
Falerii, Faliscans 135, 138, 161, 166, 197, 273–4,
    405–6, 409–13
Falernia 470
fama 479
Fanum Fortunae 446
farms, size of 359–61
Festus, and Verrius Flaccus xxiii
fetials 80, 83–4, 180
Fidenae, Fidenates xxvi, xxxvi–xxxvii, 76,
    129–33, 135
Firmum 213–14
First Macedonian War xxxiv, xxxvi, 487, 493–4,
    514, 524, 537–8, 562
First Punic War lxxiv, 163, 213, 231, 246, 272–3,
    303–4, 313–14, 317–18, 320–405 *passim*,
    418–19, 432, 435, 453, 563
  causes of 295–7, 321–31, 337, 423
First Syrian War 290
'First Triumvirate' xlv
'firsts' xl, 93, 102–3, 109, 134, 151–3, 158, 172–3,
    175, 184, 192, 218, 266, 283, 329, 332,
    342–3, 367–8, 385–6, 391, 415, 432, 495,
    579, 598
flamines 369, 391–3, 448
  flamen Dialis 391–3
  flamen Martialis 391–3
  flamen Quirinalis 391–3, 601
Flamininus *see* Quinctius
C. Flaminius (*cos* 223, 217) 389, 427, 432, 434,
    437, 441–2, 444–8, 450, 462–5
C. Flaminius (*cos*. 187) 446, 616
C. Flavius Fimbria xxi
Cn. Flavius (*cur.aed*. 304) 184, 186–8, 218, 384
Floralia 412
Floronia 476
foedus 162
foedus vs. *sponsio* 180–1
foreign gods, brought to Rome 206–7, 537–8
fortuna 361–2, 478, 622
Forum Boarium 333, 337
Forum Flaminii 446
Forum Holitorium 282
freedmen 184, 186, 443–4
Fregellae 173, 182, 254
Fregenae 386–7
Frusinates 191
Fulginiae 446

Cn. Fulvius Centumalus (*cos*. 229) 424
Cn. Fulvius Centumalus Maximus
    (*cos*. 211) 511, 515
Cn. Fulvius Flaccus (*pr*. 212) 500
M. Fulvius Flaccus (*cos*. 264) 307, 337
Q. Fulvius Flaccus (*cos*. 237, 224, 212, 209) 413,
    432, 442, 498, 507–10
Q. Fulvius Flaccus (*cos*. 179) 640, 646, 650
Cn. Fulvius Maximus Centumalus (*cos*. 298) 195
M. Fulvius Nobilior (*cos*. 189) 604–5, 607, 617,
    629, 639
C. Fundanius Fundulus (*cos*. 243) 387–9
M. Furius Camillus (*tr. mil. c.p*. 401, 398, 386,
    384, 381) xxvi, 136–40, 142–3, 145–6,
    151–2, 154, 273–4, 410, 661
P. Furius Philus (*cos*. 223) 434
P. Furius Philus (*pr*. 174) 652
L. Furius Purpurio (*cos*. 196) 565, 567–8

Gabii 81–2, 90–1
Gades 496, 531–2
Gaesatae 428–9, 434, 436
Gaius Caesar (grandson of Augustus) 151
Gala 495
Galatians 654
Gallograecians xxxix, xliii, 604–6
Gaul, Gauls xxxix, xliv, li, 148, 158–62, 166,
    194–5, 215–16, 230–1, 234–5, 310–11, 336,
    413, 426–9, 450–1, 456, 462, 483–4, 535,
    561, 565–8, 573, 578–9, 583, 588, 593,
    604–5, 620, 652, 664
  sack Rome xli, li, lxxiv, 139–44, 148, 213, 405
  see also ager Gallicus, tumultus Gallicus,
    Cenomani, Boii, Senones, Insubrians,
    Cisalpine Gauls, Comenses
Genoa lvi, 536
Gentius 656–7, 663–5
C. Genucius (*cos*. 276, 270) 305
Cn. Genucius Augurinus (*tr.mil.c.p*. 399, 396) 409
L. Genucius Aventinensis (*cos*. 365, 362) 158
geography, and the *Periochae* lvi–lvii,
    454–5, 482
Germany, Germans xxxix, 436
Gisgo 554
Glabrio *see* Acilius
gladiators 333–5, 529–30
Golasecca 433–4
Gracchus *see* Sempronius
Graccuris 633, 635
Graviscae 628–9
Greek, in the *Periochae* lvi, 498
Gulussa xlix, 649

Hadria 213–15, 217, 309
Haemus, mountain 626

Hamilcar, Carthaginian commander in Italy 565–6, 573
Hamilcar, father of Hannibal 387, 394, 398, 400, 402–3, 452, 521–2
Hampsagoras 488
Hannibal, commander in First Punic War 345–6, 351–2
Hannibal xiii, xli, 167, 275, 280, 332, 430, 435, 438, 474, 522–3, 546, 557
　swears hatred of Rome 452
　character of 464, 499
　attacks Saguntum 332, 401, 438, 452–6, 532
　crosses Ebro 402, 452–6
　crosses Pyrenees 456–8
　crosses Rhone 456–7
　crosses Alps lviii, 449, 456–8
　victory at the Trebia 459–60
　attacks Placentia and Victumulae 459
　crosses Apennines lvi–lvii, 459–60
　crosses into Etruria 460, 462
　defeats Flaminius at Lake Trasimene 445, 462, 464–5
　against Fabius Maximus 340, 466, 469–71
　winters in Capua xxxvii, 241, 488–90, 508
　alliance with Philip xxxiv, xxxvii, 485, 487, 494
　fights Marcellus at Nola 480–1, 486–7
　captures Casilinum 481–2
　besieges Gracchus at Cumae 486
　captures Tarentum 302–5, 492, 497, 517
　attempts to support Capua 498
　marches on Rome li, lxxiv, 507–11, 523
　confronts Marcellus 435, 515–19
　meets Scipio before Zama 355–6
　defeated at Zama lxiv, 552–3
　negotiates peace treaty 554
　joins Antiochus III lxviii, 579–80, 585–6, 590, 593, 598–9
　meets Scipio in Syria xliii, liii, lxviii, 587–9
　death of 621–3
Hannibalic War *see* Second Punic War
Hanno, commanders in First Punic War 345, 347–8, 396
Hanno, anti-Barcid Carthaginian 395, 452, 478, 480
Hanno (commander in Spain) 461
Hanno, lieutenant of Hannibal 498
Hanno, commander in Africa 545
'hard-core facts', in historiography lxiii–lxiv, lxvi–lxvii
haruspices 280–2, 569
Hasdrubal, commander at Panormus 377–9
Hasdrubal, son-in-law of Hamilcar 402, 452
Hasdrubal, brother of Hannibal 312, 450, 461, 484–5, 521–3, 528

Hasdrubal, son of Gisgo 549, 551–2
Heliodorus 636
M. Helvius (*pr.* 197) 578, 583
Henna 493
Heraclea, battle of 239, 248–58, 266, 268, 271–2, 277–8, 287
　conflated with Ausculum 249–50, 255–7
Hercte 366, 394
Hercules 184, 262, 512, 516
Herdonia 514
Ap. Herdonius 114
T. Herminius Aquilinus (*cos.* 506) 100
Hernici 105, 109, 113, 148, 158, 160, 166, 187
Hiero II 321–4, 326–7, 330–2, 370, 400–1, 491–2
Hierocles 321
Hieronymus xlvii, 491–2
Hippo 394
Hirpini 311–12
historicism and interpretation lxvii–lxx
historiography, representing reality lxiii–lxx
Horatii and Curiatii, duel of 79
Horatius, trial of 79
M. Horatius Barbatus (*cos.* 449) 118
Horatius Cocles xxv, 99–100, 102
P. Horatius Pulvillus (*cos.* 509, 507) 98–9
L. Hortensius (*pr.* 170) 653, 655
Q. Hortensius (dictator) 219–20, 222
Hostus 488
human sacrifice 421, 474

Iapydae xxxv
Ilipa, battle of 527–8
Iliturgi 484, 529, 633
Illyria, Illyrians 421–6, 437–41, 656–7, 663, 665
　First Illyrian War 421–6, 438, 441
　Second Illyrian War 437–41, 450
Ilvates 573
imperium, abrogation of 200–3
Indibilis 524, 535
Ingauni 617
Insubrians 428–9, 432–6, 566, 573, 578–9, 583
'intentional history' lxxiii
Interamna 183
Issa 422–3, 425, 440–1
Isthmian Games lxiv–lxv, 577, 585
Istia, Istrians 437–8, 644
Istrian War 437–8
ius Ariminense 311
Iuventas 83

Janiculum 221–2
Janus, temple of 78–9, 418
Jews 320, 637
Judaea 637, 666

GENERAL INDEX 715

Jugurtha 82, 465
C. Julius Caesar (dictator) xxxiii, xliii–xlv, lxxvii–lxxviii, 103, 385, 393
L. Julius Libo (*cos.* 267) 314
P. Junius 425
D. Junius Brutus (*cos.* 138) xxxv
L. Junius Brutus (*cos.* 509) xxxi, 91, 93–8, 127
M. Junius Brutus (*cos.* 178) 540, 595
M. Junius Brutus (*pr.* 44) 127
D. Junius Brutus Pera 334
C. Junius Bubulcus Brutus (*cos.* 291, 277) 299
D. Junius Pera (*cos.* 266) 213, 314, 334, 370
L. Junius Pullus (*cos.* 249) 380, 382–3, 386, 394
C. Junius Silanus (*cos.* AD 10) 392
M. Junius Silanus (*pr.* 212) 525
Juno xxvi, xli, 138
  temple of 410
Juno Lacinia, temple of 646
Jupiter li, 146–7, 168, 509
Jupiter Capitolinus, temple of xli, 82, 90–1, 98–9, 146–7, 281–2
Jupiter Feretrius 78, 436
Justin, and Pompeius Trogus lxvi

kingship, and Rome 91

Laberius *see* M. Calpurnius Flamma
Labicani 133, 135
Lacus Curtius 157
Lacus Velinus 407
C. Laelius (*cos.* 190) 534, 550–1, 598
C. Laetorius (*tr.pl.* 471) 112
Laevinus *see* Valerius
Lake Regillus, battle of xxxvii, 102–3
Lake Trasimene, battle of xxv, 434, 445, 462–7, 517
Sp. Larcius Rufus (*cos.* 506, 490?) 100
Lars Porsenna li, 98–102
Lars Tolumnius 129–31
Latin War 167–72
Latinius xxxvii, 107–8
Latins 80–1, 83–5, 90, 103, 105, 148
  see also Latin War
Laus Pompeia 432
lectisternium xl
legal language 122–3
leges Publiliae 172
Lentulus *see* Cornelius
Leonidas 349
Leontini 279
Lepidus *see* Aemilius
Leucas 576
lex Aquilia de damno 219
lex Canuleia xlii, 125–6, 152, 221
lex de ambitu xlii

lex Genucia 152
lex Hortensia 219-22
lex Maenia 219
lex Metilia de Fullonibus 445
lex Oppia 581, 641, 643
lex Voconia 640–4
libertas, rhetoric of 303–4, 585
Liberty, temple of 388
libri lintei 129
Licinian–Sextian rogations 150–3, 158–61, 172
M. Licinius Crassus (*cos.* 70, 55) xlv
P. Licinius Crassus (*cos.* 171) 647–8, 652–5
P. Licinius Crassus Dives (*cos.* 205) 546
P. Licinius Dives Crassus Mucianus (*cos.* 131) 391
C. Licinius Stolo (*cos.* 364/1) 150–3, 160–1
C. Licinius Varus (*cos.* 236) 416
lictors 77
Liguria, Ligurians lvi, 412–16, 432, 535, 566, 573, 588, 593, 616–18, 628–9, 644, 651, 663
  see also Apuani, Ingauni
Lilybaeum 348, 365, 394
Lipara 339, 365
Liris 254
Lissus 425, 438–40
Liternum 584
M. Livius (prefect at Tarentum) 516
Livius Andronicus 516
M. Livius Drusus (*tr. pl.* 91) lxxv
C. Livius Salinator (*cos.* 188) 596–7
M. Livius Salinator (*cos.* 219, 207) xxvii, lviii, 312, 441, 522–3, 526–7, 546–7
Livy
  and Polybius lxi–lxx
  and Sallust 253
  and Thucydides 320
  and traditions of Republican history xi, li–lii, lxxii–lxxiv
  Civil War edition of lvii, lxxvi–lxxviii
  digressions in 320–1
  scepticism of 76
  self-allusion in 361–2
  structure of history lxxiv–lxxviii
Locri, Locrians xlvii, 243, 536–7, 541–2, 610
'lost epitome' hypothesis xii–xiv, xx–xxiii, xxvii–xxviii, 402, 486–7
Lucania, Lucanians 176, 183, 187, 220–4, 226, 230–1, 233–6, 243, 258, 277–8, 286–7, 293, 299, 302, 334, 489, 499
Luccia 420–1
Luceria, Lucerians 183, 187
Lucius Caesar (grandson of Augustus) 151
Lucretia 74, 81–2, 85, 91–2, 118, 176
C. Lucretius Gallus (*pr.* 171) 647, 652–3, 655
Sp. Lucretius Tricipitinus (*cos.* 509) 92, 94

ludi Apollinares 498
Ludi Magni 107
Luna 617
Lusitania, Lusitanians xxxv, 601, 635–6
C. Lutatius Catulus (*cos.* 242) 392, 396–401, 403
Q. Lutatius Cerco (*cos.* 241) 403, 442
Lysimachus 252

Macedon, Macedonians xxiv, 239, 242, 252, 300–1, 308, 438–40, 554, 559–77 *passim*, 623, 626–30, 642, 646–8, 652–3, 656–7, 659–60, 662, 669–70
Macra 617
Sp. Maelius xxvi, 127–8
Magna Mater xlii, 208, 537–40
  temple of xxxv, xli, lviii–lix, 595
Magnesia, battle of xxvii, 599–600, 637
Mago, ambassador to Rome 271–2
Mago, brother of Hannibal xxxiii, xxxvi, lvi, 484, 531–6, 557–8, 566
Mago (commander at New Carthage) 461
Mago, lieutenant of Hannibal 478–9
Maharbal 465
maiestas 387
Maleventum *see* Beneventum
Maluginensis *see* Cornelius
Mamertines 244–5, 285, 321–4, 326–9, 423
Mamertium 328
Mandonius 524, 535
M. Manlius Capitolinus (*cos.* 392) 142–3, 148–50
P. Manlius Capitolinus (*tr.mil.c.p.* 379, 367) 152
L. Manlius Capitolinus Imperiosus (dictator 363) xlvii, 154–6
T. Manlius Imperiosus Torquatus (*cos.* 347, 344, 340) xxvi, xlvii–xlviii, li, 155–6, 158–61, 168–72, 177
T. Manlius Torquatus, executed by father xlviii, 159, 169–70, 177
T. Manlius Torquatus (*cos.* 235, 224) 417–18, 432, 442, 474, 488, 514
A. Manlius Torquatus Atticus (*cos.* 244, 241) 387, 403, 409, 418
Cn. Manlius Vulso (*cos.* 189) xxxviii, xliii, 604–5, 607–8, 616–17
L. Manlius Vulso Longus (*cos.* 256, 250) 353–4, 357–8
manumission 97–8
Marcellus *see* Claudius
L. Marcius (*tr. mil.* 211) xxiv, 247, 503–6, 532
Cn. Marcius Coriolanus xxxvii, 106–9
C. Marcius Figulus (*cos.* 162, 156) 659
Q. Marcius Philippus (*cos.* 281) 236
Q. Marcius Philippus (*cos.* 186, 169) xxiv, 659, 663

C. Marcius Rutilus Censorinus (*cos.* 310) 332
Marcius, prophecies of 498
C. Marius (*cos.* 107, 104, 103, 102, 101, 100, 86) xxi, liii, xliii, lxxv–lxxvii, 367, 523
marriage 641–2
Mars 75–6, 146, 235, 328, 392
  temple of 185
Marsi xxxiv, 187, 191–2, 195
Martial, and the 'lost epitome' xii–xiii
Masaesuli 528–9
Masinissa xliv, xlix, lxiv, lviii, 465, 494–6, 520–1, 528–9, 531–2, 534, 543–6, 550–2, 555–6, 586, 648–9
Massiva 520–1
Massylii 495, 528–9, 544
C. Matienus (*pr.* 173) 652
Mediolanum 431
Megacles 248
C. Menenius Agrippa (*cos.* 503) xxxvii, li, 105–6
mercenaries 246, 336, 347–8, 363, 398–9, 429, 494–6
Mercenary War 348, 401–3
Messana 244–5, 321–5, 327–8, 330, 347, 370, 537
Messapi 213, 234, 314, 387
Metapontum 499
Metaurus, battle of 522–3
Metellus *see* Caecilius
Mettius Fufetius 74, 79
Mevania 446
Milan lvii, lxxiii
  see also Mediolanum
Milo (Pyrrhus' lieutenant) 295, 298, 302
Milo *see* Annius
Minos 588
Minturnae 194
L. Minucius (*cos.* 458) 127–9
M. Minucius Rufus (*cos.* 221) xxxvii, xlvii, 437, 466–7, 469–71, 517
Q. Minucius Rufus (*cos.* 197) 573
Mithridates VI lxxvii, 285
Molossians 239–40
Mons Sacer 106, 123, 221–2
C. Mucius Scaevola li, 99–102
Murgantia 493
Mylae, battle of 103, 341–5, 352
Myonessus, battle of 598–9
Mytistraton 336

Nabis xxv, xxxi, xxxiii–xxxiv, 573–4, 582, 584–5, 588–9, 591–2
M. Naevius (*tr.pl.* 184) 611
names, inversion of 131
Naples, Neapolitans 174–5, 304
Narnia 194, 446
Nasica *see* Cornelius

navy, development of 231, 296, 316–17, 341–3
Nemean Games 577
Neoptolemus II 240
Nero *see* Claudius
New Carthage xxxv, 461, 512, 529, 531
Nicias (doctor) 276
Nicomedes 671
Nola, battles of xiii, xx–xxi, xxxvii, 480–1, 485–90, 492
Numa 78–9, 83–4, 628–9
Numantia xliv, liii, 181, 633
Numidia, Numidians xlix, 496, 529, 544, 550, 555, 649
Numistro 515–16
Numitor 75

Ocriculum 446
Octavia 635
Octavian *see* Augustus
Q. Ogulnius Gallus (*cos.* 269) 207
Olbia 345
Olonicus 657–8
Olympia 207
omens 145–6, 168, 463
  see also prodigies
Opimia 476
Opus 525
oracles, misleading 157–8
oratio obliqua 86–7, 89, 208–9, 569
Oreum 525
Orosius
  and the 'lost epitome' xx–xxii
  and Livy 189
  and the *Periochae* xiv–xxii, xxviii–xxx, lvii, 98, 110, 112, 120–3, 141, 180, 203–4, 291, 431, 456–7, 459, 474, 487, 499–500, 511, 521, 621
  dates in xxix
  use of sources xxii, xxviii–xxx
Ostia 80, 83–4, 386
M'. Otacilius Crassus (*cos.* 263, 246) 331, 336
Oxyrhynchus Epitome, style of 73

Paeligni 187
Paestum 292–4, 309, 334
Palaepolis 175
Palatina, tribe 444
Palladium 404, 406
Pandonia 251
Panormus xxxviii, 350, 365, 394
  battle of 369, 374, 377–9
L. Papirius 176
L. Papirius Cursor (*cos.* 293, 272) xxxv, lxxv, 169, 176–7, 182–3, 189, 196, 198–9, 302
C. Papirius Maso (*cos.* 231) 411–12, 417–18
Parthia 372, 375

patrician–plebeian conflict 103–7, 112, 114, 124–5, 133, 150–3, 158–9, 172, 188, 192, 219–22
  see also secessions
patronage 443
Paul the Deacon, and Festus xxiii
Paulus *see* Aemilius
Peace of Phoenice 537
Pelias 394–5
pentads and decades lxxiv–lxxviii
perduellio 383, 387
Pergamum 559, 636, 654, 668
Periander 308
Periochae
  adapts Livy to fit tradition 112, 121, 140–1, 156, 470, 478–9, 530, 592, 598, 620, 626, 629
  adds details to Livy xlii, 84, 89, 110, 113, 144, 156–7, 537, 578
  and chronology xlvi
  and exemplarity xi–xii, xlv–xlvi, xlviii, 96, 100, 606
  and the 'lost epitome' lix
  arbitrariness of selection 85, 113–14, 124, 135, 148, 191, 601
  audiences of lxii–lxiii
  author of xxxii–xxxiii, lv–lvii
  causation in xlvi–xlvii
  changes Livy's chronology/order xxxvi–xxxviii, 83, 85–6, 96–7, 103–5, 108, 115, 132, 138, 152, 189, 205, 207, 213, 215–16, 307, 373, 378, 387, 454–5, 475–6, 521, 533, 557–62, 572, 607–15, 623, 639, 650, 660, 663, 665
  critically engages with Livy xxiv–xxv, xlviii, lxii–lxiii, lxxii, 88, 94–5, 100, 104–5, 122, 131–2, 134, 137, 141–2, 151, 178, 181, 203–4, 320–1, 327, 352–3, 460, 467–8, 476–7, 489, 509, 545, 555–6, 582, 585, 614–15, 646
  cross-refers to other parts of Livy xxiii–xxiv, xxxi–xxxii, 84, 88–9, 131–2, 141, 169, 181, 458, 485, 497, 504–5, 536–7, 583, 600, 646, 667
  distortion of Livy 102, 454–5, 464–5, 495–6, 506, 511, 523, 544, 549–50, 578–9, 591, 594–6, 600, 605
  ethical complexities in xlix–l, 111, 126–7, 227
  ethical simplicity of xlvi–xlviii, 85, 155–6, 163, 276, 327, 356, 373, 424, 428, 435, 466, 469, 493, 498, 620, 651
  includes alternative versions 611, 619
  interest in individuals xlii–xlvi, 462
  length of books lvii–lviii
  Livian language in xxiii–xxv, liii–liv, 92, 110, 130–1, 158, 164, 468, 489–90, 521–2, 606, 638

Periochae (cont.)
　manuscript tradition of lxxix–lxxxii
　missing books lxxviii–lxxix
　narrative coherence of xxxiii–xxxvii, lxii, lxviii–lxix, 340, 540, 553, 595, 621–2, 649, 658
　non-Livian stories in xiii–xiv, xl, l–li, lviii–lix, lxxii, 89, 101, 106, 150–2, 157–8, 168, 180–1, 191–2, 509, 532, 536, 540, 574, 591, 594–5, 625, 662
　omits alternative versions l, 106, 125–6, 131, 177, 182, 420
　refers to Livy explicitly xxxix–xl, 189, 321, 453
　self-reference by 195, 306, 308, 386, 437, 469, 609
　sentence structure lii–liii
　speeches in xli
　style of lii–lv
　substitutes Livy's alternative version l, 168–9, 194–5, 455, 545
　title of xi
　uses Cicero xxvi, xxviii, 86, 128, 130–1, 277, 373–4, 474–5
　uses Cornelius Nepos 460, 465
　uses Horace 188
　uses Julius Paris xxvii, 599, 619
　uses Pompeius Trogus 627
　uses Quintilian 470
　uses Valerius Maximus xxvi–xxviii, 91, 101, 109–10, 138, 177, 195, 606, 663
　word play in 465, 482
Perseus lxxiv, 623, 626–7, 629–30, 644–7, 653, 656–7, 659–60, 664–6, 668–70
Persians 320
Q. Petillius (*tr.pl.* 187) 611
Q. Petillius Spurinus (*cos.* 176) 644
Pharsalus, battle of xliv
Pharus 440
　see also Demetrius of Pharus
Pheidias 207
Philip V xxxiv, 303, 439, 634
　makes treaty with Hannibal 485, 487, 494
　in First Macedonian War 493–4, 524–5
　makes peace with Rome 537
　in Second Macedonian War 559–62, 564–7, 569–71, 573–4, 576–7, 584–5
　in Antiochan War 594
　disputes with Rome 623
　as tyrant 625
　family tragedy of 626–30
　death of lxxiv, 629–30
Philippus *see* Marcius
Philocles 559–60, 570
Philopoemen 591, 606, 621–3
philosophical language 111

Phocis 574
Phoenicians 419
Picenum, Picentes 213–15, 307, 309–11, 370, 407, 427
Pinnes 422, 425–6, 441
pirates, piracy 161, 422–3, 437–8
Pisa 617
Placentia 446, 449–51, 459, 565, 616
plague xxxviii, xli–xlii, 114, 144, 154, 206–7, 282–3, 289
C. Plautius Venox (*cens.* 312) 186
plebiscites 219–20
Q. Pleminius xlvii, 536–7, 541–2
Plutarch, and the 'lost epitome' xiii
Po 428, 431–4, 449–50
poisoning, prosecutions for 173–4
Polybius
　attacks Philinus 295–9, 330
　geographical errors of 453–5
Polycrates 661
Polyxenidas 603
pomerium 88–9
Pometia 102
Cn. Pompeius Magnus (*cos.* 70, 55, 52) xxxv, xliii, xlv, lxxvii, 622, 639
Cn. Pompeius Strabo (*cos.* 89) xxxv
M. Pomponius (*tr.pl.* 362) xlvii, 155–6
M. Pomponius Matho (*cos.* 231) 417
M'. Pomponius Matho (*cos.* 233) 417
T. Pomponius Veientanus 497
Pontia 183
pontifices 192, 369
　pontifex maximus 367–8, 391–3, 404–5
C. Pontius 179, 182, 205
Pontius, Herennius 179, 205
Popilia 110
C. Popillius Laenas, supposed assassin of Cicero li
C. Popillius Laenas (*cos.* 172, 158) 668
M. Popillius Laenas (*cos.* 173) 651
M. Porcius Cato (*cos.* 195)
　and Third Punic War xlix–l, 643–4
　at capture of Tarentum 516
　opposes repeal of *lex Oppia* 581, 641
　campaigns in Spain 581–4
　at Thermopylae 594
　campaigns against corruption 611
　censorship of 265, 442, 619–20
　supports *lex Voconia* 640–4
　defends the Rhodians 668
M. Porcius Cato (*pr.* 54) 622
Porsenna *see* Lars li
Porta Capena li, 509
Porta Collina li, 291, 509
Posidonia *see* Paestum
postliminium 372

A. Postumius Albinus (*cos.* 242) 391–3, 442
A. Postumius Albinus (*cos.* 180) 640
L. Postumius Albinus (*cos.* 234, 229, 215) 413, 424, 483–4
L. Postumius Albinus (*cos.* 173) 633, 635–6
Sp. Postumius Albinus (*cos.* 334, 321) 179–81
P. Postumius Albinus Regillensis (*tr.mil.c.p.* 414) 133–5
L. Postumius Megellus (*cos.* 305, 294, 291) 209–10, 232–3
L. Postumius Megellus (*cos.* 262) 370
A. Postumius Tubertus (dictator 431) 132
Potitii 184
praefectus annonae 128–9
Praeneste, Praenestines 148, 254, 573
praetorship
  creation of 154
  enlargement of 390–1, 426
  praetor peregrinus 390–1
  praetor urbanus 390
prata Flaminia see campus Flaminius
priesthoods, plebeian access to 150
Prisci Latini 81, 85
prisoner exchanges 374–5, 386, 402–3
privateers, in First Punic War 394–6
Privernates 160, 166–7, 174
proconsulship, first 175
prodigies xxxix, xli–xlii, 79, 91, 114, 136–7, 157–8, 280–2, 291, 303, 356–7, 398, 527, 569, 598–90, 631–2
Proserpina 541
Prusias 622–3, 671–2
Ptolemy Ceraunus 238, 252
Ptolemy II Philadelphus 290
Ptolemy III Euergetes 362
Ptolemy V Epiphanes 559, 579
Ptolemy VI Philometor 666–7
Ptolemy VIII Euergetes 666–7
Ptolemy XIII 639
Ptolemy, son of Pyrrhus 301
publicani 497
M. Publicius Malleolus (*cos.* 232) 417
Publicola *see* Valerius
C. Publilius 176
Q. Publilius Philo (*cos.* 339, 327, 320, 315) 172–3, 175, 182
puns 97, 122, 129, 181, 203
Puteoli 584
Pydna, battle of xxvi, lxxvii, 662–3, 665–6
Pyrenees 456–8
Pyrrhic War 248–87, 296, 303, 308, 313, 316
Pyrrhus 162, 167, 198–9, 210, 234–41, 270–1, 273–7, 283, 298, 308, 316, 589
  invades Italy 227, 233–4, 237–9, 241, 243, 271, 305, 314

  in Tarentum 241
  at Heraclea 248–53, 271
  marches on Rome 251, 254–5, 277
  makes peace overtures 255–65, 271
  and his doctor 138
  at Ausculum 266–9
  in Sicily 250, 272, 277, 279–81, 290
  returns to Italy 284–5
  at battle of Beneventum 285–7
  defeated by Rome 281, 290, 311
  leaves Italy 287, 294, 305–6
  death of 295, 299–301

quaestorship
  enlargement of 316–19
  quaestor Gallicus 317
  quaestor Ostiensis 316
  quaestores classici 316–19
Quinctius, Kaeso 114
T. Quinctius 165
T. Quinctius Capitolinus Barbatus (*cos.* 471, 468, 465, 446, 443, 439) 124
L. Quinctius Cincinnatus (*cos.* 460) xxvi, 95, 114, 116–17, 124, 127–8, 359–60
T. Quinctius Crispinus 499
T. Quinctius Crispinus (*cos.* 208) 517–19
L. Quinctius Flamininus (*cos.* 192) 570–2, 576–7, 619–21
T. Quinctius Flamininus (*cos.* 198) xxv, xxxi, xxxiv, lxiv–lxv, lxviii, lxxii–lxxiii, 561, 569–74, 576–7, 582–6, 592, 622
T. Quinctius Poenus Cincinnatus (*cos.* 431, 428) 130
Quirina, tribe 407–8
quorum, in Senate 261

'rash commanders' in Livy 469
'raven' (device for naval warfare) 341, 353
Rea Silvia 75–6
Rediculus, shrine of 509
Regillus *see* Aemilius
Regulus *see* Atilius
religion, and the *Periochae* xli–xlii, lvi
Remus 75–7
rex sacrorum 369, 391
Rhegium xxxiii, 241–7, 304–7, 326
Rhodes, Rhodians 559, 561, 567, 570–1, 576, 598–602, 650, 659–60, 668–9
Rhone 456–7
right of appeal 192–3
Romulus 75–8
'round-up' passages xxxviii–xxxix, lii, 113, 123–4, 135, 148, 166, 186–7, 222, 233–7, 277–8, 299–301, 336–8, 487–9, 514, 524, 526, 574–5, 596, 628, 656–7
Rufinus *see* Cornelius

Sabines 76–7, 79, 81–2, 85, 87, 103, 105, 112–13, 118, 122, 124, 333, 407–8
Sacred Spring 466
sacrilege 381
Saguntum, Saguntines 332, 438, 452–5, 494, 532, 565
Salapia 514
Salernum 584
Sallentini 213, 234, 314, 316–17, 387
Samnium, Samnites 162–7, 173–9, 181–3, 187, 194–206, 210–13, 215, 225–6, 231, 233, 258, 263, 277–8, 284, 286, 299, 302, 311–12, 328, 335–6
  political structure 205, 212
  treaties with 161, 163, 187, 211–12
  see also Hirpini
  see also Samnite Wars
Samnite Wars xxxv
  First Samnite War 162–5, 167, 170, 175–6, 178, 195, 211
  Second Samnite War 167, 174–83, 211
  Third Samnite War lxxv, 194–206, 209, 211
Samothrace 666
Sapienati 139
Sardinia, Sardinians 345–7, 351, 402, 414–19, 426, 438, 485, 487–8, 634, 644
Sassina, Sassinates 213, 314–16
Saticulani 183, 187
Satricum, Satricans 182, 187
Saturn 170
Saturnia 623, 634
Saturninus see Appuleius
Scaevola see Mucius
Scerdilaidas 440
Scipio see Cornelius
scribes 384–5
scroll vs. codex lviii–lix
Scythia 320
secessions 103–6, 118–19, 123, 219–22
Second Macedonian War xxxiv, xxxvi, 303, 487, 493, 514, 537, 554, 559–77 *passim*, 598, 647, 657
  origin of xxxix, 559–64
Second Punic War lxxiv, 213, 246, 304, 308, 310, 313, 321, 364, 428, 430, 435, 438, 449, 452–558 *passim*, 565–6, 587, 590, 640, 660
  origin of xxxix, 401, 403, 418, 452–6
secret ballot 443
Secular Games lxxix
Seleucus IV Philopator 636–9
Semo Sancus 224
C. Sempronius Blaesus (*cos.* 253, 244) 365
C. Sempronius Gracchus (*tr.pl.* 123, 122) xxxvi, xliv–xlv, lxxvi–lxxvii, 409, 443, 634
Ti. Sempronius Gracchus (*cos.* 238) 387–8, 413

Ti. Sempronius Gracchus (*cos.* 215, 213) 485–6, 488, 492, 499–500
Ti. Sempronius Gracchus (*cos.* 177, 163) xxxi–xxxii, 608–9, 613–15, 633–6, 640, 644, 671
Ti. Sempronius Gracchus (*tr.pl.* 133) xliv–xlv, 443, 634
Ti. Sempronius Longus (*cos.* 218) 449
P. Sempronius Sophus (*cos.* 268) 309, 370
C. Sempronius Tuditanus (*pr.* 197) li, 578
M. Sempronius Tuditanus (*cos.* 240) 442
P. Sempronius Tuditanus (*cos.* 204) 546
Sena (Senogallia) 213–17, 309, 427
Senones 226–8, 233–4, 236
Sentinum, battle of 1, 194–6, 198, 203, 207, 263, 267
Sergia, tribe 408
L. Sergius Catilina (*pr.* 68) 254
C. Servilius Ahala (*mag.eq.* 439) xxvi, 127–8
M. Servilius Pulex Geminus (*cos.* 202) 670
Servius Tullius xxiv, xli, li, 74, 81, 85, 88–9, 104, 115
Setia 573
L. Sextius Sextinus Lateranus (*cos.* 366) 150–2
Sextus Tarquinius 82
Sibylline Books 207, 539–40
L. Siccius 118
Sicilian Expedition 320
Sicily xxxiii, xlvii, 270, 272, 284–5, 295, 298, 304, 320, 323–8, 335–6, 339, 341–2, 346–51, 353, 365, 370, 377–8, 380, 383, 392, 394, 399–403, 426, 435, 445, 459, 474, 485, 492–3, 514, 534
Cn. Sicinius (*pr.* 172) 647
Sidicini 163, 167
Silanus see Junius
Sinuessa 194
Siris 251
slaves, slavery xxxiii, 97, 114–15, 133, 283, 337–8, 359–60, 385, 492, 572–3, 640, 655
  see also manumission
snakes 206, 208–9
Social War xxxiv–xxxv, lxxv–lxxvi, 168, 234
Soli 601
Solon 119
Sophoniba 551–3
Sorani 183, 187
sources, and allusion lxi–lxx
Spain, Spaniards xxiv, xliv, lxxiv, 362, 401, 438–9, 452, 466, 475–6, 484–5, 487–8, 494–6, 503–6, 508, 511–12, 520–1, 524–5, 527–32, 534–5, 578, 581–3, 588, 593, 601, 623, 628–9, 631–6, 643, 652, 657
  see also Celtiberi, Lusitani, Saguntum, Vaccaei
Sparta, Spartans 218, 224, 229, 231, 300–1, 316, 350–1, 362–3, 573–4, 582–5, 591, 623

Spartacus xxxiii, 523
Spoletium 412–13
spolia opima xxxv–xxxvi, 77, 130–2, 431, 435–7
Statius Statilius 225
stereotypes 159–60, 190, 309, 339–41, 351–2, 373, 376, 378, 397, 489
Sthennius Stallius 224–5
Stoicism 371–2
Stolo *see* Licinius
Straton of Sidon 240
Suburana, tribe 444
Suessula 163
Sulci 351
Sulla *see* Cornelius
Ser. Sulpicius Galba (*cos.* 144) 670
P. Sulpicius Galba Maximus (*cos.* 211, 200) 524–6, 566–7
C. Sulpicius Galus (*cos.* 166) 662
C. Sulpicius Paterculus (*cos.* 258) 346–7, 351
C. Sulpicius Peticus (*cos.* 364, 361, 355, 353, 351) 160
P. Sulpicius Saverrio (*cos.* 279) 266
Summanus, temple of 280
Sybaris 224
Syphax 494–6, 528–9, 543–4, 546, 549–52, 554–6
Syracuse, Syracusans xli, xlvii, 244, 279, 321–2, 327, 330–2, 337, 370, 435, 491–3, 500–3, 514, 516, 537, 541, 610

Tacitus, and *Periochae* 182–3, 253
Tanaquil xlvii, 85
Tarentum, Tarentines 176, 182, 198, 220, 227, 229–38, 241, 251, 256, 260, 272–3, 277, 279, 284–5, 287, 291, 294–305, 308, 312, 327, 497–8, 514, 516–17
Tarpeia 76
Tarquinia 334
Tarquinienses 160–1, 166
Tarquinii 85
L. Tarquinius Egeri Collatinus (*cos.* 509) xxxi, 82, 93–6
Tarquinius Priscus xxvi, xlvii, 81–3, 85–9
Tarquinius Superbus 74, 81–3, 88–91, 93, 98, 102–3
Tarraco 530
Taurus mountain range 600
Telamon, battle of 427
Tellus, temple of 309
Tempestates, temple of 346
Tempsa 584
Q. Terentius Culleo 556–7
Terentius Gentianus 392–3
C. Terentius Varro (*cos.* 216) 167, 472, 474–7
Terminus 83

Teuta 421–3, 425–6
theatre *see* drama
Thebes, Thebans 653
Themistocles 274
Theoxena 625
Thermae 365–6
Thermopylae
  battle in Persian War 112, 349–51
  battle in Antiochan War 594
Thessaly 570–1, 574
Third Macedonian War lxxiv, 623, 642, 644–57, 659–65
Third Punic War xlviii–l, lvii–lviii, lxxvi, 495, 556, 581, 643–4, 648–9
  origin of xxxix
Thisbe 653
Thrace 607, 623
Thurii, Thurini 223–5, 230, 234–5, 243–4, 499, 584
Tiber 282
  Tiber island 96, 209
  flooding of 398
Tiberius, emperor lxxix, 391–3, 522
Tibur, Tiburtines 160–1, 166
Ticinus, battle of lviii, 456–8
Timochares 276
M. Titinius Curvus (*pr.* 178) 652
Transpadania 431–5
Trasimene *see* Lake Trasimene
Treaty of Lutatius 399–405, 418, 453, 455
'Treaty of Philinus' 272–3, 295–9, 326–7
Trebia, battle of lviii, 449, 459–60
Trebulani 191
tresviri epulones 579
'Trials of the Scipios' 608–15
tribes 407
  introduction of new xl, 104–5, 148, 160, 173, 183, 193, 406–8
  urban vs. rural 443–4
tribunate
  creation of 105–6
  reforms to 112
tributum 641
Tricipitinus *see* Lucretius
triumphs
  double 210–13, 314
  in *Periochae* xliii
triumviri capitales 217–18
triumviri nocturni 217–18
Troy 138, 406
Tuccia 420–1
Tullia, wife of Tarquinius Superbus 81–2, 85
Q. Tullius Cicero (*pr.* 62) xliv
Tullus Hostilius 74, 79
tumultus Gallicus 428

Tunis 357
Turnus Herdonius 74, 81–2, 90
Tusculum 367
Twelve Tables, Laws of 119–21
Tyndaris 352
tyrants, stereotypes of 492

Umbria, Umbrians l, 187, 191, 194–5, 233, 310, 314–16, 412–13
Utica 546, 549

Vaccaei 635–6
P. Valerius Falto (*cos.* 238) 413
Q. Valerius Falto (*cos.* 239) 392, 396, 403
L. Valerius Flaccus (*cos.* 195) 442
L. Valerius Flaccus (*cos.* 131) 391
L. Valerius Flaccus (*cos.* 86) xxi
M. Valerius Laevinus (*cos.* 220, 215) 494
P. Valerius Laevinus (*cos.* 280) 238–9, 248–51, 253, 277
M. Valerius Maximus Corvus (*cos.* 348, 346, 343, 335, 300, 299) 161–3, 165, 191–3
M'. Valerius Maximus Messalla (*cos.* 263) 330–1, 336, 370
L. Valerius Potitus (*cos.* 449) 118
L. (or P.) Valerius Publicola (*cos.* 509, 508, 507, 504) 98–100, 102
P. Valerius Publicola (*cos.* 460) 114
Varro *see* Terentius
Veii xxiv, xxvi, xli, 76, 81, 88, 111–13, 129–30, 133, 135–9, 142, 144–5, 410, 661
Velina, tribe 407
Veliterni 160, 166
Velitri 148
Veneti 437
Venus, temple of 198
Venusia 223, 515
Verginia 117–18, 122–3, 176
L. Verginius (*tr.pl.* 449) 118, 122–3

Vertomarus/Viridomarus 436
Vesta, shrine of 290, 404–6, 527, 631–2
    Vestals xlii, li, 110, 172, 290–2, 369, 405, 420–1, 474–6, 527, 631–2, 643
Vestini 191
Via Aemilia 446, 616
Via Amerina 411
Via Appia 183–6, 262, 312, 380, 387, 447
Via Flaminia 444–7, 616
viatores 384
Vibellius Taurea 247, 510–11
Victumulae 459
P. Villius Tappulus (*cos.* 199) 569, 589
Viminal 88
Vindicius 96–8
Viriathus xxxiii
Viridomarus *see* Vertomarus
Vitellius, emperor 254
Vitruvius Vaccus 224
Q. Voconius Saxa (*tr.pl.* 169) 640, 642–3
Volsci 81, 90–1, 105, 109, 112–14, 124, 126, 132–3, 135, 148, 162, 166–7
Volsinii 139, 221–2, 236, 278, 337–8
Volturnum 584
Volturnus 470
L. Volumnius Flamma Violens (*cos.* 307, 296) 316
Vulci 236, 278, 294

war-vote, procedures 328–9
women, defending cities 299–300
word play 344
    and etymologies 78
    see also puns

Xanthippus 355–6, 362–4

Zama, battle of lxiv, lxxvii, 552–4, 660
Zeus, temple of 638

Index of Latin

abolere 581
ad urbem 254
adamare 552
agellus 359
ampla manus 536
ampliare lv, 87
apparere 605

bellare 73

circumposita 471
clangor 142
colligere 190
condere 119
condiciones ferre 168
consecrare 78
conspirare 165–6
corripere 655

deferre 580
deformare 366
deponere 121
descendere 159
deserere 259–60
devincere 73
dies 611–12
diripere 231–2
dubio eventu 269

evocare 341, 612
excidere 544

fame laborare 127
ferox victoria 468
fidem custodire lv, 376
foedus 181
frequens senatus 261

hibernaculum 136

indignationem movere 137
iniuriis vexari 612
invadere 82
iubere 667

laborare 170–1
legationem perferre 168
legem perferre 125

manipularis 145
maxime 252
movere 288

nam 509
notabilis 547

obstringere 196
obtestari 92
opponere 468
orator 109
ortus 453

perseverare in accusatione lv, 156–7
praecludere 528
primum bellum 545
proelium 571
proferre 175–6

rapere 630
redigere 188
regnare 91
religio 154
removere 202
renovare 211
restituere 171

saepius 331
seminarium lv, 619
semita 185
sternere 184–5

triumphum ducere 343
tunc primum 218

valetudo oculorum 262
viam munire 447
vigiliae 462
vilissimus rex lv, 639
visus lv, 107
vorago 158